# *Victorious in Defeat*

# Victorious in Defeat

## THE LIFE AND TIMES OF CHIANG KAI-SHEK, CHINA, 1887–1975

Alexander V. Pantsov

Yale UNIVERSITY PRESS
New Haven & London

Translated from Russian by Steven I. Levine.

Yale University Press books may be purchased in quantity for educational, business, or promotional use. For information, please e-mail sales.press@yale.edu (U.S. office) or sales@yaleup.co.uk (U.K. office).

Set in Adobe Garamond type by IDS Infotech Ltd.
Printed in the United States of America.

Library of Congress Control Number: 2022934236
ISBN 978-0-300-26020-5 (hardcover : alk. paper)

A catalogue record for this book is available from the British Library.

This paper meets the requirements of ANSI/NISO Z39.48-1992 (Permanence of Paper).

10 9 8 7 6 5 4 3 2 1

To my wife,

Ekaterina Borisovna Bogoslovskaia,

I dedicate this book with love

# *Contents*

# *Spelling and Pronunciation of Chinese Words*

The English spelling of Chinese words and names used in this book is based on the pinyin system of romanization (use of the Latin alphabet) to represent the pronunciation of Chinese characters. I follow the modified pinyin system used by the Library of Congress, which replaces an older system with which readers may be familiar. Thus, for example, I spell the name of Chiang Kai-shek's second wife as Song Meiling, not Soong May-ling. (Both romanizations yield the same pronunciation: *Sung Meiling.*) For the same reason I spell the name of China's capital as Beijing, not Peking. Following accepted practice, however, I use the traditional English spelling of the subject of this biography, Chiang Kai-shek, not Jiang Jieshi, as well as the names of his children, Chiang Ching-kuo, not Jiang Jingguo, Chiang Wei-kuo, not Jiang Weiguo, and Chiang Yao-kuang, not Jiang Yaoguang. I also use the traditional English spelling of the family name of his grandchildren and great-grandchildren—Chiang, not Jiang, as well as the name Sun Yat-sen, not Sun Yixian, names of the cities Canton, not Guangzhou, and Taipei, not Taibei, the name of a famous Shanghai avenue, Nanking Road, not Nanjing Road, and the names of famous institutions such as Peking (not Beijing) University, Yenching (not Yanjing) University, and Tsinghua (not Qinghua) University.

The pronunciation of many pinyin letters is roughly similar to English pronunciation. However, some letters and combinations of letters need explanation:

Vowels:

A like *a* in *father*
AI like the word *eye*
AO like *ow* in *cow*
E like *e* in *end*
I like *i* in *it*
IA like *ye* in *yes*
O like *o* in *order,* except before the letters *ng,* when it is pronounced like the two o's in *moon*
U like the second *u* in *pursue* when it follows the letters *j, q, x,* and *y;* otherwise, like the double *o* in *moon,* except in the vowel combination UO the *u* is silent
Ü like the second *u* in *pursue*
YA like *ya* in *yacht*
YE like *ye* in *yet*
YI like *ee* in *feet*
When two separately pronounced vowels follow each other, an apostrophe is inserted to indicate the syllable break between them. Thus, *Xi'an,* for example, is two syllables whereas *xian* is just one.

Consonants:

C like the letters *ts* in *tsar*
G like the hard *g* in *get*
J like *j* in *jig*
Q like the letters *ch* in *cheese*
R in initial position, like the *s* in *vision;* at the end of a word, like the double *r* in *warrior*
X like the *s* in *soon*
XI like the *shee* in *sheet*
Z like the letters *dz* in *adze*
ZH like the *j* in *jockey*

*Victorious in Defeat*

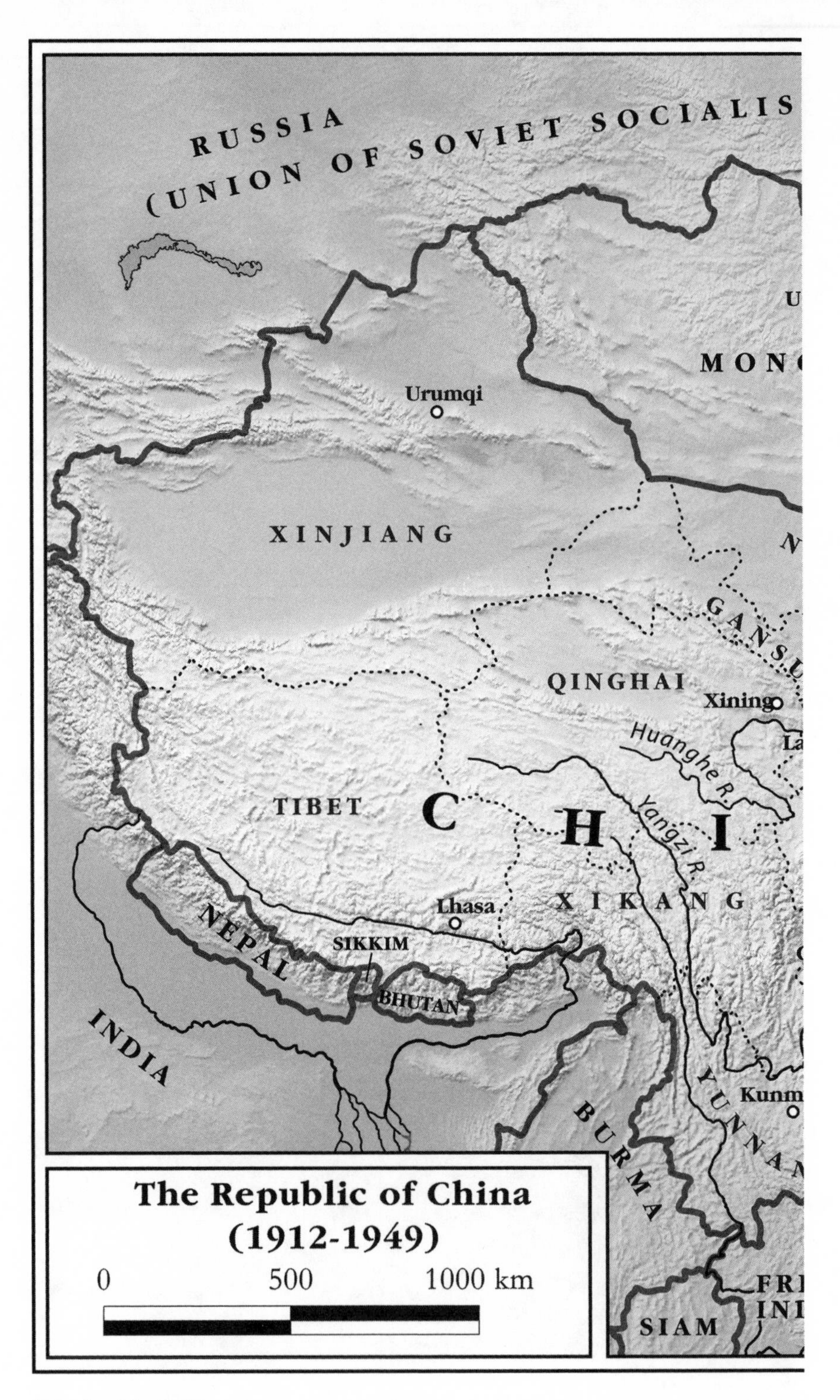


(Map by Erin Greb)

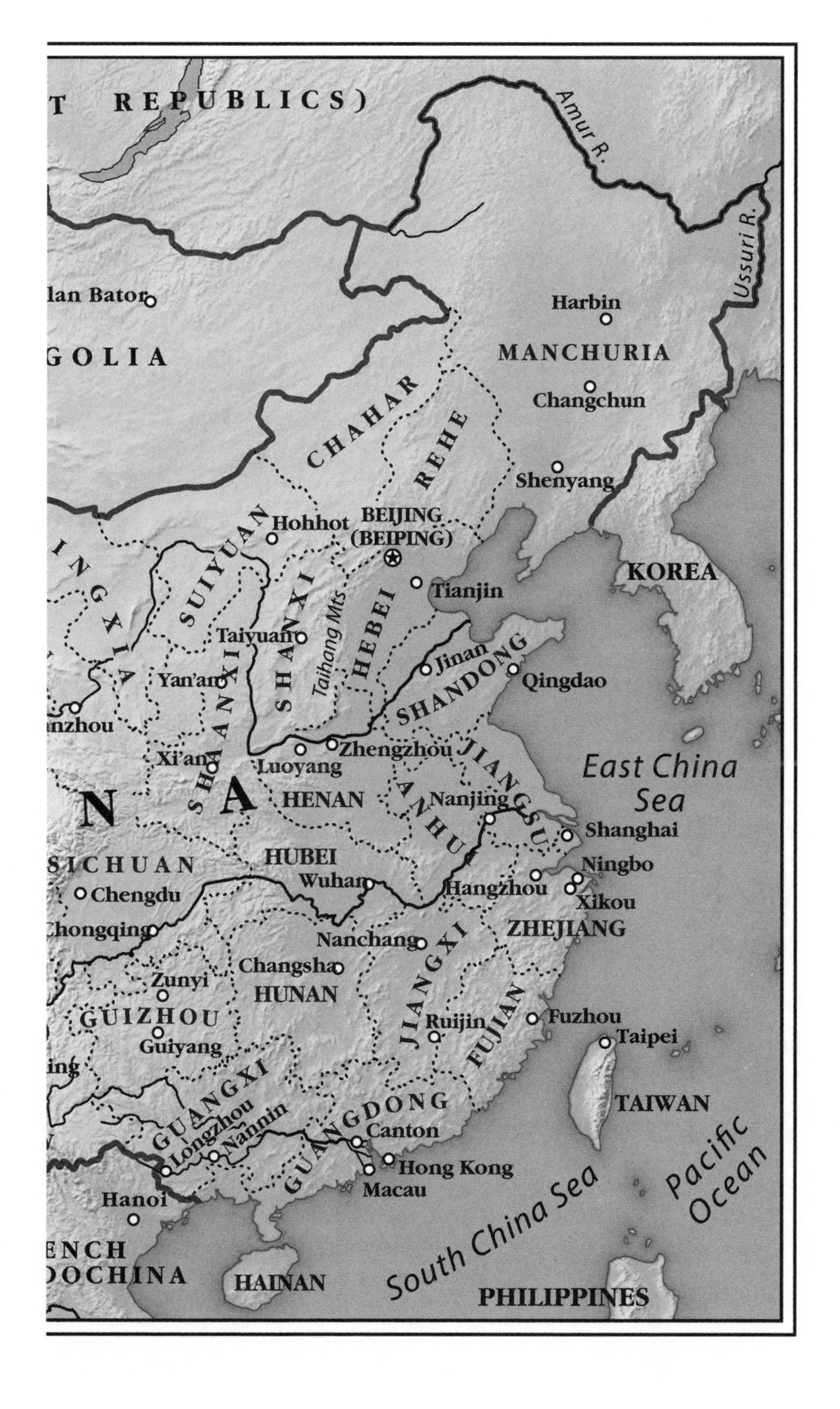
REPUBLICS)
Amur R.
Ussuri R.
Harbin
MANCHURIA
Changchun
CHAHAR
REHE
Shenyang
Hohhot
BEIJING
(BEIPING)
SUIYUAN
Tianjin
KOREA
SHANXI
Taihang Mts
HEBEI
Taiyuan
Jinan
SHANDONG
Qingdao
Yan'an
SHAANXI
Zhengzhou
JIANGSU
Xi'an
Luoyang
East China
Sea
A
HENAN
ANHUI
Nanjing
Shanghai
Ningbo
SICHUAN
HUBEI
Wuhan
Hangzhou
Xikou
Chengdu
ZHEJIANG
Nanchang
Changsha
JIANGXI
Zunyi
HUNAN
GUIZHOU
Ruijin
FUJIAN
Fuzhou
Taipei
Guiyang
GUANGXI
TAIWAN
GUANGDONG
Longzhou
Nannin
Canton
Hong Kong
Macau
Pacific
Ocean
Hanoi
South China Sea
HAINAN
PHILIPPINES

# *Introduction*

In May 1949 the North China city of Qingdao, located on the shore of the Shandong peninsula, was gripped by panic. Everyone was anticipating the day when the American warships, stationed in adjacent Jiaozhou Bay, would depart, after which the city would inevitably be seized by communist forces. A civil war was raging in China, and during the past two years the insurgent People's Liberation Army (PLA) of the communist leader Mao Zedong had repeatedly inflicted defeats on the government forces of Generalissimo Chiang Kai-shek. Everyone was afraid that the communists would carry out a slaughter even bloodier than the one that, according to rumors, had taken place in a number of Shandong cities in November 1947; in Weihaiwei alone at that time the communists had massacred several thousand peaceful inhabitants.[1] All hope was placed on the American sailors, despite the fact that, coming on shore, they had not always behaved properly toward the local inhabitants. During the four years they had been present the local authorities had received numerous complaints about their conduct.[2] But now people thought the United States Navy might intervene in the internal Chinese conflict to stop the communists. In early May, however, it became clear that the Americans were leaving, notwithstanding that, again according to rumors, on May 3 the Generalissimo himself had secretly flown into Qingdao to persuade them not to abandon the Chinese. But he was supposedly able to secure only an American promise to remain five more days in order to enable Chiang

Kai-shek to evacuate his garrison successfully.[3] The inhabitants were leaving the city in droves; excited crowds were besieging passenger ships.

However, the rumors about Chiang Kai-shek's arrival and the departure of US ships in five days were false. The Generalissimo had not flown to Qingdao in early May to hold negotiations with the commander of the American fleet.[4] There was no need for him to do so. The Americans themselves had asked the Chinese to stay in Qingdao as long as possible and had even promised to help with its defense. But not because they intended to fight the Chinese communists. They had long since decided to leave Qingdao, but they needed time to evacuate their naval base. This is the only reason they wanted Chiang to keep his troops in Qingdao.[5]

Chiang had long realized that he could not count on American military support, so in early 1949 he had begun preparations to redeploy his forces from Qingdao to the area of Nanjing and Shanghai. As for the Americans, he had decided to inform them of his departure no earlier than three days prior to the completion of the Guomindang army evacuation.[6] He was angry at them and did not trust them. On February 12, 1949, he wrote in his diaries, "The indecisiveness and helplessness of the Americans cause me pain and induce laughter. . . . [They] request that my troops remain in Qingdao and not retreat, promising me active assistance. But who can believe them?"[7]

On May 4 Chiang discussed the situation with the commander of the Twenty-first Army Corps defending Qingdao, General Liu Anqi, insisting that the troops be withdrawn as soon as possible. "We don't need to guard the gates any longer to provide for the evacuation of the Americans," he said irritably.[8] The US ships left Jiaozhou Bay on May 25, 1949, and the Guomindang garrison withdrew on June 2.[9] Qingdao fell that same day.

A week earlier the communists had seized Shanghai, the largest Chinese metropolis. Nanjing, the capital of China, had already been in their hands for a month. The troops of the PLA flowed south in a mighty stream, and the civil war was inexorably drawing to a close. Chiang Kai-shek's army was falling apart, and many of the closest associates of the Generalissimo, including several members of his family, fled the country. His main ally, the United States of America, which had spent hundreds of millions of dollars in military and financial aid to Chiang before and during the final civil war in China, ultimately also had to throw him to the mercy of fate.

Needless to say, it was Chiang Kai-shek, his government, and his generals who were most responsible for the defeat. However, his debacle also marked a defeat of the American policy in China that had been extremely contradictory. On the one hand, the Americans had rendered massive financial and military help to Chiang's regime, but on the other they had made serious mistakes that made the situation worse.

The loss of China was to some extent preconditioned by President Franklin D. Roosevelt's behavior during the Yalta Conference with Josef Stalin in February 1945, when, in effect, he sold China's Manchuria to Russia in exchange for Russian entry into the Japanese war. Moreover, he did it behind Chiang Kai-shek's back. Would the Chinese Communists have defeated Chiang Kai-shek had the Russians not occupied Manchuria and provided critical assistance to the Chinese Communist Party (CCP) at a decisive moment? We cannot know the answer for sure, but we do know that this region played an enormous role in the Communist takeover of China. It was indeed an anvil of Communist victory.[10] President Harry S. Truman, who confirmed the Yalta agreement at the Potsdam conference in July 1945, admitted the mistake in early 1946, observing that his administration "found later that we didn't need Russia there [in the war against Japan] and the Russians have been a head ache to us ever since."[11] To be sure, Roosevelt also felt bad about his own behavior in Yalta.[12]

The prime American mistake with respect to the Chinese Civil War (1946–49) was its adherence to the idea of universal democratization. The spread of "a healthy democracy" in the world was the ultimate goal of Truman's containment of the USSR.[13] But by promoting this idea in China on the eve of and during the civil war, Truman and George C. Marshall were unwittingly playing into the hands of Stalin and the CCP, who cynically deceived the world, including many Chinese liberals, by the alluring concept of Mao's New Democracy, which claimed that China needed to achieve not a socialist but a liberal and democratic revolution. The American leaders, however, never acknowledged their mistakes openly. Instead they blamed only Chiang and his corrupt regime for the loss of China.

Actually, American government and public opinion had long since turned against Chiang personally despite the massive American support rendered to his regime. A negative image of him as a "third-rate warrior" and "corrupt dictator" who parasitized on the military assistance of his allies had taken hold in the United States as early as 1943–44. Chiang was partly responsible himself, for he had indeed been blackmailing President Roosevelt and threatening to abandon resistance to Japan if the United States did not increase its military aid. At the time, China's image was not improved by the catastrophic defeats its army suffered at the front, especially in 1944, when the Japanese seized the capitals of Henan, Hunan, Fujian (for the second time; it briefly had been under their occupation from late April to early September 1941), and Guangxi provinces, 146 other cities, and over 77,000 square miles of territory, including the most important agricultural areas that supplied Free China with grain. Chiang Kai-shek's wife, the ambitious Song Meiling, who along with her nephew and niece had been guests at the White House in February 1943, also produced a negative impression on Roosevelt. So did his personal meetings with Chiang himself in Cairo, some months later in November. The president did not like the first lady of China nor Chiang, who Roosevelt suspected was dishonorable.

The view of Roosevelt and his confidants toward Chiang was also influenced by confidential reports reaching him from US Ambassador Clarence E. Gauss and some other Foreign Service and Office of Strategic Services (OSS) officers in China who despised Chiang. Other reports came from the chief of Chiang Kai-shek's allied staff, Lt. General Joseph W. Stilwell (Vinegar Joe), who was a close friend of US Army Chief of Staff Marshall. Stilwell simply hated Chiang.

In December 1943 Roosevelt ordered Stilwell to do everything possible to get rid of Chiang Kai-shek. Stilwell began to prepare a secret plan to assassinate Chiang.[14] It was never carried out, but in September 1944 Roosevelt savagely humiliated Chiang by demanding that he give "unrestricted command of all your forces" to General Stilwell.[15] Chiang perceived this as worse than anything else. "It not only was an insult to me personally, but also an act of aggression against my country," he wrote in the margins of Roosevelt's telegram to him.[16] Within a few days he openly accused the United States of practicing "a new form of imperialism."[17]

To a large degree negative information about Chiang and his regime, deliberately disseminated by many popular journalists working in China, also influenced the American leadership. It also greatly influenced Americans overall. Many of these journalists inclined to the liberal or even leftist views that were widespread in America at that time, when the country was fighting German totalitarianism and Japanese militarism. The anti-Chiang publications of Theodore White, Brooks Atkinson, Edgar Snow, T. A. Bisson, Jack Belden, Freda Utley, Thoban Wiant, Joseph Alsop, Agnes Smedley, and others about the ineffectiveness and corruption of the Chiang Kai-shek regime and the terrible living conditions of the Chinese people made a particularly strong impression. The American public was engrossed in reading anti–Chiang Kai-shek books by Harold R. Isaacs and André Malraux.[18]

On October 31, 1944, the American public was shocked by Atkinson's article published on the front page of the *New York Times* that for the first time revealed a conflict between Stilwell, who "has been eager to fight the Japanese in China," and an "increasingly unpopular" dictator, Chiang Kai-shek, the leader of "a moribund antidemocratic regime that is more concerned with maintaining its political supremacy than in driving the Japanese out of China." This regime, Atkinson claimed, was "unenlightened, cold-hearted autocratic . . . bureaucratic, inefficient, and corrupt."[19] Atkinson mainly relied on the information he received firsthand from Stilwell himself shortly after Roosevelt's recall of Vinegar Joe from China on Chiang Kai-shek's categorical demand.[20] *Life* and *Time* magazines, published by Chiang Kai-shek's friend Henry Luce, and the pro-Chinese Nationalist China Lobby in the United States tried to counter the stream of negative characterization of Chiang, but to no avail.[21]

The general public's attitude toward Chiang Kai-shek began to change with the beginning of the Cold War and the start of the final civil war in China between the Communists and the Nationalists in 1946. The menace posed by the Soviet Union and Mao Zedong made many Americans view Chiang as an ally in the global fight against an old foe: World Communism. However, the shift was temporary. As soon as Chiang began to lose the new war the American public reverted to the negative image of him as a loser and a corrupt dictator. This attitude was reinforced by documentary accounts, especially by the anti–Chiang Kai-shek *Stilwell Papers* (1948), the so-called *China White Paper* (a massive collection of US State Department documents, 1949), and the best-selling memoirs of Graham Peck, an official of the US Office of War Information (1950).[22]

After the failure of Truman's special representative George C. Marshall to carry out his mission in China (late 1945–early 1947), Truman and his administration also lost confidence in Chiang. That mission had been aimed at forestalling a Chinese Civil War and helping Chiang Kai-shek unite and democratize his country. In the aftermath of the collapse of the Marshall mission in the spring of 1947, Truman withdrew most US forces from North China, although he continued to render financial assistance when pressured by a Republican-dominated Congress. The US Marines' withdrawal from Jiaozhou Bay near Qingdao marked the final step in the American departure from China.

The negative portrayal of Generalissimo Chiang Kai-shek became a conventional theme in Western historiography. In the early 1970s the well-known American scholar Lloyd Eastman even branded Chiang a fascist;[23] the label was reflected in college textbooks.[24] This negative view of Chiang has been shared by most of his biographers, including the British journalist Jonathan Fenby, who published a major book in 2003.[25] At the same time, however, in the early 2000s the conventional negative view of Chiang began to fade. The same year Fenby published his book, the British historian Hans J. van de Ven, in *War and Nationalism in China 1925–1945,* challenged what he called "the Stilwell–White paradigm."[26] He demonstrated that Chiang Kai-shek was not an incompetent military leader and criticized instead Allied strategy in East and Southeast Asia.[27]

The declassification in late March 2006 of Chiang Kai-shek's personal diaries from 1917 to 1923 and from 1925 to 1931,[28] preserved in the Hoover Institution Archives at Stanford University, laid a new foundation for the reappraisal of Chiang.[29] Then, in April 2007 the diaries from 1932 to 1945 were opened, and in July 2008 the public was given access to the diaries from 1946 to 1955. Finally, the remaining diaries from 1956 to 1972 were declassified in July 2009.[30]

The entire set of diaries encompassing a period from 1917 to 1923 and from 1925 to July 21, 1972, was transferred to the Hoover Institution Archives from Taiwan through Canada by Chiang's elder son Chiang Ching-kuo's daughter-in-law Elizabeth Chiang Fang Chih-yi. She inherited them from her late husband, the youngest son of Ching-kuo, Eddie Chiang, who in turn had received them from his father. Worrying that the diaries could fall into the hands of the anti–Chiang Kai-shek Democratic Progressive Party (DPP) that came to power in Taiwan in 2000, Chiang Fang decided to deposit them in the Hoover Institution Archives for fifty years or until "a permanent repository is found on the territory of China."[31]

Drawing on most of these diaries as well as on many other documents, in 2009 Jay Taylor, a former China desk officer in the US State Department, continued to reverse the negative perspective on Chiang Kai-shek in his *The Generalissimo: Chiang Kai-shek and the Struggle for Modern China.*[32] However, in his zeal to correct the record he went too far in trying to overturn almost all criticism previous scholars have levied against Chiang.[33] In addition, Taylor lacked full access to the unique documentary collections of the massive Russian archives, which did not allow him to assess correctly the enormously important role that Stalin and the Soviet Union played in China and in the rise and fall of Chiang Kai-shek on the mainland.

How should one draw up a balance sheet on Chiang? The answer can hardly be unidimensional. On the one hand, Chiang was a perfidious and cunning ruler who thirsted after unlimited power and was responsible for the deaths of more than 1.5 million innocent people. On the other hand, he was a great revolutionary, a fighter for the national liberation of his innocent people, a patriot, a leading political and military figure of the twentieth century, the architect of a new, republican China, a hero of the Second World War, and a faithful ally of the countries of the anti-Hitler coalition. He was simultaneously a Christian and a Confucian and dreamed of universal equality. Moreover, unlike many other cruel rulers of the past century, such as Stalin and Mao Zedong, in the last phase of his life (1949–75) he was able to draw conclusions from the tragic mistakes of the past. After suffering defeat in the civil war, he ultimately contributed substantially to the transformation of the island of Taiwan—even though small compared to the country of China—into a flourishing state, based on the principles of the people's livelihood and social justice. To be sure, he did this through authoritarian means, but how else could one overcome the socioeconomic backwardness of the Chinese people? Is there a bloodless path from totalitarianism to democracy?

It is always difficult to overcome stereotypes, and it is particularly difficult in the case of Chiang Kai-shek. His figure is too contradictory and multifaceted. Some consider Chiang to be a fervent reactionary and even a fascist; others are convinced that he was a progressive; still others see him as a neo-Confucian; and there are those who view him as a radical revolutionary. Some deem him a Utopian; others a pragmatist. Even the Chinese Communist historians are not united in their view of this immensely important historical figure, whose significance in modern Chinese history is equal to that of his major rival Mao Zedong.

Explaining the phenomenon of Chiang Kai-shek has only now become possible after many archival documents shedding light on his life, his activity, his relations with his relatives, friends, and enemies were declassified. In addition to the Hoover Institution Archives, these documents are preserved in the Archives of Academia Historica in Taiwan, the Central Party Archives of the Guomindang, the Second Historical Archives of China in Nanjing, the Russian State Archives of Social and Political History (RGASPI, the former Central Party Archives of the Institute of Marxism-Leninism of the Central Committee of the Communist Party of the Soviet Union), the Archives of Foreign Policy of the Russian Federation (AVPR), Russian State Archives of Contemporary History (RGANI), the former Archives of the Central Committee of the Communist Party of the Soviet Union (CPSU), the National Archives of the United States, the Reading Room of the Central Intelligence Agency of the United States, the Archives of Columbia University, Oberlin College Archives, Regional Oral History Office of the Bancroft Library of the

University of California, Berkeley, the presidential libraries and museums of Franklin D. Roosevelt, Harry S. Truman, Dwight D. Eisenhower, John F. Kennedy, Lyndon B. Johnson, and Richard M. Nixon. Parts of these materials have been recently published.

Among these archival documents Chiang Kai-shek's diaries still occupy a special place. Besides the original copies housed in the Hoover Institution Archives, which I used, Chiang's diaries repose partly (1919–30 and 1934) in copies made by Chiang's secretary Mao Sicheng in the Second Historical Archives of China in Nanjing.[34] However, they are not accessible to outsiders, especially not to foreign scholars. Only a tiny group of Chinese historians enjoy privileged access.[35] In addition, photocopies of the diaries are preserved in the Taiwan Academia Historica and the Central Party Archives of the Guomindang in Taipei, and digital copies of Chiang Kai-shek's diaries circulate freely among Chinese scholars.

I also used a considerable number of documents from the unique two-volume personal file of Chiang Kai-shek as well as from the personal files of his last wife, Song Meiling, his sons, his relatives, his associates and adversaries, which are held in the Russian archives. They are also enormously significant. Equally important are numerous Russian diplomatic papers. It is this documentary material that sheds new light on Chiang Kai-shek's rise to power in the middle of the 1920s and on the principal role played by the Russians and the Comintern in this process as well as in his subsequent political career and in the Chinese revolutionary movement as a whole. Furthermore, there are numerous documents from the archives of Chiang Kai-shek and his son Chiang Ching-kuo collected in the Archives of the Taiwan Academia Historica. It is precisely from these unique materials that this biography of Chiang Kai-shek is mainly composed.

I hope this book will help readers find a proper and objective place for Chiang Kai-shek in their understanding of the history of modern China and twentieth-century world history.

PART ONE

# *"Firm as a Rock"*

CHAPTER 1

# *Descendant of Zhou Gong*

Outside the window the first light of dawn was barely showing when Wang Caiyu, the twenty-two-year-old pregnant wife of the honorable Jiang Suan, the proprietor of a salt shop in the village of Xikou (Jikou in the local dialect) in East China, began to feel contractions. So began the morning of the fifteenth day of the ninth month of the Year of the Pig on the lunar calendar. That date corresponded to the thirteenth year of the reign of the Guangxu emperor of the Manchu Qing dynasty that had ruled All-under-Heaven since 1644. According to the Gregorian calendar the date was October 31, 1887.

Suan's father immediately ordered all the family members to go at once into the courtyard; no one should be present during a birth. Moreover, he commanded Suan to seal his lips. The father of the future child should not say a single word during the birth because his words might attract the attention of evil spirits. Then he firmly shut the doors of the bedroom on the second floor of the salt shop where his daughter-in-law lay on a large, dark-red bed under a carved canopy and sent a shop assistant to fetch the midwife, the wife of his distant relative who lived not far off.

Grabbing a lighted lantern, the servant dashed headlong out of the house and soon returned with the panting midwife. Approaching the birthing mother, the midwife first lit a thick candle and then laid out around the bed all the necessary talismans: an opened umbrella, a mirror, Buddhist sutras, and the canonical Confucian texts. On a small table in front of the bed she placed a statue of the Bodhisattva Guan Yin, the protectress of birthing mothers. All around the room paper figures were hung to subdue all sorts of evil spirits.

At midday, during the Hour of the Horse, Wang gave birth to her baby.[1] The midwife showed her the crying infant. It was a boy, and the happy Wang smiled. The birth of a son was always a special event for Chinese. A male continued the family line. Her forty-five-year-old husband already had both a son and a daughter from his first, deceased wife, but this was Wang's first baby. Entering the bedroom, grandfather proudly took his grandson in his arms and announced, "Let his first, child name be Ruiyuan" (Auspicious Beginning).

Grandfather was following the tradition of his clan—the extended group of near and distant relatives that traced their descent from a common ancestor. His clan was named the Wuling Jiangs, that is, the Jiangs from the village of Xikou at the foot of Wuling Mountain, about 110 miles south of Shanghai in Fenghua county, Zhejiang province. These Jiangs believed that all the children in the Ruiyuan generation—the twenty-eighth generation starting from the clan's settlement in Wuling—should have the Chinese character "rui" (auspicious) in their names. Suan's daughter from his first marriage, who had been born in 1874, already bore the name Ruichun (Auspicious Spring); the elder son, born three years later, was Ruisheng (Auspicious Birth).

Bo Lin, the third son of Zhou Gong, the great ruler of Ancient China in the twelfth or eleventh century BCE, was considered the ancestor of the Wuling Jiangs. The great Confucius himself (551–479 BCE) saw Zhou Gong as an exemplar of virtue.[2] Zhou Gong's son, Bo Lin, received from his father the small principality of Jiang in the southeast of what is now the northern Chinese province of Henan, but after almost 600 years, in 617 BCE, it was swallowed up by the mighty southern state of Chu. Many of Bo Lin's descendants resettled in the west, in Shanxi province; others in the east, in Shandong. And all of them adopted the clan name of Jiang to commemorate their lost homeland. In the thirteenth century, during the Mongol invasion, one of the branches of the eastern Jiangs resettled in the valleys of Fenghua county in Zhejiang province, and in the seventeenth century, when the Manchus attacked, some of them moved into the depths of the county, to the eastern spurs of the Wuling mountains. There they settled in the village of Xikou, or "mouth of the river," on the right bank of the narrow, shallow stream called the Shanxi. In this village, along the single street of Wuling that ran from east to west for about a mile, members of three other clans—the Zhangs, Rens, and Songs—also lived. But the Jiangs constituted the majority, and the chiefs of their clan headed the temple where all four clans worshipped and where, starting in 1790, solemn ceremonies were conducted before the altars of the ancestors.

A child's name, or "milk name," was seen as unofficial and temporary, although sometimes it took hold, usually for girls in wealthy or educated families who were given names. In others they were simply given numbers: the first, second, etc. sister or first, second, etc. daughter. Jiang Suan's family was well-to-do, so all of his daughters would bear their child names throughout their lives. But a boy had to receive another, grown-up name that corresponded with the demands of the genealogical chronology of the clan. Such chronicles were maintained in all Chinese clans, where scribes kept records of the births and deaths of relatives as well as recorded other events connected with the activities of their fellow clan members. In every chronicle from the very beginning each generation of males was assigned its own Chinese character that had to be used in their names. The chronicle of the Jiangs from Wuling dated from 1691, and it had long since been determined that the generation of the boy Ruiyuan and his brothers would have to use the clan character *zhou* (round, full, complete). The older brother of Ruiyuan already bore the clan name Zhoukang (Complete Health).

Grandfather and father invited the local Daoist fortune-teller to their home, and he initially put the clan character with the character *jian,* which is a synonym for the character *kang* (healthy), but then, after scrutinizing the disposition of the stars, advised them to use the character *tai* (peaceful, great) in the boy's name. The result was lovely: Zhoutai (Completely Peaceful or Boundlessly Great).

In August 1903, at the age of fifteen, this boy would set off for the great port of Ningbo, some twenty-five miles from his village. There he would take the exams for the first scholarly stage *xiucai* (literally, "flourishing talent"), without which one could not even dream of occupying an official position. Before his journey he took a new name for himself that expressed his noble intentions: Zhiqing (Striving to be Honest). In 1912, by then already a well-known revolutionary, he would take yet another grandiose name, one that should be used for special ceremonial occasions: Jieshi (Firm as a Rock). He borrowed the Chinese characters "jie" and "shi" from an ancient Chinese classic—the *Yijing* (The Book of Changes), a collection of divination hexagrams and trigrams—different combinations of straight and broken lines symbolizing the various combinations of the forces of light and darkness (that is, *yang* and *yin*) used in the Zhou era (1121 or 1066–221 BCE). The commentary on the second line of the sixteenth hexagram of this book reads, *Liu er, jie yu shi, bu zhong ri, zhen ji.* ("The second SIX, divided, shows one who is firm as a rock. [He sees a thing] without waiting till it has come to pass; with his firm correctness there will be good fortune").[3] He wrote his first article under the name Jiang Jieshi in the journal *Junsheng* (Voice of the Army), which had recently begun publication. In the Cantonese dialect Jiang Jieshi sounds like Chiang Kai-shek, and that is how Jiang began to be called by that name from early 1918, when he arrived in the south at a time when the Chinese national liberation movement was developing.

Not long before this southern period, in 1917, he chose yet another name for himself that he came to like more than the others: Zhongzheng (Central and Correct). He also took this from the *Yijing* commentary on the second line of the sixteenth hexagram: '*Bu zhong ri, zhen ji', yi zhong zheng ye.* ("[He sees a thing] without waiting till it has come to pass; with his firm correctness there will be good fortune: this is shown by the central and correct position [of the line].")[4]

But this would come later; meanwhile, the Suan family continued to carry out the traditional ceremonies. The parents of the birth mother, who lived in a neighboring district beyond Xuedou Mountain and some fifteen miles from Xikou, were sent a rooster to announce the birth of their grandson. (If a granddaughter had been born, they would have been sent a hen.) The child himself was laid for several hours on a dog's litter so that he would be "healthy as a dog," and his lips were moistened with meat bouillon so he would be rich and happy. The child appeared to be healthy, and the fact that he had been born in the Year of the Pig promised a good future. As a rule, persons born in that year were generally honest and sincere, firm in their convictions and unafraid of difficulties. The mother, to be sure, had no milk at all, but Suan hired a wet nurse.[5]

Suan's family was one of the most respected in the village. It owned more than thirty *mu* of rice fields (about five acres), bamboo groves, and a number of tea bushes. Both Suan and his elder brother were considered to be rather well educated, although they had been unable to pass the exam in the competition for the *xiucai* degree. Suan leased a parcel of land and kept a salt shop which, in addition to salt, traded in wine and lime. Both salt and wine were state monopolies, but the Jiang family, making use of *guanxi* (connections) with higher-ups in the county, were able to acquire a license. The Jiangs' shop was always crowded; many people came not to make purchases but to seek advice on how to settle disputes or simply to listen to the conversation of intelligent persons.[6]

The family lived on the second floor, above the shop, which was in a courtyard planted with bamboo and jasmine. All around, as far as the eye could see, were mountains and hills covered with evergreen trees and bushes. On the bank of the river women occasionally washed clothes, and men with harpoons speared fish in the shallow water. Peace and quiet reigned. Not by chance the great Tang dynasty poet Li Bai (701–62) while, visiting these places, compared the softly babbling Shanxi to "a beautiful and shy maiden." His brilliant contemporary Du Fu (712–70) wrote, "The Shanxi contains a special beauty; I cannot forget it no matter how hard I try."[7] Not far off in the mountains was a Buddhist nunnery, Jinzhu (Golden Bamboo), and a Buddhist temple, Xuedou (Grotto in the Snow), in which a statue of a smiling Buddha Maitreya towered. (It was said that in his earthly existence Maitreya was a monk from the Fenghua district.)[8]

Chiang Kai-shek's father, Jiang Suan (a possible translation: Jiang Respectful and Devoted to Buddha; clan name, Jiang Zhaocong—Jiang Novice Sage), was born on November 10, 1842, and prior to his marriage with Wang Caiyu (Wang Colored Jade) had been married twice. His first wife, née Xu, had died, leaving him, as noted, with two children. The second, née Sun, died after less than two years of marriage. She had no children. The unfortunate Suan wanted to remain a widower, but he married again at his father's bidding. This time he was lucky. His father found him a wife who was spirited and strong. A geomancer compared the horoscopes of the two young ones, and they were surprisingly compatible. Moreover, Suan's new wife was a beauty. When Suan removed the red veil from her face before the first wedding night and looked at her for the first time, he could not restrain his delight.[9] His wife's beauty exceeded all his expectations.[10]

Despite her youth (she was born on December 17, 1864, and was just twenty-one), Wang was already a widow. After the death of her first husband, she secluded herself for a time in the Golden Bamboo nunnery, but soon another match was arranged for her. Thus, a nun's life did not suit her. She was hardworking, unaccustomed to luxury, and preferred home-spun, coarse clothing to silk robes. She was a willful woman, endowed with a sharp mind and great vitality, and she was also an excellent homemaker who knew how to weave linen and prepare tasty dishes of fish, pork, and poultry, although she herself was a vegetarian. She was skilled at pickling bamboo shoots—this delicacy was a favorite food of Chiang Kai-shek throughout his life. Chiang also loved a famous Zhejiang soup made from yellow croaker (a small fish somewhat like a perch), taro roots (which taste like potatoes and were boiled in chicken bouillon), and fatty pork cooked with pickled herbs *meigancai* (Chinese mustard).[11]

Several months after Chiang's birth, the family moved from the second floor over the salt shop to a new seven-room house built nearby in the traditional *sanheyuan* Chinese style of three buildings along three sides of a rectangular courtyard. The members of the household called it Suju (Simple Dwelling). Here is where Chiang spent his childhood. Here, too, his younger sisters and brother were born: on June 7, 1890, his sister Ruilian (Auspicious Lotus), in 1892 his sister Ruiju (Auspicious Chrysanthemum), and on October 26, 1894, his brother Ruiqing (Auspicious Youth). Unfortunately, Ruiju died when she was just a few months old.

As a child, Chiang was often sick, but when he felt well he happily ran around the village with the neighborhood boys, fought with them, played at war, swam in the Shanxi, climbed the surrounding hills, and lit bonfires. He was up to such mischief that people in the village called him Ruiyuan the Bandit.[12] "I might have drowned at any moment, and my body was always covered with burns and cuts," he recalled. Contemporary doctors would probably have diagnosed him with attention deficit hyperactivity disorder, but at the time in China no one had any understanding of such an illness. The father sat in his shop from morning till evening and had no time to spend with his son, but grandfather and especially his mother took care of him. "My grandfather always looked after me [when I was sick]. He was constantly at my bedside. . . . [And] my poor mother worried about me twice as much as other mothers about their children. . . . She loved me as if I had always remained an infant in arms," Chiang wrote.[13]

Grandfather, however, died of pneumonia when Chiang was seven years old. Chiang grieved for him greatly, cried inconsolably and was in mourning for two months. But soon new trials began. Several months later, on August 24, 1895, his father, who was only about fifty-four years old, suddenly died, and a year later, in 1896, Chiang's half brother, the twenty-year-old Ruisheng, who was now the eldest male in the family, demanded a division of the property. Chiang's mother was shocked. She had always treated him as her son even though Ruisheng had grown up in the family of his uncle, his father's elder brother, who had no sons. Even more galling was that Suan, before his death, had demanded that Ruisheng swear to take care of his stepmother and his half brothers and sister. (Chiang was nine years old, his sister was six, and Ruiqing was only two.) With tears in his eyes, Ruisheng took the oath, but he did not keep his word. Evidently, the Confucian concept of *xiao* (filial piety) was not among his virtues. He took the larger part of the property, including the shop and half of the house, its eastern wing. The other half, the western wing, in accordance with Chinese tradition, was formally divided between Suan's two other male heirs—Chiang and the infant Ruiqing; Chiang's half was named the House of Feng and Ruiqing's half the House of Gao, according to the names of two early capitals of the Zhou dynasty: Fengjing and Gaojing, located in Shaanxi province on opposite banks of the Fengshui River. Then the entire western wing began to be called the House of Fenggao.[14]

This house still stands in the village of Xikou on the bank of the Shanxi: a small, three-room, two-story wing under a curved bamboo roof with a long, open balcony wrapping around the entire second floor. Pines and cinnamon trees grew inside the courtyard.[15] Here Chiang passed his orphaned adolescence filled, in his words, with hardships and humiliations.

His mother retained a parcel of twenty *mu* from his father that she rented out. In addition, she herself worked a lot, mostly weaving linen. A bamboo grove in the mountains that also passed to her after Suan's death also yielded a small income. But she was a widow and had no *guanxi* (connections). There was no one to defend her, and therefore both she and her children were slighted by relatives and acquaintances alike. "After father died and my elder brother refused to take care of the family, everyone cheated us, and my mother quietly suffered, enduring trials and tribulations," Chiang wrote bitterly. "Often we had to pay taxes that we were not obligated to pay, and undertake public duties that we were not obligated to undertake," he continued. "To our distress none of our relatives helped us. . . . It is impossible to describe the terrible situation in which our family found itself at the time."[16] Once there was a bad harvest in the region, and two of the renters refused to pay their rent to the defenseless Mama Wang, while others demanded that she lower the rent. The unfortunate widow had to cut back on her expenditures.[17]

Being a poor orphan inevitably shaped the character of the future revolutionary. Chiang grew up as a high-strung, proud child. From very early on he began to display the instincts of a leader. He wanted to show those around him that he was better than and superior to everyone else. In children's games he always strived, with the aid of his fists, to assert his role as commander, thereby compensating for his lower social status.[18] He also liked to give speeches to his peers, actively gesticulating and acting out. Not infrequently he had severe mood swings from unrestrained exuberance to hysterical sobbing, from ambitious dreams to deep depression and self-reproach.[19] Thanks solely to the firm character of Mama Wang, who dedicated herself to the goal of making a man out of her son, Chiang was able to receive a suitable education. To the end of his life he would recall that he was indebted to his mother for everything he achieved in his youth.

In 1898 one more misfortune happened in the family: Chiang's brother Ruiqing died when he was four years old. The death of her younger son was a particularly heavy blow for his mother. She loved the littlest one most of all her children. "He was the most beautiful of us," Chiang Kai-shek recalled. "My mother bitterly mourned his death, and suffered greatly, both morally and physically."[20] After the death of Ruiqing, whom she had adored, she focused all of her love on Chiang.[21]

Chiang started school early, before he had turned six. According to him, this was his mother's decision. She was very anxious lest the restless boy come to a bad end, either by drowning or breaking his neck. Her apprehensions were well-founded. At the age of three Chiang stuck a chopstick deep down his throat. He wanted to know how far down it would go. The family had to call a doctor to save the child, who was beginning to choke. Two years later Chiang, observing a layer of ice on a large barrel of water that was outside in the cold, was unable to stay at the edge and fell under the ice. Only with great effort did he manage to get out.[22] It is no surprise that his mother, despite being a devout Buddhist, frequently resorted to taking a rod in her hands, as Chiang himself later acknowledged, so as not to "let the child get spoiled."[23]

The first educational institution to which his grandfather led the five-year-old Chiang was a private village school, where he learned to read and write. When still just a youngster, under the command of strict teachers he began to study the Confucian "Four Books" (*si shu*): *Da xue* (The Great Learning), *Zhong yong* (The Doctrine of the Mean), *Lun yu* (Analects), and *Mengzi* (Mencius). Later, he studied such canonical classics as *Li Ji* (Book of Rites), *Xiao jing* (The Classic of Filial Piety), *Chunqiu* (Spring and Autumn Annals), *Zuozhuan* (Commentary on the "Spring and Autumn Annals") and *Gu wen ci lei zuan* (Compilation of Ancient Texts).[24] These books not only cultivated the moral-ethical norms of Confucianism in him, but also taught him to express his thoughts correctly and in a literate manner. At the age of ten he wrote his first essay in classical style, dedicated to his deceased younger brother.[25]

Both his mother and his teacher, using words and the rod, instilled a love of learning and work into Chiang. In addition to studying the Confucian texts, written in the difficult ancient Chinese language *wenyan,* and reading Buddhist sutras that taught goodness, love, and respect for elders, the young Chiang helped his mother a lot around the house. "When I was a little boy," he said many years later, "I was required by my parents and teachers to do many tasks such as sweeping and mopping the floor, cooking rice and preparing food in general, and even washing dishes. If I carelessly dropped a few grains of rice, or failed to fasten my clothing properly, I was severely taken to task."[26]

In 1899, at the age of twelve, Chiang continued his studies at a school located in his maternal grandmother's house. For the first time he was separated from his mother for several months and felt this keenly. It is said that when he returned home during the summer holidays he burst into tears on seeing his beloved mother and was inconsolable. When the time came for him to return to school, he again began crying so loudly that the neighbors rushed to see what the noise was about. Everyone tried to calm him down, but he continued to sob even when he was miles from home.[27] It's not that Chiang had a difficult time at his grandmother's: she loved him very much, but his love, compassion, and gratitude toward his mother, who essentially had devoted her whole life to him, overpowered him.[28]

At his grandmother's school he began to write not only short prose essays but also verses. He did not become a poet—in his whole life Chiang wrote no more than ten short poems—but his teacher liked this first effort at versification so much that for a long time he excitedly kept lavishing praise on Chiang. Frankly, the verses he wrote hardly sparkle with brilliance. Here they are:

> I see: on the mountain
> Bamboo growing everywhere,
> On summer days it brings us
> Cool and shade.[29]

Not daring to say no to his mother, in 1901, when he was barely fourteen years old, at his mother's command Chiang entered into a marriage with Mao Fumei, a nineteen-year-old girl from a neighboring village who was born on November 9, 1882. The bride's father, like Chiang's father, was engaged in commerce, not salt and wine but rice and other products. That the bride was five years older than the groom satisfied Chiang's mother, who needed a capable helper around the house.[30] Mama Wang didn't even consider whether her son liked his bride. At that time, weddings in China were arranged by parents, and love marriages were unheard of.

But unlike his father, after the wedding celebrations, when Chiang was alone with his wife and removed the red veil from her face, he was by no means ecstatic. "I have never seen my wife's face before the wedding ceremony, and after marriage we did not get on well together," he said subsequently.[31] The bride's name meant Happy Plum Blossom, but she was deeply unhappy in her marriage to Chiang. He did not develop affectionate feelings toward her even though Fumei was far from plain-looking. She had full lips, a sweet, oval face, and a large, splendid bosom. Chiang, however, did not live with her, and soon after the wedding he returned to his studies, this time in the village school of his wife's native village. Fumei, along with a servant woman, went to live with his mother.

Chiang's new teacher was a distant relative of his wife—twenty-nine-year-old Mao Sicheng—whom Chiang would take on as his secretary in the mid-1920s. In 1936, by which time Chiang was already the national leader, Mao Sicheng wrote the best book about the first thirty-nine years of the Generalissimo: a twenty-volume chronological biography. In it he included reminiscences of his pupil that provide impressions of his character: "He considered class a stage and his fellow students marionettes. He was wild and unrestrainable. But when he was answering at the board, reading, or clenching a writing brush in his hand and thinking over his answer, even thousands of voices around could not distract him from his profound concentration. He alternated between moments of calm and outbursts, sometimes in the course of several minutes. One might think there were two different persons. I found him very intriguing."[32]

Evidently, Chiang Kai-shek's character did not change much despite his study of Confucianism and Buddhism. Chiang remained just as unbalanced as before. "He was incapable of responding normally and in due proportion to a wide range of emotional situations," one of his biographers wrote: "But he could be challenged and fulfilled when confronted with a crisis, for under such circumstances he was able not only to summon up the best qualities in himself, but also to derive maximal psychological satisfaction therefrom. He would feel more 'normal' or creative in situations that required leadership and authority, that called for heroic deeds, and that offered suitable opportunities for the projection of his anxieties and suspicion, fear and hostility."[33] With the help of Mao Sicheng he studied the *Yijing* (Book of Changes) and wrote philosophical-historical essays in classical style. He prepared for the *xiucai* examinations that were supposed to be held in Ningbo in August 1903. But to his excruciating disappointment he failed the exams. This setback made a profound impression on the proud, high-strung adolescent who had just turned fifteen, especially since his elder brother, with whom he likely had a complicated relationship, passed the examinations and received the desired degree. Most of all, Chiang was indignant at his "cruel and contemptuous treatment by the members of the commission."[34]

Chiang shut himself up and began to study even more persistently. But he did not get a second chance to take the examinations: in the course of the imperial educational reforms that were taking place at the time, the examinations were abolished. He then transferred to another, recently opened school in the district town of Fenghua that taught not only the classics but also several contemporary subjects, including arithmetic and English. His mother was against this move: she wanted him to pursue a career in commerce, but Chiang insisted. His wife went with him; he didn't want her to, but his mother demanded it.

An ancient trading center founded four thousand years ago, Fenghua had become a district seat as far back as the Tang dynasty in 738. The town was surrounded by an impressive medieval wall with iron gates that were locked at night. The streets were crowded, and sometimes one might even encounter "hairy foreign devils" as the Chinese called foreigners. These were missionaries: the first white people Chiang had ever seen.[35]

Chiang spent two years in this school and again displayed his tempestuous character by quarreling with the administration. In the spring of 1905 he and his wife moved to Ningbo, where he registered in a new, recently opened school named Golden Arrow. It had been founded by a certain Gu Qinglian, a well-educated man and graduate of the Yokohama Pedagogical Institute who had recently returned from Japan. Even though his beloved mother paid for his substantial registration fee at Golden Arrow, it would be difficult to accuse Chiang of squandering her money. This school and the exceptionally talented teacher Gu played an important role in his life. From the venerable Gu Qinglian the seventeen-year-old Chiang first heard of the need for a national revolution in China, which was under the yoke of the Manchu conquerors. Gu told him about the foremost leader of the national revolutionary movement, Sun Yat-sen.[36] He was living in Tokyo under the name Nakayama Kiroki (in Chinese this name sounds like Zhongshan Qiao).[37]

With surprise and delight Chiang listened to the inspirational stories told by his teacher about this unusual man, who was also known by the name Sun Wen (Sun the Civilized). Yat-sen (Recluse) was the sobriquet Sun used on the advice of his Christian Chinese teacher when, in 1883 or 1884, as a pupil in middle school in Hong Kong he was baptized by an American Congregationalist, Charles Robert Hager.[38]

Sun was a native of the southern province of Guangdong, where the Cantonese dialect was spoken, and therefore his sobriquet was pronounced

"Yat-sen." (The standard Chinese pronunciation was Yixian.) He was born on November 12, 1866, in a poor family in the village of Cuiheng, not far from the Portuguese colony of Macao. His mother and he moved when he was thirteen to the Hawaiian Islands—then the Kingdom of Hawaii—where his elder brother, a businessman, was living. He went to school in Hawaii, Canton, and Hong Kong. In 1892 he graduated from Hong Kong Medical College and worked in Macao and Canton, but after two years he left China again and returned to Hawaii. There, in November 1894, in Honolulu, he founded the first Chinese revolutionary society, the Xingzhonghui (Revive China Society), comprised of Chinese emigrants.[39]

Sun Yat-sen called for the revolutionary reconstruction of China's sociopolitical system according to republican principles. In the fall of 1895 members of the Society organized the first anti-Manchu uprising in Canton; it ended in defeat. Afterward, the Manchu authorities offered a substantial award for Sun Yat-sen's head. In October 1896, when Sun was in London, he was kidnapped by officials in the Chinese embassy who intended to transport him secretly to China. A wave of protest that arose in the English press compelled the unlucky kidnappers to release him after twelve days. This unsuccessful kidnapping merely increased Sun's popularity among Western liberals and the nationalistically inclined Chinese public, especially Chinese emigrants.[40]

The London episode made a strong impression on Chiang Kai-shek. As did two books that Chiang read on the recommendation of his teacher: a work by his fellow Zhejiang provincial Huang Zongxi (1610–95) (*Anticipating Dawn*) that condemned autocracy, and a collection of quotations, *Instructions for a Practical Life*, by the famous Confucian philosopher Wang Yangming (1472–1529), one of a small number of Chinese thinkers who placed personality at the forefront of his philosophical concepts.

Under the influence of what he had read and heard from his teacher, Chiang came to the conclusion that "we [young Chinese intellectuals] must, first of all, advance the great idea of our nation and define the principles of revolutionary ideology. Second, clearly formulate our conscious moral principles. . . . [And], third, become suffused with the spirit of our democratic ideas."[41]

From his teacher Chiang also learned about the enormous role of the military factor in the future Chinese revolution. Gu taught him the fundamentals of Chinese military strategy and tactics, elucidating the works of the famous military strategists Sun Zi (545–470 BCE) and Zeng Guofan (1811–72). And Gu advised Chiang to study abroad as soon as possible.[42] "As a result that year [1905] I decided to travel abroad," Chiang Kai-shek wrote in his diaries.[43]

Gu spoke a lot about his life in Japan, which in 1905 had shown the whole world that an Asian country, having cast off the yoke of absolutism and entered upon the path of modernization, could inflict defeat on a strong European power: tsarist Russia, which was caught in the grip of an absolute monarchy. At that time, September 5, 1905, the Russo–Japanese War ended. It was a war in which the Japanese fought brilliantly and defeated the Russians over Chinese concessions in Manchuria.

Like Fenghua, Ningbo, one of the largest cities of Zhejiang, had a four-thousand-year-old history. It flowered during the Tang dynasty (618–907) and continued to develop thereafter. In the center of the city Confucian, Buddhist, and Daoist temples towered under curved brick roofs, glittering in the sun. Alongside were the palaces of the Chinese aristocracy; the poor took shelter in the narrow alleys and on junks that jammed the local canals. Overall, Ningbo resembled "a labyrinth of narrow, crooked, overcrowded streets. Here and there a bridge connected one teeming section with another. The air had a fishy smell, for Ningbo is famous for the salted and dried fish it sends to all parts of east-central China."[44]

In 1905 Ningbo looked like a typical colonial port. On the northern bank of the Yuyao River, which bisected it from west to east, was a small but comfortable foreign quarter with Christian churches, two- and three-story stone houses, fashionable hotels, and expensive restaurants. Rickshaws dashed about on the wide streets, and ships from many countries unloaded at the noisy, smoky port. British colonialists forced the Qing government to open Ningbo to foreign trade along with four other ports (Canton, Xiamen, Fuzhou, and Shanghai) right after they routed the Manchus during the so-called Opium War of 1839–42. The Qing monarchy signed an unequal treaty by which, in part, it lost control over its own customs revenues, that is, it lost its economic independence. Soon the United States and France signed similar treaties, and then several other countries did as well. After the first Opium War a second one took place (1856–60) between China on one side and England and France on the other, and then a new Sino–French War over Vietnam (1884–85). The Manchus lost both of these wars also. The result was that China turned into a semicolony of the Western powers, which Japan joined in 1895 after routing the Manchus in the 1894–95 war. In September 1901 eight powers compelled the Qing to accept the Final Protocol following their collective intervention in North China aimed at suppressing the uprising of the so-called Boxers (Chinese poor peasants, masters of martial arts whose method of fighting resembled boxing). The Boxers had risen against the "foreign devils" and received support even from Empress Dowager Cixi, who was then ruling China. According to this protocol, over the course of thirty-nine years the Qings were obligated to pay an enormous indemnity of US 670 million gold dollars, including 4 percent annual interest.

At the beginning of the twentieth century China had unequal treaties with a total of eighteen powers, including even Peru, Brazil, and Mexico. Foreign merchants were not obligated to pay the internal tariffs (*lijin*) that Chinese merchants were obliged to pay on crossing provincial borders. Foreigners also had the right to create their own settlements in the ports open to them. In 1860 there were 15 such ports, and by the beginning of the twentieth century as many as 107. On Chinese territory foreigners enjoyed the right of extraterritoriality or consular jurisdiction, meaning they were not subject to Chinese courts.

Chiang Kai-shek did not fail to observe the domination by foreigners, but thoughts of an anti-imperialist revolution had not yet occurred to him. He placed all the blame for China's semicolonial position and its social degradation on the ruling Manchu dynasty, the Qing, that had conquered China in the second half of the seventeenth century. He denounced as well the corrupt Chinese officials and oligarchs who had betrayed the nation. The most prominent oligarchs possessed their own armed forces, that is, they were militarists, and, by employing their political and military power, they not only restrained the initiative of individual private entrepreneurs but also mercilessly fleeced the people. "I decided to go abroad," Chiang wrote in his diaries, "[because] I suffered from the decline of my country and the degradation of the Manchus. Moreover, I experienced orphanhood and the bitter situation of my family, which was deceived and insulted. I very much wanted to rise up and show everyone my own strength."[45]

Here, in Ningbo, Chiang Kai-shek's wife became pregnant, but she was unable to bring the fetus to term.[46] For a long time rumors floated around Xikou that she had either had a miscarriage or that she had given birth to a dead infant after Ruiyuan the Bandit had savagely beaten her because she had dared to contradict him over some matter.[47] Mama Wang, grief-stricken, was unable to come to her senses for a long time, and one of the neighbors heard her shouting at her son, "There are three things which are unfilial, and to have no posterity is the greatest of them."[48]

At the beginning of 1906 Chiang and his wife returned from Ningbo to Fenghua, where he resumed studying English. His teacher was a man named Dong Xianguang, who was of the same age as Chiang and who seven years earlier had graduated from the Anglo–Chinese College in Shanghai. In English he called himself Hollington Tong. Many years later, in October 1937, with Chiang Kai-shek's permission and making considerable use of material from Mao Sicheng, he would publish a two-volume English biography of Chiang. He remembered certain things about his pupil: "He was a serious-minded student . . . an early riser, and, after his matutinal ablutions, it was his custom to stand erect on the veranda in front of his bedroom for half an hour. During this time his lips were compressed, his features were set in determination, and he stood with his arms folded. . . . In fact, it is clear from his own diary that during those few months . . . he was formulating plans to go to Japan to study military science in order the better to equip himself for a career that was to be wholly dedicated to the nation."[49] Evidently, Chiang steeled his will, developing his masculine character and submitting himself to strict discipline. At the same time, he began to take up sports seriously to strengthen his body. Soon, in the first student athletic competitions in Ningbo, he took third prize in running. He spent his free time from studies and sports in the library, greedily consuming newspapers from Shanghai. He wanted to be up-to-date on everything that was happening in the world.[50]

In April 1906 the eighteen-year-old Chiang Kai-shek abandoned school and, full of determination, returned home and announced to his mother his intention to leave soon for Japan and enroll in a military academy. The tales of his teacher Gu and the numerous humiliations Chiang had experienced in his life, his failure in the examinations for a degree, nurtured by his pride, ambition, and his sense of purpose developed by means of his daily exercises—all came together in a conscious desire to join the ranks of revolutionaries in distant Japan who were developing bold plans for a social and political revolution. Moreover, he decided to become a soldier so he could participate more actively in the revolutionary struggle, which, inevitably, would be bloody. "I believed that if I did not go abroad, where I intended to study and to join the revolution, I would have no way out," Chiang recalled. He still knew nothing of Sun Yat-sen's revolutionary theory. In his diaries he wrote, "I understood only that I hated the *tuhao* [bloodsuckers] and the *lieshen* [evil gentry, that is, the greedy rural literati-officials] and that my enemies were evil curs and corrupt bureaucrats who oppressed orphans and widows. I could not [openly] say this in China, therefore, I wanted to leave. I believed that only by going abroad to study would I be able to fortify my strength. And although my relatives firmly opposed this, I decided to persist."[51] Money was required, and, knowing that she could not make her son change his mind, Chiang's mother amassed it. "And subsequently my late mother had to work even more than usual, skimping on everything to be able to send me the wherewithal to study," Chiang gratefully recalled.[52]

Chiang said farewell to his mother, to his unloved wife, to his relatives and acquaintances who had often demeaned him. He set off for Ningbo and then for Shanghai, some 110 miles from his native village. There he embarked on a passenger liner for the Land of the Rising Sun. From Ningbo he sent his mother his queue that he had cut off to let her know that he had set out on a revolutionary path.[53] All Chinese male subjects in the Qing empire wore long queues as a sign of submissiveness to the Manchus. When the inhabitants of his village learned that he had cut off his queue they were horrified. But his mother maintained her composure: she believed in the son she adored and feared nothing.

CHAPTER 2

# *In the Shadow of the Rising Sun*

In Japan, Chiang encountered disappointment. It turned out that neither a military nor any other kind of school—government or private—could accept him since, on March 2, 1905, the Japanese government, per agreement with the Qing, issued a decree (No. 19) prohibiting Chinese without letters of recommendation from the Manchu authorities from studying in the Land of the Rising Sun.[1] The Manchus and the Japanese wanted to secure themselves against the possibility of Chinese revolutionaries showing up in Japanese schools.

To return home ingloriously was out of the question. That would mean a loss of face. So Chiang enrolled in the Qinghua School in the Ushigome district of Tokyo, the only educational institution open to Chinese "from the street." The famous reformer and educator Liang Qichao had founded this school in July 1899 with money from Chinese emigrants. The Qing embassy had also provided financial assistance, which is why the school was named the Qinghua School, meaning the School of Qing China. In essence, the school offered preparatory courses in which the Japanese language was the main subject. One could also take classes in English, chemistry, physics, and mathematics. But Chiang enrolled only in Japanese language classes.[2]

There were many Chinese students in Japan at the time. The Japanese victory in the war with Russia had led many Chinese wishing to copy the Japanese experience in modernization to grow, not by the day but by the hour. In 1901 only 280 Chinese students were studying in the Land of the Rising Sun, but by 1905 there were 8,000 and in 1906 more than 13,000.[3] And despite the strict vetting by the Qing government many students were sympathetic to revolution. It was they who would play "a central role in undermining the dynasty."[4] Chiang Kai-shek soon met with some of them, and these encounters produced the strongest impression. Their militant patriotism inspired the hot-tempered provincial who was striving to perform heroic deeds.

He developed the closest friendship with his fellow Zhejiang provincial Chen Qimei, known also by the name Yingshi (Hero Soldier). Chen was also an orphan who experienced much grief and who arrived in Tokyo shortly after Chiang. But his letters of recommendation were all in order, and he entered the Tokyo Police Academy. He was a stately young man of twenty-nine, businesslike and resolute. Piercing eyes were concealed behind the lenses of his round eyeglasses. Almost ten years older than Chiang, he was able at once to elicit enormous respect from Chiang, who soon began to call him his elder brother. They spent all their free time together, and once, in a moment of spiritual exaltation, having made cuts on their right hands with a knife, they mingled the blood from their wounds and became blood brothers. Such kinship was considered quite natural in China, so Chiang acquired a second family along with a brother. Subsequently, the nephews of Chen Qimei, Guofu and Lifu, became the closest assistants of Uncle Kai-shek.[5]

The Hero Soldier revealed to Chiang that he had recently joined the ranks of Sun Yat-sen's revolutionary party, which Sun had organized in Tokyo a year earlier, on August 20, 1905. Chen said that Sun had named the party Zhongguo geming tongmenghui (Chinese Revolutionary Alliance) and that at the inaugural congress of this organization Sun had been chosen as president. He also related that soon after the founding of the alliance, on November 26, 1905, Sun Yat-sen, in the preface to the first issue of the party organ *Minbao* (The People), presented a radical political program: the so-called Three Principles of the People: Nationalism, Democracy, and People's Livelihood.

Chen explained that the first of these principles (Nationalism) entailed "national liberation for all of China" and "equal rights for all nationalities on the territory of China"; the second (Democracy) meant not only providing the right to vote to everyone, but also of introducing legislative initiative, referendum, and recall of officials; and the third (People's Livelihood) implied "restricting capital," that is, conversion to state property or placing under state control all of the largest and vitally important means of production—land and minerals as well as leading branches of industry—and "equalization of land rights" by means of a land tax based on the value of the land. Sun called his program socialist and sometimes even communist, having in mind that the future Chinese state would not simply be nationalist, but also social, that is, one in which there would be an extensively developed system of people's welfare.

Sun Yat-sen, however, did not envision the destruction of private property, but rather looked toward establishing a democratic state in China based on the collaboration of all classes. Sun's *étatisme* (state-centered system) was a political program aimed at ensuring state dominance in the economy and directed against oligarchic capitalism that created conditions for the exclusive enrichment of the powers that be. The true objective of the Chinese revolutionary was to employ the levers of the state to facilitate the development of a middle class in China. To Sun Yat-sen the state was a controlling and guiding force. That is why a progressive tax on the value of land was meant to play an important role in state economic policy. The introduction of such a tax, from Sun Yat-sen's perspective, might put an end to the monopolistic policy of the oligarchic bureaucratic institutions, thereby facilitating the construction of an ideal "just society" with equal opportunities and "mutual love."[6]

In the tradition of ancient Chinese philosophy familiar to all educated Chinese, Sun called this *datong* (the Grand Union). *Datong* is referred to in the classical work *Li Ji* (Book of Rites), in which Confucius is quoted as saying, "When the Grand course was pursued, a public and common spirit ruled all under the sky; they chose men of talents, virtue, and ability; their words were sincere, and what they cultivated was harmony. . . . [They labored] with their strength, disliking that it should not be exerted, but not exerting it [only] with a view to their own advantage. . . . This was [the period of] what we call the Grand Union [*datong*]."[7] Having quoted *Li Ji,* Sun Yat-sen announced, "All-under-Heaven is for everyone!"

Thus the leader presented a tripartite goal to the revolutionaries: overthrowing the Manchu's Qing dynasty, establishing a republic, and forming a national state with equal opportunities and a mixed economy under the control of state institutions. He believed in a republic with "genuine democracy," one that, unlike Western democracy, would be based not on three but five independent branches: legislative, executive, judicial, examination, and control.[8]

Sun, who frequently traveled around the world fundraising for his party, found himself in Tokyo once more at the end of 1906, and Chen Qimei suggested to Chiang that he meet with him. Chiang agreed enthusiastically. Thus on a day in November or December 1906 by prior arrangement the blood brothers, together with another friend, the Hebei native Zhang Ji—five years older than Chiang Kai-shek and already engaged in important revolutionary work such as editing the paper *The People*—arrived at the apartment of the Japanese revolutionary and philosopher Miyazaki Torazō (Tōten), a close friend of Sun Yat-sen. There the first meeting between Sun Yat-sen and Chiang Kai-shek took place.[9]

There are no documentary records of this meeting, but according to several sources the young native of Zhejiang made a good impression on Sun even though he was unable to give straight answers to any of the questions his interlocutor asked. Mostly he kept silent, feeling overwhelmed by the greatness of the leader. And this is precisely what pleased Sun Yat-sen, who could not tolerate very independent-minded persons. Sun was dictatorial by nature, and he needed people who were ready to do anything to carry out the tasks assigned them. He sensed at once that Chiang was exactly such a person: energetic, resolute, devoted, and dependable. Hearing that Chiang wanted to be a soldier, he enthusiastically supported him. "Study military science well," he advised, "[and] later you will be able to serve the revolution."[10] After the meeting he observed to Chen Qimei, "That man will be the hero of our Revolution: we need just such a man in our revolutionary movement."[11]

At the time, Chiang Kai-shek had just turned nineteen while Sun was forty. The leader of the revolution was just two years younger than Chiang's mother. But unlike Mama Wang, who had aged considerably from hard work, Sun looked younger than his years. He wore a European-style suit, a white shirt, tie, and polished shoes. His short, combed-back hair glistened with brilliantine, and his small mustache bristled handsomely. He was obviously self-confident and at the same time pensive, somehow reminding one of a Protestant pastor. He had a high forehead, and his brown eyes, "very lively and twinkling," look at one attentively. He was some five inches shorter than Chiang (Chiang was five feet seven inches; Sun was five feet two inches), but he had a larger build.[12] His charisma was palpable; he was obviously able to influence people, and Chiang departed from his meeting in a state of considerable excitation.[13]

Chiang lived in the Chinese section of Tokyo, not far from Chen Qimei. He liked Japan. The city and even the Chinese quarter were neat and charming; the streets were clean. Trams ran through the city, there were many automobiles and a countless number of rickshaws, and at night electric lamps lighted many districts. Tokyo was particularly beautiful in the spring, when the Japanese cherry trees (*sakura*) blossomed. Then it seemed as if the city streets were covered with "so much snow. . . . And when the blossoms are scattered over the ground, there is all the effect of a theatrical snowstorm."[14] Chiang kept in mind that the Land of the Rising Sun was no less greedy than European countries and the United States, that it was pillaging his homeland, and that not a few Japanese in Tokyo demonstrated their contempt for Chinese. At the same time, Japanese exhibited a kind of innate, internalized discipline and organizational capacity that impressed Chiang, who, as before, was persistently working on perfecting his character.

In the mornings he pursued his studies in school, then he rested, and in the evenings he dined with his friends in cheap Chinese restaurants while avidly discussing plans for overthrowing the Manchus. He had just one weakness: at night he loved to spend time in the red-light district, where compliant geisha calmed his revolutionary ardor for a few hours.[15]

At the end of 1906 he received a letter from his mother asking him to return home. She informed him that on the twelfth day of the twelfth month of the lunar calendar, that is, January 25, 1907, her daughter Ruilian would be married. "It is a propitious day according to the celestial almanac," she wrote, so the wedding could not be postponed.[16] As the elder brother, Chiang was obligated to be present at the ceremony. He had to leave school. His blood brother accompanied Chiang to the railroad station, where Chiang boarded the train for Nagasaki and from there sailed home.

On the day of the wedding his thickly rouged sixteen-year-old sister, wearing a long red dress—a *qipao* slit to the thigh—looked beautiful. A red veil covered her face. She seemed happy, especially since she had known her groom from childhood. He had previously served as an assistant in father Suan's salt shop. To be sure, he was not very literate, but she did not need an educated husband. They lived in connubial harmony for the next thirty-one years, up to the time of her death. They had two children, a son and a daughter. Chiang's nephew would become a military pilot, and in the late 1940s would die in battle against the communists; his niece moved to Shanghai, where she lived even after Mao Zedong came to power.[17] Her father followed Chiang Kai-shek to Taiwan.[18]

Two and a half weeks after the wedding, in the circle of his family Chiang celebrated the most important holiday in China, the lunar New Year (the Spring holiday), which came on February 13. Several days later, again parting from his mother, sister, and wife, he went off to Hangzhou, the chief city of Zhejiang province. There he intended to take the exams for accelerated six-month courses at one of the best educational institutions in China, the Baoding Academy of the Ministry of War, designed for preparatory students who wished to study in foreign military schools. The academy was not far from Beijing, but exams were held in the capitals of each of the empire's eighteen provinces; in each one for natives of the province. For Zhejiang men who had not previously served in the army, the quota was fourteen places, and there were more than seventy would-be aspirants for each place. Yet Chiang was able to pass the exams successfully and was enrolled.[19] He was very proud. Finally, his dream was coming true.

In the summer of 1907 he arrived in Baoding and began to study hard in his courses, combining lectures and field exercises with drills and physical culture. But he was not always pleased with his studies. Several classes were taught by Japanese instructors who never let slip an opportunity to demonstrate their superiority over the Chinese cadets, not only in a professional sense but also in terms of their nationality. The hot-tempered Chiang could not tolerate this, and once he lashed out at an arrogant Japanese officer who had compared Chinese to microbes. Placing a lump of earth on a table, this Japanese, who was teaching a course on hygiene, contemptuously remarked, "There are 400 million microbes in this lump, as many as there are people in China." Enraged, Chiang ran up to the Japanese and, breaking off a small fragment from the lump, parried, "And 50 million people live in Japan. Are they like 50 million of the microbes in this piece?" The officer, who had "lost face," complained to the leadership, but fortunately for Chiang the head of the academy was a patriot and took no disciplinary measures against him.[20]

After finishing the short-term courses, Chiang could go to Japan again, but this time, as a graduate of the Baoding Academy, he had a letter of recommendation from the Ministry of War. In March 1908 he was back in Tokyo, where he enrolled in the preparatory military school Shinbu Gakko (School for Advancing Military Arts), established by the Chinese government for Chinese cadets. It was located in the Chinese quarter.

At this educational institution courses were not limited to military science. Cadets studied Japanese, history, geography, mathematics, physics, chemistry, biology, and drawing. The programs in Japanese and mathematics were especially intensive.[21] Quite a few Chinese who would later gain glory in their homeland studied there: in 1904–5, Cheng Qian, the future governor of Hunan under Chiang Kai-shek who went over to the communists in August 1949; and in 1909–11, He Yingqin, the future minister of military administration under Chiang Kai-shek. A fellow classmate and close friend of Chiang Kai-shek was Zhang Qun, also a graduate of the Baoding Academy with whom Chiang became acquainted on the ship on his second trip to

Tokyo. In the 1930s he would become minister of foreign affairs in Chiang's government.

Soon after his return to Japan and his reunion with his blood brother, Chiang, in his words, felt that "if I don't join the Revolutionary Alliance, it will prove impossible to achieve my goal."[22] Thus, in 1908, recommended by Chen Qimei, he joined Sun Yat-sen's organization. Two of his other revolutionary friends also vouched for him, and during a secret ceremony he took a solemn oath of allegiance, swearing to be faithful to the Three Principles of the People.[23] Raising his right hand, he pronounced: "We shall expel the barbarians, revive China, establish a republic, and equalize land rights! May I be severely punished should I retreat before reaching this goal!"[24]

At this time Sun and his comrades in arms were organizing one armed uprising in China after another, but for the time being they kept Chiang out of these efforts. "Great hopes were placed upon me as a future warrior, therefore my comrades did not allow me [for now] to take part in military operations," he recalled.[25] In his free time he avidly read revolutionary literature that he discussed with Zhang Qun and other new friends, including Dai Jitao, an amazingly well-educated student who studied law and politics at one of the Japanese universities. His forebears were also from Zhejiang province although he himself had been born in Sichuan. Dai was four years younger than Chiang.

A militant anti-Manchu tract titled *The Revolutionary Army,* written in 1903 by Zou Rong, a Sichuanese, made an enormous impression on Chiang. It called for a violent national revolution in China, the establishment of a parliamentary system, and the introduction of a constitution. For writing this brochure the youthful Zou Rong was sentenced to hard labor that undermined his health. He died at the age of twenty. According to Chiang Kai-shek, he could not calm down for a long time after reading the book, and he even had imaginary conversations with Zou Rong about how to overthrow the Qing dynasty.[26]

Full of revolutionary aspirations, he composed verses that he sent to one of his relatives. The poem was titled "Formulating a Goal":

> A lethal vapor enshrouds the planet,
> We are weak now, with much work to do!
> I must revive our sacred country,
> Why, then, am I living like a baron in Tokyo?[27]

After spending a year in school, in the summer of 1909 Chiang went home for the holidays. But now he no longer stayed at home with his mother even though he still loved her just as much as always. Toward his wife, however, he felt nothing but irritation. Having barely touched down in Xikou, he set off for Shanghai to help Brother Chen Qimei, who had arrived there from Tokyo in late 1908 on assignment from Sun Yat-sen, to make preparations for the next uprising. Together they began to draw up plans to seize power in Shanghai as well as in their native province of Zhejiang, but nothing came of these plans. Chiang intended to return to Japan in August, but suddenly his mother arrived with his unloved wife. She demanded that her son fulfill his conjugal duty, inasmuch as the geomancer had predicted that if Fumei became pregnant that summer, she would give birth to an important official who would bestow glory on the family and the entire country. Chiang refused, but his mother then threatened to drown herself in the turbid waters of the Huangpu River on whose banks Shanghai stood. What could her poor son do? Reluctantly he fulfilled her request, but as soon as he learned that Fumei was pregnant, he sent her home to Xikou while he himself hastened to embark by ship for Tokyo.[28]

Nine months later, on April 27, 1910, on the eighteenth day of the third month of the Year of the Dog on the lunar calendar, Fumei gave birth to a boy, for whom Grandma Wang, with the help of a Daoist fortune-teller, chose two names: a child name Jianfeng, that is, He Who Shall Build the Capital of Feng, and Ching-kuo (Jingguo), He Who Shall Successfully Rule the State.[29] The latter was considered the main name and was chosen largely in accordance with the genealogical chronicle of the clan for the generation of Chiang Kai-shek's son, the twenty-ninth generation, for which the identifying Chinese character was *guo* (state). At his mother' request Chiang Kai-shek agreed to register the infant as the son of his late younger brother Ruiqing, whom his mother had loved so much.[30]

The fortune-teller's prophesy was wholly vindicated. Many years later, after Chiang Kai-shek's death, Chiang Ching-kuo became the president of the Republic of China on Taiwan, where he carried out profound economic and political reforms in the interests of the inhabitants of the island, leading the whole world to speak about the "Taiwan miracle."

Meanwhile, Chiang, after graduating along with his friend Zhang Qun from the preparatory school Shinbu Gakko in November 1910, was assigned to the Nineteenth Field Artillery Company of the Japanese Thirteenth Division. It was quartered in western Honshu in the town of Takada, where he was supposed to get practical training as a junior officer-in-training, a required condition for admission to the Japanese military academy.[31] Actually, Chiang had not done very well on his final exams; he was ranked fifty-fifth of sixty-two graduates, receiving a grade of 68 out of 100, while Zhang Qun graduated third with a grade of 95.[32] But he was accepted into the practical training, which was all that mattered.[33]

The practical training was exhausting; the food was awful (cold rice barely flavored with vegetables), but the main thing was that Chiang, a southerner, suffered terribly from the cold in the winter. He endured the forced marches in the open air through deep snow in freezing temperatures with difficulty. With his rather frail build of 5 feet 7 inches and his weight of 130 pounds, Chiang, despite his daily physical exercises, was completely exhausted by evening.[34] But he did not dare show weakness and submitted himself to an iron discipline. "It will be much harder on the field of battle than now," he said to his comrades. "We need to get used to it so we can endure everything."[35] The spring and early autumn were easier for him, although not much, and in the summer the cadets were sent home. He did not display any special ardor—"There was nothing about him that could attract attention," recalled one of his commanders—but he did everything that was required of him.[36]

But suddenly, on a day in October 1911, when Takada was again covered with snow, Chiang's blood brother sent him a telegram from Shanghai. It conveyed staggering news. On October 10, in Wuchang (in Hubei province in Central China) another anti-Qing uprising had taken place, this time, finally, a successful one. A majority of the rebels were members of the revolutionary Society for Common Progress (*gongjinhui*), which had close ties with the Revolutionary Alliance. The next day Manchu power was overthrown in Hankou and Hanyang, neighboring cities of Wuchang. Thus the three cities of Hankou, Hanyang, and Wuchang, generally known by their collective name, Wuhan, became the epicenter of revolutionary events. The spontaneous event evoked an outpouring of anti-Manchu sentiments in many cities around the country, and Chen Qimei asked Chiang to return to the homeland promptly to take part in the unfolding revolution.

Chiang was shocked. After all, he had just returned to Japan in September after the summer vacation he had spent in Shanghai with Chen, and now suddenly this.[37] Along with Zhang Qun and another Chinese cadet, he quickly applied for leave to their immediate commander, who did not object but gave them only forty-eight hours to leave Japan. Bidding them farewell, he said, "In Japan a Bushido Knight[38] who drinks water at a farewell shows he is determined not to come back alive."[39] All three Chinese cadets filled glasses of water and drained them in solemn silence.

Two days later Chiang, Zhang Qun, and an additional 118 Chinese students and cadets determined to dedicate themselves to the cause of the national liberation of their homeland were aboard a ship sailing from Nagasaki to Shanghai. Prior to departure Chiang, Zhang, and their comrades from the Nineteenth Regiment packed their uniforms and swords into a parcel and mailed it to their commander. This act signified that they were not deserting from the army but retiring honorably.[40]

CHAPTER 3

# *All-under-Heaven Is for Everyone*

Chiang, Zhang, and their comrades arrived in Shanghai on October 30, and Chiang immediately met with Chen Qimei.[1] Chen, who was coordinating all of the work in Shanghai and environs, instructed him to form a "dare to die" detachment from among the native fishermen of Chiang's home district of Fenghua who were in Shanghai at that time. The detachment was to take part in storming Hangzhou, the capital of Zhejiang. Each fisherman was offered sixteen Chinese dollars (at the time a great sum of money, as rickshaw pullers could earn no more than fifteen dollars a month), of which the fishermen immediately sent around ten dollars to their families.[2] Chiang collected 120 men with whom he set off on November 3 to carry out a revolution in Hangzhou. Before he departed he sent a farewell letter to his mother and his eldest half brother, writing that he "had decided to give his life to the revolution," and, if he perished, he asked them "to forgive him."[3]

On the night of November 4 Chiang's detachment, along with other patriots, attacked the *yamen* (office) of the Manchu governor of Zhejiang. The defending garrison surrendered almost without a fight. The entire engagement lasted forty minutes. The attackers fired only a few shots and soon celebrated their victory. On the following day the entire city of Hangzhou was in their hands.[4]

Such was Chiang's first baptism of fire, not very much like Napoleon's at Toulon, to be sure, but it was what it was! The former junior officer of the artillery regiment, like the famous artillery lieutenant from distant France 118 years earlier, had opened his path to glory at the age of twenty-four. Hangzhou was taken, after which Qing power collapsed throughout the entire province of Zhejiang, which declared its independence from Beijing.

Meanwhile, also on November 4 Chen Qimei seized Shanghai, after which he declared himself the *dudu* (governor), having also announced the independence of the city from the imperial government. He counted on a merchant militia as well as three thousand cutthroats put under his control by the municipal mafia. Both he and Sun, as well as other members of the Revolutionary Alliance, had long since maintained businesslike relations with the Shanghai bandits—the Red and especially the Green Gang, secret societies that controlled the municipal opium trade—since the municipal mafia had always hated the alien Manchus.[5] Rumors circulated that Chen Qimei himself had become a member of the Green Gang, occupying one of its leading positions, but whether this is true is unknown.[6]

After several days Chiang returned to Shanghai, where, just as in Hangzhou, the people were celebrating the fall of the alien dynasty. Flags were flown in all the windows in the Chinese quarter. The police roamed about the city carrying large scissors and forcibly sheared off men's queues, symbols of Chinese subordination to the Manchus. They wore armbands on their sleeves with the inscription "Restoration of sovereignty."[7]

The French Concession and the International Settlement that had existed in the city from 1849 and 1863, respectively, and constituted more than one-third of the city—twelve square miles of the municipal territory's thirty-five square miles—remained silent. They were waiting to see how things turned out, which did not hinder the Chinese inhabitants of the settlements, who outnumbered the foreigners ten to one, from expressing their overflowing joy on account of the revolution. Dudu Chen appointed Chiang commander of the Fifth (later renamed the Ninety-third) Regiment of the Jiangsu Army, which he himself headed.[8] This regiment had to be created from the members of mafia organizations as well as urban paupers and lumpen elements.

With the help of his blood brother, Chiang soon made his way into the municipal bandit environment.[9] And, like Chen, he too quickly became one of them. Bold, willful, and decisive, he easily became acquainted with highly placed mafiosi, having earned their respect. At the same time, he fraternized with yet another fellow provincial from Zhejiang, the antiques dealer Zhang Jingjiang, who was also a member of the criminal world. Although Zhang was ten years older than Chiang, they quickly established close relations. Zhang, a frail invalid confined to his armchair by arthritis and concealing weak eyes behind the dark lenses of his glasses, possessed a surprisingly strong, imperial character. He began to exert great influence on Chiang, and soon he and Chiang became blood brothers.

Among themselves the police in the French settlement of Shanghai, who were keeping tabs on suspicious characters, called Zhang Quasimodo, but he was so self-confident that he named himself Renjie (Outstanding Man). At times he made fun of his physical defects. "I am a cicada lying on its back," he said.[10] Zhang was not only a businessman but also an excellent artist and calligrapher and overall a widely educated man. From 1906 on he had had close relations with Sun Yat-sen and often provided financial assistance to the leader of the Revolutionary Alliance, although he inclined more toward anarchism than to the Three Principles of the People.[11]

Zhang was very rich, and his private house, not far from the Bund on Nanking Road—the central avenue of the International Settlement—was considered one of the best in Shanghai. He lived there with his four daughters (his wife had emigrated to the United States). The house was always open to Chiang, but, as in Tokyo, the future Generalissimo preferred to spend his nights in bordellos. Military service did not occupy much time, two or three hours a day; domestic matters were taken care of by a servant and a cook, and Cicada Zhang loaned him quite a lot of money as a token of friendship so that Chiang was able to indulge in various amusements.

During those days in the brothels he met a strikingly beautiful woman named Yao Yiqin (Yao Pleasant *Qin*).[12] She was the same age as he and so lovely that Chiang fell in love with her. He took her as his mistress, bestowed a new name upon her, Yecheng (Sincere Girl from the Banks of the Yechangjin River),[13] and installed her in his modest apartment in the French Concession.[14]

Meanwhile, events in China unfolded at a furious pace. On December 25, a rainy and windy Christmas day, Sun Yat-sen returned to Shanghai from abroad, where he had kept up with events in his homeland by reading foreign newspapers.[15] Four days later, forty-three delegates from eighteen provinces of the empire gathered in the city of Nanjing and by an absolute majority—sixteen of the provincial delegations voted for him—elected Sun Yat-sen as the provisional president. On January 1, 1912, he took up his post and announced the founding of the Republic of China.

China was divided. In Beijing power remained in the hands of the emperor, who depended on the support of the reactionary general Yuan Shikai, who commanded the Beiyang Army, the most powerful in the country, deployed in the north. In Nanjing Sun Yat-sen and the Nanjing assembly governed; on January 28 the assembly reorganized itself as the Provisional Senate of the Republic of China. A civil war seemed unavoidable, and the regimental commander Chiang was ready to take part in it. Like his blood brother Chen, he favored an open conflict against Yuan Shikai.

At exactly that time, the beginning of 1912, an old enemy of Chen's, one Tao Chengzhang, a pompous and self-confident young man of thirty, arrived in Shanghai. He also had made contributions to the revolution, but as the head of the Restoration Society (Guangfuhui), a rival of the Revolutionary Alliance. He was a Zhejiang man like Chiang and a graduate of the Japanese military school Seijō Gakko. Tao studied there in 1902–3 along with the future founder of the CCP, Chen Duxiu. He actively participated in the anti-Manchu movement from 1902 on, published a journal, and raised funds. But like other members of his society he was an open critic of Sun Yat-sen. Tao himself sought power, at least in Zhejiang and the neighboring province of Jiangsu, in which Shanghai is located. He announced publicly that he would put an end to Chen Qimei's absolute power in Shanghai and that of his associates in Zhejiang. Chiang subsequently asserted that Tao was not averse to becoming the *dudu* of Shanghai himself since he "wanted to destroy the organization of the Revolutionary Alliance."[16] But meanwhile, in January 1912, he ran for governor of Zhejiang, counting on the help of secret society members of districts in the province among whom he enjoyed influence. He himself was a member of the Zhejiang secret Dragon Flower Society.[17]

But he failed. He lost to a follower of the Revolutionary Alliance and, evidently fearing that now his forces and those of Dudu Chen had become unequal, he got out of harm's way via a supposed illness, admitting himself to a Shanghai hospital, the Hospital of the Holy Virgin Mary in the French Concession.

Evidently, All-under-Heaven was not for everyone and certainly not for him. Chen decided to rid himself of his rival at any price and entrusted Chiang with handling this "delicate matter." At 2 a.m. on the night of January 14, 1912, Chiang and some of his trusted companions made their way into the hospital and, bursting into Tao's room on the second floor, shot their political opponent in the head: "The Chairman [Chiang Kai-shek], angry beyond control, pulled out his pistol and killed [Tao] with one shot."[18] Later, Chiang asserted that he had dispatched Tao because he had learned of his plans to kill Chen Qimei; he "was terribly indignant" and "decided to get rid of Tao in order to defend the revolution."[19]

Learning of the assassination, President Sun Yat-sen, who had despised his rival, declared hypocritically that "our Republic will always grieve" for Tao Chengzhang, whose "contributions to the revolution were enormous." He and his minister of war, Huang Xing, even demanded that Chen Qimei "find the killer."[20] But Tao's death and the weakening of the Restoration Society played into Sun's hands. Just as in France in the late eighteenth century, in China, "like Saturn, the Revolution devours its children," degenerating into criminal-like settling of accounts.

Tao's death, however, did not help Sun much, and he soon began to lose real power. After the revolution, the role of the army began to grow precipitously, and Sun Yat-sen had no troops. In many places military leaders and military governors, conscious of their power, began to govern the surrounding territories autocratically, paying no heed to the weak president. The members of the Provisional Senate were quite moderate and had no desire to enter into conflict with the militarists, let alone with the most powerful of them commanding the strongest army in China: General Yuan Shikai. The result was that on February 13, 1912, Sun Yat-sen was compelled to tender his resignation, and the next day the members of the Senate unanimously accepted it. On February 15 they unanimously elected General Yuan as provisional president; three days earlier (on February 12) Yuan had succeeded in convincing the imperial court to capitulate. (After the deaths of the Guangxu emperor and of Empress Dowager Ci Xi in November 1908, the emperor of China was Pu Yi, who, at the time, was just six and a half years old. Guangxu's widow, Empress Dowager Long Yu, served as regent.) The Qing "entrusted" Yuan with "organizing a provisional republican government" and, for the sake of restoring order, making peace with the Revolutionary Alliance and other revolutionary organizations.[21] All these events, starting with the uprising on October 10, 1911, in Wuchang, took place in the *xinhai* year on the Chinese lunar calendar and therefore in China the revolution was called the Xinhai Revolution.

Chiang was deeply disillusioned. He still wanted to fight Yuan, and he was simply unable to understand the "stance of appeasement" of the leader of the revolution. In March 1912, exasperated, he again went to Japan. In his words, he "manifested egoism, not thinking about the overall cause," but he really had to get out of Shanghai: of course, his blood brother had no intention of "tracking him down," but the murder of Tao was of concern to the police in the French Concession, and if they came upon any traces of Chiang it might compromise both Chen and Sun himself.[22]

In Tokyo he began studying German because he had decided that at some point he would set off to study in Germany, the most advanced European country. At the same time, with his own funds he founded a journal, *Voice of the Army,* in which he published his first five political articles. In one of them, following Sun Yat-sen, he developed the idea of *datong* with reference to the whole world, insisting that after the victory of the antimonarchical revolution in China, the Great Powers would accept the Republic of China into the community of nations as an equal member. Then, he thought, "there would be a universal commonwealth, uniting all five continents without dividing them into various foreign countries. When we have established a World-Republic." Another article was devoted to tsarist Russia's penetration into Inner Mongolia, which Chinese nationalists considered part of China. Chiang called upon Chinese republicans to quickly launch a military campaign in Mongolia to repel Russian aggression and defend national unity.[23]

In Tokyo he learned that in late August–September 1912 Sun Yat-sen was conducting negotiations with Yuan Shikai to work out a joint program of action. On September 9 Sun accepted Yuan's proposal that he occupy the post of general director of railways in his government with an incredibly large annual salary of 30,000 silver Chinese dollars.[24] On October 6, at a meeting in Shanghai with members of his own party, he declared, "Many believe that he [General Yuan] is pretending to be a republican. I firmly assert that Mr. Yuan's intentions are completely sincere. . . . Mr. Yuan is a statesman, and everything he does, he does for the good of the state; we can believe this."[25]

Sun was maneuvering here, trying to seek a compromise. But Chiang simply became despondent. In December he returned to China for several days, only long enough to bring his mistress Yecheng to Japan. In early February 1913 he returned again, again for personal reasons. Before departing for Germany he wanted to celebrate the lunar New Year in his native Xikou in a warm family environment with his mother, wife, son, and lover, whom he brought along with him.[26] His wife, Fumei, and his lover, Yecheng, surprisingly got along with each other. Mama Wang also accepted her son's lover. In traditional China, men often had concubines, so there was nothing unusual about this. Chiang's mother decided to have Yecheng sleep in her room, Fumei and her son shared a second room with a woman whom Chiang had hired to teach the illiterate Yecheng how to read and write, and Chiang occupied a third room. So a space was found for all.[27]

Meanwhile, the political situation in China was apparently becoming stabilized. In the winter of 1912–13 elections were held in the country for a new legislative organ: a parliament. In these elections Sun Yat-sen's new party, which, in preparation for the elections, he established on August 25, 1912, on the foundation of the Revolutionary Alliance by uniting it with four other organizations, achieved a total victory over more than three hundred parties. The new party was named the Guomindang (GMD, Nationalist Party). In the House of Representatives (the lower chamber of parliament), it won 269 of 596 seats, or 45 percent, and in the Senate (the upper chamber) 123 of 274, or 44.8 percent.[28]

Bidding farewell to his relatives, Chiang, along with Yecheng, went to Shanghai in March, where they intended to sail to Europe. But something happened that abruptly altered their plans. At the railroad station in Shanghai on the evening of March 20, Song Jiaoren, the head of the Guomindang faction in parliament, was severely wounded by two bullets. He was on his way to Beijing to assume the position of prime minister. Two days later he died in hospital. Soon after the police found his killer. He turned out to be linked with the acting premier, one of Yuan Shikai's most trusted associates. How could one even think about studying in Germany now? Sun personally ordered Chen Qimei, the *dudu* of Shanghai, to detain Chiang Kai-shek in the city and convince him to abandon his trip to Europe.[29] Sun was now in particular need of military cadres. Chiang handed over to Chen 3,000 Chinese dollars that he had planned to use on his studies in Germany and awaited the development of events.[30]

Shocked members of the Guomindang began to openly accuse General Yuan of orchestrating the crime. Yuan didn't even consider trying to vindicate himself. He really had no desire to share power with either Sun Yat-sen or Song Jiaoren, and, having secured the support of Western powers that provided him with an enormous loan of more than 25 million pounds sterling (about 100 million US dollars), he soon began to prepare openly for civil war. At his directive, Beiyang Army troops were redeployed to strategically important centers around the country. Moreover, he replaced a number of pro-Guomindang governors.

Sun then decided to mount a second revolution—this time against Yuan. On July 12, 1913, an anti–Yuan Shikai uprising erupted in Jiangxi province under the leadership of the Guomindang governor Li Liejun, following which Jiangxi proclaimed its independence. Then the Guomindang *dudus* of Nanjing, Anhui, Hunan, Fujian, and Zhejiang declared their independence. Chen Jiongming, the military governor of Guangdong and one of Sun Yat-sen's closest associates, also came out against Yuan and declared independence. In early August an uprising began in Chongqing (Sichuan province).

Naturally, under the leadership of Chiang's blood brother, Dudu Chen, Shanghai also rebelled and declared its independence on July 18. Chiang took a very active role in the rebellion. He worked out a plan for an attack on the Shanghai arsenal, which was under the control of troops loyal to Yuan. Three times—on July 22, 28, and 29—he led attacks at the head of two battalions of Guomindang troops. But nothing came of it. His troops were subjected to massive artillery fire from Yuan Shikai's ships in the Shanghai roadstead. Opposing Chiang also, as he later recalled bitterly, were "imperialists from the territory of the settlement" as well as "compradors, *tuhao* and *lieshen,*" so he was forced to retreat.[31] Yuan's troops seized the city.[32]

Along with the "outstanding man" Cicada Zhang, Chiang sailed up the Yangzi River to Nanjing to continue the struggle there, but there too the revolutionary forces were about done for. Soon troops loyal to the president suppressed the uprising.[33] The Second Revolution had failed.

Three months later, on November 4, 1913, Yuan Shikai declared the Guomindang illegal and then dissolved the parliament. Sun Yat-sen, Chen Qimei, Chiang Kai-shek, and many other fighters against the dictatorship were forced to flee to Japan once again. Chen Qimei noted, "During the Xinhai Revolution we had almost no weapons; there were only a few hundred of us, but when the call came in Wuchang, the whole country joined the movement. That is because we had the spirit of a revolutionary party. During the battles in the *guichou* year [1913], although we controlled several provinces and had an army of one hundred thousand the bandit armies surpassed us in numbers and we were defeated. That is because we had lost the spirit of a revolutionary party."[34]

After arriving in Tokyo, Sun and other Guomindang members began to revive a revolutionary party in that image. Sun called it the Zhongguo gemingdang (Chinese Revolutionary Party). He announced its formation on July 8, 1914, at a meeting of more than 400 of his supporters, calling on them to prepare for a third revolution. Unlike the parliamentary Guomindang which Sun now considered "wholly bankrupt," because it was strongly reminiscent of "a western-style political party," the new organization was built on the principles of strict centralism and secrecy. Chiang joined it as the 102nd member.[35]

By this time Chiang was already cooperating rather closely with Sun Yat-sen. Their personal contacts were resumed in December 1913, when, according to one source, Chen Qimei, and, to another source, Cicada Zhang, the semi-mafioso friend of both Sun and Chiang, again brought them together, this time in Sun Yat-sen's apartment.[36]

Sun again showed interest in the "future hero of the revolution." Chiang already had made contributions to the revolution, but, most important, as before he was devoted to Sun. Moreover, he did not hide his readiness to destroy all of Sun's enemies, both outside as well as inside the party, if such were found. Sun could not but value this, especially since after the defeat of the second revolution the overwhelming majority of his supporters abandoned him. They even refused to join the Revolutionary Party. Only a few hundred of the several thousand of his previous comrades joined the new party, and many of those who did no longer showed their former respect toward him.[37] Subsequently, Chiang reminisced that "among those who . . . became members of the Chinese Revolutionary Party in Japan, only a very few really believed in Tsung-li's [*zongli's*, manager-in-chief's, was Sun Yat-sen's title] ideological principles. . . . They even acted in an arrogant and insulting way toward *Tsung-li*. . . . I made up my mind then and there I must, as a Party member, endeavor to vindicate our *Tsung-li*. . . . Otherwise, I wouldn't be a loyal and worthy member of the Party."[38] From then on, Chiang was especially close to Sun. Subsequently, he did actively struggle against his enemies: the dictator Yuan Shikai, the militarists who tore China into pieces after Yuan's death in 1916, and, finally, when Sun ultimately began to struggle against them, the colonial imperialists.

Following Sun Yat-sen and depending on his support, Chiang now was steadily advancing on the upward path to power. But the going was not easy. He needed to overcome the resistance of countless opponents and rivals. Hence he needed to be not only resolute but also cautious. It was not by chance that the great Chinese philosopher Zhuang Zi (369–286 BCE), one of the founders of Daoism, said, "Great Courage is not seen in stubborn bravery."[39]

## CHAPTER 4

# *Sun Yat-sen's Obstinate Pupil*

The main principle on which the Revolutionary Party was founded was personal loyalty to the leader. Sun unambiguously declared to his associates, "There are many things you do not understand. . . . You should blindly follow me."[1] He demanded that those who joined the party not only promise to sacrifice their lives and freedom "for the cause of saving China and rescuing the people," but also take an oath of allegiance and unconditional subordination to him personally.[2] This did not discomfit Chiang and his blood brother Chen; unlike many other revolutionaries they affixed their signatures to the text of Sun Yat-sen's oath and sealed them with fingers marked with red mastic.

Establishing a new party along the lines of Chinese secret societies, Sun, however, did not retreat from the struggle for democracy. Now he simply figured that progress toward this form of political system would require a lot of time. In 1905, founding the Revolutionary Alliance, he supposed that China was only six years away from democracy: three years of military dictatorship and three years of governance based on a provisional constitution restricting the voting rights of citizens; but in 1914 he declared that it was impossible to predict how long the period prior to the introduction of democracy would last. He even began to assert that during this period a constitution was not necessary and that the state would be under the "political tutelage" of his party, that is, in essence, under an overt one-party dictatorship.[3]

Sun Yat-sen's immediate goal was still armed struggle against Yuan Shikai. Toward that end, all means were good from his perspective, even help from the Japanese government, despite the fact that the "revolutionary democrat, endowed with nobility and heroism"[4] knew very well that the Japanese were striving to enslave China. But he was ready to sacrifice a lot, even Manchuria, having supported a separatist movement of local monarchists behind which Japan stood.[5]

Nor did Sun forget about preparations for new uprisings in China. In May 1914, for example, he sent Chiang Kai-shek to Shanghai and then, in the autumn, to Harbin to find out whether there was anybody there one could depend on in the struggle against Yuan Shikai. Both trips were fruitless, and Chiang, after returning to Tokyo, immersed himself in reading books. He studied all of Wang Yangming, his beloved Confucian philosopher, who affirmed the right of every person to think critically. He also read the complete works of Zeng Guofan, the victor over the Taipings: the famous uprising of rural paupers and lumpen elements as well as members of the poor Hakka (guest people) clans that raged through southern and East China in 1851–64.[6] He read so much that his vision suffered, and he had to seek treatment at an ophthalmologist. At the same time, as before, he diligently practiced gymnastics and meditated every day, tempering himself physically and spiritually.[7]

Meanwhile, on July 28, 1914, the First World War began. Yuan Shikai declared neutrality while Japan joined the Entente and in late August, along with the British, made a landing in the region of Qingdao on the Shandong peninsula. This city and the adjacent Jiaozhou Bay had been a German colony since 1898. Absorbed by the war in Europe, the Germans did not resist strongly. The Chinese army did not interfere. On November 7, 1914, Qingdao fell, now becoming a colony of Japan. The Chinese did not get involved. On January 28, 1915, the Japanese issued an ultimatum to Yuan Shikai, the so-called Twenty-one Demands, acceptance of which would have turned China into a Japanese colony.

News of the flagrant Japanese demands aroused the Chinese intelligentsia. However, Yuan Shikai, fearing an invasion of Japanese imperial troops, accepted most of the demands on May 7. This time even the parliament disagreed with him, refusing to ratify the agreement. Then, on May 25, 1915, Yuan affirmed the demands by affixing his seal. In response an anti-Japanese movement began in China, and even Sun Yat-sen, despite his earlier flirtation with the Japanese, openly criticized the treachery of Yuan Shikai, calling for "a blow against him."[8]

The moment for a third revolution had become more than favorable. So Sun sent Chen Qimei and then Chiang Kai-shek back to Shanghai once more. In the autumn of 1915 Chiang again arrived in the city, where, together with Chen, he first organized the killing of the governor and then, on December 5, initiated the next uprising, which this time also failed. The blood brothers barely managed to escape. Chiang even took ill from grief, and, having heard of this, his mother came to take care of him.[9]

Meanwhile, dissatisfaction with the policies of President Yuan continued to grow swiftly. In late December 1915 Yuan Shikai took another rash step. Following the suggestion of his American advisor, Frank Goodnow, on the last day of December 1915 he announced the restoration of the monarchy as of January 1, 1916. He declared himself the new emperor, having proclaimed the start of the *Hongxian* (Unlimited Lawfulness) era. This riled public opinion. Yunnan, Guangxi, and Guizhou, that is, the three southwestern provinces, declared their separation. Civil war again flared up. Despite the fact that Yuan, after coming to his senses, announced the liquidation of the monarchy after eighty-one days, Chiang took an active part in this war on orders from Sun Yat-sen.

In the struggle against Yuan, Japan now offered Sun full support because Yuan, under pressure from Western powers, had sabotaged fulfillment of the Twenty-one Demands. At the beginning of 1916 Sun received 1.7 million yen (equivalent at the time to US $700,000) that he used to prepare a new uprising in East China.[10] On May 5, 1916, together with a group of rebels, Chiang seized a fort along the Yangzi River, halfway between Shanghai and Nanjing. Unfortunately, both for him and for Sun, he was unable to hold it, and after five days Chiang's own soldiers, having lost hope, rebelled against him. Only by a miracle was he able to escape.[11]

Then, on May 18, 1916, Chiang received a new blow: his blood brother Chen Qimei was treacherously killed on the territory of the French Concession in Shanghai. His death was the result of an attempt on his life arranged by a provocateur. Chen was thirty-eight years old.

It is difficult to describe Chiang's grief. Two days later, speaking at the funeral ceremony, he swore to continue the mission begun by his blood brother. "This I promise you," he declared, addressing his deceased friend, "just as I promised you [earlier] 'to be another you if you died.' "[12] Later, he wrote in his diaries, "One might say that my revolutionary foundation was laid after we were defeated in the struggle against Yuan during the second year of the Republic [1913], but I was fully formed [as a revolutionary] after the assassination of Yingshi [Chen Qimei] in the fifth year of the Republic [1916]. This was the time when I began to go forward, relying on my own strength."[13] More than two weeks earlier, on May 1, 1916, Sun Yat-sen returned to Shanghai together with a strikingly beautiful young woman whom he had married in Tokyo half a year earlier. Her name was Song Qingling (Song Happy Disposition), and she was twenty-three years old. She was christened Rosamonde, but at home they called her Suzy. She was the daughter of a friend of Sun's, the Shanghai entrepreneur and Christian missionary Charlie Song (Song Jiashu), who was only three years older than Sun Yat-sen. Sun had stayed at Charlie's home in Shanghai a number of times and for long periods, so he had known Suzy as a girl. The difference in age between them was twenty-seven years.

Sun was keen on young girls. A couple of years before his marriage he had proposed to Rosamonde's older sister, the twenty-four-year-old Song Ailing (Song Friendly Disposition), also a beauty, who worked as his secretary and was only four years older than Song Qingling. At the same time, according to the testimony of friends, he did not stop frequenting Japanese bordellos. "The old boy could not keep his hands off women," recalled his close friend, the Australian journalist William Henry Donald.[14] This despite the fact that Sun had long since been legally married. It is true that he did not love his wife. His parents had arranged the match when Sun was eighteen and his bride nineteen. His wife was also a Christian, and he had three children with her: his son Sun Fo, who was just two years younger than Song Qingling (he too became a well-known revolutionary), and two daughters. He had a third daughter with one of his Japanese lovers, but Sun did not acknowledge her.[15]

The enraptured Song Qingling worshiped the great revolutionary, the Father of the Republic, whom she was accustomed from childhood to call Uncle Yat-sen. Later she said that she "didn't fall in love," but that she was moved by romanticism: she admired him as a great hero.[16] Her older sister had suggested she consider marrying Chiang Kai-shek, "the slim officer with the thin mustache" with whom Ailing had become acquainted in Tokyo at Sun Yat-sen's apartment early in 1914, but Song Qingling refused.[17] Her father, not wanting his daughter to marry an elderly, married man, locked her up in his Shanghai home. Sun promised to get a divorce, but, being a Methodist, Charlie did not recognize divorces. With the aid of a servant woman who raised a ladder to the window of her bedroom, Qingling climbed down and ran off to Sun in Tokyo. On the eve of her arrival, October 24, 1915, Sun announced his divorce from his first wife, and on the following day, October 25, Sun and Song had a modest wedding. One day later Sun Yat-sen made his new wife his secretary.[18]

Soon they went back to Shanghai. Sun Yat-sen tried to restore relations with his former friend and present father-in-law, Charlie, but the latter was unable to the end to forgive either his daughter or his friend. He died two years later. At the same time, Charlie's children approved of the marriage: Rosamonde's older sister, Ailing, whose Christian name was Nancy, her younger sister, the eighteen-year-old Meiling (Excellent Disposition), whose Christian name was Olivia, and their three brothers. The eldest, the twenty-two-year-old Song Ziwen (Song Industrious Son), was known to everyone by his Christian name, Joe, or by the initial letters of his name in what was then the system of Latin transcription: T. V.[19] They were all revolutionaries and were enormously respectful of Sun Yat-sen. They were particularly impressed with the gift Sun gave his bride at their wedding: a Browning revolver with a beautiful wooden handle. Presenting it to her, Sun said to his beloved, "There are twenty bullets in this pistol—nineteen for the enemies, and the last one, if worse comes to worst, for you."[20] This is how they all were at the time: love and revolution were inseparable.

Meanwhile, the civil war in China was continuing, but at its height, on June 6, 1916, Yuan Shikai suddenly died from uremia at the age of fifty-six. General Li Yuanhong, nicknamed Buddha, a participant in the 1911 Wuchang uprising, was chosen president. Sun Yat-sen moved the headquarters of his Revolutionary Party to Shanghai and then entered into negotiations with President Li about restoring a legal, constitutional government.[21] At the same time, he sent Chiang Kai-shek to Shandong in June, appointing him chief of staff of a future, so-called Revolutionary Army of Northeast China. Chiang did not succeed in establishing the army and was then sent to Beijing to sort out the military and political situation. But by autumn Chiang was back in Shanghai.[22]

An old friend of Chiang's, Dai Jitao, a student of law and politics with whom Chiang had become well acquainted during his second stay in Japan in 1908, returned from Tokyo to Shanghai together with Sun. Dai was much more educated than Chiang in the field of philosophy, especially Western philosophy. He was a short, frail young man with a black moustache and intelligent, ironic eyes. A member of Sun Yat-sen's party, he had taken part in the Xinhai Revolution and had served as the leader's personal secretary since 1912. After escaping to Japan in 1913, Chiang and Dai became close friends and soon, having become blood brothers, began to share an apartment. Living with them in addition to Yecheng was Dai Jitao's lover, a Japanese nurse named Shigematsu Kaneko (Goldie). Dai, like Chiang, was married, but youth had its due, and moreover Chiang and Dai had before them the example of their dissolute treasured leader Sun Yat-sen.

Following the change of political circumstances in China, however, Chiang left Tokyo in the autumn of 1915, and then, on April 27, 1916, Dai followed. It is not known whether Dai, on leaving the Japanese islands, was aware that his young nurse was three months pregnant. He probably knew because on the eve of her giving birth he sent a letter to a friend in Tokyo asking him to look after Goldie. It is true that he had no intention of living with her or acknowledging the infant since he was terrified of his lawful wife, Niu Youheng, whom, even in private, he called elder sister out of timidity and respect. Five years older than he, she had an amazingly strong character and could easily have created a grand scandal had she known about her husband's illegitimate child. She was a real *émancipée* and, moreover, was a member of the Revolutionary Party whom Sun Yat-sen greatly respected. She and Dai had a legitimate son. Therefore it was not surprising that when, in early November 1916, Dai Jitao received news that Kaneko had delivered a son he became terribly frightened. He turned to his blood brother Chiang, imploring his assistance. Chiang manifested his nobility, saying that he could adopt the child. At the end of November 1916 Dai wrote about this to his friend in Tokyo.[23]

Three years later the quiet, shy Goldie showed up at the door of Chiang's and Dai's home in Shanghai, holding the adorable, thin child by the hand.[24] She still hoped that Dai would acknowledge the child, but he hid from her on the second floor and would not even see her. After speaking with Chiang and understanding the situation, the teary-eyed woman fled, abandoning her son to the mercy of fate.[25] Keeping his word to his blood brother, Chiang adopted the child and gave him the child name of Jiangao, that is, He Who Shall Build the Capital of Gao.[26] And, in accordance with the genealogical chronicle of his own clan, he named the child Wei-kuo (Weiguo), the translation of which is the same as that of Ching-kuo: He Who Shall Successfully Rule the State.[27]

Chiang thus acquired a second son. He entrusted his mistress, Yecheng, with caring for the child, and she raised him, treating him like her own son throughout her life. Chiang brought Yecheng and his new son to his homeland, to the village of Xikou. Grandma Wang joyfully welcomed her new grandson, but Chiang's wife, Fumei, did not want the child in her home. According to Wei-kuo's reminiscences, she installed Yecheng and him in a shed where the firewood and hay were infested with fleas that attacked the uninvited guests. Sometime later Chiang's elder brother, taking pity on the unfortunates, took them into his home. They lived there for several years until they moved to Ningbo in 1924.[28]

Meanwhile, events in China were developing at a dizzying speed. President Li Yuanhong, who at first had attempted to restore the constitution his predecessor had trampled upon, under pressure from the North China militarists dissolved the parliament on June 13, 1917. Indignant at the president's conduct, the deputies decamped to Shanghai and then to Canton, where Sun Yat-sen arrived on July 17. On August 25 an emergency session of parliament convened in this southern city, and on September 1 Sun Yat-sen was elected Generalissimo of South China (formally Generalissimo of China, but of course the military government he established did not control all of the country).

China had plunged into the abyss of chaos. The armies of numerous militarists, in which destitute peasants and other unemployed persons willingly served, began fighting against each other. Western powers, interested in selling arms to China and receiving additional economic privileges from local militarists, encouraged such warfare. Based in Canton, the leader of the revolution began to prepare for a Northern Expedition against the warring oligarchs.

As for Chiang, on Sun Yat-sen's orders he remained for some time in Shanghai coordinating the activities of Sun's followers in East China and engaging in the illegal collection of financial means for the party. According to information from the municipal police of the International Settlement, on October 18, 1917, he took part in a robbery of a private house in the center of the city.[29]

From Shanghai Chiang sent Sun two operational plans for the Northern Expedition, one after the other. He proposed that the first blow be struck against forces of the local militarists of Fujian and Zhejiang in order to establish the southern government's control over the entire southern and southeastern coast.[30]

Not until early in March 1918 did Chiang arrive in the south, only after Sun, with the help of associates, the ex-governor of Guangdong Zhu Qinglan, and the southern Chinese general Chen Jiongming, had succeeded in organizing in 1917 a ten-thousand-man Guangdong army. Following Chiang Kai-shek's plan, the army took the field in Fujian, and Sun ordered Chiang to proceed at once to the city of Swatow in eastern Guangdong, where the commander in chief, Chen Jiongming, was headquartered. On March 15 General Chen appointed Chiang chief of the Operations Department of his army with the rank of colonel.[31]

As a staff member of the Guangdong Army, Chiang took part in military operations and displayed exceptional military talent, drafting several operational plans. However, a personal conflict developed between him and Chen Jiongming, an imperious man of forty, who looked like a typical rural *shenshi* (literatus). Chen had a long, slightly drooping moustache and a high forehead; he preferred a gray cotton robe to a military uniform, and he supported himself with a walking stick when he walked. He was a native of Guangdong province but belonged to the oppressed Hakka clan (guest people), as did Sun Yat-sen. His family, it is true, was not poor, unlike the majority of the members of his extended family (clan), and he had even been able to receive an excellent education. In 1899 he was awarded a *xiucai* degree, and in 1908 he graduated from the Academy of Law and Politics in Canton. Chen became a member of Sun Yat-sen's Revolutionary Alliance around the same time Chiang did, in 1908, but in 1914 he did not wish to join the conspiratorial Revolutionary Party. In his words, he "found it [the charter of the new organization] quite unsatisfactory."[32] As noted earlier, Sun Yat-sen demanded an oath of personal loyalty to himself from party members. There were a few like Chen, and it is not hard to understand their position, but Chiang Kai-shek from the outset considered it his duty to defend Sun from renegades. Therefore, not surprisingly he did not get along well with Chen, notwithstanding the fact that General Chen was now fervently supporting Sun.

Chiang Kai-shek simply didn't trust him, and moreover he was deeply offended that, from his perspective, he had been given a low rank. "I waited patiently for five years and worked persistently, and now that I am thirty years old, what have I achieved?" he wrote in his diaries. "Nothing. This morning I went to the staff headquarters of the commander in chief and was given the rank of colonel."[33]

He had obviously long since counted on becoming a general. In the spring of 1918 he had avidly read the *Memoirs* of Napoleon, whose brilliant career likely ignited his own vain aspirations.[34] He did not conceal his injured pride, and Chen soon sensed that the chief of his Operations Department was a proud and obstinate man. But Chen was clever and cunning. He understood that Chiang had *guanxi* (connections) not only with Sun but also with many other leading revolutionaries. Therefore, unlike the hot-tempered Chiang Kai-shek, he did not betray his true feelings, although at an opportune occasion he rejected operational plans drawn up by Chiang.

Many officers of the Guangdong Army also disliked Chiang and were also skeptical of his operational plans, and not only because they were trying to please the commander. They all viewed Chiang as an outsider, someone from East China. He did not know the local customs, neither the Cantonese dialect nor the Hakka language. Thus all his knowledge in the field of military science as well as his Zhejiang accent irritated them. For the time being the hard feelings did not burst into the open. But judging from Chiang's diaries, on three occasions he decided to retire, since he had "never experienced such humiliation," and three times "under the pressure of circumstances and by getting a grip" on himself he forced himself not to submit his resignation.[35]

Meanwhile, Sun Yat-sen was unable to hold on to power in the south. At the beginning of May 1918 General Lu Rongting, the head of the military clique from Guangxi, the province neighboring Guangdong, demanded the removal of the Generalissimo. The number of his troops exceeded that of Chen Jiongming's army, so Sun had no option but to retire. On June 26, accompanied by Dai Jitao, he returned to Shanghai on a Japanese postal vessel. He settled in the territory of the French Concession in an expensive, two-story private house at 29 Molière Street. Lush with greenery, the house was given to him by a patriotic Canadian Chinese.

Chiang Kai-shek, fed up with intra-army squabbles, submitted his resignation on July 31 and decamped to Shanghai in the summer of 1918.[36] But Chen Jiongming immediately requested that he return. Although he was not fond of the proud Zhejiangese, he did not want to assume responsibility for the break. He sent him several letters, ingratiating himself in every way possible. "Our army can undergo a hundred defeats, but it cannot go on without you," he wrote to him.[37] Chiang yielded to persuasion, particularly since Sun Yat-sen, who trusted Chen Jiongming, asked him to undertake a new campaign in Fujian.[38] At this time, Sun was hoping that Fujian would become the new base for the revolution.

In September 1918 Chiang was given command of the 2nd Column of the Guangdong Army that was deployed north of the Fujianese city of Zhangzhou. The column comprised four battalions numbering about 1,000 fighting men in toto. Under Chiang's command it operated quite successfully. Its soldiers penetrated the enemy's front, seized several important strategic points, and posed a direct threat to Fuzhou, the capital of Fujian. But in December Chiang contracted a fever, and in January 1919 his troops, cut off from their main force, fell into a trap and suffered a serious defeat. The Guangdong officers would not forgive Chiang for this; they began to mock him openly.[39] Chen Jiongming quickly made peace with the Fujianese.

Then in March 1919 Chiang, incensed, again went to Shanghai and from there set out for his native village Xikou to visit his mother. Three months earlier, in December 1918, she had turned fifty-five according to the Chinese system of calculation, but since he was at the front Chiang had been unable to congratulate her. Now he fulfilled his obligation. Sun Yat-sen sent Chiang's mother warm congratulations and gifts.[40]

From the village in the summer of 1919 Chiang Kai-shek, who no longer wished to serve under the command of Chen Jiongming, submitted a request to retire to Chen's deputy, one of the few with whom he was on good terms. "I tried with all my strength to help the commander [Chen], and, by helping him, help the party," he wrote, "but silently observing the development of the situation and the recent events, I believe they are not for the good of the party, the state, nor Mr. Sun. . . . I am physically and spiritually exhausted." Chiang basically complained about the absence of discipline in the army, that he was unable to get his subordinates to execute his orders, and that the army was "shot through with provincialism" (he had in mind that the officers were suspicious of outsiders).[41]

Meanwhile, on October 10, 1919, Sun Yat-sen reorganized his party yet again, now calling it the Chinese Guomindang (in 1912–14, as noted earlier, it was also called the Guomindang, but now he added the word "Chinese"). The sectarian character of the party was no longer appropriate for the situation in China. The old statutes, which had engendered disagreements, were changed. Sun Yat-sen finally deleted the chapter binding party members to swear personal allegiance to him. Yet he continued to be convinced that he embodied not only the party but also the revolution. "[T]o obey me," he insisted, "is to submit to the revolution which I advocate. And if one follows my revolution, naturally one should [also] obey me."[42] In the new party, too, he possessed all the power, retaining for himself the post of *zongli* (manager in chief).

Both Chiang and Chen Jiongming became members of the new party, but Chiang continued to mistrust General Chen. He was in a foul mood all the time and even asked Sun Yat-sen to send him on a long journey to England and the United States. He wanted to enroll in some sort of higher educational institution and study for three years. Recently, he had even resumed studying English, although he made little headway with it.[43]

He also hoped to visit Soviet Russia, whose Bolshevik experiment began to interest him at this time. Naturally, he had heard about the October Revolution and of how a civil war was raging between an enigmatic extremist party that had organized a powerful Red Army and counterrevolution supported by imperialists. He knew that in Moscow, in March 1919, the Bolshevik leaders Lenin and Trotsky had formed the Communist International (Comintern), calling on all nations to what they called the world socialist revolution. At this time Chiang's blood brother Dai Jitao had immersed himself in studying

Bolshevik theory and practice and was constantly talking about Marxism and communism.

Chiang Kai-shek was always inclined toward the radical left. The poverty and humiliation he had endured in his childhood, keen compassion toward his mother, who had worked indefatigably, and his loathing of the rich persons who had deceived his family all served to arouse his hatred of the feudal landlord class. His burning desire to put an end to shameful social injustice was sharpened by his fierce temperament as well as by the intriguing news of Bolshevik victories in the civil war in Russia that the Chinese press increasingly reported. The further he went in his studies, the more he wanted to understand how the Russian revolutionaries succeeded in defeating the counterrevolutionaries and the imperialists. Would it make sense to copy their experience?

In October 1919 he wrote in his diaries, "Unless we destroy the class of *shenshi* [rural literati], the common people will be unable to establish their power. On the path of the common people . . . stand capitalists and *shenshi*. . . . I believe that for the revolutionary renewal of society we need first to completely destroy the two middle classes—capitalists and *shenshi*."[44] Such thinking would qualify one to join the Comintern.

Sun Yat-sen too was interested in Russian affairs, although he had not yet come to entertain such thoughts. In 1918 he had simply sent a congratulatory telegram to the Soviet government in Moscow.[45] But he permitted Chiang only to travel to Tokyo, and for only three weeks, to visit his old friends and to rest. His trip whetted Chiang Kai-shek's interest in Soviet Russia. He had barely set sail from Shanghai on October 25, 1919, when he began writing an article about the relationships of various powers to the Russian worker-peasant government, and once in Japan he began to read the leftist press and books about socialism.[46] But as he explored socialist theory, he couldn't help despairing about the capacity of the Chinese people to accept it. "Enormous efforts will be required to instill [in the consciousness of the almost wholly illiterate population of China] progressive ideas of other countries," he wrote in his diaries. "It took the Japanese less than three years of reform to achieve their present position . . . [but] even ten years will not suffice for us to carry out a revolution."[47] In Japan he bought a book titled *Chronicle of the Russian Revolution* that he read with great interest on the return trip to Shanghai in mid-November 1919. In his words, it had a profound impression on him.[48]

In December 1919 a special messenger from Chen Jiongming came to meet him in Shanghai. The commander in chief of the Guangdong Army was again urgently summoning him. But Chiang was in no hurry. In Shanghai he began to study Russian every day, continued to read radical leftist journals, including *Xin qingnian* (New Youth), published on the territory of the French Concession by the well-known educator Chen Duxiu. He also discussed the views of Trotsky with Dai Jitao and another friend, the Guomindang general Xu Chongzhi, with whom he had served in Fujian.[49]

Bolshevik ideas of world revolution took possession of his consciousness. "If revolution really succeeds in one country, then other countries may closely approach [revolution] and resolve [their problems]," he wrote.[50] He decided that a trip to Russia would be his major task in 1920.[51] He was increasingly impressed with how decisively the Bolsheviks dealt with their enemies. But he understood that to achieve the kind of successes the Russian communists had, the Guomindang needed its own army. He never doubted that Chen Jiongming and the other militarists were unreliable, and therefore as early as February 1920 he suggested that a Guomindang officers academy should be established.[52] But his suggestion was not accepted at the time.

Understanding, too, that the foundation of Marxism was the doctrine of the decisive role of economic factors in the development of civilization, he read two books on economic issues: *Principles of Economics* (1890) by the famous British economist Alfred Marshall and *Principles of National Economy* (1914) by the Japanese author Tsumura Hidematsu. Reading these books only deepened his hatred of rich Chinese. "I read '[Principles of] Economics,' which upset me emotionally," he wrote in his diaries. "I think it will be impossible to set up any enterprises [in China] if Chinese businessmen cannot get rid of their bad habits."[53]

Sun Yat-sen also continued to display heightened interest in Russia. In the summer of 1920, when the Red Army was preparing to administer a final blow to the White Armies in the European part of Russia, he met in Shanghai with Alexei Potapov, a former general in the tsarist army who had been stranded in China by the October Revolution and intended to return to his homeland. Evidently assuming that Potapov would be received by leading members of the Bolshevik party, Sun asked him to convey his greetings to Lenin on his arrival in Russia. "He refrained from addressing written greetings to the Soviet government," Potapov wrote while already in Moscow, "from anticipated fears that were confirmed, that I would be subjected to search by representatives of the Entente powers."[54]

Somewhat later, in September 1920, Sun met with a representative of the Amur regional committee of the Russian Communist Party, a Chinese named

Liu Qian (Fedorov). Deeply disappointed with the state of affairs in southern China, where the troops of Chen Jiongming had been unable to achieve success by any means, Sun began to discuss seriously with the Bolshevik emissary a completely absurd plan of joining together the military efforts of the Guomindang and Soviet Russia to overthrow the Beijing government. According to Sun's agreement with Liu Qian, the Soviet Red Army would invade Xinjiang, and from there they "would be able to freely move troops to North [China]" via Sichuan. To coordinate the actions, Sun even sent his liaison to the Russian city of Blagoveshchensk, but the Bolshevik leadership did not support the plan.[55]

In November 1920 Sun Yat-sen welcomed the Soviet communist Grigorii Naumovich Voitinsky to his private house in Shanghai on Molière Street. Voitinsky, whose real name was Zarkhin, had been sent to China by the Vladivostok Department of the Far Eastern Bureau of the Russian Communist Party per agreement with the Executive Committee of the Comintern (ECCI) to establish a link with local leftist intellectuals and organize a communist movement. As Voitinsky recalled, during the course of the conversation a potential project came up: the possibility of establishing a regular link between Sun and the government of Soviet Russia in order "to unite the South China struggle with the struggle of the distant Soviet state." Sun Yat-sen, increasingly disappointed with the Western democracies that evidently were not trying to assist him, expressed the desire to maintain permanent contact with the Soviet government.[56] Chen Duxiu, the publisher of the journal *New Youth,* who four months earlier, with the help of Voitinsky, had organized the first Chinese Bolshevik circle in Shanghai, took part in the conversation.

Voitinsky had several conversations in Shanghai with the editors of the Guomindang journal *Xingqi pinglun* (Sunday Observer), including Dai Jitao. Dai and other colleagues at the journal informed Sun Yat-sen's close associates Liao Zhongkai and Zhu Zhixin, who were with Chen Jiongming's army in the Fujianese city of Zhangzhou, of the content of these conversations, and they in turn informed Sun Yat-sen.

Ever more determined to establish close ties with Soviet Russia, at this time Sun specially invited a teacher of Russian for Liao Zhongkai, Zhu Zhixin, and another of his associates, Li Zhangda, hoping that in the near future they would be able to set off for the Land of the Soviets and learn about its experience. He had made arrangements for their mission to Moscow with Potapov.[57] While their trip did not take place, "studying Russian soon became fashionable" among Guomindang leaders.[58]

Sun Yat-sen still had no intention of sending Chiang Kai-shek to Moscow. He needed the talented military man in China, so Chiang was unable to go to Russia at that time. In April 1920 Sun firmly requested that Chiang again join Chen Jiongming's army. He did not want to get involved in the personal relationships among his associates. Chiang had to submit. This time, however, he did not remain in the south for long. After just three weeks, tired of new squabbles, again he left it all and returned to Shanghai. As before, Europe beckoned, and if he couldn't go to Russia then perhaps to France. He wanted very much to go there with Liao Zhongkai and Zhu Zhixin, but Sun said no.[59] Then, as if on purpose, in early May Chiang suddenly was hospitalized with typhus for an entire month, so any sort of trip, whether to South China, Russia, or France, was out of the question.[60]

When Chiang recovered in July 1920 despite everything, on orders from Sun he again set out to join Chen Jiongming. Once again not for long. He arrived in Zhangzhou on July 16, became depressed anew, and returned to Shanghai on August 7. He was overwhelmed by anger. He had gone south four times and always to no effect. The Guangdong Army, he believed, was incapable, the officer corps was rotten with corruption; Chiang himself was still viewed as an outsider, and his relations with Chen Jiongming were still unsatisfactory. "There is no hope that the Guangdong Army will be able to fight," he wrote in his diaries, "again I want to go to Russia to become acquainted all-around with the situation [there]."[61]

In Shanghai, again, as in his youth, he immersed himself in debauchery. Later, he acknowledged: "People say that I am extremely dissolute, but they do not know that this is how I drown my profound depression."[62] His friends and associates, including his blood brothers Dai Jitao and Cicada Zhang, urged him to return to the south, but he would hear nothing of a new trip.[63] Finally, Sun Yat-sen offered him a choice: either go to Russia if he still wanted to so badly or to Sichuan to organize a revolutionary movement there, or, yet again, to Chen Jiongming's army. He let it be known that he wanted his disciple to choose Chen Jiongming. This was a test of loyalty. Chiang still had the strength to control himself. "I have an obligation to my friends and the party; my efforts should be directed toward the good of the state," he decided, and for the fifth time he set out for the south.[64]

At this time Commander in Chief Chen, at Sun Yat-sen's request, was actively preparing for a fight against the old enemies of the Guomindang: the Guangxi militarists who, as before, were occupying Canton. Sun had again decided to make this South China city, rightly considered the capital of South

China, his revolutionary base. So it was a very important moment. Chen forthwith appointed Chiang commander of the 2nd Corps. This was a general's position, so Chiang's ambition, it seemed, should have been satisfied.[65]

Chiang swiftly drew up plans for three military operations that General Chen accepted and successfully implemented. Not only was Canton taken, but the entire province of Guangdong was cleared of the Guangxi militarists. Nevertheless, the proud Chiang, considering that he had fulfilled his obligation and after submitting a new request for leave in early November 1920 again sank into a depression.

Indeed, Sun Yat-sen had difficulty asserting his sole leadership in the party. Most likely he truly valued Chiang, a talented, goal-oriented, bold officer who was at the same time "impatient, uncompromising, impulsive, and ill-tempered, periodically manifesting symptoms of psychosomatic dysfunction," that is, a psychological disorder occasioned by severe negative emotions.[66] Trying once more to bring the obstinate Chiang to his senses, Sun wrote him a brief but very significant letter in which he expressed his displeasure with his behavior:

> To my dear Elder Brother Chiang Kai-Shek [Kai-shek] [a polite form of address in premodern China],
>
> When our elder brother Chen Chiung-Ming [Jiongming] fought back to Canton, he was using all his strength to serve our party and our country. We, on our part, are using all our strength to help him. . . . [O]ur co-operation[with him] cannot be compared with any ordinary temporary alliance. . . . I trust him exactly as I did . . . Chen Chi-Mei [Qimei] at those times. . . . But you have a very fiery temper, and your hatred of mediocrity is too excessive. And so it often leads to quarrelling and difficulty in co-operating. As you are shouldering the great and heavy responsibility of our party, you should sacrifice your high ideals a little and try to compromise. This is merely for the sake of the party and has nothing to do with your personal principles. Would you, my elder brother, agree with this? Or wouldn't you?[67]

Chiang did not agree. He abandoned everything and went off to Xikou. On November 25 Sun Yat-sen set off for Canton, now free of Guangxi troops. On November 29 he again established a South China military government in this largest city of South China, located on the left (northern) bank of the Zhujiang (Pearl River), ninety miles from the British colony of Hong Kong.[68] The city, founded as far back as 214 BCE, had always been a thriving commercial center. In the early twentieth century it was no less dynamic than Shanghai, although it looked very different from the capital of East China, which, more than other Chinese cities, had been "corrupted" by Western civilization. Canton had several broad streets along which automobiles careened, electric streetlights shone here and there, and handsome modern buildings adorned the embankment. There were even six- and nine-story department stores. But these fruits of Western culture were not what gave this populous capital of South China, with its more than one and a half million people, its local flavor. Overall the city remained purely Chinese, but unlike the intellectual, prim Beijing it was multicolored and diverse.

After establishing his new government, Sun began to settle in. On December 25 Dai Jitao, apparently on orders from Sun, came to Chiang's village, requesting that he return to the south.[69] Dai declared that Chen Jiongming had now put himself wholly at the service of the party, and Sun had gone to Canton to head the military government there, the goal of which was to prepare an expedition against the northern militarists. He insisted that Chiang and others must forget about all the disagreements and stick together in the south. But Chiang was disinclined to do so and nothing came from the conversation. "To urge me to go out [to the south] and work [there]," he said, "is to urge me to shorten my life."

The blood brothers shouted at each other, and Dai slammed the door shut. Yet afterward they exchanged courteous letters that provide additional information about the character of Chiang Kai-shek and his political views at this time. In the first of these, dated January 5, 1921, Chiang confessed: "I have a bad temper and am usually lacking in good manners. . . . I become unconsciously rude, bursting out all at once."

Dai replied the following week: "When I met with your fury without apparent reason, I felt most dejected. . . . You, my Elder Brother, are extremely self-willed to an almost incorrigible extent. Whenever you are disappointed at some trifle, you let your anger go unchecked. In dealing with people in that way, you run the grave danger of courting calamity; or at least you will find it most damaging to your career."

Chiang retorted: "The complications of the situation there [in Guangdong], my Elder Brother, you could not comprehend. . . . [T]hey throw me over when they don't need me and beckon me to go back when they do. How can I bear such kind of treatment? Am I too narrow-minded? Perhaps. Although we shouldn't feel swelled-headed, neither should we consider ourselves as dirt. . . . I only said that I had a bad temper, unsuitable for society;

I must leave my friends, to live alone in the mountains or wilderness, in which case perhaps I might live longer."[70] Still, Chiang pondered the words of his blood brother. Four telegrams that Sun Yat-sen sent him from Canton over the next two months also had their effect. In addition, he received letters from other comrades in the party, who, like Dai Jitao, implored him to sacrifice his ego for the sake of the common cause.

After a difficult mental struggle, on January 20, 1921, he finally decided to go to Canton, but only when the Guangdong Army announced mobilization for a campaign into Guangxi province.[71] This would signify the start of the Northern Expedition that both he and Sun Yat-sen had fought for. Chiang even prepared a new, detailed plan for this campaign for Sun Yat-sen, this time hoping to seize Sichuan after Guangxi and then Shaanxi and Hubei. Instead of striking eastward along the coast of Fujian and Zhejiang, he now insisted upon moving west.[72] Meeting with the leader of the party in Canton, where he had finally arrived at the beginning of February 1921, Chiang again expressed his doubts about Chen Jiongming's loyalty, but Sun Yat-sen repeated what he had written in his letter: "Try to collaborate with our friends. Time is working for us."[73]

Chiang tried but not for long. After two weeks he again went off to Shanghai after submitting his resignation.[74] He left Sun Yat-sen a letter in which he emphasized his opinion of Chen Jiongming: "As for receiving orders, carrying them out at the critical moment, respecting the Party, trying to eliminate its enemies, he [Chen Jiongming] will never do so. I hope you will be able to change him and direct him."[75]

But Sun did not heed the advice of his loyal, albeit obstinate, disciple. It seemed that his bond with Chen Jiongming was firm. The cunning Chen tried so hard to convince Sun he was one of his men that he even fooled experienced agents of Soviet Russia who, at the time, were coming on exploratory visits to South China. The first of these, Lubo (the original Russian of his surname is unknown), came especially to see Chen Jiongming in the city of Zhangzhou, which Chen, in the words of several radically inclined Chinese, had turned into a real "Moscow of southern Fujian" as early as April 1920.[76] Lubo's orders were to present a personal letter from Lenin.[77] Liao Zhongkai and Zhu Zhixin took part in their meeting. The latter prepared a draft reply to Lenin for Chen Jiongming. Lubo acquainted his interlocutors with the situation in Soviet Russia, enthusiastically welcomed the development of the revolution in China, and expressed the readiness of Soviet Russia to help China in completing the nationalist revolution. Liao Zhongkai and

Zhu Zhixin reported this meeting to Sun Yat-sen.[78] In January 1921 Voitinsky also paid a visit to General Chen, this time in Canton. He treated Chen with great respect.[79] And the counselor of the Soviet diplomatic mission to China, the old Bolshevik Vladimir Dmitrievich Vilensky-Sibiriakov, in a letter to Lenin characterized Chen Jiongming as one of "the leaders of young China that was undergoing emancipation. [He] may be placed alongside Dr. Sun Yat-sen in terms of his political record of devotion to revolutionary ideas and organizational talent."[80] In December 1920 even Chen Duxiu, the well-known leftist public figure, came to Canton. By this time, as noted earlier, he had begun to collaborate actively with the Comintern. At Chen Jiongming's invitation, he served as chairman of the Guangdong Provincial People's Education Committee.[81]

On April 7, 1921, Sun Yat-sen was proclaimed emergency president of the Republic of China, and on May 5 the inauguration ceremony took place. In reality, he controlled only a part of South China, but this wording sounded more impressive. On June 13, 1921, he received a salutatory letter from People's Commissar for Foreign Affairs of Soviet Russia Georgii Vasilievich Chicherin that had been sent to him on October 31, 1920. In response, on August 28, 1921, Sun Yat-sen wrote, "I would like to establish personal contact with you and other friends in Moscow. I am extraordinarily interested in your affairs, in particular in the organization of your Soviets, your army, and education. I would like to know what you and others may inform me of these things, particularly about education. Like Moscow, I would like to instill the principles of the Chinese Republic deep in the minds of the younger generation—the toilers of tomorrow." He asked Chicherin to convey his best regards to "my friend Lenin."[82]

At the time, Chiang was in Xikou. His mother had long been sick, and he was trying to alleviate her suffering. But just then he received a telegram from Sun Yat-sen: the northern militarists had unexpectedly announced a southern campaign against the Cantonese government, and the Guomindang leader requested his help. Chen Jiongming also begged him to return. Telegrams from Sun, Chen, and other party comrades in arms followed, one after the other. On April 21 Sun informed Chiang that he had declared mobilization, as Chiang had wanted. In the latter half of May 1921 Chiang, for the seventh time, left for the south.[83] However, on the third night after his arrival he had a strange dream. A mountain entirely covered with white snow appeared before him. Since white is the color of mourning in China, Chiang was terribly upset. The dream was prophetic. The next day Chiang received a dispatch from his native village that his mother was worse. Now even Sun Yat-sen could not hold him back. On May 27 Chiang set sail from Canton and arrived in Xikou at midnight on May 31.[84] He did not take part in the conquest of Guangxi that began in June.

He was unable to help his mother, however, and was therefore deeply depressed and embittered all the time. He not only loved his mother more than anyone else on earth, but also considered her his closest friend. Now he felt that he was going to be completely alone, and he didn't feel like socializing with anyone. "I have many false friends, and few true ones," he wrote in his diaries. "[T]here are many egoists around, but far fewer who sacrifice themselves for the common good and for friends. Therefore, I crave solitude, I want to sever all ties with the outside world, but I cannot."[85] The venerable Wang died on June 14, 1921, at 7:49 in the morning in her fifty-eighth year.[86]

Chiang was completely dispirited. He looked on dully as loudly weeping relatives and neighbors who had gathered in the house carried the body in the main room on a so-called water bed, made by joining three boards. Then the women washed her. Her feet were tied together with red cord so that the deceased woman could sleep quietly and no longer be able to rise. Someone sealed the windows and set up a family altar of white paper; someone else posted a white paper with a funeral notice on the gates of the house; and yet another person hung a killed rooster over the body of the deceased so that death would no longer look in on the house. According to local beliefs, Yan Wang, the King of Death, was satisfied with two corpses. Soon, Buddhist nuns from the Golden Bamboo nunnery, where Chiang's mother had once served as a novice, arrived and chanted prayers for the repose of the deceased's soul. Everyone present placed one of their hairs in the hands of the deceased, indicating their desire to be with her at her new reincarnation. Chiang, remaining aloof, also tore hair from his head and placed it in the ice-cold hand of his mother. The next day the coffin holding the corpse was taken to a deep, cold cellar, where it would be kept until the funeral. On the advice of a geomancer (incidentally, one of the old members of the Guomindang whom Chiang had specially invited from Shanghai), the funeral should take place on November 23, the most auspicious day.[87]

Three days later Chiang received a telegram of condolences and 2,000 Chinese dollars from Sun Yat-sen as well as 1,000 from Chen Jiongming. Soon telegrams from many other comrades in the party arrived, including from the blood brothers Cicada Zhang and Dai Jitao. But Chiang was inconsolable. He contributed 10,000 Chinese dollars to the Golden Bamboo nunnery, requesting they use the money to found a nunnery school. Afterward, he dealt with all the financial questions regarding the solemn funeral on November 23. It was decided that the funeral would be held on a hilltop some two *li* west of Xikou.[88] By that day a grave should be ready and a temporary memorial erected—a permanent one would be finished in two years' time. The cost of preliminary work clearing the area and digging the grave was estimated at 3,000 to 4,000 Chinese dollars.[89]

At the end of August 1921 Chiang left for Shanghai and from there again set sail to Canton. There, over several days, he discussed the plans and timing of the Northern Expedition with Sun Yat-sen and those persons closest to him. Afterward he departed for Nanning, the capital of Guangxi province, to Chen Jiongming's headquarters. But here he was disappointed once again. General Chen did not want to launch the Northern Expedition, deeming it necessary first to shore up his position in South China.[90] Chiang once again lost self-control. "People from Guangdong and Guangxi are terribly untruthful," he wrote in his diaries. "I can't help feeling disgusted. . . . Guangdong people . . . absolutely lack any concept of morality and duty."[91]

Furious, he returned to Canton and reported the situation to Sun Yat-sen, who convened a secret meeting with his associates. There it was decided that the 2nd Corps under the command of Chiang Kai-shek himself would launch the Northern Expedition into southern Hunan at an appropriate time.[92] Then he let Chiang return to Xikou to bury his mother's body and conduct all the requisite ceremonies.

On the appointed day, November 23, the solemn funeral took place on the hill chosen by the geomancer. A grave tablet that Sun Yat-sen, Chiang's leader and mentor, at Chiang's request, had sent him for his mother's grave, was mounted into the memorial. It was inscribed, "Grave of Mother Jiang." (Her surname was Wang but Jiang [Chiang] is the family name of Chiang Kai-shek.) The characters on the stone were in the style of Sun's own calligraphy. They were engraved by Hu Hanmin and Wang Jingwei, close comrades in arms of the leader.[93] Sun was represented at the funeral by Chiang's blood nephew Chen Guofu, who conveyed to Chiang condolences from the Father of the Republic.[94]

Chen Guofu, speaking on Sun's behalf, requested that Chiang return to Guangdong as soon as possible. Sun was determined to launch the Northern Expedition.[95] Before departing, Chiang announced to Fumei and Yecheng that now, after his mother's funeral, he was divorcing them, and all the property would be divided among the sons; the management of household affairs would be given over to his nonblood relative, his aunt Sun, the younger sister of his father's second wife. Actually, he did not officially divorce Fumei since she and her relatives were adamantly opposed to it. Fumei lost her property rights but continued to live in Xikou. Things were easier with his mistress Yecheng. Chiang promised to pay her a certain subsistence sum and she agreed.[96] Chiang's eldest son, Ching-kuo, remained with his mother, and his younger son, Wei-kuo, with Yecheng. Chiang wrote a letter to both of them saying that from now on, after the death of their grandmother, he could give himself "up to the country alone." "From the age of 18 the main object of my life has been Revolution," he explained. "[I]n comparison with this supreme aim, life, death, glory, and misfortune are all as nothing to me. My only cause of disquiet was my mother's welfare," Chiang declared. "This anxiety is no longer with me."[97]

Wei-kuo wept loudly on parting from him. He wanted to go with his father and kept shouting, "Papa, papa!" He clung to Chiang's neck, and Yecheng had a hard time prying him off. Chiang was heartbroken. He loved his little adopted son more than his own son. "Wei-kuo is splendid, and Ching-kuo is pitiful," he wrote in his diaries on the eve of his departure.[98] But he had to do his duty. On December 12 Chiang again went out into the wider world.[99] His home had nothing more to offer.

PART TWO

# *The Anti-Imperialist Revolution*

CHAPTER 5

# *Canton–Shanghai–Moscow–Canton*

On the road south in December 1921 Chiang stopped in Shanghai for several days to resolve a matter important to him. He acquired a new concubine. Chiang's new mistress was just a girl: born in the Year of the Horse, August 26, 1906, she had turned fifteen three and a half months earlier. Chiang was now thirty-four, so there was a nineteen-year difference between them. The girl, whose name was Chen Feng (Chen Phoenix), was from a very wealthy Shanghai family, close acquaintances of Cicada Zhang, Chiang Kai-shek's blood brother. Chiang had first seen her two and half years earlier in Cicada's house. She was then about thirteen and quite plain-looking: very tall, thin, with an extremely large mouth and slightly protruding lower jaw. But her dark eyes penetrated into the soul. She was very demure but obviously well educated. The servants and her friends called her A Feng, meaning Little Phoenix, or, in English, Jennie.

In the future, contrary to appearances, she proved to be far from inoffensive. After Chiang left her in September 1927 to marry Song Meiling (Olivia), the third daughter of Charlie Song, Sun's friend, and the younger sister of Song Ailing and Song Qingling, she could not just let the insult pass. After Chiang's defeat in the civil war and his flight to Taiwan, in 1964 while living in Hong Kong, she would write her memoirs. First, she asserted that she was Chiang's lawful second wife (after Fumei), when in fact she was his official concubine, and, second, she told countless filthy stories about Chiang Kai-shek, Yecheng, and Song Meiling. For example, she claimed that the promiscuous sexual couplings of Ruiyuan the Bandit in Shanghai and Tokyo prior to his meeting her led to his contracting gonorrhea and, after being cured, he became infected again and transmitted the disease to her during their honeymoon. Both he and she were eventually cured, but Chiang developed epididymitis (inflammation of a tube at the back of the testicle) and was sterile for the rest of his life. She also asserted that, supposedly, Yecheng's face was terribly disfigured because her former lover, whom she left for Chiang, in revenge poured a cauldron of hot shark's fin soup over her head, badly scalding her skin. Moreover, she swore that Chiang Kai-shek never loved Song Meiling and that he married her only for political reasons and never even slept with her. In sum, according to her, for his whole life Chiang adored her alone, his proud beauty: before, during their years together, and after his break with her.[1]

Much of what she wrote is impossible to verify, but the book, published almost simultaneously in Taiwan, the PRC, and the United States in 1992–93, has the aura of a cheap romance novel that contains all the elements: blood, passion, betrayal, a sharp knife, venereal disease, and even an attempted rape of a thirteen-year-old girl by a savage bumpkin. Chiang is depicted first as a young officer dying of love, ready to cut off his finger to win a standoffish beauty, then as a vile egoist whose abandonment of a woman causes her to attempt suicide. A very few of the events described in the book do not arouse suspicion inasmuch as they can be confirmed by documents, but in general the book literally abounds with errors and flagrant falsehoods. It is simply amazing that several biographers of Chiang, such as Jonathan Fenby, unthinkingly accept as true everything contained therein.

Jennie, for example, asserts that Chiang officially married her in Shanghai on December 5, 1921, after which the young newlyweds spent three days in the Dadong (Great East) Hotel, then ten days in Xikou, Chiang's native village, then four days in Shanghai, afterward visiting Suzhou and again returning to Shanghai, where they were treated for gonorrhea for at least ten days.[2] If she is right about the banquet on December 5, then most of what she says is simply impossible since, according to his diaries, Chiang left the Dadong Hotel on December 15 at two o'clock in the afternoon for Hong Kong, where he arrived on December 18 at nine o'clock in the morning.[3] That means he had only nine days, no more, including treatment for venereal disease. Apparently, he and Jennie really did go to Xikou—at least, according to his diaries, on December 12 Chiang was in Ningbo, a stone's throw from Xikou—but all the rest is the fruit of an aggrieved woman's fantasy.[4]

The truth most likely is this. When the girl whom Chiang had an eye for reached marriageable age, at Chiang's request Cicada Zhang talked it over with her mother (Jennie's father had died on September 7, 1921), and she agreed that her daughter would go to live with the important Guomindang general, the blood brother of Zhang and comrade in arms of Sun Yat-sen, Father of the Republic. There could not have been any discussion of a legal marriage because Chiang was not formally divorced from Fumei. However, the position of a favorite concubine in old China was no less and sometimes even more important than that of an unloved wife, so there would have been no problem in that regard. Chiang made the offer, Jennie accepted, and a banquet was held in the large reception hall of the Dadong Hotel. But there was no wedding ceremony, although in her memoir Jennie narrates the contents of the "marriage certificate" supposedly signed by Chiang Kai-shek and herself and attested to by Zhang, matchmakers, her mother, and the groom's witness, Dai Jitao. But she published neither a photocopy of the document nor pictures from the purported wedding. Chiang has no mention whatsoever about this marriage in his diaries. He simply writes that he was living in Shanghai in the Dadong Hotel.[5]

Taking his new, favorite concubine with him, Chiang arrived in South China at the end of December 1921. He gave his heartthrob a new name that she liked very much: Jieru, meaning Pure and Chaste.

At this time Sun was in the city of Guilin, in Guangxi province, almost a thousand *li* northwest of Canton. There, units of the Guangdong Army loyal to him, under the command of General Xu Chongzhi, whom Sun treated like a son, were making preparations for the Northern Expedition while Sun Yat-sen was constantly in military meetings.[6] Moreover, from December 23, 1921, Sun held secret meetings in Guilin with a new representative of the Comintern, Hendricus Sneevliet, a Dutchman by birth, who was presented to Sun as Ma Lin, which is how his pseudonym, Maring, the name under which he worked in the Executive Committee of the Comintern, sounded in Chinese. In China he was also known by the pseudonyms Andreson and Philipp. He was about forty years old, very self-assured, energetic, and imposing.[7]

He came to see Sun with his interpreter, a young, intelligent-looking Chinese around twenty-three years of age, wearing big round eyeglasses. The interpreter's name was Zhang Tailei. Maring proposed to Sun the establishing of a secret alliance between the Guomindang and Soviet Russia and sending several Guomindang so-called delegates to Moscow via Germany under the guise of businessmen. He likewise proposed that the Guomindang orient itself to supporting the popular masses, establishing schools to train military cadres for the Chinese revolution, and organizing the Guomindang into a powerful political party that would unite representatives from various segments of society.[8] He gave a speech about Soviet Russia before the officers of Xu Chongzhi's army in which he emphasized that, after the civil war, the Bolshevik party, transitioning to a new economic policy aimed at partial restoration of market relations, was supposedly moving away from communism.[9]

Maring's proposals impressed Sun immensely, and he privately assured Maring that he himself was a Bolshevik.[10] Speaking in Guilin to a gathering of fellow Guangdong natives on January 4, 1922, he informed everyone that he wanted to build a state in China just like the one in Soviet Russia, that is, a "new type of republic."[11] In a letter to his comrade in arms Liao Zhongkai in Canton,[12] he explained: "Russia's economic situation as yet do not provide the necessary conditions for Communism. That is why I was quite surprised when I first heard of Communism being practiced in Russia. I have since learned with gratification from Ma Lin [Maring] that there is not much difference between Russia's New Economic Policy and our Program of Industrialization."[13] Sun was now convinced that "the principle of the equal division of property has been implemented in Russia" and that it meant that the principle of People's Livelihood that he had fought for since 1905 had been "fully put into practice there."[14]

By this time, with the assistance of Russian Bolsheviks, the communist movement in China had begun to develop. After Chen Duxiu, leaning on financial support from the Comintern representative Voitinsky, had organized the first Bolshevik circle in Shanghai in July 1920, analogous circles arose in Beijing, Changsha, Jinan, Canton, Wuhan, and even in Tokyo. (In the latter two Chinese students organized a circle.) With the help of Maring and another emissary from Soviet Russia, Boris Nikolsky—also known as Vasilii Berg, Vasilii, Vasiliev; his real name was Vladimir Abramovich Neiman—the First Congress of the CCP was convened in Shanghai and Jiaxing (Zhejiang province) in July 1921, at which Chen Duxiu was chosen as secretary of the Central Bureau. Chen did not take part in the congress since he was in Canton, where he was one of the ministers in the Guomindang government.

There were not many Chinese communists at this time, only fifty-eight, but they were all wholly resolved to transform China and place it on the path of the Soviet Bolsheviks. As early as the summer of 1920 the Comintern itself had determined to establish a united anti-imperialist front of communists and local nationalists in China as in other colonies and semicolonies where the national question, not the social question, was the most acute. Nevertheless, the first adherents of communism in China unequivocally rejected any sort of alliance with Sun Yat-sen even though their leader, Chen Duxiu, was a minister in Canton. Maring and Nikolsky tried unsuccessfully to make them understand, but to no avail.[15]

His trip to the south and his conversations with Sun and other leaders of the Guomindang, including Chen Jiongming, as well as his acquaintance with the Guomindang's achievements in organizing the workers' movement in Canton, strengthened Maring's determination to persuade the leaders of the CCP to renounce "their one-sided position regarding the Guomindang." Moreover, it occurred to Maring that the Chinese communists should join Sun Yat-sen's party in order to "engage in political activity *inside* the Guomindang." This way, he figured, the CCP would be able to connect more easily with the workers and soldiers of South China, where power was in the hands of Sun Yat-sen's supporters. Maring stressed that the CCP should not "relinquish its independence. On the contrary, the comrades should discuss what tactics to pursue inside the Guomindang. . . . The state of propaganda of these small groups [of communists] while they are not united with the Guomindang," he concluded, "is very pathetic."[16] Sun Yat-sen, along with a number of other Guomindang leaders, welcomed Maring's initiative regarding entry of communists into the Guomindang. They assured the Comintern representative that they would not impede communist propaganda inside their party. But Sun Yat-sen was pessimistic regarding interparty collaboration between the Guomindang and the CCP.[17]

Maring left Guilin in mid-January 1922, just when Chiang Kai-shek and Jennie arrived at Sun Yat-sen's headquarters.[18] Chiang probably just missed meeting Moscow's emissary, as otherwise he would have noted the meeting in his diaries. It is possible that Sun simply didn't want to let Chiang in on his political and diplomatic affairs and therefore did not introduce him to Maring. At this time, he usually tried to make use of Chiang only as a military advisor, valuing his talent as a staff officer and a strategist.

For political consultation he had Hu Hanmin and Liao Zhongkai, both frail but extraordinarily energetic and gifted. Hu, born in 1879, a brilliant publicist and intrepid revolutionary, was particularly close to Sun. Editor of *The People,* the main organ of the Revolutionary Alliance during the Xinhai Revolution, he became the military governor of Guangdong, and then, like Chen Qimei, he lost his post after opposing Yuan Shikai. Liao, who was two years older than Hu, also took part in the revolution and also boldly struggled against Yuan. Sun recognized his organizational talent. Sun also highly valued Wang Jingwei, the party's best orator, who became especially famous in 1910, when he arranged an attempted assassination of the Manchu prince-regent Zai Feng. The attempt failed, to be sure, but Wang, who was then twenty-seven years old, was sentenced to life imprisonment, and only the Xinhai Revolution freed him.[19] These three revolutionaries were Sun's brain trust from the founding of the Revolutionary Alliance, and their position in the party was above that of Chiang Kai-shek. At this time, they, and especially Liao and Wang, enthusiastically supported the development of relations between the Guomindang and Soviet Russia.[20]

Chiang arrived at Sun's headquarters full of energy and with a detailed plan for the Northern Expedition. But he soon discovered that once again there were no hopes for a military expedition. Although Xu Chongzhi and the Yunnan–Guizhou army allied to him had thirty thousand officers and men, Sun had neither sufficient resources nor arms. Chen Jiongming continued to oppose the Northern Expedition, although, meeting Sun halfway, he promised to send funds and arms. However, at the last minute he let Sun down, and at the end of March 1922 he even arranged the assassination of Sun Yat-sen's go-between who was conducting negotiations in Hong Kong to acquire arms.[21]

Chiang immediately proposed to Sun Yat-sen that he mount a punitive expedition against Chen Jiongming, who was in Canton, but Sun did not agree. He merely relieved Chen Jiongming of the positions of commander of the Guangdong Army, governor of Guangdong, minister of war affairs and minister of internal affairs in his government. He did not want to take responsibility for unleashing a war with General Chen. In April Chiang again retired; bitter and irritated once more, he left for Shanghai with Jennie, arriving there April 27.[22] From there he went to the shore of Lake Taihu in Huzhou (Zhejiang province) to visit the grave of his blood brother Chen Qimei.[23] Evidently, he wanted to vent all the grievances accumulating within him recently to his old friend.

Meanwhile, the armed conflict between Sun and General Chen was coming to a head. After receiving the order relieving him of all his positions, Chen Jiongming quickly left Canton for Huizhou, the main city in eastern Guangdong, his home territory. Not yet ready for a test of strength with Sun Yat-sen, he decided to fortify his position back home. Sun had long since exasperated Chen with his ambitions and his foolhardy desire to unify all China quickly under his control. Unlike Sun Yat-sen, Chen Jiongming believed it was impossible for now to unify China by force, and therefore he was in favor of organizing a Chinese federation, in essence an alliance of independent regions in the country. He envisioned himself as military governor of the conjoined provinces of Guangdong and Guangxi, an enormous region with a population of thirty million. In early 1922 his differences with Sun Yat-sen were so manifest that they did not escape Maring's gaze. "His relations with Sun Yat-sen [were already] very negative," Ma Lin later reported to Moscow.[24] Chen began to insist that Sun Yat-sen resign.[25]

Sun was also increasingly exasperated by General Chen. "I am the president, and ministries should subordinate themselves to me," he declared indignantly to Sergei Alekseevich Dalin, yet another representative from Moscow who visited him in late April 1922. "He has come out against me. . . . There can be no talk of compromises."[26] He even resorted to threats: "I have eight-inch guns with poisonous shells which are capable of entirely finishing their sixty battalions in three hours."[27]

On May 9 he announced the start of the Northern Expedition against the militarists in Jiangxi, and troops loyal to him under the command of Xu Chongzhi crossed the boundary into that province. Sun and his other comrades insistently called on Chiang Kai-shek to return. But he took the bit in his teeth and, nurturing his grievances, bombarded Sun and other Guomindang leaders with telegrams from Shanghai. He affirmed the need to have done with Chen Jiongming, saying it was a necessary condition for the success of the Northern Expedition. He wrote even to General Chen, calling on him "[f]or the sake of our past friendship . . . to retire once and for all or at least for the time being."[28]

It is difficult to say whether Chiang was aware that his telegrams were precisely what provoked an open conflict between Chen and Sun. Most likely he deliberately exacerbated the situation. And he did this despite repeated warnings from his comrades in the party, urging him "to desist from urging our leader to attack General Ch'en Chiung-ming [Chen Jiongming]." "[Y]our many letters and telegrams to various brothers, . . ." Hu Hanmin wrote to him, "will only cause great mischief. . . . Much ill-feeling [regarding Sun Yat-sen's intention to strike Chen Jiongming] has already been created. Worst of all, if Ch'en Chiung-ming believes these rumors, Canton will easily become a bloody battle field."[29]

That is precisely what happened. On the night of June 15–16, 1922, supporters of General Chen Jiongming, unable to stand this any longer, rose in rebellion against Sun Yat-sen. Miraculously, Sun and his wife managed to flee from the palace amid the thunder of an artillery cannonade. Song Qingling took refuge with friends in Lingnan University on the south bank of the Pearl River across from Canton. (She was pregnant, but that night she suffered a miscarriage from anxiety.)[30] Sun himself took refuge on a military vessel, the *Yongfeng,* anchored in the Canton roadstead of the Pearl River. From there, disconsolate and close to suicidal,[31] he sent a telegram to Chiang Kai-shek on June 18—in the interests of security he addressed it to Chiang's son Wei-kuo. "The situation in Canton is critical," he wrote. "There is no one to head the army. We can brook no delay. Come at once."[32] Wang Jingwei and Lin Yeming, another of Sun Yat-sen's close associates, sent Chiang similar telegrams about the coup.[33]

One can imagine how Chiang must have felt. "I predicted it! I predicted it!" he shouted. Then, turning to Jennie, he blurted out, "Pack up! We are leaving for Canton by the first ship!"[34] He then wrote to Cicada Zhang, requesting that he look after his family in the event of his death, collected 60,000 Chinese dollars from Sun's comrade in arms, the head of the Shanghai chamber of commerce, and, by June 25, together with Jennie was already on board a ship heading from Shanghai to Canton where he arrived four days later.[35]

Climbing aboard the cruiser *Yongfeng,* he saw that Sun Yat-sen could barely hold back his tears. Among all the military men who had professed loyalty to him, there was no one he could rely on now apart from Chiang. Xu Chongzhi and other generals were at the front in Jiangxi, and soon news arrived that, after seizing Canton, General Chen had attacked Xu's forces, inflicting a serious defeat upon them. The Northern Expedition had bogged down, and Sun had nowhere to turn for help. Desperate, he turned to the Americans, requesting that they dispatch troops to Canton, but the US government turned down his proposal. He tried to get in touch with Chen Jiongming, but nothing came of this.[36]

In this situation Chiang advised the only correct decision: flee at once. He stayed calm; aboard the cruiser almost every day he read Arthur Conan Doyle's *Canon of Sherlock Holmes.*[37] The ability of the great detective to concentrate in the time of chaos must have made a deep impression on him, a devout neo-Confucianist.

Sun agreed to flee, and at four o'clock in the afternoon of August 9 he, along with Song Qingling, Chiang, and Jennie departed to Hong Kong on the schooner *Moses,* provided to them by the British. From there they reached Shanghai on the morning of August 14 aboard the *Empress of Russia,* a Canadian liner.[38]

Before departing, Sun had dispatched a note to Dalin, who remained in Canton: "During these days I have thought a lot about the fate of the Chinese revolution. I am disillusioned with almost everything I believed earlier. Now I am convinced that the only true and sincere friend of the Chinese revolution is Soviet Russia. . . . In case of failure, I will go to Soviet Russia."[39]

After returning to Shanghai, Sun rapidly drew closer to Moscow. In his unequal struggle with militarism in 1922–25, Sun Yat-sen, without an army of his own, was forced to accept financial and military aid from what he perceived to be a natural ally: anti-imperialist Soviet Russia, which by then had achieved a decisive victory not only over the Whites in the civil war but also over the imperialist interventionists. The upshot was that the Bolshevik regime and the Comintern that it directed, whose goal was to achieve a world socialist revolution, became the most important players on the political stage of China.

Chiang Kai-shek also moved to the left, not by the day but the hour. One finds the following entries in his diaries from October 1921 to March 1923: "I want to open a school [in Xikou], but the local *shenshi* are strongly opposed. . . . Living in the countryside is very difficult, the common people face obstacles at every turn, there is no possibility of changing society for the better. . . . Chinese merchants are frightful snobs who despise everyone below them on the social ladder, [they are] horrible bureaucrats and liars. Seeing this, I feel hatred." He added, "I simply hate the loathsome and envious merchants." Departing from Xikou to the larger world at the end of 1921, he swore not to return there until the rural elite was destroyed down to the roots. In the depth of his soul, however, he acknowledged that this was "far from the path" that Buddha, so beloved by his mother, had pointed out to him.[40]

Returning to Shanghai with Sun, Chiang, at Sun's request, occupied himself with drafting a plan to shift the military base of the Chinese revolution to Urga, the capital of Mongolia. The plan required coordinating efforts with the Soviets inasmuch as Mongolia, which prior to the Xinhai Revolution had been under the control of the Qing empire, after 1912 found itself a de facto Russian protectorate in accordance with a secret treaty the Mongols had concluded with Tsarist Russia. After the October Revolution, White forces under Baron Roman Fedorovich von Ungern-Sternberg occupied Mongolia, and then the Red Army took over in May–August 1921. All Chinese politicians, including Sun, nonetheless considered Mongolia Chinese territory, but Sun, who was now dependent on Soviet aid, was ready for now to close his eyes to the presence of Bolshevik troops in Mongolia.[41]

Chiang's plan was unrealistic but was approved by Sun, who at the time was not in the best shape. Chiang intended to organize and arm a force of eighteen thousand to thirty thousand officers and men on Mongolian territory over the next two years. The next step would be to invade China, overthrow the Beijing government and establish control over the entire Yellow River valley and the Longhai railroad, which bisected North China from west to east.[42] Then he planned to cross the Yangzi River[43] and liberate South China.[44]

From late September to late December Sun discussed this plan, which he called "bold, innovative, and, moreover, revolutionary." He addressed the military attaché of the embassy of Soviet Russia in China, the former chief of the military academy of the Red Army Anatolii Ilyich Gekker, Maring, and Adolf Abramovich Joffe, a leading Russian Bolshevik, who arrived in Beijing in August 1922 as the head of the Soviet diplomatic mission. Joffe informed Moscow about the plan that, from his perspective, was "a fantasy," but Sun "continues to be obsessed with it."[45] In November 1922 Sun sent one of his trusted aides to Beijing to liaise with Joffe, and at the end of December posed the question starkly to Joffe: "I can move almost 100,000 from Sichuan through Gansu to Inner Mongolia. . . . CAN YOUR GOVERNMENT HELP ME VIA URGA AND, IF SO, TO WHAT DEGREE AND HOW?"[46] But the Soviet government delayed answering. And Sun continued to negotiate with Joffe, Maring, and other representatives of Soviet Russia and the Comintern. He even wrote to Lenin, Trotsky, and Chicherin.

Meanwhile, in order to win the trust of the Russians he began to hold talks with the Chinese communists regarding their entry into the Guomindang and, on this basis, establishing a united anti-imperialist front. At the beginning of September 1922 Sun accepted the first four communists into the ranks of his party, including Chen Duxiu and Zhang Tailei.[47] On January 1, 1923, he published an announcement concerning the reorganization of the Guomindang, and the following day he convened a conference on party affairs in Shanghai at which he unveiled the party program and statutes. In these documents Sun Yat-sen's Three Principles of the People were reinterpreted in a more radical fashion. Sun stressed anti-imperialism, the defense of workers' rights, and the democratic transformation of China.[48]

During all this time Chiang not only assisted the leader but also strengthened his position in the party hierarchy. In addition to drafting the military plan, on September 13, 1922, he wrote a seventy-page brochure titled "Notes on the Misadventures of the Great President Sun Yat-sen in Canton." This pamphlet took the form of a chronicle covering events from June 15 to August

15, 1922. It was published in Shanghai in October 1922, and thereafter was republished many times. It was enormously significant to Chiang. The main personages in it were Sun Yat-sen and Chiang himself—the only one of the leader's disciples who came to his assistance. At Chiang's request, Sun wrote a foreword to the brochure, and Cicada Zhang carefully wrote out its title in beautiful characters that were then reproduced on the cover. In the foreword the leader praised his faithful disciple: "When the traitor Chen rebelled, Kai-shek came to Canton to share our hardships and came onto the ship. He was next to me all the time, and many of his suggestions made me happy."[49] In order to win himself a place next to Sun Yat-sen, Chiang wittingly chose the title of the publication: it brought to mind the title of Sun's reminiscences of his kidnapping in London in 1896—in Chinese, Sun's brochure was titled "Notes on the Misadventures in London."

At the same time Chiang published a photograph of Sun and himself taken on board the cruiser: he, a young officer, was standing behind Sun, as if protecting the leader from any possible treacherous blow; both were dressed in white sailors' tunics, and their gaze, radiating courage, was directed straight ahead. Like the brochure, the photograph confirmed Chiang in the role of the closest comrade in arms of Sun Yat-sen, convincingly demonstrating Chiang's close ties (*guanxi*) with the leader.

Chiang participated in a series of military conferences in Shanghai convened by Sun Yat-sen, repeatedly suggesting plans for campaigns against Chen Jiongming, first from Fujian, then from Guangxi. On October 20, 1922, Sun dispatched him to southern Fujian, having appointed Chiang chief of staff in the army of Xu Chongzhi, who had redeployed there after his unsuccessful battles against General Chen.

But then Chiang's emotionally unbalanced character resurfaced again. Even though General Xu had always treated him as a brother—they were the same age—Chiang managed to serve under his command for just one month. On November 27 he was in Shanghai again, and from there he ran off to his native village. Most likely he was simply unable to subordinate himself to most people. Apart from his deceased mother, his late brother Chen Qimei, Sun Yat-sen, and Cicada Zhang, he acknowledged no authority figures. From childhood, noted above, he considered himself above everyone else. Now that he had become a general and a close comrade in arms of the leader, he was mostly unable to get along with anyone else, especially in the army. So he repeatedly quarreled with General Xu, first falling into depression, then becoming hysterical.

After barely recovering, a month later he again set off for Fujian in response to a new request from Sun, but once again for just a short time. By early January, after a blowup with General Xu, he returned to Shanghai and thence to Ningbo.[50] As an extremely impulsive and psychologically unbalanced man, he was simply "unable to exercise rational control over his behavior in moments of stress."[51] Once more, from nervous exhaustion as in 1914, his eyes became very painful, and he experienced a loss of vision. He had not found a place for himself, and now, on top of it all, he had an eye disease. Judging from his diaries, he was now so depressed that he began thinking seriously about committing suicide, and only his belief that "the Will of Heaven had placed upon his shoulders a mission ordained by the party" stopped him.[52]

He was indeed a difficult man, and those who valued and respected him, including Sun Yat-sen, had to exercise a great deal of patience in dealing with him. Chiang understood that his nerves were in disorder. Therefore, following a routine begun in his youth every morning, after rising at five or six o'clock, in whatever the weather he sat and meditated for half an hour in front of an open window, with his legs tucked under him and his arms folded across his chest. He was following the counsel of the neo-Confucian Wang Yangming, his favorite philosopher, who emphasized the significance of meditation for getting in touch with one's self and cultivating the positive, creative potential every cultured man could find there. Once as early as the beginning of 1920 he even asked Sun Yat-sen to write for him in his own calligraphy four characters on a sheet of paper: calmness, respect, peace, and concentration (*jing, jing, dan, yi*).[53] After writing these characters, Sun presented the poster to Chiang on the lunar New Year, February 20, and Chiang hung the sheet of paper in his house.[54]

Meanwhile, in mid-January 1923 the Guangxi and Yunnan troops that Sun had won over with a bribe of 400,000 Chinese dollars, inflicted a series of defeats on Chen Jiongming, forcing him to flee to eastern Guangdong.[55] This whetted Moscow's interest in strengthening ties with Sun. On January 17, 1923, Joffe himself came to see Sun in Shanghai. Sun Yat-sen, in talks with him, presented, in the words of the Soviet representative, his definitive military plan "from head to toe." He no longer requested either Soviet intervention in China or territory in Mongolia for his troops, but, as the future would show, neither did he disavow these plans. This time he asked merely for military and financial assistance, and therefore Joffe enthusiastically supported him. In a letter to Lenin and other leaders of the Bolshevik party, he advised them to meet Sun halfway.[56]

On January 26 Joffe and Sun together published a joint communiqué in Shanghai that read, "China enjoys the broadest sympathy of the Russian people and can count on the support of Russia." Both sides showed "full agreement in their views of Chinese–Russian relations," stressing that "at present the communist order or even the Soviet system cannot be introduced into China" due to the absence of the necessary conditions; "the most urgent and important task for China is national unification and the achievement of full national independence."[57]

A month later, on February 21, Sun returned to a liberated Canton, again heading up a local military government. He again proclaimed himself Generalissimo. On March 8, 1923, the Politburo of the Central Committee of the Russian Communist Party (Bolsheviks) (RCP[b]) finally adopted a resolution to provide "monetary support to Sun Yat-sen in the amount of approximately 2 million Mexican dollars"[58] and also to dispatch to him a group of "political and military advisors." In addition, the Politburo decided "to lay the foundation for a revolutionary army in Western China."[59]

While still in Shanghai Sun began to summon Chiang Kai-shek urgently to go with him to Canton. On February 3, 1923, he included Chiang on the staff of the supreme organ of military administration, the Military Council of the Guomindang, that he himself headed. On February 18 he appointed him chief of staff, not in the army of Xu Zhongzhi, to whom Chiang would not subordinate himself, but of his own personal headquarters.[60]

But Chiang's ailments continued to bother him. Not just physically but emotionally too. Most likely he was simply unable to escape from his regular cycle of nervous disorder, and he continually obsessed about himself and his relationship to those around him. This is evident from his diaries' entries. "My parents wanted me to become a perfect person," he wrote during these days, "but even now I am a small child, in the grip of wicked passions. . . . Who apart from Sun Yat-sen treats me with sincerity? I can count such persons on my fingers. Those whom I once trusted are no longer deserving of trust. In all things under Heaven one must rely only on oneself. In the whole world the only person close to me is Sun Yat-sen. Apart from that, are only my children. All the others are beasts evoking disgust."[61] Most likely at this time he placed his new passion, Jennie, among these animals. In any case, he didn't mention her then as someone who was close to him. Nonetheless, he took her with him to Canton when, in mid-April 1923, after urgent requests from Sun Yat-sen, Cicada Zhang, Liao Zhongkai, and other comrades in the party, he went there.

In Canton he became completely absorbed in drafting operational plans for the destruction of the forces of Chen Jiongming, who had entrenched himself in eastern Guangdong. As the chief of staff of the Generalissimo he now reported only to Sun, and one might suppose his vanity would be satisfied. Not so. Even this was too little for him. As before, he wanted all the generals and officers to accept his war plans unquestioningly, but there were still some among them who had their own ideas. Moreover, a disagreement arose between him and Liao Zhongkai, the minister of finance of the Sun Yat-sen government, on financial questions relating to the army.

The result was that on July 12 Chiang exploded, and, after shouting at Liao Zhongkai, "in a rage" he again submitted his resignation and several hours later boarded a ship with Jennie and set off for Hong Kong. From there he ran off to Shanghai yet again and thence to his native village.[62] On departing, he left a letter in which he poured out his grievances against his former friends Liao Zhongkai and General Xu Chongzhi and, as he had done repeatedly before, requested that he be sent to Russia. He declared that after returning from Moscow he would like to take any position in the army where he could do his job without interference from others. He did not specify what position he had in mind.[63]

Comintern representative Maring, who was then in Canton, was astonished. He had recently spent a lot of time with Chiang, and in one of his letters to Joffe in late July 1923 he characterized Chiang as "the most trusted assistant of Sun," "one of [his] best generals," and "one of the best members of the GMD. . . . He never strived for a particular position or took part in a struggle for office," he added. Maring tried to find out the reasons for Chiang's departure from Sun Yat-sen, but Sun did not want to talk about it. Liao Zhongkai was more or less frank: "He was exhausted from his unsuccessful struggle here in Canton, since his plans could not be implemented because of quarrels among the generals."[64]

The patient Sun Yat-sen again reached out to Chiang. On July 23, the day after Chiang Kai-shek's return to Xikou, Wang Jingwei, evidently at the request of the leader, sent Chiang a telegram, summoning him to Shanghai. Three days later, on July 26, he conveyed to him Sun's proposal: to send him to Moscow as the head of a special mission whose composition would be decided in the coming days.[65] In the end, the delegation consisted of two GMD members, including Chiang, and two Communists, one of whom—Zhang Tailei, Maring's former interpreter—is mentioned above.[66] Chiang Kai-shek's longtime dream of visiting Russia was coming true.[67]

Sun expected a great deal from this trip. First, he wanted his man to see what was going on in the USSR with his own eyes and understand the positives and negatives of the Soviet system of power. Second, he supposed that Chiang would acquaint himself with the experience of party and military construction in Soviet Russia, with organizational work in the fields of education, propaganda, and youth policy. Third, he expected Chiang to discuss with the leaders of the Russian Communist Party (Bolsheviks) and the Comintern issues regarding the transformation of the Guomindang into a mass political party and to get recommendations on ideological and organizational issues. Finally, and most important, he hoped that Chiang would convince Moscow comrades of the expediency of Sun's old military plan. Sun was still nurturing it, and, as noted earlier, he envisioned coordinated action by his troops and the Red Army against the northern militarists and, with the aid of the USSR, the creation of a new Guomindang military base in Mongolia or along its border. He had returned to this plan in recent months, even supposing that two-thirds of the material assistance Moscow had allotted to the Guomindang could go for construction of a military base in northern or western China.[68]

Chiang's delegation departed from Shanghai on August 16. The entire high command of the Shanghai Guomindang, including Wang Jingwei and Cicada Zhang as well as Jennie and both of Chiang's sons, escorted him as far as the port of Dairen (Dalian), where the delegation transferred from a ship to a train. Chiang had prepared well for his trip. On August 5 he had written a twelve-page report on the history of the Chinese revolution and the activities of the Guomindang that he intended to present to the leaders of the Bolshevik party.[69]

While Chiang was in transit, Sun sent confidential letters to Lenin, Trotsky, and Chicherin and, in mid-September, to the new USSR ambassador to China, Lev Mikhailovich Karakhan. He said straight out to Karakhan that discussion of his military plan was the main objective of Chiang Kaishek's trip.[70] He repeated this on October 6, to Mikhail Markovich Borodin, an old member of the Bolshevik party and leading official of the Executive Committee of the Comintern. The Politburo of the CC RCP (b), on Stalin's suggestion, had sent Borodin to Sun as a political advisor on July 31. "A Mongolian base attracts him most of all," Borodin reported to Moscow.[71]

Chiang and his comrades arrived in Moscow on September 2. At the Yaroslavl' Railway Station they were festively welcomed by representatives of the People's Commissariat for Foreign Affairs and on the streets of Moscow by crowds of Muscovites. Chiang was ecstatic: it seemed to him that there may have been almost as many as 250,000 people.[72]

The following day Voitinsky, then the deputy head of the Far Eastern Department of the ECCI of the Comintern, met with the delegation, and two days later Chicherin received them. Both impressed Chiang with their sincerity, as he immediately informed Sun Yat-sen by telegram. Impressed by his initial meetings, Chiang resumed studying Russian enthusiastically in his spare time and also read *Capital* by Karl Marx. "I find the first half of this work very heavy going," he wrote to Jennie, "but the second half is both profound and entrancing."[73] In the following weeks, continuing his study of Marxism, he read *The Communist Manifesto* and several other Marxist works.[74]

It seemed that everything was going well. The thirty-six-year-old Chinese general, youthful, smart looking, and not badly educated, made a most favorable impression on the Moscow leaders, especially since in every way he demonstrated the Guomindang's and his own closeness to the Bolsheviks. "Chiang Kai-shek . . . belongs to the left wing of the Guomindang and is one of the oldest members of the party," is how Sergei Ivanovich Dukhovsky, head of the Eastern Department of the People's Commissariat for Foreign Affairs characterized him. "Sun Yat-sen trusts him a lot. He is very close to us. At present he has stepped away from his military work in South China. . . . He is known in China as one of the most educated persons."[75] The portrait of his obstinate, but loyal disciple that Sun Yat-sen drew in his letters to Lenin, Trotsky, and Chicherin had a great impact on how they treated Chiang. It was so brilliant that Chiang Kai-shek could hardly keep from crying when Dukhovsky gave them to him to read.[76]

In September and the early days of October meeting followed meeting. Members of the delegation held talks with the secretary of the Central Committee of the Russian Communist Party, Jan Ernestovich Rudzutak, with Efraim Markovich Skliansky, Trotsky's deputy on the Revolutionary Military Council, with Sergei Sergeevich Kamenev, the commander in chief of the Red Army, and numerous times with Voitinsky and Maring, who had returned to Moscow. They visited the 144th Infantry Regiment of the Red Army that was deployed in Moscow, various military academies, and an air base, the Communist University of the Toilers of the East, founded by the Bolsheviks in April 1921 for Asian and African Communists, including members of the CCP and the Chinese Communist Youth League. They even made a get-acquainted excursion to Petrograd and Kronstadt that made a particularly deep impression on them.

In his talks Chiang called the Russian Communist Party the "blood sister" of the GMD, and his hosts referred to the Guomindang as their brother. At meetings Chiang proclaimed the readiness of Guomindang members "to die in the struggle against imperialism and capitalism." His hands shook, and it was evident that "he strongly and sincerely felt the words he was saying." He sang *The Internationale,* shouted "hurrah," and, after his speeches, singing, and cries, his euphoric auditors lifted him and other members of the delegation into their arms and tossed them up before carrying them to their waiting automobile.[77] Comintern officials, inspired by Chiang's leftism, suggested even that he join the Communist Party, but he put off the proposal saying that first he had to consult with Sun Yat-sen.[78]

With Skliansky and Kamenev, Chiang discussed the main question connected with the provision of military aid to the Guomindang by the USSR. Executing Sun's assignment, he explained to them the plan for new military operations in China, emphasizing that in order to implement the plan they needed to establish a northwest base for Sun Yat-sen's army either in Mongolia itself or along its border.[79] Sun had approved the final version of this plan on August 5, 1923, just eleven days prior to Chiang's departure on his trip.[80]

At this point something went wrong. Russian hospitality virtually vanished. During October and the first ten days of November the delegation did nothing but visit some factories and mills in Moscow, and neither Chicherin nor any other highly placed persons received them. Chiang was incensed. He decided that the Russians simply did not want to accept Sun Yat-sen's plan, a plan that, incidentally, Chiang Kai-shek himself had drawn up.[81] This was a serious blow to the morbidly sensitive Chiang. He sank into depression, spent days on end learning how to play the *qin* (an ancient Chinese musical instrument), and did not go outside. On October 18 he sent the Executive Committee of the Comintern a "Report on the National Movement in China and the Guomindang Party" in which, he asserted in particular, that Sun Yat-sen's third principle was practically the first step toward communism. But that same day, in response to Chicherin's proposal they meet, he said he was sick.[82]

Chiang, though still feeling offended, agreed to meet with the Commissar for Foreign Affairs three days later but was obviously out of sorts. Chicherin informed Karakhan, the USSR's ambassador to China, that evening: "The delegation is irritable, because it has too little to do and is getting nowhere."[83] Karakhan advised Chicherin "to handle Sun Yat-sen's chief of staff with kid gloves," as the people's commissar informed Stalin, Trotsky, and other party and Comintern leaders, noting, "Meanwhile, the reverse is happening. . . .

The irritability of the chief of staff has reached such an extreme that he believes we are completely ignoring them."[84]

The leaders of the Bolshevik party indeed were skeptical of Sun's and Chiang's "fantastical" military plans. But this was not the main reason for their show of unexpected coolness toward Chiang's delegation. From the outset they believed it would be much better if their own representatives—Borodin and the military specialists sent to South China in the fall of 1923—discussed with Sun everything needing discussion. Neither Chicherin nor anyone else in Moscow had an accurate picture of the military situation in China. Frankly speaking, they thought that Chiang's arrival in the USSR prior to receiving information from Borodin and the Soviet military specialists was inconvenient, but, in Chicherin's words, they "could not get rid of" Chiang, and therefore at first they held "some talks" with him simply "not to antagonize him."[85]

In October the Bolshevik leaders' focus was far from China. Just then a struggle erupted in the party between the Left Opposition, headed by the Politburo member and People's Commissar for Military and Naval Affairs Lev Davidovich Trotsky, who opposed the bureaucratic degeneration of the party hierarchy, and the majority of the Central Committee, headed by General Secretary Josef Vissarionovich Stalin. In Chicherin's words, both factions "were wholly absorbed" in preparing for a fight at the CC plenum, scheduled for October 25–27.[86] At the same time, the CC, the Executive Committee of the Comintern, and the People's Commissariat for Foreign Affairs were drawn into organizing a large-scale communist uprising in Germany. At the time, the German revolution was deemed the most serious attempt after October 1917 to ignite the fire of world revolution.

By the beginning of November 1923, however, it had become clear that both the Bolshevik putsch in Germany and the Left Opposition had lost the battle. Around then, it seems, those in the Kremlin remembered China, although they still did not accept Sun's military plan.[87] "The military plans [of Sun], and consequently the purely military requests directed at us are put off until clarification of the situation in Europe," Trotsky declared.[88] Skliansky informed Chiang and other members of the delegation of this in softer language. At the same time, the Soviets agreed to help the Guomindang train military cadres for the Chinese revolution. And, of course, also provide the GMD weapons and money.

Naturally, Chiang was not very satisfied.[89] He was constantly depressed and even asked his Soviet hosts to arrange for him to spend two weeks in a sanitorium to undergo treatment for his nerves.[90] But he then reconsidered because in early November he received bad news from Canton: Sun's new expedition against Chen Jiongming had been defeated, so he hurried home.[91]

In the final days before departure the delegation met with the chairman of the All-Union Executive Committee, Mikhail Ivanovich Kalinin, who made a poor impression on Chiang because of his lack of knowledge of international affairs, and with Anatoly Vasilievich Lunacharsky. The delegation also attended a session of the Executive Committee of the Comintern that took place under the chairmanship of the head of the committee, Grigori Yevseevich Zinoviev. They even paid a visit to Trotsky, who basically deemed it "inappropriate to meet with the Chinese general who had already met with Comrades Skliansky and the Commander in Chief [Kamenev]." Nonetheless, Trotsky yielded to Chicherin who insisted on arranging a meeting between Chiang and the people's commissar for military and naval affairs.[92]

Although Chiang, as before, praised the Bolsheviks and asserted that the GMD also "would do something on a communist foundation," one could sense that he was disillusioned. Trotsky simply infuriated him since he not only advised Sun and the Guomindang to desist as quickly as possible from military adventures and concentrate on political work in China, but also noted that in the future "the Guomindang could commence military actions not from Mongolia . . . but from the territory of its own country."

Chiang choked with anger because both he and Sun, like all Chinese, considered Mongolia to be part of China. "After this conversation, Chiang Kai-shek became angry at everyone, saying that Trotsky was betraying them," Shen Xuanlu, a communist member of the delegation, reported to the CCP CC after their return to China. "If Mongolia wants to be independent, it's necessary that we recognize this, that we give it independence, not that it do it itself." Chiang also could not "calm down, knowing that the Red Army was there [in Mongolia]." When, in Shen's words, he disagreed with Chiang, the latter almost picked a fight with him, so angry was he.[93]

A resolution on the question of the national movement in China and the Guomindang drafted by a Comintern commission headed by one of the leaders of the Bolshevik party, Nikolai Ivanovich Bukharin, evoked a new fit of anger in Chiang despite the fact that the commission was formed at the request of the Chinese side. The problem was that the Bolsheviks did not take into account the mentality of the Chinese, who were ultrasensitive about any appearance of condescension toward them. The resolution read like a mentor instructing a pupil. The Executive Committee of the Comintern instructed Sun Yat-sen on how his own Three Principles of the People should be interpreted in "the spirit of the times." The Bolsheviks expressed confidence that Sun would carry out a thoroughgoing program of anti-imperialist, national democratic revolution, the key features of which would be a call for radical agrarian revolution and the nationalization of industry.[94]

On November 28, one day prior to the departure of Chiang and his companions to China, the resolution was passed by the Presidium of the Executive Committee of the Comintern and given to the delegation. Familiarizing himself with it, Chiang wrote in his diaries: "Superficial and incorrect. They put themselves at the center of the world revolution and are swollen with conceit. Their leader 'Zinoviev' is a person capable only of destruction and not of creation. I am convinced it will soon be necessary to establish a Fourth International."[95]

In a sour mood, Chiang and the members of his delegation left Moscow for their homeland on November 29. Prior to their departure Chicherin received them again, after which the People's Commissariat for Foreign Affairs held a farewell banquet. But this did not alter Chiang's negative attitude toward the Bolsheviks. The trip to Moscow turned out to be the decisive influence on the worldview of the thirty-six-year-old revolutionary. After spending three months in Soviet Russia, Chiang, who had previously held leftist views, came to the conclusion that one must not trust the Bolshevik party.[96]

He returned to Shanghai on December 15, 1923, and, meeting that same day with Sun's closest comrades in arms, including Hu Hanmin, Wang Jingwei, and Liao Zhongkai, gave them the report on his trip to Russia that he had drafted for Sun Yat-sen. The next day he went home to his village.[97] He believed that he had executed his mission, and he no longer had any posts in the army or the Guomindang since, as noted earlier, he had resigned in July 1923. Moreover, he had to finish work on the construction of a permanent memorial on his mother's grave.[98] He could not disregard the mourning measures because he had to follow a Confucian tradition that says, "When the dead are honored and the memory of remote ancestors is kept alive, a people's virtue is at its fullest."[99]

This is what he reported to Sun:

> The Russian Communist Party, in its dealings with China, has only one aim, namely, to make the Chinese Communist Party its chosen instrument. It does not believe that our Party can really cooperate with it for long for the sake of ensuring success for both parties. It is the policy of the Russian Communist Party to turn the lands inhabited by

> the Manchus, Mongols, Moslems, and Tibetans into parts of the Soviet domain; it may harbor sinister designs even on China proper.
>
> Success in anything is absolutely impossible if one has to depend entirely on the help of others. It would be the height of folly if our people, surrendering all self-respect, should so idolize others with the expectation that they would make righteousness prevail for its own sake. Their so-called internationalism and World Revolution are nothing but Caesarism in another name, the better to hoodwink the outside world.[100]

Along with the report, he sent Sun the Comintern resolution on the question of the national movement in China and the Guomindang. Orally via Liao Zhongkai, he conveyed to Sun that one could not trust the Russians more than 30 percent. He informed Wang Jingwei likewise.

Yet to his disappointment, Sun did not heed his warnings. Moscow's assistance was indispensable to the leader of the Guomindang. That is why, at least formally, Sun accepted almost all of the Comintern's recommendations. He rejected only one of them, on the agrarian question. He would make use of the Resolution of the Presidium of the Executive Committee of the Comintern in drafting the manifesto on reorganizing the Guomindang that would be adopted at the First Congress of the party in late January 1924.

After repeated requests by Sun, Cicada Zhang, Hu Hanmin, Liao Zhongkai, and other Guomindang leaders, Chiang and Jennie went to Canton on January 16, four days before the start of the congress. Sun wanted Chiang to speak to him in person about his trip to the USSR and not limit himself to a written report. After hearing Chiang out, on January 24 Sun appointed him chair of a preparatory committee to organize a special Guomindang educational institution, an infantry officers' academy. In spite of his negative view of the Bolsheviks, Chiang, at Sun's request, had to establish the school with the help of Soviet advisors, especially since the very idea for the school had come from the Bolsheviks. In addition, they were donating 900,000 rubles for its establishment to supplement the 186,000 yuan (Chinese dollars) that Sun Yat-sen's government had scraped together.[101]

Chiang was not among the 198 delegates at the First Congress of the Guomindang that represented more than eleven thousand GMD members and officially proclaimed the formation of a national united front of the Guomindang and the CCP while preserving the independence of communists inside the GMD. But as guests he and Jennie attended the sessions that were held in the center of Canton in the auditorium of the National Guangdong Higher Normal Institute from January 20 to January 30, 1924. Nor was he among those chosen at the congress for the party organs: the Central Executive Committee (CEC) comprising forty-one persons (twenty-four members and seventeen candidates) or the Central Control Commission (CCC) of five member and five candidates.[102] Naturally, neither did he become a member of the highest party organ, the Standing Committee of the Guomindang CEC, in which Sun placed eight of his closest comrades in arms, including Liao Zhongkai, Dai Jitao, Hu Hanmin, and Wang Jingwei as well as the communist Tan Pingshan, who symbolized the existence of the united front in China.[103] Chiang was probably displeased at being passed over—Jennie wrote that he felt "small and unimportant"[104]—but his appointment as chair of the preparatory committee to organize the officers' academy improved his mood.

Prior to his arrival in Canton Chiang knew that Sun had decided to appoint him commandant of the academy. Hu Hanmin, Liao Zhongkai, and Wang Jingwei had written to him about this on December 26.[105] Initially, Sun had wanted to appoint General Cheng Qian, a graduate of the Imperial Japanese Army Academy who headed the military–political department of his headquarters, to the post. This general had organized military classes in his department, and Sun thought he would be the better candidate. But while Chiang was traveling from Moscow to Shanghai, the leader rethought the matter and decided to give Chiang the position since he was out of a job.[106] On February 3 he again inducted Chiang into the Guomindang's Military Council. By this time Sun had also designated a location for the future academy, the small island of Changzhou in the Huangpu district (Whampoa in the local dialect) in the delta of the high-water Zhujiang River, some forty *li* east of Canton. It housed buildings of the former infantry and naval academies of the Guangdong Army. The Whampoa Academy took its name from the locality.

Chiang enthusiastically tackled the job of organizing the academy, but suddenly, on February 21, he again threw everything down and, in a rage, resigned yet again. Sun accepted his resignation and appointed Liao Zhongkai as acting chair of the preparatory committee for the school.[107] What happened is that at one of the meetings of the preparatory committee Chiang berated the Soviet military advisors, again feeling they were not taking account of his views. Worst of all, his party comrades, including even Sun, failed to support him.[108]

Subsequently, Chiang explained that he had declined his appointment as commandant of the [Whampoa] Military Academy because he had "discovered how the Chinese Communists, both in words and in actions, tried to increase their importance by playing up Soviet Russia, and how some of our own Party members had been swayed by Communist doctrines." He had been "full of misgivings regarding our Party's ability to carry out the task entrusted to it by Dr. Sun."[109]

One of these party members was the forty-seven-year-old Liao Zhongkai, the most consistently leftist member of the Guomindang, formerly known in the party under the pseudonym Tufu (Death to the Rich).[110] At this time Sun himself was rather far to the left. In a long letter to the leader Chiang explained that he felt his mentor did not trust him. He reminded Sun that he had stood alongside him on the cruiser *Yongfeng* and was always ready to follow him, but he asked Sun to trust him as Sun had trusted Chen Qimei, Chiang's blood brother, who had died from an enemy's bullet. He also complained about Sun's mistrust in an equally long letter to Liao Zhongkai, after which he expressed regret that Liao "trusted the Russians too much" and did not believe what he (Chiang) said, without taking the trouble to ascertain who was right and who was not. "If this goes on," he summed up in his letter to Liao, "a crisis will inevitably arise." He explained once again that the Russians wanted to subordinate the Guomindang to themselves and that their strategic objective was to bring the CCP to power. "My impression is that the Russian party is insincere. When I told you, my Elder Brother, that one can trust the Russians only 30 percent, I did so only because you, my Elder Brother, believed the Russians so fervently that I dared not upset you completely."[111]

After an extensive exchange of correspondence, Sun ultimately met Chiang halfway. After all, he was really only trying to make use of the Russians, and certainly did not want to be under their thumb. As he explained, "[We are] acquiring its [Soviet Russia's] benefits while rejecting its evils. We may merely yoke up Soviet Russia and mount it."[112] And further: "China has no room for the coexistence of communism with Kuomintang [Guomindang]. We have to admit the communists [into our party] and convert them, and the San Min Principles [Three Principles of the People] will serve as a good melting pot."[113] While getting help from the Bolsheviks, despite all his anti-imperialism, Sun, from time to time, also sounded out the prospects for an alliance with Great Britain and the United States. Thus in February 1923 his close comrade in arms Chen Youren (alias Eugene Chen) discussed the possibility of receiving aid from the Americans with an official from the US Department of State, and in January 1924 Sun himself held talks on the same topic with the US ambassador to China. On February 20, 1923, while in Hong Kong, Sun, as if forgetting that a year earlier he had said he wanted to establish "a new type of republic modeled on Soviet Russia,"[114] told Chinese students at a local university, "[W]e must take England as our model and must extend England's example of good government to the whole of China."[115]

To accommodate Chiang's feelings, Sun removed the Whampoa Academy from under the control of the army command and the Guomindang CEC and formally placed it under Chiang himself. Finally, Chiang had the kind of position he had dreamed about: now he could act without anyone interfering in his affairs. In mid-April he returned to Canton, and on May 3 he formally assumed his duties as head of the academy.[116] That same day Sun appointed him chief of the General Staff of the Central Command of the Guangdong Army. Six days later he appointed Liao Zhongkai to serve as political commissar (in the language of the time: representative of the party) in the Whampoa Academy.[117]

On June 16 the opening ceremony for the academy was held. Chiang was photographed with Sun several times: on the tribune along with the diminutive Liao Zhongkai, a particularly civilian-looking man dressed in a white suit, and Sun's wife, Song Qingling; on the terrace of the main administrative building along with two instructors from the academy: He Yingqin, Chiang's former fellow student at the Japanese military academy, and Wang Boling; and on the same terrace, with the leader.

Chiang probably was fondest of the last photograph, in which he was alone with the leader. When he was ruling China and Taiwan it was frequently used in Guomindang propaganda. The photograph was full of symbolism: the brave, young officer in full uniform with his sword at his side standing to the right of the elderly Sun Yat-sen seated in a wicker chair. It is evident that the commandant of the Whampoa Academy is wholly resolved to defend the leader to the last drop of his blood: he looks boldly at the camera lens, his right arm bent at the elbow, his hand clenched into a fist. Chiang and Sun together. No one else around. Incidentally, both in China and Taiwan two of the other photographs were also widely disseminated, but the second one, on Chiang's orders, was retouched: the images of He Yingqin and Wang Boling were cropped out. Only one officer could guard the leader: his selfless, devoted disciple, General Chiang Kai-shek.

CHAPTER 6

# *Commandant of the Whampoa Academy*

After moving to Whampoa, Chiang and Jennie settled into three rooms on the second floor of the two-story administration building. As usual, Chiang went to sleep early and arose early (at five o'clock), did exercises in bed, meditated for half an hour by the open window, quickly ate breakfast, and then devoted himself wholly to work. He continued to be unable to check his emotions, frequently became hysterical, and when he was drilling cadets in their morning formations he screamed at them so loudly that his voice could be heard at a considerable distance. After the drills he held meetings with the officers and Soviet specialists, delivered lectures on military science, drafted schedules, drew up programs, set salaries for the instructors, and conversed with Guomindang officials who frequently dropped in at the academy. As always, he could not stand anyone interfering in his work. "I hope all my Elder Brothers," he said to his comrades in arm in the Guomindang, "will attend to their duties more and make suggestions less."[1]

Initially Jennie discharged the duties as his lone assistant, but later Chiang added other secretaries as well: all were natives of Zhejiang, his home province. The oldest among them was fifty-two-year-old Mao Sicheng, Chiang's former teacher, and the youngest was twenty-five-year-old Chen Lifu, a mining engineer graduate of the University of Pittsburgh, a likable young man with an aquiline nose (unusual for a Chinese) who was a nephew of Chiang's late blood brother Chen Qimei. Additional secretaries included Chen Bulei, a graduate of Zhejiang University, who was very businesslike and punctual and was an excellent journalist, and Shao Lizi, a short, stout man wearing big, round glasses who had been educated at the Catholic Aurora University in Shanghai and also possessed exceptional literary talent.[2] In 1925, when Shao became Chiang's secretary, he was forty-three years old and had already been a member of the CCP for five years.[3] In 1926, however, he left the Communist Party at the suggestion of Chen Duxiu in order "to concentrate on work inside the Guomindang, deflect any suspicion away from himself, and inside the Guomindang gain Chiang Kai-shek's trust . . . and play a positive role in the united front." Unaware of the real reason Shao withdrew from the Communist Party, Chiang trusted him and assigned him important tasks. Soon, Shao, under Chiang's influence, really did break with the communists and became one of the persons closest to Chiang.[4]

There were no special household expenses: Chiang did not pay either for the apartment or for food, which he always shared with his secretaries, but his salary was very substantial: 1,500 Chinese dollars a month (an enormous sum for that time; the monthly salary of Chen Duxiu, the CCP leader, was just thirty Chinese dollars).[5] Chiang sent Fumei only fifty Chinese dollars to support his eldest son; apparently he sent the same amount to Yecheng to provide for Wei-kuo, so that Jennie was able to set aside money. Later, to be sure, she said that "Kai-shek's salary . . . was hardly enough for expenses," but this is scarcely credible.[6]

According to Jennie they spent their free evenings together. They had no children. Jennie, as noted, would later blame Chiang for supposedly having been rendered sterile by gonorrhea. Jonathan Fenby and several other biographers who believed her would later write about Chiang's sterility. In the spring of 1997 the famous Taiwan artist Fan Guangdong, too, wrote about it but offered a different and sensationalist story. Unlike Jennie, he asserted that the Generalissimo had never been able to have children because, at the age of four or five he had accidentally sat on a hot stove and burned his scrotum, following which a dog, having smelled the scent of the duck's fat that Chiang's mother had applied to the burnt skin, bit him badly on the sore spot. According to Fan, it would eventually be revealed that Chiang's oldest son, Chiang Ching-kuo, was also adopted. For this he relied on an interview that Chiang's younger adopted son Wei-kuo, who had supposedly heard the story of the stove and the dog from his foster mother, Yecheng, had granted him three years before his (Wei-kuo's) death.[7]

None of these stories are confirmed by documents. There are indications that Chiang's new ("beloved," as he wrote) wife, Song Meiling, whom he had married on December 1, 1927, became pregnant at least twice but each time she lost the baby. In his diaries Chiang wrote that the first miscarriage happened on August 25, 1929, after Meiling took fright from bandits that had broken into the house at night.[8] It is confirmed by Meiling's niece Kong Lingyi, Song Ailing's oldest daughter, who recalled Meiling being pregnant after her marriage (in 1929 Lingyi was fourteen). It was also confirmed by General Chen Cheng's wife, who said to her husband that Song Meiling told her about the miscarriage.[9] The second miscarriage took place in late August 1935. At that time General Chen Cheng, who was close to Chiang Kai-shek, wrote about it to his wife.[10] After the last miscarriage Meiling was no longer able to have children.

Whatever the truth of this matter, Chiang and Jennie spent most of their evenings quietly together; their solitude was not broken by children's cries. Dinner consisted of rather ordinary dishes: rice, vegetables, fish, and sometimes meat prepared according to Ningbo-style recipes flavored with a variety of sauces.[11] Chiang washed his food down with boiled water; he did not want either tea or wine. According to Jennie, this fact was also connected with his gonorrhea. Supposedly having infected her, and feeling guilty, he applied a penance to himself: never to drink anything but boiled water.[12] That right up to his death Chiang drank only boiled water is true, but whether he did it in memory of Jennie, whom he left in 1927, is unknown.[13]

Several months after the opening of the academy, however, Chiang's and Jennie's solitary life came to an end. Liao Zhongkai's wife, He Xiangning, a good, kindhearted woman who headed the Women's Department of the Guomindang CEC, brought an approximately two-year-old orphan girl to Jennie.[14] The little girl had been living in a foundling hospital because her parents had abandoned her at birth. These people were very poor and unable to raise their daughter (it would have been a different matter had it been a son). In poor families a daughter was considered a burden. Raise her, feed her, all for nothing. When the time came, she would get married into a stranger's family. The tenderhearted He Xiangning, who treated Jennie like a younger sister and Chiang like a brother, proposed that she and Chiang adopt the orphaned girl. They were overjoyed. Chiang gave his adopted daughter the child name of Peipei, meaning Little Friend, and the formal name of Chiang Yao-kuang (Jiang Heavenly Light). Thus a lovable "little cadet" whom Chiang and Jennie doted on arrived at the Whampoa Academy.[15]

In 1924 no fewer than twenty Soviet military specialists were working in Canton, including at the Whampoa Military Academy. The academy was the most important source of cadres for the Guomindang's "party army" that in the future would be called the National Revolutionary Army (NRA). As the commandant of the academy, Chiang now had to deal with the Soviet advisors on a daily basis, but he no longer displayed any open dissatisfaction in this regard. As Sun had advised him, he simply "yoked [them] up," making use both of their battle experience and knowledge as well as the not-insignificant amount of funds the Soviet government invested in the academy. In addition to 900,000 rubles, in the course of 1925 alone, Moscow more than once transferred enormous sums "in support of the Whampoa Academy": first 100,000, then almost 400,000 rubles. If one bears in mind that initially the Sun Yat-sen government invested only 30,000 Chinese dollars per month in the academy, it is hard to overestimate the significance of Soviet aid.[16]

From May to July 1924 the Soviet advisors' group was headed by Pavel Andreevich Pavlov, who commanded a corps during the Russian civil war. But he died in a tragic accident. While transferring from a boat to a ship on the Dongjiang (Eastern River) near the city of Shilong, not far from Canton, he stumbled, fell into the water, and drowned. In October a new chief military advisor took his place: Vasilii Konstantinovich Bliukher, a prominent commander and future marshal of the Soviet Union.[17] Sun Yat-sen and he began to consider plans for military campaigns that would unite all of China under Guomindang rule. Bliukher remained in Canton until July 1925, when he returned to the Soviet Union for medical treatment.[18]

Vasilii Konstantinovich Bliukher worked in China under the pseudonym Zoi Vsevolodovich Galin—Zoi and Vsevolod were the names of his children, and Galina was the name of their mother, whom he had divorced prior to traveling to China. The Chinese called him Jialun, and he was known in the Comintern by the secret pseudonym Uralsky. The future Generalissimo quickly established good relations with this handsome, intelligent man who was about his age and who actually resembled Chiang Kai-shek. They were almost the same height, only Bliukher was somewhat stockier, and both of them had small mustaches, and soon after becoming acquainted, Chiang, like Bliukher, began shaving his head. Bliukher became Chiang's chief military advisor in the Whampoa Academy and later in the Guomindang army as a whole. "In my opinion he was an outstanding Russian general as well as a reasonable man and a good friend," recalled Chiang.[19]

Bliukher also had a high opinion of Chiang:

> One of the most devoted to Dr. Sun, the best of the party generals . . . the most competent. . . . Considered the best administrator. . . . Dr. Sun has great respect for him, and Chiang Kai-shek is the only one of the generals who is also close to Dr. Sun even in his personal life. Externally he is sharply distinguished from the others by his military bearing, and his behavior reveals him to be a military commander in the full sense of the term. He is also distinguished by his capacity for work. Demanding of himself, he is likewise demanding of his subordinates, and therefore the academy is distinguished by the presence of firm discipline within its walls. . . . The general opinion in the Guomindang CEC is that he is not only a good party member, but politically also a broadly developed person.

At the same time Bliukher also noted Chiang's negative side:

> Extremely conceited, in all respects he considered himself better than others, and he only acknowledged the authority of Sun for himself. Stubborn, and if an idea comes into his head, and he has many, then it is difficult to push him from a straight decision or change the "idea," and if one does so, it must be in such a way that the change in decision is presented to him as if it were his own.

Bliukher also noted the "absence in Chiang Kai-shek of good operational analysis of a situation.[20]

In addition to the Soviet military specialists, Chiang often met with Borodin, the chief political advisor to the Guomindang, who simultaneously was taking Maring's place as the Comintern representative in China. He was a tall, broad-shouldered man of forty with "a shaggy head" and "a thick walrus mustache." He was considered the greatest authority on all questions relating to revolution and "impressed all who met him in China as a person of exceptionally high caliber." He had been a member of the Bolshevik party since 1903 and knew Lenin and Stalin well. He spoke "in a resonantly deep, clear, unhurried, baritone voice of mid-America intonation without a trace of Russian accent, he lowered his voice into a slow basso profundo when emphasizing the importance of a certain point he was making. He was a man who gave the impression of great control and personal magnetism."[21]

But his magnetism did not work on Chiang. As a rule, Chiang decided all questions connected with the Whampoa Academy himself, consulting only with Sun Yat-sen and Bliukher. The second-ranking person at the academy was the party representative Liao Zhongkai, but he spent little time within its walls since he was concurrently a member of the Guomindang CEC, the minister of finance of the Sun Yat-sen government, the director of the workers' and then also the peasants' departments of the CEC as well as the governor of Guangdong. In general, he supplied Chiang with material assistance, obtaining the necessary funds for the academy. The cadets called him the academy mama.[22]

Political work was handled by the political department of the academy; Chiang had appointed his blood brother Dai Jitao as its head. By this time, Dai, who had been seriously attracted to Marxism in the early 1920s, had completely lost his communist illusions and become an ardent Buddhist. "Bringing communists into the party [Guomindang] is only a seasoning, a sauce, not real food," he began saying after becoming one of the leaders of the Guomindang rightists who considered communists untrustworthy and demanded either their expulsion or absorption into the GMD.[23] (The leader of the Guomindang left at that time was Liao Zhongkai, who supported the alliance with the Communist Party unconditionally; Hu Hanmin was seen as "the leader of the Middle-of-the-Road cliques," that is, the faction of the centrists.)[24]

Dai Jitao's metamorphosis had occurred in the autumn of 1923, soon after he became intimate with the likeable Zhao Wenshu, the niece of his strong-willed wife. Then he became terribly worried that his wife would find out and tried, unsuccessfully, to commit suicide. Afterward he had a vision. Setting off on a voyage on the Yangzi River, he suddenly saw a luminous white circle: the light of Buddha. He was so overjoyed that his passionate desire to live returned. He left his wife for her niece and simultaneously converted to Buddhism, rejecting materialism. To be sure, he still quaked before his wife and did not enter into a legal marriage with Wenshu. He formalized his relationship with his beloved only after the death of his wife in 1944, a year before his own death (he succeeded in committing suicide but for a different reason than before) and six years before that of his new wife. This despite the fact that Wenshu had given birth to his daughter in 1926.[25]

By mid-autumn 1924 there were 62 drill instructors and 131 administrative staff at the academy.[26] The cadets, of whom there were 1,062, underwent a six-month course of instruction. The first class (613 cadets) entered the academy in mid-May 1924 and graduated in December;[27] the second (449 men) entered in October 1924 and graduated in the summer of 1925. By October 1926 two more classes of cadets (3,875) had graduated from the academy. By then, 4,937 cadets in all had passed through the school.[28]

In mid-October 1924 academy cadets were employed in a military operation for the first time. They took part in suppressing an antigovernment mutiny of the *shangtuan* (guard detachments of the Canton merchants). These guards were popularly called paper tigers, although in reality the *shangtuan* were quite strong and numerous: according to various estimates there were six thousand, twelve thousand, or even as many as twenty-five thousand to twenty-seven thousand men. They were under the municipal General Chamber of Commerce.[29]

The conflict between Sun and the Canton merchants had begun in May 1924, when the government levied new taxes, but at that time it was limited to a strike by the merchants. Sun canceled a number of taxes and even began to court the *shangtuan*, paying them a visit and presenting them with a banner. Although the conflict did not flare up, it continued to smolder. Rumors continued to circulate through the city that the *shangtuan* were prepared to support General Chen Jiongming if he decided to attack Canton; naturally the existence of a fifth column in the city aroused Sun's fears.[30]

The dispute was exacerbated at the beginning of August by the arrival in Canton of a Norwegian ship, the SS *Hav*, with a cargo of arms ordered by Chen Lianbo, the head of the General Chamber of Commerce: 5,000 rifles, 3,000 Mauser pistols, and half a million cartridges. Sun was terribly upset and ordered Chiang to seize the shipment and store it at the Whampoa Academy, which he did. One supposes he did so enthusiastically: at the time there were almost no weapons at the academy, only 330 rifles.[31] The *shangtuan* protested mightily, even requesting assistance from representatives of the foreign powers. Sun took the bit in his teeth, however, and decided to have done with his domestic opposition. Chiang fully supported him.

On Sun's side were the Soviet specialists as well as Karakhan, the ambassador of the USSR to China, who all decided "to make wide use" of the conflict. "This is a very serious matter," Karakhan wrote to Chicherin on August 25, 1924, "because in connection with this conflict it is possible to have done with the so-called paper tigers . . . and on the other hand deal a blow to the right wing [of the Guomindang]."[32] It is logical to suppose that the Soviet side proposed this idea—at least the part of it that related to the *shangtuan*—to Sun himself.

Yet it was probably Sun who provoked the paper tigers' mutiny on October 10, 1924. Notably, the uprising took place two days after the Soviet naval vessel *Vorovsky*, arriving at Whampoa from Leningrad, delivered several artillery pieces with shells, eight thousand rifles, and ten thousand pistols and cartridges to Sun or, more precisely, to Chiang. On October 9 Chiang, who up till then would hear nothing about conceding to the *shangtuan*, decided, on orders from Sun and Hu Hanmin, to give them a portion of the confiscated weapons. But at the very moment when the *shangtuan* began unloading in the port on October 10, a column of progovernment demonstrators approached them, setting off the conflict.[33]

Sun swiftly ordered Chiang to organize a Revolutionary Committee "to resolve various urgent matters," calling on him to "learn from Russia" in everything. He also requested that weapons be distributed "to those detachments of our comrades who are ready to destroy the traitors to our cause."[34] Chiang himself commanded the troops of the Revolutionary Committee. He also became one of the three leaders of this new organ along with Sun, who became its chair (Hu Hanmin replaced Sun in this post on October 14) and Liao Zhongkai, who served as secretary.[35] Martial law was declared in the city, and on October 15 the mutiny was brutally suppressed. The entire western suburb of Canton, in which the *shangtuan* had entrenched themselves, was ransacked, and a third of it burned to the ground.[36]

This victory strengthened the position of Sun less than that of Chiang, who, on November 11, was appointed secretary of the Military Department of the Guomindang CEC,[37] in particular because after the rout of the paper tigers in mid-November 1924 Sun left Canton for Beijing, as it turned out, forever. The occasion for his trip was an invitation to take part in a peace conference to unify the country. He received it at the end of October from Marshal Feng Yuxiang, a former assistant of Wu Peifu, a militarist, who controlled North and Central China. In October 1924 Feng came out in opposition to his patron, declaring himself a supporter of Sun Yat-sen. He renamed his army the Guominjun (Nationalist Army) along the lines of Sun's party, the Guomindang, occupied Beijing, and called for an end to the civil war. At the same time, he turned to the USSR for assistance, and soon several dozen Soviet advisors arrived, followed by more than six million rubles' worth of arms. Feng's persona had long since been infused with the aura of a warrior against the traditional Confucian foundations of Chinese society. Legends surrounded him. It was said that in 1913, as either a captain or a major, he had abandoned the faith of his ancestors and had accepted Christianity in its Methodist form. Afterward, he christened his troops from the nozzle of a fire hose and forbade them from drinking alcoholic beverages, smoking opium, and oppressing the people.[38]

On November 13 Sun and his wife, Song Qingling, sailed out of Canton. They were accompanied on the journey by Wang Jingwei and his wife. The send-off turned into "a grandiose demonstration of the people of Canton," Bliukher recalled: "All of Canton to the poorest sampan was decked out with Guomindang flags.[39] The streets of the city were crisscrossed with a countless number of arches. Tens of thousands of demonstrators passed by Sun, enthusiastically greeting him. The demonstrators were seized by a revolutionary enthusiasm such as Canton had never seen before. . . . Canton was seething with activity. There were meetings and gatherings everywhere. . . . A whole series of revolutionary organizations of workers, soldiers, and students issued calls to the country to support Dr. Sun in the North."[40]All the members of the Sun Yat-sen government came to the port to wish the leader *yilu ping'an* (bon voyage). Chiang and Jennie were there, and along with Hu Hanmin and Borodin they escorted Sun and Song Qingling to Whampoa. There, the Sun couple and the Wang couple spent the night and then sailed to Hong Kong with Liao Zhongkai. Before departing, according to Chiang Kai-shek's reminiscences, Sun said to him, "I am going to Peking [Beijing]. Whether I can come back is not yet certain. Anyway, I am going there to carry on our struggle. Having seen the spirit of this Academy, I know it can carry on my revolutionary task. Even if I should die, my conscience will be at peace."[41] In Chiang's words, in the name of the government of the USSR Borodin invited Sun to visit Russia after his trip to Beijing, but Sun, after consulting with Chiang, who asserted that "he was against such a trip," declined the proposal.[42]

Dai Jitao set off for Beijing as Sun Yat-sen's secretary. As the head of the Political Department at Whampoa vacated by Dai, Chiang appointed Dai's deputy, the twenty-six-year-old communist Zhou Enlai, who had arrived in Canton in September 1924 from France, where he had organized a communist movement among Chinese emigrants. Chiang soon developed excellent relations with this intelligent young man, who was a brilliant organizer and an erudite person and, moreover, was extremely modest.[43]

In general, Chiang had no problem with communists at this time. Members of the CCP as well as the Soviet advisors considered him extremely leftist, even very procommunist. Therefore, Borodin, for example, insisted that in reorganizing the Guomindang army, emphasis should be placed on "fostering Whampoa [Academy] only." Zhou Enlai fully agreed with him. In the autumn of 1924 Borodin and the Chinese communists resolved "to raise the status of General Chiang Kai-shek so that the Whampoa forces could develop more rapidly."[44]

How wrong they were. In fact, as we know, Chiang was not in the least procommunist, but having accepted Sun's shrewd policy toward the USSR and

CCP early in 1924, he did everything possible to appear "as more Catholic than the Pope." It is true that he still had leftist inclinations and, as before, despised *tuhao* (bloodsuckers), but as Jennie correctly writes (and here she is not mistaken), Chiang the Bald, as he was called then from his habit of shaving his head, flirted with the communists basically because he badly needed Soviet arms to crush his own bloody foe Chen Jiongming once and for all. Chiang was "aggressive, stubborn, sensitive, headstrong, and quick tempered."[45] The number of offenses, real and supposed, that General Chen had inflicted upon him was already so great that Chiang was probably ready to ally with anyone available in order to destroy his enemy, who, after retreating from Canton, felt himself fully at ease on his own turf in eastern Guangdong. Arms and advisors from the USSR would help Chiang establish his own power in the Guomindang itself if Sun should die.

This is why he befriended the communists in 1924–25, striving to utilize the Communist Party as well as the Soviet advisors and the masses.[46] He himself, his cadets, and the instructors all wore red neckties, his speeches in Whampoa and outside overflowed with vows of fidelity to Soviet Russia and world revolution, and he relied on Soviet advisors and gave them, in the words of one of the CCP leaders, Zhang Guotao, "real authority in the school." Moreover, "CCP members filled most of the political instructorships and handled most of the political work."[47] Replicating the experience of the Red Army, with which he had become acquainted in the USSR, Chiang introduced the institution of political commissars among the units formed from the cadets, and even granted them "control over operational orders which gave them . . . equal rights with the commanders."[48] Finally, he gave permission to establish the communist Union of Young Soldiers in the academy. That group, to be sure, was balanced by the Guomindang Society for the Study of Sun Wenism [Sun Yat-senism]," which became the bastion of the rightist cadets.

At the end of December 1924 Sun arrived in Beijing via Shanghai, Nagasaki, and Tianjin. The sea voyage had tired him, and in Tianjin he was not feeling well. An examination revealed that he had liver cancer. He took to his bed, and for the next two and a half months was able to live only via periodic injections of morphine.[49] On March 11 he signed his testament, composed for him by Wang Jingwei, as well as a message to the Soviet Union, written by Borodin. He called on the Guomindang "to continue its work in the field of the national revolutionary movement so that China may throw off the yoke by which the imperialists have reduced China to the position of a semicolonial country." He ordered "the party henceforward to strengthen cooperation" with the USSR.[50]

Then, looking around at those present, he said, with difficulty, "I am dying. Do not forget that there are enemies all around, do not forget the danger. Do not yield to the enemy." Song Qingling, who was standing by his bed, cried loudly. Then Sun gave orders that his body be embalmed.

"After I die," he said to Wang Jingwei, "bury me on Purple [Gold] Mountain in Nanjing because Nanjing is where the Provisional Government was established.[51] Thus the 1911 Revolution will not be forgotten. In addition, my body should be permanently preserved using scientific methods."[52]

"He wanted the people to remember him," wrote Liao Zhongkai's wife, who was at Sun's bedside.

Falling into semiconsciousness, Sun repeated over and over, "Peace . . . struggle . . . saving China." The leader of the revolution died at 9:10 in the morning on March 12, 1925, in the fifty-ninth year of his life.[53]

CHAPTER 7

# *The Struggle over Sun Yat-sen's Legacy*

After Sun's death a struggle for power among various factions flared up in the Guomindang, but the rightists soon lost out. Sun's formal successor was the centrist Hu Hanmin whom the great leader himself, prior to his trip to Beijing, had appointed as acting Generalissimo. Hu became the chair of the Political Committee of the Guomindang CEC, the party's highest organ of power that coordinated and led the work of both the party and the government. The Political Committee had been established on Sun's initiative in July 1924, six months after the First Congress of the Guomindang, when Sun Yat-sen, under the influence of the Bolsheviks, decided to organize in his own party something like the all-powerful Soviet Politburo. Sun himself became its first chair. The Political Committee ranked higher in the hierarchy of power than the Standing Committee of the CEC that had been established in January 1924 and dealt only with party affairs.

In reality, however, power was concentrated in the hands of four persons: Hu Hanmin, Wang Jingwei, Liao Zhongkai, and Borodin. General Xu Chongzhi, the new commander of the Guangdong Army whose political outlook was close to that of Hu Hanmin, was also a powerful figure. Chiang, too, possessed quite a lot of authority.[1] In Sun's absence, cooperative relations among the Guomindang, the USSR, and Marshal Feng Yuxiang continued to develop.

As Sun lay dying, Chiang was in eastern Guangdong, where, starting in February 1925, troops loyal to Sun were taking part in the Eastern Expedition against Chen Jiongming. Learning of the death of his mentor, Chiang at once published an obituary. He conveyed words of grief to all the soldiers and officers and, along with Wang Jingwei and Hu Hanmin, also signed an address to all comrades in the party, swearing to fulfill the last will and testament of the leader and carry the revolution through to the end.[2]

Detachments from the Whampoa Academy also took part in the Eastern Expedition. From the end of October 1924 the Guomindang members began to call them their party army, while their enemies called them the Russian Red Army.[3] The cadets comprised two regiments that were part of the so-called Eastern front Southern Group that was under the command of General Xu Chongzhi. Bliukher was assisting him while the military advisor Vasilii Andreevich Stepanov was assisting Chiang. Stepanov wrote about Chiang:

> We [Stepanov and the Chinese Communists, including Chen Duxiu] consider Chiang Kai-shek a peculiar person with peculiar characteristics, most prominent of these being his lust for glory and power and craving to be the hero of China. He claims that he stands not only for the Chinese National Revolution but for the World Revolution. . . . To achieve this goal, power and money are required. He does not, however, use money to enrich his own pocket. . . . Chiang possesses much determination and endurance. Compared with the average Chinese, he is unusually forthright. . . . Yet he is not free from suspicion and jealousy. No one is allowed to argue with him over any matter or to act for him.[4]

At the end of March the Southern Group defeated the forces of Chen Jiongming and established its control over the eastern part of Guangdong province. In early April 1925 Chiang returned to Canton, which was throbbing with revolutionary enthusiasm just as it had been under Sun: "Multicolored signs bearing revolutionary slogans were apparent everywhere on the roads and streets. Streamers of white cloth with moving slogans in red hung at intersections. . . . The doors of most trade unions and other mass organizations were also decorated in a variety of colors."[5]

At the same time, Guangxi and Yunnan troops, which were by no means revolutionary, were quartered in the city. As noted earlier, in January 1923, for the sum of 400,000 Chinese dollars, they had chased Chen Jiongming out of Canton, bringing Sun to power. There were twenty-five thousand officers and men: five thousand from Guangxi and twenty thousand from Yunnan. During their stay in Canton they had levied taxes on all the gambling houses and opium dens, established control over the narcotics trade between Canton and Yunnan, and behaved like invaders vis-à-vis the local population, robbing and insulting the Cantonese. After Sun's death their generals aspired to gain complete power in the city, launching a campaign against the dominance of the communists, by which they meant not only members of the CCP but also Liao Zhongkai and even Hu Hanmin. Several Yunnanese officers even favored the arrest of Generalissimo Hu.[6]

At the end of April, Bliukher, Liao Zhongkai, and Chiang Kai-shek sketched the basic contours of an operation against the new enemies that represented, in the words of the Soviet ambassador Karakhan, "an even greater danger than Chen Jiongming."[7] At the beginning of June, Chiang's so-called party army, supported by other troops loyal to the Guomindang CEC, routed the Yunnanese and Guangxi forces. They took 500 officers and 16,500 men prisoners, and the Guangxi and Yunnan generals fled to Hong Kong.[8] "The Cantonese victory was undoubtedly due to the Whampoa cadets," the US consul general in Canton informed Washington.[9]

Soon after, a new group of military men came to power in Guangxi, headed by the youthful generals Li Zongren, aged thirty-five, and Bai Chongxi, aged thirty-two. It was called the new Guangxi clique. In the summer of 1925 these generals, through the mediation of the Guangxi native and head of the Instructional Department at the Whampoa Academy General Li Jishen, formed an alliance with the Guomindang, thereby uniting Guangxi and Guangdong.[10]

Meanwhile, China as a whole was experiencing a rapid upsurge of the nationalist movement, marked by the intensification of the anti-imperialist struggle of workers and students. On May 30, 1925, anti-imperialist disturbances began in Shanghai and soon gripped most of the cities throughout China. On that day British police on Nanking Road in the middle of the International Settlement shot into a crowd of Chinese who were protesting the killing five days earlier of Gu Zhenghong, a communist worker, by a Japanese. Ten people died and several dozen were wounded.[11]

The Shanghai massacre marked the start of a new patriotic upsurge, the so-called May 30 Movement of 1925. In fact, an anti-imperialist revolution had begun in China.[12] A two-day mourning period was declared in Feng Yuxiang's Nationalist Army, and Feng issued a call: "We are beginning a struggle against imperialism, and others will follow in our footsteps."[13] He urged that the coffins containing the bodies of those killed be displayed in the squares of various cities and that "the entire nation be summoned to the struggle against foreigners."[14]

The revolutionary wave engulfed Canton also. On June 19, soon after the defeat of the Yunnan and Guangxi forces, workers in Canton and Hong Kong went on strike. They were supported by laborers in the Anglo-French Concession of Shamian located on a small, eponymous island in White Goose Bay in the southwest of the city where the Zhujiang divides into two branches. On June 23 workers, students, merchants, and Whampoa cadets numbering several tens of thousands in all organized a demonstration next to the concession under the slogans, "Revenge the blood of our killed compatriots!" and "Down with imperialism." Someone fired a shot—most likely a provocateur—and the settlement police opened fire. They were supported by artillery salvos from foreign ships anchored in the roadstead. The result was that along the bank of the Zhujiang, by the bridge that linked the eastern quarter of Shamian with the Chinese district of Canton, lay 52 dead and 178 seriously wounded demonstrators. Among the dead were 20 Whampoa cadets. On Shamian there was a dead Frenchman and several wounded foreigners.[15]

In response to the new killings in China a general strike began in Hong Kong and Canton. More than 250,000 people stopped working, and a massive exodus of working people began from Shamian and Hong Kong into Canton and neighboring towns and villages. The Guomindang government began to provide all possible assistance to the strikers. A blockade of Hong Kong and Shamian was declared, and a Hong Kong–Shamian strike committee was organized by the workers' department of the Guomindang CEC.[16]

On July 1 a new cabinet of ministers was officially instituted, ambitiously named the National government of the Republic of China. Wang Jingwei became the chairman, Hu Hanmin the minister of foreign affairs, Liao Zhongkai the minister of finance, and Xu Chongzhi the minister of military affairs.

General Xu evidently, in the name of Wang Jingwei, recommended to Chiang that he join the government, but he declined the flattering proposal: "A commander who is directly subordinate to the government should not be in the government [itself]."[17] The upshot was that on July 3 he was included only in the Military Council that was also under the chairmanship of Wang Jingwei. In addition to him and Wang Jingwei, the council was comprised of Hu Hanmin, Liao Zhongkai, General Xu, and General Tan Yankai, the former governor of Hunan, a millionaire, and a member of the Guomindang since 1912, a "[d]ignified, poised, and intelligent [man],"[18] General Zhu Peide, the new commander of the Yunnanese forces and minister of armaments and material supplies, and Wu Chaoshu, the new mayor of Canton, a well-known diplomat and jurist who had been educated in the West. Wu was the only member of the leadership who knew West European and American law, which was particularly important in light of the upsurge of the anti-imperialist movement in China.

Meanwhile, since Chiang's position in the Guomindang hierarchy had become stronger, friction between him and Minister of Military Affairs Xu Chongzhi soon surfaced. In a conversation with Bliukher, Chiang even expressed dissatisfaction with General Xu, noting that Xu was a person "with whom, working for ten years and considering him a friend, in the eleventh year, you might be discarded from his circle of friends and turn out to be an idiot." The commander of the Guangdong Army, who had patronized Chiang for many years, had obviously become unnecessary to the ambitious commandant of Whampoa, whom Bliukher, on this occasion, called "a subtle schemer and far from mediocre politician."[19] Moreover, Xu was in the way, blocking Chiang's path to greater power.

At this point, Borodin helped Chiang enormously. Absolutely convinced of Chiang's procommunist inclinations, he wholly supported him in his covert struggle with Xu. This was in contrast with Bliukher, who for all his respect for Chiang, insisted on supporting General Xu Chongzhi as military leader. In the words of Zhang Guotao, the well-informed member of the CCP leadership, "The matter had been arbitrated by Moscow, and Galen's [Galin's, that is, Bliukher's] view was rejected." The latter returned to Moscow.[20]

Soviet representatives in China posed the question of increasing "the Whampoa divisions and, if circumstances permit, increasing the forces to 20,000–30,000 by January 1, 1926.[21] . . . If this turns out well, then the Guomindang government will have an army that very easily will be able to threaten the Yangzi River valley."[22] Around the same time, the Politburo of the Central Committee of the Bolshevik party adopted a resolution to approve the formation in Canton by October 1, 1925, of two new divisions and the transfer of 477,000 rubles' worth of arms to equip them.[23] With the help of Soviet comrades, Chiang was continuing to augment his forces.

The Russians were increasingly delighted with his leftism, particularly since, after twenty of his cadets were left lying at the bridge to Shamian, felled by British bullets, his anti-imperialism reached its apogee. At this time his diaries became sprinkled with anti-British entries. They would cease only after September 7, 1926, soon after his troops in the Northern Expedition seized the city of Hankou on the Yangzi River. "The English idiots and barbarians consider Chinese as trash and destroy them senselessly," he wrote on June 23, 1926, splashing his hatred onto the pages of his diaries. And for the next seventy-seven days almost every entry began with curses directed at the English. "We need to kill all the English enemies. . . . I will kill you, English enemies!" and so forth. There were 494 such entries in all.[24]

Not only Chiang but also many other leaders of the Guomindang at the time felt ever increasing indignation toward the English. Among other reasons it was the British authorities in Hong Kong, who controlled the Chinese Customs Service that withheld from both Sun and his successors that portion of customs revenues remaining after deducting the sums the British collected in payment of the indemnity placed on China by the unequal treaties. This surplus part of the customs duties they remitted to Beijing since the Beijing government was recognized internationally. All the Guomindang efforts to receive this portion of customs duties were unsuccessful. And then came the shooting.

Many Guomindang leaders also connected the intrigues of British authorities in Hong Kong to a new event that shook the whole city. At 9:50 in the morning on August 20, in front of the gates of the Guomindang CEC, Liao Zhongkai was shot. He was rushing to a meeting and had just gotten out of his car when he was felled by four bullets fired by hired assassins. He died on the way to a hospital.[25]

Several hours after the killing a joint session of the CEC, the government, and the Military Council convened, at which, on Borodin's proposal, a Special Committee composed of three persons—Wang Jingwei, General Xu, and Chiang Kai-shek—was established to investigate the crime. Borodin and Viktor Pavlovich Rogachev, the acting chief military advisor in Bliukher's absence, served as advisors to the committee, which concentrated all power in the Guomindang. Martial law was declared in Canton.

None of the committee members seemed to have any doubts that "the British were behind" the killers. After all, Liao had been the most brilliant leader of the left wing of the Guomindang, so who other than the imperialists would benefit from his death? Several hours after Liao's death, Chiang was already pointing to the British as organizers of the killing.[26] With suspicious rapidity the "customers of the killing" were located in the Guomindang itself; as Zhang Guotao wrote, "Hu Hanmin's [younger] cousin . . . and his confidantes . . . were all involved as suspects in the Liao case."[27] All of them were rightists and, as such, were opponents of Liao in the party, so "rumor had it then that Liao was assassinated by the right wing."[28]

Unfortunately for the committee, almost all the persons involved fled to Hong Kong. They managed to arrest only one of them, a former secretary of

Hu Hanmin. Borodin quickly demanded that Hu himself be arrested, and Hu was put under house arrest at the Whampoa Academy. For the sake of appearances, the chief of the Office of Public Security (OPS) in Canton was also arrested. He, too, was a member of the right wing. To be sure, both Hu and the chief were released, either for lack of sufficient evidence against them or for some other reasons. It was said that Chiang Kai-shek came to the defense of the chief of OPS, and either Chiang or Wang Jingwei, who was unnerved by everything that had happened, came to the defense of Hu. Chiang later asserted that it was he who "had decided the fate of Mr. Hu. . . . And that Borodin, Wang Jingwei, and Ruwei [Xu Chongzhi] deemed it necessary to take advantage of the moment 'to destroy Hu,' but I resolutely objected." For his part, Wang Jingwei said that it was he who saved Hu, defending him from the bloodthirsty General Xu. In his turn, Xu subsequently told Hu that he had not been killed owing only to his own intercession.[29] (The latter is hardly likely to be true: it was known that Xu hated Hu Hanmin, whom, incidentally, many in the leadership of the Guomindang disliked for his intellect and arrogance.)[30] On September 22 Hu was sent into honorable exile, to Moscow, as representative of the Guomindang CEC. Borodin was very happy; he "hoped that the Comintern would have Hu remain in Russia and not permit him to return to China."[31]

The result was that the only suspect to appear before a hastily convened special military tribunal was Hu Hanmin's former secretary. The trio of nonprofessional judges—they were all generals, not jurists—were essentially unable to prove his guilt. The accused categorically denied his participation in the assassination. Nevertheless, he was imprisoned in a fortress on Humen Island not far from Whampoa, where he remained for two and a half years until Chiang Kai-shek broke up the united front with the communists in the spring of 1927. On the day of his release, Guomindang rightists greeted him as a hero at the gates of the fortress.

Another result of the Liao Zhongkai assassination affair was the removal from power of a member of the Special Committee itself, that is, General Xu. In the course of the investigation, it was revealed that his subordinate, the commander of the First Guangdong division, was closely linked to the plotters. Chiang's party army quickly disarmed this unit, after which Xu himself lost the trust of Wang, Chiang, and Borodin. In addition, there were quite a few complaints against General Xu, a well-known bon vivant and drunkard. In early June 1925, for example, while in eastern Guangdong, without permission he abandoned the place where his troops were deployed and went to

Canton simply because he was bored in the provinces. It seemed he was not at all distraught when he learned that after his desertion General Chen Jiongming had retaken everything he and Chiang had seized during the Eastern Expedition some two months earlier.

Chiang and his cadets surrounded General Xu's residence and in the name of the government proposed to him that he go off to Shanghai to rest for a year (according to other sources for three months). But after Xu's departure, in mid-October 1925 Chiang reorganized the Guangdong Army and subordinated most of General Xu's troops to himself.[32] The deceived Xu and his comrades in arms were enraged, and Xu's younger cousin even tried to kill Chiang but was prevented from doing so by the bodyguards of the future Generalissimo.[33]

In this way the work of the Special Committee led to one outcome: the former members of the highest leadership of the Guomindang, the centrists Hu Hanmin and Xu Chongzhi, were removed from Canton. Just who benefited from this, as from the death of Liao Zhongkai? Only two persons: Wang Jingwei, whom Borodin described as the most devoted and energetic worker, and Chiang Kai-shek, "who definitely makes a good showing of being an adherent . . . of the extreme left tendency in the Guomindang."[34] The assassination of Liao Zhongkai was advantageous to many, including rightists, but the rightists got nothing from it. On the contrary, their position weakened. In the Guomindang, as Borodin, who was extremely pleased with this, expressed it, "a revolutionary dictatorship" of Wang and Chiang was established. No one knows if Wang, Chiang, and Borodin were in favor of the assassination of Liao, but there is no doubt that they made good use of this tragedy to oust the centrist and rightist leaders from power.[35] "We have removed Xu Chongzhi, Hu Hanmin," Borodin admitted, and he added that the CCP CEC had decided "to prepare military–political forces for an inevitable struggle" with the government of Hu Hanmin as far back as May 1925.[36]

All these events contributed perfectly to Moscow's policy in China that Borodin was supposed to implement: it was aimed not only at converting the CCP inside the Guomindang into a mass political organization, but also at radically transforming the class and political character of the GMD itself by having the Guomindang leftists and communists seize power inside the party. Within the framework of this policy CCP members were supposed to make use of their presence in the Guomindang to push the organization as far left as possible, or, more precisely, to transform it into a "people's (worker-peasant) party." They were supposed to do this by squeezing out "representatives of the bourgeoisie" from leadership positions and then eliminating them from the Guomindang; following this, they were supposed to subordinate their petit bourgeois allies to their own influence in order to establish, in the end, the "hegemony of the proletariat" in China—not directly via the Communist Party but through the Guomindang. This policy was put in place by the Comintern in the spring of 1925 under pressure from Stalin.[37] By the fall of that year the first successes in implementing the policy had become evident.

The discouraged rightists had tried to split the Guomindang; on November 23 they convened a separate meeting they called the Fourth Plenum of the GMD CEC, in the suburbs of Beijing, in Xishan (the Western Hills), in the Temple of Azure Clouds, where the embalmed body of Sun Yat-sen was temporarily reposing. Fourteen well-known leaders of the Guomindang demanded the expulsion of communists from the Guomindang, the sacking of Borodin, and the transfer of the CEC of the party from Canton to Shanghai. Their ideologue was Dai Jitao, who, in the summer of 1925, had published two theoretical works, *The Philosophical Foundations of Sun Wenism* [Sun Yat-senism] and *The National Revolution and the Guomindang.* In them Dai accused the communists of parasitizing the body of the GMD, inciting class violence, provoking intra-Guomindang conflicts, and luring Guomindang leftists into the CCP.

Dai also wrote a lengthy letter to his blood brother Chiang, warning him of the danger of cooperating with the CCP. But Chiang, like Wang Jingwei and many other Guomindang leaders who were supported by the communists, came out against the Western Hills faction. Chiang even recalled that in his presence Sun had supposedly said to him, "Borodin's opinion is my opinion. His opinion must be sought on all political questions." The Fourth Plenum undertaking collapsed. But the Western Hills faction, based in Shanghai, began publishing anticommunist articles in a local newspaper, *Minguo ribao* (Republican Daily).[38]

Meanwhile, in the autumn of 1925 the National government launched its Second Eastern Expedition against General Chen Jiongming. Chiang was now commander in chief of the campaign, and Rogachev his advisor. On the eve of this undertaking, August 26, 1925, troops under the control of the Guomindang were reorganized into a single NRA, comprising six corps (later, in March 1926, the Seventh Corps was added, and in June of that same year, the Eighth).[39] Chiang Kai-shek himself was commander of the First Corps, which consisted of Whampoa cadets; Tan Yankai was commander of the Second; Zhu Peide, the Third; Li Jishen, the Fourth; Li Fulin, the Fifth; and Cheng Qian, whom Sun, at one time, had wanted to appoint head of the Whampoa Academy, the

Sixth. Zhou Enlai was appointed head of the Political Department of the First Corps. Quite a few communists were also active in the other corps.[40]

Toward the end of 1925 the well-trained and heavily armed troops of the NRA, with the support of fourteen airplanes flown by Soviet flyers, routed the army of Chiang Kai-shek's sworn enemy.[41] In January 1926 local militarists on Hainan island were routed. The star of the commandant of the Whampoa Academy, who from then on began to be called Invincible within the Guomindang, began to rise rapidly.

The heightened activity of the CCP and of Soviet advisors in the Guomindang as well as the evident, seemingly steady rise of interest on the part of Guomindang leaders themselves in developing relations with the USSR were manifested in a wave of leftist, procommunist phrases at the Second Congress of the Guomindang, which took place in Canton on January 1–19, 1926. Of the 256 delegates chosen for the congress, 189 actually took part. By this time, membership in the Guomindang, according to various sources, numbered between 150,000 and 500,000.

Chiang Kai-shek was among the delegates this time. In the words of an observer, he "attracted great attention" to himself. He "showed himself to be a man of extraordinary achievement," exhibiting "the pose of an important military bulwark. Wang Ching-wei [Jingwei] and the others paled into insignificance beside him."[42] On January 6 Chiang spoke before the congress on military affairs. He was pleased to report that the NRA numbered 86,000 soldiers and officers and that, moreover, the government had six thousand cadets at its disposal. But he noted a series of problems, in particular the shortage of weapons: for the almost 90,000 soldiers there were only 60,000 rifles. He drew a lot of attention to the troops' financial allowances, stressing that their salaries were sixteen times less than that of officers and forty-five times less than that of generals. "This is hardly right," he noted.[43]

At the end of the congress, Chiang, by an overwhelming majority, was elected to the CEC of the Guomindang. Both he and Wang Jingwei received just one vote less than Hu Hanmin, who was elected unanimously despite being in exile in Moscow.[44] At the First Plenum of the CEC, January 22–25, Chiang entered the exclusive ranks of the two leading organs of the Guomindang CEC: the Standing Committee and the Political Committee (both consisting of nine persons). Besides him, the committees included, among a few others, Wang Jingwei, the chair of both organs, Tan Yankai, and Hu Hanmin (in absentia). On February 1, 1926, Chiang was also given the post of general inspector of the NRA.[45]

The revolutionary dictatorship of Wang and Chiang was gaining strength, and there was not far to go to turn the Guomindang into a "people's (worker-peasant) party." A month after its Second Congress, the Guomindang CEC made an official request to the Presidium of the Comintern Executive Committee to admit the party into the Comintern.[46]

But events did not develop in the direction Soviet advisors and Chinese communists were urgently pushing them. At a certain stage, having savored the taste of victory, they began to act in an extremely clumsy manner, trying openly to gain control of the Guomindang CEC apparatus and the National government. On this point, Chicherin, one of the sensible Soviet leaders, wrote critically at the beginning of 1926: "The Chinese Communist Party systematically substituted itself for the Guomindang, put forward its own slogans, appointed communists to leading positions, alienating even Guomindang leftists like Hu Hanmin [in fact, Hu Hanmin was a centrist]."[47] At the same time, the new chief of the South China group of Soviet military advisors was the twenty-nine-year-old corps commander Nikolai Vladimirovich Kuibyshev, an arrogant officer. He had worked in China since the end of October 1925 under the pseudonym Kisanka (the Chinese called him Ji Shanjia). After the Second Congress of the Guomindang and especially after Borodin's temporary departure for Beijing on business at the end of January 1926, he began to demonstrate his contempt for Chinese military men, including Chiang himself. He did not fail to observe that Chiang was "[b]y character . . . irresolute, but stubborn" and that "his stubbornness being of a special Chinese type, as when persons, holding some post (it happens so especially among military men), in case all does not go according to their wishes, immediately resign or simply leave, but come back again after long negotiations and entreaties." Kisanka, a man with "a steep forehead," himself was stubborn and therefore began to look down on Chiang, seeing him as a "typical 'intelligentsia' of the radical kind."[48] He supposed that Chiang "could not have obtained much success as leader of troops on the battlefield without the aid of our [Soviet] instructors."[49] Moreover, Kisanka opposed the Northern Expedition even though almost all the NRA corps commanders and Chiang himself favored an imminent campaign to the north. In this case, Kisanka proceeded from the wholly logical directives of Stalin and a majority of the Bolshevik Politburo that advancing the Guomindang army from Canton would inevitably limit the chances of radicalizing the Cantonese regime under the pretext of military necessity.[50] Underestimating the future Generalissimo, Kisanka began simply ignoring him, preferring to deal on all military questions with

Wang Jingwei, who, in addition to his other posts, filled the position of political commissar of the Whampoa Academy after the assassination of Liao. Kisanka's deputies Rogachev and Israel Razgon, who worked in China under the pseudonym Ol'gin, began acting the same way.

Wang Jingwei in turn used Kisanka and other Soviet advisors to discredit Chiang Kai-shek. Behind the superficial unanimity of the two Guomindang leaders lurked a deep mutual antipathy. To a considerable degree, as with Chiang's conflict with General Chen, this was rooted in regional differences. Wang was a proud native of Guangdong, and even though his ancestors were originally from Zhejiang he could not stand Chiang, the provincial Zhejiangese. Moreover, the two leaders possessed entirely different characters. The trim General Chiang, who despised idle talk, simply could not stand Wang Jingwei, a handsome lady killer and consummate politician. The misfortune of the Soviet military advisors and Chinese communists may be ascribed to their unequivocal support of Wang Jingwei and Kisanka.

Knowing how pathologically sensitive and irascible Chiang was, it is not difficult to understand the depth of his indignation. On January 19, 1926, he wrote in his diaries, "I am deeply unhappy with the views and actions of Rogachev and Kisanka. I treat them with sincerity, but they repay me with deceit. These are comrades with whom it is impossible to undertake joint actions." After his next meeting with Kisanka on February 7, he added, "It is perfectly clear that his heart is full of doubts, suspicion and fear [in relation to me]."

A day later he submitted his resignation, but Wang did not accept it, although "he did not express the desire" that Chiang remain. Deeply depressed, Chiang wrote in his diaries on February 11, "Soviet friends are suspicious [of me], they despise and deliberately ignore me, I don't want at all to fight against their lies and I do not accuse them, and everything that I do, I repay them with sincerity."[51] He remembered Confucius, who taught: "Put loyalty and trust above everything else; do not befriend your moral inferiors; do not be afraid to correct your mistakes."[52]

Meeting with Wang Jingwei, he complained face-to-face about Kisanka, apparently calculating that Wang would send him back to Moscow. But instead Wang advised Chiang himself to go to the USSR to rest up and study the experience of the Russian revolution and at the same time discuss his personal problems in the Comintern. Wang at once told Kisanka everything that the offended general had said about him.[53]

What could Chiang do? At first, in February 1926, he actually decided to go to Russia and asked his secretary, Chen Lifu, to accompany him. The efficient Chen even bought tickets and exchanged currency, but on the road to the port Chiang kept having second thoughts, several times ordering the chauffeur to turn back. Finally, after making up his mind once and for all, he returned home. Chen Lifu asserts that he did this after taking his (Chen's) advice to use force against his enemies.[54] At this time all those who were dissatisfied with the government's pro-Soviet course began to gather around him. He had a chance now to defeat Kisanka, Wang Jingwei, and the Chinese communists. Chiang had no intention of turning his party over to these people.

During that time he gave an interview to the *New York Times* correspondent Lewis S. Gannett who later wrote, "Chiang is a moody, tempestuous soul. He has proved himself as an administrator, but his nerves are fray."[55] It is not astonishing: with every day he felt ever more keenly that the ring of hatred encircling him was tightening. Now he saw enemies everywhere weaving intrigues behind his back. Once, returning from a banquet arranged by the Soviet advisors to mark the eighth anniversary of the founding of the Red Army, he wrote in his diaries: "Mouru [General Wang Boling, one of the rightists] said to me that there were persons [at the banquet] slandering me. I also noticed people who despise me. . . . Why was I so stupid before? I will never be so again!"[56]

On the night of March 19–20, 1926, Chiang snapped. He issued an order to arrest about fifty Chinese communists, sent troops to surround the residence of the Soviet military advisors, and declared martial law in Canton. He explained this by saying he had succeeded in uncovering a communist plot. The communists supposedly intended to kidnap him and spirit him away to Russia, where they would hold him a prisoner.[57]

There are many doubts, however, that such a plot existed. After all, in Moscow, as noted, Chiang was considered extremely leftist—more to the left than other NRA commanders. And Kisanka himself, for all his condescension toward the future Generalissimo, considered him a Jacobin.[58] It seems hardly likely that in such circumstances the Chinese communists would dare to arrest Chiang and spirit him off to Russia. Most likely Chiang himself provoked the incident. Such seems the only plausible explanation, especially if one considers what a depressed psychological state Chiang was in at that time and how much he feared losing face in front of Kisanka. Not by accident, on the eve of these events he asked his blood brother Cicada Zhang, who was living in Shanghai and serving as chair of the Standing Committee of the GMD CEC, to come to Canton promptly to play the role of supreme arbiter in intraparty affairs.[59] It is quite possible, to be sure, that, as someone suffering from a persecution mania, he really believed in a CCP plot, but there are no facts supporting this.

On the other hand, it is known that two days prior to these events the captain of the warship *Yongfeng,* which, after the death of Sun, had been renamed the *Zhongshan* (Yat-sen), the communist Li Zhilong received a verbal command from Chiang, transmitted to him via a higher officer, to bring the vessel to the Whampoa Academy, supposedly to defend it. However, when he executed the order and, once anchored at the roadstead next to the island, called Chiang, the latter declared this was the first he had heard of such an order. When the *Zhongshan* returned to Canton, Chiang suddenly branded Li Zhilong a mutineer and whipped up a story about a communist plot.[60]

At the same time, Chiang wanted to discredit Wang Jingwei, who, following the death of Liao Zhongkai, with the help of Comintern officials and Chinese communists, had become the leader of the left wing of the Guomindang. Toward that end Chiang published an October 1924 letter from Sun Yat-sen to him (Chiang). It was the letter in which Sun asked him not to include either Hu Hanmin or Wang Jingwei in the Revolutionary Committee that had been created to repel the *shangtuan.* Hu, in Sun's words, had "lost faith in the teachings" of the Russian "experiment," and Wang "likewise was not a supporter of the Russian revolution."[61]

The main thing he achieved was the quick removal of Kisanka, Rogachev, and Razgon, the return of Bliukher and Borodin, whom he trusted, and the weakening of Wang's position. However, he did not wish to worsen relations with the Soviet Union; as before he posed as a faithful disciple of Sun who was ready to fulfill all of his bequests, including friendship with the USSR.

According to a report by the Soviet advisor Alexander Ivanovich Cherepanov, Kisanka was completely stupefied and sent Chiang Kai-shek a letter, but it was returned to him with the notification that Chiang was not at home.[62] Chief of the Main Political Administration of the Red Army Andrei Sergeevich Bubnov, the head of a commission of the Bolshevik Politburo, who had been in Canton under the pseudonym Ivanovsky since February 1926 on an inspection mission and happened to find himself at the epicenter of events, visited Chiang Kai-shek to try to clarify the situation. Deep down both he and his commission recognized the connection between the events of March 20 and the Comintern's "forward line of seizing power" in the Guomindang, but they did not want to admit it openly.[63] Tossing a couple of lines to Bubnov, Chiang promised that he himself would come to see him the next morning "for more serious and in-depth discussions," but he did not follow through, thereby indicating that he was master of the situation.

Nothing could be done, so after four days Kuibyshev, Rogachev, and Razgon left Canton, as decided by Bubnov.[64] The Russians made concessions, but in the words of one of them, only "to buy time and to prepare to liquidate this general [Chiang Kai-shek]."[65] They had no intention of forgiving him for the events of March 20. They were simply biding their time. But for now the incident ended peacefully. After making his point, Chiang freed those who had been arrested and even apologized to the Soviet specialists remaining in Canton. On April 29 Borodin arrived in the southern capital of China and Bliukher showed up at the end of May. From then until the start of the Northern Expedition (July 1926) all the fundamental political matters began to be decided by the Big Three: Chiang Kai-shek, Cicada Zhang, who had come to Canton on March 22, and Borodin. Their meetings took place in Cicada's home. Borodin's house, at which meetings of the GMD leadership had previously been held, "was no longer the scene of intense activity."[66]

The result of the coup of March 20 was a notable weakening of the position not only of the communists and the Soviet advisors but also of the Guomindang leftists grouped around Wang Jingwei. The "revolutionary dictatorship" of Wang and Chiang was breaking down, and Chiang had substantially strengthened his power. On March 22 members of the government and army commanders expressed their support of him.[67] That day he wrote sarcastically in his diaries, "Those who prior to the events opposed my actions, after the events began to heed my words like Holy Scripture. How quickly people's moods change!"[68]

Wang was deeply depressed. He had long suffered from diabetes, and his political setbacks exacerbated his condition. He took to his bed; his wife, Chen Bijun, whom everyone called Becky, repeatedly summoned doctors to see him, and he refused to engage in "any sort of work-related conversations." After the dismissal of Kisanka, "whom he had supported," Wang felt that he "had lost face." He was insulted that the Russians had made concessions to Chiang, feeling that now he had "to step aside from his work for a while."[69] He wrote about this in a letter to Cicada Zhang, who was the most authoritative person closest to Chiang.[70] In May Wang went abroad for treatment via Shanghai.

By an irony of fate, his old ill-wisher, the centrist Hu Hanmin, who just a few days earlier, on April 29, had returned to Canton from Moscow via Shanghai despite attempts by the Soviet authorities to detain him, was on the same boat with Wang from Canton to Shanghai. That same day, April 29, Hu met at Whampoa with Chiang, whose actions on March 20 he heartily supported. He shared his impressions of the USSR with the future Generalissimo, asserting that the goal of the Russians was "to destroy the Guomindang from inside so as ultimately to replace the GMD with the CCP." He advised Chiang to arrest Borodin, but Chiang was probably not ready for this. Prior to the Northern Expedition it made no sense to break with the USSR. He said neither yes nor no, but that same day, striving to demonstrate his fidelity to the alliance with Russia and simultaneously show his own power yet again, he conveyed Hu Hanmin's words to Borodin, who was also visiting him in Whampoa.[71] Afterward, Hu had no choice but to leave Canton. In Shanghai he engaged in literary activity.[72]

At that time in the villages of Guangdong the so-called peasant unions (in fact, those of paupers and lumpens) that the communists had been forming there began to be disarmed. Moreover, Chiang issued a series of demands to the communists, aimed at severely circumscribing their political and organizational autonomy inside the GMD. These demands were introduced at the Second Plenum of the Guomindang CEC (May 15–22, 1926) by Chiang Kai-shek himself. Supporting the demands were Tan Yankai, Cicada Zhang, and Sun Ke (also known as Sun Fo), Sun Yat-sen's son from his first marriage, after which they were adopted. The demands included the following: a prohibition on criticizing Sun Yat-sen and his teaching; providing the chairman of the Guomindang CEC a list of communists who wanted to join the GMD; limiting the number of communists in the CEC and in provincial and municipal committees of the Guomindang to one-third of the total number of members of these committees; prohibiting communists from heading GMD CEC departments; prohibiting Guomindang members from convening meetings in the name of the Guomindang without the permission of the party leadership; prohibiting Guomindang members from taking part in activities of the Communist Party without permission; prior affirmation by a joint conference of all instructions of the CCP transmitted to its members;[73] and prohibiting Guomindang members from joining the CCP.[74] On May 1 thirty-four-year-old Chen Guofu, the oldest nephew of Chiang's late blood brother Chen Qimei, became the director of the key branch of the CEC, the Organization Department, in place of the communist Tan Pingshan, who had headed it from the time of the Second Congress. He was close to Chiang and had come to Canton from Shanghai at Chiang's request on the eve of the plenum. In the words of an eyewitness, his own brother, Chen began to search for covert communists in the ranks of the GMD in order to purge them at the right moment.[75]

Following Stalin's line, which was aimed at seizing power in the Guomindang at an appropriate moment, the Chinese communists retreated, accepting these demands. Otherwise they would have had to leave the Guomindang, but this would have buried all of Moscow's hopes to transform the GMD into a people's (worker-peasant) party.[76] The Moscow leaders and the CCP CEC were also deluded, so skillfully was Chiang maneuvering. Sometime after the coup he limited the activity not only of the communists but also of the Guomindang rightists. At Whampoa he dissolved both the communist Union of Young Soldiers and the Guomindang Society for the Study of Sun Wenism [Sun Yat-senism] and dismissed several rightists from their posts. At the end of May he even arrested one of the most fervent supporters of excluding the CCP from the GMD, the chief of police of Canton Wu Tiecheng. Moscow's main informant, Borodin, deemed this a concrete expression of the weakness of the rightist faction. He regarded the adoption by the May plenum of the Guomindang of the resolution limiting the activity of the CCP as merely a tactical step calculated "to eliminate misunderstanding" between the Communist Party and "honest Guomindang members." He even thought that "the resolution of the plenum of the C[E]C [GMD] on the communists inflicted greater damage to the rightists than to the communists."[77] "Had Dr. Sun been alive, he would also have taken certain measures to restrain the activities of the CCP," he said frankly to Zhang Guotao, a member of the CCP CEC.[78]

After the plenum Chiang gradually took the reins of power into his own hands: he headed the Military Council of the National government; the Department of Military Cadres of the Guomindang CEC; he became the commander in chief of the NRA, that is, the Generalissimo; and in early July he even became the chair of the highest organ, the Political Council of the CEC, which united the functions of the Political and the Standing Committees. After Wang Jingwei's resignation, the duties of the chair of the Political Committee were carried out by Tan Yankai, who also became the head of the National government, while Cicada Zhang chaired the Standing Committee. But now they yielded these posts to Chiang. However, he did ask Cicada Zhang to carry out his duties in the party during the Northern Expedition.[79]

Thus in the first half of 1926 Chiang, who was now thirty-eight years old, had apparently established full control of the party and the army. The irony was that his victory in the struggle for Sun Yat-sen's legacy was secured by Comintern agents in South China who, starting in 1924, had done everything to strengthen the Whampoa Academy and the position of its commandant, whom they mistakenly considered to be a leftist (Borodin, Bliukher), and then provoked a conflict with him (Kisanka, Rogachev). The outcome was that by relying on a majority of the cadets and academy graduates holding command posts in the NRA, Chiang was not only able to defeat his rivals in the GMD—Chen Jiongming, Xu Chongzhi, Wang Jingwei, and others—but also to limit the influence of those very same Soviet advisors and of Chinese communists and Guomindang leftists. The Whampoa graduates comprised the core of the armed forces of the GMD and were becoming the most powerful intraparty organization of the Guomindang.

CHAPTER 8

# *The Northern Expedition and the Split in the Guomindang*

On May 21, 1926, the Guomindang CEC published a manifesto on the situation in the country, announcing the imminent start of the Northern Expedition that Sun Yat-sen had dreamed of for so long. Some days later, on June 5, Chiang was confirmed as commander of this campaign. The total number of officers and men at that time was about 100,000. The Nationalist Army of 150,000 troops, commanded by Feng Yuxiang, who, as mentioned above, had announced his support of Sun back in October 1924, was an ally of the NRA in North China. However, in April 1926 he suffered a monumental defeat at the hands of the northern militarists. Early in May he and his family traveled to the Soviet Union where he had talks on expanding Soviet military assistance and "to await the development of events in China."[1] On the second day after his arrival in Moscow he became a member of the Guomindang, announcing this in front of Lenin's sarcophagus. He came to an agreement with the leadership of the Bolshevik party to provide him with supplementary material aid worth more than 4.3 million rubles and to augment the group of his Soviet military advisors by adding new cadres. But since he was in Moscow he was unable to provide concrete military support to Chiang Kai-shek until he returned to China in mid-September 1926.

Nonetheless, in early July 1926 the Northern Expedition became a reality. In the words of an eyewitness, it "roused the revolutionary spirit of the KMT [GMD]."[2] From the start the campaign was successful, notwithstanding the fact that the two sides were unequal in strength. The armies of the three militarist groups opposing the NRA greatly outnumbered the Guangdong forces. At the head of these three groups were General Wu Peifu in Central China, Marshal Sun Chuanfang, who had split off from Wu Peifu, in East China, and Marshal Zhang Zuolin in North and Northeast China. The armies of Wu and Sun each numbered some 200,000 fighters, while Marshal Zhang mustered 350,000 men. But Chiang Kai-shek was lucky. In February 1926 a split had occurred in the army of the Hunan governor Zhao Hengti, part of General Wu's group. General Tang Shengzhi, the commander of the Fourth Division, rose in rebellion after earlier establishing ties with the Canton government. Enlisting the support of Canton, Tang attacked General Zhao, forcing him to flee from Changsha, the capital of Hunan province. At the end of March 1926 he proclaimed himself the governor of Hunan. But he was unable to solidify his position in Changsha right away. General Wu moved troops against him, and he was obliged to leave the city. In these circumstances, on May 19 Chiang sent one of the regiments of the NRA, numbering some two thousand men, to Hunan. On June 2 Tang's division was reorganized into the Eighth Corps of the NRA, and Tang announced the start of a struggle against the English, a campaign against Wu Peifu, and the expulsion of Zhao Hengti.

On July 9, 1926, at 9:00 a.m. on the Eastern Square of Canton—which in the Ming and Qing dynasties (1368–1912) was used as a military parade ground—in the presence of no fewer than 50,000 persons, Chiang took a solemn oath of allegiance as commander in chief of the NRA. In "an impressive ceremony" greeted with thunderous ovations, he swore "to smash the northern militarists, put an end to imperialist oppression, fulfill the behest of Sun Yat-sen, and to wipe away our shame."[3] Just two days later his forces, inspired by the ideas of the nationalist revolution, scored their first major victory over the militarist Wu Peifu, after which they occupied Changsha, the capital of Hunan province. The local inhabitants, who despised Governor Zhao Hengti for his regime of terror, "welcomed [them] as heroes." Red flags were unfurled over every shop in Changsha, and "student processions, hours long" shouted communist slogans: "Down with Western Imperialism" and "Long live Russia, the Saviour of Mankind."[4]

Afterward, minor militarists, afraid of losing their troops and consequently their power and income in case they resisted, began to come over to the side of the commander in chief of the NRA, who represented, in the opinion of a contemporary, "a new type of man: able, keen, executive."[5] Chiang received them, appointed them as generals, and folded their regiments and divisions into his own armed forces. "Everywhere they want to surrender to me," he said delightedly. "Their only fear is that I may not permit them to capitulate. . . . All of them are opportunists."[6] As a result of elements of the militarists going over to the side of the NRA, its officer corps began to acquire a distinctly conservative character. Consequently, the influence of the rightists grew, and Chiang increasingly leaned toward their position. At the same time, following the movement of NRA columns into the villages and cities of Hunan and then Hubei, unrest among the lumpens and the paupers increased. That part of the rural and urban population from time immemorial had been seen by wealthy landowners as well as by ordinary peasants and merchants as the most destructive element in society. The lumpens and the paupers who joined them, hungry and ragged, wanted to dominate, humiliate, and grind into the dirt everyone who lived even slightly better than they. In conditions of revolution and war, they had a chance to repay them for their humiliation and poverty. Even though the mass of ordinary peasants was not guilty of anything, they represented the most convenient target simply because they lived side-by-side. Naturally, pauper-lumpen banditry posed a threat to the united front because the generals and officers of the NRA were from more or less affluent families. But the communists, as they had done in Guangdong, began to organize the lumpens and paupers into so-called peasant unions, striving to establish in the future their own hegemony in the revolution. As for eliminating anticommunists from the GMD, the Communist Party demonstrated its total powerlessness, since the balance of forces in the GMD was not in their favor.[7]

Meanwhile, in mid-August, at Tang Shengzhi's meeting with Chiang Kai-shek, it was decided to continue the Northern Expedition in the direction of the tri-cities of Wuhan in Hubei province; and after its seizure to move in two columns: a western column whose goal was Beijing and an eastern column directed at Nanchang, the capital of Jiangxi province. Chiang Kai-shek himself headed the eastern column and Tang Shengzhi the western. On August 17 the Northern Expedition resumed.[8]

In the autumn of 1926 the troops of the NRA scored major victories. They reached the Yangzi River valley. On September 6 the city of Hanyang was taken; the next day Hankou. Wuchang, however, held out for an entire month, and the NRA troops succeeded in taking it as late as October 10, Republic Day. Thus all of the Wuhan tri-cities were now in the hands of the NRA. The battle for Wuchang, the capital of Hubei, was particularly bloody. An eyewitness recalled that dead bodies lay everywhere, and the stench of corpses filled the air: "From a distance I could see the blackened faces of the dead, but when my horse approached the bodies, swishing its tail, the flies which were covering them, flew off, and the black faces vanished. It is impossible to describe my anguish. . . . Sitting in the saddle, shocked, I cautiously steered my horse through the bodies, making sure that he did not step on them."[9]

In September, while in Hankou, Chiang unexpectedly received a congratulatory telegram from a woman whom he had been thinking about the past several months: Song Meiling (Olivia), the younger sister of Sun Yat-sen's widow, Song Qingling. By this time he had quite cooled off toward Jennie, although he maintained normal relations with her as with Yecheng, who was bringing up his younger son Wei-kuo. Meanwhile, Soviet communists were raising and educating his older son Ching-kuo. In October 1925, under the influence of Russian acquaintances from the Soviet embassy in Beijing, he wrote to his father asking his permission to go to Moscow to study.[10] Having received approval he went to Sun Yat-sen University of the Toilers of China (UTK), which opened in the Soviet capital in November, a Comintern higher education institution that was supposed to become a "sort of educational center of the united front . . . of the CCP and the Guomindang."[11] Ching-kuo was part of a group of 119 persons, and as early as November 23 he had become a student, receiving from the administration of UTK the Russian pseudonym (for reasons of secrecy) Nikolai Vladimirovich Elizarov.[12]

For the most part Jennie lived in Canton. After the assassination of Liao Zhongkai, his widow, who, as referred to above, was well-disposed toward her, begged her and Chiang to rent a small house next to hers in the prestigious district of Dongshan (Eastern Mountains). The area was filled mostly with two-story European-style villas where all the high Guomindang officials and Soviet advisors lived. Another neighbor of Chiang and Jennie was Cicada Zhang. Somehow during a lull in the fighting Jennie left Canton and went to see Chiang. But he never stopped thinking about a new woman.

Chiang became acquainted with Song Meiling either in early December 1922 or in early January 1923 in Sun Yat-sen's private house at 29 Molière Street.[13] But at the time, as alluded to earlier, he was not in good shape: he was tired out from trips to the front in southern Fujian, where his relations with General Xu Chongzhi were in tatters. Moreover, he still loved Jennie very much, so his acquaintance with Meiling could go nowhere.

The new meeting took place in Canton on the eve of the Northern Expedition in the home of Meiling's older sister Ailing (Nancy), the wife of the business tycoon Kong Xiangxi, a consummate gentleman with sad-looking eyes concealed behind round eyeglasses. Educated in the United States—he studied at Oberlin College in Ohio and at Yale University—Kong was considered one of the best economists in China. He and his wife invited Chiang and Jennie along with other high Guomindang officials to dinner. It was a hot Saturday night, and both beautiful sisters, shapely and well-dressed in elegant silk *qipao*—long dresses with slits up to the thigh—gracefully fanned themselves. Their perfectly coiffed black hair was pulled back into buns at the back of their heads. "Indeed, they looked as if they had stepped out of a Shanghai fashion book," Jennie recalled.[14]

And here suddenly Meiling, in the full flower of her feminine beauty (she was thirty years old), made a strong impression on Chiang. In Jennie's presence, to be sure, he did not even exchange a couple of sentences with her, and we do not know whether he began thinking about a new marriage. But there is no question that he liked her very much. On July 2, 1926, soon after the meeting, he wrote in his diaries, "Meiling is going off to Shanghai, very sorry to be parted."[15]

From then on he heard nothing about her. Then in September she unexpectedly wrote to him, congratulating him on the taking of Hankou. Moreover, she called him "a hero!" He became excited and at once, forgetting about Jennie, invited her to come to him.[16] But Meiling, replying only two months later and courteously thanking him for the invitation, expressed regrets that she was unable to come: in her words, she had to take care of her mother, who lived in Shanghai.

By that time Chiang was no longer in Hankou. Even before the fall of Wuchang, realizing that the forces of General Wu Peifu were practically destroyed, in the second week of September he turned his column toward Jiangxi, against a new foe, Marshal Sun Chuanfang, yielding the glory of the conqueror of Hubei to Tang Shengzhi. Crossing the border of Jiangxi on September 22, he and his fighters within the course of a month advanced toward Nanchang, the main city of the province, which they took on November 7. The next goal of Chiang and Bliukher, who was with his forces, was clear: to seize Shanghai and Nanjing, the most important cities in East China. At the same time, the troops of General He Yingqin, who had been a fellow student of Chiang's at the Japanese military academy and an instructor at Whampoa, were moving unhurriedly through Fujian province toward Zhejiang, Chiang Kai-shek's home province.[17]

A second missive from Meiling, which Chiang received in November, soon after the new victories at the front, stirred memories of the splendid woman. Judging from the fact that Meiling continued to correspond with him, he assumed she was interested in him. And why should she not be? He was a strong, tall, handsome man whose "alert dark eyes . . . seemed to pierce through."[18] He obviously possessed charisma as a natural leader. So the ambitious, willful woman, who knew her own worth and was aiming to make a brilliant match, could not let go of him. That the new leader of the Guomindang and commander in chief of the army had excellent prospects for becoming the head of the country suited her best of all. Her eldest sister shared these views, unlike her middle sister, Qingling, the widow of Sun Yat-sen, who was never fond of Chiang and, as cited above, back in 1914 had refused to consider the possibility of marrying him. After the death of her husband, her relations with Chiang further deteriorated. According to her, sometime after the funeral, he had the gall to send a matchmaker to her. But she brushed him off since she was convinced that "it was politics, not love."[19] Learning somewhat later that Chiang was not indifferent toward her younger sister only confirmed her belief that he was a careerist. "By hook or by crook he wants to join our family, that is, the family of Sun Yat-sen," she reasoned.

Was she right? Partly. The chance to become related to the influential and wealthy Song family must have excited Chiang's imagination. He would then become Sun Yat-sen's brother-in-law and a relative of the able financiers Kong Xiangxi and Meiling's brother T. V. Song, who could come up with the funds that were indispensable for consolidating his power in the Guomindang. But simply as a woman Meiling could please Chiang. She was truly enchanting, clever, artistic, splendidly educated, and intelligent.

She had been born on March 4, 1898, in the village of Chuansha on the outskirts of Shanghai.[20] From the age of ten through sixteen she lived in America together with Qingling, in the town of Macon, Georgia, some eighty miles southeast of Atlanta. Qingling was studying there in the prestigious Wesleyan College for Women, while Meiling was taking private English lessons. Until 1909 her eldest sister, Ailing, was studying at the same college. In 1912, at the age of fourteen, she too was admitted to Wesleyan, but a year later, once Qingling had finished college and returned to China, Meiling transferred to be closer to her brother T. V. Song, who was studying in the Department of Economics at Harvard. She enrolled at Wellesley, the famous women's college located some sixteen miles west of Cambridge. In the spring of 1917 Meiling concluded her studies in her major subject, English language and literature, and was among the top thirty-three students. She was in love with America, not really surprising since she had grown up there. In her way of thinking and her upbringing she was American. "The only thing Chinese about me is my face," she said.[21] Naturally, she spoke fluent English, although with a strong southern accent she had acquired in her childhood in Georgia and which she was never able to shake.[22]

She matured early, realizing that she was attractive to men, and like many other women she adored dressing beautifully. Convinced of how irresistible she was, she only worried about her tendency to put on weight. "My one extravagance, clothes . . . my favorite motto, don't eat candy—not one piece . . . my secret sorrow being fat," she wrote in her diaries.[23] But her desire to love and be loved was interwoven from her early youth with a strong desire to achieve fame and greatness. She simply couldn't imagine marrying an ordinary man. It is said, to be sure, that prior to meeting Chiang she had some sort of relationship with one of T. V. Song's friends, a man named Liu Jiwen, and that they supposedly became engaged. But whether this was really so, no one knows for sure. Liu himself, who, incidentally, was hardly an ordinary man and who held responsible posts in the Guomindang under Sun Yat-sen, denied this.[24]

But she liked Chiang in every way. "My marriage with Chiang Kai-shek was wholly ideal," she recalled. "As a young girl I worshipped heroes." And further: "This was my chance. Together with my husband I would work, not folding my arms, to make China stronger." Moreover, she added, "I was attracted by his shining eyes. . . . I lost my heart to him."[25]

Meanwhile, Chiang's military successes increasingly disturbed Borodin. Even though, following the May 1926 plenum of the CEC, Chiang undertook no new measures against the communists, the chief political advisor was convinced that after taking Shanghai, the largest industrial and commercial center of the country, Chiang would immediately begin killing communists. In Canton, as early as the second half of October, Borodin, behind the backs of Chiang and Cicada Zhang, convened a joint meeting of the Guomindang CEC along with representatives of provincial and special municipal committees of the party, consisting mostly of leftists. At the meeting a new program was adopted in which communist demands vis-à-vis the peasant question were included: reducing rents and the usury percentage, lightening the tax burden, and prohibiting speculation. In connection with this, the first criticism was directed at Chiang and Cicada Zhang, and it was decided that Wang Jingwei, who was living in France at that time, should be asked to return from his leave. The blow against Chiang was precisely aimed.

In early November the Political Council of the CEC of the GMD adopted a resolution to transfer the site of the National government to Wuhan, and a month later the first group of ministers—a quartet of men plus Sun's widow, Qingling, all leftists—along with Borodin moved to the new location.[26] Along the road from Canton, in one of the mountain resorts in Lushan in Jiangxi province, late on the night of December 7, Borodin met with Chiang. The meeting of these two old acquaintances took place in a tense atmosphere.[27] Borodin arrived in Wuhan in a state of irritation.

He met at once with the commander of the western column, Tang Shengzhi, and informed him that he no longer trusted Chiang and that he relied solely on Tang. "He who is able honestly to implement the ideas of Doctor Sun Yat-sen, will become the greatest figure in China," he declared to the flattered general. Tang, a frail man with scant whiskers and protruding ears, a graduate of the Baoding Military Academy and a devout Buddhist, was overjoyed and replied, "I am ready to follow all of your directives."[28] Afterward Tang openly asserted many times that "Chiang Kai-shek is fatigued. It would be better for him to take a rest, since he will not be able to accomplish anything in Kiangsi [Jiangxi]. If I were to take command, I would attack not only Kiangsi but Nanjing."[29] From then on for both Tang and Borodin the struggle against Chiang became a real obsession.[30]

The CCP, the Soviet advisors as well as the leftists, or those turning into Guomindang leftists, again went on the attack in the Guomindang, trying to take over its party bureaucracy. This time the main target of attack was Chiang himself, whom the Politburo of the Central Committee of the Bolshevik party had stopped viewing as a leftist since the summer of 1926 and now considered a centrist. The communists resorted to spreading rumors: "Chiang Kai-shek intends to follow the path of Napoleon. He is a dictator." And even, contrary to the facts: "He does not want Wang Jingwei to return." In fact, Chiang had initiated a correspondence with Wang in September 1926, and several times requested his "Elder Brother" to return and assume the burden of party affairs. "My strength is little and my ability is thin," he wrote. "I cannot look after political affairs as well [as the army]." In early October he even sent his old comrade Cicada Zhang to France to meet with Wang to persuade the obstinate fellow to return. It was all in vain.[31]

Borodin actively supported these intrigues, ceasing to take into account Chiang's acute sensitivity to even the slightest manifestation of disrespect and suspiciousness. He also unleashed a campaign of slander against Cicada Zhang. He was an invalid confined to a wheelchair, so Borodin and his comrades in arms began to agitate everywhere: "Down with the Muddle-headed, Old and Feeble Chang Ching-chiang [Zhang Jingjiang]."[32] Moreover, at Borodin's initiative, on December 13 in Wuhan a so-called Provisional Joint Conference of party and government organs was convened. It assumed full power in the Guomindang regions. In this case, Borodin acted behind the backs not only of Chiang and Cicada Zhang but also of the chairman of the National government, Tan Yankai, who, along with a second group of ministers, was preparing to leave Canton. The Minister of Justice Xu Qian, one of Chiang Kai-shek's irreconcilable enemies, was chosen as chairman of the Joint Conference; three communists were on it along with Guomindang leftists.[33]

Chiang could not tolerate their assuming such a stance toward himself nor toward Tang Yankai or his blood brother Zhang, the person dearest to him. Moscow's agents were obviously playing with fire. On December 11, 1926, Cicada Zhang, Tan Yankai, and other ministers in the second group came to Chiang Kai-shek from Canton. They were understandably offended that the Provisional Joint Conference had been convened without them, and therefore they decided not to cross over into leftist Wuhan.[34] On January 1, 1927, they learned that Wuhan had been officially proclaimed the capital of Guomindang China. In response, in Nanchang on January 3 Chiang convened a meeting of the Political Council of the CEC, the highest organ of power of the Guomindang. By a majority vote it was decided "to temporarily locate the CEC of the party and the National government in Nanchang," and to make the ultimate decision on the question of the capital on March 1, at the Third Plenum of the Guomindang CEC that would be convened in the same city.[35] Then Borodin decided to make a decisive break. "On January 3, 1927, a break became unavoidable," he acknowledged subsequently. "We did [not] hold onto Chiang Kai-shek with a rotten rope, because on January 3 we already were heading toward a break with Chiang Kai-shek."[36]

On January 11, wishing to resolve the purported misunderstanding, Chiang left Nanchang for Wuhan. But after spending a week there he achieved nothing. Borodin, the communists, and the Guomindang leftists openly humiliated him. At the very first banquet on the evening of January 12, Borodin, striking up a conversation with Chiang (with T. V. Song interpreting), gruffly demanded that Chiang subordinate himself to the Wuhan government in all respects. In essence he was accusing him of aiming to become a dictator. Barely restraining his rage but making sure everyone heard him, he told Chiang a western parable about a king who, not wishing to hear others' opinions, forbade his ministers from speaking; then the ministers said to him,

"Only dogs do not speak. And if You, Your Majesty, want us not to talk, then find yourself dogs."[37] Chiang considered these words a public insult. He was so furious and offended that he could not fall asleep the whole night after the banquet, and in the morning he even wanted to commit suicide. He was so depressed from the thought that he had "lost face."[38] One of his former friends from Whampoa, a Guomindang leftist, understanding that Borodin's words would lead inevitably to a break between Chiang and the Guomindang, got drunk and cried bitterly all night long.[39]

At this point Meiling was in Wuhan. She had come with her mother and older sister Ailing in December 1926 to visit her sister Qingling (the widow of Sun Yat-sen) and her brother T. V. Song. After the death of Liao Zhongkai, T. V. Song, starting in late September 1926, headed the ministry of finance of the national government and had come to Wuhan with the first group of ministers. Like his sister Qingling, whom he greatly respected, T. V. Song at the time was an extreme leftist. That week Chiang met with him and Qingling on more than one occasion, but whether he saw Meiling is not known, as there is nothing in his diaries to that effect.

Angry and sullen, Chiang returned to Jiangxi on January 18, and in early February he launched an assault on Shanghai and Nanjing. At the same time he demanded that the Comintern leaders swiftly recall Borodin to Moscow, replacing him with whomever they wished. Chiang proposed, in particular, the famous Soviet Communists Karl Radek or Karakhan as candidates.[40] For its part, at a secret meeting on February 17 the Politburo of the Bolshevik party adopted a resolution to wholly subordinate Chiang to the Wuhan government. "The line of the C[E]C of the Guomindang [actually they had in mind Borodin's line] vis-à-vis Chiang Kai-shek we consider correct," Stalin informed Borodin. "One must take measures . . . in such a way that Borodin does not stick out, so the conflict is not seen as a struggle for influence between Borodin and Chiang Kai-shek."[41]

At the end of February, Voitinsky was in Wuhan. Seriously worried, he went to Nanchang to converse with Chiang, bypassing Borodin, but he achieved nothing. Chiang stubbornly insisted that Borodin be recalled. "All the tensions in our party are caused by Borodin," he bluntly asserted.[42] "The conflict is rooted in Wuhan. . . . Recently Borodin has begun to follow a policy of splitting the national revolutionary movement. . . . Now I am moving against him, since he is pursuing a dangerous line, leading to the existence of two governments. . . . We are ready for a break." Chiang also complained to Voitinsky that the communists were spreading rumors: "About me that I have become a militarist, that I am a dictator, that I want to break with the USSR, that I am supposedly heading toward an agreement with the Japanese."[43]

Returning to Wuhan, Voitinsky said to one of the leaders of the CCP, Zhang Guotao, "The situation is hopeless." Borodin, hearing of his talks, blamed Voitinsky, saying that his trip only "increased Chiang's arrogance, and damaged our own prestige."[44] After a stormy conversation with Borodin, Voitinsky informed Moscow of Chiang Kai-shek's putschist intentions. Alexander Emelianovich Albrecht (alias Arno), another representative of the Executive Committee of the Comintern, informed the ECCI to the same effect.[45]

Meanwhile, on February 27, Chiang released a "Manifesto" in which he declared, "A part of the members of the GMD are always in the rear, another part on the front and, therefore, because of the loss of contact, different opinions have arisen. . . . If this should continue, not only will our party break up, but the future of our revolution will be threatened. When I think about this, I feel terrible. Therefore, I am hoping that all comrades will unite, working to strengthen the power of the party and value highly all the party's principles." He renewed his proposal that "all comrades request Wang Jingwei to return from his leave to achieve unity in the ranks of the party leaders," emphasizing that "thinking about Wang Jingwei fills all my time. . . . I have decided that if Comrade Wang does not return, I will submit my resignation." He proposed convening a plenum of the Guomindang CEC as soon as possible "to decide fundamental questions." "The time has come when our party is on the verge of a split," he warned.[46] Of course, he was being disingenuous, but it was important that he not appear to be the initiator of any split.

Furthermore, in the "Manifesto" Chiang complained that the CEC "did not have a firm line" on financial questions. What was afoot was that the Wuhan government had begun limiting monetary payments to his troops, trying by hook or by crook to bend them to its will. Understanding that unless he established good relations with Minister of Finance T. V. Song he would be unable to defeat Borodin, in early March Chiang wrote a letter to Song's older sister Ailing inviting her and her mother to come to Jiangxi. She accepted the invitation and arrived at the Jiangxi port of Jiujiang, situated some 186 miles from Wuhan along the Yangzi River. But neither she nor her mother would step on shore, so Chiang had to talk with Ailing on board the steamship. He badly needed money, and he asked Ailing to convince her brother to come over to his side. According to Jennie's recollections, which in this case are basically correct,[47] Ailing agreed but bluntly said to Chiang, "I will make a bargain with you. . . . I will not only convince my brother T. V.

[Song] to leave the Hankow [Hankou] government as you wish, but will go one better. He and I will rally the leading bankers of Shanghai to back you with the necessary funds. . . . In return, you will agree to marry my sister Mei-ling [Meiling]."[48] Chiang, who was already prepared to leave Jennie for the sake of Meiling, agreed.

It remained only to speak with Jennie. It will be recalled that Chiang never discarded his women without coming to an amicable agreement with them. He provided financial support to both his wife and his official concubine. He decided to deal with Jennie exactly the same way, frankly telling her of his agreement with Ailing. Jennie was grief-stricken, but, according to her, he assured her they would not be parting forever: "[S]tep aside for five years so that I can marry Mei-ling [Meiling] Song and get the necessary [financial] help to carry on the [Northern] expedition without the support of Hankow [Hankou]! It's only a political marriage!"[49] He proposed that she go to America to study on his account, swearing that after five years, when everything had settled, he would return to her, and they would live happily to the end of their days.

Whether such a conversation actually took place we don't know, but that Jennie left Nanchang for Shanghai sometime in the third week of March 1927 is true. Chiang sent a letter to Meiling and Ailing asking them, along with other members of the Song family, to leave Wuhan at once and come to him. He loved Meiling even more. "All day today I missed younger sister Mei [as he began to call her then]," he wrote in his diaries on March 21.[50]

The political situation around Chiang continued to heat up. Soon after his secret meeting with Ailing, the Third Plenum of the Guomindang CEC took place in Wuhan on March 10–17; it stripped Chiang of all his top posts in the party, including the position of chair of the Political Council of the CEC. The Political Council was abolished and in its place the Political Committee was restored; seven persons were chosen for its Presidium, including (in absentia) Wang Jingwei as well as the communist Tan Pingshan. The plenum also repudiated the decision of the preceding plenary session that the CC would prohibit communists from heading departments of the Guomindang CEC. It also resolved to choose a new lineup for the National government in which two posts—minister of labor and minister of agriculture—would be offered to communists. Not wishing to enter into open conflict, Chiang, who was not present at the plenum, declared his support for its decisions. But polarization in the Guomindang intensified.

The deepening split was facilitated by a new upsurge of the mass movement of lumpens and paupers in the provinces occupied by the Guomindang army. "Violence had followed in their [the NRA troops] wake," an eyewitness wrote.[51] In the spring of 1927 this movement, in the words of Zhang Guotao, a member of the CEC of the CCP, reached a "stage of madness."[52] Acting no less extreme than the village lumpens and paupers were the members of the so-called workers' pickets, active in a number of cities. The lowlifes who were filling the ranks of these organizations attacked even the relatives of influential members of the Guomindang and communists![53] "The communists are getting stronger," Chen Duxiu, the leader of the party, reported to the Bureau of the CCP CEC, "and the workers' and peasants' movement is developing more and more. The temples are being confiscated, sugar and flour are being confiscated. It seems that trade is forbidden."[54]

Striving to rely on this movement in its struggle against Chiang, on March 3 the Politburo of the Central Committee of the Bolshevik party sent a directive to the CCP CEC which, however, did not arrive in China until twelve days later. The Politburo demanded that the CCP "use all its energy . . . toward ousting the Guomindang rightists, discrediting them politically and systematically removing them from leading posts . . . pursuing a policy of taking over the most important posts in the army . . . strengthening the work of Guomindang and communist cells in the army . . . adhering to a course of arming the workers and peasants, transforming the local peasant committees into actual organs of power with armed self-defense." The CCP was supposed to act under its slogans "everywhere and in all places." "A policy of voluntary semilegality is impermissible," the resolution emphasized. "The Communist Party cannot act as a brake on the mass movement. . . . Otherwise, the revolution will face a grave danger."[55]

Right after the Third Plenum, Borodin proposed to the leftist Wuhan leaders that they give a secret order to General Cheng Qian, the commander of NRA forces on the right bank of the Yangzi, to arrest Chiang Kai-shek at the first opportunity. The Chinese communists should help him do this. This was already a direct confrontation, and the Wuhan group would be taking a great risk. Although Cheng Qian was a leftist, nonetheless he had ties with Chiang. As noted above, he had studied in the same Japanese military academy as Chiang, although three years earlier, and for Chinese, with their clan consciousness, this had no little meaning. It was no surprise, then, that Cheng, although agreeing to carry out the order, failed to do so.[56] Simultaneously, the Wuhan leftists sent a secret directive to Soviet military advisors in all the NRA forces on the approaches to Shanghai: "Go for a defeat. A defeat of the Northern Expedition near Shanghai will be seen as a defeat for Chiang Kai-shek."[57] But on March 21 a popular uprising erupted in Shanghai and was victorious.

Marshal Sun Chuanfang was overthrown. Just in case, the authorities of the International Settlement hired hundreds of Chinese coolies to dig a trench around the perimeter of the concession, stretch barbed wire around it, and erect blockhouses. On the shore 6,750 American and 1,500 Japanese sailors landed to offer assistance, if necessary, to the 9,000-man garrison of the settlement. But on the evening of March 22 units of the NRA entered the Chinese districts of Shanghai, already liberated by the workers' militia, and fortunately no clashes occurred with the foreign troops.[58]

Meanwhile, instances of clashes between detachments of Chiang Kai-shek's armies and armed formations of workers and peasants became more frequent. On March 23 in Anqing, a large city in Anhui province, the Chiang Kai-shek forces attacked Guomindang leftist and communist organizations, perpetrating a real slaughter. In a number of other places they smashed trade unions.[59] It became obvious that Chiang was striving to repeat the events of March 20, 1926, but this time much more decisively.

Soon the situation in Nanjing grew worse. On March 24 a massacre of foreigners took place in the city that had been occupied the day before by NRA troops. It occurred despite the fact that, according to an eyewitness, "both Chinese and foreigners [in Nanjing] for the most part had much sympathy with the Southern forces."[60] This eyewitness had been afraid they would be robbed not by Chiang Kai-shek's soldiers, but by Sun Chuanfang's cutthroats, who were retreating from the city. But it turned out quite differently. It was the occupying soldiers of the NRA and the urban poor supporting them who began to break into the homes of foreigners, pilfering their goods and destroying whatever they couldn't carry off. The result was that many homes, schools, Nanjing University, a Presbyterian institution founded by Americans, seminaries and the US consulate were plundered and burned. Six foreign citizens, including the vice president of Nanjing University, an American missionary named John E. Williams, and one or two Catholic priests were killed. Who organized the massacre is unknown. To this day the communists and the Guomindang members accuse each other. Most likely, soldiers and local inhabitants acted simply on instinct: war always ignites animal passions. In response, Nanjing, which is located on the right bank of the Yangzi River, was subjected to shelling from English and American warships. Despite the efforts of Shanghai businessmen who served as go-betweens acting on his behalf Chiang had a hard time persuading the imperialists to accept apologies.[61]

On March 26 Chiang came to Shanghai. On April 1 Wang Jingwei returned there from abroad; at first he acted very discreetly. He even met with

Chiang in Sun's home on Rue Molière, and they decided to convene a new plenum of the CEC in Nanjing in the near future. But on April 5 Wang published a joint declaration with the leader of the CCP, Chen Duxiu, in which he called for the establishment in China of a "democratic dictatorship of all oppressed classes that were opposed to counterrevolution." This is precisely the kind of dictatorship Stalin insisted on having.[62] On that same day he secretly fled to Wuhan to meet with Borodin, to whom he declared that "he considered Chiang Kai-shek hopeless."[63]

But Stalin still played his game in China. On April 8, 1927, he wrote an inscription on one of his photos: "To Chiang Kai-shek, the Commander in Chief of the Chinese National Army. To Celebrate the Guomindang's Victory and the Liberation of China."[64] The photo was handed over to Shao Lizi, who at the time was a Guomindang representative to the ECCI. Shao was supposed to send it to China.

In the meantime supporters of Chiang Kai-shek needed to get rid of the communists as quickly as possible. And here, they figured, all means of doing so were acceptable. Chen Lifu, Chiang's secretary, recalled that "to eradicate the Communists from the Kuomintang [Guomindang], we began to plan for a party purge. . . . [A] proposal for a party purge . . . was passed unanimously by the [Central Control] committee [Commission]. . . . By now we had discovered that our party seal was in Wuhan. Without it, we could not formally announce the party purge. . . . I suggested we have a new seal made to resemble the seal on old documents. When I now reflect about that decision, I view it as radical and even improper."[65] The culmination occurred around four o'clock in the morning of April 12. Chiang had taken three million Chinese dollars from Shanghai businessmen, and his old associates, the chiefs of the Shanghai mafia organization the Green Gang, agreed to help him disarm the workers' pickets. The mafia chiefs arranged with the police of the International Settlement and the French Concession to engage in a joint action. A Shanghai committee to purge the party was established, after which Chiang unleashed a White Terror in Shanghai and other regions of East China. Chiang's soldiers and 1,500 members of the mafia, tying white rags inscribed with the mocking character *gong* (worker) on their shirt sleeves, began to arrest communists and members of the workers' militia. On the spot, without any trials or consequences, they executed them in front of frightened passersby. With one stroke of the sabre they easily cut off the heads of those arrested. Eyewitnesses reported that "it was raining that day. . . . [T]he streets of the old section of Shanghai City [that is, the Chinese quarters] literally ran with the blood of beheaded victims. . . . Heads rolled in the gutters of the narrow lanes like ripe plums, and the wary executioners wielded their swords with the monotonous rhythm of *punka wallahs*."[66] Those who were not killed in the streets were taken either to the Buddhist temple of Longhua, whose grounds were converted into a mass killing ground, or to the south railroad station, where living people were thrown into the fireboxes of steam locomotives. When the decapitated bodies were buried, the butchers, with a kind of refined brutality, joined the severed heads of women to the bodies of men and vice versa. According to ancient superstition, this would have a devastating impact on the geomancy of the victims.[67]

The exact number of those who perished is unknown. In the words of Chen Lifu, "Countless people in Shanghai died during the purge. It was a bloodthirsty war to eliminate the enemy within. I must admit that many innocent people were killed. We paid a heavy price."[68] "[But] only then was the situation in Shanghai brought under control," Chiang recalled.[69]

Three days after the coup in Shanghai, the Wuhan leftists expelled the "traitor to the revolution" Chiang Kai-shek from the party, removing him from the post of commander in chief of the NRA and openly issuing an order for his arrest. General Cheng Qian was supposed to arrest Chiang, but "the messenger with the order . . . was delayed . . . [at his headquarters] in Nanjing for a week."[70] Even had he not been held up, it was now out of the question to execute the order. An eyewitness expressed surprise: "Who would arrest Chiang when he [Chiang] himself had succeeded in arresting everybody in Shanghai?"[71]

The Wuhan leftists probably understood their weakness, acknowledging that "the split made Chiang Kai-shek" stronger than Wuhan "in every respect."[72] Therefore, in expelling Chiang from the party, they entreated, "May everyone think this over and send their curses to Chiang Kai-shek, so that, in future, no one will dare to repeat his crimes."[73] Moreover, they offered a sum of 250,000 Chinese dollars for the capture of Chiang Kai-shek and 100,000 dollars for his head.[74]

But Chiang was not concerned. In April 1927, to spite Wuhan, he again formed the Political Council of the CEC as the highest organ of the party and placed Hu Hanmin, who wholly supported his struggle against the leftists, as its head. Moreover, on April 18, 1927, at a solemn ceremony in the presence of more than 100,000 persons, Chiang and his comrades in arms proclaimed Nanjing the capital of China, asserting they were acting in accordance with Sun Yat-sen's behest. Sun, to be sure, had said nothing of the sort; as we noted above, on his death bed he had only requested that a mausoleum be constructed for him on Purple Gold Mountain on the outskirts of Nanjing. But Chiang supposed that since the leader wished to repose in Nanjing, the city should serve as the capital.[75]

Wang Jingwei and the other Guomindang leftists in Wuhan came out strongly in opposition to Nanjing and immediately began to assemble forces for a campaign against Chiang. Naturally, they received Moscow's full support. When Stalin received the news from Shanghai he immediately demanded that Shao Lizi return his photo with the flattering inscription to Chiang Kai-shek. Luckily for Stalin, Shao had not had enough time to send it to China. The photo was archived. Infuriated by Chiang's coup, the Kremlin boss decided to transform the left Guomindang into a procommunist worker-peasant party immediately. This party would lead the agrarian revolutionary movement in the countryside, arm the workers and peasants, undertake a reorganization of the army, and transform the Wuhan government into the organ of the revolutionary democratic dictatorship of the proletariat and the peasantry.[76]

This decision took concrete form in a series of directives from the Bolshevik Politburo to the Central Committee of the CCP and Comintern representatives in China, dated May 30 and June 3, 6, 9, 18, and 20, 1927.[77] On June 23 the Politburo even sent a telegram to Wang Jingwei in the hope of convincing him that "the Guomindang should support the agrarian revolution and the peasantry."[78] On June 25 the GMD leaders were sent yet another telegram with the summons to create military units of workers and peasants devoted to the revolution.[79] In this connection, the Soviets actively extended loans to the Wuhan government.

But events overtook Stalin. The National government in Wuhan was literally falling apart. One after another, generals in various cities were abandoning it and switching their support to Chiang. At the same time, because of the rupture of commercial and financial ties between the Yangzi River ports and Wuhan, industrialists and merchants in Wuhan began to vacate the city, which led to a severe economic crisis. Unemployment rose sharply. The news that Marshal Feng Yuxiang had several meetings with Chiang Kai-shek on June 19–21 in Xuzhou (Jiangsu province) to coordinate joint actions against the CCP and the northern militarists came as a heavy blow to the leftists. To win over Feng, Chiang offered to pay him two and a half million Chinese dollars monthly, starting in July. Moreover, he expressed his "burning desire to yield the post of commander in chief to Comrade Huanzhang [that is, Feng

Yuxiang, the courtesy name of the marshal]."[80] Feng gladly agreed to take the money but courteously declined the post. From Xuzhou he sent Wang Jingwei and the CEC of the Guomindang left an ultimatum demanding that they too break with the communists. "The Communist Party is responsible for all the disasters in Hunan and Hubei. The Communist Party is plotting to destroy the Guomindang," Feng asserted. He added, "The people wanted to suppress such [communist] despotism."[81] Lacking the power to alter the situation, the leadership of the Wuhan government began shifting to a more overt anticommunist policy.

At the end of June and early in July 1927 Stalin began to realize that Wang Jingwei would soon follow Chiang's path. On June 27 he acknowledged, "I'm afraid that Wuhan will lose its nerve and come under Nanking [Nanjing, that is, under Chiang Kai-shek]."[82] For a while, to be sure, he tried to maneuver, inclining to make concessions to Wang Jingwei. He was ready to recall Borodin "if Wuhan wants" and to send additional subsidies, "but only with some assurance that Wuhan will not surrender to the tender mercies of Nanking."[83] Ultimately, however, he stepped back from the idea of making concessions, and on July 8 the Executive Committee of the Comintern sent a directive to the CCP CC demanding that the communists withdraw from the National government inasmuch as the "main armed forces of Wuhan . . . have actually become an instrument of counterrevolutionaries."[84] But it was too late. On July 15, 1927, Wang Jingwei broke with the communists, and a White Terror commenced in Wuhan. The defeat of the CCP had happened.

Soon after, Borodin and Bliukher left China. Borodin, for whose head Chiang Kai-shek's supporters were offering a reward of 30,000 Chinese dollars, returned to Russia via Northwest China, which was occupied by Marshal Feng Yuxiang. Feng and the Guomindang leftists did not put any obstacles in his way. At the Hankou railroad station Wang Jingwei and Song Qingling even arranged a magnificent send-off.[85]

Bliukher left via Shanghai. Despite the rupture of the united front, Chiang kept his good feelings toward his military advisor. He even met with him to wish him a pleasant journey. On parting, he said to him, "We may have another opportunity to work together, so please do not feel so badly about leaving." "I hope, too, this is not the last time we shall see each other. So, till we meet again!" Bliukher replied.[86]

The rout of the communists, however, did not lead to an immediate unification of the two factions of the Guomindang, that of Wang Jingwei and that of Chiang Kai-shek. There was too much enmity between them. Moreover, in early August Chiang Kai-shek's position in Nanjing sharply deteriorated. Soon after conducting successful negotiations with Feng and despite the existence of a threat from Wuhan, Chiang continued the Northern Expedition, which, however, in a month ended in defeat. Chiang failed to take the city of Jinan, the capital of Shandong province, because the forces of the most powerful militarists, Zhang Zuolin and Zhang Zongchang, were supported by the Japanese, who considered Shandong their patrimony. Feng did not provide the needed assistance, and in early August Chiang's troops retreated to Nanjing, shaming Chiang greatly. Wang Jingwei took advantage of this situation by winning over to his side the Guangxi generals Li Zongren and Bai Chongxi, who had joined the Nanjing government but had their own faction in the Guomindang.[87] Having failed to unite all of China, the Guomindang seemed to be facing a new war.

In these circumstances, Chiang demonstratively announced his resignation from all his posts on August 13. On the one hand, the move might clear the air and, on the other, strengthen his influence in the Guomindang and in China itself as a noble revolutionary who was sacrificing himself for unity in the party and the country! It was precisely this element of sacrifice that Chiang emphasized in his resignation. His calculation was perfect. The Chinese press showered him with praise, declaring that "his retirement is being praised as an act of unprecedented heroism."[88]

Under these circumstances many members of the GMD, who were not in his faction, decided to put on a brave face. Marshal Feng sent Chiang a telegram imploring him to return: "You are the pillar of China to-day. Upon you China, as well as the Party, rests her hopes of salvation. Should you disregard all this, and insist upon retirement, I, Yu-hsiang [Yuxiang], cannot but do the same."[89] When Chiang did not heed his attempt at persuasion, Feng did nothing of the sort. The chief of the New Guangxi Clique Li Zongren, a supporter of Wang Jingwei, personally came to Shanghai to ask Chiang to reconsider his decision, even though he thought Chiang was "neither an acceptable field commander nor a qualified strategist"; not only that, he was "narrow, partial, stubborn, crafty, suspicious, and jealous."[90] Members of Chiang's own faction, former graduates of the Whampoa Academy, with whom he met on August 25, also asked that he remain.[91] Unlike Feng and Li, they were sincere.

But Chiang did not bend. "We soldiers, as a rule, do not understand the science of government and the laws of economics . . .," he told the former Whampoa cadets. "We must, first of all, acquire knowledge."[92] His words smacked of a sense of resentment and a large measure of sarcasm. Following Chiang, Hu Hanmin, Cicada Zhang, and several other Guomindang leaders also retired.

Chiang asked T. V. Song to go to Wuhan for talks with Wang Jingwei. According to the reminiscences of a contemporary, T. V. Song, a "clean-shaven, active young man, with slightly tinted spectacles," had "very pleasant manners and a rather engaging confidence."[93] Chiang himself, accompanied by 200 bodyguards left for the village of Xikou. Not surprisingly, his resignation was simply a tactical maneuver. He had no intention of giving in. After four days at home he met with leaders of the Society for Graduates of the Whampoa Academy, Chiang's main support in the army. This society was founded at the end of June 1926 and numbered several thousand officers who were loyal to Chiang. At the meeting it was decided to establish a journal of the society "in order to guide the masses and the cadets."[94] Afterward Chiang secluded himself in the Golden Bamboo abbey, where in the past his mother had served as a lay sister. But even there he kept his finger on the pulse of political life in China. "His 'seclusion' is a myth," wrote one of the foreign correspondents who visited him. "Even in this far wilderness, General Chiang cannot get away from the affairs of state and war that he seeks to forget for a while."[95] He spent more than a month in the abbey, frequently meeting with journalists and secretaries and sending love letters to Meiling.[96] The correspondence with his beloved made him happy, and, fearing that someone would read his diaries or for some other reason, in his diary entries he referred to her enigmatically as third younger sister or even third younger brother.

Meanwhile, on August 19 the Wuhan leftists headed by Wang Jingwei decided to relocate to Nanjing. On September 15 the leaders of various factions resolved to form a sort of Special Committee of the Guomindang CEC that would function both as the CEC as well as the CCC and the Political Council that had been dissolved. The next day the committee set to work. On September 17 a new National government and Military Council were established, bringing together the leading members of all three factions: the Western Hills—that is, the extreme right—the Wang Jingwei leftists, who depended on the Guangxi generals Li Zongren and Bai Chongxi, and the supporters of Chiang Kai-shek. The government officially invited Chiang to return to his duties.[97]

Yet complete unity was not achieved. The attempt, in T. V. Song's words, "to unite into one the contradictory and heretofore irreconcilable elements in the Guomindang was doomed to failure."[98] Wang Jingwei declined to be a member of the Special Committee and the government, Chiang remained in the Golden Bamboo abbey, and in Wuhan General Tang Shengzhi soon rebelled against Nanjing. In October, however, Tang was attacked by General Cheng Qian's troops that were loyal to the government and was forced to abandon his army and flee to Japan. But the situation in the territory under the control of the Guomindang did not improve. The following month armed conflict broke out in Guangdong between the Guomindang generals Li Zongren and Zhang Fakui, a young and very ambitious general. No fewer than ten thousand officers and soldiers died in the war. The situation further deteriorated with the defeat of the forces of Li Zongren and Bai Chongxi on the left bank of the Yangzi at Pukou, directly across from Nanjing. This battle against Marshal Sun Chuanfang posed a direct danger to the Guomindang capital. Soon Sun Chuanfang was repulsed, but the situation at the front remained complicated.[99] On top of all this, at the end of November police in Nanjing fired into a crowd of students and workers that was demanding the dissolution of the Special Committee of the CEC. Three persons died and seventy-six were wounded.[100]

At that time Chiang, in addition to contemplating the mountains in Zhejiang and thinking about state affairs, was consumed by preparations for his wedding with Meiling. On August 19, while visiting Shanghai, he had sent his former concubine Jennie and his adopted daughter Peipei, accompanied by two daughters of Cicada Zhang, to San Francisco.[101] But after Jennie reached the shores of the United States on September 8, on September 19 he officially renounced her, telling journalists that he did not know a woman "by the name of Madame Chiang Kai-shek who had arrived in San Francisco." "I divorced my legal wife in 1921 [in fact, as noted above, he had still not divorced her]," he declared, "after which I had two concubines. But this year I freed them, since I think it is not desirable to continue having concubines."[102]

In Jennie's words, learning of this from the American press, she tried to commit suicide. Ultimately, however, she reconciled herself to her fate, especially since Chiang supported her and her daughter financially. From San Francisco she and her daughter moved to New York, where she began studying at Columbia University. Little Peipei changed her surname from Chiang to Chen. After earning a master's degree, in 1933 Jennie and her daughter returned to Shanghai, where, in the late 1930s, Peipei married a Korean named An, who, as it later became clear, was a secret agent of the Japanese. After the war, in 1945 the Korean ran off, leaving his wife and two children. In 1946 Peipei married again, this time to a forty-four-year-old Communist veteran named Lu Jiuzhi, and had a daughter with him. In 1955, however, Lu was arrested on ridiculous charges and sentenced to fifteen years in jail. In 1962, when famine was stalking Communist China, Jennie moved to Hong Kong, where she lived under the name of Chen Lu (Chen Precious Jasper). Zhou Enlai, who knew her well from the years at Whampoa, gave her permission to leave. Prior to her departure, he and his wife invited her to Beijing. Respectfully calling her *shimu,* which means "wife of my teacher" (which is what the Whampoa cadets had called her), he said, "You have freedom of movement. If you don't like Hong Kong, you may return." But Jennie did not return, and throughout the years she lived in Hong Kong, Chiang paid her US $500 every three months. Soon after she moved to Hong Kong, he sent her a letter via the son of his blood brother Dai Jitao. "You have always been a good, beautiful, honest, and sincere person," he wrote. "Not for a moment have I forgotten the care you showed me in previous years when, through wind and rain, we sailed in the same boat."[103]

Jennie died on February 21, 1971, four years before Chiang's death, in her sixty-fifth year. She had written a letter to Chiang, which included the following lines: "More than 30 years ago you alone knew of my grievances. I sacrificed myself for the sake of our great country."[104] After Jennie's death, her daughter continued to receive financial support from her father and later from her brother Ching-kuo. In the autumn of 2002, by permission of the government of the PRC, Peipei, along with two of her three children—her older son Chen Zhongren and her daughter Chen Jiuli—reinterred the ashes of their mother in Shanghai, in the Park of Happiness and Longevity (Fushouyuan). Jennie's grave is planted with yellow and red flowers, and on the pedestal on which a bust of her rests is engraved her name, Chen Jieru. The characters on the stone are in Chiang Kai-shek's handwriting. On the left side, behind the monument, rises a black granite plinth on which is reproduced a famous photograph of the young Chiang and Jennie, taken in May 1926 at the Whampoa Academy. Next to it, on the right, there is a dark-red plinth on which, inscribed in Peipei's hand, are the words "Mother of the military school" (another name the cadets at Whampoa called Jennie). Peipei outlived Jennie by forty-one years. She died in Hong Kong in 2012.[105]

Chiang, after sending his concubine away and then renouncing her, became engaged to Meiling on September 26. Two days later he left for Japan, where the ill mother of his bride had gone to escape the Shanghai heat.[106] He knew that his future mother-in-law opposed the marriage for many reasons.

First, she was aware that Chiang had not officially divorced his lawful wife. In an interview with journalists on September 19, Chiang simply acted against his conscience, saying he had divorced Fumei in 1921. Meiling's mother did not want her beloved daughter to become the new concubine of a married man. Moreover, as a deeply devout Methodist, she was generally opposed to divorce. She regarded the second marriage of a man as being possible only if his spouse violated the seventh biblical commandment "Thou shalt not commit adultery."[107] At the time, like her late husband, she had been deeply upset by what she saw as the amoral marriage of her second daughter, Qingling, to Sun Yat-sen. From her perspective he too had no right to marry a second time. The situation with regard to Chiang Kai-shek was even more complicated. Unlike the leader of the revolution, Chiang was not even a Christian.

The proud Meiling, however, considered her mother's objections groundless. Chiang's first marriage, to her way of thinking, could not be considered lawful. It had not been a church wedding, and in marrying her, Chiang could accept Christianity. "I hope I may receive the blessings of my family," she said to friends. "But I am fully determined to get married in spite of opposition. I truly love the great general."[108]

Nonetheless, not wishing to worsen relations with his future mother-in-law, on October 3 Chiang paid a visit to her in Kobe. He was accompanied by T. V. Song and, in an irony of fate, by Liu Jiwen, the same young man with whom Meiling had supposedly been engaged many years earlier. At the time, Liu was serving as Chiang's secretary. Chiang at once declared to Meiling's mother that he would study the Bible with an open mind and pray sincerely so that God would guide him to a right decision. The elderly woman was deeply moved: her future son-in-law had promised to be baptized not on account of the marriage, but rather, it seemed, he was approaching the important Christian mystery in full seriousness.[109]

Chiang also informed her that he had resolved all the problems with his first, lawful wife. To do this, in late August–early September, while in his birthplace, he had discussed the matter of an official divorce with his county magistrate, with Mao Fumei, with her family, and with her elder brother. At first, neither Fumei nor her relatives agreed to the divorce. The latter said, "Fumei is a married woman, she is not a part of our family any more. As the saying goes, 'If you marry a rooster, you will be a hen all your life, if you marry a dog, you will be a dog.' As long as she is alive, she will be a member of the Chiang family, and when she dies she will be a spirit in the Chiang family." Finally, Chiang turned to one of the local elders, who settled the dispute. He declared that the divorce would not signify Fumei's break with the Chiang family; Fumei would remain the female head of the household, Ching-kuo the main heir, and Fumei's family name (Mao) would be preserved in the "Chronicle of the Jiang clan from Wuling." Chiang signed the agreement and from then on was considered divorced. Afterward, according to the stipulations of that time, over three days (September 28, 29, 30) he published a notice of his divorce under the heading "Declaration of Family Matters of Jiang Zhongzheng" in the Shanghai newspaper *Republican daily.*[110]

After receiving the blessing of his future mother-in-law, Chiang returned to Shanghai on November 10, and just three weeks later news of the forthcoming marriage of the "great general" and the beautiful Meiling flew around the world. A dispatch in the *New York Times* said that more than three thousand guests had been invited to the wedding, including no fewer than one thousand famous Chinese political figures as well as all the foreign consuls located in Shanghai.[111]

The wedding took place on December 1. Two ceremonies were conducted. The first, at three o'clock, was a modest ceremony held according to the canons of the Methodist Episcopal Church. It took place in the spacious library of his mother-in-law's house, a two-story, European-style, private brick house at 139 Seymour Road in the International Settlement.[112] The newlyweds were married by the secretary of the Chinese Organization of Christian Youth, David Yu (his real name was Yu Rizhang). Yu was a well-known figure in society, organizer of the Chinese Red Cross, and a composer who, in 1905, wrote the anti-Manchu "Militant Song of the Student Army," which soon became famous as "China's First Revolutionary Song." The second ceremony, at 4:15, was a solemn affair administered in accordance with Chinese rites. It took place in the ballroom of the most expensive hotel in Shanghai, the Dahua fandian (Majestic), not far from Nanking Road in the International Settlement. Many journalists and photographers and even movie cameramen shooting film were present. The hotel, in front of which a crowd gathered, thirsting for a glimpse of Chiang and his bride, was guarded by dozens of uniformed police and plainclothes detectives. The venerable Cai Yuanpei, the former president of Peking University, presided over the ceremony. Among the witnesses were General Tan Yankai and He Xiangning, the widow of Liao Zhongkai. The attention of the invited guests was drawn to Chiang's erstwhile foe, Wang Jingwei, and the supposed hero of the Shanghai massacre of April 12, 1927, the head of the Green Gang Du Yuesheng, whom everyone called Big-eared Du for his large ears.

Both Meiling and Chiang looked stunning. She was dressed in a silver georgette *qipao* that conformed to Western, not Chinese, tradition—in China the bride should be in red—a white lace, floor-length veil artfully sewn with orange buds, and silver slippers and stockings of the same color. In her arms she held a magnificent bouquet of red roses tied with white and silver ribbons. Chiang was in black tails and a waistcoat, striped, dark-gray trousers, a stiffly starched white shirt with a stand-up collar, and white gloves. Meiling's brother T. V. Song escorted the bride. "When I saw my beloved wife slowly sailing into the hall like a cloud in the evening sky, I felt a surge of love such as I had never experienced before, that I could hardly understand where I was," Chiang wrote in his diaries after the wedding.[113]

As cameras flashed, Chiang and Meiling bowed three times before a photographic portrait of Sun Yat-sen adorned on both sides with the flags of China and the Guomindang. The couple vowed to live in love and bowed to each other, to the witnesses, and to the guests. Then the marriage contract was read out loud, and the seal was affixed before the eyes of the assembled. Chiang and Meiling sat down in armchairs, and at once thousands of rose petals floated down on them from a basket hanging from the ceiling. Everyone, especially the newlyweds, was ecstatic. It was the biggest wedding Shanghai had ever witnessed. "All the consular bodies attended en masse, etc. But I was so dazed and frightened that I did not see anything or anyone," Meiling wrote after the wedding to her American friend from college.[114]

After the rather brief wedding ceremony, Chiang and Meiling went riding around town in an automobile and then returned to the Song home for a celebratory banquet. But by nine o'clock they shut themselves up in a small private house at 311 Ladu Street (Route Tenant de la Tour), which Chiang had rented prior to the wedding. It was a typical Chinese lane, although it was located just four blocks south of Huaihai Street (Avenue Joffre), the main avenue in the French Concession.

Judging from Chiang's diaries, he and Meiling were in seventh heaven after the wedding. "I spent today embracing Meiling," he wrote on the day after their wedding night. "This is what the sweetness of a new marriage means! No one compares to her."[115] To be sure, according to the testimony of Gardner Cowles, the founder of *Look* magazine, Meiling told him, in October 1942, that nothing had happened on their wedding night. Chiang supposedly told her that he opposed sexual relations unless their purpose was to conceive a child, and since he already had a son from a previous marriage and did not intend to have more children, there would be no sex between them.[116]

Why Meiling needed to tell this lie is unknown. Apparently, she simply wanted to justify herself before the American journalist, who, one night in November 1942, witnessed her betrayal of her husband with Wendell Willkie, the former Republican candidate for president of the United States who was visiting China at the time. There is no doubt Meiling might be attracted to Willkie—he was handsome and looked like a Hollywood actor—but she should not have lied so clumsily. We know that throughout his youth Chiang was a lady-killer. Moreover, as mentioned earlier, in 1929 Meiling suffered her first miscarriage.

The couple lived at 311 for a while until T. V. Song bought them a large house not far away on Rue Francis Garnier—he gave it to Chiang as a dowry. The two-story, detached, European-style brick house at No. 9 was situated between the house of the Kongs (Ailing and Kong Xiangxi at No. 7) and T. V. Song's own house at No. 11. Chiang and Meiling liked it very much, and Chiang named it *Ailu* (Love Hut), and Meiling wrote these characters in indelible red paint on a large boulder in the courtyard. The house, surrounded by a high wall, is still standing, but the name of the street has been changed. Since 1943 it has been called Dongping lu (Eastern Tranquility Street), and the house itself, which looks like a palace, is occupied by a middle school devoted to music.[117]

Soon, at a press conference, Chiang declared that he and his wife intended to make a nuptial trip to America "if his plans to return to the revolution" were not destined to be realized.[118] But there was no honeymoon across the ocean, not even one in China. "Most people think we had a honeymoon," Meiling complained to a female friend on January 24, 1928. "We didn't! The day after we were married, he [Chiang] began attending political meetings and seeing guests—and it has been that way ever since."[119]

On December 3, two days after the wedding, a meeting of the Preparatory Committee to convene the Fourth Plenum of the Guomindang CEC was held in Chiang's house in Shanghai. A reorganization of the highest organs of power was contemplated and therefore thirty-three leaders of the GMD, including Wang Jingwei, Tan Yankai, Cicada Zhang, the heads of the New Guangxi Clique, and others came to consult with Chiang. It was decided to dissolve the Special Committee in the very near future. The day before Feng Yuxiang and Yan Xishan, the most powerful warlords of Northwest China, sent Chiang a joint telegram requesting that he return to power. As before, Chiang's generals and officers implored him to take on the mission of savior of the nation. Not even Wang Jingwei objected. He understood that without a charismatic military leader like Chiang it would be impossible to restore order in the army and the Guomindang. On December 10, at a new meeting in Chiang Kai-shek's house, he and several other supporters who were members of the CEC openly proposed, to the surprise of many, that Chiang again assume the post of commander in chief.[120] Chiang was gratified: his main enemy had capitulated. Several days later Wang Jingwei again left, supposedly for treatment in France. Chiang and Meiling went to Hangzhou, where they spent several honeymoon days at the secluded villa *Chenglu* (Pure Hut), with an open veranda and a magnificent view of picturesque Xihu (West Lake), the main tourist site of Hangzhou.[121] The three-story villa is located on a shady lane, Nanping lu (Southern Screen Street), bordering the eastern lakeshore.[122]

On December 13 he again addressed journalists, announcing that he was resuming his duties as commander in chief for two reasons: first, "to destroy the Communist Party," and second, to complete the Northern Expedition, finishing off not only the militarists "who refuse to submit to our party as the highest authority," but also "the civilian officials-intriguers who take advantage of our internal disagreements in their own interests."[123]

On December 28 Chiang received news that the Special Committee of the CEC, since it had been unable to unify the Guomindang, had dissolved itself, and on January 2, 1928, an official telegram addressed to him arrived from the Nanjing government, requesting that he head the armed forces. On January 4 he formally accepted the invitation and set off by train from Shanghai to Nanjing. Enthusiastic crowds greeted him at every train station. General Tan Yankai, who accompanied him, said with emotion, "Today the people rejoice at your return. This offers a graphic contrast to the gloom and despondency which gripped them at the news of your retirement in August last year."[124] There were also those who were not ecstatic about meeting with "the bloody murderer of Shanghai workers." During the 7-hour, 186-mile journey from Shanghai to Nanjing unknown terrorists made two attempts to blow up Chiang's train.[125]

On January 7 Chiang resumed his duties as commander in chief of the NRA and became a Generalissimo for the second time. To mark this occasion a festive meeting was organized in Nanjing attended by more than a thousand persons. Two days later Chiang announced to the army and the nation that he was back on the job.[126]

He was forty years old. At that age Napoleon had already been wearing the emperor's crown for five years, but Chiang's path to the summit of power was also not very long. Stalin at forty was only the people's commissar for nationalities, and Hitler was just acquiring a national reputation in Germany. But Chiang had been able to unite the greater part of China, an area four times larger than France. Now he intended to commence the final stage of the Northern Expedition to Beijing and Manchuria: to dispense with his enemy Marshal Zhang Zuolin.

The games with the communists and the united front, it seemed, were over forever. Stalin and the CCP had suffered a disastrous defeat. Chiang had utterly beaten them. To isolate the communists from the USSR, twenty days prior to Chiang's return, on December 14, the Nanjing government had officially severed diplomatic relations with the Soviet Union, shutting down all Soviet consulates and trade representative offices on the territory under Guomindang control. These, in Chiang's words, were "hotbeds of Chinese Communist intrigues."[127]

Like Confucius, who at forty "had no doubts,"[128] at this age Chiang too had found his path. He had left behind him all of his radical leftist illusions. The bloody experience of the united front had served him well.

PART THREE

# *Between Scylla and Charybdis*

CHAPTER 9

# *Completion of the Northern Expedition*

Arriving in Nanjing, Chiang settled into the staff headquarters of the supreme commander of the NRA. It was located in a small building situated on a rather dirty street in the center of the city: 2 Sanyuangang district. (The building is no longer standing.) Nanjing, like other Chinese cities, was not distinguished by its cleanliness. Moreover, it was overpopulated, so that a private house could not be found even for the commander in chief. After April 18, 1927, when Nanjing was proclaimed the capital, and especially after the normalization of relations between the factions of the Guomindang, many officials, businessmen, merchants, workers, and others flocked to the city. Housing and offices were in short supply, and many officials even slept in their own offices. The city streets were so narrow and overcrowded with pedestrians and rickshaws that moved in all directions that two cars could not pass each other; there was almost no electric lighting, and the few streetlights that illuminated the main avenues were so blurred that they "provided only a dim glow, 'resembling fireflies.' "[1] "It is an awfully dirty place, absolutely terrible," Song Meiling wrote to her American friend.[2] Nanjing had to be modernized and reconstructed, transformed from a provincial city into a world capital.

Unlike Beijing (meaning Northern Capital), Nanjing (meaning Southern Capital) had been the center of the empire for only half a century, and that long ago, at the beginning of the Ming dynasty from 1368 to 1421. Founded in the fifth century BCE on the right bank of the Yangzi River at the foot of Purple

Gold Mountain—also known as Zhongshan (Bell Mountain)—it obtained municipal rights at the end of the third century BCE. Until the founding of the Ming dynasty in 1368, it served as the capital only from time to time, and then only in the context of separate kingdoms during the period of the disintegration of the country (220–581). Nonetheless, for Chinese of modern and contemporary times the name Nanjing evoked a kind of nostalgia for the capital. A majority of citizens perceived it as their "sentimental capital,"[3] because Beijing, in the course of many centuries, had been the capital of barbarians who had conquered China: first by the Jurchens (1153–1215), then the Mongols (1271–1368), then the Manchus (1644–1912). The Chinese seem to have forgotten that Beijing had also been the capital for more than 200 years of the Chinese Ming empire after Emperor Zhu Di moved it there from Nanjing in 1421.

There were many legends about Nanjing. According to one of them, on Purple Gold Mountain dwelled a great dragon who bestowed the mandate to rule on the future emperor who had been chosen by Heaven. He showed the shape of the future emperor in a purple-gold cloud that often arose over the mountain in the rays of the rising and setting sun. It is said that once the great emperor Qin Shihuang, the first emperor of All-under-Heaven, who was making a trip through the country saw his image in the cloud. Spending the night on the left bank of the Yangzi directly across from Purple Gold Mountain, early in the morning he descried his portrait in Heaven. Unable to contain his excitement, he ordered his servants to convey him to the opposite shore, where he climbed up the mountain and discovered the dragon's cave. Desiring to rule forever but afraid that in time the dragon would depict someone else in the cloud, he brought the terrible beast precious gifts.[4] But, as is well-known, this was to no avail, and he died a few years later. From that time on, the portrait of the emperor in the cloud over the mountain changed from one to another until the monarchy collapsed. One of these emperors, the founder of the Ming dynasty, Zhu Yuanzhang, whose image the dragon had reproduced several years earlier prior to Zhu's rout of the Mongols in 1368, commanded that he be buried on Purple Gold Mountain. His grave, above which towers an enormous hill, from then on became a place of pilgrimage for patriotic Chinese.[5] After the last Qing emperor, Pu Yi, renounced his throne, Sun Yat-sen too made an ascent.[6] Possibly one of the reasons Sun left instructions to be buried on this mountain was its mystical historical significance.

After his move Chiang threw himself into preparations for the Fourth Plenum of the Guomindang CEC and the final stage of the Northern Expedition. Meiling joined him somewhat later, on January 15. Since late December she had been ill (she had a serious nervous disorder), which is why she was unable to accompany her husband on his triumphal entry into Nanjing. She was still not quite well by mid-January, but she acceded to Chiang, who pleaded that he would go out of his mind without her. He probably really loved her; without Meiling he felt bad. To be sure, this does not mean he was any more gentle toward her than to other women, especially in the early period after the wedding. At the end of December 1927 Meiling left the house because of Chiang's rudeness, but only for a few hours. "My rudeness, which I was not fully aware of, was occasioned by her stubbornness and hot temper," Chiang wrote in his diaries, in self-reflection. "She felt that her illness had been caused by a lack of personal freedom. She advised me to improve my temper, which I promised her I would."[7]

Meiling's feelings that she had been insulted passed, but her desire for independence persisted. "I do not think that marriage should erase or absorb one's individuality," she wrote to her American friend at the end of January 1928. "For this reason, I want to be myself, and not as the General's wife."[8] She succeeded in this. Her character turned out to be even stronger than that of Chiang Kai-shek. At the end of February, spending some time in a hospital at the resort of Tangshan near Nanjing and more or less recovered from her illness, Meiling began to play an important role in the Nanjing government, most of all as the chief advisor and closest secretary to Chiang.[9] A year later Chiang made her a member of the Legislative Yuan, which engaged in preparing draft laws for the entire country. (Only two other women worked in this chamber.)[10]

Chiang simply could not do without her. He took her not only to meetings of the various chambers and to diplomatic receptions but also on military campaigns. "He was plainly in love," recalled the former American intelligence officer James M. McHugh. "He glanced at her from time to time with obvious pride and affection, and occasionally furtively held her hand."[11] He was terribly jealous of her, especially when she was speaking with somebody in English, of which he understood not a word.

In addition to helping Chiang in state affairs, Meiling was included in drafting plans for the architectural development of the new capital, assisting her former friend Liu Jiwen, who previously had served as Chiang's secretary but who had become mayor of Nanjing in July 1928. Liu developed a broad plan of construction, the funds for which were invested not only by the government, but also by Shanghai and foreign businessmen who realized its benefit.[12] "I see where a lot of work needs [to] be done, and I am going to see what I can do," Meiling wrote to her friend.[13] She began to raise funds for the construction of a military hospital, an orphanage for the orphans of revolutionary fighters, and a club for young warriors.

Sensing her importance in her husband's life and in that of her country as well, Meiling finally acquired, in her words, "inexplicable calm and assurance." From time to time she suffered from depression and not infrequently felt despondent, but her commanding nature helped her overcome crises. Overall, she was happy. "I thank God many times that I have the greatest blessings which any woman could have: the opportunity to lose myself in a great Will, and a husband who has the same faith that I have," Meiling wrote.[14]

Yet she had no children, and sometimes this exacerbated her depressed mood. Each of Chiang's women had a child: the first, Fumei, had a son, Ching-kuo; the second, Yecheng, had an adopted son Wei-kuo; and the third, Jennie, had an adopted daughter Peipei. But Meiling had no one. Chiang's eldest son, Ching-kuo, it is true, lived far from his mother and father in the Soviet Union, where, as noted above, he had gone as a fifteen-year-old youth in November 1925. In Sun Yat-sen University of the Toilers of China his head was whirling from the abundance of revolutionary books, and on the recommendation of his close friend Shao Zhigang, the youngest son of Chiang Kai-shek's secretary Shao Lizi, he joined the Komsomol.[15] He began to carry out party assignments, joined the editorial board of the wall newspaper *Hong qiang* (Red Wall), and in April 1927 was so shaken by the Shanghai coup that at a university meeting he denounced his father, calling him a butcher. Then he signed a letter obviously written by officials of the university or staff members of the Executive Committee of the Comintern. It said, in part, "I know only revolution and no longer recognize you as my father. . . . I am your enemy. . . . Forgive me, please, but I am simply parting company with you."[16]

Ching-kuo was also one of the first Chinese students to join the Trotskyist organization, in whose ranks he became quite active.[17] His main hero was a leading Trotskyist and the rector of Sun Yat-sen University, Karl Radek, a widely educated, erudite man who possessed great oratorical talents and a surprising sense of humor. Ching-kuo was so impressed with Radek that he even imitated him by wearing glasses and smoking a pipe as he did, although he had perfect eyesight and did not smoke.[18] However, after he joined the Trotskyist organization it was smashed by the Soviet political police (OGPU) in November 1927, and he made a sharp break from the Opposition. In the words of his partner, the Trotskyist Qi Shugong (alias Nikolai Alekseevich

Nekrasov), Ching-kuo "became frightened by our active Trotskyist work."[19] On the advice of several classmates Ching-kuo wrote an official statement about his break with the Trotskyists.[20]

In Moscow in late December 1926 or early 1927 he married a young student named Feng Funeng (pseudonym Nezhdanova). She was the daughter of Feng Yuxiang, so the marriage was useful to both Chiang and Feng. They became fathers-in-law. But after several months, in late 1927, Ching-kuo broke with his wife: Marshal Feng, like Chiang Kai-shek, turned out to be "a bloody dog," but Ching-kuo's wife, who understood nothing about politics, did not want to condemn her father. On May 25, 1928, along with her brother Feng Hongguo, who, incidentally, was also a former supporter of Trotsky, and her younger sister Feng Fufa (both of them had studied at UTK under the pseudonyms Sobinov and Sobinova), she left for China.[21] Ching-kuo was assigned to Leningrad, to the N. G. Tolmachev Military Political Academy (MPA).[22]

Fumei suffered terribly from being separated from her son. She too understood nothing about politics and only wished that her adored little son return. As before, she was living in Xikou in the Chiang family home. When Song Meiling and Chiang visited Xikou, she and her relatives treated them courteously. They did not cause any scandals, although Chiang had been very afraid that one might erupt and, on the eve of the visit, asked his older brother to test the soil. Meiling also treated Fumei well; they hit it off. Fumei engaged a local chef to prepare Chiang's favorite dishes every day, the ones his mother used to make: taro root in chicken broth and roast pork with Chinese mustard grass (*meigancai*). Meiling usually ate Western food, but she liked this village fare. Fumei asked only one thing of Chiang: to return her son.[23] But that was precisely what Chiang was unable to do.

Occasionally he saw his second son Wei-kuo. In 1926, when Wei-kuo was ten, Yecheng took him from Ningbo to Shanghai, which, at first, the boy liked very much. The movies particularly impressed him. But soon, as he later recalled, walking through the streets of the French Concession, he saw a sign in front of the gates of one of the parks: "Entrance prohibited to dogs and Chinese." Experiencing a feeling of wounded self-pride for the first time, he conceived a hatred for the "foreign devils."[24] In 1927, soon after the forthcoming marriage of his father with Song Meiling was announced, Yecheng, by arrangement with Chiang Kai-shek, took Wei-kuo to her native town of Suzhou, where Chiang soon bought them a house for 20,000 Chinese dollars. Moreover, every month he paid his former concubine 120 Chinese dollars, no small sum at that time. In Suzhou, Wei-kuo attended the middle school attached to Dongwu University, founded by American missionaries in 1900.[25]

The main problem facing Chiang as soon as he arrived in Nanjing was attracting three generals with big armies of their own to join him in the second stage of the Northern Expedition. The generals were Feng Yuxiang, who was lording it over Henan, Shaanxi, and Gansu; Yan Xishan, the ruler of Shanxi; and Li Zongren, the leader of the New Guangxi Clique. Lacking the support of these most important militarists, he could not count on victory in a war against Zhang Zongchang, the master of Shandong, Sun Chuanfang, and the Manchurian oligarch Zhang Zuolin, who controlled Beijing.

He succeeded in reaching an agreement with Feng rather quickly. Feng had his own claims on Zhang Zuolin. Early in 1926 the Manchurian militarist had chased him out of Beijing. Complications did not arise with Li Zongren either. By this time Li had become disillusioned with Wang Jingwei, who turned out to be not very capable. "Wang Ching-wei [Jingwei] was really nothing more than a 'flower vase,' " recalled Li Zongren, ". . . good only for exhibition but of little practical value." Moreover, "he was not so clever" as Chiang.[26] As for Yan Xishan, he too ultimately supported the plan for a new military expedition despite some of his officers' inclination toward Zhang Zuolin. He initially tried to convince Chiang that it would be best to reach an agreement with the Manchurian marshal. Yan went over to the Guomindang side later than the others, in June 1927, and then only formally, fearing he would lose power in his province, and therefore he was not very reliable. In China it was said that he simply "raised [the Guomindang] flag and changed his signboard."[27]

On February 2–7, 1928, the Fourth Plenum of the CEC took place in Nanjing in the building of the CEC of the Guomindang (16 Dingjiaoqiao), on the north side of town, not far from the exquisitely beautiful Xuanwu Lake.[28] Thirty-one persons participated in it, but two of the most powerful Guomindang leaders after Chiang were not there—neither Wang Jingwei nor Hu Hanmin attended. Both of them were abroad: Hu, like Wang, had complicated relations with Chiang, so until things were sorted out he too decided to travel.[29]

Chiang gave a speech at the opening of the plenum. "I hope," he said, "that all the comrades-members of the CEC will be unanimous in achieving . . . [the following] goals: destroy the Communist Party, fulfill Sun Yat-sen's behest, destroy militarism and imperialism, complete the Northern Expedition, and recognize the highest political goal of implementing the great program of state construction." In this connection he emphasized that "the rebirth of our party is the key to the rebirth of China."[30] The plenum formally expelled the communists and the extreme leftists from the Guomindang, but without deciding to terminate the party membership of Sun's widow, Song Qingling, who was also very leftist. The alliance with the USSR was officially broken.

At the end of the plenum a new CEC comprised of thirty-six members and three candidate members was chosen. Tan Yankai, the head of the government, became chair of the CEC. A newly revived Standing Committee of the CEC was established consisting of nine members. Chiang was again confirmed as commander in chief of the NRA and was chosen as a member of the Standing Committee and chair of the Organization Committee. A month later he was appointed chair of the highest organ of Guomindang power, the Political Council of the CEC. The plenum emphasized that "the National Government, consisting of forty-nine persons, work under the guidance and control of the Guomindang CEC."[31] Chiang Kai-shek again headed the Military Council of the government.[32]

At this time preparations for the final stage of the Northern Expedition were in full swing, and at the beginning of April 1928 Chiang was able to announce the start of a new advance to the north. The NRA was divided into four army groups. Chiang himself commanded the First Army Group, Feng Yuxiang the Second, Yan Xishan the Third, and Li Zongren the Fourth. As the latter recalled, "After a long pause, the Northern Expedition was formally resumed. . . . According to the plan the revolutionary troops were supposed to advance to the north in four columns. . . . Our general offensive began at the end of April 1928."[33] The First Army Group had 290,000 men; the Second, 310,000; the Third, 150,000; and the Fourth, 240,000. The total, therefore, was about a million officers and men. Their opponents, Zhang Zuolin, Sun Chuanfang, and General Zhang Zongchang, together had approximately the same number.[34]

Chiang's forces advanced in the most dangerous direction: from the southeast, the region of Nanjing-Shanghai, toward the city of Jinan, the capital of Shandong province, and farther toward Beijing. The troops of Marshal Sun Chuanfang and General Zhang Zongchang directly confronted them, but they did not represent the main threat. Shandong was the economic and political sphere of interest of Japan. The Japanese imperial troops were stationed there, and after the bloody incident in Nanjing in March 1927 the Japanese subjects who were living in Jinan and several other cities were panic-stricken in the face of the Guomindang army. Yan and Feng, respectively, were advancing on Beijing from the west and the southwest, and Li Zongren from the south.

Chiang routed Marshal Sun's main forces rather quickly and took Jinan on May 1. But within several hours 600 additional Japanese troops arrived from Qingdao to bolster the Japanese garrison of 3,539 men. All the foreigners living in North China, including Americans, were relieved, hoping the Japanese soldiers would not permit a repetition of the Nanjing incident.[35]

But on May 3 bloody clashes occurred between Japanese and Chinese soldiers. The Japanese side, naturally, blamed the Chinese, and the Chinese blamed the Japanese. Everything might have calmed down, and Chiang might have quickly resumed the campaign, but the Japanese garrison commander, Lt. General Fukuda, decided to teach the Chinese a lesson. On May 7 this arrogant veteran commander, without the permission of the Japanese government, sent Chiang an ultimatum demanding that he severely punish "all high military officers who are connected with the incidents," disarm the NRA "soldiers who have offered resistance to the Japanese troops," and remove the Guomindang army twenty *li* (about seven miles) from the city and the Jinan-Qingdao railroad. He demanded a reply within twelve hours.[36]

Not wishing to complicate relations with Japan, whose intervention might lead to the defeat of the Northern Expedition, Chiang partially accepted the demands, hoping for a compromise, but his response was delayed since he had received the ultimatum on May 8. Fukuda did not wait, and early on the morning of May 8 he ordered his soldiers to attack Chiang's forces, numbering about five thousand officers and men, in order to rid the city of them entirely. The fighting lasted three days, with the result that many sections of the city were destroyed while 3,254 Chinese servicemen and peaceful inhabitants were killed and 1,450 wounded. The Japanese lost 236 soldiers. An eyewitness reported that "on the sidewalks, in the doorways, and often in the middle of the thoroughfares, lay Chinese dead, in uniforms and civilian clothes, of all ages and both sexes. . . . Tsinan [Jinan], on that hot May afternoon, had shown me wholesale massacre in new and shocking forms: human flesh blasted by shrapnel, the dead too long untended in the dust or in slimy gutters, the mangled bodies of children gnawed by rats the night before."[37] "The army of the dwarfs [the degrading name the Chinese called the Japanese] attacked Jinan mercilessly," Chiang wrote in his diaries on May 10. "Every day I will arise at 6:00 in the morning and recall the national shame." Four days later he added, "Every day I will think of a new way to destroy the dwarfs."[38] In Chiang's mind Japan had long since replaced England as the main enemy.

The Chinese sent a formal protest to the League of Nations, and the Japanese did the same thing. Each side had its own version of the conflict. Meanwhile, Chiang's troops had to detour around Jinan and find a place to cross the Yellow River rather than passing through the city and then across a bridge on the railroad. The capital of Shandong remained in the hands of the Japanese for a long time. Only after complicated negotiations, at the end of March 1929 a compromise was reached, and on May 20 of that year the Japanese evacuated both Jinan as well as all of Shandong.[39]

The events in Jinan held Chiang up. This might have been the Japanese intention. They feared Chiang, who was known for his anti-imperialism, more than they did Yan Xishan, who did not permit anti-Japanese demonstrations on the territory he controlled.[40] Be that as it may, it was not until May 30 that Chiang linked up with Yan Xishan in the city of Shijiazhuang, about 186 miles from Jinan. After discussing the situation with Yan, he granted him the glory of being the future conqueror of Beijing, probably in order not to irritate the Japanese. In advance, on May 4, he even appointed Yan commander of the Beijing and Tianjin garrisons of the NRA. Soon after, early on the morning of June 6, 1928, the troops of General Yan entered Beijing and completed their occupation in two days.[41] Six days later Tianjin fell.

Zhang Zuolin withdrew to Manchuria, but on June 4 around five o'clock in the morning on the outskirts of his capital, Shenyang, he was mortally wounded by officers of the Japanese Kwantung Army that was stationed in Manchuria.[42] A group of nationalistic officers under the command of Colonel Komoto Daisaku, with the help of Korean engineers, blew up the train on which he was entering the city. Seeking to place all of Manchuria under the control of the Kwantung Army, Komoto and his comrades calculated that it would be easier for them to reach a deal not with Zhang Zuolin but with his eldest son, the Young Marshal Zhang Xueliang, a well-known bon vivant, alcoholic, and drug addict.[43] Zhang Zuolin is "[t]he most widespread cancer working against Japan's policy on Manchuria-Mongolia," Komoto thought. "If we succeed in overthrowing him, by whatever means, there will be no difficulty later in arranging a reconciliation since Chang Hsüeh-liang [Zhang Xueliang] is so inexperienced."[44] Like Fukuda in Jinan, the Kwantung officers acted on their own responsibility—they even cut their own divisional commander off from the means of communications—showing yet again that the Japanese military was "much stronger than the Japanese government in Tokyo." And when the head of the government, Tanaka Giichi, tried to pin responsibility on the guilty, under pressure from the military he was forced to leave his post.[45]

The day before the assassination, June 3, Zhang Zuolin's ally, Marshal Sun Chuanfang, retired. Abandoning his troops, he fled to the Chinese city of Dairen

(Dalian) that was under the control of the Japanese. Twelve days later, on June 15, the National government announced the unification of the country.

On June 20 Beijing, at the suggestion of Chiang's former secretary Chen Lifu, was renamed Beiping (Northern Peace). In this case the Guomindang followed the example of the founder of the Ming dynasty, Zhu Yuanzhang. In 1368 while based in Nanjing, Zhu renamed the former capital Beiping. At the same time, the former capital province Zhili (meaning "Directly Subordinate") was renamed Hebei, which means "North of the Yellow River."[46]

On July 6, accompanied by Yan Xishan, Feng Yuxiang, and Li Zongren, Chiang and Meiling arrived in Beiping. Chiang was very nervous: after all, it was he who had succeeded in doing what his great teacher had only dreamed of. He coolly greeted the many people who had come to greet him and who had spent the whole night at the railroad station in anticipation of his arrival. He waved his hat, and uttered something like "Thank you, good, good."[47] Then, along with Meiling, Yan, Feng, and Li as well as other commanders of the NRA and members of the Guomindang CEC, he immediately set off for Xishan (the Western Hills), where the coffin containing the embalmed body of Sun Yat-sen temporarily lay in repose in the Temple of Azure Clouds. Chiang approached the sarcophagus while the others stayed behind. Meiling held Chiang's umbrella, shielding him from the burning rays of the sun. Chiang gazed at Sun's corpse, which lay under a glass cover. He lightly touched the coffin and, unable to restrain his emotions, began sobbing. Looking at him, many of those present also began to sob, and even the corpulent Marshal Feng and the bewhiskered General Yan, who looked like a walrus, began to sniffle. Only the inscrutable General Li Zongren, his eyes concealed behind dark glasses, did not shed even a tear. Marshal Feng approached Chiang and tried to calm him, but he could not stop his mournful crying for a long time. Feng finally led him, still sobbing, from the temple.[48]

The Northern Expedition had concluded. The leaders of the Guomindang were afraid to continue toward Manchuria. A move like that threatened an inevitable confrontation with Japan, which viewed the northeastern provinces of China as its patrimony. The Guomindang hoped for a peaceful reunification, and they were lucky. The Young Marshal Zhang Xueliang did not forgive the Japanese for killing his father. On July 1 he announced an end to the armed conflict with Nanjing, promising not to obstruct the unification of the country. On July 25 Chiang met with his representatives in a restaurant in Beiping. He promised Manchuria a high degree of autonomy if the Young Marshal reunited it with China.

At the same time, he sent his own representative to Zhang. Learning of this, the Japanese consul in Shenyang warned Zhang that if he entered into a union with Nanjing, Japan might invade Manchuria. Zhang, thin and pale from ingesting morphine, which he could not do without, began shaking with anger. "I am a Chinese," he said. "Therefore, of course, I proceed from the interests of China. And I wish to cooperate with the National government in order to fully unite China." "The honorable governor and I are good friends. I consider you the son of my younger brother.[49] And I must warn you: your point of view is dangerous," said the consul, shaking his head. But Zhang parried: "I am the same age as your emperor.[50] That is all I can reply, Your Excellency."[51]

In Nanjing in August 1928 the next plenum—the Fifth Plenum of the Guomindang CEC—was convened and passed resolutions on political matters. There was discussion about the need to reorganize the government. Several months later, in early October the Political Council, in the name of the CEC, announced the end of the period of military rule as of January 1, 1929, and proclaimed a new six-year stage of development—of so-called political tutelage by the Guomindang over the state and society. In other words, an open dictatorship of the ruling party was established in China, differing little from that which existed at the time in the USSR.

That China should be under the political tutelage of the party after military unification, it will be recalled, had been stated in 1914 by Sun Yat-sen, who believed that a direct transition to democracy was impossible in a backward country. At the First Congress of the Guomindang, Sun, under the influence of Soviet advisors in developing this idea, even put forth a striking four-character slogan: *yi dang zhi guo* (the Party Rules the State).[52] On October 4, 1928, "The Organic Law of the National Government of the Republic of China" was promulgated. In accordance with Sun Yat-sen's behest regarding the division of power into five autonomous branches, the government consisted of five *yuan* (chambers): executive, legislative, judicial, examination, and control. The Executive Yuan comprised several ministries, commissions, the Military Council, and some other offices. The representatives of all the chambers formed the State Council, the highest organ of the National government, whose members numbered variously between twelve and sixteen.[53]

The government was wholly subordinate to the party and "in fact . . . was no more than the highest executive organ of the Kuomintang [Guomindang]."[54] The congress of the GMD was declared the highest organ of power in the country, and between sessions the highest organ was the plenums of the CEC, and between the plenums it was the Political Council of the CEC of the GMD.

Obviously, the system was in no way different from that of the Bolsheviks. Following Sun, his heirs continued scrupulously to copy the Soviet experience of party–state construction that demonstrated, or so it seemed, its effectiveness.[55]

Chiang Kai-shek occupied the top position in the hierarchical system. He became the chair of the Political Council of the CEC, chair of the National government and the State Council, chair of the Military Council of the Guomindang CEC, and commander in chief of the armed forces of the Republic of China (Generalissimo).

His allies also occupied important places. Marshal Feng became the minister of military administration, General Yan the minister of internal affairs, Tan Yankai headed the Executive Yuan, Hu Hanmin, who had just returned to China, on September 3, the Legislative Yuan, Wang Chonghui, the former first minister of foreign affairs in the government of Sun Yat-sen, the Judicial Yuan, Cai Yuanpei, the Examination Yuan, and Dai Jitao, the Control Yuan. Dai was particularly useful to Chiang. He was not only devoted to the Generalissimo but was also brimming with ideas: "His mind was like a fast-producing factory whose manufactured goods had to flow continuously because there was no storage space."[56] On October 10, 1928, Chiang Kai-shek and the other members of the new government took their oaths of office at a solemn ceremony.

Several months earlier, in July 1928, the *duban* (ruler) of Xinjiang pledged his support for the peaceful unification of the fatherland, and on December 29 the Young Marshal accepted the Three Principles of the People, signifying his loyalty to the Nanjing government. Two days later Chiang formally appointed him commander of the "Northeast border forces," in other words, of the Manchurian army.[57] Only Tibet remained independent from the time the last Chinese soldier left Lhasa early in 1913, after the collapse of the Qing empire. In late 1929–early 1930 Chiang began a correspondence with the Dalai Lama, suggesting he recognize the sovereignty of China, if only formally. Soon his representatives arrived in Lhasa, but the talks that began went nowhere.[58] To be sure, this did not bother the National government; it simply looked upon Tibet as part of a united China, especially since not a single state recognized Tibet's independence.

By the end of the 1920s the new flag of the Republic of China began to be unfurled over almost all of the cities in All-under-Heaven: it was red, symbolizing the revolutionaries' suffering in the struggle to unite the country, and in the upper left-hand corner it had the blue banner of the Guomindang with a white sun and twelve rays (for the number of months in a year).

CHAPTER 10

# *Triumphs and Defeats*

The conclusion of the Northern Expedition and the establishment of a one-party Guomindang dictatorship in China did not lead, however, to the victory of the anti-imperialist revolution. China remained dependent on many foreign powers both politically and economically. The unequal treaties were not abolished.

Unresolved problems regarding treaties concluded between the tsarist government and the Qing remained, even with the USSR, despite the fact that back on July 4, 1918, Bolshevik Commissar for Foreign Affairs Chicherin had announced the intention of the Soviet leadership to denounce them.[1] On May 31, 1924, the USSR's ambassador to Beijing, Karakhan, had signed an "Agreement on General Principles for the Settlement of the Questions Between the Union of Soviet Socialist Republics and the Republic of China" that declared that "all Treaties . . . affecting the sovereign rights or interests of China, are null and void."[2] The problem was that on a number of points Chicherin's declaration and Karakhan's agreement remained on paper, since the Bolsheviks were simply unable to abrogate all the treaties. Several of them touched on territorial questions; according to the unequal Aigun Treaty of 1858, for example, tsarist Russia seized over 230,000 square miles from the Qing empire north of the Amur River, and in the Beijing Treaty of 1860 another 154,000 square miles (all in the Ussuri region). In 1881 Russia acquired more territory (8,880 square miles), this time in western Xinjiang. In this connection, the

Qing signed the Treaty of Saint Petersburg. How could the Bolsheviks annul these agreements? They did not even hasten to return to China the Chinese Eastern Railroad (CER) and its contiguous right of way, built by the Russians in Manchuria by secret treaty with the Qing in 1896–98.[3] Nor did they want to withdraw troops from Outer Mongolia, which they had occupied in 1921. The only thing they actually did, following the Americans who had done this back in 1908, was to refuse their share of the Boxer indemnity and, as the first in the world on their own initiative, renounce their right to extraterritoriality and consular jurisdiction in China (that is, their citizens' immunity from prosecution in Chinese courts). Until then only Germany and Austria-Hungary had ceased to enjoy this right, and not of their own will but because of their defeat in the First World War. Only Spain, of its own accord in December 1927 and following the example of the USSR, renounced its right of extraterritoriality in China.[4]

Thus the situation remained complicated. And although the National government, on June 15, 1928, announced that it was beginning a new struggle to achieve equality in the international arena, it recognized that this struggle would not be easy. Not only was it necessary to compel all the powers to liquidate their right of extraterritoriality and consular jurisdiction, but also to compel them to provide China full tariff autonomy; in addition, they had to withdraw their troops and naval forces from China, stop freely sailing in China's internal and coastal waters, and return to China all the concessions, settlements, and colonial possessions.[5] Nonetheless, on July 18 Chiang announced in Beiping his intention to reach agreement with the foreigners on abolishing all the unequal treaties over the next three years.[6]

He actually succeeded in achieving a lot toward this end. On July 25, 1928, the Guomindang government succeeded in concluding a treaty with the United States on restoring tariff autonomy to China in commercial dealings with that country. It was signed by T. V. Song and the American consul in China, John V. A. MacMurray.[7] By the end of the year eleven European countries had renounced their tariff privileges in China, and in May 1930 Japan did likewise. This was an enormous success for Chinese diplomacy even though the new tariffs levied by the National government on major imported goods were, on average, only 2.5–5 percent higher than the old ones. Only on alcohol, cigarettes, and several other luxury items did the Chinese introduce high taxes, from 27.5 to 50 percent.[8]

Moreover, in 1928 Portugal, Belgium, Denmark, and Italy responded to the appeal by the National government to do away with extraterritoriality and consular jurisdiction, and Mexico followed in 1929. In 1929–31 England liquidated its concession in Xiamen (Fujian) and Zhenjiang (then the capital of Jiangsu province) and also returned to China its colony of Weihaiwei in northern Shandong. Belgium also returned its concession in Tianjin. But neither England nor the United States made any moves to renounce the right of extraterritoriality and consular jurisdiction. France, Japan, Sweden, Peru, and Brazil also continued to make use of this right.[9] Negotiations on other questions regarding China's unequal status proceeded with difficulty.

At the same time, in the spring and summer of 1929, relations with the USSR sharply deteriorated. Learning that the Executive Committee of the Comintern was planning to convene a secret conference on the grounds of the Soviet consulate in Harbin, Zhang Xueliang ordered his soldiers to seize the consulate building.[10] During the raid, found documents revealed that the ECCI was using the offices of the CER for its own interests as a link to provide assistance to the CCP. Zhang had officials of the consulate arrested, and he seized the CER in July. In Nanjing Chiang Kai-shek closely followed what was happening to see how the matter would end. He did not intervene in the conflict.

Soon troops of the Red Army under the command of Bliukher, whom Chiang knew very well, crossed the border into Manchuria and attacked Zhang Xueliang from the land and the air.[11] Stalin was so angry with Zhang Xueliang that on October 7, 1929, he wrote a letter to his closest comrade in arms, Vyacheslav Mikhailovich Molotov, asserting the need "to think about *organizing* an uprising by a *revolutionary* movement in Manchuria." He wanted to form "two double regiment brigades, chiefly made up of Chinese," evidently, those living in the USSR,

> and send them into Manchuria with the following assignment: . . . to occupy Harbin and, after gathering force, to declare Chang Hsueh-liang [Zhang Xueliang] overthrown, establish a revolutionary government (massacre the landowners, bring in the peasants, create soviets in the cities and towns, and so on). . . . This we can and, I think, should do. No "international law" contradicts this task. It will be clear to everyone that we are against war with China, that our Red Army soldiers are only defending our borders and have no intention of crossing into Chinese territory, and if there is a rebellion inside Manchuria, that's something quite understandable, given the atmosphere of the regime imposed by Chang Hsueh-liang.[12]

Stalin, however, did not try to implement this plan. In December 1929 Zhang Xueliang returned the CER to the Soviet Union. Otherwise, it is entirely likely that Manchuria would have become one of the constituent republics of the Soviet Union.

All these events played out to Chiang's advantage; he made skillful use of the conflict on the CER to further inflame anti-Soviet and anticommunist moods in Chinese society, and he tried to suggest to the Young Marshal that without his support he would be unable "to stand on two feet."[13] As a result of these events the Chinese government had to restore extraterritorial rights to Soviet citizens in China, but this was done secretly so as not to provide a pretext to Western powers and Japan to sabotage negotiations to cancel these rights.[14]

Complicated relations with the leading imperialist powers and with the USSR compelled Chiang to seek allies among countries that also experienced the weight of imperialism, especially among those that had lost the First World War. From the late 1920s Germany was at the center of his attention: "Unlike the Soviets [it] had neither domestic political allies [like the CCP] nor Great Power interests in China."[15]

Chiang, as mentioned earlier, had long been interested in Germany and at one point, in 1912–13, had even studied German and intended to go there to study. Now he took into account that in the 1920s Germany, deprived of the possibility of rearming itself by provisions of the Versailles Peace Treaty, had become the main seller of arms to China, supplying 42 percent of China's arms imports. Moreover, in Germany there was a large number of professional military cadres who became unemployed because of the reduction in the army and navy.[16]

At the end of December 1927 Chiang appointed Max Bauer, a German colonel who had come to China a month and a half earlier, as his political, economic, and military advisor. A gallant artillery officer who had served during the world war on the German general staff and had been awarded the highest Prussian decoration, the Order of Merit, in December 1916, Bauer had been recommended by General Li Jishen, whom the colonel had worked for in Canton for a couple of weeks. He was fifty-nine and full of energy and grandiose plans. He endeared himself to Chiang because, like Chiang, he rejected both imperialism and communism, saying, "Each nation must develop its own socialism, its own form of government." Bauer assured Chiang that he approved of the ideas of Sun Yat-sen and could benefit the Guomindang, a party that, from his perspective, "will be victorious because its goals conform to the direction of China's natural development."[17] Chiang observed that Bauer greatly resembled Bliukher: he had the same fleshy face, small moustache, and strong-willed look. Possibly this as well influenced the Generalissimo's choice.

Going back to Germany in March 1928, Bauer assembled a group of military specialists and returned to Nanjing in November of that year. Twenty-five officers accompanied him; their task included training several model divisions of the NRA. These divisions were not only supposed to be well drilled but also equipped with the latest German arms. Toward that end, Bauer established a Commercial Department in the Chinese embassy in Berlin tasked with purchasing arms and industrial materials in Europe. In 1928 the first two Chinese officers went to study at the Dresden Infantry Academy.[18]

Chiang respected Bauer immensely, but unfortunately for Chiang the colonel died from smallpox on May 6, 1929.[19] Another German nationalist officer, the sixty-three-year-old Colonel Hermann Kriebel, became Chiang's chief advisor. He had commanded a Nazi militia, taken part in Hitler's putsch in Munich in November 1923, and even shared the same cell with Hitler in Landsberg fortress in southern Bavaria. But Chiang didn't like him. Like the Soviet advisor Kisanka, Kriebel was exceedingly arrogant; moreover, unlike Bauer he devoted a lot of time to working out tactical problems rather than reorganizing the NRA.[20] At Chiang Kai-shek's request, he soon returned to Germany. Chiang then tried to enlist as his advisor Field Marshal Erich Ludendorff, the former chief of staff of the German army during the world war (who, incidentally, had also taken part in Hitler's beer hall putsch). However, he declined, and instead another famous general, Georg Wetzell, who had headed the general staff of the Reichswehr in 1926–30, came to Nanjing in May 1930. New German officers followed him, and the number of German advisors in Chiang's army grew from forty in May 1930 to fifty in December and to ninety in 1934.[21]

The German military advisors worked diligently to help Chiang create the five model divisions and plan the most important military campaigns against all of his domestic enemies. The latter was extremely significant in that following the conclusion of the Northern Expedition there was still no peace in the country.

After formal unification of China a strict system of centralized rule was introduced along an administrative territorial principle (province–county). China was divided into twenty-eight provinces and two territories (Inner Mongolia and Tibet) that were also formally subordinate to the center. Nevertheless, war among the militarist clans that fully controlled their own territories continued in 1929 and 1930. Only now all the oligarchs paraded under the banner of a single party, the Guomindang. Every oppositionist to Chiang in the GMD "declares its loyalty to the principles of the Kuomintang [Guomindang] or Nationalist Party," a contemporary wrote, [and] "every one of the armies fighting against Nanking [Nanjing] is flying the Kuomintang Party flag."[22]

In February–April 1929 all southern China was drawn into a war between Chiang Kai-shek and a group of Guangxi militarists led by the generals Li Zongren and Bai Chongxi, who were supported by both general Li Jishen, the master of Guangdong, and Wang Jingwei's adherents. The catalyst for this new war was a conference on demobilization that Chiang convened in Nanjing in January 1929. Twenty-two high-level commanders of the NRA took part. Chiang presided. Over the course of twenty-five days the participants discussed the draft of a force reduction plan but came to no conclusion: "The conference was a failure: it was a disaster!"[23] The generals were unreceptive to Chiang's plans to reorganize the army by reducing the number of their own troops.[24]

Li Zongren and Bai Chongxi were especially dissatisfied. The former, a "small, sturdy, and ugly" general, felt that he himself was "capable of replacing Chiang Kai-shek at the helm of state." And he truly gave the impression of a man who possessed "moral and physical courage to an unusual degree. . . . [He was] very ambitious." His younger partner Bai was also unbelievably ambitious and energetic. "Tall, well-built, with a high intellectual forehead," he was lame in his left leg. He was Muslim but willingly drank wine and ate pork, which strengthened his authority among the Guangxi troops that were mainly non-Muslims.[25] Both generals were talented commanders and had no intention of subordinating themselves to Chiang. Together with other oligarchs they began spreading the rumor that Chiang was striving to establish a personal dictatorship in China.[26]

Were they correct? Was Chiang really trying to become a Chinese Napoleon? Probably yes. But after all someone had to hold China together in one piece as it was repeatedly falling apart. China, where militarists continued to dominate as before, only nominally recognized the power of the center. China was a country where capitalism had still not touched all aspects of society, where there was no common market, where every stage of economic history was present in the economy, and where the economic and social life of a significant mass of the population, 97 percent of whom were illiterate, was confined within stable, local boundaries.[27]

Despite their ambition Li and Bai soon lost out. By April Chiang's army of 100,000 men had gained the upper hand over their sixty-thousand-man force, and they had lost control of the provinces of Central China and Guangdong that they had ruled before. A month earlier, at the Third Congress of the Guomindang that took place in Nanjing from March 15 to 27, where 406 delegates representing 422,000 members of the party attended, the splittists Li and Bai were expelled from the party forever. So, too, was General Li Jishen (he was even arrested) as were the active supporters of Wang Jingwei: Chen Gongbo, Gan Naiguang, and Gu Mengyu. Wang himself, who was still abroad, received a written warning but was still chosen as a member of the CEC; this was Chiang's wish: the members of the CEC were personally chosen by him in agreement with Hu Hanmin, and although Hu never liked Wang he had to yield to Chiang.[28]

But a peace was not achieved at this congress either. In May 1929 a new war erupted, this time between Chiang and Marshal Feng Yuxiang, who left his post as minister of military administration in the Nanjing government and returned to his home turf in Henan. On May 23 the Guomindang CEC permanently expelled Feng from the party.[29] But General Yan Xishan, who also fled from Nanjing, came out in support of the splittist.

While fighting these wars, Chiang continued his efforts to further legitimize his regime. An important role in this effort, as he conceived it, would be the reinterment of Sun Yat-sen's body in the grandiose Mausoleum in Nanjing on the spur of Purple Gold Mountain along with a sharp increase in the cult of the Great Teacher. The transfer of Sun's body to the vault of the Mausoleum in Nanjing, like his cult that Chiang and his comrades in arms promoted in no lesser degree than the Bolsheviks did the cult of Lenin, were naturally intended to turn the spotlight on Chiang Kai-shek's power, conferring additional authority and sacredness upon it.[30] In March 1929 the Third Congress of the Guomindang declared the teachings of Sun Yat-sen the ideology of the entire nation. That declaration marked the beginning of the transformation of the deceased leader into virtually an object of religious worship: "This Congress is of the opinion that education hereafter must aim at the creation of a new culture based on the *San Min Chu I* (*sanminzhuyi,* Three Principles of the People). . . . Instead of adopting *a laissez-faire policy,* as was done before, a strictly nationalist educational policy must be inaugurated."[31] After this, not only in educational institutions but in all other organizations of Guomindang China weekly meetings were held at which Sun Yat-sen's "Testament" was read out loud and discussed.[32] Even at Yenching University, an American Christian university in Beiping, traditional religious classes were replaced by political ones based on the teachings of Sun Yat-sen.[33]

As early as January 1929 a commission was established to organize the interment. Naturally, Chiang Kai-shek was the chair. Typically, neither Wang Jingwei nor Feng Yuxiang nor Li Zongren nor Yan Xishan was included on the commission, obviously because of disagreement over the question of demobilization. On May 10 a special train with twelve cars painted in the white and blue colors of the Guomindang flag departed from Nanjing on its way to Beiping. Its intention was to take the coffin holding Sun's body and convey it to Nanjing.

Prior to the departure of the sarcophagus to Nanjing on May 26, Sun's body was dressed in new clothes, and 207 professional pallbearers carried it to the railway station. About 300,000 city dwellers saw Sun off on his final journey in Beiping. Over one hundred artillery salutes were fired, and military orchestras in various parts of the city played funeral marches. According to official statistics, no fewer than a million Chinese took part in meetings organized along the route taken by the train. The gathering in Jinan was especially large: more than a hundred thousand persons attended.

Song Qingling, Sun's widow, who had returned from abroad at Chiang's invitation, accompanied the coffin from Beiping. An extreme leftist, as a mark of protest against the anticommunist coups she had gone to the USSR at the Comintern's expense at the end of August 1927, spending most of her time in Moscow.[34] There she expressed her hatred toward "the bloody dog" Chiang Kai-shek in every way possible.[35] She also took part in the work of the Anti-Imperialist League, a left-wing organization supported by the Comintern, and was even drawn into the secret Comintern network. Returning to her homeland in May 1929 and settling in Shanghai after a while under the code names Madam Suzy and Leah, she secretly began to provide information to Soviet spies and agents of the Comintern. She also took part in conspiratorial financial operations, acting as a go-between transferring large sums from the Comintern to leaders of the CCP.[36]

Chiang greeted the train at the Jiangsu provincial border. He was afraid to go to Beiping, which was under the control of Feng Yuxiang. At Pukou station, on the left bank of the Yangzi where the railroad terminated, the sarcophagus was transferred to a warship that conveyed it to Nanjing. There it was greeted by artillery salvos and funereal music while overhead three airplanes sent by Zhang Xueliang performed a flyby.

The city was festooned with Chinese and Guomindang flags. The coffin was displayed for three days (May 29, 30, and 31) in the CEC of the Guomindang. It was in that building on December 29, 1911, that Sun Yat-sen had been chosen as the provisional president of the Republic of China. In front of the entrance a long line of people wishing to bid farewell to the leader formed. Chiang and his closest advisors decided to entomb Sun's sarcophagus in a mausoleum, contrary to the last will of the deceased. They explained that the body had begun to show signs of decomposition. But there may have been a different reason. As explained above, the members of Sun's family were Christians, and Chiang himself was ready to accept God. Thus to preserve the embalmed body of the former leader who, incidentally, was also a Christian and put it on display for all to see was something they simply could not do, unlike the atheistic Bolsheviks. On May 31 Sun's family and those close to him, including Chiang, conducted a ceremony during which the coffin containing the body was covered with a lid.

The following day, June 1, 1929, Sun's body was reinterred in the majestic Mausoleum made of white and blue granite and marble (colors of the Guomindang). To construct it the government spent, according to various estimates, from 1 to 6 million Chinese dollars. Four hundred and ten broad steps led up to the enormous palace on the hill, along whose sides towered mighty pines, cypresses, and gingko trees. Over the entrance to the sepulcher glittered the gilded Chinese characters *tian di zheng qi* (universal harmony) in the calligraphy of Sun Yat-sen. Six other characters formed the words *minzhu, minquan,* and *minsheng* (Nationalism, Democracy, and People's Livelihood)—that is, the Three Principles of the People—in the calligraphy of Cicada Zhang, the old member of the party whom Chiang, as before, looked on with the greatest respect. The same 207 professional pallbearers, dressed in short blue jackets emblazoned on front and back with the white sun, the symbol of the Guomindang, carried the coffin to the top of the hill. Chiang, wearing a white robe and black jacket with a mourning band on his sleeve, walked in front while a sea of people—party and state officials, military officers, representatives from all the provinces as well as organizations of workers, peasants, students, and entrepreneurs—followed behind the pallbearers. Then came detachments of Guomindang pioneers in white and blue neckties; funereal music played, and artillery salvos thundered.

After the coffin had been placed inside the Mausoleum, Chiang and everyone else present bowed before it three times; wreaths were placed upon it and funeral speeches were given. Then, precisely at noon, Nanjing observed three minutes of silence while Chiang and one of Sun's foreign friends representing diplomats from eighteen countries, with the help of laborers, hoisted the sarcophagus into the tomb. Song Qingling shut the door.[37]

Unfortunately for Chiang, in September 1929 the situation in the country deteriorated yet again. In Central China General Zhang Fakui rose in rebellion. Several militarists who had provided assistance to Chiang in his war against Li Zongren and Bai Chongxi also rebelled against the government. Wang Jingwei had incited them to clash with Chiang. On October 1, 1929, two of them, Yu Zuobo and Li Mingrui, intruded into Guangdong from Guangxi.[38] Then Wang Jingwei himself arrived in Hong Kong from Europe; in 1928 his supporters had come together in an intra-Guomindang faction of the so-called reorganizationists, who were demanding reform in the Guomindang and liberalization of the Guomindang regime.[39] Wang also became involved in the struggle against Chiang. On the eve of his arrival, September 29, he and eleven other reorganizationists published a list of ten of Chiang Kai-shek's supposed crimes, all pointing to Chiang's attempt to establish a personal dictatorship. "All his [Chiang's] doings were aimed at his personal interest. He considered the nation as his private property," they asserted, calling for a general armed uprising against him.[40]

At the end of October 1929, in an article published in the main organ of the Guomindang CEC *Zhongyang ribao* (Central Newspaper), Chiang for the first time defined his policy priorities, repeating a sentence of Zhao Pu (922–992), a famous political figure from the Northern Song: "Before we fight the external enemy, we must first establish peace inside the country."[41] When, in November 1929, former units of General Xu Chongzhi quartered in Fujian rebelled, Chiang had to expel his old acquaintance from the party along with several other leading Guomindang members who supported the mutiny.[42] Only toward the end of 1929 did the Generalissimo succeed in overcoming his opponents. He was lucky in that "the rebellions breaking out against him took place at quite convenient intervals: convenient in allowing him to devote his whole time to dealing with them one by one."[43]

On December 12, 1929, at the request of the Guangdong and Canton committees of the party, Chiang expelled Wang Jingwei from the Guomindang forever.[44] But in response to this, General Yan Xishan, whose army comprised some two hundred thousand officers and men, rebelled again. And Chiang was compelled to fight once more.

Yan Xishan seized Beiping and again renamed it Beijing. Chiang immediately expelled him, too, from the party, but the mutineer demanded a convocation of a National Assembly, and on June 18, 1930, his troops occupied Tianjin. On September 9 a separatist government headed by Yan and including Wang Jingwei, Feng Yuxiang, and Li Zongren was established in Beiping.[45] Among the major players in the military arena only the Manchurian Young Marshal Zhang Xueliang remained loyal to Chiang Kai-shek. After the assassination of his father and the unification of the country, he viewed Chiang as his elder brother. On September 20, 1930, he forced Yan Xishan to flee from Beiping and then transferred his own headquarters there from Shenyang.[46]

Chiang appointed the Young Marshal deputy commander in chief—that is, deputy of himself—and on September 24, Chiang assumed one more important position: chairman of the Executive Yuan in place of Tan Yankai, who had passed away two days earlier. After this, he decided to finish off Feng Yuxiang—the latter commanded more than two hundred thousand troops while Chiang's forces numbered some 700,000–800,000 men.[47] At the head of the advance guard attacking Feng he placed Yang Hucheng, a thirty-seven-year-old general whose round eyeglasses and high forehead gave him the appearance of a *shenshi* (a member of the rural literati). On October 29, 1930, Yang seized Xi'an, Feng Yuxiang's stronghold, and Chiang at once appointed him governor of Shaanxi province. Feng, entrenching himself in southwestern Shanxi with his battered army—only about fifty thousand of his two-hundred-thousand-man force remained—tried again to establish contact with the communists and the USSR. According to one of the Soviet intelligence officers, Feng sent his man to Shanghai, and that person "mixed around [our] party," but neither Stalin nor the leadership of the CCP wanted anything to do with him.[48]

In the 1930 war the model divisions of the NRA, trained by the German advisors, took part for the first time, and General Wetzell played a decisive role in planning the operations.[49] Nonetheless, the war was particularly difficult. A contemporary wrote, "Disunion, strife, destruction, disrupted trade, forced levies upon peasantry and towns, shocking treacheries and the open use of money for the purchase of 'loyalties'—these are the silent features of the 1930 war, just as they have been, in lesser degree, the silent features of the wars which have been recurring with appalling frequency since the year 1911."[50] Overall in the war of 1930 more than 240,000 men were killed or wounded.[51]

Only by means of a colossal exertion of force and with the aid of the Young Marshal did Chiang finally succeed in achieving victory in his armed conflicts with the militarists. The triumphs served to strengthen his belief in

God. In October 1930, near Kaifeng, Henan province, during one of the fiercest battles against the superior forces of Feng Yuxiang, Chiang's troops were on the brink of defeat. Stopping by at one of the Catholic churches, Chiang addressed God, promising to be baptized if he defeated his enemy. Suddenly it started snowing heavily, and the snowstorm turned into a full-scale blizzard. His opponents' movements were hampered, and Chiang was able to acquire reinforcements from Nanjing, which enabled him to win the battle.

After returning to Shanghai on October 23, 1930, he was baptized according to the rites of the Methodist church in the home of his mother-in-law.[52] From then on his faith in God was unshakable, although it is doubtful he could be called a true follower of Christ. The great summons of the Sermon on the Mount ("Resist not evil" and "Love your enemies")[53] found no echo in his heart. Chiang's opponents called him an Old Testament Christian, mindful that instead of Christian truths he was guided by the commandments given by the Lord to Moses: "Breach for breach, eye for eye, tooth for tooth."[54] One of his enemies even said spitefully that in his Methodist Christianity Chiang Kai-shek was methodical in one thing only: madness.[55]

While waging war against comrades in his party who repeatedly betrayed him, Chiang at the same time clashed with armed opposition on the part of Soviet agents in China, that is, members of the CCP nurtured by Moscow. In February 1928, at the Fourth Plenum of the Second Guomindang CEC, Chiang Kai-shek and other Guomindang leaders had expelled members of the CCP from their party, but this was a formal gesture. The CCP as such was no longer within the Guomindang. By this time the communists had organized a series of armed insurrections against the Guomindang in response to the White Terror. On the night of July 31–August 1, 1927, they rose in rebellion in several units of Zhang Fakui's army in Nanchang. Zhou Enlai, the communist who formerly headed the political department at Whampoa and was in the First Corps of the NRA, led the uprising. One of the military organizers was the forty-three-year-old Zhu De, a talented commander and member of the Communist Party since 1922. He was also a Sichuanese Hakka (guest people) who, as was mentioned earlier, were northern clans that had settled in the southern provinces centuries earlier but never assimilated with the local population.

Numbering some twenty thousand officers and men, the rebels, after pillaging the city, departed on the third day heading toward Guangdong to announce the formation of a new revolutionary government. But in late September–early October they suffered a crushing defeat in the vicinity of Swatow (eastern

Guangdong), where they had gone to receive a shipment of arms from the USSR that the Bolsheviks had sent them by sea from Vladivostok. In early September 1927 the thirty-four-year-old Mao Zedong, one of the founders of the Communist Party, organized an armed uprising of paupers, destitute peasants, soldiers, and miners that also ended in failure. Chiang had known Mao since the mid-1920s from the time when Sun Yat-sen, at the First Congress of the Guomindang, had made Mao, who had become widely known in China as a talented propagandist and organizer, a candidate member of the CEC of the GMD.

Both Mao and Zhu ultimately retreated to the same high-mountain region of Jinggang (literally, "wells and ridges") on the Hunan–Jiangxi border. There the first Soviet district was established. Meanwhile, in December 1927 communists under the command of Maring's former interpreter Zhang Tailei, who had accompanied Chiang Kai-shek to Moscow in the autumn of 1923, and the Comintern representative Heinz Neuman (aliases Moritz, Gruber, and Maozi [Hairy]) organized an armed uprising in Canton. It too was unsuccessful. Several Soviet operatives who had been involved in organizing it were arrested and executed. Zhang Tailei also died.

The White Terror and the adventurist policy of uprisings generally turned out very badly for the Communist Party. By the end of 1927 it had lost about four-fifths of its members, declining from some fifty-eight thousand to ten thousand members.[56] Under these conditions, not only Mao and Zhu but also many other communists were compelled to retreat to the countryside. There, in areas that were difficult to access, they began a new struggle under the slogan of the Soviets that had been dictated to them by Moscow. They began to confiscate land from everyone who possessed it, including ordinary peasants, dividing it equally among all local inhabitants, including paupers and lumpens. Understandably, such an indiscriminate division turned a sizable part of the peasantry against them, but also garnered the support of the more radical strata of society: the lumpens, the paupers, and members of the poor rural Hakka clans. On account of these groups the CCP's guerrilla army and the CCP itself began to grow again.

In early 1929 Mao and Zhu led their troops out of the Jinggang region they had ravaged, and spent a year roaming around Jiangxi, where as in Jinggang, they engaged in pillaging and killing. In October 1930 they settled at the junction of Jiangxi, Fujian, and Guangdong provinces. This territory was known informally in China as Hakka country because it was densely inhabited by these outsiders. From this area, which was called the Central Soviet

Area (CSA), they began to make forays into neighboring districts, small towns, and villages of southern Jiangxi and western Fujian.

Other communists engaged in plundering and killing in the provinces of Anhui, Hubei, Guangxi, and Guangdong. A tendency was clearly observable in the Communist Party in the slogan "Only killing and only burning," so that the killing of "exploiting elements" and "the burning of towns" turned into "the rallying cry."[57] As a contemporary wrote,[58] "Starting with the 'Red Eyebrows' and the 'Yellow Turbans' (great peasant uprisings at the beginning of our era), over the course of centuries China has often burned with the fires of terrible peasant insurrections. And the insurrection that, like a fire on the steppe, is burning now across the Chinese provinces throughout the country, still is very redolent of traditional Chinese Jacqueries."[59] In addition to the CSA in the years 1927–30 Soviets were established in the western parts of Hubei and Hunan, in the Hunan-Hubei-Jiangxi and the Hubei-Henan-Anhui regions, in northwestern Guangxi and western Fujian. The Chinese Red Army totaled about fifty-four thousand men.[60]

The central leadership of the CCP, however, worked underground in Shanghai. Chen Duxiu, whom Stalin mostly blamed for the defeat of the CCP in the summer of 1927, had long since ceased being head of the party, which was now led by others. Starting in the summer of 1928 the fifty-year-old Xiang Zhongfa, a famous leader of the workers' movement and former shipbuilding worker, along with the comparatively young intellectuals Li Lisan and Zhou Enlai (both of whom were a little over thirty years old in 1930) headed the party.

As before, the main financial streams flowed into the party from Moscow. In 1930 this subvention amounted to millions of rubles and dollars. Under these conditions the leaders of the CCP, as before, had to pay close attention to the directives of their Moscow bosses. When the Tenth Plenum of the Executive Committee of the Comintern (July 1929) clearly pointed to "symptoms of a new revolutionary upsurge" in the world, asserting that "right opportunism" was the main danger supposedly threatening all the communist parties, the leaders of the CCP decided to be "holier than the Pope," and they began to prepare for the seizure of power in China.

Then suddenly at the end of October 1929 the collapse of the New York stock market sharply exacerbated the situation. To many communists in China, as to those in Moscow, it seemed that Marx's and Lenin's prophesy about the inevitable collapse of world capitalism was fast approaching. The economic crisis directly impacted the Chinese economy, though not as strongly as the economies of developed countries.[61] Changes in the value of silver on the world market had an especially large impact. The Chinese monetary system was based on a silver standard, unlike that of the overwhelming majority of countries (Mexico and the British colony of Hong Kong were exceptions). In 1929–31 the value of silver on the world market fell sharply, resulting in a rapid depreciation of the Chinese dollar. In 1930 alone silver was almost 40 percent cheaper, falling from 21.6 cents per ounce to 14.5. The result was that in September 1930, 3.6 Chinese dollars bought 1 American gold dollar, but in early June 1931 it took 4.7 Chinese dollars. Customs revenues fell by 12 percent and foreign trade turnover by at least one-third. The budgetary deficit was 143 million Chinese dollars.[62] There was a catastrophic rise in prices. In early September 1929 a *picul*[63] of rice cost fifteen and a half Chinese dollars, but by June 1930 the price was twenty-one to twenty-three.[64] Inequality in property increased. All this turmoil occurred against the background of new wars and the further intensification of conflict among various oligarchic factions.

On June 11, 1930, the leaders of the CCP adopted a resolution "On the New Revolutionary Upsurge and Initial Victory in One or Several Provinces." It was written by Li Lisan and exhorted communists to promptly initiate a revolutionary struggle for power by seizing large cities in China. As it turned out, the leaders of the Communist Party were mistaken in their calculations: the storming of cities failed. But this new war compelled Chiang—who was making efforts to preserve the unity of the country—to begin in earnest to resolve the communist problem once and for all.

After achieving victory in a drawn-out war against Marshal Feng Yuxiang and the master of Shanxi province Yan Xishan, in October–December 1930 Chiang launched a powerful offensive against the Soviet regions in Jiangxi. The military operation carried out by the Ninth Corps of the NRA and supplementary units totaling some 100,000 men was called the First Anticommunist Campaign or the First Bandit Suppression Campaign. General Lu Diping, the governor of Jiangxi, was the commander. But the Guomindang forces lost. Mao and Zhu employed tactics that were later called people's war. Mao expressed it in the pithy formula of "the enemy advances, we retreat; the enemy camps, we harass; the enemy tires, we attack; the enemy retreats, we pursue."[65] The victory was impressive. Mao's army destroyed more than fifteen thousand of the enemy's officers and men, seized a large number of prisoners, more than ten thousand rifles and even one radio transmitter, which, however, no one knew how to operate. A division commander named Zhang Huizan was taken prisoner. He was decapitated, his head affixed to a board, and then floated down one of the tributaries of the Ganjiang. It was thought that the head would eventually wind up in Nanchang, the capital of Jiangxi province, situated on the Ganjiang, right into the hands of Chiang Kai-shek, who was there.[66] Chiang acknowledged: "The situation [in early December 1930] was extremely critical. Our fate was hanging, so to speak, by a single hair."[67]

Following this first punitive campaign, Mao's forces succeeded in repelling two more that were organized by Chiang Kai-shek in April–May and July–September 1931, respectively, even though Chiang had thrown his best forces against the terrorists. The second campaign was personally headed by the new Minister of Military Administration, General He Yingqin, who was very close to Chiang. The third was led by Chiang himself. All were failures. A brutal, protracted war against the communists had become a reality and Chiang's major preoccupation.

A contemporary wrote, "By 1931, Communism had assumed the status of a national problem in China. . . . The curse of China is its ineffectiveness; the Chinese Communists were not ineffective."[68] On July 22, 1931, Chiang repeated in his diaries what he had already written in the *Central Newspaper* a year and half earlier: "Before we fight the external enemy, we must first establish peace inside the country."[69] This time he had in mind not the suppression of Feng Yuxiang and other splittist-militarists, but that of the communists. The next day he spoke about this project in an address to the nation.[70]

Chiang's chief military advisor, General Wetzell, was directly involved in planning the punitive campaigns against Mao, but he too could do nothing about the communists. Exasperated, he began to vent his spleen on the Chinese generals, sharply accusing them of ineptitude in conducting military operations.[71] The upshot was that he turned everyone against him, including Chiang, who began looking for a replacement. In March 1932 he found one in the person of retired Lt. General Hans von Seeckt, who had commanded the ground forces of the Reichswehr in 1920–26. Seeckt, who turned sixty-six in April 1932 (he was born in the same year as Sun Yat-sen), was invited to China. A year later, in May 1933, after Hitler's accession to power on January 30 of that year, Seeckt arrived in Shanghai and then Nanjing, where over a four-day period he conversed with Chiang Kai-shek, who was ecstatic about him. Seeckt was tactful but firm: he told Chiang that the army was the foundation of power and that its effectiveness depended not on numbers, but on the qualifications of its soldiers and especially its officers. Chiang agreed on all points, and Seeckt was received in Nanjing, according to his own words, "as a military Confucius, the wise teacher."[72]

In November 1933 Seeckt agreed to become Chiang's chief military advisor, and in April of the following year he took up his post, replacing Wetzell. The first thing he did was to reduce the number of advisors to forty-five (a year later that number had grown to sixty-one), keeping only the best of them.[73] Then he expanded ties with German industrialists, securing an increase in German arms to China in exchange for Chinese raw materials. For several years the Germans became the main suppliers of modern arms to Chiang Kai-shek.

Only in the field of aviation technology were the Germans unable to compete. In this regard, the Americans and the Italians became Chiang's main partners. In the fall of 1933 Mussolini even sent a group of military advisors, engineers, and mechanics to China. It was headed by Colonel Roberto Lordi, whom Chiang appointed his chief air force advisor, and Nicola Galante, an air force engineer. In 1934, in Jiangxi, not far from Nanchang, an Italian aviation school was set up for 202 Chinese pilots and 800 air force engineers, and a Flight Academy was opened in Loyang (Henan province).[74] Twenty-five Chinese engineers traveled to Italy to study. In the summer of 1935 Il Duce sent Chiang Kai-shek a three-engine airplane as a personal gift.[75] But at the same time Mussolini, without Chiang Kai-shek's consent, recalled Lordi and replaced him with Colonel Silvio Scaroni.[76] Chiang was irritated, but Scaroni turned out to be a helpful aide, and Chiang appointed him as his chief advisor. In 1935–36 an aviation factory was constructed not far from Nanchang as well as an airfield at which ten airplanes were based, including Chiang Kai-shek's personal bomber.[77] A few years earlier, in 1932, the Americans had founded an aviation academy in China.[78]

Chiang now stepped up the anticommunist terror in the cities. On his order, his blood nephew Chen Lifu organized a special Investigation Section in the Organization Department of the Guomindang CEC—a sort of analogue of the Soviet OGPU—that engaged in exposing communists.[79] But this was not enough for Chiang. Ascribing particular importance to the work of the special services, he established another such organ inside the National government. It was headed by a certain Dai Li, another fellow provincial of Chiang's from Zhejiang, a rather young man (he was born in 1897 and thus was just three years older than Chen Lifu). Chiang wanted his special services to compete against each other. This was generally his style of leadership. Like other dictators, he liked to pit his subordinates against each other and, giving them analogous tasks, "maintained ultimate power by balancing these forces."[80] This, however, did not bother Chen Lifu. "We will do our work as though we are Chiang's eyes and ears," he explained to his associates the need for two analogous departments. "To rule out incorrect information, Chiang needs two sets of eyes and ears."[81]

As a result of the activity of Chen Lifu and Dai Li many leading communists were behind bars. "*A nightmarish situation with failures, provocation after provocation, failure after failure,*" a Soviet intelligence agent reported to Moscow.[82] In Hankou on April 24, 1931, Gu Shunzhang, a candidate member of the CCP Politburo who headed a secret (special) section of the Central Committee, was arrested. His department was responsible for organizing Red Terror in cities controlled by the Guomindang government. Afraid of being shot, this professional killer with the manners of a Shanghai playboy, gave the police all the addresses and signals for secret rendezvous of the CC Politburo and the Jiangsu and Hubei party committees. In May and June more than three thousand Chinese communists were arrested, and many of them were shot. Only by a miracle did Zhou Enlai, one of the leaders of the CCP, escape arrest. But Xiang Zhongfa, the general secretary of the CC, was not so lucky. He was seized and, unable to withstand torture, provided information. Yet this did not save his life. The Guomindang preferred to execute such a prominent communist, even one who had been broken.

In the early 1930s the Guomindang special services began active cooperation with the authorities in the international settlements. In 1931 an agreement was concluded whereby police agents of the Guomindang could freely enter the territory of the concessions in Shanghai and carry out arrests of Chinese for various reasons.[83] The settlement police ceased being tolerant, so that now not only Chinese but also foreign communists had nowhere to hide. As a result of Gu Shunzhang's betrayal, two officials of the secret International Liaison Department (ILD) of the Executive Committee of the Comintern, Yakov Matveevich Rudnik and Tatyana Nikolaevna Moiseenko-Velikaia, were behind bars in mid-June 1931. Together with their three-year-old son Dmitrii (alias Jimmy), they had been living in Shanghai as the Noulens couple. They were the conduit by which the Comintern supplied funds to the Central Committee of the CCP via the dummy company Metropolitan Trading Co. Thus their arrest undermined the financial security of the CCP, whose urban organizations depended primarily on Comintern subsidies. From August 1930 to May 1931 the Executive Committee of the Comintern paid out more than US $25,000 gold dollars monthly to the CCP CC.[84] (The monthly payout was five thousand dollars more than in 1929.)

Meanwhile, in the spring of 1931 relations between Chiang and representatives of the intraparty opposition soured yet again. The reason was that on

February 28 Chiang had arrested Hu Hanmin, whom he had deceived via a dinner invitation to his home. Hu and Chiang had become alienated a few months before that, in November 1930, when Hu Hanmin opposed Chiang's decision to appoint Zhang Xueliang's subordinate a minister of the National government. Shortly thereafter Hu evoked the Generalissimo's displeasure by sharply criticizing his plans to convene a National Assembly, a sort of parliament, to adopt a Provisional Constitution for the Republic of China that would grant Chiang additional powers: namely, to appoint the chairs of all branches of government and all ministers. The National Assembly, whose membership was to include members of the Guomindang as well as nonparty members, would demonstrate "popular support" for the Chiang Kai-shek regime and constitute the first step in preparing for the transition from the period of political tutelage to constitutional rule. Chiang's opponents, including Wang Jingwei, Yan Xishan, and Feng Yuxiang, were insisting on the adoption of a Provisional Constitution. So that for Chiang to convene a National Assembly was a rather skillful maneuver to neutralize the opposition.

But Hu considered it an inappropriate moment to convene an assembly since the period of political tutelage was not yet over. He did not want to get involved in Chiang Kai-shek's tactical games, and Chiang, as had happened before, flew into a rage. He began to yell, but Hu, in response, also raised his voice: at that point one of Sun Yat-sen's disciples (Chiang) arrested another (Hu).[85]

The following day, February 29, Hu Hanmin, the old member of the Guomindang, was transported to the Tangshan mountains, where he was placed under house arrest near one of Chiang's residences. The head of the Guomindang, who had tired of the opposition, could not forgive the disobedience even to the head of the Legislative Yuan! And this was understandable: the leader of the party that, under the slogan "political tutelage," had established its dictatorship in the country could not rule the party other than by using dictatorial methods. His teacher, Sun Yat-sen, also was no democrat, and by the early 1930s the effectiveness of the total power of a leader was attested to not only by the Soviet experience, but also the Italian, Turkish, Hungarian, and Polish. Moreover, the idea of "führerism" was increasingly taking hold in Germany too. Here is what Chiang had to say about it:

> It should be realized that, theoretically, no member of the Revolutionary Party may enjoy absolute freedom of personal movement. . . . [F]ew leaders had personal freedom in the broader sense of the term. It is for the freedom of the country and the nation, and not for personal

> liberty, that we are striving. Should individuals insist upon their full liberty it would be almost impossible for the nation to attain the coveted status of equality with other nations. . . . A Revolutionist is subject to constant discipline and regulation. He must obey the orders of the Party and abide by the laws. . . . [I]t [is] incumbent upon him to sacrifice his liberty for the sake of the Revolution.[86]

But the arrest of the head of the Legislative Yuan led to opposite results than those Chiang had hoped for. A quartet of highly respected associates of Sun Yat-sen, members of the CCC of the Guomindang, demanded that Chiang resign. In response to Chiang Kai-shek's arbitrary rule, a new coup took place in Canton in May in which Chiang's old foe, Wang Jingwei, convened a so-called emergency session of the Guomindang CEC. He then formed a separatist National government in which, in addition to him, such well-known leaders of the GMD as generals Li Zongren and Tang Shengzhi, as well as Sun Fo, Sun Yat-sen's son from his first marriage, took part. Sun Fo was a resolute man of forty and well educated, but "like many sons of famous fathers, [he had] an undistinguished personality."[87] A new military conflict flared up. In the summer of 1931 Chiang deployed troops against the Cantonese mutineers. At the beginning of June he expelled Sun Yat-sen's son from the party, along with several senior Guomindang members who were supporting Canton.[88]

Meanwhile, a National Assembly was convened. In the sessions that were held in the new assembly hall of the Nanjing State Central University in May 5–17, 1931, 447 delegates participated, including the Panchen Lama, who was then involved in a conflict with the Dalai Lama and therefore was living in China. Only 44 of the delegates represented the Guomindang CEC and the National government. At the opening session of the assembly Chiang declared that the Chinese nation rejected contemporary political theories such as fascism, communism, and liberal democracy and was striving to develop its own political system based on ancient traditions and laws. As one might expect, he received the full support. On May 12 the National Assembly adopted the Provisional Constitution for the Period of Political Tutelage, confirming the exclusive right of Guomindang members to rule the country and educate the people politically.[89]

But new trials awaited Chiang. Problems connected with the civil war of 1931 were exacerbated by catastrophic floods in Central and East China. Downpours and a powerful monsoon resulted in rising waters in thousands of rivers and lakes, including the Yangzi. A territory the size of England and half of Scotland was inundated. No fewer than fifty-three million people were without shelter or means of existence. By the end of July the entire city of Wuhan was flooded, causing the loss of housing for three-hundred thousand city dwellers.[90] Half of the capital itself was flooded. A journalist who was visiting Nanjing at the time recalled that "[water standing in the streets] stank. Backwaters of the flood were thick with rotting corpses. I stayed at the old Bridge House Hotel, the lower floor of which was under water. . . . There were mosquitoes in swarms, and fat carrion flies crawled over everything."[91]

On top of all this, at the end of 1931 the rate of exchange of the Chinese dollar increased by 90 percent because England and Japan shifted to the silver standard. But since the Chinese economy was tied to cheap imports, this development in turn had a negative influence on the economy, leading to a recession. Industrial enterprises and commercial establishments shut down, and unemployment sharply increased. According to certain data, in 1931 there were seventy million unemployed in China.[92] In Shanghai almost one-third of the three and a half million urban population was without work, and in Nanjing, Beiping, Tianjin, and Qingdao about half of the employable population lacked the means of subsistence.[93]

It is simply amazing that in such a situation, without enjoying a single day of peace, Chiang Kai-shek and his government succeeded in focusing on something other than war, natural disasters, the economic crisis, and the struggle in the international arena for a successful conclusion of the national revolution. Yet back in October 1929 Chiang had passed a law that allowed workers to join together in labor unions "[in order] to secure and improve working conditions and life." And in December of that same year a Factory Law introduced the eight-hour workday and prohibited child labor.[94]

In general, no matter how strange it may seem, it was the Guomindang and by no means the Communist Party at the time that must be seen as the workers' party in China, not only because Chiang Kai-shek strived to satisfy the basic interests of hired labor, but also because of the social composition of this organization. In 1929 a plurality of members of the Guomindang were workers: 29 percent. The intelligentsia was also well represented with 25.7 percent, the military with 23 percent, and students somewhat less with 10.5 percent, while peasants and merchants constituted 7.5 and 4.3 percent, respectively.[95] In the CCP at this time the overwhelming majority were peasants as well as rural lumpens and paupers: they were 80 percent. According to various data, workers were all of 2 to 7 percent.[96]

The Chiang Kai-shek government also tried to provide real assistance to rural laborers. On July 28, 1928, for example, the Guomindang passed a law on confiscating land, giving the government the right to purchase via eminent domain private land "to carry out projects having social utility as well as to equalize landownership with the goal of developing agriculture and improving the conditions of life of the peasantry."[97] On January 24, 1929, regulations were adopted regarding the provision of assistance to rural inhabitants to build irrigation works to defend against floods, and a year later a law regarding rivers provided for partial compensation to persons who had suffered losses from natural disasters. Finally, a Land Law was promulgated on June 30, 1930, that lowered rents to 37.5 percent. This was indeed a real revolution since at the time rents in many places were 60–70 percent. The law derived from the basic principles of the Guomindang's agrarian policy that had been formulated in November 1928: "Liquidation of the Monopolization of Land by the Few and Equalization of Land Rights, Utilizing Increases in the Price of Land for the National Wealth in Accordance with Sun Yat-sen's Testament."[98] No one was permitted to collect either taxes or rent in advance. Starting in February 1928, on Chiang Kai-shek's initiative, measures were taken to develop a cooperative movement among the peasantry. An important step was the adoption of a law on peasant unions in December 1930, according to which peasants and farmworkers received full rights to create organizations based on principles of mutual aid.[99] Three years later the China Peasant Bank was founded with initial capital of four million Chinese dollars and began to offer cheap credit to peasants.[100]

Not surprisingly many of these laws existed on paper only since Chiang lacked the power to compel large landowners and militarists to implement them.[101] Nevertheless, it is impossible not to see that Chiang Kai-shek was trying everything possible, albeit gradually, to implement Sun Yat-sen's principle of the People's Livelihood.

In the early 1930s Chiang Kai-shek's government succeeded in taking steps to establish state control of the cultivation of silkworms and the production of silk, to stabilize the yuan (Chinese dollar), to standardize taxes, measures and weights, to introduce a strictly centralized system of higher education, to work out comprehensive rules for entrance exams in higher educational institutions, and even to get to work building new roads. In 1926 there were only about 1,300 miles of modern highways, but by 1930 there were 31,700. And this was accomplished even though 80 to 85 percent of the annual budget was allotted for military expenditures.[102] In 1932 the government abolished internal tariffs (*lijin*).

By 1932 Nanjing was totally transformed. An eyewitness who visited the city five years after it had been seized by the Guomindang wrote in her diaries,

> I almost get lost in the unfamiliarity of new, wide streets with promises of sidewalks—a new thing under the sun in China. Countless new houses and business buildings of all sorts have been built within less than a year, and parts of the city, which used to be truck gardens, unsettled hillsides or grave land, have been transformed into populous city streets. . . . [W]e begin to see our dream of running water and a proper sewer system coming true. . . . [L]ast year the immense stadium was completed just in time for the Far Eastern Olympics in October[103]—the games which did not come off on account of the Manchurian trouble and threat of war.[104]

At the same time, in the four years 1928–31, despite all his efforts, Chiang had not succeeded in establishing his personal totalitarian dictatorship in either the party or the country. What kind of dictator was he if his opponents repeatedly threw whole armies into battle against him and, after being defeated, rose again like a phoenix from the ashes? The year 1931 was critical: Chiang failed to defeat the Cantonese. Nor was he able to smash Mao Zedong, and in Shanghai the CCP CC and representatives of the Comintern continued to function deep underground. The country, in fact, was not united.

Then, at the most difficult moment, Japanese troops invaded Northeast China on September 18, 1931. By late autumn all of Manchuria, a territory with a population of thirty million people, was under Japanese control. Indeed, heaven itself was taking up arms against Chiang, but it was not so easy to break this man. He always remembered the words of Confucius: "A gentleman can indeed find himself in distress, but only a vulgar man is upset by it."[105]

CHAPTER 11

# *"For a New Life!"*

China could not resist a powerful country like Japan, which possessed modern military forces. It remained industrially underdeveloped, and its army lacked a sufficient quantity of the most modern weapons; moreover, neither the Guomindang nor China itself was united. In such a situation a reckless leader could lead the nation to catastrophe. Moreover, it should be borne in mind that to a certain degree the Chinese themselves were responsible for what had happened in Manchuria. From 1907 on Chinese patriots repeatedly resorted to economic boycotts in dealing with the Japanese. By the early 1930s there had already been eight national campaigns to boycott Japanese goods. The most powerful ones had been the campaign of 1915 in response to the Twenty-one Demands the Japanese had addressed to Yuan Shikai; the 1919 campaign in response to the Japanese position on Qingdao—the Japanese refused to return the city to China after WWI; the 1925 campaign in response to the killing of a communist worker in Shanghai by a lone Japanese; and the 1928–29 campaign in response to the massacre in Jinan.

The Chinese did not boycott only Japanese goods. In 1905 there was a widespread boycott of American goods, and in 1909 and 1925–27 of British products. But boycotts were more often directed at the Japanese.[1] A majority of Chinese simply could not reconcile themselves to having their country exploited by these "dwarfs," whom they had always looked down upon as inferior beings. After all, the Japanese, who had begun to create their civilization as late as the sixth century CE, had borrowed so much from Imperial China: the principles of statecraft, the written language, and philosophy.

In July 1931 a new boycott of Japanese goods began after a pogrom against Chinese in Korea. Over the course of ten days Koreans, instigated by the Japanese, destroyed Chinese shops and restaurants in various cities on the peninsula; 143 Chinese merchants were killed, 343 were wounded, and 72 disappeared without a trace.[2] Korea at the time was a Japanese colony, so Japanese bore responsibility for the carnage; however, this was not an ideal time for China to boycott them. Japan, like all the industrialized countries, was experiencing a severe depression: from 1929 to 1931, even without the boycott Japanese exports declined by half, its GNP by 18 percent, and capital investment by one-third. Contraction was happening everywhere: more than a million persons filled the ranks of the unemployed, many small companies were ruined, and because of a sharp drop in the price of silk and rice many Japanese peasants became paupers. Moreover, in 1931 famine broke out in northern Japan because of a bad harvest.[3] And now they suffered a boycott of their goods.

What particularly disturbed the Japanese was that this new Chinese so-called economic war was not spontaneous: the boycott was deliberately organized and directed by the leadership of the Guomindang. It was henceforth adhering to the principles of revolutionary diplomacy and conducting a policy of import substitution, moreover, exclusively vis-à-vis Japanese goods. Chiang and his associates welcomed British and American imports. After the Jinan events of 1928 a pro-American faction headed by Chiang's relatives Song Meiling, T. V. Song, and Kong Xiangxi as well as Minister of Foreign Affairs Wang Zhengting was dominant in the Nanjing government.

As perceived by the Japanese, the boycott of 1931 was preceded by a series of other unfriendly measures on the part of the Nanjing government. On February 1, 1931, China introduced a protectionist tariff on imported cotton yarn and cloth (mostly from Japan), and then raised taxes on the products of foreign enterprises located in China (the majority of which were also Japanese). In addition, all goods entering the Chinese market from the Manchurian city of Dairen (Dalian), which had been under Japanese occupation since 1905, also became subject to higher taxes as goods of purportedly foreign manufacture.[4]

The 200,000 Japanese living in Manchuria, half of whom were women, were increasingly concerned about their safety.[5] They were living amid a Chinese and Manchu population that in the early 1930s comprised thirty million people in Northeast China. Moreover, the economic depression hit the

Japanese in Manchuria very hard. Massive layoffs occurred on the South Manchurian Railroad that belonged to Japanese capital, and small- and medium-sized Japanese enterprises began to go belly-up.

The Japanese in Manchuria were particularly frightened by a declaration of the Chinese Ministry of Internal Affairs on May 4, 1931, which asserted that the Chinese government, continuing its struggle to achieve equality in the international arena, as of January 1, 1932, was unilaterally rescinding the right of extraterritoriality and consular jurisdiction of foreigners. After which the ministry intended to return all foreign settlements, leased territories, and railroads constructed by foreigners (including the CER) to China as well as prohibit foreign ships from sailing in Chinese coastal and inland waters. On the following day, May 5, Chiang made a similar declaration when he opened the National Assembly.[6]

The officers of the Kwantung Army, a majority of whom were from peasant and urban commercial strata in Japan, were badly upset by news of the economic crisis in their homeland. They also reacted very negatively to the desire of the Minseito, the Japanese ruling party that had come to power in the 1930 elections, to strive for friendly relations with China. From the perspective of the Kwantung Army officers, this was a betrayal of the interests of the Japanese in Manchuria, whom the Minseito, in their words, treated like stepchildren. What's more, they were indignant at the plans of the Minseito to reduce expenditures on the armed forces.[7]

A group of Kwantung Army officers decided to intervene in the situation. Like their predecessors in 1928, they acted at their own risk, directly bucking discipline. On September 18, 1931, several officers, on their own initiative, showed up at the Shenyang train station, where at one o'clock in the afternoon a train arrived carrying General Tatekawa. An emissary from the Japanese minister of the army, he was bearing an order prohibiting the Kwantung Army from undertaking any actions against the Chinese side. The officers dragged Tatekawa to a restaurant, made him drink too much, and left him in the charge of Japanese geisha.[8] The result was that the general was unable to transmit the order to the army command in time, and while he was luxuriating in the embraces of beautiful women, at 10:20 in the evening several Japanese officers blew up the roadbed of the CER on the northern outskirts of Shenyang, although causing only light damage.[9] Then the command of the Kwantung Army accused Chinese of being responsible for this "terrible sabotage." Japanese soldiers then attacked the Shenyang garrison, and by the morning of the following day, supported by Japanese youth in Shenyang assembled in militarized groups, seized the entire city. At the same time, Changchun, the capital of the Manchurian province of Jilin was seized.[10]

Chiang, who was then in Nanchang, the capital of Jiangxi province—where he was directing the third punitive expedition against the communists—was shocked, even though he had known that Japanese provocations were imminent. "Last night the dwarf bandits attacked the Shenyang arsenal without any reason, and fifteen minutes later I received news that they had seized our [cities] Shenyang and Changchun," he wrote in his diaries on September 19, 1931. He went on,

> They want to make use of the traitorous coup in Guangdong to split the country and seize the Northeastern provinces. The domestic disturbances will not cease, the traitors lack any pity in their hearts for the suffering country, and the people have no feelings of patriotism, society is not organized, and the government is not strong. If one speaks of this people, they are not living at all according to the rules of the contemporary world, and the situation is exacerbated by natural cataclysms and disasters brought about by bandits. The only one I trust is my own heart that loves my country. At this moment I clearly realize that a crisis is approaching and the only thing left for me is to serve [the homeland] with all my strength until the last day of my life.[11]

Chiang delivered an address to the nation, calling upon the people to unite around the government. "There was but one China . . . and it could have only one national reconstruction," he declared.[12]

During these events the master of Manchuria, the Young Marshal Zhang Xueliang, was in Beiping. On September 18 he was discharged from the Rockefeller clinic, where he had long been under treatment for dependency on narcotics, complicated by typhus. That evening after dinner he went to the theater to listen to Beijing opera, in which the famous actor Mei Lanfang was playing the lead female role. (In Chinese operas all the female roles are performed by men.) The news he received late at night about the events in Shenyang and Changchun completely demoralized him. Soon the Japanese inflicted a new blow on his pride: they demonstratively sent him 417 boxes with things from his Shenyang residence. He got in touch with Chiang, not knowing what to do. The main units of his army were not in Manchuria at the time but in North China. Should he go to Shenyang and Changchun? Taking everything into consideration, Chiang ordered him not to resist, hoping to settle the incident peacefully.[13] On September 21 his government sent a protest to the League of Nations while taking the strictest measures to defend Japanese subjects in China.[14]

At the same time, despite his war against the Chinese communists Chiang began efforts to normalize relations with the USSR. He needed an ally against Japan, and the Soviet Union was best suited to play that role. After occupying Manchuria, the Japanese posed a potential threat both to the CER and to the USSR, and Chiang understood that Stalin would have to take this into account in his geopolitical calculations. The Germans were continuing to help China, but only the USSR, which directly bordered Manchuria, could intervene in the conflict, at least to defend their own CER if the Japanese threatened it. A conflict between the Soviet Union and Japan would be the optimal outcome of the situation in Chiang's view. In September 1931 the former Soviet consul in Dairen (Dalian), Ivan Ivanovich Shebeko (who also went by Zhurba or Shurba) wrote to the 2nd Eastern Department of the People's Commissariat for Foreign Affairs: "The Chinese are trying to provoke recognition [*sic*] that the USSR is bringing in troops to the CER, since the Japanese incursion is directed against both the USSR and against China. . . . The prevailing opinion is that the USSR by virtue of its very position must somehow counteract Japan."[15]

In discussions with Deputy Commissar for Foreign Affairs Karakhan (September 20–29), Mo Dehui, the Chinese director of the CER, who was in fact Chiang's plenipotentiary in Moscow, repeatedly tried to test the soil by raising the question of cooperation between China and the USSR in opposing Japanese aggression.[16]

But Stalin tried to avoid a conflict with the Japanese. On September 20, 1931, the Soviet Politburo resolved to "postpone adopting decisions on diplomatic steps [vis-à-vis China] in connection with the occupation of Southern Manchuria and Mukden [Shenyang] by Japanese troops until receipt of additional information."[17] Stalin evidently wanted Chiang to make some sort of concession to him. Demanding a cessation of the war against the communists was out of the question, but the leader of the Bolsheviks might receive something else. On December 16, 1931, Song Qingling, who (as discussed earlier) was working for the Comintern, on instructions from the Moscow leadership met with Chiang in Nanjing and proposed exchanging his son Ching-kuo for the Soviet agents Rudnik and Moiseenko-Velikaia (the Noulens couple).

At that time Chiang Ching-kuo was a graduate student at the International Lenin School in Moscow. A year earlier he had graduated from the N. G. Tolmachev Military Political Academy in Leningrad, afterward worked for a time as a metalworker in the Dynamo factory in Moscow, then taken part in Soviet collectivization. In 1930 he became a candidate member of the Bolshevik party, and as one of the ten thousand communists that the party threw into establishing the collective farms, he worked from May to November 1931 as chair of the October Revolution Collective Farm in the village of Korovino in the Moscow region.[18]

Chiang missed Ching-kuo a lot. From January 1931 on, sad entries appear in his diaries about how he considered himself not only a bad son but also a bad father: "I don't know how to be kind to my children. I regret that. . . . I miss Ching-kuo very much. I am bad because I am not taking care of him."[19] But he acted as Stalin did twelve years later, when the Soviet leader refused to exchange his son Yakov, taken captive by the Nazis during the Second World War, for the Nazi Field Marshal Paulus.[20] Even though his wife, Meiling, asked him to agree to the exchange,[21] he refused Song Qingling, saying that "he would hand over both [Noulens] to a civilian court, and he could not do otherwise."[22] "Madam Sun [Song Qingling] wanted me to free the officials of the Eastern Department of the Soviet Communist Party. But I told her their crimes had already been fully proven, but she insisted that I free them, suggesting they be exchanged for Ching-kuo," Chiang wrote in his diaries that same day. "I would sooner agree that Ching-kuo not return home or that he be killed in Soviet Russia, but I will never exchange criminals for my own son. . . . How could I . . . break the law?"[23]

Song Qingling was indignant, and that same evening, December 16, 1931, she met secretly with the Soviet military intelligence agent Richard Sorge, who was living in China under the pseudonym Johnson, and in Moscow was known by the code name Ramsay.[24] She had maintained contact with him from the time of his arrival in Shanghai in January 1930. During their meeting she "requested 100 good communists, who should be sent to Nanjing; she wanted to secure weapons for them, and she herself wanted to take the Noulens [couple] from prison in a government vehicle."[25] This proposed venture went nowhere. On August 19, 1932, Rudnik (Noulens) was sentenced to death, although this ruling was subsequently changed to life imprisonment. His wife, too, was given a life sentence. Immediately afterward, however, the secretary of the Executive Committee of the Comintern, Josef Aronovich Piatnitsky (code name Mikhail), requested that Sorge ask Song Qingling (Leah) to get in touch with well-known leaders of the Guomindang, including Cai Yuanpei and Sun Fo, to secure the release of the Noulens (in Piatnitsky's ciphered telegram they were referred to as the "sick ones" in the interests of secrecy).[26] That is what Sorge probably did. But in the Guomindang leadership no one could help them. They were freed only after five years during an amnesty, and in 1939 they returned to their homeland.[27]

How difficult it was for Chiang to govern the country when his own sister-in-law, whom everyone in China called the mother of the state (because she was the widow of the father of the state Sun Yat-sen),[28] was engaging in criminal activity, collaborating with agents of the Fourth (Intelligence) Directorate of the Soviet Red Army, arming communists, and trying to free persons who had committed crimes against the state.

Moreover, she was doing this at China's most critical moment. Chiang failed to secure the peace he had hoped for. The anti-Japanese movement in China rose to a new level. Its center was in Shanghai. In the part of the city inhabited by Japanese known as Little Tokyo, large and small character posters (*dazibao* and *xiaozibao*) appeared saying, "Kill Japanese!" and "Down with Japanese imperialism!" Shanghai students commandeered a train and came to Nanjing, where they attacked the Foreign Ministry building, demanding active measures against Japan. They seized Minister of Foreign Affairs Wang Zhengting and almost killed him.

But Chiang remained composed. "With unity even 1,500 students of this university can defeat Japanese imperialism," he declared, on visiting Central University in Nanjing. "But without unity 400,000,000 people would be unable to present a strong front."[29] "[We will] never surrender and never sign unequal treaties with Japan," he assured students at a school in his native village of Xikou.[30] To his closest associates, he said bitterly, "The responsibility of revolution has fallen upon my shoulders. Given my knowledge of ourselves and of our enemies, I must not act irresponsibly to disappoint our Chairman [Sun Yat-sen] and our martyrs, our country and our people. . . . All that I can do [now] is to sustain humiliation and carry a heavy burden."[31] But students continued to organize demonstrations and protest strikes, demanding war with Japan. In mid-December 1931 no fewer than seventy thousand students from various parts of the country came to Nanjing and attacked the Guomindang CEC, the printing house of the party, the *Central Newspaper,* and other government institutions.

Taking advantage of the situation, the Cantonese putschists headed by Wang Jingwei asserted that Chiang had sold out to the Japanese "dwarfs," and again demanded his resignation. For the sake of unity in the country and the Guomindang, Chiang was forced to enter into talks with Canton. He freed Hu Hanmin, who had suffered from high blood pressure for a long time, entreating him to go to Wang.[32] And via Hu's mediation, in October 1931 representatives of the various factions, meeting at the home of Sun Fo, Sun Yat-sen's son, began discussing how to resolve the crisis. During the discussions Hu Hanmin demanded that Chiang resign at once and leave China forever. Chiang refused and, indignant, returned to Nanjing. "I swear before the portrait of Dr. Sun Yat-sen, and before the people and the country, that I will adhere to the *yo-fa* [*yuefa*] [the Provisional Constitution] if I must die for it," he asserted.[33] A bit later in his diaries he angrily wrote, "The flesh of the traitor Hu Hanmin does not deserve to be eaten."[34]

But it was necessary to find a compromise. From November 12 to 23, 1931, Chiang convened the Fourth Congress of the Guomindang in Nanjing, at which a resolution was adopted to readmit to the party all those who had been expelled from it since the Second Plenum of the CEC (that is, since February 1928), including Wang Jingwei, Marshal Feng Yuxiang, and Generals Yan Xishan, Li Jishen, and Li Zongren. In his speech to the congress Chiang declared that unification of the party was the only way to resolve the critical situation. Afterward a Special Committee on the Japanese Question was established, headed by Dai Jitao and Minister of Military Administration He Yingqin. Moreover, the 381 delegates resolved to make September 18 a Day of National Mourning.

Almost simultaneously in Canton (in November–December) and in Shanghai (in early December), Sun Fo and Wang Jingwei, respectively, convened their own separate Fourth Congresses of the Guomindang. As at Chiang Kai-shek's congress, they too elected CECs of the party. In this situation, in order to unite the party once and for all, Chiang proposed to his opponents that a unifying First Plenum of all three CECs be convened in Nanjing. But Sun Fo, speaking on December 10 in the name of the opposition, demanded Chiang's resignation prior to December 20 as a precondition.[35]

Understanding that further resistance would be useless, Chiang, on December 15, decided once again to give up all his posts.[36] "[He] simply had made too many enemies and thus for the second time was forced to step down at the peak of his powers," recalled Chen Lifu.[37]

Chiang and his wife departed for his native Xikou. At the end of December the First Unified Plenum of the CEC took place. Chiang did not participate, but he was chosen in absentia as one of the nine members of the Standing Committee of the CEC of the Guomindang. The plenum, on the recommendation of the Guomindang CEC, chose Lin Sen, an old associate of Sun, to head the government, and Sun Fo to head the Executive Yuan.[38]

Meanwhile, in January 1932 a direct threat was posed to Shanghai. Japanese naval officers, serving on ships cruising along the Yangzi River, tried to repeat the exploit of their Kwantung comrades. They felt free to do so because the Japanese government, unaware of the events of September 18, was forced after the fact to approve the actions of the Kwantung army, even awarding those who took part in the events. The commander of the Kwantung Army also expressed his approval even though his officers had acted without his orders.

In this situation, at an emergency session the National government of China resolved once again to ask Chiang to return and lead the country. Lin Sen and Sun Fo sent him an official invitation. Even the head of the Cantonese, Wang Jingwei, who was then in a hospital in Shanghai, understood that they could not manage without Chiang, who wielded authority in the army. Japan was threatening to subdue all of China, and preparations had to be made for the future war. Checking out of the hospital, Wang set off for Hangzhou to the villa *Chenglu* on the eastern shore of the lovely West Lake (Chiang had spent several days there with Meiling after their wedding). Wang met there with Chiang on January 17, 1932. After discussing the situation, they arrived at a compromise solution. Chiang would return to lead the armed forces again, Wang would replace Sun Fo as head of the Executive Yuan, and Sun Fo would become the chair of the Legislative Yuan.[39]

Returning to Nanjing on the evening of January 22, Chiang at once met at home with his closest associates to review the situation. Since October 1929 he and Meiling had lived in a new residence, a two-story, European-style redbrick house specially built for them. The house was right next to the Central Infantry Academy, established on the foundation of the former Whampoa Academy in March 1928 (presently 3 Huangpu Street).[40] Chiang loved this house, calling it *Qilu* (Hut of Repose), but Meiling wanted to live outside of town. They had a country house seventeen miles from Nanjing at the spurs of the Tangshan mountains, near hot springs—a stone house with a small courtyard planted with magnolias at 3 Wenquan Street, Tangshan. But it did not suit Meiling. First, it was right in the center of the village of Tangshan, neighboring two other cottages, and, second, it was too small, just three rooms on one floor and two stone baths in the basement. It had been built in 1920 by one of the descendants of Tao Yuanming, the great Chinese poet of the fourth to fifth century CE, and was therefore named *Taolu* (Tao's Hut).[41] Cicada Zhang, who had purchased the house from its owner, presented it as a wedding gift to Chiang and Meiling. Both Meiling and Chiang were there only rarely. In May 1931 Hu Hanmin was placed under house arrest in the adjacent cottage and remained there until the middle of July, after which Chiang had him transferred to Kong Xiangxi's house. In October 1931, as noted earlier, Chiang freed him in connection with the Japanese aggression in Manchuria.[42] Yielding to Meiling's persuasion, Chiang had a new country house built in 1934: a luxurious three-story, colonnaded, yellow stone palace under a curved green brick roof that cost 360,000 yuan. He gave it to Meiling on her birthday, March 4. Situated not far from Sun's Mausoleum, in the woods on the spurs of Purple Gold Mountain, the house came to be called Meiling's Palace. The couple moved there in the summer of 1936.[43]

But that was to come later. In the meantime, on January 27, 1932, Chiang learned that Admiral Shiozawa, commanding the Japanese fleet in the Shanghai region, had issued an ultimatum to the mayor of Shanghai, demanding that he end the anti-Japanese boycott. The Japanese fleet did not want to be outdone by the army, and the pretext for the ultimatum was that the evening before Chinese hooligans in Zhabei, the workers' quarter on the north bank of the small Wusong River (also known as Suzhou Creek), had beaten up several Japanese monks. Even though the next day the mayor accepted the admiral's demands and had even shut down anti-Japanese organizations, Shiozawa decided to teach the Chinese a lesson. "I'm not satisfied with conditions in Chapei [Zhabei]," he told a correspondent of the *New York Times.* "There are 600,000 excited Chinese in the Chapei district of Shanghai, and the most of them are violently anti-Japanese. About 6,000 helpless Japanese civilians have their homes and shops in Chapei."[44]

At eleven o'clock on the night of January 28, 1932, he issued an order to storm Chapei. But unlike what occurred in Shenyang, in Shanghai the sailors who landed on the shore encountered fierce resistance from the Nineteenth Route Army that had been redeployed there from Guangdong by Wang Jingwei back in late 1930. Then at midnight on January 28–29, 1932, Shiozawa gave the order to bomb Zhabei from the air. This was the first bombing of urban living quarters in history. The planes flew low, precision bombing peaceful inhabitants who were fleeing in terror. After several hours of bloody bombing, not a single building in Zhabei was left undamaged, and thousands of people had been killed or wounded; refugees flooded the International Settlement.[45] But the mayhem did not in the slightest disturb Shiozawa, a fifty-year-old admiral "who in looks and in manner seemed to be one of the kindest and mildest of men." "I see your American newspapers have nicknamed me the Baby-Killer," he observed to the same *New York Times* correspondent four days after the operation began. "But after all, they should give me some credit. I used only 30-pound bombs, and if I had chosen to do so I might have used the 500-pound variety."[46]

Five years later the whole world would be shocked by just such a bloody bombing of the Basque city of Guernica by Germany's Condor Legion, one of the squadrons of the Luftwaffe. And thanks to the genius of Picasso, Guernica would be remembered right up to the present. Alas, few outside of China now remember the no-less-cruel bombing of Zhabei.

Chiang sent his best troops to the aid of the Nineteenth Army: two divisions of the Fifth Army, including the First Model Division, trained by the Germans. "No sacrifice is too great to make in giving them [the Nineteenth Army] support," he wrote in an order. "The glory to the Nineteenth Route Army is the glory to China."[47]

At the same time, understanding that his troops would not defeat the Japanese, Chiang and his government quickly evacuated to the city of Luoyang (Henan province), where he convened a meeting of the members of his cabinet and the military. It was decided to commence negotiations with the Japanese to settle the situation in Shanghai, on the basis of a directive formulated by Wang Jingwei, the head of the Executive Yuan: "Resistance on the one hand and negotiations on the other." In other words, resisting while negotiating. Both elements of this formula were important. It was impossible for a weak China to resist without conducting negotiations, but it was likewise impossible to conduct negotiations without resisting, as the country might quickly lose its independence.[48] The troops of the Nineteenth Army resisted the Japanese, thereby demonstrating to the enemy what Chinese were capable of; now it was time for the diplomats to resolve the problem. They accomplished this in May 1932, arranging for the Japanese to withdraw troops from Zhabei. However, the Chinese in turn demilitarized all of Shanghai and its environs, which liberal public opinion adamantly opposed. The diplomat who signed the truce, later badly beaten by students, was hospitalized. Chiang did not return to Nanjing until December 1932.[49]

Meanwhile, on February 5, 1932, the Japanese seized Harbin, and on February 18 Manchuria, an area one-sixth the size of the United States, was proclaimed independent of the Nanjing government. On March 1 the founding of so-called Manchukuo (the State of Manchuria) was announced, and on March 9, in Changchun, which six days later was renamed Xinjing (New Capital), the Japanese proclaimed Pu Yi, the last scion of the Qing dynasty, whom they had brought with two of his wives from Tianjin where he lived, as the Supreme Ruler of this purported state. Two years later, on March 1, 1934, the Japanese renamed Manchukuo as Manzhou da diguo (The Great Empire of the Manchus). Pu Yi, under the reign name Kangde (Peace and Virtue), was proclaimed the emperor of the "great empire."[50]

The Japanese government tried in every way to emphasize the supposed independence of Manchukuo not only from Nanjing but also from Tokyo. Yet they failed to convince world opinion or eclipse Chinese diplomacy, which consistently repeated that Manchuria was an inalienable part of China. The League of Nations censured the aggressors.[51] But in spring and autumn 1932 Stalin in essence recognized the independence of Northeast China by starting negotiations on the sale of the CER to the new authorities in Manchuria: in reality, the Japanese.[52] He decided as well to allow the opening of a Manchukuo consulate in Blagoveshchensk, which was done in 1932; approved the replacement of Chinese members of the CER management with officials nominated by the Manchukuo government; allowed Japanese troops to be transported on the railroad; and began to supply aviation fuel to the Japanese under a five-year agreement.[53] A number of Japanese officers at the time were on probationary service in the Soviet Red Army, and not only were they not asked to return to their homeland, but their contracts were extended for a year. The Soviet Union did not endorse the League of Nations resolution on the Japanese–Chinese conflict.[54]

At the same time, Stalin agreed to restore diplomatic relations with China, fearing that exercising "coolness" in this matter might just push "Nanjing into the embrace of Japan. This question," he emphasized, "like the question of our relations with America, is directly related to the question of a Japanese attack on the USSR. If Japan, owing to our excessive coolness and rudeness to the Chinese, gains control over Nanjing and forms a united front with it, and if America is neutral, a Japanese attack against the USSR will be accelerated and guaranteed. Therefore, coolness toward Nanjing . . . should not turn into rudeness and rejection, should not deprive them of the hope for the possibility of rapprochement."[55] This minimalist reasoning was not enough for Chiang. Judging by information from Soviet intelligence, one can conclude that in early June 1932 the Generalissimo began to express interest not only in exchanging ambassadors with the USSR but also in simultaneously concluding a nonaggression treaty with the Soviet Union. He needed such a treaty to compel Stalin to recognize officially that Manchuria was a part of China because it should be included in the territories of the Republic of China that the Soviet government negotiated with Nanjing concerning nonaggression.[56] On June 29 the Chinese delegate to the Council of the League of Nations, Yan

Huiqing, addressed an official communication to Maxim Maximovich Litvinov, the commissar for foreign affairs of the USSR, proposing the conclusion of a nonaggression treaty.[57] But as Molotov and Kaganovich, members of the Soviet Politburo, rightly observed, this treaty might hamper the establishment "of relations with Manchukuo that we [USSR] need."[58]

At the time, Stalin was disinclined to conclude a nonaggression treaty, but he did restore diplomatic relations with China on December 12, 1932. In April 1933 the Soviet ambassador Dmitrii Vasilievich Bogomolov arrived in Nanjing. Forty-two years old, he was an experienced diplomat: from 1927 to 1929 ambassador to Poland and, from 1929 to 1932, embassy counselor of the Soviet embassy in London. On May 2 he presented his diplomatic credentials to Lin Sen, chair of the Nanjing government.[59]

At the first reception at the Soviet embassy on November 7, 1933, in honor of the October Revolution almost all the leaders of the Guomindang attended, some 150 persons, including Wang Jingwei and Chiang's brother-in-law Minister of Finance Kong Xiangxi. But Chiang was absent. Probably for a valid reason: he was on an inspection tour in Changsha, the capital of Hunan. However, on precisely that day, he praised the assembled provincial Guomindang officials for having "not only wholly rid Hunan province of bandits, but also helping neighboring provinces to eradicate them."[60] Needless to say, he was referring to communists. He was indicating that the restoration of relations with the USSR did not signify an end to the civil war.

Both Chiang and Stalin were playing a double game. While aiming for an alliance with the USSR to contain Japan, the Nanjing leader was at the same time continuing his persistent battle against the CCP; and the Moscow leader, even while agreeing to develop friendly diplomatic relations with China, was not only helping the CCP as before, but also smoothing the way for relations with Chiang's mortal enemies, Manchukuo and Japan.[61] In correspondence with friends, Stalin referred to Chiang as a petty crook,[62] but he himself was no better.

The occupation of Manchuria and incursion into Shanghai signaled only the beginning of Japanese aggression in China. Japan continued its expansion in North China. In March 1933 Japanese soldiers seized the northern Chinese province of Rehe, which bordered Manchuria on the south. At the same time, Japan left the League of Nations.

It is difficult not to agree with one of Chiang's biographers who wrote that from the leader of the nation "it required super-human strength to swallow

. . . [the] great insult whilst the whole country was crying out for war. But he [Chiang] chose to act against popular sentiment and took the whole responsibility upon his own broad shoulders."[63] In May 1933 Chiang made a new truce with the Japanese, this time in North China. In Tanggu, a small town not far from Tianjin, his delegation signed a humiliating agreement to establish a one-hundred-kilometer (sixty-two-mile) demilitarized zone south of the Chinese Great Wall. In reality, Japanese troops came within fifteen miles of Beiping and thirty-six miles of Tianjin. It was no secret to anyone, including Chiang, that, notwithstanding the truce, the Japanese annexationist plans extended to all of North China.

No matter how humiliating the truces with Japan were and no matter how strongly they undermined Chiang's personal authority in the eyes of patriotic public opinion, they afforded the Nanjing government an indispensable breathing space to finish off the communist movement. On June 1, 1933, Chiang wrote in his diaries, "The agreement in Tanggu essentially has no analogues, the text is shameful, the helplessness [of our] representatives matches the cowardice at the front, I can't get over the shame. But once the agreement with the enemy was signed, I could not but bear personal responsibility [for it]."[64]

On the very next day he again turned his attention to opposing the Communist Party in Jiangxi, where only by a miracle did the Ninth Division escape a crushing defeat. The very ill Young Marshal, whose troops, as before, had been deployed in North China but did not engage the Japanese, was made the scapegoat for the shameful defeat in Rehe. Even though Chiang himself was essentially following a policy of appeasing the aggressor, nevertheless, in March 1933 he placed all the blame on the drug addict and demanded his resignation. Zhang Xueliang submitted and called on his officers and soldiers to follow the commands of the Generalissimo from there on and "support the government unanimously."[65] He himself left for Shanghai, where, along with two of his wives, also drug addicts, he started a new, intensive course of treatment for his drug dependency that in the end cured him.

Afterward he went to Europe, where he traveled for six months with William Henry Donald, "an incredible, ruddy, sandy-haired Australian" who was a former friend of Sun Yat-sen and was now serving as Zhang's advisor.[66] Zhang not only rested but also searched for possible allies against Japan. In Italy he held talks with Mussolini, whom he praised as an outstanding man.[67] Mussolini's daughter Edda helped him arrange this meeting. She was Zhang's lover, whom he had somehow managed to charm in Shanghai, where her husband, Count Ciano di Cortellazzo, a future Italian minister plenipotentiary in China and then minister of foreign affairs, was serving as consul general. But Mussolini had nothing critical to say about militarist Japan. Then Zhang traveled to Germany, where he met with Hitler and Goering. Nothing came of that either, so Zhang departed for France, where he crossed paths with Litvinov. Hoping now to receive assistance from the communists, he asked Litvinov to arrange a trip for him to the Soviet Union but was rebuffed. As before, Stalin did not want to complicate his relations with Japan. Moreover, in February 1933 the Kremlin boss even approved the opening of another Manchukuo consulate on Soviet territory, in Chita. There were already five Soviet consulates in Manchukuo.[68] On May 2, 1933, Litvinov transmitted a proposal to the Japanese ambassador to the USSR, Ota, to resume negotiations for the sale of the CER to Manchukuo that had been broken off in the past year. On June 26, 1933, a USSR representative in Tokyo discussed this issue anew.[69]

During the previous year it seemed that Chiang Kai-shek's struggle against the Chinese communists was beginning to bring at least partial successes. This time he was able to inflict defeat on one of their formations, the 16,000-man Fourth Front Chinese Red Army. It was operating in the region of Hubei–Henan–Anhui under the command of Zhang Guotao, one of the founders of the CCP. Chiang, who had come to Hankou at the time, personally commanded a 630,000-man army that encircled the Hubei–Henan–Anhui Soviet region. But he did not succeed in totally defeating Zhang Guotao. In early October 1932, after breaking through the blockade, Zhang led his troops to the west, into northern Sichuan and southern Shaanxi. Chiang's forces pursued them, but units of the Fourth Front, traversing more than five thousand *li* (fifteen hundred miles) and losing 40 percent of their men ("It had been a nightmarish battle of retreat," Zhang Guotao recalled)[70] in early 1933 still managed to consolidate its hold in the Sichuan–Shaanxi region.[71]

Chiang next concentrated his efforts on the Central Soviet Area in Jiangxi. From late February to the end of March 1933 he conducted the fourth punitive expedition. But here his forces, at whose head he had placed Minister of Military Administration He Yingqin, again tasted the bitterness of defeat. The local communists, as before, employed Mao Zedong's tactic of "luring the enemy in deep." "The enemy advances, we retreat; the enemy camps, we harass; the enemy tires, we attack; the enemy retreats, we pursue": this was the magic formula that saved the CCP.[72]

At the end of September 1933 Chiang launched a new, fifth punitive expedition, throwing a million-man army against the "red bandits" of the Central Soviet Area. This time he himself led the forces, transferring his headquarters to the "ugly foreignized" town of Guling (Ox Peak) in the Lushan mountains, which were in the north of Jiangxi province not far from the city of Jiujiang. The town was "much frequented by missionaries escaping from the heat of the plains. It was quite a big place, with room for conferences and meetings."[73] From 1934, not far from this town, in the woods was another of Chiang's family country homes, which he named *Meilu* (Meiling's Hut or the Beautiful Hut).[74] It was also known as the Cottage on the Bridge of the Goddess of Mercy Guan Yin. This two-story stone villa, surrounded by greenery, had been built in 1903 and given to Chiang's wife by her friend, an English missionary who had acquired it in 1922. From the windows of the villa and the second-story balcony a beautiful view opened up, one that, in the words of a visitor to the villa, made "Switzerland look mild."[75] But the view did not distract Chiang from his gloomy thoughts. He had come to the house on the bridge of the Goddess of Mercy to exterminate the communists mercilessly once and for all. A difficult war lay before him, and he understood that Mao simply could not win for a fifth time.

Two English journalists visited Chiang there: Peter Fleming, a special correspondent of the London *Times,* and Gerald York, a correspondent of the Reuters Agency. Both were struck by the Spartan setting of the "small bungalow" that was guarded by just six soldiers bearing submachine guns. In Fleming's words, Chiang received them in "a small room, modestly furnished in European style. On the walls hung cheap reproductions only of religious content. ("Steel engravings of Christ and the Virgin," York added.)[76] The furniture was simple, unattractive, and old. The home of the Generalissimo of the army of the Republic of China looked entirely unbefitting his status." Chiang, dressed in a dark blue gown, looked incredibly gaunt to his guests. "He came into the room quietly, and stood quite still, looking at us," Fleming recalled. "He was a rather more than average height, and unexpectedly thin. His complexion was dark, his cheek bones high and prominent, and he had a jutting, forceful lower lip like a Habsburg's.[77] His eyes were . . . large, handsome, and very keen—almost aggressive. His glances had a thrusting and compelling quality which is very rare in China, where eyes are mostly negative and noncommittal, if not actually evasive."[78]

Fleming and York were basically interested in two questions: "How soon did he [Chiang Kai-shek] expect to see the Red areas cleared up and the problem of Communism in China solved?" and "When might we see a *rapprochement* between China and Japan?" Chiang immediately replied that he would finish off the communists by Christmas, that is, by December 25, 1933, and he would never compromise on the Manchurian question. Then he gave the Englishmen one of those "glances, of the kind of which prompts an involuntary self-accusation of some grave sartorial omission. We trooped down the garden path feeling very small."[79] "He is the most impressive Chinese that I have met," York summed up.[80]

Chiang's German advisors drew up a plan for a campaign that would conclude with smothering the Chinese Soviet Republic by constructing along its borders several thousand blockhouses, powerful stone forts, at a distance of two to three kilometers (1.2–1.8 miles) from each other. Having decided to finish off the CCP once and for all, Chiang was cautious. Most of all he was in no hurry. Soldiers entered into the depths of the "red zone" slowly, at the rate of two to three *li* (that is, one to one and half kilometers or about one mile) per day, consolidating their position at each new line. From twelve to sixteen airplanes daily bombed Red Army positions, dropping about three thousand bombs every month.[81] Time passed and the ring tightened. One of Chiang's generals characterized the tactics as, "Drain the pond to catch the fish." Along with military measures, Chiang used political ones. Moreover, he laid special stress on the latter: 30 percent of the efforts on war and 70 percent on politics. Everywhere in the recovered territories the traditional rural system of mutual control (*baojia*) was revived and local peasant militias (*mintuan*) were reestablished. Large rewards were offered for the capture of leaders of the Communist Party. For Mao's head, for example, 250,000 Chinese dollars.[82]

But soon new difficulties arose. In November 1933 the troops of the Nineteenth Army rebelled against Chiang. These were the former defenders of Shanghai whom Chiang had redeployed to Fujian after signing the truce with Japan. In Fuzhou, the capital of the province, the so-called People's Revolutionary Government of the Republic of China, headed by Li Jishen, the Guangdong general who was a longtime adversary of Chiang Kai-shek, was proclaimed on November 22. The troops of the Nineteenth Army were mostly Guangdong men. The "minister of foreign affairs" of the new government was the Guomindang leftist Eugene Chen, whose ancestors were also from Guangdong. The rebels announced their withdrawal from the Guomindang and the establishment of a new Productive People's Party. Their program was not only sharply anti–Chiang Kai-shek but also anti-Japanese and, moreover, anti-imperialist. The leaders of the rebels declared that they were for democracy, against any kind of dictatorship, and in favor of state control of the economy and the redistribution of land in the interests of the starving peasants. Instead of fighting against the CCP, they began cooperating with it, but they were unable to hold out for long.[83] In January 1934 Chiang suppressed the rebellion and then returned to dealing with the CCP.

In February 1934, in order to eradicate communism, at the initiative of Meiling, Chen Lifu and William Henry Donald, formerly the advisor to the Young Marshal, who had returned with him from Europe and gone over to the service of Chiang Kai-shek,[84] a comprehensive program of national cultural revival was drawn up. The object of this plan was to restore the lost Confucian norms of ethics and morality.[85] Chiang fully supported it and emphasized that satisfying the spiritual needs of people seeking a new life depends on the government to a certain degree, especially its system of education, economic policies, and measures in defense of the entire population.[86]

On February 19, 1934, in Nanchang, where the Generalissimo's headquarters were then located, Chiang announced at a mass meeting the launch of a new movement called For a New Life![87] Afterward a wave of meetings and demonstrations in support of the movement engulfed the country. To a certain degree its initiators imbued it with a religious character, striving to instill in the consciousness of the people ideals that in equal measure were part traditional Chinese philosophy and part Christianity.[88]

The main ideas of the movement were expressed in what became a popular four-character slogan: *li, yi, lian, chi* (courtesy, duty, honesty, and self-mindedness).[89] This slogan was borrowed from the tract of a great ancient Chinese philosopher, Guan Zi (Guan Zhong, 720–645 BCE), that Chiang had attentively read in early 1934. "The four virtues," he asserted, "are the essential principles for the promotion of morality. . . . The main object of the New Life Movement is to substitute a rational life for the irrational. . . . [O]ur people must have military training. As a preliminary, we have to acquire the habits of orderliness, cleanliness, simplicity, frugality, promptness, and exactness. We have to preserve order, emphasize organization, responsibility, and discipline, and be ready to die for the country at any moment."[90] In the framework of the movement, beginning in Jiangxi, on the borders of the Central Soviet Area and then quickly extending to other provinces, campaigns unfolded to promote brotherhood, order in the family, cleanliness, and hygiene. These campaigns were intended to contrast with the uncivilized behavior of the so-called filthy Communists.[91] Police in the cities began to closely monitor passersby to make sure they didn't spit, litter, or even smoke on the streets.[92]

Measures were also taken against the trade in opium, the scourge that was deeply affecting Chinese society. Despite the fact that the opium trade had long been prohibited one could easily buy opium everywhere. No one had really been fighting to eradicate the opium trade. Merchants were simply taxed. Donald, shocked by such an outrage, wrote in a letter to Song Meiling in the spring of 1934, "[T]he statue of Dr. Sun Yat-sen overlooked the biggest opium shop in Hankou. On the shop's window was a large sign that read: 'CHEAP SALE OF OPIUM—THOSE WHO MAKE EXTRA LARGE PURCHASES WILL BE GIVEN FREE TICKETS IN THE NATIONAL GOVERNMENT LOTTERY' ."[93] Only after this did Chiang issue a decree commencing a real struggle against the opium trade. However, it was not particularly successful. Donald suggested that Chiang and Meiling introduce strict measures against opium dealers and corrupt officials, including shooting them, but Chiang was simply unable to follow this advice: he would have had to shoot millions of people. So he basically limited himself to using propaganda. In November 1934 Song Meiling did open a center for drug addicts in Xi'an.[94] So-called foot soldiers of the new movement were members of the newly organized Scouts of China General Association. Primary and junior high school students enlisted in this organization patrolled the streets to "make sure public spaces were hygienic and pedestrians wore clean, decent clothes."[95]

The experience gained in the nationwide movement was put into practice by graduates of the Whampoa Academy, two thousand of whom had joined together on January 1, 1929, to form the puritanical officers' Whampoa Alumni Society to Establish the Will (Huangpu tongxue lizhishe).[96] This society was founded on the model of the conservative officers' organization of Japan Kaikosha (March Together Society), established in 1877.[97] Chiang became the honorary head of the society; absolute loyalty to him was defined as the foundational postulate of the Lizhishe. Song Meiling was chosen as a member of the board of directors. Board members were supposed to serve as exemplary moral models for the entire nation. They were forbidden to drink, smoke, or gamble. The headquarters of the society was initially located not far from Chiang Kai-shek's residence *Qilu*, on the grounds of the Whampoa Academy. In 1931 it moved into a luxurious private residence, 307 Zhongshan Avenue, at the intersection of Huangpu Street and Zhongshan Avenue. Chiang often visited this building, in which he had an office. The New Life Museum is presently located in this building. Chiang devised the slogan for this organization: *li ren li ji, ge ming ge xin* ("Strengthening the will of others, strengthen oneself; carrying out revolution, reform oneself.")[98]

In China at that time there were, in addition to the Lizhishe, a number of other quasimilitary organizations, participation in which meant unquestioning devotion to the leader, that is, to Chiang. The majority of the members were graduates of the officers' academy. All of them treasured swords given to them by Chiang Kai-shek at graduation. Carved into the swords were the words "Conquer or Be Conquered."[99] The members of these organizations came to be known as the Whampoa Clique.

The largest of these fellowships was the Society for Vigorous Practice of the Three Principles of the People (Sanminzhuyi lixingshe), founded in February 1932 with Chiang's direct participation.[100] It had more than half a million members, most no older than forty, who swore not only to put into practice the Three Principles of the People, but also to revive "the Chinese race." Deeply conspiratorial, this Praetorian Guard of Chiang's, under the command of such devoted generals as his fellow provincials Chen Cheng and Hu Zongnan, operated through its own legal organizations: the Blue Shirts Society (Lanyishe),[101] the Revolutionary Army Comrades Association (Geming junren tongzhi hui), the Revolutionary Youth Comrades Association (Geming qingnian tongzhi hui), and the Renaissance Society (Fuxingshe). They were all very closely related to each other.[102] Moreover, there was the CC clique (*CC pai*), established by the brothers Chen Guofu and Chen Lifu, which was close to the ideology of the Lixingshe but at odds with it.

Several of these organizations, judging by their political aims, structure, and activities, resembled Mussolini's Black Shirts or Hitler's Brown Shirts. Not infrequently they beat up, kidnapped, and even killed opponents of Chiang Kai-shek, and their members called Chiang *lingxiu* (leader or führer), inflating his cult of personality with all their might—Chiang himself, incidentally, encouraged it.[103] They borrowed a lot from external attributes of the fascists and the Nazis: for example, their rhetoric, their torch-light processions and musical marches; and the Blue Shirts Society, numbering fourteen thousand members, even openly called on Chiang to imitate Mussolini and Hitler.[104] But neither Chiang nor members of his organizations ever sought to substitute fascism or Nazism for Sun Yat-senism, nor in any case did they wish to reject "*the traditional social and political philosophy of the Kuomintang [Guomindang].*"[105]

This outlook was clearly demonstrated by the New Life Movement, during which Chiang, while acknowledging that the ideas of the movement were consonant with the principles followed by the powerful "contemporary Italy and Germany," nonetheless appealed to Chinese tradition, that is, to the moral-ethical norms of Confucianism, though intermixed, to be sure, with Christian ethics.[106] He demanded the strengthening of discipline and law and order on the foundation of the authentically Chinese clan customs and norms of respect for elders and the authority of those in power. "We should not imitate the superficialities of the West nor plagiarize the Doctrine of Might of the Imperialist nations. . . . My hope lies in the revival of our old national traits," Chiang said.[107] Meiling added, "Each nation . . . has sought to find a way out of stagnation into normalcy. . . . Italy has its Fascism, Germany its Nazism, the Soviet Union its first and second five-year plans, and America its New Deal."[108]

Indeed, Chiang, Marshal Zhang Xueliang, and many other leaders of the Guomindang were following with interest and envy how Il Duce and then the Führer were subordinating their peoples to their dictatorial rule and how, having aroused the Italians and the Germans, lifted them from their knees. W. H. Donald, who was visiting Italy and Germany with the Young Marshal, was also ecstatic about the fascist–Nazi experiment. After returning to China and switching from serving Zhang Xueliang to Chiang as his chief advisor, Donald also recommended to the Generalissimo that he revive the spirit of the nation in China as Il Duce and the Führer had done in their countries.[109] In February 1933, during Kong Xiangxi's visit to the Vatican, Pope Pius XI, an admirer of Mussolini, also "advised the Chinese government to base the reorganization of the country on the fascist corporative system introduced in Italy by that man of Providence called Mussolini."[110] Around that time Mussolini was indeed very famous in China. The Shanghai press praised him as "a soldier, an orator, a statesman, a farmer, [and] a flyer." Even the great Chinese artist Xu Beihong called him Visionary.[111]

There was nothing surprising about this. In the late 1920s and early 1930s the fascist and Nazi experiments attracted the attention of Chiang and his companions in arms, just as Bolshevism had done in its time. They never doubted that a weak China needed a totalitarian dictatorship. On July 23, 1933, Chiang, for example, told his officers that Italy, Germany, and Turkey were developing rapidly because their rulers had put forward the "collective slogan" "Labour! Create! Military force!"[112] In 1933 Chiang sent four officials to Italy to study the fascist system of governing.[113]

Chiang wanted to make China, which had broken into pieces, powerful and strong, and he tried therefore to create in his country the kind of socioeconomic system that would enable China to become united. Yet China lacked a common economic market, and there existed, as before, various military cliques that time and again opposed the central government. Moreover, the middle class was undeveloped, the greater part of the population was illiterate and terribly poor, and the unification of the country on democratic and liberal principles was impossible. Only a dictatorship in the hands of a single party, strictly centralized and hierarchical, could unite China. Such a party needed a great leader whose countrywide, unlimited cult would aid in the consolidation of society. From Chiang's perspective, the state security agencies, which must fully control the political and intellectual life of citizens, should serve the same objective. And for the sake of that same unity, it followed that private property should be placed under strict state control and be partially nationalized so that the economy could be developed from above along centralized plans. "It is perfectly within the right of the Party or Government to restrict, whenever circumstances demand, the personal liberty of any individual," Chiang asserted. "This principle is applicable to all, regardless of their position, their past record, or the nature of the responsibility with which they are entrusted."[114] Furthermore "[he] believed that unless everyone has absolute trust in one man, we cannot reconstruct the nation and we cannot complete the revolution."[115]

Does it resemble a fascist perspective? Yes, but first, unlike Mussolini and Hitler, Chiang accomplished very little of this program; he was not even able to unify China. Second, it was Sun Yat-sen who, long before Mussolini and Hitler, called for a regime of political tutelage in China, that is, an openly one-party dictatorship, subordinating both the party and society to his personal power. It was Sun who demanded that all large and critical means of production either be converted into state property or put under state control. In other words, everything that Chiang was trying to do accorded with the teachings of Sun Yat-sen, not those of Mussolini and Hitler.

The communists always tried to accuse Chiang of fascism and even Nazism, but it didn't turn out well for them. Here, for example, is what the chief Comintern representative in China, Artur Ernst Ewert, wrote to Moscow in early December 1932:

> Chiang Kai-shek is organizing a fascist group inside the Guomindang —"the Blue Shirts Association." . . . This organization puts forth the following national socialist slogans:
>
> 1. Agrarian reform ("to equalize the ownership of land"[116]).
> 2. Struggle against foreign aggressors against the unequal treaties.
> 3. Development of industry (foreign loans for these goals; part of them to be used in support of the fascist organization).

4. "Elimination of conflict between workers and capitalists."
5. Strengthening the army and reorganizing it on the basis of universal military service.
6. Gender equality, etc.[117]

Yes, what a terrible Nazi-fascist organization Chiang Kai-shek created, if it had strived to achieve such goals! Gender equality seems particularly "Nazi," does it not?

To a certain extent the perverse reaction of the Comintern representative to the traditionalist New Life Movement is explicable in terms of the fact that Chiang at that time sharply increased his anticommunist propaganda, which reached the summit of bitterness. "In the last several months," Chiang informed the nation in 1934, "their [the communists] all-consuming flame has become higher than ever before. . . . The villages through which they passed are drowning in blood. They are destroying everyone, men and women, old people and children. . . . They are doing things that human beings are incapable of doing. No one has done such things in the last two-hundred years. When I speak of such things, my heart contracts in pain, and when I think of such things, my hair stands on end."[118] No one doubts that the communists created mayhem: they burned the houses of better-off peasants, seized their property, and even killed those they deemed landlords and kulaks. But Chiang's officers and soldiers were equally cruel. They were like inquisitors destroying heresy with fire and sword. Thus, it is unlikely that Chiang, who was inured to violence, had his heart contract in pain or his hair stand on end. Especially since, as it will be recalled, he had no hair on his head; he shaved his head.

In the course of the fifth punitive expedition Chiang began to achieve his goal. As the Chinese communist Yang Song subsequently recalled, Chiang "during the fifth campaign was smarter than us; he learned from all the old experience."[119] Bleeding profusely and losing one battle after another, the Chinese Red Army retreated into the depths of the Central Soviet Area. By the summer of 1934 their situation was critical: "A dangerous condition in the CSA," Ewart reported to Moscow on June 2. "There is no hope in the near future for a radical change in our favor. . . . Our losses are enormous. Desertion is growing."[120] Stalin sent "the Chinese comrades" 200,000 rubles[121] (about 150,000 Chinese dollars at the current rate of exchange). He could do no more.[122]

In October 1934 units of the Central Red Army began to break through the blockade, and at the very beginning of November they emerged into southern Hunan. At the time they numbered only slightly more than 86,000. The goal of the campaign that would get the name "the Long March" had not been thought through to the end. They wanted only to escape from the cauldron. It seemed that once outside the lines of the blockade, everything would become clear. There was no radio link with the Executive Committee of the Comintern. Nor was there any communication with other Soviet areas, and no one knew what was going on there. Only one thing was more or less clear: they had to move in a westerly direction, toward the border area where Guangxi, Hunan, and Guizhou intersected and which, according to the communists' intelligence, was "free of enemy fortifications."[123] The route was chosen very precisely: through districts densely populated by the guest people (Hakka), who welcomed the Red Army as their liberators.[124] Due to their support, in December, after traversing almost two thousand *li,* the Red Army entered Guizhou province. Guomindang troops, in pursuit, did not risk attacking the main Red force. They were afraid of a rebellion by the Hakka people, who lived apart, according to their own clan laws, and did not recognize the authority of the Guomindang *bendi* (native inhabitants).[125]

By forcing the Reds westward, Chiang relieved the tension in East and Southeast China. Moreover, in pursuit of the CCP forces, his army finally began to subordinate to his government in Nanjing remote regions heretofore only nominally under the control of the central authority. Entering Guizhou, for example, Chiang's troops immediately replaced the local governor, and Chiang, who personally came to Guiyang, the capital of the province, compelled the former governor to fly to Nanjing. In his place Chiang appointed one of his own generals. "Thus," General Li Zongren recalled, "it developed that in their westward march the Communists . . . turned Kweichow [Guizhou] over to him [Chiang]."[126] In the middle of December 1934 Chiang flew to Chengdu, the capital of Sichuan, and there too replaced the governor of the province, this time appointing in his place one of the local militarists, General Liu Xiang, who had fully demonstrated his loyalty. This was a mistake, however, as Liu Xiang soon began to establish his own order in Sichuan.

Nevertheless, the year 1934 did not end badly for Chiang. The Great Depression, it seemed, was over. The economy was growing, and foreign capital investment was increasing. An end to the civil war against the communists appeared to be in sight; the communists were retreating toward the foothills of Tibet. Relations with the Japanese, who were basically observing the truce in Shanghai and North China, were more or less normalizing, although they were in control of Manchuria and Rehe. In 1934 Japan did succeed, however, in breaking the diplomatic blockade of Manchukuo. In March, El Salvador recognized the government of Pu Yi, and was followed by the Dominican Republic and the Vatican, but this had little effect. The League of Nations continued to condemn the aggressor.

In September 1934 Chiang assigned his secretary, Chen Bulei, the task of writing an article on Sino–Japanese relations for him. He wanted to explain to the Japanese government that a failure to end its aggressive policy might lead to the victory of evil forces (meaning the communists) throughout all of East Asia. The article proved to be rather pointed, and Chiang decided not to publish it under his own name. Xu Daolin, secretary of Chiang Kai-shek, was listed as the author. It appeared in December 1934 in the double issue (11–12) of the Shanghai journal *Waijiao pinglun* (Foreign Review) under the title "Enemy? Friend" and was later printed as a pamphlet.[127] The Japanese government did not react to the article but refrained from making new provocations. Subsequently the article was included in Chiang Kai-shek's collected works.

After New Year's on the Gregorian calendar, January 1, 1935, Chiang flew to his native Xikou for several days. He had earned a rest.

## CHAPTER 12

# *Playing with Stalin*

In 1935 the situation around China worsened again. Despite the fact that on March 19 the Soviet Politburo adopted a resolution to activate relations with China, asserting "the absolute respect of the Soviet Union for the sovereign rights, integrity, and inviolability of its territory," four days later the USSR sold the Chinese Eastern Railroad to Manchukuo (in reality to Japan) for 140 million yen (at the then current rate of exchange slightly more than US $40 million).[1] At almost the same time the Politburo considered it "expedient . . . to conclude a nonaggression pact [with China]," but this was not already enough for Chiang.[2] The situation in North China was heating up more and more, and the threat of a full-scale war with Japan was becoming more obvious by the day.

In June the Kwantung Army intruded into Eastern Hebei and, at the same time, provoked an armed incident in northern Chahar province and began penetrating Suiyuan province.[3] On July 4 Minister of Finance Kong Xiangxi informed Ambassador Bogomolov of the Nanjing government's desire to conclude not a nonaggression treaty but a mutual assistance treaty with the USSR.[4]

While the Soviets were considering this, Chiang was forced to make further concessions to the Japanese. In his name, on July 6 Minister of Military Administration He Yingqin concluded a new (secret) agreement with the aggressors, essentially giving them approval to establish a so-called Autonomous (in practice pro-Japanese) Anticommunist Government of Eastern Hebei. By the terms of the agreement all Guomindang troops, including the army of Zhang Xueliang, would be withdrawn from Hebei.[5] The northern Chahar incident was resolved just as shamefully: by the demilitarization of Chahar province. At the end of November 1935 the Anticommunist Government of Eastern Hebei, encouraged by the Japanese, declared its independence from Nanjing.

At this time Zhang Xueliang was in Hankou. After the Young Marshal had returned from his European trip in December 1933, Chiang appointed him one of the leaders of the campaign to exterminate the communist bandits in Central China. But he was not happy with these new duties. In Europe he had failed to secure support in the struggle against Japan and was depressed. Apparently, the Young Marshal had become disillusioned with the capacity of the Chinese nation to defend its right to independence. In the summer of 1934 Donald wrote to H. B. Elliston, the editor of the *Washington Post,* "The Young Marshal thinks only the methods of the Bolsheviks will do anything—chop the heads off a million or so. He says that the only thing to do is to hand the country over to some foreign power and let them run it for twenty-five years or so."[6]

By foreign power, however, Zhang Xueliang did not have Japan in mind. He continued to hate it as before. But Chiang would not let him fight the "dwarfs." On the contrary, in the summer of 1935 he redeployed the main forces of the Northeast Army—numbering some 160,000—from Hebei and Hubei to the northwest, to the provinces of Gansu and Shaanxi, where Mao's forces, completing the Long March, were heading. Zhang received a new post as deputy commander in chief "to eradicate communist bandits in Northwest China." Chiang appointed himself as commander. Zhang had to move to Xi'an, the capital of Shaanxi, which was then under the control of Yang Hucheng, who had routed Feng Yuxiang in late October 1930. General Yang, who commanded the 60,000-man Seventeenth Field Army (also known as the Northwest Army), also served as governor of Shaanxi from October 1930. In June 1933, however, by decision of Chiang, he yielded the post of governor to the former secretary of the Generalissimo and one of his most trusted subordinates, Shao Lizi. The change hardly pleased General Yang, especially since Shao's wife, "an energetic and ambitious woman" who was terribly corrupt and sold positions in exchange for bribes, began to meddle in provincial affairs. General Yang complained about her to Chiang, but to no effect.[7] However, Shao Lizi and his wife were concerned only with civilian matters while military power in the province remained entirely in Yang's hands, especially since, starting in 1931, he also headed the so-called Shaanxi pacification administration. Zhang Xueliang did not intend to dispute Yang Hucheng's position, although his troops were much stronger than those of the Seventeenth Army. Both the Young Marshal and the general were strongly anti-Japanese, so they soon got along well with each other.

Meanwhile, Stalin continued to maneuver. He did not want to sign a mutual assistance pact with China because he was not eager to be drawn into a Sino–Japanese war, but he was afraid that Chiang would capitulate to the Japanese after concluding an anticommunist alliance with them. If that happened, not only would the CCP face the threat of complete destruction, but there would be a real danger of Japan, who relied on the resources of China, attacking the Soviet Union. Beginning in 1934 Stalin regularly received information from the Foreign Department of the Joint State Political Directorate (OGPU) and military intelligence of a probable Japanese incursion into the USSR. In the summer of 1934 the Mexican consul in Shanghai, Mauricio Fresco, informed the Soviets that "according to intelligence from Italian circles, Chiang Kai-shek had received news that Japan would start a war against the USSR in one to two months."[8] The report from the Mexican diplomat was not borne out, but tension on the Far Eastern borders of the USSR did not slacken.

Chiang also continued to maneuver, as he had earlier in trying to draw the USSR into conflict with Japan. He became increasingly convinced that to a decisive degree China's fate would depend on the outcome of the approaching Second World War that, as he saw it, would begin with a clash between Japan and the USSR.[9] At the same time, he understood very well that Stalin needed an alliance between China and the USSR in the future world war no less than he himself did.

Stalin thus had to deal with many circumstances. He tried consistently, via his ambassador, to instill in Chiang Kai-shek's mind the thought that "an agreement between the USSR and China was incomparably more advantageous to China than to the Soviet Union."[10] Nonetheless he realized that he did not hold all the trump cards. Chiang Kai-shek held quite a few of them. The question was who would use them and when to compel his partner to make concessions.

Sometime after being informed of Kong Xiangxi's proposal, Stalin replied to Chiang in his own distinctive way. From July 25 to August 20, 1935, in the Hall of Columns of the House of the Unions in Moscow the Seventh World Congress of the Comintern took place: at this convention the policy of the world communist movement was officially changed. Fearing German and Japanese invasions of the USSR, Stalin commanded foreign communists to abandon their struggle to overthrow their ruling classes and instead organize new united fronts with them: in the West, antifascist; in the East, anti-Japanese. Naturally, the idea of a new united front in China did not occur to Stalin in response to Kong Xiangxi's appeal. The decisions of the Seventh World Congress had been prepared earlier, starting in mid-1934, but they accurately reflected the Kremlin leader's dual policy vis-à-vis Chiang Kai-shek.[11] Despite the normalization of diplomatic relations and ongoing negotiations between Moscow and Nanjing regarding various pacts—nonaggression, mutual assistance—the Seventh Congress directed by Stalin made it crystal clear that the Comintern and the CCP intended to establish a united front in China with whomever it wished, only not with Chiang Kai-shek or other leaders of the Guomindang.

On October 1, 1935, the Comintern's Chinese language newspaper in Paris, the *Jiuguo bao* (National Salvation), in the name of the Chinese Soviet government and the Central Committee of the CCP, published "An Appeal to All Compatriots Regarding Resistance to Japan and National Salvation." The article called on all citizens of China to cease their civil strife, unite, and struggle against Japan. The document, dated August 1, 1935, had been drafted in July by a delegation of the CCP and the Comintern headed by Wang Ming (real name Chen Shaoyu), an ambitious young man of thirty, a member of the Politburo of the CCP CC since 1931, and approved by the Secretariat of the Executive Committee of the Comintern on September 24. Chiang Kai-shek, Wang Jingwei, Zhang Xueliang, and several other "national traitors" were excluded from the list of "compatriots." In the appeal they were labeled "disgraceful dregs" "with human faces, but hearts of beasts."[12]

Naturally, Chiang was not pleased with this document. It was obvious that Stalin was playing with him, like a cat with a mouse, first giving him hope for assistance in the struggle against Japan, then threatening a worsening of relations and continuation of the civil war. Just then, on October 4, the Japanese government gave the Chinese ambassador to Japan a document containing three principles for stabilizing the situation in East Asia. They were formulated by Minister of Foreign Affairs Hirota Koki. The Japanese demanded, first, that Chiang cease all anti-Japanese propaganda in China and stop depending on the Europeans and Americans; second, recognize the independence of Manchukuo; and third, in alliance with the Japanese imperial army, smash the communists in Northwest China.[13]

In theory Chiang was not opposed to receiving help from the Japanese in his struggle against the CCP, but he did not intend to surrender his independence. He adhered to this position even though, in the autumn of 1935, both the American and the British governments began to pressure him to become a realist and recognize Manchukuo.[14] But for Chiang, a staunch patriot and revolutionary, such a step was unacceptable. Instead, he decided again to clarify the position of the USSR. On October 19 he sent Kong Xiangxi to Ambassador Bogomolov, and Kong "secretly" informed the Soviet ambassador that that very evening the Generalissimo would be coming to his house to see him (Kong), and that the ambassador could come too if he wished. Naturally, Bogomolov would not let slip such an opportunity, and he met privately with Chiang that evening. Chiang straightforwardly proposed concluding a secret military agreement with the Soviet Union. In passing, he hinted that Japan was offering him a military alliance against Bolshevism but he didn't want that.[15]

Everything was perfectly clear, but Stalin was in no hurry to reply. Chiang, too, was content to wait, especially since just then problems flared up again inside the Guomindang. On November 1, 1935, an attempted assassination of Wang Jingwei occurred—as mentioned earlier, he had been serving as head of the Executive Yuan since January 1932, per an agreement with Chiang.

Various conflicts had erupted in the past three and a half years between the two ambitious leaders of the Guomindang. The first had occurred in August 1932, when Wang, in a perpetually gloomy frame of mind after the establishment of Manchukuo, finally exploded, demanding that Zhang Xueliang resign. He sent Zhang a hysterical letter blaming him for the loss of Manchuria and his unwillingness to defend Rehe Province. At the time, Chiang did not want to alienate the Young Marshal, whereupon Wang, supported by other members of the cabinet of ministers, demonstratively resigned. He had a right to be offended since Zhang had violated the government directive expressed in the formula "Resistance on the one hand and negotiations on the other," and Chiang had not punished him. Wang had obviously lost face.[16] T. V. Song, Chiang's brother-in-law, became the acting head of the Executive Yuan. Wang left for Shanghai and, later, in October, for France, fearing an assassination attempt by Chiang Kai-shek's Blue Shirts. The conflict came to an end a year later, after the shameful defeat in Rehe. In the spring of 1933 Zhang Xueliang finally stepped down at the request of Chiang Kai-shek himself. Only after this did Wang Jingwei return to China, and this time headed not only the Executive Yuan but also the post of minister of foreign affairs.[17] Again, with Chiang's full support, he pursued the same policy with respect to Japan: "Resistance on the one hand and negotiations on the other," but from the autumn on he began to emphasize the second dimension. Chiang did likewise. The two of them concluded, first, that they had to finish off the Communist Party, and, second, that active resistance to the Japanese could wait. Therefore he, too, no less than Chiang, began to evoke the hatred of patriotically inclined Chinese who accused both Chiang and Wang of taking the path of appeasing the Japanese "dwarfs."

It seemed that the Chiang-Wang coalition at the time was "firmer than ever,"[18] but that was really not so. Trying to whitewash the Generalissimo in the eyes of the public, his closest associates—especially Chen Guofu, Chen Lifu, and other members of the CC clique as well as the pro-Western faction headed by T. V. Song and Kong Xiangxi—began to spread rumors that Wang headed a pro-Japanese faction in the Guomindang. This was probably done at Chiang's directive or with his approval in order to shift responsibility for the policy of appeasement onto Wang alone. In reality Chiang was a greater proponent of this policy than Wang Jingwei.[19]

That is why Wang was a target of the attempted assassination. The assault took place during a photo session in the building of the Guomindang CEC just before the opening of the fourth session of the Sixth Plenum of the CEC. More than one hundred members of the CEC were lined up in front of the photographers when one of the photo correspondents cried out, "Death to the traitor of the motherland!" and shot Wang four times. Wang was wounded in the cheek, the left arm, and the spine. The fourth bullet missed. He was hospitalized, and the terrorist, wounded by Wang's bodyguard, was arrested. At Chiang's request, the head of one of the two secret services, Dai Li—who in China was called the Chinese Himmler—personally interrogated the terrorist. He ascertained that the man was an officer named Sun Fengming, a graduate of the Whampoa Academy who had served as a company commander in the Nineteenth Army during the Japanese attack on Shanghai.[20] He had wormed his way into the ranks of the journalists in order to kill Chiang Kai-shek, whom he considered the main enemy of the people. But to his disappointment Chiang had not taken part in the photo session, so Sun Fengming shot Wang Jingwei instead. According to Chen Lifu, Chiang was not feeling well before the session while others claimed he was in the toilet.[21] The next day the terrorist was executed, and his wife and sister-in-law were also shot along with several dozen other persons who were supposedly involved in the plot.

Chiang was beside himself.[22] Most of all because the incident cast a shadow on him. Naturally, Wang and his wife had some questions. Why was Chiang not at the photo session? How could the terrorist obtain an entry permit to the Guomindang CEC? Was he not acting under the orders of Chiang's own secret services? After all, he was a Whampoa graduate. Naturally, Chiang did all he could to convince Wang and his wife of his innocence, and they supposedly accepted his explanations—but a residue of doubt remained.

In Wang Jingwei's absence, on November 12, 1935, the sixty-ninth birthday of the great Sun, Chiang convened the Fifth Congress of the Guomindang. This forum, lasting eleven days, until November 22, was a real congress of unity. Even General Yan Xishan came to Nanjing to take part in it. In addition to 405 delegates with voting rights, 103 members of the CEC and the CCC took part as well as about 150 guests invited by the CEC and the National government. They represented 520,000 members of the party.

The main question was to work out a policy toward Japan. On November 19 Chiang himself delivered a report on this, formulating the following principle: "We shall not forsake peace until there is no hope for peace. We shall not talk lightly of sacrifice until we are driven to the last extremity, which makes sacrifice inevitable."[23] In other words, he let everyone know that for now he was not giving up his policy of appeasing the Japanese aggressors, but he did not intend to surrender to them. This declaration was his response to Hirota's three principles.

In elections for the new CEC, Chiang received the largest number of votes; Wang Jingwei was in second place, and in third was Hu Hanmin, who had been abroad since June 1935. Yet, by agreement with Chiang, the venerable Hu, Chiang Kai-shek's old opponent, was chosen as chair of the Standing Committee of the CEC. In the face of creeping Japanese aggression, Chiang had to unite all the leaders of the Guomindang around himself. It was not by chance that Chiang's old enemy, Wang Jingwei, received the key post of chair of the Political Council of the CEC, which controlled the government. Chiang himself became the sole deputy chair of both the Standing Committee of the CEC and the Political Council.[24] He demonstratively expressed the wish that the venerable Hu return as soon as possible to the homeland. On his instruction Minister of Finance Kong Xiangxi even sent Hu Hanmin 40,000 Chinese dollars for travel expenses, and in late December Hu left the French city of Lyons for home. On arriving in Canton, however, he firmly refused to go any further, to Nanjing, because he did not want to cooperate with Chiang Kai-shek. In this connection, Chiang wrote in his diaries, "I have heard that Hanmin is cursing the policy of the C[E]C and asserting that he will not come to Nanjing, people suppose that this is a misfortune, so what should I do: be quiet or rejoice?"[25]

Chiang didn't consider Hu Hanmin's absence from Nanjing a misfortune, although he preferred to have his enemy nearby in order to control him more easily.[26] Hu never did come to Nanjing, leaving the post of chairman of the Standing Committee of the CEC vacant. On May 9, 1936, at seven o'clock in the evening, he suffered a massive stroke, and three days later this famous comrade in arms of Sun Yat-sen died at the age of fifty-seven.[27]

Not long before that, in the spring of 1936, after spending half a year in the hospital, Wang Jingwei, together with his wife again departed to convalesce in Europe. Doctors had been unable to remove the bullet from his spine, and he was suffering both physically and emotionally.[28]

Thus neither of Chiang's opponents was able to fill the highest posts in the Guomindang. It is not known whether Chiang was involved in the death of Hu and the attempt on Wang Jingwei or was simply very lucky; Chiang's biographers do not believe he was guilty, although they have no proof of that.[29] Yet there is no doubt he was a big winner after the elimination of his rivals. Even formally all the power was now in his hands, as he was the lone deputy of the chair of the Standing Committee of the CEC and of the chair of the Political Council. After the Fifth Congress, in December 1935, for the second time he became the head of the Executive Yuan, in place of Wang Jingwei and Kong Xiangxi.[30] Chiang appointed Zhang Qun, his close friend and fellow student at the Baoding Academy and the Japanese Shinbu Gakko, as minister of foreign affairs in place of the wounded Wang.

While Chiang Kai-shek was busy at the congress, good news finally arrived from the Soviet Union. On November 19, the Deputy People's Commissar for Foreign Affairs in charge of Far Eastern affairs, Boris Spiridonovich Stomoniakov, informed Bogomolov that the USSR had agreed to sell weapons to Chiang. A month later, on December 14, Stalin, via Stomoniakov and Bogomolov, hinted to Chiang his readiness to discuss a secret military alliance with him. But unequivocally he stated that this potentiality depended on Guomindang relations with the CCP: "Without the implementation of a united military front of Chiang Kai-shek's troops with the units of the Chinese Red Army a serious struggle against Japanese aggression is impossible."[31]

Who would say that? It was the Chinese communists themselves, following Stalin's policy, who did not want a united front with Chiang. Most likely

Stalin was trying to compel Chiang Kai-shek to enter into negotiations with the communists first, notwithstanding their openly anti–Chiang Kai-shek position. In other words, he wanted Chiang to capitulate to him and the CCP.

According to a decision from Moscow, one of the secret agents of the Comintern Executive Committee, the son of Guomindang leftist Eugene Chen, who, as noted above, had served in 1933 as the minister of foreign affairs of the People's Revolutionary Government in Fujian, using his family ties (*guanxi*), met with leading members of the Guomindang to acquaint them with the Comintern's united front policy: those present included the chair of the Control Yuan Yu Youren, Feng Yuxiang, Sun Fo, Kong Xiangxi, T. V. Song, and the deputy chair of the Legislative Yuan Ye Chucang. Yu Youren, Sun Fo, and Feng Yuxiang informed Chiang of these meetings, and he decided to establish a small commission to study the problem.[32]

Although he had no intention of yielding, Chiang had long understood that he had to hold talks not only with the USSR, but also with the CCP. But he himself wanted to push the communists, who were on the verge of total defeat, into capitulating. Back in November 1935 he had begun building a bridge to the CCP, having secretly assigned his blood nephew Chen Lifu "to conduct negotiations with both the Chinese Communists and the Soviet Union."[33] Through intermediaries Chen was able to establish contact with some of the workers in the underground organizations of the CCP in Shanghai and Beiping, and his people initiated talks with them. At the same time, at T. V. Song's request, Song Qingling made contact with the Shanghai communists.[34]

At this point, Stalin's chances of getting Chiang himself to capitulate suddenly soared. In December 1935 a wave of anti-Japanese student protests rolled across China. It started in Beiping on December 9 and quickly spread to almost all the large cities in China. Crowds of students everywhere demanded that Chiang organize resistance to Japan, and various patriotic organizations of the Chinese intelligentsia quickly sprang up.[35] Chiang was in a tough position, and Stalin hoped he would become more compliant.

But the Chinese leader continued to play his own game. On December 19, 1935, he again met with Bogomolov in order to seek a compromise on the question of the CCP. He conveyed to Moscow a request to utilize as the foundation of Chinese–Soviet relations the principles formulated in the joint communiqué of Sun Yat-sen and Joffe of January 26, 1923. This document, as discussed earlier, plainly asserted that "at present the communist order or even the Soviet system cannot be introduced into China because of the absence of the necessary conditions."[36] It was a clever move, but Stalin did not respond to the request.

Then, on Christmas Day, December 25, Chiang sent Chen Lifu and Zhang Chong, the director of the Organization Department of the Guomindang CEC, on a secret mission to the USSR, but it ended inconclusively: Chen and Zhang turned back halfway there because Stalin did not want to meet with them.[37]

Chiang did not give up. After the New Year he ordered another trusted person, Deng Wenyi, the organizer of the Renaissance Society (Fuxingshe), to meet with Wang Ming, the head of the CCP delegation to the Comintern. Deng and Wang had *guanxi:* in 1925–27 they had both studied at the same Sun Yat-sen University in Moscow (incidentally, Chiang Kai-shek's son Chiang Ching-kuo was a student there too). Deng studied under the pseudonym Zatsepin, and Wang was Ivan Andreevich Golubev.[38]

Deng, who at the time was serving as military attaché of the Chinese embassy in Moscow, met with Wang three times between January 17 and 23. He made no secret of the fact that he had been sent by Chiang who "sincerely" and "for a long time had wanted to hold talks with the Red Army." In his words, Chiang was offering any form of a united front: either the CCP could again enter the Guomindang or it could continue to exist independently. The Generalissimo even offered to supply ammunition, weapons, and rations to the Communist Party, but he requested that the Soviet government be disbanded and the Red Army reorganized into the NRA. In this connection, Deng noted that Chiang wanted to send him (Deng) to Sichuan or Shaanxi to meet with the leaders of the CCP CC, but he was afraid "since there was no advance agreement from the Red Army side."

Pan Hannian, the Deputy Commissar for Foreign Affairs of the Chinese Soviet Republic, took part in the conversations. It was decided that Deng along with Pan "would head for Nanking for talks with Chiang Kai-shek," and then from Nanjing to the Soviet areas for discussions with Mao Zedong and other CCP leaders on "concrete measures for resisting Japan and national salvation." On January 23 Pan Hannian sent a letter to Chiang guaranteeing Deng Wenyi's personal safety in the territory of the Soviet areas.[39] The day before, Chiang, having been informed by Deng Wenyi of the success of the negotiations, told Bogomolov that he "considered it possible to reach an agreement with the [Chinese] Communist Party" but requested that the USSR "use its authority to convince the Red Army to recognize the actual government [in Nanjing]." But Bogomolov and then Stalin (via Stomoniakov) let Chiang know that the USSR was "unable to undertake or carry out" mediation between him and the CCP,[40] again pushing him to take the initiative.

By this time the CCP was weakened. Still, it was not destroyed. At the end of October 1935 the Chinese communists concluded their Long March. On October 22, in the tiny village of Wuqizhen in northern Shaanxi province, Mao Zedong announced the Long March had ended. Overall, the communists had marched 12,000 *li* (about 5,000 miles) from southeast to Northwest China.[41] Mao, to be sure, announced that they had gone 25,000 *li* (10,000 miles), which sounded more heroic. Of the 86,000 commanders and soldiers who had broken through the encirclement in October 1934, no more than 5,000 made it to the village. Yet one could not speak about the crushing defeat of the CCP.

The communists began to settle into a new Soviet area on the Shaanxi–Gansu–Ningxia border. There was still no radio link with the Comintern, so they knew nothing about the anti-Japanese united front policy. In February 1936 their troops invaded Shanxi province, where again, as they had done in the Central Soviet Area, they began looting and killing everyone they considered to be an exploiter. Otherwise, they could not have survived. Northern Shaanxi, where they ended up, was the poorest region of China. Moreover, in 1928–33, for several years prior to the arrival of Mao's forces, more than half a million people had died of starvation there. In many villages all children under the age of ten had died. Northern Shaanxi was almost depopulated, and those who survived were struggling through a miserable existence.[42] There was nothing the communists could take from them. Shanxi, the neighboring province of Shaanxi, was a different matter, as in Shanxi there were provisions to be had.

Chiang had to respond to the communists' banditry. Without breaking off his negotiations with Moscow and the CCP, he mobilized all his forces to surround and destroy Mao's forces in Shanxi.[43] The communists were compelled to return to neighboring Shaanxi.

Meanwhile, Chiang learned that on February 9, 1936, *Leningradskaia pravda* (Leningrad Truth) published a letter from his eldest son Ching-kuo to his mother, in which, as after the April 12, 1927, coup, Ching-kuo stigmatized his father in the worst terms: "What should be done, mother," the letter said,

> if your husband, Chiang Kai-shek, barbarously destroys thousands and tens of thousands of our brothers, betrays our people, and sells out

> the interests of the Chinese nation? . . . Now Chiang Kai-shek is propounding the theories and moral codes of Confucius. . . . [But] could it be, mama, that you don't remember who dragged you down from the second story by your hair? Was it not he? Whom you begged on your knees not to expel you from your home? Was it not he? Who drove my grandmother into the grave with his insults and beating? Not he? . . . Every honest Chinese must . . . struggle relentlessly against Chiang Kai-shek.[44]

On February 14 Chiang wrote in his diaries, "I received news that my son Jing [Ching-kuo] placed in a Moscow [actually Leningrad] newspaper a letter to his mother, in which he slandered his own father. I think the letter was fabricated, therefore, my heart is at ease."[45]

Chiang was correct: the letter really was false. It had been written on November 23, 1935, by Wang Ming, the head of the CCP delegation to the Comintern.[46] According to Ching-kuo, when he learned of its publication he got sick and spent thirteen days in the hospital.[47]

At this time Ching-kuo, who, as discussed above, from the time of his admission to Sun Yat-sen University of the Toilers of China in Moscow in November 1925, had gone under the Russian name of Nikolai Vladimirovich Elizarov, was living in the Urals, in Sverdlovsk. He was transferred there in November 1932, after graduate studies at the International Lenin School, and was serving as an assistant to the head of the No. 1 Mechanical Section of the Ural Machine Factory. In 1933 or 1934 he had become acquainted there with a fair-haired girl and orphan, the Komsomol member Faina Ipatievna Vakhreva, who was seven years younger than he.

Vakhreva had been born on May 15, 1916, in the village of Gavrilov-Yam, not far from Yaroslavl, where her parents, Ipatii Federovich and Ekaterina Petrovna, as well as her sister Anna, who was seventeen years older than she, worked in a linen spinning mill belonging to the merchant A. A. Lokalov. According to various sources, Ipatii Federovich, a Belorussian by nationality, had moved to Gavrilov-Yam from the city of Orsha. In Belorussian his name was pronounced Vakhrava, but, having moved to Central Russia—first to Vladimir province and then to Yaroslavl province—he changed it to sound Russian. Faina's mother died when Faina was six years old, in 1922, and her father in 1931. Faina was brought up by Anna, her "sister-mother."[48] Her family also had a nursing baby, a little brother, but he died soon after the death of Faina's mother. The same year her father died, Anna was sent to study in the

Machine Building Institute in the city of Sverdlovsk, and the fifteen-year-old Faina went with her. Faina initially studied in a technical school and after two years began to work as a lathe operator at the Ural Machine Factory. According to Ching-kuo, he fell in love with her at first sight. On March 15, 1935, after he had already been serving half a year as deputy editor of the factory newspaper *Za tiazheloie mashinostroenie* (For Heavy Industry), they got married. The young couple lived in communal apartment No. 19, at 4 Red Partisans Street, two steps from the factory. On December 14, 1935, their first child was born, to whom Ching-kuo gave the child name Ailun (He Who Loves Virtue), and Faina gave him the then modish name Eric. He was premature and weighed only a little more than 3.3 pounds, but Faina and Jiang tended to him. Thus Chiang had his first grandson, of whom he knew nothing, however, at that time.

On December 7, 1936, Ching-kuo was promoted from a candidate to a full member of the party, and in early 1937 he was appointed deputy director of the Organization Department of the Sverdlovsk Municipal Soviet.[49] He was recognized as a good person, and in a reference regarding him it was stressed that he "takes most active part in political life . . . stands out as a solid party man, a Bolshevik, actively upholding the general line of our party in all the work that he does."[50]

In publishing a false letter from Ching-kuo to his mother, Wang Ming presumably was not acting on his own. He must have received permission from the highest level, that is, from Stalin, because from 1925 on, the leader exercised personal control over all matters pertaining to relations with China. Evidently, Stalin once again wanted to wave his trump card in front of Chiang, who was in no hurry to capitulate. But the result was the opposite: Chiang did not take fright and continued to pursue the communists.

By this time Mao and other leaders of the party had acquainted themselves with the basic resolutions of the Seventh Comintern Congress. There was still no radio link with Moscow, but in mid-November 1935 a messenger from the CCP delegation to the Comintern, the old communist Lin Yuying (pseudonym Zhang Hao) arrived in Wayaobao, the capital of the Soviet area in northern Shaanxi. He brought Comintern documents, including the "August 1 Declaration." The leaders of the CCP discussed the documents over several days and approved them, because they were bound by Comintern discipline and, as always, depended on Moscow for financial and military support.

On November 25, 1935, the Central Committee of the CCP published an appeal to their fellow countrymen. It proposed that "all parties, factions, armies, societies, unions and various mass organizations, prepared to offer resistance to Japan, swiftly discuss conditions and methods for jointly repulsing Japanese aggression."[51] The next day Mao Zedong first addressed a proposal for a truce and joint operations against the Japanese to one of the commanders of the Northeast Army that was deployed in Shaanxi.[52] In essence, this was a goodwill gesture toward the commander of that army, Zhang Xueliang. It was to him that the message was addressed. One month later, on December 25, the Politburo of the CCP CC adopted "A Resolution on the Current Political Situation and the Tasks of the Party" that pointed the communists toward establishing "the broadest national united front." In conformity with the decision of the Comintern, the resolution was directed not only to Japanese imperialism but also to another "main enemy," "the chief national traitor Chiang Kai-shek."[53]

In December 1935 the Chinese communists established contact with General Yang Hucheng, who agreed in principle with the idea of an anti-Japanese united front, and in early 1936 they also sent a liaison to Zhang Xueliang. The liaison was a commander of one of the regiments of the Northeast Army whom they had taken prisoner two months earlier and whom the communists had subjected to their own propaganda. He conveyed to the Young Marshal the CCP CC's proposal to transform the civil war between the Red Army and the Northeast Army into an anti-Japanese war. According to Zhang Xueliang's later confession, the communists "touched his heart," which is not surprising. We know how he felt about the Japanese. By that time he had managed to establish contact with several members of the Communist Party in Shanghai, trying to explore the possibility of joint action with the CCP in the struggle against Japan. Soon Li Kenong, the head of the Liaison Bureau of the CCP CC (this is what the intelligence service of the Communist Party was called) met with Zhang Xueliang in the hamlet of Luochuan in northern Shaanxi province. In secret negotiations Zhang Xueliang did not agree just to one communist proposal: to struggle together also against Chiang Kai-shek.[54]

At the same time these negotiations were proceeding, on February 27 two members of the Shanghai organization of the Communist Party arrived in Wayaobao carrying a proposal to the leaders of the CCP from Chen Lifu, who was probably acting on Chiang's order, to begin direct consultations.[55] Unable to ask for Moscow's advice, Mao and his comrades, on their own recognizance, decided at a new session of the Politburo in late March 1936 not to rebuff Nanjing but rather to put forth a condition: the establishment of a government of national defense and a United Anti-Japanese Army.[56] On March 21 Kong Xiangxi "secretly" informed the Soviet ambassador that Chiang Kai-shek "is already holding talks with the Communist Party about a united front" and that "he is personally hoping for success."[57]

True, this meant little. Chiang took no further steps toward organizing a united front with the CCP, and the leaders of the CCP also did nothing concrete. But the communists ramped up their negotiations with Zhang Xueliang. On April 9 Zhou Enlai met with the Young Marshal in a Catholic church in the northern Shaanxi city of Yan'an. The talks took place in a friendly atmosphere, but Zhang continued to insist that the communists change their relations with Chiang. When Zhou replied evasively, the Young Marshal then offered a compromise formula: instead of the slogan "Oppose Chiang and oppose Japan" to call on the Chinese people: "To put pressure on Chiang and oppose Japan."

By midsummer 1936 Zhou and Zhang had met two more times, and Zhou finally agreed, but without consulting Mao and other CCP leaders, to change the party's slogan. Zhou and Zhang both burst into tears of joy, and Zhang soon sent the communists a substantial sum of money from his personal funds.[58]

But this too meant nothing. The Chinese communists stubbornly continued their anti–Chiang Kai-shek line, using every opportunity to weaken him. Thus on June 12 and 13 they published two declarations supporting the southwest militarists Chen Jitang, Li Zongren, and Bai Chongxi, who a week earlier had rebelled yet again against Chiang Kai-shek, declaring an "anti-Japanese campaign to the north."[59] The communists called this campaign a national revolutionary war "against the chief of the national traitors—Chiang Kai-shek."[60]

Stalin and the Comintern expressed dissatisfaction with the behavior of the CCP leaders in the conflict between Chiang and the southwestern militarists. But they did so rather late (on August 15, 1936) and in confidence.[61] So Chiang did not know about the complaint. But the treacherous conduct of the communists inevitably affected the Generalissimo's attitude toward negotiations, not only with the CCP but with the USSR as well. These negotiations had borne no real fruit. Moreover, on March 12, 1936, the USSR also badly harmed its relations with China by signing a protocol for mutual assistance with the Mongolian People's Republic (Outer Mongolia), providing for mutual support in case of war.[62] As indicated earlier, Chinese considered Mongolia a part of China, so Chiang naturally perceived this protocol as an unfriendly act. On April 7 and 11 his Ministry of Foreign Affairs sent official protests to the government of the USSR.[63]

Even commercial and economic relations between China and the USSR developed weakly. In 1935 commodity trade with the Soviet Union amounted to no more than US $9.5 million, whereas it was more than $247 million with the United States, China's chief trading partner; $182 million with Japan; $125 million with England; and almost $120 million with Nazi Germany.[64]

The promises of arms deliveries from the USSR remained unfulfilled, and Germany remained the main supplier of arms to China. In February 1936 China signed a very favorable credit agreement with the Nazis for 100 million Chinese dollars. The Germans agreed to provide this money to the Chinese for the purchase of arms in their country in exchange for supplying the Reich with raw materials, wolfram especially. In late June 1936 Chiang sent a large delegation of athletes to take part in the Berlin Olympics. They were accompanied by twenty-nine officials headed by Dai Jitao himself, the head of the Examination Yuan. Even though the Chinese athletes lost in all the competitions, not winning even a single medal, Chiang considered the trip a success: it was "a new level of [China's] international recognition."[65] Dai Jitao was received by Hitler as well as by Hjalmar Schacht, the head of the Reichsbank, Baldur von Schirach, the leader of the Hitler Youth, and Bernhard Rust, the Reichsminister of science, education, and national culture. Dai was very impressed by his meetings and talks, and, speaking before the Chinese athletes, he recommended that they cultivate in themselves the "great spirit" of the German people. (At this Olympics the Germans took first place in the unofficial medal count.)[66]

In July 1936, as a contribution to developing bilateral relations, the Nazis awarded Chiang Kai-shek the Honorary Sabre and Kong Xiangxi the Order of the Red Cross. Chiang's new chief military advisor, Alexander von Falkenhausen, who had replaced Seeckt in March 1935, like Seeckt did everything he could to train several model divisions for Chiang Kai-shek's army as quickly as possible. Chiang had known him since the summer of 1934, when Falkenhausen began to serve as chief of staff to Seeckt, and he respected this "cultivated, sympathetic, and musical" man[67] no less than he had Seeckt, who had left his post due to illness.[68]

In the summer of 1936 one of the chief lobbyists for China in Nazi Germany, General Walter von Reichenau, even proposed that Chiang sign a German–Chinese anti-Comintern pact, promising to increase military aid substantially.[69] Reichenau two years later occupied Czechoslovakia, seized Paris in 1940 as well as Kyiv and Kharkov in 1941, and bore the chief responsibility for the mass execution of Kievan Jews in the infamous ravine Babi Yar. In July 1936 the Nazis even signed a barter agreement with Chiang worth 100 million Reichsmarks (at the prevailing rate of exchange, more than US $40 million), and then new trade agreements for the supply of arms. In the short period between August 1934 and October 1937 several such agreements were concluded, for a total sum of 389 million Reichsmarks (about US $157 million).[70]

Although Chiang did not enter into a political alliance with the Nazis, his friendly relations with Hitler were very useful in his game with Stalin and the CCP. Not only could he frighten Stalin with this relationship, as with a hypothetical alliance with Japan, but by relying on support from the Germans he could blackmail the Kremlin chief by continuing his war against the CCP. Thus Chiang's maneuvers were no less subtle than Stalin's tricks.

Therefore, it is not surprising that in June 1936, after the rout of Mao's forces in Shanxi, Chiang launched a new offensive against the main Soviet area that embraced the north of Shaanxi and parts of the neighboring provinces of Gansu and Ningxia. On his orders, the commander of the Eighty-sixth Division of the Guomindang army, Gao Shuangcheng, suddenly attacked the communists and seized their capital, Wayaobao. The communists had to flee to the town of Bao'an, almost 300 *li* west of Wayaobao.[71]

In a strategic sense this changed nothing. The Chinese Red Army grew steadily and already comprised more than 25,000 fighters, and the population of the Soviet area of Shaanxi–Gansu–Ningxia was about half a million. The communists continued to play successfully with Zhang Xueliang, even proposing him as chair of the Northwest Government of National Defense that they were planning to establish. Moreover, they began to consider admitting him covertly into the Communist Party. Zhang himself expressed a desire to become a communist.[72]

Possibly the communists would have admitted him if, at the very end of June 1936, the Comintern's radio station had not succeeded in establishing a radio link with them. On August 15 the Secretariat of the Executive Committee of the Comintern transmitted Stalin's latest directives to the leaders of the CCP. They were received by General Secretary of the Executive Committee of the Comintern Dimitrov in a conversation with the Kremlin leader at the end of July. These directives were the basis of a telegram from the Secretariat of the Executive Committee of the Comintern to the Secretariat of the CCP CC, the text of which had been drafted by the Executive Committee of the Comintern in the last week of July and approved by Stalin on August 13. Most likely it was not received in China earlier than August 17.[73] This telegram clearly indicated that Stalin had begun to worry about the increasingly close relations between the Chinese Generalissimo and the Nazis. Chiang's obvious disinclination to make any concessions to the Soviet Union and the CCP on the question of the united front also disturbed him.

Stalin categorically forbade the admission of the "unreliable ally" Zhang Xueliang into the Communist Party and demanded that Mao and other leaders of the CCP enlarge the scale of the united front and change the CCP's negative attitude toward Chiang Kai-shek. Understandably, he said nothing about the fact that he himself had earlier demanded of the CCP that it conduct a struggle on two fronts, the Japanese and Chiang Kai-shek. The telegram said: "We think that it is wrong to put Chiang Kai-shek on a level with the Japanese aggressors. . . . For serious armed resistance to Japan, the participation of Chiang Kai-shek's army, or the greater part of it, is necessary. . . . For these reasons we consider it necessary that the Chinese Communist Party and the command of the Red Army officially propose entering into negotiations with the Guomindang and Chiang Kai-shek regarding a cessation of military actions and conclusion of a concrete agreement for joint struggle against the Japanese aggressors."[74] Mao and other CCP leaders were most likely not surprised by Moscow's change of course vis-à-vis Chiang. They already knew about it from Pan Hannian, the same person who, along with Wang Ming, had held talks in Moscow in January 1936 with Deng Wenyi, the military attaché of the Chinese embassy. After coming to Nanjing in April 1936 for talks with the Chen brothers Guofu and Lifu, and Zhang Chong about the united front, Pan maintained his link with the Comintern, using a personal code. At the request of the Guomindang officials he went to Bao'an, the new CCP capital, on August 8 to ascertain the attitude of Mao and other leaders concerning the united front. And he acquainted the party leaders with Moscow's new line regarding Chiang.[75] Naturally, observing intra-Comintern discipline, they enthusiastically supported this line. On August 10 they adopted a resolution to "recognize Nanjing as a great revolutionary force of the nationalist movement."[76] And fifteen days later they dutifully sent a letter to the Guomindang CEC proposing a cessation of the civil war and the start of negotiations.[77] "The essence of our policy is unity with Chiang Kai-shek in resistance to Japan," Mao declared following this turn of events.[78]

On September 1, 1936, Zhou Enlai sent a letter to Chen Guofu and Chen Lifu, his old acquaintances from the first united front, in which, in the name of the CCP CC, he proposed to the Guomindang that they should unite "with the

Soviet Union and with the Chinese Communist Party to fight against Japan."[79] After this, Chiang Kai-shek decided to give the communists a last chance to capitulate. Chen Lifu and Zhang Chong informed Zhou of Chiang's demands, which, if implemented, would induce Chiang to agree to end the civil war. The CCP would have to "strive to fulfill completely Dr. Sun's *San Min Chu I* [*sanminzhuyi,* Three Principles of the People] . . . abolish its policy of sabotage and sovietization, which aims at overthrowing the National government . . . stop the forcible confiscation of landlord property . . . abolish all existing soviets . . . abolish the name and insignia of the Red Army, which will be reorganized as the National Revolutionary Army and subject to control by the government's Military Commission [Council] to make ready to fight the Japanese."[80]

The communists agreed to everything but voiced a demand of their own: start a war against Japan. That was precisely what Chiang could not accept. The main reason was that he could not allow the CCP to impose their will upon him, the leader of the nation. He believed that he alone had the right to decide when the moment for self-sacrifice had finally come. As Ambassador Bogomolov reported to Moscow, Chiang could make up his mind about allying with the communists "only on the eve . . . of war with Japan and in connection with an agreement with the Sov[iet] Union."[81] At the end of 1936 he was still not ready for a war with Japan.

Chiang simply did not trust the communists, and he could hardly be blamed for this. After all, like many other anticommunists in both Asia and Europe, he was convinced that "the Comintern was always the most inveterately untruthful institution in the champion untruthful country [USSR]."[82] Therefore, rather than signing something with the CCP, he decided to finish it off in its lair, gathering his forces for a new, sixth punitive expedition.[83] Just then, in mid-September, he succeeded by dint of great efforts, including bribes, to resolve the problem of the southwestern militarists, compelling them to end their mutiny. Now he was able once again to deploy all his forces against the communists.

The knockout blow against the Communist Party was to be delivered by the Young Marshal Zhang Xueliang and General Yang Hucheng, whose forces, as noted above, were based along the borders of the Shaanxi–Gansu–Ningxia Soviet area. On October 22, 1936, Chiang flew from Nanjing to Xi'an, the capital of Shaanxi province, to coordinate the last anticommunist campaign. But there, on October 26, he received an appeal from forty-six leaders of the Communist Party sent to him and to the generals of the Guomindang troops stationed in the northwest. This time the communists requested an end to the offensive against the Red Army and again proposed direct talks about forming a united front against the Japanese aggressors.[84] Chiang, however, regarded their appeal as a deception. The communists, he asserted, "are undoubtedly international puppets [that is, agents of the USSR], and will sacrifice the Chinese people."[85] The Young Marshal did not see it that way and tried to persuade Chiang to end the punitive expedition and unite with the CCP. Chiang exploded in anger, shouting at him and rejecting his proposal as capitulation. "[Zhang Xueliang] understands nothing, and my heart is in pain from this," he wrote in his diaries.[86]

On October 29 he flew to Luoyang (Henan province), where two days later he celebrated his fiftieth birthday (by Western calculations he was still forty-nine but Chinese count the nine months spent in the womb, so he had every reason for the jubilee). Celebrations took place all around the country, and Chiang published an appeal to his fellow citizens in which, after describing his difficult childhood and acknowledging yet again his love for his mother, he asked his fellow citizens to help him achieve "his mother's instruction": to achieve the liberation of the Chinese nation.[87] At the request of Meiling, who was ill in Shanghai (she had developed an ulcer), he sent a plane to fetch her so she could spend his birthday with him. There were many guests at the festive table, including Zhang Xueliang and even Chiang's former foe Marshal Feng Yuxiang, and for each of them Meiling personally sliced a piece of a cake. The cake was decorated with fifty candles. Chiang again recalled his mother and grieved that he had been unable to follow her instructions. That same day Chiang and Meiling attended a military parade in honor of the celebrant. There was a twenty-one-gun salute, and everyone there bowed three times to Chiang.[88]

Apart from Meiling there were no other relatives at the banquet. Meiling's sisters, Chiang's sisters-in-law, were in Nanjing: his brother-in-law Kong Xiangxi was lying in bed with a high fever—he was suffering from schistosomiasis, and there was something wrong with his heart—so his wife, Song Ailing, was with him.[89] To Song Qingling, Chiang's birthday not only was not a holiday but the very worst of days. Chiang's brothers-in-law, T. V., T. L., and T. A. Song, were also unable to come. Nor were his children. Ching-kuo was still in Sverdlovsk, and Chiang's younger son Wei-kuo, on the very eve of the jubilee, October 21, and under the patronage of General von Reichenau, had left to acquire a military education in Nazi Germany. He sailed from Shanghai on the German ocean liner *Potsdam*.[90] He aimed to accomplish what Chiang himself, who had dreamed of traveling to Germany in his youth, had been unable to do. According to Wei-kuo's recollections, his father, seeing him off, said, "China should learn from a country that is solid, not fancy. We cannot do things yet in the fancy way. . . . Germany is the only country from which we can learn something. They can give us the base from which to develop our own style: firm and solid."[91] Wei-kuo congratulated his father in a telegram from Singapore.[92]

The greatest celebrations took place in the capital, where 200,000 persons, led by the chair of the government Lin Sen, gathered at the airport, and enthusiastically watched as 35 airplanes, soaring in the sky, wrote Chiang's official name, Zhongzheng. For Chiang's jubilee, funds were collected throughout China to purchase new airplanes, and by the end of October seventy-two had already been bought, and contracts for an additional thirty or so were being drawn up.[93]

The idea of collecting money to buy planes came from Song Meiling, who was an airplane enthusiast. On Donald's recommendation, her grateful husband soon appointed her, on November 9, 1936, head of the government aviation commission. This was a wise step. There was no airplane industry in China, and what was required of the head of the commission was basically the ability to negotiate with Western partners. In that capacity the charming Song, who spoke fluent English, could be very useful.

On October 31, even though it was Chiang's birthday, Zhang Xueliang again had an unpleasant conversation with him about the need for a united front with the CCP. Marshal Feng Yuxiang, who took part in the conversation, supported him. But Chiang flared up as usual and cursed them. "If one speaks of the forces of the Northeast Army in Xi'an, then their spirit and discipline have been undermined by the propaganda of the communist bandits," he wrote in his diaries that day. "Hanqing [Zhang Xueliang's honorific name] has no firm foundation."[94]

Chiang may have believed that he, like Confucius, having attained the age of fifty, "knew the will of Heaven,"[95] and was therefore absolutely right about everything and had no need to listen to the advice of either the young or old marshals. He would have been better off had he followed the example of Confucius's favorite pupil, Zi Lu (542–480 BCE), who, if one can believe Mencius, always rejoiced when he was told "he had a fault."[96]

The room in which Chiang Kai-shek was born. (Photo by the author)

Chiang Kai-shek's house in the village of Xikou. (Photo by the author)

Chiang Kai-shek, his mother, Mao Fumei (his first wife), and his son Ching-kuo (late 1910). (Courtesy of Academia Historica)

Chiang Kai-shek shortly after he joined Sun Yat-sen's party, the Chinese Revolutionary Alliance (Tokyo, 1908). (Courtesy of Academia Historica)

Chen Qimei, Chiang's closest friend and "blood brother." (Courtesy of Academia Historica)

Sun Yat-sen and Song Meiling. (Courtesy of Academia Historica)

Chiang Kai-shek when he was Commandant of Whampoa Academy (May, 12, 1924). (Courtesy of Academia Historica)

Guomindang leaders at the official opening of the Whampoa Academy. On the stage (*left–right*): Liao Zhongkai, Chiang Kai-shek, Sun Yat-sen, Song Qingling. The man in the white suit to the right of the stage is Sun Yat-sen's bodyguard, Morris Abraham Cohen (Changzhou Island, June 16, 1924). (Courtesy of Academia Historica)

Photo of Stalin that he sent to Chiang Kai-shek four days before the rout of the communists. The inscription reads: "To Chiang Kai-shek, the commander in chief of the Chinese National Army. To celebrate the Guomindang's victory and the liberation of China" (April 8, 1927). (Courtesy of the Russian State Archives of Social and Political History)

Wedding photograph of Chiang Kai-shek and his second wife, Song Meiling (Nanjing, December 1, 1927). (Courtesy of Academia Historica)

Chiang Kai-shek at the front during the Civil War (1932). (Courtesy of Academia Historica)

Chiang Kai-shek and Song Meiling celebrate Chiang's fiftieth birthday, according to the Chinese system of calculation (Luoyang, October 31, 1936). (Courtesy of Academia Historica)

Zhang Xueliang. (Courtesy of the Hoover Institution Archives)

Marco Polo Bridge, where the Sino–Japanese War began on July 7, 1937. The city of Wanping is in the background. (Photo by the author)

Chiang Kai-shek and Song Meiling (*third from right*), who is standing between her sisters Song Ailing (*to her left*) and Song Qingling (*to her right*) (Chongqing, 1940). (Courtesy of Academia Historica)

Chiang Kai-shek during his inspection tour in Sichuan Province (January 2, 1941). (Courtesy of Academia Historica)

Chiang Kai-shek in Chongqing (October 10, 1943). (Courtesy of Academia Historica)

Chiang Kai-shek and Song Meiling in India. Seated between them is Victor Alexander John Hope, governor-general and viceroy of India; Hope's wife, Doreen Maud Milner, is seated to Chiang's left (New Delhi, February 10, 1942). (Courtesy of Academia Historica)

Chiang Kai-shek with General Joseph Warren ("Vinegar Joe") Stilwell (March 6, 1942). (Courtesy of Academia Historica)

The Cairo Conference. Seated from left to right: Chiang Kai-shek, US President Franklin Delano Roosevelt, British Prime Minister Winston S. Churchill, Song Meiling (November 27, 1943). (Courtesy of Academia Historica)

Chiang Kai-shek with (*left–right*) China's Minister of Foreign Affairs T. V. Song, General Albert C. Wedemeyer, and General Patrick J. Hurley (Chongqing, November 1, 1944). (Courtesy of Academia Historica)

Chiang Kai-shek and General Claire Lee Chennault, commander of the US Fourteenth Air Force (March 24, 1945). (Courtesy of Academia Historica)

Chiang Kai-shek and Song Meiling with (*standing behind them, left–right*) General Chen Cheng, future governor of Taiwan; Chiang's son Ching-kuo; and Chairman of the Executive Yuan T. V. Song (Chongqing, October 3, 1945). (Courtesy of Academia Historica)

Chiang Kai-shek and Mao Zedong during negotiations on the peaceful unification of China (Chongqing, Fall 1945). (Courtesy of Academia Historica)

Chiang Kai-shek receiving reports on the course of the civil war against the Communists (May 1947). (Courtesy of Academia Historica)

Chiang Kai-shek, president of the Republic of China (Nanjing, May 20, 1948). (Courtesy of Academia Historica)

Chiang Kai-shek and Song Meiling with various family members, including Chiang Ching-kuo (*second row, far left*), Chiang Wei-kuo (*second row, second from left*), and Faina Chiang (*second row, fourth from left*), on the eve of Chiang's seventieth birthday, according to the Chinese system of calculation (Taipei, October 10, 1956). (Courtesy of Academia Historica)

Chiang Kai-shek delivers an appeal to eradicate "the Communist bandits" and return to the mainland (Taipei, November 12, 1962). (Courtesy of Academia Historica)

Chiang Kai-shek on his eighty-seventh birthday, according to the Chinese system of calculation (Taipei, October 1973). (Courtesy of Academia Historica)

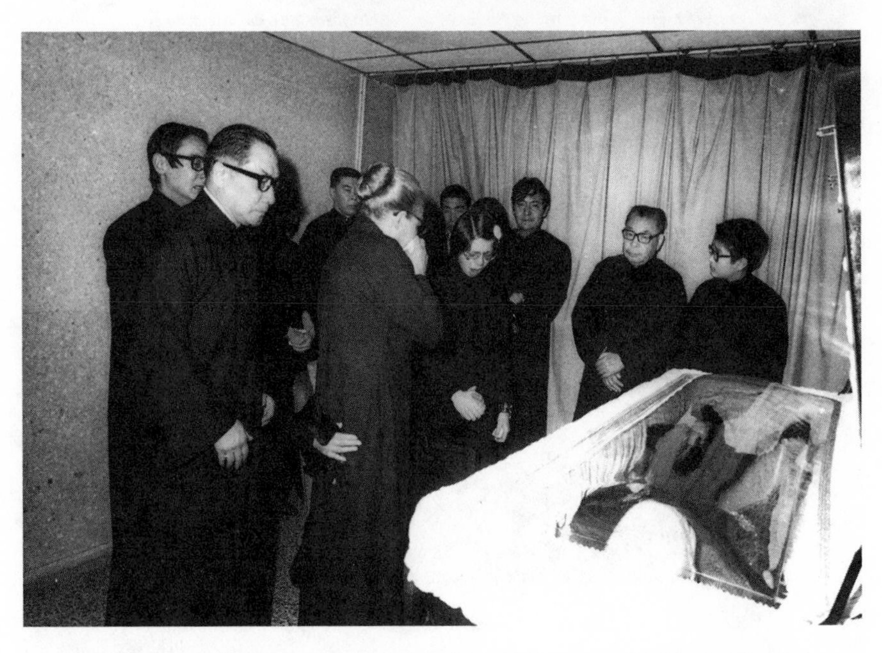

The late Chiang Kai-shek's relatives bid him farewell. (Courtesy of Academia Historica)

PART FOUR

# *Pro et Contra*

CHAPTER 13

# *Captivity in Xi'an*

The international situation continued to deteriorate. In November 1936 Germany, which Chiang considered a friendly country, signed an anti-Comintern pact with Japan.[1] The act was not directed at China, but it laid the foundation for the development of a strategic partnership between the Nazis and the Japanese, especially given that several months earlier the Germans had concluded a commercial treaty with Manchukuo, in essence thereby recognizing its faux independence.[2] Also in November 1936 the situation in Suiyuan province sharply deteriorated when the Mongolian khans, instigated by the Japanese, launched an offensive against Chiang's forces. A powerful anti-Japanese movement again surfaced in Chinese society, weakening Chiang Kai-shek's position.

Under these circumstances, Chiang had to rout the CCP as soon as possible in order to strengthen his position in negotiations with Stalin. Stubborn and authoritarian as he was, he wished to be victorious so that in future he could dictate his conditions to both the USSR and the vanquished CCP. "The cunning plans of the Russian ambassador and the red bandits still do not change, their goal is to keep me from getting stronger," he wrote in his diaries.[3]

Meanwhile, the disappointed Zhang Xueliang, after returning to Xi'an, met with Yang Hucheng, told him about his unsuccessful talks with Chiang, and asked for his advice. He felt that just as in Luoyang he had been doused with a bucket of cold water. The words of the Generalissimo, pronounced as always in his shrill Ningbo accent, kept sounding in his ears: "Those who are in favor of an alliance with the great traitors [communists] are worse than Yin Rugeng."[4] The general fell silent, and then he uttered something that initially struck Zhang like a bolt of lightning: "Next time when Mr. Chiang comes to Xi'an, do what they did in antiquity—*bingjian*."

The word meant "remonstration with the help of soldiers." *Bingjian* or *qiangjian* (remonstration with the help of force) was spoken of in the ancient commentaries to the classic Chinese chronicle *Chunqiu* (Spring and Autumn Annals). According to it, in the seventh century BCE Yu Quan, one of the commanders of the state of Chu, advanced his troops and arrested the ruler, Wen Wang, to compel him to correct his mistakes. He meant no harm to the head of state but, as a patriot, simply had recourse to the ultimate argument, trying to bring pressure to bear on the ruler. In a token of his loyalty to Wen Wang, he cut off his leg, after which the chastened ruler corrected his mistakes and even raised Yu Quan's rank. Zhang Xueliang did not want to cut off his leg, but the noble idea of *bingjian* stuck in his mind.

The final drop emptying Zhang's cup of patience was the arrest on November 23, 1936, by Chiang Kai-shek's police of seven patriotic organizers of the All-China National Salvation Association. The eighth organizer was Chiang's sister-in-law Song Qingling, but, needless to say, no one dared to arrest her. Zhang was shocked, and on November 27 he wrote a letter to Chiang imploring the Generalissimo to allow him and his troops to take part in the anti-Japanese struggle and to send his army to Suiyuan for this purpose. The day before he had already dispatched one of the units of his army to this province but without Chiang's permission.[5]

On December 3 Zhang again flew to Luoyang, where Chiang was assembling his generals and officers to discuss plans for the sixth anticommunist campaign. But, upon meeting with the Generalissimo, Zhang again failed to find a common language. Zhang Xueliang implored him to release the patriots, and Chiang again exploded: "You are the only one in the whole country who sees things as you do. I am the revolutionary government; what I do is revolution!"[6]

That day Japanese army marine units landed in the city of Qingdao, initiating a penetration into Shandong province. Stunned, Chiang decided to take immediate measures toward routing the CCP, stubbornly considering this, as he had before, a necessary condition for starting a war with Japan.[7] The next morning, December 4, he and forty-nine members of his staff drove to Xi'an to deal with the situation developing in the Northeast Army. He was in a fighting mood: during almost the whole trip he was rereading *The Art of War,* the treatise by the ancient Chinese philosopher Sun Zi.[8] The Young Marshal left for Xi'an after the Generalissimo.

Chiang arrived in Xi'an or, to be more precise, in the hamlet of Huaqingchi (Beautiful and clean hot springs) in the northwest suburbs that evening at nine o'clock. He loved to lodge there in the antique residence of the Tang dynasty emperor Xuanzong (Li Longji), surrounded on all sides by picturesque hills and famed for its mineral springs. For some reason he liked the one-story, rather gloomy *Wujianting* (Five-room Pavilion) in the southwestern wing of the park complex.

On December 5 he delivered a hysterical speech to the cadets of the Xi'an Military Academy, appealing to them to smash the red bandits, and two days later, according to the reminiscences of the Young Marshal, the Generalissimo shouted at him again: "Except in the Northwest and except for you, Chang Hsüeh-liang [Zhang Xueliang], no one dares talk with me in the manner as you did and none dare criticize me. I am the Generalissimo; I do not err; I am China; and China cannot do well without me!"[9] "Mr. Chiang was very stubborn, very conservative, too conservative," Zhang Xueliang recalled many years later. "If one could imagine himself the emperor, then he was the emperor. . . . He could allow no one to undermine his authority. I undermined his authority."[10]

After four days the situation in Xi'an worsened. In response to a speech on December 8 by the Japanese minister of war threatening China anew, the next day, the one-year anniversary of the anti-Japanese demonstrations in Beiping, more than ten thousand students came out on the streets. They demanded an end to the civil war and the unification of all forces against Japan. Along the road from Xi'an to Chiang Kai-shek's residence the students were met by police, who opened fire on them. Two students were wounded. By mere chance they were children of one of the officers of the Northeast Army.[11] But the students continued their procession, and a while later, on the bridge across the Wei River not far from the residence, their path was blocked by troops. A massive loss of life was avoided only because the Young Marshal rushed to the scene and with tears in his eyes begged the students to turn back. "As a patriotic military man," he said to the students, "[I] also wish to engage in anti-Japanese resistance." He promised he would repeat students' demands to Chairman Chiang Kai-shek. "Trust me," he said. "If you trust me, I will answer you in a week." Following Zhang, many students also burst into tears.[12]

The next day Chiang received the Young Marshal in his pavilion. Zhang Xueliang began to plead for the students, but Chiang, furious once again, began to shout at him as usual: "The only way to deal with these patriotic youth is with machine guns!" Devastated, Zhang Xueliang returned home. That same evening Chiang received Yang Hucheng, but they too failed to achieve a mutual understanding. Before going to bed, Chiang wrote in his diaries, "My heart is not at peace. . . . I feel bitterness and indignation."[13]

Zhang and Yang Hucheng understood that it was no longer possible to endure the willful Chiang Kai-shek, who had simply left them no choice. Yu Xuezhong, the commander of the Second Army and governor of Gansu, who was also in Xi'an, supported them. Yang and Yu were so indignant at Chiang's behavior that they did not even attend the farewell dinner the Generalissimo gave on the evening of December 11; he intended to fly out from Xi'an the next day, Saturday the twelfth.[14] The cautious Zhang Xueliang, however, did come to the dinner, but Chiang noticed that he was excited and confused and simply not himself. Before going to bed Chiang pondered this, prayed to God, and decided to be on guard. As the great military strategist of All-under-Heaven Zhuge Liang (181–234 CE) said, "Preparedness against the unexpected is a way of good government."[15] Afterward, Chiang calmed down and fell asleep.[16]

When he awoke, dawn had already broken. His watch showed it was five thirty. He arose, did his usual half hour of calisthenics, and was getting ready to dress when suddenly he heard gunshots. He thought that bandits, possibly communists, were attacking the residence. Throwing a light gown over his nightshirt (he never wore pajamas), he jumped out of the window, ran to a fence, climbed over it, badly injuring his side, and then jumped into a ditch that encircled the residence. He was wracked by a terrible pain. On falling from a nine-meter height, he had severely struck his coccyx on the frozen ground. Barefoot after losing his slippers but heedless of the icy wind, he ran along the path into the hills. Two servants followed him. Climbing farther up into the snow-covered hills, Chiang discovered a narrow crevice in one of the hills and took refuge within it. Later he would say that God had pointed out the hiding place to him.[17] He did not know what had happened at his residence. He could not conceive that he was being attacked by soldiers whom the Young Marshal had sent to arrest him.

Parting with Chiang after dinner, at one o'clock on the night of December 12, Zhang Xueliang had assembled the highest officers of the Northeast Army at his headquarters and informed them of his intention to resort immediately to *bingjian* (remonstration with the help of soldiers). Afterward he issued an order to the chief of his personal guard, the twenty-six-year-old Captain Sun

Mingjiu to set out at the head of a detachment of 120 troops to Huaqingchi and arrest Chiang Kai-shek. But he emphasized: "If our plan succeeds, we might be alive tomorrow, but if it fails, we might not be alive."[18]

At five-thirty in the morning Captain Sun's detachment arrived on station and approximately half an hour later attacked Chiang's residence. They engaged in a battle with Chiang's guards, killing forty of his eighty bodyguards and gendarmes. As a result they lost time and gave Chiang the opportunity to flee.[19] They did not find him until nine o'clock in the morning. Barefoot and pitiful, he was shaking severely from the cold and at first was unable to say even a word. In his haste, he had forgotten his false teeth.[20] The captain saluted Chiang Kai-shek in accordance with military protocol. Then, with difficulty, Chiang finally mumbled: "If you are my comrades, shoot me now and finish it all."

"We will not shoot," replied Sun, with tears rolling down his cheeks. "We only ask you to lead our country against Japan. Then we shall be the first to cheer our Generalissimo."

"Call Marshal Chang [Zhang] here, and I will come down," Chiang Kai-shek said.

"Marshal Chang is not here. The troops are rising in the city; we came here to protect you."

Hearing these words, the Generalissimo, it seemed, calmed down and requested a horse be brought to him so he could descend the hill.

"There is no horse here," Sun replied. "But I will carry you down the mountain on my back."

And he went down on his knees before Chiang Kai-shek. After a brief delay the Generalissimo scrambled up onto the captain's broad back. Taking the Generalissimo to a car, the chief of Zhang Xueliang's guard said at the end, "The past is past. From now on there must be a new policy for China."

"I am sure," Chiang Kai-shek said sarcastically, "that Marshal Chang has an excellent policy for China."

"This is a time of national crisis," Sun parried. "We hope the Generalissimo will receive the demands of the people."

"I am always ready to consider the demands of Marshal Chang," Chiang Kai-shek pronounced.

"The one urgent task for China is to resist Japan. This is the united demand of the men of the Northwest. Why do you not fight Japan, but instead give the order to fight the Red Army?"

"I never said that I would not fight Japan," replied Chiang indignantly.

"But the Tungpei [Dongbei, Northeast] army demands that you fight Japan as soon as possible, for their homes have been seized by the enemy, and all China suffers because of their loss."

"I am the leader of the Chinese people," Chiang suddenly burst out. "I represent the nation. I think that my policy is right, not wrong."

"If you represent the Chinese people," said Sun, "why do you not resist Japan? This is the demand of the whole Chinese nation. How can you claim to represent them when you do not carry out their demands?"

"I am a revolutionary," the Generalissimo said, terminating the dispute. "I am always ready to sacrifice myself. I have never changed my views; and even though you hold me prisoner, my spirit will never submit to another's."[21]

Meanwhile, soldiers from Yang Hucheng's army arrested the civil governor of Shaanxi province, Shao Lizi, who had given the order to disperse the student demonstration of December 9, his wife, who was wounded during her arrest, as well as persons in Chiang Kai-shek's retinue. Then, on the ancient Bell Tower (Zhonglou) constructed in the center of the city in the 1380s during the reign of Zhu Yuanzhang, founder of the Ming Dynasty, an enormous poster was hung supporting the victory of the supposed "United anti-Japanese forces."

By ten thirty that morning Chiang was brought to Xi'an, to Yang Hucheng's headquarters, where, to his surprise, he was greeted not only by Zhang Xueliang and Yang Hucheng, but also by a military orchestra and a guard of honor. Zhang and Yang evidently meant him no harm and were acting in strict accordance with the tradition of *bingjian.* But Chiang as always was unable to control himself. He began to yell hysterically at Zhang: "If you are my subordinate, take me out of here immediately. If you are not my subordinate, shoot me now."

Turning aside, Zhang said, "You are really stubborn."[22]

Chiang was placed under house arrest, and the mutineers sent an open appeal containing eight demands to the Guomindang CEC, the chair of the Nanjing government Lin Sen, and to other state officials and editors of various newspapers: reorganization of the government on a democratic basis; cessation of the civil war; release of all political prisoners, in the first place the seven patriots arrested in Shanghai; the development of a mass patriotic movement; provision of political freedoms to popular organizations; fulfillment of the behests of the *zongli* (Sun Yat-sen); and the prompt convening of a conference on national salvation. It was transmitted by telegraph on December 12 and on the following day published in the Xi'an newspaper *Jiefang ribao* (Liberation Daily).[23] On December 12 Marshal Zhang also sent personal messages to Chiang's brother-in-law Kong Xiangxi, the second-ranking person in the government, and to the Generalissimo's wife, Meiling. He tried to calm her, declaring that it was only a matter of "asking Mr. Jie [Chiang Kai-shek] to remain temporarily in Xi'an."[24]

Meanwhile, soldiers in the city went on a rampage of pillaging that did not abate for three days. The servicemen in the Northwest Army set the tone. Almost all the banks, including the Young Marshal's main bank, warehouses, and stores were emptied. Similar rampages occurred in Lanzhou, the capital of Gansu, the home ground of General Yu Xuezhong, who supported the mutiny.[25]

Prior to the arrest of Chiang, most likely right after Zhang Xueliang's meeting with the highest officers of the Northeast Army, that is, around two o'clock in the morning, a CCP representative at Zhang Xueliang's headquarters, Liu Ding, sent an urgent coded telegram to the communist leaders in Bao'an informing them about Zhang's decision to arrest Chiang.[26] Sometime later, between three and five o'clock in the morning, Zhang Xueliang himself sent a top priority telegram to Mao Zedong and Zhou Enlai: "Acting in the interests of the Chinese nation and from the perspective of resisting Japan, heedless of consequences, today we have arrested Chiang Kai-shek in order to compel him to release the patriots, reorganize, and unite the government. What do the elder brothers think about this? Please respond quickly."[27]

The leaders of the Communist Party were ecstatic upon receiving this. All of the words about a united front with Chiang Kai-shek were immediately forgotten. At a mass meeting the communists adopted a resolution demanding a "mass trial" to judge Chiang as a traitor; in Bao'an there was "wild jubilation."[28] According to Zhang Guotao's reminiscences, "Some of us [leaders of the CCP] said, 'It serves Chiang Kai-shek right!' Others said, 'Bravo, Chang Hsue-liang [Zhang Xueliang]. . . .' Mao Tse-tung [Zedong] . . . was laughing like mad."[29]

At midnight on December 12 Mao and Zhou radioed a reply to Zhang, saying that Zhou Enlai intended to go to Xi'an "to discuss the big plan."[30] Twelve hours earlier, at noon, they forwarded Zhang Xueliang's telegram to the Secretariat of the Executive Committee of the Comintern.[31]

There it was received but not deciphered until the thirteenth. Dimitrov also rejoiced. "The optimistic, favorable assessment of Zhang Xueliang. The Sov[iet] Union should respond with restraint and boldly react to the anti-Soviet campaign in connection with the events in Xi'an," he wrote in his diaries.[32]

But his enthusiasm collapsed after he read the editorial in the main Soviet newspaper, *Pravda* (Truth) on the morning of December 14. There Zhang Xueliang's uprising was characterized as intrigues on the part of "pro-Japanese elements in China" who were employing "all means to facilitate Japanese imperialism's aim of enslaving the country." A similar thought was published in another Soviet newspaper, *Izvestiia* (News).[33] The same papers published a TASS (Telegraph Agency of the Soviet Union) statement refuting information of the Japanese news agency Dōmei Tsushin (United News Agency) that Zhang Xueliang supposedly was receiving support from the USSR. Dimitrov understood that this was the position of Stalin, who had also received news about the events in Xi'an on December 13.[34] Therefore, he immediately changed his point of view and convened a meeting to discuss Chinese affairs with his most trusted associates. Afterward he wrote a letter to Stalin placing blame for the arrest of Chiang Kai-shek not only on Zhang Xueliang, but also on the leaders of the CCP, evidently trying to distance himself from them: "It is hard to imagine that Zhang Xueliang undertook his adventurist action without coordinating with them or even without their participation."[35] To confirm this he even sent Stalin a report from one of the leading persons in the Communist Party.

But Stalin probably already knew about Dimitrov's initial, joyful reaction to the arrest of Chiang Kai-shek (the Deputy People's Commissar for Foreign Affairs Stomoniakov witnessed how enthusiastic Dimitrov had been, and he might have reported this to him). Several hours later, at midnight, Stalin called Dimitrov. Without concealing his irritation, Stalin asked, "Are the events in China taking place with your sanction?"

"No!" a frightened Dimitrov exclaimed.

"This is the greatest gift that one could give Japan."

"That is how we, too, see these events."

"What's with your Wang Ming? Is he a provocateur? He wanted to send a telegram saying they should kill Chiang Kai-shek."

The flabbergasted Dimitrov said he knew nothing about this.

"I will send you this telegram!" Stalin said, slamming down the phone.[36]

Whether there was a telegram is not known. Probably not, but Stalin was obviously dissatisfied with the position of the Comintern leadership. After all, the execution of Chiang would inevitably exacerbate the civil war in China, making the country easy prey for Japanese imperialism, which, in the future, relying on Chinese resources, could strike a blow against the USSR. Moreover, Stalin understood that Wang Jingwei might take over from Chiang, and this did not bode well at all. While undergoing treatment in Germany, Wang had met with Hitler. Stalin did not know what they had talked about, but he had grounds for fearing that if Wang came to power China might join the anti-Comintern alliance.[37]

The euphoria in the CCP from Chiang's arrest had not abated. On December 15 the Politburo of the Central Committee of the CCP sent a pointed letter to the Nanjing government and the Guomindang, that read, "With regard to the demands [of the Xi'an mutineers], there is nothing to say but approval. . . . Is it permissible for patriots and leaders of the Guomindang to submit without principle to Chiang Kai-shek and the pro-Japanese faction that cringes before Japan and oppresses the people. . . . If you want to dissociate yourselves from Chiang Kai-shek and the pro-Japanese faction, you must show resolve and accept the demands of Zhang Xueliang and Yang Hucheng—end the war that has begun, remove Chiang Kai-shek from his position, and hand him over to a people's court."[38] (The communist leaders were not embarrassed that neither Marshal Zhang nor General Yang had demanded Chiang's dismissal or handing over to a court; it was enough that they, the communists, wanted this.)

But ultimately they succeeded in conforming to the Kremlin's policy dictated by Stalin. On December 16, in his office in the Kremlin, Stalin discussed the situation with Dimitrov, Secretary of the Comintern ECCI Dmitrii Zakharovich Manuilsky, and four members of the Politburo of the Bolshevik party: Molotov, Kaganovich, Voroshilov, and Ordzhonikidze. After this a directive from the Secretariat of the Executive Committee of the Comintern was dispatched to the Central Committee of the CCP, ordering the Chinese communists to come out "decisively for a peaceful resolution of the conflict" on the basis of reorganizing the government by means of including within it "several representatives of the anti-Japanese movement, supporters of China's territorial integrity and independence," guarantees of "the democratic rights of the Chinese people," an end to "the policy of destroying the Red Army," and the establishment of "cooperation with it in the struggle against Japanese aggression" as well as "cooperation with those states that sympathize with the liberation of the Chinese people from the offensives of Japanese imperialism [that is, with the USSR]."[39]

This enciphered telegram arrived in Bao'an on either December 17 or December 18. Due to some technical difficulties, however, parts of it did not transmit. Mao was not able to read the entire text until December 20.[40] But this changed nothing. By then he and other CCP leaders had acquainted themselves with the article in *Pravda* and the TASS statement, which left no doubts about the position of Stalin and the Comintern. Moreover, they had read the appeal of the Xi'an mutineers to the Guomindang CEC and the Nanjing government, and it must have been clear to them that neither Zhang nor General Yang intended to judge and execute Chiang Kai-shek. Their goal was simply a romantic *bingjian,* that is, "a remonstration with the help of soldiers."

Late on the night of December 17 Zhou Enlai arrived in Xi'an. After meeting with Zhang Xueliang he sent a telegram to Mao and other CCP leaders in which he proposed a compromise formula: "In order to avert the attack of the Chiang Kai-shek faction, ease our split with Nanjing, and promote an all-China [patriotic] movement, it would be possible for tactical reasons to say that we will guarantee Chiang's safety, but [in this connection] make a declaration that if Nanjing deploys troops and unleashes a civil war, Chiang's safety will not be guaranteed."[41] On the 18th the Central Committee of the CCP sent an appeal to the Guomindang CEC phrased in the spirit of Zhou's telegram. The statement contained an appeal to establish an anti-Japanese united front on the basis of the democratization of the Nanjing regime. The following day the CCP CC and the Soviet government of China sent another letter to Nanjing and Xi'an calling on both sides to settle the conflict peacefully.[42] Meanwhile, Zhou met with General Yang, who thought that Chiang could be freed only if he affixed his signature under the eight points formulated in the mutineers' address of December 12.[43]

All this time Chiang was in a foul mood, lying on a bed wrapped in a blanket. He barely touched his food despite the urging of Zhang Xueliang, who repeatedly excused himself for the forced inconvenience. Unlike Yang Hucheng, he was not happy to have involved himself in this dangerous business. The looting carried out by the soldiers of the Northwest Army greatly disturbed him, and he was terribly frightened by Chiang's obstinacy. Therefore, he wanted to wrap up the *bingjian* as quickly as possible and kept begging Chiang to provide at least an oral commitment to end the civil war and head a unified countrywide resistance to Japan.[44] But Chiang would not even discuss this. "Either for your own sake or for the sake of the nation, the only thing for you to do is to repent at once and escort me back to Nanjing," he told the Young Marshal. "You must not fall into the trap set by the Communists. Repent now before it is too late."[45]

At this time the Guomindang leaders in Nanjing were deciding what to do. They learned of Chiang's arrest at one o'clock in the afternoon of December 12 and soon received Zhang and Yang's demands. Meiling and Kong

Xiangxi were in Shanghai and therefore received news of the events in Xi'an only at eight o'clock that night.[46] They departed for Nanjing immediately, deciding that the first to fly to Xi'an would be Chiang's advisor, Donald, a close friend of Chiang's for three years. Donald, as discussed earlier, had also been an advisor to the Young Marshal, and Meiling knew he still had influence over Zhang Xueliang. They were most concerned about whether Chiang was alive. Donald had no doubt that Chiang was alive, and therefore Meiling, Kong Xiangxi, and T. V. Song immediately favored a peaceful resolution of the conflict as long as their relative's life was preserved. Without Chiang Kai-shek their family would lose all of its power. However, they encountered resistance from Minister of Military Administration He Yingqin, the willful and decisive general who had begun to transfer troops to the border of Shaanxi province with the aim of punishing the mutineers. Warplanes began patrolling over Xi'an, repeatedly threatening to begin a bloody bombardment. General He was apparently not very worried about Chiang's safety. In the worst-case scenario he himself could lead the country. Looking steadily into Meiling's eyes, General He repeated over and over again: "He [Chiang Kai-shek] is dead, and we will give the order to attack." Assuming the duties of the Generalissimo, he immediately dismissed Zhang Xueliang from all his posts, thereby placing him outside the law. Only by dint of great efforts were Chiang Kai-shek's relatives able to convince the militant commander to wait while they conducted negotiations with Zhang Xueliang.[47]

By Monday, December 14, Donald was already in Xi'an, and at five o'clock in the afternoon he visited Chiang, who was still being held in Yang Hucheng's residence in the center of town, in the so-called Yellow Palace, a massive one-story building with a colonnade (it now houses the People's Government of Shaanxi province). He found Chiang lying on a wooden bed, wrapped in a hooded blanket and turned toward the wall. There was nothing in the room apart from the bed, a pair of twig brooms in the corner, and a honey bucket. Donald, who didn't speak Chinese, addressed Chiang in English: "Greetings, Gissimo!" He always called him this, humorously abbreviating Chiang's title of Generalissimo. Incidentally, in the same way he called Meiling "Missimo," from the words madame and generalissimo.

Chiang immediately turned over, sat up on the bed, and began sobbing. "I knew you would come," he said. Zhang Xueliang translated.[48]

The room was rather gloomy and unfit for habitation, and Donald, with Zhang's approval, therefore persuaded Chiang to move to a more suitable place: the private house of General Gao Guizi, the commander of the Eighty-fourth

Division of the Northwest Army, built just three years earlier. The next day, December 15, Donald flew to Luoyang to call Meiling and calm her since the connection to Xi'an was not working. He really was a good friend. Learning that her husband was alive, Meiling sent Chiang a telegram: "I implore you to agree to resist Japan, you don't need to die in the arms of the enemy."[49]

On December 20 T. V. Song flew into Xi'an. Meeting him, Zhang said at once that he was ready to settle everything peacefully and escorted him to the Generalissimo. T. V. Song handed Chiang a letter from Meiling which read, "Should T. V. fail to return to Nanking [Nanjing] within three days I will come to Shensi [Shaanxi] to live and die with you."[50] Chiang again began to cry bitterly, and T. V. Song had to calm him down, saying that "the whole world was concerned and sympathizes with him." He tried to cheer up the Generalissimo. They discussed the probability of a military operation by government troops against Xi'an, and Chiang said this was "the only way." But T. V. Song vehemently objected, noting that an attack against the mutineers would not only exacerbate the civil war but create a mortal danger to the life of Chiang himself, notwithstanding Zhang's assurances. He was not mistaken. That evening Zhang Xueliang told him frankly that "if war once broke out on a large scale, the committee [of the rebels] had decided to hand the Generalissimo to the communists for safekeeping."[51]

T. V. Song understood the sarcastic hint. He was very alarmed. On the morning of December 21 he met with Chiang again. Chiang gave him three wills, to the people, to his wife, and to his two sons, and asked Song to show them to Marshal Zhang. His readiness to die but not to compromise surprised Donald, who believed that Chiang "would act stubbornly," yet neither Donald nor T. V. Song was able to make him change his mind. At midday they flew off from Xi'an to Nanjing.[52]

Prior to their departure Chiang implored T. V. Song not to allow Meiling to come to Xi'an, but she had decided to come to persuade Zhang Xueliang to free her husband quickly. There was a rumor that at sometime in the 1920s Meiling and Marshal Zhang had had a love affair.[53] Whether this is true is not known, but that the Young Marshal's pulse quickened in his meetings with the first lady of China is a fact. That is why Meiling decided to use all of her charm to help out her husband. "Mr. Donald had laid the foundations, T. V. had built the walls, and it would be I who would have to put on the roof," she thought, having in mind negotiations for a peaceful settlement of the Xi'an Incident.[54] T. V. Song supported her decision, figuring that only she would be able to make an impression on the stubborn Generalissimo.[55]

Meiling flew to Xi'an on December 22, accompanied by T. V. Song, Donald, the chief of the secret services Dai Li, and another general. Before takeoff she held out a small revolver to Donald. "Shoot me if hostile troops seize me when we land," she requested.[56] But no one arrested her. The Young Marshal himself met her at the gangway, courteously greeted her, and escorted her to her husband. Seeing her, Chiang was unable to restrain his emotions. "I thought I was dreaming," he recalled. Under Meiling's influence, he finally agreed to several demands of the putschists: "reshuffle the government, hold a national salvation conference three months from now, reorganize the Kuomintang [Guomindang], and approve an alliance with Russia and cooperation with the Communist party."[57] He instructed T. V. Song to conduct negotiations with Zhang, but he categorically refused to sign any document. He gave only oral promises.[58]

On December 23 T. V. Song met with Zhou Enlai in both the morning and afternoon, and Meiling met with him in the afternoon. After lengthy negotiations the next morning with both Zhang and Yang they were finally able to work out a solution that was acceptable to all sides, laying the foundation for the formation of a new united front, reorganization of the government, and resistance to Japan. It was decided to end the civil war, legalize the Communist Party, and, after a while, redesignate the Red Army as one of the units of the NRA.[59]

On the evening of December 24 Zhou Enlai visited Chiang Kai-shek.[60] This was their first meeting since 1926. Back then Zhou had been serving under Chiang at the Whampoa Academy, but now he addressed Chiang Kai-shek courteously, but with dignity. "Mr. Chiang! We have not seen each other for ten years. You have noticeably aged." Chiang nodded his head, sighed, then suddenly decided to remind Zhou that he was his commander, even if in the past. At issue was that Chinese, with their clan mentality and relations between elders and the young both inside and outside of the family, had a sacral, unchangeable character. "Let the lord be a lord; the subject a subject; the father a father; the son a son," said Confucius.[61]

Chiang said, "Enlai, you are my subordinate and must follow my orders."

Zhou parried: "If Mr. Chiang is able to change the policy expressed in the formula, 'Before we fight the external enemy, we must first establish peace inside the country,' end the civil war, unite the country to resist Japan, not only will I follow the orders of Mr. Chiang, but even our Red Army will be able to come under the command of Mr. Chiang."[62]

Chiang understood everything and quickly ended the conversation, saying, "The suppression of Communists will stop, there will be an alliance with the Red Army to resist Japan." He added that the unification of China will be brought about, and the unified country will be under his (Chiang's) leadership. He also appointed T. V. Song, Song Meiling, and Zhang Xueliang as his plenipotentiary representatives "in discussing the solution of all the problems" with Zhou. Chiang promised that upon his return to Nanjing he would negotiate directly with Zhou Enlai. T. V. Song urgently convinced Zhou to believe Chiang.[63] Chiang then told Zhou he was tired, and Zhou left him, saying on parting, "Rest, Mr. Chiang, we will still have time to talk." Chiang nodded and said, "Good, good."[64]

Everything seemed to be progressing smoothly toward a happy ending, but on December 24, when rumors about the negotiations and imminent release of Chiang reached officers of the Northeast and Northwest armies, many of them were indignant and demanded that Chiang give written assurance he would fulfill the demands addressed to him on December 12. On the night of December 24 a stormy conflict erupted between Zhang Xueliang and Yang Hucheng regarding the release of Chiang. Yang too did not want to release the Generalissimo without written guarantees. "It's perfectly clear that he'll cut off our heads," he shouted. Early on the morning of December 25 officers delivered a threatening letter to T. V. Song that declared it would be better to die than to let Chiang go. Understanding what the rebels risked if they "allowed the Generalissimo to go having received only oral promises from him," T. V. Song informed Chiang of the letter.[65] Chiang, terribly frightened, asked his brother-in-law to beg Zhang Xueliang to release him that very day.

The charming Meiling asked the same of the Young Marshal, and the upshot was that he decided to present the beautiful lady with a Christmas present. He declared that he himself would escort her and her husband to Luoyang and then to Nanjing.[66]

Just after ten o'clock in the morning on December 25 Zhou Enlai paid another visit to Chiang. They came to an agreement that the Communist Party would stop disturbing the unity of the country, the Chinese Red Army would subordinate itself to Chiang as the supreme commander, and Chiang in return would end his anticommunist campaigns. Chiang invited Zhou, as soon as he had had "a good rest," to come to Nanjing to continue the negotiations.[67]

The Generalissimo seemed to be candid. In Zhou Enlai's words, "There was a real change in Chiang Kai-shek's attitude. . . . He was sincere."[68] Deep down, however, Zhou was tormented by doubts, and he regretted that Zhang Xueliang intended to go to Nanjing with Chiang. "Zhang has been poisoned by old operas like *Lianhuantao,*" Zhou said later to his comrades in arms.[69]

"He, like a monkey, is playing at being a kind of Chinese Robin Hood, displaying great patience and magnanimity. He not only released the scoundrel, but even admitted his own guilt!"[70]

In the meantime, T. V. Song asked Zhou to talk things over with General Yang so he would not place any obstacles in the way of freeing the Generalissimo. "He [Chiang] made it clear that if he did not depart today, then he would simply not want to leave," T. V. Song said. Zhou went at once to see Yang, who, after prolonged persuasion, finally agreed not to detain Chiang any longer.[71] Before departing, Chiang read Zhang Xueliang and Yang Hucheng a short lecture in which he acknowledged his errors and let them know he bore them no ill will.[72]

Later in the day Zhang Xueliang, having made sure that Chiang, Meiling, Donald, and T. V. Song were seated in three vehicles, took them to the airport. The cars drove directly onto the apron of the airfield and stopped in front of the Young Marshal's plane. It was a Boeing, and sitting at the controls was an American pilot, Royal Leonard. Zhang sat in the second officer's seat, Meiling sat in another armchair in the cockpit, and Chiang, T. V. Song, and Donald climbed into the main cabin. Before sitting down in the airplane, Chiang said to Zhang, "Up to today, you would have been responsible for the outbreak of civil war; henceforth, it is I who will take responsibility if it breaks out again. From now on I will never engage in the suppression of Communists. I admit my past mistakes, but you must also admit yours."[73] While he was speaking, Meiling impatiently fidgeted in her armchair. "Are you ready to go?" she asked Leonard in English when Chiang finally finished. The pilot glanced at her and could not hide his delight. "One of the most beautiful Chinese women I had ever seen was sitting in the left-hand front seat of the cabin," he recalled several years later.[74]

"Yes," he nodded his head. "Any time."

"Okay," said the excited Meiling. "Get out of here! Let's get going!"

It was four o'clock in the afternoon when the plane took off.

They arrived in Luoyang in an hour and twenty minutes.[75] "Thanks to the Almighty who protected me," Chiang wrote in his diaries.[76] The next morning, after resting, they flew to Nanjing. This time Chiang, Meiling, and Donald flew on Chiang Kai-shek's personal Junkers with a German crew. They landed in the capital at 12:20 p.m. to the explosion of firecrackers and the joyful cries of a crowd of thousands who had come to meet them at the airport. Zhang Xueliang and T. V. Song arrived two hours later on the Boeing, and when Zhang emerged from the plane the crowd boiled over with hatred. Soldiers and secret service agents had to form a living corridor to enable Zhang to pass through. Otherwise he would have been torn to pieces. Tears streamed down Zhang's face, but he walked through the crowd with his head held high.[77] At the exit from the airport he was arrested and taken under guard to T. V. Song's house. On December 31, 1936, breaking all his promises, Chiang Kai-shek handed the rebellious marshal over to a court martial. The Young Marshal knew where he was going and really, like the hero of antiquity Yu Quan, sacrificed himself.[78] On December 19, in a private letter to a correspondent of the London *Times,* David Frazer, he wrote that he was ready to follow Chiang to Nanjing, "if a dispassionate and fair tribunal is possible. . . . I will take the punishment meted out, be it even a sentence of death," he assured him.[79]

On December 31 Zhang was sentenced to a ten-year prison term and deprivation of civil rights for an additional five years. Till the end of his days he thought that Chiang himself, having forgiven him, had saved him from being shot.[80] But that he was not executed was owing chiefly to the energetic protection of Meiling, who afterward also demonstrated her concern: she sent him money, clothing, and medicines; and once, when her beloved dog had puppies, even sent him one of the litter.[81] After five days, on January 5, 1937, he was transferred and put under house arrest, where he would languish for many years. On January 13 he was taken from Nanjing to Xikou, Chiang's native village, where he stayed for several days, but on January 24 he was taken higher up into the mountains, where he was installed in a gloomy, one-story, barracks-like pavilion (his museum is there now). The setting was Spartan, but the prisoner was allowed to read, write, take walks, and even meet with two of his wives (one month with one of them; the next month with the other). He was guarded by thirty soldiers.

By an irony of fate, his cheerless prison was adjacent to the Buddhist temple Xuedou (Grotto in the Snow), on whose grounds an enormous statue of a smiling Buddha Maitreya towered.[82] Did this wise Teacher not smile upon Zhang? Looking at the statue, the Young Marshal could only smile back sadly: in 1937 he was only thirty-six years old, but his career ended.

In November 1946, soon after the start of a new war with the Communist Party, Chiang sent Zhang, who at the time was living under guard in the suburbs of Guiyang, the capital of Guizhou province, to Taiwan. At first he was settled in a small private house in the hills in Xinzhu, eighty miles south of Taipei. Then, twelve years after Chiang's own flight to Taiwan, in August

1961 he was transferred to the foothills of the Yangming Mountains in the outskirts of the Taiwan capital. (There are museums in both places.)[83] Six years earlier, in 1955, he was baptized, having become a fervent Methodist. He was not released until 1990, as an old man of almost ninety.

After his release, many distinguished persons attended a banquet in his honor arranged by Zhang Qun, the former foreign minister of China. Among the guests was the chair of the Executive Yuan of Taiwan, Hao Baicun. Deng Yingchao, the widow of Zhou Enlai (who had died in January 1976) sent Zhang Xueliang a congratulatory telegram from Beijing, and Song Meiling, who was then living in New York, sent a bouquet of flowers. The former Young Marshal was deeply moved and, replying to the congratulations, said, "At age ninety, my eyesight and hearing have deteriorated, but I have not yet become senile. If the government and the nation need me, I would like to devote myself even more than I did during my youth."[84] But the government and people of Taiwan probably did not need him, and in 1994 Zhang, together with one of his wives (the second had died by then), moved to Honolulu, where he died of pneumonia on October 14, 2001, at the age of one hundred.[85]

As for his coconspirator, Northwest Army commander Yang Hucheng, he, like Gansu general Yu Xuezhong, was relieved of all his posts on January 5, 1937. A month later Xi'an was occupied by the forces of General Gu Zhutong, who was loyal to Chiang. General Yang was not arrested, however. In June Chiang sent him abroad, along with his wife and young son. After the start of the full-scale war between China and Japan on July 7, 1937, General Yang asked Chiang to allow him to return to take part in the anti-Japanese struggle, but he was rebuffed. So he had no recourse but to travel. He visited the United States, England, France, Germany, Czechoslovakia, Austria, Switzerland, and Spain. But in November 1937 he couldn't hold back, and on his own responsibility he returned to China. As soon as he arrived in Hong Kong on November 26 he was followed by Chiang's secret agents. Soon Chiang himself called General Yang, inviting him to come to Nanchang to meet with him. But when General Yang and his family arrived in China, they were arrested on the spot. From then on they were held in prisons, first in Hunan, then in Hubei, then Guizhou, then Sichuan. At the end of November 1946 his wife went on a hunger strike; she died in February 1947. And on September 6, 1949, before leaving Mainland China, Chiang Kai-shek gave a secret order to eliminate both General Yang as well as his two children, a son and a daughter. All three were killed in a Chongqing prison along with Yang's secretary as well as the latter's wife and young son.[86] Obviously, Chiang had never forgiven Yang Hucheng who, unlike Zhang Xueliang, had not wanted to release him in Xi'an.

Having returned to Nanjing and still far from having recovered from his ordeal, Chiang, on that very day, December 26, was deeply mortified upon receiving a disturbing telegram from his niece in Xikou reporting that his elder brother, Ruisheng, was dying. What had happened was that hearing of the arrest of his brother by the Xi'an mutineers, Ruisheng became so upset that he suffered a stroke.[87] For two weeks the village doctor battled to save his life but could do nothing. On the evening of December 26 Chiang sent the best doctors to him, but it was too late. On December 27 he died. As was the practice, the coffin with his body was transferred to a deep, cold cellar, there to await the funeral.

There had not always been cordial relations between the brothers. As recounted above, for a long time Chiang could not forgive Ruisheng for having treacherously divided the property after their father's death and for not helping his mother. But bygones were bygones, and Chiang had long since forgiven him, especially since, according to Confucian rules, the younger brother always had to respect the elder, particularly if he, like Ruisheng, was the head of the family. Chiang was inconsolable. "Alas!" he wrote in his diaries. "We were three brothers, and now only I alone remain. At a difficult time my sick elder brother's heart faltered from fear, and this led to his quick demise. But he received news of my release from captivity, and this probably relieved him."[88]

On December 29 Chiang again submitted a request to be relieved of all his posts, asserting that as commander in chief he was responsible for the conduct of his subordinates in Xi'an and should share the blame with them. This was an elegant, distinctly Chinese gesture: the entire country would be bound to admire Chiang's modesty. Naturally, the members of the Guomindang CEC unanimously declined his request, but he still submitted it twice more. Needless to say, this was in vain, and he was simply granted a three-month leave.[89] Chiang needed a rest. According to several reports, as the result of "an injury occurred during his unfortunate jump from a window during the events in Xi'an and as the result of a cold his bad legs got worse," he suffered "a contusion of the shinbone," and doctors feared he would require "an amputation of the leg." But all turned out well: massages helped restore normal circulation in his legs.[90]

On January 2, 1937, Chiang came to Xikou to bid farewell to his brother. It was decided to delay the official funeral until spring. It took place on April

15.[91] In addition to Chiang and Meiling, the attendees were leading members of the Guomindang, including Lin Sen, the head of the government, Minister of Military Administration He Yingqin, Marshal Feng Yuxiang, and General Yan Xishan as well as Chiang's old friend, the Shanghai mafioso Du Yuesheng, who, as referred to earlier, was called Big-eared Du. More than a thousand tables were set for those from all around who had come to bid farewell to the Generalissimo's brother. The funeral was solemn and sumptuous. More than twelve thousand yuan were spent on it.[92]

Three days after the funeral Chiang and his wife left Xikou for Hangzhou. The next day, April 19, they received good news from Shanghai. At last his eldest son, Ching-kuo, and Ching-kuo's wife and son had arrived there on a Soviet ship from Vladivostok. How did it happen that Ching-kuo had managed to leave the USSR, moreover with his whole family? He himself supposed that the letter to Stalin he had written at the start of 1937, "begging . . . to send him home" had played a certain role.[93] But this is doubtful. His fate was a matter of high politics, and Stalin was hardly inclined toward sentimentalism.

Stalin decided to return Ching-kuo to China because, following the peaceful resolution of the Xi'an Incident, a quick unification of the Guomindang and the CCP on an anti-Japanese united platform had not followed, and Stalin was understandably dissatisfied. Violating all the agreements, Chiang, after his release, continued to prepare for the sixth anticommunist campaign. At the end of December new military forces began actively to gather on the borders of the Soviet area in northern Shaanxi. In response, the Central Committee of the CCP also began "to prepare determinedly for a [new] war" with the Guomindang.[94]

Stalin had to intervene again, and on January 19, 1937, via the Comintern, he first of all warned Mao that the peaceful resolution of the Xi'an events "could be undermined not only owing to the intrigues of the Japanese imperialists and their agents, who are trying in every way to ignite a civil war, but as a result of the mistaken steps of your party."[95] At the same time, he instructed Dimitrov to send Mao Zedong a directive in the form of a separate letter saying that for the sake of the united front it was necessary "to shift from the Soviet system [in China] to a system of national revolutionary rule on democratic principles."[96] This would be a great concession to Chiang Kai-shek.

Furthermore, with the help of the Moscow leaders the Central Committee of the CCP composed a telegram to the Third Plenum of the Fifth Guomindang CEC, scheduled to convene on February 15. It promised to end the policy of nationwide armed rebellion aimed at overthrowing the National government. The Chinese communists likewise expressed their readiness to rename the Soviet government the government of the Special Region of the Republic of China and the Red Army into the National Revolutionary Army, declaring they would be subordinate to the Central Government of the Guomindang and to the Military Council in Nanjing. They agreed as well to introduce a democratic system of general elections in the Special Region and end the confiscation of landlords' land.[97] They dispatched this telegram to Nanjing on February 10.[98]

But Chiang and other members of the Guomindang CEC deemed that the time was not yet ripe to accept the proposals of the Chinese communists. On February 21, in response to their too vague promises, they approved the Resolution for Complete Eradication of the Red Menace.[99] It contained the following four demands:

1. The organization and command of the nation's armed forces must be unified before there can be any effective control and operation. The simultaneous existence of armed forces that follow entirely incompatible political ideologies is impermissible. Therefore, the so-called Red Army and its units under various specious names should be completely abolished.
2. The unitary administrative power is a prerequisite to national unification. The existence of two administrations side by side is impermissible. Therefore, the so-called Soviet government and other organizations detrimental to unification should be completely abolished.
3. Communism is absolutely incompatible with the Three People's Principles, which are dedicated to saving the nation and the people. It is against the interests of the Chinese people, their opportunity of livelihood and their way of life. Therefore, it must cease its operation.
4. Class struggle is based on the interests of a single class. Its method is to divide society into so many opposite classes and then set them hating and killing one another. It necessarily resorts to fighting over the control of the masses and to armed uprisings, resulting in social disorders and general sufferings. Therefore, it must cease.[100]

Three days before, Chiang wrote in his diaries, "It is necessary to struggle resolutely and to the end against the inhumane theories of the Communist Party, the communists' amoral way of life, and their anarchistic, anti-national isms."[101]

That same day he delivered a report to the plenum on the events in Xi'an,[102] and members of the plenum were given his "Notes on a Two-Week

Stay in Xi'an." The "Notes," which were then translated into several foreign languages, had been prepared by Chiang's secretary, Chen Bulei.[103] At Chiang's request, he composed them in the form of a diary that the Generalissimo supposedly kept during his incarceration—in order to lend greater veracity to history. In reality, Chiang's diary entries during his incarceration in Xi'an are much more lapidary than the notes compiled by Chen Bulei.[104]

Around this time, January 20, 1937, General Secretary of the Comintern Executive Committee Dimitrov received a message from an official of the Soviet embassy in China, a certain Nikonov. Chiang Kai-shek, he reported, supposedly sent a letter to Hitler pledging "to fully cooperate with Germany even to the point of including China in a possible struggle against the USSR."[105] Then the chargé d'affaires of the USSR in China, Ivan Ivanovich Spil'vanek, informed the Deputy Commissar for Foreign Affairs Stomoniakov that "the German ambassador to Nanjing . . . proposed to the MFA [Ministry of Foreign Affairs] that China join the Japanese–German [anti-Comintern] agreement."[106] Stalin had reason to be concerned.

Meanwhile, a new campaign against the communists did not follow, and Stalin, having sent the CCP US $800,000 at the beginning of March and promising another like sum,[107] evidently decided to make a magnanimous gesture toward the Chinese Generalissimo by returning his son to him. Stalin might also have supposed that Ching-kuo, a communist, might be able to convince his father to enter into an alliance with the USSR and the communists to repulse Japanese aggression. In any case, Stalin evidently was calculating that Ching-kuo's return home might avert the renewal of civil war in China.

Formally, Ching-kuo's departure was in response to an indirect request from Chiang Kai-shek, transmitted via Meiling through the Chinese Ambassador to the USSR Jiang Tingfu back in November 1936. According to Jiang Tingfu's recollections, prior to his departure for Moscow Meiling told him that "the Generalissimo wished very much that his son, Chiang Ching-kuo, would return to China."[108] Jiang Tingfu conveyed this request to Stomoniakov, and he sent it up the chain of command. But Stalin procrastinated, making his decision no earlier than mid-February 1937.[109] On February 23 either Wang Ming once again or someone else from the Executive Committee of the Comintern wrote another letter in Chiang Ching-kuo's name to his father. It said, "I joyfully . . . celebrate that you, my father, are taking all measures to unite China. . . . I wholly sincerely wish, hand-in-hand with you, to struggle for a united, independent, powerful China. . . . In a few weeks I will depart from Moscow with my wife and son."[110]

Whether this letter was sent or whether a different letter, written by Ching-kuo himself, was sent by diplomatic pouch prior to his departure, is not known.[111] But what *is* known is that on March 8 the Soviet Politburo resolved: "No objection to Chiang Kai-shek's son's trip to China if he himself agrees."[112] On the very next day Ching-kuo received a telegram from the Executive Committee of the Comintern requesting that he come to Moscow from Sverdlovsk at once. On March 10 the General Secretary of the Executive Committee of the Comintern Dimitrov wrote in his diaries, "Summon [here] the son of Chiang Kai-shek and send to China."[113] He evidently executed an order from the Kremlin leader. On Stalin's instructions, Ambassador Bogomolov, who was in Moscow at this time, also met with Ching-kuo, after which Ching-kuo sent for Faina to come to Moscow.[114]

Prior to their departure for China on March 26 by railroad via Vladivostok —Stalin himself was in charge of their itinerary—Ching-kuo was given money to buy his wife decent clothes and other necessities as well as to buy the train tickets. Moreover, he was given hard currency: US $120 for travel expenses.[115] Ching-kuo solemnly swore to follow the instructions of the Bolshevik leaders. He secretly revealed these instructions to his closest friends in Sverdlovsk when they came to the train station to say farewell to him and Faina for the last time. One of Ching-kuo's acquaintances, Sukhikh, wrote to the administration of the Commissariat for Internal Affairs (NKVD) of the Sverdlovsk region and to the Municipal Party Committee at the end of July 1937: "On *Elizarov*'s departure for China while the train stopped at Sverdlovsk, Anikeev and Pavlov from Uralmash went to meet him. At the train station he beckoned Anikeev to the side and said that he was going on a special mission from Moscow to his father in China, that soon a war between Japan and China would start, and since my father Chiang Kai-shek is conducting an unstable policy, I must exert influence upon him. He is going to China with his wife."[116] How really naïve the informer was to notify the local NKVD and the party officials of Ching-kuo's words. Three days later Ching-kuo sent a telegram to Dimitrov: "I send you my most heartfelt Bolshevik greeting from the road. All of your instructions will be fulfilled."[117] On April 12 he sailed from Vladivostok to Shanghai. Ten days earlier Ambassador Bogomolov informed Chiang's blood nephew Chen Lifu that Chiang's son would soon arrive in Shanghai.[118]

After twelve years Ching-kuo again set foot on Chinese soil. From Shanghai he, his wife, and his son, accompanied by the mayor of Hangzhou, who had met them at the dock, left that same day, April 19, by train for Hangzhou, where his father was at the time. But Chiang did not want to meet with him.

His son had still not asked his forgiveness for having repeatedly renounced him and, moreover, he was a communist. On April 20 Chiang left Hangzhou for Shanghai to get several sore teeth extracted. He had long had many problems with his teeth, and several of them needed to be pulled,[119] but it is doubtful he needed to go to Shanghai for that procedure. Had he wanted, he could either have gone to a dentist in Hangzhou or summoned any Shanghai dentist to his home. Hence there is no doubt that his departure was done for effect. Chen Lifu advised Ching-kuo to write to his father, apologizing and requesting admission to the Guomindang.[120] Ching-kuo did this, and Chiang finally received him in his Hangzhou residence *Chenglu* on April 30, directly after his return from Shanghai.

It is said that when the prodigal son entered the room where Chiang was awaiting him, he went down on his knees before his father and kowtowed three times. After this they spoke about the future, and Ching-kuo said that he had progressive ideas and wanted to put them into practice in China. Chiang advised him to first brush up on his Chinese—Ching-kuo spoke and wrote fluently in Russian but had forgotten many Chinese characters—and also to study the Chinese classics anew: Confucius, Mencius, Wang Yangming, and other philosophers as well as the works of Sun Yat-sen.[121] He wanted his son to return to the bosom of Chinese culture.

Then Chiang presented Ching-kuo to his new mother, Meiling, who secretly slipped him an envelope with money. For his part Ching-kuo handed his father and his new mother gifts from Moscow that he had chosen along with Ambassador Jiang Tingfu. He gave Chiang a desk set made of ebony Ural marble and an astrakhan fur coat to Meiling. Then Faina and little Eric-Ailun were introduced to Chiang and Meiling. Both Chiang and Meiling liked their daughter-in-law and grandson very much. Probably on that same day Chiang gave Faina a Chinese name, calling her Fangniang, which means Beautiful Girl. Apparently, Eric-Ailun then received a new name too—a clan name—from his grandfather. Chiang named him Xiaowen. Eric-Ailun's generation was the thirtieth of the Wuling Jiangs, denoted by the Chinese character *xiao*. It means "filial piety," and *wen* means "civilized," "educated." In other words, his name was wholly in keeping with Confucian canons. Possibly that day but perhaps later, at the request of Chiang and Meiling, Ching-kuo and Faina agreed to have their son baptized. At his christening they gave him the name Allen, and from then on everyone in the family called him that.

Only later, when he was alone in the evening, Chiang wrote in his diaries: "Son Ching-kuo returned home from Russia. No reason to be surprised that, after being cut off from each other in the past, flesh and bones are again reunited after twelve years. The spirit of my late mother can now rest in peace."[122]

Having reconciled with his father, Ching-kuo now could pay a visit to his mother Fumei. At the beginning of May, he, his wife, and his son finally arrived in Xikou. Weeping with joy, Fumei was looking at him and her grandson. She also liked her daughter-in-law, who was very modest and quiet. Faina was quiet largely because she didn't speak Chinese, but she became talkative after several years, having mastered the Ningbo dialect. The only thing Ching-kuo's mother did not like was Faina's Chinese name. "No, this will simply not do," she said. "How can she be a girl if she is married?" We need to change her name to Fangliang (Neat and Virtuous).[123] Ching-kuo was very pleased. He and then all of China began to call Faina by her new name, Fangliang.

At Fumei's request, a new wedding, Chinese style, was arranged for her son and Faina. Faina was dressed in a beautiful red, silk dress with slits up to the thighs (*qipao*), embroidered with flowers and enormous dragons. Ching-kuo wore a three-piece suit.[124] Many relatives and friends were invited, and Faina prepared several Russian dishes—with great difficulty because the village mischief makers had put wet brushwood in the oven. It was a custom at Chinese weddings to play tricks on the bride, so everyone laughed gaily.

The fair-haired, modest, and hardworking Faina made a very good impression on the local people. The only thing that surprised them was that several days after the wedding she suddenly appeared at the riverbank dressed in a bathing suit. A crowd of idlers spilled out onto the bank to look at Chiang Kai-shek's "naked" daughter-in-law. But Fumei chased them away, explaining that that was how women in the West bathe.[125]

The newlyweds moved into a detached brick house that Chiang had had built on the outskirts of Xikou in 1930. The one-story, three-room private house, located on the bank of the Shanxi River, is distinguished even now from the other houses in the village because it is built in a Western style with a flat roof, surrounded by a low parapet and stone stairs going down to the river. The house had all the conveniences: even a toilet and bathroom. Ching-kuo spent half a year there on this visit, after which he went to work in Nanchang. There he wrote a short book of reminiscences, *My Days in Soviet Russia.*[126] And on February 15, 1938, Faina gave birth to a daughter whom the happy grandfather proposed in a letter to his son the next day be named Xiaozhang.[127] *Xiao* (filial piety) as mentioned earlier, is the Chinese character of Chiang Kai-shek's grandchildren's generation. In the given context the character "zhang" has a dual interpretation: first, it is close in meaning to the character *wen* (educated, civilized), and there is even an expression *wenzhang* (literally, text and chapter); second, it can be translated as "following the rules," "organized." There certainly can be no doubt about the Confucian meaning of Chiang's granddaughter's name. Ching-kuo and Faina agreed, but between themselves they began calling their daughter Emma.[128] At her christening she was given the name Amy.

Chiang's younger son Wei-kuo, after arriving in Berlin in early December 1936, initially enrolled in intensive language classes at the University of Berlin, where he studied for barely four months. During his studies he almost got into serious trouble when the landlord of his apartment, a certain Baron von Stengel, denounced him to the Gestapo, supposedly for not respecting the Führer and sympathizing with the communists. Wei-kuo was able to put a stop to this and moved to a different apartment. Several months later, in November 1937, under the name Wego, he was enrolled in the mountain infantry division of the Wehrmacht and soon was made a noncommissioned officer.[129]

Chiang Kai-shek, after completing his lengthy leave of absence, returned to his official duties on May 27, 1937. The day before he had arrived at his summer home, *Meilu*, located, as noted above, not far from the town of Guling in the Lushan Mountains (in northern Jiangxi province). Here, on June 8, he resumed his face-to-face negotiations with Zhou Enlai, the representative of the CCP. Taking part in them from the CCP side were such leading communists as Lin Boqu and Bo Gu, and on the Guomindang side, Meiling, T. V. Song, and Zhang Chong, the director of the Organization Department of the CEC of the Guomindang.

The first round of negotiations had taken place on March 26 in Hangzhou, but at that point the sides agreed on very little. At that meeting Chiang had expressed his conviction that, because of strong opposition from veteran members of the Guomindang, cooperation between the communists and his party was out of the question. Only in principle did he give his consent to ending the civil war.[130] But the new round of negotiations in Lushan, which continued until June 15, was more successful. An official agreement to end the civil war was achieved, and Sun Yat-sen's Three Principles of the People were proclaimed as the foundation for cooperation. But not all the important questions were resolved. Chiang and T. V. Song insisted, for example, that the CCP "not become too numerous" and that its growth should not "create large difficulties for Chiang [Kai-shek]."[131] There was no agreement on this point. Nor did Chiang succeed in getting Mao Zedong to go abroad, a denouement Chiang wanted very much.[132]

Six weeks earlier, in early April, Chiang had held secret talks in Shanghai with Ambassador Bogomolov.[133] In exchange for an alliance with the CCP, he wanted to secure an agreement with the government of the USSR to provide material support to the Guomindang. He was very desirous of concluding a treaty of mutual assistance with the Soviet Union in the event of war, but Stalin, naturally, did not want to get drawn into the Japanese–Chinese conflict. On April 12 Bogomolov informed the new Chinese Minister of Foreign Affairs, Wang Chonghui, that instead of a treaty of mutual assistance Moscow was seeking a prompt start to negotiations with Nanjing on a nonaggression pact.[134]

The two sides continued to discuss possible variants, but neither Chiang nor Stalin was in a hurry to conclude a pact. Chiang continued to hold discussions with the communists. Stalin at this point was convinced that Japanese policy in the Far East had somewhat softened. Bogomolov, who had repeatedly reported to the Soviet People's Commissariat for Foreign Affairs that "a 'peaceful period' [in Japanese–Chinese relations] would continue for a long time. . . . They [the Japanese] are not ready for a 'big' war in China," had inclined Stalin to this thought.[135] Soviet intelligence informed Stalin along the same lines.

Apparently, Chiang also nurtured the hope that Japan would not decide to attack China. From April 1936 on, his chief military advisor, von Falkenhausen, suggested to him that the Land of the Rising Sun "is trying to avoid risks" in China. The German general even considered it possible that the Chinese army could commence an offensive against Japanese positions in China: to insert saboteurs and guerrillas into Manchuria and Japan itself and attack Japanese garrisons in Hankou, Shanghai, North China, and the west coast of Korea. He assessed China's chances of victory in a future war to be high, believing that the Chinese were fully capable of thrusting the Japanese back north of the Great Wall.[136]

But both Stalin's Soviet informants and Chiang's German advisor were wrong, which quickly became evident. In midsummer 1937 the Japanese dealt a new blow to Chiang Kai-shek's army, this time in the vicinity of Beiping. Chinese troops resisted but were unable to defeat the aggressor. Thus began a broadscale war that many in China and on Taiwan consider the beginning of the Second World War.

CHAPTER 14

# *A Moment of Self-Sacrifice*

It is difficult to blame Chiang for lack of foresight or excessive faith in his German advisor von Falkenhausen. Chiang knew that the Japanese had concentrated their forces not far from Beiping and Tianjin: his secret agents informed him of that. Moreover, on April 17, an American acquaintance, a correspondent for the *New York Times* who had just returned from a trip to Manchukuo, told him this in Guling. He informed Chiang that he had observed large contingents of Japanese troops being redeployed from the north to the south of Manchuria and that they were being concentrated along the Chinese border.[1] But Chiang also possessed other information, namely, that the Japanese had just increased the number of their troops along the border with the USSR by twenty thousand, probably in preparation to attack the Soviet Union jointly with Germany.[2]

The Generalissimo looked tired to his American guest. After his unfortunate fall from the wall in Huaqingchi on December 12, 1936, he suffered continuous pain in his spine even though he wore a corset. Neither foreign nor Chinese doctors were able to help him, assuring him that even an operation would be of no benefit.[3] But nevertheless he was now fully determined to fight the Japanese. At any rate, he firmly declared to his guest that "this time he would not yield again to the Japanese pressure but would fight to the finish."[4]

An excessively proud man, Chiang was psychologically wounded by the events in Xi'an. After all, in Xi'an in essence he lost face, and for this not only

Marshal Zhang and General Yang had to answer but the Japanese "dwarfs" as well. Chiang's cup of patience was all but empty; barely a single drop remained.

The radioed message he received early on the morning of Thursday, July 8, 1937, proved to be the last drop. It said that the previous night, July 7, around eleven o'clock an armed clash had occurred between Japanese and Chinese troops in the vicinity of Lugouqiao, a bridge across the Yongding River, some thirty *li* southwest of Beiping. The Yongding River (River of Eternity) had earlier been called the Lugouhe (Black Ditch River), hence the unharmonious name of the bridge, which in reality is very beautiful. It was constructed of white stone and decorated on both sides with some five hundred carved fierce-looking stone lions. Foreigners called the bridge, which had been built in the twelfth century, the Marco Polo Bridge, since the great traveler had referred to it in his book, noting that it "is a very fine stone bridge, so fine indeed, that it has very few equals."[5]

The clash of arms was quite ordinary. It began when the commander of a small Japanese detachment quartered on the right bank of the river in accordance with the terms of the 1901 Boxer Protocol wound up the maneuvers he had planned for that day.[6] He appealed to the commander of the Chinese garrison, which was situated in the town of Wanping on the left bank of the river, for permission to allow his soldiers into the town to search for a missing Japanese serviceman. The Chinese officer refused, and shooting commenced. It is difficult to say whose nerves snapped first, but each side accused the other of opening fire. At first it was rifle fire, but then the Japanese began shelling the Chinese positions with artillery salvos. The Chinese responded. The next day everything calmed down, and the missing soldier showed up: he had spent the night in a Chinese brothel.[7] Thus everything that followed could probably have been avoided.

But Chiang, learning of what happened, reacted according to his true nature and exploded. He had always been unbalanced, as noted earlier, and periods of depression alternated with sharp bursts of rage. At this moment his reaction was undoubtedly aggravated by his physical condition, made worse by his post-Xi'an syndrome. Instead of forgetting about the incident, he decided to act.

On the morning of July 8, after receiving the news from Beiping, he convened an urgent working meeting with a number of military and civilian Guomindang leaders. Many important officials were in Guling at the time, first, because Chiang Kai-shek was there and, second, because it was unbearably hot in Nanjing. In the mountains the fresh air, scented with pines, brought a light, refreshing coolness: "After the intense, damp heat of the valley the air was wonderfully sweet and pure. Flowers grew richly on the hillsides, tall tiger lilies and the little white-fringed parnassia."[8] Among others, Wang Jingwei, who had returned in January 1937 after being treated abroad, was spending time in Guling. He had heart trouble but was very active.[9]

That day, July 8, Chiang issued several orders, including to General Song Zheyuan, the commander of the Twenty-ninth Army, whose forces had clashed with the Japanese at Marco Polo Bridge. He told Song to fortify Wanping and not retreat no matter what. Moreover, he ordered Chief of Staff General Cheng Qian to deploy additional troops to the north.[10] That night he wrote in his diaries, "The dwarf bandits have arranged a provocation at Lugouqiao. 1. Taking advantage of the fact that I have not completed preparations [for war], do they want me to capitulate? 2. [Do they want] to create difficulties for Song Zheyuan? Do they want to turn North China into an independent [state]? 3. I have decided: we need to fight, hasn't the time come? 4. This time the dwarfs, having started a war, will not succeed in making use of the initiative."[11] He wanted the initiative to lie with him. Hence he moved additional troops to the north, into the area of the Beiping–Hankou and Tianjin–Pukou railroads, knowing full well that the Japanese would be riled by the maneuver. An advance into North China violated the terms of the May (1933) Tanggu Agreement, according to which a one-hundred-kilometer (sixty-two-mile) demilitarized zone had been established south of the Great Wall.[12]

In Guling on July 9 he gave a two-hour speech to a closed meeting of Guomindang leaders, saying that he was sending six divisions north and that China would fight.[13] The next day he wrote in his diaries, "Their [the Japanese] goal is not limited [to Lugouqiao]. . . . I have already actively moved troops to the north and am ready for war."[14] Nonetheless, Chiang believed he should not make a formal declaration of war until that became absolutely necessary.[15]

No matter how strange it may seem, unlike Chiang, the Japanese premier at the time, Prince Konoe Fumimaro, who had headed the emperor's government from early June 1937, was not fully determined to start a real war. On July 9 Konoe, a very cautious person, rejected a request from the minister of war to send an additional five divisions to North China. At the suggestion of Major General Kanji Ishiwara, who feared that Japan might get "bogged down in China just as Napoleon had in Spain," Konoe ordered that an airplane be prepared in case he had to fly to China for negotiations with Chiang.[16]

But this peaceful give-and-take did not last long. The aggressive military faction in the Japanese government had its way, and two days later Konoe announced the dispatch of troops to North China, not five divisions but three. Meanwhile, he too was in no hurry to declare war, aiming for now only to establish Japanese control over part of North China—from Beiping to Tianjin to Baoding. That accomplished, it would be the moment to present Chiang with peace terms that would lead to the loss of Chinese independence. There were relatively few Japanese troops in this part of China—no more than 130,000.[17] The Japanese were aware that if they started full-scale military operations they would be unable to seize all of China.

By July 12 new Japanese troops had landed in Tianjin. Chiang discussed the situation with Wang Jingwei, with whom he had probably begun to repair relations right after the latter's return from Europe. In February 1937 Chiang had even nominated Wang Jingwei to the post of chair of the Standing Committee of the Guomindang CEC but had not then received support from other authoritative leaders of the party.[18] Like Chiang, Wang, in a bitterly anti-Japanese mood because of the events on Lugouqiao, expressed his readiness to fight. But as before he did not reject the possibility of peace negotiations, staying true to his formula "resistance on the one hand and negotiations on the other."[19] However, he was resolutely opposed to a united front with the communists: "Such a step [a united front] is tantamount to drinking poison in the hopes of quenching one's thirst."[20]

On July 17 Chiang delivered another speech to high-ranking officials of the party and the government, this time intended to be published in the press. He reminded them that two years earlier, in November 1935, at the Fifth Congress of the Guomindang, he had said that "while there was the slightest hope for peace, we would not abandon it; so long as we had not reached the limit of endurance, we would not talk lightly of sacrifice." Then he declared that "once that stage is reached, we can only sacrifice and fight to the bitter end. Only a determination to sacrifice ourselves to the uttermost can bring us ultimate victory." He rejected all hopes for compromise, stressing that peace is possible only on the basis of preserving the territorial integrity of China and respecting its sovereign rights.[21]

On the morning of July 20 this address was distributed by the Central News Agency of the Republic of China.[22] Four days later Chiang wrote to his son in Xikou, "You don't have to bother about the invasion of China by the Japanese, for I am sure of finding a way to subdue them."[23]

Chiang's speech of July 17, however, had no effect on the Japanese. They figured he was bluffing, and on July 26 they attacked Beiping.[24] Three days later, on Chiang's orders, Song Zheyuan abandoned Tianjin, withdrawing south to Baoding, and the next day Tianjin fell. Chiang was shocked: "The dwarf-bandits easily took Beiping and Tianjin, this was beyond all expectations. But if today they did this so easily, is it impossible to be sure that some other day they will just as easily be defeated?"[25]

He decided to choose that day and a new place himself from which he would be able to teach the Japanese a lesson. In early August he decided to shift military operations from the North China plain to Shanghai. Apparently von Falkenhausen recommended this move. Both he and Chiang believed it would be easier for the lightly armed Chinese troops to conduct military actions on the city streets rather than in the expanses of North China.[26] Moreover, opening a front in Shanghai, the center of the economic interests of Anglo-American investors, might lead to direct intervention into the conflict by Western powers. That more than anything might force the Japanese to curtail military actions in China since the Land of the Rising Sun was not ready yet for open conflict with the West. Finally, Chiang calculated that a war in Shanghai would stymie the rapid Japanese offensive in North China.

His younger son Wei-kuo subsequently wrote about this plan: "On Aug[ust] 7, 1937, when he adopted the sustained strategy, President Chiang decided . . . 'to concentrate our main force in east China to assume an offense against the enemy in Shanghai, so as to force the Japanese army to operate on a line from east to west along the Yangtze [Yangzi] River.' . . . It was one of the outstanding achievements of the Generalissimo Chiang's strategic direction to alter the Japanese army's line of operations."[27] It is striking that neither Wei-kuo, von Falkenhausen, nor Chiang Kai-shek himself was bothered that a result of this "outstanding achievement" was that Chiang condemned to death tens of thousands and perhaps hundreds of thousands of peaceful inhabitants of Shanghai, a city in which he intended to trap the Japanese. They were not bothered either that the city itself, the largest industrial, commercial, and cultural center in China, would be destroyed, perhaps razed.

On that day, August 7, once back in Nanjing, Chiang convened a new secret meeting of the highest leadership dedicated to questions of defense. Sternly looking around the hall, his voice cracking, he nervously addressed the assembled: "So, comrades, we need a decision. Do we fight, or shall we be destroyed?"[28] He asked those who wanted to resist Japan to stand. Everyone stood, including Wang Jingwei. "The decision to fight has been taken," he wrote in his diaries that night.[29]

Having chosen Shanghai as the main locus of battle, Chiang quickly sent major forces to the city: 450,000 officers and men, including two of his best divisions, armed and trained by the Germans.[30] He also issued orders that the lower Yangzi River be mined in three places and that over twenty ships be sunk in the Yangzi near Nanjing to block entry into the Grand Canal.[31] As in his redeployment of troops to the north in July, he understood very well that he was violating an agreement he had reached earlier with the Japanese. In this case, it had been concluded in March 1932 after the Japanese attack on Shanghai at the beginning of that same year. According to that agreement, as mentioned earlier, the Chinese did not have the right to station troops in Shanghai or its vicinity. In other words, Chiang again was deliberately creating a provocation.[32]

The Japanese demanded that Chiang withdraw his troops, but he ignored the demand. They asked for help from representatives of the foreign governments, but they were powerless. Then it became clear to everyone that a new massacre in Shanghai was unavoidable.[33]

In response to Chiang's actions, the Japanese, first, began to evacuate their citizens living in the Shanghai district of Hankou (Little Tokyo). They numbered some 30,000. Second, they reconfigured the golf course on the eastern outskirts of the International Settlement as an air strip. And, third, they began actively redeploying troops from the North China front to Shanghai. At the beginning of August there were 5,000 Japanese soldiers and sailors in the city; by August 9 there were 8,000. The number of Japanese warships in the roadstead at Shanghai grew from three to twelve in the same period. Two days later sixteen more Japanese ships were approaching Shanghai, and by Friday, August 13, there were thirty-two fighting craft along the riverbank.[34] Among them was the flagship, the battleship *Izumo,* which had distinguished itself in 1905 in the famous Battle of Tsushima in the Russo–Japanese War. The muzzles of its artillery guns were turned toward the city districts.

In Shanghai the day before, August 12, panic had already set in: thousands of Chinese, remembering the Japanese bombardment of January 1932, streamed into the International Settlement on the bridge across the Wusong River. The crowd stretched for ten miles. "We were soon sardined in a ten-mile stream of Chinese heading for the Shanghai International Settlement—the one island of safety," recalled an eyewitness. "Our speed was the speed of those hurrying sandaled or slippered feet. . . . My feet were slipping . . . on blood and flesh. Half a dozen times I knew I was walking on the bodies of children or old people sucked under by the torrent, trampled flat by countless feet."[35]

That same day the Chinese mayor of Shanghai fled from the city, and the authorities of the Settlement began to distribute the refugees anywhere they could—to warehouses, offices, stores, movie theaters—but still there was not enough space. Thousands of people spent the night on the streets, in parks, and in alleys.[36]

At 9:15 on the morning of Friday, August 13, the shooting started. As on July 7 at the Marco Polo Bridge, it was not clear who opened fire first. That same day at four o'clock in the afternoon Chiang received ambassadors from several Western powers, saying that "China had no desire to precipitate hostilities [with Japan]; that China desired peace."[37] But precisely at four the Japanese commenced an artillery bombardment of Shanghai from their vessels. The Chinese responded.[38] Chiang was beside himself. "Drive the enemy into the sea, block off the coast, and resist landings," he ordered his troops.[39]

The next day, on Saturday, Chinese planes took off to attack Japanese ships. Their main target was the *Izumo.* But one of the pilots, frightened by the heavy fire from the ships' antiaircraft guns, dropped two bombs on the territory of the International Settlement, one on the famous Bund, the other on the Palace Hotel. Either 728 or 729 people were killed and 861 wounded. Soon another Chinese pilot mistakenly dropped two bombs not far from the New World Amusement Park in the northwest sector of the French Concession, killing 1,011 people and wounding 570 (according to other figures, more than 3,000 were killed and wounded).[40]

The world had never seen anything like this. An eyewitness recalled that "dust, smoke and noise blotted our eyes and thoughts. We were showered with debris. . . . I . . . raced into a Bund magically cleared of refugees. On the corner a decapitated Sikh policeman lay with his arms outstretched as though against oncoming traffic. . . . Heads, arms, legs lay far from mangled trunks. For the full long stretch of both buildings, pavements and roadways were littered with bodies."[41] On this accursed Sabbath, the peaceful city dwellers paid a high price for the "outstanding achievement of the strategic plan" of their Generalissimo.

The devastation was only the beginning. Japanese soldiers and sailors landed on the shore, and the fighting shifted to the streets of the city. It was accompanied by Japanese carpet bombing of urban quarters from both ships and airplanes. Meanwhile, several days later, pursuing a flexible policy, Konoe, via Minister of Foreign Affairs Hirota, asked the German ambassador to Tokyo to act as a mediator in peace negotiations with Chiang Kai-shek. But nothing came of this undertaking.[42]

At the beginning of September the Japanese quickly redeployed an additional 100,000 troops from the North China front and Taiwan, which had been under Japanese occupation since 1895, to Shanghai.[43] The battle continued for three months. The Chinese soldiers resisted heroically, but they lacked sufficient arms, cartridges, and shells. The Japanese dominated the air. The Chinese quarters were almost totally destroyed, and tens of thousands of totally innocent persons perished. In addition to peaceful citizens, more than 187,000 Chinese officers and soldiers fell in battle or were wounded in this Chinese version of the Battle of Stalingrad. On average two thousand servicemen died every day. And even though Chiang demanded that his troops attack "without regard for casualties and to defend . . . positions to the last man," he had to admit defeat.[44] In early November 1937 some 400,000 Chinese soldiers withdrew from the city. On November 11 Japanese soldiers shouting *banzai!* began to enter the city, completing their occupation the next day. Some 350,000 city dwellers managed to flee from Shanghai, but the majority of the four million peaceful inhabitants of the city were under occupation, in the hands of ruthless enemies who established a reign of terror. The Japanese were embittered. More than 42,000 Japanese servicemen had perished in the battle for the city.[45]

On the eve of taking the city, the Japanese government, calculating that the Chinese army could no longer recover, again turned to the Germans—this time through both their ambassador to Tokyo and ambassador to Nanjing—requesting German mediation in peace negotiations with Chiang Kai-shek. Konoe's tactics, as before, were to incline Chiang toward peace after inflicting a series of defeats on him. His victory in Shanghai was the most important part of this strategic plan.

On November 5, 1937, a week before the city fell, the German ambassador to China transmitted the Japanese peace conditions to Chiang: Inner Mongolian autonomy, expansion of demilitarized zones in North China and Shanghai, termination of the anti-Japanese campaign, joint struggle against communism, lowering tariffs on Japanese goods, and respecting the rights of foreign subjects. Chiang rejected them decisively.[46] The Japanese did not persist; for now they had the forces needed to achieve new victories.

Chiang's defeat along all fronts was not surprising. Notwithstanding the bravery of Chinese soldiers and their numerical superiority—the Chinese army numbered 2,378,970 servicemen, while the Japanese army amounted to several hundred thousand—they could not overcome the enemy either on the broad North China plain or in the narrow city streets.[47] In the words of Chiang Wei-kuo, "With its better equipment, full strength, and long- and well-trained cadres and troops, one Japanese division at the beginning of war could fight our three full-fledged divisions. . . . The combat strength of Japanese 51 divisions was equal to that of Chinese 153 reorganized divisions."[48] Before the start of the war, China had 177 military aircraft, but by late 1937 they were almost all destroyed. There were only 70 tanks, almost no modern artillery, only 76 medium- and small-caliber antiaircraft guns, and 48 field artillery and almost no shells.[49] Ambassador Bogomolov correctly reported to Stalin on August 26, 1937, that the Chinese "had barely enough military equipment for three months of war."[50] At this time Chiang himself assessed China's chances in the war against Japan pessimistically—in the event that no one came to his aid, he figured that China could hold out for no more than six months.[51]

But the international situation did not favor China since neither the United States nor England was ready to offer Chiang real assistance. Moreover, the United States, despite the policy of neutrality it had proclaimed since the end of August 1935, was actively helping the Japanese, supplying them with arms as well as certain strategic materials such as scrap metal, steel, and, most important, oil, which the Japanese almost entirely lacked. The Americans' supply of oil covered 80 percent of the needs of the Land of the Rising Sun.[52] In this case the United States was following the terms of the American–Japanese Treaty of Trade and Navigation of 1911, establishing the principle of most favored nation with regard to trade between the United States and the Japanese empire. Great Britain and France, which also valued their commercial ties with the Japanese and feared a future war on two fronts—against Germany, the threat from which was growing ever more palpable, and against Japan—did not hasten to help China. On the eve of the war, in May–June 1937, in London the British even were conducting negotiations with the Japanese about recognizing the latter's rights in North China. Although these negotiations went nowhere, nevertheless, Bogomolov, for example, considered that "to a certain degree they freed the hands of the Japanese in north China."[53] He did not hide his opinion from the Chinese side.

Chiang knew all this, and that is why, on August 7, 1937, expressing his readiness to fight, he acknowledged that "in spirit, the United States and Britain would help us morally, but as the Italian case shows, they're not reliable."[54] The unreliability of the West was soon confirmed by both the League of Nations and the nine-power Brussels Conference held in November 1937 in connection with the start of the war in China.[55] Neither the League of

Nations nor any of the leading countries of the world could do anything about Japan. Chiang's reference to Italy was on the mark. In 1936–37 Mussolini cut off aid to China completely, taking offense at Chiang, who joined the sanctions imposed on Italy by the League of Nations in response to the Fascists' invasion of Ethiopia in October 1935. But Chiang had to condemn Italy for this act of aggression because it was a " 'pernicious example to Japan' that was preparing to invade China." At the request of Chiang, Kong Xiangxi met with Scaroni to subtly advise him to convey this thought in a personal telegram to Mussolini without informing the Italian ambassador. Chiang asked Il Duce "to resolve as soon as possible the question of Ethiopia"; otherwise it would be impossible for Italy "to fulfill its business engagements undertaking with China."[56] By that time Italians had sold over 130 training and bombing aircraft to China, and several hundred Chinese pilots and engineers had taken classes in Italy and China.[57] In 1937 only one well-known Italian, Alberto De Stefani, a former minister of finance in Mussolini's government and a member of the Grand Council of Fascism, was actively working for Chiang Kai-shek, as his economic advisor.[58]

The Nazis, however, continued to supply military aid to China. In the summer and autumn of 1937 Hitler demonstrated his sympathy toward Chiang Kai-shek in every way possible. In September, in the lobby of the Nazi party congress in Nuremberg, he pressed the hand of the Chinese ambassador for a long time, expressing his admiration for Chiang Kai-shek's bravery.[59] Chiang Wei-kuo was introduced to the Führer as "the son of the Chinese Generalissimo." According to Wei-kuo's recollections, Hitler warmly greeted him and asked that he give his regards to his father.[60] Evidently on Chiang's instructions, in September 1937 Chiang's brother-in-law Kong Xiangxi, who was in Germany undergoing treatment, sent a letter to Hitler, replete with polite phrases, imploring the Führer not to support Japan. He assured the Führer that China had much more in common with the Reich than Japan did. In China, as in Germany, there was an authoritarian regime headed by a single nationalist party and a strong leader. In Japan there was a rotting parliamentary system.[61] Although he did not receive a reply, in November Hitler nevertheless responded to Chiang's request to allocate new arms worth 50 million Reichsmarks (a little more than US $20 million). Overall, in 1937 China received 37 percent of all German arms exports for a sum of 83 million Reichsmarks (about US $32 million), while Japan, to which the Nazis also sold arms, received 13 percent—a sum of about 11 million Reichsmarks (slightly more than US $4 million). Soon the Führer agreed to supply China with additional arms worth 100 million Reichsmarks (more than US $40 million). Despite Japan's furious protests, German military advisors continued to work in China—there were forty-six at the start of the war—as well as almost fifteen hundred German civilian specialists. Germany invested 400 million Reichsmarks in China (more than US $160 million).[62]

Yet Chiang did not fully trust the Nazis. He probably did not know that on August 16, 1937, Hitler had told his ministers of foreign affairs and defense that in principle he was devoted to the idea of cooperating with Japan, but he knew that in April 1936 and June 1937 Germany had concluded trade agreements with Manchukuo and, on September 4, 1937, had supplied Pu Yi a credit of 100 million Reichsmarks in exchange for the supply of Manchurian goods to the Reich.[63] Hitler was not alone in playing a double game with Chiang in Manchuria: Stalin's Manchuria policy was also provocative. Thus, while receiving German arms, Chiang could close his eyes to Hitler's unfriendly conduct regarding the question of Manchukuo just as he had closed them to Stalin's analogous behavior. But he could not forget that the Führer had signed an anti-Comintern pact with the Japanese. He also knew that in Berlin on January 30, 1937, and in Nuremberg on September 6, notwithstanding his cordiality toward Wei-kuo and the Chinese ambassador, the Führer noted that Japan was making every effort to combat "the Comintern Movement" and to ward off "an attack on the civilized world."[64] All this contributed to Chiang's anxiety regarding the prospects for Chinese–German cooperation.

Taking into account China's complicated international situation in early August 1937, Chiang realized that it was no longer possible to put off signing a formal nonaggression pact with the Soviet Union. As discussed above, Chiang very much wanted to conclude a treaty of mutual assistance with the USSR in order to draw it into the war, but in the end he was forced to agree to a nonaggression pact, as the cautious Stalin insisted. At this juncture the Kremlin leader did not want to bind himself with written obligations to assist but wanted a formal guarantee that the Soviet arms sold to China would not be used against the USSR.

Stalin was a dangerous player, and the unhappy experience of the united front in the 1920s served as a reminder to Chiang not to lower his guard. But at that specific moment—Chiang understood this very well—only Stalin could help China quickly and without delay by all possible means. This was not because he had any sympathy for the Chinese Nationalists, but because the defeat of Chiang Kai-shek and China's subordination to Japan could lead to the destruction of the CCP and, most important of all, to a Japanese attack on the USSR. Thus Chiang and Stalin had a common enemy, and Chiang could still hope that the Soviet Union would not only help him with arms and funds but would ultimately intervene in the Japan–China conflict and deal a preemptive blow to the Kwantung Army.

Chiang knew that Stalin was ready to begin assisting at once. Four and a half months prior to the outbreak of war, on March 8, 1937, the Soviet Politburo had adopted a resolution "agreeing to sell the Nanjing government airplanes, tanks, and other military-technical supplies for 50 mil. Mexican dollars [almost US $14 million], with delivery over a two-year period, and a term of 6 years." In return, China was to pay for these goods by supplying strategic raw materials of equivalent value to the USSR.[65] Three weeks after the events at Marco Polo Bridge, the Soviet government, at Chiang Kai-shek's request, revisited the resolution, and decided "1. To increase the supply of arms [to China] with a credit of 100 miln. [as in original text] Chi[nese] dollars [that is, approximately US $28 million], offer the Nanjing government 200 airplanes with equipment and 200 tanks on the conditions earlier stipulated, with delivery in the course of one year. 2. Propose that the Nanjing government allow a small group of our military officers to come to Nanjing to become acquainted with the needs of the Chinese army. 3. Agree to accept for training here a group of Chinese pilots and tankists."[66] This is just what Chiang Kai-shek needed. That is why, driven to an extreme by the Japanese, he made a deal with Stalin. The deal, as he well understood, was that in return for Stalin's help he had to legalize the CCP and its Red Army.

In mid-August 1937 a draft treaty was quickly agreed to. On the initiative of the Soviet side it was decided that the treaty would enter into force the moment it was signed, without wasting time on formal ratification, and would be in effect for five years.[67] At Stalin's request, Chiang agreed that upon signing the nonaggression pact, his Minister of Foreign Affairs Wang Chonghui would make an oral gentleman's declaration that "during the term of operation of the nonaggression treaty . . . the Republic of China will not conclude any other treaty with a third power on so-called joint actions against communism that, in practice, is directed against the USSR." In return, at the request of the Chinese side and with Stalin's agreement, Bogomolov declared that the USSR "would not conclude any kind of nonaggression treaty with Japan."[68] The treaty was signed in Nanjing on August 21, 1937 at ten o'clock in the evening by Wang Chonghui and Bogomolov.

The next day, August 22, Chiang issued an order to incorporate the Chinese Red Army into the organization of the NRA under his command. The

Chinese Workers and Peasants Red Army was renamed the Eighth Route Army. Soon the government of the so-called Special Border Region of the Republic of China, as the territories controlled by the Communist Party in Northwest China now began to be called, was confirmed. The Special Border Region with a new capital, the city of Yan'an, included eighteen districts in the provinces of Shaanxi, Gansu, and Ningxia. A month later, on September 22, a declaration of the Communist Party recognizing the leading role of the Guomindang was published, and on the twenty-third a declaration by Chiang Kai-shek concerning the formation of an anti-Japanese united front of all political parties in China.

But problems persisted with regard to actual unification of the GMD and the CCP. Chief among them was that neither Chiang Kai-shek nor Mao Zedong trusted each other, and in essence neither of them wanted a genuine united front. "We must not allow [the communists] to be too independent," Chiang wrote in his diaries two months prior to the formation of the united front.[69]

He was prepared to tolerate the Chinese communists because he desperately needed Soviet arms. And he understood that as long as China was waging war against the Japanese, "Russia will not allow [the Chinese] Communist Party to carry out a revolution."[70] Furthermore, he continued to count on an intervention by the Soviet army into Manchuria, pressing ever more insistently the idea of a Soviet–Japanese war in conversations with Soviet representatives.

"Counting on a Japanese–Soviet war remains Chiang Kai-shek's idée fixe as before," Bogomolov reported to Moscow earlier, on July 17. "In a recent conversation with Lepin[71] he again expressed the opinion that from the Japanese point of view the basic problem is not the Chinese, but the Soviet problem."[72] In August, Guomindang personnel began to bombard Soviet representatives with requests to intervene in the war—either directly or "to carry out some sort of movement of Soviet troops along the Manchurian border 'to divert the attention of Japan away from China.' " On August 1 Jiang Tingfu, China's ambassador to the USSR, addressed such a proposal to People's Commissar Litvinov, and the following day Sun Fo, chair of the Legislative Yuan and the son of Sun Yat-sen, made a similar request to Bogomolov.[73] On August 28 Chiang himself asked Bogomolov to convey to Stalin his request not only to speed up the delivery of Soviet airplanes but also to allow Soviet flyers "to join the Chinese army as volunteers."[74] In the autumn General Yang Jie, who was leading the Chinese delegation in Moscow in secret negotiations about military procurement, addressed a request to the leadership of the USSR to join in the anti-Japanese war.

He conveyed this to Commissar for Defense Kliment Efremovich Voroshilov, saying this was a personal request from Chiang Kai-shek. In response, Voroshilov advised Chiang to restore order in his own army and take control of all the generals and military governors. "At the present time CKS [Chiang Kai-shek] must become a dictator," he asserted, explaining, "He should cut off the head of any general who tries to evade fulfilling his obligation."[75]

Voroshilov's words made a lot of sense: the NRA, as before, was a conglomeration of military cliques, and the generals did not always obey the orders of the higher-ranking commanders. They were afraid of losing their troops, the source of their power and wealth, in battles. This was also one of the reasons for Chiang Kai-shek's failures at the front. As mentioned earlier, however, Chiang was unable to become a dictator like Stalin and Hitler, as his opponents were too varied and numerous: from communists to militarists who, even in a moment of mortal danger, supported his government only provisionally.

Localism manifested itself even during the battle for Shanghai. Thus, in the words of the British consul general, the fifty-thousand-man Chinese army, deployed in the south of Zhejiang, did not enter into the battle because the provincial authorities feared there would be no one left to defend their territory. Zhang Xueliang's former troops, which had been transferred from Xi'an to the city of Wuxi in Jiangsu province, north of Shanghai, behaved even worse. Not desiring to help the Generalissimo, who had arrested their commander, they simply refused to let pass transports with arms for the defenders of the Chinese Stalingrad who were shedding their blood. "Provincialism dies hard," the consul general concluded. "One can sympathize with Chiang Kai-shek's desire for a national army."[76]

Meanwhile, on September 14 Yang Jie's delegation reached an agreement with the Soviets on military deliveries. Over a month (from September 25 to October 25) 225 airplanes should arrive in China. The official agreement regarding a financial credit to China for the purchase of these planes had not yet been signed. The first such agreement would be concluded on March 1, 1938, and not for US $14 million or US $28 million, but for US $50 million. By that time 282 airplanes had been ferried across to China, and as stipulated in the agreement, the Soviets in all would supply China with 297 airplanes, 82 tanks, 425 cannon and howitzers, 1,825 machine guns, 400 motor vehicles, 360,000 shells, 10 million rifle rounds, and other war materiel.[77]

The day before Shanghai fell, November 11, 1937, General Yang Jie was granted an audience with Stalin. Naturally, he made use of the opportunity to ask the leader of the USSR directly to enter the Japan–China war. At that point Stalin suddenly and unexpectedly did not reject such a possibility, declaring instead that "the USSR would enter the war" when "Japan begins to defeat" China.[78] It is difficult to say why he did this: all the available documents show that he had no intention of taking part in this war.

One can only imagine how happy Chiang Kai-shek was when General Yang Jie, returning to China, reported Stalin's words to him. Immediately (on November 25, 1937) he wrote a letter to the Kremlin leader—the first in a series of letters that would follow. Naturally, he warmly thanked Stalin "for moral and material support" and assured him of his "friendly feelings." Not satisfied with just one letter, the next day he wrote a second, again asking the Kremlin leader to decide "the question of sending Your troops" to China. Evidently, he thought to strike while the iron was hot.[79]

On December 1 the first Soviet planes landed in Nanjing: twenty-five I-16 fighters under the command of the famous flyer Gavriil Mikhailovich Prokofiev, who five months earlier had been awarded the title of Hero of the Soviet Union for participating in the civil war in Spain.[80] Several hours later twenty Soviet SB bombers landed.[81] Chiang was glad, but he noted bitterly in his diaries: "Alas, too late, although they can still be used."[82]

Two days later, December 3, he received new peace proposals from Japan, again transmitted to him by the German ambassador to China. The Japanese now demanded that he recognize Manchukuo, the independence of Inner Mongolia, and the presence of Japanese troops in North China, expand the demilitarized zone, develop economic cooperation, jointly fight against communism, and terminate the anti-Japanese campaign.[83]

In order to induce Stalin to join the war against Japan quickly, Chiang at once informed the new military attaché of the Soviet embassy about this proposal.[84] The attaché was division commander Mikhail Ivanovich Dratvin, whom Chiang had known since the mid-1920s when Dratvin had served as an advisor at the Whampoa Academy.[85] Dratvin had just arrived in Nanjing with the first group of Soviet military specialists and, among other tasks, had begun to fulfill the duties of chief Soviet military advisor to Chiang. Dratvin immediately informed Moscow of his conversation with Chiang, and only after Chiang received new assurances from Moscow of its support for China did the Generalissimo give a negative response to the German ambassador.[86]

Chiang's determination to fight to the death remained unshakable; he had taken the bit in his teeth. Such was his character: wild and unrestrained. As in his distant childhood, when an "explosive moment" replaced "a moment of calm," he was no longer able to control himself and went full speed ahead.[87] All doubts and thoughtful weighing of pros and cons went out the window. He awaited the reply from Moscow only because he was bluffing: he needed to instill in Stalin the idea that he could easily end the war if the Soviet Union did not give him sufficient aid. In reality, he would agree to peace with the aggressor only if the Japanese restored the status quo existing before the Marco Polo Bridge incident. Some might see this as stubbornness, others as heroism.

## CHAPTER 15

# *Blood and Ashes*

As Chiang awaited Stalin's reply, his troops suffered another loss, this time in the capital itself, Nanjing. The city, located 600 *li* (175 miles) up the Yangzi River from Shanghai, was under direct threat right after the fall of China's Stalingrad. That is why, by the end of November 1937, Chiang had decided to evacuate the government headed by the veteran Lin Sen deep to the rear, to the city of Chongqing; the military headquarters was moved to Wuhan. Both cities were situated along the Yangzi River but farther upstream from Nanjing, to the west. Chongqing was over 1,000 miles upstream, in Sichuan province, and Wuhan about 500 miles in Hubei province.

In Nanjing in mid-November Chiang held three military conferences to discuss the defense of the city. Not all the participants considered it necessary to hold on to the capital, which was difficult to defend. The enemy could surround it from three sides, and the Yangzi River would impede the withdrawal of Chinese units from the fourth side. The Guangxi generals Li Zongren and Bai Chongxi strongly insisted on yielding the city without a fight, arguing that after the rout in Shanghai the army had lost its fighting spirit and needed a respite. They suggested declaring the city "undefended" to avoid giving the Japanese an excuse for repressing the peaceful population. Von Falkenhausen supported them.[1] But Chiang, afraid of losing face, decided to defend the capital. "The Mausoleum of the Father of the State is located here," he declared. "And we must defend it."[2]

One can understand Chiang's perspective: the leader could not lightly yield his capital to the enemy even though Nanjing had no strategic significance and its defense was doomed to fail. This city was the symbol of New China. Nevertheless Chiang's decision to defend it to the end was obviously mistaken. It exacted a colossal number of victims from both the Chinese military and especially the civilian population.

Soviet flyers, including Prokofiev, also took part in the battle for Nanjing, but they could not alter the outcome either. On December 7, after amassing a large number of artillery, airplanes, and tanks, the Japanese attacked the city. Chinese forces were able to hold out for only five days, and during that time lost 70,000 killed (their daily loss was seven times that of the losses in Shanghai).

Chiang himself and Meiling fled the city early on the morning of December 7. After rising at four o'clock they prayed to God, and by five-thirty they were aboard a plane for the two-and-a-half-hour flight to the town of Guling, situated, as noted above, in the Lushan Mountains of Jiangxi. Stepping out of the plane, Chiang eagerly inhaled the pure air. "How peaceful here," he wrote in his diaries that night. "I am spiritually at ease, and my thoughts are in order."[3] His advisor Donald, who flew in with them, recalled they were "never thinking of adversity or defeat." They simply strolled along the mountain paths, "never discussing the startling events of the war, never bothering about it."[4]

However, the situation in the capital had become horrifying. On December 8 the mayor of Nanjing fled. By then everything that could be taken out—for the most part works of culture and art—had been sent to Chongqing. Afterward, soldiers began to set on fire or blow up buildings. Universal chaos reigned in the city. People tried to escape the siege, but they were unable to get across the nearly mile-wide Yangzi River. The streets were filled with people who were no longer paying attention to the cannonade. Bloody battles were raging in the approaches to the city. On the evening of December 12 General Tang Shengzhi, the commander of the Nanjing troops, issued an order to retreat. Late that same night he himself sailed from the city on a small cutter.[5] At two in the afternoon of December 13 Japanese soldiers entered the city.

All foreigners, with the exception of about thirty persons, had left the city in the fall. Those who remained—businessmen, missionaries, and doctors—took measures to establish a so-called Safety Zone in the central part of the city around the US embassy.[6] They enclosed a territory of over one and a half square miles with white flags and red crosses, declaring it was neutral and setting up a refugee camp there. In order to administer and guard the zone they established an international committee. They hoped the Japanese, fearing diplomatic complications, would not risk entering the zone. After all, in that space was the embassy of the United States.[7] In addition, within the Safety Zone were the Nanjing committee of the International Red Cross, the embassy of Italy, the diplomatic mission of the Netherlands, the international and German clubs, and the American-run Jinling Women's College.[8] As the occupants soon found out, however, the zone was not wholly safe. The international committee conducted repeated negotiations with the Japanese but received only evasive responses or oral promises not to seize the zone.

Before the fall of the city as many as 200,000 Chinese gathered in the zone—the population of Nanjing at the start of the war was one million—and soon thereafter another fifty thousand crowded in. The zone quickly turned into an overpopulated ghetto where masses of people huddled together wherever they could: in deserted buildings, cellars, dugouts, trenches, hastily constructed huts, and even on the streets under the open skies. There were no sanitary facilities, and the stench was unbearable. Worst of all, the Japanese frequently intruded into the zone, and despite the firm protests of members of the international committee and often their actual heroic resistance they killed and raped refugees.[9]

Nevertheless, those who took refuge in the zone, sojourning there until the middle of February 1938, had at least some chance of surviving.[10] The other inhabitants of Nanjing might as well have been in hell. What they encountered cannot be called anything other than carnage. Over the course of at least six weeks Japanese soldiers and officers, intoxicated with victory, embittered by the resistance of the Chinese army, and exhausted from the endless, bloody battles—a majority of the soldiers who had taken Nanjing also participated in the battle for Shanghai—literally massacred the inhabitants of Nanjing. At the same time, as if mocking them, everywhere declarations were posted proclaiming that the Japanese were the only friends of the Chinese.[11]

"No one expected anything like this," a foreign eyewitness wrote. "With the coming of the Japanese soldiers we thought . . . peace would come. . . . But the surprise of surprises came to us all. Robbery, looting, torture, murder, rape, burning—everything that can be imagined was carried out from the very beginning without any limit. Modern times have nothing to surpass it. Nanjing has been almost a living hell. . . . Soldiers have taken anything they wanted, destroyed what they did not want, raped women and girls openly and publicly by the scores and hundreds."[12] A note from December 19, 1937, read as follows: "The horror of the last week is beyond anything I have ever experienced. I never dreamed that the Japanese soldiers were such savages. It has been a week of murder and rape. . . . They not only killed every prisoner they could find but also a vast number of ordinary citizens of all ages. Many of them were shot down like the hunting of rabbits in the streets. There are dead bodies all over the city."[13] The end result was that in six weeks of massive terror the Japanese, according to various estimates, killed thousands of innocent people.[14]

Chiang was not indifferent on this account. On December 16, 1937, he sent a message to the nation in which he took responsibility for the surrender of the capital.[15] Learning of the scale of the Nanjing tragedy, he wrote in his diaries on January 22, 1938, "The cruel killings and monstrous rapes committed by the dwarf bandits have still not ceased. The enemy stubbornly moves into the interior [of the country]. . . . [T]he sufferings of my fellow countrymen are enormous."[16] One month earlier, on December 24, 1937, he had sent a message to President Franklin Roosevelt of the United States requesting aid, but Roosevelt promised nothing concrete.[17]

At the same time, Chiang gave an interview to a German correspondent, declaring that "the Chinese people are full of resolve to resist." In this connection, he noted—probably deliberately because, as discussed earlier, he wanted to provoke a conflict between Japan and the USSR—that he was receiving an adequate quantity of military provisions and weapons from the Soviet Union. Stalin was furious: after all, Soviet arms were being supplied to China unofficially. But, after thinking it over, the Kremlin leader calmed down: at that time it was important to him that Chiang continue to resist Japan. Therefore, he wrote to Molotov and Voroshilov, "Chiang-Kaishek [*sic*] has not acted very cautiously—but to hell with him." Both Molotov and Voroshilov agreed with sending Chiang to the Devil.[18]

Meanwhile, on December 26, 1937, in Wuchang, where Chiang had arrived on December 14, the German ambassador visited him again and transmitted a third draft of the Japanese peace terms. It was practically the same as the other two: the Japanese added only one demand: that China pay "an appropriate indemnity." Two days later Chiang informed the new Ambassador of the USSR Ivan Trofimovich Luganets-Orel'sky (real surname Bovkun) of this, once again trying to scare Stalin. "The situation is such," he said, bluffing, "that if the USSR does not come out openly to assist China with military force, then China's defeat is inevitable. . . . Within Chinese public opinion . . . the mood is beginning to grow stronger that inasmuch as hopes for military action on the part of the USSR have proved unfounded, defeat is inevitable and it is better to support a pro-Japanese government."[19] Chiang expounded on this thought for over two and a half hours. Luganets-Orel'sky, the son of a blacksmith, "the solidly built man with a body like Hercules,"[20] listened attentively. (He combined the office of ambassador with the duties of the resident of Soviet foreign intelligence.)[21]

Seeking to frighten other countries, too, in order to compel them to aid China, Chiang ordered that the Japanese peace terms be sent as well to the governments of the United States, Great Britain, and France. It was obvious that he was bluffing: on December 27, speaking before a session of the Supreme National Defense Council, he, after informing his subordinates of Japan's demands, let them know that under no circumstances was he intending to accept them. "Today there can be no peace without surrender, no survival [of the nation] without resistance," he declared.[22] Two days before New Year's he wrote in his diaries, "Now the most dangerous thing is to end the war and begin talking about peace."[23]

Nonetheless, he instructed Kong Xiangxi, who was advising him not to reject mediation by the Germans, to hold talks with the Japanese in order to buy time. But the Japanese had lost patience, and on January 16, 1938, Konoe declared that from then on he would have no dealings with the government of Chiang Kai-shek. The Japanese then turned to forming puppet governments in North and East China. In response, Chiang recalled his ambassador from Tokyo. But then the Japanese recalled theirs.[24] Diplomatic relations between Japan and China were severed.[25]

Paying tribute to China, which was continuing to resist Japan despite colossal defeats and countless victims, the American news magazine *Time,* published by Henry Luce, a fervent sympathizer with China, on January 1, 1938, proclaimed Chiang Kai-shek and Meiling "Man and Wife of the Year." Chiang was depicted in a Chinese gown but with a felt hat in his left hand, and Meiling was wearing an austere, western-style dress. For some reason they were shown against a background of Roman-like columns, perhaps to make them more accessible to Western readers.

At this time Chiang, who was in Wuchang in the Hubei provincial capital, began making plans for the defense of the Wuhan tri-cities, the de facto capital of the country. It possessed not only political but also enormous strategic significance. The city is located at the intersection of the two most vital transportation arteries of China, the Yangzi River, flowing from west to east, and the Beiping–Canton railroad.[26] Wuhan was also one of the largest megalopolises in the country. About two million people lived there, including several hundred thousand refugees. "How to hold Wuhan?" Chiang wrote in his diaries on January 1, 1938. "We have to make the dwarf bandits understand that they will not succeed in swallowing up China, they need to know how difficult that is so they will stop."[27]

On January 10 he flew to Kaifeng, the former capital of the Song dynasty (960–1127), located 280 miles north of Wuhan. The next day he convened another meeting of the high command. He was in a rage and issued an order to arrest General Han Fuju, the governor of Shandong province, who had surrendered the city of Tai'an to the enemy without a battle. The general was handed over to a court martial and several days later was shot. Chiang resolutely demanded that military discipline be strengthened and that all forces be mobilized to defend the Wuhan region.[28] Twenty days later he wrote to Roosevelt again, requesting that he intervene in the war.[29] But the Americans adhered to their policy of neutrality.

The Soviet Union at this point provided Chiang with a great deal of aid in the defense of Wuhan. In the words of Jiang Tingfu, the former Chinese ambassador to the USSR, "Moscow was more pro-Chinese, both in diplomacy and in the supplying of military equipment, than either Washington or London."[30] Initially Dratvin and then, from July 1938, the new chief military advisor who replaced him, Aleksandr Ivanovich Cherepanov (pseudonym Chagin), whom Chiang also knew from the 1920s, took part along with his staff officers in drafting plans for military operations. Dozens of military advisors were already embedded in fighting units at the front.[31] In January–February 1938, 31 Soviet bombers landed at the Wuhan aerodrome, and at the same time 40 fighters arrived in Nanchang. By mid-February 100 Soviet airplanes were stationed in the tri-cities region. Overall, by early September the Chinese had acquired 123 SB-bombers and 105 I-16 and 133 I-15 fighters from the USSR. From May through October 1938 Soviet aviation destroyed more than 100 Japanese airplanes and more than 70 military and transport vessels. But not a few of the flyers perished. Of the entire complement (602 airplanes)[32] in the arsenal of the Chinese army in the summer of 1938 only 87 remained by October 28, 1938.[33]

In March the first Soviet tanks arrived: 40 T-26 battle tanks along with instructors. Soon, with the help of Soviet advisors, the first mechanized division in the Chinese army was formed. In April the first Soviet artillery pieces arrived.[34] On July 1 a new agreement that again gave US $50 million in credit to China was signed in Moscow. According to the agreement, the USSR would supply China with 180 airplanes, 300 artillery pieces, 1,500 light machine guns,

500 heavy machine guns, 300 trucks, aviation motors, spare parts, shells, cartridges, and other war materiel.[35]

But this was not enough for Chiang. Throughout 1938 he asked Stalin over and over to increase his assistance with arms and advisors, making further efforts to draw the USSR into war with Japan. Moreover, he implored Stalin to conclude either a secret military alliance or a mutual aid treaty; to issue a joint political declaration or even simply exchange notes about friendship. His ambassador, Jiang Tingfu, told Chiang that this made no sense: Stalin would not enter the war. But Chiang, infuriated and refusing to accept this negative appraisal, recalled Jiang, and replaced him with Yang Jie.[36] For his part, Chiang insistently promised Stalin that henceforth he would always follow the lead of Soviet foreign policy. Starting in early June 1938 he repeatedly asked Stalin to send Bliukher as his chief military advisor, someone with whom he had had excellent relations in the 1920s. In June 1938 Chiang proposed even that Stalin invite him to Moscow "to discuss these questions."[37]

Stalin, however, while regularly assuring him that "everything possible would be done to help the great Chinese people," refused to enter the war or to sign a secret military agreement or a new treaty; nor would he issue a declaration.[38] He did not wish to exchange notes about friendship or send Bliukher to China.[39] Or receive Chiang in Moscow.

Yet it would be difficult to overestimate the importance of Soviet assistance to China, inasmuch as just then Chiang's relations with his other ally, Nazi Germany, deteriorated sharply. What Hitler had told his party members back on August 16, 1937, now came to pass: from February 1938 he began to openly support Japan. His decision was not due only to racial considerations.[40] It was because Hitler could not forgive Chiang Kai-shek for drawing close to the Bolsheviks, despite the fact that the minister of foreign affairs of China, prior to publication of the text of the pact with the USSR, had assured the ambassador of Germany (and similarly the ambassadors of France, Great Britain, the United States, and Italy) that the pact did not indicate a departure from the traditional anticommunist policy of the Chinese government.[41] At the same time, the Führer had no doubts about Japan's anti-Sovietism. The close cooperation between Germany and Japan developed precisely on an anti-Soviet platform. Hitler also had economic reasons. The impressive victories of the Japanese army, which had occupied an enormous swath of China, led the Führer to express interest in developing broad commercial ties with Japan. Now he could receive the Chinese raw materials he needed from the Japanese.

On February 20, 1938, Hitler officially recognized Manchukuo, declaring that "no matter when and no matter how the events in the Far East come to their ultimate conclusion, in its position of defense against Communism, Germany will always regard and value Japan as a safeguarding factor—namely, in safeguarding human civilization."[42] (Three months earlier, on November 29, 1937, Manchukuo was recognized by Mussolini, who, on November 6, had joined the Japanese-German anti-Comintern pact.)

Chiang was dismayed.[43] In March 1938, trying to make a good impression on Hitler, he congratulated him via the German ambassador on the Anschluss, the seizure of Austria. Incidentally, Chiang's younger son Wei-kuo participated in the Austrian campaign as a noncommissioned officer in an infantry division of the Wehrmacht, something that both Chiang and Hitler knew. In October of that year Wei-kuo and his division took part in the German invasion of Sudeten, after which he was enrolled in the Munich officers' academy.[44] In the March letter Chiang asked the Führer to sell him twenty bombers, and in April 1938 Kong Xiangxi again sent a new friendly letter to Hitler.

But neither Chiang nor Kong achieved anything. At the end of April Hitler issued an order to stop supplying arms to China and demanded that all German military advisors—at that time there were thirty-two—return to Germany. Not all of them obeyed. Seven remained, but the majority of them left China via Hong Kong in the next two months. The last of them, including von Falkenhausen, left the country on July 5, 1938.[45] At the same time, the German ambassador was recalled to Berlin. Three days before their departure, Chiang invited them all to a farewell banquet during which he warmly thanked them for their service. The Japanese government expressed its gratitude to Berlin.[46]

The deterioration of relations with Germany was unpleasant, but Chiang had no time to nurse his hurt feelings. Throughout the spring, summer, and early fall of 1938 he exerted every effort to strengthen the Wuhan military base. From March 29 to April 1 he convened an Emergency National Congress of the Guomindang in the building of Wuhan University in Wuchang. (It had opened in Chongqing, but Chiang had not gone there; all the other sessions were held in Wuchang.)[47] Participating were 272 delegates invited by the CEC of the party (under wartime conditions, elections were not possible). Zhou Enlai was invited as an observer, representing the CCP. At this critical moment Chiang wanted to unite all the forces of the country. On the last day of the congress, Chiang gave a speech titled "On the War of Resistance against Japan and the Party's Perspectives" in which he emphasized that the anti-Japanese war was a continuation of the revolution.[48]

The congress invested Chiang with truly dictatorial powers, appointing him to the newly created post of *zongcai* (general director, leader).[49] His old enemy Wang Jingwei was chosen as deputy *zongcai* in order to more or less balance various factions. The "Manifesto" and the "Program of Armed Resistance and National Reconstruction" adopted by the congress were rather vague overall but expressed the main point: China would never bow before the aggressors. All the delegates, it seemed, agreed with this. Both documents called for closer cooperation among all parties of the country in resisting the Japanese, and the "Program" spoke of the need to establish a new council "for the people to participate in the affairs of state."[50]

The council, called the National Political Council (NPC), was established in early July 1938. It included two hundred persons, half of whom were not members of the Guomindang. It had no power but provided an opportunity for the various parties to set forth their views, thereby serving as a consultative organ of the anti-Japanese united front for Chiang's government. Seven communists, including Mao Zedong, became members of the NPC, but Mao never took part in its work, as he never traveled to Wuhan. Moreover, the CCP had its own representation in Wuhan, the so-called Changjiang Bureau of the CCP CC (Changjiang is another name for the Yangzi River).[51]

All this time Chiang was terribly busy. He not only took part in various military and political activities and delivered lectures and speeches, but also worked out plans for military operations. He often visited the fronts, connecting by telephone or radio with commanders of war zones and commanders of individual units. It seemed that he had "a hundred pairs of hands and eyes. . . . How his whipcord body generated such energy was a mystery," an eyewitness marveled.[52] Probably it was only now, during the defense of Wuhan, that he came to himself, recovering from the first unexpected defeats and turning into "a more determined and effective leader."[53]

Meiling also was not sitting idly by; she was engaged in establishing orphanages for the homeless children who were flooding into Wuhan. The city was overflowing with refugees who were living on the sidewalks or on the banks of the Yangzi River. Beggars went from house to house seeking alms. Here and there soldiers marched along the streets, coolies dashed about dragging someone's belongings. An unbearable noise and din arose from the streets, punctuated periodically by sirens that warned of approaching enemy aircraft. After the all-clear signal, writhing bodies lay everywhere, and heartrending cries of the wounded could be heard.[54]

Chiang grew even thinner, drawn in the face, and he began to look much older than his years. The Soviet military advisor Aleksandr Yakovlevich Kalyagin, who saw him for the first time early in the summer of 1938, recalled: "The side door swung open, and a man of medium height appeared, dressed in a khaki uniform without insignia. . . . He walked slowly, stooping . . . an old man's gait . . . a frail figure, robed in an intentionally simple uniform, with limp hands and darting eyes."[55] Nevertheless, one sensed in him a kind of vitality, although it was noticeable that he was tense, like a wild animal in a moment of danger. Another eyewitness, an English journalist, wrote, "My main impression of Chiang Kai-shek . . . was of his vitality, his alertness, his sincere confidence, and the inscrutability of that smiling, lean, and handsome countenance. He has the slimness and grace of movement. . . . [H]e is extremely dignified and courteous, but one has the impression that he never relaxes and is continually vigilant. His eyes are his most striking feature: large, very dark and bright, extremely intelligent, completely unrevealing of his personality. . . . He appears . . . more a seventeenth-century Puritan than a twentieth-century dictator."[56]

Meanwhile, the war in China was continuing, and it seemed it would never end. In the spring, however, there was encouraging news from the front: in March–April Chinese forces under the command of Generals Zhang Zhizhong and Li Zongren inflicted major defeats on the Japanese in battles near the cities of Linyi and Taierzhuang in southern Shandong province. But these battles had no influence on the course of the war. After seizing all the major centers in the north and east of China—including, on May 19, the city of Xuzhou, an important junction on the Longhai railroad (running from west to east) and the Beiping–Pukou railroad (running from north to south)—the Japanese "dwarfs," at the end of May, began advancing rapidly on the Longhai line to Zhengzhou, the capital of Henan province, another major transportation junction but located at the intersection of the Longhai and Beiping–Hankou railroads.

On June 6 they seized Kaifeng, located just forty-seven miles east of Zhengzhou. The situation was critical. Chiang, who was in Zhengzhou from May 12, understood that the city would fall in a few days.[57] The seizure of Zhengzhou might quickly lead to the fall of Wuhan. It seemed that no human forces could stop the Japanese. Then Cheng Qian, the commander of the

First War Zone located along the Beiping–Hankou railroad (and concurrently the chair of the Henan provincial government) proposed a truly audacious and mind-boggling plan to Chiang: to blow up the dams along the Yellow River, which was especially high after torrential rains. the objective was to create an artificial flood on the enormous territory of the Great China Plain in order to stop the Japanese "dwarfs."[58]

The plan seemed effective from a military perspective, but it doomed hundreds of thousands of those same compatriots whom Chiang so pitied in his diaries to famine, ruin, and death. Nonetheless, Chiang approved it. On June 9 a couple of thousand soldiers, each one promised a reward of two thousand yuan, executed the terrible assignment, blowing up dams some ten miles north of Zhengzhou, thirty miles from the front line. The operation was conducted in total secrecy: none of the local inhabitants was forewarned so that the Japanese would not learn of it.

A powerful torrent of water over 600 feet wide and nearly 5 feet high and heading in a southeasterly direction inundated the land. The Yellow River changed course and, sweeping away everything in its path, roared toward the Huai River, which flowed between it and the Yangzi River in Anhui province. As a result, 21,000 square miles in Central China—44 counties in the provinces of Henan, Anhui, and Jiangsu—were flooded; some five million people lost their livestock.[59] According to various estimates, from 500,000 to more than 890,000 people perished.[60] In other words, with his own hands Chiang killed many more peaceful Chinese than the Japanese "dwarfs" had in Nanjing.

Joseph Goebbels, learning of this, said Chiang Kai-shek's actions were "much more barbaric" than those of the Japanese.[61] To be sure, from his lips the condemnation of Chiang Kai-shek rang hollow. In pursuit of their own goals, not a single dictator—neither Hitler, Stalin, nor Mao Zedong—was ever deterred by the prospect of sacrificing hundreds of thousands of innocent victims. Yet it is also true that none of them ever drowned hundreds of thousands of their peaceful inhabitants. Chiang's actions had no historical analogues.[62]

Chiang himself knew he had committed a crime. Therefore on June 11 he sent a secret telegram to Cheng Qian that read, "We need to tell the people that enemy airplanes bombed the dams on the Yellow River."[63] Neither Chiang nor Cheng ever acknowledged what they had done, and Guomindang propaganda, per Chiang's order, stubbornly placed the blame on the Japanese.

God sits in judgment of Chiang, especially since, from a military point of view and even taking into account that the flooding actually impeded the

Japanese offensive against Wuhan for five months, the action was not particularly effective. In mid-June the Japanese launched a new offensive toward Wuhan, this time along the Yangzi, south of the flooding. On June 15 they took Anqing, a major city in Anhui province 105 miles upriver from Nanjing, and on July 26 the river port of Jiujiang. Here they carried out a new massacre of the peaceful population, aimed at terrorizing the Chinese. After they seized Canton on October 22, 1938, in a swift, unexpected operation the fate of Wuhan was sealed. They cut off the Canton–Wuhan railroad that linked China, via Hong Kong, with most of the countries in the world.

"The fall of Canton has exposed our flank," Chiang explained to Donald. "Now we must leave."

"He spoke of the loss of a city as if it was the loss of a piece in a chess match," Donald thought.

But Chiang, as if reading his thoughts, added, "I am not disturbed by the loss of cities. If we lose too many, we will build some more."[64]

Donald was shocked by this comment not knowing that Chiang was simply repeating Stalin's thought, conveyed to him by Sun Fo after a conversation with the Kremlin leader: "The main thing is . . . not to be afraid to yield one or another city. This has no significance in the course of a struggle."[65]

Wuhan fell on October 25, 1938. More than half a million Chinese soldiers and officers died or were wounded during its defense, but there was no panicked flight.[66] Chiang was able to organize an orderly withdrawal of his main forces to the west.[67] Before leaving the city and without hurrying, he inspected the troops lined up along the embankment from an open car. But at the same time he issued another terrible order: destroy Wuhan thoroughly so it would not fall into the hands of the enemy.[68]

Chiang and his wife flew from frosty, snowbound Wuhan to the south, again to the mountains but this time not to Guling but to the little town of Nanyue, situated in the Hengshan mountains, 105 miles south of Changsha, the capital of Hunan province. He and Meiling were the last of the high command to depart from the smoke-shrouded city, leaving at ten o'clock on the night of October 24.[69] They reached Nanyue, which means South Mountain, more or less calmly. But several days later, fearing that the Japanese would soon take Changsha—it was only 220 miles from Wuhan—Chiang suddenly panicked and, unable to control himself, committed yet another terrible crime: he ordered the governor of Hunan, General Zhang Zhizhong, to burn Changsha to the ground if the Japanese were drawing close to it.[70]

Zealous subordinates, thinking the city would fall tomorrow if not today, set Changsha on fire on the night of November 12. None of them thought to forewarn the sleeping inhabitants. The ancient city, founded three thousand years earlier, burned throughout November 12 and 13. A doctor in an American hospital who was an eyewitness, wrote, "For two days and nights the roar of the fire, the pall of smoke and the wanton destruction were the three most pressing things in my consciousness. . . . The heat was terrific. . . . [The doctors] saw fire being set; poor fellows trying to drag themselves out of the hospital doors and windows on their elbows; sick and wounded soldiers burned alive in that hospital unit."[71] From twenty to thirty thousand people died in the fire.[72]

But the Japanese did not take Changsha. Chiang, after coming to his senses, managed to emerge unscathed. Meiling sent a letter to the American hospital in Changsha saying that she and the Generalissimo were terribly depressed by what had happened and that the arson had not been performed on the orders of the Generalissimo. Chiang placed the blame on the local military. The garrison commander, who was one of Chiang's blood brothers, the commander of one of the regiments, and the chief of the municipal police were arrested and shot, and the Hunan governor, General Zhang Zhizhong, was forced to retire.[73]

In this tragic moment Chiang obviously betrayed the ancient rule of the great Chinese military commander of the Tang era Li Jing (571–649): "To be awesome and yet caring makes a good balance."[74]

CHAPTER 16

# *The Protracted War*

From November 25 to 28 Chiang, who was still in Nanyue, convened the largest military conference since the start of the war to sum up the disappointing results and work out strategy and tactics for the future. As always, he radiated determination to continue resisting, despite the colossal losses in personnel and equipment. Various sources claimed that the number of killed, wounded, and missing-in-action among officers and men was from 1 to 1½ million. The Japanese had seized half the territory of China proper, including the most developed areas in North, East, and South China, the major cities and lines of communication. China had lost up to 90 percent of industrial capacity as well as 80 percent of tax revenues.[1] Chiang firmly believed in ultimate victory and starting from late October even contemplated whether he should formally declare war against Japan. However, he did not because he encountered serious opposition among the members of his government.[2] In his opening speech to the conference in Nanyue he asserted that with the fall of Wuhan only the first stage of the war had concluded. And now China had entered the second stage, in which "we will shift from defense to offense and from defeat to victory."[3]

In effect this was a response to Konoe's radio address to the Japanese people three weeks earlier, on November 3, in which the Japanese premier set forth principles for the so-called New Order in East Asia. On this occasion Konoe proposed establishing equal cooperation among the Japanese empire,

China, and Manchukuo, asserted that Tokyo had no material claims on the Republic of China, and promised to annul Japanese concessions and extraterritorial rights in China. He only wanted to fight against communism and Western imperialism along with the Chinese and Manchurians.[4]

Rejecting Konoe's proposals, Chiang Kai-shek devoted singular attention to the need to develop guerrilla warfare in the Japanese rear. He asked Zhou Enlai and Ye Jianying, the chief of staff of the communists' Eighth Route Army, who were present at the conference, to help the Guomindang train cadres for this war. Soon, guerrilla warfare courses were begun in Nanyue, courses to which even one of the Soviet military advisors was assigned.[5]

Chiang had spoken earlier about the need to conduct guerrilla warfare. The first time was on August 2, 1937, at a meeting of his general staff, after which he returned repeatedly to this theme. But until the fall of Wuhan this question had not been translated into practice since Chiang basically did not understand how to wage such a war. He simply thought to redeploy several units and subunits to the enemy rear to conduct regular actions there like soldiers at the front. Many generals, however, were contemptuous of this plan, supposing that those sent to the Japanese rear would actually be avoiding real fighting and "saving their hides." Therefore, the idea of war behind Japanese lines became extremely unpopular among officers who did not want to lose face.

But with the fall of Wuhan and the Japanese occupation of an enormous part of the country, Chiang sharpened the question anew. The fact of the matter was that the Japanese lacked sufficient troops to occupy every square mile of Chinese earth; they controlled only the more pivotal cities and other strategic objectives, including lines of communication. Thus there remained territory in the rear to which their power did not extend. That is where Chinese guerrillas could operate.

In March 1939 Chiang succeeded in breaking the condescending attitude of his officers to guerrilla warfare, and the Nationalists finally began sending a large number of troops behind the front lines and divided the Japanese rear into five war zones (overall, ten war zones were organized in China). But to the end Chiang failed to realize that war in the enemy's rear could not be either positional or mobile but only people's war. He did not try to organize the people into irregular fighting units.[6]

This approach was different from that of the communists who were involved in developing people's war in the enemy's rear, fully applying experience accumulated during the period of the Soviet movement. Generally, Mao did not want to take part in either positional or mobile warfare against the Japanese so long as the leadership of the Generalissimo was in play. He did not refuse to assist friendly regular forces, but from his perspective the Eighth Route Army could and should conduct guerrilla or mobile-guerrilla military actions—what he dubbed sparrow warfare—in the Japanese rear, independent of the Guomindang and thereby taking the initiative into its own hands. Such a method of warfare, he thought, would be "more free, livelier and effective."[7] Stalin gave him the same advice. "[The Eighth Route Army] tactics," he said, "should . . . entice the opponent, draw him deep into the country and strike him in the rear. You need to blow up the lines of communication, the railroads, bridges [used by] the Japanese army."[8] Both Mao and Stalin supposed that the anti-Japanese war would be protracted. One had to be patient and wait, Mao explained, until the Japanese army exhausted its strength.[9] He continued to follow his beloved rule: "The enemy advances, we retreat; the enemy camps, we harass; the enemy tires, we attack; the enemy retreats, we pursue."

At the beginning of 1939, according to Japanese data, 300,000 guerrillas were already operating north of the Yangzi behind Japanese lines, 100,000 in Central China and 250,000 in the areas between Shanghai, Nanjing, and Hangzhou. The Chinese gave other figures, asserting that 2½ million armed patriots were operating behind the front lines. According to a Dutch intelligence agent living in Shanghai, in 1939 from 800,000 to 1 million guerrillas were fighting in the Japanese rear. Some were acting under the leadership of the Guomindang, some under the communists.[10]

Like Mao and Stalin, Chiang began to think the war against Japan would be protracted.[11] Therefore he began to devote an enormous amount of attention not only to developing and arming his military forces, but also to the training and education of leading cadres for the party. "Cadres decide everything," he wrote in his diaries on November 15, 1938. "The achievement of a political line, strategy and tactics of the party is linked in the closest way with how strong the party cadres are, how much the forces of the party are alienated, how well the cadres are connected to the masses, how much practical experience do the cadres possess, and how high is their level of theoretical preparation."[12]

He was quoting Stalin again, this time the speech Stalin gave in the Kremlin Palace to graduates of the military academies on May 4, 1935.[13] He appears to have been quite interested in everything the Soviet leader said, not passing up the opportunity to learn from him. The next year he even planned a conference with the slogan "Cadres decide everything." "Politics is more important than military affairs. . . . Spirit is more important than material," he declared at a meeting in Nanyue.[14]

On December 1, 1938, he flew from Hunan to Guilin in northeastern Guangxi and a week later arrived in Chongqing, his new capital. He chose the city, located in Sichuan province, not by accident, considering above all its strategic position on the banks of China's main water artery, the Yangzi River, at its confluence with another broad river, the Jialing (River Flowing Between Beautiful Hills). The latter rises in the north of China, in Shaanxi. Squeezed on two sides by these rivers, the city rises on steep hills along a narrow peninsula that looks like a parrot's beak. It was rather distant from the front—more than five hundred miles, and, moreover, the approaches to it were blocked by mountain ridges and riparian gorges, the Sanxia (Three Gorges), separating Sichuan from the rest of China.

Chongqing had been founded in the eleventh century BCE, but it was given its current name, meaning Double Happiness, two thousand years later in the twelfth century. The name was conferred on it by Zhao Dun, a prince of the Southern Song dynasty who administered the city, to mark two joyful events in his life: his forty-second birthday and the news that the very old emperor had appointed him his successor. Apart from its strategic significance, the city had little to commend it. It was a "desolate, damp, cheerless spot."[15] It immediately struck newly arrived persons as "an amazingly unfortunate site for human habitation, since there is no level land. One becomes a goat in the effort to get anywhere."[16] By December 1938 the city was terribly overcrowded with refugees from every corner of China. The municipal population had increased by 2.3 times—from 480,000 in July 1937 to 1.1 million.[17] This explosion of residents made all the urban problems worse: food supply, housing, communal apartments, sanitary, ecological, transportation, and public health. Crime rose sharply.

From morning until night almost all of the four hundred city streets and alleys swarmed with people making a racket in various dialects. A great many of the new inhabitants lived on the streets, sleeping, eating, taking care of their needs. The police were unable to establish order. There were beggars everywhere, emaciated, ragged, filthy vagrants. Some sat on the curbs, others followed passers-by, clutching their clothes. "Along the streets corpses sprawled out, and no one collected them. . . . The police paid no attention to them."[18] Many of the beggars were sick with leprosy "and forgivably spiteful; you hurried to find money in your purse; if not quick enough, they touched your shrinking skin."[19] Hordes of rats ran through the streets.[20] The stench of human excrement scattered about filled the air.

Nine months of the year Chongqing was covered by clouds that loosed a constant light drizzle, and the streets turned into gutters along which streams of turbid, stinking swill flowed into the Yangzi and the Jialing rivers. At that time the rays of the sun penetrated the thick smog so rarely that in China it was said that "when the sun shines in Chungking [Chongqing], even the dogs bark in fear."[21] On summer days the temperature reached 104 degrees with almost 100 percent humidity, causing both people and animals to gasp for breath.

Martha Gellhorn, Ernest Hemingway's wife, who was visiting China's wartime capital in 1941, wrote that Chongqing looked like "a grayish brown expanse of rubble . . . shapeless, muddy, a collection of drab cement buildings and poverty shacks, the best feature a lively market."[22] Hemingway did not like the city either. "Life in Chongqing is unbelievably difficult and unpleasant," he wrote.[23] However, foreigners as well as wealthy Chinese lived outside the city limits, south of the Yangzi in the Huangshan (Yellow Mountain) district. There, too, were hills, but pine trees and cypresses grew upon them and the air was clean and fresh. This was an area of summer cottages where neither the noise nor the dirt of the city penetrated.

Naturally, Chiang and his wife settled in Huangshan, especially since they loved nature and especially green hills and mountains. In preparation for their arrival the government had purchased summer houses from their owners. Thus in addition to the Chiang couple several other highly placed officials settled in this comfortable place, including Chiang's brother-in-law Kong Xiangxi, who, starting in January 1938, again headed the Executive Yuan. He was then living alone because his wife Ailing, Meiling's older sister, along with her third sister Qingling, Sun Yat-sen's widow, was in Hong Kong. Chiang's old friend and mentor Cicada Zhang was not there either. Instead of accompanying everyone to Chongqing, he left besieged Wuhan for Switzerland to receive treatment. After a year Zhang traveled to New York, where he remained thereafter. At the end of the war Chiang would call on him to return to China, but he did not. Not long afterward, on September 3, 1950, he died of heart disease at the not very advanced age of seventy-three. He is buried in Ferncliff Cemetery in Hartsdale, north of New York.

Chiang missed his old friend, but he had much business to attend to. During the war his summer house on the south bank of the Yangzi, at 23 Huangshan, became the headquarters of Chinese resistance to Japan. The detached, three-story, ten-room house in a dense pine forest was constructed in a fusion of Chinese and Western styles. At one time belonging to a banker, it was located at the summit of Huangshan, actually a low hill just 1,640 feet above sea level. A comfortable bomb shelter was built in the basement, a matter of no small importance.

Chiang Kai-shek also had a residence in the city, actually two. One was in the center of town on a small side street, De'an li (Morality and Tranquility Alley). It was a two-story detached house with columns, at Number 101, next door to the representative office of the Communist Party where Zhou Enlai worked when he visited Chongqing. Nearby was the building of the counterintelligence and other secret services of the Chinese government, which, as before, were headed by Dai Li, "the Chinese Himmler." The second residence was located in the southern suburbs, in the Xiaoquan Hotel (Small Spring), occupied at the time by students and teachers of the Political University of the Guomindang CEC. Since Chiang often went there for various reasons, they built a small pavilion for him in a Western style, where he both rested and worked.

But Chiang loved his summer house in Huangshan, which he named the Cavern in the Clouds, best of all, evoking one of the writings of the great Tao Yuanming:

> A cloud has taken up residence in a cavern,
> and has no wish to fly up to Heaven.
> A bird is exhausted from flying
> and returns home, barely breathing.[24]

The people of Chongqing, however, called his residence Eagle's Nest, the name of Hitler's Bavarian chalet, but Chiang did not like the comparison.[25]

Chiang's residences were guarded by several dozen soldiers under the command of the chief of his personal guard, Walter Franz Maria Stennes, one of the seven former German military advisors who had not wanted to return to their homeland in July 1938. Stennes, who had been one of the organizers of the Nazi party and its storm troops, had broken with Hitler in the early 1930s; in 1933, after the Führer had come to power, he was forced to flee. He lived in China, working for Chiang Kai-shek. A brave man in his forties and Aryan in appearance, he was "a big blond German," who enjoyed the full confidence of Chiang and his wife.[26] Unfortunately for them, they did not know that in March 1939 Stennes had offered his services to Soviet intelligence, after which he began supplying secret information to Moscow. The Russians gave him the code name Friend.[27]

Despite the war and his relocation to Chongqing, Chiang, as always, adhered to a strict daily regimen.[28] He arose as always at five o'clock and first prayed to God and read the Bible given to him by his mother-in-law. Then he meditated in front of an open window for half an hour, did calisthenics, and washed with icy water, not allowing anyone into his room. Then he cried out, "Wei!" and an orderly appeared, giving him a hot towel. Chiang dried himself, then he drank a glass of warm boiled water. He never drank tea or coffee, as mentioned above. Then he went out to breathe some fresh air, either humming or muttering something under his breath. Invariably he did this when going for a stroll. After an hour and a half he was served a light breakfast of either vegetables, noodles, or rice gruel, which he ate before going to work in his office. At one in the afternoon he dined with his wife, eating rice, a bit of meat, and salted vegetables. Then he slept until three o'clock, again took a walk, and then went to his office. At six in the evening he went for a third walk, this time with Meiling. At seven thirty he was served supper, again, like his breakfast and dinner Spartan simple, to which Chiang usually invited several guests. "The Generalissimo liked to watch people eating, having formed the conviction that people reveal themselves in the private ceremony of meals," one of his biographers wrote. "He liked people to eat fast with scarcely any outward movement of their features and with disdain for the food."[29] After supper he either worked again till late at night or, as occurred more often in Chongqing, watched a film with Meiling and guests. Before going to bed he wrote briefly in his diaries about the events of the day, and if he didn't manage to do this, he did so the next morning. At ten o'clock he prayed and then went to bed.[30]

Chiang demanded that those who attended him always follow the prescribed routine, and he often got angry at lackadaisical subordinates. He was very strict, rarely smiled, and never joked with service personnel. He did not like new clothes and often issued orders that the old ones be mended. Knowing their boss's stern, irascible nature, everyone in the house was afraid of him, except for Meiling. She went to sleep at one or two in the morning and got up at eleven. She forced herself to wake up for fifteen minutes when Chiang awoke before dawn so they could pray to God together. But then she went back to sleep. She liked to dress beautifully, eat well, dance and joke; she smoked long Russian cigarettes provided to her by the TASS correspondent Vladimir Nikolaevich Rogov. She enjoyed drinking expensive wine and playing bridge (Chiang preferred Chinese checkers). Everyone around her adored her. In sum, she was quite unlike her rather boring husband.[31]

Meanwhile, Chiang, on December 9, 1938, the day after his arrival, conducted a meeting of the Supreme National Defense Council at which he repeated what he had said in Nanyue: This is a protracted war, we will not surrender.[32] "His resolve to continue the war was firm," an eyewitness recalled.[33]

Among those who took part in the conference was the Number 2 man in the party and the state, Wang Jingwei, the deputy *zongcai.* After the surrender of Nanjing Wang was depressed all the time. The loss of Wuhan and especially of Canton, near where he was born, bothered him a great deal. In a private conversation with Chiang, he shared his thoughts that the time had come to sit down at the negotiating table with the Japanese. He believed that China did not know "how to sustain the war" and Japan "how to end the war," and Konoe had noticeably softened his demands on China.[34] Wang, as before, was acting on the formula "Resistance on the one hand and negotiations on the other." But Chiang did not agree, even though he knew this was not the position of Wang alone, but also that of many other party leaders, including even Kong Xiangxi and Chen Lifu, his close comrades in arms.[35] There existed even a group named the Low-Key Club that constantly agitated against "war hysteria." Wang Jingwei had close ties with the members of this club.[36]

Nevertheless, Wang continued to insist. He had two main arguments. The first was that continuing resistance would lead to the destruction of the Chinese nation and, second, that owing to the indifference of the Western powers China was under the control of the USSR. Dictating its will to Chiang via its military assistance, the Russians were clearing the path for the advent to power of the Communist Party. But Chiang, it seemed "completely failed to understand the difficult situation in which the country found itself . . . unthinkingly rejecting proposals for peace."[37] During the conversation, he could not restrain himself and flared up as the conversation turned stormy.

Wang was squelched, but a week later he again paid a visit to "the blind optimist," as he and his supporters referred to Chiang Kai-shek among themselves. However, it too came to nothing.[38] Jiang Tingfu, China's former ambassador to the USSR, recalled it: "When I went to his [Wang Jingwei's] residence, I found him downcast. He told me that the Generalissimo was completely against his views."[39] At this time, Chiang's position strengthened notably. On December 15, Roosevelt decided to provide China with an initial loan of $25 million. It could not be used for the purchase of American arms because the United States continued to maintain an isolationist policy.[40] But the loan itself testified to a change in the US position toward the Japanese–Chinese conflict.[41] "The American loan is a most powerful blow against the enemy," Chiang wrote in his diaries.[42]

Thereupon Wang decided to act on his own and enter into open negotiations with the Japanese without Chiang's approval.[43] He realized he might be subjecting himself to universal condemnation, but he was prepared, in his own words, "to be a sacrifice" in the name of saving China.[44] On December 18, two days after his last meeting with Chiang and having sent his children abroad earlier, Wang, his wife, and his close comrades in arms flew out of Chongqing. They went first to Kunming, the capital of Yunnan, where Wang turned for support to the local governor, Long Yun. But Long was equivocal, and the next day Wang and his supporters flew to Hanoi in North Vietnam and from there they moved to one of the neighboring mountain resorts.[45] Learning of Wang's flight, Premier Konoe, on the evening of December 22, made a new declaration, proposing peace "to those far-sighted Chinese who share in our ideals and aspirations." The peace would rest on the basis of just three principles: a relationship of neighborly friendship, common defense against Communism, and economic cooperation.[46]

Meanwhile, Chiang, on December 21, informed of Wang Jingwei's flight, lost sleep.[47] He did not know how much solid support Wang had in the party and the army. Most of all he was worried about whether Yunnan and Guangdong would revolt. The next day he held meetings with high-ranking army officers: in all he was able to talk with more than eighty generals.[48] But his anxiety turned out to be in vain. Despite their merely formal subordination to the Generalissimo, the governors of Yunnan and Guangdong did not support Wang. On December 26 Chiang officially rejected Konoe's three principles, and so informed the Western powers.

Three days later, however, Wang Jingwei sent a "peace telegram" to his former comrades in Chongqing, openly stating that Konoe's principles were a reasonable basis for negotiations.[49] In response, after bowing to the spirit of the late Sun Yat-sen (apparently in order to secure his support) early on the morning of January 1, 1939, Chiang convened a meeting of the Standing Committee of the Guomindang CEC to discuss Wang's action. He suggested sending the traitor a warning, explaining that he should not swallow "the Japanese bait." The majority of the committee members present, understanding what the *zongcai* actually wanted, demanded the expulsion of Sun Yat-sen's closest disciple from the party forever, while stripping him "of all posts in the party and elsewhere." Chiang immediately declared a dinner break until two thirty in the afternoon, after which, having resumed the discussion, he pretended he was submitting to the opinion of the majority. "Wang Jingwei must be expelled from the ranks of the GMD and deprived of all his positions," he asserted, "since he is 90 percent a traitor." Hence, having performed his role, he suggested they vote: "Who is for expulsion?" Of the sixty-eight members of the Standing Committee, sixty-four raised their hands (according to another source, of sixty present, fifty-eight raised their hands). Among those who did not agree with the decision was Kong Xiangxi, who said it would be better to reprimand Wang, and if he did not change his mind then expel him.[50]

Informing the Soviet ambassador of this action on January 2, Sun Fo observed that Wang Jingwei was the Chinese Trotsky. "You expelled your Trotsky, and we expelled our Trotsky—Wang Jingwei."[51] Luganets-Orel'sky, who, on Stalin's instructions, had been trying to win over the Chinese in the struggle against Trotskyism,[52] was likely satisfied with this comparison. Several days later, Chiang himself frankly wrote in his diaries, "That Wang fled is a blessing for the party and the country."[53]

Indeed, in the aftermath of Wang's flight Chiang's position in the party, the army, and the country was strengthened. At the Fifth Plenum of the Guomindang Fifth CEC that took place in Chongqing from January 21 to 30, 1939, Chiang was awarded a new position: he became not only the *zongcai* but also the chair of the Supreme National Defense Council, thereby uniting the leadership of the party and the army.[54] On February 10 he sent someone to Hanoi to persuade Wang to go somewhere farther away, for example, to France, and he even gave him a foreign passport and 500,000 yuan for the road. Wang firmly refused.[55]

Chiang then issued a secret order to the head of the special services to eliminate the traitor—just as Stalin did to Trotsky.[56] On March 21, 1939, the assassins entered Wang's bedroom, emptied their automatic weapons on the person sleeping in the bed, and quickly disappeared. To Chiang's great disappointment, Wang escaped death. For some reason or other, the night before he had switched bedrooms with his secretary. The poor young man paid with his life for being loyal to his boss. Wang, frightened that Chiang would not stop at this, sailed from Vietnam at the end of April for a less dangerous place, Japanese-occupied Shanghai.[57]

Wang was luckier than Trotsky, whom Stalin's agent would mortally wound a year and a half later, but Wang's fate too was unenviable. Arriving in Shanghai on May 5, 1939, he put himself in the hands of the Japanese. His romantic dream of a "good-neighborly peace" with the aggressor crashed on the rocks of crude reality. From then on only one path was open to him: to become a Japanese puppet. This he did by beginning the process of establishing a pro-Japanese government.[58]

Meanwhile, a patriotic upsurge was growing in Chongqing. Every morning the national anthem blared over the radio and in the evening the sound of bugles everywhere, accompanying the lowering of the national flag.[59] In movie theaters "prior to the showing of films, images of the national flag waving and photographs of party and state leaders were projected on the screen. Everyone had to stand and listen in silence to the national anthem."[60] The New Life Movement was unfolding in the city, and efforts were being made to solve municipal problems. "Thousands of workmen toiling night and day, bored and blasted shelters into Chungking [Chongqing]'s rock foundations," an eyewitness recalled, "and from those excavations came blocks of stone for the construction of the new factories, shops, offices, and private dwellings."[61] The opium trade, which had been flourishing until then, was strictly prohibited. All residents were ordered to dress simply, observe hygiene, and abide by rules of morality. Mixed gender public baths, which had long been flourishing in Chongqing, were closed, the sale of alcohol stopped, it was forbidden to spit on the streets and to hold sumptuous banquets, including on wedding and funeral days. Women, except for prostitutes, were not allowed to wear high heels. Streets were given revolutionary names: Sun Yat-sen Street, Zhongzheng (that is, Chiang Kai-shek) Street, Nationalism Street, Democracy Street, People's Livelihood Street (Sun Yat-sen's Three Principles of the People).[62] From time to time Chiang himself drove around Chongqing to check on the uniforms of military and police officers and to ensure they behaved properly or if there were any "other inadequacies in the city's appearance."[63] New roads and sidewalks were built, and construction began on an aqueduct to bring water from the Yangzi and Jialing rivers into the city. This was a real revolution in that a wonder like an aqueduct was something the city's residents had never seen. Long lines of coolies carrying water buckets on shoulder yokes and climbing stone steps up to the city had supplied the needs of residents.[64]

Life in Chongqing, as throughout Sichuan and other free regions of China, was gradually returning to normal. The rich province of Sichuan, the most populous in China, with a population then of about fifty million people, was essentially self-sufficient, that is, it could feed itself. To be sure, it had no raw cotton and was entirely lacking modern industry, but all problems could be solved. Cotton began to be brought in from elsewhere, and translocated factories resumed production. Chiang did not even encounter any difficulties with the local authorities who had previously controlled Sichuan. The Generalissimo was simply lucky. The Sichuan militarist Liu Xiang, who had only grudgingly accepted Chiang's authority, died on January 20, 1938, not long before Chiang's arrival in Chongqing. "This is good fortune for the country," Chiang wrote in his diaries that day, noting that although he was "deeply saddened" by the passing of Liu Xiang, "now Sichuan could be united and lay the foundation for the war of resistance."[65] He was laying that foundation, but he faced many difficulties. On November 9, 1940, he wrote in his diaries, "The old warlords in Sichuan are incompetent and useless. They are greedy and cowardly. It is indeed most pitiful and troublesome. I cannot be either tolerant or harsh, I only have to advance slowly to see the results."[66]

From time to time Chongqing was bombed by the Japanese. The first and the most terrible of all took place in early May 1939. "An armada—the biggest I had ever seen in China—passed directly overhead," recalled an Australian correspondent: "I scaled a cliff, edged through a blazing slum area, and reached the old walled city. Heavily wounded people were crawling to the exits. A man with a pulped face was charging blindly into walls and telephone posts. . . . Dead and dying were everywhere and screams came from bashed, burning buildings whose flames luridly illuminating the ghastly scene."[67] As a result of this terrible bombing, which went on for two days, the number of residents in the central part of the city was reduced by almost half.[68] "Chongqing has become one vast cemetery," said a horrified French missionary.[69] By mid-September 1939 the Japanese had made thirty flights over the city, each one of which brought new destruction and victims. The energy supply was frequently damaged and the water supply cut off.[70]

In addition to all of the current difficulties, in the spring of 1939, Chiang's relations with his main ally, Stalin, began to deteriorate. On the surface everything appeared to be normal as the USSR continued to supply China. Soviet pilots did everything they could to defend Chongqing. It was not their fault that Japanese bombers were still able to get through. But Chiang sensed that something had gone wrong: in the spring of 1939 Stalin unexpectedly began to delay signing a third agreement on a loan, the largest yet, for US $150 million.

Until then everything had seemed just fine. At the Fifth Plenum of the Guomindang CEC in January 1939 Chiang had declared that the Soviet Union was China's best friend. He expressed his hope that China, the USSR, the United States, England, and France would form a front of peaceful countries to oppose the aggressive bloc of Japan, Germany, and Italy.[71] On March 22, in connection with the departure to Moscow of Ambassador Luganets-Orel'sky (on leave "for 2–2.5 months"), Chiang gave him a letter for Stalin.[72] In part he wrote, "It is my unshakable opinion that over the course of the coming fifty years the USSR and China should be closely linked in a united front." He emphasized that he was counting on the $150 million loan "to cover our deficiency in war materiel," and, moreover, he again proposed to conclude a supplementary treaty, this time under the rubric of "a general pact to defend peace in the Far East."[73] At the same time, he dispatched Sun Fo to Moscow as his special ambassador with plenipotentiary power and as his personal representative to sign the loan agreement. Sun and Luganets-Orel'sky flew out of Chongqing on the same plane on March 25 and arrived in Moscow on April 7.

Stalin treated Sun Fo exactly as he did Mao Zedong ten years later: he settled him into a dacha on the outskirts of Moscow and ignored him.[74] Chiang repeatedly requested of various officials that Stalin grant Sun an audience, and Sun himself insistently asked also, but Stalin declined to meet him, citing various pretexts.[75] Luganets-Orel'sky, for example, informed Sun Fo that Stalin "is not in Moscow."[76] In fact, he was in the city.[77] Only five weeks later, on May 15, 1939, Stalin received Chiang's envoy.[78] Yet the meeting was a mere formality. Although Stalin promised to provide supplies, he was in no hurry to sign a new loan agreement with Sun nor would he consider the question of a new pact. Possibly that is why at the start of the meeting he requested that there be no stenograph of the conversation, and at the end he took away the writing pad on which the interpreter, Sergei Leonidovich Tikhvinsky, had been taking notes during the conversations.[79] The next day, Molotov, in whose office an audience with Sun took place, shamelessly informed him that inasmuch as "information regarding our conversation that took place recently in the evening has become known to outsiders, the Soviet government has decided to extend and, consequently, put off, pending further developments, the current negotiations over sending Soviet aid to China."[80]

Chiang supposed that the distinct change in the USSR's policy toward China was due to the appointment in May 1939 of Molotov as people's commissar for foreign affairs, in place of Litvinov. Owing to some inexplicable naivete, Chiang seemed to think that people's commissars in the Soviet Union could influence the political direction of the country.[81] He was mistaken. Most likely Stalin's behavior was linked to the fact that it was precisely in the spring of 1939 that relations between the Guomindang and the Chinese communists in Hebei, in the Japanese rear area, sharply deteriorated.[82]

By its very nature an alliance of two formerly mortal enemies could not last, and in conditions where communist and Guomindang troops were forced to act side by side in the Japanese rear, a deep split between them was unavoidable. After all, the local peasants could not feed everyone—the Japanese, the communists, and the Guomindang—and thus friction, that is, armed conflicts between CCP and GMD troops foraging for fodder and provisions, were inevitable. Starting in late 1938 Chiang repeatedly tried to settle the communist problem. He insisted on a strict delineation of war zones in the Japanese rear, demanded that Mao and Zhu De, the commander of the communist Eighth Route Army, unfailingly execute all his orders. He repeatedly suggested that the communists either join the Guomindang or agree to dissolve both parties and establish a single organization under the name Republican or Socialist.[83] At Chiang's request of June 3, 1938, the Guomindang's CCC restored the GMD membership of Chen Duxiu, Zhang Guotao, Zhou Enlai, Mao Zedong, and twenty-six other present and former members of the Communist Party. These men had joined the Guomindang earlier, during the period of the first united front in the 1920s.

But all of Chiang's importuning was in vain. That same day, June 3, Mao and other members of the CCP rejected the decision of the Guomindang CCC, declining to have their party membership reinstated.[84] Following the course set by the enlarged Politburo meeting in Luochuan in August 1937, they continued to conduct operations in the Japanese rear area independent of Chiang Kai-shek. Understanding that China by itself would be unable to defeat Japan, Mao used the time to establish as many CCP military bases as possible on the territories seized by the Japanese. By 1940 there were already more than ten such bases. For propaganda purposes the communists called them liberated areas, although in reality they hadn't liberated anyone: there were no Japanese in most villages behind the front lines.[85]

Though Chiang was outraged, he did not stop funding the Eighth Route Army because this aid had been stipulated in the August 1937 agreement: 675,000 Chinese dollars per month.[86] But sometimes his nerves snapped, and he began taking certain anticommunist measures, mostly, it is true, limited to the area of propaganda. He prohibited, for example, the sale of books about the Eighth Route Army and ordered the distribution of anticommunist leaflets. But as soon as he enacted these measures Soviet representatives immediately informed Moscow of Chiang's terrible anticommunism. In response Stalin wanted to teach the Chinese Generalissimo a lesson by continuing to drag out the process of concluding the loan agreement.

At the same time, Stalin, for a different reason and by other means, also taught Ambassador Luganets-Orel'sky a lesson. At the end of May Stalin ordered his arrest, which was carried out while the ambassador was staying in

Tskhaltubo in Georgia in a sanatorium belonging to the People's Commissariat for Internal Affairs. Soon his wife was also taken into custody. On July 8 both were killed—there was no investigation or trial—their heads smashed in with a hammer on a train from Tskhaltubo to Tbilisi. Their corpses were dragged into an automobile, and Stalin's agents plunged it down an embankment, staging an automobile accident. Soon it was announced that the Ambassador of the USSR to China, Comrade I. T. Luganets-Orel'sky, and his wife, N. V. Luganets-Orel'skaia, perished in an untimely automobile accident near Tskhaltubo. On July 14 a solemn funeral was held for them in Tbilisi.

According to several sources, the murder of the ambassador who was also the intelligence chief was arranged in such a strange manner because, in addition to discharging his immediate duties, he controlled the narcotics trade in China, most likely on Moscow's orders. Hence if he had been openly declared an enemy of the people, his Chinese associates might have gone into hiding. At least this is what appears in the file of Chief of the Soviet Secret Services Lavrentii Pavlovich Beria, preserved in the Federal Security Bureau archive. But what this all means and why Luganets-Orel'sky was arrested is not known.[87]

Stalin nevertheless approved an agreement for a new loan to China of US $150 million, which was signed on June 13, 1939. Three days later a commercial treaty between the USSR and the Republic of China was concluded, and four days after that contracts were signed by which the Soviet Union would supply China with military technology and other supplies to resist Japanese aggression.[88]

On June 17, 1939, three weeks before the murder of Luganets-Orel'sky, Stalin, in his office in the Kremlin, received the future new ambassador and station chief of Soviet foreign intelligence in China: senior major of state security thirty-four-year-old Aleksandr Semenovich Paniushkin.[89] "You have to try your hand at diplomatic work," he said to the comparatively young man who was then chief of the 3rd (operational) special division of the People's Commissariat for Internal Affairs, whose jurisdiction included external surveillance of persons under suspicion, searches, and arrests. Prior to Paniushkin's departure for China, that is, prior to July 10, Stalin met with him twice more to define his assignments.[90]

In the words of the future ambassador, the leader said to him, "The Soviet Union going forward will categorically provide moral support to China and, unconditionally, fulfill its obligations according to the Soviet–Chinese nonaggression treaty and the credit agreements to supply arms and materiel."[91] He may indeed have said that, but he was evidently in no hurry to fulfill his obligations, especially since, in June 1939 in the Japanese rear area in Hebei province, a full-scale battle took place between the 120th Division of the Eighth Route Army and Guomindang troops.[92] Although the latter were thoroughly defeated, and their commander fled from the province along with the governor, Stalin could not help being irritated with Chiang Kai-shek since it turned out that the Soviet arms he had supplied to Chiang were being used against the communists. Therefore, the Kremlin boss began to delay their shipment.

On July 30, 1939, Chiang Kai-shek wrote a letter to Voroshilov, noting that "according to rumors all of the arms you have promised to China have not yet been sent,"[93] but he achieved nothing. The first consignment of arms from the new loan—250 artillery pieces, 500 motor vehicles, 500,000 artillery shells, 50,000 rifles, and 2.1 million cartridges—arrived in China several months later.[94]

Meanwhile, both at the front and in the rear Soviet military servicemen continued to work actively in China. In October 1939 there were eighty military advisors in country and more than 3,500 other specialists.[95] One of them was Andrei Andreevich Vlasov, the future lieutenant general who in July 1942 went over to serve the Nazis. He had been assigned to Chongqing from Kyiv under the pseudonym Volkov in November 1938. After working for several months as a military advisor to Yan Xishan in Shanxi province in May 1939 he was appointed chief of staff to Chief Military Advisor Cherepanov. He was on assignment until the end of November 1939 and succeeded Cherepanov when he returned home at the end of June 1939 and prior to the arrival of the new chief military advisor, division commander Kuzma Maximovich Kachanov (pseudonym Volgin) in October of that year. Thus over the course of three and a half months Vlasov served as acting chief advisor to Chiang Kai-shek. As he had with Dratvin, Cherepanov, and would have with Kachanov, Chiang developed a very good personal relationship with Vlasov.[96]

Relying on the experience of Soviet advisors and specialists, Chiang, in April, July, and September 1939, attempted three breakthroughs on the front but all failed. The Japanese, however, got lucky once again in May 1939 and seized the capital of Jiangxi, the city of Nanchang.[97]

Meanwhile, in China the news that, on August 23, the Soviet Union had concluded a nonaggression treaty with Nazi Germany reverberated like thunder in a clear blue sky. In China, as everywhere else in the world, nothing was known of the secret protocol to the treaty.[98] But Chiang was highly upset because it might doom his idea of creating the front of peaceful countries alluded to earlier. He had placed great hopes on this front, especially since, starting in April 1939, Anglo–French–Soviet negotiations had been taking place in Moscow on concluding a treaty of mutual assistance, and their successful conclusion did not seem far off.[99] He simply did not know what to think, so he invited the new Soviet ambassador to dinner on August 25 and plied him with questions about what the Soviet–German treaty signified and what would happen with the Anglo–French–Soviet negotiations. Chiang was also troubled by the question of whether the Soviet Union, under the influence of Germany, might conclude a similar treaty with Japan. He asked Paniushkin to elucidate Stalin's views on these matters. Also at his request, Sun Fo and General Yang Jie, China's ambassador to Moscow, tried to clarify Stalin's perspective on the possibility of concluding a Soviet–Japanese treaty.[100]

Paniushkin was meeting with the Generalissimo for the second time since his arrival in China. He remembered Chiang as trim, neat, "with a penetrating look from small eyes and a closely cropped graying mustache." Chiang's movements struck him as being "slow, deliberate. In the very first minutes of the [first] conversation, I understood that before me was an experienced Oriental politician."[101]

In early September Chiang revived his proposal to Stalin to conclude a mutual assistance treaty. He thought such a treaty would pull the rug out from under Japan, as it would not be able to conclude a nonaggression treaty with the USSR. But Stalin, after again refusing to sign such a treaty, wrote a response to Chiang via Paniushkin: "We don't understand why Chiang Kai-shek is anxious. Rumors that Japan proposed a nonaggression pact to the USSR and that negotiations about this are going on are without any foundation."[102]

When the Second World War erupted in Europe Chiang understood very well what had served as the catalyst. On September 5, obviously not without Chiang's knowledge, Kong Xiangxi declared to the Soviet ambassador that "Germany could not have attacked Poland if France, England, and the USSR had reached an agreement among themselves. . . . The USSR could put an end to the war with a strong word."[103]

On September 11 Chiang Kai-shek himself, after receiving a report about partial mobilization in the Soviet Union, directly asked Paniushkin the following question: "What position does the USSR hold with respect to this country [Poland]?" He emphasized that "the Chinese Government has not yet taken any decisions on this question, but . . . pub[lic] sympathies are on the side of Poland, which has been subjected to aggression."[104] The ambassador, as frantic as a cat on a hot tin roof, unconvincingly muttered, "The USSR will adhere to benevolent neutrality with respect to Poland."[105]

Either he was lying or he had not been informed of Stalin's plans, but six days later, on September 17, the Soviet Union attacked Poland, entering the Second World War on the side of Hitler. Following the division of Poland almost along the Curzon line, the Führer and Stalin, on September 28, signed another treaty, this one on friendship and the border.[106] Chiang's expectations about drawing the USSR into the Japanese–Chinese war collapsed: Japan was the closest ally of Germany—and Germany was now the new friend of the USSR.

Chiang was shocked: "This morning Soviet troops attacked Polish territory under the pretext that the Polish government had collapsed . . . but at the same time they declared that they were maintaining neutrality in the German–Polish war as before. Isn't this ridiculous? Yesterday they reached an agreement with Japan, and today they attacked Poland.[107] Their principles and convictions have nothing in common with international norms of morality."[108]

A week later in a new conversation with the Soviet ambassador, Chiang informed him of his supposition that "Germany and the USSR had agreed upon the division of Poland." He did not try to conceal his sympathy for the brave Polish soldiers.[109] There was nothing he could do, however, since he was still dependent upon Soviet military aid. "Yes, in the international arena we must compromise with the USSR," he wrote in his diaries, "but news of the Soviet aggression against Poland pains the hearts of all moral persons in the world."[110]

Pain or no pain, in September 1939, with the help of Soviet military advisors, Chiang's forces succeeded in repulsing the enemy's 120,000-man offensive against Changsha. It was a great victory. During the month-long battle the Chinese wiped out 40,000 officers and men of the enemy, one third of the army that attacked Changsha.

But at the end of November the Japanese, after making a sudden landing on the coast of Guangxi province, seized the city of Nanning. Just prior to this, disturbing news had reached Chiang from Moscow: the Japanese ambassador to the USSR had proposed to Molotov on September 9, 1939, that he sign a Soviet–Japanese commercial treaty and, on October 4, a provisional agreement on trade and navigation. Chiang was upset. On two occasions, November 13 and 21, he requested that Paniushkin inform the Soviet government that it should not have "any commercial dealings with Japan." But on November 16 Stalin agreed to conclude a commercial treaty with Japan.[111] Chiang Kai-shek could never accuse Stalin of boring him!

On November 30, 1939, the Kremlin boss presented him with a new, unpleasant surprise. After securing Germany's support, he suddenly attacked Finland.

This was more serious than Poland in that it placed Chiang Kai-shek in a terribly difficult position. In the League of Nations, the Argentine government, supported by a majority of Latin American states, soon raised the question of expelling the Soviet Union from membership in that organization. As luck would have it, China was one of the states possessing veto power in the League Council. It could not permit the expulsion to occur, but if it exercised its veto, China, like the USSR, would be isolated internationally. After all, it was not just the Latin American countries but also the Western democracies that pointedly disapproved of the actions of the Soviet Union. Moreover, the British and the French were even considering plans to send a joint expeditionary force to fight against the Russians and bomb the oil fields in Baku.[112] On December 14, the day the vote was taken, the Chinese delegate, Wellington Koo, abstained.[113] Even though representatives of eight other states also abstained while twenty-eight voted in favor of expulsion, Stalin, not surprisingly, viewed the action of the Chinese delegate in particular as betrayal.

None of Chiang's clumsy excuses or references to technical obstacles helped. Nor did a hypocritical statement he made, conveyed via his special representative General He Yaozu on December 30, 1939, help bring Stalin around. The statement asserted that "public opinion in China, putting itself in the position of the Soviet Union, recognizes as wholly correct those measures that the USSR adopted on the Baltic Sea to implement its peaceful policy from the moment war erupted in Europe."[114]

Then, in addition to everything else, in the northern province of Shanxi, in the Japanese-controlled area, large-scale clashes between communist and Guomindang troops broke out again. Tens of thousands of officers and men were involved. Worst of all is that the battles took place during a new winter offensive by Chiang Kai-shek's army, the very largest, for which Chiang had mobilized 450,000 troops. This offensive, organized in Central China, proceeded with varying degrees of success because the Chinese suffered from a colossal shortage of weapons. In the entire army, then numbering 4½ million officers and soldiers, there were only 1.6 million rifles, 68,762 submachine guns, 17,700 machine guns, 5,884 mortars, and 2,650 artillery of assorted calibers.[115] On top of this there were now clashes with the communists. Because of the friction with the Communist Party, the governor of Shanxi, General Yan Xishan, was unable to take part in the offensive and even entered into negotiations with the Japanese to rout the communists with their help. But still nothing came of this, and the communist troops scored a new, convincing victory over the Guomindang forces.[116]

The fighting was not the end of it. Around this same time, communist guerrillas in southern Hebei, under the command of Liu Bocheng and Deng Xiaoping, after establishing their own bank in October 1939, began large-scale printing of their own paper currency that circulated widely in North China. Such a development might undermine the financial–economic system of the country.[117] What was more, in 1939, according to certain sources, Mao Zedong began to regularly sell to the Japanese secret intelligence information about conditions in Guomindang territory.[118]

Then, on December 12, Japanese aviation bombed Chiang's native village of Xikou for the first time. His father's house was destroyed, and his first wife, Mao Fumei, was heavily injured when a wall collapsed on her. She died the next day at just fifty-seven years of age. Chiang was deeply saddened, but he was unable to go to her funeral. On December 13, right after learning of her death, he asked Ching-kuo to make all the arrangements for the funeral.[119] Ching-kuo immediately went to Xikou and, after burying his mother, had a tombstone erected over her grave inscribed with four characters in his own hand: *yi xue xi xue* (blood will be washed away with blood).[120]

At the front, on December 16, Chinese troops achieved a victory, recapturing Kaifeng from the enemy, although they were unable to hold on to it. Ultimately, by the spring of 1940, after fighting 960 battles and 1,340 minor skirmishes, they were forced to retreat along almost the entire front after losing 200,000 soldiers and even allowing the Japanese to penetrate more than another 185 miles into the interior of the country, up to the city of Yichang on the Yangzi River. Now the enemy was only a little over 300 miles from Chongqing. But the Japanese imperial army was unable to surmount this distance. The front stabilized, and the Japanese did not undertake any general offensive against Sichuan or Chongqing.[121] They merely continued to bomb the Chinese capital, executing 268 raids in 1939–41[122] and turning Chongqing into the most intensively bombed city in world history.[123]

In January 1940 Chiang Kai-shek began new negotiations with representatives of the Communist Party to fully delineate a division of territory in the Japanese rear area. A wide-scale war with Mao was the last thing he needed. This, incidentally, even Soviet historians understood in the 1970s, regardless of their overall negative attitude toward Chiang Kai-shek.[124] They, too, had to acknowledge that Chiang was not the guilty party in the conflicts between the Communist Party and the Guomindang in 1939–40. First, Chiang could gain nothing from provoking quarrels with Stalin since, for all the pros and cons, the USSR remained the chief arms supplier to China; and, second, because Chiang knew that at this time Wang Jingwei was proceeding rapidly in establishing his regime in Nanjing. The dissolution of the anti-Japanese united front would play into Wang's hands. Wang Jingwei's puppet government would come into being on March 30, 1940.

The negotiations proceeded slowly. Not until mid-June did Chiang Kai-shek and Zhou Enlai, who again was representing the CCP, apparently succeed in reaching an agreement. It stipulated that all communist troops operating south of the old channel of the Yellow River would be withdrawn to the north.[125]

But at that very time, in July, Molotov received a proposal from the Japanese ambassador to the USSR to conclude a neutrality agreement which, in essence, was aimed at China. The ambassador explained that neutrality meant the USSR would refrain from "providing aid to the Chongqing government." Molotov shamelessly told the Japanese that "all talk about [Soviet] aid to China was ungrounded." He did not deny that earlier the USSR had provided China aid "in personnel, arms, and airplanes." "But," he noted, "it is a different situation now." Thus the Number 2 man after Stalin let China's mortal enemy know that Moscow was not opposed to discussing an agreement with Tokyo behind Chiang Kai-shek's back.[126]

Molotov knew what he was talking about. Without Stalin's approval he would never have made such a statement. The Kremlin leader was probably inclined then to change partners in the Far East in the near term. At least he began to apply the brakes more firmly to arms shipments to China.[127]

Naturally, the delay in deliveries alarmed the Chinese. In September 1940 the counselor of the Chinese embassy in the USSR, Liu Zerong,[128] complained to the People's Commissariat for Foreign Affairs that not a single question addressed by [our] ambassador to the People's Commissariat for Foreign Trade has been decided. Perhaps this is the general attitude toward Chinese affairs. Our ambassador Shao Lizi[129] . . . came here in a very upbeat mood, but at present he is deeply depressed."[130]

Chiang Kai-shek was no less distressed. In early September 1940 he wrote in his diaries: "I need to telegraph Stalin and ask what, after all, [is going on]. (He has replied neither to the telegram transmitted via Ambassador Pan [Paniushkin] and the main advisor, nor to the letter transmitted by Ambassador Shao. Has he received them, has he read them? I think intensely about Chinese–Soviet relations, is receipt of material aid at this time generally possible?)"[131]

Meanwhile, in 1940 Chiang's relations with his closest friend and advisor Donald became extremely complicated due to the war in Europe. As of September 3, 1939, Australia was in a state of war with Germany, so Donald began to voice strongly anti-Nazi sentiments in an attempt to sway Chiang in the same direction. But the Generalissimo was very cautious, especially with regard to the Soviet–German pact, and observed to Donald: "I am not at war with Germany."

"I am," Donald replied, now understanding that it was time to part.

Just at this time he had a difficult conversation with Meiling, to whom he pointed out in his characteristic bluntness the unacceptable behavior of members of her family, who were noted for their corrupt deals and speculation on the currency market. In a burst of anger the first lady of China said to him, "Donald, you may criticize the government or everything in China, but there are some persons even you cannot criticize!"[132]

Corruption and larceny always existed in China, even under the Guomindang. On June 30, 1932, for example, Chiang wrote in his diaries, "Old Party members are corrupt, they do not know their own past and are quick to make a chaos." On August 5 of the same year he named corruption in China "the second object of the revolution" (the liquidation of the unequal treaties being the first and the reactionary forces the third). And on September 1 he once again complained that "all Party members are terribly corrupt. All new Party members are either depraved or worthless careerists."[133]

But the unlawful enrichment of those in power including, first of all, members of Chiang's family, was especially unacceptable from a moral perspective during wartime. However, Meiling and Chiang himself did not wish to intervene, viewing the situation as unexceptional. When one of the foreign journalists remarked to Meiling that the communists were probably the least corrupt of everyone in China, Madame Chiang irritably exclaimed, "Incorrupt, yes; but that's because they haven't got power yet!"[134]

That Chiang was not corrupt is beyond doubt, but Chiang' brother-in-law Kong Xiangxi, who served as minister of finance from 1933 on, and Kong's wife, Ailing, could hardly be considered innocent. They flaunted their wealth indecently. After meeting Ailing at a reception, Martha Gellhorn said she reminded her "of stout rich vulgar matrons in Miami Beach hotels. . . . I remember her dress as one of the most beautiful I have ever seen. It was the classic Chinese model . . . of black velvet. The little buttons that close these gowns from collar to knee are usually made of silk braid; hers were button-size diamonds. She said she had ruby and emerald buttons too."[135]

In 1941 Kong and Ailing in particular became objects of intense criticism in both the Chinese and foreign press. "I was amazed by the almost universal dislike for Madame Kung [Kong]," an eyewitness who lived in Chongqing in the second half of 1941 recalls. "Everybody believed that she controlled one particular bank, through which she bought American dollars just before each new, steep fall in the value of the Chinese dollar."[136] In 1942 one of Kong's protégés was even executed on charges of corruption, and in 1943 several more of his associates were arrested.[137] But Chiang never launched an investigation of Kong.

In the meantime, in May 1940 Donald abandoned the Chiangs and with them China, his second homeland. Over the course of two years, he sailed around the Pacific Ocean in his yacht *Meihua* (which can be translated either as Beautiful Flower or Flower of Meiling) until, in January 1942, he was taken prisoner by the Japanese in Manila. They did not know whom they had seized, as Donald concealed his name. He returned to China only after the war and soon died in Shanghai on November 9, 1946, precisely when Chiang needed him more than ever.[138]

Who knows, but wise advice from his old friend at that crucial time might have saved Chiang and, with him, China, from the catastrophe that befell them. Three years later, in October 1949, Chiang lost his last war with the communists, and China wound up in the vise of the communist dictatorship. It is unlikely, however, that Donald could have saved him during the last civil war. Chiang and his wife should have listened to him earlier, in the spring of 1940, when the honest advisor directly pointed out to them the terrible tumor that was devouring their government: the corruption of those in power. During the ensuing years of the anti-Japanese war, this tumor would fatally metastasize and, along with other factors, lead to the downfall of their regime. Thus it is difficult not to agree with an eyewitness, the American flyer Claire Lee Chennault, who recalled, "It was a tragedy for all China in 1940 when Donald's attempt to rout reactionaries from their high places in the Kuomintang [Guomindang] government failed, and he was banished from his place behind the Generalissimo's chair. Donald was an implacable foe of Oriental graft and inefficiency."[139]

One cannot ignore the truth of Confucius, who said, "Failure to cultivate moral power, failure to explore what I have learned, incapacity to stand by what I know to be right, incapacity to reform what is not good—these are my worries."[140]

PART FIVE

# *China's Destiny*

CHAPTER 17

# *Ave Maria*

The complication in relations with the Soviet Union naturally distressed Chiang, but he took it as a given. "Russia's foreign policy has obviously changed radically, and we need not [any longer] hope for their help," he wrote in his diaries at the start of 1940.[1] He sized up the situation soberly, especially since he became convinced at the time that he would soon garner a new friend, the United States.

The American government had begun taking steps to constrain Japan's aggression in the Far East in July 1939. It was then that good news from Washington arrived in Chongqing. President Franklin D. Roosevelt received congressional authorization to abrogate in six months the American–Japanese trade and navigation treaty of 1911 by which the United States supplied the Japanese with strategic raw materials.[2] However, the Americans, following their isolationist policy fielded only a small army consisting at the end of 1939 of half a million officers and soldiers, including reserves.[3] The United States still did not want to intervene in the conflict and therefore continued to avoid any actions that might draw them into it, in particular refusing to sell weapons to the Chinese.

Yet by early 1940, around the time the annulment of the trade treaty with Japan was to come into effect, a change occurred in American public opinion. Seventy percent of Americans, outraged by Japanese atrocities in China and ashamed that their government had helped the aggressors in the initial years of the war, began expressing a desire to punish Japan, employing "naval forces if necessary."[4] These bellicose inclinations reanimated the ever-growing fears of American citizens regarding possible Japanese incursions into Southeast Asia, an important source of raw materials for American industry.

The alliance between the Japanese and the Nazis, who had unleashed the Second World War, likewise elicited strong dissatisfaction on the part of the American public and government. That is why the US ambassador to Japan, Joseph Clark Grew, back in April 1939, had told the editor of the *Tokyo nichi nichi shimbun* (Tokyo Daily News) that "if Japan turns out to be in the same camp with Germany, it will be difficult for our two countries to maintain peaceful relations."[5]

Chiang Kai-shek also nurtured hopes for a serious exacerbation of Anglo–Japanese relations, especially because Great Britain was already fighting Japan's ally, Nazi Germany. (The United Kingdom declared war on Germany on September 3, 1939.) In the spring of 1940 Chiang's hopes began to materialize. On March 7 Roosevelt extended a second loan to him, this time for US $20 million. Although this was not a lot of money and again was not designated for arms purchases, Chiang was heartened. "The American loan is not much," he wrote in his diaries, ". . . but it can't be called worthless in a moral sense, since it obviously deals a blow to Wang [Jingwei]'s false organization."[6] At almost the same time, the British were launching a program of arming and training thirty thousand Chinese guerrillas.[7]

In June 1940 Chiang sent his brother-in-law T. V. Song to Washington to seek substantial assistance for China's war effort. Song was accorded the status of a personal representative of the Generalissimo. Very soon after arriving in Washington he commenced a whirlwind of activity, making full use of the China Lobby in the American establishment. In this connection, on Chiang's instruction he repeatedly informed the powers-that-be in Washington that the amount of American assistance would determine whether the government of China would continue its resistance to the enemy. Both he and Chiang were bluffing again. Chiang Kai-shek had no intention of surrendering to the Japanese under any conditions, but he needed to extract as much as he could from American banks. In that regard the tactic of intimidation was optimal.[8] "If, as before, the US[A] stands on the sidelines and does not promptly intervene [in the conflict]," Chiang wrote in a telegram to T. V. Song on the same day Song arrived in Washington, "there will be negative effects on our war against [Japanese] aggression."[9] Next, through the US ambassador to China, Chiang informed Roosevelt that he feared "the defiant Communists" even "more than the Japanese army"; in other words, he was trying to frighten him with the specter of communist revolution.[10]

In the summer and fall of 1940 Chiang faced a sharp deterioration in the international situation. On June 22 Hitler's army routed France, and the latter's Indochina colonies were basically left without a master. It was evident that Japan would not let slip the opportunity to take advantage of the situation. That is precisely what occurred just three months later. On September 22 the Japanese imperial army began to occupy Vietnam, and five days later Japan signed the Tripartite Pact with the Nazis and the Italian fascists, aimed at the United States and its allies: it was now formally in the same camp with them. Roosevelt and his closest advisors concluded that the United States "would be drawn into the war eventually."[11]

All of these events increased Chinese sympathy toward the United States, especially after November 30, 1940, the day the Japanese recognized the government of Wang Jingwei. To spite the Japanese and express solidarity with Chiang Kai-shek, Roosevelt offered Chiang the largest loan yet: US $100 million, half of which Chiang could use for so-called general purposes, including, at long last, the purchase of arms in the United States. The other half was designated to stabilize the Chinese currency.[12]

Roosevelt simultaneously authorized the sale of military aircraft to China as well as the dispatch of American volunteer airmen, despite Article 1 of the US Constitution, which prohibits officers of the United States from serving in foreign armies. This is what Chiang wanted most of all, hoping that the Americans would help him defend Chongqing. In October he had sent another of his relatives to Washington to resolve these problems: Air Force Major General Mao Bangchu, the thirty-six-year-old nephew of Chiang's first wife, Mao Fumei. Mao was not only a member of the family, but also Chiang's student at the Whampoa Military Academy and a classmate of Ching-kuo (Mao's first cousin) at Sun Yat-sen University in Moscow.

Claire Lee Chennault, the retired American air force captain who had served since June 1937 as a civilian advisor to Meiling (she, as noted earlier, headed the Chinese air force), accompanied Mao on the trip. (Mao Bangchu had met Chennault at an air show in Miami during his first trip to the United States and invited him to visit China.) Chennault had been discharged into the reserves of the American air force in the spring of 1937 because of his deteriorating health. He suffered from chronic bronchitis, deafness, and low blood pressure. He could no longer fly, but doing so was not demanded of him in China. Mao Bangchu, Chiang Kai-shek, and Meiling valued him most of all as an expert aviator and extremely talented organizer. Until mid-1940 he was occupied in training Chinese flyers and forming a foreign air legion. Nothing came of the latter undertaking, but now the energetic Chennault, with the aid of General Mao, T. V. Song, and the China Lobby in Washington began work on establishing a purely American squadron of the Chinese air force.[13] Meiling fully supported him, and Chennault was entranced by her. "She will always be a princess to me," he wrote in his diaries.[14] Meiling liked him also; he was tall, strong, decisive—a real macho man. Therefore, she pointedly called him Colonel, even though he was only a retired captain.[15]

Chennault and Mao informed the American officials with whom they met of the terrible state of the Chinese air force. Although China had 480 air force pilots, they had only 37 fighters and 31 bombers of Russian design. There was no antiaircraft artillery at all. At the same time, they added, the Japanese had 968 airplanes in China and 120 in Indochina.[16]

Chennault and Mao had to overcome enormous difficulties because in the United States at this time a Eurocentric view of the Second World War dominated. It was thought that "Hitler must first be defeated via the Atlantic and Europe, and after that it will be relatively easy to deal with the Far East."[17] Therefore, all available planes were being sent to England.

But in mid-December 1940 Chiang's envoys had a good chance of achieving success. On December 17 Roosevelt announced a program to help countries that were fighting against aggressors: it was called the Lend-Lease program. It was mostly designed for Great Britain, but its extension to China was not precluded, especially since Roosevelt had enormous sympathy for China and its people. He had inherited this feeling from his mother and uncle, who had once lived in China along with their father (his grandfather), a major opium trader.[18]

In late January 1941, at the suggestion of T. V. Song, Roosevelt sent his own man to Chongqing to investigate the financial situation in China, including inflation as well as possible Lend-Lease deliveries. Song asked him to send the former secretary of commerce Harry Hopkins, but Roosevelt chose one of his own economic advisors, Lauchlin Bernard Currie. After returning in early March, Currie recommended the inclusion of China in the Lend-Lease program even though Chiang Kai-shek had demonstrated his strong disinclination to deal with economic problems and inflation. Chiang was convinced that market prices could be stabilized by force, by executing the most egregious speculators. He had the mayor of Chengdu shot. The only thing that interested him at the moment was direct military and financial aid from the United States.[19]

The situation in China at the time remained complicated. The Japanese were no longer advancing, but after the battles of 1939 and 1940 the territory of free China shrank, though not by much. Only 47.5 percent of the population lived there; no fewer than two hundred million Chinese were in occupied territory. The financial–economic situation in Guomindang regions continued to deteriorate, so Chiang's disinclination to deal with these problems was a mistake. The prices of basic commodities rose catastrophically—the price index in June 1941 compared to that of July 1937 was 3,214 percent—and the level of inflation remained very high. At the end of 1940 one American dollar fetched sixteen Chinese dollars while before the war the exchange rate was 1:3.3. In Chongqing the interruption in deliveries of rice was keenly felt. Expenditures on the army, comprised of 3,856,000 officers and men in 1941, consumed two-thirds of the budget.[20]

What Chiang considered much more important was that in early 1941 the United States finally decided to send China the initial complement of one hundred P-40B planes (the famous Tomahawks). On March 11, 1941, the United States Congress passed the Lend-Lease Act, and on March 15 Roosevelt issued a declaration: "China . . . expresses the magnificent will of millions of plain people to resist the dismemberment of their Nation. China, through the Generalissimo, Chiang Kai-shek, asks our help. America has said that China shall have our help."[21] Twenty days later T. V. Song presented a concrete request to the Americans to supply China with 1,000 airplanes, including 300 bombers, as well as enough modern weapons to equip thirty divisions. In addition, he asked for other military materiel via the Lend-Lease program.[22] On April 26, 1941, Roosevelt informed Chiang that he had approved the transfer to China of Lend-Lease goods worth US $45 million. On May 6 he declared that the defense of China was vitally important to the defense of the United States.[23]

Thus in the spring and summer of 1941 Chiang clearly defined the United States as his main ally. Chiang would have been able to celebrate, counting the weeks to the start of the US–Japan war, but for one circumstance. After occupying Vietnam, the Japanese cut the line that linked China to the outside world via the port of Haiphong, leaving the Chinese only one "road of life": the Burma road, which ran from Kunming to Rangoon, the capital of the British colony of Burma. From Rangoon north to the Burmese town of Lashio there was a railway, but after that a dirt road through the mountains, a narrow ribbon twisting through the sheer cliffs. On July 12, 1940, however, Winston Churchill, the new prime minister of Great Britain who had replaced Neville

Chamberlain two months earlier, closed a 116-mile stretch of the road for three months during the rainy season. In October he reopened it, and in December he offered Chiang a commercial loan of five million pounds sterling.[24] But no one knew whether Churchill would close the road again in the rainy season of 1941. Meanwhile, Stalin finally approved the execution of contracts, and from the end of 1940 to June 1941 more than 250 Soviet airplanes and, in roughly the same period, 300 trucks and 250 artillery pieces, 200,000 shells and other equipment arrived in China.[25]

But at precisely this time relations between the Guomindang and the CCP again became strained. The new crisis began in July 1940 when the communists launched an offensive against Guomindang troops in Central China, operating under the command of the Jiangxi provincial governor Han Deqin and the Anhui provincial governor Li Pinxian. By this time the communist Eighth Route Army had routed the Guomindang guerrilla detachments in North China. Now another communist army, the New Fourth Army, composed of 15,000 soldiers and headed by the veteran warriors Ye Ting and Xiang Ying, began attacking those Nationalists operating south of the old Yellow River channel. The attacks began just when Zhou Enlai and Chiang Kai-shek, meeting in Chongqing, had apparently reached an agreement demarcating the territories occupied by communist and Guomindang troops in the Japanese rear. On October 19, 1940, Chiang ordered Ye Ting to redeploy the New Fourth Army north of the old Yellow River channel. But right at this time, in October, this army defeated the troops of the Guomindang governor of Jiangsu province, taking more than 8,000 officers and soldiers prisoner. On October 31 General Bai Chongxi told Paniushkin that "the communists . . . are behaving entirely illegally and improperly. . . . We cannot stand these endless frictions, conflicts, and clashes that cause enormous harm to our forces."[26]

But in December fresh conflicts occurred between the New Fourth Army and the Guomindang forces. Consequently, on January 6, 1941, nine Guomindang divisions attacked the headquarters column of the New Fourth Army, and over the course of nine days, with "unprecedented ferocity," totally obliterated it.[27] Ye Ting was taken prisoner, and Xiang Ying was killed.

The next day Paniushkin, along with a new military attaché, Vasilii Ivanovich Chuikov, who arrived in China just before New Year in 1941, and several other Soviet representatives met with Zhou Enlai and Ye Jianying, the chief of staff of the Eighth Route Army, to discuss the incident. The men were troubled: no one knew how to react. Should they begin a struggle against Chiang Kai-shek or not? The belligerent General Chuikov proposed that at least in their political activity the Communist Party should "indicate that C[hiang] K[ai-]sh[ek] was the guilty one in all these events," but Paniushkin disagreed. "We must maintain cooperation," he said. The discussion was somehow garbled, and Paniushkin asked Zhou and Ye not to inform Mao Zedong of their (the representatives of the USSR) "personal assessment of the developing situation." There was actually nothing to convey: they had made no sort of assessment.[28]

On January 25 Paniushkin, acting on Stalin's instructions, met with Chiang Kai-shek to ascertain whether Chiang would continue the war against the New Fourth and Eighth Route Armies. According to Soviet historians, Chiang tried to avoid answering, and the Soviet ambassador had to repeat the question three times. Only then did Chiang promise to settle the matter peacefully.[29] Chiang described this meeting differently in his diaries: "The Russian ambassador, executing the orders of his government, asked me about the incident with the New Fourth Army. . . . I cut him off sharply. He lapsed into embarrassed silence and withdrew." Chiang further wrote that the "strategy of the Chinese communists is to use Russia's assistance to China as a political weapon to suppress the center [that is, the Guomindang CEC] and the anticommunist tendency. Their plan may be called an extremely stupid fantasy. [Nevertheless] from the very start of the war of resistance they wanted with the help of intrigues to crush the Center, dreaming of seizing power."[30] Following this, Chiang issued an order to blockade the Shaanxi–Gansu–Ningxia Special Region where the CCP government was located.

Under these circumstances it was senseless to wait for new military contracts with the USSR, and on February 2 Chiang wrote a letter to Stalin that was delivered by Kachanov, who was returning to the Soviet Union.[31] He emphasized the significance of the USSR's moral rather than its material support of China.[32] He assessed the situation correctly. The deliveries of Soviet arms in late 1940–early 1941 were the last ones. Did that matter? In February 1941 the first American fighters were ready to be sent to China.[33] And Chiang could depend on Chennault's success in recruiting 250 pilots from the United States.[34] Therefore, he could get along quite well with only moral support from Stalin.

But unexpectedly, late on the night of April 13, 1941, Chiang received terrible news from Moscow: the Soviet government, without having informed him, had signed a neutrality pact with Japan. It included an article which, in essence, precluded the USSR from providing assistance to China as well as a declaration whereby the USSR recognized the territorial integrity of Manchukuo, and

Japan that of Mongolia.[35] This was a violation of all the moral obligations of the USSR, especially since, just two days earlier, Paniushkin had assured Chiang that, notwithstanding the visit to Moscow of Japanese Foreign Minister Matsuoka Yōsuke—who had arrived there on April 8—the Soviet Union "would not sacrifice the interests of a friendly power for selfish considerations and that the Soviet Government was only extending to Matsuoka the usual diplomatic courtesy."[36]

There is no doubt that Chiang later received a report that on the evening of April 13 Stalin had personally escorted Matsuoka to the Yaroslavl' Railway Station, where the Japanese foreign minister was departing. Matsuoka himself had not expected such an honor. This step was quite extraordinary: never before and never again did Stalin escort foreign visitors. The train was delayed for an hour because it was waiting for Stalin. When he arrived he led Matsuoka into the station restaurant, where, together with Molotov, they got him drunk. Then, after embracing the drunken Japanese and whispering in his ear, "You are an Asiatic, and I am also an Asiatic, we should unite," Stalin led him to the coach. He literally dragged him into the train before the eyes of the entire diplomatic corps that was assembled on the platform. Emerging from the train, he asked in a loud voice where Schulenburg, the German ambassador, was. Finding him, Stalin approached the ambassador, embraced him, and said, "We must remain friends, and you must do everything now for this!" Then he turned toward the acting German military attaché, Hans Krebs, and "having made sure in advance that he was German," said to him, "We must remain friends with you in any case."[37]

Chiang could not have known that during Stalin's conversation with Matsuoka in the Kremlin the day before, Stalin had told the Japanese minister that he was a "staunch supporter of the Axis,[38] and an opponent of England and America."[39] But what Chiang did know was already quite enough. The Kremlin dictator had shown the whole world that his friendship with Japan and Germany was now his highest priority.

That whole day, April 13, was a disaster for Chiang. At dinner he and Meiling planned a meeting with Hemingway and Gellhorn, who were in Chongqing on journalistic business. Gellhorn represented the mainstream magazine *Collier's Weekly*, and Hemingway had a contract with the modest New York newspaper *PM*.[40] Chiang and Meiling were supposed to receive the guests, but Chiang did not have his false teeth. What had become of them no one knows (they were either broken or lost), but facts are facts: he was forced to receive his guests toothless. At first, everything went smoothly since Meiling, as usual, presided over the conversation. She tried to charm the famous author. Chiang listened silently, only rarely inserting a short *hao* (good). "He was thin, straight-backed, impeccable in a plain gray uniform and looked embalmed," Gellhorn recalled later. But when the conversation turned to the New Fourth Army Incident, and Ernest and Martha intimated that they did not believe the official Guomindang version, he could not restrain himself and broke in saying the incident was insignificant. Since his guests did not agree with him, he repeated himself four times, expatiating on the theme. Martha's eyes opened wide at the sight of the Generalissimo's bare gums. Noticing this, Chiang changed the topic of the conversation, which obviously had produced an unpleasant impression on him as it had on his guests as well.[41]

Then that evening the bad news from Moscow arrived. Now it was Chiang Kai-shek's turn to view Stalin as a traitor. He wrote in his diaries, "Russia and Japan signed an agreement on neutrality at 2:00 p.m. in Moscow.[42] In it, I heard, is mutual recognition of the territorial integrity of two pseudo-states—Manchuria and Mongolia. Russia has already made a habit of harming others. One must expect this. . . . This will strike the largest blow to trust in Russia in the world."[43]

On April 19 he told Paniushkin, "The people and army of China . . . received news of the conclusion of the pact . . . very sharply and painfully. . . . [O]ur people and army are very shocked." Barely restraining his indignation, he added, "I would like to hope that if the USSR would undertake any steps vis-à-vis Japan, it would not be a secret for us." The ambassador was taken aback: "What do you have in mind?"[44] Chiang had never spoken so sharply to him before.

Three weeks later, on May 12, after receiving from his intelligence service notice that Germany intended to attack the USSR in a month and a half, Chiang conceivably informed not Stalin but Roosevelt (in their secret correspondence with him, Chiang and his wife used the general code name Segac). Yet this information reached Moscow from the Soviet agent Stennes (Friend), Chiang's bodyguard.[45] However, as one might suppose, Stalin did not believe it.

Nevertheless, in June 1941, when the Soviet Union became the target of aggression from one of its new "friends," Nazi Germany, Chiang expressed unconditional support for the USSR; this despite the fact that his resentment of Stalin for having signed the treaty with Japan behind his back never abated. Now Chongqing and Moscow were in the same camp, fighting against the Axis powers. Although each was fighting on its own front against its own enemy, Chiang Kai-shek understood very well that as a result of the Soviet Union's entry into the Second World War "a bright hope awaited all mankind."[46] On July 3, responding to Germany's and Italy's recognition of the government of Wang Jingwei, he severed diplomatic relations with these countries.[47]

Meanwhile, Chiang Kai-shek's fears regarding the communist threat to his regime did not diminish, especially after he had read the testimony of Ye Ting, the commander of the New Fourth Army, who had been arrested and interrogated. Ye asserted, "The Third International in Moscow is 'directing' the actions of the Eighth Route Army of the Chinese Communist Party"; they aimed at "expanding their influence and forces in the [Japanese] occupied regions" as well as "prolonging Japanese–Chinese enmity."[48] Only at the very start of the Soviet–German war did Chiang Kai-shek hope that the USSR and the Chinese communists "would calm down."[49] But he quickly realized this would not happen. That is why he had good reason to say to the American journalist Theodore White, "The Japanese are a disease of the skin, the Communists are a disease of the heart."[50]

If only he had known that on July 3, 1941, the Soviet Politburo adopted a resolution authorizing the Executive Committee of the Comintern to allocate "one million American dollars in support of the CC of the Chinese Communist Party."[51] Nazi aircraft were bombing Murmansk, Orsha, Mogilev, Smolensk, Kyiv, Odessa, and Sevastopol, and Stalin decided to send a million American dollars to the Central Committee of the CCP.[52] But Stalin no longer had either money or arms for Chiang Kai-shek.[53] On October 24, 1941, the Kremlin boss coldly informed Chiang that he could no longer provide him with military aid.[54] In February 1942 Chuikov and the other Soviet military specialists left China.

By this time the Americans were in high gear, making deliveries to Chongqing despite the fact that the Lend-Lease agreement with China was not signed until June 2, 1942.[55] Up to the end of 1941 this aid program had provided Chiang about US $26 million, which constituted 1.7 percent of the total value of all goods (more than one and a half billion dollars) sent to all of the friendly combatant countries. (As before, priority was given to Great Britain, which, in the same period, received thirty times more, as well as to the USSR after Nazi Germany's attack on the Soviet Union. But in the summer of 1941 a program to train Chinese flyers was launched in Arizona.)[56]

On April 15, 1941, the American volunteer pilots received Roosevelt's permission to join Chennault's squadron. Thus the American Volunteer Group (AVG), comprising the first 110 retired fighter pilots, came into being. Soon Chennault received permission from the president to form a second group of 100 bomber pilots as well as 181 gunners and radiomen.[57]

In July 1941 Chennault, Meiling's energetic advisor, returned to Chongqing to "report on the incredible success of the American project to the Generalissimo."[58] Then he left for Burma, where an AVG training center was established. The first squadron arrived in Burma and then the second, and in mid-December the newly formed third, which also numbered 100 pilots. They were called Flying Tigers because they painted the prows of their Tomahawks with terrifying shark's teeth, just as the British Royal Air Force flyers in Libya. Why they were called tigers instead of sharks is not known, and even Chennault himself could not answer that question.[59]

Unfortunately for Chiang, due to lengthy training in Burma and the drawn out transfer of airplanes, not until December 20, 1941, were American volunteers able to enter into battle in the skies over Kunming.[60] But they fought bravely, no worse than Soviet flyers. However, unlike the latter, who never exceeded the "bounds of morality" from obvious fears of having to deal with the NKVD, the flyers from the United States spent all their free time with Chinese prostitutes, which evoked the disapproval of the Chinese authorities.[61]

Along with Chennault, another long-awaited guest of Chiang's arrived in Chongqing: his new political advisor, Owen Lattimore, who was sent to China by the president of the United States. Lattimore was a well-known China expert and former editor of the journal *Pacific Affairs.* Chiang himself had requested that a political advisor be sent to him, but it was Currie who, after securing Roosevelt's agreement, selected Lattimore. It turned out that one could not have wished for a better person.

Unlike Chiang's other foreign advisors, Lattimore, a forty-year-old scholar, historian, and political scientist, not only knew China well but also could express himself fluently in Chinese. Up to the age of twelve he had lived first in Shanghai, then Baoding, and after that in Tianjin, where his father taught English, French, and German. He even understood Chiang Kai-shek's accent more or less because his Chinese nanny was a native of the same area as Chiang. Overall, he could be very useful to the Generalissimo. Chiang's and Roosevelt's intention was to have him play a special role of secret liaison between them. In doing so he would be short-circuiting the diplomatic services of the United States, which, in Lattimore's words, neither Roosevelt nor Chiang fully trusted. Chiang consulted with him on all issues, and at his request Lattimore composed Chiang's messages to Roosevelt. After Chiang edited them they were dispatched to Washington, not to the president himself but to Currie. Currie deciphered them and then personally handed them to Roosevelt.

This was called a hot line. The code which Lattimore and Currie used was held by only two persons: Meiling in Chongqing and Currie in Washington.

Lattimore was settled into the western, picturesque quarter of the city in T. V. Song's private house, situated on a high bluff over the Jialing River. Currie had previously lived in this house. It was vacant, as its owner was in Washington. Although the American scholar had very liberal views and got along well with Mao Zedong and other communist leaders whom he had visited in June 1937, he quickly established good rapport with Chiang and Meiling.[62] The Generalissimo and his wife valued the fact that Lattimore tried his utmost not only to help them wrest as much aid as possible from the United States, but also to convince Roosevelt to recognize China as an equal great power. He enthusiastically supported both the Chinese war against Japanese imperialism and the national liberation struggle of China in general. Roosevelt's response to Lattimore's suggestion to recognize China, however, was silence. He did not want to come into conflict with his main ally, Great Britain, whose government feared that, after the war, recognizing China as a great power might encourage the movement for national liberation in India, a colony of Great Britain.[63]

Meanwhile, an American military mission headed by General John Magruder arrived in Chongqing in October 1941 to oversee deliveries from the Lend-Lease program. Chiang and Meiling developed a good working relationship with the general, who had served as the US military attaché in Beiping.[64] Magruder remained in Chongqing until June 1942, while Lattimore left in mid-January 1942. Despite his liberalism, Lattimore formed an entirely positive impression of Chiang. "Having known Chiang Kai-shek personally," he recalled many years later, "I still think that he was a great man. He certainly was no saint, but neither was he a total villain. He was a man who was not only patriotic, but according to his own lights, revolutionary. He wanted to change Chinese society . . . [but] has in some ways an antiquated mode of thinking . . . half feudal and militaristic and half modern in his mentality."[65] It is hard not to agree with this assessment. Equally valid is Lattimore's assertion that even during the anti-Japanese war Chiang Kai-shek could not become a dictator in the true sense of the word, even though the war demanded the maximum centralization of power. Chiang was simply not in a position to subordinate all the local militarists to himself, and "[b]eing a Chinese military politician who had come up on top, he had to keep balancing one faction against another," in both the party and the army.[66]

Nor did Chiang always succeed in controlling even his family. There was nothing he could do about either of Meiling's sisters, the ultra-leftist widow of Sun Yat-sen and the corrupt wife of Kong Xiangxi. He could not even subordinate his own wife to his power, allowing her to interfere in any matters. He was accustomed to relying on her, but when she went too far and became too dominant he never reprimanded her. He simply let it pass. He conducted serious conversations with Lattimore only after Meiling had gone to sleep. Until then, sitting in his armchair and mostly keeping quiet, he observed how his self-confident spouse monopolized the conversation.[67]

With his sons, however, he was domineering. He certainly did his best to display fatherly concern for them. Even prior to the start of the Second World War he was fearful for his younger son, who, as mentioned earlier, was studying at the officers' academy in Munich. The deterioration of relations with Nazi Germany might lead Wei-kuo to become a hostage like his older brother had been in Soviet Russia. When Wei-kuo graduated in Munich, Chiang demanded that he leave right away for America. There Chiang found a place for him at the Army Air Corps Tactical School at Maxwell Air Force Base in Alabama. Wei-kuo, obeying his father, left the Reich in mid-September 1939,[68] exactly two weeks after the German invasion of Poland.[69] He soon became the first Chinese enrolled in the Tactical School.[70] After a while, however, at the request of the Americans he transferred to another military base, Fort Knox, in Kentucky, where he began to share with his American colleagues what he had learned in Germany. He returned to China on October 27, 1940.

At Chiang's request, Ching-kuo, who had not seen his brother in fifteen years, met him at the pier in Hong Kong. He took Wei-kuo to a hotel right away, where they spent the whole night drinking beer and socializing. The next day he took Wei-kuo to see "mama" Meiling, who was in Hong Kong for medical treatment.[71]

Wei-kuo and Meiling met for the first time. For some reason Chiang had never tried to acquaint them with one another. Of course, rumors had reached her that her husband had an adopted son whose mother was Japanese and whose father was a "Guomindang political figure." In 1939 the American journalist John Gunther had retold these stories in his book *Inside Asia*.[72] Meiling acquired the book and kept it in her personal library. It is not known whether she asked Chiang about these rumors and was interested in finding out who Wei-kuo's biological father was, but in all likelihood she was curious. At the time they met, she probably knew that her "new child" was the son of Dai Jitao and Goldie Kaneko. Judging by Wei-kuo's reminiscences and Chiang's diaries entries, "mother" and "son" liked each other. Chiang wrote about their meeting: "I heard that mother and son met in Hong Kong and liked each other very much, I am very happy. . . . I feel that the Almighty's grace is boundless."[73]

Chiang's children and wife were supposed to arrive in Chongqing by his birthday on October 31, according to the Gregorian calendar. He had specially requested that they join him because he wanted everyone gathered together at the festive table. But they were delayed in Hong Kong. That evening an aggrieved Chiang wrote, "Wife promised to return today, but I have not yet seen her. She did not call, and I don't know where she is."[74]

Meiling did not return for quite some time, but both of Chiang's sons finally came to see their father in Chongqing on November 3. Chiang was overjoyed to see them, especially Wei-kuo, whom he hadn't seen in four years and who, as noted earlier, had always been his favorite. He kept him by his side, bombarding him with questions about Germany and America. Wei-kuo in turn gave him a large number of secret materials he had been able to carry away from Fort Knox. Chiang was satisfied: America and Japan were rapidly moving toward war in the Pacific, and these documents might be very important.[75] He kept his beloved Wei-kuo with him for an entire month, and not until early December 1940 did he send him to Wei-kuo's older brother in the city of Ganzhou, in southern Jiangxi province, to meet his sister-in-law, his nephew, and his niece.

Ching-kuo along with his family had moved to this provincial city in March 1939, after working for a year in Nanchang as deputy chief of the provincial security department. His father had appointed him to this post at the request of the local governor. Ching-kuo had joined the Guomindang back in January 1938, and in the spring of that year he was made a major general. In Nanchang he lived alone for almost a year; the city was frequently bombed, and therefore Faina and the children remained in the village with his mother. She spent her days riding around on a bicycle or in an automobile, meanwhile learning both the official North Chinese dialect as well as the local Ningbo one. She was bored in the absence of her husband, who rarely was able to visit her, about once in three months.[76] But in March 1939, on the eve of the seizure of Nanchang by the Japanese, Ching-kuo, in the interest of security, was transported 250 miles south, to Ganzhou. Faina and the children followed him there. In Ganzhou Ching-kuo headed the department of security for the entire administrative region of southern Jiangxi, a territory of nearly 9,000 square miles, embracing eleven counties with a population of more than 1.6 million people. In addition, he fulfilled the duties of commissar—that is, special representative of the governor—in this region.[77] In other words, he held all the local power in his hands. He uprooted banditry; judged and laid down the law;

fought against prostitution, opium smoking and gambling; implemented agrarian reform; lowered rent payments by 25 percent and redistributed land; delivered lectures at courses for young cadres; published newspapers; and conducted a campaign to eradicate illiteracy. In 1941 he even drafted a three-year economic development plan for the region.[78] Every day he rose at four or five o'clock and, since he was so burdened with work, went to bed at two o'clock in the morning. Meanwhile, Faina began working as the director of an orphanage for three- to fifteen-year-old children, and within four years her pupils numbered more than six hundred.[79]

Wei-kuo became acquainted with his brother's work, made friends with Faina, and enjoyed getting to know his nephew and niece. He also visited his foster mother Yao Yecheng, Chiang Kai-shek's former lover, to whom, as noted above, he was very attached. She also lived in Ganzhou. Afterward, he and Ching-kuo went to Zhejiang, the province next to Jiangxi, to their native village Xikou, where they bowed before the graves of their ancestors. They did so just in time because half a year later, on April 22, 1941, the Japanese captured Xikou, and, in order to harm Chiang's geomancy, they destroyed the tombs of his blood relatives.[80] Wei-kuo did not return to Chongqing until December 24, just before Christmas. In early 1941 Chiang Kai-shek sent him off to Xi'an to join the army of one of his loyal generals.[81]

Chiang's joy at meeting his children, however, did not ease the pain in his heart caused by his separation from Meiling. She had gone to Hong Kong for medical treatment on October 6, 1940, and refused to return despite Chiang's repeated requests. She was truly sick. Chongqing's oppressive climate was obviously not good for her; she repeatedly caught colds and even ordered medicines from America to treat her respiratory illnesses. Moreover, Meiling was terribly frightened of the bombing, and her nerves were on edge from fear; she suffered from insomnia. When one of the bombs exploded on the lawn in front of their in-town house, shattering all the windows, the first lady of China simply panicked. "The bombers are constantly circling over us," she wrote to her former classmate. "They come in formation—in droves—looking like enormous black crows. Thud, thud, thud! They are dropping bombs now on the other side of the river. I cannot see the explosions as I am on the Huang-Shan [Huangshan] side. My husband and I are living in the hills since our Chungking [Chongqing] house is no longer habitable. The Japs know this house also, since that traitor Wang Ching-wei [Jingwei] once visited us here, and told them of our whereabouts. . . . Heavens, how we lack planes here! We have enough trained pilots, but a deplorable scarcity of planes."[82] In addition to everything else, Meiling suffered from severe back and neck pains, which her doctors diagnosed as displacement of the vertebrae. Her condition was connected to an automobile accident in which she and Donald were involved in the fall of 1937, when they were traveling along the Shanghai front. A rear tire burst and the passengers were thrown onto the road. Donald got off easy, but it turned out that Meiling had broken a rib.[83] Evidently her spine was also injured, but her doctors at the time did not consider it significant. The rib healed well, but her spine gave her more and more trouble.

If that was not enough, Meiling suffered from a severe toothache, and the dentists in Chongqing had been unable to determine its cause.[84] Most likely the pain was related to her nervous system. That is why she had left for Hong Kong in early October 1940, and Chiang had to celebrate his birthday according to the lunar calendar without her (that year, the fifteenth day of the ninth month according to the lunar calendar fell on October 15) as well as his birthday according to the Gregorian calendar.[85]

Meiling's illnesses, however, were just one of the reasons for her long separation from her husband. She was away for more than four months and did not return to Chongqing until February 12, 1941. Another, probably, was jealousy. Meeting with Wei-kuo, she suddenly began to doubt that he was her husband's adopted son. Perhaps because it seemed to her that Wei-kuo resembled Chiang Kai-shek or perhaps for some other reason. But she evidently felt she had been deceived.[86]

Jealousy, aggravated by her illnesses, combined to make her hate Chongqing. In a letter she wrote on April 10, 1941, to her American friend who wanted to visit her after she returned to Chongqing, Meiling wrote, "There is not *one* single amusement place, or any sort of social life [here]. Nothing but sheer, wearying, heartbreaking work between air raids. The heat, and the rain are not romantic." She complained about the poor conditions of life, the repulsive food, the deficient water supply, and illnesses.[87]

These complaints were not so much the whining of a spoiled and capricious noblewoman as the cry of a tired, sick woman. After she returned to Chongqing malaria and dengue fever, an acute viral disease, were added to all her woes. Her skin was covered with rashes, and her lymph nodes swelled up.[88] She had had a skin problem before. As early as August 1932 Chiang complained in his diaries that his "wife's skin was very itchy."[89] In a photograph with Hemingway and Gellhorn taken in April 1941 she appears emaciated and exhausted, especially next to the well-fed, smiling American man. Yet she still looks dazzlingly beautiful.

Nevertheless, Meiling remained in Chongqing, and she forgave Chiang, though not immediately. For what? He was not guilty of anything. But, as they say in China, *hao nan bu gen nü dou* (a wise man does not quarrel with a woman). Chiang chose not to strain his relations with Meiling, especially since her character was much stronger than his. Evidently he succeeded somehow or other in convincing her that Wei-kuo was not his son, and by April 1941 their domestic life had returned to normal. Chiang was in seventh heaven.[90] On March 31 he wrote in his diaries, "In the family there is peace, love, and union between husband and wife, mother and children—this is the foundation of happiness in life, renewal of the body and peace of mind, I offer prayers."[91]

He did not know, however, that soon after returning, Meiling, for some reason known only to herself (treachery? malice? intrigue?), suggested to the unsuspecting Wei-kuo, who had returned to his father in Chongqing, that in his spare time he read Gunther's book. Possibly she wanted to test the young man's reaction or provoke him to have a conversation with Chiang Kai-shek. But Wei-kuo showed restraint, although he was shocked. No rumors about his birth had reached him, and he was convinced that he was Chiang's natural son. For some reason he imagined that the "political figure in the Guomindang," named in the book as his father, was most likely Dai Jitao, Chiang Kai-shek's blood brother. Wei-kuo visited him to ask about it. But Dai simply laughed and, bringing a mirror and a portrait of Chiang from another room, asked Wei-kuo to compare whom he resembled. Wei-kuo shifted his glance from the portrait to Dai Jitao and then to his own reflection, and said, "I seem to look more like father [that is, Chiang Kai-shek]."

Again bursting out in laughter, Dai Jitao asked, "Well, shall we leave it at that?"

Wei-kuo had no more questions. But after returning home, somewhat confused, he thought, "In the final analysis, both father and uncle are great men, to be the son of either one of them is honorable."[92] He said nothing to either Meiling or Chiang about this conversation.

Meanwhile, in mid-November 1941 troubling news reached Chiang: Roosevelt had expressed his willingness to reach an agreement with the Japanese "dwarfs" to settle issues in dispute peacefully. The Generalissimo was shocked. It had seemed that everything was pointing toward an American–Japanese war, especially since the president of the United States had frozen Japanese assets in American banks. Now suddenly Roosevelt was discussing a modus vivendi, temporary peaceful coexistence, with Japan. Even Churchill was surprised. He wrote to Roosevelt, "Of course, it is for you to handle this business and we certainly do not want an additional war. There is one point that disquiets us. What about Chiang Kai-shek? Is he not having a very thin diet? Our anxiety is about China. If they collapse our joint danger would enormously increase."[93]

Chiang knew nothing about Churchill's secret telegram to Roosevelt. Feeling that the liberal West was betraying him, he became hysterical. He asked Lattimore to send an urgent telegram to Washington saying that "his [Chiang's] reliance on America is the foundation of his whole national policy." He hinted that if Roosevelt reconciled with the Japanese, the act would forever undermine the prestige of the United States in China, just as the closing of the Burma road had undermined the prestige of England. Moreover, he asked Lattimore to warn Roosevelt that American–Japanese detente would strengthen the regime of Wang Jingwei and weaken the position of the Chinese National government. Lattimore informed Currie that "he had never really seen Chiang Kai-shek agitated before."[94]

Chiang's anxiety did not abate until four o'clock in the morning on December 8, 1941, when he was awakened by a telephone call from Hollington Tong, the deputy director of the Department of Propaganda of the Guomindang CEC who had been his teacher in early 1906 in the district school in Fenghua. Tong informed him of stupendous news: three hours earlier Japanese warplanes had attacked the US naval base at Pearl Harbor in Hawaii. The intensive bombing had lasted for two hours and twelve minutes. Five battleships and 3 cruisers had been sunk, 177 airplanes destroyed, over 2,000 servicemen killed, and another 2,000 or so wounded or missing in action.[95] At almost the same time the Japanese attacked the British colonies of Hong Kong, British Malaya, and Singapore.[96]

No matter how terrible the casualties, Chiang could not help but feel relief: the most powerful countries on earth, the United States and Great Britain, had joined the war against Japan. This meant not only that victory over the most fearsome foe was getting closer, but also that China, joining the ranks of its allies, would finally be able to secure the status of a great power. Unable to contain his excitement, Chiang placed one of his favorite records on the gramophone—*Ave Maria*—by Johann Sebastian Bach and Charles Gounod. Sitting in his armchair, he began listening and experienced bliss. When the record finished he replaced it with another—also *Ave Maria* by Franz Schubert. He loved both versions.

There was no urgency at present: from now on the fate of China would be decided on the fronts of the Pacific war.

CHAPTER 18

# *Playing with Roosevelt*

No matter how beautiful the music, Chiang did not delight in it for long. Everyone was awaiting his response and therefore, four hours later, he convened an emergency session of the Standing Committee of the Guomindang Executive Committee in his office in the city. A decision was made to propose promptly to the United States, Great Britain, and the USSR the establishment of a military coalition, conclusion of a treaty of alliance, and joint declaration of war against Germany, Italy, and Japan.[1] Later that day Chiang presented these proposals to the American and Soviet ambassadors.[2] He had a separate meeting with Paniushkin at which he tried to convince him (and, through him, Stalin) of the need to deal a preemptive blow against Japan. The conversation with Paniushkin got nowhere. Just three days earlier Soviet troops had begun their counteroffensive near Moscow, and a simultaneous war with Japan was something Stalin could contemplate only in a nightmare. Thus that evening Chiang invited only the military attachés of the United States and the United Kingdom to a meeting of his War Council, informing them that China would share all the misfortunes of war with their countries. He also called for the establishment of a joint military command under the leadership of the United States.[3]

The following day, December 9, 1941, the Chinese government officially declared war on Japan as well as on Germany and Italy. Until then it had been in an undeclared war with Japan. A day before, the United States and the

United Kingdom also declared war on Japan, and on December 11 Germany and Italy declared war against the United States. The result was that the China–Japan front became a military theater of the Second World War.

At this time Japanese armed forces numbered about two and a half million service personnel, of which more than 600,000 were in China and 230,000 in the Pacific Ocean area. The United States, England, and the Dutch East Indies (Indonesia) together could muster 370,000 officers and soldiers against them. The Chinese army was the largest numerically: 3,819,000 men, but, as before, it was not very effective. Of the 316 Chinese divisions, only 30 of the best were Chiang's own troops, the others being controlled by their regional commanders, former militarists.[4] Thus before issuing an order to a commander Chiang had to consider, "Is this an order this man will obey, or will he sabotage it?"[5]

Well aware of his own army's weakness and its string of endless failures at the front, Chiang experienced mixed feelings of sympathy and schadenfreude at the news of the initial defeats of his allies. On December 10, he wrote in his diaries,

> Apparently eight-tenths of Anglo-American naval forces in the Pacific Ocean have been destroyed. This is the inevitable result of the excessive chatter, as well as the total unpreparedness of the Anglo-American armed forces. But, if one speaks of the situation in the world as a whole and of the consequences [of this event] for the war in the Far East, then it's entirely possible to gain benefit from catastrophe. From now on England and the United States must concentrate all their forces to resolve first of all the problem with the Japanese bandits in the Far East, that is, they will no longer place China and the Far East in second place [after Europe].[6]

Roosevelt soon suggested that Chiang Kai-shek convene a military conference in Chongqing consisting of representatives of the allied powers to work out a joint strategy.[7] Chiang set about this task enthusiastically. But the conference, which took place on December 23, revealed disagreement between Chiang and the commander of British forces in India, General Archibald Wavell. A week earlier Japanese troops had invaded Burma. On December 24 Chiang, fearing they would be able to seize control of the "lifeline" that connected China with the rest of the world, made a proposal to Wavell. His plan was to deploy two Chinese armies numbering 80,000 men to Burma to aid the British. Wavell reportedly replied, "We British would consider it a disgrace to have Chinese troops liberate Burma for us."[8] Chiang was very offended, especially since, like all Chinese, he considered northern Burma to be Chinese territory illegally taken from China by the British in the 1880s.

Chiang in general was hypersensitive. By the end of 1941 his nerves were utterly shattered because of new trouble in the family. The daughter of Kong Xiangxi and Ailing, Meiling's beloved niece Lingjun (alias Lingwei)—whom the family called Jeanette—had returned in mid-December from Hong Kong, which had been attacked by the Japanese. She brought with her not only numerous servants, but also seven dogs and puppies. She and her retinue occupied the entire cabin of the airplane Chiang had sent to evacuate the publisher of China's oldest newspaper, *Dagong bao* (Impartial Daily), from Hong Kong. But because of the dogs there was no room on the plane for the publisher. The incident would have passed without notice, but when the howling troop alighted at the Chongqing airport the editor in chief of *Impartial Daily,* who had come to meet the publisher, was so outraged that he wrote an editorial that kicked up a storm.[9] The Kong family had long had a bad reputation in China, and now this scandal came along.

Naturally, in time the dustup faded, but many people retained a bitter aftertaste. Jeanette, absolutely clueless and acting as if nothing had happened presented one of the setter puppies to her uncle and aunt as a gift. The dog was charming, and Chiang and Meiling were delighted with him, especially since they happened to love dogs. But the scandal cast a shadow over the gift, which, however, did not affect the puppy's fate. Chiang became enamored of the dog and began taking his walks only with him.[10]

Meanwhile, in Washington in late December Roosevelt and Churchill were holding a series of meetings under the code name Arcadia. The outcome was the publication on January 1, 1942, of a "Declaration of the United Nations," a term introduced by the president of the United States. It was signed by representatives of twenty-six member countries of the antifascist coalition. Of special significance to Chiang, as to all of China, was that the signature of the Chinese representative, T. V. Song, who had become the new minister of foreign affairs of China on December 23, 1941, was the fourth one on the list. It appeared directly after the signatures of Roosevelt, Churchill, and Litvinov, who was then deputy people's commissar for foreign affairs and the ambassador of the USSR to the United States. The remaining signatures were in alphabetical order of the other countries. Did Chiang know that Roosevelt had initially placed China second after the United States in the list of signatories and only afterward substituted the United Kingdom, evidently fearing

Churchill's displeasure?[11] Possibly. But the inclusion of China in the quartet of leading allied powers in itself was compelling, as it represented a great victory for China's national revolution.

One day earlier Roosevelt had proposed to Chiang that he assume the position of commander in chief of allied forces in the China Theater, which included parts of Thailand and Indochina in addition to China. On January 3 Chiang accepted the proposal, requesting that a high-ranking general be dispatched to him to serve as chief of the allied general staff. He wished to include representatives of the United States, China, Great Britain, and Holland in this general staff.

Three weeks later, summing up the month, he proudly wrote in his diaries, "After the publication of the joint declaration of twenty-six states, the United States, England, the USSR, and China were officially made the center, the result is that our country has become one of the four great powers. Moreover, after I agreed to become commander in chief of the China Theater, including Vietnam and Siam [Thailand], the prestige and place [of our] country and every citizen has really strengthened to an incredible degree, such as has never before been in history. . . . We no longer need fear anything."[12] In January 1942 Roosevelt agreed to provide Chiang a fourth, and the largest, loan of US $500 million, and on February 7 Congress approved this decision. With such credit one could boldly continue the war until achieving victory. Especially to the beautiful sounds of *Ave Maria.*

Inspired by Roosevelt's support, Chiang decided to put the British in their place, making them face up to the new status of the Republic of China.[13] The British, it is true, also helped China financially within their more limited means. On February 3, for example, they agreed to provide 50 million pounds sterling.[14] Yet they continued to treated China as a third-rate power.[15] Thus in February 1942 Chiang and Meiling visited India, a British colony. In the suburbs of Calcutta they conversed for five hours with the sworn enemy of the British, the leader of the Indian national liberation movement, Mahatma Gandhi. Chiang did so despite a request from the governor-general of India, Victor Alexander John Hope, conveyed via the British ambassador to China, Archibald Clark Kerr, that he desist from taking such a step. The Generalissimo was evidently intoxicated with his new role as a revolutionary who had just transformed his state into a great power. He wanted to act as a mediator between Gandhi and the British. He wished to show the latter that without him they would be unable to convince the father of the Indian nation to support them in the anti-Japanese struggle. When Gandhi agreed "not to harm the war against Japan," Chiang Kai-shek could not hide his delight.[16]

Chiang's and Meiling's meeting with Jawaharlal Nehru, the chair of the Indian National Congress, a nationalist party whose outlook was close to that of the Guomindang, was equally successful. On February 21 on Radio Calcutta Meiling read Chiang's address to the Indian people. In it the Generalissimo openly called on the British to grant the Indians freedom "as soon as possible"—the following day the address was published in India.[17] Chiang was convinced that the colonial peoples of Asia and the Pacific could be mobilized in the struggle against Japan only if Great Britain and Holland gave them "real political power."[18]

That same day Chiang and Meiling returned to China, but on March 1 they were traveling again. This time they flew to Burma, where they wanted to clarify the situation that had deteriorated following the humiliating defeat in late February of British colonial forces at the bridge across the Sittang River in the south of Burma. They arrived at the Burmese town of Lashio, situated at the gates of the "lifeline." Two days later Lt. General Joseph Warren Stilwell flew in: Roosevelt had just appointed him as Chiang's chief of the allied general staff.[19]

Chiang was acquainted with this American. Starting in 1911 Joe Stilwell had come to China four times on long assignments, and in 1935–39 he had served as military attaché in the American embassy. In total, he had lived in China for more than ten years. He was a tall, gaunt man of about sixty, an experienced and resolute commander. Roosevelt had appointed him to the post on January 23 at the suggestion of Chief of Staff of the U.S. Army George C. Marshall Jr., and Chiang was to meet him again. He could be of enormous help: in addition to executing the duties of chief of staff, he was supposed to command all the American soldiers in the China Theater. Regrettably, Stilwell was exceedingly hot-tempered and gruff, "difficult to deal with, impatient and at times caustic," which earned him the nickname Vinegar Joe among his troops.[20] Chiang paid no attention to that. Stilwell was obliged to submit himself to Chiang as commander in chief, and Chiang hoped they would get along.

Unfortunately for Chiang, he did not know that Stilwell was ill-disposed toward him. Vinegar Joe had long since formed an impression of Chiang as a completely incompetent warrior and in his diaries called the Generalissimo "a goddamned fool."[21] Even Chiang's voice—"sharp, clipped staccato"—irritated him.[22] Not long before his arrival in Burma, while flying across the Atlantic and discussing with his subordinates the fraught relations between Chiang and General Wavell, he happily picked up a joke of two younger officers, one of whom noted that Chiang's position was "too shaky to harbor grudges" against the British.

"With the mess China's in today, he's . . ." said one fellow as he searched for the right comparison.

". . . like a peanut perched on top of a dung heap," the other jokester suggested.

Stilwell burst out laughing.

"Not a bad description of the old boy, The Peanut."[23]

Everyone doubled over in laughter, amused by the crude put-down. From then on Stilwell often referred to the Generalissimo, behind his back, as the Peanut. For Meiling, both he and his American subordinates came up with the more decorous nickname Snow White. They called Chiang Kai-shek's seven chief generals by the names of the dwarfs in the fairy tale.

The meeting in Lashio, however, went very well. Chiang and Meiling greeted Stilwell warmly. Two days later the three of them were back in Chongqing, but the situation in Burma then flared up anew. This time it was in connection with the Japanese army's seizure on March 6 of Rangoon, the capital of the country. Rangoon was where American Lend-Lease cargo was being delivered from the United States. British troops began a headlong retreat, and even Churchill was forced to observe that the "violence, fury, skill, and might of Japan has far exceeded anything we had been led to expect."[24] Things had not gone according to the whims of Wavell, who, incidentally, became deeply depressed. The British agreed to Chiang's proposal to send two of his best armies to Burma.

That same day, March 6, Chiang offered Stilwell command of these armies, the Fifth and the Sixth, and instructed his generals to take orders from the American. "General Stilwell will command you, and I will command Stilwell. Isn't General Stilwell my chief of staff?"

Stilwell was pleasantly surprised and already prepared to change his opinion of Chiang, writing in his diaries, "He seems willing to fight and is fed up with the British retreat and lethargy. Also, extremely suspicious of their motives and intentions. . . . It was a relief to find that the G-mo contemplates command in Burma for me. . . .[25] Never before has a foreigner been allowed any control over Chinese troops. . . .[26] He had a lot of good sense in his talk."[27]

Stilwell had no warm feelings toward the British either, viewing them as "sons of bitches" and "mongrels" for having abandoned Rangoon. On March

11 he flew to Burma, where he spent six days sizing up the situation. After returning, he presented a tactical operational plan to Chiang, proposing to airlift Chinese troops to Burma in order to establish a defensive line about 175 miles north of Rangoon.

It was then that friction between them began to develop. Everything the American proposed, Chiang rejected, asserting the need to construct a defensive line in central Burma, that is, at a distance of approximately 375 miles north of Rangoon. Naturally, Chiang considered himself more knowledgeable about military affairs than Vinegar Joe.

Stilwell returned to Burma in a bad mood, while Chiang had to shift his attention to family affairs again. In March 1942 Jeanette performed yet another stunt. Taking a walk in the outskirts of Chongqing, she came across an attractive youth and on the spot shamelessly propositioned him. The young man politely refused her, perhaps taking Jeanette for a homosexual man, since she often wore masculine attire. Enraged, Jeanette ordered her four bodyguards to give the ingrate a thrashing, which they did. The young man turned out to be the son of Bai Chongxi, one of the leaders of the Guangxi military clique and deputy chief of staff of Chiang Kai-shek's army. General Bai made a big fuss over the incident, and Chiang again had to calm the waters.[28]

In late March 1942 Chiang's older son Ching-kuo brought him a new surprise. Unexpectedly coming to see him in Chongqing on March 27, he informed his father that almost a month earlier (March 1), he (Chiang) had again become a grandfather, twice over, with the birth of twin boys, named Li Er and Shi Er (Handsome Boy and Lion Cub). Like his older grandson Allen, the twins were born prematurely, shy of seven months, and therefore they were also called Damao and Xiaomao (Big Kitten and Little Kitten).[29] It was a joyful event for the fifty-five-year-old grandfather, but it turned out that the new grandsons were not Fangliang's (Faina), Ching-kuo's lawful wife, but his mistress's, a certain Zhang Yaruo, whom Chiang had not known of. Neither had Meiling.

That Ching-kuo had a mistress did not surprise Chiang. He himself had had not a few in his day, but the delicacy of the situation derived from the fact that Faina, a foreigner, was not accustomed to the Chinese tradition of polygamy, and if she learned of her husband's infidelity that might create a scandal. This would not only damage the Generalissimo's prestige but also complicate the political situation in the country.

After thinking it over, Chiang changed the strange names of his grandsons Li Er and Shi Er, which, according to Ching-kuo, his mistress had given them from the name of the street on which she lived, Lishi lu (Handsome Lion Street). He named them in accordance with the genealogical chronicle of his own clan: Xiaoyan and Xiaoci.[30] As specified earlier, the thirtieth generation of the Wuling Jiangs had to include the character *xiao* (filial piety) and the character *yan* means "strict" while the character *ci* means "good." Later, at their christening, the children were also given Western names: John and Winston. But Chiang strictly forbade giving his new grandsons his family name and demanded that their surnames be Zhang, that of their mother. Learning of this, Ching-kuo's mistress became depressed: she understood that her children would be denied the right of inheritance.[31]

She was a beautiful but naïve woman. In December 1939, when she and Ching-kuo met, she was already twenty-six, but she looked eighteen: petite, voluptuous, with an oval face and Cupid's bow–shaped lips. She had been born in 1913, in the village of Wucheng in northern Jiangxi in a family of *shenshi* (rural literatus). Her child name was Maoli (Enchanting Plum), and it fitted her perfectly. At seventeen she was married off, and she had two sons from this marriage, but six years later, for some reason or other, her husband committed suicide. When the Japanese came, in March 1939, she went south to Jiangxi, to Ganzhou, leaving her children in the care of her mother. Her head filled with romantic ideas, and she decided to devote herself wholeheartedly to the heroic struggle for the liberation of the Fatherland. So in Ganzhou she enrolled in courses for young cadres. Several months later, in November, at a large municipal gathering, she first saw Ching-kuo.[32] Naturally, she was taken at once by the young handsome, genial man who, it turned out, was Chiang Kai-shek's son.

After completing her courses, Yaruo began working in the local administration, and it was there that Ching-kuo himself took notice of her and soon invited her to serve as his secretary. What followed is obvious. The romance lasted for almost two years, in complete secrecy from Faina, who was also living in Ganzhou with the children. This continued despite the fact that Faina knew Yaruo well and even occasionally asked her to look after her children, Eric-Allen and Emma-Amy, when she had to be away for a while. At Faina's request, Yaruo even helped her study Chinese.

Was Ching-kuo attracted to Yaruo because she did not at all resemble Faina, who was also a pretty woman but obviously of a Slavic type? Or perhaps, in the words of the Russian poet Vladimir Mayakovsky, he wanted "to steep" his "clangor in softness, in woman."[33] The submissive, voluptuous Yaruo (which means Obedient) answered that desire more than Faina did.

Faina's character, after all, was no less strong than that of Meiling. Or perhaps he was simply drawn "to the strawberry patch"? The affair was probably fired by mutual passion. He tenderly called her Huiyun (Bright Cloud), and she called him Huifeng (Strong Wind), names deriving from the Chinese expressions *fengyun jihui* and *fengyun buli* ("the wind and the cloud meet" and "the wind and the cloud never part").

In October 1941 the romance ended after Yaruo, with a sinking feeling, told her lover she was pregnant. Ching-kuo panicked on the spot. Giving her a princely sum of money, he turned Yaruo over to her friend Gui Changde, who escorted her to Guilin, in northern Guangxi province some distance from Ganzhou. Gui's brother, a district magistrate, lived not far from that city.

After the birth of the twins Ching-kuo arrived in Guilin, gave her more money, but, realizing that he would not succeed in keeping the birth of the children a secret, set off at once to see his father in Chongqing. Apparently after putting everything in order, he returned to Ganzhou, to his lawful wife.

Yaruo and the twins remained in Guilin. In August 1942 she noticed she was being followed. Then, after someone forced the lock, broke into her house and carried off some things, she decided to go to the police. The chief of police himself received her and not only carefully heard her out but also ordered tea for her and then stationed a guard at her house. Everything seemed to be going well, but soon after the visit to the police precinct, Yaruo had a severe attack of diarrhea accompanied by acute stomach spasms. She was wracked with pain. Frightened to death, Gui Changde called the doctors, and Yaruo was hospitalized, placed in a separate ward. The faithful Gui spent the whole night with her.

By the morning of August 15 the patient was getting better. A doctor came, introduced himself as Wang, the most common surname in China, and said he needed to give her an injection. She held out her left arm, he quickly administered an injection and left, without saying another word. No one knew what sort of injection it was and for what illness. "Doctor Wang" did not reappear. Soon Yaruo, grasping her left arm with her right hand, cried out, "I feel awful. I can't see anything!" A doctor asked Gui Changde's brother, who was in the ward, to run out to the street and buy ice, but the ice was not needed: when it was brought in Yaruo was dead. Her friends were given a certificate saying that she had died of "blood poisoning."[34]

There is no doubt she was killed, but it is not clear on whose orders. Several persons accused Ching-kuo despite the fact that he suffered from Yaruo's death to the end of his life, and before his own death he whispered her name in his sleep. Others blame his classmate at Sun Yat-sen University, a certain Huang Zhongmei, who studied in Moscow under the pseudonym Malyshev,[35] and worked under Ching-kuo in the Ganzhou security service. He supposedly did so on his own initiative because his boss and friend needed to save face. This version is quite plausible, especially since Huang Zhongmei was subsequently arrested and executed by the Guomindang secret services. Perhaps because he killed Yaruo?

Most likely, however, it was none other than Chiang Kai-shek who was responsible for the murder. He was identified, for example, by a former official of the Guomindang secret service, General Gu Zhengwen, who spoke about the matter in a 2004 interview. The old spymaster also accused the Generalissimo's close comrade in arms Chen Lifu, his blood nephew, of complicity in the murder.[36] It is hard not to believe a man like Gu, especially since he spoke about this dramatic event three years before his death.

Whatever the truth of the matter, it is evident that Chiang, after giving names to his new grandsons, did not want his son's adultery to be revealed to the public. He was afraid of a scandal that might become international in scope. Hence he was not open about the matter even privately. In his diaries on July 6, 1944, two years after the birth of his grandsons, he wrote, "My wife received a lot of anonymous letters, including ones slandering me. One of them, judging by the expressions, was written by an Englishman. These letters not only defame me, but also both of my sons Jing and Wei. A great deal of slander is about my son Jing—that he has a mistress in Chongqing, and that she gave birth to his twins which were given to her mother to raise. All of this gossip is fodder for the Communist Party, and for the British and the Americans, who use it not only to undermine the people's faith in me, but also to discredit fully my family."[37]

Obviously, Chiang was dissembling. In the gossip that he referred to, the only falsity was that Ching-kuo's mistress lived in Chongqing. Everything else was true, including the rumor that the infants had been handed over to their grandmother. Certain that her daughter had been killed, she did everything she could to protect them. She even registered them under different dates of birth.[38] Possibly this is why up to now there is confusion in the historiography: some authors cite their date of birth as March 1, others as March 13, yet others as May 2, and a fourth group as May 21.[39] This despite the fact that from 2008 to 2014 the elder of the twins, Zhang (Jiang) Xiaoyan, held one of the most important posts in the Republic of China, deputy chair of the

Guomindang CEC. The younger twin, Zhang (Jiang) Xiaoci, was also, until his death in 1996, a member of the CEC of the party and rector of Suzhou University in Taipei. It is interesting that Zhang (Jiang) Xiaoyan's passport still indicates his date of birth as May 2, 1942, even though in August 2002 he received a copy of his birth certificate from the Second People's Hospital of Guilin, the former Guangdong provincial hospital.[40] He and his brother had been born there, attesting that they were born on March 1, 1942.[41]

Meanwhile, the conflict between Stilwell and Chiang flared up. Taking note that the Generalissimo did not support his chief of staff in all matters, many Chinese generals began to sabotage the American's orders. On March 31, 1942, the enraged Stilwell wrote in his diaries, "The Chinese commanders . . . feel, of course, the urgent necessity of pleasing the Generalissimo, and if my suggestions or orders run counter to what they *think* he wants they offer endless objections. . . . I can't shoot them; I can't relieve them; and just talking to them does no good."[42]

The next day he gave a description of Chiang himself: "Chiang K'ai-shek [Kai-shek] has been boss for so long and has so many yes-men around him that he has the idea he is infallible on any subject. . . . He is not mentally stable, and he will say many things to your face that he doesn't mean fully or exactly. . . . [I]t is patently impossible for me to compete with the swarms of parasites and sycophants that surround him."[43] In early April Chiang and Meiling paid a visit to Stilwell in Burma, trying to reduce the growing tension. Chiang told Stilwell he even had the right to dismiss and discipline any Chinese officer. The matter seemed closed: photographs taken on April 7 do not reveal any tension among them: all three are smiling broadly.

But the situation soon changed owing to the crushing defeat that British and Chinese forces suffered in Burma in early May. Stilwell, along with the remains of the army he led, was forced to make his way to India on foot in a twenty-day hike through the jungles. He did not return to Chongqing until early June 1942, terribly emaciated (he had lost over twenty pounds) and embittered. He blamed Chiang for the defeat, for not replying to his telegrams, and for sending senseless orders from Chongqing: for example, not to retreat to India but to the Chinese border, where Stilwell believed Chinese troops might be surrounded.[44] In reality, Stilwell himself made strategic mistakes in Burma that contributed to the defeat, so Chiang was unable to forgive the American general.[45]

For several days Stilwell almost never went out, holing up in his residence—the same house that belonged to T. V. Song, where Currie and Lattimore had been guests before (the address was 3 Jialing Village).[46] From the windows of this beautiful modern house and especially from the roof a captivating view opened out of the Jialing River valley and the surrounding hills, but Vinegar Joe did not feast his eyes on the landscape. Ever more negative descriptions of Chiang appeared in his diaries, even malicious attacks against him: "The Chinese government is a structure based on fear and favor, in the hands of an ignorant, arbitrary, stubborn man. It is interlaced with family and financial ties and influences, which could easily tear it to pieces if pulled out. . . . He [Chiang] can hurdle logic and reason by using his 'intuition'; he dismisses proven principles and methods by saying that Chinese psychology is different . . . and his obstinacy refuses discussion. He has lost all habit of discussion, in fact, because everybody around him is a Yes-man. No one dares tell him an unpleasant truth, because he gets mad. He's in a hell of a fix."[47] Then, on June 15, the conflict exploded into the open. Conversing with Chiang, Stilwell suddenly could not control himself and began raging. Meiling had to calm him down. Chiang restrained himself, but three days later he poured out his indignation in a letter to T. V. Song in Washington.[48] A week later he openly expressed his dissatisfaction with US policy. At just that time Roosevelt decided to send American troops, based in India, to North Africa to assist the British who were fighting against the best German commander, Field Marshal Erwin Rommel. Offended that, from his perspective, the Americans were not taking into account the interests of the anti-Japanese war, Chiang, via Stilwell, demanded that, by the end of August, Roosevelt send three American divisions to the India–Burma border, provide at least 500 airplanes to China, and ship up to 5,000 tons of supplies monthly. Otherwise, he hinted at the possibility of surrendering to the enemy. Chiang asked Stilwell to pose a question to Roosevelt: "Is the U.S. interested in maintaining the Chinese theater?"[49]

Stilwell deemed this to be an ultimatum, as he irritably told Meiling, whom he often called Madamissimo, La Grande Dame, or even "Madam Empress" behind her back. He did not want to transmit any sort of ultimatum to the president, especially since the defeat in Burma had led to the closure of the "lifeline" and the almost complete blockade of China. During 1941 the monthly supply to China had grown from 4,000 to almost 15,000 tons of American goods,[50] and now even 5,000 tons seemed unrealistic. All that remained was an air link with China across India and the Himalayas. Stilwell told Meiling he was a soldier, not a "rubber stamp" or a "postal agency." She grew angry and told Chiang. A scandal arose, and Vinegar Joe even took ill. He had sharp stomach pains all night and had to run to the john repeatedly.

But Roosevelt supported his lieutenant-general, and the conflict apparently died down. In his diaries, however, Stilwell began to refer to Chiang as Peanut only. In a letter to his wife he jocularly referred to Chinese officials (officialdom) as "Officialdumb."[51]

In September, Roosevelt informed Chiang that although he could not send him 500 planes, he would send 265 and then try to increase the scale of supply shipments to 5,000 tons.[52] The shrewd Meiling tried to smooth over the contradictions between her husband and Vinegar Joe. Sometimes she even spoke up for Stilwell, who, starting in October only showed up in Chongqing for short visits since Chiang had granted him full control of Chinese forces stationed in India.

Soon Chiang ignored Stilwell entirely for a while because more problems arose on the family front. In early October Meiling suddenly started an affair with a high-ranking guest who had come to Chongqing: Roosevelt's personal representative, the former Republican Party candidate for president Wendell Willkie, who was embarked on a world tour. In November 1940 he had lost to Roosevelt by a huge margin, getting only 82 electoral votes to the sitting president's 449. But Willkie was not despondent and intended to run again in the next election in 1944. He had a shot at the presidency. He was very handsome, attractive to women, and in 1940, of the fifty million people who had gone to the polls, almost twenty-two-and-a-half-million had voted for him.[53]

Willkie spent six days in China and met with Chiang and Meiling several times, talking about everything from the industrialization of China to the war on the Soviet–German front. Chiang captivated him: "The Generalissimo, both as a man and as a leader, is bigger even than his legendary reputation. . . . When he is not in military uniform, he wears Chinese dress, and this accentuates the impression he makes of a scholar—almost a clerical scholar—rather than a political leader. He is obviously a trained listener, used to the task of picking other men's brains. He nods his head when he agrees with you, with continuous soft little ya-ya's; it is a subtle form of compliment, and one that disarms the man he is talking to. . . . He is undoubtedly sincere, and his dignity and personal imperturbability have something almost severe in quality."[54] But the fifty-year-old ladies' man Willkie liked Meiling, "one of the most beautiful, intelligent, and sexy women."[55] He was so enticed by her that, without giving it much thought, he seduced the forty-five-year-old beauty from under the nose of the Generalissimo.[56] Remembering the fling after he returned to the States, he nevertheless asserted only that his talks with Chiang Kai-shek's wife were geared only to "solve the problems of the universe."[57]

Perhaps. But judging from the story of the founder of *Look* magazine, Gardner Cowles, who accompanied Willkie on the trip, these problems were not foremost. He wrote,

> One evening back in Chungking [Chongqing] the Generalissimo gave an enormous reception for us. . . . About an hour later [after the start of the festivities] . . . Wendell . . . whispered that he and the Madame were disappearing in a few minutes and that I was to take his place and cover up for them as best I could. Sure enough, ten minutes later they were gone.
>
> I stationed myself alongside the Generalissimo and unleashed a flurry of questions about China every time I felt his attention wandering. He [Chiang] stayed at the reception for another hour and then suddenly clapped his hands to summon his aide. He was leaving, and I decided to do the same. My aide took me back to the [T. V.] Song house where we were staying. . . . I wondered where Wendell and the Madam had gone. By nine o'clock I began to worry. . . . Shortly after dinner there was a great clatter in the courtyard. The Generalissimo stormed in, visibly furious. He was accompanied by three bodyguards, each carrying a little Tommy gun. Trying to restrain his rage, the Generalissimo bowed coldly and I returned the bow.
>
> "Where is Willkie?" he asked.

Cowles replied that he had no idea. Chiang searched the house, but, finding no one, he left. It seemed he had calmed down.

Willkie showed up at four in the morning, satisfied like "a young college student after a successful night with a girl." He told Cowles of his adventure, saying that "there was never anything like this before," and "[i]t was the only time . . . he had ever been in love." He added that he had convinced the "Madam" to go to Washington with him. Cowles exploded. He said that "[Willkie's] wife and son would probably meet him at the airport in Washington" and that "the presence of the Madam would be a considerable embarrassment." He could not understand how Willkie would be able now to run for the presidency in 1944.

After thinking it over, Willkie agreed and asked Cowles to find Meiling and hush up the matter: "She had an apartment on the top floor of the Women's and Children's Hospital in town." (That is where the rendezvous took place.) But Cowles's visit to Meiling was not entirely successful. Hearing that Willkie had reconsidered taking her with him, Snow White ran up to the cofounder of *Look* and, not hiding her fury, raked both of his cheeks with her long fingernails.[58]

What happened afterward nobody knows, but though Meiling did not fly to the States on the same plane with Willkie, neither he nor she wished to break off relations. Before leaving, Willkie officially invited Madamissimo to visit America in the near future. "With wit and charm, a generous and understanding heart, a gracious and beautiful manner and appearance, and a burning conviction [in the rightness of her cause], she is just what we need as a visitor," he said to Kong Xiangxi and his wife Ailing.[59]

Meiling's trip to the States was presented to Chiang as a boon for China. Reluctantly, he agreed. Possibly he simply refused to believe in the liaison between his wife and the candidate for president of the United States, or perhaps he sacrificed himself for the common good. Most likely it was the latter. Meiling did not try hard to conceal the liaison. On the day Willkie flew out from Chongqing, she again met with him alone: they spent almost an hour and a half together. Not only did she go to the airport to see him off, but in full view of everyone she rushed to embrace him, and Willkie planted a passionate kiss on her lips.[60] Little did he know that in China it was considered improper for even a husband and wife to show affection in public.

After a short time, Meiling told her husband that she urgently needed to go to the United States "for treatment." And the doctors immediately diagnosed a clutch of illnesses she was suffering, thereby convincing Chiang that she could be cured only in the States.

There is no doubt that Meiling was not fully healthy, but it is not known whether she was so ill that she urgently needed to be hospitalized in a clinic in New York. In any event, in mid-November 1942 she flew off to the United States for a long time. She took her favorite niece, Jeanette, with her, her secretary Pearl Chen, physicians, three nurses, and the deputy director of the Department of Propaganda of the Guomindang CEC, Hollington Tong, as her personal press secretary. She was carried into the plane on a stretcher so that no doubts would arise about her tenuous physical condition.[61]

Meanwhile, as the year 1943 arrived, it brought China great news: on January 11 the United States and Great Britain abrogated their unequal treaties with China and concluded new agreements. Chiang devoted two works to this event: *China's Destiny*, published on March 10, specially timed for the eighteenth anniversary of Sun Yat-sen's death,[62] and *Chinese Economic Theory*, published soon thereafter. Both books were intended to answer the question of how the Republic of China would develop in the new international conditions. Chiang formulated his own paradigm of social progress, presenting an ultra-etatist interpretation of the social and political ideas of Sun Yat-sen's Three Principles of the People: Nationalism, Democracy, and People's Livelihood. He in fact set forth a New Authoritarianism, calling for strengthening state control over the economy and private property in the spirit of Oriental Despotism.[63] This was a system of state monopoly, limiting foreign investments and collectivizing the peasantry as well as tightening the Guomindang political regime and eradicating dissidents.[64]

On Chiang's instructions, the drafts of both works were prepared by Tao Xisheng, a forty-four-year-old former professor who had taught at a number of universities, including Peking University. In December 1938 Tao had followed Wang Jingwei to Hanoi, after which, from August 1939 to January 1940, he was a member of Wang Jingwei's version of the Standing Committee of the CEC of the Guomindang and director of its Department of Propaganda. But then he fled to Hong Kong, where he went public with an exposure of the puppet regime and its secret treaties with the "Japanese dwarfs." He moved to Chongqing early in 1942, after the fall of Hong Kong, and Chiang, forgiving him his betrayal and valuing him as a talented publicist, made Tao his new secretary.

Chiang ascribed more importance to the first book, *China's Destiny,* which he assigned Tao Xisheng to write soon after he learned of the intention of the United States and Great Britain to abrogate the right of extraterritoriality in China in the coming year.[65] Tao received the order on October 10, 1942, on the thirty-first anniversary of the 1911 Revolution. He produced a draft at the beginning of 1943, and Chiang himself carefully edited it. He was very satisfied with the result, he said.[66]

The initial printing was 200,000 at a subsidized price of ten Chinese cents per copy to accelerate its distribution. The book was immediately included in university programs and taken as a kind of catechism for members of the Guomindang. Just ten days later Chiang himself personally requested that it be taught in all middle schools and that all middle school principals report how they intended to accomplish this task. After another ten days Chiang decided that all the high-ranking officers should study it.[67] By the end of 1943 it had been reprinted two hundred times.

Then the Chinese Ministry of Information distributed its English digest in New York. An English-language newspaper published in Chengdu, *West China Missionary News,* printed separate parts of it. The Chinese government did not publish the entire English translation despite the fact that it too was ready in 1943. Meiling, who had returned from the States on July 4 after a seven-month absence, advised her husband not to publish the book given its openly anti-Western and antiliberal contents. Chiang's American advisor, a Presbyterian missionary named Francis Wilson Price, also expressed some doubts.[68] He pointed to the "mentality of British and American people."[69] Several of Meiling's comments were taken into consideration by Chiang Kai-shek on the republication of the book in Chinese in January 1944. But an English edition did not come out in China at that time either.[70]

Governments of Western countries were likewise disinclined to publish the book. The US Department of State made its own translation but preserved the manuscript in its archives under a Top Secret seal. In January 1946 six congressmen requested the State Department to provide them with the text, but they were told that the proper moment for it to circulate had not yet come.

Two completed English-language translations appeared in New York three years after the second Chinese edition. Both books came out in early 1947. The first one, the very same Guomindang edition that had been prepared in 1943, was accompanied by enthusiastic commentaries made by a famous Chinese American journalist Lin Yutang.[71] The second, the new one, was supplemented by harsh accusations branding Chiang a fascist by an American Stalinist, Philip Jaffe, one of the publishers of a pro-Communist journal *Amerasia*. Jaffe even compared Chiang's book to *Mein Kampf*.

In 1947 Jaffe published the first English-language translation of *Chinese Economic Theory*. It too was accompanied by vicious remarks.[72] At the time, a decisive civil war between the CCP and the Guomindang was taking place in China, and Jaffe's comments had a clear political connotation. All Western liberals viewed Chiang Kai-shek's books as Nazi scribbling or, at least, literature that insults a reader.[73] Even some Sinologists viewed Chiang Kai-shek's books as fascistic, reactionary, and xenophobic and its ideas Utopian and dubious.[74]

But what were they really? Can Chiang's authoritarianism be equated with fascism or considered Utopian? By no means. In his books Chiang sought to demonstrate that China was not ready for any kind of democracy. Moreover, he asserted that Western ideology and politics were alien to China due to the peculiar characteristics of its historical development. A large part of the lengthy *China's Destiny* and of the relatively short *Chinese Economic Theory* is dedicated to a thoroughgoing critique of the West, including Western principles of the market economy. But is this fascism or Utopianism?

Sun Yat-sen himself had repeatedly written essentially the same thing. Both Sun and Chiang knew the history and philosophy of China very well, and they had no doubt that a Chinese type of civilization differed radically from the Western one. The Chinese economy had always been based on collective or state property ownership whereas the economy of Western countries had always been built on private property ownership. In other words, the Chinese government had always played a leading role in the economy. It had always striven to monopolize the main means of production such as land, its natural and water resources, and the irrigation system. In emphasizing this fact, Chiang Kai-shek referred to numerous Chinese economists, including Guan Zhong (720–645 BCE), Shang Yang (390–338 BCE), Fan Zhongyan (989–1052), Wang Anshi (1021–86), and Zhang Juzheng (1525–82). These scholars served at different courts, but they all emphasized the supremacy of the state over the individual. "The theories of the aforementioned economists differed, but their origins and objectives were similar," Chiang noted. "None was based on man's wants—particularly on the wants of any special individual or individuals. All were based on man's nature and all their objectives were national planning and the people's livelihood. To attain their objectives all of them centered their efforts on [state] economic planning and control [of the market]."[75]

This idea was precisely what Chiang intended to bring to life, rejecting Adam Smith's liberal Western theory of *laissez-faire la nature* as inapplicable to China. But Sun Yat-sen also wrote about this: "Social problems should not as a rule be left to resolve themselves. When left untended to grow by themselves, trees inevitably branch out and spread, and so will social problems."[76]

Rejecting Western values, Chiang justifiably paid attention to the fact that Chinese, by virtue of the specific characteristics of the economic development of All-under-Heaven, were collectivists in terms of their social psychology. That's why, he asserted, "the traditional Chinese philosophy . . . [is] based on the idea that men are not individual, separate entities, not each a single 'I,' but each a part of the plural 'We.' "[77]

That is why, expounding Sun Yat-sen's ideas, Chiang Kai-shek believed that in the future ideal Chinese society private property would be put under strict state control as it had been in the sacred past; the government would prevent the emergence of private capitalist monopolies and promote economic planning; all land property rights would be equalized as the government would expropriate differential ground rent; and the peasants would work in collective farms that would resemble military settlements in which all males would form military regiments, a sort of people's militia (*mintuan*).

Furthermore, the state would serve as a mediator settling disputes between employers and employees and elaborate a welfare system to benefit the poor. "The economic duties of a government are to support the people—the people's livelihood—on the one hand, and to protect the people—national defense—on the other," asserted Chiang, insisting that only in this way could China achieve the Great Harmony or the Grand Union (*datong*), which "embodies the final economic goal of the Three People's Principles."[78] In essence, such steps were a matter of peacefully constructing state socialism in China, that is, the very same kind of society that Sun Yat-sen had envisioned.

Thus Chiang never deviated from the basic ideas of his teacher. Sun Yat-sen too had proceeded from the need "to preserve . . . the traditions of state regulation" and affirmed the superiority of "the Ch[inese] civilization . . . over the Western one."[79]

Chiang's program undoubtedly corresponded to the economic and social characteristics of China, but Chiang overestimated the possibilities opening for his country in connection with the granting of full independence to it by the liberal West. Abrogation of the unequal treaties in no way indicates that Chiang, in the name of the Chinese government, could freely advance theories that ran counter to the liberal values accepted in the democratic West. Especially at a time when a bloody world war was being fought between totalitarianism—associated in the popular consciousness with the political regimes of Germany, Italy, and Japan—and democracy, whose main champions at the time were seen not only as the United States and Great Britain, but also, paradoxically, the USSR.

Chiang made a political mistake, an especially unforgivable one, because three years earlier, in late 1939–early 1940, Mao Zedong had put forth a diametrically opposite interpretation of the ideas of Sun Yat-sen. The CCP leader expounded on his intention to implement the so-called theory of New Democracy on coming to power. The leader of the CCP spoke of the need to implement liberal democratic reforms in China, and he renounced the struggle for a socialist dictatorship. He promised to fully respect the rights of private proprietors, to stimulate national entrepreneurship, and to attract foreign investors under strict state control. Moreover, he called for lowering taxes, developing a multiparty system, establishing a coalition government, and instituting democratic freedoms. The New Democracy differed from old-style Western democracy, according to Mao, because it would be implemented under the leadership of the Communist Party. However, the party was no longer presenting itself as the political organ of the working class but rather as the organization of the united revolutionary front striving to unite "all the revolutionary people." Postrevolutionary China, Mao affirmed, would not be a dictatorship of the proletariat but a republic of "a joint dictatorship of all revolutionary classes"; in the economy of the new country, state, cooperative, and private capitalist property would coexist.[80]

The sociopolitical views of Mao and Chiang were thus radically different, at least on paper. The publication of Chiang's books was largely a reaction to Mao Zedong's "New Democracy." "They are a great force that in the future will really stabilize the national ideology and will strike the CCP a heavy blow," wrote Chiang in his diaries.[81] But in the eyes of Chinese and Western liberals Mao Zedong appeared in the guise of a democrat while Chiang did so as a dictator.

Chiang obviously underestimated the degree of influence of democratic ideas on Chinese public opinion. Yet China in the first half of the twentieth century was hardly a country that had never heard of democracy. Many factors at the time stimulated a substantial renewal of Chinese political culture. Among them was the victory of the antimonarchical Xinhai Revolution of 1911; the proclamation of a republic on January 1, 1912; elections to the first parliament and parliamentary debates; the struggle between Sun Yat-sen and Yuan Shikai and the latter's plans to restore the monarchy; the anti-Japanese movement of May 4, 1919; the mass boycotts of foreign goods; as well as the cooperation and confrontation between the Communist Party and the Guomindang in the period of the first united front of 1924–27. All these events strengthened the democratic leanings of the Chinese intelligentsia, and it was this segment of society that was the first to accept New Democracy enthusiastically. It was no accident that in December 1939, while working on the concept of New Democracy, Mao, on behalf of the CCP CC, worked out a special decision on attracting intelligentsia to the side of the party.[82]

In reality, however, Mao Zedong's theory was not strategic but tactical in nature and based on deception. The New Democratic maneuver was intended to enable the CCP to greatly expand its mass base by means of winning over to its side representatives of intermediate strata who opposed any sort of dictatorship, whether communist or Guomindang. It was aimed at preparing conditions for the subsequent seizure of power in China.

Such a maneuver had been suggested to Mao back in November 1937 by Stalin, who was working intensively then on developing new tactics for the entire world communist movement. Stalin was trying to deceive not merely the Chinese intelligentsia and Chiang Kai-shek but the entire bourgeois West.

He wanted to make them all believe that all the communist parties, apart from the CPSU, starting from the Seventh Congress of the Comintern (July–August 1935), had renounced the struggle for socialism, substituting for this goal the idea of constructing a humane society of "People's (or New) Democracy."[83]

In other words, the paradigm of social progress formulated by Mao Zedong was a fiction. Neither Mao nor the majority of his supporters intended to implement it. Their goal was to weaken the Guomindang, label Chiang Kai-shek a dictator, and present themselves as authentic democrats.

But Chiang apparently did not fully understand this. Therefore, he vainly counterposed his own strategic program to Mao's purely tactical ideas. And while Mao was skillfully deceiving both Chinese and world public opinion, constantly affirming the need for a prompt transition to "constitutional rule," Chiang, underestimating the powerful polarization between the world forces of totalitarianism and democracy that had occurred in the course of the war, stubbornly insisted, in essence, that the period of political tutelage had not been completed. This assertion evoked dissatisfaction from the constantly growing circles of liberals, not only in China but also in the democratic West.

The response of Western liberals to Chiang's elaborations was especially dangerous. Chiang Kai-shek's prestige in the democratic West began to weaken at the same time Mao Zedong's began to grow. This imbalance was facilitated by the numerous publications by Western journalists about the ineffectiveness and corruption of the Chiang Kai-shek regime and the terrible living conditions of the Chinese people. The anti-Chiang publications of Theodore White, Brooks Atkinson, Edgar Snow, T. A. Bisson, Jack Belden, Freda Utley, Thoban Wiant, Joseph Alsop, Agnes Smedley, and others made a particularly strong impression. All of them testified in one voice and, moreover, assured the world that the Chinese communists had nothing in common with Marxism-Leninism.[84] In this connection, especially revealing was an article by T. A. Bisson, who asserted that there were two Chinas, a democratic China ruled by the Communist Party and a feudal China ruled by Chiang Kai-shek.[85] The result was that the "dismal dictator" Chiang and his regime were steadily "losing points," in the eyes of many Americans losing out to the liberal nationalist Mao and his supposed popular government.

A negative image of Chiang Kai-shek and his regime also gradually took shape in the White House. The change was owing partly to the influence of the liberal and leftist press and partly on the basis of confidential information arriving from Stilwell; Ambassador Clarence Edward Gauss, who despised Chiang;[86] Second Secretary of the Embassy John Stewart Service; and others.

Visiting Chiang again in the autumn of 1942, Lattimore also expressed his dissatisfaction with the Generalissimo for shifting the burden of the war against Japan to the United States.[87] At the same time, Roosevelt's close friend and former bodyguard, Captain Evans Carlson, who had visited the CCP headquarters in the city of Yan'an in North Shaanxi in May 1938, reported to the president of the United States that Mao was a "dreamer, of course; a genius," and the "Chinese Communist group (so-called) is not communistic in the sense that we are accustomed to use the term. . . . I would call them a group of Liberal Democrats, perhaps Social-Democrats (but not of the Nazi breed). They seek equality of opportunity and honest government. . . . It is not Communism according to the connotation with which they [the people of America] are familiar."[88] That the Chinese Communist movement was more "a national and agrarian awakening than an international or proletarian conspiracy," Willkie reported upon his return to Washington.[89]

Meiling's American tour likewise contributed more than a little to the drop in Chiang's prestige and that of his government. The ambitious madame wanted not only to improve her health but also to have a good time. She had already captured Willkie's heart, and now she wanted to continue the affair as well as captivate all of America. To secure unconditional and broad support for her country from the United States, she dreamed of producing an impression on Americans both as a woman and as a central political figure. The aim was noble, but Meiling evidently overestimated her charm.

The Roosevelts, husband and wife, who initially greeted Madame Chiang very cordially, toward the end of her stay did not know how to get rid of her. At first, the petite ill woman evoked their natural sympathy. Eleanor Roosevelt, who visited her in the Presbyterian Medical Center of Columbia University, even felt "a desire to help her and take care of her" as if Meiling had been her "own daughter" (Eleanor Roosevelt was fourteen years older than Meiling).[90] After checking herself out of the hospital, Madame Chiang, on the Roosevelts' invitation, moved into the White House on February 17, 1943. However, the president and his wife soon became very disenchanted. By this time Roosevelt knew via a memorandum of January 15, 1943, presented by J. Edgar Hoover, the director of the Federal Bureau of Investigation, that "the Songs have been depicted as 'money mad' and their desire to secure additional funds appears to prompt their every move." Hoover accused the entire Song clan of a "giant conspiracy" whose aim was the appropriation of the credits released for Lend-Lease. The Song organization, he wrote, was said to be "very closely knit and ruthlessly operated. . . . Anyone 'getting out of hand' is either bought off or exterminated." The brains of the group, in his words, was Madame Chiang's sister Ailing, the wife of the minister of finance and director of the Central Bank Kong Xiangxi. Hoover expressed his suspicion that the real goal of Madame Chiang's visit to the United States was not medical treatment but control over the financial streams from America to China.[91]

The puritanically inclined Roosevelts were astonished by the luxury that was Meiling's preferred lifestyle. She showed off her jewelry and did not want to sleep on the cotton sheets with which her bed in the White House was made up.[92] She had brought with her from China four sets of silk sheets and demanded that the maid change them every day.[93] Her twenty-three-year-old niece Jeanette and twenty-six-year-old nephew Kong Lingkan (alias Kong Lingkai and David), who had come to visit their aunt from Harvard, did not behave very modestly either. They too took up residence in the White House, to the dismay of the servants, whom Meiling's relatives treated "like Chinese coolies," and to the embarrassment of the Roosevelts. In the words of the president's wife, they "did not want to be at all friendly," as if "bearing some grudge" toward them. Jeanette made the worst impression, putting on airs that she was the direct descendant of Confucius and dressing every day in male attire. At first the president mistakenly called her "My boy." The Roosevelts were also surprised by the unexpected cruelty of the superficially "good, soft, and fragile" Meiling. At dinner one evening, in answer to the president's question, "What would you do in China with a labor leader like John Lewis?"[94] the diminutive Madame silently slid her finger across her throat.[95] When, at the end of February 1943, Meiling finally left the White House and returned to New York, Roosevelt, according to Vice President Henry A. Wallace, "always had his fingers crossed" when referring to her.[96]

In New York Meiling occupied an entire floor in the fashionable Waldorf-Astoria Hotel and spent whole days visiting expensive stores on Fifth Avenue. Willkie inundated her with flowers and visited her repeatedly, but their affair broke off in mid-April 1943, soon after the publication of his book about his world travels. It's not known whether the book was responsible for the rupture or something else: in the book, it is true, he refers to Meiling only in ecstatic tones. Soon after the breakup, Meiling, in a private conversation with Roosevelt, called her former lover a "perpetual adolescent."[97] A year later Willkie ran in the new presidential race but dropped out in the primaries. Soon after, on October 8, 1944, he died of a heart attack.

In the meantime, on May 26, 1943, Lauchlin Currie received a report from his informant that checks to the tune of $370,000—that is, contributions collected by Meiling in America—had been deposited in the account of her nephew David Kong. On June 10, according to new information, the money was transferred to Meiling's personal account, which then totaled US $800,000.[98]

The longer Meiling stayed in the States, the more her "dirty linen" became known, not just to American counterintelligence but also to reporters. Toward the end of her stay the press was screaming about the whims and wealth of the madame from China. In America itself at that time the average standard of living was not high, and during wartime the government had even introduced price controls and rationing of consumer goods. What's more, Meiling displayed her provocative extravagance at a time when, in her homeland, according to dispatches from *Time* correspondent Theodore White, there was a terrible famine, whose epicenter was in Henan province. Americans were horror struck to read reports about the deaths of hundreds of thousands of persons,[99] and instances of mass cannibalism.[100] They instinctively asked the question, "How can Chiang Kai-shek's wife not be ashamed to flaunt her wealth?"

One of Meiling's biographers, Laura Tyson Li, accuses Lauchlin Currie of inspiring a campaign against Meiling, hinting that he was acting at the behest of the Kremlin inasmuch as he was a "secret Soviet agent."[101] This is doubtful, however. Even if Currie really was working for Moscow, for which there is some evidence though dubious, it was not he who actually transferred the donations collected by Meiling into the accounts of her nephew David Kong and then to that of Meiling herself.[102]

It would be unfair to consider all of Meiling's visit a failure. Her artfully crafted, impassioned speech to Congress on February 18, 1943, together with press conferences and numerous presentations from Boston to Los Angeles, facilitated growing American sympathy toward China in its struggle for independence. But Meiling did not achieve any concrete results. Her charm did not work on Roosevelt, and he did not make her any concrete promises. On the contrary, the president only smiled at her attempts to engage him in conversations on politics.[103] He gave her the opportunity to speak at various meetings, to talk on all issues, including military strategy, to make the case that the Allies should first defeat Japan and only then Germany, and to call for an increase in American aid to China. But it was evident that he did not consider her the authoritative ruler of China, leaving the resolution of concrete matters to a personal meeting with Chiang Kai-shek. When her sojourn was nearly at an end, Roosevelt was so tired of her that he even observed to a congressman that it would be best if this prima donna returned home soon so that "these irritations might subside."[104]

Overall, Madame's prolonged American tour did more harm than good, although upon her return to Chongqing in early July 1943 Meiling spoke at a press conference of the "enormous spiritual lift" she had felt from the "spontaneous goodwill" shown by the American people.[105] But this was putting up a bold front.

Roosevelt began to ponder the idea of having a personal meeting with Chiang, who by then held all the most important positions in China. In August 1942, after the seventy-five-year-old Lin Sen died, Chiang also assumed the post of chairman of the government.[106] Roosevelt had long wanted to invite Chiang to discuss overall war strategy at one of the summit meetings taking place among the heads of the Allied powers.[107] But because of the opposition of Churchill, who did not want to recognize China as a great power,[108] Chiang had not been invited either to the Casablanca conference in Morocco in January 1943 or to the summit in Quebec City in Canada in August of that year. Chiang was terribly offended but could do nothing.

He vented his dissatisfaction in his diaries[109] and also took out his anger on Stilwell, with whom, by the autumn of 1943, his relations were on the brink of rupturing. In early October, via T. V. Song, Chiang requested that Roosevelt recall the obstinate general. The president of the United States did not object but, wishing to ease the tension, he invited Chiang to take part in the next Allied meeting in Cairo in November. This invitation to Chiang was delivered by Major General Patrick J. Hurley, the former secretary of war in the United States, whom Roosevelt sent specially to Chongqing for this purpose.[110] It was expected that not only Churchill but Stalin too would come to the Cairo meeting. Stalin, however, declined, not wanting to irritate the Japanese by meeting Chiang. After all, the USSR and Japan had signed a neutrality pact. Roosevelt also invited Molotov, but he too, of course, did not come. Therefore, it was decided that Roosevelt and Churchill would meet with Stalin immediately after Cairo in Teheran.[111] Chiang accepted enthusiastically. He even decided not to send Stilwell away.

The Generalissimo arrived in Cairo on November 21. Naturally, he traveled together with Meiling, although she was sick again. In addition to a skin rash, she had conjunctivitis and stomach problems for which she was taking some sort of medication.[112] Chiang worried about his wife, but he was in an elated mood. This was the first time in history that a leader of China would participate as an equal in a summit meeting with the heads of the two leading powers.

The conference was brief: four days, from November 23 to 26, but for Chiang and for China it had colossal meaning. Chiang could finally meet with Roosevelt and Churchill, both in formal and informal settings. He could form his personal opinion of them as well as decide a number of crucial problems. He liked Roosevelt but not Churchill at all: "He is a politician of the English type, a classic example of the Anglo-Saxon nation. With respect to his ideas, his moral qualities, and his character, by no means can he be placed alongside President Roosevelt. He is a narrow minded and slippery egotist and a stubborn man."[113]

Curiously, Churchill, on the contrary, formed a rather positive impression of Chiang while Roosevelt did not. The president was displeased that Chiang tried to extract from him as much money and arms as he could with no intention of employing them against the Japanese. On the eve of the conference, Chiang had written in his diaries that he would refrain from making any requests to the American president, but on November 26 he dispatched his wife to visit Roosevelt in order to "wangle out" of him a whopping one billion gold dollars.[114]

Roosevelt felt that Chiang wanted to deceive him, "to squirrel away" the funds and arms for the postwar struggle against the communists.[115] Believing that Chiang was sabotaging the war effort against the Japanese, Roosevelt, understandably, did not intend "to pull his [Chiang's] chestnuts out of the fire."[116] During the meeting in Cairo he did everything he could to persuade Chiang to avoid conflict with the communists and focus his efforts on the struggle against the Japanese. He even posited a condition for further support of China, requesting that Chiang "form a unity government, *while the war was still being fought,* with the Communists in Yan'an." Chiang promised to do so if Roosevelt would guarantee that the USSR would respect the borders of Manchuria and that the British and other foreigners would not have special rights in Hong Kong, Shanghai, and Canton. Roosevelt agreed.[117]

After the Cairo conference, at dawn on November 27 Roosevelt and Churchill flew to Teheran, asking Chiang and Meiling to remain in Cairo. They planned to return there to further coordinate strategy with them after the Teheran summit with Stalin. But the couple refused and flew home from Cairo that day.[118] After arriving in Teheran, Roosevelt informed Stalin of his agreement with Chiang Kai-shek regarding the communists and his request that the USSR respect the borders of Manchuria. The Soviet leader nodded his head in agreement to all of this.[119]

But upon returning to Cairo late on the night of December 2, Roosevelt again began to doubt Chiang's reliability. Four days later he summoned Stilwell, who had also been present at the summit, to tell him everything that he, Stilwell, thought about Chiang. One can easily imagine what Vinegar Joe had to say to the president. Roosevelt ordered him to do everything possible to ensure that "China would continue to fight," adding, "And if Chiang goes completely bankrupt, support somebody else."[120] Stilwell interpreted the president's words as an order to prepare a plan to assassinate Chiang, to have it ready and put it into effect at an appropriate moment. Returning from the summit, he informed his deputy, Colonel Frank Dorn that "the Big Boy's fed up with Chiang and his tantrums, and said so."[121] Two weeks later a plan was ready. But Stilwell did not receive an order from Washington to execute it.

Meanwhile, Chiang, suspecting nothing, returned safely to Chongqing, satisfied with the results of the summit. The final declaration included a paragraph having great meaning to the Chinese: "All the territories Japan has stolen from the Chinese, such as Manchuria, Formosa [Taiwan], and the Pescadores, shall be restored [after the war] to the Republic of China."[122] Both Roosevelt and Churchill agreed to this.

This was Chiang Kai-shek's finest hour. The Generalissimo was proud and happy, not noticing that during the meeting in Cairo seeds of mistrust toward Chiang himself and to his regime—sown both prior to and during Meiling's visit—were growing rapidly in Roosevelt's mind.[123] It is regrettable that after returning home from Cairo, Chiang did not call to mind the words of the wise Lao Zi: "To withdraw oneself when the work proceeds—this the Dao of heaven."[124]

CHAPTER 19

# *The Bitter Taste of Victory*

On the evening of December 7, six days after returning to Chongqing, Chiang dined with his oldest son in Huangshan. They were quietly conversing when a secret telegram from Roosevelt was handed to Chiang. The telegram read that in late spring 1944 the Allies were planning Operation Overlord, that is, a landing in Normandy. Roosevelt and Churchill had agreed to this in Teheran with Stalin, who insisted on opening a second front against Nazi Germany.[1]

Chiang was deeply disappointed. Only a few days earlier in Cairo Roosevelt had assured him that in the spring of 1944 the Allies would carry out a landing in the south of Burma, an operation code-named Buccaneer. Its objective was to break the blockade of China by reestablishing British control over the Burmese "lifeline." Roosevelt had discussed the details with Chiang Kai-shek without the approval of Churchill, who was dead set against making a landing in Burma. It is not surprising, then, that in Teheran Churchill supported Stalin; the president had no recourse but to agree with his main partners in the anti-Hitler coalition. He now proposed to Chiang that Operation Buccaneer be put on hold until November 1944.[2]

Unable to restrain himself, on December 8–9, 1943, Chiang dashed off a pointed letter to Roosevelt, again threatening to surrender to the Japanese: "If the Chinese army and people now know of the radical change in policy and strategy, they would be so disheartened that, I fear, this would impact China's ability to continue the war." He also noted that the Japanese would not fail to take advantage of the situation, and while the Allies were occupied with the war in Europe they would undoubtedly begin "a general offensive against China . . . in the coming year." Understanding that Roosevelt would not act contrary to Stalin and Churchill, he called on the president of the United States to demonstrate "sincere concern about the Chinese military theater." In a communication that was just short of an ultimatum, he asked Roosevelt to compensate for the change of plans by granting him [Chiang] a loan of one billion gold dollars, doubling the number of American planes in China, and increasing the delivery of supplies across the Himalayas to 20,000 tons per month.[3] He did not wait for an answer; on December 17, obviously apprehensive, he sent Roosevelt a new, calmer letter, agreeing to postpone Operation Buccaneer until November 1944. At the same time, he again implored the president to provide him with financial support and planes as soon as possible.[4]

Roosevelt replied curtly on December 18: "I spoke with the Treasury Department and will telegraph you on Monday [December 20]."[5] Indeed, on that day he dispatched an extended reply via Stilwell that Chiang received the following evening. Considering that the Americans had already increased deliveries across the Himalayas by severalfold—in December 1943 they ferried almost thirteen-and-a-half thousand tons to China, twice as much as for all of 1942[6]—the president rejected Chiang's request. He also rejected the request to double the number of American planes in China. With regard to the loan he wrote that the issue was still "being worked on by the Treasury Department and I will wire you very soon,"[7] although on December 18, he had received a categorical response from the Treasury Department reporting in black and white that "[a] loan to China . . . could not be justified."[8] Incidentally, the phrase that the issue concerning the loan was "being worked on by the Treasury Department and I will wire you very soon" was inserted into the text of the letter by the president himself. In the draft of the letter prepared by his secretaries, it said that this issue "is now receiving my serious consideration and will be made the subject of a later message."[9]

This news disappointed Chiang because he desperately needed either the Burmese "lifeline," dollars, or preferably both so that, in the first place, he could stop the catastrophic rate of inflation that was threatening Free China with economic collapse. In a letter to Roosevelt on December 9, 1943, he had written frankly that "China's economic situation was more critical than the military."[10] He understood that as early as the fall of 1942 and his assessment was correct.[11] In 1939 wholesale prices in Chongqing, where the economic situation was not the worst, increased by 99 percent compared to 1938; in 1940 the increase was 301 percent; in 1941, 144 percent; in 1942, 154 percent; and in 1943 an additional 192 percent. By comparison, the annual rate of inflation in the United States was 9.6 percent, in England 4.4 percent, and in Nazi Germany for the entire period 1939–43 prices rose only by 10 percent.[12]

Retail prices increased even more drastically. A resident of Chongqing wrote,

> The war had begun in 1937 with the Chinese currency stable at three Chinese dollars to the American dollar. The exchange rose, officially, to six to one, by 1939; prices stayed in line, doubling. By the spring of 1940, however, prices had doubled again; and again by late fall of that year. By June 1941 . . . prices were sixteen times higher than prices at the war's outbreak . . . in the fall of 1942, they were thirty-two times higher; and then, by winter 1942, they doubled to sixty-four times the prewar mark. . . . The official rate of exchange had been raised to 20 Chinese dollars to 1 U.S. dollar by the time America entered the war [on December 8, 1941]. But as the Chinese currency shriveled in value, the true rate of exchange became 100 to 1; then 200 to 1 by early 1944.[13]

In January 1943 Chiang Kai-shek's government established strict price controls—their ceiling should not exceed the price levels of November 30, 1942—but this only made the situation worse since many goods began to disappear from the shelves and businesses shut down. Who would want to sell at a loss? A piece of cloth, for example, officially cost less than the cotton from which it was made.[14]

Chiang resorted to repressive measures, shooting speculators, fighting the black market, and confiscating goods being sold at higher than mandated prices. But real prices continued to rise: from November 1942 to January 1943 they rose by 12 percent and by the end of December 1943 by more than 200 percent. The cost of living in Chongqing from July 1937 to the end of 1938 rose 40 percent; from January 1939 to December 1942 by 48 times; and in 1943 alone, it increased by 208 times.[15]

The primary cause of inflation was the terrible deficit in the state budget due to the war. Unable to pay for expenses for the army, armaments, capital construction, officials' wages, and other budgetary items, the government put ever more unsecured paper money into circulation. In 1943, for example, forty-two billion Chinese dollars were printed, twice as much as in 1942.[16]

Another cause was the great influx of paper money from the Japanese-occupied territories. Where the Japanese conquered huge parts of China, they began to collect *fabi,* the Chinese banknotes first issued in 1935 as a result of the British financial assistance. But after the beginning of the Pacific war they could no longer use them in the international market, so they began to smuggle this money to purchase goods in the GMD- and CCP-controlled areas.[17] "Prices go up rapidly, fabi is flowing to the rear areas from the occupied territories," wrote Chiang in his diaries.[18]

No less significant a role was played by the reduction of trade and consumer goods resulting from the Japanese blockade of China and its occupation of a large part of its territory. Another key factor was the increase in consumer demand on account of the influx of refugees: in the short period from 1937 to 1940 the population of Free China increased by one-fourth. What's more, because of the opposition of regional authorities, the government was unable to arrange centralized collection of taxes from territories that were formally under its control.[19]

Inflation expanded the scale of corruption that permeated society from top to bottom. The seriousness of the problem is attested to by the fact that in late 1943 the secret police of Dai Li, the "Chinese Himmler," uncovered a plot by young officers who were planning to arrest Chiang Kai-shek in Kunming after his return from the Cairo conference. Their plan was to force him to cleanse the government of corrupt officials, in the first place Kong Xiangxi, Minister of Military Administration He Yingqin, and the brothers Chen Guofu and Chen Lifu. This was probably an attempt at a new *bingjian* (remonstration with the help of soldiers), but it failed and several hundred officers were arrested. Their leaders, including sixteen generals, were shot.[20]

Chiang simply didn't know what to do. How could he put a stop to corruption when, for example, in the city of Chengdu in 1943 prices compared to prewar were 174 times greater, and wages, even for professors, only nineteen times greater? For salaried employees there were only two ways out of their position: either to steal or take bribes. "No official could remain honest for long, . . ." an eyewitness recalled. "What the famine had done to peasants in Honan [Henan], the inflation was doing to the middle class of the cities and universities: wiping out all loyalties [to the Guomindang], denying all effort except to survive."[21]

How could one stop corruption in the armed forces if the National government was unable to supply soldiers with either money or food? By 1944 servicemen, including generals, almost everywhere on the front lines were trading with the enemy, especially with the servicemen of the puppet troops, with whom they could find a common language. Moreover, they mercilessly fleeced the local population, which often led to peasant uprisings. In addition, officers and veteran soldiers harassed recruits, among whom, beginning in August 1944, were young middle school students. They beat them, confiscated their food and pay, and even killed them. Not infrequently soldiers died from exhaustion.[22]

On the first day of the New Year, 1944, Chiang began his diaries with a quotation from Confucius: "Kong Zi [The Master] said to [Zi] Zhang:[23] 'He who cultivates the five treasures and eschews the four evils is fit to govern. A gentleman is generous without having to spend; he has ambition but no rapacity; he has authority but no arrogance; he is stern but not fierce.' "[24] As an example of such a gentleman he cited his eldest son. But there were very few officials like Ching-kuo, who tried mightily to transform southern Jiangxi into a model region and who, as noted earlier, regularly rose at four or five o'clock and went to bed at two in the morning.[25] That is why Chiang placed all his hopes for overcoming the financial crisis on help from the United States.

On January 5, 1944, Roosevelt finally informed the Generalissimo that the Treasury Department had turned down the billion-dollar loan.[26] Deeply offended, Chiang did not reply for ten days and then delivered a curt response to Ambassador Gauss. He first said that the US Treasury Department was not acting as it should with an ally, and, second, that if the Americans did not want to provide a billion-dollar loan they should pay for the upkeep of their troops based in China as well as construct and repair the air bases and other military facilities. Moreover, they should pay at the official rate of exchange of twenty Chinese dollars to one American dollar.[27] He was simply unable to control himself and, handing over the letter, "seriously warned" the ambassador that "the situation now is incomparably worse than last year . . . and . . . if the U.S Treasury Department does not provide money to China, then the U.S. army in China must rely on its own forces, beginning March 1, 1944." He added that China "is not a petty thief or a highwayman." That declaration elicited a smile from the ambassador and from George Atchison Jr., the embassy counselor who was accompanying him. Paying them no attention, Chiang threatened that his country was facing "inevitable economic and political collapse."[28]

Needless to say, Chiang's resentment made no impression whatsoever on the president of the United States. The Americans did not refuse to pay for their forces in China, but the demand to calculate expenses at the unrealistic rate of 20:1 was naturally unacceptable. Gauss, relying on the opinion of an American advisor to the Chinese government, proposed that Chiang accept a rate of 60:1 or 75:1, which would also be to America's disadvantage but nevertheless more realistic.[29]

On January 20 Roosevelt wrote courteously to Chiang Kai-shek, noting "there may be danger that we may fail adequately to work out our common problems and may rush into decisions which would not be in the interests of either of our people." He informed Chiang that the US government would spend about US $25 million on the upkeep of its troops in China but not a cent more. Roosevelt said nothing about the exchange rate, simply letting Chiang know that he would not exceed the amount he stated.[30] Maintaining the 20:1 exchange rate would mean that American servicemen in China (of whom there were several thousand) would not be able to make ends meet and would inevitably leave the country.[31]

The issue of the exchange rate thus remained unresolved: Minister of Finance Kong Xiangxi agreed to raise it only twice. But this did not satisfy the Americans. The upshot was that the Chinese themselves had to provide for the upkeep of the American troops during the three spring months of 1944, to the tune of fifteen billion Chinese dollars.[32] The actual exchange by this time was 230:1.[33] "Chinese currency is doing such fantastic things," wrote an eyewitness.[34]

Kong Xiangxi flew to Washington in June 1944 for further discussions of financial problems. However, in the White House this lover of expensive cigars was treated with disrespect and contempt. Not only because they knew about his rampant corruption, but also because, from the perspective of the Americans working with him, this dumpy, fat man was a poor economist—on the level of a moneychanger on the Bund in Shanghai. An American advisor said, "The trouble with China is not that the Generalissimo doesn't understand economics, but that his Minister of Finance doesn't either." In an interview with the journalist Theodore White, Kong exclaimed, "Inflation, inflation! You American reporters talk about our inflation all the time. There is no inflation in China! If people want to pay twenty thousand dollars for a fountain pen, that's their business, it's not inflation. They're crazy, that's all. They shouldn't pay it."[35] One must feel sorry for Chiang for having such a minister of finance and director of the Central Bank. By the way, Chiang himself frequently complained in his diaries about Kong's (and T. V. Song's) inadequate "financial assistance."[36]

Meanwhile, in the spring of 1944 the situation on the Chinese front worsened catastrophically. In April the Japanese made a breakthrough on the Henan front, launching a rapid offensive, and Chiang once again had to focus exclusively on military matters. The plan of the Japanese "dwarfs" was clear: to take full control of the Beiping–Hankou and Wuchang–Canton and Henan–Guilin railroads to secure for the army and civilian population of Japan an uninterrupted supply of raw materials, above all, oil sourced in Southeast Asia. This mobilization stemmed from the fact that, starting in the summer of 1942, the Japanese suffered one defeat after another in the Pacific at the hands of the Americans. Japanese cargo ships were unable to effectively carry out their mission of transporting freight. Allied airpower was sinking Japanese tankers, and by late 1943 Japanese sealift capacity had been reduced by 77 percent. They had to switch routes urgently. On November 22, 1943, the Japanese drafted a plan for a campaign to unite the northern territories of China with the southern. They wanted to seize an enormous territory, from the Yellow River basin to Indochina. Moreover, they needed to obliterate the Chinese airfields in Hunan and Guangxi provinces, from which General Chennault's air force was carrying out daring raids on the Japanese rear.[37] This was "the largest campaign ever undertaken by the Japanese army in its history."[38]

In December 1943 the operation was given the name Ichigo (No. 1), and in mid-April 1944 the Japanese imperial forces, numbering 140,000, began the first stage by crossing the Yellow River. Chiang was caught by surprise even though he had supposed that the Japanese could start to advance into South China; on March 27 he wrote to Roosevelt that this advance might threaten Chongqing itself.[39] Until the very last moment, however, he did not believe that the Japanese would resume such a large-scale offensive in China. After all, on March 8, 1944, they had attacked India from Burmese territory, apparently launching a broad Indian operation. Who would have thought that this was a diversionary maneuver, or that the Japanese would aim their main blow against Henan?[40] Even when he received a report about military actions in the vicinity of the Yellow River, he refused to believe this was serious, writing in his diaries, "The enemy bandits in Henan are once again undertaking idiotic actions."[41]

That these actions were definitely not idiotic became clear very soon. The army of one of his most loyal generals, Tang Enbo, deployed to Henan was literally smashed to pieces. More than 20,000 officers and men were killed and wounded in one month. In May the Japanese attacked the city of Luoyang and seemed on the verge of taking it any day. Panicked, Chiang stayed by his telephone for hours on end, repeatedly issuing orders not only to General Tang, but also, over his head, to Tang's subordinates. He became particularly religious in those days, and several times daily he prayed to God, asking his protection. In his dreams he began looking for portents from above. On May 14, after seeing a bright moon and stars in a dream, he decided that God was telling him of the approaching light at the end of a tunnel. When he learned that an unexpected deluge on the field of battle had bogged down Japanese tanks, he interpreted this as help from the Almighty. He swore before the Creator that if the Japanese failed to take Luoyang and were defeated he would have his eldest son christened, which he had not done before.[42]

But the Japanese took Luoyang on May 26 and rushed south into Hubei and then Hunan. They also struck a blow in the west and began advancing toward Xi'an. Chiang lost his appetite and couldn't sleep. His best troops, defending Shaanxi, fled from the field of battle. Chiang shot three of his divisional commanders and wrote in his diaries, "If Tongguan[43] and Xi'an fall, it will be hard for us to repair the situation overall."[44] Luckily for Chiang, the Japanese were not planning to capture Xi'an. Their objective at this stage was Changsha, the capital of Hunan. After routing Chiang's best forces, they halted the offensive toward Xi'an. Chiang breathed a sigh of relief and gave thanks to God.[45]

But it was too early for him to drop his guard. Increasing the number of their army via reinforcements to 326,000, the Japanese began rapidly advancing into Central China. At the end of May they attacked Changsha and captured it on June 18, after which they reached the important rail junction of Hengyang in southern Hunan province. Chiang Kai-shek's troops had been unable to offer any real resistance.

Observing developments in China with alarm, Roosevelt sent Vice President Henry A. Wallace to China to survey the situation. He had several meetings with Chiang and Meiling from June 21 to June 24.[46] One of his missions was to secure a commitment from Chiang to bring about true unity in China to provide effective resistance to Japan. On Roosevelt's instruction, Wallace directly raised with Chiang the issue of terminating the feud with the communists. He even requested permission to visit the Special Region, but Chiang firmly refused.

Wallace was extremely disappointed with the economic, political, and military situation in China and in reports to Roosevelt, he emphasized that "I feel you should be prepared to see . . . all of East China including all the forward American air bases in Japanese hands, within 3 or 4 weeks." He proposed sending to China, in place of Stilwell, who, he thought, should focus only on Burmese affairs, "an American general officer of the highest caliber in whom political and military authority will be at least temporarily united." In his words, when he discussed this problem in China, "the name of General [Albert] Wedemeyer has been strongly recommended" to him. Since October 1943 Wedemeyer had been serving as deputy chief of staff of the Southeast Asia theater of military operations.[47]

Roosevelt agreed to place an American general at the head of Chinese and American forces, but he did not want to replace Stilwell. Therefore, on July 6, 1944, he sent Chiang an urgent telegram, proposing that he immediately recall Stilwell from northern Burma, where, since October 1943, Anglo-American-Chinese troops were again waging fierce battles against the Japanese. Stilwell was to take full control of all armed forces in China. Roosevelt informed Chiang that he was promoting Stilwell to general of the army. "I think I am fully informed of your feelings regarding General Stilwell," he wrote, "but . . . I know no one else who possesses the capacity, strength, and resolution to stop the catastrophe that is threatening China and our general plans for victory over Japan." In this connection, to be sure, he added that Vinegar Joe would be directly subordinate to the Chinese Generalissimo, but the phrase was probably just a formality.[48]

The president expressed his "sincere assurance" that Chiang Kai-shek "would not take offence from the sincerity" of his words. But he was mistaken. Chiang was terribly indignant, deeming Roosevelt's message "interference in Chinese domestic affairs."[49] What he found particularly insulting was that he received the telegram on July 7, the seventh anniversary of the beginning of the war. Of course, this was a coincidence. Roosevelt had not aimed to offend Chiang in this way, but the Generalissimo was humiliated.[50]

That same evening he drafted a reply, saying that command of the Chinese forces in China was not the same as that in northern Burma, and therefore to appoint Stilwell "in haste" would not do: "There must be a preparatory period."[51] He rebuffed Roosevelt's proposal, and the president noted in reply: "The situation with its danger to our common cause calls for quick action."[52] Stilwell, observing the situation in China, was shocked at the lack of talent of the Chinese military and, as usual, blamed Chiang Kai-shek, the Peanut, for everything. "Over in China things look very black. . . . If this crisis were just sufficient to get rid of the Peanut, without entirely wrecking the ship, it would be worth it."[53]

On top of everything, problems flared up again in Chiang's family. After returning from the United States, Meiling was always in a bad mood. Her illnesses, real and imagined, did not go away. She hated Chongqing, and everything irritated her. It is not surprising that she found it hard to live with Chiang, and he with her. The public took notice. The first couple of All-under-Heaven found it harder and harder to conceal their strained relations. Rumors began sprouting around Chongqing that the Generalissimo had taken a sixteen-year-old mistress. People knowingly shrugged their shoulders: "What do you expect? Madam is barren and Chiang wants more children." Others gossiped that Jennie, his former concubine, had returned to him and that was why he was ditching Meiling.

It is hardly likely that all these bits of gossip were true, although Chiang was not always a faithful husband—he could, for instance, visit a brothel but only secretly.[54] The gossip certainly did not help the family situation. In the summer of 1944, in order to refute the stories, Chiang and Meiling held a press conference for foreign journalists in the courtyard of their house. The Generalissimo denied all the rumors about his private life, asserting that, as a result of the rumors "the future of [the] revolution [was] jeopardized."[55] He sounded sincere, and many people, including even those who wished him ill, believed him. However, the American ambassador informed Washington of "an extremely serious split" between Chiang and Meiling. According to him, Meiling often spoke bitterly of "all the trouble she has had with him," and Madame Kong told foreigners that her sister's problems "weighed heavily on her mind."[56]

It was thus not surprising when, on July 9, taking Ailing with her as well as the devoted Jeanette, her nephew Kong Lingjie (Louis), four servants, a chef, and a secretary, Meiling flew out of Chongqing, abandoning her husband at the most difficult moment.[57] She flew to Rio de Janeiro for some unfathomable reason. There were no good doctors there who might help her, and the climate in Brazil did not facilitate her recovery. According to some reports, Meiling had major investments in Brazil, and the family of Kong Xiangxi, one of the wealthiest in China, owned a great deal of land there.[58] If this is true, it explains a lot: for example, why she took Ailing with her, why her visit was secret, and why neither the American ambassador to Brazil nor the Brazilian minister of foreign affairs knew anything about it. Meiling spent a month in Rio and in early September flew to New York, this time really for medical treatment. She went to the same medical center at Columbia University where she had stayed before. She also was treated at the Johns Hopkins University clinic in Baltimore. But she did not recover her health, and in October she moved to a seventeen-room house on the banks of the Hudson

River, where Jeanette and Meiling's nephew David lived with her. She spent more than an entire year in the United States and did not return home until September 1945, fourteen months after her departure from Chongqing.[59]

Chiang, meanwhile, continued to pray. On July 21 he wrote in his diaries, "Heavenly Father, I am sunk in a deep well, I see only four dark walls, my body is severely wounded. If You do not hold out your hand to me, I am afraid, I will not be able to fulfill the mission God has given me, and I will be eternally ashamed." Four days later he promised God that if he "grants victory" to his troops at Hengyang he will erect an enormous iron cross on the summit of Nanyue Mountain in Hunan on the occasion of his sixtieth birthday according to the Chinese reckoning, October 31, 1946. He repeated this on July 31, swearing, moreover, that if he was victorious he would have his entire Tenth Army baptized.[60]

He put the blame for the defeats on his own shoulders. True, he did it only in his private diaries: "In spite of the fact," he wrote, "that the last five years were my golden period in which I could thoroughly solve diplomatic problems with Russia and America as well as political problems with the Communists and other domestic issues, I still was not able to use that time. I hesitated and did not make decisions but when I made the ones, I regretted and did not dare to implement them. It is an unwise behavior termed as 'Beat a snake but not kill it, a neglected sore becomes a serious illness.' How extremely ignorant and stupid I am!"[61]

In those days, in addition to the Bible, every evening Chiang read from *Streams in the Desert* by the American female evangelist Lettie Burd Cowman (1870–1960), who wrote the book when her husband, Charles, was gravely ill.[62] Suffering deeply from the ill health of her beloved one and wishing to have some peace of mind, the poor woman daily wrote down thoughts inspired by her reading of Holy Scripture as well as quotations from the Bible and the sermons of well-known evangelists. It constituted a kind of diary comprising 366 short chapters (one for each day of a leap year) that were titled "January 1," "January 2," and so on. Cowman took the title of her diary from the Book of the Prophet Isaiah: "In the wilderness shall waters break out, and streams in the desert."[63] The book was first published in the United States in 1925, and the Chinese translation in Shanghai in December 1939.

It is not hard to understand why Chiang liked this work. Like Cowman, he tried to find in religion an explanation for his suffering and defeats, eagerly seeking a way out of his tragic situation. He made the first reference to *Streams in the Desert* in his diaries on July 12, 1944: "God shows the path to tranquility."[64]

Then, reading the appropriate chapter per day, he cited her more and more often. A typical quotation read, "Our trials are a good opportunity for God to test us. But we often view them as obstacles. We would be able to achieve peace and inspiration if we knew that each and every one of these trials is a path that God has chosen to show us His love."[65]

One can understand Chiang. The only thing left to him during this time was to count on God. On the one hand, the Japanese were assailing him; on the other, Roosevelt was pressing him, demanding that he hand over command to Stilwell and strengthen the united front with the communists. Mao Zedong's dabbling in New Democracy produced so many marvelous fruits that Roosevelt began seriously to contemplate cooperating with the CCP. At the end of July 1944 an American mission arrived in Yan'an to meet Mao. It included officials from the State Department, the Pentagon, and the Office of Strategic Services, the precursor of the Central Intelligence Agency. The mission was headed by Colonel David D. Barrett, a short, stout man of about fifty, who had once been an assistant military attaché in Chongqing. He was considered to be a specialist in Chinese affairs, he knew the history and culture of China very well, and he spoke fluent Chinese. Next in rank in the group was the second secretary of the US Embassy in Chongqing, John Stewart Service, "our expert on Chinese communism," as Ambassador Gauss called him. Soon after, in early August, a second group, headed by the diplomat Raymond P. Ludden, arrived. Following these experts, Americans frequently visited Yan'an and even began organizing trips to several "liberated areas." Overall, by the end of July 1945 there were thirty-two members of the so-called American Observer Group in Yan'an.[66]

The conclusion that Barrett and many other members of the missions drew from conversations with Mao and their own observations was the following: "Politically, any orientation which the Chinese Communists may once have had toward the Soviet Union seems to be a thing of the past. The Communists have worked to make their thinking and program realistically Chinese, and they are carrying out democratic politics which they expect the United States to approve and sympathetically support." The members of the missions persistently advised the American leadership to reorient themselves to the Chinese Communists, warning that they might turn back toward the Soviet Union "if they are forced to in order to survive American-supported Kuomintang [Guomindang] attack.[67]

At the time, Stalin and Molotov were working over the Americans diplomatically, no less masterfully and skillfully than Mao and his comrades. On

June 10, 1944, for example, Stalin said to W. Averell Harriman, the US ambassador to the USSR, that the Chinese Communists are not real Communists, but "Margarine Communists" and that "the Generalissimo was committing an error in disputing over ideological questions rather than employing them against the Japanese." In the beginning of September 1944 the utterly befuddled Roosevelt sent his representatives to Moscow specially to clarify "Russia's relations to the Chinese Communists and Russia's position toward China." They were received by Molotov, who also asserted, "Some of these people [poor Chinese] called themselves 'Communists' but they had no relation whatever to communism. . . . The Soviet Government could not be blamed in any way for this situation nor should it be associated with these 'Communist elements.' "[68] In the fall of 1944 the Soviets, via the chargé d'affaires of the USSR in China, Tikhon Fedotovich Skvortsov-Tokarinin, even proposed arranging a meeting between Stalin and Chiang Kai-shek to demonstrate Moscow's reorientation to the Guomindang.[69]

Meanwhile, on August 8, 1944, Hengyang fell, and the Japanese rapidly advanced toward Guangxi along the Hengyang–Guilin railroad. Two days later Chiang received another unpleasant message from Roosevelt, insisting on the prompt resolution of the issue of designating Stilwell as the de facto commander of all Allied forces in China. To smooth over the conflict between Vinegar Joe and Chiang, the president proposed sending to China as his personal representative, General Hurley, who had made a big impression on Chiang during his first trip to Chongqing. Along with Hurley, he wanted to send Donald M. Nelson, the head of the War Production Board, to study the economic situation.[70]

Reeling from defeats at the front as well as Roosevelt's demands, Chiang wrote in his diaries, "I underestimated the strength of the Japanese. . . . There's nothing more to say about that, my sufferings and anger have no limit. . . . How can our army continue to be called an army? How can foreigners not despise us? This might compel me to hand over the training and command of the whole army to Stilwell."[71] On August 12 he agreed to appoint Stilwell as commander and to receive Hurley and Nelson.[72] Roosevelt was satisfied.[73]

In reality, Chiang's pride would not allow him to hand over command, although he himself was quite unable to do anything about the Japanese. During this period, he again considered committing suicide.[74] This terrible thought vanished as quickly as it had come, however, not because he remembered divine punishment but because he decided his country and his people could not get along without him. On August 11 he wrote in his diaries, "If I live another day, the country will live another day. . . . And if, yielding to pessimism and sorrow, I do away with myself, the country and the people will [also] inevitably perish."[75]

In defense of Guangxi, he threw in his Ninety-third Army, the majority of whose officers were graduates of the Whampoa Military Academy. One tank battalion and one artillery battalion were attached to it. But Japanese forces from Canton and Vietnam came to the aid of the Japanese imperial armies invading Guangxi from Hunan. The Ninety-third Army shamefully fled.[76]

Meanwhile, Roosevelt anxiously awaited information as to when Chiang would at last make a final decision about Stilwell.[77] But the Generalissimo kept dragging it out. Then, in mid-September, Chief of Staff of the U.S. Army George C. Marshall received a secret telegram from Stilwell himself. He had just visited Guilin, in Guangxi province, where he had been involved in evacuating American personnel. "Situation [in] that area now [is] hopeless," Stilwell wrote. "The place will then become another rat trap, like Changsha and Hengyang. . . . We are getting out of Kweilin [Guilin] now, and will have to get out of Liuchow [Liuzhou] as soon as the Japs appear there. The disaster south of the Yangtze [Yangzi] is largely due to lack of proper command—the usual back seat driving from Chunking [Chongqing]. The trouble continues to be at the top."[78]

Roosevelt was not in Washington at the time; he was taking part in a regular summit in Quebec City. Marshall forwarded him Stilwell's letter and recommended sending Chiang a telegram in the form of an ultimatum, the text of which he had already drafted. The telegram contained a demand to immediately place "General Stilwell in unrestricted command of all your [Chiang's] forces" given that "we are faced with the loss of a critical area in East China with possible catastrophic consequences."[79] Roosevelt signed it on September 16,[80] and two days later (September 18) he sent the text to Stilwell, who was to deliver it to Chiang Kai-shek.

Receiving the telegram the next day, Vinegar Joe could not restrain his joy, and at 5:40 p.m. at Huangshan, in Hurley's presence, he handed over the "bundle of paprika" to Chiang Kai-shek. Chiang was overwhelmed, and after hearing the translation, in a sinking voice he said just two words: "I understand" and terminated the audience.[81]

Left alone, barely containing his rage, he wrote in the margins of Roosevelt's telegram, "This cable is tantamount to an ultimatum. *It not only is an insult to me personally, but also an act of aggression against my country.* Since the beginning of my revolutionary career, although both Japan and the Soviet Union have made excessive threats against me, but nothing they have done was ever as unacceptable as this one. . . . This is a blight in Roosevelt's political career, and an indelible disappointment in Sino–American history."[82] He made the following entry in his diaries: "From the time on July 7 of this year I received Roosevelt's telegram that insulted our country, again, for the third time, I am suffering shame and pain. . . . This cannot be endured. . . . Why is God compelling me to experience shame and pain. . . . Roosevelt's telegram is the greatest humiliation in my life and in the life of the country in recent times."[83]

In addition to everything else, he was pained once again that the telegram from Washington had been dispatched on a special day: this time, on September 18, the Day of National Mourning, so named because that was the day in 1931 when the Japanese commenced their occupation of Manchuria. Of course this was a coincidence, like the telegram of July 7, but Chiang Kai-shek was so depressed that he literally came to hate Roosevelt.

Stilwell, returning home, gleefully wrote, "*Private. 9/19/44. Peanut's Waterloo.*"[84, 85] Finally, he could take pleasure in the view of Chongqing, glittering with lights. "The harpoon hit the little bugger right in the solar plexus, and went right through him," he exulted.[86]

But he celebrated prematurely. Chiang Kai-shek did not want to endure humiliation, especially not from Roosevelt. He could not openly express his dissatisfaction with the president of the United States but nothing inhibited him from venting his rage at Vinegar Joe. On September 20 he asked Minister of Foreign Affairs T. V. Song to inform Hurley and Nelson of his thoughts about the stain left by the telegram; this time "on American democracy and on the traditional principles of equality and freedom in the world." T. V. Song was also tasked with explaining to Roosevelt's emissaries that "the Chinese army cannot abide humiliation from foreigners, and the Chinese people do not want foreigners to look on them as slaves."[87]

On September 21 Chiang withdrew to Huangshan for several days to ponder what to do. He did not share his thoughts even with his sons, who were then living with him. Finally, on September 23, he arrived at a decision: remove Stilwell from China. The next morning he informed T. V. Song, and that evening Hurley, who the following day sent an aide-mémoire to Roosevelt.[88] In this note, he said, in part, "I agree to the choice of an American general officer as Commander in Chief of the Chinese–American forces fighting against Japan in China; I will place under his command all Chinese field armies and air forces; and will concurrently appoint him Chief of Staff of the China

Theater. . . . I cannot, however, confer this responsibility upon General Stilwell, and will have to ask for his resignation as Chief of Staff of the China Theater and his relief from duty in this area."[89] On September 26 he wrote about his decision to his wife and Kong Xiangxi, who were then in the United States. Then he ordered Kong not to ask for any more American aid, so as not to provide further cause for ridicule.[90]

On October 2 he convened a session of the Standing Committee of the Guomindang CEC, at which he gave, in his words, a complete and accurate report on what had happened. He was very excited, and, thumping his fist on the table, he exclaimed, "General Stilwell 'must go'. . . . [I]f there is to be an American commander in chief in China, he must be under the Generalissimo's command. . . . [N]ow it seems that the Americans are trying to infringe on China's sovereignty in another direction. . . . This is a new form of imperialism; if we agree, then we should be nothing but puppets; we might just as well go over to Wang Jingwei. . . . [W]e can get along without them [the Americans]—without their help." One of those present at the meeting said that Chiang acted as "though he were crazy."[91]

Roosevelt did not object, although he expressed his "surprise and regret" that Chiang had reexamined their previous agreement regarding Stilwell. He said that under these conditions "the United States Government should not assume the responsibility involved in placing an American officer in command of your ground forces throughout China."[92] He asked Patrick J. Hurley to ascertain whom Chiang wanted in place of Stilwell as commander of the allied staff. Chiang named three generals, the first among them Dwight Eisenhower. But Roosevelt did not go along with these candidates, and then, in mid-October, Chiang remembered Wedemeyer.[93] Roosevelt agreed, and on October 18, via Hurley, he informed Chiang of Stilwell's recall and the appointment of Wedemeyer.[94] Chiang was satisfied by this information.[95]

On October 21 Stilwell left China forever. Before his departure, Chiang wanted to award him one of the highest military orders of the Republic of China: Order of the Sacred Tripod with Blue Ribbon. Hearing of this, Stilwell wrote in his diaries, "Told him to stick it up his [it's obvious where to; in the published edition of the diaries there is a dash.]"[96] Sun Yat-sen's widow, who, as mentioned earlier, hated Chiang Kai-shek, cried on parting, and Clarence Gauss, the American ambassador, "enraged and disgusted," retired. At the request of the Chinese side, on November 23 Roosevelt appointed Hurley, with whom Chiang had developed good relations, as ambassador.[97] Hurley took up the position on December 11.[98]

Meanwhile, Chiang Kai-shek's army continued to suffer defeats, and he continued to pray to God, seeking secret portents in the Bible. On October 31, his birthday, while reading the Book of the Prophet Ezekiel, he rejoiced, finding the following words in chapter 39: "After that they have borne their shame, and all their trespasses whereby they have trespassed against me, when they dwelt safely in their land, and none made them afraid. When I have brought them again from the people, and gathered them out of their enemies' lands, and am sanctified in them in the sight of many nations."[99] Chiang took this prophecy as being addressed directly to him. "The lost lands will be returned, and peace and happiness will come to the state," he wrote in his diaries.[100]

On November 11, however, the Japanese seized the largest cities in Guangxi province—Guilin and Liuzhou—and then, sweeping aside everything in their path, they invaded the provinces of Guizhou and Sichuan. They were speedily advancing at the rate of thirteen and a half miles per day. The Americans in Chongqing had already made evacuation plans, and they took all necessary precautions to protect Chiang against the contingency of a parachute landing by the Japanese to kidnap the Generalissimo.[101] To top off these failures, Chennault's air force mistakenly bombed the headquarters of one of the Chinese armies, killing more than a thousand servicemen and a large number of civilians.[102]

Arriving in Chongqing on November 1, Wedemeyer found there was nothing he could do to help Chiang, although he tried. "Tall and imposing, smooth, able and ambitious,"[103] he had served with American forces in Tianjin in 1930–32 and then, in 1936–38, studied at a German military academy in Berlin. Initially the short-tempered Chiang was suspicious of Wedemeyer, above all because he was by nature reserved and responded coolly to Chinese cordiality.[104] Unlike Stilwell, the new chief of staff from the start was impressed by Chiang, whom he characterized as the "small, graceful, fine-boned man with black, piercing eyes and an engaging smile."[105] He did not alter his positive opinion of Chiang in the future, was markedly courteous toward him, and, although he did not conceal his negative feelings about the organization of the Chinese army, he never disputed Chiang's authority. Within two weeks of his arrival Chiang noted in his diaries, "This is a sincere man, pleasant, straightforward, and attentive. . . . He is the complete opposite of Stilwell. He works intensely and well. Here is a model for our military."[106]

Unexpectedly, joyful news came to Chiang in these difficult days. Strangely enough, it came from Japan. At 4:20 p.m. on November 10, 1944, in the clinic of the Imperial University of Nagoya, Chiang's sworn enemy, Wang Jingwei, died at the age of sixty-one. Wang had been unable to recover fully from the serious wound to his spine he had suffered as a result of the assassination attempt on him on November 1, 1935. Surgeons could not extract the bullet, his wound hurt all the time and, in August 1943, became seriously inflamed. An operation was performed in a Japanese military hospital in Nanjing, but it did not help. In March 1944 he was transported to Nagoya, Japan, where a new operation was performed. But on November 9 American bombers raided Nagoya, and Wang was carried to a shelter that was barely heated and poorly ventilated. He caught a cold there, became feverish, and died the next day.[107] "Although this does not affect the overall situation," Chiang noted in his diaries, "it is good for the party and the country."[108]

In the third week of November Roosevelt irritated Chiang Kai-shek yet again, demanding that he cashier the corrupt Kong Xiangxi from the post of minister of finance.[109] It's not known precisely what he wrote to Chiang, but in late November Chiang noted in his diaries, "Roosevelt's words regarding Yongzhi [the courtesy name of Kong Xiangxi] are contemptuous, offensive, and shameless."[110] Nonetheless, he relieved Kong of this position but retained him as deputy chair of the Executive Yuan and director of the Central Bank of China. (Kong was also director of the Peasant Bank and the Bank of China.)

By early December the situation had deteriorated so badly that on December 2 Wedemeyer advised Chiang to prepare to move the capital to Kunming. He was certain that Chongqing would fall. But Chiang firmly rejected this proposal, and Wedemeyer then declared that he would remain with Chiang, which moved him greatly.[111] Fortunately for Chiang, the Japanese halted 185 miles short of Chongqing. The objectives of Operation Ichigo had been achieved, and the Japanese no longer had enough forces to assault the Chinese capital.

The results of the Japanese offensive were disastrous for Chiang's army. It had lost 750,000 officers and men killed or wounded as well as 23,000 tons of arms, enough for 40 divisions, 7 air force bases, and 36 airfields in the provinces of Hunan and Guangxi. The Japanese had also dealt a heavy blow to the Chinese economy, occupying the capitals of Henan, Hunan, Fujian (for the second time), and Guangxi provinces, 146 other cities, and over 77,000 square miles of territory, including the productive agricultural areas that supplied Free China with grain. It is hard not to concur with the historian Ch'i Hsisheng, who wrote, "By the end of 1944, the government [of Chiang] no longer possessed an effective fighting machine for the defense of China proper."[112]

Indeed, 1944 was not the best year in the life of Chiang Kai-shek, and on December 31 he addressed the nation, describing the preceding months as "a year of great trial and danger."[113] Six days earlier, on Christmas Day, he had transferred command of all Chinese ground forces to General He Yingqin, whose headquarters were located in Kunming, the capital of Yunnan province. Wedemeyer was occupied with the reorganization and retraining of troops, trying to correct what he called "a multitude of errors committed in the past," but not calculating, to be sure, that the Chinese would soon be able to conduct offensive operations.[114]

Nevertheless, in early 1945 a turning point occurred on the Burma front. On January 21 China's X Force, which had been trained earlier by Stilwell at a base in India and had fought in northwest Burma since October 1943, joined with China's Y Force, which had entered northeast Burma in April 1944. With the support of the British and the Americans, these armies wrested all the northern regions of Burma from the Japanese, securing uninterrupted delivery of supplies in the new "lifeline" from northeast India through Burma to Kunming. The Americans had begun building this road back in December 1942 as an alternative to the Burmese "lifeline" the Japanese had seized. Chinese soldiers also took part in its construction. The conjunction of the two Chinese armies was a great event, one that a Chinese correspondent reported as follows: "X + Y = V [victory]."[115] On January 26 Roosevelt congratulated Chiang Kai-shek, who then graciously named the new route from India to China the Stilwell Road.[116] Around this time a decisive turning point occurred in the war in the Pacific. In January 1945 the Americans landed in the Philippines, and in February they took the capital, Manila. It became clear to both Chiang and his people that the collapse of Japan was not far off.

But victories over Japan were clouded in that same month by another summit of the heads of the three powers of the anti-Hitler coalition—the USSR, the United States, and Great Britain—in Yalta. Stalin, Roosevelt, and Churchill, secluded from the whole world and, most important, behind Chiang Kai-shek's back, concluded an agreement at the expense of China. In return for Soviet entry into the war against Japan in two or three months after its victory over Germany, the Soviet Union was supposed to receive a series of concessions in China. It was done under the pretext of restoring the rights belonging to Russia that had been "violated by the treacherous attack of Japan in 1904." Specifically, "the commercial port of Dairen [Dalian] shall be internationalized, the preeminent interests of the Soviet Union in this port being safeguarded and the lease of Port Arthur [Lüshun] as a naval base of the USSR restored," while the Chinese Eastern and South Manchurian railroads would be "jointly operated" by the USSR and China, again while safeguarding "the preeminent interests of the Soviet Union."[117] Also agreed was that the status quo, that is, independence, of Mongolia would be maintained.[118] In other words, as Chiang wrote later, "China's sovereignty in Outer Mongolia and administrative integrity in Manchuria were sacrificed in return for Soviet Russia's entry into the war against Japan."[119]

Chiang had anticipated something like this. Three days before the signing of the secret Yalta Agreement, on February 8, he had posed this question in his diaries: "Won't Roosevelt make a deal with the British and the Russians against me?"[120] On his instructions, Chiang Ching-kuo consulted with Skvortsov-Tokarinin, the chargé d'affaires of the USSR, asking whether "issues regarding the Far East were discussed at the [Crimean] conference." But Skvortsov, who himself probably knew nothing, stated, "As is evident from the declarations that were made, such problems were not discussed at the conference."[121]

Chiang had hoped that Roosevelt would inform him of the results of the conference, but the agreement was secret and therefore the president did not reveal the truth even to his new vice president, Harry S. Truman, or to other close associates and members of Congress. He simply lied to Hurley, his ambassador to China, and only when Hurley accidentally found out about the agreement did he admit he had dissembled.[122]

Roosevelt had, of course, betrayed Chiang, but his concessions to Stalin are understandable. In the first instance he was thinking not of China but of the lives of American soldiers, many of whom might be saved by the entry of the USSR into the war. Barely a month before the Yalta Conference, on December 30, 1944, he learned from the director of the Manhattan Project—the super-secret program to build a nuclear weapon—Lt. General Leslie R. Groves Jr., that the first atomic bomb would not be ready before early August 1945, and the second only toward the end of the year.[123] Therefore, Groves could not accurately tell whether the United States would be able to employ it against Japan or, if it did, whether it would suffice to ensure victory. Nonetheless, in early April 1945 when Hurley visited him in the White House Roosevelt, who was gravely ill by this time, felt bad not only physically but also morally—because of Yalta—and therefore asked Hurley to fly to London and Moscow to put the situation right.[124]

By then Chiang had learned of the Yalta Agreement from his ambassador to the United States, who had informed him on the morning of March 15 via a telegram. It sent Chiang into a rage. He wrote in his diaries, "I learned that Roosevelt and Stalin unilaterally discussed the Far East. . . . If this is so, the ideals [for which we have been fighting] of this anti-Japanese war are becoming illusory."[125] Chiang learned additional details from Hurley's reports after the ambassador returned to Chongqing from his trip to London and Moscow. Neither Churchill nor Stalin wanted to change anything, and on April 25 Chiang again gave vent to his feelings in his diaries: "In the morning I was reflecting on international problems, mostly on Hurley's visit to England and Russia, I feel incredible sadness and anger."[126]

By then Roosevelt was no longer alive. He had died at 3:35 p.m. on April 12, 1945, from a stroke at the age of sixty-three. Chiang greeted news of the president's death with sorrow, despite the fact that their recent relations had been rocky. On April 13 he wrote in his diaries,

> Today at 6:00 a.m. I learned of the death of President Roosevelt. . . . This event will have an enormous influence on the world and the further development of the international situation. But, from my perspective, in the last year Roosevelt's foreign policy has obviously made a turn. He catered to England, feared Russia, and humiliated China. Right up to the point of yielding to Russia's demand regarding Lüshun [Port Arthur]. This is very sad. But after his death, U.S. policy toward China will further worsen. Roosevelt appeased Russia and in an unprincipled way only defended the Chinese Communist Party. But he acted within limits, and he had certain principles and ideals.[127]

Such was his epitaph.

The Americans were continuing to achieve victories over the Japanese, which reconciled Chiang somewhat to Roosevelt's Yalta betrayal. In April several joyful events occurred in the Chiang family. On Easter, April 1, the very day American soldiers, launching Operation Iceberg, landed on Japan itself on the island of Okinawa, his son Ching-kuo and his nephew from his younger sister, air force pilot Zhu Peifeng, were baptized in Chiang's city residence in Chongqing. Chiang was incredibly happy. "This is really an important day for my family," he wrote in his diaries. "This is a great comfort in my life. I proposed to Ching-kuo that he himself choose the day of baptism, and he is happy at the christening. At home every evening over the course of a year, he and I knelt and prayed, repeatedly calling upon the Holy Spirit. I believe that from now on the Holy Spirit will surely bestow victory and prosperity to my country and my family. I thank the Almighty for His grace."[128] Ching-kuo's entire family and his younger brother Wei-kuo with his wife, the twenty-seven-year-old beauty Shi Jingyi, who came from one of China's best-known families, were present at the christening. Wei-kuo had met Shi in Xi'an, courted her for a long time, and on February 6, 1945, having earlier obtained the blessing of his father and stepmother, married. General Hu Zongnan, the commander of the First War Zone, had attended the wedding in Xi'an. Chiang Kai-shek had been unable to come, but he sent a handwritten greeting card in his own calligraphy: "May everything in your family be well, may there be peace and well-being in your family." Ching-kuo represented Chiang, and upon his return he told his father all about the ceremony.[129]

Toward the end of the month, on April 25, Faina Jiang presented Chiang with another grandson, on whom the satisfied Generalissimo bestowed the handsome name Xiaowu (*xiao,* as noted earlier, means "filial piety" and *wu* means "martial"). That day Chiang wrote in his diaries, "Today at 7:00 in the morning . . . my second grandson was born.[130] If my late mother were alive, she would be incredibly happy. I praise the Lord for his grace."[131] At his baptism the baby was given the name Alexander (in the family everyone called him Alex or Aili).[132]

During this time Chiang often visited Ching-kuo's family, which had moved to Chongqing. He loved to play with his grandchildren. He also continued to pray with his son and discuss *Streams in the Desert.* Meanwhile, the military situation in the China War Theater continued to be far from satisfactory, notwithstanding the Japanese defeats in the Pacific and in northern Burma. Until early May 1945 Chiang Kai-shek's armies were suffering defeats throughout China. In late March some 70,000 Japanese troops launched new, successful offensives in southwest Henan, northern Hebei, and western Hunan. Not until May 8, the same day Germany signed an act of unconditional surrender, were Chiang's troops able to stop the enemy and mount a counterattack. On May 11 they seized Fuzhou, the capital of Fujian; on May 27, Nanning; on June 28, Liuzhou; and on July 27, Guilin.[133]

But there could be no talk of a general offensive so far. On August 1, 1945, Wedemeyer reported to Marshall that "currently throughout the Theater [of military actions] we are adhering to an Active Defense. . . . In the meantime we are feverishly deploying troops and supplies in preparation for Carbonado [the operation to liberate Canton and Hong Kong]. . . . There should be approximately twenty Chinese divisions equipped and trained to conduct a credible offensive in September."[134]

But suddenly the war ended. On August 6, 1945, at 8:15 in the morning, American pilots, on orders from the new president, Harry S. Truman, dropped the first atomic bomb on the peaceful Japanese city of Hiroshima. Truman sought to end the war quickly to save the lives of his soldiers. More than 65,000 Japanese died and about 70,000 were wounded, constituting 60 percent of the municipal population. On August 9, at 11:01 a.m., American pilots dropped a second bomb, this one on Nagasaki. More than 35 percent of the population suffered, while 39,000 were killed and 25,000 were wounded.

At midnight on August 9 Soviet troops had crossed the Manchurian border and attacked the Kwantung Army. It was a severe blow to Japan, although Emperor Hirohito and the Japanese government were most shaken by the US atomic bombs. On August 10 Radio Tokyo announced that the Imperial Cabinet of Ministers was prepared to accept terms of surrender.[135]

Four days later, at nine o'clock in the evening, Hirohito signed an imperial edict of unconditional surrender.[136] The next day, on August 15, at noon Tokyo time (August 14, at ten o'clock in the evening Washington time), the emperor announced the country's surrender on the radio. He explained that he took this action because "the enemy has begun to employ a new and most cruel bomb, the power of which to do damage is, indeed, incalculable, taking the toll of many innocent lives. Should we continue to fight, it would not only result in an ultimate collapse and obliteration of the Japanese nation, but also it would lead to the total extinction of human civilization."[137]

Chiang wrote in his diaries, "This morning I received the text of the unconditional surrender of the enemy state. I feel only profound gratitude to the Almighty for His enormous grace and wisdom in time of war. It is completely incomprehensible how the words from the ninth chapter of Psalms are coming to pass."[138] This chapter reads, in part, "Thou hast rebuked the heathen, thou hast destroyed the wicked, thou hast put out their name for ever and ever. O thou enemy, destructions are come to a perpetual end: and thou hast destroyed cities; their memorial is perished with them. . . . And he shall judge the world in righteousness, he shall minister judgment to the people in uprightness."[139] God may have helped Chiang defeat his enemy but did so through the hands of the Americans (in the first place) as well as Soviet soldiers. Despite the colossal sacrifices—China, according to a moderate estimate, lost no fewer than thirteen to fourteen million people[140]—Chiang Kai-shek's army could not have defeated the Japanese military machine by itself. When the emperor read the proclamation of surrender, his troops were still occupying more than half the territory of China proper.

Several hours before Hirohito's speech, in Moscow, late on the night of August 14, Soviet–Chinese negotiations that had been underway for a month and a half were concluded, resulting in the signing of a Soviet–Chinese Treaty of Friendship and Alliance based on the Yalta Agreement between the USSR, the United States, and Great Britain. In Chongqing it was six o'clock in the morning on August 15. The Soviet Union recognized the territorial integrity of China, including Manchuria. A special agreement that complemented the treaty granted the Soviets the right to have a naval base in Northeast China for a period of thirty years in the city of Lüshun (Port Arthur), control of the port in the city of Dalian (Dal'nii, Dairen), and joint control of the Chinese Eastern and South Manchurian railways, now renamed the Chinese Changchun Railway. In supplementary notes that accompanied the treaty China recognized the independence of Outer Mongolia (the Mongolian People's Republic) within its existing borders.[141]

The treaty noticeably favored the Soviet Union: Stalin himself said it was unequal.[142] Chiang also acknowledged that "during the Moscow negotiations we [Chinese] had to make . . . important concessions."[143] But Chiang had no choice. On the eve of the Soviet–Chinese negotiations, on June 14, two weeks before a Chinese delegation headed by T. V. Song and Chiang Ching-kuo[144] left for Moscow, Truman ordered his ambassador to China to inform Chiang "of the Soviet conditions." He also let him know that the United States wanted him to accept them. The ambassador was "to inform the Generalissimo that the Government of the United States would support the Yalta Agreement." Truman personally and in complete secrecy informed Stalin of this.[145]

This imperialist treaty was signed by two founding members of the United Nations Organization, whose representatives, including T. V. Song, had just participated (April 25–June 26, 1945) in the international conference in San Francisco that adopted the UN charter. On October 24, 1945, these two countries would even become permanent members of the Security Council. This treaty was the only one of its kind in history.

Stalin literally compelled Chiang to agree to the treaty, first winning him over by promising his unconditional support vis-à-vis the communists and then threatening to break off negotiations. After the first round of talks, T. V. Song felt completely worn out and, taking advantage of a break in the negotiations at the end of July, returned to Chongqing. He told Chiang that he refused to sign the treaty and did not want to return to Moscow.[146] At the time he held two principal positions: chair of the Executive Yuan (it was in that capacity that he was negotiating with Stalin) and minister of foreign affairs. As such, he, along with Molotov, was supposed to affix his signature to the treaty and agreements. But after returning to Chongqing he resigned from the latter post. Chiang accepted his resignation, but persuaded T. V. Song to continue the negotiations, saying that "he would personally assume responsibility for the future treaty."[147] He appointed Wang Shijie, former director of the Propaganda Department of the Guomindang CEC as the new minister, whose duty would be to sign the treaty and agreements. However, this did not save T. V. Song from being labeled a "traitor to the Motherland" by a patriotically inclined Chinese public that perceived the treaty and agreements as a new instance of humiliation for China.[148]

Meanwhile, on August 17 the commander in chief of American forces in the Pacific Theater (he was also the Supreme Commander of the Allied Powers), General Douglas MacArthur, issued General Order No. 1, approved by Truman two days earlier. It said, in part, that all Japanese forces in China—with the exception of Manchuria—on Taiwan, and in Indochina north of the sixteenth parallel must surrender only to the forces of Chiang Kai-shek. The territory of China where Japanese troops were present was divided into fifteen zones, for each of which a commander was appointed. It was to him that the appropriate Japanese troops must surrender, and after the act of surrender they were to turn over all their arms and equipment. Northern Vietnam was the sixteenth zone. As for Manchuria, on that same day, August 17, by agreement with MacArthur, the high command of the Kwantung Army handed over a document of unconditional surrender to Soviet forces.[149]

On September 2, aboard the American battleship *Missouri* in Tokyo Bay, Japan's formal act of unconditional surrender was signed. The main ceremony accepting the act of unconditional surrender of all Japanese armed forces in China was held on September 9 at nine o'clock in the morning in the building of the Central Infantry Academy in Nanjing. At this solemn service General He Yingqin, the commander of ground forces, accepted the surrender in the name of the Chinese army. The date and time of the ceremony were chosen deliberately, as, according to Chinese popular belief, the number nine, repeated several times, brings success.[150]

All of China rejoiced. Chiang wrote in his diaries,

> Today . . . the Day of victory. However, the lost territories of the Northeast are still in the hands of the Russian army, and in every important region of Xinjiang sit puppets of Russia. Bandits are running wild, and military and political leaders are incompetent, the army retreats when it wants to and cannot execute orders. . . . The issue of Outer Mongolia is still not resolved. The country is terribly humili-

> ated, it may be said that from the time of the anti-Japanese war the situation has never been as dangerous as it is today. People are rejoicing, but I feel terrible shame. Alas, although the war of resistance ended in victory, our revolution has still not achieved success. If we don't defeat the Third International[151] and do not wipe out the communist bandits, the revolution cannot achieve victory.[152]

The long, arduous war with Japan was over, but a new battle was beginning: that against the communists, who were thirsting for power.

CHAPTER 20

# *New Trials*

The clashes between communist and Guomindang forces that repeatedly occurred during the Second World War had intensified on the eve of its ending. The question was who would accept the surrender of Japan, where, and when. On August 11, three days before Hirohito announced the cessation of hostilities, the commander of the Communist Party's forces, Zhu De, issued an order calling for an offensive on all fronts in order "to be prepared to accept the surrender."[1] In response, Chiang Kai-shek demanded that the communists "remain where they were until further orders [were given]," and on August 14 he invited Mao to come to Chongqing for talks.[2] Mao did not reply, but, with respect to the order to remain in their positions, he and Zhu De sent Chiang a radiogram demanding that he revoke his order and acknowledge his mistake.[3]

The situation favored the communists inasmuch as Chiang's forces were stationed far from the areas under Japanese occupation, and it was precisely in those areas, the Japanese rear, that the Communist Party was active. Therefore Chiang's major headache at the time was to transport his armed forces rapidly to North, Northeast, and East China. He requested even that Stalin postpone the scheduled date for the Soviet army departure from Manchuria because the Americans could not help him redeploy his troops until October 1945.[4]

On August 20 and August 23 Chiang sent Mao two more invitations to talks.[5] On August 23 Zhu De's forces in Hebei province occupied the major city of Kalgan (Zhangjiakou), located 120 miles northwest of Beiping. In response, General He Yingqin, who was responsible for all matters connected to the surrender, demanded that the Japanese return to the city and hold it until Guomindang forces could reach it.[6] He did so in complete accordance with the policy General MacArthur, who had received relevant instructions from Washington, was following in China at the time. "It was perfectly clear to us that if we told the Japanese to lay down their arms immediately and march to the seaboard the entire country would be taken over by the Communists," Truman recalled in the mid-1950s. "So the Japanese were instructed to hold their places and maintain order."[7]

But the Americans and the Nationalists did not take into account that this order would only exacerbate an already difficult situation. Therefore, to avert a broad-scale civil war the direct mediation of Truman and Stalin was required at that juncture. Neither the new boss in the White House nor the boss of the Kremlin, who were allies at this time, wanted a violent conflict in China, fearing it might easily jeopardize the worldwide peace that had been won with such effort.[8]

Unlike Roosevelt, however, Truman at the time harbored few illusions about either the Soviet Union or the CCP. He admitted that the only time he "liked the little son of a bitch [Stalin]" was at their first meeting in July 1945 at the Potsdam Conference, because Stalin seemed "honest—but smart as hell."[9] "At the time we were anxious for Russian entry into the Japanese war," Truman recalled early in 1946. "Of course, we found later that we didn't need Russia there [in this war] and the Russians have been a head ache to us ever since."[10] Truman was acquainted with the information about Mao, "the democrat independent of the USSR," that was arriving in Washington from American special service agents, diplomats, and journalists; but he remained a greater pragmatist than Roosevelt. The son of a simple farm family, he was in no hurry to believe everything the communists said. "Neither Marshall nor I was ever taken in by the talk about the Chinese Communists being just 'agrarian reformers,' " he recalled in the mid-1950s.[11] Moreover, in the summer of 1945 intelligence officers in Washington who were analyzing the dispatches of their colleagues from China as well as an enormous amount of other material about the CCP, informed him: "The Chinese Communists *are* Communists. . . . The 'democracy' of the Chinese Communists is Soviet democracy. . . . The Chinese Communist Movement is part of the international Communist movement, sponsored and guided by Moscow."[12]

Responding to American public opinion, Truman hastened to bring the 113,000 American soldiers home from China as soon as possible. These servicemen had come to China to assist the Chinese in repatriating about three million Japanese citizens, including a million and a half former soldiers and sailors of the imperial army and navy "who had surrendered, but had not been defeated."[13] A new civil war might delay the process of repatriation, and with it the presence of American soldiers in China. Also, like many people in the United States at the time, Truman felt a measure of guilt for America's failure to have helped Chiang Kai-shek in the 1920s and 1930s overcome the de facto fragmentation of his country. Such neglect had made China an easy prize for Japanese aggressors and, by virtue of this, it pushed the Japanese toward the Pacific Ocean.[14] "We should rehabilitate China and create a strong central government there," Truman wrote to Secretary of State James Byrnes at this time, although he did not mail the letter for some reason.[15] It was Truman, via Ambassador Hurley, who compelled Chiang to write to Mao three times proposing talks.

Stalin also did not want a new war in China, given that in his geopolitical calculations in 1945–49 he had to take into account the US monopoly on nuclear weapons. Unprepared to resist a nuclear attack from the United States, he had to make every effort to avoid provoking Washington.[16] Moreover, he did not want to risk what he had already received from the United States and Great Britain at Yalta and from the treaty in Moscow with Chiang by providing unconditional support to Mao Zedong. His tactical conduct, however, was not always consistent, changing in response to circumstances. From the end of August until mid-September 1945 Soviet soldiers and officers in Manchuria, which their army had occupied, actively supported Chinese communists in penetrating the region. Precisely with the support of Soviet soldiers Chinese communist forces had seized the mountain pass, Shanhaiguan, in the vicinity of the Great Wall on the route from North China to Manchuria. After this victory they had entered the cities of Jinzhou, Shenyang, and a number of other cities in Manchuria. By mid-November 1945 about 130,000 CCP troops were in Northeast China.[17] But at the same time, Stalin expressed doubts about Chinese communists' ability to take power, and, insisting that Mao go to Chongqing, he advised the CCP leader "to come to a 'temporary agreement' with Chiang." His explanation constituted nothing better than an assertion that "a new civil war might lead to the destruction of the Chinese nation."[18]

Mao was terribly despondent over such treachery on the part of the leader and teacher, but he had to acquiesce. At eleven o'clock in the morning on August 28, Mao, along with Zhou Enlai and another CCP official, Wang

Ruofei, flew from Yan'an to Chongqing. He did not believe the talks would succeed, and during the flight he said to his comrades, "It is quite possible the talks will yield no results."[19] Accompanying the communist leaders were Chiang's representative, General Zhang Zhizhong, and Ambassador Hurley, who had arrived in Yan'an the day before and were organizing the talks.[20] Like many liberals in the State Department, Hurley perceived the Chinese Communists as "good people who were seeking reforms." "Of course," he said, "the fact that their political party has their own armed forces is very unpleasant, however, but it is necessary to create a democratic base to eliminate this situation, so the Communists will peacefully cooperate and help Chiang Kai-shek in the common struggle."[21] Chiang met with Mao at nine-thirty that same evening at a banquet. They were markedly convivial, smiling, shaking hands, and even drinking to peace and cooperation. They didn't talk about business.

At the talks the next day Chiang wanted to discuss with his old foe the many issues connected with the unification and democratization of China. At the Sixth National Congress of the Guomindang that had taken place in Chongqing on May 5–21, 1945, meeting the Americans and his other allies halfway, he had even, at least formally, touched on the issue of "eliminating one-party rule in China."[22] He proposed terminating the period of political tutelage after the war ended, convening a National Assembly, introducing constitutional rule in the country, and even eliminating Guomindang party cells in the army. The 579 delegates, representing 6,920,000 members of the Guomindang, voted to convene the National Assembly on November 12, 1945, evidently figuring that the war would be over by then.[23]

Intending to discuss all these issues with the leader of the communists, Chiang wanted to put special emphasis on the need for military and administrative-territorial unification of the country as the key to further democratization. "Concerning political demands, here one may show exceptional patience," he believed, "but with regard to the issue of complete unification of the armies, it is impossible to yield an inch."[24]

Yet it was precisely with respect to merging Communist Party troops into Chiang's army and handing over power in the purportedly liberated areas to the National government that Mao and the other communist leaders were unwilling to do. They were convinced that such actions would "inevitably lead to the liquidation of the CCP and its armed forces."[25] Mao even refused to reduce the number of his troops, which then comprised 1.2 million soldiers. In addition to the Shaanxi–Gansu–Ningxia Special Region, he demanded that five provinces in North China be handed over to the Communist Party.

This latter proposal, however, did not indicate that he intended to divide China permanently, as some historians contend.[26] Neither the Korean, the future Vietnamese, nor the German–Austrian variations suited him. He simply wanted to build up his strength in the north in order to seize all of China more easily later on; though he didn't voice these thoughts aloud. He constantly reiterated the need for prompt democratization, the release of all political prisoners, holding general elections, and the formation of a coalition government.[27]

Chiang was not opposed to democratization, but he believed that general elections were too complicated an undertaking for which one had to make preparations. The demand to hand over five provinces to the communists he viewed as "the division of China into two parts—two states," and not surprisingly he was unwilling to give up the territory. Whether he understood Mao's proposal as being purely tactical in nature is unknown.[28] He prayed devoutly, asking the Almighty to enlighten Mao Zedong and show him the path of the peaceful unification of the motherland.[29] Either God was not listening or the atheist Mao did not heed the voice of the Lord.

Mao spent forty-three days in Chongqing, met frequently with Chiang and other Guomindang leaders as well as with representatives of liberal public opinion, and even signed a peace agreement. But he did not abandon the struggle for power. He was simply bowing to Stalin, understanding perfectly well that his confrontation with the Guomindang could succeed only if the CCP received military and economic aid from the USSR. Chiang was also ready to fight, dreaming only of destroying the Communist Party. The Guomindang would never "abdicate to a loose combination of parties," he thought in the depths of his soul.[30] This was the same frame of mind Churchill's representative in China had. He believed that "there is only one answer to communists, and this answer is victory on the field of battle."[31] Overall, the talks could lead nowhere, and that is just where they led: in the words of Mao Zedong, "an enormous distance between the sides was revealed."[32] The only document signed was a formal declaration saying that civil war was unacceptable. Chiang promised to extend democratic freedoms to the people, convene a multiparty Political Consultative Conference to discuss the question of a National Assembly, and ultimately to terminate the period of political tutelage.[33]

But even as formal peace talks were being held in September–October 1945 the communist field army of the Shanxi–Hebei–Shandong–Henan military region, under the command of Liu Bocheng and Deng Xiaoping and following Mao's orders, carried out a successful operation on the Shanxi–

Hebei border to accept Japanese surrender. It executed this operation, in Mao's words, "to put pressure on the GMD and force it to be more compliant in the negotiations."[34] Hastening to consolidate the success, Mao Zedong ordered Liu and Deng to conduct a blocking maneuver against Guomindang troops that were advancing north. Again their army was victorious.[35] In essence, these actions initiated the real civil war.

Stalin began to worry, fearing direct intervention by the United States. Thus in mid-September he ordered General Rodion Yakovlevich Malinovsky, the commander of Soviet forces in Manchuria, not to turn over to Chinese Communist troops a portion of the arms of the Kwantung Army that Soviet soldiers had seized.[36] But in early October 1945 he again decided to help the Chinese Communists and to turn the Japanese trophy arms over to them. Moreover, he refused to allow the Guomindang army to land in the port of Dalian on the pretext that it was a commercial port, not a military one. He directed Soviet troops to permit the armed forces of the CCP to occupy two additional ports in southern Manchuria. The result was that Guomindang forces were completely blocked from landing in Manchuria. On November 17 the communists in Shenyang convened a sort of Congress of Representatives of the Peoples of Manchuria, at which a Coalition Autonomous Council of Manchuria was proclaimed. It was to be headed by Zhang Xueliang, chosen in absentia because he was being held captive by Chiang Kai-shek. All of these actions contravened one of the agreements signed in Moscow on August 14, 1945: Soviet troops were obligated to turn over to the National government of China all power in the territories they occupied.[37]

Chiang sent his son Ching-kuo to Manchuria as a representative of the Chinese Ministry of Foreign Affairs "jointly with the Soviet Command to implement on the spot a treaty transferring Manchuria to the Central Government and request that the Soviet Command provide assistance to the Generalissimo's headquarters in Changchun to facilitate the entry of troops of the Central Government to ensure order in Manchuria." But when Ching-kuo requested that the Soviet representatives allow him to visit Shenyang, Harbin, and other cities in Manchuria, they refused to allow him to enter, and what's more they did so, in his words, "in a rude manner."[38] The Soviets' treatment of Chiang's other representatives in Manchuria, such as Xiong Shihui, whom Chiang had appointed the head of Northeast Headquarters, and Zhang Jia'ao, who was in charge of economic affairs, was equally rude.

Stalin did not want to advertise his participation in the Chinese civil war, although he evidently began to consider the war a reality. In November 1945, he again reversed his policy, and "the level of cooperation and support for the Communist troops dropped to a new low."[39] Nor did he want to step forward as a mediator between the CCP and the Guomindang, instead formally declaring his "noninterference in the internal affairs of China."[40]

Chiang took advantage of the situation, and in November 1945 issued orders to retake Shanhaiguan from the Communists. His troops did so quickly, and by the end of November they also took Jinzhou, a city at the northern end of the Liaoxi Corridor connecting North China and Manchuria.[41] But all of Chiang's new attempts to resolve the problem of transporting Guomindang troops to Manchuria itself failed. Stalin did not even permit Chiang to transport his troops via the Chinese Changchun Railroad, and he did not approve the formation in Manchuria of Guomindang military units composed of the local population. Chiang simply could not advance north from Jinzhou: he understood that, in spite of all of Stalin's tactical maneuvers, in the end the Soviet dictator would without fail support one side of the conflict: Mao.

Chiang was bewildered. If this weren't enough, the impulsive American ambassador Patrick J. Hurley suddenly submitted his resignation, which came as a surprise not only to Chiang but also to Truman. Hurley had returned to Washington in late September for consultations. On November 27, less than two hours after he had assured Truman that "there was reason to hope that China's problems might be solved," he declared to the press that State Department careerists were pursuing pro-Communist policies in China. He handed reporters "a letter of resignation" he had prepared a day earlier.[42] Under the label of careerists he had in mind in particular the former second secretary of the American Embassy John Stewart Service, whom he had already dismissed in April 1945. After returning to the United States, Service had turned over to Philip Jaffe, the editor of the journal *Amerasia,* secret State Department documents that expressed sympathy toward the communists. Jaffe published these, after which he, Service, and four other persons were arrested by the FBI. Before long they were released under various pretexts, and Service was assigned to work in Japan, so it seemed that Hurley's demarche was rather too late.[43] "See what a son-of-a-bitch [Hurley] did to me," Truman exclaimed, addressing his cabinet, who had gathered for their weekly luncheon.[44] He was both furious and confused because he didn't know whom to appoint in Hurley's place.

Secretary of Agriculture Clinton Anderson pointed a way out by proposing the candidacy of General Marshall, the US Army former chief of staff, a hero of the Second World War whom Churchill once called "the true architect of victory." Marshall had retired just six days earlier, but Truman called and asked him to go to China. "Yes, Mr. President," Marshall replied laconically and hung up the phone abruptly.[45]

Initially Chiang was very upset. He wanted to see Wedemeyer, whom he regarded highly, as ambassador in place of Hurley. But Truman was not sending Marshall to China as ambassador, although he elevated him to that rank. The post of ambassador remained vacant. Marshall was supposed to play the role of the president's special representative, tasked by Truman with "convincing the Chinese government to convene a national conference of representatives of the major political groupings to effect the unification of China and simultaneously facilitate an end to clashes, particularly in North China." The president of the United States even allowed Marshall to threaten Chiang that "a China disunited and torn by civil strife could not be considered realistically as a proper place for American assistance."[46]

Marshall was sixty-five years old. Around six feet tall, thin, slightly stooped, with ash-colored, shortly cropped hair, and piercing blue eyes, he impressed those around him. There was a kind of aura surrounding him that made many people feel reverent. Churchill called him "the noblest Roman."[47] The future secretary of state Dean Acheson wrote that "a powerful force directed at you emanated from him. His figure radiated energy that magnified the sound of his voice, a low and sharp staccato. He elicited respect. Authority and tranquility emanated from him."[48]

Marshall once knew China fairly well, as he had served there, in Tianjin, along with Stilwell in 1924–27, and even spoke a little Chinese.[49] But his impression of Chiang Kai-shek and his associates was basically derived from reports by his friend Stilwell, whom, as noted above, he always supported. Many years later Marshall denied that Stilwell's relations with Chiang colored his picture of Nationalist China; he claimed that he had been and still was "fond of Chiang Kai-shek."[50] His wife, Katherine, pitied the Generalissimo because of his troubles but thought he was cute.[51] But Marshall, in fact, was inclined to be critical of Chiang even before his arrival in China on December 21, 1945. Later he repeatedly voiced as many put-downs of Chiang as Stilwell had. Before leaving the United States, he had met with W. H. Donald, who let him in on the Chiang family secrets. Donald pointedly told him of the powerful influence exerted on Chiang by his sister-in-law Nancy-Ailing, Mei-ling's corrupt older sister and the wife of Kong Xiangxi. Ailing had such a strong character that even within the Song family they said of her, "If elder sister had been born a man, the Generalissimo would already be dead, and she would be ruling China."[52] She subjected both Kong Xiangxi and her younger sister Meiling to her influence, and it was through them that she usually acted on Chiang Kai-shek.[53] Although Donald defended Chiang, asserting that the Generalissimo himself was not at all corrupt but was simply not strong enough to stand up to his sister-in-law, Marshall's critical view of Chiang's regime inevitably hardened.

On the eve of the arrival of Truman's special representative, Chiang made a short trip to Beiping and then to Nanjing, where he met with Marshall.[54] In Beiping he spoke before a crowd of schoolchildren, who were so excited by a flood of patriotic feelings that they surrounded him in a dense crowd and did not let him descend from the platform. They reached out their hands toward him, made a lot of noise, and grabbed the flaps of his clothes. A happy reception awaited him in Nanjing too. After arriving in the city, the first thing he did was to offer a prayer to the Almighty for having bestowed victory upon him and allowing him to return peacefully to the old capital. Then he went directly from the airfield to the Military Academy, where he had lived earlier, and met there with generals and officers. In a fine hand he wrote a placard for one of the auditoriums: "The Hall of Christ's Victory Song." He was accompanied on the trip by Ching-kuo, with whom he visited the Mausoleum of Sun Yat-sen on Purple Gold Mountain in Nanjing to bow before the remains of the great teacher; he also visited other points of interest. On the way back from Nanjing he stopped in Wuhan.[55]

For a time these trips diverted him, but Chiang was unable to relax completely. He was constantly worried by the unceasing conflict with the CCP and wanted to find out what Stalin's true aims in China were. Through the new ambassador of the USSR, Apollon Aleksandrovich Petrov—who replaced Paniushkin in the spring of 1945—in November he had requested that the Kremlin leader receive his eldest son as his [Chiang's] personal representative.[56] By this time Ching-kuo had become his father's most trusted proxy. In the words of Song Qingling, Chiang's other sister-in-law, it would be "difficult to find another person who enjoyed such broad powers as Chiang Ching-kuo."[57] Stalin, too, knew of Ching-kuo's growing role. It was not by chance that in the summer of 1945, on the occasion of the arrival in Moscow of a Chinese delegation headed by T. V. Song, he raised a toast both to Chiang and to Chiang Ching-kuo as "Chiang Kai-shek's successor."[58]

Ching-kuo left Chongqing on Christmas Day, December 25, 1945, and Stalin accorded him two lengthy audiences—on December 30 (one hour and forty minutes) and January 3 (one hour and thirty minutes)—but made no promises to him. He demonstratively received him as a private person: he specifically ordered that the airport at which Ching-kuo landed should not be adorned with the flags of the USSR and China, that there be no honor guard, no national anthems, and that those greeting him not be in parade dress. He housed Ching-kuo like a tourist in the Hotel National at his own expense (he was given an ordinary room, No. 200).[59] During their talks he basically made excuses by saying he knew little about the situation in China and almost nothing about the CCP. He even asked Ching-kuo if China was a republic. He pretended not to know what the Communists in China wanted. To Ching-kuo's repeated requests that he advise the Chinese Communists to cooperate with the Guomindang, he replied several times that "the Chinese Communists do not submit to the Russian Communists" and "do not ask for advice." He said further that "the Soviet government . . . is dissatisfied with their behavior" and "they know that the Soviet government does not agree with them." "If they ask for advice, it will be given to them, but now God knows," he noted profoundly, adding that, from his perspective, "the Communists are rather inscrutable." But what kind of thoughts they were concealing, he, Stalin, according to his words, of course, did not know. Stalin spoke unflatteringly of Mao: "Mao Zedong is a peculiar person and a peculiar Communist. He goes about in the villages, avoids the cities, and is not interested in them." "He, Com[rade] Stalin, does not understand this," wrote the stenographer.[60]

The "Great Leader and Teacher" was putting on a good performance. Meeting the Soviet ambassador on the eve of New Year, 1946, Chiang decided to go for broke, telling him to inform Stalin that he was amenable even to the peaceful coexistence in China of the armed forces "of various parties and tendencies" as long as they submitted to the orders of the commander in chief.[61]

Marshall was now working furiously, meeting with numerous Chinese politicians and aiming all his efforts at getting the Nationalists and the Communists to sit down again at the negotiating table. In conversations with him, the Communists and a majority of members of other parties and nonparty persons reviled the Guomindang, while Chiang and his supporters cursed the Communist Party. But Marshall did not go into details. He tried to carry out his mission at whatever price since he was accustomed to winning.

His effort achieved the desired effect. Nineteen days after his arrival, on January 10, 1946, Marshall succeeded in convincing Chiang to agree to a truce. The communists, too, signed the agreement. The truce, to be sure, did not apply everywhere nor was it consistently observed, but Marshall was satisfied. He thought that his mission had begun to bear fruit. A Political Consultative Conference convened in Chongqing on January 10 with the participation of eight members of the Guomindang, seven Communists, fourteen representatives of liberal parties, and nine nonparty persons. It adopted a resolution calling for the convocation four months later, on May 5, of a National Assembly to adopt a constitution. That was the anniversary of the day in 1921 when Sun Yat-sen had been inaugurated in Canton as the emergency president of the Republic of China.[62]

But this was all just a formality. It was impossible to unify China via negotiations since, as before, there were various military groupings among which the Communist Party was just one, although the most aggressive. The country still lacked a national common market, and the mass of the illiterate population, understanding nothing about democracy, elections, or constitutions, lived as they had for hundreds of years in their closed-off village communities. Wedemeyer, who understood China well, wrote,

> China is not prepared for a democratic form of government with 95 per cent of her people illiterate and for many other cogent reasons. The inarticulate masses of China desire peace and are not particularly interested in or aware of the various ideologies represented. An opportunity to work, to obtain food and clothing for their families and a happy peaceful environment are their primary concern.
>
> *Conditions here could best be handled by a benevolent despot or a military dictator, whether such a dictator be a Communist or a Kuomintang [Guomindang] matters very little. From my observation practically all Chinese officials are interested [only] in their selfish aggrandizement.*[63]

How could one forget what Churchill said to Hurley in April 1945 (he could have said the same thing to Marshall): "You are quite a strange person. They [the Chinese] have been unable to unite in the course of 5,000 years, and you [via negotiations] want to unite them in three months."[64] The centrifugal tendencies in China could be overcome only by force. Mao had long since expressed this in his vivid formula: "Political power is obtained from the barrel of a gun."[65]

Chiang Kai-shek thought just as Mao did, therefore, yielding to Marshall's attempts at persuasion, he nevertheless wrote in his diaries, "Marshall wholly fails to understand that they [the communists] are absolutely insincere. . . . These last few days I have been in a dismal mood, I am ashamed.

The communist bandits are unrestrained, they howl like a pack of dogs. I know that past matters are unresolved."[66]

Both the communists and the Nationalists continued to violate the truce. Marshall was initially inclined to place the blame on the Guomindang, then on the Communist Party, and afterward again on the Guomindang. On February 2, 1946, Chiang wrote in his diaries, "I spoke with Marshall. Perhaps he is gradually beginning to become aware of the fraudulence of the Chinese communists. . . . Zhou Enlai . . . told Marshall that the CCP is pro-American, not pro-Soviet. This is so surprising, I don't know what to say!" And this is what he jotted down in late February: "Although Marshall understands me well enough, the influence of the rhetoric of the communists on him is especially strong. Americans are easily deceived, it is not difficult to make fools of them. This is true even of such hardened warriors as Marshall. . . . I cannot stop worrying about the fate of the world."[67]

Truman was also obsessed with worrying about the fate of the world, but, like a majority of Americans, he saw the salvation of humanity in democratization. He did not know China and its distinctive characteristics and, unlike Wedemeyer, he did not understand it. Moreover, until he was almost thirty, the future president of the United States was generally prejudiced against Chinese. In his own words, he hated both them and Japanese. "I think this is [my] racial prejudice," he wrote to his future wife on June 22, 1911.[68] In time he overcame this prejudice, but he never developed a serious interest in studying China. After receiving Marshall's report that the first stage of his mission had been successfully completed, he wrote to him on February 2, 1946, "It looks as if the Chinese program is working out exactly as planned."[69]

On March 15 Marshall, pleased with his progress, returned to Washington for consultations with the president. He thought the time had come to shore up the peace process in China with a large sum of money and therefore requested a credit of $500 million. While he was absent the situation in China spun out of control, largely because of the deterioration of Chinese–Soviet relations regarding Manchuria.

Until the spring of 1946 Chiang continued to hope that Stalin would implement the Treaty of Friendship and Alliance and help establish the authority of the Guomindang government in Northeast China on the eve of the Soviet withdrawal. To secure enough time to transfer his military units to Manchuria, he twice asked the Kremlin dictator to delay the withdrawal of Soviet armed forces from the region: at first until January 3, 1946, and then until February 1. But he received no help. Moreover, the occupation forces stayed in Northeast China even after February 1 ("due to winter conditions and bad weather"). While they were there they engaged in brazen pillage: under the guise of acquiring "war trophies" they dismantled large industrial enterprises, including the Anshan Metallurgical Complex and the Manchuria Airplane Manufacturing Company in Harbin. They shipped these pilfered items to the Soviet Union, while also appropriating the property of Japanese citizens as well as that of Chinese.[70] The Soviet soldiers were unable or unwilling to distinguish between Chinese and Japanese. Colonel Robert Rigg, who inspected the situation in 1946, estimated that the Soviets, for instance, had taken 296 pieces of machinery out of 333 from the Hitachi plant and 96 percent of the machinery of the Manchurian Electric Wire Company.[71]

The result, according to various estimates, was that the economy of Manchuria suffered a loss of from $858 million to $2.236 billion American dollars.[72] Both the Guomindang and the Chinese public began to express open aversion toward the conduct of the Soviet army. The people were especially disturbed by the frequent instances of rape perpetrated by Soviet soldiers against Japanese as well as Chinese women. Sometimes enraged inhabitants killed Soviet soldiers for this.[73] In February–March 1946 massive, vehemently anti-Soviet student demonstrations took place in Chongqing, Shanghai, Nanjing, and Canton. The scale of pillaging and violence was so horrendous that even the Northeast Bureau of the CCP Central Committee eventually expressed its dissatisfaction.[74]

Chiang succumbed to these moods and began to pursue a shortsighted policy toward the USSR. On March 6, 1946, the Ministry of Foreign Affairs of the Republic of China issued a protest regarding the pillaging of Manchuria and demanded the swift evacuation of the Soviet army.[75] Did Chiang Kai-shek understand then that the Chinese Communists would step in to replace the Russians? Probably not. He figured on occupying the cities vacated by the Soviets himself, depending on support from the United States. But he miscalculated.

A week later, on March 13, Stalin began withdrawing his troops, a process that concluded on May 3. Feeling offended by Chiang, he simultaneously called on the Chinese Communists to act decisively and freely, and he criticized them for showing excessive courtesy toward the United States.[76] First, he secretly notified the Chinese Communists about the imminent withdrawal two days before it commenced.[77] Second, the Soviet army began to give enormous assistance to the CCP in redeploying its troops to Manchuria, handing over to them the remaining arms of the Kwantung army and even some German, Czechoslovak, and Soviet weapons.[78]

The Americans tried to help Chiang Kai-shek transport his troops to North, Northeast, and East China and expended the enormous sum of $300 million on this effort.[79] (For comparison, during the Second World War they spent a total of $846 million on Lend-Lease deliveries to China.)[80] But they could not make use of the main Manchurian ports, Dalian and Port Arthur, that remained under Soviet occupation. Nevertheless, on March 13 the Guomindang army took Shenyang, the largest city in Manchuria, located about 140 miles northeast of Jinzhou.[81]

By this time relations between the Soviet Union and the United States had soured considerably, and a Cold War had erupted. Early in 1946 Truman had written in an unmailed letter to his secretary of state, James F. Byrnes, "I'm tired of babysitting the Soviets," after which the Americans pursued a policy of containing the USSR.[82] Stalin acted the same way. On February 9, at a preelection meeting of voters in the Stalin electoral district of Moscow, he delivered a rather critical speech about his former allies.[83] On March 5, with Truman's approval and in his presence, Churchill, during a visit to the United States, assailed Stalin's policy in Eastern Europe on the occasion of his receipt of an honorary doctorate from Westminster College in Fulton, Missouri.

Mao then launched a new attack, ordering a blow against Guomindang troops in Manchuria that was to begin on March 12 with an advance on Siping. After taking this city in southern Manchuria—halfway from Shenyang to Changchun—on March 18 the Communists proceeded north to Changchun, the capital of Jilin province, from which the Soviet army had withdrawn. Again, the Communists were victorious and followed up this victory in the second half of April by occupying the major cities of Changchun and Harbin.[84] They began to transform Manchuria, rich in oil, gas, and coal, into their military base.[85]

Chiang was indignant. "The Communist bandits have openly seized Changchun . . . violated the agreement on stopping the war, and caused distress in the state," he wrote in his diaries. "Russia is openly airlifting aid to the Communist bandits, and is constantly transporting soldiers of the communist bandits from Harbin and Changchun by railroad. They [the Russians] have decided to divide the Northeast [of China], and establish a puppet regime in Northern Manchuria from their Communist bandits."[86]

Given this new situation, Chiang concluded that the Americans could no longer refrain from helping him. On Saturday, April 13, he wrote in his diaries, looking forward to Easter, which that year fell on April 21: "Beginning from this week's Easter everything can be transformed from bad to good."[87] However, he did not take into consideration the depth of the democratic delusions of Truman and his entourage. The Americans stubbornly stuck to their line. Instead of providing Chiang immediate military aid, they continued to insist upon peaceful regulation of the conflict and carrying out democratic reforms in China. After returning to Chongqing in April, Marshall openly told Chiang Kai-shek that the right wing of the Guomindang was having a baleful influence on him and that if Chiang continued to listen to the military hawks, it would lead to China's collapse, as had occurred in Japan.[88]

But Chiang did not listen to him. "In the second half of the day, I discussed policy toward the Communists with Marshall," he wrote in his diaries on April 22. "As before, he pressured me, advising me to compromise, but I again clearly set forth my position." And further: "He [Marshall] does not know that if I now make concessions to the Communist bandits, it would be tantamount to my submission to Russia and capitulation to her."[89]

Chiang was convinced he could defeat the Communists in three months, so the war flared up. Fortunately for Chiang, he began to score victories over Mao Zedong. His troops, numbering 4.305 million, exceeded the army of the communists, which numbered no more than 1.2 million officers and soldiers, as noted earlier.

On April 29, Chiang frankly laid out to Marshall his view of the kind of policy the United States should follow in China:

> [You] need to reexamine relations with Russia and the [Chinese] Communists. And do this promptly. You face the question of whether to passively withdraw from East Asia or actively intervene [in events], and playing the leading role [in them]. You mustn't withdraw passively as you did on September 18 [1931]. Your withdrawal led to the tragedy of the Second World War. If the United States and Great Britain had used force against Japan, undertaking active measures, Japan would have given in, and the tragedy of war would have been avoided. The situation in East Asia now is the same. Now one should not engage in empty blathering with the Communists. Instead, gathering one's strength, one must switch to active measures. And unambiguously declare your resolve to provide assistance to our Central Government. Then the [Chinese] Communists and Russia can be defeated. Otherwise the United States will find it extremely difficult to maintain its preeminent authority in East Asia which would undoubtedly lead to a Third World War.[90]

But Marshall and Truman were apparently not frightened by the specter of a Third World War, so they continued to work toward ending the Chinese civil war. Meanwhile, on May 3, 1946, Chiang and his wife returned from Chongqing to Nanjing. Two days later the entire National government followed. Nanjing again became the capital of the Republic of China.

Chiang was happy to return from the more than eight-year-long evacuation. He settled in once more at his beloved *Qilu* (Hut of Repose) on Huangpu Street, on the campus of the Central Infantry Military Academy. Every morning he set out by car on the ten-minute drive to his office on Changjiang (Yangzi) Avenue, in the Zizhao Palace. It was a handsome five-story, yellow brick building constructed in 1935 in the guise of a three-tiered pyramid for the then chairman of the government, Lin Sen. Thus it was named in his honor (Zizhao was Lin Sen's honorific name). His office was a spacious but spartanly furnished room in the right wing of the second floor; its lone window looked out over a garden planted with tall trees: a fragrant viburnum, pines, and cedars.[91]

Nanjing gradually reacquired its former appearance, new home construction was proceeding everywhere, and buildings destroyed by the war were undergoing repair. In various Chinese cities in the spring of 1946 trials of Wang Jingwei's major assistants were underway. Most of them, including Chen Gongbo, who had become head of the puppet regime in March 1944 after Wang's departure for medical treatment in Japan, were sentenced to death by firing squad. Chiang pardoned only one of them: Zhou Fohai, the former deputy of Wang and Chen, commuting his death sentence to life imprisonment. Old ties were at work. Zhou Fohai had been an old friend of Dai Li, the "Chinese Himmler" who had headed all of the secret services of the Chinese government for many years. Dai, as it happens, had died in an air crash seven months before the trial, on March 17, 1946, but Chiang, obviously in Dai's memory, spared Zhou from execution.[92]

A terrible fate, from the viewpoint of Chinese, befell the chief criminal, Wang Jingwei. The victors committed an outrage against his remains, which, according to an ancient belief, would have a devastating influence on his geomancy. Three months prior to Chiang's return, in January 1946, by order of ground forces commander General He Yingqin, who had received the go-ahead from Chiang, Wang's grave, located not far from the Mausoleum of Sun Yat-sen on Purple Gold Mountain, was blown up. In December 1945, when Chiang and his son visited Nanjing, it was still there, but now in its place, on the low hill Meihuashan (Plum Blossom Hill), was a small gazebo encased in grape vines. Sun Fo, the son of Sun Yat-sen, had ordered this built. In 1947 the gazebo was also taken down, and in its place, again by decision of Sun Fo, a rather elegant pavilion under a curved brick roof was constructed.[93]

On May 6, 1946, soon after his arrival in Nanjing, Chiang received an invitation from Stalin to visit Moscow. The invitation, given to him by Ching-kuo, had been transmitted via Nikolai Vasilievich Roshchin, the military attaché of the embassy of the USSR. Chiang courteously declined on the pretext that the situation in China was extremely serious.[94] As the American historian Steven I. Levine wrote, "He tried to avoid bilateral Soviet–Chinese negotiations, preferring multi-lateral diplomacy in which American support could compensate for China's weakness."[95]

Meanwhile, the war continued. On May 19, after a forty-day battle with the Communists, the Nationalists retook Siping. On May 23, at noon, they captured Changchun. The main Communist forces retreated to Harbin and the Korean border.[96] They were greatly weakened. Zhou Enlai later said to the Soviet ambassador Petrov that at that time the troops had "only two cartridges per soldier."[97] That same day, on May 23, at four o'clock in the afternoon, Chiang and his wife arrived in Shenyang, where they stayed in the former Japanese General Consulate. Chiang was excited. "The speed of retaking Changchun and the terrible collapse of the Communist bandits are beyond imagination. Does the Lord protect me? Should I still be surprised after what happened?" he wrote in his diaries.[98] He and Meiling spent ten days in Shenyang and Changchun.

Chiang's chief of the General Staff, Chen Cheng, believed that the Communists would be totally crushed in three to six months.[99] But Chiang understood that the farther advance to the north might irritate the Soviets, who considered North Manchuria their special sphere of interest. In late April he wrote in his diaries that "after the conquest of Sipingjie [Siping] we will not go north. At first we will clear South Manchuria, Shenyang, and consolidate heavy industrial areas and Beiping–Shenyang Railroad."[100] There were additional reasons to halt the advance: first, in Chiang's rear, in North and Central China, there were many communist troops inhibiting his freedom of maneuver; second, the American technology that was part of Guomindang military equipment got bogged down on the springtime Manchurian roads; and, third, after their defeat near Siping, the communist troops, dug in north of the Songhua (Sungari) River, and, as before, receiving enormous assistance from the USSR, primarily resorted to guerrilla warfare, relying on their bases in agricultural districts.[101]

In early June 1946 Marshall was again able to achieve a truce. But it did not last long. It was impossible to put the genie of war back in the bottle from whence it had sprung. On June 26 Chiang Kai-shek launched a new campaign against the communists, this time in North and Central China. In a final attempt to bring Chiang to his senses, in late July 1946 the American government placed an embargo on shipments of weapons to Chiang's army. But even this had no effect on him.

In July 1946 Truman appointed a new ambassador to China, John Leighton Stuart, a famous China expert and missionary who had been born and lived in that country (with interruptions) for fifty-two years. Stuart had headed the American-financed Yenching University in Beijing since January 1919. Marshall had prompted Truman to appoint Stuart to the ambassadorship, sensing Chiang's mistrust of himself and thinking that by teaming up with Stuart—who, incidentally, was a personal friend of Chiang and Meiling—it would be easier for him to influence the Generalissimo.[102] Stuart was already rather old, having just turned seventy, but this did not trouble either Truman or Marshall. The latter had become acquainted with Stuart in April 1946 in Nanjing, after his return from the United States, and since then had cooperated closely with him. Stuart's candidacy received unanimous support from the United States Senate as well as full approval from Chiang Kai-shek. Everyone hoped that Stuart, of all persons, an American by extraction and a Chinese in spirit, would be able to help Chiang solve difficult problems. After presenting his credentials at Chiang's summer home in the Lushan mountains town of Guling, Stuart told the Generalissimo that he wanted to maintain his relationship not as an American official but on the basis of their long friendship.[103]

But in that same month of July the civil war flared up again. Simultaneously, under the pretext of needing to centralize power under wartime conditions, Chiang did everything he could to strengthen his personal dictatorship, eliminating dissidents. He was not, however, behind the most notorious assassinations that took place in July in Kunming (Yunnan province). The secret police there assassinated two leaders of the Democratic League, a procommunist organization of Chinese intellectuals established in 1944, including the famous poet Wen Yiduo. Chiang himself was shocked by this killing and immediately demanded that the assassins be found in order to counter any Communist use of this event in their propaganda.[104] But the assassinations did in fact provoke an enormous reaction, in China and abroad; even more persons expressed their opposition to Chiang and the Guomindang, and liberal Western public opinion in particular began to criticize him even more intensely.

Chiang and the Americans increasingly failed to see eye-to-eye. "The Generalissimo's attitude and actions were those of an old-fashioned warlord, and, as with the warlords, there was no love for him among the people," noted Truman.[105] Chiang wrote in his diaries, "The Americans are very naïve by nature, they are ridiculous like children."[106] On August 10 the president of the United States sent Chiang a letter expressing the "grave concern" of the American people in regard to "the rapidly deteriorating political situation in China." He emphasized that from his perspective Marshall's "efforts have apparently proved unavailing." He blamed "extremist elements, equally in the Kuomintang [Guomindang] as in the Communist party," and, hinting that he might terminate aid if Chiang did not rectify the situation, he called on the Generalissimo to inform him in the near future of something encouraging.[107] Chiang did not heed Truman. Meeting Marshall six days later in Guling, he bluntly asserted that "the Communists were violating all aspects of the truce" and "by its recent military actions in the field has openly declared itself to a policy of force." He explained that the situation had changed and the Chinese Communists "were now working close in hand with the Soviet Government." Marshall tried to object, noting that "there has been much on the Government side in the way of indication of a policy of force," but Chiang did not listen to him, saying he "had no faith in the Communists' intentions to keep any agreement." "At present the Generalissimo, it seems, is evidently inclined toward a policy of force as the only acceptable solution" Marshall concluded, and after a while he wrote to Truman that he and Stuart were stymied.[108]

Yet the American government still backed Chiang despite Truman's and Marshall's growing dissatisfaction with his regime. This resulted in a loss of sympathy toward the US by China's so-called middle forces, in particular Chinese liberal intellectuals, who opposed Guomindang dictatorship and now gravitated toward Mao's New Democracy.[109]

In the fall Chiang announced his intention to retake Kalgan from the communists. In response, the communists warned that they would consider an attack on the city in Hebei as an official declaration of civil war. Hearing this, Marshall immediately threatened Chiang that he would ask Truman to cut off all economic and military aid to China and recall him (Marshall) home. On October 5 he wrote to Truman who, since April 1946, had been pondering the idea of appointing Marshall secretary of state in place of the ailing Byrnes.[110] But that same day, meeting with Marshall, Chiang declared that the latter's threat "had upset him more than anything else in many years," stressing that he "could not even contemplate" his departure. But he did not agree with Marshall's proposal to stop the war. The next day, however, bowing to pressure from Marshall and Stuart, he promised to end military actions in the Kalgan region. But he did not keep his promise, as on October 10 the Nationalists took Kalgan.[111]

Marshall was beside himself. Visiting Chiang Kai-shek, he said to him, "You have broken agreements, you have gone counter to plans. People have said you were a modern George Washington, but after these things they will never say it again." He understood that his words sounded undiplomatic, and therefore he asked Meiling, who was acting as interpreter, not to translate them if she thought they were too tactless. But the Generalissimo's wife decided that Chiang needed to hear them.[112] Chiang listened silently, lifting and lowering the toes of his boots as he always did when he was nervous. But he made no reply: he remained convinced that he was right and that victory over the communists was imminent.

It seemed that he had reason to think that. After bloody battles, the Communist forces by the end of 1946 withdrew from 165 cities and other populated areas, comprising 67,200 square miles.[113] Chiang Kai-shek carried out a broad offensive on all fronts, from Shaanxi province in the west to the shores of the Pacific Ocean in the east. He also continued the war in Manchuria.

The Americans, however, considered Chiang Kai-shek's actions to be "overambitious," and they warned that such a military campaign would "plunge China into economic chaos and eventually destroy the National Government." Indeed, Chiang, by extending the front, had exposed his "communications to attack by Communist guerrillas"; his soldiers were compelled either "to retreat or to surrender their armies together with the munitions which the United States has furnished them."[114]

What the Americans said made sense. Chiang Kai-shek's army had no advantage over Mao's forces other than material. In terms of morale, it had essentially lost. Chiang himself quickly grasped this. In 1947 he would acknowledge that even though his troops "were ten times richer than the communist army in terms of military-supply replacements, such as food, fodder, and ammunition . . . [i]t cannot be denied that the [revolutionary] spirit of most commanders is broken." Unlike the officers and soldiers of the CCP, the Nationalists entirely lacked the will to fight. This, in essence, was the cause of Chiang Kai-shek's misfortune. He sent divisions and armies into battle, but his generals, as before, often tried to avoid engagements, being "concerned only with preserving their *shi li* (military strength and resources)."[115] They viewed their units in the first instance as the source of their own political influence in society and enrichment. Corruption and regionalism continued to flourish in all units. In various places the Guomindang bureaucrats and generals "used opportunities of takeover [former Japanese-occupied areas] to benefit themselves by confiscating businesses" of Chinese owners, acts that alienated the local population.[116]

The situation was not the least bit better than it had been in Stilwell's time, when, in 1944, he wrote, "He [Chiang] can't see that the mass of Chinese people welcome the Reds as being the only visible hope of relief from the crushing taxation, the abuses of the Army and [the terror of] Tai Li's [Dai Li's] Gestapo. Under Chiang Kai-shek they [the masses] now begin to see what they may expect. Greed, corruption, favoritism, more taxes, a ruined currency, terrible waste of life, callous disregard of all rights of men."[117] Closely following the situation in China, Truman was forced to say in an informal conversation with a group of American publishers that everything in China was "very, very bad."[118]

Meanwhile, in mid-October 1946 Chiang and Meiling visited Taiwan, the former province of China annexed by Japan in 1895. The Portuguese, in the sixteenth century, named it Ilha Formosa (Beautiful Island). On August 15, 1945, as soon as Japan surrendered, Chiang appointed General Chen Yi, then the governor of Fujian province, governor of Taiwan. After the Americans transported Chiang Kai-shek's troops to Taiwan, on October 25, 1945, Chen Yi received what was by now just the formal surrender from the local Japanese governor-general. In fact, that is why Chiang and Meiling flew to Taiwan in October 1946, their first joint trip to the island: they wanted to take part in the celebrations on the first anniversary of Taiwan's return to the bosom of the Motherland. In Taipei, the capital of the province, the Chiangs stayed in the most beautiful place on the island: in the Caoshan (Grass Mountains) in the northern suburb of the city, near the mineral hot springs. Chiang noted that although Japanese influence on the island was still profound, he liked much about the island: nature and especially the absence of communist organizations. The minuscule Taiwan Communist Party had ceased to exist in 1931, and from then on Communist ideas evoked no response in the hearts either of the Taiwanese (that is, Chinese born on the island) or the Chinese who had come over from the mainland. The standard of living there under the Japanese was much higher than under Chiang on the mainland.[119] "Taiwan may be called virgin territory. We must build it up, and turn it into a model province for our country," Chiang wrote in his diaries.[120]

Soon after Chiang and Meiling returned to Nanjing, on November 4, China and the United States signed a Treaty of Friendship, Trade, and Navigation that was important to Chiang. The treaty was completely balanced: the United States was given no privileges in China. But the treaty was soon subjected to severe criticism by Chinese and Soviet communists. In Yan'an they even lowered the flag to half-mast for three days, and Mao declared November 4 "a day of national humiliation." The accusations were without foundation, and the only thing about which one might reproach Chiang, and even then only theoretically, was that the treaty allowed citizens of the United States to build industrial enterprises in China and invest capital in Chinese industry. Moreover, it extended most favored nation status to Americans. But that was something any country could be afforded in China, and even Mao himself, who was then promoting New Democracy, advocated attracting capital into the Chinese economy. The communists, however, did not care whether their criticism was justified. They made use of the treaty to ignite a powerful anti-American campaign aimed at accelerating the withdrawal of American forces from China. Chiang was also a target, being accused of "selling out China to American imperialism."[121] Then, on December 24, a student in Beiping asserted that she had been raped by an American soldier. Throughout China organizations sprang up "to protest the violence of American forces in China," and signatures were collected to change Chinese policy toward the United States. The upshot was that by June 1, 1947, Truman had withdrawn almost all of his forces from China. At Chiang's request only 6,800 men remained, comprising groups of advisors and guard units.[122]

On November 15, 1946, Chiang convened the Constitutional National Assembly in Nanjing. It was initially planned for May 5 but was not held on schedule. The communists boycotted it. They deemed it illegal inasmuch as the elections were conducted according to a Guomindang script. Zhou Enlai, who until then had been cooperating with Marshall (that was probably why Americans in Chongqing nicknamed him Cherry, while other members of the CCP delegation were called Poplars), demonstratively flew back to Yan'an.[123] His actions indicated that the Communist Party would no longer hold formal talks with the Guomindang. Representatives of the Democratic League and several leading nonparty politicians did not take part in the Constitutional National Assembly either. Nevertheless, it was not homogeneous. Fifty percent of the 1,355 delegates were in opposition to the Guomindang.[124]

On Christmas Day, December 25, the Constitutional National Assembly adopted the Constitution of China, which was promulgated on January 1, 1947. It was based on the teachings of Sun Yat-sen about the division of powers into five independent branches: legislative, executive, judicial, examination, and control; it proclaimed that the Republic of China was a "democratic republic of the people, for the people, by the people founded on the Three Principles of the People."[125] A series of articles in the Constitution guaranteed civil rights and freedoms, including the universal and equal right to choose members of parliament and local organs of power (on reaching twenty years of age) and to be elected to these organs of power (at twenty-three years of age). The president and vice president were elected for six-year terms and were limited to two such terms. Overall, it was a fully democratic document. Stuart said it "exceeded all his expectations."[126]

But the civil war was continuing, and there was no reason for Marshall to remain in China. On January 3, 1947, Truman directed Secretary of State Byrnes to recall him to Washington. While Marshall was en route Truman appointed him the new secretary of state. Before departing, Marshall told Chiang he did not believe the Generalissimo would win the war. He noted that the communists could wage a war of attrition, cutting the Nationalists' lines of supply and communication at will while Chiang's troops tried to hold on to the cities.[127]

Marshall had no right to humiliate Chiang. It was not only Chiang and Mao, but also the Americans themselves who bore responsibility for the failure of their mediation in the negotiations between the Nationalists and communists aimed at "unifying and democratizing China." Stalin simply outplayed Truman, purposefully giving him the role of lone mediator despite the fact that both the Americans and Chiang had repeatedly asked Stalin to assume the role of mediator as well.[128] But the determination of the United States to play the role of Messiah in the dissemination of democratic values to the entire world compelled Washington to pull Stalin's chestnuts from the fire. It was Stalin himself who, as noted above, during the anti-Japanese war had advised the CCP to pose as a main proponent of democracy in China in contrast with the totalitarian Guomindang. Thus American intervention in Chinese affairs (Hurley's and Marshall's mediation) could only strengthen the position of the CCP—just as the formal nonintervention of the USSR served to demonstrate that the Soviets supposedly had nothing in common with the "margarine communists" of China. It was difficult to prove that Stalin was actually helping arm the communists. Any investigation demanded time and effort, which neither the Americans nor Chiang Kai-shek possessed. Moreover, Stalin persistently denied everything, asserting that he was not interfering in Chinese domestic affairs.

In essence, by forcing Chiang Kai-shek to compete with the communists in their propagandistic game of "democratic" tricks, Marshall unwittingly played into Stalin's hands. From this perspective, his mission was not simply unsuccessful but actually disastrous. Not only did he fail to avert a civil war in China, but he strengthened the position of Mao and Stalin. At the same time, it is difficult not to agree with Steven I. Levine, who writes that there was a positive kernel in the Marshall mission: the representative of the US president was able to negate the possibility of an open confrontation between America and the USSR in China, and he also delayed, insofar as was possible, a full-scale civil war.[129]

Be that as it may, Marshall's departure freed the hands of both Chiang Kai-shek and Mao Zedong. China irrevocably plunged into the abyss of civil war, among the most bitter of all those that China had ever experienced. In the war Chiang faced an enemy that was much stronger than the Japanese, one that relied not only on their own armed forces, but also on support of the multimillion mass of the Chinese people as well as the backing of the USSR, one of the most powerful countries in the world. This enemy was not striving to turn Chiang Kai-shek into a puppet and push him to surrender, but positing as its goal the total destruction of his regime.

The war was a matter of life and death. Chiang wagered everything he had on it.

PART SIX

# *"Victory Will Come with Determination"*

CHAPTER 21

# *Catastrophe*

In the latter half of 1946 the economic situation in China sharply deteriorated. The war was consuming from 70 to 90 percent of the greatly inflated budget, and Chiang continued to insist, as he had during the years of the Second World War, on printing ever more paper money. From September 1945 to February 1947 the exchange rate of the yuan fell thirty times. In January 1947 alone it lost more than twice its value, falling from 7,700 yuan per dollar to 18,000. In 1947 monthly inflation was 26 percent. On March 1, 1947, T. V. Song, who disagreed with this policy, submitted his resignation, and Chiang replaced him as head of the Executive Yuan.[1] This was bold but shortsighted. By concentrating all power in his own hands, Chiang Kai-shek was exposing himself to the criticism of the people who were suffering from inflation and rising prices. Chiang soon realized that rather quickly, and, on Marshall's recommendation, he yielded the position to a friend from his youth and one of his most trusted associates, Zhang Qun, who was considered a liberal among the Guomindang higher-ups.[2]

The crisis continued to deepen. An eyewitness reported that "inflation was creating tremendous financial insecurity. . . . Inflation was so severe that the pile of money that would purchase three eggs in the morning would buy only one egg by the afternoon. People carried their money in carts, and the price of rice was so high that citizens who in ordinary times would never have dreamed of stealing were beginning to break into grain shops and make off with what they could."[3] A bottle of Coca-Cola that cost ten cents in American currency sold for a million yuan.[4]

Taking the bit in his teeth, Chiang sabotaged all proposals to carry out reforms, both economic (including agrarian and tax reforms) as well as political. He said he would implement them but in fact did nothing. As early as mid-September 1946 the Nationalists announced the start of agrarian reform, including lowering taxes, expanding agricultural credits, and even redistributing land, but this declaration was never put into effect. Chiang simply did not want to enter into conflict with the Americans, who were insisting on reforms, but he considered it impossible to carry them out at the time and therefore put them off until after the war.

He employed repressive measures against all opponents, just as he always had. The worst repression occurred in Taipei in February–May 1947. Soldiers and police were deployed against demonstrators who were condemning the corruption of Guomindang officials, the centralization of the economy, unemployment, inflation, and price rises. Chen Yi, the governor of the province, had the full support of Chiang, who deemed it necessary to maintain peace and order on Taiwan, relying on "military force."[5] As a result of the confrontations that began on February 28, several thousand persons died on this beautiful island that Chiang and Meiling had liked so much. According to CIA estimates, the death toll was from 10,000 to 20,000, and 3,000 fled from the island.[6] The "virgin territory" was covered in blood, and any public reference to the massacre was considered a crime against the state.

In late February 1947 Chiang addressed the members of his Military Council several times, demanding decisive victory. He needed a spectacular offensive.[7] But on March 7 Truman told the members of his Cabinet that "Chiang Kai-shek will not fight it out. [The] Communists will fight it out—they are fanatical. It would be pouring sand in a rat hole [to give aid] under present conditions." Secretary of State Marshall fully supported him: "He [Chiang Kai-shek] is losing about forty percent of his supplies to the enemy [since his troops fight poorly]. If the percentage should reach fifty percent he will have to decide whether it is wise to supply his own troops." However, the secretaries of defense and of the navy as well as General Douglas MacArthur, the uncrowned king of Japan who commanded Allied occupation forces in that country, disagreed. MacArthur voiced the view of this group of military men most succinctly: the Guomindang is not "the best" but "on our side."[8]

Nevertheless, on March 12, 1947, Chiang Kai-shek's air force bombed Yan'an itself, the capital of the communists, and the nearby caves in which the

Communist Party leaders were living. Several days later the troops of Hu Zongnan, who had suggested to Chiang Kai-shek that he conduct this operation, occupied the city. But this was Chiang's last triumph. Mao successfully prepared to depart, withdrawing the main forces of his army from the city, although even the members of Chiang's Military Council were not informed of the secretive operational plan. Hu Zongnan's secretary, who was a CCP agent, had informed Mao of the plan to attack Yan'an in advance.[9]

By the summer of 1947 communist troops began an offensive against enemy positions. Chiang panicked. In late May he wrote in his diaries, "Military, economic and social affairs are all in deep crisis. The major problem is that the high-ranking generals at the front are ignorant and negligent, they underestimate the enemy. But they still do not know that they are ignorant and incompetent."[10] However, he did not lose hope. "Yesterday I was sad," he wrote the next day. "But I analyzed possible countermeasures against the bandits, and I felt they could be effective, therefore I slept well for more than seven hours. At present this is a really good omen." Chiang was counting very much on help from the Almighty.[11] But in June 1947 he unleashed a tirade of fury and rage against his generals and officers: "If we speak about the level of most officers' spirit and morality, knowledge and ability, and the level of understanding of ourselves and of the enemy, then we today should long ago have been defeated by the bandit army."[12]

At his request the procurator of the Supreme Court issued an order for the arrest of Mao Zedong, after which all communists were declared "traitors to the Chinese nation."[13] But a turning point had already come in the war. Understanding that the communists would soon be able to rout Chiang, in late May 1947 the American administration lifted the embargo on the delivery of arms to China, ten months after it had been imposed. Up to the end of 1949 the United States would not only supply Chiang with goods via Lend-Lease, but also with credits and loans amounting to about $2 billion (more than to any country in Western Europe after the Second World War). Moreover, it would sell China weapons worth $1.2 billion.[14] Yet even this support would not radically change the situation.

In June 1947 the US Ambassador Stuart told the Soviet Ambassador Petrov that "the Chinese government is becoming weaker and weaker. This is noticeable in military, economic, and psychological terms. The economic crisis is deepening, financial difficulties are causing mistrust of the government, and the growth of mistrust in the government in turn is the most important psychological factor influencing military affairs. Defeatist moods are growing in government circles. . . . Chiang Kai-shek must undertake decisive and essential reforms. Otherwise he needs . . . to go abroad or into retirement."[15] At the same time, Marshall said frankly to representatives of the American business elite, "I have tortured my brain and I can't now see the answer [to the question of what to do about China]."[16]

Truman also did not know what to do. From July 1946 through June 1947 Chiang's troops had lost 780,000 officers and men and, with the addition of local defense forces, 1.12 million overall.[17] In order to assess the political, economic, psychological, and military situation in the country, Truman, in July, sent General Wedemeyer, much beloved by Chiang, who had been back in the States since May 1946, on a trip to China.[18]

After conducting inspections over the course of two months, prior to departing for Washington Wedemeyer felt compelled to tell Chiang the truth, especially since Chiang asked him to do so: "To regain and maintain the confidence of the people, the Central Government will have to effect immediately drastic, far-reaching political and economic reforms. . . . It should be accepted that military force in itself will not eliminate communism."[19] He pointedly criticized the widespread corruption, hapless military command, and repressive government that had lost the trust of the people.[20]

In the meantime, Chiang's army continued to suffer defeats in Manchuria, which Chiang had reason to consider "our key industrial base." He was in a bad mood. "The reports of failure come down just like snowflakes," he wrote.[21] Chiang was humiliated by Wedemeyer, but he decided to improve the political situation. From November 21 to November 23, in the regions under his control, elections to the Chinese National Assembly (the constitutional parliament) were held. The delegates elected numbered 2,961. The communists and the democrats boycotted the elections, but that was of their own doing. Several leftist leaders of the Guomindang also did not take part in the elections, including Sun Yat-sen's widow Song Qingling, Liao Zhongkai's widow He Xiangning, Marshal Feng Yuxiang, and General Li Jishen. In November 1947 these persons gathered in Hong Kong at the so-called First Congress of the Left Guomindang, and, on January 1, 1948, they announced the creation of a new party, the Revolutionary Committee of the Chinese Guomindang. It "would strive to overthrow the dictatorial regime of Chiang Kai-shek."[22] Chiang's sister-in-law Song Qingling became its honorary chair.

Soon more than sixty representatives from various circles in Shanghai sent a request to the American government via the American ambassador Stuart to compel Chiang Kai-shek to step down. They wanted to replace him with

Zhang Qun. Learning of this, Chiang wrote in his diaries, "The intelligentsia as a whole and [even] a large number of well-known persons, consider foreigners as some sort of saints, believing that our country's policies should change in accordance with the position of foreign states. They lack national self-consciousness."[23] On February 7, 1948, Feng Yuxiang addressed an open letter to Chiang, now directly calling on him "to retire, promptly leave the country, and give everything to the people." Furthermore, Feng demanded that Chiang seek asylum in another country, preferably "in Argentina."[24]

The actions of the dissenters played into the hands of the communists, and Chiang expelled them from the party.[25] In Nanjing, on March 29, 1948, in a massive palace on Changjiang Avenue, not far from Zizhao Palace, the first session of parliament convened, tasked with electing the president and vice president of the Republic of China.

Two months prior to its convening, Guangxi general Li Zongren, with whom Chiang had long had far from smooth relations, announced his intention to run for vice president while indicating his support for Professor Hu Shi, a well-known philosopher and diplomat and a nonparty person, for president. Possibly in the context of an intensifying civil war, this would have been the best option. Even Chiang began thinking it over. He didn't want Li Zongren to be elected and persuaded him to withdraw his candidacy.[26] He had slotted Sun Fo, the son of Sun Yat-sen, for the post of vice president, but he was ready to agree to the nomination of Hu Shi. Probably, in the depth of his heart, he wanted to become president, but weighing all the pros and cons, on March 31 he offered the post to Professor Hu. Hu accepted immediately. Chiang was rather taken aback by Hu's acceptance. It is common knowledge that in China it is considered improper to accept a proposal on the first offer. On April 1 Chiang received Zhang Qun, the chair of the Executive Yuan, to consult with him once more about Hu Shi. In principle Zhang had no objections to the nomination of Professor Hu, although he noted that Hu had a difficult character.[27]

However, participants in the next plenum of the CEC and the CCC of the Guomindang that met on the morning of Sunday, April 4, did not want Hu Shi for the post of president. On instructions from the plenum, the following afternoon the question was discussed by members of the Standing Committee of the CEC, a majority of whom voted for the *zongcai* (the leader) of the party, Chiang Kai-shek, for the post of president. At the session on April 6 the members of the CEC and the CCC nominated Chiang for president.

On April 19 the delegates of the Chinese National Assembly, among which Guomindang members predominated, overwhelmingly voted for Chiang

Kai-shek as president for a six-year term. He received 2,430 of 2,699 votes, or 90 percent, and his formal opponent, the chair of the Executive Yuan Zhang Qun received just 269 votes (or 10 percent). On assuming the position Chiang promised "to instill our people with democratic skills, and, thereby, put our country on the road to authentic democracy."[28]

Chiang's authority, however, was not indisputable. Notwithstanding the fact that Chiang had let everyone know in unambiguous terms that he wanted to see Sun Fo as the second-ranking person in the government, he encountered opposition even from among the Guomindang deputies. A majority of votes for this important post went to General Li Zongren. He received 1,438 votes of 2,761, or 52.1 percent, while Sun Fo received 1,295 votes (46.9 percent). Twenty-eight votes were deemed invalid.[29]

According to an eyewitness, when Chiang learned about the election of Li, he "was so infuriated" that "he kicked over the radio set from which he had heard the news and did not calm down for hours."[30] Clearly, he was furious because the deputies had ignored his wish. But they voted for General Li, first of all, because he bribed many of them: the going price for one vote was a hundred million yuan and up.[31] Another reason was that, unlike the Generalissimo, Li was considered to be a supporter of democratic reforms. At least, he himself asserted all the time that "the severe domestic political and economic crisis in China was caused by the political-administrative decay of the Guomindang system. This system was dominated by prominent bureaucrats who were unconcerned about the interests of the people. Therefore, solving China's domestic problems had to begin with introducing general reforms aimed at improving the government system, cleansing it of corruption, arbitrariness, bribery, and other social illnesses."[32]

One day before the election of Chiang as president, the members of the National Assembly, by a decision of the Standing Committee of the GMD CEC adopted on April 5, inserted into China's Constitution several supplementary "Temporary Provisions Effective During the Period of National Mobilization for Suppression of the Communist Rebellion." These articles gave the president the right to declare martial law, extend without limit his term in power, and also take other emergency measures in the interests of national security.[33]

Meanwhile, the Nationalist forces were falling apart literally before one's eyes. By the beginning of February 1948, their losses already amounted to 1,977,000 men, and new reinforcements could not compensate for the reduction in the army. The number of Chiang's troops shrank to 3,650,000 (according to figures from He Yingqin, it was four million); at the same time Mao's forces grew to 2.8 million (according to He Yingqin 2.2 million).[34] By the middle of March the Guomindang army in Manchuria controlled only Shenyang, Changchun, and some territory in the south of this region.[35] On April 21, 1948, the communists retook Yan'an.

Chiang ranted and raved. A majority of officers "do not use their brains and are unwilling to study," he fulminated, "[and] . . . the brains of most of our soldiers are actually asleep." "It is only because everything in China is backward and there is a shortage of talent that you, with minuscule abilities, bear such heavy responsibilities," he shouted at his generals.[36] But they were powerless to make things better. The morale of the soldiers continued to decline precipitously. Theft and corruption flourished in all units. The vestiges of regionalism and militarism remained strong. Chiang, in his own words, was no longer able to do anything about his corrupt military or his venal bureaucrats. "If I make . . . changes," he said to one of his American friends, "the Government collapses and the Communists [will] take over."[37]

Even the inauguration on May 20, 1948, did not dissipate Chiang Kai-shek's dark thoughts. That evening he wrote in his diaries,

> Today I became president, but my heart is uneasy, and my mood depressed. I feel enveloped in gloom and am sad as never before. Whenever I think of the future of the country, of the sufferings of the people, and of my responsibilities toward the revolution, I worry that I will be unable to do anything. Ever since I was elected [president], I have thought all the time of retiring, but today, taking up my duties, I am thinking about it particularly intensely. . . . The members of the party are greedy and concerned only with the struggle for power, they do not think about the history of the revolution or the interests of the people. Party discipline is lacking, and a concept such as party spirit is totally lost. How can we exist in the present circumstances and defeat the communist bandits? I feel powerless, and the only thing remaining to me is to resolve to retire.[38]

He and his closest comrades in arms tried their best to bring the Americans into the conflict, stressing that "the struggle for China constitutes a part of the larger plan of resistance to Russian totalitarianism" and that "China is playing the role of advance post of the Third World War."[39] Nothing came of this. Truman did not change his policy.

Distrusting Truman and thinking he might intervene in the Chinese conflict at any time and employ nuclear weapons against the communists, in June 1948 Stalin issued an order to begin a blockade of West Berlin, in an effort to divert the Americans' attention away from China. Truman fell for the trick and for a certain time actually did shift his attention to Berlin.[40]

The government's inability to stimulate economic development also became painfully obvious. In the spring of 1948 the government was forced to introduce food ration cards in all the big cities, and, in order to increase grain reserves, initiated compulsory purchase of grain at lowered prices.[41] This latter measure alienated the better-off peasants, the Guomindang's natural ally. By August 1948 the cost of rice had risen tenfold compared to May.[42] To rectify the situation, Chiang Kai-shek put gold yuan into circulation. It was exchanged for three million of the old yuan (one US dollar equaled four gold yuan). But this did not help either. The new yuan quickly became devalued like the old one.[43] An eyewitness noted in his diaries in the middle of October 1948, "By now there can be no doubt of the collapse of the new currency, despite deceptive statements from Finance Minister Wong Yun-wu [Wang Yunwu] . . . that the gold yuan has been a brilliant success. We thought prices astronomical a couple of week ago; in comparison with today's they seem reasonable. Prices of most everyday products have tripled, quadrupled, or even quintupled since mid-September, and most of this rise has taken place in the last ten days. Despite this phenomenon, the government clings to its artificial exchange rate of US $1: GY [gold yuan] $4."[44] Another eyewitness wrote in November, "The new currency which started out so hopefully just three months ago is being inflated even faster than the old Chinese National Currency."[45]

The cities were crammed with refugees, the worst situation being in the capital. An American woman living in Nanjing testified that "the situation here is very bad. There are shortages of flour, rice, sugar, and firewood. . . . Stores are shutting down. Refugees are pouring in from the north. People are starving."[46] Enterprises everywhere were going broke, unemployment was increasing rapidly, here and there antigovernment strikes of workers and student demonstrations were occurring. Overall, Chiang Kai-shek was losing both on the front and in the rear. His domestic policy was evoking dissatisfaction from a broad swath of the population. Another American, a Presbyterian missionary, asserted, "The present set-up does not have the confidence or loyalty of any considerable group at all in China; many people think the Communists would do a much better job, and even those who don't hold any brief at all for the Communists have an equal lack of enthusiasm for the Kuomintang [Guomindang], and think that any change might have a chance of bettering things."[47] At the same time, the Associated Press reported that the "nationalist troops who have not been paid regularly" often looted "food stores."[48]

Chiang tried to save face. He addressed the nation by radio, calling for a "movement for industriousness and economy toward the goals of national reconstruction," in order "to reduce consumption in public and private life to a minimum . . . and to increase production and military power to the highest possible level." He called on the nation "to work diligently and live frugally" in order "to conserve the limited resources of China" and "suppress the communists in the near term." He frankly stressed that "China faces two new serious threats." One of them is the "rebellion of the Chinese communists everywhere, and the other economic ruin and social injustice."[49]

He also gave an interview to the government's English-language newspaper *Beiping Chronicle* claiming that "press reports of recent price increases and rush purchases were 'greatly exaggerated.' " He blamed "the people in general and intellectuals in particular for allowing themselves to be 'bewitched' by Communist propaganda [and urged] a cooperative stand to assist the government in achieving unity of the purpose and action."[50] In early November 1948 he wrote in his diaries, "Recently the military and economic situation has drastically deteriorated, and the intellectuals, in particular left-leaning professors and journalists, violently slander [the government]. . . . The hearts of the people are not at peace, they are building up more and more resentment. This [is] the result of the thirty-two-year systematic campaign of the communist bandits, aimed at discrediting me. This is a poisonous weed that kills more effectively than weapons."[51] In this difficult time, the single bit of good news for Chiang Kai-shek was the birth of another grandson. He was given the name Xiaoyong (*xiao* means "filial piety" and *yong* means "brave"). At his christening he received the name Edward, the family called him Eddie. Faina gave birth on October 27, 1948. "This is consolation in grief," Chiang wrote in his diaries the next day.[52]

He directed his oldest son to bring about order at least in the Shanghai region, the most important economically. Ching-kuo, with his characteristic energy, set to the task, starting the so-called Tiger Hunt to root out corruption and speculation by the harshest measures. He became de facto the "economic czar of Shanghai"[53] and arrested over three thousand people in two weeks. But unexpectedly he discovered that one of the main speculators was his cousin, Meiling's nephew David Kong. Without giving it much thought, Ching-kuo placed him under house arrest. Meiling immediately intervened. Chiang himself did not stay on the sidelines. He was upset that David's arrest had attracted the attention of the press, including that of both the Guomindang and the opposition. The matter of David cast a shadow on Chiang himself, and he could not allow this. Under his father's pressure, Ching-kuo was forced to release his cousin. In return, David Kong turned in US $6 million to the treasury and left China for good. He moved to the States, where, one year earlier, in August 1947, his parents had resettled (Kong Xiangxi formally had arrived there as Chiang Kai-shek's personal representative).[54]

Another speculator turned out to be Du Weiping, the elder son of Chiang's old friend Du Yuesheng (Big-eared Du), the godfather of the Shanghai mafia. But in this case Chiang Kai-shek backed his son. "My son Jing arrested and transferred to the court the Shanghai biggest money dealer Rong Hongyuan and Du Yuesheng's son," he wrote in his diaries. "One can say that he dealt with this matter decisively."[55] Big-eared Du had to publicly apologize for his son's wrongdoing. "I brought him up improperly," he declared.[56] The younger Du was sentenced to several months in jail, but in early November 1948 Ching-kuo had to resign.[57]

Meanwhile, over the course of three months, from September 1948 to January 1949, communist troops carried out their three largest strategic operations. One was in Manchuria (the Liao–Shen Campaign), another in East China (the Huai–Hai Campaign), and the third in the vicinity of Beiping–Tianjin (the Ping-Jin Campaign). The outcome was that 1.5 million of Chiang Kai-shek's officers and men were put out of commission, and several large cities were occupied.[58]

In late November 1948 Meiling again set out for the United States, deploying her charm in an effort to convince Truman's government to provide urgent aid to China. Chiang had fervently hoped that Truman, whom he had not seen as a reliable ally, would lose the 1948 election. But he won, and on the next day, November 3, Chiang wrote down a few bitter lines in his diaries: "After Dewey's[59] defeat, my country's diplomatic situation became worse, the people's hearts were shaken, the society is not calm, and we will face drastic changes in the future."[60] But he and his wife had no choice but to continue to deal with Truman. That's why as early as a few days after Truman's reelection Chiang sent a message to him begging him to help. "Now the CCP troops are approaching Nanjing and Shanghai," he wrote, "if we fail to stop their advance now, then the democratic countries would lose all of China." He sought to explain his defeat by attributing it to "Soviet violation of the Sino-Soviet Treaty" and warned: "Now the reaction to the urgent situation depends upon your sympathy and quick decision."[61] However, neither his letter nor Meiling's charm helped.

On December 10, 1948, Chiang invoked his right to declare martial law in the country. He declared it in the core areas of China, with the exception of the western provinces (Xinjiang, Tibet, Xikang and Qinghai) as well as in Taiwan. But this did not help either. He had to do something else.

All this time, starting in May when he first considered retiring, Chiang did not stop thinking about it. He thought that the Lord God Himself was counseling him to do this.[62] In the meantime, many Guomindang leaders wavered, lost faith in the possibility of victory, and began demanding that Chiang renew peace negotiations with the communists. The vice president of China, Li Zongren, was the head of this group. Members of the Executive Yuan supported him. On June 17 generals from the Guangxi clique, headed by Li Zongren and Bai Chongxi, addressed a request to Chiang Kai-shek that he step down.[63] On November 19 Chiang received the news from his chief of staff General Xue Yue that more than two hundred high-ranking party and state officials had signed a petition demanding that he step down. Although Chiang himself had already definitely decided to retire, the news disheartened him.[64]

On December 16, when the US government expressed the hope that Chiang would retire of his own accord, he felt terribly offended.[65] Two days later, summing up the past week's events, he wrote angrily in his diaries,

> It is likely that the embassy of the United States is the main headquarters of the anti-China forces that are trying to overthrow Chiang. . . . Over the past two years the American government and Marshall have consistently followed an anti-Chiang policy. . . . They have fully exposed themselves. This is a terrible insult to our country. These little boys think that ultimately, under their pressure, I cannot but retire. These arrogant people do not know my character, Chinese history and culture, and want to subordinate me to their economic and material power. They do not yet know that I have steeled my spirit and my faith.[66]

It was impossible for him to delay stepping down any longer, but Chiang really had no intention of handing real power over to anyone. He decided to withdraw from affairs of state only formally, after appointing his Vice President Li Zongren merely acting president. Given that Li was an advocate of peace negotiations with the communists, Chiang decided to give him the opportunity of occupying himself with this. Chiang did not want any sort of peace deal with the communists or to dirty his hands by negotiating with the enemy. But he needed time to regroup his forces. With the aid of Sun Fo, the son of Chiang Kai-shek's mentor Sun Yat-sen, he worked out the plan for negotiating with the Communists, but it was Li Zongren, whom both Chiang and Sun did not like, who was perfectly cast for the unenviable role of negotiator.[67] At the same time, in order to limit Li's power, on December 23 Chiang reorganized the government, appointing Sun Fo, who had lost to Li Zongren in the election for vice president in April 1948, as chair of the Executive Yuan.[68]

On the evening of January 3, 1949, Chiang paid an unexpected visit to Li Zongren at his home and spoke with him for half an hour about his (Chiang's) retirement.[69] During that time he proposed that Li take over his post, but Li Zongren did not agree immediately. He first wanted to make sure that he would receive American support and backing from the Guomindang elite in order to feel independent from Chiang Kai-shek.[70] The US representatives, "overjoyed to see Jiang [Chiang] go," promised a huge amount of aid.[71]

Mao, however, did not want to negotiate. He was ready to discuss only the surrender of the Guomindang army. On January 14 he announced his eight-point peace proposal that left no room for negotiation: he demanded the abolishment of the Guomindang regime and the handover of state power to "a democratic coalition government," that is, to the Communist Party.[72] That evening Chiang wrote in his diaries, "After 10:00 [p.m.] son Jing informed me of the eight peace proposals announced by bandit Mao Zedong this evening as the basis for negotiations. He really showed no repentance at all, and he wants to carry out the rebellion until the end. We must immediately announce his proposals to let the army and the people know who is responsible for the war."[73]

In this environment, on January 16, 1949, Chiang Kai-shek visited the Mausoleum of Sun Yat-sen, bowed three times before the tomb of the Teacher, as if asking his blessing, and in the evening he hosted an official dinner for leaders of the party and the government. Five days later, on January 21, at a session of the Standing Committee of the CEC, he announced his retirement. Many of the committee members were shocked, and numerous attendees wept. At four o'clock that afternoon he flew off to Hangzhou.[74] That night he wrote in his diaries, "Only now do I feel calm. I thank the Almighty for His grace, for helping me to step away from my affairs so easily. This is truly happiness." The next day he flew to his native village of Xikou, where at once he visited his mother's grave to bow before her ashes.[75]

General Li Zongren, who became the acting president, immediately suspended martial law and entered into negotiations with the communists. But nothing came of them. On January 31, 1949, per agreement with General Fu Zuoyi, who had been defending Beiping but betrayed Chiang, units of the communist army entered the city without firing a shot. The communists then published a list of forty-five people they considered to be war criminals and demanded they be arrested immediately before a truce could be worked out. Among the forty-five people on the list were Chiang, Meiling, Ching-kuo, and T. V. Song. General Li tried his best to reach an agreement with the communists and even signed an order releasing their old friend Zhang Xueliang from custody. By this time Zhang had been transferred to Taiwan, but despite having retired Chiang continued to hold power in his hands and countermanded the order. In early March representatives of Li Zongren visited Chiang in Xikou to persuade him to go abroad, but he refused. It was then that he issued a secret order to transfer China's gold reserves to Taiwan. He appointed his son Ching-kuo to direct this operation. According to various sources more than 112.38 tons of gold and an enormous amount of silver were shipped out from Shanghai. At the same time, more than US $15,270,000 were transferred to banks in the United States.[76] On April 20 Li Zongren was forced to reject the demands of the communists.[77]

The communists then struck at Nanjing. An eyewitness wrote, "The peace negotiation between Nationalist Vice President Li Tsung-jen [Li Zongren] and the Chinese Communists collapsed suddenly on Wednesday [April 20]. That night there was heavy bombardment across the Yangtse [Yangzi] River." On April 22 evacuation began: "Planes shuttled overhead all day long moving out party and government officials and others who wished to leave and could find the money for [a] ticket. . . . There is real fear here of rioting and looting."[78] The next day the communists took the city.

Li Zongren fled to his native land, Guilin, in Guangxi province. Earlier, on February 5, the Guomindang government had relocated to Canton. Even earlier, on January 24, T. V. Song had left for Hong Kong. From there he would sail to Paris in May, and in early June, like Kong Xiangxi and his wife, he would settle in the States. On June 10, 1949, the Shanghai Chamber of Commerce would demand that the Guomindang government return T. V. Song and Kong Xiangxi to China to be remanded to court for trial on charges of corruption, machinations in the Chinese stock market, and monopolizing what they called "normal channels of trade," but no one heeded these demands.[79] In March 1949 Sun Yat-sen's son, Sun Fo, abandoned Chiang. He and his wife left for Hong Kong, and in 1951, like T. V. Song before them, moved to France and then to the United States.[80]

Everything was falling apart. Even foreigners who lived in China "together with the Chinese population, though in a considerably less degree . . . suffered increasingly from maladministration by most of the dominant figures of the Nationalist regime."[81] Under these circumstances Chiang decided to take power into his own hands again. On April 25 he visited the grave of his beloved mother for the last time. He stood there a long time, head bowed and whispering words of farewell, and then he turned around and left Xikou forever. That same day he traveled to the port city of Ninghai, located south of the city of Ningbo. A warship awaited him there, on which, accompanied by Ching-kuo, he set sail for Shanghai to undertake its defense.[82] But the largest megalopolis of the country fell on May 27, as the Second and Third Field Armies of the communists, under the command of Liu Bocheng, Deng Xiaoping, and Chen Yi (not to be confused with the Guomindang governor of Taiwan Chen Yi—their given names are written with different Chinese characters), in the course of a week routed the two-hundred-thousand-man Guomindang force that was defending the city.

Chiang was not present at the fall of Shanghai. Early in May he sailed out of the besieged city to one of the Pescadores Islands in the Taiwan Strait and from there, at the end of May, to Taiwan. Realizing that the war on the mainland was drawing to a close, he decided to ascertain whether it would be possible to dig in on the island. He wrote in his diaries that he "very much wanted to make it a Three Principles of the People province."[83] Five months earlier, at the end of December 1948, he had appointed General Chen Cheng, who was loyal to him, as the new governor of Taiwan. Early in 1949 Chen had initiated agrarian reform, lowering rents from 50–75 percent to 37.5 percent and releasing peasants from their debts. In May 1949 he proclaimed martial law on the island to put a stop to the subversive activities of the communists. That month Chiang received a letter from his old friend General Wedemeyer advising him to create on Taiwan "a base of [further] operation and the most effective government devoted to promoting the welfare of the islanders."[84]

In June Chiang arrived in Canton, where he organized an eleven-person Supreme Political Committee of the Guomindang with himself as the head and Li Zongren his deputy. This committee in essence replaced the government. General Yan Xishan formally became head of the Executive Yuan and also a member of the Supreme Political Committee. Then Chiang again left for Taiwan and from there, on July 10, he paid a visit to the Philippines to make an agreement with the Philippine president to jointly repel the communist danger. He received support, at least verbally. Several days later he was back in Canton, where, on July 16, he reported on his successful negotiations in the Philippines. That same day at a joint session of the Political and Standing Committees of the Guomindang CEC, a new organ of power—the Emergency Supreme Council—was established, also headed by Chiang Kai-shek with Li Zongren as his deputy.[85]

But neither Chiang nor Li nor the other members of all committees were able to do anything any longer. No one and nothing could save the Guomindang. The communist forces flowed south in a mighty stream. No longer able to change anything, Chiang poured out his indignation in an open letter to Guomindang members, asserting that the current shameful defeat is the result of the "notorious factional struggles" in the party from its founding in 1905.[86]

On July 21 Chiang again flew to Taipei, where, on August 1, he established his new headquarters in Caoshan.[87] A week later he set off on another trip abroad, this time to South Korea, to discuss the issue of a joint struggle against communism with the president there. There, too, he received assurances of unconditional support.[88] Afterward, in a speech marking the fourth anniversary of the liberation of Taiwan from the Japanese colonizers, Chiang declared that "Formosa is meant to be the bastion of resistance to the plans of Russian imperialism, and is already such a bastion."[89]

On the mainland the situation worsened by the day. On August 23 Chiang arrived in Canton, convened an urgent military conference, and two days later flew to Sichuan, where he visited Chongqing and Chengdu, and then, in mid-September, again flew to Canton to direct its defense. By this time, early September, the Guomindang government had moved to Chongqing again, as it had during the Second World War. Chiang went from Canton to Xiamen, in Fujian province, in late September, and from there he flew to Taipei.[90]

Meanwhile, on October 1 in Beijing, which had received its former name ten days earlier, on the central square of Tiananmen, Mao Zedong proclaimed the founding of the Central People's Government of the People's Republic of China. The next day the Soviet Union recognized this government and broke diplomatic relations with Chiang Kai-shek.[91] Several Western journalists opined that Chiang would immediately declare war against the USSR, but that did not happen. Chiang simply asserted that "the Third World War has already begun."[92]

On October 14 Canton fell. On November 14 Chiang flew to Chongqing from Taipei, but at the end of the month he fled to Chengdu, the last bastion of resistance on Mainland China. On December 5 he gave an interview to representatives of the press, asserting that "the struggle on Chinese territory will continue at any price, regardless of the sacrifices," but just two days later the National government of China moved from Chengdu to Taipei.[93] But not everyone. President Li Zongren left Guangxi for the United States on the pretext of treatment for gastritis.[94] He would supposedly receive treatment for fifteen years, and in 1965, on the eve of the Cultural Revolution, he was pardoned by Mao Zedong and returned to China. He died of pneumonia in Beijing on January 30, 1969.

In the meantime, at two o'clock in the afternoon on December 10, the Generalissimo, along with his eldest son Ching-kuo (Meiling was still in America), were among the last to board a plane in Chengdu, which at once began to taxi down the runway. The number of the airplane—219—and the two characters painted on its side—Meiling—glistened in the rays of the sun. Chiang had named the plane in honor of his wife. Through the window he watched the buildings of the airport pass by, then the fields and rice paddies, and soon Chiang was able to view the entire city of Chengdu quickly receding from him. Lifting off, the plane headed east. Chiang saw the glow of flames. Below a battle was raging, yet its outcome was not in doubt. The storming of the capital of Sichuan province that the communists had begun early that morning was powerful. That Chengdu, the last surviving stronghold of the Nationalists on the mainland, would fall was inevitable. The battle for Mainland China was lost, but Chiang did not want to think about that. His will remained unbroken. He was flying to the island of Taiwan to continue the struggle against the communists, firmly recalling the words of Sun Yat-sen: "Final victory belongs to those who fight until the last."[95]

CHAPTER 22

# *Taiwan's Prisoner*

The island of Taiwan (Formosa), whose beauty so impressed the Portuguese, lies 112 miles off the southeast coast of China. Stretching 245 miles from north to south, it is rather narrow across; at its widest it is 90 miles from east to west. Its shape on the map looks like a large papaya floating in the ocean. The island is about 14,000 square miles in area, but only one-third is suited for agriculture: basic agricultural crops include rice, sugar cane, pineapples, and tea. Two-thirds of the island are hills and mountains covered with evergreen trees, palm trees, bamboo, cypress, fir, and camphor trees. Along the shores stretch the undergrowth of mangrove trees. The climate is tropical and humid. June to August is the rainy season, when a constant light drizzle turns into a downpour from time to time. The rain brings a bit of cooling in the summer, the hot season when temperatures of 86–95 degrees Fahrenheit are common. The rest of the year is warm, around 75 degrees, and dry. Overall, Taiwan is a typical tropical island, a paradise.

Until the mid-sixteenth century there were almost no Chinese there. Austronesian aboriginals, who look entirely different from their neighbors from China, were the masters of the island.[1] But then migration from Mainland China began, intensifying especially during the era of the Qing dynasty, which incorporated Taiwan into the Chinese empire in 1683. Prior to that, the Dutch established themselves on the southwestern coast in the sixteenth century, and then the Portuguese in the north. In the early 1660s, when almost all China was under the rule of the Manchus, the Chinese naval commander Zheng Chenggong (1624–62), who hated both the Qing and the Europeans, defeated the Dutch colonists and on the site of the Dutch colony founded a Chinese state called Dongning (Eastern Peace). But it lasted for only twenty-two years and fell under the blows of the Qing.

For a long time Taiwan was administered as part of Fujian province, but in 1887 the Qing carved it out as a separate province. In 1895 it was seized by the Japanese, who routed the Chinese Empire in the war of 1894–95. Taiwan became a colony of Japanese imperialism and remained so until China's victory in the Second World War.

Colonial rule left a deep impression on the way of life and the social and economic conditions of the island population, which, prior to the Second World War, numbered slightly more than five million persons. Among them more than 4.7 million were native Taiwanese, that is, Chinese born on Taiwan; Japanese, more than 250,000; Chinese, about 45,000, who came in the twentieth century; and aborigines, about 150,000, who had long since been relocated to the mountains by the Chinese who occupied the fertile valleys.[2] The Japanese not only exploited their subjects but also civilized them. They established civil order, stabilized the currency, undertook a cadastre—a complete land survey—and invested money in infrastructure, hydropower, and mechanized agriculture. They developed the educational system (in 1937 more than half a million Taiwanese children were enrolled in school, and more than four thousand young men and women were enrolled in higher education); organized peasant associations and credit unions; introduced a system of elections for local and rural administration (by 1939 more than 286,000 Taiwanese men, twenty-five years old and up, received the right to vote). In sum, prior to the Second World War, Taiwan was prospering. The income level of the population was steadily growing. Between 1926 and 1930 the annual growth in GNP was more than 8 percent, and in 1931–35, despite the world economic crisis, it was 5.21 percent.[3] Edgar Snow, an American journalist who visited the island in 1930, recalled that "it was a colony, of course, but the administration seemed free of graft and people seemed secure in their homes and property as long as they obeyed the law. The land was clean and prosperous, beggars were rare, public services including sanitation and health were good, there were numerous schools, and Formosa had a higher standard of living and a higher percentage of literacy than any province of China."[4] By mid-1949, that is, when Chiang Kai-shek's troops began their flight to Taiwan—the first streams of refugees headed there immediately after the Communists had crossed the Yangzi River in late May 1949—the population of the island had already grown to 6.5 million. The majority, as before, were native-born Taiwanese whose ancestors had emigrated from the mainland (basically from Fujian and Guangdong provinces) in the sixteenth to nineteenth centuries. The new migrants, who had come from the mainland in the twentieth century, or, as the Taiwanese called them, the people from Tang Mountain (Tang Mountain was the Taiwanese term for the Chinese mainland), already numbered more than 60,000. The former masters of Taiwan, the aborigines, numbered about 200,000.[5]

With the arrival of Chiang Kai-shek's troops and civilian refugees, the population of the island increased by more than 1.5 million. More than 600,000 of these people were seen as "the flower of the nation": professors, engineers, technicians, and professional administrators. In the words of the American specialist Neil H. Jacoby, they constituted "an increment of human talent in a relatively small country without parallel."[6] This provided the foundation for the rapid development of Taiwan.

Chiang Kai-shek himself and his eldest son arrived in Taipei, after a six-and-a-half-hour flight from Chengdu, at 8:30 p.m. on December 10. An automobile was waiting for them at the ramp. It was unusually quiet. Taipei was as different from frontline Chengdu "as Heaven from earth." Chiang happily breathed the pure air, sat down in the car, and set off for the nearby Caoshan. There, on the slope of a hill covered with evergreen trees, some ten miles north of the city was situated the house where he had stayed a number of times already. Chiang called it *Caolu* (Grass Hut). That night he went to sleep around midnight.[7]

He loved the house, which had been built many years before for the future emperor of Japan Hirohito who had visited Taiwan. From its windows a marvelous view opened out onto the neighboring hills and fields. The following year he would move in the spring to a more spacious house located on the spur of the Caoshan. It was in the northern district of Shilin (Forest of Warriors) in a large park complex whose address is 60 Fulin Street, Taipei. From time to time, however, he would continue to come back to *Caolu* to breathe in the mountain air. In March 1950 he came up with the idea of renaming the Caoshan Mountains that he liked so much as Yangming Mountains, in honor of his favorite philosopher, Wang Yangming. On March 31 the provincial government of Taiwan adopted a resolution to this effect that came into force a month later.[8]

Because of his love for the Yangming Mountains, a Taipei newspaper described him as "the decrepit old man of the Caoshan" and even as "A bandit hiding in tall grass." This newspaper represented the interests of the native Taiwanese, who disliked the people from Tang Mountain after the bloody events of February 28, 1947. Chiang was enraged, demanded that the paper be shut down and the author of the article arrested.[9] Many years after Chiang's death, in early 2007, the Caoshan xingguan museum, that is, the Caoshan Villa, was opened in this house, but shortly thereafter, in April, it burned to the ground. Now there is only a restaurant and an exhibition hall on this site with pictures of Chiang Kai-shek.[10]

All that, however, would come later. Meanwhile, after resting in *Caolu* for one day, on December 12 Chiang received the chief of counterintelligence in the Ministry of Defense[11] Mao Renfeng, to discuss a plan for organizing a countrywide guerrilla movement on the territories of China occupied by the communists. On December 13 he mapped out the immediate tasks: "1. Reducing and reorganizing the Central government; 2. Reorganizing the Central [Executive] Committee [of the Guomindang]; 3. Reorganizing and holding elections for the provincial government of Taiwan; 4. Unifying central and local organs; and 5. Appointing [Wu] Guozhen as acting chair of the provincial government of Taiwan to sound out the attitude of the United States toward providing aid to China."[12] At that time the fifth task was the crucial one for Chiang. Without aid from the United States his regime would inevitably collapse in the near future. Even the most optimistic pro-Chiang commentators predicted its fall by the end of 1950.[13] That is precisely why Chiang had nominated Wu Guozhen (also known as K. C. Wu) for the governorship of Taiwan. A diplomat and political leader, K. C. Wu, who had a doctorate in political science, was the former mayor of Chongqing, deputy minister of foreign affairs in 1943–45, and the mayor of Shanghai (1945–49). Educated in the United States, where he defended his dissertation at Princeton in 1926, K. C. Wu was at ease among Americans and therefore could be more useful to Chiang than anybody else.[14] On December 15 Chen Cheng divested himself of the authority of the governor and K. C. Wu was appointed in his place.[15]

On Christmas Day Chiang, together with Ching-kuo and his family, traveled to the picturesque Riyuetan (Sun Moon Lake), located in the very center of Taiwan in the mountains. Its name derived from its shape: the eastern part of the lake was round like the sun while the western part was long and thin, like the crescent moon. Chiang, his son, daughter-in-law, and grandsons stayed in a comfortable private house named Hanbi (Jasper) on a small peninsula on the northern shore of the lake. (There is a hotel there at present.) "Nice scenery, heart and soul gradually calm down," Chiang wrote in his diaries.[16] They spent the whole day on the lake in a small boat, strolled around the small island of Lalu situated in the middle of the lake, and in the evening gathered around the Christmas tree at the holiday table. After praising God and dining, they watched a film.

The idyllic rest continued the next day. Chiang rose, thanked the Almighty for having helped him escape from Xi'an thirteen years earlier, and then went to pass out Christmas presents for his son, daughter-in-law, and grandsons. Then all of them went for another stroll, and Chiang even caught a fish, which he had done very rarely in his life. He hooked a large fish that the Chinese call *quyaoyu* (that looks like a long carp). It was prepared for dinner, and Chiang liked it so much that, hearing of this, everyone on Taiwan thereafter began calling it "president fish." The family members and servants were very glad, and they unanimously asserted that this was an auspicious catch, a good omen indicating that the coming year would be a happy one.[17]

But Chiang understood that even a large fish was not big enough to satisfy his desires. There were too many of them. "This past year everything has fallen completely apart—the party, the state, the economy, the army, foreign policy, and education . . . and there is no hope at all," he wrote that day in his diaries.[18]

He was not quite right, however. The fish fulfilled at least one of his desires: Chiang very much wanted Meiling to return promptly from the United States, and on January 13, 1950, she arrived, and he was able to embrace her again. Although many people, including her sister Ailing and even Roosevelt's widow, Eleanor, tried to dissuade Meiling from going to Taiwan, she nevertheless decided to share her husband's fate. In her own words, at dawn she suddenly heard a Voice saying, "All is right," and after that she had no further doubts. At once she rushed to her elder sister's bedroom (Meiling lived in the Kongs' house) and declared that God had ordered her to return home.[19]

Chiang was indescribably happy, and as soon as Meiling got off the plane he took her at once to a nearby country home in the village of Daxi (Big Brook), about thirty minutes from the airport.[20] He loved this place, whose natural beauty reminded him of his native Xikou. Along the road, he clasped her hand tightly while she poured out her story to him of her mission to the United States. Unfortunately for them, a failed mission.

President Truman, now thoroughly disillusioned with Chiang Kai-shek and considering his regime "about the rottenest government that ever existed," did not want to help him anymore.[21] "Let the dust settle," he decided as he began to study the possibility of rapprochement with Communist

China.[22] At just this time a conflict between the leader of the Yugoslavian communists, Josip Broz Tito, and Stalin broke out. Both Truman and his State Department were hoping for a similar split between Stalin and Mao in the near future. The specter of Titoism began to stir the minds of American politicians, many of whom resurrected the fable of "a democratic Mao." They were ready to sacrifice Taiwan in the cause of winning over the leader of the CCP and the Titoization of New China.

On December 30, 1949, Truman approved National Security Council Resolution No. 48/2, which emphasized that "the United States should continue the policies of avoiding military and political support of any non-Communist elements in China," but "should exploit, through appropriate political, psychological and economic means, any rifts between the Chinese Communists and the USSR and between the Stalinists and other elements in China."[23]

On January 5, 1950, President Truman, speaking to journalists in the White House, delivered an open "Statement on Formosa," emphasizing that "the United States Government will not pursue a course which will lead to involvement in the civil conflict in China. Similarly, the United States Government will not provide military aid or advice to Chinese forces on Formosa."[24] On January 12 and 16 Secretary of State Dean Acheson repeated the same words.[25] Chiang was shocked.[26]

At the same time, a version of a proclamation declaring the independence of Formosa as neither Communist nor Nationalist was being carefully considered in Washington. There were many games going on. Agents of the United States established contacts with Chinese liberals who had emigrated to Hong Kong and linked up with pro-American military officers in Chiang Kai-shek's army. In the first instance they met with General Sun Liren, the commander of Guomindang forces on Taiwan, and at the same time they were holding talks with Taiwan nationalists based in Tokyo.[27] In this connection, Truman even met with T. V. Song, who, it will be recalled, had fled to America. From the summer of 1949 Song had been living in Manhattan, at 1133 Park Avenue, not far from Central Park and the Metropolitan Museum. According to various sources, Truman unequivocally offered him aid if he agreed to head the regime on Taiwan: "If you agree, we will put you in power." It is said that T. V. Song was tempted and even composed a list of the new government comprising fifty names. But his sister Meiling, who was also in New York at the time, and members of the Kong family found out. They were all outraged at his treachery, and David Kong even said he would kill the scoundrel. But Meiling stopped him: "After all," she said, "he is your uncle."[28]

Whether this story is true or not is uncertain, but that the Americans themselves were contemplating various plans for an attempt on Chiang's life at this time is true.[29] But none of the plans was carried out. In any case, at the end of February 1950 the position of the United States began to change. On February 14, in Moscow, Mao and Stalin had signed a Treaty of Friendship, Alliance and Mutual Assistance with a term of thirty years.[30] And thus the hope that Mao would take the Titoist path dissipated.

Meanwhile, Chiang and Meiling took pleasure in each other's company after a long separation. Now they resumed praying together. Chiang experienced such a spiritual uplift that he sat down to write a work titled "The Survival of China and the Question of Success or Failure of the Nations of the East in the Struggle for Freedom and Independence."[31] He didn't finish it, however, so it was never published.

At the same time, Chiang Kai-shek consolidated his official positions on Taiwan. In February 1950, despite insistent requests from a number of Guomindang leaders that he return to the motherland, the acting president of China, General Li Zongren, decided to remain in the United States for health reasons, as he informed Taipei. Then, at the request of members of the highest party and government organs, on March 1 Chiang Kai-shek returned to the post of president. The next day, at a reception of more than two thousand officials, he announced the basic principles of his program: "In the military field: to consolidate the base on Taiwan in preparation for the eventual recovery of the mainland. 2. In international relations: from self-reliance to the formation of an anticommunist alliance with the democratic countries. 3. In the economic field: to practice austerity, to increase productivity and to implement Dr. Sun's Principle of People's Livelihood. 4. In the political field: to protect fundamental human rights and the rule of law."[32] "The communists have turned China over to a Russian cabal," he added. "China is on the threshold of its greatest catastrophe throughout its five-thousand-year history."[33]

Two days later Chiang and Meiling greeted a crowd of 100,000 citizens who had assembled in the square in front of the Presidential Office Building to express their delight at Chiang's return to the post of president.[34] It is possible that many of the people gathered on the square really were happy, although it was not they who had voted for Chiang, who was simply returning to the position to which deputies of the National Assembly had elected him on April 19, 1948.

Beforehand, in February 1950, on his own initiative, the former commander of United States Naval Forces Western Pacific (the Seventh Fleet),

Admiral Charles M. Cooke Jr., nicknamed Savvy, arrived in Taipei. He had been retired since May 1948 and, after arriving in Taiwan, offered his services to Chiang. Chiang had known him since 1946, respected him as a talented military commander, and therefore gladly made him his advisor. He trusted him so much that in the spring of 1950 he accepted Cooke's revisionist proposal to evacuate Guomindang troops from the Zhoushan Islands located close to the Zhejiang city of Ningbo.

At that time, in addition to Taiwan, Chiang Kai-shek's forces still controlled not only these islands, but also the Dachens, located just south of the Zhoushans, across from the city of Taizhou in Zhejiang province; the Mazu (Matsu) Islands; Jinmen (Quemoy) and the Pescadores in the Taiwan Strait; and Hainan island in the South China Sea. But in early May 1950 the communists seized Hainan. They could just as easily have taken the Zhoushan islands, which lay just 1 nautical mile from the coast of the PRC but almost 350 miles from Taiwan. That is precisely why Cooke thought it was necessary to abandon the farther islands and concentrate all forces on the defense of Taiwan and other islands in the strait. On May 16 Chiang evacuated 150,000 officers and men from these islands, yielding them to the communists without a fight.[35] But that same day he declared that he would defend Taiwan, either dying in battle or committing suicide. "I will keep my word," he added.[36] Around the same time, he and Meiling addressed the women of China, calling on them "to use their influence in the family for the struggle against communism."[37]

Cooke fully supported Chiang, but after the fall of Hainan panic set in among the inhabitants of Taiwan, including foreigners. Everyone was expecting a communist invasion and the inevitable seizure of the island no later than the middle of July 1950. American diplomats on Taiwan believed that Chiang's government would run off to Manila or Seoul in the very near future.[38] In Washington voices were again heard demanding either replacement of Chiang by General Sun Liren—in secret messages to the Department of State he assured them he was ready to take power at any minute—or placing Taiwan under the rule of the United Nations or returning Taiwan to Japan or subordinating the island to General MacArthur, who was still commanding Allied occupation forces in Japan. According to several sources, Chiang himself was ready to leave if Truman would defend Taiwan from the communists. He even personally invited MacArthur to Taiwan.[39]

But on June 25, 1950, the international situation, and with it the position of Chiang Kai-shek, changed dramatically. On that day North Korean communists, via an agreement with Stalin, unleashed a war against South Korea, one of the allies of the United States.[40] This event is what saved Taiwan. Truman understood that it was necessary to save all his friends in East Asia, including Chiang Kai-shek, who were threatened by the communist invasion.

The welcome news that war had begun in Korea was given to Chiang by Ching-kuo, who since July 1949 had headed the Guomindang's secret services.[41] Chiang saw this development as a second Pearl Harbor,[42] a gift of fate.[43] Several hours later the U.N. Security Council, convened by request of the United States, censured the North Koreans. The resolution expressing that censure was adopted by a vote of nine in favor. Only one country abstained, Stalin's bête noire, Yugoslavia; there were no votes against because the Soviet Union was boycotting the session. Two days later the Security Council, again in the absence of the Soviet representative, approved the use of international armed forces against the Korean People's Army (KPA), and soon fifteen countries took part in repelling the aggressor; fifty-three countries voted in favor of the use of force.[44] That same day, June 27, Truman sent the US Seventh Fleet into the Taiwan Strait to block any attempts by the Chinese communists to seize the island. In this connection, he stressed, "The occupation of Formosa by Communist forces would be a direct threat to the security of the Pacific area and to the United States forces performing their lawful and necessary functions in this area."[45]

Two days later Chiang expressed the desire to take part in the Korean War, seeking agreement from the Americans to send 33,000 of his own troops (two divisions) to Korea under the command of General Sun Liren, who, unknown to Chiang, was secretly making plans to overthrow him. To do so he was prepared to evacuate the islands of Jinmen (Quemoy) in the Taiwan Strait, in close proximity to the city of Xiamen in Fujian province.[46] He requested that the Americans fully arm these divisions and train them in modern warfare over a two-year period. According to the testimony of then assistant secretary of state for Far Eastern affairs, Dean Rusk, "The whole idea was an illusion." Chiang understood that the Americans would reject his proposal because sending Guomindang troops to Korea could jeopardize the security of Taiwan itself. But he wanted to demonstrate his fidelity to his duty as an ally.[47] Truman was initially well-disposed toward this idea, but under the influence of Secretary of State Acheson and the chiefs of staff he ultimately rejected it.[48]

Soon, at the end of July 1950, MacArthur flew in to see Chiang. But not in order to take over leadership of the island. Rather, he wanted to find out if Chiang could defend the island militarily and to express his fervent support of the Generalissimo. He acted on his own initiative without clearing his visit with Truman or the State Department.

MacArthur had long sympathized with Chiang Kai-shek, and from the fall of 1948 he had persistently asserted to the Truman administration that "the strategic interests of the United States will be in serious jeopardy if Formosa is allowed to be dominated by a power hostile to the United States."[49] At the end of May 1950 he compared Taiwan to "an unsinkable aircraft carrier and submarine tender" that under no circumstances should be surrendered to the communists.[50] On the eve of the Korean War he repeated his favorite comparison, calling on Washington to take "political, economic, and military measures . . . to prevent the fall of Formosa."[51]

Now he had flown into Taipei. "It was a great pleasure for me to meet my old comrade-in-arms of the last war, Generalissimo Chiang Kai-shek," he recalled. "His indomitable determination to resist the Communist domination aroused my sincere admiration."[52] Chiang discussed with MacArthur his proposal to send Guomindang troops to Korea, but MacArthur, who initially nurtured the idea, ultimately rejected it. He did not want Chiang to dissipate his forces. On the contrary, he urged Chiang to do everything necessary to fortify Taiwan.[53]

After returning to Tokyo, MacArthur dispatched his deputy, General Alonzo Fox, on a three-week inspection tour of Taipei to determine what arms the Guomindang army needed. Fox recommended providing Chiang with $158.2 million of arms, but Truman did not agree to allocate the funds.[54] The incensed MacArthur, believing that the president had again unfairly "conceived a violent animosity toward Chiang Kai-shek,"[55] this time in front of the annual meeting of the Veterans of Foreign Wars, declared that Taiwan is "an unsinkable aircraft carrier" that must be fortified.[56]

Only after Mao, following Stalin's wishes, on October 19, 1950, sent four field armies and three artillery divisions to Korea to the aid of the North Korean communists, did Truman become inclined to arm Taiwan. Striking while the iron was hot, in late December 1950 Chiang openly addressed the United States, calling on it "to provide leadership to all the peoples and governments of Asia that are now fighting to preserve their freedom." He stressed that "the most pressing task today is to find the means to prevent the spread to other parts of Asia of the fire begun by the communists in Korea. This is the fundamental condition for thwarting the Soviet imperialist policy aimed at achieving world domination."[57]

In February 1951 Truman finally decided to allot $71.2 million for Taiwan's military needs. That was still a modest sum, but the first step is the hardest.[58]

In subsequent years US military aid to Chiang rapidly increased, and by April 1955 it amounted to $948 million.[59] Starting in the spring of 1951 a group of American military advisors headed by a hero of the Pacific War, Major General William C. Chase, began working in Taipei. By the end of 1951 it comprised 360 persons. At the same time, American bases began to be constructed on the island.[60]

Having undertaken the defense of Taiwan, however, the Americans posed strict conditions to Chiang: Chase's group would wholly control the island's military budget. Otherwise Truman would refuse to arm Chiang's regime. Chiang was outraged by this ultimatum and could not sleep because of the indignation he felt—but he had to accept it.[61] Without help from the United States he simply could not survive and therefore no longer even dream of equality in relation to America.[62]

Had Truman not continued to snub Chiang politically, his resentment would not have mattered. Under pressure from the British, who, in early January 1950, had recognized the People's Republic of China as the sole legal government of China, Truman agreed, for example, that the representatives of Chiang Kai-shek not be invited to sign the peace treaty with Japan in San Francisco in September 1951. This affront occurred notwithstanding the fact that Guomindang China had borne on its shoulders the basic burden of the war against Japan. Behind Chiang's back the United States and Great Britain agreed not to invite any Chinese to San Francisco because the British did not recognize the Nationalists and the Americans did not recognize the Communists. Apprised of this, a stunned Chiang protested, but he was ignored.[63] Then the president of Taiwan decided to go on a hunger strike. On September 9, the day that representatives of forty-nine nations signed the peace treaty—among which not only China was missing but also, for various reasons, the USSR, Mongolia, Korea, Burma, and India—he refused to eat breakfast.[64]

Not until April 28, 1952, did the Republic of China sign a bilateral peace treaty with Japan (without annexes or reparations), after the Japanese, bypassing all proprieties, received from the Americans and the British the illegal right to choose with whom they would sign a treaty, with Chiang or with Mao. They chose Chiang.[65] Meanwhile Chiang focused on implementing a whole series of reforms in Taiwan, several of which he had outlined in December 1949. The chief ones were economic—agrarian and industrial.

Several years later these reforms inspired people around the world to speak of "the Taiwan miracle." Chiang himself provided the theoretical foundation of these reforms, radically revising the previous economic views he had systematically expounded in *China's Destiny* and *Chinese Economic Theory.* In place of the state taking over the economy, he now advocated privatization, acknowledging that at the present stage of the development of Chinese society that is what was needed. He called this society exactly what Deng Xiaoping would call it later on: *xiaokang,* that is, a society of "moderate prosperity" or a "relatively well-off society."[66] "In this society goods are produced for profit, and people work for wages," in contrast to the ideal society of *datong* (the Grand Union), in which "the goal of production is the satisfaction of the needs of the population. . . . [L]abor serves all society and is not labor for the sake of wages." The society of *datong* still embodied the ultimate economic goal of the Three Principles of the People, of the Guomindang, and of Chiang himself, but China itself was not yet ready for it from Chiang's perspective. "By comparing two stages of the development of society—xiaokang and datong," he said, "it becomes clear that construction . . . proceeds along the steps of a ladder—from . . . [*xiaokang* to *datong*]. The task of our revolution and of national reconstruction must move forward on the steps of this ladder, in order to achieve a society of freedom and peace . . . [*datong*]."[67]

General Chen Cheng, the former governor of Taiwan whom Chiang appointed as head of the Executive Yuan on March 15, 1950, played an enormous role in implementing these ideas. In June 1951 the reduction of agricultural land rent to 37.5 percent that he had initiated in early 1949 had been carried out everywhere and was put into law. Chen then began the second phase of agrarian reform, allowing tenants who worked public lands—that is, land that had previously been the property of Japanese colonists and then had become the property of the Taiwan government—to purchase them on an installment plan over a ten-year period at below-market prices (they had to pay 250 percent of the value of the annual harvest from this land). By July 1952, more than 150,000 families of former tenants became landowners. In early 1953 the third stage of reform began. Under the slogan "Land to those who till it," farmers were given not only the remaining public land, but also surplus land from the large landowners (according to a new law, one could not have more than 2.84 hectares of irrigated land and 5.68 hectares of unirrigated land). Those who lost surplus land received compensation from the government in the form of land bonds as well as the stocks of several state enterprises—again at the rate of 250 percent of the value of the annual harvest from the land.[68]

The overall result of the reform was that more than 70 percent of all cultivated land was transferred to rural tillers, and 86 percent of farmers became landowners. This led to an increase in their material well-being, the rapid growth of the middle class, and development of the consumer market; all of these programs gave a powerful boost to both agriculture and industry.[69] At the same time, measures were taken to supply the countryside with technical equipment as well as to develop a health and educational system for the rural population. The result was that by 1952 the prewar level of production was restored, and, compared to 1948, the yield of rice per hectare had increased by 19 percent. By 1959 the yield of rice per hectare had increased by a further 31 percent. Farmers' incomes also increased: by 1952 by 81 percent; and by 1959 by a further 50 percent.[70]

As in agriculture, the industrial reform was aimed at increasing the numbers of the middle class and at strengthening its position in the economy. From the early 1950s Chiang and his government began the broad-scale privatization of state enterprises: the widespread elimination of all monopolies that had become pervasive during the administration of the first Guomindang governor of the island, General Chen Yi (1945–47). Chen had tried to let the state take over everything possible, including trade and production of camphor oil, matches, wine, and cigarettes, thereby making life impossible for petty proprietors.[71] It was precisely this policy that, along with corruption, inflation, price increases, and unemployment had led to the bloody events of February 28, 1947.

But now Chiang and Chen Cheng were working to create a society of *xiaokang* in the cities as well. In the twelve years from 1951 to 1963, the share of private companies increased from 45 to 62 percent. The number of private firms increased from 68,000 to 227,000.[72] In 1953 the first four-year plan for economic development was adopted. It was directed toward completing the reconstruction of the country and further increasing the production of rice, fertilizer, and electric power.[73]

Closely related to the agrarian and industrial reforms was the financial reform that Chiang carried out in close cooperation with the Americans and using their credits; from 1950 to April 1955 US economic aid to Taiwan totaled US $527 million.[74] This reform was implemented by a special Economic Stabilization Board that adopted measures to strengthen the Taiwan currency, the New Taiwan dollar put into circulation in June 1949. By the end of 1954 prices on basic goods had stabilized overall, the pace of inflation had slowed drastically, and, with the help of American grants, the budget deficit was easily covered.[75]

Party reform, which began in August 1950, also was of particular importance. Chiang had long been contemplating such renovation, having concluded, under the influence of defeats at the hands of the communists, that the Guomindang had lost spirit and that the members of the party lacked "discipline and even more . . . standards of right and wrong." "Never, in the history of China, or abroad," he said, "has there been a revolutionary party as decrepit and degenerate as we are today."[76] Both the party and its youth organization, he regretted, are "mere empty shells, without any real strength." Comparing the Guomindang to the Communist party, he came to the disturbing conclusion that "nowhere are our methods or actions the equal of theirs," because "most of our cadres do not use their brains and are unwilling to study, are neither careful nor reliable . . . and thus we sink in defeat."

He referred favorably to the Maoist *zhengfeng*—the wide-scale purge of the Communist Party—carried out in 1942–45. Barely having established himself on Taiwan, he tried to do something similar. "If only we can study everything of theirs [the communists] and comprehend everything of theirs, we can then have assurance of annihilating them," he believed.[77]

Chiang presented a draft of party reform as early as July 1949 at a meeting with members of the CEC of the Guomindang in Canton, but at the time, for understandable reasons, it was impossible to implement the reform. Now, in 1950, he began to implement it: first of all, in May he required all members of the central organs of the party to swear an oath personally to him, following Sun Yat-sen, who had also demanded this. On July 22 he dissolved the CEC and the CCC, chosen by the Sixth Congress of the Guomindang in 1945, as well as the Standing Committee of the CEC. On August 5 he formed a Central Reorganization Commission consisting of sixteen persons chosen by him and working under his control. These were the persons most loyal to him, notably his eldest son Ching-kuo as well as the chair of the Executive Yuan Chen Cheng. Chiang did not include any of the old militarists or any leaders of the former intraparty factions in the commission because he had become disillusioned with them. He had lost confidence even in his blood nephews, Chen Lifu, who would soon leave for the United States, and Chen Guofu, who was ill with tuberculosis and could not take part in political activities. He died in a Taipei hospital on August 25, 1951.

Chiang appointed twenty-nine distinguished members of the CEC and CCC to the newly organized Central Advisory Committee (Zhongyang pingyi weiyuanhui), a special organ that permitted elderly leaders who did not wish to be pensioned off to withdraw from active work and not lose face. The members were directly subordinate to Chiang.[78] (In September 1982 Deng Xiaoping, for the same reasons, would follow this example by establishing a CCP Central Advisory Commission [Zhongyang guwen weiyuanhui].)

At the same time, instead of the purely territorial primary party units that had existed up till then, local party organizations began to be established on the territorial-production principle, as the communists did. These party cells were assigned ideological-educational as well as organizational functions.

Chiang made the party members study the documents of the Maoist *zhengfeng* movement, specially published in the context of the campaign to reorganize the Guomindang. He made it their responsibility to engage in criticism and self-criticism at party meetings as well as to hold meetings with members of the public to ascertain their needs. Chiang also introduced courses to raise the educational level of Guomindang members. Everyone was required to pay membership dues.

The so-called Institute of Revolutionary Practice (in essence a Higher Party School) was established in the Yangming Mountains for middle- and higher-level party, government, and military cadres. Chiang himself was its president, and Chiang Ching-kuo its director. During the period of reorganization 3,075 students studied there. The course of instruction lasted from four to six weeks. A series of educational programs was established for other party cadres and for rank-and-file members of the Guomindang everywhere. By the beginning of 1952 more than 40 percent of the 282,000 Guomindang members on Taiwan had a middle or higher education. A disciplinary committee was established to carry out a purge, and in the period between August 1950 and August 1952 more than a thousand violations of discipline by party members were brought to light. A number of them were expelled, some forever and some temporarily.[79]

Nonetheless, the party grew by 210,533 persons: from 72,426 in 1950 to 282,959 in 1952. Members of the Guomindang constituted 3.5 percent of 8,128,000 inhabitants of the island. In essence, this was a new, young, militant party. Persons under forty years of age constituted 80 percent of its members, 226,367, and almost 40 percent, 112,000, served in the army. A sizable number of the members, 83,300, almost 30 percent, were workers and peasants. Few women were in the Guomindang—only 5.6 percent.[80]

Having completed the party reorganization, Chiang, in October 1952, was able to convene the Seventh Congress of the Guomindang. This forum, which took place on October 10–20 in the suburbs of Taipei in the Yangming Mountains, was not a national one, although it was called that for propaganda purposes. Taking part in it were 200 delegates as well as 325 invited guests, including 173 members or candidate members of the CEC and 98 members or candidate members of the CCC, selected at the Sixth Congress. Members of the Central Reorganization Commission also attended.[81]

The congress adopted a revised statute of the Guomindang in which the reorganized party was defined as revolutionary-democratic, affirming the Leninist principle of democratic centralism borrowed from the communists. It dissolved the Central Reorganization Commission, merged the CEC and CCC into a single Central Committee, and approved the Platform of Struggle against Communism and Resistance to Russia proposed by Chiang Kai-shek. The platform defined the CCP and the USSR as the two main enemies of Free China. "We will fight against Russian aggression and Chinese Communists for the restoration of the territorial integrity of the Republic of China," the document proclaimed.[82] The ideas of the platform were the foundation for the new party program that was approved by the congress.

The congress elected thirty-two members of the Central Committee, including Chen Cheng and Chiang Ching-kuo and sixteen candidate members. It confirmed the forty-eight members of the Central Advisory Committee selected by Chiang Kai-shek. Among the latter were Meiling as well as such well-known Guomindang leaders as Wang Shijie, He Yingqin, Hu Zongnan, Zhang Qun, Yu Youren, and Yan Xishan.

The highest organ of the party again became the reestablished Standing Committee of the CC, elected at the First Plenum of the Central Committee and completely revamped. It comprised ten persons, including Chen Cheng and Chiang Ching-kuo. An official chair of this committee was not elected, but usually Chiang Kai-shek would preside at its sessions. He was not formally a member of the Standing Committee, but at the congress itself he had been reelected as *zongcai* (general director, leader).[83]

It was only the composition of the National Assembly and the Legislative and Control Yuans that Chiang was unable to revamp. These representative organs had been formed as a result of national elections, and Chiang thus considered it unacceptable to change their composition until new nationwide elections were held in China. Elections were possible only after the Guomindang returned to power on the mainland. This presented a legal conundrum. The members of the assembly and the two organs of government were aging, but Chiang Kai-shek was unable to replace them for political reasons. Instead, in early 1951 elections were held for county and municipal organs of power, and in December members of the county and municipal assemblies formed a Taiwan Provisional Provincial Assembly.[84]

Simultaneously, a reform of the military was being conducted in the early 1950s, one element of which was the restoration of the system of political commissars in the military that had been done away with after the Northern Expedition and the strengthening of ideological-political education and party control over commanders. The absence of proper education, Chiang believed, had led to a weakening of "the will to fight the enemy." The "fighting spirit was entirely lost. And, especially, [the troops] were ignorant of the need to protect and unite with the people, even unrestrainedly harassing them, so that military discipline was completely nonexistent."[85] In April 1950 Chiang appointed his son Ching-kuo as head of the Main Political Directorate of the Ministry of Defense. Ching-kuo, however, soon developed strained relations with General Chase, the chief of the group of American military advisors. General William Chase was dissatisfied with the undemocratic role the Main Political Directorate, which he viewed as the Guomindang secret service, played in the army. He demanded that it be placed under the control of his group. But Chiang sided with his son, and Chase, having achieved nothing, retired at the end of July 1955.[86]

The reorganization of the army was also successful. By the autumn of 1953 the armed forces of Taiwan had been cut in half to 600,000 (from twenty to ten armies) and refitted with American arms.[87] Its combat efficiency improved: the American advisors and instructors knew their business. At the same time, Ching-kuo organized a mass campaign to enroll military servicemen into the Guomindang in order to turn Taiwan's army into a party army. The campaign was conducted energetically, and by 1954 one-third, or 210,000, of the officers and men were members of the party.[88]

All these reforms took place against the background of the strengthening of authoritarian rule by the Guomindang and colossal expenditures on defense—up to 70 percent of the annual budget.[89] Chiang and his retinue refused to accept that the civil war was over. For them it was ongoing both before and after the Americans had begun guaranteeing their security. Therefore Chiang's promise to observe basic human rights remained unfulfilled. Not only was martial law in force on Taiwan, but the harshest form of White Terror was established, directed against the "red danger." The Guomindang secret services directed by Ching-kuo uncovered communists, spies, and saboteurs everywhere, even among generals and their wives. Many thousands of persons were arrested during the first ten years of the terror. No fewer than 2,000 people were shot, while 8,000 received harsh prison sentences. Many were thrown into a concentration camp, established by Ching-kuo's order on Lüdao Island (Green Island), situated southeast of Taiwan. The camp bore the derisive name of The New Life Institute.[90]

General Sun Liren, whose conspiratorial plans evidently became known to Chiang, was one of the victims of the terror. In June 1954 he was removed from the post of commander in chief of the armed forces and appointed to a secondary position of chief of Chiang Kai-shek's personal staff. In August of 1955 he was placed under house arrest. He was freed and rehabilitated thirteen years after Chiang's death, in March 1988.

In April 1953, after an unsuccessful attempt on his life, the liberal governor of Taiwan, K. C. Wu, retired. He and his wife fled to the United States. On February 27, 1954, he sent an open letter to the deputies of the Taiwan National Assembly in which he condemned one-party rule, the conversion of the national army into a party army, the institution of political commissars, the wave of White Terror of Chiang Ching-kuo's special services, and the violation of human rights and freedom of speech. In response, the official Taiwan press unleashed a wave of accusations against K. C. Wu of treason and corruption. The former governor did not hold his tongue but in fact intensified his attack on the terrorist regime of Chiang Kai-shek. He began writing letters to Chiang and giving interviews to American journalists. Chiang expelled him from the party, but in order to reduce the wave of criticism against him he allowed K. C. Wu's son, who had remained a hostage on Taiwan, to be reunited with his parents in the summer of 1954.[91] General Sun Liren and K. C. Wu were members of the top party organ, the Central Committee, elected in October 1952 at the Seventh Congress of the Guomindang, but their lofty party status could not protect them.

After reorganizing the party and consolidating his position, Chiang for the first time could really enjoy dictatorial power. All of his former opponents, generals, militarists, and communists could no longer threaten him. At the end of 1952 he again proposed that the Americans send Taiwan troops to Korea, this time to fight against Mao Zedong's forces, and he declared that in 1953 he would complete the preparation of his own troops to invade Mainland China.[92] For various reasons he did not send troops either to Korea or to the PRC, and in 1954 he declared that the invasion of the continent might be delayed "for a year or two." He linked it to the Third World War, which he believed was inevitable.[93]

In February 1954, in an interview with Reuters news agency he declared that he did not want to be reelected president for a second term (the elections were supposed to take place the following month). He expressed the desire to become premier or commander in chief of the armed forces. For the position of president, he recommended, as he had in 1948, the nonparty Hu Shi.[94]

This was his usual game. In March Chiang again ran for president. Of the 1,575 deputies in the National Assembly, 1,507, or 95.7 percent, voted for him. For the post of vice president, 1,417 deputies of the 1,569 voting, or 90.3 percent, voted for Chen Cheng, whom Chiang Kai-shek had nominated.[95] Any candidate in a truly democratic election could envy such a result, but Taiwan, like China in 1948, when Chiang received 90 percent of the vote, was not democratic. The impressive results are not surprising.

As for the Chinese communists, one year after the end of the war in Korea, on September 3, 1954, they commenced intensive shelling of the Guomindang-controlled islands of Jinmen (Quemoy), where 50,000 Nationalist troops were stationed (in addition to its 5,000 inhabitants), and of the Dachen Islands (15,000 troops) situated off the coast of the PRC. The communists did not intend to seize the islands. In fact, they considered Chiang's military presence on these offshore islands useful in helping to unify the Chinese people to struggle for the fulfillment of the party's plans. In addition, it was necessary to show the world the fighting spirit and growing might of the Chinese army.

Mao, however, showed an excess of zeal. The shelling of the islands led Dwight D. Eisenhower, a war hero and the Republican president of the United States who had won the election in November 1952, to sign a Mutual Defense Treaty with Taiwan in December 1954. The meaning of that document to Chiang and his regime would be difficult to overestimate. The treaty emphasized that the United States and Taiwan would jointly repel "armed attack and communist subversive activities." In exchange, however, Chiang had to promise not to attempt to seize Mainland China without the agreement of the United States. Moreover, at the end of January 1955 the US Congress, by an overwhelming majority (there were only six nay votes in both houses of Congress), authorized the president "to employ the Armed Forces of the United States as he deems necessary for the specific purpose of securing and protecting Formosa and the Pescadores against armed attack."[96]

Even though the islands of Jinmen (Quemoy) and Mazu (Matsu) were not included in the defense zone, their omission changed little. The main point was that by signing the treaty the United States demonstrated to the USSR and the PRC that it would defend Taiwan as if it were a part of its own territory. Chiang was inexpressibly happy, and even more so when, in March 1955, he received word that the chief of naval operations in the United States, Admiral Robert B. Carney, had told journalists that war with the PRC was imminent and that some in the American military were pressuring the president "to destroy Red China's military potential and thus end its expansionist tendencies."[97]

Even though the much-too-indiscreet Carney was soon relieved of his command by Eisenhower, Chiang Kai-shek could remain absolutely calm. In August 1955 the number of American advisors on Taiwan grew to 2,347 men, which made this unit the largest group of US advisors in the world.[98] Under Washington's wing, Chiang was completely secure.

CHAPTER 23

# *Under Washington's Wing*

Meanwhile, Chiang's personal life took its own course. He and Meiling spent most of their time at the villa in Shilin on the spur of the Yangming Mountains. They lived in a spacious, two-story house under a brick roof with a glass terrace on the first floor and an overhanging glassed-in balcony on the second. There is now a museum there with a one-hundred-yuan entrance fee (a bit more than three US dollars).

The windows of the house looked out over a park. When he rested, Chiang loved to sit on the terrace and, looking out at the trees growing in front of the house, take pleasure in the peace and quiet. His office and bedroom were on the second floor. Meiling's bedroom was adjacent, separated from her husband's by a bathroom. As he always did, Chiang rose very early, now at six o'clock, wiped himself with a hot towel, and drank a glass of warm boiled water. In his whole life he never altered this routine. After the glass of warm water, he prayed with Meiling, then meditated, at eight o'clock ate a light breakfast, then worked, ate lunch at 12:30 or 1:30, then took a nap, walked, worked, ate a light supper at seven o'clock, relaxed (he very much liked to watch films, especially those produced in Taiwan), then wrote in his diaries, prayed at ten o'clock, then went to bed at eleven. If he was unable to finish his diary entries at night, he would continue them the next morning. Everything was precise, in military fashion.[1]

As before his routine differed from that of the Bohemian Meiling, who was always suffering from illnesses, usually skin diseases, allergy, and insomnia. She lay in bed for long periods, smoked menthol cigarettes, and watched television.[2] She fell asleep toward morning and slept until dinner. Husband and wife remained close to each other, they called each other Dar, short for "darling," walked together in the park, went golfing and played chess. They enjoyed growing flowers and feeding goldfish in the pond. In fact, Chiang gave each fish a name, and if any one of them did not swim over to feed, he asked Meiling, "Where has [so-and-so] fish gone today?" Moreover, he loved dogs, and there were always two sheep dogs living in their home. Chiang fed them, took them for walks, and trained them. He was especially fond of a dog he called Bai Lang (White Wolf), probably in memory of a famous Chinese Robin Hood who bore that name. In 1913 Bai Lang had risen in rebellion against Yuan Shikai. Not unlike many marriages, the couple, however, often quarreled.[3]

Not far from the house, situated in the northern part of the park complex, they built a small, red-brick temple they called Kaige tang (Song of Victory temple). That is what he had called the chapel in honor of the victory over Japan that was in his residence in Nanjing. Here husband and wife prayed every Sunday morning. Usually, their children and relatives as well as Christian members of the government and the top leadership of the Guomindang took part in the services. On Wednesday afternoons Meiling organized group prayers and Bible discussions with her women friends.[4]

To Chiang's surprise, after moving to Taiwan Meiling amused herself with landscape painting. Earlier she had never painted, but suddenly she began spending many hours in this occupation and even took painting lessons three times a week. Chiang was skeptical of her new hobby, and occasionally grumbled, "If you had any talent in painting, you would have discovered it before. You'll never be any good at it at your age."[5] Chiang was wrong. Meiling actually learned to paint well.

In addition to Shilin, the Chiangs, according to official information, had an incredible number of villas: thirty-three. (According to unofficial information disseminated by members of the Democratic Progressive Party, they had forty-six.[6] The latter figure is apparently an exaggeration but, whatever the precise number, there were obviously many.) They were scattered across the whole island: one of them was located even on the Pescadores Islands. Chiang and Meiling loved nature and from time to time traveled around the country visiting their out-of-town residences.

Meiling did not always accompany her husband. Sometimes illness or sometimes nostalgia for her relatives living in America compelled her to forsake her husband. Sometimes she went away because she was burdened by the steadily worsening relations with her eldest stepson. After she had abandoned Chiang at the most difficult moment for him, in July 1944, and had gone abroad, Ching-kuo became Chiang's alter ego. After returning to China in September 1945, Meiling engaged in a struggle with Ching-kuo for influence over the Generalissimo. For a while it seemed that she had won, but after she left her husband again in November 1948 for a long period of time, Ching-kuo invariably stayed close to his father. Chiang simply could not do without him, and, after resettling in Taiwan, he began preparing Ching-kuo to become his successor. Ching-kuo held a number of positions in the party, the army, and the secret police. From October 1952 he directed the newly established Chinese Anticommunist National Salvation Youth Corps, whose formal chair was Chiang Kai-shek himself.[7] It was Ching-kuo who, at his father's request, introduced the harshest White Terror on Taiwan, evoking the hatred of such liberals as K. C. Wu, the governor of the island. After returning from the States, Meiling vainly tried to recoup her power, repeatedly complaining to Chiang about Ching-kuo and even using K. C. Wu against her stepson. But she failed to drive a wedge between father and son. Chiang did not want to hear anything negative. In February 1952, when K. C. Wu openly told Chiang that he should not retain Ching-kuo as head of the secret police, the Generalissimo bawled him out, saying that he had a headache and telling K. C. Wu to shut up.[8]

Unlike Meiling, who frequently traveled to the States, Ching-kuo was always at his father's side—through grief and through joy. He worshipped his father and was ready to fulfill his every command. Ching-kuo's wife Faina, his granddaughter Amy, and his grandsons Allen, Alex, and Eddie also enveloped Chiang in tenderness and concern. Chiang loved to spend time with them, and they visited him often.

Chiang also had good relations with his younger son Wei-kuo, but he and his wife, Shi Jingyi, had no children. Shi Jingyi, whom Wei-kuo married on February 6, 1945, was unable to bear children. She had nine miscarriages in eight years. After the last miscarriage, deeply depressed and while her husband was on a mission in Japan she took a huge dose of sleeping pills, wishing to commit suicide or simply struggling with the insomnia that tormented her. She died on March 21, 1953. Greatly upset, Wei-kuo returned home immediately. In honor of his wife he later established a primary school. All the members of the family deeply sympathized with him, and after the funeral Chiang said to him, "Losing your wife in the prime of life is terrible. There are no especially important matters in our country right now, therefore you should make use of the opportunity to return to your studies." Wei-kuo left for the United States, where he was enrolled in a study group at the infantry staff headquarters.

Around this time rumors were circulating in Taiwan that it was actually Chiang Kai-shek who had forced poor Jingyi to commit suicide, not because she had been unable to give birth to a grandson but because her father, a textile manufacturer, was involved in a corruption scandal in which he supplied the army with shoddy military uniforms. There were also rumors that Jingyi had been killed. Some said on Chiang's orders, others on Ching-kuo's, supposedly after learning that she was mixed up in the theft either of American goods earmarked for the army or of hard currency.[9] But it is doubtful that all this gossip can be believed. A year later, Chiang said to Wei-kuo that "being by oneself in the prime of life cannot last too long. Otherwise family traditions will be destroyed. If the opportunity arises, you should marry again."[10]

Soon at a soiree at the Sino-German Society for Cultural and Economic Relations Wei-kuo met a beautiful girl named Qiu Ruxue, whose Christian name was Ellen. She was eighteen years younger than he, but they had a lot in common. Like him, she loved Germany, where she had been born. Her mother was German. Ellen's father, a Chinese engineer and future professor at the National Taiwan University, had met her in Hanover when he was working on his doctoral dissertation at the University of Leibnitz.

Ellen had regular features, fine eyebrows, full lips, luxuriant dark hair, and a captivating smile. Wei-kuo introduced her to his foster mother, Yecheng, who was living in Taizhong, and to his father. Both of them liked her. In 1955 Wei-kuo and Ellen became engaged, and two years later, after Ellen had finished her studies in Japan, they were married. In 1958 Wei-kuo was appointed commander of the First Tank Division, quartered not far from Taipei, in the town of Hukou. In 1961 he was made a lieutenant general.[11]

Meanwhile, extremely serious events were happening in the political life of Taiwan. In the first half of 1955 intensive shelling of Jinmen (Quemoy) and the Dachen Islands from Chinese territory continued. Chiang Kai-shek's forces responded by bombarding the outskirts of the city of Xiamen in Fujian province. Every day a communist invasion of Taiwan was expected. Eisenhower seriously discussed with members of his administration the option of employing small atomic bombs against military objectives in the PRC to stop the aggressor.[12]

Unlike his predecessor Truman, Eisenhower was well-disposed toward Chiang, viewing him as a close ally, even if "proud and sometimes stubborn." But he was one of the "fearless leaders."[13] As before, the Americans wholly controlled Taiwan's military budget, but Eisenhower chose not to slight Chiang, as Truman had done. Moreover, he supposed that "to protect the prestige of Chiang and the morale of his forces, any alteration in military and political planning [in Taiwan] should obviously be developed under his leadership; above all, there must be no basis for public belief that the alterations came about through American intervention or coercion."[14]

At the same time, Eisenhower did everything in his power to defend Taiwan. In August 1954, prior to the conclusion of the Mutual Defense Treaty, he declared at a press conference that "any invasion of Formosa would have to run over [our] Seventh Fleet."[15]

But he understood: "If we get into a general war, the logical enemy will be Russia, not China, and we'll have to strike there [against Russia]."[16] But this was something he didn't want to happen at all. Therefore, on the one hand, he let the Chinese and the Soviet communists know that he might use nuclear weapons to defend Taiwan; on the other hand, on the advice of Secretary of State John Foster Dulles, he proposed a compromise with Chiang: hand over to the communists the small Dachen Islands, which were two hundred nautical miles from Taiwan, but strengthen the defense of the major islands.

Chiang was forced to agree, and on February 4 American ships began evacuating Guomindang troops from the Dachen Islands, an operation that took one week. Dulles on March 15 and Eisenhower on March 16 declared they would use nuclear weapons in the event of a general war in Asia.[17] "I see no reason why they shouldn't be used just exactly as you would use a bullet or anything else," Eisenhower explained to journalists.[18]

In response, the communists also made concessions. At a conference of twenty-nine Asian and African states held in Bandung, Indonesia, in April 1955 Zhou Enlai, who was then both the premier and foreign minister of the PRC, declared that the Chinese people did not want a conflict with the United States, and he offered to sit down at the negotiating table with the Americans. He also did not rule out "the peaceful liberation of Taiwan."[19] The Taiwan crisis was resolved for a time, and the Americans even began talks at the consular level in Geneva with the Chinese communists (later the meetings were moved to Warsaw and shifted to the ambassadorial level).

Less than a year later Chiang, like the rest of the world, learned the stunning news of the so-called secret speech that the impulsive Soviet political leader Nikita S. Khrushchev—the successor to Stalin, who had died three years earlier—delivered from the tribune at the Twentieth Congress of the Communist Party of the Soviet Union on February 25, 1956. Khrushchev exclaimed that the deceased leader and teacher of all the communists of the world was a terrible criminal, a person who had done innumerable evil deeds, including the annihilation of millions of innocent Soviet citizens. Chiang himself considered Stalin a criminal but was naturally struck to hear this from the lips of the new Soviet leader and closest ally of Mao. Of course, Chiang could not stand Khrushchev any more than he had Stalin, but neither could he disagree with Khrushchev's assessment of the former Kremlin dictator. By no means, however, did he trust Khrushchev in any other regard, especially when he learned that in his report to the Twentieth Congress, Khrushchev had not only spoken of "the possibility of preventing war in the present era," but also expounded the Stalinist thesis of "peaceful coexistence between two systems."[20] "In appearance, Khrushchev has modified Stalinism," Chiang recalled. "Stalin believed that war was inevitable, and considered war as the highway to Communist domination of the world. On the contrary, Khrushchev maintained that war was not inevitable; he adopted 'stop all wars' as his slogan. In substance, however, Khrushchev's 'peaceful coexistence' campaign . . . is a repetition of Stalin's 'United Front' of 1935–1939."[21]

Chiang wanted very much to convey this thought to the entire world, to share with the peoples of the free world his own bitter experience of dealing with the communists who, he believed, were always deceiving him. With the aid of his secretaries he began working diligently on a book of reminiscences and reflections. He finished it on December 1, 1956, the twenty-ninth anniversary of his marriage with Meiling and one month after his seventieth birthday (bearing in mind that Chinese count the nine months spent in the womb as one year). He titled his book *Soviet Russia in China: A Summing Up of the Thirty-Year Experience of China's Relations with Soviet Communists* and dedicated it to the "sacred memory of our [with Meiling] dearly beloved mothers, the late Madame Chiang, née Wang, and the late Madame Soong [Song], née Nie [Ni]." In the book he emphasized that he and his wife had failed in "not living up to the lofty ideals instilled in us by our mothers through our childhood training."[22]

Not everything in Chiang's narrative stands up to criticism. Like all losers, Chiang Kai-shek tried to vindicate himself to a degree and depicted Mao and the USSR as devils incarnate. Sometimes his memory failed him, and in some cases he openly dissembled. Still, regardless of these shortcomings he succeeded in setting forth a truthful history of the Chinese national liberation movement. He summarized its struggle on two fronts: against Western and Japanese imperialism and the especially aggressive Soviet expansionism. If Chiang Kai-shek managed to be victorious over the first enemy, he was defeated by the second.

In addition to the basic historical memoir in the book that undoubtedly is of great interest, Chiang also included theoretical sections: "The Successes and Failures of the World's Struggle Against Communism" and "The Communists' Strategy for World Revolution." But they are verbose and uninteresting from either a historical or philosophical perspective. Such also is the impression left by the appendix in the book, "A Study of Dialectics."

Throughout the book ran the thought that it was impossible to trust the communists at all. It was necessary to prepare for a national revolution against Communism in the Far East that would also point "a way to the defeat of the Soviet bloc and to the lifting of the Iron Curtain without a world war. . . . This is also the only way to rebuild world peace and to safeguard human freedom."[23]

The book was published promptly, on Christmas Day, December 25, 1956, and its entire printing was bought up by members of the Guomindang. Subsequently, it was repeatedly reprinted on Taiwan. In 1957 the first American edition was published under the title *Soviet Russia in China: A Summing Up at Seventy,* followed by German and many other editions.

Ten months after the appearance of the first Taiwan edition of the book, the Eighth National Congress of the Guomindang convened in Taipei October 10–23, 1957. Addressing the congress, Chiang declared that the Guomindang would be able to suppress the Chinese Communists as the result of a counterattack in the coming two to three years.[24] The meeting was attended by 372 delegates and 202 guests, representing 509,864 members of the party. Since the Seventh Congress in 1952 the Guomindang had grown by 226,905 persons. As before, 80 percent of the members, or 407,891 persons, were people under the age of forty. Workers and peasants now comprised 26 percent (132,565 persons), that is, 4 percent less than in 1952. Overall, Guomindang members constituted 5.1 percent of the almost ten million inhabitants of the island.[25]

The delegates at the congress again unanimously elected Chiang as *zongcai* (general director, leader). Restoring the post of deputy *zongcai* that had been abolished after the treason of Wang Jingwei, the delegates confirmed Chen Cheng, who had been nominated by Chiang, in that position. Chiang Ching-kuo was elected once again to be a member of the Central Committee, which, in addition to him, comprised 49 persons. Of these, 39 were elected by the congress and 10 added personally by Chiang, to whom the new party statutes, adopted at the congress, had accorded that right. Also elected were 25 candidate members of the CC. And 76 members of the Central Advisory Committee, selected by Chiang, were confirmed, Meiling once again among them. At the First Plenum of the CC following the congress, Ching-kuo again became a member of its Standing Committee. Fourteen others in addition to him were elected as members of this highest organ.[26]

Just several months later came confirmation of the main thesis of Chiang's book of reminiscences, namely, that it was impossible to believe the communists. In August 1958 a serious crisis erupted again in the Taiwan Strait. This time the Chinese communists subjected the island of Jinmen (Quemoy) and the Mazu (Matsu) archipelago in the Taiwan Strait to a powerful bombardment. At the time one-third of Chiang Kai-shek's ground forces were stationed there. Chiang declared this to be "attacks against America's first line of defense in Asia." Eisenhower again came to Chiang's aid, reaffirming his decision to employ small atomic weapons against PRC military objectives in case of a communist invasion of Taiwan territory.[27] All US armed forces in the region were put on alert. But this time, too, Mao did not intend to seize the islands. In China at that time the Great Leap Forward was unfolding. It was a gigantic effort to construct communism by doubling industrial and agricultural production in one year. The leaders of the Communist Party therefore believed it was especially vital to intensify the atmosphere of a military camp to raise the enthusiasm of the Chinese population.

The Chinese communists continued their bombardment over the next twenty years—to be sure, only on odd-numbered days, but why on those days is not known—and Chiang Kai-shek and the Americans eventually had to learn to accept this. "Asking the Chinese Communists for a ceasefire is only deceiving ourselves," Chiang asserted in October 1958. "The desire to achieve a ceasefire will never be realized."[28] On the advice of Eisenhower, he simply reduced the size of his armed forces on Jinmen (Quemoy) and the Mazu (Matsu) Islands even though he didn't want to do so.

Eisenhower continued to support Chiang thereafter as well, not only with demonstrations of force but materially. Up to the end of his presidential term, January 20, 1961, he provided Taiwan with more than one billion dollars in economic aid alone. Additional hundreds of millions were spent on the military needs of the island.[29] In August 1959, for example, the Americans transferred thirty-six missile launchers to Taiwan and a large number of ground-to-air nuclear-capable Nike-Hercules missiles.[30]

To Chiang the missiles were extremely crucial. A grave situation had developed in Red China in 1959, both in connection with the failure of the Great Leap and with an uprising of Tibetans demanding independence. Chiang again began considering the possibility of invading the mainland. On March 7, 1959, five days before the uprising in Tibet, in an interview with the Italian newspaper *Corriere della sera* (Evening Herald), he stated, "If an uprising occurs on Chinese soil, we will not sit idly by. We will make a landing on the continent and we will win the battle. I think the Soviet Union will not intervene in this matter under any circumstances, since it is afraid of getting bogged down in China as happened to the Japanese. Moreover, I am convinced the Soviet Union will not employ nuclear weapons, because it knows that might provoke a world war. . . . The Soviet Union doesn't want war, at least, not right now. That is the only point on which I agree with Khrushchev."[31] The Tibetan uprising, which began on March 12, was harshly suppressed by communist troops, and despite offering moral support for the rebels, Chiang Kai-shek did not invade the continent. The spiritual leader of Tibet, the Dalai Lama, fled to India, and Chiang, with American assistance, continued to strengthen the defenses of Taiwan. He contended yet again that "a counterattack against Mainland China is our duty," while emphasizing that this task "is 70 percent a political task and only 30 percent military."[32] His bold talk enabled him to rally the Guomindang and the NRA.

The year 1960 was especially consequential in the life of Chiang Kai-shek. First, in March, on the basis of "Temporary Provisions Effective During the Period of National Mobilization for Suppression of the Communist Rebellion" adopted in 1948 and then extended, the National Assembly elected Chiang to a third term as president (though initially, as noted previously, the Constitution of the Republic of China did not allow a president to be elected a third time). Three months before the election, on December 23, 1959, Chiang gave a speech before two thousand Guomindang activists in which he said he "opposed changing the constitution."[33] This statement was for show only. Washington, not understanding this, welcomed the decision, supposing that Chen Cheng would replace Chiang. The Americans even intended to invite Chen Cheng to visit the United States.[34] But Chiang quickly regrouped and received 98.1 percent of the deputies' votes in the election (1,481 of 1,509). General Chen Cheng, ran for vice president again and received 91.8 percent (1,381 of 1,505).[35] Chiang could celebrate victory once more. At 12:30 in the afternoon, despite the rain, thousands of people gathered in front of the Presidential Office Building.

They held portraits of Chiang with the caption, "We will follow Chiang to the mainland."[36]

The second momentous event was the visit to Taiwan of Chiang's main ally, Eisenhower, along with his son and daughter-in-law. It was the first visit of an American president to China and therefore had historic meaning (even though Eisenhower was in Taipei for less than twenty-four hours). He arrived on the afternoon of June 18 on a helicopter that lifted off one of the ships of the Seventh Fleet. He held two talks with Chiang Kai-shek and Meiling and spoke before an enormous crowd of city folk assembled in the square in front of the Presidential Office Building in the center of Taipei. According to official data, more than half a million people were present.

Chiang was indescribably happy in welcoming Eisenhower, a man who had done so much to strengthen Taiwan. Ordinary Taiwanese also expressed genuine joy. On the trip from Songshan Airport to Chiang Kai-shek's residence both sides of the broad avenue were filled with a sea of people, joyfully waving small Chinese and American flags. Among them were specially transported Guomindang representatives from Jinmen (Quemoy) and the Mazu (Matsu) Islands. People were dancing and lively music played everywhere.[37]

Chiang met Eisenhower at the airport, wearing a dress military uniform with the Order of Blue Sky and White Sun on his left breast. He loved this order very much even though it was only the second-highest award in the Republic of China. He also had the highest order—of National Glory—which he was awarded on October 10, 1943, the anniversary of the 1911 Revolution—but he wore it rarely. The Order of Blue Sky and White Sun he had received in 1930 for uniting the country as a result of the Northern Expedition. He prized the award greatly.

Now in his seventy-third year, he looked quite fit for his age. He was tanned and had a handsome gray mustache and lively eyes. He had become a bit stooped, and his voice was no longer a sharp staccato. Meiling, who went to the airport with her husband, was, as always, irresistible, looking nothing like a woman of sixty-two. Elegant and delicate, she was dressed in a light blue *qipao.* She made a most positive impression on the American president.[38] Although she did not wear it, she too held the Order of Blue Sky and White Sun, which Chiang had conferred on her after the Cairo conference for her contribution to the talks with Roosevelt.

Chiang and Meiling had met Eisenhower before, in November 1943 in Cairo, but at that time he was only a member of the American delegation. Now, in Chiang's eyes, he was the leader of the entire free world and his chief ally. To be sure, Chiang was upset that Eisenhower had done nothing to defend the president of South Korea, the eighty-four-year-old Syngman Rhee. He had been ousted from his position in March 1960 as a result of massive demonstrations by the liberally inclined intelligentsia over the falsification of elections held in South Korea. The Americans merely helped Syngman Rhee flee to Hawaii.

Naturally, the overthrow of the South Korean dictator upset Chiang, not only because he considered Syngman Rhee a friend, but also because he feared that the Americans, in the event of similar demonstrations by Taiwanese liberals, might betray him as they had Rhee. Chiang was also upset by events in Turkey, where, in May 1960, popular demonstrations toppled another US ally, the prime minister of the country. Eisenhower wrote in his memoirs that Chiang told him that communists, both Soviet and Chinese, undoubtedly stood behind all these uprisings, and he was fearful that a similar upheaval would take place in Japan. He was absolutely convinced that Khrushchev and Mao were working hand in hand and that their goal was to undermine stability in Asia, "the weakest link in defense of the Free World." He did not believe the disagreements between the CPSU and the CCP that were then becoming visible were real, assuring Eisenhower that "Mao could never afford to split off from the Soviet Union, for he owed his own power to Kremlin support."[39] How wrong he was. It was precisely at that time that the dispute between Mao and Khrushchev had passed the point of no return.

In speeches and conversations with Chiang and Meiling, Eisenhower again emphasized "America's steadfast solidarity" to Chiang personally and to his government, and he said the Beijing regime was nothing other than "warlike and tyrannical." The Joint Communiqué published on June 19 citing the results of the visit observed that "taking note of the continuing threat of Communist aggression against the free world in general and the Far Eastern free countries in particular, the two Presidents expressed full agreement on the vital necessity of achieving closer unity and strength among all free nations."

A lot of attention was accorded to economic issues in Taiwan. Chiang spoke about the successes, and Eisenhower "expressed the admiration of the American people for the progress achieved by the Republic of China in various fields in recent years and gave assurance of continuing United States assistance."[40]

It was not for nothing that Eisenhower expressed admiration. Taiwan's economy was on an upsurge. The first four-year plan (1953–56) had been successfully fulfilled. In 1952 the growth in GDP was 12.3 percent, and from 1953 to 1956 it rose to 37 percent; in terms of per capita growth it was 17 percent. The second four-year plan of 1957–60 had almost been completed, and it was clear that GDP would grow by a further 31 percent and on a per capita basis by 13 percent.[41] Stores and markets in Taiwan were full of goods. This situation was quite unlike that of the PRC, where, as a result of the Great Leap, millions of people were dying of famine.

In 1960 two momentous events occurred in Chiang Kai-shek's family: almost simultaneously two weddings were held. In April, Allen, the eldest son of Ching-kuo and Faina, married Xu Naijin (Christian name Nancy), a fellow student at the University of California in Berkeley. (Allen and his sister Amy had gone to study in America in December 1959.) Like Wei-kuo's second wife, Nancy was half-German and a beauty, like all the women in the Chiang family. But her beauty was not the main point. Nancy was a person of very strong character, and her marriage to Allen was a stroke of good fortune for the whole family. After coming to America, Allen began to drink a lot, and his future bride literally had to drag him away from bars by force. Only after he was married did he settle down for a while. He and his wife lived in a charming two-story house at 1095 Keeler Avenue in north Berkeley, not far from the university.[42]

Four months later, on August 11, 1960, Chiang's granddaughter Amy also got married. She married a man named Yu Yanghe, who was much older than she (by fourteen years) and, moreover, thrice divorced. He was a very interesting person, however, a former military pilot who had conducted more than thirty aerial combat missions against the Japanese. He was the son of Chiang Kai-shek's minister of defense, Yu Dawei. Nevertheless, Ching-kuo, who adored Amy and hoped for something better for her, was displeased with this marriage. After all, as a Christian Chiang Kai-shek's eldest son was opposed to divorce. Yet he had to reconcile himself to it. The newlyweds began living quietly in Oakland, California, in a small apartment, No. 204, at 5939 Telegraph Avenue, one of the main streets. Their apartment was about a twenty-minute drive south from Allen's house.[43]

At the end of 1960, however, unpleasant news reached Chiang, not familial but political, although politics had long since become his family matters. In the US presidential election of November 1960, the Republican candidate, Vice President Richard M. Nixon, lost to the young Democrat John F. Kennedy. In that Nixon lost by the minuscule margin of only seventeen-hundredths of a percent, the defeat was particularly distressing. Chiang had suffered a great deal at the hands of the Democrats, while Republicans, Eisenhower in the first instance, were basically well-disposed toward him. Chiang felt bad for Nixon, whom he knew personally. In 1953 Eisenhower had sent Nixon to Taiwan, and the vice president had conversed for seven hours with Chiang and Meiling, who was serving as interpreter. Nixon and Chiang liked each other, and Nixon subsequently recalled that he was "impressed by his [Chiang's] high intelligence and his total dedication to the goal of freeing the Chinese people from Communist domination."[44]

Nevertheless, in 1949, as a young congressman, Kennedy had shown himself to be a friend of the Chinese Nationalists by criticizing Truman's China policy even though they were in the same party. "This is the tragic story of China, whose freedom we once fought to preserve," he said on January 30, 1949, understanding that the victory of the Communists was obvious. "What our young men had saved, our diplomats and our President have frittered away."[45] However, Chiang was not optimistic about Kennedy's position on Taiwan. He feared that Kennedy might sacrifice Taiwan for the sake of developing relations with the PRC and possibly might support the admission of Maoist China to the UN.

Chiang was not far from the truth. Dean Rusk, who had become secretary of state in Kennedy's administration in January 1961, pressed the notion of two Chinas.[46] Chiang did not know that Eisenhower, on leaving the White House, told Kennedy that "although he would support him on foreign policy in general, he would strongly oppose any attempt by the new administration to recognize Peking [Beijing] and seat Mainland China at the United Nations." Nor did Chiang know that with his thin margin of victory in the election, Kennedy "was extremely cautious about selecting issues on which to do battle."[47] But he demonstrated caution only at the start of his presidential term. Most likely he simply had no time to make fundamental changes in China policy. According to the reminiscences of his special assistant, Arthur M. Schlesinger Jr., Kennedy by no means rejected the idea of two Chinas and of recognizing the PRC. "It really doesn't make any sense—the idea that Taiwan represents China," he said to members of his administration in 1961, while putting off recognition of the PRC until after US congressional elections in November 1962.[48]

In 1961 Kennedy succeeded only in getting the very reluctant Chiang to order his representative on the UN Security Council to abstain on a vote to admit Mongolia to the UN. Chiang was dissatisfied with Kennedy's behavior on this question because, as before, he viewed the Mongolian People's

Republic as a part of China, despite the old, 1945 treaty with the Soviet Union, which he understandably considered inoperative. Nevertheless, he had to submit to the president of the United States.

Chiang was not pleased either that in 1962 Kennedy openly informed both the USSR and China that he would not support Chiang in any of his "adventures" vis-à-vis Mainland China. This offended the elderly Generalissimo, who believed that a friend should not "openly inform an enemy that the United States would not help" its own ally.[49]

Meanwhile, in 1961, joyful events were again occurring in Chiang's family. On March 21 a daughter was born to Chiang's grandson Allen and his wife, Nancy. She was Chiang Kai-shek's first great-granddaughter. In accord with family tradition she was named Youmei. The character *you* ("brotherhood") was for the thirty-first generation of the Wuling Jiangs, and the character *mei* means "plum blossom." Her full name was Youmei Margarita Faina Maria. She was named Margarita in honor of her maternal grandmother, and Faina in honor of her paternal grandmother, and Maria was the name she received upon her christening.

The girl was born in Taipei, and Chiang and Meiling were happy to hold their great-granddaughter in their arms. She became their favorite. On June 30, in accordance with Chinese tradition, they arranged a party to celebrate her hundredth day. But soon Allen, Nancy, and Youmei left for the United States so that Allen and Nancy could continue their studies. Within three years, sadly, Allen again began drinking and, while driving his car while intoxicated, had an accident in a suburb of Oakland. He was deported from the United States, and Nancy and Youmei returned to Taiwan with him.

Ching-kuo (before he became president of Taiwan in 1978) and Faina also loved to drink, especially while eating Russian hors d'oeuvres. They delighted in Russian food and vodka and generally everything Russian. Ching-kuo and Faina even spoke to each other in Russian. But neither Ching-kuo nor Faina (who died on December 15, 2004, at the age of eighty-eight) became alcoholics.[50]

In May 1961 Chiang's granddaughter Amy gave birth to his first great-grandson. He was named Zusheng, which means Voice of the Ancestors. He was born in San Francisco. His paternal grandmother, like Youmei's maternal grandmother, was German. Amy's future father-in-law, Yu Dawei, met this woman in Germany during his studies in the early 1920s. They fell in love with each other, had a child (Amy's future husband), and intended to marry, but they didn't succeed in doing so. The parents of the fiancée not only denied permission for their daughter to marry a Chinese, but even demanded that she give up her son. So Yu Dawei took him to China, where Amy's husband grew up.

The great-grandson was not in Chiang Kai-shek's family line, since he was born to his granddaughter. But this did not influence Chiang's relationship with him. The Generalissimo was a loving grandfather, quite unlike Mao Zedong incidentally, who was almost indifferent to his children and grandchildren. He loved lively family picnics on Yangming Mountains and festive meals; sometimes he would cook for the whole family, usually fried rice. He loved to stroll with his children along mountain paths, wearing a long gown and carrying a walking stick, while declaiming the verses of Tang dynasty poets: Li Bai, Du Fu, Wang Wei, and Meng Haoran.[51]

In May 1961 good news came from Washington. Kennedy sent Chiang a letter assuring him that "the United States as before would honor its obligations to the Nationalists according to the Mutual Defense Treaty, adhere to the position of not recognizing Communist China, oppose seating Communist China in the UN, support the representation of Nationalist China in the UN, and be faithful to its promise to provide Nationalist China economic aid."[52] This letter was handed to Chiang by Vice President Lyndon B. Johnson, who visited Taipei with his charming wife, Lady Bird, as well as Kennedy's sister and her husband. His visit on May 14–15 lasted for twenty-three hours.

Everything would have been fine, but in the early 1960s Chiang began to have serious health problems. He needed an operation to remove growths on his prostate gland, and in 1962 an anxious Meiling wrote to her brother T. V. Song requesting that he find a good urological surgeon in the States. T. V. Song quickly set to the task, and the surgeon who came to Taiwan performed the operation successfully. But after the operation it took Chiang a long time to fully recover. Meiling was very nervous and asked her favorite niece, Jeanette, to come from New York to cheer her up. Jeanette settled in at the park complex of Shilin, next to the Chiangs, in a two-story house named the Guest Lodge. At Meiling's request, she took charge of managing the entire estate and demanded that servants call her General Manager Kong. It is said that from then on even Chiang himself and Ching-kuo began calling her that. As before, she dressed in masculine clothes, and the servants, who hated her because of her overbearing character, gossiped behind her back that she preferred women to men when it came to love affairs.[53] Meiling tried to marry her off but to no effect.[54]

In the spring of 1963 Kennedy again raised Chiang's ire. At the end of April the president and his secretary of state, Dean Rusk, announced at a press conference their intentions to improve relations with the PRC.[55] Chiang was beside himself. Only the birth of another grandson on May 22, 1963, improved his mood. The new grandson, Chiang's last, after a long wait was from Wei-kuo. The pleased grandfather named him Xiaogang (*xiao,* as noted earlier, means "filial piety" and *gang* means "strong" or "firm").[56] At his baptism the child was given the name Gregory. He was two years younger than Youmei, the daughter of his first cousin, and Zusheng, the son of his first cousin.

The birth of another grandson could not long distract Chiang from his baleful thoughts. In July 1963, out of pique at Kennedy, he decided on a dangerous gambit: to begin secret talks with the Soviet Union on a joint anti-Maoist platform. By then he knew that Khrushchev's conflict with Mao was serious and long-lasting, and therefore he decided to join forces with him for a possible joint blow against the PRC. At Chiang's direction the relevant Taiwan services began to test the water, but nothing came of it at this time.[57]

Meanwhile, in the autumn of 1963 Chiang convened the Ninth Congress of the party. At the forum, which took place on November 11–22, there were 996 participants (600 delegates and 396 guests), representing 667,000 members of the Guomindang. Since the Eighth Congress in 1957 the party had added 157,136 members. Younger members up to forty years of age now constituted slightly more than 70 percent (more than 472,000). Workers and peasants were 23 percent (more than 150,000), that is, 3 percent less than in 1957. Overall, Guomindang members composed 5.8 percent of the more than eleven million inhabitants of the island.[58]

Although Chiang was in his seventy-seventh year, he was again unanimously elected *zongcai.* Chen Cheng again became his deputy, and Chiang Ching-kuo a member of the Central Committee. (The latter included seventy-four persons: 60 elected and 14 appointed by Chiang Kai-shek.) The number of candidate members of the Central Committee was increased from 25 to 35, and members of the Central Advisory Committee, chosen by Chiang, from 76 to 144 (Meiling again was one of the members). At the first CC plenum after the congress, Chiang Ching-kuo was again given a place among the 15 members of the Standing Committee.[59] Chiang gave a speech at the congress in which he said that at present the Chinese Nationalists were as strong as they have not "been since the 1911 Revolution."[60] On Chiang's proposal, the congress adopted a Program of Anticommunism and National Construction, the foundation of which was the idea of uniting all Chinese inside and outside Taiwan in a Chinese Anticommunist National Construction Alliance.[61]

On the morning after the congress Chiang received news that evoked mixed feelings in him. On November 22, at twelve thirty in the afternoon, an attempt was made on the life of President Kennedy. He died in hospital a half hour later. Chiang was not fond of Kennedy, as mentioned. From the beginning of November 1963 his coolness turned to hostility after South Vietnamese President Ngo Dinh Diem was assassinated. Chiang possibly didn't know for certain that the CIA was involved in the assassination, but rumors that Kennedy was culpable in the death of the Saigon dictator must have reached him.[62]

A year later, at the request of Kennedy's younger brother Robert, Chiang wrote a short reminiscence (four pages in the English translation) of Kennedy. It was designated for a memorial library to the deceased. Chiang diplomatically noted that during the presidential campaign of 1960 he had "begun to develop great respect for his [Kennedy's] abilities, his great talent, youthful energy and ability to find a way out of any situation." He declared even that he "considered President Kennedy a 'second Lincoln' among presidents of the United States." Not because Kennedy too was killed but because he "tried to restore freedom and hope to the billion people who were enslaved by the Communists."[63]

As for the new president of the United States, Lyndon B. Johnson, Chiang had apparently formed good relations with him from the time of his visit to Taiwan on May 15, 1961. When Johnson flew into Taipei, Chiang initially treated him coolly because he thought that as a member of Kennedy's entourage Johnson had come to read him and Meiling "lectures or to berate them, or to bring them bad news of an imminent decrease in aid from the United States."[64] But it soon became clear this was not the case. Like Eisenhower before him, Johnson formed a good impression of Chiang, Meiling, and the situation on Taiwan, emphasizing the "great successes" achieved by the Taiwanese regime in the economic realm, and in particular "in the achievement of land reform and developing the irrigation system" as well as in education. He did not neglect to call attention to the rise in the standard of living of Taiwanese: "The Communists can never count on success where peasants own their own land."[65]

Unfortunately for Chiang, Johnson also turned out to be "a tough nut."[66] On May 28, 1964, without prior consultation with Chiang, the chief of the State Department News Division, Richard I. Phillips, announced that the United States would be terminating its economic assistance to Taiwan from June 1965 "because of the healthy economic growth of the Republic of China on Taiwan."[67] In the summer of 1965 the American ambassador Admiral Jerauld Wright declared that Taiwan had ultimately graduated from US assistance. He also said that Taiwan's growth was "one of marvels of the present age."[68] In February 1966 *Reader's Digest* praised the "Asian's newest economic miracle" on Taiwan, which proved "the wisdom of depending mainly upon private enterprise for economic growth."[69] By 1970 military assistance would also decrease from $100 million to $30 million a year. News reached Chiang that Johnson also decided to continue Kennedy's policy of building bridges to the PRC.[70]

All this was quite disturbing, especially since the international situation in East Asia soon sharply deteriorated. At three o'clock in the afternoon on October 16, 1964, the Chinese communists carried out a successful experiment of a nuclear weapon on the Malan test site in the Lop Nor desert of Xinjiang. Chiang was terribly upset, although he gave no outward sign of it. He had long since supposed that Mao Zedong would be able to make an atomic bomb, and therefore, in December 1958, he had ordered the start of work on his own Taiwanese bomb.[71] The order was secret—even from the Americans because they did not want to see nuclear weapons proliferation.

The Taiwanese did not succeed in creating a bomb earlier or at the same time as the communists. Therefore, Chiang Kai-shek, on the one hand, stepped up work on producing a nuclear weapon and, on the other hand, asked the new president of the United States to allow him to send groups of saboteurs to Mainland China to destroy PRC atomic sites. He deemed this "the only way to put an end to the nuclear threat and take a step toward destroying a regime that had brought innumerable calamities to our region."[72] Johnson did not permit him to do this.

In 1964–65 the Americans became increasingly mired in South Vietnam, where communist guerrillas, both local and those infiltrating from North Vietnam, were waging war against the government supported by the United States. After the death of Ngo Dinh Diem on November 2, 1963, a succession of presidents took over in Saigon until June 14, 1965, when, with American help, General Nguyen Van Thieu established himself firmly in power. But even after Thieu took power the military and political situation in South Vietnam remained critical. On July 28, 1965, Johnson decided to send a large contingent of American forces there. The Americans became completely mired in Indochina and could not even consider Chiang's plans regarding Mao.

A year earlier, in a letter to Johnson, Chiang had warned the American president that getting involved in the Indochina war would only evoke Vietnamese hatred for America and that the Americans would confront the prospect of a protracted war of attrition. He tried to talk Johnson out of taking such a rash step, but Johnson did not listen to him.[73] Then Chiang proposed sending his own troops to Vietnam but was rebuffed. His proposal was purely formal in character, like his offer to send two divisions to Korea. Actually, he thought the Vietnamese should resolve their own affairs.[74]

Meanwhile, 1966 was approaching, the year of the fourth election of Chiang as president of Taiwan. Chiang was seventy-eight years old now, and it is not clear why he needed to be elected to another six-year term. The National Assembly could simply declare him president-for-life. Even the Americans understood very well that elections on Taiwan were a profanation. But in the contemporary world, where democracy is a generally recognized value, all dictators evidently like to be elected. Once every few years they need to receive confirmation that all the people, or at the very least the entire parliament, loves them.

Alas! How far all of them are from the gentlemen of antiquity, of whom Confucius said: "A gentleman makes demands on himself; a vulgar man makes demands on others."[75]

CHAPTER 24

# *Sorrow and Hope*

In February 1966, prior to the elections for president, Chiang once more displayed his tact by declaring he did not want to run. In accordance with Chinese tradition, he had to demonstrate his modesty again. But the central organs of the Guomindang nominated him and he was "forced" to agree. In the March elections he received 1,405 of 1,425 votes of the deputies to the National Assembly (98.6 percent). General Chen Cheng had died on March 5, 1965, so Chiang nominated a new candidate, Yan Jiagan, for vice president. Yan Jiagan, known in the West as C. K. Yen was a sixty-year-old chemist by education. He had held various governmental positions since 1950, including minister of the economy and finance. In late December 1963 he had replaced the ailing Chen Cheng as chairman of the Executive Yuan. In the voting for vice president C. K. Yen received 782 of 1,416 votes (55.2 percent).[1]

According to a report by an Associated Press correspondent, the election of Chiang Kai-shek "served as a cause for celebration throughout Nationalist China." On the streets of Taipei and other cities there were fireworks displays, people danced in the streets, and congratulated each other. A crowd of some 25,000 gathered in the center of Taipei, sang songs to the accompaniment of dozens of brass bands, one after the other, and then, splitting up into columns, marched "through the streets of the capital under festive flags."[2]

It is difficult to say whether Chiang Kai-shek would have received a majority of votes and whether people would have rejoiced in his victory had the elections on Taiwan been democratic. Many native-born Taiwanese, as noted, could not forgive him for the slaughter of 1947. The local people, moreover, were unhappy that Nationalists who had come over from the mainland dominated all the powerful government institutions. "People from Tang Mountain," that is, mainlanders, were also a majority of 70 percent in the party itself.[3] Yet a majority of those living on the island had to admit that in the past fifteen years—from the time the Guomindang government had moved to Taiwan—their lives had notably improved. Between 1951 and 1965 the rate of growth of Taiwan's economy was second only to Japan's in Asia. The average annual growth of GNP was 7.6 percent and 4.2 percent on a per capita basis. Even in 1956, when a powerful typhoon inflicted great damage on the national economy, GNP grew by 4 percent. From 1951 to 1963 the production of agricultural products increased by 82 percent and industrial production by an impressive 324 percent. The share of industrial output in overall GNP grew from 28 to 49 percent. In the mid-1960s the Taiwan authorities began to establish Special Economic Zones (SEZs) very similar to the ones that, thirteen years later, Deng Xiaoping would authorize, obviously copying Chiang Kai-shek's experiment. To attract foreign investment these special zones created an ideal investment climate, and goods produced were neither taxed nor subject to tariffs. Foreign or joint enterprises established in these zones had to produce goods for export. The currency market was also stabilized at a rate of one US dollar to forty Taiwan dollars. Such successes would have been impossible without colossal financial, economic, and military aid from the United States, which, between 1951 and 1965, amounted to the enormous sum of 1,443.3 billion American dollars.[4] Moreover, it is doubtful that Taiwan would have achieved such progress had the Americans not guaranteed its security.

Yet the policies of Chiang Kai-shek himself naturally played the decisive role. After all, it was under him that farmers received land and urban residents had an opportunity to secure cheap credit and freely conduct business without fearing arbitrary police intervention, official corruption, or fierce competition from state or private monopolies.

By this time successes were also achieved in the social sphere, in the first instance in public health and education. By 1963 Taiwanese health authorities had wholly eliminated the epidemics of malaria and had succeeded in reducing the mortality rate from tuberculosis by 75 percent. As a result of the development of a system of comprehensive education, the percentage of literacy increased from 57 to 76 percent. The percentage of the urban population increased from 31 percent in 1955 to 35 percent in 1963. Newspaper circulation increased from 350,000 to 750,000, and 490 of every thousand Taiwanese had radios compared with only 31 of every thousand in 1951. The percentage of Taiwanese with private telephones also rose, from 29 per ten thousand to 121 per ten thousand. Improvement in the conditions and quality of life led to a growth in the birth rate to 3.3 percent per annum. The life expectancy of men rose from 51.7 years to 65.2 years, and that of women from 54.7 to 67.6 years. By 1965 the population of the island had reached 12.6 million.[5]

The people on Taiwan knew very well that their standard of living was higher than that of their counterparts in Communist China. Every day they heard about how their compatriots were dying from hunger after the Great Leap. And suddenly came news of a Great Proletarian Cultural Revolution, beginning in April 1966. Anxious Taiwanese read with horror about crowds of youth in the PRC who, incited by Mao Zedong, were wrecking universities and other educational and cultural centers as well as monuments of a thousand-year-old civilization and religious sacred places. They defiled the tomb of Confucius and other historical figures, overthrew the authorities, and called for world revolution. The contrast with tranquil Taiwan was obvious. Moreover, Maoist China, wrapped in the flames of the Cultural Revolution and already presenting a threat to their country, had become completely unpredictable. All of these occurrences induced the people of Taiwan to rally around the Guomindang and its leader.

Chiang knew how to play on the mood of his people. He always instilled in them the thought that an anti-Maoist revolution would soon break out on the mainland, and the Chinese people, enslaved by the communists, would seek sanctuary under the wing of the Guomindang. Chiang made use of every opportunity to undermine Mao's regime. On October 7, 1966, he called on all Christians in the world "to unite against the Beijing government that is using the Red Guards to destroy freedom of religion in Mainland China." He demanded that "a fierce blow be struck against the Chinese Communists."[6] What he had in mind by "a fierce blow" is unknown, but in any case his appeal didn't sound very Christian.

Three days later Chiang delivered a radio address to officers and soldiers of the PRC army, calling on them to rise against the Beijing authorities. He declared that in the event of an uprising he could deploy his troops to the mainland "in the course of eight hours" and promised that all the participants in an uprising would enjoy "the same kind of rewards and treatment accorded his own soldiers."[7] Unfortunately for Chiang Kai-shek his American protectors again refused to support his bellicose plans. Moreover, on July 12, 1966, Johnson even openly called for peace with the PRC, proclaiming that "lasting peace can never come to Asia as long as the 700 million people of mainland China are isolated . . . by their rulers from the outside world."[8] Meanwhile, the Americans continued to conduct talks with the Chinese communists in Warsaw at the ambassadorial level: 134 meetings were held between 1955 and 1968.

Nixon, who launched his second election campaign for president in the spring of 1967, also failed to inspire hope in Chiang for a change in US policy. In October 1967, in an article published in the journal *Foreign Affairs,* Nixon, to the surprise of Chiang Kai-shek, who had always viewed this leading Republican as his friend, expressed a desire to improve relations with Mao.[9] The publication of the article had a terrible impact on the elderly Chiang. He was very upset, but he didn't stop hoping that Nixon—who had visited Taiwan a number of times since 1953 as the personal guest of the Chiangs and had friendly relations with them,[10] would not betray them on entering the White House. He wanted Nixon to continue Eisenhower's policy of firmly defending Taiwan's interests. According to several sources, Chiang supported Nixon's campaign strenuously and even contributed a substantial sum to the coffers of the Republican Party.[11] But a year later, in the summer of 1968, the elderly leader of the Guomindang decided to try again to reach a mutual understanding with the USSR. By this time Khrushchev, in October 1964, had lost power, and Chiang began to place his hopes in the new Soviet leader, Leonid Ilych Brezhnev. Especially since April 1965 Soviet diplomats working at the UN had tried to establish a dialogue with a Taiwanese representative in that organization. At that time Chiang had displayed caution and nothing had come of it, but in July 1968 he gave a secret order to one of the secretaries of the Taiwan embassy in Mexico to establish an appropriate contact with Soviet diplomats. That person began talks with the first secretary of the embassy of the USSR, who, in one of their conversations and evidently on the order of a higher-up, said that the Chinese problem was the "principal headache" of the Soviet government. "We have recognized our previous mistaken policies on China," he stated.[12]

The resulting talks took place against the background of Chiang's ever-increasing disappointment with the United States. In August 1968, shortly after his nomination, Nixon, Chiang's friend, declared, "We must not forget China. We must always seek opportunities to talk with her. . . . We must not only watch for changes. We must seek to make changes."[13] In November

Nixon won the presidential election, and Chiang began waiting for him to reexamine the declarations he had made during the election campaign. But that didn't happen.

Nixon indeed was very interested in normalizing relations with Beijing. The reality was that by the 1970s the American war in Vietnam had reached a full impasse, and he badly needed Beijing's help. He knew that sooner or later American troops would have to be withdrawn from Indochina, but he didn't want this to look like a defeat. It was very important to him that the Vietcong (the South Vietnamese guerrillas) and North Vietnam extend some sort of guarantee to the pro-American Saigon regime. Only then could he give the order to evacuate "with a clear conscience." That is why he needed Mao. He wanted Mao to pressure his Vietnamese comrades to make concessions. In the same way, Nixon counted on using Moscow, too, promising the Soviets détente and food aid in return for their help in resolving the problem of Vietnam.[14]

On October 19, 1968, Chiang wrote in his diaries, "I feel universally humiliated. Particularly I feel infinitely deceived and betrayed by the United States—an unprecedented dishonor of both the nation and my family. If I failed to awaken myself to the reality, to make up my mind, then the recovery of the mainland would be hopeless and I would eventually become a guard dog of America. I would thus be ashamed to face the nation, the people, and the spirits of my ancestors! A boundless shame for me! The only option that I have is to break with the Americans and to start all over again, so as to save and support my government. This would not be too late."[15] Taking another few steps in this direction, Chiang might really have become a friend of Russia. In October 1968 a KGB official, Victor Evgenievich Louis, came to Taipei under the cover of working as a correspondent for the British newspaper *Evening News.* Chiang personally gave permission for him to visit because he was very desirous that the talks end successfully. On his instructions, all the meetings with Louis were controlled by Ching-kuo, who, on October 29, met personally with the Moscow envoy. Louis told Ching-kuo directly that Moscow would support the Guomindang in an invasion of the PRC, but he posed one condition: the Nationalists, after returning to the mainland, would permit the existence of a pro-Soviet CCP. Chiang was disappointed on hearing this news. After already having suffered much at the hands of Kremlin leaders, who repeatedly tried to deceive him, he approached this suggestion with suspicion. In the end, he decided that the new Soviet leaders wanted to use the Guomindang to defeat their enemy (in this case Mao Zedong), after which they would bring to power a new puppet in China: a pro-Moscow CCP. He did not break off the talks, however, and his representative, Wei Jingming, who headed the Department of Information in the Taiwan government, met twice more with Louis, not in Taiwan but in Europe: in May 1969 in Rome and in October 1970 in Vienna.

Chiang wanted the USSR to provide Taiwan with offensive weapons and at no cost but nothing came of this. He knew why. His intelligence service informed him that the Soviet leadership was not of one mind regarding the question of establishing an alliance with the Republic of China on an anti-Maoist platform. Only two members of the Politburo actively supported an alliance with Chiang, Arvid Yanovich Pel'she and Aleksandr Nikolaevich Shelepin. The former was the chair of the Party Control Commission and the latter the chair of the All-Union Central Council of Trade Unions. But Aleksei Nikolaevich Kosygin, the chair of the Council of Ministers, was resolutely opposed, wanting to restore relations with the PRC. The result was that Brezhnev made no decision, while Chiang lost interest in the USSR and ordered that the talks end.[16]

Doubtless nothing would have come out of these meetings with Louis, even had Kosygin not opposed an alliance with Taiwan. After all, Chiang Kai-shek had never actually decided to launch an invasion of Mainland China because he had no chance of defeating Mao, who possessed nuclear weapons. In March 1969, it is true, he conceived the hope that the Soviet Union would help him not only with weapons but also with actions, that is, by striking a blow against nuclear sites in Maoist China. An armed conflict had broken out between the USSR and China at that time. Soviet and Chinese border troops entered into battle over Damansky (Zhenbao) Island in the Ussuri River. Both sides suffered dozens of killed and wounded. Chiang, who avidly began to follow the development of events, instructed Taiwan's mass media to change its hostile view of the USSR. The entire Taiwan press slowly began to express sympathy toward the Russians in their conflict with the PRC.[17] Chiang did not know that at the time members of the Soviet Politburo were actually contemplating the option of destroying Chinese nuclear objectives, and the USSR Minister of Defense Andrei Antonovich Grechko was insisting on initiating an atomic attack on industrial centers in China. But the Generalissimo, whom experience had made wise, supposed this was a possibility. Brezhnev, however, was indecisive and eventually merely issued a command to carry out a large-scale attack on Chinese territory with Grad artillery pieces to a depth of twelve miles. New clashes took place in April, May, June, and

August 1969, both in the Far East and in the Xinjiang sector of the border. But those clashes marked the end of the matter.

Meanwhile, in late March 1969 Chiang convened the Tenth Congress of the Guomindang. It took place from March 29 to April 9 in the majestic Sun Yat-sen palace, erected three years earlier in the Yangming Mountains. Taking part in it were 1,198 persons, including 596 delegates representing 919,327 members of the party. Since the Ninth Congress in 1963 the party had grown by 252,327 persons. Workers and peasants still constituted 23 percent of the members, and, as before, there were few women, only slightly more than earlier at 9 percent. Data on the number of younger party members below forty was not provided, but those below thirty-five constituted 39 percent. Among party members, 56 percent had higher and medium-level education.[18] Chiang presided over the opening and closing sessions. In his speech on March 29 he called on all members of the Guomindang and citizens of the country to fulfill three tasks: "Carry out all-around reforms, and lay a firm foundation for revival; rally together as one to eradicate the Communist bandits; and give birth to a New China based on the ethical, democratic, and scientific Three Principles of the People."[19]

The congress adopted new party statutes by which the post of deputy *zongcai* (general director, leader) was eliminated. A new organ was established, the Presidium of the Central Advisory Committee, composed of eleven persons. Meiling was one of its members along with other distinguished veterans, including Sun Fo, He Yingqin, Zhang Qun, and Chen Lifu, who had returned to Taiwan from the United States in 1966. The Central Advisory Committee itself was expanded from 144 to 154 members. The Central Committee was likewise enlarged from 74 to 99 members and from 35 to 51 candidate members. Chiang, naturally, was unanimously elected as *zongcai* again. Ching-kuo, as before, was included on the Central Committee and elected to its Standing Committee, now consisting of 21 members, at its First Plenum following the congress.[20]

The congress, as usual, went well, and there were no surprises, nor could there be since the members of the party were accustomed to subordinating themselves to the leaders. But the international situation remained trying. On the eve of the congress more bad news came from Washington. On March 27 the new US secretary of state, William P. Rogers, testifying before the Senate Committee on Foreign Relations, said, "One could hardly consider how to proceed on such fundamental matters as the Middle East, Viet-Nam [Vietnam], and disarmament without paying careful contemplation of our relations with the other so-called superpower [the Soviet Union] and the potential power of Communist China. . . . We . . . continue to look forward to a time when we can make progress toward a useful dialogue to reduce tensions, resolve our differences, and move to more constructive relations [with China]."[21] But now Ching-kuo, who, on January 25, 1965, had assumed the post of minister of defense in Taiwan and had become deputy chair of the Executive Yuan on July 1, 1969, dealt with relations with the United States. Chiang became particularly close to him while at the same time cooling vis-à-vis his younger son Wei-kuo. The change in feelings was connected to the fact that on January 21, 1964, a certain General Zhao Zhihua suddenly launched an antigovernment uprising in the small town of Hukou, not far from Taipei. Zhao had replaced Wei-kuo as commander of the First Tank Division in 1963. Wei-kuo then took over the duties of rector of the General Staff Ground Forces Academy. Zhao was quickly arrested by his own subordinates and nothing came of the mutiny, but Chiang was unable to forgive Wei-kuo for having recommended the future rebel for the post of division commander. Wei-kuo was deeply upset that he had let his father down and bitterly said to his acquaintances, "I am not put on the same level as the pig and the dog." Wei-kuo, as stated above, had been born in the Year of the Dragon (1916), Chiang in the Year of the Pig (1887), and Ching-kuo in the Year of the Dog (1910).[22]

Chiang now spent a lot of time in the Yangming Mountains. In 1969 he decided to build a new residence, somewhat higher in the mountains than his old *Caolu.* It was called Zhongxing binguan (Renaissance villa). On September 19, 1969, around five o'clock in the afternoon, he and Meiling got into an automobile accident on a mountain road. The culprit, the driver of an American jeep, suddenly came speeding around a curve. The lead car of Chiang's convoy stopped abruptly to avoid a head-on collision, and his luxurious Cadillac, following behind, smashed into its rear. Chiang and Meiling were not wearing seat belts; they were thrown up and hit their heads hard against the top of the vehicle. Then they were flung forward, directly against the steel partition that separated the passenger compartment from the driver. Meiling hurt her arms and legs, and Chiang, who was in his eighty-second year, smashed his face, causing his false teeth to fly out of his mouth. He was seriously injured, and both he and Meiling were taken to the nearest veterans' hospital.

For a long time Meiling was unable to stand on her feet and spent several months in bed. Chiang's trauma soon passed, but after a while his doctor, Xiong Wan, discovered a heart murmur in one of his heart arteries. From then on, Chiang began to be unwell, frequently complaining about pains and a burning sensation in his rib cage. His physician, an experienced man who had been with him since 1943, understood that Chiang had a damaged aortic valve. He did whatever he could, but Chiang's age and the nervous stress that resulted from the accident left the Generalissimo with little to no chance of recovery. He again developed problems with his prostate gland. He had another operation, but it was unsuccessful, and he often had blood in his urine.[23]

Both the incident and Chiang's illness were state secrets, as is the practice in authoritarian and totalitarian countries. Even the Americans heard of the accident only half a year later. Nixon expressed his sympathy to Chiang and Meiling as late as mid-November 1969.[24] Nixon's delayed sympathy was appreciated, but both Chiang and Meiling would have preferred that, in place of the empty words of support the president of the United States uttered he would stop genuflecting to Maoist China. But he didn't stop. At the end of 1969 Nixon, on whom they had counted so much, withdrew the US Seventh Fleet from the Taiwan Strait, and in early October 1970, in an interview with *Time* magazine, he even expressed his desire to visit the PRC. "If there is anything I wanted to do before I die, it is to go to China," he said. "If I don't, I want my children to."[25] A year later, in April 1971, at the invitation of Chinese table tennis officials acting on the personal orders of Mao, a table tennis team from the United States traveled to China from the Japanese city of Nagoya, where the thirty-first world table tennis championship matches were being held. On April 14 the Americans—as well as ping-pong players from Canada, Colombia, England, and Nigeria who were taking part in the competition and were invited along with the Americans—were festively received in the Chinese parliament. Languages around the world were enriched by a new expression: "ping-pong diplomacy."[26] Soon afterward, on July 9, 1971, Nixon's special representative, Henry A. Kissinger, the president's national security advisor, arrived in Beijing via Pakistan. For three days he conversed with Zhou Enlai and officials of the PRC Ministry of Foreign Affairs behind closed doors. On July 15, 1971, by prior agreement, a joint Sino–American communiqué on the talks was made public. That same day Nixon emphasized that his national security advisor had brought him an invitation from Premier Zhou that he accepted with pleasure.[27]

The news virtually knocked Chiang off his feet and was followed by a succession of ever more bad news. In early October the governor of California, Ronald Reagan, arriving in Taipei on assignment from Nixon, tried to explain to Chiang that the Americans had to allow the PRC into the UN.

Chiang was given a choice: either agree to dual Chinese representation of the PRC and Taiwan in the UN or voluntarily withdraw. Under pressure from Meiling, the ailing Chiang preferred to save face, and on October 25, 1971, the Taiwan delegation left the UN building and a delegation from the PRC took its place. An appropriate resolution to this effect was adopted by the General Assembly. The American representative, who, until then had defended Taiwan's rights, withdrew his objections. Four months later, on February 21, 1972, the president of the United States and his wife, Pat, arrived in Beijing, where Nixon was received by Mao. Afterward, on February 28 a joint Sino–American communiqué was published that, in addition to setting forth various positions of the two sides on a range of issues in international politics, emphasized that "progress toward the normalization of relations between China and the United States is in the interests of all countries."[28]

In March 1972 Chiang ran for president for the last time. He was now eighty-five, but that probably did not bother the members of the central organs of the Guomindang. Initially both the Central Advisory Committee and then the Central Committee unanimously nominated him, in order, as they put it, "to satisfy the general desire of the Chinese people."[29] No one asked the Chinese people, of course, but this bothered no one, including, most likely, the Chinese people themselves. Chiang received 1,308 of 1,316 votes, that is, 99.4 percent. This was his best result in all the years of taking part in elections! C. K. Yen ran a second time for vice president and received 1,095 of 1,307 votes or, 83.8 percent.[30]

Real power, however, was already in the hands of Ching-kuo, who in May 1972 replaced C. K. Yen as chair of the Executive Yuan. Chiang had almost entirely stepped away from affairs of state, and in July 1972 he became seriously ill. After accidentally catching cold and despite receiving intensive care, he not only failed to get better but began to get worse. His attending physician wrote, "I remember once at Sun Moon Lake, Mr. Chiang asked me in to chat, and I noticed at once something wrong with his speech. It seemed to me he had suffered a slight heart attack." The doctor now became worried, and Chiang was transported to his new residence Zhongxing binguan high up on the Yangming Mountains. It was cooler there, but unfortunately for Chiang *fengshui* (the organization of space in accordance with Daoist concepts) turned out to be inauspicious, and as he was strolling about one day Chiang suddenly felt a heaviness in his legs. He stopped, unable to take another step. The doctors and bodyguards carried him back home and put him in bed. But he kept getting worse. Xiong suggested he be hospitalized, and

Chiang agreed. "Good, I will go to the hospital," he said in a slurred voice, but he was unable to stand up. His legs turned to jelly, and he pitched forward into the doctor's arms. Xiong gave him an injection and revived him but had to withhold hospitalization. A group of physicians arrived from the neighboring veterans' hospital, and Chiang began to be treated at home. On the evening of July 21 he made a regular entry into his diaries that turned out be his last: "We shall take revenge for the shame.[31] Today I am very tired, and my soul is uneasy. This afternoon Anguo came to see me.[32] Then I rode with Ching-kuo along mountain roads."[33] The next morning Chiang came down with pneumonia and began to gasp for breath. At five o'clock in the afternoon he fell into a coma. On August 6 he was carefully transported to the veterans' hospital, to ward no. 6. Meiling, Chiang's devoted niece Jeanette, and Ching-kuo moved into the adjacent rooms.

Meanwhile, a wave of diplomatic recognition of the PRC was taking place around the world. In September 1972 Prime Minister Tanaka of Japan visited Mao, and diplomatic relations were established between the PRC and the Land of the Rising Sun. A month later an exchange of ambassadors took place between the PRC and the Federal Republic of Germany and, later on, with many other countries.

But by now Chiang did not know what was happening in the world, as he was lying on his bed, unconscious. He was constantly surrounded by doctors, headed by Xiong Wan, but they were powerless. At Dr. Xiong's suggestion, the well-known cardiologist Paul Yu (Yu Nangeng), who headed the cardiology department at the University of Rochester Medical Center in New York, was invited to come from America.[34] But he could do nothing either. Chiang was slowly dying. His arterial pressure was high, and he was having a very hard time breathing.[35]

Chiang emerged from the coma half a year later, in January 1973. The first thing he did after regaining consciousness was to call for Ching-kuo. He wanted to discuss affairs of state with him. Thereafter, Ching-kuo came to report to him every evening. As soon as the sun began setting, Chiang would ask his doctors, "Has Ching-kuo come?" If the answer was "yes," he would order dinner. He did not dine without Ching-kuo. If Wei-kuo dropped in to the ward, Chiang would allot him a few minutes and then say, "Good, there is nothing to discuss, you may go!"[36]

In mid-1973 he became better and could now get out of bed. They began taking him in a wheelchair to the hospital courtyard. But he still spent several more months in the hospital, and not until December 22, 1973, did the doctors give permission for him to be taken to his urban residence in Shilin.[37] Meiling, Jeanette, and Ching-kuo as well as all his attending physicians and nurses also moved there. Since the patient was improving every day, Paul Yu returned to New York, but Dr. Xiong consulted with him daily by telephone.

During the time Chiang was ill, Meiling was also hospitalized, although this news was kept from him. Cancer was discovered in her mammary gland, and she had to have part of a breast removed.[38] Strong by nature, however, Meiling survived the disease. On March 25, 1974, she was even able to attend a farewell dinner marking the departure from Taiwan of US Ambassador Walter P. McConaughy. At her wish, Chiang also attended the dinner, in a wheelchair, emaciated, and deathly pale. On call in the next room was the entire medical staff with an oxygen tank and medicines.[39] But help was not needed, as Chiang sat through the entire dinner till the end. He never appeared in public again.

Until April 1975, however, he actually felt not bad at all, both physically and spiritually, and his mind continued to work well.[40] Every day Meiling came to see him at lunch, as Ching-kuo did every evening, and Chiang enjoyed their company. Once he asked his wife and son to come together to see him, then join their hands and swear to love each other after his death. They fulfilled his request.[41]

The crisis came at the beginning of April. Suddenly the peaks on the electrocardiogram went flat. Chiang's heart had stopped beating. The doctors immediately added medicine to the IV line, and his heart resumed beating. Chiang regained consciousness and in a weak voice asked a nurse to read him verses of the Tang poets that spoke of a traditional event in China: the holiday commemorating the deceased (*qingming jie*) that was observed on April 4–6. And the nurse read him the verses of Du Mu (803–52) titled *Qingming:*

> On Qingming heavy rain is falling
> Delirious, I wander along paths, my soul thirsting for God.
> "Tell me, please, where can I drink my fill of wine?"
> "In Xinghua,"[42] the young shepherd points out the road.[43]

On April 5, contrary to his habit, Ching-kuo came to see his father in the morning. He asked how he had spent the night. Chiang replied that he had slept very well.

"You go and rest up," he said.

Ching-kuo left but he went to work, not to rest. All day he felt out of sorts.[44] Not for nothing. At eight o'clock in the evening Chiang again took a turn for the worse. He had a heart attack. His heart stopped for a second time. Dr. Xiong injected him in the heart. The spiking lines on the electrocardiogram resumed but soon they flattened out. Xiong injected him again. At that moment Meiling and Ching-kuo entered the room. Chiang's heartbeat, then stopped. Xiong turned to Meiling and said, "You see, we cannot save him, perhaps we should stop trying?"

But Meiling commanded, "No! Continue!"

For another half hour the hapless Xiong tried to revive Chiang, and finally Meiling said, "Stop!" At the very same time, outside the window lightning flashed and a terrible storm broke out, torrential streams of rain splattered on the ground, a hurricane wind howled, rattling the palms. The storm was pure coincidence but still very symbolic.

The Generalissimo had died in his eighty-eighth year.

Those trying to save Chiang had forgotten to look at their watches, so when Chiang's secretary asked the doctor, "What time did the honorable gentleman die?" he could not answer. But to tell the truth, he was frightened. It was already around two in the morning on April 6. Dr. Xiong thought for a moment, then, recalling that he had begun to revive Chiang three hours earlier, replied, "At 11:50 p.m., April 5."[45]

# *Epilogue*

It's impossible not to love Taipei. It has everything: ultramodern commercial centers, broad boulevards, and one of the tallest skyscrapers in the world, Taipei 101, which is 1,667 feet tall, and luxurious, well-known Western hotels. And, at the same time, there are bustling night markets with innumerable colorful stalls selling traditional Chinese food and consumer goods, and hole-in-the-wall eating places where one can try snake meat and anything one's heart and stomach desires. In addition, cozy parks, gardens, and embankments; narrow alleys in commercial districts with endless rows of restaurants and all kinds of shops; Buddhist, Confucian, and Daoist temples and shrines under curved roofs; and splendid history and art museums, including the Gugong, the best museum of Chinese art in the world (on fleeing the mainland, the Nationalists took with them all the finest artistic works). All of this bathed in tropical greenery and set in a multicolored sea of flowers, palm and camphor trees towering above.

Founded relatively recently—two hundred years ago—Taipei lies in a broad valley on a bend of the Danshui (Tamsui) River (Bright River). The Jilong (Keelung) River (River Flowing from the District of Jilong) winds around it from the north, and the Xindian River (River Flowing from the District of Xindian) from the south. Both are tributaries of the Danshui. On all sides along the horizon stretch mountains whose slopes are densely covered with evergreen shrubs that, from a distance, look like giant broccoli.

Many Japanese-style buildings are in the city center. Prominent among them is the rose-colored six-story Presidential Office Building with a 197-foot tower over the front entrance. It has a rectangular shape and an interior courtyard divided by a wall into two equal parts. If one views the palace from above it looks like this: 日. In both Japanese and Chinese this is the character for "sun," the first character in the Japanese word *Nippon* and in the Chinese *Riben* (both of which mean Japan). The Japanese constructed two such buildings, both for the governors-general of their colonies, one in the Korean capital Seoul and the other in Taipei. But only one has survived. The palace in Seoul was destroyed after Korea was liberated in 1945. The office of the Chinese governor was initially located here in the Taipei palace after the defeat of Japan, and in March 1950 Chiang Kai-shek moved into it after returning to the post of president of the Republic of China.

Now the first floor of the building is a free museum. It is only open from nine in the morning to noon on weekdays, but earlier visitors may circumnavigate the entire perimeter of the building, look into both interior courtyards, and peruse a photo gallery of Taiwan's history. Entry onto other floors is permitted only to guests of the head of state or officials in the administration. A broad staircase leads from the entrance to the second floor. Located there, as before, is the office of the president, by now the seventh to occupy that office. The current president is a woman named Tsai Ing-wen. She is the first woman president in the history of the island, and the first in whose veins flows not only Chinese but also aboriginal blood. She is the second president who is not a member of the Guomindang. Since 2014 she has been the chair of the Democratic Progressive Party.

A lot has changed since the death of Chiang. Martial law has long since been lifted. Chiang's son Chiang Ching-kuo, who was elected president three years after the death of his father, ended it on July 15, 1987. Genuinely democratic elections to the National Assembly have been held since 1991, to the Legislative Yuan since 1992, and since 1996 for the presidency. The Guomindang has lost the presidential election four times. The Democratic Progressives defeated Chiang's party in 2000, 2004, 2016, and 2020.

Would Chiang have been upset to learn of this? Of course. After all, the Guomindang was his child. And would he have reinstated martial law to put an end to this "outrage"? Possibly. He was harsh, authoritarian, and hot-tempered. On his way to power, he never took pity on people. He unleashed the White Terror in China in 1927, and in the 1950s, on Taiwan, tens of thousands of dissidents were arrested and killed on his orders. In 1947, with his approval, Governor Chen Yi conducted a massacre in Taiwan. (Not until 1987 was it permitted to speak publicly about this.) Also unforgettable are the military crimes he committed during the Sino–Japanese war, and how he condemned to death no fewer than one and a half million civilians by shifting military operations to Shanghai, by destroying the dams on the Yellow River, and by reducing Changsha to ashes. Also well known is that it was he who established a corrupt, oligarchic regime in China that pushed China toward revolution in 1949. Chiang is much to blame for bringing the communists to power in China.

On the other hand, he drew lessons from the defeat on the mainland and laid the social, economic, and cultural-ethical foundations on Taiwan for its current democracy. In the end, he broke with oligarchy and implemented agrarian and other economic reforms, secured a very high rate of economic growth, and encouraged the growth of the middle class that constitutes the majority of Taiwanese society. He led Taiwan to the top among developing countries with respect to the standard of living, implemented Sun Yat-sen's Principle of People's Livelihood, equalized property rights for all citizens, and guaranteed national security for the country and its people. In sum, it was he who pointed the Taiwanese to the path that led to their political freedom. Perhaps he would even have accepted democracy in its current form? Who knows?

Chiang himself could not answer this question. As of April 16, 1975, he reposed in a black granite sarcophagus in a modest mausoleum on the shore of Lake Cihu (Mercy Lake), forty miles southwest of Taipei and close to his beloved villa Daxi. The nature of these places, as mentioned earlier, reminded him of the surroundings of his native village of Xikou. That is why he wished to have his mausoleum built here.

The people of Taiwan and the world were informed of his demise eleven hours after his death, on April 6, 1975. The coffin with the body of the deceased was placed in the monumental Sun Yat-sen Memorial House in the center of Taipei. During the eleven days of bidding him farewell, no fewer than two million persons—about one of every six in Taiwan—passed by the coffin. Chiang lay covered with a flag of the Republic of China, and next to him in the coffin were his favorite books: the Bible, Sun Yat-sen's *Three Principles of the People*, a collection of Tang poetry, and *Streams in the Desert.* Hundreds of thousands of people came to escort Chiang on his final journey. Many knelt down on their knees or prostrated themselves along the road from the center of Taipei to the mausoleum on the shore of Lake Cihu. The funeral procession proceeded for three hours.[1]

Now one can take a cheap Taipei taxi and get to Lake Cihu from downtown Taipei in an hour. A narrow path leads the visitor along the shore through a dense tropical forest. Palm trees rise here and there, young bamboo protrudes from the ground, and a gentle breeze wafts from the still surface of the small lake. After walking for ten minutes one will see a small stone stele with the inscription Cihu lingqin (Mausoleum of Cihu) in the undergrowth of the tropical foliage. In two more minutes the gates of a small pavilion appear. It is constructed in the traditional style of a quadrangular courtyard (*siheyuan*) with an interior courtyard and one-story structures along the perimeter. Directly beyond the gates is a carved, dark red, lacquered wood screen, with two characters—*fu* (happiness) on the outer side, and *shou* (longevity) on the inner side. The screen shields the entrance. One cannot go straight through but rather around it to the right or left. This is also a tradition. The entrance is closed not to visitors but to evil spirits because the latter, as is well known, can travel only in straight lines. One walks around the screen and follows along a balustrade to the central room. In front of it on the right is a small engraved inscription in three languages (Chinese, English, and Japanese): "Please bow before the portrait of Chiang Kai-shek, show respect. Thank you." The doors to the room are open, and at its center stands a black granite sarcophagus. In front of it is a massive yellow cross, and on the wall behind it a portrait of Chiang. Along the wall to left and right are four armchairs, apparently for high-ranking guests. One can stand there quietly, not hurried along, as in Mao's mausoleum. But there are far fewer visitors here than in the Memorial Hall to the Great Helmsman.

The same path leads one back to the entrance, beside which, on a broad lawn, is a memorial park where several dozen statues of the late Generalissimo are displayed. Black, gray, brown, even bright green. Here is Chiang dressed in a semimilitary service jacket. Sun Yat-sen wore a similar jacket, hence the name Sun Yat-sen jacket. Here Chiang is standing, leaning on a cane, here he is sitting in an armchair wearing a Chinese gown, here in a military uniform with epaulets, and there with a book.[2] These sculptures were brought to the mausoleum from all around the country. Here, at least, only the wind and the rain pose any threat to them. Now, in many other places in Taiwan, after the DPP came to power, statues of Chiang have been destroyed. Democracy, as always, begins with the demolition of monuments.

For the majority of young Taiwanese today, Chiang Kai-shek is a bloody dictator who, at best, deserves to be forgotten, if not hated. Youth looks to the future, creating new heroes. And they ignore the fact that without Chiang not only would there not be a prosperous Taiwan, but also there would have not been a successful Northern Expedition of 1926–28; suppression of the militarists; unification of the country; victory in the national revolution; abolition of the unequal treaties; restoration of Chinese control over customs; liquidation of the rights of extraterritoriality and consular jurisdiction of the foreign powers; safeguarding of China's independence and organization of resistance to a superior foe during the fourteen years of Japanese aggression; establishment of alliance relations with the leading countries of the West during the Second World War; and universal recognition of China as one of the five Great Powers. To be sure, Chiang did not transform China into one of the geopolitical centers of the world. That was done by his historic adversary Mao Zedong, who, in the 1960s, situated China equidistant from the two superpowers: the United States and the Soviet Union. But what Chiang did accomplish was enough for one lifetime.

Thus, with or without monuments, Chiang Kai-shek will always remain in the history of China and Taiwan as a great national revolutionary. One can judge him on many counts; he committed mistakes and crimes, but he was a man of his times and of his society. He battled throughout his life. First, with the Manchus, then with the militarists, with the Communists, and with the Japanese. He ruled China longer than anybody else in the twentieth century—nearly half a century, but until his move to Taiwan he rarely had a single day of peace. Even after fleeing to Taiwan, he always had to prepare for war, to strengthen the defense of the island, and take a stand against communism.

He wanted very much not to go down in history as an ordinary dictator. "If I die as a dictator," he said to Ambassador Hurley in May 1945, "I will go down in history, like all dictators, but if I can establish peace, democracy, and unity in the country, I will die as a great leader."[3] Nonetheless, not all of Chiang's descendants publicly take pride in the late Generalissimo, often not wishing to advertise their kinship with him. They live in a different world, many of them in the West, in a liberal environment where dictators are not much liked.

Those who knew Chiang Kai-shek well and were proud of him have long since died. His eldest son, Chiang Ching-kuo, on January 13, 1988 (he is buried not far from his father, also in a small mausoleum), and his younger son, Wei-kuo, on September 22, 1997. Meiling died on October 23, 2003. After her husband's death, she moved back to her beloved New York, closer to her blood relatives. Despite her chronic illnesses, she lived into her 106th year. She was buried in a marble burial vault in the Ferncliff Mausoleum of Ferncliff Cemetery in New York state. The Kong family burial vault, located next to Meiling's, holds the remains of her eldest sister, Nancy (Ailing), who died in 1973; her brother-in-law Kong Xiangxi, who died in 1967; her niece Jeanette, who died in 1994; and her nephews David and Louis, who died in 1992 and 1996, respectively. Not far from them are the burial vaults of Meiling's brothers, T. V. Song (died in 1971) and T. L. Song (died in 1987), as well as that of Chiang's old friend Cicada Zhang. Five years after Meiling's death, her oldest niece Kong Lingyi (Rosamonde) was buried in Meiling's crypt.[4]

Death has not spared the majority of Chiang's grandchildren. Only two of the seven are alive at present: his granddaughter Amy (Xiaozhang), the daughter of Chiang Ching-kuo and Faina Vakhreva, who lives in California, and his grandson John (Xiaoyan), the son of Chiang Ching-kuo and Zhang Yaruo, who lives in Taipei.

All fourteen of Chiang's great-grandsons and great-granddaughters are living, one of whom, Youmei Margarita Faina Maria, the daughter of Eric-Allen, Ching-kuo's oldest, is a poet and artist living in London. She is the oldest member of the family.

Chiang Kai-shek requested that after his death his body not be committed to the earth. He believed the time would come when the Guomindang would defeat the communists, the National government would return to China, and then his body would be transported to Nanjing, the nation's capital, where it would be buried with honors next to his Teacher, Sun Yat-sen, on the slopes of Purple Gold Mountain.

Therefore the small mausoleum in Cihu is temporary. In front of the entrance on both sides of the gates an honor guard of soldiers in steel helmets, parade uniforms, and white gloves stands at attention. They firmly grip their rifles with fixed bayonets. The keen-eyed soldiers safeguard the tranquility of the deceased Generalissimo. Chiang sleeps soundly in his granite coffin. He is waiting to return to Nanjing.

# *Acknowledgments*

This book would never have seen the light of day without the financial support of the Chiang Ching-kuo Foundation for International Scholarly Exchange as well as the Edward and Mary Catherine Gerhold Chair in the Humanities in the United States. I express my sincere gratitude to both of these foundations.

It also gives me great pleasure to express my profound gratitude to my friend and translator of this book, Steven I. Levine. Without his benevolent assistance this book would never have been published.

I also want to thank my other friends and acquaintances in various countries who helped me at different stages of the writing and publishing of the book: Yurii Nikolaevich Arabov, Nikolai Sergeevich Arinchev, Daria Aleksandrovna Arincheva, Richard Ashbrook, Peter W. Bernstein, Ekaterina Borisovna Bogoslovskaia, Andy Carlson, Chen Hongmin, Chen Luyun, Ch'en San-ching, Chen Wei, Ch'en Yung-fa, Georgii Iosifovich Cherniavsky, Cui Jinke, James DeGrand, Joseph W. Esherick, Feng Hailong, Fujishiro Kaori, Huang Tsu-chin, Guo Bin, Erin Greb, Liubov' Spiridonovna Kaliuzhnaia, Lawrence Kenney, Irina Nikolaevna Kondrashina, Liudmila Mikhailovna Kosheleva, Madeline G. Levine, Li Jifeng, Li Kan, Li You, Li Yuzhen, Lin Hsiao-ting, Liu Ke-ch'i, Liu Yuyi, Lü Fang-shang, Ma Zhendu, Stephen MacKinnon, Larisa Nikolaevna Malashenko, Anthony Mughen, Nina Stepanovna Pantsova, Andrei Vital'evich Petrov, R. Christian Philipps, Dexter Roberts, Larisa Aleksandrovna Rogovaia,

Svetlana Markovna Rosental, Jeffrey Schier, John Sexton, Valerii Nikolaevich Shepelev, Boris Vadimovich Sokolov, Irina Nikolaevna Sotnikova, Grigorii Ivanovich Spichak, Kristen Stapleton, David He Sun, Yurii Tikhonovich Tutochkin, Hans J. van de Ven, Aleksandr Iur'evich Vatlin, Wang Qisheng, Wang Wen-lung, Xiao Ruping, Yu Min-ling, and Yang Tianshi.

# *Appendix 1: Chronology of the Life of Chiang Kai-shek*

| | |
|---|---|
| 1887<br>October 31 | In the village of Xikou, Fenghua county, Zhejiang province, a son Ruiyuan (his second, clan name is Zhoutai) is born in the family of Jiang Suan, a shopkeeper, and his wife, Wang Caiyu. |
| 1893 | Is enrolled in a private primary school in his native village. |
| 1895<br>Summer | Father dies. |
| 1901 | Marries a girl named Mao Fumei (born November 9, 1882), at his mother's request. |
| 1903<br>August | Changes his name to Zhiqing (Striving to Be Honest).<br>He fails the *xiucai* (flourishing talent) exam.<br>Enrolls in a county school in the city of Fenghua. |

| | |
|---|---|
| 1905 | |
| Spring | Enrolls in a new school, Golden Arrow, in the city of Ningbo. He becomes acquainted with the ideas of Sun Yat-sen, the leader of the Chinese national democratic movement. |
| 1906 | |
| | Travels to Japan. He enrolls in the Qinghua School and becomes acquainted with his fellow countryman Chen Qimei, a member of Sun Yat-sen's Chinese Revolutionary Alliance. |
| November or December | Meets with Sun Yat-sen on the recommendation of Chen Qimei. |
| 1907 | |
| Summer | After returning from Japan, joins the preparatory group of those wishing to study in foreign military schools, taught in intensive six-month courses at the Baoding Military Academy. |
| 1908 | |
| March | Returns to Japan, where he enrolls in the preparatory military academy Shinbu Gakko (School for Advancing Military Arts). |
| 1908 | |
| | On the recommendation of Chen Qimei, joins Sun Yat-sen's Revolutionary Alliance. |
| 1909 | |
| Summer | Returns to China to prepare for an uprising against the Qing monarchy. |
| 1910 | |
| April 27 | Birth of son Ching-kuo. |
| November | Finishes at Shinbu Gakko and begins practice as a junior officer-in-training in the Nineteenth Field Artillery Company of the Japanese Thirteenth Division in the city of Takada (Honshu island). |
| 1911 | |
| October 10 | An antimonarchical uprising takes place in Wuchang, initiating the bourgeois Xinhai Revolution. |

| | |
|---|---|
| Late October | Sails to Shanghai to take part in the revolution. |
| November | Heads a "dare to die" detachment composed of fishermen from Fenghua county that storms Hangzhou, the capital of Zhejiang province. |
| December | Meets Yao Yiqin (Yecheng) (born August 26, 1887) and takes her as his concubine. |

1912

| | |
|---|---|
| January 1 | Proclamation of the Republic of China. Sun Yat-sen elected provisional president. |
| January 14 | Kills Tao Chengzhang, an opponent of Sun Yat-sen and Chen Qimei. |
| February 12 | Manchu emperor Pu Yi renounces the throne. |
| February 13 | Sun Yat-sen submits his resignation. |
| February 15 | General Yuan Shikai is elected provisional president. |
| March | Again leaves for Japan. He chooses a new name for himself: Jieshi (Firm as a Rock). Publishes a journal *Junsheng* (Voice of the Army). |
| August 25 | Sun Yat-sen founds the Nationalist Party (Guomindang). Chiang joins it. |

1913

| | |
|---|---|
| February | The Guomindang is victorious in parliamentary elections. Chiang returns to China. |
| Summer | Conflict between Sun Yat-sen and Yuan Shikai. Sun begins second revolution: against Yuan Shikai; Chiang takes part. |
| November | Yuan Shikai outlaws the Guomindang. Chiang again flees to Japan. |

1914

| | |
|---|---|
| July 8 | Sun founds a new party, the Chinese Gemingdang (Chinese Revolutionary Party). Chiang joins it. |

1914–15

| | |
|---|---|
| November–May | After the start of the First World War, Japan, as a member of the Entente, occupies Germany's colony in China, the port of Qingdao, after which it presents an ultimatum to Yuan Shikai aimed at transforming China into a Japanese colony. Yuan Shikai's acceptance of Japanese demands triggers an anti-Japanese patriotic movement in China. |

| | |
|---|---|
| 1915 | |
| Autumn–Winter | Participates in a new uprising against Yuan Shikai in Shanghai. |
| 1916 | |
| May 18 | Chen Qimei is killed as the result of an attempt on his life. |
| June 6 | Yuan Shikai dies. In China a years-long struggle for power begins among regional military cliques. |
| 1917 | |
| | Chooses yet another name for himself: Zhongzheng (Central and Correct). |
| September 1 | Sun Yat-sen is elected as Generalissimo of South China. |
| November 7–8 | The Bolshevik party under the leadership of Lenin and Trotsky seizes power in Petrograd. A socialist revolution takes place in Russia. |
| 1918–19 | |
| | Takes part in battles in the south of China on the side of Sun Yat-sen in the Guangdong Army, but he has a series of conflicts with his commanding officer, Chen Jiongming. |
| 1919 | |
| | Adopts the son of his friend Dai Jitao. He names him Wei-kuo and turns him over to his mistress Yecheng to be raised. |
| March | In Moscow the First Congress of the Communist International (Comintern), a worldwide organization of Bolsheviks whose goal is to carry out a world socialist revolution, is held. |
| May 4 | In Beijing a mass student movement begins against the transfer to Japan of the former German colony in China (Qingdao) by the Entente Powers. Following this, a new upsurge of patriotic, anti-Japanese feelings occurs in China. |
| October 10 | Sun Yat-sen reorganizes the Chinese Revolutionary Party into the Chinese Guomindang. |
| 1920–21 | |
| | Attracted to Bolshevism and dreams of visiting Soviet Russia. |

| | |
|---|---|
| 1921 | |
| April 7 | In Canton, Sun Yat-sen is proclaimed emergency president of the Republic of China. He would be inaugurated in a month, on May 5. |
| June 14 | Mother dies. |
| July 23–31 | The First Congress of the Chinese Communist Party is held in Shanghai and Jiaxing. |
| December | Takes a new mistress, Jennie Chen Feng (Jieru) (born August 26, 1906). |
| 1922 | |
| June 15–16 | Supporters of Chen Jiongming mutiny against Sun Yat-sen in Canton. |
| June 29–August 14 | Helps Sun Yat-sen flee from Canton to Shanghai. |
| 1923 | |
| January 26 | Sun Yat-sen and the head of a Soviet diplomatic mission to China, Adolf Abramovich Joffe, sign a declaration in Shanghai by which the USSR pledges support to the Guomindang. |
| February 21 | After the seizure of Canton by militarist forces friendly to Sun Yat-sen, Dr. Sun returns to that city, where he heads a South Chinese government. |
| April | Moves to Canton. |
| August 16 | On Sun Yat-sen's instruction, goes to Moscow as head of a Guomindang delegation. |
| September–November | Holds talks with Bolshevik leaders on assistance to the Guomindang. He becomes disillusioned with Bolshevism and concludes that the Bolsheviks want to take over China. |
| 1924 | |
| January 20–30 | The First Congress of the Guomindang takes place in Canton and proclaims a national united front between the Guomindang and the Chinese Communist Party. Chiang attends its sessions as a guest. |
| January 24 | Sun Yat-sen appoints Chiang as chair of a preparatory committee to organize an infantry offices' academy (Whampoa Academy). |
| May 3 | Assumes duties as head of the Whampoa Academy. |
| October 15 | Suppresses a mutiny of the *shangtuan* (armed militia of the Cantonese merchants). |

| | |
|---|---|
| 1925 | |
| February–March | Takes part in the First Eastern Expedition against Chen Jiongming. |
| March 12 | Sun Yat-sen dies. |
| May 30 | British police on Nanking Road in Shanghai shoot at Chinese demonstrators. The national revolution begins in China. |
| June | Guangxi and Yunnan militarists' troops stationed in Canton are dispersed. |
| August 20 | Sun Yat-sen's comrade in arms Liao Zhongkai dies as the result of an attempt on his life. Wang Jingwei and Chiang Kai-shek come to power. |
| August 26 | Becomes commander of the First Corps of the National Revolutionary Army of the Guomindang. |
| October | Sends his son, Ching-kuo, to study in the USSR. |
| Autumn–Winter | Leads the Second Eastern Expedition against Chen Jiongming. |
| 1926 | |
| January 1–19 | Takes part in the work of the Second Congress of the Guomindang in Canton. Elected a member of the Central Executive Committee of the GMD. After the congress, he enters the Standing Committee and the Political Committee of the CEC. |
| March 20 | Carries out a bloodless coup in Canton, removes Wang Jingwei from power. |
| May | Becomes commander in chief (Generalissimo) of the National Revolutionary Army. |
| Early July | Becomes chair of the Political Council of the Guomindang CEC and launches the Northern Expedition. |
| 1927 | |
| March 22 | Chiang Kai-shek's troops enter Shanghai. |
| April 12 | Unleashes a bloody White Terror in Shanghai and other regions of East China. |
| April 18 | Declares Nanjing the capital of China. |
| July 15 | Wang Jingwei breaks the united front with the communists. |

| | |
|---|---|
| August 13 | Due to factional conflict within the Guomindang, resigns all his posts. |
| December 1 | Marries Song Meiling (born March 4, 1898). |
| **1928** | |
| January | Moves to Nanjing and again becomes commander in chief (Generalissimo) of the National Revolutionary Army. |
| February | Again becomes chair of the Political Council of the Guomindang CEC. |
| April | Continues the Northern Expedition, and on June 15 brings it to a successful conclusion. |
| October 10 | Becomes chair of the government of the Republic of China. |
| December | Manchuria peacefully unites with China. |
| **1929** | |
| January 1 | The Political Council of the Guomindang CEC announces the beginning of the period of political tutelage of the Guomindang over the state and society. |
| February–March | Wages war against the Guangxi militarists. |
| May | Wages war against Feng Yuxiang. |
| September–December | Wages war against Zhang Fakui, Yu Zuobo, Li Mingrui, and the "reorganizationists." |
| **1930** | |
| February–December | Wages war against Yan Xishan. |
| October | Wages war against Feng Yuxiang. |
| October 23 | Baptized according to the protocols of the Methodist Church. |
| November 24 | Becomes chair of the Executive Yuan. |
| Late 1930–early 1931 | Chiang Kai-shek's forces carry out the first punitive expedition against the Central Soviet Area in Southeast China and are defeated. |
| **1931** | |
| April–May | Chiang Kai-shek's forces carry out the second punitive expedition against the Central Soviet Area and are defeated. |

| | |
|---|---|
| July–September | Chiang Kai-shek's forces carry out the third punitive expedition against the Central Soviet Area and are defeated. |
| September 18 | Japan's Kwantung Army begins its occupation of Manchuria. |
| December 15 | Because of interfactional conflict within the Guomindang, Chiang again resigns from all his posts. |
| **1932** | |
| January 22 | At request of the government, Chiang returns to Nanjing and again heads the army. |
| January 28–March 3 | Sino–Japanese armed clashes in Shanghai. |
| **1933** | |
| February–March | Chiang Kai-shek's forces carry out the fourth punitive expedition against the Central Soviet Area and are defeated. |
| September–October 1934 | Chiang Kai-shek's forces carry out the fifth punitive expedition against the Central Soviet Area and are victorious. Chinese communist forces begin the Long March. |
| **1934** | |
| Spring | Inaugurates the New Life Movement throughout the country. |
| **1935** | |
| July–August | The Seventh Congress of the Communist International takes place in Moscow; it adopts a policy of establishing a new, anti-Japanese united front in China. |
| October | Chinese communists complete the Long March in Northwest China. |
| December 16 | Again becomes chair of the Executive Yuan. |
| **1936** | |
| June–September | Wages war against the southwestern militarists. |
| September | Prepares for the sixth anticommunist expedition. |
| October | Sends his younger son Wei-kuo to Germany for a military education. |
| December 12 | Arrested by his subordinates in the city of Xi'an (the Xi'an Incident). |

| | |
|---|---|
| December 25 | Freed after giving a verbal assurance to "reshuffle the government, hold a national salvation conference three months from now, reorganize the Kuomintang [Guomindang], and approve an alliance with Russia and co-operation with the Communist party." |
| **1937** | |
| April 19 | Elder son Ching-kuo and his family return from the USSR. |
| July 7 | Japan initiates a large-scale war against China. |
| August 13 | Shifts military actions against Japan to Shanghai. |
| September 22–23 | Formation of a new united front with the Chinese Communist Party. |
| December 13 | The Japanese seize Nanjing. |
| **1938** | |
| January 1 | Steps down as chair of the Executive Yuan. |
| March 29—April 1 | Convenes an All-China Emergency Congress of the Guomindang in Wuhan, at which he is elected *zongcai* (general director, leader) of the Guomindang. |
| June | Orders destruction of dams on the Yellow River to stop the movement of the Japanese army. |
| October 25 | Wuhan falls. |
| November | Fearing that the Japanese will capture Changsha, orders that the city be burned. |
| December 11 | Again becomes chair of the Executive Yuan. |
| December 29 | Wang Jingwei goes over to the side of the Japanese. |
| **1939** | |
| September 1 | Start of the Second World War. |
| **1940** | |
| October 27 | Younger son Wei-kuo returns to China. |
| **1941** | |
| January 6 | Guomindang troops destroy the headquarters column of the Communist New Fourth Army. |
| March | Roosevelt decides to provide Lend-Lease aid to China. |
| April 13 | The USSR signs a neutrality treaty with Japan. |
| June 22 | Nazi Germany attacks the Soviet Union. |
| December 7 (8) | Japan attacks the United States. |

1942

| | |
|---|---|
| January 1 | Publication of the Declaration of the United Nations. China is included as one of four leading powers. |
| January 3 | Accepts Roosevelt's proposal to assume the position of commander in chief of allied forces in the China Theater of War. |
| February | Chiang and his wife visit India and meet with Gandhi and Nehru. Calls upon the British to grant freedom to India "as soon as possible." |
| March | Lieutenant General Joseph W. Stilwell arrives in China as Chiang Kai-shek's chief of the allied general staff. |

1943

| | |
|---|---|
| January 11 | The United States and Great Britain abrogate the unequal treaties with China. |
| March | Publishes the books *China's Destiny* and *Chinese Economic Theory.* |
| August 1 | Again becomes chair of the government of the Republic of China. |
| November 21–27 | Chiang and his wife take part in the three-power Cairo Conference (USA, Great Britain, China). |

1944

| | |
|---|---|
| April–December | The Japanese conduct the Ichigo offensive, seizing Central China, approaching within 185 miles of Chongqing, China's wartime capital. |
| October 18 | Roosevelt recalls Stilwell from China because of his conflicts with Chiang. |
| November 1 | Chiang's new chief of the allied general staff, General Albert Wedemeyer, arrives in China. |

1945

| | |
|---|---|
| April 25–June 26 | China's representative T. V. Song takes part in the international conference in San Francisco that adopts the UN Charter. |
| June 25 | Steps down as chair of the Executive Yuan. |
| August 6 | The United States drops an atomic bomb on Hiroshima. |

| | |
|---|---|
| August 9 | Soviet troops cross into Manchuria. The United States drops an atomic bomb on Nagasaki. |
| August 14 (15) | Japan surrenders. |
| Late August–mid-October | Holds peace talks with Mao Zedong in Chongqing. |
| October 24 | China enters the UN Security Council as one of five permanent members possessing a veto power. |
| December 21 | US president's special representative George Catlett Marshall Jr. begins mediation between the Chinese Communist Party and the Guomindang. His mediation mission fails and is abandoned January 8, 1947. |

1946

| | |
|---|---|
| June | Start of a new, wide-scale civil war. |

1947

| | |
|---|---|
| February 28 | Per agreement with Chiang Kai-shek, Taiwan governor Chen Yi suppresses massive antigovernment demonstrations on the island. |

1948

| | |
|---|---|
| April 19 | Elected president of the Republic of China. |
| May 20 | Resigns from the post of chair of the government of the Republic of China. |
| December 10 | Declares martial law throughout the main territory of China. |

1949

| | |
|---|---|
| January 21 | Retires as president because of defeats in the war with the communists. |
| April–May | Forces of the Chinese Communist Party take Nanjing and Shanghai. |
| May 19 | Per agreement with Chiang, Chen Cheng, the new governor of Taiwan, declares martial law on the island. |
| October 1 | Mao Zedong proclaims the founding of the People's Republic of China. |
| December 10 | Flies from Chengdu to Taiwan with his eldest son, Ching-kuo. |

| | |
|---|---|
| 1949–51 | Taiwan governor Chen Cheng carries out the first phase of land reform. |
| 1950 | Initiates massive privatization of state enterprises and social reforms. At the same time, he establishes a regime of terror in Taiwan, aimed at the "Red menace." |
| March 1 | Returns to the post of president of the Republic of China. |
| June 25 | The Korean War begins. |
| June 27 | Truman sends the US Seventh Fleet into the Taiwan Strait to defend Taiwan. |
| 1950–52 | |
| | Reforms the Guomindang and carries out military reform. |
| 1951–53 | |
| | Carries out the two final stages of land reform on Taiwan. |
| 1952 | |
| October | Leads the Seventh Congress of the party. Reelected *zongcai.* |
| 1954 | |
| March 22 | Elected president of the Republic of China for a second time. |
| September–April 1955 | Chinese Communists shell Taiwan's offshore islands of Jinmen (Quemoy) and Dachen. |
| December 2 | United States and Taiwan sign a Mutual Defense Treaty. |
| 1955 | |
| January 29 | The US Congress authorizes the president to use armed force to defend Formosa and the Pescadores Islands "as he deems necessary." |
| 1956 | |
| December 25 | Publishes a book of reminiscences titled *Soviet Russia in China.* |
| 1957 | |
| October | Leads the Eighth Congress of the party. Reelected *zongcai.* |

| | |
|---|---|
| 1958 | |
| February 18 | Mao Zedong and the PRC announce a policy of "more, faster, better, and more economically" as the new, general line of the party in socialist construction. Three months later the Second Session of the Eighth Congress of the CCP confirms this policy. The Great Leap begins. |
| Late August | Mao Zedong orders the start of artillery bombardment of the Nationalist-occupied offshore islands of Jinmen (Quemoy) and Mazu (Matsu) in the Taiwan Strait. |
| Winter | Onset of massive famine in the PRC as a result of the Great Leap. |
| 1959 | |
| Late August | Armed conflict on the Sino–Indian border. |
| 1960 | |
| March 21 | Elected for a third time as president of the Republic of China. |
| April | Public polemics begin between the CCP and the CPSU. |
| May 14–15 | Chiang receives US president Dwight Eisenhower. |
| 1963 | |
| July | On Chiang's orders, Taiwan's secret service begins to test the waters for holding secret talks with the USSR. |
| November | Leads the Ninth Congress of the party. Reelected *zongcai.* |
| 1964 | |
| October 16 | The PRC conducts a successful test of a nuclear weapon. |
| 1966 | |
| March 21 | Elected for a fourth term as president of the Republic of China. |
| May 16 | The Great Proletarian Cultural Revolution begins in the PRC. |
| 1968 | |
| July | Approves secret talks between Taiwan and Soviet representatives. |

| | |
|---|---|
| 1969 | |
| March 2 and 15 | Armed conflicts on Damansky (Zhenbao) Island between Soviet and Maoist border guards. |
| March–April | Leads the Tenth Congress of the party. Reelected *zongcai.* |
| September 19 | Involved in an automobile accident with his wife, after which doctor detects a heart murmur as result of damage to aorta. |
| 1971 | |
| October 25 | Taiwan voluntarily withdraws from the UN. The PRC occupies its place. |
| 1972 | |
| February 21 | US President Richard Nixon arrives in the PRC, converses with Mao. |
| February 28 | A joint Sino–American communiqué is published in Shanghai, foreshadowing the normalization of relations between the two countries. |
| March 21 | Elected for a fifth term as president of the Republic of China. |
| Early July | Becomes gravely ill. |
| July 21 | Makes final entry in his diaries. |
| July 22 | Falls into a coma. |
| 1973 | |
| January | Emerges from coma. |
| 1974 | |
| March 25 | Receives a foreign visitor for the last time, US Ambassador Walter P. McConaughy. |
| 1975 | |
| April 5 (approx. 11:50 p.m.) | Dies from a heart attack. |

# *Appendix 2: Chiang Kai-shek's Genealogy*

### *PARENTS*

Father (twenty-seventh generation of the Jiang clan named "zhao"—"novice"): Jiang Suan (Zhaocong) (November 10, 1842–August 24, 1895).
Mother: Wang Caiyu (December 7, 1864–June 14, 1921).

### *WIVES*

First wife: Mao Fumei (November 9, 1882–December 13, 1939). Married in 1901.
Second wife: Olivia Song Meiling (March 4, 1898–October 23, 2003). Married December 1, 1927.

### *OFFICIAL CONCUBINES*

First concubine: Yao Yecheng (August 26, 1887–1966).
Second concubine: Chen Jieru (August 26, 1906–February 21, 1971).

### *CHILDREN*

First child (from his first wife): a son, Chiang Ching-kuo (twenty-ninth generation of the Jiang clan named "guo" ["kuo"]—"state") (April 27, 1910–January 13, 1988).
Chiang Ching-kuo's first wife: Feng Funeng (1911–72). Married late December 1926 or early 1927. Divorced in late 1927.

Chiang Ching-kuo's second wife: Faina Ipatievna Vakhreva (Jiang Fangliang) (May 15, 1916–December 15, 2004). Married March 15, 1935.

Chiang Ching-kuo's mistress: Zhang Yaruo (1913–August 15, 1942).

Second child: Adopted son Chiang Wei-kuo (twenty-ninth generation of the Jiang clan named "guo" ["kuo"]—"state") (October 6, 1916–September 22, 1997).

Chiang Wei-kuo's first wife: Shi Jingyi (September 23, 1924–March 21, 1953). Married February 6, 1945.

Chiang Wei-kuo's second wife: Ellen Qiu Ruxue (born 1934). Married on February 3, 1957.

Third child: adopted daughter Chiang (Chen) Yao-kuang (about 1922–2012).

Chiang (Chen) Yao-kuang's first husband—An unknown Korean named An. Married in the late 1930s, disappeared in 1945.

Second husband: Lu Jiuzhi (1902–February 12, 2008). Married in 1946.

*GRANDCHILDREN*

Thirtieth generation of the Jiang clan named "xiao" ["kuo"]—state:

Grandson (from Chiang Ching-kuo and Jiang Fangliang): Eric (Alan) Jiang Xiaowen (December 14, 1935–April 14, 1989).

Jiang Xiaowen's wife: Nancy Xu Naijin (1937–August 20, 2005). Married in 1960.

Granddaughter (from Chiang Ching-kuo and Jiang Fangliang): Emma (Amy) Jiang Xiaozhang (born February 15, 1938).

Jiang Xiaozhang's husband: Yu Yanghe (December 2, 1924–May 19, 2010). Married August 11, 1960.

Grandson (from Chiang Ching-kuo and Zhang Yaruo): John Zhang (Jiang) Xiaoyan (born March 1, 1942).

Zhang (Jiang) Xiaoyan's wife: Huang Meilun. Married in 1970.

Grandson (from Chiang Ching-kuo and Zhang Yaruo): Winston Zhang (Jiang) Xiaoci (March 1, 1942–February 24, 1996).

Zhang (Jiang) Xiaoci's wife: Zhao Shende.

Grandson (from Chiang Ching-kuo and Jiang Fangliang): Alexander Jiang Xiaowu (April 25, 1945–July 1, 1991).

Jiang Xiaowu's first wife: Wang Zhangshi (born 1951). Married in 1969. Divorced in 1975.

Jiang Xiaowu's second wife: Michelle Cai Huimei (born 1959). Married April 11, 1986.

Grandson (from Chiang Ching-kuo and Jiang Fangliang): Edward Jiang Xiaoyong (October 27, 1948–December 22, 1996).

Edward Jiang's wife: Elizabeth Fang Zhiyi (born 1949). Married July 23, 1973.

Grandson (from Chiang Wei-kuo and Qiu Ruxue): Gregory Jiang Xiaogang (born May 22, 1963).

Jiang Xiaogang's wife: Wang Yihui. Married in 1987.

Grandson (from Chen Yao-kuang and An): Chen Zhongren.
Grandson (from Chen Yao-kuang and An): Chen Xiaoren (died 2009).
Granddaughter (from Chen Yao-kuang and Lu Jiuzhi): Chen Jiuli.

### *GREAT-GRANDCHILDREN*

Thirty-first generation of the Jiang clan named "you"—"brotherhood."
Granddaughter (from Jiang Xiaowen): Margarita Faina Maria Jiang Youmei (born March 21, 1961).
Grandson (from Jiang Xiaozhang): Theodore Yu Zusheng (born in May 1961).
Granddaughter (from Jiang Xiaowu): Jiang Youlan (born January 19, 1972).
Grandson (from Jiang Xiaowu): Jiang Yousong (born July 23, 1973).
Grandson (from Jiang Xiaoyong): Demos Jiang Youbo (born September 10, 1976).
Grandson (from Jiang Xiaoyong): Edward Jiang Youchang (born November 9, 1978).
Grandson (from Jiang Xiaoyong): Andrew Jiang Youqing (born June 14, 1990).
Granddaughter (from Jiang Xiaogang): Jiang Youjuan (born 1992).
Grandson (from Jiang Xiaogang): Jiang Youjie (born in 1994).
Granddaughter (from Jiang Xiaoyan): Vivian Jiang Huilan (born 1970).
Granddaughter (from Jiang Xiaoyan): Jiang Huiyun.
Grandson (from Jiang Xiaoyan): Wayne Jiang Wan'an (born December 26, 1978).
Grandson (from Jiang Xiaoci): Jiang Jingsong (born 1960).
Granddaughter (from Jiang Xiaoci): Jiang Jingju (Jiang Youju).

### *BROTHERS*

Twentieth-eighth generation of the Jiang clan named "rui"—"auspicious."
Elder brother: Jiang Ruisheng (January 3, 1875–December 27, 1936).
Jiang (Jiang) Ruisheng's first wife: née Sun.
Jiang (Jiang) Ruisheng's second wife: née Zhang.
Jiang (Jiang) Ruisheng's third wife: née Dan.
Younger brother: Jiang Ruiqing (October 26, 1894–98).

### *SISTERS*

Twentieth-eighth generation of the Jiang clan named "rui"—"auspicious."
Jiang Ruichun (1874–October 31, 1947).
Jiang Ruichun's husband: Song Zhouyun (late 1860s or early 1870s–early 1930s). Married in 1889.
Jiang Ruilian (June 7, 1890–1937).
Jiang Ruilian's husband: Zhu Zhishan (late 1890s–1971). Married January 25, 1907.
Jiang Ruiju (1892).

# *Notes*

## *INTRODUCTION*

1. See *Foreign Relations of the United States* (hereafter *FRUS*), *1947*, 7:360 (Washington, DC: U.S. Government Printing Office, 1947).
2. On this complaint see Xiaobing Li and Hongshan Li, eds., *China and the United States: A New Cold War History* (Lanham, MD: University Press of America, 1998), 201.
3. Cм.: http://news.sina.com.cn/o/2013-06-13/114427386720.shtml.
4. See Zhang Rong, "Jiang Jieshi ceng liang ci lai Qingdao haibin sanbu youren renchu" (Chiang Kai-shek Visited Qingdao Twice, Walked Along the Beach, Nobody Recognized Him), *Qingdao ribao* (Qingdao Daily), May 23, 2014.
5. Chiang Kai-shek, *Riji* (Diaries), February 12, 20, 28, 1949, Hoover Institution Archives at Stanford University (hereafter Hoover Archives), box 47, folder 10.
6. See ibid., January 29, 31, February 4, 5, 10, 1949, Hoover Archives, box 47, folders 9 and 10.
7. Ibid., February 12, 1949, Hoover Archives, box 47, folder 10.
8. Ibid., May 4, 1949, Hoover Archives, box 47, folder 13.
9. See *FRUS 1948*, 9:1209 (Washington, DC: U.S. Government Printing Office, 1974). See also Jonathan B. Chavanne, "The Battle for China: The U.S. Navy, Marine Corps and the Cold War in Asia, 1944–1949" (PhD diss., Texas A&M University, 2016), 247.
10. See Steven I. Levine, *Anvil of Victory: The Communist Revolution in Manchuria, 1945–1948* (New York: Columbia University Press, 1987).
11. Harry S. Truman, *Strictly Personal and Confidential: The Letters Harry Truman Never Mailed,* ed. Monte M. Poen (Boston: Little, Brown, 1982), 33, 40; Harry S. Truman,

*Off the Record: The Private Papers of Harry S. Truman,* ed. Robert H. Ferrell (Columbia: University of Missouri Press, 1980), 53. See also David McCullough, *Truman* (New York: Simon & Schuster, 1992), 418–19.

12. See Furuya Keiji, *Chiang Kai-shek: His Life and Times* (New York: St. John's University Press, 1981), 823.
13. "President Harry S. Truman's Address before a Joint Session of Congress on March 12, 1947," in Harry S. Truman, *Public Papers of the Presidents of the United States: Harry S. Truman, 1947* (Washington: Government Printing Office, 1963), 176–80.
14. See Charles F. Romanus and Riley Sunderland, *Stilwell's Command Problems* (Washington, DC: Office of the Chief of Military History, Department of the Army, 1956), 72.
15. George C. Marshall, "Memorandum for the President and Proposed Message from the President to the Generalissimo, September 16, 1944," in *Franklin D. Roosevelt Papers as President: Map Room Papers, 1941–1945,* Franklin D. Roosevelt Presidential Library & Museum, box 10, 53–56/220.
16. Quoted from Ch'i Hsi-sheng, *The Much Troubled Alliance: US–China Military Cooperation During the Pacific War, 1941–1945* (Singapore: World Scientific, 2016), 563. Emphasis added by Chiang Kai-shek.
17. *FRUS 1944,* 6:265–66 (Washington, DC: U.S. Government Printing Office, 1967).
18. See Stephen R. MacKinnon and Oris Friesen, *China Reporting: An Oral History of American Journalism in the 1930s and 1940s* (Berkeley: University of California Press, 1987), 161–68; Kenneth E. Shewmaker, *Americans and Chinese Communists, 1927–1945: A Persuading Encounter* (Ithaca: Cornell University Press, 1971), 239–62; Harold R. Isaacs, *The Tragedy of the Chinese Revolution,* with an introduction by Leon Trotsky (London: Secker and Warburg, 1938); André Malraux, *Man's Fate,* trans. Haakon Maurice Chevalie (New York: Modern Library, 1934).
19. See Brooks Atkinson, "Long Stem Seen, Stilwell Breaks Stems from Chiang Refusal to Press War Fully," *New York Times,* October 31, 1944. The final part of the article appeared on p. 4.
20. See *New York Times,* January 27, 1984.
21. See Alan Brinley, *The Publisher: Henry Luce and His American Century* (New York: Alfred A. Knopf, 2010), 296–300; Patricia Neils, *China Images in the Life and Times of Henry Luce* (Savage, MD: Rowman & Littlefield, 1990), 119–52.
22. See Joseph W. Stilwell, *The Stilwell Papers,* arranged and edited by Theodore H. White (New York: Schocken Books, 1972); Graham Peck, *Two Kinds of Time* (Boston: Houghton Mifflin, 1950).
23. See Lloyd E. Eastman, "Fascism in Kuomintang China: The Blue Shirts," *China Quarterly* 49 (January–March 1972): 4, 20; Lloyd E. Eastman, *The Abortive Revolution: China under Nationalist Rule 1927–1937* (Cambridge: Harvard University Press, 1974), 36.
24. See Jeremy E. Taylor and Grace C. Huang, "'Deep Changes in Interpretive Currents'? Chiang Kai-shek Studies in the Post-Cold War Era," *International Journal of Asian Studies* 9, no. 1 (January 2012): 106. On "fascism" in China, also see Maggie Clinton, *Revolutionary Nativism: Fascism and Culture in China, 1925–1937* (Durham: Duke University Press, 2017), 209–10; Brian Tsui, *China's Conservative Revolution: The*

*Quest for a New Order, 1928–1949* (Cambridge: Cambridge University Press, 2018), 5–6.

25. See Jonathan Fenby, *Generalissimo: Chiang Kai-shek and the China He Lost* (London: Free Press, 2003). Thereafter references will be made to the American edition: Jonathan Fenby, *Chiang Kai-shek: China's Generalissimo and the Nation He Lost* (New York: Carrol & Graft, 2004).
26. *The Stilwell Papers* were edited and published by Theodore H. White.
27. See Hans J. van de Ven, *War and Nationalism in China 1925–1945* (London: RoutledgeCurzon, 2003).
28. The diary for 1924 is lost.
29. See Hoover Institution Archives Staff, "An Inventory of the Chiang Kai-shek Diaries 1917–1972" (manuscript).
30. According to the will of the Chiang family some pages of the diaries have not been declassified and will be kept private until 2035.
31. Fang-shang Lu [Lü] and Hsiao-ting Lin, "Chiang Kai-shek's Diaries and Republican China: New Insights on the History of Modern China," *Chinese Historical Review* 15, no. 2 (Fall 2008): 331.
32. See Jay Taylor, *The Generalissimo: Chiang Kai-shek and the Struggle for Modern China* (Cambridge: Harvard University Press, 2009).
33. Many reviewers have pointed to this. See, for instance, reviews by R. Keith Schoppa, Aaron William Moore, Andrew J. Nathan, Arthur Waldron, Charles W. Hayford, Roger Thompson, Joseph W. Esherick, Yu Min-ling, Huang Ko-wu, and other scholars who published correspondently in *Journal of Asian Studies, English Historical Review, New Republic, China Brief, H-Diplo, Journal of Historical Biography, Chinese Historical Review, Hanxue yanjiu* (Sinological Studies), and *Journal of Modern Chinese History.*
34. For a comparison of Chiang Kai-shek's original diaries and Mao Sicheng's copies, see Ma Zhendu, "Chiang Kai-shek's Diary: A Comparison between the Original and Copies Compiled by Mao Sicheng—Using Entries from July 1926 as Examples," *Journal of Modern Chinese History* 5, no. 2 (December 2011): 247–60.
35. Author's interviews with the director of the Second Historical Archives Ma Zhendu in Nanjing, June 3, 2017, and Professor Yang Tianshi, Research Fellow of the Institute of Modern History of the PRC Academy of Social Sciences, in Taipei, June 20, 2017.

## 1. *DESCENDANT OF ZHOU GONG*

1. In traditional China the day was divided into twelve two-hour periods which, like the years in the twelve-year cycle, were named after animals. The time from 11:00 a.m. to 1:00 p.m. was called the Hour of the Horse.
2. See Confucius, *The Analects of Confucius,* trans. and notes Simon Leys (New York: W. W. Norton, 1997), 29, 36, 93; L. S. Perelomov, *Konfutsii: Lun Yu* (Confucius: Lunyu) (Moscow: Izadatel'skaia firma "Vostochnaia literatura" RAN, 1998), 347, 409.
3. *Zhou Yi,* [Song] Zhu Xi zhu ([Book] of Changes of the Zhou Era), with commentary by [Song] Zhu Xi) (Shanghai: Shanghai guji chubanshe, 1995), 57; Ch'u Chai with Winberg Chai, eds., *I Ching: Book of Changes,* trans. J. Legge (New Hyde Park, NJ: University Books, 1964), 91. Emphasis added.

4. *Zhou Yi*, [Song] Zhu Xi zhu, 58; *I Ching*, 288. Emphasis added.
5. Information about the birth and early days of the life of Chiang Kai-shek is based on the author's impressions on visiting the village of Xikou on August 8, 2009, and materials from the Xikou Museum of the Jiang family. See also Chiang Kai-shek, *Riji* (Diaries), June 1919 and January 1, 1920, Hoover Archives, box 1, folder 18 and box 2, folder 4; Letter from one of Chiang Kai-shek's relatives to the author, October 26, 2014; Mao Sicheng, *Minguo shiwu nian yiqian zhi Jiang Jieshi xiansheng* (Mr. Chiang Kai-shek Before 1926) (Hong Kong: Long men shudian, 1965), 7–8; Wang Tiancang, *Xikou fengguang* (Xikou Scenery) (Ningbo: Ningbo chubanshe, 2003); Cui Xiaozhong, *Qingnian Jiang Jieshi* (Young Chiang Kai-shek) (Beijing: Huawen chubanshe, 2003), 2–14; Chen Bulei, *Jiang Jieshi xiansheng nianbiao* (Chronological Biography of Mr. Chiang Kai-shek) (Taipei: Zhuanji wenxue chubanshe, 1978), 1–2; Wan Renyuan and Fang Qingqiu, eds., *Jiang Jieshi nianpu chugao* (Draft Chronological Biography of Chiang Kai-shek), 1:1 (Beijing: Dang'an chubanshe, 1992); Cheng Shuwei et al., *Jiang Jieshi mishi* (Secret History of Chiang Kai-shek) (Beijing: Tuanjie chubanshe, 2007), 9–10; Furuya, *Chiang Kai-shek*, 3–4.
6. See Yang Shubiao and Yang Jing, *Jiang Jieshi zhuan (1887–1949)* (Biography of Chiang Kai-shek [1887–1949]) (Hangzhou: Zhejiang daxue chubanshe, 2008), 1–2; Taylor, *The Generalissimo*, 10–11; Hollington K. Tong, *Chiang Kai-shek: Soldier and Statesman: Authorized Biography*, 1:2–3 (Shanghai: China Publishing Co., 1937).
7. Wang, *Xikou fengguang* (Xikou Scenery), 135; Du Fu, *Du Fu quanji* (Complete Works of Du Fu) (Hong Kong: Guangzhi shuju, [195?]), 84.
8. See Wang, *Xikou fengguang* (Xikou Scenery), 81–85, 132–33, 135.
9. In traditional China brides were dressed entirely in red because that is the color of prosperity and good fortune.
10. See Hsieh Shou-kang, *President Chiang Kai-shek: His Childhood and Youth* (Taipei: China Cultural Service, [1954]), 15–16; Cui, *Qingnian Jiang Jieshi* (Young Chiang Kai-shek), 10.
11. See the letter from one of Chiang Kai-shek's relatives to the author, November 13, 2014; Chiang Kai-shek, "Xian bi Wang tai furen shilüe" (Brief Biography of the Late Mother, Mrs. Wang), in Chiang Kai-shek, *Jiang zongtong yanlun huibian* (Collected Works of President Chiang), 24:63–64 (Taipei: Zhongzheng shuju, 1956); Cheng, *Jiang Jieshi mishi* (Secret History of Chiang Kai-shek), 5–9; the author's impressions on visiting Xikou village, August 8, 2009.
12. See "Mao Fumei," *Zhongguo baike zai xian* (Chinese Internet Encyclopedia), http://www.zwbk.org/MyLemmaShow.aspx?zh=zh-tw&lid=263253.
13. Chiang, "Xian bi Wang tai furen shilüe" (Brief Biography of the Late Mother, Mrs. Wang), 63. On the solicitous relationship of Chiang's grandfather toward him, see the latter's reminiscences, published in S. I. Hsiung, *The Life of Chiang Kai-shek* (London: Peter Davies, 1948), 7–9.
14. See Chiang, *Riji* (Diaries), August 1929, Hoover Archives, box 2, folder 11; Hsiung, *The Life of Chiang Kai-shek*, 17; Wang, *Xikou fengguang* (Xikou Scenery), 30–31; Chen, *Jiang Jieshi xiansheng nianbiao* (Chronological Biography of Mr. Chiang Kai-shek), 3.
15. The author's impressions on visiting the village of Xikou, August 8, 2009.

16. Chiang, *Riji* (Diaries), 1917, Hoover Archives, box 1, folder 1; Chiang Kai-shek, "Bao guo yu si jin" (My Debt to the Country and My Thoughts about My Mother), in Chiang, *Jiang zongtong yanlun huibian* (Collected Works of President Chiang), 24:69.
17. See Hsieh, *President Chiang Kai-shek*, 29–33, 37.
18. See Tong, *Chiang Kai-shek: Soldier and Statesman*, 1:11.
19. See Pichon P. Y. Loh, *The Early Chiang Kai-shek: A Study of His Personality and Politics, 1887–1924* (New York: Columbia University Press, 1971), 9.
20. Chiang, "Xian bi Wang tai furen shilüe" (Brief Biography of the Late Mother, Mrs. Wang), 64–65.
21. See ibid., 64. See also Chiang's other reminiscences of his mother published in his collected works: Chiang, *Jiang zongtong yanlun huibian* (Collected Works of President Chiang), 24:68–72, 141–42.
22. See Mao, *Minguo shiwu nian yiqian Jiang Jieshi xiansheng* (Mr. Chiang Kai-shek Before 1926), 8.
23. Chiang, "Xian bi Wang tai furen shilüe" (Brief Biography of the Late Mother, Mrs. Wang), 63.
24. There are 49 chapters in *Li Ji*. *Da xue* and *Zhong yong*, which are parts of the Four Classical Books, are two chapters from this treatise published as separate books.
25. See Chen, *Jiang Jieshi xiansheng nianbiao* (Chronological Biography of Mr. Chiang Kai-shek), 2–3; Hsiung, *The Life of Chiang Kai-shek*, 38.
26. Quoted from Tong, *Chiang Kai-shek: Soldier and Statesman*, 1:6.
27. See Mao, *Minguo shiwu nian yiqian zhi Jiang Jieshi xiansheng* (Mr. Chiang Kai-shek Before 1926), 14.
28. Chiang's reminiscences of his maternal grandmother are published in Hsiung, *The Life of Chiang Kai-shek*, 10–12.
29. Quoted from Mao, *Minguo shiwu nian yiqian zhi Jiang Jieshi xiansheng* (Mr. Chiang Kai-shek Before 1926), 14, translated by Steven I. Levine.
30. Incidentally, unlike the overwhelming majority of Chinese women at the time, including Chiang Kai-shek's mother, Fumei did not bind her feet every day, and therefore she was able to work very efficiently.
31. Quoted from Ch'en Chieh-ju, *Chiang Kai-shek's Secret Past: The Memoir of His Second Wife*, ed. and with an introduction by Lloyd E. Eastman (Boulder, CO: Westview Press, 1993), 31–2; see also Chiang, *Riji* (Diaries), 1917; Jay Taylor, *The Generalissimo's Son: Chiang Ching-kuo and the Revolutions in China and Taiwan* (Cambridge: Harvard University Press, 2009), 5–6.
32. Mao, *Minguo shiwu nian yiqian zhi Jiang Jieshi xiansheng* (Mr. Chiang Kai-shek Before 1926), 16.
33. Loh, *The Early Chiang Kai-shek*, 12–13.
34. Mao, *Minguo shiwu nian yiqian zhi Jiang Jieshi xiansheng* (Mr. Chiang Kai-shek Before 1926), 16.
35. Taylor, *The Generalissimo*, 11.
36. Chiang, *Riji* (Diaries), 1917.
37. It is said that Sun arbitrarily chose the pseudonym Zhongshan, under which he became particularly well known in Mainland China, when, after arriving in Tokyo in 1897, he

registered in a hotel. He glanced at a Japanese newspaper that was lying on the registration counter and his gaze fell upon two characters *zhong* (middle), the first character in the word *Zhongguo* (China), and *shan* (mountain or mountains). So he took the name Zhongshan (Nakayama). The character *qiao*, or in Japanese *kiroki* (woodcutter) that he adopted somewhat later, in addition to its literal meaning, in Japanese also has an indirect, somewhat deprecatory meaning of "modest person." The result was thoroughly in the Confucian spirit—"A Modest Man in the Chinese Mountains."

38. For Charles R. Hager's recollections of his meetings with Sun Yat-sen and Sun's christening, see Charles R. Hager, "Doctor Sun Yat Sen: Some Personal Reminiscences," in Lyon Sharman, *Sun Yat-sen: His Life and Its Meaning: A Critical Biography* (New York: John Day, 1934), 382–87.
39. For more about Sun Yat-sen, see Marie-Claire Bergère, *Sun Yat-sen* (Stanford: Stanford University Press, 1998).
40. See Sun's reminiscences of this: Sun Yat-sen, *Kidnapped in London: Being the Story of My Capture, Detention at, and Release from the Chinese Legation* (Bristol, UK: Simpkin, Marshall, Hamilton, Kent, 1897).
41. Quoted from Cui, *Qingnian Jiang Jieshi* (Young Chiang Kai-shek), 45.
42. Chiang, *Riji* (Diaries), 1917; Mao, *Minguo shiwu nian yiqian zhi Jiang Jieshi xiansheng* (Mr. Chiang Kai-shek Before 1926), 17.
43. Chiang, *Riji* (Diaries), 1917.
44. Harry A. Franck, *Marco Polo Junior: The True Story of an Imaginary American Boy's Travel-adventures All over China* (New York: Century, 1929), 26; See also Zhe Fu, ed., *Ningbo jiu ying* (Old Pictures of Ningbo) (Ningbo: Ningbo chubanshe, 2004).
45. Chiang, *Riji* (Diaries), 1917.
46. See "Mao Fumei," *Zhongguo baike zai xian* (Chinese Internet Encyclopedia).
47. See Cui, *Qingnian Jiang Jieshi* (Young Chiang Kai-shek), 34.
48. Mama Wang was citing the ancient Chinese Confucian philosopher Mencius (372–289 BCE). For the English translation, see Mencius, *The Works of Mencius,* trans. with critical and exegetical notes, prolegomena, and copious indexes by James Legge (New York: Dover, 1970), 313.
49. Tong, *Chiang Kai-shek: Soldier and Statesman,* 1:vii.
50. See ibid., 1:vii–viii, 12.
51. Chiang, *Riji* (Diaries), 1917.
52. Chiang, "Xian bi Wang tai furen shilüe" (Brief Biography of the Late Mother, Mrs. Wang), 63.
53. Mao, *Minguo shiwu nian yiqian zhi Jiang Jieshi xiansheng* (Mr. Chiang Kai-shek Before 1926), 18.

## 2. *IN THE SHADOW OF THE RISING SUN*

1. Chiang, *Riji* (Diaries), 1917; Yamada Tatsuo, "Jiang Jieshi jiyi zhong zhi Riben liuxue" (Chiang Kai-shek's Reminiscences about Studying in Japan), in Huang Zijin and Pan Guangzhe, eds., *Jiang Jieshi yu Xiandai Zhongguo de xingsu* (Chiang Kai-shek and the Formation of Contemporary China), 1:9–10 (Taipei: Zhongyang yanjiuyuan jindaishi yanjiusuo, 2013).

2. See Yamada, "Jiang Jieshi jiyi zhong zhi Riben liuxue" (Chiang Kai-shek's Reminiscences about Studying in Japan), 6–7.
3. See Wenxin Zheng, "Sun Yat-sen and Japan, 1895–1915," MA thesis (Bowling Green, OH, 1998), 67; Marius B. Jansen, *The Japanese and Sun Yat-sen* (Cambridge: Harvard University Press, 1954), 112; Huang Fuqing, *Qing mo liu zhi xuesheng* (Chinese Students in Japan in the Late Qing Dynasty) (Taipei: Zhongyang yanjiuyuan jindai-shi yanjiusuo, 2010), 17.
4. Jansen, *The Japanese and Sun Yat-sen,* 112.
5. See Ch'en Li-fu, *The Storm Clouds Clear over China: The Memoir of Ch'en Li-fu, 1900–1993* (Stanford: Stanford University Press, 1994), 23; on Chen Qimei, see Qin Xiaoyi, ed., *Chen Yingshi xiansheng jinian ji* (Collection in Memory of Chen Yingshi) (Taipei: Jingxiao chu zhongyang wenwu gongyingshe, 1977); Mo Yongming and Fan Ran, *Chen Yingshi jinian* (Chronology of the Life of Chen Yingshi) (Nanjing: Nanjing daxue chubanshe, 1991).
6. See Sun Yat-sen, *Prescriptions for Saving China: Selected Writings of Sun Yat-sen,* ed., with an Introduction and Notes by Julie Lee Wei, Ramon H. Myers, Donald G. Gillin, trans. Julie Lee Wei, E-su Zen, Linda Chao (Stanford: Hoover Institution Press, [1994]); Chiang Kai-shek, *Riji* (Diaries), 1917; Hsieh, *President Chiang Kai-shek,* 58–63; Chen Xiqi, ed., *Sun Zhongshan nianpu changbian* (Large Chronological Biography of Sun Zhongshan), 2 vols. (Beijing: Zhonghua shuju, 1991); Duan Yunzhang and Ma Qingzhong, eds., *Sun Zhongshan cidian* (Dictionary of Sun Zhongshan) (Guangzhou: Guangdong renmin chubanshe, 1994).
7. Ch'u Chai and Winberg Chai, eds., *Li Chi: Book of Rites: An Encyclopedia of Ancient Ceremonial Usages, Religious Usages, Religious Creeds, and Social Institutions,* trans. James Legge, 1:364–66 (New Hyde Park, NY: University Books, 1967).
8. See Sun Yat-sen, *Izbrannye proizvedeniia* (Selected Works), 2nd ed., revised and expanded (Moscow: Nauka, 1985), 118–20; see also Paul Linebarger, *The Political Doctrines of Sun Yat-sen: An Exposition of the San min chu i* (Baltimore: Johns Hopkins University Press, 1937); Bergère, *Sun Yat-sen;* David J. Lorenzo, *Conceptions of Chinese Democracy: Reading Sun Yat-sen, Chiang Kai-shek and Chiang Ching-kuo* (Baltimore: Johns Hopkins University Press, 2013).
9. In the literature on Chiang Kai-shek several dates for this meeting are indicated: 1905, 1906, 1907, 1908, and 1909. But Sun was not in Japan in either 1908 or 1909, and in 1905 Chiang was still studying in China. In his diaries Chiang himself indicates that he became acquainted with Sun the year he arrived in Japan, that is, in 1906. Considering that Sun was in Tokyo on that trip from October 9, 1906, to March 4, 1907, and that Chiang, as discussed below, left Japan no later than the beginning of January 1907, one must conclude that the meeting of the two revolutionaries could have taken place only in late 1906.
10. Quoted from Hsieh, *President Chiang Kai-shek,* 70.
11. Quoted from Tong, *Chiang Kai-shek: Soldier and Statesman,* 1:16.
12. On Sun Yat-sen's appearance, see David Strand, *An Unfinished Republic: Leading by Word and Deed in Modern China* (Berkeley: University of California Press, 2011), 33; Fernand Farjenel, *Through the Chinese Revolution: My Experience in the South and North: The Revolution of Social Life: Interviews with Party Leaders: An Unconstitutional*

*Loan—The Coup d'État* (New York: Frederick A. Stokes, 1916), 252; S. A. Dalin, *Kitaiskie memuary: 1921–1927* (Chinese Memories: 1921–1927) (Moscow: Nauka, 1975), 109; Minge zhongyang xuanchuanbu, ed., *Huiyi yu huainian—Jinian Sun Zhongshan xiansheng wenzhang xuanji* (Memoirs and Warm Reminiscences—Selected Articles in Memory of Mr. Sun Zhongshan) (Beijing: Huaxia chubanshe, 1986).

13. See Hsieh, *President Chiang Kai-shek*, 70; Jin Guo, *Jiang Jieshi yu Jiang Jingguo, Jiang Weiguo* (Chiang Kai-shek, Chiang Ching-kuo and Chiang Wei-kuo) (Beijing: Dongfang chubanshe, 2009), 15.
14. Walter Del Mar, *Around the World Through Japan* (London: A. and C. Black, 1903), 141.
15. See Hsieh, *President Chiang Kai-shek,* 69; Taylor, *The Generalissimo,* 18.
16. Quoted from Hsieh, *President Chiang Kai-shek,* 63.
17. Cui, *Qingnian Jiang Jieshi* (Young Chiang Kai-shek), 14.
18. Chiang Kai-shek's brother-in-law died in Taiwan in 1971.
19. Chiang, *Riji* (Diaries), 1917.
20. See Mao, *Minguo shiwu nian yiqian zhi Jiang Jieshi xiansheng* (Mr. Chiang Kai-shek Before 1926), 21–22.
21. See Yamada, "Jiang Jieshi jiyi zhong zhi Riben liuxue" (Chiang Kai-shek's Reminiscences about Studying in Japan), 11.
22. Chiang, *Riji* (Diaries), August 1929, Hoover Archives, box 7, folder 1.
23. Ibid.
24. Quoted from Khe Hsian-nin (He Xiangning), *Vospominaniia o Sun Yat-sene* (Reminiscences of Sun Yat-sen), trans. Yu. M. Garushiants (Moscow: Progress, 1966), 24.
25. Chiang, *Riji* (Diaries), 1917.
26. Ibid.
27. Guoshiguan (Academia Historica), document no. 002-050101-00001-002. See also Mao, *Minguo shiwu nian yiqian zhi Jiang Jieshi xiansheng* (Mr. Chiang Kai-shek Before 1926), 24. Translated by Steven I. Levine.
28. See Cui, *Qingnian Jiang Jieshi* (Young Chiang Kai-shek), 34.
29. Chiang Kai-shek's home in Xikou, as pointed out earlier, was called Fenggao, from the names of two earlier capitals of the Zhou dynasty, Fengjing and Gaojing.
30. See Chiang, *Riji* (Diaries), 1917; Taylor, *The Generalissimo,* 19; Taylor, *The Generalissimo's Son,* 6–7; Jin, *Jiang Jieshi yu Jiang Jingguo, Jiang Weiguo* (Chiang Kai-shek and Chiang Ching-kuo, Chiang Wei-kuo), 12; Wang, *Xikou Fengguang* (Xikou Scenery), 31.
31. Chiang, *Riji* (Diaries), 1917.
32. Even Chiang Kai-shek's Japanese was not as good as Zhang Qun's. Subsequently, Chiang would sometimes use Zhang as his interpreter from Japanese.
33. See Yamada, "Jiang Jieshi jiyi zhong zhi Riben liuxue" (Chiang Kai-shek's Reminiscences about Studying in Japan), 11–12.
34. Ibid., 15.
35. Quoted from Mao, *Minguo shiwu nian yiqian zhi Jiang Jieshi xiansheng* (Mr. Chiang Kai-shek Before 1926), 24. See also Chiang, *Riji* (Diaries), 1917.
36. See the reminiscences of his commander cited in Hsiung, *The Life of Chiang Kai-shek,* 58–61.

37. Chiang, *Riji* (Diaries), August 1929.
38. The Bushido (literally "Way of the Warrior") is a military code of a Japanese samurai.
39. Quoted from Hsiung, *The Life of Chiang Kai-shek,* 66.
40. See Tong, *Chiang Kai-shek: Soldier and Statesman,* 1:17.

### 3. *ALL-UNDER-HEAVEN IS FOR EVERYONE*

1. See Mao, *Minguo shiwu nian yiqianlai zhi Jiang Jieshi xiansheng* (Mr. Chiang Kai-shek Before 1926), 26.
2. See Ying Mengqing, "Fenghua yumin canjia guangfu Hangzhou gansidui ji" (Notes on the Dare-to-die Detachment of Fenghua Fishermen that Took Part in the Restoration of Sovereignty in Hangzhou), in Zhongguo renmin zhengzhi xieshanghui Zhejiang sheng weiyuanhui wenshi ziliao yanjiu weiyuanhui, ed., *Zhejiang xinhai geming huiyilu* (Reminiscences of the Xinhai Revolution in Zhejiang) (Hangzhou: Zhejiang renmin chubanshe, 1981), 186–92.
3. Chiang, *Riji* (Diaries), 1917.
4. See Yang Tianshi, *Dizhi de zhongjie: Jianming Xinhai geming shi* (End of Imperial Rule: Brief History of the Xinhai Revolution) (Changsha: Yuelu shushe, 2011), 328–30.
5. On the Xinhai Revolution in Shanghai, see Shanghai shehui kexueyuan lishi yanjiusuo, ed., *Xinhai geming zai Shanghai shiliao xuanji* (zengdingben) (Collection of Selected Materials on the History of the Xinhai Revolution in Shanghai), expanded ed. (Shanghai: Shanghai renmin chubanshe, 2011); Yao Fan, *Hu jun dudu—Xinhai geming zhong de Chen Yingshi* (Military Dudu of Shanghai: Chen Yingshi during the Xinhai Revolution) (Shanghai: Shanghai wenyi chubanshe, 1982).
6. See Brian G. Martin, *The Shanghai Green Gang: Politics and Organized Crime, 1919–1937* (Berkeley: University of California Press, 1996), 79–80, 242.
7. See Stella Dong, *Shanghai: The Rise and Fall of a Decadent City* (New York: Perennial, 2000), 86–88.
8. Chiang, *Riji* (Diaries), August 1929 and February 10, 1931, Hoover Archives, box 7, folder 18 and box 8, folder 3.
9. See Martin, *The Shanghai Green Gang,* 80–81.
10. Quoted from Jonathan D. Spence and Chin Anping, *The China Century: A Photographic History of the Last Hundred Years* (New York: Random House, 1996), 99.
11. On Zhang Jingjiang, see Zhang Jiangzhi, *Zhang Jingjiang zhuan* (Biography of Zhang Jingjiang) (Wuhan: Hubei renmin chubanshe, 2004); *Zhang Jingjiang xiansheng baisui jinian ji* (Memorial Collection on the Centenary of Zhang Jingjiang) (Taipei: Shijie she, 1976); Nelson Chang et al., *The Zhangs from Nanxun: A One Hundred and Fifty Year Chronicle of a Chinese Family* (Denver: CF Press, 2010).
12. The *qin* is an ancient Chinese musical instrument.
13. Yechangjin is the name of a canal in Jiangsu province, on the banks of which was the native hamlet of Chiang's passion; it is now part of the city of Suzhou.
14. See Cui, *Qingnian Jiang Jieshi* (Young Chiang Kai-shek), 87–88.
15. See Earl Albert Selle, *Donald of China* (New York: Harper & Brothers, 1948), 108.
16. Chiang, *Riji* (Diaries), February 20, 1931, Hoover Archives, box 8, folder 3.

17. See Mary Backus Rankin, *Early Chinese Revolutionaries: Radical Intellectuals in Shanghai and Chekiang, 1902–1911* (Cambridge: Harvard University Press, 1971), 151–54.
18. Quoted from Loh, *The Early Chiang Kai-shek,* 27. See also Tao Chengzhang, *Tao Chengzhang ji* (Works of Tao Chengzhang) (Beijing: Zhonghua shuju, 1986); Zhongguo renmin zhengzhi xieshanghui Zhejiang sheng weiyuanhui wenshi ziliao yanjiu weiyuanhui, *Zhejiang Xinhai geming huiyilu* (Reminiscences of the Xinhai Revolution in Zhejiang), 21; R. Keith Schoppa, *Chinese Elites and Political Change: Zhejiang Province in the Early Twentieth Century* (Cambridge: Harvard University Press, 1982), 148–49.
19. Chiang, *Riji* (Diaries), February 20, 1931.
20. Zhejiang sheng xinhai geming shi yanjiu hui, Zhejiang sheng tushuguan, eds., *Xinhai geming Zhejiang shiliao xuanji* (Collection of Selected Materials on the History of Zhejiang during the Xinhai Revolution) (Hangzhou: Zhejiang renmin chubanshe, 1982), 357.
21. Quoted from Jonathan D. Spence, *The Search for Modern China,* 3rd ed. (New York: W. W. Norton, 2013), 254. See also S. L. Tikhvinsky, ed., *Novaia istoriia Kitaia* (Modern History of China) (Moscow: Nauka, 1972), 502; Chen Xiqi, ed., *Sun Zhongshan nianpu changbian* (Large Chronological Biography of Sun Zhongshan), 1:654–61 (Beijing: Zhonghua shuju, 1991).
22. Chiang, *Riji* (Diaries), 1917, August 1929 and February 20, 1931.
23. Chiang, *Riji* (Diaries), 1917, August 1929; Hsiung, *The Life of Chiang Kai-shek,* 74.
24. See Selle, *Donald of China,* 132.
25. Quoted from Tikhvinsky, *Novaia istoriia Kitaia* (Modern History of China), 513; see also Chen, *Sun Zhongshan nianpu changbian* (Large Chronological Biography of Sun Zhongshan), 1:714–35.
26. See Mao, *Minguo shiwu nian yiqian zhi Jiang Jieshi xiansheng* (Mr. Chiang Kai-shek before 1926), 28.
27. See Cui, *Qingnian Jiang Jieshi* (Young Chiang Kai-shek), 88–89.
28. The election, needless to say, was not universal. Only men over twenty-one who owned property worth at least five hundred Chinese dollars or who paid annual tax of two Chinese dollars could vote, amounting to forty million persons, or about 10 percent of the population. See Spence, *The Search for Modern China,* 266.
29. Chiang, *Riji* (Diaries), 1917, August 1929 and February 20, 1931.
30. Ibid., August 1929.
31. A comprador is a local entrepreneur and middleman who has business relations with foreign colonialists and imperialists, helping them exploit the resources of his own country. In China at the time there was no sharp distinction between the national bourgeoisie and the comprador. All business that was the property of the nationally inclined bourgeoisie was nonetheless closely linked with the foreigners.
32. Chiang, *Riji* (Diaries), August 1929 and February 20, 1931. See also Furuya, *Chiang Kai-shek,* 52–53.
33. Chiang, *Riji* (Diaries), August 1929 and February 20, 1931.
34. Quoted from Chiang Kai-shek, "Chen Yingshi xiansheng guichou hou zhi geming jihua ji shilüe" (The Revolutionary Plans and Brief Biography of Mr. Chen Yingshi after the Guichou Year), in Chiang, *Jiang zongtong yanlun huibian* (Collected Works of President Chiang), 24:31.

35. See George T. Yu, *Party Politics in Republican China: The Kuomintang, 1912–1924* (Berkeley: University of California Press, 1966), 118; Furuya, *Chiang Kai-shek,* 56–57.
36. See Cui, *Qingnian Jiang Jieshi* (Young Chiang Kai-shek), 74–75.
37. See Bergère, *Sun Yat-sen,* 259.
38. Quoted from Furuya, *Chiang Kai-shek,* 57.
39. *The Sacred Books of China: The Texts of Taoism,* book 1, trans. James Legge (Oxford: Clarendon Press, 1891), 189.

## 4. *SUN YAT-SEN'S OBSTINATE PUPIL*

1. Quoted from Bergère, *Sun Yat-sen,* 257.
2. Quoted from Yu, *Party Politics in Republican China,* 119.
3. See Bergère, *Sun Yat-sen,* 257.
4. This is what Lenin called Sun Yat-sen. V. I. Lenin, "Democracy and Narodism in China," *V. I. Lenin, Collected Works,* 18:165 (Moscow: Progress, 1975).
5. See Bergère, *Sun Yat-sen,* 256–69; Tong, *Chiang Kai-shek: Soldier and Statesman,* 1:61.
6. The Hakka (guest people) were clans from the north of China that had resettled in the southern provinces many centuries earlier under pressure from the steppe nomads, but they had not assimilated with the local population (*bendi*), native inhabitants who despised and exploited them.
7. См.: Chiang, *Riji* (Diaries), 1917, August 1929 and February 21, 1931; Mao, *Minguo shiwu nian yiqian zhi Jiang Jieshi xiansheng* (Mr. Chiang Kai-shek Before 1926), 30–31, 33–34; Hsiung, *The Life of Chiang Kai-shek,* 81–82; Hsieh, *President Chiang Kai-shek,* 106–9.
8. Quoted from Wei Hongyun, *Sun Zhongshan nianpu (1866–1925)* (Chronological Biography of Sun Zhongshan [1866–1925]) (Tianjin: Tianjin renmin chubanshe, 1979), 55.
9. See Chiang, *Riji* (Diaries), August 1929 and February 20, 1931; Mao, *Minguo shiwu nian yiqian zhi Jiang Jieshi xiansheng* (Mr. Chiang Kai-shek Before 1926), 34–35; Loh, *The Early Chiang Kai-shek,* 29, 130; Hsiung, *The Life of Chiang Kai-shek,* 86–87; Tong, *Chiang Kai-shek: Soldier and Statesman,* 1:42–44.
10. See Bergère, *Sun Yat-sen,* 264–65.
11. Chiang, *Riji* (Diaries), August 1929 and February 20, 1931; Mao, *Minguo shiwu nian yiqian zhi Jiang Jieshi xiansheng* (Mr. Chiang Kai-shek Before 1926), 36; Hsiung, *The Life of Chiang Kai-shek,* 88.
12. Quoted from Hsiung, *The Life of Chiang Kai-shek,* 91.
13. Chiang, *Riji* (Diaries), August 1929.
14. Quoted from Hannah Pakula, *The Last Empress: Madame Chiang Kai-shek and the Birth of Modern China* (New York: Simon & Schuster, 2009), 56; see also Selle, *Donald of China,* 66, 139, 140, 143.
15. See Bergère, *Sun Yat-sen,* 250; "Dr. Sun Yat-sen Museum Tells Story of Dr. Sun's First Wife, Lu Muzhen (With Photos)," http://www.info.gov.hk/gia/general/201204/20/P201204200485.htm.
16. Quoted from Edgar Snow, *Journey to the Beginning* (New York: Random House, 1958), 88.

17. See Taylor, *The Generalissimo,* 27.
18. See Snow, *Journey to the Beginning,* 88; Pakula, *The Last Empress,* 63–65.
19. Two other, younger brothers, who did not play an important role in Chiang's life as Meiling, Ailing, Qingling, and T. V. Song, were named T. L. Song and T. A. Song.
20. Quoted from "The Song Qingling House Museum Exhibition in Shanghai," http://www.huaxia.com/zhwh/whrd/2011/02/2300913.html.
21. See Hsiung, *The Life of Chiang Kai-shek,* 95.
22. See Chen, *Jiang Jieshi xiansheng nianbiao* (Chronological Biography of Mr. Chiang Kai-shek), 7.
23. See Yan Lu, *Pre-understanding Japan: Chinese Perspectives, 1895–1945* (Honolulu, HI: University of Hawai'i Press, 2004), 146–47, 287; Shen Shiming and Xu Yong, eds., *Sun Zhongshan yu Huzhou ren* (Sun Zhongshan and People from Huzhou) (Beijing: Tuanjie chubanshe, 2001), 367–69.
24. At the time Chiang and Dai were living together again; Chiang on the first floor of the small private house and Dai on the second.
25. See Chen, *Chiang Kai-shek's Secret Past,* 73–75.
26. It will be recalled that Chiang Kai-shek's house in Xikou was called Fenggao, after the names of two early capitals of the Zhou dynasty: Fengjing and Gaojing. Chiang Kai-shek's eldest son already bore the child name Jianfeng (He Who Shall Build the Capital of Feng).
27. The literal translation of the characters *jing* and *wei* are "the longitude" and "the latitude." The character *guo* means "state." The meaning is: Ching-kuo will rule the state from north to south (the longitude), and Wei-kuo from west to east (the latitude). Such were the ambitious names Chiang Kai-shek bestowed on his children.
28. See Wang Shichun, *Qianshan duxing: Jiang Weiguo de ren sheng zhi lü* (The Solitary Path among a Thousand Mountains: The Life Path of Chiang Wei-kuo) (Taipei: Tianxia wenhua, 1996), 20; Chiang Wei-kuo and Liu Fenghan, *Jiang Weiguo koushu zizhuan* (The Autobiography of Chiang Wei-kuo as Told by Himself) (Beijing: Zhongguo dabaike quanshu chubanshe, 2008), 1, 43.
29. See Loh, *The Early Chiang Kai-shek,* 133.
30. See Wan and Fang, *Jiang Jieshi nianpu chugao* (Draft Chronological Biography of Chiang Kai-shek), 1:27; Hsiung, *The Life of Chiang Kai-shek,* 97–98.
31. See Chiang, *Riji* (Diaries), March 5, 15, 1918, and February 21, 1931, Hoover Archives, box 1, folder 4 and box 8, folder 3; Mao, *Minguo shiwu nian yiqian zhi Jiang Jieshi xiansheng* (Mr. Chiang Kai-shek Before 1926), 50, 52.
32. Quoted from Leslie H. Dingyan Chen, *Chen Jiongming and the Federalist Movement: Regional Leadership and Nation Building in Early Republican China* (Ann Arbor: University of Michigan Press, 1999), 65.
33. Chiang, *Riji* (Diaries), March 15, 1918, Hoover Archives, box 1, folder 4.
34. Ibid., April 24–30 and May 1, 1918, Hoover Archives, box 1, folders 5 and 6.
35. Ibid., June 25, 1918, Hoover Archives, box 1, folder 7.
36. Ibid., July 26, 31 and August 21, 1918, Hoover Archives, box 1, folder 8 and 9.
37. Quoted from Hsieh, *President Chiang Kai-shek,* 116. See also Wan and Fang, *Jiang Jieshi nianpu chugao* (Draft Chronological Biography of Chiang Kai-shek), 1:32–33.

38. Chiang, *Riji* (Diaries), August 29, 1918, Hoover Archives, box 1, folder 9.
39. See Mao, *Minguo shiwu nian yiqian zhi Jiang Jieshi xiansheng* (Mr. Chiang Kai-shek Before 1926), 67–73, 75; Tong, *Chiang Kai-shek: Soldier and Statesman,* 1:53; Chiang, *Riji* (Diaries), March 7 and 8, 1919, Hoover Archives, box 1, folder 15.
40. See Wan and Fang, *Jiang Jieshi nianpu chugao* (Draft Chronological Biography of Chiang Kai-shek), 1:32–33.
41. Quoted from ibid., 35–36. See also Tong, *Chiang Kai-shek: Soldier and Statesman,* 1:52–54.
42. Quoted from Yu, *Party Politics in Republican China,* 157; see also Bergère, *Sun Yat-sen,* 279.
43. See Chiang, *Riji* (Diaries), various entries of late 1918–the first half of 1919, Hoover Archives, box 1, folders 13–18; Hsieh, *President Chiang Kai-shek,* 118; Zhang Xiuzhang, *Jiang Jieshi riji jiemi* (Chiang Kai-shek's Diaries Reveal Secrets) (Beijing: Tuanjie chubanshe, 2007), 24.
44. Chiang, *Riji* (Diaries), October 12, 1919, Hoover Archives, box 2, folder 1.
45. The text of Sun Yat-sen's telegram to Moscow has not been found. For the reply of the Soviet government over the signature of the People's Commissar for Foreign Affairs of Soviet Russia G. V. Chicherin, see A. A. Gromyko, ed., *Dokumenty vneshnei politiki SSSR* (Documents of the USSR Foreign Policy), 1:415–16 (Moscow: Politizdat, 1957).
46. Chiang, *Riji* (Diaries), October 23, November 5, 16, 27–29, December 1, 2, 6–8, and 12, 1919, Hoover Archives, box 2, folders 1–3; Zhang, *Jiang Jieshi riji jiemi* (Chiang Kai-shek's Diaries Reveal Secrets), 24.
47. See Chiang, *Riji* (Diaries), November 2–3, 1919, Hoover Archives, box 2, folder 2.
48. Ibid., November 16, 1919, Hoover Archives, box 2, folder 2.
49. Ibid., November 27–December 12, 1919, January 8, February 26, and March 18, 1920, Hoover Archives, box 2, folder 2–6.
50. Ibid., March 14, 1920, Hoover Archives, box 2, folder 6.
51. Ibid., various entries of 1920, Hoover Archives, box 2, folders 4–15.
52. Ibid., February 24, 1920, Hoover Archives, box 2, folder 5.
53. Quoted from Yang Tianshi, "Perspectives on Chiang Kai-shek's Early Thoughts from His Unpublished Diary," in Mechthild Leutner et al., eds., *The Chinese Revolution in the 1920s: Between Triumph and Disaster* (London: RoutledgeCurzon, 2002), 78.
54. A. Potapov, "O doktore Sun Yat-sene, byvshem pervom presidente Kitaiskoi respubliki," Russian State Archives of Social and Political History (hereafter RGASPI), collection 514, inventory 1, file 6, sheet 35; see also M. L. Titarenko et al., eds., *VKP(b), Komintern i Kitai: Dokumenty* (The CPSU, Comintern and China: Documents), 1:46 (Moscow: AO "Buklet," 1994).
55. Titarenko, *VKP(b), Komintern i Kitai: Dokumenty* (The CPSU, Comintern and China: Documents), 1:42–44, 60; Chen, *Chen Jiongming and the Federalist Movement,* 233–34.
56. G. Voitinsky, "Moi vstrechi s Sun Yat-senom" (My Meetings with Sun Yat-sen), *Pravda* (Truth), March 15, 1925.
57. See Titarenko, *VKP(b), Komintern i Kitai: Dokumenty* (The CPSU, Comintern and China: Documents), 1:46; Khe, *Vospominaniia o Sun Yat-sene* (Reminiscences of Sun

Yat-sen), 60; Jiang Yihua, *Guomindang zuopai qizhi—Liao Zhongkai* (Banner of the Left Guomindang Liao Zhongkai) (Shanghai: Shanghai renmin chubanshe, 1985), 69–70.

58. Khe, *Vospominaniia o Sun Yat-sene* (Reminiscences of Sun Yat-sen), 60.
59. Chiang, *Riji* (Diaries), April 26, 1920, Hoover Archives, box 2, folder 5.
60. Ibid., May 1, 16–27 and June 6, 1920, Hoover Archives, box 2, folders 8 and 9.
61. Ibid., July 19, 1920, Hoover Archives, box 82, folder 10.
62. Quoted from Mao, *Minguo shiwu nian yiqian zhi Jiang Jieshi xiansheng* (Mr. Chiang Kai-shek Before 1926), 247.
63. Chiang, *Riji* (Diaries), August 7, 31 and September 15, 1920, Hoover Archives, box 2, folders 11 and 12.
64. Ibid., September 22, October 1, 3 and 5, 1920, Hoover Archives, box 2, folders 12 and 13.
65. Ibid., October 20, 1920, Hoover Archives, box 2, folder 13.
66. Loh, *The Early Chiang Kai-shek,* 32.
67. Quoted from Hsiung, *The Life of Chiang Kai-shek,* 115–16.
68. See Sheng Yonghua, ed., *Song Qingling nianpu (1893–1981)* (Chronological Biography of Song Qingling), 1:174 (Guangzhou: Guangdong renmin chubashe, 2006). On the history of Canton, see Alexander V. Pantsov with Steven I. Levine, *Mao: The Real Story* (New York: Simon & Schuster, 2012), 131–32.
69. Chiang, *Riji* (Diaries), December 25, 1920, Hoover Archives, box 2, folder 15.
70. Quoted from Hsiung, *The Life of Chiang Kai-shek,* 118–24.
71. Chiang, *Riji* (Diaries), January 12, 1921, Hoover Archives, box 2, folder 16.
72. See Hsiung, *The Life of Chiang Kai-shek,* 124–28; see also Chiang, *Riji* (Diaries), January 6–11 and 13 January 1921, Hoover Archives, box 2, folder 16.
73. Quoted from Hsieh, *President Chiang Kai-shek,* 122.
74. Chiang, *Riji* (Diaries), February 19 and 20, 1921, Hoover Archives, box 2, folder 17.
75. Quoted from Hsieh, *President Chiang Kai-shek,* 123.
76. Quoted from Bergère, *Sun Yat-sen,* 295.
77. See Jiang, *Guomindang zuopai qizhi—Liao Zhongkai* (Banner of the Left Guomindang Liao Zhongkai), 69.
78. Ibid.
79. See Titarenko, *VKP(b), Komintern i Kitai: Dokumenty* (The CPSU, Comintern and China: Documents), 1:60.
80. Ibid., 1:73.
81. See Pantsov with Levine, *Mao,* 101.
82. Sun, *Izbrannye proizvedeniia* (Selected Works), 300.
83. Chiang, *Riji* (Diaries), March 3, 27, April 3, 4, 17, 21, 27, 28, May 1, 2, 5, 17, and 21, 1921, Hoover Archives, box 2, folders 18–20.
84. Ibid., May 24, 27, and 31, 1921, Hoover Archives, box 2, folder 20.
85. Ibid., June 21, 1921, Hoover Archives, box 2, folder 21. See also May 28, 1920, Hoover Archives, box 2, folder 20.
86. Ibid., June 14, 1921, Hoover Archives, box 2, folder 21.
87. See "Jiang Jieshi quan kao zong mu hao fengshui" (Chiang Kai-shek Buried His Mother Strictly According to Fengshui), http://www.csxxly.com/lywh_detail/

newsId=6.html; interview with scholar at Institute of Modern History of Academia Sinica Yu Min-ling in Taipei, September 22, 2015.

88. *Li* is a Chinese measure of distance equal to 0.31 mile.
89. See Chiang, *Riji* (Diaries), June 17, 19, 20, 23, 26, 27, July 22, 25, 26, and August 5, 1921, Hoover Archives, box 2, folders 21–23.
90. See Lü Fangshang, ed., *Jiang Zhongzheng xiansheng nianpu changbian* (Large Chronological Biography of Mr. Jiang Zhongzheng), 1:146 (Taipei: Guoshiguan, 2014).
91. Chiang, *Riji* (Diaries), October 1, 1921, Hoover Archives, box 3, folder 2.
92. See Lü, *Jiang Zhongzheng xiansheng nianpu changbian* (Large Chronological Biography of Mr. Jiang Zhongzheng), 1:146.
93. See Mao, *Minguo shiwu nian yiqian zhi Jiang Jieshi xiansheng* (Mr. Chiang Kai-shek Before 1926), 136.
94. Ibid.
95. See Wan and Fang, *Jiang Jieshi nianpu chugao* (Draft Chronological Biography of Chiang Kai-shek), 1:73.
96. See Chiang, *Riji* (Diaries), November 28, 1921, Hoover Archives, box 3, folder 3; Cui, *Qingnian Jiang Jieshi* (Young Chiang Kai-shek), 55–56.
97. Quoted from Hsieh, *President Chiang Kai-shek,* 130–31.
98. Chiang, *Riji* (Diaries), November 28, 1921, Hoover Archives, box 3, folder 3. See also ibid., September 3, 7, 8, and 10, 1921, Hoover Archives, box 3, folder 1.
99. See Mao, *Minguo shiwu nian yiqian zhi Jiang Jieshi xiansheng* (Mr. Chiang Kai-shek Before 1926), 137.

## 5. *CANTON–SHANGHAI–MOSCOW–CANTON*

1. See Ch'en, *Chiang Kai-shek's Secret Past,* 83–85; The author's impressions on visiting the grave of Chen Jieru in the Park of Happiness and Longevity (Fushouyuan) in Shanghai, April 23, 2016.
2. See Ch'en, *Chiang Kai-shek's Secret Past,* 21–22, 35–85.
3. There are numerous errata in Jennie's book. For example, she asserts that after the "wedding" celebration on December 5, 1921, she and Chiang spent no less than a month in East China and on December 1 (!) 1921 sailed from Shanghai via Hong Kong to Canton, from which on December 10 (!) they arrived at Sun Yat-sen's headquarters in Guilin (Guangxi province).
4. Chiang, *Riji* (Diaries), December 12, 15, and 18, 1921, Hoover Archives, box 3, folder 4; Mao, *Minguo shiwu nian yiqian zhi Jiang Jieshi xiansheng* (Mr. Chiang Kai-shek Before 1926), 137.
5. Chiang's biographer Jay Taylor has already drawn attention to the lack of a photocopy of a marriage certificate and any reference to a wedding in Chiang Kai-shek's diaries. See Taylor, *The Generalissimo,* 604–5.
6. See Ch'en, *Chiang Kai-shek's Secret Past,* 117.
7. For Maring's personal dossier in the Comintern archive, see RGASPI, collection 495, inventory 244, file 176.

8. Some historians, to be sure, express doubt that Maring and Sun Yat-sen discussed the question of a military academy. See A. G. Yurkevich, *Moskva–Kanton, 1920-e: Pomoshch' SSSR Gomindanu i dve strategii ob"edineniia Kitaia* (Moscow–Canton, 1920s: USSR Aid to the Guomindang and Two Strategies for Uniting China) (Moscow: OOO "Variant," 2013), 96–97.
9. See "Otchet tov. Maringa Kominternu: Iul' 1922 g." (Com. Maring's Report to the Comintern: July 1922), RGASPI, collection 514, inventory 1, file 20, sheets 85–91; Zhang Tailei, *Zhang Tailei wenji* (Works of Zhang Tailei), 1:330 (Beijing: Renmin chubanshe, 1981); *Zhongguo geming shi jiangyi* (Lectures on the History of the Chinese Revolution) (Beijing: Zhongguo renmin daxue chubanshe, 1983), 98; Harold Isaacs, "Documents on the Comintern and the Chinese Revolution," *China Quarterly* 45 (January–March 1971): 103–4; Lin Hongnuan, "Zhang Tailei," in Hu Hua, ed., *Zhonggongdang shi renwu zhuan* (Biographies of Persons in the History of the CCP), 4:81–82 (Xian: Shaanxi renmin chubanshe, 1985); Guangdong renmin lishi bowuguan, ed., *Zhonggong "sanda" ziliao* (Documents of the Third CCP Congress) (Guangzhou: Guangdong renmin chubanshe, 1985), 12; Tony Saich, *The Origins of the First United Front in China: The Role of Sneevliet (Alias Maring),* 1:81, 216–46, 252, 317–23; 2:928 (Leiden: Brill, 1991).
10. See Saich, *The Origins of the First United Front in China,* 1:317.
11. Sun, *Izbrannye proizvedeniia* (Selected Works), 303.
12. Quoted from Chiang Chung-cheng (Chiang Kai-shek), *Soviet Russia in China: A Summing-up at Seventy,* trans. under the direction of Madame Chiang Kai-shek, revised, enlarged ed. with maps (New York: Farrar, Straus and Cudahy, 1957), 17.
13. A program for the industrialization of China was set forth by Sun Yat-sen in his work *The International Development of China,* which came out in 1920.
14. Sun, *Izbrannye proizvedeniia* (Selected Works), 303–4.
15. For more details, see Pantsov with Levine, *Mao,* 89, 92–93, 98–100, 102–6; Alexander V. Pantsov and Daria A. Arincheva, *Zhizni i sud'by pervykh kitaiskikh kommunistov: Sbornik statei k 100-letiiu Kompartii Kitaia* (Lives and Fates of the First Chinese Communists: A Collection of Articles Dedicated to the 100th Anniversary of the Chinese Communist Party) (Moscow: IDV RAN, 2021).
16. "Otchet tov. G. Maringa Kominternu: Iul' 1922 g." (Com. Maring's Report to the Comintern: July 1922), 90–91.
17. See Jiang Huaxuan, "Dangde minzhu geming gangling de tichu he guogong hezuo celüede jige wenti" (Several Questions Connected with the Party's Program for the Democratic Revolution and Defining the Strategy for Guomindang–CCP Cooperation), *Jindaishi yanjiu* (Studies in Modern History), no. 2 (1985): 116.
18. See Saich, *The Origins of the First United Front in China,* 1:80; Mao, *Minguo shiwu nian yiqian zhi Jiang Jieshi xiansheng* (Mr. Chiang Kai-shek Before 1926), 143.
19. Rumors circulated that Wang had avoided execution only because, as a very handsome man, the Manchu princess had taken a liking to him.
20. See Zhou Yue and Chen Hongmin, *Hu Hanmin pingzhuan* (Biography of Hu Hanmin) (Guangzhou: Guangdong renmin chubanshe, 1989); Chen Fulin and Yu Yanguang, *Liao Zhongkai nianpu* (Chronological Biography of Liao Zhongkai) (Changsha: Hunan chubanshe, 1991); Chen Ruiyun, *Jiang Jieshi yu Wang Jingwei* (Chiang Kai-shek

and Wang Jingwei) (Beijing: Tuanjie chubanshe, 2009); Chen Dawei, *Wang Jingwei da zhuan* (Large Biography of Wang Jingwei) (Beijing: Huawen chubanshe, 2010).

21. The son of Chen Jiongming, in his investigative but not entirely objective work about his father, insists that this killing was arranged by Sun Yat-sen himself, whose followers simultaneously undertook a series of attempts on the life of Chen Jiongming himself. See Chen, *Chen Jiongming and the Federalist Movement,* 169–71. His assertions, however, are not supported by facts.
22. See Mao, *Minguo shiwu nian yiqian zhi Jiang Jieshi xiansheng* (Mr. Chiang Kai-shek Before 1926), 147–49; Ch'en, *Chiang Kai-shek's Secret Past,* 95–96; Zheng Chuangqi, *Jiang Jieshi quan jilu: 1887–1975* (Complete Collection of Writings about Chiang Kai-shek: 1887–1975), 1:105 (Beijing: Wenhua chubanshe, 2009).
23. See Chiang Kai-shek, *Jiang Zhongzheng zongtong wu ji: Ai ji* (Five Diaries of President Jiang Zhongzheng: Diaries about Love) (Taipei: Guoshiguan, 2011), 6.
24. Saich, *The Origins of the First United Front in China,* 1:321.
25. See Bergère, *Sun Yat-sen,* 302.
26. Quoted from Dalin, *Kitaiskie memuary* (Chinese Memoirs), 110.
27. Quoted from Bergère, *Sun Yat-sen,* 302.
28. Quoted from Ch'en, *Chiang Kai-shek's Secret Past,* 99.
29. Ibid., 103.
30. Khe, *Vospominaniia o Sun Yat-sene* (Reminiscences of Sun Yat-sen), 68.
31. Ibid., 65.
32. Quoted from Mao, *Minguo shiwu nian yiqian zhi Jiang Jieshi xiansheng* (Mr. Chiang Kai-shek Before 1926), 154.
33. Chiang, *Riji* (Diaries), June 18, 1922, Hoover Archives, box 3, folder 10.
34. Quoted from Ch'en, *Chiang Kai-shek's Secret Past,* 108.
35. See Chiang, *Riji* (Diaries), June 18–29, 1922, Hoover Archives, box 3, folder 10.
36. See Loh, *The Early Chiang Kai-shek,* 71; Bergère, *Sun Yat-sen,* 303.
37. See Chiang, *Riji* (Diaries), July 15–23, 1922, Hoover Archives, box 3, folder 11.
38. See ibid., August 9, 10, 13, and 14, 1922, Hoover Archives, box 3, folder 12.
39. Quoted from Dalin, *Kitaiskie memuary* (Chinese Memoirs), 134.
40. Chiang, *Riji* (Diaries), October 28, 1921, November 28, 1922, and February 3, 1923, Hoover Archives, box 3, folders 2, 14 and 18; Yang Tianshi, *Jiang shi midang yu Jiang Jieshi zhenxiang* (Chiang's Secret Archive and the True Face of Chiang Kai-shek) (Beijing: Shehui kexue wenxian chubanshe, 2002), 21, 22.
41. See Titarenko, *VKP(b), Komintern i Kitai: Dokumenty* (The CPSU, Comintern and China: Documents), 1:98–103, 153–54.
42. From the western city of Lanzhou, the capital of Gansu province (known in antiquity as Long) to the eastern city of Haizhou on the shore of the Yellow Sea.
43. See Chen, *Chen Jiongming and the Federalist Movement,* 234.
44. Chiang Kai-shek's plan in essence developed an idea of Sun Yat-sen's regarding the intrusion of the Red Army into China. Sun first articulated the plan in September 1920. As noted above, he then proposed that the Bolsheviks invade Xinjiang.
45. Titarenko, *VKP(b), Komintern i Kitai: Dokumenty* (The CPSU, Comintern and China: Documents), 1:126–29, 131, 132, 139; Saich, *The Origins of the First United Front in China,* 1:352–53.

46. Titarenko, *VKP(b), Komintern i Kitai: Dokumenty* (The CPSU, Comintern and China: Documents), 1:153. In the Russian translation of the original message the question was written in capital letters.
47. See Chang Kuo-t'ao, *The Rise of the Chinese Communist Party 1921–1927: Volume One of Autobiography of Chang Kuo-t'ao* (Lawrence: University Press of Kansas, 1972), 260; Xu Yuandong et al., *Zhongguo gongchandang lishi jianghua* (Lectures on the History of the CCP) (Beijing: Zhongguo qingnian chubanshe, 1982), 36.
48. See Zou Lu, *Zhongguo guomindang shigao* (An Outline History of the Chinese Guomindang) (Changsha: Minzhi shuju, 1931), 345–48.
49. Sun Wen (Sun Yat-sen), "Preface," in Chiang Kai-shek, *Sun da zongtong Guangzhou mengnan ji* (Notes on the Kidnapping of Great President Sun in Canton) (Shanghai: Minzhi shuju, 1922), supplementary insert.
50. Wan and Fang, *Jiang Jieshi nianpu chugao* (Draft Chronological Biography of Chiang Kai-shek), 1:102, 105, 108, 112.
51. Loh, *The Early Chiang Kai-shek,* 51.
52. Chiang, *Riji* (Diaries), February 17, 1923, Hoover Archives, box 3, folder 18; Mao, *Minguo shiwu nian yiqian zhi Jiang Jieshi xiansheng* (Mr. Chiang Kai-shek Before 1926), 220.
53. Mao, *Minguo shiwu nian yiqian zhi Jiang Jieshi xiansheng* (Mr. Chiang Kai-shek Before 1926), 85.
54. The author's observation from a visit to Chiang Kai-shek's summer home *Taolu* in Tangshan on June 4, 2017.
55. See Donald S. Sutton, *Provincial Militarism and the Chinese Republic: The Yunnan Army, 1905–25* (Ann Arbor: University of Michigan Press, 1980), 274.
56. Titarenko, *VKP(b), Komintern i Kitai: Dokumenty* (The CPSU, Comintern and China: Documents), 1:188–204.
57. I. F. Kurdiukov et al., eds., *Sovetsko-kitaiskie otnosheniia, 1917–1957: Sbornik dokumentov* (Soviet–Chinese Relations, 1917–1957: A Documentary Collection) (Moscow: Izd-vo vostochnoi literatury, 1959), 65.
58. Mexican dollars circulated in China along with yuan (Chinese dollars) and were exchanged at the rate of one-to-one.
59. Titarenko, *VKP(b), Komintern i Kitai: Dokumenty* (The CPSU, Comintern and China: Documents), 1:206.
60. See Mao, *Minguo shiwu nian yiqian zhi Jiang Jieshi xiansheng* (Mr. Chiang Kai-shek Before 1926), 186, 189; Wan and Fang, *Jiang Jieshi nianpu chugao* (Draft Chronological Biography of Chiang Kai-shek), 1:117.
61. Chiang, *Riji* (Diaries), March 10, 1923, Hoover Archives, box 3, folder 19; Mao, *Minguo shiwu nian yiqian zhi Jiang Jieshi xiansheng* (Mr. Chiang Kai-shek Before 1926), 220.
62. Chiang, *Riji* (Diaries), July 12, 14–20, 21, and 22, 1923, Hoover Archives, box 3, folder 23; Mao, *Minguo shiwu nian yiqian zhi Jing Jieshi xiansheng* (Mr. Chiang Kai-shek Before 1926), 200.
63. See Loh, *The Early Chiang Kai-shek,* 86–87.
64. Saich, *The Origins of the First United Front in China,* 1:697.
65. See Chiang, *Riji* (Diaries), July 26–28, 30, 31 and August 5, 1923, Hoover Archives, box 3, folder 23; box 4, folder 1; Chiang, *Soviet Russia in China,* 19.

66. A month after the delegation's arrival in Moscow, another Guomindang member joined it, arriving from Europe. Thus the number of delegates increased to five.
67. Sun originally wanted to send Zhang Ji, an old member of the Guomindang to Moscow, but then reconsidered. See Saich, *The Origins of the First United Front in China,* 2:552.
68. See ibid., 2:545, 552.
69. See Guoshiguan (Academia Historica), document no. 002-010100-00001-001.
70. See Allen S. Whiting, *Soviet Policies in China, 1917–1924* (New York: Columbia University Press, 1954), 243; Louis Fischer, *Men and Politics: An Autobiography* (Westport, CT: Greenwood Press, 1946), 138.
71. Titarenko, *VKP(b), Komintern i Kitai: Dokumenty* (The CPSU, Comintern and China: Documents), 1:331.
72. Chiang, *Riji* (Diaries), August 16–31, September 1 and 2, 1923, Hoover Archives, box 4, folders 1 and 2.
73. Quoted from Ch'en, *Chiang Kai-shek's Secret Past,* 133.
74. Chiang, *Riji* (Diaries), September, 3, 5, 6, 15, 21, 22, 24, October 3, 4, 7, 10, 18, 20, 22, November 1–3, 9, 16, and 22, 1923, Hoover Archives, box 4, folders 2–4.
75. Titarenko, *VKP(b), Komintern i Kitai: Dokumenty* (The CPSU, Comintern and China: Documents), 1:261.
76. See Chiang, *Riji* (Diaries), October 13, 1923, Hoover Archives, box 4, folder 3.
77. See Titarenko, *VKP(b), Komintern i Kitai: Dokumenty* (The CPSU, Comintern and China: Documents), 1:263–64.
78. See Mao, *Minguo shiwu nian yiqian zhi Jiang Jieshi xiansheng* (Mr. Chiang Kai-shek Before 1926), 244.
79. Ibid., 255, 257–60, 307, 331.
80. The text of the plan, preserved in the Taiwanese archives, was first published with several excisions, in the book Lü, *Jiang Zhongsheng xinsheng nianpu changbian* (Large Chronological Biography of Mr. Jiang Zhongzheng), 1:202–4.
81. Titarenko, *VKP(b), Komintern i Kitai: Dokumenty* (The CPSU, Comintern and China: Documents), 1:346.
82. See ibid., 268–73; Chiang, *Riji* (Diaries), October 16–21, 1923, Hoover Archives, box 4, folder 3.
83. A. I. Kartunova, ed., *Perepiska I. V. Stalina i G. V. Chicherina s L. M. Karakhanom: Dokumenty, avgust 1923 g.-1926 gg.* (Correspondence of J. V. Stalin and G. V. Chicherin with L. M. Karakhan: Documents, August 1923–1926) (Moscow: Natalis, 2008), 95.
84. Titarenko, *VKP(b), Komintern i Kitai: Dokumenty* (The CPSU, Comintern and China: Documents), 1:277–78.
85. Kartunova, *Perepiska I. V. Stalina i G. V. Chicherina s L. M. Karakhanom* (Correspondence of J. V. Stalin and G. V. Chicherin with L. M. Karakhan), 80, 95.
86. Ibid., 99.
87. See Titarenko, *VKP(b), Komintern i Kitai: Dokumenty* (The CPSU, Comintern and China: Documents), 1:278–82, 306–8, 346–49, 355; Kartunova, *Perepiska I. V. Stalina i G. V. Chicherina s L. M. Karakhanom* (Correspondence of J. V. Stalin and G. V. Chicherin with L. M. Karakhan), 95, 99.

88. Titarenko, *VKP(b), Komintern i Kitai: Dokumenty* (The CPSU, Comintern and China: Documents), 1:278.
89. See, for example, Chiang's letter to H. Maring of November 12, 1923, published in Saich, *The Origins of the First United Front in China,* 1:702–3.
90. See Titarenko, *VKP(b), Komintern i Kitai: Dokumenty* (The CPSU, Comintern and China: Documents), 1:282; Chiang, *Riji* (Diaries), November 5 and 12, 1923, Hoover Archives, box 4, folder 4.
91. Chiang, *Riji* (Diaries), November 5, 12, and 17, 1923, Hoover Archives, box 4, folder 4.
92. Titarenko, *VKP(b), Komintern i Kitai: Dokumenty* (The CPSU, Comintern and China: Documents), 1:308; Kartunova, *Perepiska I. V. Stalina i G. V. Chicherina s L. M. Karakhanom* (Correspondence of J. V. Stalin and G. V. Chicherin with L. M. Karakhan), 99.
93. Titarenko, *VKP(b), Komintern i Kitai: Dokumenty* (The CPSU, Comintern and China: Documents), 1:346–48.
94. This resolution was first published in 1969. See *Kommunist* (Communist), no. 4 (1969): 12–14.
95. Chiang, *Riji* (Diaries), November 28, 1923, Hoover Archives, box 4, folder 4.
96. See Chiang, *Soviet Russia in China,* 24.
97. Chiang, *Riji* (Diaries), December 13–16, 1923, Hoover Archives, box 4, folder 5.
98. See Hsiung, *The Life of Chiang Kai-shek,* 179; Wang Guangyuan, *Jiang Jieshi zai Huangpu* (Chiang Kai-shek at Whampoa) (Beijing: Zhongguo wenshi chubanshe, 2009), 1.
99. Confucius, *The Analects of Confucius,* 4.
100. Chiang, *Soviet Russia in China,* 23–24.
101. See Titarenko, *VKP(b), Komintern i Kitai: Dokumenty* (The CPSU, Comintern and China: Documents), 1:341; Kartunova, *Perepiska J. V. Stalina i G. V. Chicherina s L. M. Karakhanom* (Correspondence of J. V. Stalin and G. V. Chicherin with L. M. Karakhan), 157; M. I. Sladkovsky, ed., *Noveishaia istoriia Kitaia 1917–1927* (Contemporary History of China 1917–1927) (Moscow: Nauka, 1983), 159; Yurkevich, *Moskva–Kanton, 1920-e* (Moscow–Canton, 1920s), 97–98; Hsiung, *The Life of Chiang Kai-shek,* 183.
102. See Luo Jialun et al., eds., *Geming wenxian* (Documents of the Revolution), 8:92–97 (Taipei: Zhongguo guomindang dangshi shiliao bianzuan weiyuanhui, 1955).
103. See A. V. Pantsov and M. F. Yuriev, "Ustanovlenie sotrudnichstva mezhdu KPK i Sun Yat-sen v 1921–1924 gg.: K istorii obrazovaniia edinogo antiimperialisticheskogo fronta" (Establishment of Cooperation between the CCP and Sun Yat-sen in 1921–1924: On a History of the Formation of the Anti-imperialist United Front), in L. S. Tikhvinsky, ed., *Sun Yat-sen, 1866–1986: K 120-letiyu so dnia rozhdeniia: Sbornik statei, vospominanii i materialov* (Sun Yat-sen, 1866–1986: On the 120th Anniversary of His Birth: Collection of Articles, Reminiscences and Materials) (Moscow: Nauka, 1987), 161–62.
104. Ch'en, *Chiang Kai-shek's Secret Past,* 137.
105. See Mao, *Minguo shiwu nian yiqian zhi Jiang Jieshi xiansheng* (Mr. Chiang Kai-shek Before 1926), 218–19.

106. See *Nanfang dushu bao* (Southern Capital), Shenzhen, September 16, 2014; interview with Ch'en Yung-fa in Taipei, July 9, 2015.
107. See Mao, *Minguo shiwu nian yiqian zhi Jiang Jieshi xiansheng* (Mr. Chiang Kai-shek Before 1926), 232; Chen and Yu, *Liao Zhongkai nianpu* (Chronological Biography of Liao Zhongkai), 245; for a photocopy of Sun Yat-sen's order, see Luo Jialun et al., eds., *Geming wenxian* (Documents on the Revolution), 10: photograph no. 3 (Taipei: Zhongguo guomindang dangshi shiliao bianzuan weiyuanhui, 1955).
108. See Loh, *The Early Chiang Kai-shek,* 91–92; Mao, *Minguo shiwu nian yiqian zhi Jiang Jieshi xiansheng* (Mr. Chiang Kai-shek Before 1926), 233–45.
109. Chiang, *Soviet Russia in China,* 25.
110. See He, *Vospominannia o Sun Yat-sene* (Reminiscences of Sun Yat-sen), 35.
111. Mao, *Minguo shiwu nian yiqian zhi Jiang Jieshi xiansheng* (Mr. Chiang Kai-shek Before 1926), 233–45.
112. Quoted from C. Martin Wilbur, *Sun Yat-sen: Frustrated Patriot* (New York: Columbia University Press, 1976), 175.
113. Quoted from Chiang Kai-shek's statement in H. G. W. Woodhead, ed., *The China Year Book 1928* (Tientsin: Tientsin Press, 1928), 1382.
114. Sun, *Izbrannye proizvedeniia* (Selected Works), 303.
115. Quoted from Wilbur, *Sun Yat-sen,* 144.
116. Sun signed the order appointing him one day earlier. For a photocopy of Sun Yat-sen's order, see Luo, *Geming wenxian* (Documents on the Revolution), 8: photograph no. 4.
117. See Mao, *Minguo shiwu nian yiqian zhi Jiang Jieshi xiansheng* (Mr. Chiang Kai-shek Before 1926), 256; Lü, *Jiang Zhongzheng xiansheng nianpu changbian* (Large Chronological Biography of Mr. Jiang Zhongzheng), 1:246; Chen Yipei et al., eds., *Huangpu junxiao shiliao, 1924–1927 (xu bian)* (Documents on the History of the Whampoa Academy, 1924–1927 [Supplementary Collection]) (Guangzhou: Guangdong renmin chubanshe 1994), 1; Chen and Yu, *Liao Zhongkai nianpu* (Chronological Biography of Liao Zhongkai), 257.

## 6. *COMMANDANT OF THE WHAMPOA ACADEMY*

1. Quoted from Hsiung, *The Life of Chiang Kai-shek,* 184.
2. See Ch'en, *Chiang Kai-shek's Secret Past,* 139–40, 166–67; Ch'en, *The Storm Clouds Clear over China,* 23–25, 47; Chen Bulei, *Chen Bulei huiyilu* (Memoirs of Chen Bulei) (Taipei: Zhuanji wenxue chubanshe, 1981), 70–72; "Chen buzhang Lifu xiaozhuan" (Short Biography of Department Head Chen Lifu), Zhongguo di er lishi dang'anguan (Second Historical Archives of China), document no. 718/5/6/040; the author's impressions on visiting the Whampoa Academy, December 13, 1987; Zhang Ruide, *Wusheng de yaojiao: Jiang Jieshi de shicongshi yu zhang shi Zhongguo* (Silent Key Point: Chiang Kai-shek's Personal Secretariat and Wartime China) (Taipei: Taiwan shangwu, 2017), 51–52.
3. See personal file of Shao Lizi, RGASPI, collection 495, inventory 225, file 1358, sheets 22–27 reverse; Zhongguo renmin zhengzhi xieshang huiyi quanguo weiyuanhui wenshi ziliao yanjiu weiyuanhui bangongshi, ed., *Heping laoren Shao Lizi* (Peaceful

Oldster Shao Lizi) (Beijing: Wenshi ziliao chubanshe, 1985), 238–39; Panzuofu (A. V. Pantsov), "Gongchan guoji dang'an zhong de Shao Lizi wenjian" (Documents on Shao Lizi in the Comintern Archive), *Zhonggong chuangjian shi yanjiu* (Studies on the History of Founding the CCP), no. 1 (2016): 121–34.

4. Du-Nin (Yang Zhihua), "Biografiia Shao Lizi i ego politicheskie vzgliady: 8 iulia 1940 g." (Biography of Shao Lizi and His Political Views: July 8, 1940), RGASPI, collection 495, inventory 225, file 1358, sheets 12–18.
5. See Pantsov with Levine, *Mao,* 116.
6. Ch'en, *Chiang Kai-shek's Secret Past,* 166.
7. See *Shangye zhoukan* (Trade Weekly), September 23, 1997; http://www.boxun.com/forum/lishi/652.shtml.
8. See Chiang, *Riji* (Diaries), August 26, 29, 31, September 2–4, 6, and 17, 1929, Hoover Archives, box 7, folders 1 and 3. See also Zhu Baoqin and Li Nin, *Song Meiling nianpu* (Chronological Biography of Song Meiling) (Beijing: Dongfang chubanshe, 2019), 141; "24 in Plot to Slay Chinese President," *New York Times*, September 7, 1929.
9. See Dou Yingtai, *Jiang Jieshi bi xia de fenghu xueyue* (Romantic Themes Under a Pen of Chiang Kai-shek) (Hong Kong: Zhonghe chuban, 2015), 340; Chen Cheng, *Chen Cheng xiansheng shuxin ji: Jiashu* (Collection of Chen Cheng's Letters: Family Letters Volume), 1:228 (Taipei: Guoshiguan, 2006).
10. See Chen, *Chen Cheng xiansheng shuxin ji: Jiashu* (Collection of Chen Cheng's Letters: Family Letters Volume), 336; Lü Fang-shang et al., *Jiang Jieshi de qinqing, aiqing yu youqing* (Jiang Jieshi's Family, Lovers, and Friends) (Taipei: Shibao wenhua chuban qiye gufen youxian gongsi, 2011), 25, 75, 132–33, 260, 267–68; Letter from Wang Qisheng of Beijing University to the author, February 10, 2020; Zhu and Li, *Song Meiling nianpu* (Chronological Biography of Song Meiling), 186.
11. Ningbo, it will be recalled, is a big city in Zhejiang, Chiang Kai-shek's home province.
12. See Ch'en, *Chiang Kai-shek's Secret Past,* 85, 167.
13. The author's interview with one of Chiang Kai-shek's relatives, March 19, 2015.
14. He Xiangning headed the Women's Department of the Guomindang CEC from August 14, 1924, to June 18, 1925. See Liu Weikan, ed., *Zhongguo guomindang zhiming lu (1894–1994)* (List of Officials of the Chinese Guomindang [1894–1994]) (Beijing: Zhonghua shuju, 2014), 30; Chen Shan, *He Xiangning nianpu* (Chronological Biography of He Xiangning) (Nanning: Guangxi renmin chubanshe, 2016), 83. So it is only during that period that she could have brought the little girl to Chiang and Jennie.
15. See Chen Jieru, *Chen Jieru huiyilu quan yi ben: Jiang Jieshi Chen Jieru de hunyin gushi* (Complete Text of Chen Jieru's Reminiscences: The Story of Chiang Kai-shek and Chen Jieru's Family Life), 1 (Taipei: Zhuanji wenxue, 1992); http://baike.baidu.com/view/4185179.htm?fromtitle=%E9%99%88%E7%91%B6%E5%85%89&fromid=1284160&type=syn.
16. See Titarenko, VKP(b), *Komintern i Kitai: Dokumenty* (The CPSU, Comintern and China: Documents), 1:570–71; Hsiung, *The Life of Chiang Kai-shek,* 183.
17. Taylor tells us that "Blucher" (must be Bliukher), "commander of the Soviet Far Eastern forces," arrived in China "at Chiang's request" as "his chief of staff." Chiang,

Taylor says, "had met" Bliukher in Siberia and "immediately liked" him (Taylor, *The Generalissimo,* 171). Everything is incorrect here. First, Chiang could never have met "a commander of the Soviet Far Eastern forces" Bliukher in Siberia because in 1923, when Chiang was crossing this region by train, Bliukher was a commander of the Soviet Red Army First Corps and served in Petrograd. Second, Chiang never asked Sun to invite Bliukher because he did not know him at all and so could not like him. Finally, Bliukher did not arrive as Chiang's chief of staff but as the chief military advisor to Sun Yat-sen.

18. See A. I. Kartunova, ed., *V. K. Bliukher v Kitae: 1924–1927: Novye dokumenty glavnogo voennogo sovetnika* (V. K. Bliukher in China: 1924–1927: New Documents of the Chief Military Advisor) (Moscow: Natalis, 2003), 15.
19. Chiang, *Soviet Russia in China,* 51.
20. Kartunova, *V. K. Bliukher v Kitae* (V. K. Bliukher in China), 148–50.
21. Fischer, *Men and Politics,* 139; Jiang Song Meiling (Madame Chiang Kai-shek-Song Meiling), *Yu Baoluoting tanhuade huiyilu* (Recollections of Conversations with Borodin) (Taipei: Liming wenhua shiye gufen youxian gongsi, 1976), 12–13.
22. "Caizhengbu caizheng shiliao chenlieshi" (Exhibition of Materials on the History of Finances of the Ministry of Finance of the Republic of China), http://museum.mof.gov.tw/ct.asp?xItem=3421&ctNode=63&mp=1.
23. Quoted from Khe, *Vospominaniia o Sun Yat-sene* (Reminiscences of Sun Yat-sen), 90.
24. Chang, *The Rise of the Chinese Communist Party 1921–1927,* 1:446.
25. See Yan, *Pre-understanding Japan,* 287; Yu Fangde, "Dai Jitao yu ta de san qiqin" (Dai Jitao and His Three Lovers), http://www.sjfx.com/qikan/bkview.asp?bkid=39447&cid=69428; Li Yongming and Fan Xiaofang, *43 zhanfan de houbansheng* (The Second Half of the Lives of 43 War Criminals) (Wuhan: Hubei renmin chubanshe, 2008), 77; Fan Xiaofang, Bao Dongbo, and Li Quanlu, *Jiang Jieshi de guoce guwen Dai Jitao* (Dai Jitao, Political Advisor to Chiang Kai-shek) (Beijing: Tuanjie chubanshe, 2011), 92–97.
26. See Kartunova, *V. K. Bliukher v Kitae* (V. K. Bliukher in China), 148.
27. Various sources give different numbers for the first class of cadets. The most frequently cited figure is 500, but, according to documents from the school itself, it was 613.
28. See Richard D. Landis, *The Origins of Whampoa Graduates Who Served in the Northern Expedition* (Seattle: Far Eastern and Russian Institute, University of Washington, 1964), 150, 152.
29. See M. F. Yuriev, *Revoliussiia 1925–1927 gg. v Kitae* (The Revolution of 1925–1927 in China) (Moscow: Nauka, 1968), 43; A. I. Cherepanov, *Zapiski voennogo sovetnika v Kitae* (Notes of a Military Advisor in China), 2nd ed. (Moscow: Nauka, 1976), 143; Kartunova, *Perepiska I. V. Stalina i G. V. Chicherina s L. M. Karakhanom* (Correspondence of J. V. Stalin and G. V. Chicherin with L. M. Karakhan), 316.
30. "Fifth column" is a term from the history of the Civil War in Spain (1936–39) meaning the agents of General Francisco Franco (1892–1975) in revolutionary Madrid, on which four columns of Franco's troops were advancing.
31. See Yuriev, *Revoliutsiia 1925–1927 gg. v Kitae* (The Revolution of 1925–1927 in China), 47; Yurkevich, *Moskva–Kanton, 1920-e* (Moscow–Canton, 1920s), 140.

32. Kartunova, *Perepiska I. V. Stalina i G. V. Chicherina s L. M. Karakhanom* (Correspondence of J. V. Stalin and G. V. Chicherin with L. M. Karakhan), 316.
33. For more details, see Yurkevich, *Moskva–Kanton, 1920-e* (Moscow–Canton, 1920s), 140–46.
34. Sun, *Izbrannye proizvedeniia* (Selected Works), 695–96. See also Mao, *Minguo shiwu nian yiqian zhi Jiang Jieshi xiansheng* (Mr. Chiang Kai-shek Before 1926), 312–13, 317.
35. Following Borodin's advice, Sun sent Chiang a letter in which he proposed not to put either Hu Hanmin or Wang Jingwei on the Revolutionary Committee, on the grounds that the former had "lost faith in the teachings" of the Russian "experiment," and the latter supposedly "likewise was not a supporter of the Russian revolution." But Chiang did not agree.
36. See Kartunova, *V. K. Bliukher v Kitae* (V. K. Bliukher in China), 75; Cherepanov, *Zapiski voennogo sovetnika v Kitae* (Notes of a Military Advisor in China), 148.
37. See Mao, *Minguo shiwu nian yiqian zhi Jiang Jieshi xiansheng* (Mr. Chiang Kai-shek Before 1926), 334.
38. See G. Davis, *China's Christian Army: A Story of Marshal Feng and His Soldiers* (New York: Christian Alliance, 1925), 7; M. Broomhall, *General Feng: "A Good Soldier of Christ Jesus"* (London: China Inland Mission, 1923), 11; M. Ch'eng, *Marshal Feng—The Man and His Work* (Shanghai: Kelly & Walsh, 1926), 9; Feng Lida, *Wode fuqin Feng Yuxiang jiangjun* (My Father General Feng Yuxiang) (Chengdu: Sichuan renmin chubanshe, 1984), 92.
39. Sampans, literally "three boards," were houseboats that served as the dwelling places of poor people of Canton.
40. Kartunova, *V. K. Bliukher v Kitae* (V. K. Bliukher in China), 92.
41. Quoted from Chiang, *Soviet Russia in China,* 35. See also Mao, *Minguo shiwu nian yiqian zhi Jiang Jieshi xiansheng* (Mr. Chiang Kai-shek Before 1926), 334.
42. Chiang, *Soviet Russia in China,* 35; Ch'en, *Chiang Kai-shek's Secret Past,* 150.
43. See Fan, Bao, and Li, *Jiang Jieshi de guoce guwen Dai Jitao* (Dai Jitao, Political Advisor to Chiang Kai-shek), 111–12; Kartunova, *V. K. Bliukher v Kitae* (V. K. Bliukher in China), 149: *Nanfang zhoumo* (Southern Weekend), June 1, 2006; Ch'en, *Chiang Kai-shek's Secret Past,* 159–60; Yuan Xiaolun, *Zhou Enlai yu Jiang Jieshi* (Zhou Enlai and Chiang Kai-shek) (Beijing: Guangming ribao chubanshe, 1994), 9–57.
44. Chang, *The Rise of the Chinese Communist Party*, 1:450–51.
45. Ch'en, *Chiang Kai-shek's Secret Past,* 158.
46. C. Martin Wilbur and Julie Lien-ying How, *Missionaries of Revolution: Soviet Advisers and Nationalist China 1920–1927* (Cambridge: Harvard University Press, 1989), 706.
47. Chang, *The Rise of the Chinese Communist Party,* 1:450–51.
48. Kartunova, *V. K. Bliukher v Kitae* (V. K. Bliukher in China), 160–61.
49. See Titarenko, *VKP(b), Komintern i Kitai: Dokumenty* (The CPSU, Comintern and China: Documents), 1:521.
50. Sun, *Izbrannye proizvedeniia* (Selected Works), 741–42.
51. The Purple Gold mountain, located on the eastern outskirts of Nanjing, is 1,400 feet high.

52. Quoted from Charles D. Musgrove, *China's Contested Capital: Architecture, Ritual, and Response in Nanjing* (Honolulu: University of Hawai'i Press, 2013), 127–28.
53. Quoted from Khe, *Vospominaniia o Sun Yat-sene* (Reminiscences of Sun Yat-sen), 97–98; see also *Chronology of Dr. Sun Yat-sen: The Founding Father of the Republic of China* (Taipei: Dr. Sun Yat-sen Memorial Hall, [1972]), 21.

## 7. *THE STRUGGLE OVER SUN YAT-SEN'S LEGACY*

1. See Wilbur and How, *Missionaries of Revolution,* 608; Titarenko, *VKP(b), Komintern i Kitai: Dokumenty* (The CPSU, Comintern and China: Documents), 2:101.
2. See Lee Hun-ju, *A Brief Biography of the Late President Chiang Kai-shek* [Taipei, 1987], 9.
3. See Yurkevich, *Moskva–Kanton, 1920-e* (Moscow–Canton, 1920s), 150; Titarenko, *VKP(b), Komintern i Kitai: Dokumenty* (The CPSU, Comintern and China: Documents), 1:536.
4. Wilbur and How, *Missionaries of Revolution,* 705–6.
5. Chang, *The Rise of the Chinese Communist Party,* 1:448.
6. See Sutton, *Provincial Militarism and the Chinese Republic,* 285–87.
7. Kartunova, *Perepiska I. V. Stalina i G. V. Chicherin s L. M. Karakhanom* (Correspondence of J. V. Stalin and G. V. Chicherin with L. M. Karakhan), 548.
8. See "Zhongyang zhixing weiyuanhui zhi haineiwai tongzhi gao taoping Yang, Liu jingguo dian" (Telegram from the CEC of the Guomindang to Comrades in and outside of the Country on the History of the Suppression of Yang [Ximin] and Liu [Zhenhuan]), in Luo Jialun et al., eds., *Geming wenxian* (Documents of the Revolution), 11:287–88 (Taipei: Zhongguo guomindang dangshi shiliao bianzuan weiyuanhui, 1956); Kartunova, *V. K. Bliukher v Kitae* (V. K. Bliukher in China), 315–420; Yuriev, *Revoliutsiia 1925–1927 gg. v Kitae* (The Revolution of 1925–1927 in China), 219–23.
9. Quoted from Chen, *Chen Jiongming and the Federalist Movement,* 253.
10. See Diana Lary, *Region and Nation: The Kwangsi Clique in Chinese Politics, 1925–1937* (London: Cambridge University Press, 1974), 56–58.
11. See Yuriev, *Revoliutsiia 1925–1927 gg. v Kitae* (The Revolution of 1925–1927 in China), 159–67.
12. See Pantsov with Levine, *Mao,* 143–44.
13. Quoted from Yuriev, *Revoliutsiia 1925–1927 gg. v Kitae* (The Revolution of 1925–1927 in China), 212.
14. Lt. Henry A. Allen (V. M. Primakov), *Zapiski volontera: Grazhdanskaia voina v Kitae* (Notes of a Volunteer: The Civil War in China) (Moscow: Nauka, 1967), 59.
15. See Chiang, *Riji* (Diaries), June 23, 1925, Hoover Archives, box 4, folder 11; Yuriev, *Revoliutsiia 1925–1927 gg. v Kitae* (The Revolution of 1925–1927 in China), 228; Hsiung, *The Life of Generalissimo Chiang Kai-shek,* 221; Taylor, *The Generalissimo,* 49.
16. See Chen and Yu, *Liao Zhongkai nianpu* (Chronological Biography of Liao Zhongkai), 339.
17. Chiang, *Riji* (Diaries), June 21, 1925, Hoover Archives, box 4, folder 11.
18. Ch'en, *The Storm Clouds Clear over China,* 86.
19. Kartunova, *V. K. Bliukher v Kitae* (V. K. Bliukher in China), 129–30.

20. Chang, *The Rise of the Chinese Communist Party,* 1:459.
21. In light of the fact that, in October 1925, the number of troops attached to the Whampoa Academy comprised about six thousand men, the planned increase in two months would be no less than four or five times.
22. Kartunova, *Perepiska I. V. Stalina i G. V. Chicherina s L. M. Karakhanom* (Correspondence of J. V. Stalin and G. V. Chicherin with L. M. Karakhan), 549. See also Titarenko, *VKP(b), Komintern i Kitai: Dokumenty* (The CPSU, Comintern and China: Documents), 1:638.
23. See Titarenko, *VKP(b), Komintern i Kitai: Dokumenty* (The CPSU, Comintern and China: Documents), 1:573–74.
24. Chiang, *Riji* (Diaries), June 23, 1925–September 7, 1926, Hoover Archives, box 4, folder 11–box 5, folder 3.
25. Khe, *Vospominaniia o Sun Yat-sene* (Reminiscences of Sun Yat-sen), 105–7; Mao, *Minguo shiwu nian yiqian zhi Jiang Jieshe xiansheng* (Mr. Chiang Kai-shek Before 1926), 491.
26. Chiang, *Riji* (Diaries), August 20, 1925, Hoover Archives, box 4, folder 13.
27. See Chang, *The Rise of the Chinese Communist Party,* 1:460.
28. Ch'en, *The Storm Clouds Clear over China,* 35.
29. Quoted from Xiao Jie, *Jiang Jieshi yu Hu Hanmin* (Chiang Kai-shek and Hu Hanmin) (Beijing: Tuanjie chubanshe, 2009), 29.
30. See Ch'en, *The Storm Clouds Clear over China*, 85.
31. Chang, *The Rise of the Chinese Communist Party,* 1:461. See also He, *Vospominaniia of Sun Yat-sene* (Reminiscences of Sun Yat-sen), 108.
32. See Cherepanov, *Zapiski voennogo sovetnika v Kitae* (Notes of a Military Advisor in China), 285–88; Ch'en, *Chiang Kai-shek's Secret Past,* 162–65; Te-kong Tong and Li Tsung-jen, *The Memoirs of Li Tsung-jen* (Boulder, CO: Westview Press, 1979), 148.
33. See Ch'en, *Chiang Kai-shek's Secret Past,* 198–99.
34. Titarenko, *VKP(b), Komintern i Kitai: Dokumenty* (The CPSU, Comintern and China: Documents), 2:101 (Moscow, 1996).
35. Quoted from Chang, *The Rise of the Chinese Communist Party,* 1:457, 461–62.
36. Titarenko, *VKP(b) Komintern i Kitai: Dokumenty* (The CPSU, Comintern and China: Documents), 2:101; 1:555–56. See also Hu Hanmin, *Hu Hanmin zizhuan* (Autobiography of Hu Hanmin) (Taipei: Zhuanji wenxue chubanshe, 1969), 93.
37. For more details, see Alexander Pantsov, *The Bolsheviks and the Chinese Revolution 1919–1927* (Honolulu: University of Hawai'i Press, 2000), 211–12.
38. See Yuriev, *Revoliutsiia 1925–1927 gg. v Kitae* (The Revolution of 1925–1927 in China), 265–78; C. Martin Wilbur, *The National Revolution in China, 1923–1928* (Cambridge: Harvard University Press, 1983), 30–31; Taylor, *The Generalissimo,* 53.
39. The decision to reorganize "in the future" the Guomindang troops into a single National Revolutionary Army was made as early as June 15, 1925. See Chen Shan, *He Xiangning nianpu* (Chronological Biography of He Xiangning), 95.
40. See Mao, *Minguo shiwu nian yiqian zhi Jiang Jieshi xiansheng* (Mr. Chiang Kai-shek Before 1926), 463, 492–94; Zhang Xianwen, ed., *Zhonghua minguo shigang* (Studies

in the History of the Republic of China) (Zhengzhou: Henan renmin chubanshe, 1985), 231–32; Yuriev, *Revoliutsiia 1925–1927 gg. v Kitae* (The Revolution of 1925–1927 in China), 239–41; Alexander V. Pantsov and Steven I. Levine, "Chinese Comintern Activists: An Analytic Biographic Dictionary" (manuscript), 290.

41. See Chen, *Chen Jiongming and the Federalist Movement,* 255; See also Cherepanov, *Zapiski voennogo sovetnika v Kitae* (Notes of a Military Advisor in China), 288–315.
42. Chang, *The Rise of the Chinese Communist Party,* 1:479.
43. Mao, *Minguo shiwu nian yiqian zhi Jiang Jieshi xiansheng* (Mr. Chiang Kai-shek Before 1926), 589–94.
44. It is revealing that in declaring the results of the balloting, the secretary of the session, the communist Wu Yuzhang, by agreement with Wang, placed Hu's name after the names of Wang Jingwei and Chiang Kai-shek. See Chang, *The Rise of the Chinese Communist Party,* 1:708.
45. See Zhang, *Zhonghua minguo shigang* (Studies in the History of the Republic of China), 248–51; Titarenko, *VKP(b), Komintern i Kitai: Dokumenty* (The CPSU, Comintern and China: Documents), 2:42, 58.
46. See RGASPI, collection 514, inventory 1, file 168, sheet 219.
47. Kartunova, *Perepiska I. V. Stalina i G. V. Chicherina s polpredom SSSR v Kitae L. M. Karakhanom* (Correspondence of J. V. Stalin and G. V. Chicherin with L. M. Karakhan), 586.
48. The "rock-ribbed" Bolsheviks viewed the radical "intelligentsia" as unreliable and untrustworthy fellow travelers.
49. Wilbur and How, *Missionaries of Revolution,* 608–9. See also V. V. Vishniakova-Akimova, *Dva goda v vostavshem Kitae, 1925–1927: Vospominaniia* (Two Years in Revolutionary China, 1925–1927: Memoirs) (Moscow: Nauka, 1965), 237.
50. See Pantsov, *The Bolsheviks and the Chinese Revolution 1919–1927,* 91–93.
51. Chiang, *Riji* (Diaries), January 19, February 7 and 11, 1926, Hoover Archives, box 4, folders 18 and 19.
52. Confucius, *The Analects of Confucius,* 42.
53. Chiang, *Riji* (Diaries), February 19, 1926, Hoover Archives, box 4, folder 19; Chiang, *Soviet Russia in China,* 38.
54. See Chiang, *Riji* (Diaries), February 13 and 19, 1926, Hoover Archives, box 4, folder 19; Ch'en, *The Storm Clouds Clear over China,* 27–28.
55. Lewis S. Gannett, "Chiang Kai-shek, Leader of the Cantonese Revolutionists, Extends His Sway by a Series of Unexpected Victories," *New York Times,* November 14, 1926.
56. See Chiang, *Riji* (Diaries), February 23, 1926, Hoover Archives, box 4, folder 19; Hsiung, *The Life of Chiang Kai-shek,* 241.
57. See Jiang Zhongzheng, "Jiangshu Zhongshan jian shijian jingguo" (On the History of Events on the Cruiser Zhongshan), in Luo Jialun et al., eds., *Geming wenxian* (Documents on the Revolution), 9:85–86 (Taipei: Zhongguo guomindang dangshi shiliao bianzuan weiyuanhui, 1955); Jiang Zhongzheng, "Jiangshu Zhongshan jian Li Zhilong shijian jingguo xiangqing" (On the Historical Details of Events on the Cruiser Zhongshan and on Li Zhilong), ibid., 87–94; Chiang, *Soviet Russia in China,*

39–40; Ch'en, *The Storm Clouds Clear over China,* 28–30; Ch'en, *Chiang Kai-shek's Secret Past,* 176–85.

58. See Wilbur and How, *Missionaries of Revolution,* 608.
59. See Ch'en, *The Storm Clouds Clear over China,* 35.
60. See Yuriev, *Revoliutsiia 1925–1927 gg. v Kitae* (The Revolution of 1925–1927 in China), 312–13.
61. Sun, *Izbrannye proizvedeniia* (Selected Works), 695. See also Chang *The Rise of the Chinese Communist Party,* 1:503.
62. Cherepanov, *Zapiski voennogo sovetnika v Kitae* (Notes of a Military Advisor in China), 376.
63. For the report by Bubnov (Ivanovsky) as well as his letter to Borodin about the events of March 20, preserved in RGASPI, see Titarenko, *VKP(b), Komintern i Kitai: Dokumenty* (The CPSU, Comintern and China: Documents), 1:139–52, 157–62, 208–27. The secretary of the Far Eastern Bureau of the Executive Committee of the Comintern Moisei Grigorievich Rafes (1883–1942), who was in Canton in late July–August of that year, also recognized this. See "Report of Com. Rafes at closed session on the Chinese question, November 26, 1926," RGASPI, collection 495, inventory 165, file 71, sheet 4.
64. See Titarenko, *VKP(b), Komintern i Kitai: Dokumenty* (The CPSU, Comintern and China: Documents), 2:152–53; Chiang, *Riji* (Diaries), March 19–22, 1926, Hoover Archives, box 4, folder 20.
65. Titarenko, *VKP(b), Komintern i Kitai: Dokumenty* (The CPSU, Comintern and China: Documents), 2:153.
66. Chang, *The Rise of the Chinese Communist Party,* 1:507.
67. Chiang, *Riji* (Diaries), March 22, 1926, Hoover Archives, box 4, folder 20.
68. Ibid.
69. Titarenko, *VKP(b), Komintern i Kitai: Dokumenty* (The CPSU, Comintern and China: Documents), 2:153–54.
70. See Hsiung, *The Life of Chiang Kai-shek,* 245.
71. It is amusing that Borodin returned to Canton from Beijing via Shanghai also on April 29 and on the same ship as Hu Hanmin. During the passage, Hu was able to tell him that after March 20 "many do not approve of Chiang Kai-shek."
72. See Chang, *The Rise of the Chinese Communist Party,* 1:506, 511, 709; Hu, *Hu Hanmin zizhuan* (Autobiography of Hu Hanmin), 96–97; Xiao, *Jiang Jieshi yu Hu Hanmin* (Chiang Kai-shek and Hu Hanmin), 42.
73. The decision to organize a joint conference comprising five representatives of the GMD CEC and representatives of the CCP CEC with the participation of Borodin was also taken at the May (1926) plenum of the Guomindang CEC. However, it remained only on paper.
74. See RGASPI, collection of unsorted documents. The text adopted by the plenum is in Cherepanov, *Zapiski voennogo sovetnika v Kitae* (Notes of a Military Advisor in China), 403–4; Zhongguo di er lishi dang'anguan, ed., *Zhongguo guomindang di yi, er ci quanguo daibiaodahui huiyi shiliao* (Materials on the History of the First and Second Congresses of the Guomindang), 2:714–15 (Nanjing: Jiangsu guji chubanshe, 1986). See also Chiang, *Soviet Russia in China,* 40–41.

75. See Ch'en, *The Storm Clouds Clear over China,* 37.
76. For more details see Pantsov, *The Bolsheviks and the Chinese Revolution 1919–1927,* 91–92.
77. Titarenko, *VKP(b), Komintern i Kitai: Dokumenty* (The CPSU, Comintern and China: Documents), 2:231.
78. Quoted from Chang, *The Rise of the Chinese Communist Party,* 1:508.
79. Yuriev, *Revoliutsiia 1925–1927 gg. v Kitae* (The Revolution of 1925–1927 in China), 320–21; Pang Xianzhi, ed., *Mao Zedong nianpu, 1893–1949* (Chronological Biography of Mao Zedong, 1893–1949), 1:165 (Beijing: Renmin chubanshe/Zhongyang wenxian chubanshe, 2002); Zhang Renjie, *Zhang Jingjiang xiansheng wenji* (Collection of Works of Zhang Jingjiang) (Taipei: Zhongguo guomindang zhongyang weiyuanhui dangshi weiyuanhui; Jingxiaochu zhongyang wenwu gongyingshe, 1982), 5–6.

## 8. *THE NORTHERN EXPEDITION AND THE SPLIT IN THE GUOMINDANG*

1. See Titarenko, VKP(b), *Komintern i Kitai: Dokumenty* (The CPSU, Comintern and China: Documents), 2:228, 281.
2. Chang, *The Rise of the Chinese Communist Party,* 1:520.
3. Chiang Kai-shek, *Jiang zongtong yanlun huibian* (Collected Works of President Chiang), 8:224 (Taipei: Zhengzhong shuju, 1956). See also Chiang, *Riji* (Diaries), July 9, 1926, Hoover Archives, box 5, folder 1; Chang, *The Rise of the Chinese Communist Party,* 1:520; Ch'en, *Chiang Kai-shek's Secret Past,* 204.
4. Ruth Altman Greene, *Hsiang-Ya Journal* (Hamden, CT: Archon Books, 1977), 44–45.
5. Ibid., 46.
6. Quoted from Hsiung, *The Life of Chiang Kai-shek,* 252.
7. For more details, see Pantsov with Levine, *Mao,* 167–76.
8. See Yuriev, *Revoliutsiia 1925–1927 gg. v Kitae* (The Revolution of 1925–1927 in China), 323–38; Chang, *The Rise of the Chinese Communist Party,* 1:520–36; Angus W. McDonald Jr., *The Urban Origins of Rural Revolution: Elites and the Masses in Hunan Province, China, 1911–1927* (Berkeley: University of California Press, 1978), 229–36.
9. Ch'en, *The Storm Clouds Clear over China,* 43.
10. See Chiang, *Riji* (Diaries), July 2, 1926, Hoover Archives, box 4, folder 15.
11. D. A. Spichak, *Kitaiskii avangard Kremlia: Revoliutsionery Kitaia v moscovskikh shkolakh Kominterna (1921–1939)* (The Chinese Vanguard of the Kremlin: Revolutionaries of China in the Moscow Schools of the Comintern [1921–1939]) (Moscow: "Veche," 2011), 75.
12. Ibid., 80, 83; Chiang Ching-kuo, *Jiang Jingguo riji* (Diaries of Chiang Ching-kuo) (Beijing: Zhongguo wenshi chubanshe, 2010), 8–11; Chiang Ching-kuo, *My Days in Soviet Russia* [Taipei, 1963], i–ii, 1–3.
13. See Pakula, *The Last Empress,* 169.
14. Ch'en, *Chiang Kai-shek's Secret Past,* 188.
15. Chiang, *Riji* (Diaries), July 2, 1926, Hoover Archives, box 5, folder 1.

16. Ch'en, *Chiang Kai-shek's Secret Past,* 210.
17. See Peter Worthing, *General He Yingqin: The Rise and Fall of Nationalist China* (Cambridge: Cambridge University Press, 2016), 70–76.
18. Barbara W. Tuchman, *Stilwell and the American Experience in China, 1911–45* (New York: Macmillan, 1971), 93.
19. Quoted from Snow, *Journey to the Beginning,* 85.
20. On Song Meiling's grave at Ferncliff Cemetery in New York state there is the date February 12, 1898; some authors give a date of March 23, 1899, but most researchers rely on a date that appears on her passport, issued in 1907: March 4, 1898.
21. Quoted from Thomas A. DeLong, *Madame Chiang Kai-shek and Miss Emma Mills: China's First Lady and Her American Friend* (Jefferson, NC: McFarland, 2007), 6.
22. On Meiling's early years, see Pakula, *The Last Empress,* 16–26; Laura Tyson Li, *Madame Chiang Kai-shek: China's Eternal First Lady* (New York: Atlantic Monthly Press, 2006), 5–40; He Husheng and Yu Zejun, *Song Meiling da zhuan* (Large Biography of Song Meiling), 1:26–48 (Beijing: Wenhua chubanshe, 2007), http://www.wellesley.edu/studentlife/aboutus/handbook/academic/otherhonors.
23. Quoted from Pakula, *The Last Empress,* 25.
24. See Tyson Li, *Madame Chiang Kai-shek,* 61. See also Dou Yingtai, *Song Meiling yu Liu Jiwen de chulian* (The First Love of Song Meiling and Liu Jiwen) (Beijing: Tuanjie chubanshe, 2005).
25. Quoted from Tyson Li, *Madame Chiang Kai-shek,* 82; Pakula, *The Last Empress,* 169.
26. See Pang, *Mao Zedong nianpu, 1893–1949* (Chronological Biography of Mao Zedong, 1893–1949), 1:169–72; Yuriev, *Revoliutsiia 1925–1927 gg. v Kitae* (The Revolution of 1925–1927 in China), 416; Vera Vladimirovna Vishnyakova-Akimova, *Two Years in Revolutionary China, 1925–1927,* trans. by Steven I. Levine (Cambridge: East Asian Research Center, Harvard University, 1971), 243–71; Chang, *The Rise of the Chinese Communist Party,* 1:532–72.
27. See Chiang, *Riji* (Diaries), December 17, 1926, Hoover Archives, box 5, folder 6; Chang, *The Rise of the Chinese Communist Party,* 1:557–58; Titarenko, *VKP(b), Komintern i Kitai: Dokumenty* (The CPSU, Comintern and China: Documents), 2:920.
28. Quoted in Chang, *The Rise of the Chinese Communist Party,* 1:557.
29. Quoted from Wilbur and How, *Missionaries of Revolution,* 772.
30. General Tang, a former militarist, was no sort of leftist. In Voitinsky's words he was no "more reliable [a] factor in revolution than Chiang Kai-shek and only played at revolution, hoping for support from the USSR to seize power in the NRA." Titarenko, *VKP(b), Komintern i Kitai: Dokumenty* (The CPSU, Comintern and China: Documents), 2:602.
31. Hsiung, *The Life of Chiang Kai-shek,* 263–64.
32. Quoted from Ch'en, *The Storm Clouds Clear over China,* 49.
33. See Fenby, *Chiang Kai-shek,* 127.
34. See Lü Fangshang, ed., *Jiang Zhongsheng xiansheng nianpu changbian* (Large Chronological Biography of Mr. Jiang Zhongzheng), 2:2 (Taipei: Guoshiguan, 2014).
35. Ibid., 2:3.

36. Titarenko, *VKP(b), Komintern i Kitai: Dokumenty* (The CPSU, Comintern and China: Documents), 2:922.
37. Quoted from Chen Gongbo, *Kuxiao lu (yi jiu er wu zhi yi jiu san liu)* (Somber Notes [1925–1936]) (Beijing: Xiandai shiliao biankanshe, 1981), 71.
38. Chiang, *Riji* (Diaries), January 12 and 13, 1927, Hoover Archives, box 5, folder 7.
39. See Chen, *Kuxiao lu* (Somber Notes [1925–1936]), 72.
40. See Cherepanov, *Zapiski voennogo sovetnika v Kitae* (Notes of a Military Advisor in China), 517.
41. Titarenko, *VKP(b), Komintern i Kitai: Dokumenty* (The CPSU, Comintern and China: Documents), 2:619–20.
42. Chiang, *Riji* (Diaries), February 24, 1927, Hoover Archives, box 5, folder 8.
43. "Zapis' besedy t. Grigoriia [Vointinskogo] s Chan Kai-shi ot 24 fevralia 1927 g." (Record of a Conversation between Com. Grigorii [Voitinsky] and Chiang Kai-shek, February 27, 1927), RGASPI, collection 514, inventory 1, file 240, sheets 12–13. See also Titarenko, *VKP(b), Komintern i Kitai: Dokumenty* (The CPSU, Comintern and China: Documents), 2:630–31.
44. Quoted from Chang, *The Rise of the Chinese Communist Party,* 1:571.
45. See Titarenko, *VKP(b), Komintern i Kitai: Dokumenty* (The CPSU, Comintern and China: Documents), 2:630–31, 628.
46. A. V. Bakulin, *Zapiski ob ukhan'skom periode kitaiskoi revoliutsii (iz istorii kitaiskoi revoliutsii 1925–1927 gg.)* (Notes on the Wuhan Period of the Chinese Revolution [From the History of the Chinese Revolution of 1925–1927]) (Moscow-Leningrad: Giz, 1930), 212–14.
47. See Liu Hongzhe, "1927 nian Jiang Jieshi yu Song Ailing 'Jiujiang tanhua' tanwei—Qian lun 'Chen Jieru huyilu' de shixue jiazhi" (Brief Analysis of the "Jiujiang Conversations" of Chiang Kai-shek and Song Ailing in 1927, or On the Historical Value of the "Reminiscences of Chen Jieru"), *Jiujiang xueyuan xuebao (shehui kexue ban)* (Bulletin of Jiujiang University [Social Sciences Issue]), 30, no. 2 (161) (2011): 63–65.
48. Ch'en, *Chiang Kai-shek's Secret Past,* 238.
49. Ibid.
50. Chiang, *Riji* (Diaries), March 21, 1927, Hoover Archives, box 5, folder 9.
51. Green, *Hsiang-Ya Journal,* 56.
52. Chang, *The Rise of the Chinese Communist Party,* 1:606.
53. For more details, see Pantsov with Levine, *Mao,* 176.
54. Titarenko, *VKP(b), Komintern i Kitai: Dokumenty* (The CPSU, Comintern and China: Documents), 2:688.
55. RGASPI, collection 17, inventory 162, file 4, sheets 71–72. See also Titarenko, *VKP(b), Komintern i Kitai: Dokumenty* (The CPSU, Comintern and China: Documents), 2:632–33, 732.
56. See Chang, *The Rise of the Chinese Communist Party,* 1:581–82.
57. Titarenko, *VKP(b), Komintern i Kitai: Dokumenty* (The CPSU, Comintern and China: Documents), 2:732.
58. See Tuchman, *Stilwell and the American Experience in China, 1911–45,* 131.
59. See Ch'en, *The Storm Clouds Clear over China,* 53–54.
60. Anna Moffet Jarvis, "Letters from China 1920–1949" (manuscript), [1974], 5.

61. See ibid., 5–15; Ch'en, *The Storm Clouds Clear over China,* 51.
62. "Sovmestnoe zaiavlenie predsedatalia Natsional'nogo pravitel'stvo Van Tsinveia i General'nogo secretaria TsIK KPK Chen Dusiu o prodolzhenii sotrudnichestvo KPK i Gomindana. 5 aprelia 1927" (Joint Declaration of the Chairman of the National government Wang Jingwei and the General Secretary of the CCP CEC Chen Duxiu on Continuing Cooperation between the CCP and the Guomindang. April 5, 1927 g.), in M. I. Sladkovsky, ed., *Dokumenty po istorii Kommunisticheskoi partii Kitaia 1920–1949 gg. (v chetyrekh tomakh)* (Documents on the History of the Chinese Communist Party 1920–1949 [in four volumes]), vol. 1, book 3, 173 (Moscow: IDV AN SSSR, 1981).
63. Titarenko, *VKP(b), Komintern i Kitai: Dokumenty* (The CPSU, Comintern and China: Documents), 2:684.
64. See RGASPI, collection of unsorted documents.
65. Ch'en, *The Storm Clouds Clear over China,* 56–59.
66. Indian servants waving fans.
67. *China: A Century of Revolution,* PBS Documentary, part 1: *China in Revolution,* Ambrica Production, 2007; Ch'en, *Chiang Kai-shek's Secret Past,* 248; Dong, *Shanghai,* 183–85.
68. Ch'en, *The Storm Clouds Clear over China,* 62. See also Martin, *The Shanghai Green Gang,* 106–8.
69. Chiang, *Soviet Russia in China,* 47.
70. Titarenko, *VKP(b), Komintern i Kitai: Dokumenty* (The CPSU, Comintern and China: Documents), 2:683–84, 687, 700.
71. Bakulin, *Zapiski ob ukhan'skom periode kitaiskoi revoliutsii (iz istorii kitaiskoi revoliutsii 1925–1927 gg.)* (Notes on the Wuhan Period of the Chinese Revolution), 115.
72. Titarenko, *VKP(b), Komintern i Kitai. Dokumenty* (The CPSU, Comintern and China: Documents), 2:684.
73. "Deklaratsiia Ts[i]K Guomindanga ob iskliuchenii Chan Kai-shi iz partii" (Declaration of the C[E]C of the Guomindang on the expulsion of Chiang Kai-shek from the Party), in Bakulin, *Zapiski ob ukhan'skom periode kitaiskoi revoliutsii (iz istorii kitaiskoi revoliutsii 1925–1927 gg.)* (Notes on the Wuhan Period of the Chinese Revolution), 246.
74. See Hsiung, *The Life of Chiang Kai-shek,* 266.
75. See Musgrove, *China's Contested Capital,* 27–29, 36.
76. See M. L. Titarenko, ed., *Kommunisticheskii Internatsional i kitaiskaia revoliutsiia: Dokumenty i materialy* (The Communist International and the Chinese Revolution: Documents and Materials) (Moscow: Nauka, 1986), 116–33.
77. See RGASPI, collection 17, inventory 162, file 5, sheets 8–9, 29–30, 33–34, 36–38, 42, 49–51. These telegrams were first published in 1996. See Titarenko, *VKP(b), Komintern i Kitai: Dokumenty* (The CPSU, Comintern and China: Documents), 2:763–64, 770–71, 774–75, 804–5.
78. See RGASPI, collection 17, inventory 162, file 5, sheet 46. See also Titarenko, *VKP(b), Komintern i Kitai: Dokumenty* (The CPSU, Comintern and China: Documents), 2:803.
79. See RGASPI, collection 17, inventory 162, file 5, sheet 54. See also Titarenko, *VKP(b), Komintern i Kitai: Dokumenty* (The CPSU, Comintern and China: Documents), 2:817.
80. Chiang, *Riji* (Diaries), June 19, 1927, Hoover Archives, box 5, folder 12. See also ibid., June 20–21, 1927, Hoover Archives, box 5, folder 12; Zhao Suisheng, *Power by Design: Constitution-Making in Nationalist China* (Honolulu: University of Hawai'i Press,

1996), 97–98; Feng Yuxiang, *Wo suo renshi de Jiang Jieshi* (The Chiang Kai-shek as I Remember Him) (Harbin: Beifang wenyi chubanshe, 2010), 25–28.

81. Quoted from Titarenko, *VKP(b), Komintern i Kitai: Dokumenty* (The CPSU, Comintern and China: Documents), 2:819; James E. Sheridan, *Chinese Warlord: The Career of Feng Yü-hsiang* (Stanford: Stanford University Press, 1966), 228.
82. Lars T. Lih et al., eds., *J. V. Stalin's Letters to V. M. Molotov 1925–1927,* trans. Catherine A. Fitzpatrick (New Haven: Yale University Press, 1995), 136–37.
83. Ibid., 137.
84. RGASPI, collection 17, inventory 162, file 5, sheets 65–66. This directive was first published in 1996. See Titarenko, *VKP(b), Komintern i Kitai: Dokumenty* (The CPSU, Comintern and China: Documents), 2:842–43.
85. See Dan N. Jacobs, *Borodin: Stalin's Man in China* (Cambridge: Harvard University Press, 1981), 284–86.
86. Quoted from Chiang, *Soviet Russia in China,* 52.
87. See Zhao, *Power by Design,* 98–99.
88. Quoted from ibid., 100. See also Hsiung, *The Life of Chiang Kai-shek,* 276–81.
89. Quoted from Lü, *Jiang Zhongzheng xiansheng nianpu changbian* (Large Chronological Biography of Mr. Jiang Zhongzheng), 1:124–25; Tong, *Chiang Kai-shek: Soldier and Statesman,* 1:179.
90. Tong and Li, *The Memoirs of Li Tsung-jen,* 192, 220.
91. See Lü, *Jiang Zhongzheng xiansheng nianpu changbian* (Large Chronological Biography of Mr. Jiang Zhongzheng), 1:127.
92. Quoted from Tong, *Chiang Kai-shek: Soldier and Statesman,* 1:191.
93. Arthur Ransome, *The Chinese Puzzle* (Boston: Houghton Mifflin, 1927), 64. For a brief biography of T. V. Song, see Zhongguo di er lishi dang'anguan (The Second Historical Archives of China), document no. 718/5/6/002–003.
94. Chiang, *Riji* (Diaries), August 18–21, 1927, Hoover Archives, box 5, folder 14.
95. Quoted from Tong, *Chiang Kai-shek: Soldier and Statesman,* 1:180.
96. See ibid., 1:180–84; Pakula, *The Last Empress,* 179.
97. See Lü, *Jiang Zhongzheng xiansheng nianpu changbian* (Large Chronological Biography of Mr. Jiang Zhongzheng), 2:130–31.
98. Quoted from Titarenko, *VKP(b), Komintern i Kitai: Dokumenty* (The CPSU, Comintern and China: Documents), 3:200.
99. See Yurkevich, *Moskva–Kanton 1920-e* (Moscow–Canton, 1920s), 323–24; Zhao, *Power by Design,* 101–3; Tong, *Chiang Kai-shek: Soldier and Statesman,* 1:195.
100. See Musgrove, *China's Contested Capital,* 40.
101. *New York Times,* August 20, 1927.
102. *San Francisco Chronicle,* September 20, 1927.
103. Quoted from Cui, *Qingnian Jiang Jieshi* (Young Chiang Kai-shek), 174.
104. Quoted from ibid., 175.
105. See ibid., 168–78; Lu Xingsheng, *Xiang qian zou, bie huigu: Lu Xingsheng baogao wenxue xuan* (March Forward, Don't Look Back: Selected Reports by Lu Xingsheng on Literature) (Beijing: Duli zuojia, 2015), 336–45; the author's impressions on visiting Chen Jieru's grave in the Park of Happiness and Longevity (Fushouyuan) in Shanghai, April 23, 2016.

106. Chiang, *Riji* (Diaries), August 16 and 28, 1927, Hoover Archives, box 5, folder 14.
107. Exodus 20:14. The Methodist church is particularly strict on this point. See John James Tigert, ed., *The Doctrines and Discipline of the Methodist Episcopal Church, South, 1902* (Nashville: Publishing House of the Methodist Episcopal Church, South, 1902), 62.
108. *New York Times,* September 22, 1927.
109. Elmer T. Clark, *The Chiangs of China* (New York: Abingdon-Cokesbury Press, 1943), 78–80.
110. See Cui, *Qingnian Jiang Jieshi* (Young Chiang Kai-shek), 56–57.
111. See *New York Times,* November 26 and December 2, 1927.
112. At what is presently No. 369 Shaanxi North Road.
113. Chiang, *Riji* (Diaries), December 1, 1927, Hoover Archives, box 5, folder 18.
114. Quoted from Delong, *Madame Chiang Kai-shek and Miss Emma Mills,* 77.
115. Chiang, *Riji* (Diaries), December 2, 1927, Hoover Archives, box 5, folder 18.
116. See Gardner Cowles, *Mike Looks Back: The Memoirs of Gardner Cowles, Founder of Look Magazine* (New York: Gardner Cowles, 1985), 90.
117. See *New York Times,* December 2, 1927; *Renmin ribao* (People's Daily), August 1, 2003; Clark, *The Chiangs of China,* 81; the author's impressions on visiting Shanghai, April 23, 2016.
118. *New York Times,* December 2, 1927.
119. Quoted from DeLong, *Madame Chiang Kai-shek and Miss Emma Mills,* 77.
120. See Shi Quansheng et al., *Nanjing guomin zhengfu de jianli* (Formation of the Nanjing National Government) (Zhengzhou: Henan renmin chubanshe, 1987), 148, 152; Chen Dawei, *Wang Jingwei da zhuan* (Large Biography of Wang Jingwei) (Beijing: Huawen chubanshe, 2010), 77–78.
121. See Chiang, *Riji* (Diaries), December 12, 1927, Hoover Archives, box 5, folder 18; the author's impressions on visiting Hangzhou, April 21, 2016.
122. Now the street is named Nanshan Road, and the number of the villa is 189.
123. Jiang Zhongzheng, "Duiyu shijue de tanhua—Minguo shi liu nian shi er yue shi san ri zai Shanghai zhaodai xinwen jizhe zhi yanci" (Conversation on the Present Moment—Speech at a Press Conference in Shanghai, December 13, 1927), in Luo Jialun et al., eds., *Geming wenxian* (Documents on the Revolution), 16:110 (Taipei: Zhongguo guomindang dangshi shiliao bianzuan weiyuanhui, 1959). See also Tong, *Chiang Kai-shek: Soldier and Statesman,* 1:198–99.
124. Quoted from Furuya, *Chiang Kai-shek,* 236.
125. See Lü, *Jiang Zhongzheng xiansheng nianpu changbian* (Large Chronological Biography of Mr. Jiang Zhongzheng), 1:158; see also Chiang, *Riji* (Diaries), January 4, 1927, Hoover Archives, box 5, folder 19.
126. Lü, *Jiang Zhongzheng xiansheng nianpu changbian* (Large Chronological Biography of Mr. Jiang Zhongzheng), 1:160; Chiang, *Riji* (Diaries), January 9, 1927, Hoover Archives, box 5, folder 19; Shi, *Nanjing guomin zhengfu de jianli* (Formation of the Nanjing National Government), 153.
127. Chiang, *Soviet Russia in China,* 55.
128. Confucius, *The Analects of Confucius,* 6.

## 9. *COMPLETION OF THE NORTHERN EXPEDITION*

1. Quoted from Musgrove, *China's Contested Capital,* 57. See also Jarvis, "Letters from China 1920–1949," 3–4.
2. Quoted from DeLong, *Madame Chiang Kai-shek and Miss Emma Mills,* 79.
3. William Edgar Geil, *Eighteen Capitals of China* (London: Constable, 1911), 196.
4. See ibid., 192, 194.
5. The author's impressions on visiting Nanjing, November 29, 1987.
6. See Henrietta Harrison, *The Making of the Republican Citizen: Political Ceremonies and Symbols in China, 1911–1929* (New York: Oxford University Press, 2000), 41–42.
7. Chiang, *Riji* (Diaries), December 29, 1927, Hoover Archives, box 5, folder 18; Pakula, *The Last Empress,* 184.
8. Quoted from DeLong, *Madame Chiang Kai-shek and Miss Emma Mills,* 77.
9. See Chiang, *Riji* (Diaries), January 4, 5, 8–16, 18, 28, and February 19–21, Hoover Archives, box 5, folders 19 and 20; Pakula, *The Last Empress,* 187.
10. In general, there were very few women in the Guomindang government: 2.75 percent in all. Strangely, most, twenty-two, were in the Ministry of War.
11. Quoted from Tyson Li, *Madame Chiang Kai-shek,* 86. On James M. McHugh, see Wang Chengzhi and Chen Su, *Archival Resources of Republican China in North America* (New York: Columbia University Press, 2016), 137–38.
12. See Ransome, *The Chinese Puzzle,* 116.
13. Quoted from DeLong, *Madame Chiang Kai-shek and Miss Emma Mills,* 79.
14. Quoted from Tyson Li, *Madame Chiang Kai-shek,* 91.
15. Shao Zhigang studied at the University of the Toilers of China under the pseudonym Mirsky. See *Lichnoe delo Mirskogo (Shao Czhi-gana)* (Personal file of Mirsky (Shao Zhigang), RGASPI, collection 495, inventory 225, file 1982.
16. Quoted from V. P. Galitsky, *Tszian Tszingo: Tragediia i triumf syna Chan Kaishi* (Chiang Ching-kuo: The Tragedy and Triumph of Chiang Kai-shek's Son) (Moscow: RAU-Universitet, 2002), 57.
17. See "Beseda t. Kotel'nikova s Khabarovym" (Conversation of Com. Kotel'nikov with Khabarov), RGASPI, collection 514, inventory 1, file 1031, sheet 13; Chiang, *My Days in Soviet Russia,* 8–9.
18. See Zhou Yan et al., *Chen Yu zhuan* (Biography of Chen Yu) (Beijing: Gongren chubanshe, 1988), 117. On Karl Radek as a rector of UTK, see Alexander V. Pantsov, "Karl Radek—Sinilogist," in Alexander V. Pantsov, ed., *Karl Radek on China: Documents from the Former Secret Soviet Archives* (Leiden: Brill, 2021), 1–15.
19. "Pokazanie tov. Nekrasova" (Deposition of Com. Nekrasov), RGASPI, collection 514, inventory 1, file 1012, sheet 2.
20. See Chiang, *Jiang Jingguo riji* (Diaries of Chiang Ching-kuo), 19–25; Chiang, *My Days in Soviet Russia,* 13.
21. See *Lichnoe delo Fen Hun-go* (Personal File of Feng Hongguo), RGASPI, collection 495, inventory 225, file 1341, sheets unnumbered; *Lichnoe delo Fen Fu-nen* (Personal File of Feng Funeng), ibid., file 2034, sheets unnumbered.

22. For more details, see A. V. Pantsov, *Mao Tsze-tun* (Mao Zedong), 2nd, rev. ed. (Moscow: "Molodaya gvardiya," 2012), 441; Spichak, *Kitaiskii avangard Kremlia* (The Chinese Vanguard of the Kremlin), 110–12.
23. See Cui, *Qingnian Jiang Jieshi* (Young Chiang Kai-shek), 59–60.
24. Chiang and Liu, *Jiang Weiguo koushu zizhuan* (The Autobiography of Chiang Wei-kuo as Told by Himself), 1, 45–46. The inscription on the sign might have stipulated ten rules governing the park (the park was not located in the French Concession but the International Settlement), including "1. The Gardens are reserved for the foreign community . . . 4. Dogs and bicycles are not admitted." Robert A. Bickers and Jeffrey N. Wasserstrom, "Shanghai's 'Dogs and Chinese Not Admitted' Sign: Legend, History, and Contemporary Symbol," *China Quarterly* 142 (June 1995): 446.
25. Wang, *Qianshan duxing* (The Solitary Path among a Thousand Mountains), 47–48; Chiang and Liu, *Jiang Weiguo koushu zizhuan* (The Autobiography of Chiang Wei-kuo as Told by Himself), 1, 46, 48; Jin, *Jiang Jieshi yu Jiang Jingguo, Jiang Weiguo* (Chiang Kai-shek and Chiang Ching-kuo, Chiang Wei-kuo), 95.
26. Tong and Li, *The Memoirs of Li Tsung-jen*, 235.
27. See Donald G. Gillin, *Warlord: Yen Hsi-shan in Shansi Province: 1911–1949* (Princeton: Princeton University Press, 1967), 104–6; Li Maosheng et al., *Yan Xishan quan zhuan* (Complete Biography of Yan Xishan), 1:403–21 (Beijing: Dangdai Zhongguo chubanshe, 1997).
28. At present No. 10 Hunan Road.
29. See Zhou and Chen, *Hu Hanmin pingzhuan,* 309.
30. Quoted from Lü, *Jiang Zhongzheng xiansheng nianpu changbian* (Large Chronological Biography of Mr. Jiang Zhongzheng), 1:170.
31. Luo Jialun et al., eds., *Geming wenxian* (Documents of the Revolution), 22: photograph 1 (Taipei: Zhongguo guomindang dangshi shiliao bianzuan weiyuanhui, 1959).
32. See Shi, *Nanjing guomin zhengfu de jianli* (Formation of the Nanjing National Government), 156–57.
33. Tong and Li, *The Memoirs of Li Tsung-jen,* 246.
34. See Shi, *Nanjing guomin zhengfu de jianli* (Formation of the Nanjing National Government), 159.
35. See Harumi Gato-Shibata, *Japan and Britain in Shanghai, 1925–1931* (New York: St. Martin's Press, 1995), 71–72; Tang Peiji, ed., *Zhongguo lishi dashi nianbiao: Xiandai* (Chronology of Events in Chinese History: Contemporary History) (Shanghai: Shanghai cishu chubanshe, 1997), 120.
36. *Tsinan Affair*, 1:42 (Shanghai: International Relations Committee, 1928).
37. Hallett Abend, *My Life in China: 1926–1941* (New York: Harcourt, Brace, 1943), 80.
38. Chiang, *Riji* (Diaries), May 10 and 14, 1928, Hoover Archives, box 6, folder 4.
39. See Luo Jialun et al., eds., *Geming wenxian* (Documents of the Revolution), 19:3504–3657 (Taipei: Zhongguo guomindang dangshi shiliao bianzuan weiyuanhui, 1959); Gato-Shibata, *Japan and Britain in Shanghai, 1925–1931,* 75–76; Tang, *Zhongguo lishi dashi nianbiao: Xiandai* (Chronology of Events in Chinese History: Contemporary History), 120; Donald A. Jordan, *The Northern Expedition: China's National Revolution*

*of 1926–1928* (Honolulu: University Press of Hawaii, 1976), 159–61; William Fitch Morton, *Tanaka Giichi and Japan's China Policy* (New York: St. Martin's Press, 1980), 117–28; H. G. W. Woodhead, ed., *The China Year Book 1929–30* (Tientsin: Tientsin Press, 1930), 881–93; Shi, *Nanjing guomin zhengfu de jianli* (Formation of the Nanjing National Government), 162.

40. "The Japanese played a really dirty trick on Chiang Kai-shek," Alexander Emel'ianovich Al'brecht, agent of the Comintern Executive Committee, reported to Moscow. "At the decisive moment, they compelled him to retreat, and opened the road to his rivals Feng and Yan Xishan." M. L. Titarenko et al., eds., *VKP(b), Komintern i Kitai: Dokumenty* (The CPSU, the Comintern and China: Documents), 3:447 (Moscow: AO "Buklet," 1999). See also Gillin, *Warlord,* 108–9.
41. See Jordan, *The Northern Expedition,* 166; Shi, *Nanjing guomin zhengfu de jianli* (Formation of the Nanjing National Government), 165.
42. Kwantung (more properly Guandong) is the name of the southern extremity of the Northeast Chinese Liaodong peninsula, on which are located the cities of Dalian (Dal'nii, Dairen) and Lüshun (Port Arthur). Here, on August 1, 1906, following its victory in the Russo–Japanese War, the Japanese government created the Kwantung Army. This force was to defend the newly acquired rights in Manchuria that Japan had acquired, in the first place safeguarding the South Manchurian Railway that Japan began building four months later.
43. See Heben Dazuo (Komoto Daisaku), "Heben Dazuo wei cehua 'Huanggutun shijian' zhi Jigu Lianjie deng han liangjian (1928 nian 4 yue)" (Two Messages from Komoto Daisaku to Isogai Rensuke on the Plans for the Huanggutun Incident [April 1928]), *Minguo dang'an* (Republican Archive), no. 3 (1998): 3–5; Heben Dazuo (Komoto Daisaku) et al., *Wo shasile Zhang Zuolin* (I Killed Zhang Zuolin) (Changchun: Jilin wenshi chubanshe, 1986); Morton, *Tanaka Giichi and Japan's China Policy,* 130–31. Several years ago an article appeared in the Russian press claiming that agents of Stalin killed Zhang Zuolin, but the author's arguments are unpersuasive. See Dmitrii Prokhorov, "'Liternoe delo' marshala Zhan Zolinia" (The "Lettered File" of Marshal Zhang Zuolin), *Nezavisimoe voennoe obozrenie* (The Independent Military Review), August 1, 2003.
44. Quoted from Morton, *Tanaka Giichi and Japan's China Policy,* 130.
45. See Neil Boister and Robert Cryer, eds., *Documents on the Tokyo International Military Tribunal: Charter, Indictment and Judgment* (New York: Oxford University Press, 2008), 112, 1004–5; Yoshihisa Tak Matsusaka, *The Making of Japanese Manchuria, 1904–1932* (Cambridge: Harvard University Asian Center, 2001), 344–48.
46. See Ch'en, *The Storm Clouds Clear over China,* 99.
47. Quoted from David Strand, *Rickshaw Beijing: City People and Politics in the 1920s* (Berkeley: University of California Press, 1989), 11.
48. See Ch'en, *The Storm Clouds Clear over China,* 79; Tong and Li, *The Memoirs of Li Tsung-jen,* 257; Feng, *Wo suo renshi de Jiang Jieshi* (The Chiang Kai-shek as I Remember Him), 35; Lary, *Region and Nation,* 116.
49. The Japanese consul was born in 1860 and Zhang Zuolin in 1875.
50. Emperor Hirohito and Zhang Xueliang were born in the same year, 1901.

51. Quoted from Chiang Kai-shek, *Jiang zongtong milu: zhong-ri guanxi bashi nian zhi zhengyan* (Secret Notes of President Chiang: The True Face of Eighty Years of Sino–Japanese Relations), 7:95–96 (Taipei: Zhongyang ribao she, 1974).
52. Sun Yat-sen, *Sun Zhongshan quanji* (Complete Works of Sun Zhongshan), 9:97 (Beijing: Renmin chubanshe, 1986).
53. See Jin Dequn, ed., *Zhongguo xiandai shi ziliao xuanji* (Selected Documents on Contemporary Chinese History), 3:35–39 (Beijing: Zhongguo renmin daxue chubanshe, 1988); Min-Ch'in T. Z. Tyau, *Two Years of Nationalist China* (Shanghai: Kelly and Walsh, 1930), 36–37 (a chart between these pages).
54. Tong, *Chiang Kai-shek: Soldier and Statesman,* 1:318.
55. See *The Organic Law of the National Government of the Republic of China* (New York: China Institute of America, 1928); "The Organic Law of the National Government of the Republic of China," in Chao-chu Wu, *The Nationalist Program for China* (New Haven: Yale University Press, 1929), 81–89; Jin, *Zhongguo xiandai shi ziliao xuanji* (Selected Documents on Contemporary Chinese History), 3:34; Paul Myron Anthony Linebarger, *Government in Republican China* (Westport, CT: McGraw-Hill, 1938), 163–64; Jiajin Liangzi (Ieshika Ryuko), *Jiang Jieshi yu Nanjing Guomin zhengfu* (Chiang Kai-shek and the Nanjing National Government) (Beijing: Shehui kexue wenxian chubanshe, 2005), 116.
56. Ch'en, *The Storm Clouds Clear over China,* 87.
57. See Jin, *Zhongguo xiandai shi ziliao xuanji* (Selected Documents on Contemporary Chinese History), 3:20–22; Shi, *Nanjing guomin zhengfu de jianli* (Formation of the Nanjing National Government), 168–69.
58. See Melvyn C. Goldstein, *A History of Modern Tibet, 1913–1951: The Demise of the Lamaist State* (Berkeley: University of California Press, 1989), 58–64, 213–21.

## 10. *TRIUMPHS AND DEFEATS*

1. See Chiang, *Soviet Russia in China,* 13–14.
2. *Russian Review* 3, no. 20 (October 15, 1925): 416; Kurdiukov, *Sovetsko–kitaiskie otnoshniia, 1917–1957* (Soviet–Chinese Relations, 1917–1957), 83.
3. For the unseemly measures that tsarist officials resorted to in order to incline the Chinese toward signing the agreement to build the CER, see the reminiscences of Count S. Yu. Witte, the Russian minister of finance. Count S. Yu. Witte, *Vospominannia: Tsarstvovanie Nikolai II* (Reminiscences: Reign of Nicholas II), 1:37–55, 57, 3rd ed. (Berlin: "Slovo," 1924).
4. See Woodhead, *The China Year Book 1929–30,* 854–55.
5. See Edmund S. K. Fung, "Chinese Nationalists and Unequal Treaties 1924–1931," *Modern Asian Studies* 21, no. 4 (1987): 809.
6. M. I. Sladkovsky, ed., *Noveishaia istoriia Kitaia 1928–1949* (Contemporary History of China 1928–1949) (Moscow: Nauka, 1984), 9.
7. "Treaty Regulating Tariff Relations between China and the United States," in Wu, *The Nationalist Program for China,* 110–12.
8. See Sladkovsky, *Noveishaia istoriia Kitaia 1928–1949* (Contemporary History of China 1928–1949), 15.

9. See Fung, *Chinese Nationalists and Unequal Treaties 1924–1931,* 810–11.
10. See Zhongguo guomindang zhongyang dangshiguan (The Central Party Archives of the Guomindang), General Division, document 588/22.
11. For details, see Michael M. Walker, *The 1929 Sino–Soviet War: The War Nobody Knew* (Lawrence: University Press of Kansas, 2017).
12. Lih, *Stalin's Letters to Molotov 1925–1936,* 182. Emphasis added by Stalin.
13. See John B. Powell, *My Twenty-five Years in China* (New York: Macmillan, 1945), 173–76; George Alexander Lensen, *The Damned Inheritance: The Soviet Union and the Manchurian Crisis 1924–1935* (Tallahassee, FL: Diplomatic Press, 1974), 32–171; Aron Shai, *Zhang Xueliang: The General Who Never Fought* (New York: Palgrave Macmillan, 2012), 22.
14. For more details, see Bruce A. Elleman, "The End of Extraterritoriality in China: The Case of the Soviet Union, 1917–1960," *Republican China,* no. 2 (1996): 65, 76–78.
15. William Kirby, *Germany and Republican China* (Stanford: Stanford University Press, 1984), 44. See also Robyn L. Rodriguez, "Journey to the East: The German Military Mission in China, 1927–1938" (PhD diss., Ohio State University, 2011).
16. See Yu Maochun, *The Dragon's War: Allied Operations and the Fate of China, 1937–1947* (Annapolis, MD: Naval Institute Press, 2006), 1.
17. Kirby, *Germany and Republican China,* 50.
18. Ibid., 52–62; John P. Fox, "Max Bauer: Chiang Kai-shek's First German Military Adviser," *Journal of Contemporary History* 5, no. 4 (1970): 21–44; Pan Qichang, *Bainian Zhong-De guanxi* (One Hundred Years of Sino-German Relations) (Beijing: Shijie zhishi chubanshe, 2006), 79–85.
19. After his death, rumors circulated in China that he had been poisoned by one of his Chinese enemies.
20. See Billie K. Walsh, "The German Military Mission in China, 1928–38," *Journal of Modern History* 46, no. 3 (1974): 505–6.
21. See ibid., 506; Titarenko, *VKP(b), Komintern i Kitai: Dokumenty* (The CPSU, the Comintern and China: Documents), 3:1146, 1294.
22. Hallett Abend, *Tortured China* (New York: Ives Washburn, 1930), 47.
23. Hsiung, *The Life of Chiang Kai-shek,* 301.
24. See Shi, *Nanjing guomin zhengfu de jianli* (Formation of the Nanjing National Government), 179–85.
25. Eugene William Levich, *The Kwangsi Way in Kuomintang China 1931–1939* (Armonk, NY: M. E. Sharpe, 1993), 7, 14.
26. See Titarenko, *VKP(b), Komintern i Kitai: Dokumenty* (The CPSU, Comintern and China: Documents), 3:545.
27. To be sure, the Dutch historian Frank Dikötter says there was no need for Chiang to unify China as there was no particular harm, in his opinion, from the fragmentation of the country and the civil wars, but his preposterous point of view is hardly convincing. See Frank Dikötter, *The Age of Openness: China before Mao* (Berkeley: University of California Press, 2008), 7–13.
28. See Huang Meizhen and Hao Shengchao, eds., *Zhonghua minguo shi shijian renwu lu* (Dictionary of Events and Persons in the History of the Republic of China) (Shanghai: Shanghai renmin chubanshe, 1987), 171–72; Hsiung, *The Life of Chiang Kai-shek,* 293; Ch'en, *The Storm Clouds Clear over China,* 82.

29. See Liu Yisheng, "Guomindang kaichu dangji xianxiang shulun" (Brief Essay on the Phenomenon of Guomindang Expulsion from the Party), *Shixue yuekan* (Historical Science Monthly), no. 5 (1997): 45.
30. See in detail Chen Yunqian, *Chongbai yu jiyi—Sun Zhongshan fuhao de jianguo yu chuanbo* (Worship and Memory—Construction and Dissemination of the Symbol of Sun Yat-sen) (Nanjing: Nanjing daxue chubanshe, 2009); Li Gongzhong, *Zhongshanling: Yige xiandai zhengzhi fuhao de dansheng* (Sun Yat-sen's Mausoleum: The Birth of a Modern Political Symbol) (Beijing: Shehui kexue wenxian chubanshe, 2009).
31. Quoted from Tyau, *Two Years of Nationalist China,* 452.
32. See Wang Liping, "Creating a National Symbol: The Sun Yat-sen Memorial in Nanjing," *Republican China,* no. 2 (1996): 47–48.
33. See Philip West, "Liberal Persuasions and China: Soong Meiling and John Leighton Stuart," in Samuel C. Chu, ed., *Madame Chiang Kai-shek and Her China* (Norwalk, CT: EastBridge, 2005), 61.
34. The journey to Moscow of Song Qingling and the former minister of foreign affairs of the Wuhan government Eugene Chen cost the Comintern about ten thousand rubles. See Titarenko, *VKP(b), Komintern i Kitai: Dokumenty* (The CPSU, Comintern and China: Documents), 3:74.
35. See her letters to Chiang, published in *Pravda* (Truth), December 24, 1927.
36. See Pantsov with Levine, *Mao,* 311.
37. See Mildred Merland, "Motion Picture Film on the State of Burial of Sun Yat-sen, President of China, in Nanking, 1929," Hoover Archives; Wang, *Creating a National Symbol,* 46–52; Abend, *Tortured China,* 64 and 65 (a photograph between these pages); Henry Francis Misselwitz, *The Dragon Stirs: An Intimate Sketch-Book of China's Kuomintang Revolution 1927–29* (Westport, CT: Harbinger House, 1941), 241–44; the author's impressions on visiting Sun Yat-sen's mausoleum in Nanjing, June 3, 2017.
38. See Alexander V. Pantsov with Steven I. Levine, *Deng Xiaoping: A Revolutionary Life* (New York: Oxford University Press, 2016), 63.
39. See Jin, *Zhongguo xiandai shi ziliao xuanji* (Selected Documents on Contemporary Chinese History), 3:445–69.
40. Quoted from Hsiung, *The Life of Chiang Kai-shek,* 295–96.
41. Quoted from Huang Daoxuan, "Jiang Jieshi 'rang wai bi xian an nei' fangzhen yanjiu" (A Study of Chiang Kai-shek's Policy "Before We Fight the External Enemy, We Must First Establish Peace Inside the Country"), *Kangri zhanzheng yanjiu* (Studies on the War of Resistance Against Japan), no. 2 (2000): 31–32.
42. See Liu, *Guomindang kaichu dangji xianxiang shulun* (Brief Essay on the Phenomenon of Guomindang Expulsion from the Party), 45; Cai Dejin and Wang Sheng, *Wang Jingwei shengping jishi* (Chronological Biography of Wang Jingwei) (Beijing: Zhongguo wenshi chubanshe, 1993), 126–27.
43. Hsiung, *The Life of Chiang Kai-shek,* 296.
44. See Liu, *Guomindang kaichu dangji xianxiang shulun* (Brief Essay on the Phenomenon of Guomindang Expulsion from the Party), 45; Cai and Wang, *Wang Jingwei shengping jishi* (Chronological Biography of Wang Jingwei), 127–28.
45. Jin, *Zhongguo xiandai shi ziliao xuanji* (Selected Documents on Contemporary Chinese History), 3:285–86.

46. It is amusing that, wishing to emphasize that their government was established for the long term, the Beijing mutineers announced their organization at nine o'clock in the morning on September 9, that is, the ninth month of the year 1930, the nineteenth year of the proclamation of the Republic. They figured that the number nine, repeated four times, would bring them success. In Chinese the number nine sounds like the word "long," or "a long time." But they survived for just eleven days.
47. See Sladkovsky, *Noveishaia istoriia Kitaia 1928–1949* (Contemporary History of China 1928–1949), 22–23; Titarenko, *VKP(b), Komintern i Kitai: Dokumenty* (The CPSU, Comintern and China: Documents), 3:992–93.
48. See Titarenko, *VKP(b), Komintern i Kitai: Dokumenty* (The CPSU, Comintern and China: Documents), 3:1265.
49. See Kirby, *Germany and Republican China,* 110.
50. Abend, *Tortured China,* 47–48.
51. See Tong, *Chiang Kai-shek: Soldier and Statesman,* 1:306.
52. See James Burke, *My Father in China* (New York: Farrar & Rinehart, 1942), 346–47.
53. The Gospel According to Saint Matthew 5:39, 44.
54. Leviticus 24:20.
55. Quoted from Burke, *My Father in China,* 347.
56. For more details, see Pantsov with Levine, *Mao,* 185–205.
57. *Stenograficheskii otchet VI s"ezda Kommunisticheskoi partii Kitaia* (Stenographic Report of the Sixth Congress of the Chinese Communist Party), 2:151, 4:183 (Moscow: Institute of Chinese Studies Press, 1930); Zhou Enlai, *Selected Works of Zhou Enlai,* 1:195–96 (Beijing: Foreign Languages Press, 1981).
58. A. Ivin, *Sovietskii Kitai* (Soviet China) (Moscow: Molodaia gvardiia, 1931), 35.
59. Jacquerie was the uprising of French peasants in 1358. The name derives from a derisive term the nobility applied to peasants: Jacques Bonhomme.
60. See A. M. Grigoriev, *Kommunisticheskaia partiia Kitaia v nachal'nyi period sovetskogo dvizheniia (iul' 1927 g.–sentiabr' 1931 g.)* (The Chinese Communist Party in the Initial Period of the Soviet Movement [July 1927–September 1931]) (Moscow: IDV AN SSSR, 1976), 338.
61. See Tim Wright, "Coping with the World Depression: The Nationalist Government's Relations with Chinese Industry and Commerce, 1932–1936," in John Fitzgerald, ed., *The Nationalists and Chinese Society 1923–1937: A Symposium* (Parkville: History Department, University of Melbourne, 1989), 136–37; Shiroyama Tomoko, *China during the Great Depression: Market, State, and the World Economy, 1929–1937* (Cambridge: Harvard University Asian Center, 2008).
62. See Titarenko, *VKP(b), Komintern i Kitai: Dokumenty* (The CPSU, Comintern and China: Documents), 3:1361–64, 1472.
63. A *picul* is a measure of weight equal to 133 lbs.
64. Titarenko, *VKP(b), Komintern i Kitai: Dokumenty* (The CPSU, Comintern and China: Documents), 3:601, 917.
65. Stuart R. Schram, ed., *Mao's Road to Power: Revolutionary Writings 1912–1949,* 3:155–56 (Armonk, NY: M. E. Sharpe, 1995).
66. See Pang, *Mao Zedong nianpu, 1893–1949* (Chronological Biography of Mao Zedong, 1893–1949), 1:330–31; Philip Short, *Mao: A Life* (New York: Henry Holt, 1999), 257.

67. National Archives of the United States, document 893.00PR Nanking/21.
68. Peter Fleming, *One's Company: A Journey to China* (New York: Charles Scribner's Sons, 1934), 183.
69. Chiang, *Riji* (Diaries), July 22, 1931, Hoover Archives, box 8, folder 8.
70. See Lü Fangshang, *Jiang Zhongzheng xiansheng nianpu changbian* (Large Chronological Biography of Mr. Jiang Zhongzheng), 3:470 (Taipei: Guoshiguan, 2014); Huang, "Jiang Jieshi 'rang wai bi xian an nei' fangzhen yanjiu" (A Study of Chiang Kai-shek's Policy "Before We Fight the External Enemy, We Must First Establish Peace Inside the Country"), 32–33; Xiong Zongren, "Rang wai bi xian an nei" zai pipan (New Critique of the Expression "Before We Fight the External Enemy, We Must First Establish Peace Inside the Country"), *Kangri zhanzheng yanjiu* (Studies on the War of Resistance against Japan), no. 4 (2001), 31.
71. See Kirby, *Germany and Republican China,* 110.
72. Quoted from ibid., 118.
73. See ibid., 124; Walsh, *The German Military Mission in China, 1928–38,* 507.
74. See Ger Teitler and Kurt W. Radtke, eds., *A Dutch Spy in China: Reports on the First Phase of the Sino–Japanese War (1937–1939)* (Leiden: Brill, 1999), 63–64; Claire Lee Chennault, *Way of a Fighter* (New York: G. P. Putman's Sons, 1949), 36–37.
75. See Shirley Ann Smith, *Imperial Designs: Italians in China, 1900–1947* (Madison, NJ: Fairleigh Dickenson University Press, 2012), 125.
76. Michele Fatica, "The Beginning and the End of the Idyllic Relations between Mussolini's Italy and Chiang Kai-shek's China (1930–1937)," in Maurizio Marinelli and Giovanni Andornino, eds., *Italy's Encounters with Modern China: Imperial Dreams, Strategic Ambitions* (New York: Palgrave Macmillan, 2014), 101, 106–7; Smith, *Imperial Designs,* 124–25.
77. See Fleming, *One's Company,* 235; Gerald Yorke, *China Changes* (New York: Charles Scribner's Sons, 1936), 208; S. L. Tikhvinsky, ed., *Russko–kitaiskie otnosheniia v XX veke: Dokumenty i materialy* (Russo–Chinese Relations in the Twentieth Century: Documents and Materials), vol. 4, book 1, 524 (Moscow: "Pamiatniki istoricheskoi mysli," 2000). For more details, see Scaroni's memoirs: Silvio Scaroni, *Missione Militare Aeronautica in Cina* (Air Force Military Mission in China) (Maggio: Ufficio storico, 1970).
78. See Chennault, *Way of a Fighter,* 36–37; Smith, *Imperial Designs,* 124.
79. See Ch'en, *The Storm Clouds Clear over China,* 65.
80. Parks M. Coble, "The Soong Family and Chinese Capitalists," in Chu, *Madame Chiang Kai-shek and Her China,* 74.
81. Ch'en, *The Storm Clouds Clear over China,* 67.
82. Titarenko, *VKP(b), Komintern i Kitai: Dokumenty* (The CPSU, Comintern and China: Documents), 3:1270.
83. See Patricia Stranahan, *Underground: The Shanghai Communist Party and the Politics of Survival, 1927–1937* (Lanham, MD: Rowman & Littlefield, 1998), 108.
84. See Frederick S. Litten, "The Noulens Affair," *China Quarterly* 138 (June 1994): 492–512; Frederic Wakeman Jr., *Policing Shanghai 1927–1937* (Berkeley: University of California Press, 1995), 151–60, 253–54; Nie Rongzhen, *Nie Rongzhen huiyilu* (Reminiscenses of Nie Rongzhen), 1:118, 126–28 (Beijing: Jiefangjun chubanshe, 1983).

85. See Yang Tianshi, *Zhaoxun zhenshi de Jiang Jiieshi: Jiang Jieshi riji jiedu* (In Search of the True Chiang Kai-shek: Analyzing Chiang Kai-shek's Diaries), 1:177–200 (Hong Kong: Sanlian shudian, 2008).
86. Quoted from Tong, *Chiang Kai-shek: Soldier and Statesmen*, 1:314.
87. Ransome, *The Chinese Puzzle*, 65.
88. See Sladkovsky, *Noveishaia istoriia Kitaia 1928–1949* (Contemporary History of China 1928–1949), 23–24; Liu, *Guomindang kaichu dangji xianxiang shulun* (Brief Essay on the Phenomenon of Guomindang Expulsion from the Party), 45.
89. See H. G. W. Woodhead, ed., *The China Year Book 1932* (Nendeln/Liechtenstein: Kraus Reprint, 1969), 688–90; Jiajin, *Jiang Jieshi yu Nanjing guomin zhengfu*, 112; Tong, *Chiang Kai-shek: Soldier and Statesman*, 1:316.
90. See Chris Courtney, "The Dragon King and the 1931 Wuhan Flood: Religious Rumors and Environmental Disasters in Republican China," *Twentieth-Century China*, no. 2 (2015): 84; Titarenko, *VKP(b), Komintern i Kitai: Dokumenty* (The CPSU, Comintern and China: Documents), 3:1472.
91. Abend, *My Life in China: 1926–1941*, 155.
92. See Titarenko, *VKP(b), Komintern i Kitai: Dokumenty* (The CPSU, Comintern and China: Documents), 3:1472.
93. See Mark Elvin and G. William Skinners, eds., *The Chinese City between Two Worlds* (Stanford: Stanford University Press, 1974), 10.
94. See V. I. Khor'kov, ed., *Rabochee dvizhenie v Kitae (1927–1931): Nankinskii gomindan i rabochii vopros: Dokumenty i materialy* (The Workers' Movement in China [1927–1931]: The Nanjing Guomindang and the Worker Question: Documents and Materials) (Moscow: Nauka, 1982), 73–82, 86–96.
95. See Abend, *Tortured China*, 50.
96. Grigoriev, *Kommunisticheskaia partiia Kitaia v nachal'nyi period sovetskogo dvizheniia (iul' 1927 g.–sentiabr' 1931 g.)* (The Chinese Communist Party in the Initial Period of the Soviet Movement [July 1927–September 1931]), 359; He Yizhong, "Da geming shibai hou zhonggongdangyuan de 'zhengshou' yundong" (Movement to "Expand" the Number of Communists after the Failure of the Great Revolution), *Shilin* (History Review), no. 1 (2012): 123.
97. Quoted from A. A. Pisarev, *Gomindan i agrarno-krest'ianskii vopros v Kitae v 20–30-e gody XX v.* (The Guomindang and the Agrarian-peasant Question in China in the 1920s and 1930s) (Moscow: Nauka, 1986), 104–5.
98. Quoted from ibid., 116.
99. See ibid., 115–27.
100. See Frederic Wakeman Jr., "A Revisionist View of the Nanjing Decade: Confucian Fascism," in Frederic Wakeman Jr. and Richard Louis Edmonds, eds., *Reappraising Republican China* (New York: Oxford University Press, 2000), 166.
101. For more details, see A. V. Meliksetov, *Sotsial'no-ekonomicheskaia politika Gomindana v Kitae (1927–1949)* (The Socioeconomic Policy of the Guomindang in China [1927–1949]) (Moscow: Nauka, 1977), 47–82.
102. See Tong, *Chiang Kai-shek: Soldier and Statesman*, 1:317; Fenby, *Chiang Kai-shek*, 182–83; Grigoriev, *Kommunisticheskaia partiia Kitaia v nachal'nyi period sovetskogo*

*dvizheniia (iul' 1927 g.–sentiabr' 1931 g.)* (The Chinese Communist Party in the Initial Period of the Soviet Movement [July 1927–September 1931]), 174.

103. The first Far Eastern Olympic Games were held in 1913 in Manila. In all, there were ten such games, three of which were staged in Shanghai (1915, 1921, and 1927).
104. Jarvis, "Letters from China 1920–1949," 16.
105. Confucius, *The Analects of Confucius,* 75.

## 11. *"FOR A NEW LIFE!"*

1. See C. F. Remer and William B. Palmer, *A Study of Chinese Boycotts: With Special Reference to Their Economic Effectiveness* (Baltimore: Johns Hopkins University Press, 1933). 22.
2. See Woodhead, *The China Year Book 1932,* 605–12.
3. See James L. McClain, *Japan, A Modern History* (New York: W. W. Norton, 2002), 405–7.
4. Donald A. Jordan, *Chinese Boycotts versus Japanese Bombs: The Failure of China's "Revolutionary Diplomacy," 1931–32* (Ann Arbor: University of Michigan Press, 1991), 2–15, 31–32, 34–36, 331–34.
5. See Matsusaka, *The Making of Japanese Manchuria, 1904–1932*, 414.
6. See Sadako N. Ogata, *Defiance in Manchuria: The Making of Japanese Foreign Policy, 1931–1932* (Berkeley: University of California Press, 1964), 18–19; T. A. Bisson, "The United States and the Far East: A Survey of the Relations of the United States with China and Japan—September 1, 1930 to September 1, 1931," *Pacific Affairs,* no. 1 (1932): 67–68.
7. Quoted from Ogata, *Defiance in Manchuria,* 38.
8. There is a suspicion that Tatekawa allowed himself to be lured into the restaurant since he sympathized with the plans of the Kwantung officers to seize Manchuria. See Craig Collie, *The Reporter and the Warlords* (Sydney: Allen & Unwin, 2013), 186.
9. The roadway was almost undamaged. Ten minutes after the explosion a train passed over that section of the railroad without delay.
10. See *Hostile Activities of Japanese Troops in the Northeastern Provinces of China (From September 18, 1931, to November 7, 1931),* 1:1, 13 (S.I: s.n., 1931).
11. Chiang, *Riji* (Diaries), September 19, 1931, Hoover Archives, box 8, folder 10.
12. Quoted from Hsiung, *The Life of Chiang Kai-shek,* 306.
13. See Selle, *Donald of China,* 266–70; Collie, *The Reporter and the Warlords,* 186; Abend, *My Life in China: 1926–1941,* 150–51.
14. See Hollington K. Tong, *Chiang Kai-shek: Soldier and Statesman: Authorized Biography,* 2:326 (Shanghai: China Publishing, 1937).
15. Quoted from R. A. Mirovitskaia, "Sovetskii Soiuz i Kitai v period razryva i vosstanovleniia otnoshenii (1928–1936 gg.)" (The Soviet Union and China during the Period of the Rift and the Restoration of Relations), *Informatsionnyi biulleten' IDV AN SSSR* (Information Bulletin of the Institute of the Far East, Academy of Sciences, USSR), no. 67 (Moscow: IDV AN SSSR 1975), 77; see also S. L. Tikhvinsky, ed., *Russko–kitaiskie otnosheniia v XX veke: Dokumenty i materialy* (Russo–Chinese Relations in the Twentieth Century: Documents and Materials), 3:777 (Moscow: "Pamiatniki istoricheskoi mysli," 2010).

16. See A. A. Gromyko, ed., *Dokumenty vneshnei politiki SSSR* (Documents of the USSR Foreign Policy), 14:527–28, 533–35, 544–48 (Moscow: Politizdat, 1968).
17. M. L. Titarenko et al., eds., *VKP(b), Komintern i Kitai: Dokumenty* (The CPSU, Comintern and China: Documents), 4:68 (Moscow: AO "Buklet," 2003).
18. See Chiang Ching-kuo, *Jiang Jingguo riji* (Diaries of Chiang Ching-kuo), 30–39; Pantsov, *Mao Tsedun* (Mao Zedong), 441.
19. Quoted from Taylor, *The Generalissimo's Son,* 59.
20. See Svetlana Alliluyeva, *Twenty Letters to a Friend,* trans. Priscilla Johnson McMillan (New York: Harper & Row, 1967), 161.
21. See Taylor, *The Generalissimo's Son*, 59.
22. Titarenko, *VKP(b), Komintern i Kitai: Dokumenty* (The CPSU, Comintern and China: Documents), 4:112.
23. Chiang, *Riji* (Diaries), December 16, 1931, Hoover Archives, box 8, folder 13.
24. On Sorge in China, see Su Zhiliang, ed., *Zuoerge zai Zhongguo de mimi shiming* (Sorge's Secret Mission in China) (Shanghai: Shanghai shehui kehui chubanshe, 2014).
25. Titarenko, *VKP(b), Komintern i Kitai: Dokumenty* (The CPSU, Comintern and China: Documents), 4:112.
26. A. G. Fesiun, ed., *Delo Rikharda Zorge: Neizvestnye dokumenty* (The Richard Sorge Case: Unknown Documents) (Moscow: "Letnii sad," 2000), 69.
27. See E. Prudnikova, *Rikhard Zorge: Razvedchik No. 1?* (Richard Sorge: Spy No. 1?) (Saint Petersburg: Neva, 2004), 73–77.
28. The CEC of the Guomindang officially proclaimed Sun the founding father of the Republic of China on April 1, 1940. Prior to that, in China he was unofficially called Guofu (Father of the State).
29. Quoted from Tong, *Chiang Kai-shek: Soldier and Statesman,* 2:334.
30. Quoted from Taylor, *The Generalissimo,* 97.
31. Quoted from Wakeman Jr., "A Revisionist View of the Nanjing Decade: Confucian Fascism," 153–54.
32. See Chiang, *Riji* (Diaries), March 5, 1931, Hoover Archives, box 8, folder 4.
33. Quoted from Tong, *Chiang Kai-shek: Soldier and Statesman,* 2:328.
34. Chiang, *Riji* (Diaries), November 25, 1931, Hoover Archives, box 8, folder 12.
35. See Huang and Hao, *Zhonghua minguo shi shijian renwu lu* (Dictionary of Events and Persons in the History of the Republic of China), 209–11; Li Songlin et al., eds., *Zhongguo guomindang dashiji (1894.11–1986.12)* (Chronology of the Chinese Guomindang [November 1894–December 1986]) (Beijing: Jiefangjun chubanshe, 1988), 587–90.
36. See Jin, *Zhongguo xiandai shi ziliao xuanji* (Selected Documents on Contemporary Chinese History), 3:360–61.
37. Ch'en, *The Storm Clouds Clear over China,* 109–10.
38. See Hsiung, *The Life of Chiang Kai-shek,* 307–8; Lin Youhua, *Lin Sen nianpu* (Chronological Biography of Lin Sen) (Beijing: Zhongguo wenshi chubanshe, 2011), 205, 209.
39. See Hsiung, *The Life of Chiang Kai-shek,* 399; Chiang, *Riji* (Diaries), January 17, 1932, Hoover Archives, box 36, folder 1; Lü, *Jiang Zhongzheng xiansheng nianpu changbian* (Large Chronological Biography of Mr. Jiang Zhongzheng), 3:593.

40. The author's impressions on visiting Nanjing, June 2, 2017.
41. The author's impressions on visiting Chiang Kai-shek's summer home *Taolu* in Tangshan, June 4, 2017.
42. Ibid.; Zhou and Chen, *Hu Hanmin pingzhuan* (Biography of Hu Hanmin), 311.
43. The author's impressions on visiting Meiling's Palace in Nanjing, June 3, 2017.
44. Quoted from Abend, *My Life in China: 1926–1941,* 187.
45. For more details on Japanese aggression in Shanghai, see Donald A. Jordan, *China's Trial by Fire: The Shanghai War of 1932* (Ann Arbor: University of Michigan Press, 2001); Jarvis, "Letters from China 1920–1949," 15.
46. Quoted from Abend, *My Life in China: 1926–1941,* 192–93.
47. Quoted from Tong, *Chiang Kai-shek: Soldier and Statesman,* 2:340.
48. See Wang Ke-wen, "Wang Jingwei and the Policy Origins of the 'Peace Movement,' 1932–1937," in David P. Barrett and Larry N. Shyu, eds., *Chinese Collaboration with Japan, 1932–1945: The Limits of Accommodation* (Stanford: Stanford University Press, 2001), 22–23.
49. See Hsiung, *The Life of Chiang Kai-shek,* 310–11.
50. For details, see the biography of Pu Yi: Pu Yi, *From Emperor to Citizen,* trans. W. J. F. Jenner (New York: Oxford University Press, 1987), 215–62.
51. See The Earl of Lytton, *Lessons of the League of Nations Commission of Enquiry in Manchuria* (London: Constable, 1937).
52. Begun in the spring of 1932, negotiations on this matter were, however, quickly broken off at the initiative of the Japanese.
53. See G. M. Adibekov and Haruki Wada, eds., *VKP(b), Komintern i Iaponiia: 1917–1941 gg.* (The AUCP(b), the Comintern and Japan, 1917–1941) (Moscow: ROSSPEN, 2001), 79–82, 84, 85, 91, 98; Titarenko, *VKP(b), Komintern i Kitai: Dokumenty* (The CPSU, Comintern and China: Documents), 4:165; Tikhvinsky, *Russko–kitaiskie otnosheniia v XX veke* (Russo–Chinese Relations in the Twentieth Century), 3:79–80, 83, 84, 87–88, 99–100; A. Sidorov, "Problema zakliucheniia pakta of nenapadenii v sovetsko–itaiskikh otnosheniiakh (1932–1937 gg.)" (The Problem of Concluding the Sino–Soviet Non-Aggression Pact [1932–1937]), *Problemy Dal'nego Vostoka* (Far Eastern Affairs), no. 1 (2009): 123; Mirovitskaia, "Sovetskii Soiuz i Kitai v period razryva i vosstanovleniia otnoshenii (1928–1936 gg.)" (The Soviet Union and China during the Period of the Rift and the Restoration of Relations), 155.
54. See Adibekov and Wada, *VKP(b), Komintern i Iaponiia: 1917–1941 gg.* (The AUCP(b), the Comintern and Japan: 1917–1941), 81, 100.
55. O. V. Khlevniuk et al., eds., *Stalin i Kaganovich: Perepiska: 1931–1936 gg.* (Stalin and Kaganovich: Correspondence: 1931–1936) (Moscow: ROSSPEN, 2001), 199–200.
56. Nikolai Nikolaevich Krestinsky, the First Deputy of the People's Commissar for Foreign Affairs, wrote about this to the secretary of the Central Committee of the AUCP(b), Lazar Moiseevich Kaganovich.
57. See Tikhvinsky, *Russko–kitaiskie otnosheniia v XX veke* (Russo–Chinese Relations in the Twentieth Century), 3:96.
58. Khlevniuk, *Stalin i Kaganovich: Perepiska* (Stalin and Kaganovich: Correspondence), 160, 163. See also Tikhvinsky, *Russko–kitaiskie otnoshennia v XX veke* (Russo–Chinese Relations in the Twentieth Century), 3:97, 108–9.

59. See Lin, *Lin Sen nianpu* (Chronological Biography of Lin Sen), 235. For more details on Bogomolov, see V. V. Sokolov, "'Zabytyi diplomat' D. V. Bogomolov (1890–1938)" (A "Forgotten Diplomat" D. V. Bogomolov [1890–1938]), *Novaiia i Noveishaia Istoriia* (Modern and Contemporary History), no. 3 (2004): 165–95.
60. Quoted from Lü, *Jiang Zhongzheng xiansheng nianpu changbian* (Large Chronological Biography of Mr. Jiang Zhongzheng), 3:771.
61. See Titarenko, *VKP(b), Komintern i Kitai: Dokumenty* (The CPSU, Comintern and China: Documents), 4:171; Kurdiukov, *Sovetsko–kitaiskie otnoshniia: 1917–1957* (Soviet–Chinese Relations, 1917–1957), 156–57.
62. See Lih, *Stalin's Letters to Molotov 1925–1936,* 229.
63. Hsiung, *The Life of Chiang Kai-shek,* 310.
64. Chiang, *Riji* (Diaries), June 1 and 2, 1933, Hoover Archives, box 36, folder 18.
65. Selle, *Donald of China,* 281.
66. Chennault, *Way of a Fighter,* 33.
67. Zhang Xueliang must have constantly heard praise in regard to Mussolini from his father, the late Zhang Zuolin, who was excited that the "great" Il Duce's name in Chinese sounded close to that of his own: "Mu Zuolin." See Shirley Ann Smith, *Imperial Designs,* 114.
68. The USSR proposed that Manchukuo also open five consulates in the Soviet Union, but that never happened.
69. See Khlevniuk, *Stalin i Kaganovich: Perepiska* (Stalin and Kaganovich: Correspondence), 305; Tikhvinsky, *Russko–kitaiskie otnoshennia v XX veke* (Russo–Chinese Relations in the Twentieth Century), 3:161–69, 171–76, 676–81; Mirovitskaia, "Sovetskii Soiuz i Kitai v period razryva i vosstanovleniia otnoshenii (1928–1936 gg.)" (The Soviet Union and China during the Period of the Rift and the Restoration of Relations), 74; Selle, *Donald of China,* 284–85; Harriet Sergeant, *Shanghai* (London: Jonathan Cape, 1991), 5; James M. Bertram, *Crisis in China: The Story of the Sian Mutiny* (London: Macmillan, 1937), 108.
70. Chang Kuo-t'ao, *The Rise of the Chinese Communist Party 1921–1927: Volume Two of Autobiography of Chang Kuo-t'ao* (Lawrence: University Press of Kansas, 1972), 316.
71. See A. S. Titov, *Iz istorii bor'by i raskola v rukovodstve KPK 1935–1936 gg.* (On the History of Struggle and Split in the Leadership of the CCP 1935–1936) (Moscow: Nauka, 1979), 21.
72. Pantsov with Levine, *Mao,* 268.
73. Enid Saunders Candlin, *The Breach in the Wall: A Memoir of the Old China* (New York: Macmillan, 1973), 207.
74. The author's impressions on visiting the *Meilu* villa, June 11, 2017.
75. Quoted from Tyson Li, *Madame Chiang Kai-shek,* 273.
76. Yorke, *China Changes,* 180.
77. The Habsburgs were a dynasty of Austro–Hungarian monarchs (1526–1918).
78. Fleming, *One's Company,* 225.
79. Ibid., 226–27. Emphasis added by Peter Fleming.
80. Yorke, *China Changes,* 180.
81. See Titarenko, *VKP(b), Komintern i Kitai: Dokumenty* (The CPSU, Comintern and China: Documents), 4:479.

82. See Pantsov with Levine, *Mao,* 272.
83. See Huang and Hao, *Zhonghua minguo shi shijian renwu lu* (Dictionary of Events and Persons in the History of the Republic of China), 235–36; Sladkovsky, *Noveishaia istoriia Kitaia 1928–1949* (Contemporary History of China 1928–1949), 78–81; Yorke, *China Changes,* 253–90.
84. Chiang and Meiling paid much attention to Donald in early 1934 when he, as an advisor to Zhang Xueliang and accompanying the latter, met with them in a restaurant in Hangzhou. They quickly established close, confidential relations with him even though the Australian did not speak Chinese. Meiling willingly played the role of interpreter. In late 1934, at Chiang's invitation, Donald became his unofficial advisor. Both Chiang and Meiling valued his friendship and called him simply Don.
85. See Nie, *Nie Rongren huiyilu* (Reminiscences of Nie Rongren), 1:187; Otto Braun, *A Comintern Agent in China 1932–1939,* trans. Jeanne Moore (Stanford: Stanford University Press, 1982), 40–43, 75–76; Violet Cressy-Marcks, *Journey into China* (New York: E. P. Dutton, 1942), 166.
86. See Chiang Kai-shek, *The New Life Movement in China,* trans. Madame Chiang Kai-shek (Calcutta: Chinese Ministry of Information, 1942), 7.
87. See Zhang, *Wusheng de yaojiao* (Silent Key Point), 17.
88. See Hsiung, *The Life of Chiang Kai-shek,* 315.
89. Translation of the terms is by Song Meiling. See Song Mei-ling, *General Chiang Kai-shek and the Communist Crisis: Madame Chiang Kai-shek on the New Life Movement* (Shanghai: China Weekly Review Press, [1937]), 58–59.
90. Chiang, *The New Life Movement in China,* 9, 17, 19.
91. See Tsui, *China's Conservative Revolution,* 15.
92. See Peter Fleming, *News from Tartary: A Journey from Peking to Kashgar* (London: Jonathan Cape, 1936), 49.
93. Selle, *Donald of China,* 294.
94. National Archives of the United States, document 893.114 Narcotics/912.
95. Tsui, *China's Conservative Revolution,* 95.
96. Chiang, *Riji* (Diaries), January 1, 1929, Hoover Archives, box 6, folder 12; Frederic E. Wakeman Jr., *Spymaster: Dai Li and the Chinese Secret Service* (Berkeley: University of California Press, 2003), 52–53; Van de Ven, *War and Nationalism in China 1925–1945,* 165.
97. *Kaiko* (in Chinese *xie xing*) is an expression from an ancient collection of Chinese poetry, *Shijing* (The Book of Poetry), in the line "Yu zi xie xing" (I will march along with you). *The Chinese Classics,* with a trans., critical and exegetical notes, prolegomena, and copious indexes by James Legge, vol. 4, book 1 (Oxford: Clarendon Press, 1893), 202. Emphasis added by the author.
98. The author's impressions on visiting the Lizhishe Museum in Nanjing, June 10, 2017.
99. Lu [Lü] and Lin, "Chiang Kai-shek's Diaries and Republican China: New Insights on the History of Modern China," 337.
100. The expression *lixing* (to practice with vigor) was taken from the ancient Chinese classic *Zhongyong* (The Doctrine of the Mean), which says, "The Master said: 'To

be fond of learning is to be near to knowledge. To practice with vigor is to be near to magnanimity. To possess the feeling of shame is to be near to energy." *The Chinese Classics*, with a trans., critical and exegetical notes, prolegomena, and copious indexes by James Legge, 1:407 (Oxford: Clarendon Press, 1893).

101. Another name of which is "The Detachment of Those Who Wear Cotton [that is, simple] Clothes" (*buyituan*).

102. See Wakeman Jr., "A Revisionist View of the Nanjing Decade: Confucian Fascism," 143–55.

103. See Jeremy E. Taylor, "The Production of the Chiang Kai-shek Personality Cult, 1929–1975," *China Quarterly* 185 (March 2006): 99.

104. See William Kirby, "The Internationalization of China: Foreign Relations at Home and Abroad in the Republican Era," in Wakeman Jr. and Edmonds, *Reappraising Republican China,* 195; Wakeman Jr., "A Revisionist View of the Nanjing Decade: Confucian Fascism," 142.

105. Maria Hsia Chang, "'Fascism' and Modern China," *China Quarterly* 79 (September 1979): 558. Emphasis added by Maria Hsia Chang; see also Maria Hsia Chang, *The Chinese Blue Shirt Society: Fascism and Developmental Nationalism* (Berkeley: University of California Press, 1985), 29.

106. Chiang, *The New Life Movement in China,* 18.

107. Quoted from Pakula, *The Last Empress,* 250.

108. Song, *General Chiang Kai-shek and the Communist Crisis,* 55. For a scholarly comparison of Fascism, Nazism, and the New Deal, see Wolfgang Schivelbusch, *Three New Deals: Reflections on Roosevelt's America, Mussolini's Italy, and Hitler's Germany, 1933–1939* (New York: Metropolitan Books, 2006).

109. See Selle, *Donald of China,* 296–97.

110. The fascist corporative system was based on principles of statism, that is, the right of the state to control the economy and society totally in the name of the entire nation.

111. Quoted from Fatica, "The Beginning and the End of the Idyllic Relations between Mussolini's Italy and Chiang Kai-shek's China (1930–1937)," 89, 91–92, 94.

112. Quoted from Wakeman Jr., "A Revisionist View of the Nanjing Decade: Confucian Fascism," 169.

113. See Fatica, "The Beginning and the End of the Idyllic Relations between Mussolini's Italy and Chiang Kai-shek's China (1930–1937)," 96.

114. Quoted from Tong, *Chiang Kai-shek: Soldier and Statesman,* 1:314.

115. Quoted from Fenby, *Chiang Kai-shek,* 226.

116. In English in the original text.

117. Titarenko, *VKP(b), Komintern i Kitai: Dokumenty* (The CPSU, Comintern and China: Documents), 4:221.

118. Quoted from Hsiung, *The Life of Chiang Kai-shek,* 313–14.

119. RGASPI, collection of unsorted documents.

120. See Titarenko, *VKP(b), Komintern i Kitai: Dokumenty* (The CPSU, Comintern and China: Documents), 4:602.

121. Ibid., 4:613.

122. Jay Taylor claims that in 1933 "a clandestine Comintern organization in Shanghai" bought "an airplane" or even "a heavy airplane" for the Chinese Communists in the Central Soviet Area. See Taylor, *The Generalissimo,* 101, 106. However, the documents he refers to do not confirm this. They say only that the Soviet envoys in Shanghai requested money from Moscow for purchasing such a plane (not the heavy one), but there is nothing about the purchase. See Titarenko, *VKP(b), Komintern i Kitai: Dokumenty* (The CPSU, Comintern and China: Documents), 4:357, 459, 486, 489–90. At the same time, it is well known from many sources that the Chinese Communists in the 1930s had no airplanes.
123. Braun, *A Comintern Agent in China 1932–1939,* 90.
124. Mary S. Erbaugh, "The Secret History of the Hakkas: The Chinese Revolution as a Hakka Enterprise," *China Quarterly* 132 (December 1992): 937–68.
125. See Pantsov with Levine, *Mao,* 275–77.
126. Tong and Li, *The Memoirs of Li Tsung-jen,* 297.
127. See Chen San-ching, *Sifenxi ban lunshi* (Articles on History Written on the Bank of Sifen Creek) (Hong Kong: Jiuzhou chubanshe, 2013).

## 12. *PLAYING WITH STALIN*

1. See Mirovitskaia, "Sovetskii soiuz i Kitai v period razryva i vosstanovleniia otnoshenii (1928–1936 gg.)" (The Soviet Union and China during the Period of the Rift and the Restoration of Relations), 155.
2. Quoted from Sidorov, "Problema zakliucheniia pakta o nenapadenii v sovetsko-kitaiskikh otnosheniiakh (1932–1937 gg.)" (The Problem of Concluding a Sino–Soviet Non-Aggression Pact [1932–1937]), 127.
3. In 1948 both Chahar and Suiyuan were incorporated into Inner Mongolia.
4. See A. A. Gromyko, ed., *Dokumenty vneshnei politiki SSSR* (Documents of the USSR Foreign Policy), 18:437 (Moscow: Politizdat, 1973).
5. See Huang and Hao, *Zhonghua minguo shi shijian renwu lu* (Dictionary of Events and Persons in the History of the Republic of China), 250.
6. Quoted from Selle, *Donald of China,* 301.
7. See Tikhvinsky, *Russko–kitaiskie otnosheniia v XX veke* (Russo–Chinese Relations in the Twentieth Century), 3:742.
8. See RGASPI, collection 558, inventory 22, file 187, sheet 24. See also Pantsov, *Mao Tsedun* (Mao Zedong), 420.
9. Chiang, *Riji* (Diaries), March 14, 1936, Hoover Archives, box 38, folder 11.
10. A. A. Gromyko, ed., *Dokumenty vneshnei politiki SSSR* (Documents of the USSR Foreign Policy), 19:723 (Moscow: Politizdat, 1974).
11. These decisions were drawn up on the initiative of the Bulgarian communist Georgii Dimitrov (his full name and family name was Georgi Dimitrov Mikhailov), whom Stalin had made the general secretary of the Executive Committee of the Comintern at the Seventh Comintern Congress.
12. Van Min (Wang Ming), *Sobranie sochinenii* (Collected Works), 3:364 (Moscow: IDV AN SSSR, 1985).

13. Stephen Lyon Endicott, *Diplomacy and Enterprise: British China Policy 1933–1937* (Vancouver: University of British Columbia Press, 1975), 118.
14. See Taylor, *The Generalissimo,* 113.
15. See Gromyko, *Dokumenty vneshnei politiki SSSR* (Documents of the USSR Foreign Policy), 18:537–38.
16. See Wang, "Wang Jingwei and the Policy Origins of the 'Peace Movement,' 1932–1937," 24.
17. See Akira Odani, "Wang Ching-wei and the Fall of the Chinese Republic, 1905–1935" (PhD diss., Brown University, 1976), 109, 111–12; Tong, *Chiang Kai-shek,* 2:342–43.
18. Odani, "Wang Ching-wei and the Fall of the Chinese Republic, 1905–1935," 112. See also Wang, "Wang Jingwei and the Policy Origins of the 'Peace Movement,' 1932–1937," 29.
19. See Wang, "Wang Jingwei and the Policy Origins of the 'Peace Movement,' 1932–1937," 29–32.
20. See Wakeman Jr., *Spymaster,* 182–86.
21. See Ch'en, *The Storm Clouds Clear over China,* 115; Wakeman Jr., *Spymaster,* 182.
22. Chiang, *Riji* (Diaries), November 1 and 2, 1931, Hoover Archives, box 8, folder 2.
23. Quoted from H. G. W. Woodhead, ed., *The China Year Book 1936* (Nendeln/Liechtenstein: Kraus Reprint, 1969), 169–70.
24. See Zhongguo guomindang zhongyang weiyuanhui dangshi weiyuanhui, ed., *Zhongguo guomindang zhiming lu* (List of Officials of the Chinese Guomindang) (Taipei: Guomindang dangshi hui chuban, 1994), 124, 131.
25. Chiang, *Riji* (Diaries), February 16, 1936, Hoover Archives, box 38, folder 10.
26. The author's interview with Ch'en Yung-fa in Taipei, June 20, 2017.
27. Chiang, *Riji* (Diaries), December 12, 1936, Hoover Archives, box 39, folder 5; see also Zhou and Chen, *Hu Hanmin pingzhuan* (Biography of Hu Hanmin), 310–11.
28. See Odani, "Wang Ching-wei and the Fall of the Chinese Republic, 1905–1935," 139.
29. The author's interviews with Li Jifeng of Nanjing University in Nanjing, June 1, 2017, and with Yang Tianshi, Research Fellow of the Institute of Modern History of the PRC Academy of Social Sciences, in Taipei, June 19, 2017.
30. After the attempt on Wang Jingwei's life, Kong Xiangxi carried out the duties of the chair of the Executive yuan for just over a month.
31. Gromyko, *Dokumenty vneshnei politiki SSSR* (Documents of the USSR Foreign Policy), 18:602.
32. Titarenko, *VKP(b), Komintern i Kitai: Dokumenty* (The CPSU, Comintern and China: Documents), 4:960–62.
33. See Ch'en, *The Storm Clouds Clear over China,* 121.
34. Zhonggong zhongyang wenxian yanjiu shi, ed., *Zhou Enlai nianpu (1898–1949) (*xiudingben*)* (Chronological Biography of Zhou Enlai [1898–1949], [revised ed.]) (Beijing: Zhongyang wenxian chubanshe, 1998), 307; Zhu Yuzhi and Cai Lesu, eds., *Mao Zedong yu 20 shiji Zhongguo* (Mao Zedong and Twentieth-century China) (Beijing: Qinghua daxue chubanshe, 2000), 109–10.

35. For more details, see John Israel, *Student Nationalism in China 1927–1937* (Stanford: Stanford University Press, 1966), 111–56; John Israel and Donald Klein, *Rebels and Bureaucrats: China's December 9ers* (Berkeley: University of California Press, 1976), 87–104.
36. See Gromyko, *Dokumenty vneshnei politiki SSSR* (Documents of the USSR Foreign Policy), 18:599.
37. See Ch'en, *The Storm Clouds Clear over China,* 121–23.
38. The personal files of Deng Wenyi and Wang Ming are held in the Russian State Archives of Social and Political History. See RGASPI, collection 495, inventory 225, files 1711 and 3.
39. See Titarenko, *VKP(b), Komintern i Kitai: Dokumenty* (The CPSU, Comintern and China: Documents), 4:941–59.
40. Gromyko, *Dokumenty vneshnei politiki SSSR* (Documents of the USSR Foreign Policy), 19:35, 36, 723.
41. See Ed Jocelyn and Andrew McEwan, *The Long March: The True Story Behind the Legendary Journey that Made Mao's China* (London: Constable, 2006), 326–27.
42. See Agnes Smedley, *China Fights Back: An American Woman with the Eight Route Army* (New York: Vanguard Press, 1938), 8–9, 19–20; Janice R. MacKinnon and Stephen R. MacKinnon, *Agnes Smedley: The Life and Times of an American Radical* (Berkeley: University of California Press, 1988), 183.
43. Chiang, *Riji* (Diaries), February 23, 24, 29, March 5, 7, 8, 11–16, 19, 20, 22, 25–28, 30, 31, 1936, Hoover Archives, box 38, folders 10 and 11.
44. Yang You-cheng, "Pis'mo syna Chan Kai-shi k materi" (Chiang Kai-shek's Son's Letter to His Mother), *Leningradskaia Pravda* (Leningrad Truth), February 9, 1936.
45. Chiang, *Riji* (Diaries), February 14, 1936, Hoover Archives, box 38, folder 10.
46. The draft of the letter is preserved in one of the Russian archives. See Galitsky, *Tszian Tszingo* (Chiang Ching-kuo), 129–32.
47. See Chiang Ching-kuo, *My Days in Soviet Russia* [Taipei, 1963], 27–29.
48. This is what Faina called Anna in her letters to her.
49. See Pantsov, *Mao Tsedun* (Mao Zedong), 441–42; Chiang Ching-kuo, *Jiang Jingguo riji* (Diaries of Chiang Ching-kuo), 39–46; the author's interview with one of Chiang Kai-shek's relatives, March 19, 2015; letter from one of Chiang Kai-shek's relatives to the author, December 1, 2016; RGASPI, collection of unsorted documents; personal questionnaires and the autobiographies of Chiang Ching-kuo and Anna Vakhreva as well as Faina's letters to Anna from China preserved in various archives in Russia and first published in Galitsky, *Tszian Tszingo* (Chiang Ching-kuo), 113–57.
50. Tikhvinsky, ed., *Russko–kitaiskie otnosheniia v XX veke* (Russo–Chinese Relations in the Twentieth Century), vol. 4, book 2 (Moscow: "Pamiatniki istoricheskoi mysli," 2000), 342.
51. M. I. Sladkovsky, ed., *Dokumenty po istorii Kommunisticheskoi partii Kitaia 1920–1949 gg. (v chetyrekh tomakh)* (Documents on the History of the Chinese Communist Party, 1920–1949 [In Four Volumes]), vol. 2, book 5 (Moscow: IDV AN SSSR, 1981), 45.
52. See Pang, *Mao Zedong nianpu, 1893–1949* (Chronological Biography of Mao Zedong, 1893–1949), 1:490.

53. Sladkovsky, *Dokumenty po istorii Kommunisticheskoi partii Kitaia 1920–1949 gg.* (Documents on the History of the Chinese Communist Party, 1920–1949), vol. 2, book 5, 57.
54. See Zhang Xueliang, "Chang Hsueh-liang's Self-examination over the Sian Incident," in Chiang Kai-shek, *A Fortnight in Sian;* Soong Chiang Mayling (Madame Chiang Kai-shek), *Sian: A Coup d'Etat,* 2nd ed. (Taipei: China Publishing, 1986), 74–76; Titarenko, *VKP(b), Komintern i Kitai: Dokumenty* (The CPSU, Comintern and China: Documents), 4:1024–25; *Zhonggong zhongyang wenxian yanjiu shi, Zhou Enlai nianpu (1898–1949)* (Chronological Biography of Zhou Enlai [1898–1949]), 1:306; Itoh Mayumi, *The Making of China's War with Japan: Zhou Enlai and Zhang Xueliang* (New York: Palgrave Macmillan, 2016), 108, 115–19; Yang Kuisong, *Shiqu de jihui? Kangzhan qianhou guogong tanpan shilu* (Lost Chance? Notes on Negotiations between the Guomindang and the CCP Before and After the War of Resistance Against Japan) (Beijing: Xinxing chubanshe, 2010), 10–16.
55. They came through the mediation of Song Qingling. Song was able to make a false pass for one of them that, at her request, was signed by T. V. Song and Kong Xiangxi.
56. See Zhonggong zhongyang wenxian yanjiu shi, *Zhou Enlai nianpu (1898–1949)* (Chronological Biography of Zhou Enlai [1898–1949]), 1:307, 309.
57. Gromyko, *Dokumenty vneshnei politiki SSSR* (Documents of the USSR Foreign Policy), 19:724.
58. See "Chang Hsueh-liang's Self-examination over the Sian Incident," 76; Itoh, *The Making of China's War with Japan,* 120–231, 126–28.
59. See Pang, *Mao Zedong nianpu, 1893–1949* (Chronological Biography of Mao Zedong, 1893–1949), 1:551–52; Sladkovsky, *Dokumenty po istorii Kommunisticheskoi partii Kitaia 1920–1949 gg.* (Documents on the History of the Chinese Communist Party, 1920–1949), vol. 2, book 5, 93–94.
60. Sladkovsky, *Dokumenty po istorii Kommunisticheskoi partii Kitaia 1920–1949 gg.* (Documents on the History of the Chinese Communist Party, 1920–1949), vol. 2, book 5, 93.
61. See Titarenko, *VKP(b), Komintern i Kitai: Dokumenty* (The CPSU, Comintern and China: Documents), 4:1070.
62. See Gromyko, *Dokumenty vneshni politiki SSSR* (Documents of the USSR Foreign Policy), 19:136–37.
63. See Kurdiukov, *Sovetsko–kitaiskie otnosheniia: 1917–1957* (Soviet–Chinese Relations, 1917–1957), 158; Tikhvinsky, *Russko–kitaiskie otnosheniia v XX veke* (Russo–Chinese Relations in the Twentieth Century), 3:524–26.
64. See Woodhead, *The China Year Book 1936,* 131–32.
65. Andrew D. Morris, *Marrow of the Nation: A History of Sport and Physical Culture in Republican China* (Berkeley: University of California Press, 2004), 176.
66. See Liang Hsi-Huey, *The Sino-German Connection: Alexander von Falkenhausen between China and Germany 1900–1941* (Amsterdam: Van Gorcum, 1978), 110–11; Andrew Morris, "'I Can Compete!' China in the Olympic Games, 1932 and 1936," *Journal of Sport History,* no. 3 (1999): 550–61; Fan, Bao, and Li, *Jiang Jieshi de guoce guwen Dai Jitao* (Dai Jitao, Political Advisor to Chiang Kai-shek), 176.

67. Candlin, *The Breach in the Wall,* 283.
68. Seeckt died in Berlin a year and a half after returning from China, December 28, 1936.
69. See Kirby, *Germany and Republican China,* 137, 144, 299.
70. See Arthur N. Young, *China and the Helping Hand 1937–1945* (Cambridge: Harvard University Press, 1963), 18.
71. See Pantsov with Levine, *Mao,* 296.
72. See Titarenko, *VKP(b), Komintern i Kitai: Dokumenty* (The CPSU, Comintern and China: Documents), 4:1055, 1058, 1068; Fenby, *Chiang Kai-shek,* 279.
73. Enciphered telegrams from Moscow to China usually reached the addressee in two days. And in rare cases in one day. The same was true for enciphered telegrams from China to Moscow. The time lapses were due to the absence of a direct radio link as well as the fact that decryption and verification took a lot of time. See F. I. Firsov, *Sekretnye kody istorii Kominterna 1919–1943* (Secret Codes in the History of the Comintern 1919–1943) (Moscow: AIRO-XX/Kraft+, 2007).
74. Titarenko, *Kommunisticheskii Internatsional i kitaiskaia revoliutsiia* (The Communist International and the Chinese Revolution), 268; see also Alexander Dallin and F. I. Firsov, *Dimitrov and Stalin 1934–1943: Letters from the Soviet Archives,* trans. Vadim A. Staklo (New Haven: Yale University Press, 2000), 101–5; Titarenko, *VKP(b), Komintern i Kitai: Dokumenty* (The CPSU, Comintern and China: Documents), 4:1060–64, 1067–71.
75. See Itoh, *The Making of China's War with Japan,* 128.
76. Stuart R. Schram, ed., *Mao's Road to Power: Revolutionary Writings 1912–1949,* 5:323–32 (Armonk, NY: M. E. Sharpe, 1999); Jin Chongji, ed., *Zhou Enlai zhuan (1898–1976)* (Biography of Zhou Enlai [1898–1976]), vol. 1, 2nd ed. (Beijing: Zhongyang wenxian chubanshe, 2009), 349.
77. See Sladkovsky, *Dokumenty po istorii Kommunisticheskoi partii Kitaia 1920–1949 gg.* (Documents on the History of the Chinese Communist Party, 1920–1949), vol. 2, book 5, 98–111.
78. Schram, *Mao's Road to Power,* 5:334.
79. For a photograph of the letter, see Ch'en, *The Storm Clouds Clear over China,* 118–19. See also Chiang, *Soviet Russia in China,* 72. It is true that Chen Lifu and Chiang Kai-shek write that Zhou sent this letter on September 1, 1935, which seems unlikely. In the first place, on September 1, 1935, Zhou was seriously ill with malaria, and along with Mao and the majority of other leaders of the CCP was in the midst of the Songpan marshes in northern Sichuan. He was in no condition for anything other than recovering his health and getting out of the marshy quagmire. There was no way for him to send a letter from this dreadful place. Moreover, in September 1935 neither Zhou nor Mao nor anyone else in the CCP could propose to the GMD CEC "to unite with the USSR and the Chinese Communist Party to struggle against Japan" since this went against the policy of the Comintern.
80. Quoted from Ch'en, *The Storm Clouds Clear over China,* 120.
81. RGASPI, collection 146, inventory 2, file 3, sheet 28. See also Georgi Dimitrov, *Dnevnik 9 mart 1933–6 fevruari 1949* (Diary, March 9, 1933–February 6, 1949) (Sofia: Universitetsko izdatelstvo "Sv. Kliment Okhridski," 1997), 117.

82. Quoted from Khlevniuk, *Stalin i Kaganovich: Perepiska* (Stalin and Kaganovich: Correspondence), 524. These words were those of a correspondent for *Gazeta Polska* (The Polish Newspaper) published on August 13, 1935, reporting on the Seventh Comintern Congress.
83. Chiang, *Riji* (Diaries), August 29, 31, September 2, 12, 14, 20, 23, 26, 30, October 10, 12, 18, 23, 29, 31, November 5, 7, 15, 16, 28, and 29, 1936, Hoover Archives, box 39, folders 1–4.
84. See Pang, *Mao Zedong nianpu, 1893–1949* (Chronological Biography of Mao Zedong, 1893–1949), 1:602–3.
85. Quoted from Lü Fangshang, *Jiang Zhongzheng xiansheng nianpu changbian* (Large Chronological Biography of Mr. Jiang Zhongzheng), 5:169 (Taipei: Guoshiguan, 2014).
86. Chiang, *Riji* (Diaries), October 28, 1936, Hoover Archives, box 39, folder 3.
87. See Hsiung, *The Life of Chiang Kai-shek,* 373–78.
88. See ibid., 318–19; Tong, *Chiang Kai-shek,* 2:433–34; Pakula, *The Last Empress,* 251.
89. Schistosomiasis is a dangerous illness caused by a schistosome—a parasite similar to a flat worm that is found in the reservoirs of south and east China. This illness causes pareses or paralysis that frequently leads to a fatal outcome.
90. Chiang, *Riji* (Diaries), October 21, 1936, Hoover Archives, box 39, folder 3.
91. Quoted from Kirby, *Germany and Republican China,* 147. For more details, see Wang, *Qianshan duxing* (The Solitary Path among a Thousand Mountains), 60, 63–71; Chiang and Liu, *Jiang Weiguo koushu zizhuan* (The Autobiography of Chiang Wei-kuo as Told by Himself), 51–60; Martin Bernd, *Deutsch–chinesische Beziehungen 1928–1937: "Gleiche" Partner unter "ungleichen" Bedingungen: Eine Quellensammlung* (Sino–German Relations 1928–1937: "Equal" Partners under Dissimilar Conditions: A Source Collection) (Berlin: De Gruyter Akademie Forschung, 2003), 471–79.
92. Guoshiguan (Academia Historica), document no. 002-040300-00001-012.
93. See Tong, *Chiang Kai-shek,* 2:432; Lin, *Lin Sen nianpu* (Chronological Biography of Lin Sen), 376–78.
94. Chiang, *Riji* (Diaries), October 31, 1936, Hoover Archives, box 39, folder 3.
95. Confucius, *The Analects of Confucius,* 6.
96. Mencius, *The Works of Mencius,* 205.

## 13. *CAPTIVITY IN XI'AN*

1. Despite the China Lobby in Germany, Hitler generally treated the Chinese with contempt, placing them on the same racial level as black people. As for Japanese, he wrote in his book *Mein Kampf* that they were a nation "under Aryan influence," and he welcomed Japan's struggle against the "machinations of international Jewry." See Kirby, *Germany and Republican China,* 140.
2. See ibid., 143; Tikhvinsky, *Russko–kitaiskie otnosheniia v XX veke* (Russo–Chinese Relations in the Twentieth Century), 3:761.
3. Chiang, *Riji* (Diaries), November 15, 1936, Hoover Archives, box 39, folder 4.
4. In 1935 Yin Rugeng (1883–1947) headed the pro-Japanese "Autonomous Anticommunist Government of Eastern Hebei."

5. See Wu Tien-wei, *The Sian Incident: A Pivotal Point in Modern Chinese History* (Ann Arbor: Center for Chinese Studies, University of Michigan, 1976), 60–62.
6. Quoted from ibid., 63.
7. Cм.: Chiang, *Riji* (Diaries), December 3, 1936, Hoover Archives, box 39, folder 5.
8. Ibid., December 4, 1936, Hoover Archives, box 39, folder 5.
9. Quoted from Wu, *The Sian Incident,* 71. See also Zhang Xueliang and Tang Degang, *Zhang Xueliang koushu lishi* (History of Zhang Xueliang Told by Himself) (Taiyuan: Shanxi renmin chubanshe, 2013), 153.
10. Zhang and Tang, *Zhang Xueliang koushu lishi* (History of Zhang Xueliang Told by Himself) (Taiyuan), 154.
11. See Edgar Snow, *Red Star over China* (London: Victor Gollancz, 1937), 409; Wu, *The Sian Incident,* 72.
12. Quoted from Itoh, *The Making of China's War with Japan,* 136.
13. Zhang and Tang, *Zhang Xueliang koushu lishi* (History of Zhang Xueliang Told by Himself) (Taiyuan), 153; Chiang, *Riji* (Diaries), December 10, 1936, Hoover Archives, box 39, folder 5.
14. See Zhang Xueliang and Wang Shujun, *Zhang Xueliang de jinsheng jinshi* (Life of Zhang Xueliang), 2:268–69 (Beijing: Tuanjie chubanshe, 2011).
15. Zhuge Liang and Liu Ji, *Mastering the Art of War,* trans. and ed. Thomas Cleary (Boston: Shambhala, 1989), 43.
16. See Lü, *Jiang Zhongzheng xiansheng nianpu changbian* (Large Chronological Biography of Mr. Jiang Zhongzheng), 5:197.
17. See Abend, *My Life in China: 1926–1941,* 233–34.
18. Quoted from Itoh, *The Making of China's War with Japan,* 137. See also Zhang and Wang, *Zhang Xueliang de jinsheng jinshi* (Life of Zhang Xueliang), 2:269–70.
19. See Hollington K. Tong, *Chiang Kai-shek's Teacher and Ambassador: An Inside View of the Republic of China from 1911–1958: General Stilwell and American Policy Change Towards Free China* (Bloomington, IN: Arthur House, 2005), 61–62.
20. He was able to receive a new set of false teeth only ten days later. Meiling brought it to him.
21. Quoted from Bertram, *Crisis in China,* 134–37. See also Snow, *Red Star over China,* 412.
22. Quoted from Itoh, *The Making of China's War with Japan,* 144.
23. For the text of the document, see Zhang and Wang, *Zhang Xueliang de jinsheng jinshi* (Life of Zhang Xueliang), 2:278–79; Zhu Wenyuan, ed., *Xi'an shibian shiliao* (Documents on the History of the Xi'an Incident), 1:58–59 (Taipei: Guoshiguan, 1993).
24. "Telegram from Zhang Xueliang to Song Meiling, December 12, 1936," in Yang Tianshi, *Jiang Jieshi yu guomin zhengfu* (Chiang Kai-shek and the Nationalist Government) (Beijing: Zhongguo renmin daxue chubanshe, 2007), 478.
25. See Wu, *The Sian Incident,* 80–81.
26. See Tong Xiaopeng, *Zai Zhou Enlai shenbian sishi nian* (Forty Years I Served by the Side of Zhou Enlai), 1:16 (Beijing: Huawen chubanshe, 2015). It must have been the telegram which Mao's secretary Ye Zilong remembered two characters from: *bing* (soldier) and *jian* (remonstration). For some reason he mistakenly asserted that it was a missive from Zhang Xueliang and Yang Hucheng. See Ye Zilong, *Ye Zilong huiyilu*

(Reminiscences of Ye Zilong) (Beijing: Zhongyang wenxian chubanshe, 2000), 38–39. On Liu Ding, see Wu Dianyao, *Liu Ding zhuan* (Biography of Liu Ding) (Beijing: Zhongyang wenjiao chubanshe, 2012).

27. Quoted from Zhang Yongbin, *Zhang Xueliang da zhuan* (Large Biography of Zhang Xueliang), 1:325 (Beijing: Tuanjie chubanshe, 2001). See also Pang, *Mao Zedong nianpu, 1893–1949* (Chronological Biography of Mao Zedong, 1893–1949), 1:620; Itoh, *The Making of China's War with Japan,* 145.
28. Edgar Snow, *Random Notes on Red China (1936–1945)* (Cambridge: East Asian Research Center, Harvard University, 1957), 1.
29. Chang, *The Rise of the Chinese Communist Party,* 2:480.
30. Quoted from Pang, *Mao Zedong nianpu, 1893–1949* (Chronological Biography of Mao Zedong, 1893–1949), 1:620; see also Itoh, *The Making of China's War with Japan,* 145.
31. See Yang Kuisong, *Xi'an shibian xin tan: Zhang Xueliang yu zhonggong guanxi yanjiu* (A New View of the Xi'an Incident: A Study of Zhang Xueliang's Links with the CCP) (Xi'an: Shaanxi renmin chubanshe, 2012), 306.
32. RGASPI, collection 146, inventory 2, file 3, sheet 29. See also Dimitrov, *Dnevnik* (Diary), 118.
33. "Sobytiia v Kitae" (Events in China), *Pravda* (Truth), December 14, 1936; "Vosstanie Chzhan Siue-liana" (Zhang Xueliang's Uprising), *Izvestiia* (News), December 14, 1936.
34. In general, outside of China the Xi'an events became known only on the morning of December 13. Japanese newspapers were the first to publish reports.
35. Titarenko, *VKP(b), Komintern i Kitai: Dokumenty* (The CPSU, Comintern and China: Documents), 4:1085.
36. RGASPI, collection 146, inventory 2, file 3, sheet 30. See also Dimitrov, *Dnevnik* (Diary), 118.
37. See Itoh, *The Making of China's War with Japan,* 154.
38. Quoted from A. S. Titov, *Materialy k politicheskoi biografii Mao Tsze-duna* (Materials for a Political Biography of Mao Zedong), 2:293 (Moscow: IDV AN SSSR, 1970).
39. Titarenko, *Kommunisticheskii Internatsional i kitaiskaia revoliutsiia* (The Communist International and the Chinese Revolution), 270; RGASPI, collection 270, inventory 2, file 3, sheet 30. See also Dmitrov, *Dnevnik* (Diary), 118.
40. See Jin Chongji, ed., *Mao Zedong zhuan (1893–1949)* (Biography of Mao Zedong [1949–1976]), 1:433 (Beijing: Zhongyang wenxian chubanshe, 2003).
41. Jin, *Zhou Enlai zhuan (1898–1976)* (Biography of Zhou Enlai [1898–1976]), 1:365 (photocopy of archival document).
42. See Pang, *Mao Zedong nianpu, 1893–1949* (Chronological Biography of Mao Zedong, 1893–1949), 1:625, 627; Sladkovsky, *Dokumenty po istorii Kommunistcheskoi partii Kitaia 1920–1949 gg.* (Documents on the History of the Chinese Communist Party, 1920–1949), vol. 2, book 5, 137–38.
43. See Itoh, *The Making of China's War with Japan,* 152, 157–58, 161–62.
44. See Zhang, "Chang Hsueh-liang's Self-examination over the Sian Incident," 78; Tang, *Zhongguo lishi dashi nianbiao: Xiandai* (Chronology of Events in Chinese History: Contemporary History), 320; Chiang Kai-shek, "The Day I Was Kidnapped," in Dun J. Li, ed., *The Road to Communism: China since 1912* (New York: Van Nostrand Reinhold, 1969), 135–41.

45. Chiang, *Soviet Russia in China,* 74.
46. See Selle, *Donald of China,* 319; Chen, *Chen Bulei huiyilu* (Memoirs of Chen Bulei), 116; Itoh, *The Making of China's War with Japan,* 146.
47. See Selle, *Donald of China,* 319–20; "Song Meiling's Telegram to Zhang Xueliang, December 13, 1936," in Yang, *Jiang Jieshi yu guomin zhengfu* (Chiang Kai-shek and the Nationalist Government), 480.
48. Quoted from Selle, *Donald of China,* 319, 326.
49. Quoted from Jin, *Zhou Enlai zhuan (1898–1976)* (Biography of Zhou Enlai [1898–1976]), 1:368.
50. Quoted from Chiang Kai-shek, "A Fortnight in Sian: Extracts from a Diary," in General and Madame Chiang Kai-shek, *General Chiang Kai-shek: The Account of the Fortnight in Sian When the Fate of China Hung in the Balance* (New York: Doubleday, Doran, 1937), 164.
51. T. V. Song, "TVS Diary of Xi'an Incident, 1936," in T. V. Soong Papers, Hoover Archives, box 59, folder 22, 1–3; for a Chinese translation of T. V. Song's diary, see Lin Bowen, *Zhang Xueliang, Song Ziwen dang'an da jiemi* (Big Secrets Uncovered in the Archives of Zhang Xueliang and Song Ziwen) (Taipei: Shibao wenhua chuban qiye gufen youxian gongsi, 2007), 207–23.
52. Song, "TVS Diary of Xi'an Incident, 1936," 1, 4.
53. See Itoh, *The Making of China's War with Japan,* 167–68.
54. Mayling Soong Chiang (Mme Chiang Kai-shek), "Sian: A Coup d'État," in General and Madame Chiang, *General Chiang Kai-shek: The Account of the Fortnight in Sian When the Fate of China Hung in the Balance,* 89.
55. Song, "TVS Diary of Xi'an Incident, 1936," 3–4.
56. Quoted from DeLong, *Madame Chiang Kai-shek and Miss Emma Mills,* 94.
57. Zhou, *Selected Works of Zhou Enlai,* 1:86.
58. See ibid.; Jin, *Zhou Enlai zhuan (1898–1976)* (Biography of Zhou Enlai [1898–1976]), 1:372.
59. See Song, "TVS Diary of Xi'an Incident, 1936," 6–11. Zhou Enlai informed the CCP CC about this on December 25, 1936. See Zhou, *Selected Works of Zhou Enlai,* 1:88–99.
60. Chiang, *Riji* (Diaries), December 23 and 24, 1936, Hoover Archives, box 39, folder 5.
61. Confucius, *The Analects of Confucius,* 57.
62. Quoted from Jin, *Zhou Enlai zhuan (1898–1976)* (Biography of Zhou Enlai [1898–1976]), 1:375.
63. Zhou, *Selected Works of Zhou Enlai,* 1:89–90.
64. Quoted from Jin, *Zhou Enlai zhuan (1898–1976)* (Biography of Zhou Enlai [1898–1976]), 1:375.
65. Song, "TVS Diary of Xi'an Incident, 1936," 11, 12.
66. Zhang and Tang, *Zhang Xueliang koushu lishi* (History of Zhang Xueliang Told by Himself) (Taiyuan), 152. Kong Xiangxi on his part also asked Zhang for "a splendid Christmas gift to the nation." Quoted from Soong Chiang, *Sian: A Coup dÉtat,* 107.
67. Cm.: Chiang, *Riji* (Diaries), December 25, 1936, Hoover Archives, box 39, folder 5; T. V. Song, "TVS Diary of Xi'an Incident, 1936," 13–14; Lü, *Jiang Zhongzheng*

*xiansheng nianpu changbian* (Large Chronological Biography of Mr. Jiang Zhongzheng), 5:211–12.

68. Zhou, *Selected Works of Zhou Enlai,* 1:90.
69. The Beijing opera *Lianhuantao,* based on a Chinese novel from the Qing era, tells the story of a romantic robber, Dou Erdun, freeing his enemy Tianba, a man who had been his friend in the past, from captivity, even though Tianba had challenged him as a thief.
70. Quoted from Luo Ruiqing, Lü Zhengcao, and Wang Bingnan, *Zhou Enlai and the Xi'an Incident: An Eyewitness Account: A Turning Point in Chinese History* (Beijing: Foreign Languages Press, 1983), 86.
71. Song, "TVS Diary of Xi'an Incident, 1936," 14.
72. See ibid., 15; Chiang, "A Fortnight in Sian," 177–84.
73. Quoted from Zhou, *Selected Works of Zhou Enlai,* 1:90.
74. Royal Leonard, *I Flew for China* (Garden City, NY: Doubleday, Doran, 1942), 105.
75. See Chiang, *Riji* (Diaries), December 25, 1936; Chiang, "A Fortnight in Sian," 175. According to another source they arrived in Luoyang at four-thirty in the afternoon. Song, "TVS Diary of Xi'an Incident, 1936," 15.
76. Chiang, *Riji* (Diaries), December 25, 1936.
77. See Leonard, *I Flew for China,* 108–9.
78. See Zhang and Tang, *Zhang Xueliang koushu lishi* (History of Zhang Xueliang Told by Himself) (Taiyuan), 151, 152; Zhang Xueliang and Tang Degang, *Zhang Xueliang koushu lishi* (History of Zhang Xueliang Told by Himself) (Taipei: Yuan liu chubanshe ye gufen youxian gongsi, 2009), 287–88.
79. Quoted from Bertram, *Crisis in China,* 154.
80. Chiang Kai-shek actually did petition for pardoning Zhang Xueliang, but this was an empty formality. Feng Yuxiang also requested that the Young Marshal be pardoned.
81. See Zhang and Tang, *Zhang Xueliang koushu lishi* (History of Zhang Xueliang Told by Himself) (Taiyuan), 151–52; Zhang and Tang, *Zhang Xueliang koushu lishi* (History of Zhang Xueliang Told by Himself) (Taipei), 288; Itoh, *The Making of China's War with Japan,* 1684; DeLong, *Madame Chiang Kai-shek and Miss Emma Mills,* 96.
82. The author's impressions on visiting Zhang Xueliang's first place of confinement in Xikou, August 8, 2009.
83. The author's impressions on visiting the places in Taiwan where Zhang Xueliang was confined, June 20, 2018.
84. Quoted from Itoh, *The Making of China's War with Japan,* 221.
85. For a detailed account of Zhang Xueliang's life after the Xi'an Incident, see Zhang Yongbin, *Zhang Xueliang da zhuan* (Full Biography of Zhang Xueliang), vol. 2 (Beijing: Tuanjie chubanshe, 2001).
86. See Yang Han, *Xi'an shibian, banian kangzhan yu Yang Hucheng* (The Xi'an Incident, the Eight-Year War of Resistance, and Yang Hucheng) (Taipei: Fengyun shidai, 2016), 369–70; Yang Han, *Yang Hucheng yu Xi'an shibian* (Yang Hucheng and the Xi'an Incident) (Beijing: Dangdai Zhongguo chubanshe, 2014).
87. See Cui, *Qingnian Jiang Jieshi* (Young Chiang Kai-shek), 19.
88. Chiang, *Riji* (Diaries), December 27, 1936, Hoover Archives, box 39, folder 5.

89. Hsiung, *The Life of Chiang Kai-shek,* 332.
90. "Pis'mo Nikonova G. Dimitrovu ot 20 ianvaria 1937 g." (Nikonov's Letter to G. Dimitrov of January 20, 1937), in Galitsky, *Tszian Tszingo* (Chiang Ching-kuo), 179; Tikhvinsky, *Russko–kitaiskie otnosheniia v XX veke* (Russo–Chinese Relations in the Twentieth Century), 3:743.
91. Chiang, *Riji* (Diaries), April 2, 7, 10, and 15, 1937, Hoover Archives, box 39, folder 10.
92. See Cui, *Qingnian Jiang Jieshi* (Young Chiang Kai-shek), 19–20.
93. Chiang, *My Days in Soviet Russia,* 32.
94. Pang, *Mao Zedong nianpu, 1893–1949* (Chronological Biography of Mao Zedong, 1893–1949), 1:639.
95. Titarenko, *Kommunisticheskii Internatsional i kitaiskaia revoliutsiia* (The Communist International and the Chinese Revolution), 270.
96. Ibid., 272; RGASPI, collection 146, inventory 2, file 3, sheets 25, 41; Dimitrov, *Dnevnik* (Diary), 122.
97. See *Kangri minzu tongyi zhanxian zhinan* (Directives on the Anti-Japanese National United Front) (n.p., n.d), 55–56.
98. See Sladkovsky, *Dokumenty po istorii Kommunisticheskoi partii Kitaia 1920–1949 gg.* (Documents on the History of the Chinese Communist Party, 1920–1949), vol. 2, book 5, 141–42; Pang, *Mao Zedong nianpu, 1893–1949* (Chronological Biography of Mao Zedong, 1893–1949), 1:650–52.
99. See Hsiung, *The Life of Chiang Kai-shek,* 334.
100. Quoted from Chiang, *Soviet Russia in China,* 80.
101. Chiang, *Riji* (Diaries), February 18, 1937, Hoover Archives, box 39, folder 8.
102. For Chiang's report, see Xibei daxue lishixi Zhongguo xiandai shi jiaoyanshi, Xi'an dizhi xueyuan Zhonggong dangshizu, Balujun Xi'an banshichu jinianguan eds., *Xi'an shibian ziliao xuanji* (Selected Documents on the History of the Xi'an Incident) (Xi'an: Xibei daxue lishi xi Zhongguo xiandai shi jiaoyanshi, 1979), 511–13.
103. Chen Bulei also edited Meiling's reminiscences of the mutiny in Xi'an. See Chen, *Chen Bulei huiyilu* (Memoirs of Chen Bulei), 120; Gu Siyong, *Liang dai bei ge: Chen Bulei he ta de nüer Chen Lian* (The Sad Song of Two Generations: Chen Bulei and His Daughter Chen Lian) (Beijing: Tuanjie chubanshe, 2005), 85–87; Wang Taidong, *Jiang Jieshi de di yi wendan Chen Bulei* (Jiang Jieshi's First Speechwriter—Chen Bulei) (Beijing: Tuanjie chubanshe, 2011), 172–82.
104. Chiang, *Riji* (Diaries), December 13–25, 1936, Hoover Archives, box 39, folder 5.
105. "Pis'mo Nikonova G. Dimitrovu ot 20 ianvariia 1937" (Nikonov's Letter to G. Dimitrov of January 20, 1937), in Galitsky, *Tszian Tszingo* (Chiang Ching-kuo), 177.
106. Tikhvinsky, *Russko–kitaiskie otnosheniia v XX veke* (Russo–Chinese Relations in the Twentieth Century), 3:761.
107. See Titarenko, *VKP(b), Komintern i Kitai: Dokumenty* (The CPSU, Comintern and China: Documents), 4:1098.
108. Quoted from Jiang Tingfu, *The Reminiscences of Tsiang T'ing-fu (1895–1965)* (New York: Chinese Oral History Project, East Asian Institute of Columbia University, 1975), 213.

109. A few scholars (most notably Steve Tsang) assert that as early as December 24, 1936, Stalin let Chiang know that he would allow his son to return to China soon. They alleged that he did it via Zhou Enlai. However, their sources seem dubious. See S. Tsang, "Chiang Kai-shek's 'Secret Deal' at Xian and the Start of the Sino–Japanese War," *Palgrave Communications* 1, 14003 (2015), https://doi.org/10.1057/palcomms.2014.3.
110. "Pis'mo Tszian Tszingo Chan Kai-shi ot 23 fevralia 1937 g." (Chiang Ching-kuo's Letter to Chiang Kai-shek of February 23, 1937), in Galitsky, *Tszian Tszingo* (Chiang Ching-kuo), 173–74.
111. Before departing, Ching-kuo really did write a letter to his father and handed it to the Soviet Ministry of Foreign Affairs with a request that it be delivered to the addressee. But what was in it and was that the one sent and, if it was, whether it reached Chiang Kai-shek is not known.
112. Tikhvinsky, *Russko–kitaiskie otnosheniia v XX veke* (Russo–Chinese Relations in the Twentieth Century), vol. 4, book 1, 40.
113. RGASPI, collection 146, inventory 2, file 3, sheet 49; Dimitrov, *Dnevnik* (Diary), 124.
114. See Tikhvinsky, *Russko–kitaiskie otnosheniia v XX veke* (Russo–Chinese Relations in the Twentieth Century), vol. 4, book 1, 44; as well as the explanation of Anna Vakhreva given to the Visa and Registration Department of the Worker-Peasant Militia Administration of Saratov oblast, June 25, 1938, in Galitsky, *Tszian Tszingo* (Chiang Ching-kuo), 158.
115. Tikhvinsky, *Russko–kitaiskie otnoshenii v XX veke* (Russo–Chinese Relations in the Twentieth Century), 3:774.
116. RGASPI, collection of unsorted documents. Emphasis in original.
117. Ibid.
118. Tikhvinsky, *Russko–kitaiskie otnosheniia v XX veke* (Russo–Chinese Relations in the Twentieth Century), vol. 3, 633; vol. 4, book 2, 342.
119. Chiang, *Riji* (Diaries), April 21, 22, 24, and 25, 1937, Hoover Archives, box 39, folder 10; Lü, *Jiang Zhongzheng xiansheng nianpu changbian* (Large Chronological Biography of Mr. Jiang Zhongzheng), 5:278.
120. See Taylor, *The Generalissimo's Son,* 79–80.
121. See ibid., 79–80; the author's impressions on visiting the village of Xikou on August 8, 2009.
122. Chiang, *Riji* (Diaries), April 30, 1937, Hoover Archives, box 39, folder 10.
123. Xiao Ruping, *Jiang Jingguo zhuan* (Biography of Chiang Ching-kuo) (Hangzhou: Zhejiang daxue chubanshe, 2012), 80.
124. A photo of the newlyweds is published in the book by Liao Yanbo and Chen Yiming, *Jiang shi jiazu shenghuo mishi* (Secret History of the Life of the Chiang Clan) (Taipei: Haodu chuban, 2007), 155.
125. See Taylor, *The Generalissimo's Son,* 81.
126. The author's impressions on visiting the village of Xikou on August 8, 2009.
127. See Chiang Kai-shek's Letter to Chiang Ching-kuo of February 16, 1938, in Chiang Ching-kuo, *Calm in the Eye of a Storm* (Taipei: Li Ming Cultural Enterprise, 1978), 124.

128. See the letters from Faina Jiang to Anna Vakhreva of mid-October 1938, April 3, 1943, and November 7, 1947, as well as Chiang Ching-kuo's letter to Anna Vakhreva of November 7, 1947, in Galitsky, *Tszian Tszingo* (Chiang Ching-kuo), 147–49, 151–53, 154–57.
129. See Wang, *Qianshan duxing* (The Solitary Path among a Thousand Mountains), 64–65, 68–70; Chiang and Liu, *Jiang Weiguo koushu zizhuan* (The Autobiography of Chiang Wei-kuo as Told by Himself), 53–60; Liang, *The Sino–German Connection,* 139.
130. See Titarenko, *VKP(b), Komintern i Kitai: Dokumenty* (The CPSU, Comintern and China: Documents), 4:1103–4.
131. Ibid., 1120; see also Zhonggong zhongyang wenxian yanjiu shi, *Zhou Enlai nianpu (1898–1949)* (Chronological Biography of Zhou Enlai [1898–1949]), 1:399–401.
132. Chiang, *Riji* (Diaries), June 17, 1937, Hoover Archives, box 39, folder 12.
133. See Tang, *Zhongguo lishi dashi nianbiao: Xiandai* (Chronology of Events in Chinese History: Contemporary History), 329.
134. See Sidorov, "Problema zakliucheniia pakta o nenapadenii v sovetsko-kitaiskikh otnosheniiakh (1932–1937 gg.)" (The Problem of Concluding a Sino–Soviet Non-Aggression Pact [1932–1937]), 132.
135. Tikhvinsky, *Russko–kitaiskie otnoshenii v XX veke* (Russo–Chinese Relations in the Twentieth Century), 3:654, 642.
136. See Liang, *The Sino-German Connection,* 104; Donald S. Sutton, "German Advice and Residual Warlordism in the Nanking Decade: Influences on Nationalist Military Training and Strategy," *China Quarterly* 91 (September 1982): 401–2; John P. Fox, *Germany and the Far Eastern Crisis 1931–1938: A Study in Diplomacy and Ideology* (Oxford: Clarendon Press, 1982), 234.

## 14. *A MOMENT OF SELF-SACRIFICE*

1. See *FRUS: Diplomatic Papers, 1937,* 3:121–22 (Washington, DC: Government Printing Office, 1954); Abend, *My Life in China: 1926–1941, 244–5.* Abend gives the wrong date for his visit to Chiang Kai-shek: June 28.
2. Chiang, *Riji* (Diaries), June 17, 1937.
3. See *FRUS 1937,* 3:122.
4. Abend, *My Life in China: 1926–1941,* 245.
5. Marco Polo, *The Book of Ser Marco Polo, the Venetian, Concerning the Kingdoms of Marvels of the East,* trans. Colonel Sir Henry Yule, 3rd ed. (New York, Charles Scribner's Sons, 1929), 2:4.
6. Article IX of this treaty, signed between the Qing government and the eight powers after their suppression of the Boxer Rebellion, permitted the foreign occupation of a series of inhabited points in the region of Peking (Beijing) and Tianjin. See "Settlement of Matters Growing Out of the Boxer Uprising (Boxer Protocol)," in Charles I. Bevans, ed., *Treaties and Other International Agreements of the United States 1776–1949,* 1:307 (Washington, DC: Department of State, 1968).
7. See *FRUS 1937,* 3:129–30, 149; Taylor, *The Generalissimo,* 145; Lü, *Jiang Zhongzheng xiansheng nianpu changbian* (Large Chronological Biography of Mr. Jiang

Zhongzheng), 5:334; Rana Mitter, *Forgotten Ally: China's World War II, 1937–1945* (Boston: Houghton Mifflin Harcourt, 2013), 85; Dong, *Shanghai,* 251.

8. Candlin, *The Breach in the Wall,* 208.
9. Chiang, *Riji* (Diaries), June 18 and July 7, 1937, Hoover Archives, box 39, folders 12 and 13; Chen, *Kuxiao lu* (Somber Notes), 256.
10. See Lü, *Jiang Zhongzheng xiansheng nianpu changbian* (Large Chronological Biography of Mr. Jiang Zhongzheng), 5:334–35.
11. Chiang, *Riji* (Diaries), July 8, 1937, Hoover Archives, box 39, folder 13.
12. See *FRUS 1937,* 3:138; Marius B. Jansen, *Japan and China: From War to Peace, 1894–1972* (Chicago: Rand McNally, 1975), 394.
13. Chiang, *Riji* (Diaries), July 9, 1937, Hoover Archives, box 39, folder 13; *FRUS 1937,* 3:138.
14. Chiang, *Riji* (Diaries), July 10, 1937, Hoover Archives, box 39, folder 13.
15. See ibid., July 12, 1937, Hoover Archives, box 39, folder 13.
16. See Mitter, *Forgotten Ally,* 85; John Hunter Boyle, *China and Japan at War 1937–1945: The Politics of Collaboration* (Stanford: Stanford University Press, 1972), 51–52, 59.
17. See Mitter, *Forgotten Ally,* 89.
18. Chiang, *Riji* (Diaries), January 25, February 14, 18, 19, and 20, 1937, Hoover Archives, box 39, folders 7 and 8.
19. See Odani, "Wang Ching-wei and the Fall of the Chinese Republic, 1905–1935," 142–43; Wang, "Wang Jingwei and the Policy Origins of the 'Peace Movement,' 1932–1937," 36.
20. Quoted from Boyle, *China and Japan at War 1937–1945,* 189.
21. Chiang Kai-shek, *The Collected Wartime Messages of Generalissimo Chiang Kai-shek 1937–1945,* 1:22, 24 (New York: John Day, 1946).
22. See *FRUS 1937,* 3:216–18.
23. Chiang, *Calm in the Eye of a Storm,* 124.
24. See Boyle, *China and Japan at War 1937–1945,* 51.
25. Chiang, *Riji* (Diaries), review of July 1937 events, Hoover Archives, box 39, folder 13.
26. See Sutton, "German Advice and Residual Warlordism in the Nanking Decade," 402–3.
27. General Wego W. K. Chiang, *How Generalissimo Chiang Kai-shek Won the Eight-Year Sino-Japanese War* (Taipei: Li Ming Culture Enterprise, 1979), 31, 33.
28. Quoted from Mitter, *Forgotten Ally,* 95. See also Van de Ven, *War and Nationalism in China 1925–1945,* 197; Liu Weikai, "Guofang huiyi yu guofang lianxi huiyi zhi zhaokai yu yingxiang" (Convening the Conference on National Defense Issues and the Joint Conference on Issues of Defense and Their Influence), *Jindai Zhongguo* (Contemporary China), no. 163 (2005): 50–51; Chennault, *Way of a Fighter,* 42. Chennault gives an incorrect date for the conference.
29. Chiang, *Riji* (Diaries), August 7, 1937, Hoover Archives, box 39, folder 14.
30. See Sutton, "German Advice and Residual Warlordism in the Nanking Decade," 402.
31. See Jarvis, "Letters from China 1920–1949," 19.
32. Ch'i Hsi-sheng, *Nationalist China at War: Military Defeats and Political Collapse, 1937–45* (Ann Arbor: University of Michigan Press, 1982), 41–42; Jensen, *Japan and China,* 395.

33. See *FRUS 1937*, 3:351, 379–80, 383, 391, 392, 398.
34. See ibid., 379, 396; Van de Ven, *War and Nationalism in China 1925–1945*, 197.
35. Rhodes Farmer, *Shanghai Harvest: A Diary of Three Years of the China War* (London: Museum Press, 1945), 41–42.
36. See *FRUS 1937*, 3:380; Dong, *Shanghai*, 254.
37. Quoted from *FRUS 1937*, 3:398.
38. Ibid., 404; Chen Xiaoqing et al., *Kangri shiwu nian: yige shidai de ceying: Zhongguo 1931–1945* (Fifteen Years of the War of Resistance: A Silhouette of an Epoch: China 1931–1945), 2nd ed. (Guilin: Guangxi shifan daxue chubanshe, 2008), 173.
39. Quoted from Van de Ven, *War and Nationalism in China 1925–1945*, 197. See also Tong and Li, *The Memoirs of Li Tsung-jen*, 324.
40. See *FRUS 1937*, 3:406–9; Farmer, *Shanghai Harvest*, 44–49; Dong, *Shanghai*, 253–54.
41. Farmer, *Shanghai Harvest*, 46.
42. See Fox, *Germany and the Far Eastern Crisis 1931–1938*, 243–44.
43. See Mitter, *Forgotten Ally*, 101.
44. Quoted from Dong, *Shanghai*, 254.
45. For more details, see Peter Harmsen, *Shanghai 1937: Stalingrad on the Yangtze* (Philadelphia: Casemate, 2013); Mitter, *Forgotten Ally*, 126.
46. See Fox, *Germany and the Far Eastern Crisis 1931–1938*, 260–66; John W. Garver, *Chinese–Soviet Relations 1937–1945: The Diplomacy of Chinese Nationalism* (New York: Oxford University Press, 1988), 27.
47. At the time, the Chinese army (not counting reserves) was the largest in the world. The army of the USSR was second, Italy's third, France's fourth, and Germany's fifth. The Japanese army was eighth, and the Americans were in eleventh place.
48. Gen. Chiang Wei-Kuo, *How the China Mainland Was Lost* (Taipei: Armed Forces University, 1979), 29–31.
49. See B. G. Sapozhnikov, *Kitai v ogne voiny (1931–1950)* (China in the Fires of War [1931–1950]) (Moscow: Nauka, 1977), 83; A. Ya. Kalyagin, *Po neznakomym dorogam (Zapiski voennogo sovetnika v Kitae)* (Along Alien Roads [Notes of a Military Advisor in China]), 2nd, expanded ed. (Moscow: Nauka, 1979), 98, 102; A. M. Dubinsky, *Sovetsko–kitaiskie otnosheniia v period iapono–kitaiskoi voiny 1937–1945* (Soviet–Chinese Relations in the Period of the Japanese–Chinese War 1937–1945) (Moscow: "Mysl,'" 1980), 66–68.
50. Tikhvinsky, *Russko–kitaiskie otnosheniia v XX veke* (Russo–Chinese Relations in the Twentieth Century), 3:667.
51. See Wang, "Wang Jingwei and the Policy Origins of the 'Peace Movement,' 1932–1937," 36.
52. See William R. Nester, *Japanese Industrial Targeting: The Neomercantilist Path to Economic Superpower* (New York: St. Martin's Press, 1991), 140.
53. Tikhvinsky, *Russko–kitaiskie otnosheniia v XX veke* (Russo–Chinese Relations in the Twentieth Century), vol. 4, book 1, 60, 65; A. A. Gromyko, ed., *Dokumenty vneshnei politiki SSSR* (Documents of the USSR Foreign Policy), 20:271, 301–3 (Moscow: Politizdat, 1976).
54. Quoted from Mitter, *Forgotten Ally*, 94.

55. The nine powers that, on February 6, 1922, had signed the Washington Treaty guaranteeing the territorial integrity of China—Belgium, the British Empire, China, Italy, the Netherlands, Portugal, the US, France, and Japan—were supposed to take part in this conference. But Japan refused to participate. The ninth power invited to the conference was the USSR.
56. Quoted from Fatica, "The Beginning and the End of the Idyllic Relations between Mussolini's Italy and Chiang Kai-shek's China (1930–1937)," 106.
57. See ibid., 99.
58. See Guido Samarani, "Italians and Nationalist China (1928–1945): Some Case Studies," in Anne-Marie Brady and Douglas Brown, eds., *Foreigners and Foreign Institutions in Republican China* (London: Routledge, 2013), 234–50; Guido Samarani, "The Evolution of Fascist Italian Diplomacy During the Sino–Japanese War, 1937–1943," in David P. Barrett and Larry N. Shyu, eds., *China in the Anti-Japanese War, 1937–1945: Politics, Culture, and Society* (New York: Peter Lang, 2001), 65. One other Italian of whom we have information, Petro Cabutti, worked in a factory in Nanchang (apparently as an engineer), but he returned home to Turin in December 1937. See Zhongguo di er lishi dang'anguan (The Second Historical Archives of China), document no. 718/4/169/90.
59. See Liang, *The Sino–German Connection,* 122.
60. See Wang, *Qianshan duxing* (The Solitary Path among a Thousand Mountains), 64–65, 68–70; Chiang and Liu, *Jiang Weiguo koushu zizhuan* (The Autobiography of Chiang Wei-kuo as Told by Himself), 53–60; Liang, *The Sino–German Connection,* 139.
61. See Yu, *The Dragon's War,* 4; Kirby, *Germany and Republican China,* 234, 238; Young, *China and the Helping Hand 1937–1945,* 18; Liang, *The Sino–German Connection,* 122.
62. See Liang, *The Sino–German Connection,* 122, 126; Harald von Waldheim, "Germany's Economic Position in the Far East," *Far Eastern Survey* 6, no. 6 (1937): 9–65; Fox, *Germany and the Far Eastern Crisis 1931–1938,* 241.
63. See Fox, *Germany and the Far Eastern Crisis 1931–1938,* 169–70, 240, 248.
64. Adolf Hitler, *Adolf Hitler Collection of Speeches 1922–1945* (n.p., n.d.), 355, 375.
65. Tikhvinsky, *Russko–kitaiskie otnosheniia v XX veke* (Russo–Chinese Relations in the Twentieth Century), vol. 4, book 1, 40.
66. Ibid., vol. 3, 658; vol. 4, book 1, 68, 71.
67. Ibid., vol. 3, 659–61.
68. Ibid., vol. 4, book 1, endpaper.
69. Chiang, *Riji* (Diaries), July 27, 1937, Hoover Archives, box 39, folder 13.
70. Ibid., December 7, 1937, Hoover Archives, box 39, folder 18.
71. Eduard Davydovich Lepin (1889–1938) was a corps commander and served as military attaché at the embassy of the USSR in 1934–37.
72. Tikhvinsky, *Russko–kitaiskie otnosheniia v XX veke* (Russo–Chinese Relations in the Twentieth Century), vol. 4, book 1, 66.
73. Ibid., 79; Gromyko, *Dokumenty vneshnei politiki SSSR* (Documents of the USSR Foreign Policy), 20:742.
74. Tikhvinsky, *Russko–kitaiskie otnosheniia v XX veke* (Russo–Chinese Relations in the Twentieth Century), vol. 4, book 1, 101.

75. Ibid., 137–38.
76. Quoted from Sutton, "German Advice and Residual Warlordism in the Nanking Decade," 406.
77. See Gromyko, *Dokumenty vneshnei politiki SSSR* (Documents of the USSR Foreign Policy), 20:748; Sokolov, "'Zabytyi diplomat' D. V. Bogomolov (1890–1938)" (A "Forgotten Diplomat" D. V. Bogomolov [1890–1938]), 194; Tikhvinsky, *Russko–kitaiskie otnosheniia v XX veke* (Russo–Chinese Relations in the Twentieth Century), vol. 4, book 1, 212–14; book 2, 603.
78. Tikhvinsky, *Russko–kitaiskie otnosheniia v XX veke* (Russo–Chinese Relations in the Twentieth Century), vol. 4, book 1, 155–56.
79. Ibid., 159–60, 163.
80. At the time, Stalin was supporting the Popular Front government in Spain in its fight against the rebellious general Francisco Franco.
81. See S. V. Sliusarev, "V vozdushnykh boiakh nad Kitaem" (In Air Battles over China), in Yu. V. Chudodeev, ed., *Po dorogam Kitaia 1937–1945: Vospominaniia* (Along Chinese Roads 1937–1945: Reminiscences) (Moscow: Nauka, 1989), 97.
82. Chiang, *Riji* (Diaries), December 1, 1937, Hoover Archives, box 39, folder 18.
83. See Tikhvinsky, *Russko–kitaiskie otnosheniia v XX veke* (Russo–Chinese Relations in the Twentieth Century), vol. 4, book 1, 166; Fox, *Germany and the Far Eastern Crisis 1931–1938,* 271–74.
84. In September 1937, the military attaché Lepin and Ambassador Bogomolov were recalled from China; soon both were arrested on the charge that they "informed the leadership incorrectly." Moreover, they were accused of Trotskyism. They were then both shot and rehabilitated twenty years later.
85. See Wilbur and How, *Missionaries of Revolution,* 582.
86. See Tikhvinsky, *Russko–kitaiskie otnosheniia v XX veke* (Russo–Chinese Relations in the Twentieth Century), vol. 4, book 1, 524. For the report of the German ambassador about his meeting with Chiang on December 3, 1937, see Erwin Wickert, ed., *The Good Man of Nanking: The Diaries of John Rabe,* trans. John E. Woods (New York: A. A. Knopf, 1998), 259–61.
87. Mao, *Minguo shiwu nian yiqian zhi Jiang Jieshi xiansheng* (Mr. Chiang Kai-shek Before 1926), 16.

## 15. *BLOOD AND ASHES*

1. See Tong and Li, *The Memoirs of Li Tsung-jen,* 326–27; Zhang Xueji and Xu Kaifeng, *Bai Chongxi da zhuan* (Large Biography of Bai Chongxi) (Hangzhou: Zhejiang daxue chubanshe, 2012), 319–22.
2. Quoted from Lü, *Jiang Zhongzheng xiansheng nianpu changbian* (Large Chronological Biography of Mr. Jiang Zhongzheng), 5:430. See also Walsh, *The German Military Mission in China, 1928–38,* 509.
3. Chiang, *Riji* (Diaries), December 7, 1937.
4. Quoted from Selle, *Donald of China,* 341–42.
5. See Mitter, *Forgotten Ally,* 130–31; Taylor, *The Generalissimo,* 151.

6. Unlike Shanghai, Nanjing had no International Settlement where Chinese citizens could legally shelter under the protection of foreigners.
7. The Embassy of the United States was empty, however. All its officials had evacuated to the gunship *Panay,* which was anchored in the roadstead of Nanjing. But this did not save them from the fires of war. On December 12, 1937, Japanese aircraft sank the *Panay;* afterward the Japanese apologized and even paid compensation.
8. Jinling (Gold Mountain) is an ancient name for Nanjing.
9. See Minnie Vautrin, *Terror in Minnie Vautrin's Nanjing: Diaries and Correspondence, 1937–38* (Urbana: University of Illinois Press, 2008), 81–83; Hu Hua-ling, *American Goddess of the Rape of Nanking: The Courage of Minnie Vautrin* (Carbondale: Southern Illinois University Press, 2000), 77, 78.
10. See Zhang Xianwen, ed., *Nanjing da tusha: zhongyao wenzheng xuanlu* (The Nanjing Massacre: A Collection of Assorted Documentary Evidence) (Nanjing: Fenguang chubanshe, 2014); Wickert, *The Good Man of Nanking,* 168–206.
11. See Harold J. Timperley, *Japanese Terror in China* (Freeport, NY: Books for Libraries Press, 1938), 27; Diana Lary and Stephen MacKinnon, eds., *Scars of War: The Impact of Warfare on Modern China* (Vancouver: UBC Press, 2001), 84. 87.
12. Timperley, *Japanese Terror in China,* 58.
13. Martha Lund Smalley, ed., *American Missionary Eyewitnesses to the Nanking Massacre, 1937–1938* (New Haven: Yale Divinity School Library, 1997), 23.
14. In historiography the number of victims varies from 13,000 to almost 400,000. See Daqing Yang, "Convergence or Divergence: Recent Historical Writings on the Rape of Nanjing," *The American Historical Review,* 104, no. 3 (June 1999): 850-53; Iris Chang, *The Rape of Nanking: The Forgotten Holocaust of World War II* (New York: Basic Books, 1997), 139; Bian Xuyue, *Kangri zhanzheng shiqi Zhongguo renkou sunshi wenti yanjiu (1937–1945)* (A Study of the Losses of the Chinese Population during the Period of the Anti-Japanese War [1937–1945]) (Beijing: Hualing chubanshe, 2010), 167–72; James Yin and Shi Young, *The Rape of Nanking: An Undeniable History in Photographs* (Chicago: Innovative Publishing Group, 1996), v, xi; Sun Zhaiwei, ed., *Nanjing da tusha* (The Nanjing Massacre) (Beijing: Beijing chubanshe, 1997).
15. See Chiang, *The Collected Wartime Messages of Generalissimo Chiang Kai-shek 1937–1945,* 12:49–52.
16. Chiang, *Riji* (Diaries), January 22, 1938, Hoover Archives, box 39, folder 20.
17. See *FRUS 1938,* 3:6–7, 832–33 (Washington, DC: U.S. Government Printing Office, 1938).
18. For Stalin's original resolution, see RGASPI, collection 558, inventory 11, file 324, sheet 21. It was first published in Tikhvinsky, *Russko–kitaiskie otnosheniia v XX veke* (Russo–Chinese Relations in the Twentieth Century), vol. 4, book 1, 180.
19. Chiang, *Riji* (Diaries), December 14 and 26, 1938, Hoover Archives, box 39, folder 18; Fox, *Germany and the Far Eastern Crisis 1931–1938,* 278–79; Tikhvinsky, *Russo–kitaiskie otnosheniia v XX veke* (Russo–Chinese Relations in the Twentieth Century), vol. 4, book 1, 181–82.
20. A. I. Cherepanov, "Itogi Uhanskoi operatsii," (Notes on the Wuhan Campaign), in Chudodeev, *Po dorogam Kitaia 1937–1945* (Along Chinese Roads 1937–1945), 15.

21. See L. M. Mlechin, *Istoriia vneshnei razvedki: Kar'ery i sud'by* (The History of Foreign Intelligence: Careers and Fates) (Moscow: ZAO Tsentrpoligrapf, 2008), 398.
22. Quoted from Garver, *Chinese–Soviet Relations 1937–1945,* 28. See also Chiang, *Riji* (Diaries), December 27, 1938, Hoover Archives, box 39, folder 20.
23. Chiang, *Riji* (Diaries), December 30, 1937, Hoover Archives, box 40, folder 2.
24. See H. G. W. Woodhead, ed., *The China Year Book 1939* (Shanghai: *North China Daily News and Herald,* 1939), 426; Yang Tianshi, *Zhaoxun zhenshi de Jiang Jiieshi: Jiang Jieshi riji jiedu* (In Search of the True Chiang Kai-shek: Analyzing Chiang Kai-shek's Diaries), 1:169–70 (Chongqing: Chongqing chubanshe, 2015); Garver, *Chinese–Soviet Relations 1937–1945,* 28–30.
25. Subsequently, both the Japanese and Chinese sides tried to initiate efforts to begin peace negotiations. During the duration of the war, the Japanese, for example, made twenty-nine proposals toward that end. Various officials from the two sides even met with each other secretly in Hong Kong or exchanged letters, but nothing came of all of this.
26. The Beiping–Canton railroad consisted of two railroads that were not connected: the Beiping–Hankou and the Wuchang–Canton railroads, since there was no railroad bridge across the Yangzi until 1957.
27. Chiang, *Riji* (Diaries), January 1, 1938, Hoover Archives, box 39, folder 20.
28. See ibid., January 11, 1938, Hoover Archives, box 39, folder 20; Lü, *Jiang Zhongzheng xiansheng nianpu changbian* (Large Chronological Biography of Mr. Jiang Zhongzheng), 5:461.
29. See *FRUS 1938,* 3:59–61.
30. Jiang, *The Reminiscences of Tsiang T'ing-fu (1895–1965),* 210.
31. See Cherepanov, *Zapiski voennogo sovetnika v Kitae* (Notes of a Military Advisor in China), 604–7.
32. The Chinese also bought airplanes from other countries, but not as many as from the USSR. From May to October 1938, they acquired 211 from Western Europe.
33. See Sliusarev, "V vozdushnykh boiakh nad Kitaem" (In Air Battles over China), 99; Tikhvinsky, *Russko–kitaiskie otnosheniia v XX veke* (Russo–Chinese Relations in the Twentieth Century), vol. 4, book 2, 587, 599.
34. See A. Ya. Kalyagin, "Bitva za Uhan" (Battle for Wuhan), in Yu. V. Chudodeev, ed., *Na kitaiskoi zemle: Vospominaniia sovetskikh dobrovol'tsev 1925–1945* (On Chinese Soil: Recollections of Soviet Volunteers 1925–1945) (Moscow: Nauka, 1977), 175; Kalyagin, *Po neznakomym dorogam* (Along Alien Roads), 99–100, 103.
35. See Tikhvinsky, *Russko–kitaiskie otnosheniia v XX veke* (Russo–Chinese Relations in the Twentieth Century), vol. 4, book 1, 263–66; book 2, 603.
36. See Jiang, *The Reminiscences of Tsiang T'ing-fu (1895–1965),* 211–12.
37. See Tikhvinsky, *Russko–kitaiskie otnosheniia v XX veke* (Russo–Chinese Relations in the Twentieth Century), vol. 4, book 1, 198, 199, 238, 241, 245, 253, 256, 258, 260–62, 273, 277–78, 281–82, 285, 291, 292, 295, 298, 300, 302, 303, 311, 314, 317, 319, 328, 332, 343, 353.
38. Ibid., 243.
39. On October 22, 1938, on Stalin's order, Bliukher was arrested and executed eighteen days later. Subsequently, Stalin explained to Sun Fo why he had Bliukher shot:

"for succumbing to the charms of a Japanese woman spy." Chiang, *Soviet Russia in China*, 52.

40. The Führer, as noted earlier, always viewed the Japanese as a nation "under Aryan influence," but he despised the Chinese.
41. Tikhvinsky, *Russko-kitaiskie otnosheniia v XX veke* (Russo-Chinese Relations in the Twentieth Century), vol. 4, book 1, 105.
42. Adolf Hitler, *Collection of Speeches 1922–1945*, 420.
43. See Woodhead, *The China Year Book 1939*, 413.
44. See Wang, *Qianshan duxing* (The Solitary Path among a Thousand Mountains), 71–75; Chiang and Liu, *Jiang Weiguo koushu zizhuan* (The Autobiography of Chiang Wei-kuo as Told by Himself), 59–65; Liang, *The Sino–German Connection*, 134.
45. In 1958, on the occasion of his eightieth birthday, Chiang awarded von Falkenhausen, who was then living in the Federal Republic of Germany, with one of the highest military honors of the Republic of China, the Order of the Sacred Tripod with Blue Ribbon. Von Falkenhausen died in 1966 at the age of eighty-eight.
46. See Yu, *The Dragon's War*, 4–5; Kirby, *Germany and Republican China*, 235; Liang, *The Sino–German Connection*, 134; Walsh, *The German Military Mission in China, 1928–38*, 511–12; Fox, *Germany and the Far Eastern Crisis 1931–1938*, 314, 317–18, 330–31.
47. See Zeng Jingzhong, "Youguan Guomindang linshi quanguo daibiaodahui zhi yantao" (Study of the All-China Emergency Congress of the Guomindang), *Minguo dang'an* (Republican Archive), no. 4 (2001): 81–89; Lü, *Jiang Zhongzheng xiansheng nianpu changbian* (Large Chronological Biography of Mr. Jiang Zhongzheng), 5:500; Wang Chaoguang, "Kangzhan yu jianguo: Guomindang linshi quanguo daibiao dahui yanjiu" (The War of Resistance and State Construction: A Study of the All-China Emergency Congress of the Guomindang), in Lü Fangshang, ed., *Zhanzheng de lishi yu jiyi* (War in History and Memory), 2:191–210 (Taipei: Guoshiguan, 2015).
48. See Li, *Zhongguo guomindang dashiji (1894.11–1986.12)* (Chronology of the Chinese Guomindang [November 1894–December 1986]), 595–96; Lü, *Jiang Zhongzheng xiansheng nianpu changbian* (Large Chronological Biography of Mr. Jiang Zhongzheng), 5:501–2; Wang Liangjing, "Zhongguo guomindang zongcai zhidu de zhan qian yunnian yu zhan shi jianli" (Establishment of the Zongcai System in the Chinese Guomindang before the War and Its Creation during the War), in Lü, *Zhanzheng de lishi yu jiyi* (War in History and Memory), 2:211–34.
49. *Zongcai* literally means the person who makes the major decisions.
50. Milton J. T. Shieh, *The Kuomintang: Selected Historical Documents 1894–1969* (New York: St. John's University Press, 1970), 189.
51. For details, see Meng Guanghan et al., eds., *Guomin canzhenghui jishi* (Records of the National Political Council) (Chongqing: Chongqing chubanshe, 1985), 1:41–255; Chiang, *The Collected Wartime Messages of Generalissimo Chiang Kai-shek 1937–1945*, 1:71–75.
52. Farmer, *Shanghai Harvest*, 104.
53. Stephen R. MacKinnon, *Wuhan, 1938: War, Refugees, and the Making of Modern China* (Berkeley: University of California Press, 2008), 130.
54. See Freda Utley, *China at War* (New York: John Day, 1939), 43–49.
55. Kalyagin, *Po neznakomym dorogam* (Along Alien Roads), 42–43.

56. Utley, *China at War,* 244–45.
57. Chiang, *Riji* (Diaries), May 12, 1938, Hoover Archives, box 39, folder 24; MacKinnon, *Wuhan, 1938,* 35.
58. According to another source, this plan was proposed by Chiang's "blood nephew" Chen Guofu. See Ma Zhengdu, *Kangri zhong de Jiang Jieshi* (Chiang Kai-shek during the War of Resistance) (Beijing: Jiuzhong chubanshe, 2013), 121.
59. According to another source, it was twelve and a half million. See He Husheng, *Banian kangri zhong de Jiang Jieshi 1937–1945* (Chiang Kai-shek during the Eight-Year War of Resistance 1937–1945) (Beijing: Taihai chubanshe, 2011), 63.
60. See Diana Lary, "Drowned Earth: The Strategic Breaching of the Yellow River Dyke, 1938," *War in History* 8, no. 2 (2001): 197–207; Diana Lary, "The Waters Covered the Earth: China's War-induced Natural Disasters," in Mark Selden et al., eds., *War and State Terrorism: The United States, Japan, and the Asia-Pacific in the Long Twentieth Century* (Lanham, MD: Rowman & Littlefield, 2004), 143–70; Diana Lary, *The Chinese People at War: Human Suffering and Social Transformation, 1937–1945* (New York: Cambridge University Press, 2010), 44–78; Micah S. Muscolino, *The Ecology of War in China: Henan Province, the Yellow River and Beyond* (New York: Cambridge University Press, 2015), 26–31; He, *Banian kangri zhong de Jiang Jieshi, 1937–1945* (Chiang Kai-shek during the Eight-Year War of Resistance, 1937–1945), 63.
61. Quoted from Kirby, *Germany and Republican China,* 245.
62. This history is unique even if one considers the legend as being true that on May 2, 1945, executing the order of the by-now-deceased Hitler, the Nazis supposedly blew up the metro tunnel under the Landwehr Canal. According to the legend, from fifteen to twenty thousand Germans who were taking refuge from Soviet bombers died. The number, obviously, does not compare with the Chinese inundation. A majority of historians are not convinced that the Nazis were connected to this event.
63. Quoted from He, *Banian kangri zhong de Jiang Jieshi 1937–1945* (Chiang Kai-shek during the Eight-Year War of Resistance 1937–1945), 63.
64. Quoted from Selle, *Donald of China,* 345.
65. Tikhvinsky, *Russko–kitaiskie otnosheniia v XX veke* (Russo–Chinese Relations in the Twentieth Century), vol. 4, book 1, 199.
66. The Japanese lost more than a hundred thousand.
67. See MacKinnon, *Wuhan, 1938,* 42.
68. See Farmer, *Shanghai Harvest,* 180; Hsiung, *The Life of Chiang Kai-shek,* 340.
69. See Leonard, *I Flew for China,* 206–9; Chiang, *Riji* (Diaries), October 25, 1938, Hoover Archives, box 39, folder 29.
70. See MacKinnon, *Wuhan, 1938,* 24, 42, 129–30; He, *Banian kangri zhong de Jiang Jieshi 1937–1945* (Chiang Kai-shek during the Eight-Year War of Resistance 1937–1945), 110.
71. See Green, *Hsiang-Ya Journal,* 114.
72. Diana Lary, *China's Republic* (New York: Cambridge University Press, 2007), 120.
73. See Green, *Hsiang-Ya Journal,* 114; Zhang Zhizhong, *Zhang Zhizhong huiyilu* (Reminiscences of Zhang Zhizhong), 1:262–93 (Beijing: Wenshi ziliao chubanshe, 1985); Farmer, *Shanghai Harvest,* 196.
74. Zhuge and Liu, *Mastering the Art of War,* 82.

## 16. *THE PROTRACTED WAR*

1. See Jiang, *The Reminiscences of Tsiang T'ing-fu (1895–1965),* 229; Tikhvinsky, *Russko–kitaiskie otnosheniia v XX veke* (Russo–Chinese Relations in the Twentieth Century), vol. 4, book 1, 384, 412; Cherepanov, *Zapiski voennogo sovetnika v Kitae* (Notes of a Military Advisor in China), 645; Taylor, *The Generalissimo,* 162.
2. See Chiang, *Riji* (Diaries), October 28, 1938, Hoover Archives, box 39, folder 29; Wang Qisheng, "Kangzhan chuqi de 'he' sheng" (Voice About "Peace" in the Initial Period of the War of Resistance), in Lü Fangshang, ed., *Zhanzheng de lishi yu jiyi* (War in History and Memory), 1:153 (Taipei: Guoshiguan, 2015).
3. Chiang Kai-shek, *Xian zongtong Jiang gong quanji* (Complete Works of the Late President Mr. Chiang), 1:1171–77 (Taipei: Zhongguo wenhua daxue chubanbu, 1984); Lü, *Jiang Zhongzheng xiansheng nianpu changbian* (Large Chronological Biography of Mr. Jiang Zhongzheng), 5:635; Xie Rudi, *Jiang Jieshi de peidu suiyue: 1937–1946* (Chiang Kai-shek's Sojourn in the Provisional Capital: 1937–1946) (Shanghai: Wenhui chubanshe, 2010), 3; Kalyagin, *Po neznakomym dorogam* (Along Alien Roads), 299–300. Kalyagin gives the wrong date for the conference: November 22.
4. See Boyle, *China and Japan at War 1937–1945,* 192.
5. See Xie, *Jiang Jieshi de peidu suiyue* (Chiang Kai-shek's Sojourn in the Provisional Capital), 3–4.
6. See Zhang Shiying, "Kangzhan shiqi guojun tongshibu duiyu youjizhang de gouxiang yu zhixing" (Concepts of the Unified Command of the National Army Relating to Guerrilla Warfare and Its Implementation during the War of Resistance), in Lü, *Zhanzheng de lishi yu jiyi* (War in History and Memory), 1:195–221.
7. See Pang Xianzhi, ed., *Mao Zedong nianpu, 1893–1949* (Chronological Biography of Mao Zedong, 1893–1949), 2:14–16 (Beijing: Renmin chubanshe/Zhongyang wenxian chubanshe, 2002); Stuart R. Schram, ed., *Mao's Road to Power: Revolutionary Writings 1912–1949,* 6:43, 51–52, 179–92, 319–90 (Armonk, NY: M. E. Sharpe, 1999).
8. See RGASPI, collection 146, inventory 2, file 3, sheets 64–66; Dimitrov, *Dnevnik,* 130. Emphasis in original.
9. Mao Zedong, *Mao Zedong wenji* (Works of Mao Zedong), 2:8–10 (Beijing: Renmin chubanshe, 1993).
10. See Teitler and Radtke, *A Dutch Spy in China,* 247–48.
11. Chiang, *The Collected Wartime Messages of Generalissimo Chiang Kai-shek 1937–1945,* 1:127–28.
12. Chiang, *Riji* (Diaries), November 13 and 15, 1938, Hoover Archives, box 40, folder 1.
13. See *Pravda* (Truth), May 6, 1935.
14. Quoted from Xie, *Jiang Jieshi de peidu suiyue* (Chiang Kai-shek's Sojourn in the Provisional Capital), 3.
15. Selle, *Donald of China,* 346.
16. John King Fairbank, *Chinabound: A Fifty-Year Memoir* (New York: Harper & Row, 1982), 202. See also Robert Payne, *Chiang Kai-shek* (New York: Weybright and Talley, 1969), 233–34.
17. See Zhang Jin, "'Xin du' yihuo 'jiu du': Kangzhan shiqi Chongqing de chengshi xingxiang" ("New Capital" or "Old Capital": The Urban Appearance of Chongqing

during the War of Resistance), in Lü, *Zhanzheng de lishi yu jiyi* (War in History and Memory), 3, 32.

18. Ibid., 37.
19. Martha Gellhorn, *Travels with Myself and Another* (New York: Dodd, Mead, 1978), 55.
20. Local inhabitants thought there were more than two million rats in the city—but who was counting them?
21. Quoted from Farmer, *Shanghai Harvest,* 206.
22. Gellhorn, *Travels with Myself and Another,* 26, 55. See also Theodore H. White, *In Search of History: A Personal Adventure* (New York: Harper & Row, 1978), 66–69.
23. Letter from Ernest Hemingway to Henry Morgenthau, Secretary of Treasury, July 30, 1941, in Henry Morgenthau Jr., *Morgenthau Diary (China),* 1:460 (Washington, DC: U.S. Government Printing Office, 1965).
24. Tao Yuanming, "Guiqiu lai xici" (Return Home), https://baike.baidu.com/item/%E5%BD%92%E5%8E%BB%E6%9D%A5%E5%85%AE%E8%BE%9E. Translated by Steven I. Levine.
25. See Payne, *Chiang Kai-shek,* 235.
26. Chennault, *Way of a Fighter,* 58.
27. See A. Pronin, "Sovetnik Chan Kaishi" (Chiang Kai-shek's Advisor), *Trud* (Labor), March 11, 2000; S. Maslov, "Drug sovetskoi razvedki" (A Friend of Soviet Intelligence Service), in V. N. Karpov, ed., *Rassekrecheno vneshnei razvedkoi* (Declassified by Foreign Intelligence Service) (Moscow: OLMA-PRESS, 2003), 6–48; S. Maslov, "Kak nashi s drugom Gitlera v rasvedku khodili" (How Our People Cooperated in Intelligence Work with a Friend of Hitler), *Komsomol'skaia pravda* (Communist Youth Truth), April 18, 2004; Jerrold Schechter and Leona Schechter, *Sacred Secrets: How Soviet Intelligence Operations Changed American History* (Washington, DC: Brassey's, 2002), 15.
28. See Tao Baichuan, ed., *Jiang zhuxi de shenghuo he shengguan* (Life and the Life Views of Chairman Chiang) (Chongqing: Zhong zhou chubanshe, 1944).
29. Payne, *Chiang Kai-shek,* 236.
30. See ibid., 234–38; Tong, *Chiang Kai-shek: Soldier and Statesman,* 2:582; Xie, *Jiang Jieshi de peidu suiyue* (Chiang Kai-shek's Sojourn in the Provisional Capital), 97–98, 102; Jiang, *The Reminiscences of Tsiang T'ing-fu (1895–1965),* 221.
31. See Xie, *Jiang Jieshi de peidu suiyue* (Chiang Kai-shek's Sojourn in the Provisional Capital), 99–100, 102; Farmer, *Shanghai Harvest,* 226–27; Lu [Lü] and Lin, "Chiang Kai-shek's Diaries and Republican China: New Insights on the History of Modern China," 337; Roger B. Jeans, ed., *The Marshall Mission to China, 1945–1947: The Letters and Diary of Colonel John Hart Caughey* (Lanham, MD: Rowman & Littlefield, 2011), 171.
32. Chiang, *Riji* (Diaries), December 9, 1938, Hoover Archives, box 40, folder 2; Lü, *Jiang Zhongzheng xiansheng nianpu changbian* (Large Chronological Biography of Mr. Jiang Zhongzheng), 5:643; Xie, *Jiang Jieshi de peidu suiyue* (Chiang Kai-shek's Sojourn in the Provisional Capital), 5–7.
33. Quoted from Wang, "Kangzhan chuqi de 'he' sheng" (Voice about "Peace" in the Initial Period of the War of Resistance), 152. See also Chiang, *Riji* (Diaries), December 9, 1938.
34. Quoted from Boyle, *China and Japan at War 1937–1945,* 209.

35. See *Lichnoe delo Kun Sian-si* (Personal File of Kong Xiangxi), RGASPI, collection 495, depository 225, file 40, sheets 7, 8, 11–13.
36. See Boyle, *China and Japan at War 1937–1945,* 166–93; Tikhvinsky, *Russko–kitaiskie otnosheniia v XX veke* (Russo–Chinese Relations in the Twentieth Century), vol. 4, book 1, 378–79.
37. Quoted from Wang, "Kangzhan chuqi de 'he' sheng" (Voice about "Peace" in the Initial Period of the War of Resistance), 154.
38. Chiang, *Riji* (Diaries), December 16, 1938, Hoover Archives, box 40, folder 2.
39. Jiang, *The Reminiscences of Tsiang T'ing-fu (1895–1965),* 223.
40. The loan was granted to cover the cost of exporting American agricultural and industrial goods to China and importing Chinese tung oil into the United States.
41. See Generalissimo Chiang Kai-shek, *Resistance and Reconstruction: Messages during China's Six Years of War 1937–1943,* 4th ed. (New York: Harper & Brothers, 1943), xvii; Young, *China and the Helping Hand 1937–1945,* 82; Michael Schaller, *The U.S. Crusade in China, 1938–1945* (New York: Columbia University Press, 1979), 28; Arthur N. Young, *China's Wartime Finance and Inflation 1937–1945* (Cambridge: Harvard University Press, 1965), 103.
42. Chiang, *Riji* (Diaries), December 17, 1938, Hoover Archives, box 40, folder 2.
43. Wang Jingwei's supporters were already conducting secret negotiations with the Japanese. Italy served as a go-between.
44. Quoted from Wang, "Wang Jingwei and the Policy Origins of the 'Peace Movement,' 1932–1937," 35.
45. See Gerald E. Bunker, *The Peace Conspiracy: Wang Ching-wei and the China War, 1937–1941* (Cambridge: Harvard University Press, 1972), 114–15; Tikhvinsky, *Russko–kitaiskie otnosheniia v XX veke* (Russo–Chinese Relations in the Twentieth Century), vol. 4, book 1, 379, 382–83.
46. Konoe Fumimaro, "Statement by the Japanese Prime Minister (Prince Konoye), December 22, 1938," https://history.state.gov/historicaldocuments/frus1931–41v01/d332.
47. Chiang, *Riji* (Diaries), December 16 and 21–31, 1938, Hoover Archives, box 40, folder 2.
48. Ibid., December 23 and 24, 1938, Hoover Archives, box 40, folder 2; Wang, "Kangzhan chuqi de 'he' sheng" (Voice about "Peace" in the Initial Period of the War of Resistance), 154.
49. See Boyle, *China and Japan at War 1937–1945,* 221–24.
50. See Chiang, *Riji* (Diaries), January 1, 1939, Hoover Archives, box 40, folder 4; Tikhvinsky, *Russko–kitaiskie otnosheniia v XX veke* (Russo–Chinese Relations in the Twentieth Century), vol. 4, book 1, 381, 383; Wang, "Kangzhan chuqi de 'he' sheng" (Voice about "Peace" in the Initial Period of the War of Resistance), 156.
51. See Tikhvinsky, *Russko–kitaiskie otnosheniia v XX veke* (Russo–Chinese Relations in the Twentieth Century), vol. 4, book 1, 383.
52. See ibid., 252, 322, 325, 371.
53. Chiang, *Riji* (Diaries), January 7, 1939, Hoover Archives, box 40, folder 4.
54. See Zhu Wenyuan et al., eds., *Zhonghua minguo jianguo bainian da shiji* (Large Chronology of the Republic of China for One Hundred Years from Its Founding), 1:358 (Taipei: Guoshiguan, 2012).

55. Ibid.
56. Stalin gave an order to liquidate Trotsky twice—in 1937 (the order was not executed) and then in March 1939, exactly the same time as Chiang did in regard to Wang Jingwei. See Pavel Sudoplatov and Anatoli Sudoplatov with Jerrold L. and Leona P. Schecter, *Special Tasks: The Memoirs of an Unwanted Witness: A Soviet Spymaster* (Boston: Little, Brown, 1994), 64, 67.
57. See Yang Tianshi, "Zai lun Long Yun he Wang Jingwei chutao shijian: qian shu Long Yun de huangyan yu liangmian xingwei" (Once More on Long Yun and Wang Jingwei's Fleeing the Country, or about the Lies and Duplicity of Long Yun), in Lü, *Zhanzheng de lishi yu jiyi* (War in History and Memory), 2:405; Boyle, *China and Japan at War 1937–1945,* 28–232; Wakeman Jr., *Spymaster,* 337–38; Tikhvinsky, *Russko–kitaiskie otnosheniia v XX veke* (Russo–Chinese Relations in the Twentieth Century), vol. 4, book 1, 427.
58. See Boyle, *China and Japan at War 1937–1945,* 232–37.
59. See White, *In Search of History,* 72.
60. See Zhang, "'Xin du' yihuo 'jiu du'" ("New Capital" or "Old Capital"), 47.
61. Farmer, *Shanghai Harvest,* 208.
62. See Zhang, "'Xin du' yihuo 'jiu du'" ("New Capital" or "Old Capital"), 48, 51–52; White, *In Search of History,* 71.
63. Tsui, *China's Conservative Revolution,* 1.
64. See White, *In Search of History,* 68; Violet Cressy-Marcks, *Journey into China* (New York: E. P. Dutton, 1942), 87.
65. Chiang, *Riji* (Diaries), January 20, 1938, Hoover Archives, box 39, folder 20. See also ibid., Miscellaneous, January 22, 1938, Hoover Archives, box 40, folder 2.
66. Ibid., Miscellaneous, November 9, 1940, Hoover Archives, box 40, folder 14.
67. Farmer, *Shanghai Harvest,* 230–31. See also Chiang, *Riji* (Diaries), May 4, 1939, Hoover Archives, box 40, folder 8.
68. See Zhang, "'Xin du' yihuo 'jiu du'" ("New Capital" or "Old Capital"), 33.
69. Quoted from Fenby, *Chiang Kai-shek,* 351.
70. See ibid., 353; V. I. Chuikov, *Missiia v Kitae: Zapiski voennogo sovetnika* (Mission in China: Notes of a Military Advisor) (Moscow: Nauka, 1981), 103.
71. See Tikhvinsky, *Russko–kitaiskie otnosheniia v XX veke* (Russo–Chinese Relations in the Twentieth Century), vol. 4, book 1, 393.
72. Ibid., 404.
73. Ibid., 411–13.
74. For Stalin's treatment of Mao during the latter's visit to the USSR in December 1949–February 1950, see Pantsov with Levine, *Mao,* 368–73.
75. See Tikhvinsky, *Russko–kitaiskie otnosheniia v XX veke* (Russo–Chinese Relations in the Twentieth Century), vol. 2, book 1, 424–25, 426, 428, 430, 432 436–40.
76. Ibid., 432.
77. The author's interview with L. M. Kosheleva, a staff member of the Russian State Archives of Social and Political History, in Moscow, October 10, 2017.
78. See Tikhvinsky, *Russko–kitaiskie otnosheniia v XX veke* (Russo–Chinese Relations in the Twentieth Century), vol. 4, book 1, 446–47.

79. For brief reminiscences of this meeting, see S. L. Tikhvinsky, *Kitai v moei zhizni (30–90 gg.)* (China in My Life [1930s–1990s]) (Moscow: Nauka, 1992), 16–17; S. L. Tikhvinsky, *Vozvrashchenie k "Vorotam nebesnogo spokoistviia"* (Return to "the Gates of Heavenly Peace") (Moscow: "Pamiatniki istoricheskoi mysli," 2002), 38–40. For Stalin taking away Tikhvinsky's notepad, see V. V. Sokolov, "Dve vstrechi Sun Fo s I. V. Stalinym v 1938–1939 gg." (Sun Fo's Two Meetings with Stalin in 1938–1939), *Novaia i noveishaia istoriia,* no. 6 (1999): 24.
80. Tikhvinsky, *Russko–kitaiskie otnosheniia v XX veke* (Russo–Chinese Relations in the Twentieth Century), vol. 4, book 1, 447.
81. Ibid., 440.
82. See Sladkovsky, *Noveishaia istoriia Kitaia 1928–1949* (Contemporary History of China 1928–1949), 195.
83. See Tikhvinsky, *Russko–kitaiskie otnosheniia v XX veke* (Russo–Chinese Relations in the Twentieth Century), vol. 4, book 1, 378, 385–86, 409; book 2, 602.
84. See Liu, *Guomindang kaichu dangji xianxiang shulun* (Brief Essay on the Phenomenon of Guomindang Expulsion from the Party), 46.
85. See A. V. Pantsov, "Obrazovanie opornykh baz 8-i Natsional'no-revoliutsionnoi armii v tylu iaponskikh voisk v Severnom Kitae" (Establishment of Eighth Route Army Base Areas in the Japanese Rear in North China), in M. F. Yuriev, ed., *Voprosy istorii Kitaia* (Problems of Chinese History) (Moscow: Izdatel'stvo MGU, 1981), 41–48.
86. See Tikhvinsky, *Russko–kitaiskie otnosheniia v XX veke* (Russo–Chinese Relations in the Twentieth Century), vol. 4, book 1, 581.
87. See Mlechin, *Istoriia vneshnei razvedki* (The History of Foreign Intelligence), 400–407.
88. See Tikhvinsky, *Russko–kitaiskie otnosheniia v XX veke* (Russo–Chinese Relations in the Twentieth Century), vol. 4, book 1, 451–61; book 2, 611.
89. See Mlechin, *Istoriia vneshnei razvedki* (The History of Foreign Intelligence), 124.
90. See "Posetiteli kremlevskogo kabineta I. V. Stalina: Zhurnaly (tetradi) zapisi lits, priniatykh pervym gensekom: 1924–1953: Alfavitnyi ukazatel" (Visitors to the Kremlin Office of J. V. Stalin: Journals [Notebooks] Entries of Persons Received by the First General Secretary: 1924–1953: An Alphabetic Guide), *Istoricheskii Arkhiv* (Historical Archive), no. 4 (1998): 138.
91. A. S. Paniushkin, *Zapiski posla: Kitai 1939–1944 gg.* (Notes of an Ambassador: China 1939–1944) (Moscow: IDV AN SSSR, 1981), 3.
92. See Sladkovsky, *Noveishaia istoriia Kitaia 1928–1949* (Contemporary History of China 1928–1949), 195.
93. Tikhvinsky, *Russko–kitaiskie otnosheniia v XX veke* (Russo–Chinese Relations in the Twentieth Century), vol. 4, book 1, 477.
94. Ibid., 610.
95. Ibid., 567; Sladkovsky, *Noveishaia istoriia Kitaia 1928–1949* (Contemporary History of China 1928–1949), 190.
96. See Sven Steenberg, *Vlasov* (New York: Knopf, 1970), 9–11; Catherine Andreyev, *Vlasov and the Russian Liberation Movement: Soviet Reality and Émigré Theories* (Cambridge: Cambridge University Press, 1987), 21.

97. See Lü Fangshang, *Jiang Zhongzheng xiansheng nianpu changbian* (Large Chronological Biography of Mr. Jiang Zhongzheng), 6:47 (Taipei: Guoshiguan, 2014).
98. The secret protocol established in part a new Soviet–German border by dividing Poland and the Baltic states in the event of war between Germany and the USSR with these countries.
99. Chiang, *Riji* (Diaries), August 23 and 24, 1939, Hoover Archives, box 40, folder 11; Tikhvinsky, *Russko–kitaiskie otnosheniia v XX veke* (Russo–Chinese Relations in the Twentieth Century), vol. 4, book 1, 480, 482, 484, 489.
100. Chiang, *Riji* (Diaries), August 25, 1939, Hoover Archives, box 40, folder 11; Tikhvinsky, *Russko–kitaiskie otnosheniia v XX veke* (Russo–Chinese Relations in the Twentieth Century), vol. 4, book 1, 485–88, 490, 494; Paniushkin, *Zapiski posla* (Notes of an Ambassador), 8–9.
101. Paniushkin, *Zapiski posla* (Notes of an Ambassador), 8. Paniushkin incorrectly gives the date of the dinner as August 26.
102. Tikhvinsky, *Russko-kitaiskie otnosheniia v XX veke* (Russo-Chinese Relations in the Twentieth Century), vol. 4, book 1, 499.
103. Ibid., 498.
104. Zhou Enlai in October 1939 said the same to a Comintrern representative: "In China they consider Germany and the Soviet Union to be aggressive towards Poland." Quoted from Elizaveta Kishkina, *Iz Rossii v Kitai: Put' dlinnoiu v sto let: Memuary* (From Russia to China: A One-Hundred-Year Path: Memoirs) (Moscow: OOO Mezhdunarodnaia izdatel'skaia kompaniia "Shans," 2018), 205.
105. Tikhvinsky, *Russko-kitaiskie otnosheniia v XX veke* (Russo-Chinese Relations in the Twentieth Century), vol. 4, book 1, 504.
106. The Curzon Line was the Soviet–Polish border presented to the Bolshevik government by the British Minister of Foreign Affairs Lord George Nathaniel Curzon in the name of the Entente on July 10, 1920. It ran from Grodno via Brest to the Carpathians west of Lvov. The Soviet–German border of 1939 diverged toward the west of the Curzon Line only in the region of Belostok (Białystok) which was under Soviet occupation.
107. Regarding an agreement with Japan, Chiang had in mind the signing of an armistice between the USSR and Japan following the conflict in the region of the Khalkin-Gol River (Mongolian People's Republic) in May–September 1939. Chiang had calculated that this conflict would lead to a Japanese–Soviet war, but it was settled September 15 (16).
108. Chiang, *Riji* (Diaries), September 17, 1939, Hoover Archives, box 40, folder 12.
109. Tikhvinsky, *Russko-kitaiskie otnoshniia v XX veke* (Russo-Chinese Relations in the Twentieth Century), vol. 4, book 1, 521.
110. Chiang, *Riji* (Diaries), September 17, 1939.
111. See ibid., November 13, 1939, Hoover Archives, box 40, folder 14; Tikhvinsky, *Russko–kitaiskie otnosheniia v XX veke* (Russo–Chinese Relations in the Twentieth Century), vol. 4, book 1, 501, 529, 535, 538, 550, 561.
112. See Geoffrey Roberts, *The Soviet Union and the Origins of the Second World War: Russo–German Relations and the Road to War, 1933–1941* (New York: St. Martin's Press, 1995), 113.

113. See Garver, *Chinese–Soviet Relations 1937–1945,* 99–100.
114. Tikhvinsky, *Russko–kitaiskie otnosheniia v XX veke* (Russo–Chinese Relations in the Twentieth Century), vol. 4, book 1, 556, 556.
115. See Ch'i, *Nationalist China at War,* 59.
116. See Sladkovsky, *Noveishaia istoriia Kitaia 1928–1949* (Contemporary History of China 1929–1949), 196; Van de Ven, *War and Nationalism in China 1925–1945,* 241.
117. See Pantsov with Levine, *Deng Xiaoping,* 112; Tikhvinsky, *Russko-kitaiskie otnosheniia v XX veke* (Russo-Chinese Relations in the Twentieth Century), vol. 4, book 1, 579.
118. See Yuan Tengyu (Endo Homare), *Mao Zedong goujie rijun de zhenxiang: lai zi ri die de huiyi yu dang'an* (The True Story of Mao Zedong's Secret Collaboration with the Japanese Army: From the Memoirs of Japanese Spies and Archives) (Deer Park, NY: Mingjing chubanshe, 2016).
119. See Chiang, *Riji* (Diaries), December 13, 1939, Hoover Archives, box 40, folder 15.
120. See Cui, *Qingnian Jiang Jieshi* (Young Chiang Kai-shek), 63–66.
121. See Ch'i, *Nationalist China at War,* 53–63; Hsiung, *The Life of Chiang Kai-shek,* 341; Van de Ven, *War and Nationalism in China 1925–1945,* 234–46.
122. They did this right up until August 1943, when defeats in the war in the Pacific drew their attention away from Chongqing.
123. See Zhang, "'Xin du' yihuo 'jiu du'" ("New Capital" or "Old Capital"), 33.
124. See Sladkovsky, *Noveishaia istoria Kitaia 1928–1949* (Contemporary History of China 1928–1949), 197.
125. See Jin, *Zhou Enlai zhuan (1898–1976)* (Biography of Zhou Enlai [1898–1976]), 1:518–33.
126. See Tikhvinsky, *Russko–kitaiskie otnoshenii v XX veke* (Russo–Chinese Relations in the Twentieth Century), vol. 4, book 1, 599–602.
127. See Garver, *Chinese–Soviet Relations 1937–1945,* 103–4.
128. Liu Zerong (also known as Liu Shaozhou, 1892–1970) was rather well known in the USSR. He spent his childhood and youth in Russia, where his father was a successful tea merchant, and graduated from the St. Petersburg Polytechnic Institute prior to the February Revolution of 1917. Subsequently, he headed the Union of Chinese Emigrants for three years in Russia, and, in 1919 and 1920, on the invitation of the People's Commissariat for Foreign Affairs, he took part in the First and Second Congresses of the Comintern as a nonvoting representative. He was acquainted with many Bolshevik leaders, including Lenin.
129. Shao Lizi, Chiang's former secretary, came to the USSR as the new Chinese ambassador on June 7, 1940. He replaced Yang Jie, who retired because of disagreements with Chiang about the Soviet–Finnish war. Nine years later, in Hong Kong, General Yang was assassinated.
130. Tikhvinsky, *Russko–kitaiskie otnosheniia v XX veke* (Russo–Chinese Relations in the Twentieth Century), vol. 4, book 1, 617. For Shao Lizi's sojourn in Moscow, see his memoirs: Shao Lizi, "Chushi Sulian de huiyi" (Memoirs of My Mission as an Ambassador in the Soviet Union), *Wenshi ziliao xuanji* (Selected Documents of Literature and History), no. 60 (1979): 181–94.
131. Chiang, *Riji* (Diaries), September 4, 1940, Hoover Archives, box 40, folder 25.

132. Quoted from Selle, *Donald of China,* 349.
133. Chiang, *Riji* (Diaries), June 30, August 8, and September 1, 1932, Hoover Archives, box 36, folders 6, 8, 9.
134. Quoted from Utley, *China at War,* 198.
135. Gellhorn, *Travels with Myself and Another,* 56.
136. Owen Lattimore and Fujiko Isono, *China Memoirs: Chiang Kai-shek and the War against Japan* (Tokyo: University of Tokyo Press, 1990), 142.
137. See Edwin Pak-wah Leung, ed., *Political Leaders of Modern China: A Biographic Dictionary* (Westport, CT: Greenwood Press, 2002), 78.
138. See John Ritchie, ed., *Australian Dictionary of Biography,* 8:317–18 (Carton, Victoria: Melbourne University, 1981).
139. Chennault, *Way of a Fighter,* 34.
140. Confucius, *The Analects of Confucius,* 29.

## 17. *AVE MARIA*

1. Chiang, *Riji* (Diaries), January 4, 1940, Hoover Archives, box 40, folder 17. See also ibid., March 1940, Hoover Archives, box 40, folder 19.
2. See Tuchman, *Stilwell and the American Experience in China, 1911–45,* 206.
3. See E. Eastman Irvine, ed., *The World Almanac and the Book of Facts for 1940* (New York: New York World-Telegram, 1940), 849; "The National WWII Museum: New Orleans," https://www.nationalww2museum.org/students-teachers/student-resources/research-starters/research-starters-us-military-numbers.
4. Quoted from Tuchman, *Stilwell and the American Experience in China, 1911–45,* 207.
5. Joseph C. Grew, *Turbulent Era: A Diplomatic Record of Forty Years, 1904–1945,* 2:1209 (Boston: Houghton Mifflin, 1952).
6. Chiang, *Riji* (Diaries), March 3, 1940, Hoover Archives, box 40, folder 19.
7. See Van de Ven, *War and Nationalism in China 1925–1945,* 233; Chiang, *Resistance and Reconstruction,* xix; Schaller, *The U.S. Crusade in China, 1938–1945,* 32–33.
8. For more details, see Lin Hsiao-ting, "Reassessing Wartime U.S.–China Relations: Leadership, Foreign Aid, and Domestic Politics, 1937–1945," *NIDS Military History Studies Annual,* no. 16 (2013): 121–38; Tai-chun Kuo and Hsiao-ting Lin, *T. V. Soong in Modern Chinese History: A Look at His Role in Sino-American Relations in World War II* (Stanford: Stanford University Press, 2006), 5–10; Tai-chun Kuo, "A Strong Diplomat in a Weak Polity: T. V. Soong and Wartime US–China Relations, 1940–1943," *Journal of Contemporary China,* no. 18 (29) (March 2009): 219–31.
9. Quoted from Kuo, "A Strong Diplomat in a Weak Polity," 220.
10. Quoted from Young, *China and the Helping Hand 1937–1945,* 135. See also *FRUS 1940,* 4:429–30 (Washington, DC: U.S. Government Printing Office, 1955).
11. Quoted from Tuchman, *Stilwell and the American Experience in China, 1911–45,* 214.
12. See Franklin D. Roosevelt, *The Public Papers and Addresses of Franklin D. Roosevelt with a Special Introduction and Explanatory Notes by President Roosevelt: 1940 Vol.* (New York: Random House, 1941), 587; Chiang, *Resistance and Reconstruction,* xx; Schaller, *The U.S. Crusade in China, 1938–1945,* 36–37; Young, *China's Wartime Finance and Inflation, 1937–1945,* 105.

13. See Chennault, *Way of a Fighter,* 3–52.
14. Ibid., 35.
15. DeLong, *Madame Chiang Kai-shek and Miss Emma Mills,* 102; Joseph W. Alsop with Adam Platt, *"I've Seen the Best of It": Memoirs* (New York: W. W. Norton, 1992), 147.
16. See Young, *China and the Helping Hand 1937–1945,* 141.
17. Robert P. Newman, *Owen Lattimore and the "Loss" of China* (Berkeley: University of California Press, 1992), 66.
18. See Elliot Roosevelt, *As He Saw It* (Westport, CT: Greenwood Press, 1974), 158; Stilwell, *The Stilwell Papers,* 251; Roger J. Sandilands, *The Life and Political Economy of Lauchlin Currie: New Dealer, Presidential Adviser, and Development Economist* (Durham: Duke University Press, 1990), 108–9; Robert Dallek, *Franklin D. Roosevelt and American Foreign Policy, 1932–1945* (New York: Oxford University Press, 1995), 29.
19. See Sandilands, *The Life and Political Economy of Lauchlin Currie,* 107–12; Newman, *Owen Lattimore and the "Loss" of China,* 56; Tyson Li, *Madame Chiang Kai-shek,* 162.
20. See Chuikov, *Missiia v Kitae* (Mission to China), 85, 86, 88, 90.
21. Quoted from *United States Relations with China: With Special Reference to the Period 1944–1949* (New York: Greenwood Press, 1968), 26.
22. See Young, *China and the Helping Hand 1937–1945,* 142–43.
23. See ibid., 144; *United States Relations with China,* 26; T. V. Soong Papers, Hoover Archives, box 34, folder 34.
24. See Young, *China and the Helping Hand 1937–1945,* 137.
25. See Tikhvinsky, *Russko–kitaiskie otnoshenii v XX veke* (Russo–Chinese Relations in the Twentieth Century), vol. 4, book 1, 626; Garver, *Chinese–Soviet Relations 1937–1945,* 38.
26. Tikhvinsky, *Russko–kitaiskie otnosheniia v XX veke* (Russo–Chinese Relations in the Twentieth Century), vol. 4, book 1, 624, 626; See also Sladkovsky, *Noveishaia istoriia Kitaia 1928–1949* (Contemporary History of China 1929–1949), 198.
27. Tikhvinsky, *Russko–kitaiskie otnoshniia v XX veke* (Russo–Chinese Relations in the Twentieth Century), vol. 4, book 1, 627.
28. Ibid., 628.
29. See Sladkovsky, *Noveishaia istoriia Kitaia 1928–1949* (Contemporary History of China 1929–1949), 201.
30. Chiang, *Riji* (Diaries), January 25, 1941, Hoover Archives, box 41, folder 7.
31. Military attaché Chuikov replaced Kachanov in the post of chief military advisor.
32. Tikhvinsky, *Russko–kitaiskie otnosheniia v XX veke* (Russo–Chinese Relations in the Twentieth Century), vol. 4, book 1, 635.
33. See Chennault, *Way of a Fighter,* 100.
34. See Young, *China and the Helping Hand 1937–1945,* 149–50.
35. For the text of the pact and the declaration, see B. N. Slavinsky, *Pakt o neitralitete mezhdu SSSR i Iaponiei: Diplomaticheskaia istoriia, 1941–1945* (The Pact on Neutrality between the USSR and Japan: A Diplomatic History, 1941–1945) (Moscow: TOO "Novina," 1995), 102, 104; for an English translation, see Boris Slavinsky, *The Japanese–Soviet Neutrality Pact: A Diplomatic History, 1941–1945,* trans. Geoffrey Jukes (London: RoutledgeCurzon, 2004), 55–56.

36. Chiang, *Soviet Russia in China,* 96.
37. Quoted from Yu. Fel'shtinsky, ed., *Oglasheniyu podlezhit: SSSR-Germaniia, 1939–1941: Dokumenty i materialy* (Must Be Announced: The USSR and Germany, 1939–1941: Documents and Materials) (Moscow: Moskovskii rabochii, 1991), 318. See also A. Pantsov, "Pochemy Iaponiia ne napala na Sovetskii Soiuz?" (Why Did Japan Not Attack the Soviet Union?), https://echo.msk.ru/programs/victory/560650-echo/; Chuikov, *Missiia v Kitae* (Mission to China), 123.
38. Axis Powers—from the term the Berlin–Rome Axis—the military alliance between Italy and Germany to which Japan and several other profascist states later joined.
39. Fel'shtinsky, *Oglasheniyu podlezhit* (Must Be Announced), 318.
40. See Jeffrey Meyers, *Hemingway: A Biography* (New York: Harper & Row, 1985), 356–57; James M. Hutchisson, *Ernest Hemingway: A New Life* (University Park: Pennsylvania State University Press, 2016), 176; Peter Moreira, *Hemingway on the China Front: His WWII Spy Mission with Martha Gellhorn* (Washington, DC: Potomac Books, 2006), 14–15. Moreira mistakenly cites April 14 as the date when the Chiang couple met with the Hemingway couple.
41. Gellhorn, *Travels with Myself and Another,* 57–58; Chiang, *Riji* (Diaries), April 13, 1941, Hoover Archives, box 41, folder 10; letter from Ernest Hemingway to Henry Morgenthau, Secretary of Treasury, July 30, 1941, 460–61.
42. In fact, the neutrality pact was signed at 2:45 p.m.
43. Chiang, *Riji* (Diaries), April 13, 1941.
44. Tikhvinsky, *Russko-kitaiskie otnosheniia v XX veke* (Russo–Chinese Relations in the Twentieth Century), vol. 4, book 1, 646.
45. See *FRUS 1941,* vol. 4 (Washington, DC: U.S. Government Printing Office, 1956), 187; Schechter and Schechter, *Sacred Secrets, 16.*
46. Chiang, *Riji* (Diaries), June 24, 1941, Hoover Archives, box 41, folder 12.
47. See Tikhvinsky, *Russko–kitaiskie otnosheniia v XX veke* (Russo–Chinese Relations in the Twentieth Century), vol. 4, book 1, 648; Liang, *The Sino-German Connection,* 165.
48. *FRUS 1941,* vol. 5 (Washington, DC: U.S. Government Printing Office, 1941), 480.
49. Chiang, *Riji* (Diaries), June 23, 1941, Hoover Archives, box 41, folder 12.
50. Quoted from White, *In Search of History,* 116. Two months earlier one of the Guomindang officials said the same thing to Hemingway. See letter from Ernest Hemingway to Henry Morgenthau, Secretary of Treasury, July 30, 1941, 458. On Chiang's usage of the words "a disease of the heart and a disease of the skin," see also Shao-kang Chu, "Chiang Kai-shek's Position on Resisting Japan: An Analysis of 'Domestic Stability Takes Precedence Over Resisting Foreign Invasion' Policy, 1928–1936" (PhD diss., University of British Columbia, 1999), 202–4.
51. RGASPI, collection 17, inventory 162, file 36, sheet 41.
52. See Tikhvinsky, *Russko-kitaiskie otnosheniia v XX veke* (Russo–Chinese Relations in the Twentieth Century), vol. 4, book 1, 241; Dallin and Firsov, *Dimitrov and Stalin 1934–1943,* 142–44: Firsov, *Sekretnye kody istorii Kominterna 1919–1943* (Secret Codes in the History of the Comintern 1919–1943), 374.
53. "Telegram from Chiang Kai-shek to T. V. Song of January 28, 1942," in T. V. Soong Papers, Hoover Archives, box 36, folder 1.

54. See Garver, *Chinese–Soviet Relations 1937–1945*, 108.
55. See *United States Relations with China*, 26; *FRUS 1941*, 5:635–36, 642.
56. See Young, *China and the Helping Hand 1937–1945*, 147.
57. See Chennault, *Way of a Fighter*, 100–104, 111; Young, *China and the Helping Hand 1937–1945*, 149–50; Charles R. Bond Jr. and Terry A. Anderson, *A Flying Tiger's Diary* (College Station: Texas A&M University Press, 1984), 18.
58. Chennault, *Way of a Fighter*, 106.
59. Ibid., 135–36.
60. In April 1942 the AVG would be folded into the newly formed Fourteenth Air Force of the United States, which would operate in China and Burma. Chennault would return to active military duty, and he was appointed its commander. In March 1943 he would be named major general.
61. See Lattimore and Isono, *China Memoirs*, 101.
62. See ibid., 56–63.
63. See ibid., 3–7, 75–151; Newman, *Owen Lattimore and the "Loss" of China*, 57–83.
64. See Charles F. Romanus and Riley Sunderland, *Stilwell's Mission to China* (Washington, DC: Office of the Chief of Military History, Department of the Army, 1953), 28–29, 31–32, 41–49; William G. Grieve, *The American Military Mission to China, 1941–1942: Lend-Lease Logistics, Politics and the Tangles of Wartime Cooperation* (Jefferson, NC: McFarland, 2014).
65. Lattimore and Isono, *China Memoirs*, 135, 136, 138.
66. Ibid., 143.
67. See ibid., 138–39.
68. About thirty Chinese students and cadets left Germany along with him, including Kong Xiangxi's son Louis, who set off for Scotland.
69. See Liang, *The Sino–German Connection*, 160.
70. See Wang, *Qianshan duxing* (The Solitary Path among a Thousand Mountains), 76–78; Chiang and Liu, *Jiang Weiguo koushu zizhuan* (The Autobiography of Chiang Wei-kuo as Told by Himself), 64–67.
71. Chiang, *Riji* (Diaries), October 27 and November 9, 1941, Hoover Archives, box 40, folders 26 and 27.
72. See John Gunther, *Inside Asia* (New York: Harper & Brothers, 1939), 199.
73. Chiang, *Riji* (Diaries), November 3, 1941, Hoover Archives, box 40, folder 27. See also Wang, *Qianshan duxing* (The Solitary Path among a Thousand Mountains), 81–84.
74. Chiang, *Riji* (Diaries), October 31, 1940, Hoover Archives, box 40, folder 26.
75. Ibid., November 17, 1940, Hoover Archives, box 40, folder 27.
76. "Pis'mo Fainy Vakhrevoi svoei sestre Anne: oktiabr' 1938" (Faina Vakhreva's Letter to Her Sister Anna of October 1938), in Galitsky, *Tszian Tszingo* (Chiang Ching-kuo), 147–49.
77. See Li Songlin and Chen Taixian, *Jiang Jingguo da zhuan 1910–1988* (Large Biography of Chiang Ching-kuo 1910–1988), 1:61 (Beijing: Tuanjie chubanshe, 2011).
78. See Harrison Forman, "Gissimo Junior," *Collier's*, July 31, 1943, 61–62; Jiang, *The Reminiscences of Tsiang T'ing-fu (1895–1965)*, 214; Xu Haoran, *Jiang Jingguo zai Gan'nan* (Chiang Ching-kuo in Southern Jiangxi) (Taipei: Xinchao she, 1993).

79. See “P’is’mo Fainy Vakhrevoi svoei sestre Anne: 3 marta 1943” (Faina Vakhreva’s Letter to Her Sister Anna of March 3, 1943), in Galitsky, *Tszian Tszingo* (Chiang Ching-kuo), 152–53.
80. Chiang, *Riji* (Diaries), April 23, May 7, and September 20, 1941, Hoover Archives, box 41, folders 10, 11 and 15.
81. Ibid., December 7 and 24, 1940, Hoover Archives, box 40, folder 28; Wang, *Qianshan duxing* (The Solitary Path among a Thousand Mountains), 81–95, 97.
82. Quoted from DeLong, *Madame Chiang Kai-shek and Miss Emma Mills,* 134.
83. See Selle, *Donald of China,* 340.
84. See DeLong, *Madame Chiang Kai-shek and Miss Emma Mills,* 142–43.
85. Chiang, *Riji* (Diaries), October 6, 15, and 31, 1940, Hoover Archives, box 40, folder 26.
86. See Yang, *Zhaoxun zhenshi de Jiang Jieshi* (In Search of the True Chang Kai-shek) (Chongqing), 1:475–85.
87. DeLong, *Madame Chiang Kai-shek and Miss Emma Mills,* 144. Emphasis added by Meiling.
88. See Tyson Li, *Madame Chiang Kai-shek,* 165.
89. Chiang, *Riji* (Diaries), August 22, 1932, Hoover Archives, box 36, folder 8.
90. Ibid., November 9, 30, December 28, 1940, January 13, 26, 30, 31, February 4, 12, 23–25, March 6, 9, 27 and 29, 1941, Hoover Archives, box 40, folder 27; box 40, folder 28; box 41, folder 7; box 41, folder 8; box 41, folder 9.
91. Ibid., March 31, 1941, Hoover Archives, box 41, folder 9.
92. Quoted from Wang, *Qianshan duxing* (The Solitary Path among a Thousand Mountains), 85–86.
93. Warren F. Kimball, ed., *Churchill & Roosevelt: The Complete Correspondence,* 1:277–78 (Princeton: Princeton University Press, 1984).
94. *FRUS 1941,* 4:651–52. See also Lattimore and Isono, *China Memoirs,* 158–59; “Telegram from Chiang Kai-shek to T. V. Song of November 25, 1941,” in T. V. Soong Papers, Hoover Archives, box 34, folder 34.
95. Chiang, *Riji* (Diaries), December 8, 1941; Lü, *Jiang Zhongzheng xiansheng nianpu changbian* (Large Chronological Biography of Mr. Jiang Zhongzheng), 6:675; Brian Crozier with Eric Chou, *The Man Who Lost China: The First Full Biography of Chiang Kai-shek* (New York: Charles Scribner’s Sons, 1976), 228; Jean Edward Smith, *FDR* (New York: Random House, 2007), 534–36.
96. See *FRUS 1941,* 4:733.

## 18. *PLAYING WITH ROOSEVELT*

1. See Zhang, *Wusheng de yaojiao* (Silent Key Point), 272.
2. The British ambassador was not in Chongqing then; he received the proposal the next day.
3. Chiang, *Riji* (Diaries), December 8, 1941, Hoover Archives, box 41, folder 18; *FRUS 1941,* 4:736–40; “Telegrams from Chiang Kai-shek to T. V. Song, December 8 and 10, 1941,” in T. V. Soong Papers, Hoover Archives, box 34, folder 34.
4. See Chuikov, *Missiia v Kitae,* 238, 250; Romanus and Sunderland, *Stilwell’s Mission to China,* 35.

5. Lattimore and Isono, *China Memoirs,* 143.
6. Chiang, *Riji* (Diaries), December 10, 1941, Hoover Archives, box 41, folder 18.
7. See Susan Butler, ed., *My Dear Mr. Stalin: The Complete Correspondence between Franklin D. Roosevelt and Joseph V. Stalin* (New Haven: Yale University Press, 2005), 55; "Telegram from Chiang Kai-shek to T. V. Song of December 20, 1941," in T. V. Soong Papers, Hoover Archives, box 34, folder 34.
8. Quoted from Furuya, *Chiang Kai-shek,* 721. See also Lü, *Jiang Zhongzheng xiansheng nianpu changbian* (Large Chronological Biography of Mr. Jiang Zhongzheng), 6:690. Chiang Kai-shek's future chief of allied staff, the American general Joseph W. Stilwell, learning of this, wrote in his diary, "He [Wavell] didn't want the dirty Chinese in Burma." Stilwell, *The Stilwell Papers,* 31. Later, Wavell explained his position to Churchill: "Obviously better to defend Burma with Imperial troops than with Chinese, and the Governor particularly asked me not to accept more Chinese for Burma than absolutely necessary." Quoted from Van de Ven, *War and Nationalism in China 1925–1945,* 29–30.
9. Thereafter, the Chiang's government forced *Impartial Daily* "to correct" this editorial. See L. Sophia Wang, "The Independent Press and Authoritarian Regimes: The Case of the Dagong bao in Republican China," *Pacific Affairs* 67, no. 2 (Summer 1994): 237.
10. See Xie, *Jiang Jieshi de peidu suiyue* (Chiang Kai-shek's Sojourn in the Provisional Capital), 101.
11. See Furuya, *Chiang Kai-shek,* 722.
12. See Chiang, *Riji* (Diaries), late January 1942, Hoover Archives, box 42, folder 6.
13. As noted above, he passionately hated the British ever since June 1925, when more than fifty Chinese who were taking part in an anti-imperialist demonstration at a bridge to the Anglo–French Concession in Shamian in Canton—including twenty cadets from the Whampoa Academy—fell, mortally wounded by the bullets of English soldiers.
14. Chiang had asked for one hundred million but accepted half.
15. See Young, *China's Wartime Finance and Inflation, 1937–1945,* 112–13; Young, *China and the Helping Hand 1937–1945,* 441–42.
16. The next day Chiang wrote in his diary, "After the meeting with Mr. Gandhi yesterday, I was not disappointed in his position. It may be due to my excessive enthusiasm." Chiang, *Riji* (Diaries), February 19, 1942, Hoover Archives, box 42, folder 7. Four months later, in a letter to Chiang, Gandhi explained his position: "I am anxious to explain to you that my appeal to the British power to withdraw from India is not meant in any shape or form to weaken India's defense against the Japanese." But he stressed that India would not be able to support China actively unless the British power "end immediately the unnatural connection between Britain and India." Mahatma Gandhi, *Non-violence in Peace & War,* 1:424, 426 (Ahmendabad: Navajivan Publishing House, 1948).
17. Chiang Kai-shek, *The Collected Wartime Messages of Generalissimo Chiang Kai-shek 1937–1945,* 2:668 (New York: John Day, 1946); T. V. Soong Papers, Hoover Archives, box 36, folder 1. See also Chiang, *Riji* (Diaries), February 5–28, 1941, Hoover Archives, box 42, folder 7; Qin Xiaoyi, ed., *Zongtong Jiang gong dashiji changbian chugao* (First

Draft of Large Chronological Biography of Mr. President Chiang), 5:1862–65 (Taipei: Zhongzheng wenjiao jijinhui chubanshe, 1978).

18. "Telegram from Chiang Kai-shek to T. V. Song of March 15, 1942," in T. V. Soong Papers, Hoover Archives, box 34, folder 34. See also "Telegram from Chiang Kai-shek to T. V. Song of June 22, 1942," in ibid., T. V. Soong Papers, Hoover Archives, box 36, folder 1.
19. See Qin, *Zongtong Jiang gong dashiji changbian chugao* (First Draft of Large Chronological Biography of Mr. President Chiang), 5:1869–72.
20. In addition to his difficult character, Stilwell had one other defect: he was almost blind. During the First World War an explosive burst seriously injured his left eye, to such a degree that he could not see the fingers of his hands at a distance of three feet. His right eye was also extremely nearsighted, so Stilwell had to wear glasses all the time. Chiang's military advisors from the United States were unusual: one was almost deaf (Chennault), the other was almost blind (Stilwell). However, both played outstanding roles in the anti-Japanese war.
21. Quoted from Tuchman, *Stilwell and the American Experience in China, 1911–45,* 153.
22. Stilwell, *The Stilwell Papers,* 49.
23. Quoted from Dorn, *Walkout with Stilwell in Burma,* 23.
24. Quoted from Romanus and Sunderland, *Stilwell's Mission to China,* 84–85.
25. G-mo—abbreviation from Generalissimo.
26. Stilwell was mistaken. In 1860–64 the Englishman Charles George Gordon (1833–85) commanded the Imperial Chinese "Ever Victorious Army" in battles against the Taipings.
27. Stilwell, *The Stilwell Papers,* 50–51, 55–56.
28. See Frank Dorn, *Walkout with Stilwell in Burma* (New York: Thomas Y. Crowell, 1971), 47–48; Alsop with Platt, "I've Seen the Best of It," 162.
29. Damao and Xiaomao also mean "Big Hairy One" and "Small Hairy One." These epithets are meant very affectionately; many in China name their newborn children after the soft, downy hair on their heads.
30. In the early 2000s Xiaoyan, who had been collecting materials about his mother for many years, would affirm that his father informed Chiang not about his and his brother's birth, but that their mother was pregnant, moreover, at the latter's request. In his words this occurred not in March 1942 but in October 1941. Ching-kuo indeed visited his father in October and early November 1941, but it is doubtful he informed him of Yaruo at that time. It is even more doubtful that Yaruo requested he do this. She became pregnant in August 1941, and had Chiang wanted, in October she could still have had an abortion. Why would she and Ching-kuo take such a risk? And it is quite improbable that in October 1941 Chiang would give the future twins names (as Jiang Xiaoyan also insisted, he had). How could he possibly have known that Yaruo would give birth to two boys?
31. See Chiang, *Riji* (Diaries), March 27, 1942, Hoover Archives, box 42, folder 8; Mao Jiaqi, *Jiang Jingguo de yisheng he ta de sixiang yanbian* (The Life of Chiang Ching-kuo and the Evolution of His Views) (Taipei: Taiwan shangwu yinshuguan, 2003), 102; Taylor, *The Generalissimo's Son,* 107.

32. See Zhang Su, "Jiang Jingguo yu Zhang Yaruo" (Chiang Ching-kuo and Zhang Yaruo), in Zhengxie Jiangxi sheng weiyuanhui, Zhengxie Ganzhou shi weiyuanhui wenshi ziliao yanjiu weiyuanhui, eds., *Jiang Jingguo zai Gan'nan* (Chiang Ching-kuo in Southern Jiangxi) (Nanchang: Zhengxie Jiangxi sheng weiyuanhui, Zhengxie Ganzhou shi weiyuanhui wenshi ziliao yanjiu weiyuanhui, 1989), 349.
33. Vladimir Mayakovsky, "The Cloud in Trousers," in Vladimir Mayakovsky, *The Bedbug and Selected Poetry,* trans. Max Hayward and George Reavey (Cleveland: Meridian Books, 1960), 65.
34. See Jiang Xiaoyan, *Jiang jia men wai de haizi* (The Children Behind the Gates of the Chiang House), 3rd ed. (Hong Kong: Jiuzhou chubanshe, 2012), 4, 25, 37, 51–68, 70; Xiao, *Jiang Jingguo zhuan* (Biography of Chiang Ching-kuo), 80–82; Zhang, "Jiang Jingguo yu Zhang Yaruo" (Chiang Ching-kuo and Zhang Yaruo), 356–58; Hu Xing, *Jiang Jingguo yu Zhang Yaruo zhi lian* (Love between Chiang Ching-kuo and Zhang Yaruo) (Zhengzhou: Zhengzhou wenyi chubanshe, 2009); Taylor, *The Generalissimo's Son,* 107–9.
35. See "Lichnoe delo Huan Czhun-meiia" (Personal File of Huang Zhongmei), RGASPI, collection 445, inventory 225, file 1941.
36. See Wang Xingfu, *Zhengzhi shashou Chen Lifu* (Political Killer Chen Lifu) (Shijiazhuang: Hebei renmin chubanshe, 2006), 128.
37. Chiang, *Riji* (Diaries), July 6, 1944, Hoover Archives, box 43, folder 19.
38. See Taylor, *The Generalissimo's Son,* 108.
39. See letters of October 18 and 19, 2017, to the author from Chen Hongmin and Xiao Ruping of Zhejiang University as well as from Yang Tianshi, Research Fellow of the Institute of Modern History of the PRC Academy of Social Sciences.
40. See letters to the author, dated October 18 and 21, 2017, from Liu Keqi, the producer of the project "Two Jiangs," who accompanied Zhang (Jiang) Xiaoyan on a trip to Hangzhou in September 2017.
41. See Jiang, *Jiang jia men wai de haizi* (The Children Behind the Gates of the Jiang House), 25; letter of October 18, 2017, to the author from Wang Wenlun, the director of the Guomindang Central Party Archives, who is familiar with the personal file of Zhang (Jiang) Xiaoyan.
42. Stilwell, *The Stilwell Papers,* 76. Emphasis added by Stilwell.
43. Ibid., 80.
44. Ibid., 82–83, 85, 93, 94, 116.
45. Chiang, *Riji* (Diaries), May 6, 1942, Hoover Archives, box 42, folder 10. For Stilwell's mistakes, see Van de Ven, *War and Nationalism in China 1925–1945,* 30–33.
46. Now it is 63 Jialing New Road. The Stilwell Museum is located there.
47. See Stilwell, *The Stilwell Papers,* 115, 133.
48. See Qin, *Zongtong Jiang gong dashiji changbian chugao* (First Draft of Large Chronological Biography of Mr. President Chiang), 5:1951–53.
49. Stilwell, *The Stilwell Papers,* 119. See also Ch'i Hsi-sheng, *The Much Troubled Alliance,* 261–62.
50. See Edward R. Stettinius Jr., *Lend-Lease: Weapon for Victory* (New York: Macmillan, 1944), 113.

51. Stilwell, *The Stilwell Papers,* 131.
52. See ibid., 121–23, 131, 152.
53. See Smith, *FDR,* 479.
54. Wendell L. Willkie, *One World* (New York: Simon & Schuster, 1943), 55.
55. Cowles, *Mike Looks Back,* 89.
56. Willkie was known as a womanizer. Having previously visited Russia and Iran, he also managed to find lovers there.
57. Willkie, *One World,* 57.
58. Cowles, *Mike Looks Back,* 88–89. See also Drew Pearson, *Drew Pearson Diaries: 1949–1959* (New York: Holt, Rinehart and Winston, 1974), 388; Samuel Zipp, *The Idealist: Wendell Willkie's Wartime Quest to Build One World* (Cambridge: Harvard University Press, 2020), 196–98.
59. Willkie, *One World,* 58.
60. See Pearson, *Drew Pearson Diaries,* 388; Steve Neal, *Dark Horse: A Biography of Wendell Willkie* (Garden City, NY: Doubleday, 1984), 256.
61. See Tyson Li, *Madame Chiang Kai-shek,* 193.
62. Sun, as noted earlier, died on March 12, 1925.
63. Chiang himself did not call his program "New Authoritarianism." This definition would be introduced into Chinese political science later, in the mid-1980s, by a number of Chinese reformers such as Wu Jiaxiang, Zhang Bingjiu and others, who advocated enlightened authoritarianism in the PRC. Nevertheless, it is not difficult to note much in common between Chiang's views and those of these Chinese reformers.
64. See Jiang Zhongzheng, *Zhongguo zhi mingyun* (China's Destiny) (Chongqing: Zhengzhong shuju, 1943); Jiang Zhongzheng, *Zhongguo jingji xueshuo* (Chinese Economic Theory) (Chongqing: Zhongguo zhengfu junshi weiyuanhui yuanzhang shicongshi, 1943).
65. See Tao Tailai and Tao Jinsheng, *Tao Xisheng nianbiao* (Chronological Biography of Tao Xisheng) (Taipei: Lianjing, 2017), 196–97.
66. See Chiang, *Riji* (Diaries), April 2, 1943, Hoover Archives, box 43, folder 3.
67. See ibid., March 20, 30, and 31, April 25, and October 30, 1943, Hoover Archives, box 43, folders 2, 3, and 9.
68. On Francis Wilson Price, see H. McKennie Goodpasture, "China in an American Frank Wilson Price: A Bibliographical Essay," *Journal of Presbyterian History (1962–1985)* 49, no. 4 (Winter 1971): 352–64.
69. See Chiang, *Riji* (Diaries), May 23, 1943, Hoover Archives, box 43, folder 4.
70. See Lin Yutang, "Introduction," in Chiang Kai-shek, *China's Destiny,* trans. Wang Chung-hui, with an introduction Lin Yutang (New York: Macmillan, 1947), viii; Philip Jaffe, "The Secret of 'China's Destiny,'" in Chiang Kai-shek, *China's Destiny and Chinese Economic Theory.* With Notes and Commentary by Philip Jaffe (New York: Roy Publishers, 1947), 18–21. See also Fenby, *Chiang Kai-shek,* 400–401; Taylor, *The Generalissimo,* 260–61.
71. See Chiang, *China's Destiny,* trans. Wang Chung-hui, with an introduction by Lin Yutang.
72. See Chiang, *China's Destiny and Chinese Economic Theory.* With Notes and Commentary by Philip Jaffe.

73. See Shewmaker, *Americans and Chinese Communists, 1927–1945;* Fairbank, *Chinabound,* 252–53.
74. See Melikstov, *Sotsial'no-ekonomicheskaia politika Gomindana v Kitae* (The Socioeconomic Policy of the Guomindang in China), 166–70; see also the discussion of Meliksetov's book published in the journal *Narody Azii i Afriki* (Peoples of Asia and Africa), no. 5 (1975): 180–208.
75. See Chiang, *China's Destiny and Chinese Economic Theory.* With Notes and Commentary by Philip Jaffe, 258.
76. Sun, *Izbrannye proizvedeniia* (Selected Works), 116.
77. Chiang, *China's Destiny and Chinese Economic Theory.* With Notes and Commentary by Philip Jaffe, 245.
78. Ibid., 273, 289–92.
79. G. D. Sukharchuk, "Sun Yat-sen," in M. L. Titarenko, ed., *Dukhovnaiia kul'tura Kitaia: Entsiklopediia* (Spiritual Culture of China: Encyclopedia), 2nd ed., 1:399 (Moscow: Izdatel'stvo "Vostochnaia literatura," 2011). See also G. D. Sukharchuk, *Sotsial'no-ekonomicheskie vzgliady politicheskikh liderov Kitaia pervoi poloviny XX v.: sravnitel'nyi analiz* (Socioeconomic Views of Political Leaders in China in the First Half of the Twentieth Century: A Comparative Analysis) (Moscow: Nauka, 1983).
80. Stuart R. Schram, ed., *Mao's Road to Power: Revolutionary Writings 1912–1949,* 7:330–69 (Armonk, NY: M. E. Sharpe, 2005).
81. Chiang, *Riji* (Diaries), December 7, 1943, Hoover Archives, box 34, folder 34.
82. See Schram, *Mao's Road to Power,* 262–64.
83. For more details, see Pantsov with Levine, *Mao,* 316–17, 331–32; A. V. Pantsov and D. A. Arincheva, "Novaia demokratiia Mao Tszeduna i Novyi avtoritarizm Chan Kai-shi: Dve paradigmy obshchestvennogo progressa Kitaia serediny XX veka" (Mao Zedong's New Democracy and Chiang Kai-shek's New Authoritarianism: Two Paradigms of Social Progress in Mid-twentieth Century China), *Problemy Dal'nego Vostoka* (Far Eastern Affairs), no. 1 (2014): 109–18; Yalishanda Panzuofu (A. V. Pantsov), *Dui Yang Kuisong jiaoshou guanyu "Mao Zedong zhuan" shuping de huiying* (Reply to Professor Yang Kuisong's Review of "Biography of Mao Zedong"), *Jindaishi yanjiu* (Studies in Modern History), no. 6 (2017): 105–21.
84. See Shewmaker, *Americans and Chinese Communists, 1927–1945,* 239–62.
85. See T. A. Bisson, "China's Part in a Coalition War," *Far Eastern Survey* 12, no. 14 (July 14, 1943): 139.
86. Gauss knew Chiang very well. He had worked in China since 1912 as vice-consul, consul, consul general, and, since 1941, as ambassador.
87. See Lattimore and Isono, *China Memoirs,* 167.
88. Evans Fordyce Carlson, *Evans F. Carlson on China at War, 1937–1941* (New York: China and Us, 1993), 23, 37, 49.
89. Willkie, *One World,* 57.
90. Eleanor Roosevelt, *This I Remember* (New York: Harper & Brothers, 1949), 283.
91. Quoted from Tyson Li, *Madame Chiang Kai-shek,* 218.
92. Meiling asserted that cotton made her allergic. Probably so, but she gave the impression of disdaining the bedclothes in the White House.

93. See Lillian Rogers Parks with Francez Spatz Leighton, *My Thirty Years Backstairs at the White House* (New York: Fleet, 1961), 96–97.
94. John L. Lewis (1880–1969) was president of the United Mine Workers of America from 1920 to 1960 and was a thorn in Roosevelt's side.
95. Quoted from Roosevelt, *This I Remember,* 284–85.
96. Quoted from Tyson Li, *Madame Chiang Kai-shek,* 209.
97. Quoted from ibid., 227.
98. See ibid., 217; Dorn, *Walkout with Stilwell in Burma,* 74.
99. Overall in Henan from one to three million persons starved to death in 1942–43.
100. See Theodore H. White, "The Desperate Urgency of Flight," *Time,* October 26, 1942; Theodore H. White, "Until the Harvest Is Reaped," *Time,* March 22, 1944; White, *In Search of History,* 144–56; Kathryn Edgerton-Tarpley, "Saving the Nation, Starving the People? The Henan Famine of 1942–1943," in Esherick and Combs, *1943: China at the Crossroads,* 323–64.
101. See Tyson Li, *Madame Chiang Kai-shek,* 216–17.
102. The accusations against Currie were made during the period of McCarthyism in connection with investigations into the reason for the so-called "loss of China," that is, the defeat of American policy in that country as a result of the coming to power of the Chinese Communist Party. But the matter faded away because of the unreliability of the evidence and did not arise again until the late 1990s, when a number of American historians returned to this theme, asserting that Currie was listed in the archives of Soviet intelligence under the code name "Page." Their arguments, however, lack sufficient documentary foundation.
103. See Tyson Li, *Madame Chiang Kai-shek,* 199.
104. Quoted from ibid., 234.
105. Quoted from ibid., 237.
106. Lin Sen died on August 1, 1943, at 7:04 p.m. due to injuries received in an automobile accident that happened on May 10. See Lin, *Lin Sen nianpu* (Chronological Biography of Lin Sen), 677–78.
107. See "Telegram from Chiang Kai-shek to T. V. Song of July 19, 1943," in T. V. Soong Papers, Hoover Archives, box 34, folder 34.
108. See T. V. Soong Papers, Hoover Archives, box 29, folder 9.
109. Chiang, *Riji* (Diaries), August 22, 1943, Hoover Archives, box 43, folder 7.
110. See Schaller, *The U.S. Crusade in China, 1938–1945,* 148.
111. See Butler, *My Dear Mr. Stalin,* 181–85; G. V. Priakhin, ed., *Perepiska Predsedatelia Soveta Ministrov SSR s prezidentami SshA i prem'er-ministrami Velikobritanii vo vremia Velikoi Otechesvennoi voiny 1941–1945 gg.: Perepiska s U. Cherchilem i K. Etli: iiul' 1941 g.–noiabr' 1945 g.; Perepiskas s F. Ruzvel'tom i G. Trumenom: avgust 1941 g.–dekabr' 1945 g.* (Correspondence of the Chairman of the Council of Ministers of the USSR with the Presidents of the USA and the Prime-ministers of Great Britain during the Great Patriotic War 1941–1945: Correspondence with W. Churchill and C. Atlee, July 1941–November 1945; Correspondence with F. Roosevelt and H. Truman, August 1941–December 1945), 2:167 (Moscow: Voskresen'e, 2005); Winston S. Churchill, *Closing the Ring* (Boston: Houghton Mifflin, 1951), 317, 320; Roosevelt, *As He Saw It,* 131; Lin Hsiao-ting, "Chiang Kai-shek and the Cairo Summit," in Esherick and

Combs, *1943: China at the Crossroads*, 428–30; Keith Sainsbury, *The Turning Point: Roosevelt, Stalin, Churchill, and Chiang Kai-shek, 1943: The Moscow, Cairo, and Teheran Conferences* (Oxford: Oxford University Press, 1985), 126–27.

112. See Chiang, *Riji* (Diaries), November 5, 7, 14, 19–21, 1943, Hoover Archives, box 43, folder 10.
113. Ibid., November 25, 1943, Hoover Archives, box 43, folder 10.
114. See Taylor, *The Generalissimo*, 254–55.
115. See Guo Rongrao, ed., *Jiang weiyuanzhang yu Luosifu zongtong zhan shi tongxun* (Correspondence between Chairman Chiang and President Roosevelt during the War), trans. Guo Rongrao (Taipei: Zhongguo yanjiu zhongxin chubanshe, 1978), 184; *FRUS 1943: China* (Washington, DC: U.S. Government Printing Office, 1957), 455; Lin, "Chiang Kai-shek and the Cairo Summit," 444–45, 448, 450.
116. Dorn, *Walkout with Stilwell in Burma*, 74. See also Roosevelt, *As He Saw It*, 129.
117. Roosevelt, *As He Saw It*, 164. Emphasis added by Elliot Roosevelt.
118. See Churchill, *Closing the Ring*, 328.
119. See Roosevelt, *As He Saw It*, 80.
120. Quoted from Romanus and Sunderland, *Stilwell's Command Problems*, 72.
121. Quoted from Dorn, *Walkout with Stilwell in Burma*, 76.
122. *FRUS: The Conferences at Cairo and Tehran, 1943* (Washington, DC: U.S. Government Printing Office, 1943), 448.
123. Chiang, *Riji* (Diaries), December 4, 1943, Hoover Archives, box 43, folder 11.
124. Hans-Georg Moeller, *Daodejing (Laozi): A Complete Translation and Commentary* (Chicago: Open Court, 2007), 23.

## 19. *THE BITTER TASTE OF VICTORY*

1. See *FRUS 1943: China*, 178; Chiang, *Riji* (Diaries), December 7, 1943. For the original of Roosevelt's letter, see letter from Franklin D. Roosevelt to Chiang Kai-shek, December 6, 1943, in *Franklin D. Roosevelt Papers as President: Map Room Papers, 1941–1945*, Franklin D. Roosevelt Presidential Library & Museum, box 10, no. 24–26/152, http://www.fdrlibrary.marist.edu/_resources/images/mr/mr0060.pdf.
2. See Chiang, *Riji* (Diaries), November 26, 1943, Hoover Archives, box 43, folder 10; Churchill, *Closing the Ring*, 328.
3. *FRUS 1943: China*, 180–82; Chiang, *Riji* (Diaries), December 8 and 9, 1943, Hoover Archives, box 43, folder 11.
4. See Romanus and Sunderland, *Stilwell's Command Problems*, 77.
5. Letter from Franklin D. Roosevelt to Chiang Kai-shek, December 18, 1943, in *Franklin D. Roosevelt Papers as President: Map Room Papers, 1941–1945*, Franklin D. Roosevelt Presidential Library & Museum, box 10, no. 24–26/152.
6. See *United States Relations with China*, 27.
7. See letter from Franklin D. Roosevelt to Chiang Kai-shek, December 20, 1943, in *Franklin D. Roosevelt Papers as President: Map Room Papers, 1941–1945*, Franklin D. Roosevelt Presidential Library & Museum, box 10, no. 24–26/152; Chiang, *Riji* (Diaries), December 8 and 9, 1943.

8. *United States Relations with China,* 489.
9. "Proposed Message from Franklin D. Roosevelt to Chiang Kai-shek, December 20, 1943," in *Franklin D. Roosevelt Papers as President: Map Room Papers, 1941–1945,* Franklin D. Roosevelt Presidential Library & Museum, box 10, no. 24–26/152.
10. *FRUS 1943*: China, 181.
11. See Chiang, *Riji* (Diaries), September 17, 1942, Hoover Archives, box 42, folder 14.
12. See Matthew T. Combs, "Chongqing 1943: People's Livelihood, Price Control, and State Legitimacy," in Esherick and Combs, *1943: China at the Crossroads,* 290, 300.
13. White, *In Search of History,* 162–63. For more details, see Chang Kia-ngau, *The Inflationary Spiral: The Experience in China, 1939–1950* (Cambridge: MIT Press, 1958); Chou Shun-hsin, *The Chinese Inflation 1937–1949* (New York: Columbia University Press, 1963); Jarvis, "Letters from China 1920–1949," 64.
14. See Combs, "Chongqing 1943," 293–96.
15. See ibid., 293–94, 299, 322.
16. See *FRUS 1943*: China, 480.
17. See Sherman Xiaogang Lai, "Chiang Kai-shek versus Guomindang's Corruption in the Republic Era," in Qiang Fang and Xiaobing Li, eds., *Corruption and Anticorruption in Modern China* (Lanham, MD: Lexington Books, 2018), 81.
18. Chiang, *Riji* (Diaries), September 17, 1942.
19. See Willkie, *One World,* 62–63; Combs, *Chongqing 1943,* 302–3.
20. See *FRUS 1944*, 6:312–13, 319–25, 335–36, 439.
21. White, *In Search of History,* 165–66.
22. See Ch'en Yung-fa, "Chiang Kai-shek and the Japanese Ichigo Offensive, 1944," in Laura De Giorgi and Guido Samarani, eds., *Chiang Kai-shek and His Time: New Historical and Historiographical Perspectives* (Venice: Edizioni Ca'Foscari, 2017), 38, 66–69; *FRUS 1944*, 6:160–61.
23. Zi Zhang (Zhuansun Shi [504–? BC]), Confucius's disciple.
24. Chiang, *Riji* (Diaries), January 1, 1944, Hoover Archives, box 43, folder 13. For the translation of Confucius's quotation, see Confucius, *The Analects of Confucius,* 100.
25. "Pis'mo F. I. Vakhrevoi svoei sestre A. I. Vakhrevoi: 3 marta 1943 g." (F. I. Vakhreva's Letter to Her Sister A. I. Vakhrevoi, March 3, 1943," in Galitsky, *Tszian Tszingo* (Chiang Ching-kuo), 152.
26. See *FRUS 1944*, 6:827–29.
27. Ibid., 835–37.
28. Chiang, *Riji* (Diaries), January 15, 1944, Hoover Archives, box 43, folder 13.
29. See *FRUS 1944*, 6:839.
30. Ibid., 6:859.
31. See Romanus and Sunderland, *Stilwell's Command Problems,* 300.
32. See *FRUS 1944*, 6:860; Romanus and Sunderland, *Stilwell's Command Problems,* 301.
33. See Romanus and Sunderland, *Stilwell's Command Problems,* 300; Jarvis, "Letters from China 1920–1949," 53–55.
34. Jarvis, "Letters from China 1920–1949," 64.
35. Quoted from White, *In Search of History,* 162–63. See also *FRUS 1944*, 6:428, 452, 456.

36. Quoted from Lu [Lü] and Lin, "Chiang Kai-shek's Diaries and Republican China: New Insights on the History of Modern China," 335.
37. See Ch'i, *Nationalist China at War,* 70–72.
38. Ch'en, "Chiang Kai-shek and the Japanese Ichigo Offensive, 1944," 39.
39. See Van de Ven, *War and Nationalism in China 1925–1945,* 33–34, 53–54.
40. See Ch'en, "Chiang Kai-shek and the Japanese Ichigo Offensive, 1944," 39–40.
41. Chiang, *Riji* (Diaries), April 22, 1944, Hoover Archives, box 43, folder 16.
42. See ibid., May 14, 1944, Hoover Archives, box 43, folder 17.
43. Tongguan is a city along the banks of the Yellow River on the way to Xi'an.
44. Chiang, *Riji* (Diaries), June 15, 1944, Hoover Archives, box 43, folder 18.
45. See ibid., June 14 and 15, 1944, Hoover Archives, box 43, folder 18.
46. See *United States Relations with China,* 549–59.
47. *FRUS 1944,* 6:234–37. See also letter from Henry A. Wallace to Chiang Kai-shek, June 27, 1944, in T. V. Soong Papers, Hoover Archives, box 36, folder 1.
48. Letter from Franklin D. Roosevelt to Chiang Kai-shek, July 6, 1944, in *Franklin D. Roosevelt Papers as President: Map Room Papers, 1941–1945,* Franklin D. Roosevelt Presidential Library & Museum, box 10, no. 104–105/220, http://www.fdrlibrary.marist.edu/_resources/images/mr/mr0061.pdf.
49. Chiang, *Riji* (Diaries), July 7, 1944, Hoover Archives, box 43, folder 19.
50. See ibid., September 19, 1944, Hoover Archives, box 43, folder 21.
51. Letter from Chiang Kai-shek to Franklin D. Roosevelt, July 8, 1944, in *Franklin D. Roosevelt Papers as President: Map Room Papers, 1941–1945,* Franklin D. Roosevelt Presidential Library & Museum, box 10, no. 102–103/220; *FRUS 1944,* 6:121.
52. Letter from Franklin D. Roosevelt to Chiang Kai-shek, July 13, 1944, in *Franklin D. Roosevelt Papers as President: Map Room Papers, 1941–1945,* Franklin D. Roosevelt Presidential Library & Museum, box 10, no. 99–100/220.
53. Stilwell, *The Stilwell Papers,* 306–7.
54. See Lu [Lü] and Lin, "Chiang Kai-shek's Diaries and Republican China: New Insights on the History of Modern China," 332.
55. Quoted from White, *In Search of History,* 159.
56. Quoted from Tyson Li, *Madame Chiang Kai-shek,* 254.
57. See Yang, *Zhaoxun zhenshi de Jiang Jieshi* (In Search of the True Chang Kai-shek) (Chongqing), 1:501–25.
58. See *Lichnoe delo Kun Sian-si* (Personal File of Kong Xiangxi), sheet 6.
59. See Tyson Li, *Madame Chiang Kai-shek,* 257, 262.
60. Chiang, *Riji* (Diaries), July 21, 25, and 31, 1944, Hoover Archives, box 43, folder 19.
61. Ibid., Miscellaneous, July 1944, Hoover Archives, box 43, folder 19. Sherman Xiaogang Lai incorrectly translates this quote.
62. A copy of this book with notes by Chiang Kai-shek is preserved in the library of the Institute of Modern History of the Academia Sinica in Taiwan. I am grateful to Ch'en Yung-fa for drawing my attention to it.
63. The Book of the Prophet Isaiah, 35:6.
64. Chiang, *Riji* (Diaries), July 12, 1944, Hoover Archives, box 43, folder 19.

65. Ibid., July 29, 1944, Hoover Archives, box 43, folder 19. The original reads, "Our trials are great opportunities. Too often we look on them as great obstacles. It would be a haven of rest and an inspiration of unspeakable power if each of us would henceforth recognize every difficult situation as one of God's chosen ways of proving to us His love." Mrs. Charles E. Cowman, *Streams in the Desert* (Grand Rapids, MI: Zondervan, 1996), 227.
66. See David D. Barrett, *Dixie Mission: The United States Army Observer Group in Yenan, 1944* (Berkeley: University of California Press, 1970); Carrole J. Carter, *Mission to Yenan: American Liaison with the Chinese Communists 1944–1947* (Lexington: University Press of Kentucky, 1997); P. P. Vladimirov, *Osobyi raion Kitaia 1942–1945* (Special Region of China 1942–1945) (Moscow: APN, 1975), 306–7, 313, 626; John Paton Davies Jr., *Dragon by the Tail: American, British, Japanese, and Russian Encounters with China and One Another* (New York: W. W. Norton, 1972), 402–3.
67. Joseph W. Esherick, ed., *Lost Chance in China: The World War II Despatches of John S. Service* (New York: Random House, 1974), 308, 309. See also Joseph Alsop, "The Feud between Stilwell and Chiang," *Saturday Evening Post,* vol. 222, no. 28 (January 1, 1950): 48.
68. Quoted from Tikhvinsky, *Russko–kitaiskie otnosheniia v XX veke* (Russo–Chinese Relations in the Twentieth Century), vol. 4, book 2, 39; *FRUS 1944*, 6:97, 255.
69. See *FRUS 1944*, 6:667.
70. Letter from Franklin D. Roosevelt to Chiang Kai-shek, August 9, 1944, in *Franklin D. Roosevelt Papers as President: Map Room Papers, 1941–1945,* Franklin D. Roosevelt Presidential Library & Museum, box 10, no. 88/220.
71. Chiang, *Riji* (Diaries), August 10, 1944, Hoover Archives, box 43, folder 20.
72. See *FRUS 1944*, 6:141.
73. See ibid., 6:148–49.
74. See Ch'en, "Chiang Kai-shek and the Japanese Ichigo Offensive, 1944," 56.
75. Chiang, *Riji* (Diaries), August 11, 1944, Hoover Archives, box 43, folder 20.
76. See Ch'en, "Chiang Kai-shek and the Japanese Ichigo Offensive, 1944," 57–58.
77. Letter from Franklin D. Roosevelt to Chiang Kai-shek, September 9, 1944, in *Franklin D. Roosevelt Papers as President: Map Room Papers, 1941–1945,* Franklin D. Roosevelt Presidential Library & Museum, box 10, no. 65–66/220.
78. Letter from Joseph W. Stilwell to George C. Marshall, September 15, 1944, in ibid., no. 65–66/220.
79. George C. Marshall, memorandum for the President and Proposed Message from the President to the Generalissimo, September 16, 1944, in ibid., 53–56/220.
80. See *FRUS 1944*, 6:157–58.
81. Stilwell, *The Stilwell Papers,* 333.
82. Quoted from Ch'i, *The Much Troubled Alliance,* 563. Emphasis added by Chiang Kai-shek.
83. See Chiang, *Riji* (Diaries), September 19, 1944, Hoover Archives, box 43, folder 21.
84. Waterloo is the village not far from Brussels where Napoleon lost his last battle, June 18, 1815.
85. Quoted from Ch'i, *The Much Troubled Alliance,* 561. Emphasis added by Stilwell.

86. Stilwell, *The Stilwell Papers,* 333.
87. Chiang, *Riji* (Diaries), September 20, 1944, Hoover Archives, box 43, folder 21.
88. Ibid., September 22, 24, and 25, 1944, Hoover Archives, box 43, folder 21.
89. Chiang Kai-shek, "Aide Mémoire," in *Franklin D. Roosevelt Papers as President: Map Room Papers, 1941–1945,* Franklin D. Roosevelt Presidential Library & Museum, box 11, no. 120/178, http://www.fdrlibrary.marist.edu/_resources/images/mr/mr0066.pdf.
90. See Ch'i, *The Much Troubled Alliance,* 569–70.
91. *FRUS 1944*, 6:265–66.
92. Ibid., 6:165.
93. See letter from Patrick J. Hurley to Franklin D. Roosevelt, October 15, 1944, in *Franklin D. Roosevelt Papers as President: Map Room Papers, 1941–1945,* Franklin D. Roosevelt Presidential Library & Museum, box 11, no. 105/178.
94. See letter from Franklin D. Roosevelt to Chiang Kai-shek, October 18, 1944, in *Franklin D. Roosevelt Papers as President: Map Room Papers, 1941–1945,* Franklin D. Roosevelt Presidential Library & Museum, box 10, no. 21–23/220.
95. See letter from Franklin D. Roosevelt to Chiang Kai-shek, October 18, 1944, in ibid., no. 17–20/220.
96. Stilwell, *The Stilwell Papers,* 346.
97. John S. Service, "State Department Duty in China, The McCarthy Era, and After, 1933–1977, An Oral History Conducted 1977–1978 by Rosemary Levinson," Regional Oral History Office, Bancroft Library, University of California, Berkeley, 1981, 302; *FRUS 1944*, 6:185–86, 700.
98. See *FRUS 1944*, 6:198, 207–8.
99. The Book of the Prophet Ezekiel 39:26, 27.
100. Chiang, *Riji* (Diaries), October 31, 1944, Hoover Archives, box 43, folder 22.
101. See Jeans, *The Marshall Mission to China, 1945–1947,* 52.
102. Chiang, *Riji* (Diaries), November 29 and December 2, 1944, Hoover Archives, box 43, folders 23 and 24.
103. Tuchman, *Stilwell and the American Experience in China, 1911–45,* 429.
104. See Chiang, *Riji* (Diaries), November 6, 1944, Hoover Archives, box 43, folder 23.
105. Albert C. Wedemeyer, *Wedemeyer Reports!* (New York: Henry Holt, 1958), 277.
106. Chiang, *Riji* (Diaries), November 16, 1944, Hoover Archives, box 43, folder 23.
107. See Chen, *Jiang Jieshi yu Wang Jingwei* (Chiang Kai-shek and Wang Jingwei), 196–97.
108. See Chiang, *Riji* (Diaries), November 11, 1944, Hoover Archives, box 43, folder 23.
109. See Leung, *Political Leaders of Modern China,* 78.
110. Chiang, *Riji* (Diaries), November 25, 1944, Hoover Archives, box 43, folder 23.
111. Ibid., December 2, 4–7, and 9, 1944, Hoover Archives, box 43, folder 24.
112. Ch'i, *Nationalist China at War,* 80. See also He, *Banian kangri zhong de Jiang Jieshi 1937–1945* (Chiang Kai-shek during the Eight-Year War of Resistance 1937–1945), 305.
113. Chiang, *The Collected Wartime Messages of Generalissimo Chiang Kai-shek 1937–1945,* 2:814.

114. Letter from Albert C. Wedemeyer to T. V. Song, December 31, 1944, in T. V. Soong Papers, Hoover Archives, box 9, folder 21.
115. Quoted from He, *Banian kangri de Jiang Jieshi 1937–1945* (Chiang Kai-shek during the Eight-Year War of Resistance 1937–1945), 306–7.
116. See letter from Franklin D. Roosevelt to Chiang Kai-shek, January 26, 1945, in *Franklin D. Roosevelt Papers as President: Map Room Papers, 1941–1945,* Franklin D. Roosevelt Presidential Library & Museum, box 10, no. 2/3; letter from Chiang Kai-shek to Franklin D. Roosevelt, February 1, 1945, in ibid., box 10, no. 1/3.
117. *FRUS: Conferences at Malta and Yalta, 1945* (Washington, DC: U.S. Government Printing Office, 1945), 984.
118. The Chinese still considered Mongolia to be a part of China and hoped to get it back.
119. Chiang, *Soviet Russia in China,* 125.
120. Chiang, *Riji* (Diaries), February 2, 1945, Hoover Archives, box 44, folder 3.
121. Tikhvinsky, *Russko–kitaiskie otnosheniia v XX veke* (Russo–Chinese Relations in the Twentieth Century), vol. 4, book 2, 20.
122. See Furuya, *Chiang Kai-shek,* 822–23.
123. See "The Commanding General, Manhattan District Project (Groves), to the Chief of Staff, United States Army (Marshall), War Department, Washington, December 30, 1944," https://history.state.gov/historicaldocuments/frus1945Malta/d262.
124. See Furuya, *Chiang Kai-shek,* 823.
125. Chiang, *Riji* (Diaries), March 15, 1945, Hoover Archives, box 44, folder 4.
126. Ibid., April 25, 1945, Hoover Archives, box 44, folder 5. See also Davies Jr., *Dragon by the Tail,* 394–95.
127. Chiang, *Riji* (Diaries), April 13, 1945, Hoover Archives, box 44, folder 5.
128. Ibid., April 1, 1945, Hoover Archives, box 44, folder 5.
129. Ibid., February 10, 1945, Hoover Archives, box 44, folder 3; Hu Zongnan, *Hu Zongnan xiansheng riji* (Diary of Mr. Hu Zongnan) (Taipei: Guoshiguan, 2015), 433; Wang, *Qianshan duxing* (The Solitary Path among a Thousand Mountains), 70.
130. As mentioned earlier, Chiang did not recognize children from Chiang Ching-kuo's deceased mistress.
131. Chiang, *Riji* (Diaries), April 25, 1945.
132. "Pis'mo Fainy Jiang Anne Vakhrevoi ot 7 noiabria 1947 g. i pis'mo Chiang Ching-kuo Anne Vakhrevoi ot 7 noiabria 1947" (Faina Jiang's Letter to Anna Vakhreva of November 7, 1947, and Chiang Ching-kuo's Letter to Anna Vakhreva of November 7, 1947), in Galitsky, *Tszian Tszingo* (Chiang Ching-kuo), 154–57.
133. Chiang, *Riji* (Diaries), May 28, 1945, Hoover Archives, box 44, folder 6; Tang, *Zhongguo lishi dashi nianbiao: Xiandai* (Chronology of Events in Chinese History: Contemporary History), 463–64.
134. Quoted from Ch'i, *The Much Troubled Alliance,* 679–80.
135. See Priakhin, *Perepiska Predsedatelia Soveta Ministrov SSSR s prezidentami SshA i prem'er-ministrami Velikobritanii vo vremia Velikoi Otechestvennoi voiny 1941–1945 gg.* (Correspondence of the Chairman of the Council of Ministers of the USSR with the Presidents of the USA and the Prime-ministers of Great Britain during the Great Patriotic War 1941–1945), 2:610, 645.

136. See Hirohito, *Dnevnik imperatora Showa* (Diary of the Showa Emperor) (n.p., n.d.), 52.
137. Emperor Hirohito, "Accepting the Potsdam Declaration," Radio Broadcast, https://www.mtholyoke.edu/acad/intrel/hirohito.htm.
138. Chiang, *Riji* (Diaries), August 15, 1945, Hoover Archives, box 44, folder 9.
139. The Book of Psalms, Psalm 9.
140. See, for instance, Xiaobing Li, "Anticorruption Policy and Party Politics: The Lost Political Battle and the Fate of the GMD," in Fang and Li, *Corruption and Anticorruption in Modern China,* 104; Mitter, *Forgotten Ally,* 5. The most recent Chinese study gives a much bigger number—more than fifty million. See Bian, *Kangri zhanzheng shiqi Zhongguo renkou sunshi wenti yanjiu (1937–1945)* (A Study of the Losses of the Chinese Population during the Period of the Anti-Japanese War [1937–1945]), 442.
141. See Kurdiukov, *Sovetsko-kitaiskie otnosheniia, 1917–1957* (Soviet–Chinese Relations, 1917–1957), 196–203; for documents on the course of Soviet–Chinese negotiations in June–August 1945, see "Moscow Notes," in T. V. Soong Papers, Hoover Archives, box 63, folder 1; "Draft of the Soong/Stalin Meeting Minutes," in ibid., box 63, folder 2; Tikhvinsky, *Russko–kitaiskie otnosheniia v XX veke* (Russo–Chinese Relations in the Twentieth Century), vol. 4, book 2, 71–161, 164–69, 173–87; Foo Yee Wah, *Chiang Kai-shek's Last Ambassador to Moscow: The Wartime Diaries of Fu Bingchang* (New York: Palgrave Macmillan, 2011), 188–205.
142. Quoted from A. M. Ledovsky, *SSSR i Stalin v sud'bakh Kitaia: Dokumenty i svidetel'stva uchastnika sobytii: 1937–1952 gg.* (The USSR and Stalin in the Fate of China: Documents and Testimonies of a Participant in the Events: 1937–1952) (Moscow: "Pamiatniki istoricheskoi mysli," 1999), 61. See also "Zapis' besedy tovarishcha Stalina I. V. s Predsedatelem Tsentral'nogo narodnogo pravitel'stva Kitaiskoi Narodnoi Respubliki Mao Tsze-dunom 17 dekabria 1949 g." (Note of a Conversation between Comrade J. V. Stalin with the Chairman of the Central People's Government of the People's Republic of China Mao Zedong on December 16, 1949), RGASPI, collection 558, inventory 11, file 329, sheets 9–17; "Zapis' besedy I. V. Stalin s Predsedatelem Tsentral'nogo narodonogo pravitel'sva Kitaiskoi Narodnoi Respubliki Mao Tsze-dunom 22 ianvria 1950 g." (Notes of a Conversation between J. V. Stalin and the Chairman of the Central People's Government of the People's Republic of China Mao Zedong on January 22, 1950), ibid., sheets 29–38; *Cold War International History Project* (hereafter *CWIHP*) *Bulletin,* no. 6–7 (1995/1996): 5–9; Niu Jun,"The Origins of the Sino–Soviet Alliance," in O. Arne Westad, ed., *Brothers in Arms: The Rise and Fall of the Sino–Soviet Alliance: 1945–1963* (Stanford: Stanford University Press, 1998), 70.
143. Chiang, *Soviet Russia in China,* 135.
144. According to Song Qingling, Sun Yat-sen's widow, T. V. Song was formally the head of the delegation, but Chiang Ching-kuo was actually in charge.
145. Priakhin, *Perepiska Predsedatelia Soveta Ministrov SSSR s prezidentami SshA i prem'er-ministrami Velikobritanii vo vremia Velikoi Otechestvennoi voiny 1941–1945 gg.* (Correspondence of the Chairman of the Council of Ministers of the USSR with

the Presidents of the USA and the Prime-ministers of Great Britain during the Great Patriotic War 1941–1945), 2:598.

146. See Tikhvinsky, *Russko–kitaiskie otnosheniia v XX veke* (Russo–Chinese Relations in the Twentieth Century), vol. 4, book 2, 144–45, 219.
147. Ibid., 150.
148. See ibid., 218–19, 224.
149. See ibid., 610–12.
150. See He, *Banian kangri de Jiang Jieshi 1937–1945* (Chiang Kai-shek during the Eight-Year War of Resistance 1937–1945), 317, 319–20.
151. Chiang was referring to the ideology of communism. Organizationally, the Third (Communist) International was disbanded by Stalin in May 1943.
152. Chiang, *Riji* (Diaries), September 9, 1945, Hoover Archives, box 44, folder 10.

## 20. *NEW TRIALS*

1. Quoted from Zhonggong zhongyang wenxian yanjiu shi, ed., *Zhu De nianpu* (Chronological Biography of Zhu De) (Beijing: Renmin chubanshe, 1986), 274.
2. Chiang, *Soviet Russia in China,* 129; Chiang, *Riji* (Diaries), August 15, 1945, Hoover Archives, box 44, folder 9.
3. Quoted from Zhonggong zhongyang wenxian yanjiu shi, *Zhu De nianpu* (Chronological Biography of Zhu De), 276.
4. Tikhvinsky, *Russko–kitaiskie otnosheniia v XX veke* (Russo–Chinese Relations in the Twentieth Century), vol. 4, book 2, 303.
5. Chiang, *Riji* (Diaries), August 15, 20, and 23, 1945, Hoover Archives, box 44, folder 9.
6. See Suzanne Pepper, *Civil War in China: The Political Struggle 1945–1949,* 2nd ed. (Lanham, MD: Rowman & Littlefield, 1999), xi.
7. Harry S. Truman, *Memoirs,* 2:62 (Garden City, NY: Doubleday, 1956).
8. See Dieter Heinzig, *The Soviet Union and Communist China 1945–1950: The Arduous Road to the Alliance* (Armonk, NY: M. E. Sharpe, 2004), 51–125.
9. The Potsdam Conference of the leaders of the three powers that defeated Germany (the USSR, United States, and Great Britain) took place from July 17 to August 2, 1945.
10. Truman, *Strictly Personal and Confidential,* 33, 40; Truman, *Off the Record,* 53. See also McCullough, *Truman,* 418–19.
11. Truman, *Memoirs,* 2:90.
12. Lyman P. Van Slyke, ed., *The Chinese Communist Movement: A Report of the United States War Department, July 1945* (Stanford: Stanford University Press, 1968), 1, 258.
13. See S. L. Tikhvinsky, ed., *Russko–kitaiskie otnosheniia v XX veke* (Russo–Chinese Relations in the Twentieth Century), vol. 5, book 1 (Moscow: "Pamiatniki istoricheskoi mysli," 2005), 221–22, 225–26.
14. See Douglas J. Macdonald, *Adventures in Chaos: American Intervention for Reform in the Third World* (Cambridge: Harvard University Press, 1992), 77.
15. Truman, *Strictly Personal and Confidential,* 40.
16. See A. V. Torkunov, *Zagodnochnaia voina: Koreiskii konflikt 1950–1953* (The Enigmatic War: The Korean Conflict 1950–1953) (Moscow: ROSSPEN, 2000), 6–29.

17. Cm.: Harold M. Tanner, *The Battle for Manchuria and the Fate of China: Siping, 1946* (Bloomington: Indiana University Press, 2013), 56; Harold M. Tanner, *Where Chiang Kai-shek Lost China: The Liao–Shen Campaign, 1948* (Bloomington: Indiana University Press, 2015), 31.
18. Pantsov with Levine, *Mao,* 346.
19. Quoted from Hu Qiaomu, *Hu Qiaomu huiyi Mao Zedong:* zengdingben (Hu Qiaomu Remembers Mao Zedong: Expanded ed.) (Beijing: Renmin chubanshe, 2014), 404–5.
20. See Pang Xianzhi, ed., *Mao Zedong nianpu, 1893–1949* (Chronological Biography of Mao Zedong, 1893–1949), 3:16 (Beijing: Renmin chubanshe/Zhongyang wenxian chubanshe, 2002).
21. Quoted from Tikhvinsky, *Russko–kitaiskie otnosheniia v XX veke* (Russo–Chinese Relations in the Twentieth Century), vol. 4, book 2, 39, 45.
22. Ibid., 34.
23. See Li, *Zhongguo guomindang dashiji (1894.11–1986.12)* (Chronology of the Chinese Guomindang [November 1894–December 1986]), 597–98.
24. Chiang, *Riji* (Diaries), August 28, 1945, Hoover Archives, box 44, folder 9.
25. Quoted from Tikhvinsky, *Russko–kitaiskie otnosheniia v XX veke* (Russo–Chinese Relations in the Twentieth Century), vol. 4, book 2, 214.
26. See Sergey Radchenko, "Lost Chance for Peace: The 1945 CCP–Kuomintang Peace Talks Revisited," *Journal of Cold War Studies* 19, no. 2 (Spring 2017): 84–114. For a critique of Radchenko's views see https://networks.h-net.org/node/28443/discussions/1552174/h-diplo-article-review-751-lost-chance-peace-1945-ccp-kuomintang.
27. See Tikhvinsky, *Russko–kitaiskie otnosheniia v XX veke* (Russo–Chinese Relations in the Twentieth Century), vol. 4, book 2, 229, 230–33.
28. Ibid., 233.
29. Chiang, *Riji* (Diaries), August 28, 1945.
30. Quoted from Fenby, *Chiang Kai-shek,* 454.
31. Quoted from Herbert Feis, *The China Tangle: The American Effort in China from Pearl Harbor to the Marshall Mission* (Princeton: Princeton University Press, 1953), 411.
32. Quoted from Tikhvinsky, *Russko–kitaiskie otnosheniia v XX veke* (Russo–Chinese Relations in the Twentieth Century), vol. 4, book 2, 232.
33. See Sladkovsky, *Noveishaia istoriia Kitaia 1928–1949* (Contemporary History of China 1929–1949), 253.
34. Tikhvinsky, *Russko–kitaiskie otnosheniia v XX veke* (Russo–Chinese Relations in the Twentieth Century), vol. 4, book 2, 266.
35. See Yang Shengqun and Yan Jianqi, eds., *Deng Xiaoping nianpu: 1904–1974* (Chronological Biography of Deng Xiaoping: 1904–1974), 1:577 (Beijing: Zhongyang wenxian chubanshe, 2010); Christopher R. Lew, *The Third Chinese Revolutionary Civil War, 1945–1949: An Analysis of Communist Strategy and Leadership* (London: Routledge, 2009), 23–24.
36. See Heinzig, *The Soviet Union and Communist China 1945–1950,* 87.

37. See Tikhvinsky, *Russko–kitaiskie otnosheniia v XX veke* (Russo–Chinese Relations in the Twentieth Century), vol. 4, book 2, 256–88, 294, 296–302, 305–7.
38. Ibid., 300.
39. See Tanner, *The Battle for Manchuria and the Fate of China,* 57.
40. See Ledovsky, *SSSR i Stalin v sud'bakh Kitaia* (The USSR and Stalin in the Fate of China), 185, 207.
41. See Tanner, *Where Chiang Kai-shek Lost China,* 35–36.
42. See Truman, *Memoirs,* 2:65–66.
43. For details, see Subcommittee to Investigate the Administration of the Internal Security Act and Other Internal Security Laws of the Committee on the Judiciary, United States Senate, *The Amerasia Papers: A Clue to the Catastrophe of China,* 2 vols. (Washington, DC: U.S. Government Printing Office, 1970).
44. Quoted from McCullough, *Truman,* 475. See also *FRUS 1945*: China, 7:722–26 (Washington, DC: U.S. Government Printing Office, 1967).
45. Quoted from Truman, *Memoirs,* 2:66.
46. *FRUS 1945*, 7, 726, 764–65. See also Tikhvinsky, *Russko–kitaiskie otnosheniia v XX veke* (Russo–Chinese Relations in the Twentieth Century), vol. 5, book 2, 137.
47. Quoted from McCullough, *Truman,* 533.
48. Dean Acheson, *Present at the Creation: My Years in the State Department* (New York: W. W. Norton, 1969), 140–41.
49. See George C. Marshall, *George C. Marshall: Interviews and Reminiscences for Forrest C. Pogue,* rev. ed. (Lexington, VA: George C. Marshall Research Foundation, 1991), 118; Katherine Tupper Marshall, *Together: Annals of an Army Wife* (New York: Tupper & Love, 1946), 285.
50. Marshall, *George C. Marshall: Interviews and Reminiscences for Forrest C. Pogue,* 607.
51. See Jeans, *The Marshall Mission to China, 1945–1947,* 255.
52. Cited from Alsop, "The Feud between Stilwell and Chiang," 18.
53. See ibid., 18, 41.
54. See George C. Marshal, *Marshall's Mission to China: December 1945–January 1947: The Report and Appended Documents,* 1:6 (Arlington, VA: University Publications of America, 1976).
55. Chiang, *Riji* (Diaries), December 16–24, 1945, Hoover Archives, box 44, folder 13.
56. See Tikhvinsky, *Russko–kitaiskie otnosheniia v XX veke* (Russo–Chinese Relations in the Twentieth Century), vol. 4, book 2, 294–95, 311, 313, 319, 321.
57. Quoted from ibid., 142–43.
58. Quoted from ibid., 147.
59. See ibid., 322–23; Galitsky, *Tszian Tszingo* (Chiang Ching-kuo), 168.
60. Ledovsky, *SSSR i Stalin v sud'bakh Kitaia* (The USSR and Stalin in the Fate of China), 15–39.
61. Tikhvinsky, *Russko–kitaiskie otnosheniia v XX veke* (Russo–Chinese Relations in the Twentieth Century), vol. 4, book 2, 340.
62. See Sladkovsky, *Noveishaia istoriia 1928–1949* (Contemporary History of China 1929–1949), 256.
63. Quoted from Truman, *Memoirs,* 2:63. Emphasis in the original.

64. Quoted from Tikhvinsky, *Russko–kitaiskie otnosheniia v XX veke* (Russo–Chinese Relations in the Twentieth Century), vol. 4, book 2, 40.
65. Schram, *Mao's Road to Power: Revolutionary Writings 1912–1949,* 3:31.
66. Chiang, *Riji* (Diaries), January 19 and 21, 1946, Hoover Archives, box 45, folder 2. See also Macdonald, *Adventures in Chaos,* 82.
67. Chiang, *Riji* (Diaries), February 2 and 28, 1946, Hoover Archives, box 45, folder 3.
68. Letter from Harry S. Truman to Bess Wallace, June 22, 1911, in Harry S. Truman Presidential Library & Museum, https://www.trumanlibrary.org/whistlestop/study_collections/trumanpapers/fbpa/index.php?documentVersion=both&documentid=HST-FBP_1–21_01&pagenumber=3.
69. Quoted from Macdonald, *Adventures in Chaos,* 85.
70. See Tikhvinsky, *Russko–kitaiskie otnosheniia v XX veke* (Russo–Chinese Relations in the Twentieth Century), vol. 5, book 1, 66–67, 71–74, 76–79, 85, 98; book 2, 394–95, 481–82.
71. See Tanner, *The Battle for Manchuria and the Fate of China,* 31.
72. See Chiang, *Soviet Russia in China,* 168–71; Tikhvinsky, *Russko–kitaiskie otnosheniia v XX veke* (Russo–Chinese Relations in the Twentieth Century), vol. 4, book 2, 293, 310, 335–36, 553; Tikhvinsky, *Russko–kitaiskie otnosheniia v XX veke* (Russo–Chinese Relations in the Twentieth Century), vol. 5, book 2 (Moscow: "Pamiatniki istoricheskoi mysli," 2005), 480, 484–85; Donald G. Gillin and Ramon H. Mayers, eds., *Last Chance in Manchuria: The Diary of Chang Kia-ngau,* trans. Dolores Zen, with the assistance Donald G. Gillin (Stanford: Stanford University Press, 1989), 85, 152, 197, 230, 253, 254.
73. See Tanner, *The Battle for Manchuria and the Fate of China,* 32.
74. See ibid., 31.
75. See Odd Arne Westad, *Cold War and Revolution: Soviet–American Rivalry and the Origins of the Chinese Civil War: 1944–1946* (New York: Columbia University Press, 1993), 152.
76. See Heinzig, *The Soviet Union and Communist China 1945–1950,* 98.
77. See Tanner, *The Battle for Manchuria and the Fate of China,* 103.
78. See Ledovsky, *SSSR i Stalin v sud'bakh Kitaia* (The USSR and Stalin in the Fate of China), 9.
79. See *Foreign Aid by the United States Government 1940–1951* (Washington, DC: U.S. Government Printing Office, 1952), 27.
80. Incidentally, American aid to Great Britain in the Second World War amounted to $29 billion while the USSR received more than $11 billion.
81. Tang, *Zhongguo lishi dashi nianbiao: Xiandai* (Chronology of Events in Chinese History: Contemporary History), 483.
82. Truman, *Strictly Personal and Confidential,* 41.
83. I. V. Stalin, *Sobraniye sochinenii* (Collected Works), 16:5–16 (Moscow: Izd-vo "Pisatel,' 1997).
84. See Tang, *Zhongguo lishi dashi nianbiao: Xiandai* (Chronology of Events in Chinese History: Contemporary History), 483–85; Tanner, *The Battle for Manchuria and the Fate of China,* 109.

85. See Levine, *Anvil of Victory,* 78–79.
86. Chiang, *Riji* (Diaries), April 20, 1946, Hoover Archives, box 45, folder 5.
87. Ibid., April 13, 1946, Hoover Archives, box 45, folder 5.
88. See Macdonald, *Adventures in Chaos,* 91.
89. Chiang, *Riji* (Diaries), April 22, 1946, Hoover Archives, box 45, folder 5. For a critique of Marshall's position vis-à-vis Chiang Kai-shek, see also Herbert Hoover, *Freedom Betrayed: Herbert Hoover's Secret History of the Second World War and Its Aftermath* (Stanford: Stanford University Press, 2011), 696.
90. Chiang, *Riji* (Diaries), April 29, 1946, Hoover Archives, box 45, folder 5.
91. The author's impressions on visiting the Palace of Zizhao in Nanjing, June 7, 2017.
92. See Boyle, *China and Japan at War 1937–1945,* 332–33.
93. See Wen Shaohua, *Wang Jingwei zhuan* (Biography of Wang Jingwei) (Beijing: Tuanjie chubanshe, 2016), 311–14; Chen, *Jiang Jieshi yu Wang Jingwei* (Chiang Kai-shek and Wang Jingwei), 198–99; the author's impressions on visiting Wang Jingwei's place of burial, June 8, 2017.
94. See Chiang, *Riji* (Diaries), May 6–8, 11, 21, and 31, 1946, Hoover Archives, box 45, folder 6; Larry I. Bland, ed., *The Papers of George Catlett Marshall,* 5:553–54 (Baltimore: Johns Hopkins University Press, 2003).
95. Steven I. Levine, "A New Look at American Mediation in the Chinese Civil War: The Marshall Mission in Manchuria," *Diplomatic History,* no. 3 (1979): 356.
96. See in detail Tanner, *The Battle for Manchuria and the Fate of China;* Odd Arne Westad, *Decisive Encounters: The Chinese Civil War: 1946–1950* (Stanford: Stanford University Press, 2003), 48.
97. Tikhvinsky, *Russko–kitaiskie otnosheniia v XX veke* (Russo–Chinese Relations in the Twentieth Century), vol. 5, book 1, 191.
98. Chiang, *Riji* (Diaries), May 23, 1946, Hoover Archives, box 45, folder 6.
99. See Tanner, *Where Chiang Kai-shek Lost China,* 40.
100. Chiang, *Riji* (Diaries), April 20, 1946, Hoover Archives, box 45, folder 5.
101. See Tanner, *The Battle for Manchuria and the Fate of China,* 172, 175, 186, 188, 215–21.
102. See McCullough, *Truman,* 508.
103. See John Leighton Stuart, *Fifty Years in China: The Memoirs of John Leighton Stuart, Missionary and Ambassador* (New York: Random House, 1954), 162–66.
104. See Chiang, *Riji* (Diaries), July 17, 18, 20, 23, 25–27, 29, 31, 1946, Hoover Archives, box 45, folder 8. See in detail Yang Kuisong, "Jiang Jieshi bing fei 'Li Wen can'an' de muhou zhushizhe" (Chiang Kai-shek Was Not the Man Who Gave a Secret Order to Kill Li and Wen), https://read01.com/aEQGKO.html#.YOVX8C-cbxs.
105. Truman, *Memoirs,* 2:90.
106. Chiang, *Riji* (Diaries), August 3, 1946, Hoover Archives, box 45, folder 9.
107. *FRUS 1946,* 10:2–3 (Washington, DC: U.S. Government Printing Office, 1946).
108. Ibid., 51, 53, 187.
109. See in detail Thomas D. Lutze, *China's Inevitable Revolution: Rethinking America's Loss to the Communists* (New York: Palgrave Macmillan, 2007).

110. See Dwight D. Eisenhower, *The Eisenhower Diaries* (New York: W. W. Norton, 1981), 363.
111. Chiang, *Riji* (Diaries), October 5, 1946, Hoover Archives, box 45, folder 11; Macdonald, *Adventures in Chaos,* 99; Tikhvinsky, *Russko–kitaiskie otnosheniia v XX veke* (Russo–Chinese Relations in the Twentieth Century), vol. 5, book 1, 171, 213.
112. Quoted from Marshall, *George C. Marshall: Interviews and Reminiscences for Forrest C. Pogue,* 607.
113. See Westad, *Decisive Encounters,* 61.
114. *United States Relations with China,* xv.
115. Quoted from Lloyd E. Eastman, "Who Lost China? Chiang Kai-shek Testifies," *China Quarterly* 88 (December 1981): 658, 660.
116. Li, "Anticorruption Policy and Party Politics," 105–6, 108; Westad, *Decisive Encounters,* 70, 148–49.
117. Stilwell, *The Stilwell Papers,* 317.
118. Quoted from McCullough, *Truman,* 508.
119. See K. M. Tertitsky and A. E. Belogurova, *Taivanskoe kommuniusticheskoe dvizhenie i Komintern (1924–1932 gg): Issledovanie: Dokumenty* (The Taiwanese Communist Movement and the Comintern [1924–1932]: Research: Documents) (Moscow: AST, Vostok-Zapad, 2005); *China Quarterly* 189 (March 2007): 218–19; Snow, *Journey to the Beginning,* 37–38.
120. Chiang, *Riji* (Diaries), October 22 and 26, 1946, Hoover Archives, box 45, folder 11.
121. See *Far Eastern Quarterly* 7, no. 4 (1948): 354–67.
122. See Chiang, *Soviet Russia in China,* 186–87; Tikhvinsky, *Russkokitaiskie otnosheniia v XX veke* (Russo–Chinese Relations in the Twentieth Century), vol. 5, book 1, 286–87.
123. See Jeans, *The Marshall Mission to China, 1945–1947,* 23.
124. Tang, *Zhongguo lishi dashi nianbiao: Xiandai* (Chronology of Events in Chinese History: Contemporary History), 5.
125. See Xie Ruizhi, *Zhonghua minguo xianfa* (Constitution of the Republic of China), 6th ed. (Taipei: Huatai chubanshe, 1994), 1.
126. Quoted from Tikhvinsky, *Russko–kitaiskie otnosheniia v XX veke* (Russo–Chinese Relations in the Twentieth Century), vol. 5, book 1, 214.
127. See Truman, *Memoirs,* 2:88–89.
128. See Ledovsky, *SSSR i Stalin v sud'bakh Kitaia* (The USSR and Stalin in the Fate of China), 207.
129. See Levine, "A New Look at American Mediation in the Chinese Civil War," 349, 374–75.

## 21. *CATASTROPHE*

1. See Macdonald, *Adventures in Chaos,* 92, 100, 107.
2. See *Dos'e k lichnomu delu Chzhan Tsiunia* (Dossier to the Personal File of Zhang Qun), RGASPI, collection 495, inventory 225, file 134, sheets 5, 9, 14, 16.
3. Li Zhisui, *The Private Life of Chairman Mao: The Memoirs of Mao's Personal Physician,* trans. Tai Hung-chao (New York: Random House, 1994), 37.

4. See Winthrop Knowlton, *My First Revolution* (White Plains, NY: EastBridge, 2001), 40.
5. Chiang, *Riji* (Diaries), March 15, 1947, Hoover Archives, box 46, folder 6.
6. For details, see Lai Tse-han, Ramon H. Myers, and Wei Wou, *A Tragic Beginning: The Taiwan Uprising of February 28, 1947* (Stanford: Stanford University Press, 1991); Wang Xiaobo, ed., *Chen Yi yu er er ba shijian* (Chen Yi and the February 28 Incident) (Taipei: Haixia xueshu chubanshe, 2004); Neil L. O'Brien, *An American Editor in Early Revolutionary China: John William Powell and the China Weekly/Monthly Review* (New York: Routledge, 2003), 36–41; "Taiwan Midterm Prospects: Interagency Intelligence Memorandum," https://www.cia.gov/library/readingroom/docs/CIA-RDP84B00049R000701970017-5.pdf.
7. Westad, *Decisive Encounters,* 147.
8. Quoted from Macdonald, *Adventures in Chaos,* 105, 107–8, 110.
9. See Westad, *Decisive Encounters,* 150–52.
10. Chiang, *Riji* (Diaries), May 21, 1947, Hoover Archives, box 46, folder 8.
11. Ibid., May 22, 1947, Hoover Archives, box 46, folder 8.
12. Quoted from Eastman, "Who Lost China?," 661.
13. Furuya, *Chiang Kai-shek,* 893–94.
14. See *United States Relations with China,* xv; *Foreign Aid by the United States Government 1940–1951,* 14, 22, 27.
15. Quoted from Tikhvinsky, *Russko–kitaiskie otnosheniia v XX veke* (Russo–Chinese Relations in the Twentieth Century), vol. 5, book 1, 327–28.
16. Quoted from MacDonald, *Adventures in Chaos,* 112.
17. See Tikhvinsky, *Russko–kitaiskie otnosheniia v XX veke* (Russo–Chinese Relations in the Twentieth Century), vol. 5, book 1, 364.
18. See Wedemeyer, *Wedemeyer Reports!,* 382–95. Before Wedemeyer left China in 1946, Chiang Kai-shek awarded him with one of the highest military honors of the Republic of China, the Order of Blue Sky and White Sun with Grand Cordon. The same award was also given to Chennault. On behalf of the United States Wedemeyer decorated Chiang with a Distinguished Service Medal.
19. *United States Relations with China,* 258.
20. See ibid., 257–58; Wedemeyer, *Wedemeyer Reports!,* 387, 391–95, 467; *FRUS 1947,* 7:759–61 (Washington, DC: U.S. Government Printing Office, 1972); John J. McLaughlin, *General Albert C. Wedemeyer: America's Unsung Strategist in World War II* (Philadelphia: Casemate, 2012), 158–60.
21. Quoted from Westad, *Decisive Encounters,* 172, 177.
22. *Lichnoe delo Fen Yu-siana* (Personal File of Feng Yuxiang), RGASPI, collection 514, inventory 225, file 2882, sheet 13.
23. Chiang, *Riji* (Diaries), January 19, 1948, Hoover Archives, box 46, folder 17.
24. *Lichnoe delo Fen Yu-siana* (Personal File of Feng Yuxiang), sheet 8.
25. See ibid., sheet 15.
26. See Chiang, *Riji* (Diaries), April 3, 1946, Hoover Archives, box 46, folder 20.
27. See ibid., January 15, March 30, 31 and April 1, 1946, Hoover Archives, box 46, folders 17, 19, and 20.

28. *Lichnoe delo Chan Kai-shi* (Personal File of Chiang Kai-shek), RGASPI, collection 495, inventory 225, file 120, sheet 12.
29. See Christian Schafferer, *The Power of the Ballot Box: Political Development and Election Campaigning in Taiwan* (Lanham, MD: Lexington Books, 2003), 49, 51.
30. Levich, *The Kwangsi Way in Kuomintang China 1931–1939,* 13.
31. See Tikhvinsky, *Russko–kitaiskie otnosheniia v XX veke* (Russo–Chinese Relations in the Twentieth Century), vol. 5, book 1, 414, 418, 436.
32. Ibid., 219; *Lichnoe delo Chan Kai-shi* (Personal File of Chiang Kai-shek), file 120, sheet 7; file 120/2, sheet 60.
33. See Jiang Yongjing and Liu Weikai, *Jiang Jieshi yu guogong he zhan: 1945–1949* (Chiang Kai-shek, Peace Negotiations and War between the Guomindang and the CCP: 1945–1949) (Taiyuan: Shanxi renmin chubanshe, 2013), 225–50.
34. See Tikhvinsky, *Russko–kitaiskie otnosheniia v XX veke* (Russo–Chinese Relations in the Twentieth Century), vol. 5, book 1, 402; Wu Qinjie, ed., *Mao Zedong guanghui dicheng dituji* (Atlas of Mao Zedong's Glorious Historical Path) (Beijing: Zhongguo ditu chubanshe, 2003), 81; *Lichnoe delo Wan Shi-tse* (Personal File of Wang Shijie), RGASPI, collection 495, inventory 225, file 145, sheet 19.
35. See Westad, *Decisive Encounters,* 178.
36. Quoted from Eastman, "Who Lost China?," 659.
37. Quoted from Macdonald, *Adventures in Chaos,* 120.
38. Chiang, *Riji* (Diaries), May 20, 1948, Hoover Archives, box 46, folder 21.
39. *Lichnoe delo Chen Li-fu* (Personal File of Chen Lifu), RGASPI, collection 495, inventory 224, file 131, sheets 23, 24.
40. See Sudoplatov and Sudoplatov, with Schecter, *Special Tasks,* 210–11.
41. See A. V. Meliksetov, ed., *Istoriia Kitaia* (History of China) (Moscow: MGU, 1998), 582–88; Spence, *The Search for Modern China,* 473–80.
42. See Macdonald, *Adventures in Chaos,* 122.
43. See Liliane Willens, *Stateless in Shanghai* (Hong Kong: China Economic Review, 2010), 206.
44. Derk Bodde, *Peking Diary: A Year of the Revolution* (New York: Henry Schuman, 1950), 32. See also Ralph and Nancy Lapwood, *Through the Chinese Revolution* (Westport, CT: Hyperion Press, 1954), 39.
45. Jarvis, "Letters from China 1920–1949," 115.
46. Knowlton, *My First Revolution,* 67–68.
47. Jarvis, "Letters from China 1920–1949," 115.
48. Dorothy Jacobs-Larkcom, *As China Fell: The Experiences of a British Consul's Wife 1946–1953* (Elms Court: Arthur H. Stockwell, 1976), 151.
49. *Lichnoe delo Chan Kai-shi* (Personal File of Chiang Kai-shek), file 120, sheets 28–29.
50. Ibid., 32–33.
51. Chiang, *Riji* (Diaries), November 5, 1948, Hoover Archives, box 47, folder 6.
52. Ibid., October 28, 1948, Hoover Archives, box 47, folder 5.
53. Roy Rowman, *Chasing the Dragon: A Veteran Journalist's Firsthand Account of the 1949 Chinese Revolution* (Guilford, CT: Lyons Press, 2004), 164.

54. See Chiang, *Riji* (Diaries), October 9, November 3–5, 10–12, 24, and 27, 1948, Hoover Archives, box 47, folder 5, 6; *Lichnoe delo Kun Sian-si* (Personal File of Kong Xiangxi), sheet 9; Willens, *Stateless in Shanghai,* 206–7; Taylor, *The Generalissimo,* 387; Li, "Anticorruption Policy and Party Politics," 110–11.
55. Chiang, *Riji* (Diaries), September 9, 1948, Hoover Archives, box 47, folder 4.
56. Quoted from Yang Tianshi, "Jiang Jieshi yu Jiang Jingguo de Shanghai 'da hu'" (Chiang Ching-kuo and the 'Tiger Hunt' in Shanghai), in Yang Tianshi, *Zhaoxun zhenshi de Jiang Jiieshi: Jiang Jieshi riji jiedu* (In Search of the True Chiang Kai-shek: Analyzing Chiang Kai-shek's Diaries), 3:304 (Hong Kong: Sanlian shudian, 2014).
57. See Seymour Topping, *Journey between Two Chinas* (New York: Harper & Row, 1972), 51.
58. See in detail Lew, *The Third Chinese Revolutionary Civil War, 1945–1949;* Tanner, *Where Chiang Kai-shek Lost China;* Westad, *Decisive Encounters,* 192–211. For a personal account of the Huai–Hai Battle by an American eyewitness, see Topping, *Journey between Two Chinas,* 24–48.
59. Thomas E. Dewey (1902–1971) was the governor of New York from 1943 until 1954 and the Republican candidate in the 1944 and 1948 presidential elections.
60. Chiang, *Riji* (Diaries), November 3, 1948, Hoover Archives, box 47, folder 6.
61. Quoted from Westad, *Decisive Encounters,* 198.
62. Cм.: Chiang, *Riji* (Diaries), May 21 and 22, 1948, Hoover Archives, box 46, folder 21.
63. Cм.: ibid., June 17, 1948, Hoover Archives, box 47, folder 1.
64. Ibid., November 19, 1948, Hoover Archives, box 47, folder 6.
65. Ibid., December 16, 1948, Hoover Archives, box 47, folder 7.
66. Ibid., December 18, 1948, Hoover Archives, box 47, folder 7.
67. See Westad, *Decisive Encounter,* 216.
68. Cм.: Chiang, *Riji* (Diaries), December 23, 1948, Hoover Archives, box 47, folder 7.
69. Cм.: ibid., January 3, 1949, Hoover Archives, box 47, folder 9.
70. Cм.: Westad, *Decisive Encounter,* 215. Westad gives an erroneous date of Chiang's visit to Li.
71. Ibid.
72. https://www.cctv.com/special/756/1/49913.html.
73. Chiang, *Riji* (Diaries), January 14, 1949, Hoover Archives, box 47, folder 9.
74. *Lichnoe delo Chan Kai-shi* (Personal File of Chiang Kai-shek), file 20, sheet 58.
75. Chiang, *Riji* (Diaries), January 21 and 22, 1949, Hoover Archives, box 47, folder 9; Wang Guangyuan, *Jiang Jieshi zai Taiwan* (Chiang Kai-shek on Taiwan) (Beijing: Zhongguo wenshi chubanshe, 2008), 12.
76. See *Lichnoe delo Chan Kai-shi* (Personal File of Chiang Kai-shek), file 10, sheets 59, 60; Eastman, "Who Lost China?" 662.
77. See Furuya, *Chiang Kai-shek,* 902–3.
78. Knight Biggerstaff, *Nanking Letters, 1949* (Ithaca: Cornell China–Japan Program, 1979), 15–16.
79. Quoted from *Lichnoe delo Kun Sian-si* (Personal File of Kong Xiangxi), sheet 6.
80. See Wang, *Jiang Jieshi zai Taiwan* (Chiang Kai-shek on Taiwan), 25.
81. O'Brien, *An American Editor in Early Revolutionary China,* 125.

82. See Chiang, *Riji* (Diaries), April 25, 1949, Hoover Archives, box 47, folder 12; *Lichnoe delo Chan Kai-shi* (Personal File of Chiang Kai-shek), file 120, sheet 66.
83. Chiang, *Riji* (Diaries), May 7, 1949, Hoover Archives, box 47, folder 13.
84. Quoted from Lin Hsiao-ting, *Accidental State: Chiang Kai-shek, the United States, and the Making of Taiwan* (Cambridge: Harvard University Press, 2016), 90.
85. See *Lichnoe delo Chan Kai-shi* (Personal File of Chiang Kai-shek), file 120, sheets 8, 9, 58–59, 77, 78; file 120/2, sheets 58, 59; *Lichnoe delo Chen Li-fu* (Personal File of Chen Lifu), sheet 16; *Dos'e k lichnomu delu Chzhan Tsiunia* (Dossier to the Personal File of Zhang Qun), sheet 32.
86. Quoted from Lai, "Chiang Kai-shek versus Guomindang's Corruption in the Republic Era," 73.
87. See *Lichnoe delo Chan Kai-shi* (Personal File of Chiang Kai-shek), file 120, sheets 80, 83, 85; *Lichnoe delo Wan Shi-tse* (Personal File of Wang Shijie), sheet 46; *Lichnoe delo Gu Czhen-gana (Zatsepina)* (Personal File of Gu Zhenggang), RGASPI, collection 495, sheet 225, file 25, sheet 6.
88. See *Lichnoe delo Chan Kai-shi* (Personal File of Chiang Kai-shek), file 120, sheets 84, 86–88; Lü Fangshang, "Zongcai de 'shounao waijiao': 1949 nian Jiang Zongzheng chufang Fei Han" (The Zongcai's "Summit Diplomacy": Jiang Zhongzheng's 1949 Visits to the Philippines and South Korea), in Wu Zusheng and Chen Liwen, eds., *Jiang Zongzheng yu Minguo waijiao* (President Chiang and the Diplomacy of the Republic), 2:1–37 (Taipei: Guoli Zhongzheng ji nian tang guanli chu, 2013).
89. *Lichnoe delo Chan Kai-shi* (Personal File of Chiang Kai-shek), file 120, sheet 100.
90. See ibid., sheets 91–93, 96–98, 120.
91. See Tikhvinsky, *Russko–kitaiskie otnosheniia v XX veke* (Russo–Chinese Relations in the Twentieth Century), vol. 5, book 1, 188.
92. See *Lichnoe delo Chan Kai-shi* (Personal File of Chiang Kai-shek), file 120, sheets 17, 98.
93. Ibid., sheet 102; Stephen P. Gibert and William M. Carpenter, *America and Island China: A Documentary History* (Lanham, MD: Rowman & Littlefield, 1989), 77.
94. See Tong and Li, *The Memoirs of Li Tsung-jen*, 544–46.
95. Quoted from *Lichnoe delo Chan Kai-shi* (Personal File of Chiang Kai-shek), file 120, sheet 46.

## 22. *TAIWAN'S PRISONER*

1. Austronesians are the indigenous peoples of Taiwan, Indonesia, the Philippines, Timor-Leste, Singapore, and many other islands in the Pacific as well as of Malaysia. They speak Austronesian languages.
2. See John J. Metzler, *Taiwan's Transformation: 1895 to the Present* (New York: Palgrave Macmillan, 2017), 13.
3. See ibid., 15; Neil H. Jacoby, *Evaluation of U. S. Economic Aid to Free China, 1951–1956* (Washington, DC: Bureau of the Far East, Agency for International Development, 1966), 17–18, Table VI-1, 19.
4. Snow, *Journey to the Beginning*, 37–38.

5. See Wakabayashi Masahiro, Liu Jinqin, and Matsunaga Masaesu, *Taiwan baike* (Taiwan Encyclopedia) (Tokyo: Yiqiao chubanshe, 1996), 45.
6. Jacoby, *An Evaluation of U. S. Economic Aid to Free China, 1951–1956,* 20.
7. See Chiang, *Riji* (Diaries), December 10, 1949, Hoover Archives, box 47, folder 20.
8. The author's impressions on visiting Chiang Kai-shek's residence in Shilin on July 7, 1997 and Yangming Mountains on July 8, 2012; Li Yiping et al., *Shilin guandi* (Shilin Residence), 3rd ed. (Taipei: Taipei shi wenhua ju, 2016).
9. See *Zilu wanbao* (Independence Evening Newspaper), November 17, 1950; Wang Guangyuan, *Jiang Jieshi zai Taiwan* (Chiang Kai-shek on Taiwan), 27–28; Cao Lixin, *Taiwan baoye shihua* (Sketches on the History of Newspapers on Taiwan) (Hong Kong: Jiuzhou chubanshe, 2015), 119.
10. The author's impressions on visiting *Caolu,* July 8, 2012.
11. In 1946 China's Ministry of Military Administration was renamed Ministry of Defense.
12. Chiang, *Riji* (Diaries), December 13, 1949, Hoover Archives, box 47, folder 20.
13. See John W. Garver, *The Sino–American Alliance: Nationalist China and American Cold War Strategy in Asia* (Armonk, NY: M. E. Sharpe, 1997), 19.
14. In May 1949, Wedemeyer had already advised Chiang to replace Chen Cheng with K. C. Wu.
15. Chiang, *Riji* (Diaries), December 15, 1949, Hoover Archives, box 47, folder 20.
16. Ibid., December 24, 1949, Hoover Archives, box 47, folder 20.
17. See Wang, *Jiang Jieshi zai Taiwan* (Chiang Kai-shek on Taiwan), 73.
18. Chiang, *Riji* (Diaries), December 25, 1949, Hoover Archives, box 47, folder 20.
19. Madame Chiang Soong Mei-ling, *The Sure Victory* ([Westwood, NJ]: Fleming H. Revell, 1955), 22–24.
20. See Chiang, *Riji* (Diaries), January 13, 1949, Hoover Archives, box 47, folder 9.
21. Quoted from Lin, *Accidental State,* 128.
22. Garver, *The Sino–American Alliance,* 11.
23. *FRUS 1949,* vol. 7, book 2 (Washington, DC: U.S. Government Printing Office, 1976), 1218–19.
24. http://china.usc.edu/harry-s-truman-%E2%80%9Cstatement-formosa%E2%80%9D-january-5–1950.
25. See Gibert and Carpenter, *America and Island China: Documentary History,* 88–92.
26. Chiang, *Riji* (Diaries), January 6 and 13, 1950, Hoover Archives, box 48, folder 2.
27. See Lin, *Accidental State,* 7–9.
28. Quoted from Wang, *Jiang Jieshi zai Taiwan* (Chiang Kai-shek on Taiwan), 79.
29. See Lin, *Accidental State,* 7, 120–21, 129, 171; Yang Tianshi, "Taiwan shiqi Jiang Jieshi yu Meiguo zhengfu maodun" (Contradictions between Chiang Kai-shek and the American Government during Chiang's Time on Taiwan), a lecture delivered at Zhejiang University, May 31, 2017.
30. See Kurdiukov, *Sovetsko–kitaiskie otnosheniia, 1917–1957* (Soviet–Chinese Relations, 1917–1957), 219–20.
31. Chiang, *Riji* (Diaries), January 15, 1949, Hoover Archives, box 48, folder 2.
32. Quoted from Furuya, *Chiang Kai-shek,* 913–14. See also *Lichnoe delo Chan Kai-shi* (Personal File of Chiang Kai-shek), file 120, sheets 56, 236.

33. *Lichnoe delo Chan Kai-shi* (Personal File of Chiang Kai-shek), file 120, sheet 57.
34. See Chiang, *Riji* (Diaries), March 3, 1950, Hoover Archives, box 48, folder 4.
35. See Lin, *Accidental State,* 151–52.
36. *Lichnoe delo Chan Kai-shi* (Personal File of Chiang Kai-shek), file. 120, sheet 54.
37. Ibid., sheet 229.
38. See Lin, *Accidental State,* 154–55.
39. See *Lichnoe delo Chan Kai-shi* (Personal File of Chiang Kai-shek), file 120, sheet 47; George F. Kennan, *Memoirs 1950–1963* (Boston: Little, Brown, 1972), 54, 58; Lin, *Accidental State,* 157.
40. For more details, see Pantsov with Levine, *Mao,* 374–79.
41. See Taylor, *The Generalissimo,* 435.
42. It is interesting that Chiang himself intended to provoke a war on the Korean peninsula, hoping that it would lead to a radical change in United States policy in the Far East, including with respect to Taiwan. Beginning in March 1950 he had been planning to send his secret agents to South Korea with this goal in mind.
43. See Lin, *Accidental State,* 173.
44. See Korean Institute of Military History, *The Korean War,* 1:244–73 (Lincoln: University of Nebraska, 2000); Gordon F. Rottman, *Korean War Order of Battle: United States, United Nations, and Communist Ground, Naval, and Air Forces, 1950–1953* (Westport, CT: Praeger, 2002), 117–24.
45. *FRUS 1950*, 7:202 (Washington, DC: U.S. Government Printing Office, 1976).
46. See Lin, *Accidental State,* 165.
47. See Dean Rusk, *As I Saw It* (New York: W. W. Norton, 1990), 175–76.
48. See Acheson, *Present at the Creation,* 412; *Lichnoe delo Chan Kai-shi* (Personal File of Chiang Kai-shek), file 120, sheet 47.
49. *FRUS 1950*, 7:161.
50. Quoted from Peter Lowe, *The Origins of the Korean War,* 2nd ed. (London: Longman, 1997), 175.
51. *FRUS 1950*, 7:162, 164–65.
52. Douglas MacArthur, *Reminiscences* (New York: McGrow-Hill, 1964), 339.
53. See *Lichnoe delo Chan Kai-shi* (Personal File of Chiang Kai-shek), file 120, sheets 225, 363, 364.
54. See Lin, *Accidental State,* 175.
55. MacArthur, *Reminiscences,* 341.
56. See "General MacArthur's Message on Formosa," in Harry S. Truman Presidential Library & Museum, https://www.trumanlibrary.org/whistlestop/study_collections/achesonmemos/view.php?documentVersion=both&documentid=67–4_25&documentYear=1950&pagenumber=7; Truman, *Memoirs,* 2:430.
57. *Lichnoe delo Chan Kai-shi* (Personal File of Chiang Kai-shek), RGASPI, collection 495, inventory 225, file 120, sheet 40.
58. See Lin, *Accidental State,* 175, 189.
59. See *FRUS 1955–57*, 2:457 (Washington, DC: U.S. Government Printing Office, 1986).
60. See "MAAG—Saga of Service," *Taiwan Today,* March 13, 2018; Lin, *Accidental State,* 11.

61. See Chiang, *Riji* (Diaries), July 26, 1951, Hoover Archives, box 49, folder 2.
62. See Lin, *Accidental State,* 189–95.
63. See *Lichnoe delo Chan Kai-shi* (Personal File of Chiang Kai-shek), file 120, sheet 38.
64. See Chiang, *Riji* (Diaries), September 9, 1951, Hoover Archives, box 49, folder 4.
65. The peace treaty was signed in Taiwan, at three o'clock at Tapei Hotel. See Chiang, *Riji (*Diaries), April 28, 1952, Hoover Archives, box 49, folder 12. See also Karl Lott Rankin, *China Assignment* (Seattle: University of Washington Press, 1964), 115–18.
66. For Deng Xiaoping's version of *xiaokang,* see Pantsov with Levine, *Deng Xiaoping,* 366.
67. Quoted from Meliksetov, *Istoriia Kitaia* (History of China), 652.
68. See Ch'en Ch'eng, *Land Reform in Taiwan* (Taipei: China Publishing, 1961), 191–212.
69. See ibid., 82; Hsiao Tseng, *Land Reform in the Republic of China* (Taipei: Conference on the History of the Republic of China, 1981), 8–9; Metzler, *Taiwan's Transformation,* 42.
70. See Ch'en, *Land Reform in Taiwan,* 42–43, 84; Jacoby, *An Evolution of U. S. Economic Aid to Free China, 1951–1956,* 20.
71. See Lai, Myers, and Wei, *A Tragic Beginning,* 87–89; Lin, *Accidental State,* 40, 45.
72. See Jacoby, *An Evolution of U. S. Economic Aid to Free China, 1951–1956,* 23.
73. See *Lichnoe delo Chan Kai-shi* (Personal File of Chiang Kai-shek), file 120, sheets 183–86.
74. See *FRUS 1955–1957,* 2:457.
75. See Jacoby, *An Evolution of U. S. Economic Aid to Free China, 1951–1956,* 25; Metzler, *Taiwan's Transformation,* 43; Meliksetov, *Istoriia Kitaia* (History of China), 653; Samuel P. S. Ho, "Economics, Economic Bureaucracy, and Taiwan's Economic Development," *Pacific Affairs* 60, no. 2 (Summer 1987): 226–47.
76. Quoted from Eastman, "Who Lost China?," 658. See also Bruce J. Dickson, "The Lessons of Defeat: The Reorganization of the Kuomintang on Taiwan, 1950–52," *China Quarterly* 133 (March 1993): 63.
77. Quoted from Eastman, "Who Lost China?," 661–62.
78. See *Lichnoe delo Chan Kai-shi* (Personal File of Chiang Kai-shek), file 120, sheets 225, 361, 365; Liu, *Zhongguo guomindang zhiming lu (1894–1994)* (List of Officials of the Chinese Guomindang [1894–1994]), 193–99.
79. See Dickson, "The Lessons of Defeat," 63–64, 68–71, 76–79; Lin, *Accidental State,* 181.
80. See Zou Lu, *Zhongguo guomindang gaishi* (General History of the Chinese Guomindang) (Taipei: Zhongzheng shuju, 1958), 98; Luo Jialun et al., eds., *Geming wenxian* (Documents of the Revolution), 77:190 (Taipei: Zhongguo guomindang dangshi shiliao bianzuan weiyuanhui, 1978); Chen Pengren, ed., *Zhongguo guomindang dangwu fazhan shiliao—Dangwu gongzuo baogao* (Historical Materials on the Chinese Guomindang Party Work Development—Reports on Party Work) (Taipei: Jindai Zhongguo chubanshe, 1997), 239; letter from Wang Qisheng of Beijing University to the author, April 2, 2018; letter from the director of the Guomindang Central Party Archives, Wang Wenlun, to the author, April 2, 2018; Dickson, "The Lessons of Defeat," 79–81.

81. See Guoshiguan (Academia Historica), document nos. 008-011002-00025-004 and 008-011002-00025-005.
82. Shieh, *The Kuomintang,* 249.
83. See Liu, *Zhongguo guomindang zhiming lu (1894–1994)* (List of Officials of the Chinese Guomindang [1894–1994]), 200–212.
84. See Lin, *Accidental State,* 182.
85. Quoted from Eastman, "Who Lost China?," 663.
86. "Conflict between Chiang Kai-shek and General Chase over the Position of Chiang's Sons," CIA-RDP82-00457R008900600002-0, https://www.cia.gov/library/readingroom/docs/CIA-RDP82–00457R008900600002–0.pdf.
87. See Lin, *Accidental State,* 192.
88. See Dickson, "The Lessons of Defeat," 75.
89. See Lin, *Accidental State,* 189.
90. See Metzler, *Taiwan's Transformation,* 29–30; Taylor, *The Generalissimo,* 423; Tyson Li, *Madame Chiang Kai-shek,* 347.
91. See George H. Kerr, *Formosa Betrayed* (Boston: Houghton Mifflin, 1965), 422–24, 480–86.
92. See *Lichnoe delo Chan Kai-shi* (Personal File of Chiang Kai-shek), file 120, sheets 32–35.
93. Ibid., sheet 168.
94. See ibid., sheet 172.
95. See Schafferer, *The Power of the Ballot Box,* 51; Zhang Shanke, *Taiwan wenti da shiji: 1945.8–1987.12* (Chronology of the Taiwan Question: August 1945–December 1987) (Beijing: Wenhua chubanshe, 1988), 91.
96. "Text of Joint Resolution on Defense of Formosa," in Dwight D. Eisenhower, *Mandate for Change: 1953–1956: The White House Years* (Garden City, NY: Doubleday, 1963), 608.
97. Quoted from Dwight D. Eisenhower, *Ike's Letters to a Friend 1941–1958,* ed. Robert Griffith (Lawrence: University Press of Kansas, 1984), 147.
98. See "MAAG—Saga of Service."

## 23. *UNDER WASHINGTON'S WING*

1. See Xiong Wan, *Jiang Jieshi siren yisheng huiyilu* (Reminiscences of Chiang Kai-shek's Personal Physician) (Beijing: Tuanjie chubanshe, 2009), 130; Richard Nixon, *Leaders* (New York: Warner Books, 1982), 244.
2. The author's impressions on visiting Chiang Kai-shek's residence in Shilin, July 7, 1997; Li, *Shilin guandi* (Shilin Residence), 91.
3. See Shi Yonggang and Fang Xu, *Jiang Jieshi hou zhuan: Jiang Jieshi Taiwan 26 nian zhengzhi dili* (The Last Part of Chiang Kai-shek's Biography: The Political Geography of Chiang Kai-shek's Twenty-six Year Sojourn on Taiwan) (Beijing: Tuanjie chubanshe, 2013), 101; Tyson Li, *Madame Chiang Kai-shek,* 338, 340; Li Songlin, *Jiang Jieshi de wannian suiyue* (The Last Years of Chiang Kai-shek) (Beijing: Tuanjie chubanshe, 2013), 454–62.

4. See Li, *Shilin guandi* (Shilin Residence), 64–66; Chiang, *The Sure Victory,* 29.
5. Quoted from Li Tyson, *Madame Chiang Kai-shek,* 339.
6. See Shi and Fang, *Jiang Jieshi hou zhuan* (The Last Part of Chiang Kai-shek's Biography), 6; Li Qunshan, "Jiang Jieshi zai Tai xingguan zhi chutan (1919–1975" (Initial Analysis of Chiang Kai-shek's Villas on Taiwan, 1919–1975), in Lü Fangshang, ed., *Jiang Jieshi de richang shenghuo* (Chiang Kai-shek's Daily Life) (Taipei: Zhengda chubanshe, 2012), 163–214; Wen Yuan and Wang Feng, *Wo zai Jiang Jieshi fuzi shenbian de rizi* (Days I Served by the Side of Chiang Kai-shek and His Son) (Taipei: Shibao chuban qiye gufen youxian gongsi, 2015), 84–99.
7. See Yang Bichuan, *Taiwan xiandai shi nianbiao (1945 8 yue–1994 9 yue)* (Chronological Tables of Contemporary Taiwan History [August 1945–September 1994]) (Taipei: Yiqiao chubanshe, 1996), 37.
8. See "Dr. K. C. Wu's Views on the Police State and General Chiang Ching-kuo," in Kerr, *Formosa Betrayed,* 484.
9. See Wang, *Qianshan duxing* (The Solitary Path among a Thousand Mountains), 92–95; Chiang and Liu, *Jiang Weiguo koushu zizhuan* (The Autobiography of Chiang Wei-kuo as Told by Himself), 70–72; the author's interview with Ch'en Yung-fa and his wife, Ch'en Lu-yun, in Taipei, June 15, 2017; http://hottopic.chinatimes.com/20160301004669–260812.
10. Quoted from Chiang and Liu, *Jiang Weiguo koushu zizhuan* (The Autobiography of Chiang Wei-kuo as Told by Himself), 73.
11. See Wang, *Qianshan duxing* (The Solitary Path among a Thousand Mountains), 367; Chiang and Liu, *Jiang Weiguo koushu zizhuan* (The Autobiography of Chiang Wei-kuo as Told by Himself), 72–75.
12. See Eisenhower, *The Eisenhower Diaries,* 296; Eisenhower, *Mandate for Change,* 476.
13. See Eisenhower, *Mandate for Change,* 462; Dwight D. Eisenhower, *Waging Peace: 1956–1961: The White House Years* (Garden City, NY: Doubleday, 1965), 296.
14. Eisenhower, *Mandate for Change,* 612.
15. Ibid., 463.
16. Ibid., 464.
17. See ibid., 467, 477.
18. Quoted from Stephen E. Ambrose, *Eisenhower: Soldier and President* (New York: Simon & Schuster, 1990), 383.
19. *Renmin ribao* (People's Daily), April 24, 1954.
20. Stalin had first expressed his thoughts about the possibility of "peaceful coexistence" in April 1952, replying to questions from the editors of provincial American newspapers. "The peaceful coexistence of capitalism and socialism is fully possible in the presence of a mutual desire to cooperate, a readiness to fulfill obligations undertaken, and observance of the principles of equality and non-interference in the domestic affairs of other states." Stalin, *Sobraniye sochinenii* (Collected Works), 16:224.
21. Chiang, *Soviet Russia in China,* 184.
22. Ibid., 1.
23. Ibid., 341–42.
24. See *Lichnoe delo Chan Kai-shi* (Personal File of Chiang Kai-shek), file 120, sheet 87.

25. See Guoshiguan (Academia Historica), document nos. 008-011002-00060-004 and 008-011002-00060-005; Luo et al., *Geming wenxian* (Documents of the Revolution), 77:190; Chen, *Zhongguo guomindang dangwu fazhan shiliao* (Historical Materials on the Chinese Guomindang Party Work Development), 158; letter from Wang Qisheng of Beijing University to the author, April 2, 2018; letter from the director of the Guomindang Central Party Archives, Wang Wenlun, to the author, April 2, 2018.
26. See Liu, *Zhongguo guomindang zhiming lu (1894–1994)* (List of Officials of the Chinese Guomindang [1894–1994]), 213, 214, 216; Li, *Zhongguo guomindang dashiji (1894–11–1986.12)* (Chronology of the Chinese Guomindang [November 1894—December 1986]), 602; Yang, *Taiwan xiandai shi nianbiao (1945 nian 8 yue 1994 nian 9 yue)* (Chronological Tables of Contemporary Taiwan History), 75.
27. *Lichnoe delo Chan Kai-shi* (Personal File of Chiang Kai-shek), file 120, sheet 142. See also Eisenhower, *Waging Peace,* 295.
28. *Lichnoe delo Chan Kai-shi* (Personal File of Chiang Kai-shek), file 120, sheet 141.
29. See Shannon Tiezzi, "How Eisenhower Saved Taiwan," *The Diplomat,* July 29, 2015; Taylor, *The Generalissimo,* 495; *Lichnoe delo Chan Kai-shi* (Personal File of Chiang Kai-shek), file 120, sheet 134.
30. See *Lichnoe delo Chan Kai-shi* (Personal File of Chiang Kai-shek), file 120, sheets 122, 140.
31. Ibid., sheets 124, 132–34.
32. Ibid., sheet 126.
33. Ibid., sheet 125. See also 126–29.
34. See ibid., 130–31.
35. See Schafferer, *The Power of the Ballot Box,* 51; Zhang, *Taiwan wenti da shiji* (Chronology of the Taiwan Question), 187.
36. See *Lichnoe delo Chan Kai-shi* (Personal File of Chiang Kai-shek), sheet 95.
37. See "Eisenhower F. E. Tour State Visit to the Republic of China: Documentary Produced by the China Movie Studio," https://www.youtube.com/watch?v=WDYG1XUheVI.
38. See Eisenhower, *Waging Peace,* 565.
39. Ibid., 564.
40. Dwight D. Eisenhower, *Public Papers of the Presidents of the United States: Dwight D. Eisenhower,* vol. 8: *1960–61* (Washington, DC: Office of the Federal Register National Archives and Records Service General Services Administration, 1961), 503–11.
41. See Jacoby, *An Evolution of U. S. Economic Aid to Free China, 1951–1956,* 22; http://www.nationsencyclopedia.com/Asia-and-Oceania/Taiwan-ECONOMIC-DEVELOPMENT.html.
42. See Guoshiguan (Academia Historica), document no. 002-080200-00643-092; "Chiang's Grandchild as a Coed," *Life* 46, no. 20 (May 18, 1959): 147, 149, 150; the author's impressions on visiting Berkeley, February 25, 2016.
43. See Guoshiguan (Academia Historica), document no. 002-080200-00644-029; the author's impressions on visiting Berkeley and Oakland, February 25, 2016.
44. Richard Nixon, *RN: The Memoirs of Richard Nixon* (New York: Grosset & Dunlap, 1978), 126.

45. Quoted from Joseph Keeley, *The China Lobby Man: The Story of Alfred Kohlberg* (New Rochelle, NY: Arlington House, 1969), 410.
46. See *Lichnoe delo Chan Kai-shi* (Personal File of Chiang Kai-shek), file 120, sheet 128; Arthur M. Schlesinger Jr., *A Thousand Days: John F. Kennedy in the White House* (Boston: Houghton Mifflin, 1965), 483.
47. Rusk, *As I Saw It,* 283.
48. Quoted from Schlesinger Jr., *A Thousand Days,* 483.
49. See *Lichnoe delo Chan Kai-shi* (Personal File of Chiang Kai-shek), file 20, sheets 51–52, 55–58; Taylor, *The Generalissimo,* 514–15.
50. The author's interview with one of the relatives of Chiang Kai-shek, March 19, 2015; Weng Yuan, "Jiang Fangliang hao jiuliang" (Jiang Fangliang Loved to Drink), https://tw.ixdzs.com/read/19/19131/p70.html.
51. See Taylor, *The Generalissimo,* 504.
52. *Lichnoe delo Chan Kai-shi* (Personal File of Chiang Kai-shek), file 120, sheets 60–61.
53. Jeanette indeed preferred women to men, although in fact she was bisexual. But in China there had always existed "tolerance of sexual ambiguity," so the servants could gossip about her behavior but most likely did not despise her for this. On homosexuality in China, see Anne-Marie Brady, "Adventurers, Aesthetes and Tourists: Foreign Homosexuals in Republican China," in Brady and Brown, *Foreigners and Foreign Institutions in Republican China*, 146; Tse-lan D. Sang, *The Emerging Lesbian: Female Same-Sex Desire in Modern China* (Chicago: University of Chicago Press, 2003).
54. See Li, *Shilin guandi* (Shilin Residence), 44; Tyson Li, *Madame Chiang Kai-shek,* 382, 385–86.
55. Quoted from Xiang Zhai and Ruping Xiao, "Shifting Political Calculation: The Secret Taiwan–Soviet Talks, 1963–1971," *Cold War History* 15, no. 4 (2015): 535.
56. See Chiang and Liu, *Jiang Weiguo koushu zizhuan* (The Autobiography of Chiang Wei-kuo as Told by Himself), 75–76; Guoshiguan (Academia Historica), document no. 002-050101-00117-169-180.
57. See Zhai and Xiao, "Shifting Political Calculation," 539–40.
58. See Guoshiguan (Academia Historica), document nos. 008-011002-00078-004 and 008-011002-00078-005; Luo et al., *Geming wenxian* (Documents of the Revolution), 77:259; Chen, *Zhongguo guomindang dangwu fazhan shiliao* (Historical Materials on the Chinese Guomindang Party Work Development), 239; letter from Wang Qisheng of Beijing University to the author, April 2, 2018; letter from the director of the Guomindang Central Party Archives, Wang Wenlun, to the author, April 2, 2018.
59. See Liu, *Zhongguo guomindang zhiming lu (1894–1994)* (List of Officials of the Chinese Guomindang [1894–1994]), 223–27; Li, *Zhongguo guomindang dashiji (1894.11–1986.12)* (Chronology of the Chinese Guomindang [November 1894–December 1986]), 603.
60. *Lichnoe delo Chan Kai-shi* (Personal File of Chiang Kai-shek), file 120, sheet 46.
61. For more details, see Li Songlin and Zhu Zhinan, *Zhonggong heping jiejue Taiwan wenti de lishi kaocha* (A Historical Analysis of How the CCP Will Resolve the Taiwan Question via Peaceful Means) (Beijing: Jiuzhou chubanshe, 2014), 57–58.

62. See Taylor, *The Generalissimo,* 519–20.
63. Chiang Kai-shek, "Oral History Statement, 11/22/1964," John F. Kennedy Presidential Library and Museum, https://www.jfklibrary.org/Asset-Viewer/Archives/JFKOH-CKS-01.aspx.n text 1932]
64. See Sarah McLendon, *My Eight Presidents* (New York: Wyden Books, 1978), 94. See also Margot Knight, "Interviews with Sarah McClendon for the Washington Press Club Foundation as Part of Its Oral History Project Women in Journalism" (Washington, DC, 1991), 92.
65. *Lichnoe delo Chan Kai-shi* (Personal File of Chiang Kai-shek), file 120, sheet 60. See also Schlesinger Jr., *A Thousand Days,* 541.
66. See in detail Xin Hua, *"Jiban" yu "fuchi" de kunjing: Lun Kennidi yu Yuehanxun shiqi de Meiguo dui Tai zhengce (1961–1968)* (Between "Encumbrance" and "Support": On the US Policy Toward Taiwan Under the Kennedy and Johnson Administrations [1961–1968]) (Shanghai: Shanghai renmin chubanshe, 2008).
67. *Department of State Bulletin,* vol. L, no. 1303 (June 15, 1964): 934.
68. Nick Cullather, "'Fuel for the Good Dragon': The United States and Industrial Policy in Taiwan, 1950–1965," in Peter L. Hahn, and Mary Ann Heiss, eds., *Empire and Revolution: The United States and the Third World since 1945* (Columbus: Ohio State University Press, 2001), 242.
69. Quoted from ibid.
70. See Zhai and Xiao, *Shifting Political Calculation,* 535.
71. See Taylor, *The Generalissimo,* 502, 520, 529.
72. *Lichnoe delo Chan Kai-shi* (Personal File of Chiang Kai-shek), file 120, sheet 45.
73. See Taylor, *The Generalissimo,* 526.
74. See *FRUS 1964–68,* 30:47 (Washington, DC: U.S. Government Printing Office, 1998).
75. Confucius, *The Analects of Confucius,* 77.

## 24 *SORROW AND HOPE*

1. See Schafferer, *The Power of the Ballot Box,* 51; Zhang, *Taiwan wenti da shiji* (Chronology of the Taiwan Question), 271.
2. *Lichnoe delo Chan Kai-shi* (Personal File of Chiang Kai-shek), file 120, sheet 42.
3. See Chen, *Zhongguo guomindang dangwu fazhan shiliao* (Historical Materials on the Chinese Guomindang Party Work Development), 239.
4. See Yang Bichuan, *Taiwan xiandai shi nianbiao* (Chronological Tables of Contemporary Taiwan History), 111.
5. See Jacoby, *An Evolution of U. S. Economic Aid to Free China, 1951–1956,* 22–32.
6. *Lichnoe delo Chan Kai-shi* (Personal File of Chiang Kai-shek), file 120, sheet 41.
7. Ibid., sheet 39.
8. Lyndon B. Johnson, *The Essentials for Peace in Asia* (Washington, DC: Department of State, 1966), 10–11.
9. See Richard Nixon, "Asia after Viet Nam," *Foreign Affairs* 67, no. 1 (1967): 111–25.
10. Nixon, *Leaders,* 242.

11. See Tyson Li, *Madame Chiang Kai-shek,* 398–99.
12. Quoted from Zhai and Xiao, *Shifting Political Calculation,* 542.
13. Quoted from Henry Kissinger, *White House Years* (Boston: Little, Brown, 1979), 164.
14. See George Donelson Moss, *Vietnam: An American Ordeal,* 6th ed. (Upper Saddle River, NJ, 2006), 377–78; James C. Thomas, "The Secret Wheat Deal," http://thislandpress.com/2016/12/06/the-secret-wheat-deal/.
15. Quoted from Zhai and Xiao, *Shifting Political Calculation,* 544.
16. See ibid., 545–56.
17. See *Lichnoe delo Chan Kai-shi* (Personal File of Chiang Kai-shek), file 120, sheet 19.
18. See Luo et al., *Geming wenxian* (Documents of the Revolution), 77:313; Chen, *Zhongguo guomindang dangwu fazhan shiliao* (Historical Materials on the Chinese Guomindang Party Work Development), 337–38; letter from Wang Qisheng of Beijing University to the author, April 2, 2018; letter from the director of the Guomindang Central Party Archives, Wang Wenlun, to the author, April 2, 2018.
19. Quoted from Ma Quanzhong, ed., *Taiwan ji shi liushi nian* (Sixty-Year Chronicle of Taiwan) (Taipei: Taiwan xuesheng shuju, 2010), 115.
20. See ibid., 115–16; Liu, *Zhongguo guomindang zhi ming lu (1894–1994)* (List of Officials of the Chinese Guomindang [1894–1994]), 237–42.
21. William P. Rogers, *United States Foreign Policy, Some Major Issues: A Statement by Secretary Rogers before the Senate Committee of Foreign Relations* (Washington, DC: Department of State, 1969), 8.
22. The author's interview with Ch'en Yung-fa and his wife, Ch'en Lu-yun, in Taipei, June 15, 2017.
23. See Xiong, *Jiang Jieshi siren yisheng huiyilu* (Reminiscences of Chiang Kai-shek's Personal Physician), 133; Wang Feng, *Jiang Jishi siwang zhi mi* (The Riddle of Chiang Kai-shek's Death) (Beijing: Tuanjie chubanshe, 2009), 19–22.
24. See Tyson Li, *Madame Chiang Kai-shek,* 400.
25. *Time,* October 5, 1970.
26. See Pantsov, *Mao Tsedun* (Mao Zedong), 716.
27. See Nixon, *RN: The Memoirs of Richard Nixon,* 544.
28. Quoted from Kissinger, *White House Years,* 1492.
29. *Lichnoe delo Chan Kai-shi* (Personal File of Chiang Kai-shek), file 120, sheet 12.
30. See Schafferer, *The Power of the Ballot Box,* 51; Zhang, *Taiwan wenti da shiji* (Chronology of the Taiwan Question), 388.
31. Chiang often began his entries with this sentence-incantation. Till the end of his days he remained a patriot who painfully suffered humiliation whenever any of the great powers inflicted it upon his country.
32. Dai Anguo (1913–84) was the son of Dai Jitao.
33. Chiang, *Riji* (Diary), July 21, 1972, Hoover Archives, box 76, folder 26.
34. On Dr. Yu, see Bruce Lambert, "Paul Yu, 75, Leading Cardiologist, and Physician to Chiang Kai-shek," *New York Times,* October 12, 1991.
35. See Xiong, *Jiang Jieshi siren yisheng huiyilu* (Reminiscences of Chiang Kai-shek's Personal Physician), 134–35.
36. Quoted from ibid., 135–36.

37. See Ye Bangzong, *Jiang Jieshi shiweizhang huiyilu* (Reminiscences of the Head of Chiang Kai-shek's Bodyguards) (Beijing: Tuanjie chubanshe, 2012), 59.
38. See ibid., 137.
39. See Tyson Li, *Madame Chiang Kai-shek,* 416–17.
40. Xiong, *Jiang Jieshi siren yishng huiyilu* (Reminiscences of Chiang Kai-shek's Personal Physician), 137.
41. See Tyson Li, *Madame Chiang Kai-shek,* 418.
42. There are more than thirty inhabited places in China named Xinghua. Which one Du Mu had in mind is not known. In contemporary Chinese *Xinghua* simply means a place where good wine is sold.
43. Du Mu, "Qingming," in Zhang Mei, *Du Mu* (Beijing: Wuzhou chuanbo chubanshe, 2006), 121. Translated by Steven I. Levine.
44. Quoted from Chiang Ching-kuo, *Mei tai si qin* (Reminiscences of My Parents in the Summer House under the Plum Tree) (Taipei: Zhengzhong shuju, 1976), 1.
45. Quoted from Xiong, *Jiang Jieshi siren yisheng huiyilu* (Reminiscences of Chiang Kai-shek's Personal Physician), 138.

## *EPILOGUE*

1. See *Lichnoe delo Chan Kai-shi* (Personal File of Chiang Kai-shek), file 120/2, sheet 2.
2. The author's impressions on a number of visits to Chiang Kai-shek's mausoleum in Cihu.
3. Quoted from Tikhvinsky, *Russko–kitaiskie otnosheniia v XX veke* (Russo–Chinese Relations in the Twentieth Century), vol. 4, book 2, 60. General Wedemeyer would later claim that Chiang said the same thing to him also. See Taylor, *The Generalissimo,* 593, 698.
4. The author's impressions on visiting the Ferncliff Mausoleum of Ferncliff Cemetery on November 18, 2019.

# *Bibliography*

## *PRIMARY SOURCES*

### Archival Sources

Alexander V. Pantsov's Private Archive.
The Archives of Foreign Policy of the Russian Federation (AVPR).
Bureau of Investigation of the Ministry of Legislation on Taiwan.
Columbia University Archives.
Dwight D. Eisenhower Presidential Library & Museum.
Franklin D. Roosevelt Presidential Library & Museum.
Guoshiguan (Academia Historica).
Harry S. Truman Presidential Library & Museum.
Hoover Institution Archives at Stanford University.
John F. Kennedy Presidential Library & Museum.
Lyndon B. Johnson Presidential Library & Museum.
National Archives of the United States.
Oberlin College Archives.
Reading Room of the Central Intelligence Agency of the United States.
Regional Oral History Office, the Bancroft Library of University of California, CA.
Richard Nixon Presidential Library & Museum.
Russian State Archives of Contemporary History (RGANI).
Russian State Archives of Social and Political History (RGASPI).
Zhongguo di er lishi dang'anguan (The Second Historical Archives of China).
Zhongguo guomindang zhongyang dangshiguan (The Central Party Archives of the Guomindang).

Printed Documents

Adibekov, G. M., and Haruki Wada, eds. *VKP(b), Komintern i Iaponiia: 1917–1941 gg.* (The AUCP(b), the Comintern and Japan: 1917–1941). Moscow: ROSSPEN, 2001.

Atkinson, Brooks. "Long Stem Seen, Stilwell Break Stems from Chiang Refusal to Press War Fully." *New York Times,* October 31, 1944.

Bakulin, A. V. *Zapiski ob ukhan'skom periode kitaiskoi revoliutsii: iz istorii kitaiskoi revoliutsii 1925–1927 gg.* (Notes on the Wuhan Period of the Chinese Revolution [From the History of the Chinese Revolution of 1925–1927]). Moscow-Leningrad: Giz, 1930.

Banac, Ivo, ed. *The Diary of Georgi Dimitrov 1933–1949.* Translated by Jane T. Hedges et al. New Haven: Yale University Press, 2003.

Bevans, Charles I., ed. *Treaties and Other International Agreements of the United States 1776–1949.* Vol. 1. Washington, DC: Department of State, 1968.

Bickers, Robert, et al. *Picturing China 1870–1950: Photographs from British Collections.* Bristol: Iles, 2007.

Biggerstaff, Knight. *Nanking Letters, 1949.* Ithaca: Cornell China–Japan Program, 1979.

Bisson, T. A. "China's Part in a Coalition War." *Far Eastern Survey* 12, no. 14 (July 14, 1943): 135–41.

———. "The United States and the Far East: A Survey of the Relations of the United States with China and Japan—September 1, 1930 to September 1, 1931." *Pacific Affairs,* no. 1 (1932): 67–68.

Bland, Larry I., et al., ed. *The Papers of George Catlett Marshal.* 7 vols. Baltimore: Johns Hopkins University Press, 2003.

Bodde, Derk. *Peking Diary: A Year of the Revolution.* New York: Henry Schuman, 1950.

Boister, Neil, and Robert Cryer, eds. *Documents on the Tokyo International Military Tribunal: Charter, Indictment and Judgment.* New York: Oxford University Press, 2008.

Bond, Charles R., Jr., and Terry A. Anderson. *A Flying Tiger's Diary.* College Station: Texas A & M University Press, 1984.

Burr, William, ed. *The Kissinger Transcripts: The Top Secret Talks with Beijing and Moscow.* New York: New Press, 1998.

Butler, Susan, ed. *My Dear Mr. Stalin: The Complete Correspondence between Franklin D. Roosevelt and Joseph V. Stalin.* New Haven: Yale University Press, 2005.

"Caizhengbu caizheng shiliao chenlieshi" (Exhibition of Materials on the History of Finances of the Ministry of Finance of the Republic of China). http://museum.mof.gov.tw/ct.asp?xItem=3421&ctNode=63&mp=1.

Carlson, Evans Fordyce. *Evans F. Carlson on China at War, 1937–1941.* New York: China and Us, 1993.
Chen Cheng. *Chen Cheng xiansheng riji* (Diaries of Chen Cheng). 3 vols. Taipei: Guoshiguan, 2015.
———. *Chen Cheng xiansheng shuxin ji: Jiashu* (Collection of Chen Cheng's Letters: Family Letters). 2 vols. Taipei: Guoshiguan, 2006.
———. *Land Reform in Taiwan.* Taipei: China Publishing, 1961.
Chen Pengren, ed. *Zhongguo guomindang dangwu fazhan shiliao—Dangwu gongzuo baogao* (Historical Materials on the Chinese Guomindang Party Work Development—Reports on Party Work). Taipei: Jindai Zhongguo chubanshe, 1997.
Chen Yipei et al., eds. *Huangpu junxiao shiliao, 1924–1927 (xu bian)* (Documents on the History of the Whampoa Academy, 1924–1927 [Supplementary Collection]). Guangzhou: Guangdong renmin chubanshe, 1994.
Chiang Ching-kuo. *Jiang Jingguo riji* (Diaries of Chiang Ching-kuo). Beijing: Zhongguo wenshi chubanshe, 2010.
Chiang Kai-shek. *All We Are and All We Have: Speeches and Messages Since Pearl Harbor: December 9, 1941–November 17, 1942.* New York: John Day, [1943].
———. *China's Destiny.* Translated by Wang Chung-hui. With an Introduction by Lin Yutang. New York: Macmillan, 1947.
———. *China's Destiny and Chinese Economic Theory.* With Notes and Commentary by Philip Jaffe. New York: Roy Publishing, 1947.
———. *The Collected Wartime Messages of Generalissimo Chiang Kai-shek 1937–1945.* 2 vols. New York: John Day, 1946.
———. "Duiyu shijue de tanhua—Minguo shi liu nian shi er yue shi san ri zai Shanghai zhaodai xinwen jizhe zhi yanci" (Conversation on the Present Moment—Speech at a Press Conference in Shanghai, December 13, 1927). In Luo Jialun et al., eds., *Geming wenxian* (Documents on the Revolution), 16:108–13. Taipei: Zhongguo guomindang dangshi shiliao bianzuan weiyuanhui, 1959.
———. "A Fortnight in Sian: Extracts from a Diary." In General and Madame Chiang Kai-shek, *General Chiang Kai-shek: The Account of the Fortnight in Sian When the Fate of China Hung in the Balance,* 118–76. New York: Doubleday, Doran, 1937.
———. *A Fortnight in Sian: Extracts from a Diary;* Soong Chiang Mayling (Madame Chiang Kai-shek). *Sian: A Coup d'Etat.* 2nd ed. Taipei: China Publishing, 1986.
———. *Generalissimo Chiang Speaks: A Collection of His Addresses and Messages on the War of Resistance.* Hong Kong: Pacific Publishing, 1939.
———. "The Generalissimo's Admonition to Chang Hsueh-liang and Yang Hu-chen Prior to His Departure from Sian." In General and Madame Chiang

Kai-shek, *General Chiang Kai-shek: The Account of the Fortnight in Sian When the Fate of China Hung in the Balance,* 177–84. New York: Doubleday, Doran, 1937.

———. *Jiang Jieshi xiansheng kangzhan jianguo mingyan chao* (Famous Speeches of Mr. Chiang Kai-shek on the War of Resistance and National Construction). Shanghai: Shangwu yinshuguan, 1945.

———. "Jiangshu Zhongshan jian Li Zhilong shijian jingguo xiangqing" (On the Historical Details of Events on the Cruiser Zhongshan and on Li Zhilong). In Luo Jialun et al., eds., *Geming wenxian* (Documents on the Revolution), 9:87–94. Taipei: Zhongguo guomindang dangshi shiliao bianzuan weiyuanhui, 1955.

———. "Jiangshu Zhongshan jian shijian jingguo" (On the History of Events on the Cruiser Zhongshan). In Luo Jialun et al., eds., *Geming wenxian* (Documents on the Revolution), 9:85–86. Taipei: Zhongguo guomindang dangshi shiliao bianzuan weiyuanhui, 1955.

———. *Jiang Zhongzheng xiansheng dui ri yanlun xuanji* (Selected Works of Mr. Jiang Zhongzheng on Japan). Taipei: Caituan faren Zhongzheng wenjiao jijinhui chuban, 2004.

———. *Jiang Zhongzheng zifanlu* (Jiang Zhongzheng's Self-Analysis). 3 vols. Hong Kong: Xianggang zhonghe chuban youxian gongsi, 2016.

———. *Jiang Zhongzheng zongtong wu ji* (Five Diaries of President Jiang Zhongzheng). 6 vols. Taipei: Guoshiguan, 2011.

———. *Jiang zongtong milu: Zhong ri guanxi bashi nian zhengyan* (Secret Notes of President Chiang: Testimony about 80 Years of Sino–Japanese Relations). 15 vols. Taipei: Zhongyang ribao, 1974–78.

———. *Jiang zongtong yanlun huibian* (Collected Works of President Chiang). 24 vols. Taipei: Zhengzhong shuju, 1956.

———. *The New Life Movement in China.* Translated by Madame Chiang Kai-shek. Calcutta: Chinese Ministry of Information, 1942.

———. *President Chiang Kai-shek's Selected Speeches and Messages 1937–1945.* Taipei: China Cultural Service, n.d.

———. *Resistance and Reconstruction: Messages during China's Six Years of War 1937–1943.* 4th ed. New York: Harper & Brothers, 1943.

———. *Sun da zongtong Guangzhou mengnan ji* (Notes on the Kidnapping of the Great President Sun in Canton). Shanghai: Minzhi shuju, 1922.

———. *Xian zongtong Jiang gong quanji* (Complete Works of the Late President, Mr. Chiang). 3 vols. Taipei: Zhongguo wenhua daxue chubanshe, 1984.

———. *Zhongguo jingji xueshuo* (Chinese Economic Theory). Chongqing: Zhongguo zhengfu junshi weiyuanhui yuanzhang shicongshi, 1943.

———. *Zhongguo zhi mingyun* (China's Destiny). Chongqing: Zhengzhong shuju, 1943.

———. *Zongtong Jiang gong ai si lu* (Sorrowful Notes on Mr. President Chiang). 3 vols. Taipei: Zongtong Jiang gong ai si lu bian zuan ziaozu, 1975.

———. *Zongtong yanlun xuanji* (Selected Works of the President). 4 vols. Taipei: Zhonghua wenhua chuban shiye weiyuanhui, 1953.
"Chiang Kai-shek Is Dead in Taipei at 87; Last of Allied Big Four of World War II." *New York Times*, April 6, 1975.
"Chiang's Grandchild as a Coed." *Life* 46, no. 20 (May 18, 1959): 147, 149, 150.
Chiang Soong Mei-ling, Madame. *The Sure Victory.* [Westwood, NJ]: Fleming H. Revell, 1955.
*China: A Century of Revolution: PBS Documentary.* 3 parts. Ambrica Production, 2007.
"Conflict between Chiang Kai-shek and General Chase over the Position of Chiang's Sons." CIA-RDP82–00457R008900600002-0. https://www.cia.gov/library/readingroom/docs/CIA-RDP82–00457R008900600002–0.pdf.
Dallin, Alexander, and F. I. Firsov. *Dimitrov and Stalin 1934–1943: Letters from the Soviet Archives.* Translated by Vadim A. Staklo. New Haven: Yale University Press, 2000.
Dimitrov, Georgi. *Dnevnik 9 mart 1933–6 fevruari 1949* (Diary, March 9, 1933–February 6, 1949). Sofia: Universitetsko izdatelstvo "Sv. Kliment Okhridski," 1997.
"Documents of the Decision." In Ernest May, *The Truman Administration and China, 1945–1949*, 51–99. Philadelphia: J. D. Lippincott, 1975.
"Dr. K. C. Wu's Views on the Police State and General Chiang Ching-kuo." In George H. Kerr, *Formosa Betrayed*, 480–86. Boston: Houghton Mifflin, 1965.
"Dr. Sun Yat-sen Museum Tells Story of Dr. Sun's First Wife, Lu Muzhen (With Photos)." http://www.info.gov.hk/gia/general/201204/20/P201204200485.htm.
Dun, J. Li, ed. *The Road to Communism: China since 1912.* New York: Van Nostrand Reinhold, 1969.
Eisenhower, Dwight D. *The Eisenhower Diaries.* New York: W. W. Norton, 1981.
———. *Ike's Letters to a Friend 1941–1958.* Ed. Robert Griffith. Lawrence: University Press of Kansas, 1984.
———. *Public Papers of the Presidents of the United States: Dwight D. Eisenhower.* Vol. 8: *1960–61.* Washington, DC: The Office of the Federal Register National Archives and Records Service General Services Administration, 1961.
Eisenhower, Dwight D., and John Foster Dulles. *The Communist Threat in the Taiwan Area.* Washington, DC: Department of State, [1958].
"Eisenhower F. E. Tour State Visit to the Republic of China: Documentary Produced by the China Movie Studio." https://www.youtube.com/watch?v=WDYG1XUheVI.
Esherick, Joseph W., ed. *Lost Chance in China: The World War II Dispatches of John S. Service.* New York: Random House, 1974.
Eudin, Xenia, and Robert C. North. *Soviet Russia and the East, 1920–1927: A Documentary Survey.* Stanford: Stanford University Press, 1957.

Fel'shtinsky, Yu., ed. *Oglasheniyu podlezhit: SSSR-Germaniia, 1939–1941: Dokumenty i materialy* (Must Be Announced: The USSR and Germany, 1939–1941: Documents and Materials). Moscow: Moskovskii rabochii, 1991.

Fesiun, A. G., ed. *Delo Rikharda Zorge: Neizvestnye dokumenty* (The Richard Sorge Case: Unknown Documents). Moscow: "Letnii sad," 2000.

*Foreign Aid by the United States Government 1940–1951.* Washington, DC: U.S. Government Printing Office, 1952.

*Foreign Relations of the United States.* 431 vols. Washington, DC: U.S. Government Printing Office, 1947–73.

Forman, Harrison. "Gissimo Junior." *Collier's*, July 31, 1943, 61–62.

Gandhi, Mahatma. *Non-violence in Peace & War.* Vol. 1. Ahmendabad: Navajivan Publishing House, 1948.

Gannett, Lewis S. "Chiang Kai-shek, Leader of the Cantonese Revolutionists, Extends His Sway by a Series of Unexpected Victories." *New York Times,* November 14, 1926.

General and Madame Chiang Kai-shek. *General Chiang Kai-shek: The Account of the Fortnight in Sian When the Fate of China Hung in the Balance.* New York: Doubleday, Doran, 1937.

Gibert, Stephen P., and William M. Carpenter. *America and Island China: A Documentary History.* Lanham, MD: Rowman & Littlefield, 1989.

Gillin, Donald G., and Ramon H. Mayers, eds. *Last Chance in Manchuria: The Diary of Chang Kia-ngau.* Translated by Dolores Zen, with the Assistance of Donald G. Gillin. Stanford: Stanford University Press, 1989.

*Gongfei huoguo shiliao huibian* (Collection of Materials on the History of the Communist Bandits Who Brought Misfortune to the Country). 6 vols. Taipei: Zhonghua minguo kaiguo wu shi nian wenxian biancuan weiyuanhui, 1964.

Gromyko, A. A., ed. *Dokumenty vneshnei politiki SSSR* (Documents of USSR Foreign Policy). 20 vols. Moscow: Politizdat, 1957–76.

Guangdong renmin lishi bowuguan, ed. *Zhonggong "sanda" ziliao* (Documents of the Third CCP Congress). Guangzhou: Guangdong renmin chubanshe, 1985.

Guo Rongrao, ed. *Jiang weiyuanzhang yu Luosifu zongtong zhan shi tongxun* (Correspondence between Chairman Chiang and President Roosevelt during the War). Translated by Guo Rongrao. Taipei: Zhongguo yanjiu zhongxin chubanshe, 1978.

"Guomindang yi da dangwu baogao xuanzai" (Selected Reports on Party Affairs, Submitted to the First Guomindang Congress). *Geming shi ziliao* (Materials on the Revolutionary History), no. 2 (1986): 28–35.

Heben Dazuo (Komoto Daisaku). "Heben Dazuo wei cehua 'Huanggutun shijian' zhi Jigu Lianjie deng han liangjian (1928 nian 4 yue)" (Two Messages from Komoto Daisaku to Isogai Rensuke on the Plans to Create the Huanggutun Incident [April 1927])." *Minguo dang'an* (Republican Archive), no. 3 (1998): 3–5.

Hirohito, Emperor. "Accepting the Potsdam Declaration." Radio Broadcast. https://www.mtholyoke.edu/acad/intrel/hirohito.htm.

———. *Dnevnik imperatora Showa* (Diary of the Showa Emperor). N.p., n.d.

Hitler, Adolf. *Adolf Hitler Collection of Speeches 1922–1945*. N.p., n.d.

*Hostile Activities of Japanese Troops in the Northeastern Provinces of China (From September 18, 1931, to November 7, 1931)*. Vol. 1, S.I: s.n., 1931.

Hsiao Tso-liang. *Power Relations Within the Chinese Communist Movement, 1930–1934*. Vol. 2. Seattle: University of Washington Press, 1967.

Isaacs, Harold. "Documents on the Comintern and the Chinese Revolution." *China Quarterly* 45 (March 1971): 100–115.

Jarvis, Anna Moffet. "Letters from China 1920–1949." (Manuscript), [1974].

Jeans, Roger B., ed. *The Marshall Mission to China, 1945–1947: The Letters and Diary of Colonel John Hart Caughey.* Lanham, MD: Rowman & Littlefield, 2011.

Jin Dequn, ed. *Zhongguo xiandai shi ziliao xuanji* (Selected Documents on Contemporary Chinese History). 3 vols. Beijing: Zhongguo renmin daxue chubanshe, 1988.

Johnson, Lyndon B. *The Essentials for Peace in Asia.* Washington, DC: Department of State, 1966.

*Kangri minzu tongyi zhanxian zhinan* (Directives of the Anti-Japanese National United Front). N.p., n.d.

Kartunova, A. I. *Perepiska I. V. Stalina i G. V. Chicherina s L. M. Karakhanom: Dokumenty, avgust 1923 g.–1926 gg.* (Correspondence of J. V. Stalin and G. V. Chicherin with L. M. Karakhan: Documents, August 1923–1926). Moscow: Natalis, 2008.

———, ed. *V. K. Bliukher v Kitae, 1924–1927: Novye dokumenty glavnogo voennogo sovetnika* (V. K. Bliukher in China, 1924–1927: New Documents on the Chief Military Advisor). Moscow: Natalis, 2003.

Khlevniuk, O. V., et al., eds. *Stalin i Kaganovich: Perepiska: 1931–1936 gg.* (Stalin and Kaganovich: Correspondence: 1931–1936). Moscow: ROSSPEN, 2001.

Khor'kov, V. I., ed. *Rabochee dvizhenie v Kitae (1927-1931): Nankinskii gomindan i rabochii vopros: Dokumenty i materialy* (The Workers' Movement in China [1927–1931]: The Nanjing Guomindang and the Worker Question: Documents and Materials). Moscow: Nauka, 1982.

Khrushchev, N. S. *Doklad N. S. Khrushcheva o kul'te lichnosti Stalina na XX c'ezde KPSS: Dokumenty* (N. S. Khrushchev's Report on Stalin's Cult of Personality at the 20th CPSU Congress: Documents). Moscow: ROSSPEN, 2002.

———. *Report of the Central Committee of the Communist Party of the Soviet Union to the 20th Party Congress.* Moscow: Foreign Languages Publishing House, 1956.

———. *Speech before a Closed Session of the XXth Congress of the Communist Party of the Soviet Union on February 25, 1956.* Washington: U.S. Government Printing Office, 1957.

Kimball, Warren F., ed. *Churchill & Roosevelt: The Complete Correspondence.* 3 vols. Princeton: Princeton University Press, 1984.

Konoe Fumimaro. "Statement by the Japanese Prime Minister (Prince Konoye), December 22, 1938." https://history.state.gov/historicaldocuments/frus1931–41v01/d332.

Kurdiukov, I. F., et al., eds. *Sovetsko–kitaiskie otnosheniia, 1917–1957: Sbornik dokumentov* (Soviet–Chinese Relations, 1917–1957: A Documentary Collection). Moscow: Izd-vo vostochnoi literatury, 1959.

Lambert, Bruce. "Paul Yu, 75, Leading Cardiologist, and Physician to Chiang Kai-shek." *New York Times,* October 12, 1991.

Ledovsky, A. M. *SSSR i Stalin v sud'bakh Kitaia: Dokumenty i svidetel'stva uchastnika sobytii: 1937–1952 gg.* (The USSR and Stalin in the Fate of China: Documents and Testimonies of a Participant in the Events: 1937–1952). Moscow: "Pamiatniki istoricheskoi mysli," 1999.

Lenin, V. I. *Polnoe sobranie sochinenii* (Complete Collected Works). 55 vols. Moscow: Politizdat, 1963–78.

———. *Selected Works.* 12 vols. New York: International Publishing, 1943.

Li Xiaobing et al., eds. "Mao Zedong's Handling of the Taiwan Strait Crisis of 1958: Chinese Recollections and Documents." *CWIHP Bulletin,* nos. 6–7 (1995/1996): 208–26.

Lih, Lars T., et al., eds. *Stalin's Letters to Molotov 1925–1936.* Translated by Catherine A. Fitzpatrick. New Haven: Yale University Press, 1995.

Luo Jialun et al., eds. *Geming wenxian* (Documents of the Revolution). 117 vols. Taipei: Zhongguo guomindang dangshi shiliao bianzuan weiyuanhui, 1953–89.

Lytton, Earl of. *Lessons of the League of Nations Commission of Enquiry in Manchuria.* London: Constable, 1937.

Maevsky, V. "Gruboye narusheniye svobody moreplavaniya v otkrytom more" (The Gross Violation of the Freedom of Sailing in the Open Sea). *Pravda* (Truth), June 26, 1954.

Mao Zedong. *Mao Zedong wenji* (Works of Mao Zedong). 8 vols. Beijing: Renmi chubanshe, 1993–99.

———. *Mao Zedong xuanji* (Selected Works of Mao Zedong). 3 vols. Beijing: Renmin chubanshe, 1951–52.

———. *Mao Zedong xuanji* (Selected Works of Mao Zedong). Vol. 4. Beijing: Renmin chubanshe, 1960.

———. *Selected Works of Mao Tse-tung.* Vols. 1–3. Peking: Foreign Languages Press, 1967.

———. *Selected Works of Mao Tse-tung.* Vol. 4. Peking: Foreign Languages Press, 1969.

Marshall, George C. *Marshall's Mission to China: December 1945–January 1947: The Report and Appended Documents.* 2 vols. Arlington, VA: University Publications of America, 1976.

Meng Guanghan et al., eds. *Guomin canzhenghui jishi.* (Records of the National Political Council). 2 vols. Chongqing: Chongqing chubanshe, 1985.

*Military Situation in the Far East: Hearings before the Committee on Armed Services and the Committee on Foreign Relations, United States Senate, Eighty-Second Congress, First Session, to Conduct an Inquiry into the Military Situation in The Far East and the Facts Surrounding the Relief of General of the Army Douglas MacArthur from His Assignments in That Area.* Washington, DC: U.S., Government Printing Office, 1951.

Morgenthau, Henry, Jr. *Morgenthau Diary (China).* 2 vols. Washington, DC: U.S. Government Printing Office, 1965.

"The National WWII Museum: New Orleans." https://www.nationalww2museum.org/students-teachers/student-resources/research-starters/research-starters-us-military-numbers.

Nixon, Richard. "Asia after Viet Nam." *Foreign Affairs* 67, no. 1 (1967): 111–25.

*The Organic Law of the National Government of the Republic of China.* New York: China Institute of America, 1928.

"The Organic Law of the National Government of the Republic of China." In Chao-chu Wu, *The Nationalist Program for China,* 81–89. New Haven: Yale University Press, 1929.

Panzuofu (Pantsov, A. V.) "Gongchan guoji dang'an zhong de Shao Lizi wenjian" (Documents on Shao Lizi in the Comintern Archive). *Zhonggong chuangjian shi yanjiu* (Studies on the History of Founding the CCP), no. 1 (2016): 121–34.

Pearson, Drew. *Drew Pearson Diaries: 1949–1959.* New York: Holt, Rinehart and Winston, 1974.

"Posetiteli kremlevskogo kabineta I. V. Stalina: Zhurnaly (tetradi) zapisi lits, priniatykh pervym Gensekom: 1924–1953: Alfavitnyi ukazatel'" (Visitors to the Kremlin Office of J. V. Stalin: Journals [Notebooks] Entries of Persons Received by the First General Secretary: 1924–1953: An Alphabetic Guide). *Istoricheskii Arkhiv* (Historical Archive), no. 4 (1998): 1–203.

Priakhin, G. V., ed. *Perepiska Predsedatelia Soveta Ministrov SSR s prezidentami SshA i prem'er-ministrami Velikobritanii vo vremia Velikoi Otechesvennoi voiny 1941–1945 gg.: Perepiska s U. Cherchilem i K. Etli: iiul' 1941 g.–noiabr' 1945 g.; Perepiska s F. Ruzvel'tom i G. Trumenom: avgust 1941 g.–dekabr' 1945 g.* (Correspondence of the Chairman of the Council of Ministers of the USSR with the Presidents of the USA and the Prime-ministers of Great Britain during the Great Patriotic War 1941–1945: Correspondence with W. Churchill and C. Atlee, July 1941–November 1945; Correspondence with F. Roosevelt and H. Truman, August 1941–December 1945). 2 vols. Moscow: Voskresen'e, 2005.

Qin Feng and Wan Kang. *Jiang jia sifang zhao* (Private Photos of Chiang Family). Hangzhou: Zhejiang daxue chubanshe, 2013.

Rogers, William P. *United States Foreign Policy: Some Major Issues: A Statement by Secretary Rogers before the Senate Committee of Foreign Relations.* Washington, DC: Department of State, 1969.

Roosevelt, Franklin D. *The Public Papers and Addresses of Franklin D. Roosevelt with a Special Introduction and Explanatory Notes by President Roosevelt: 1940.* New York: Random House, 1941.

Saich, Tony. *The Origins of the First United Front in China. The Role of Sneevliet (Alias Maring).* 2 vols. Leiden: Brill, 1991.

———, ed. *The Rise to Power of the Chinese Communist Party: Documents and Analysis.* Armonk, NY: M. E. Sharpe, 1996.

Schram, Stuart R., ed. *Mao's Road to Power: Revolutionary Writings 1912–1949.* 7 vols. Armonk, NY: M. E. Sharpe, 1992–2005.

Shanghai shehui kexueyuan lishi yanjiusuo, ed. *Xinhai geming zai Shanghai shiliao xuanji* (zengdingben) (Collection of Selected Materials on the History of the Xinhai Revolution in Shanghai). Expanded ed. Shanghai: Shanghai renmin chubanshe, 2011.

Shieh, Milton J. T. *The Kuomintang: Selected Historical Documents 1894–1969.* New York: St. John's University Press, 1970.

Sladkovsky, M. I., ed. *Dokumenty po istorii Kommunisticheskoi partii Kitaia 1920–1949 gg. (v chetyrekh tomakh)* (Documents on the History of the Chinese Communist Party 1920–1949 [In Four Volumes]). Moscow: IDV AN SSSR, 1981.

Smith, Wesley M. "Wesley Smith Papers: Letters from China 1937–1950." (Manuscript).

"Sobytiia v Kitae" (Events in China). *Pravda* (Truth), December 14, 1936.

Song Meiling. *General Chiang Kai-shek and the Communist Crisis: Madame Chiang Kai-shek on the New Life Movement.* Shanghai: China Weekly Review Press, [1937].

"The Song Qingling House Museum Exhibition in Shanghai." http://www.huaxia.com/zhwh/whrd/2011/02/2300913.html.

Spence, Jonathan D., and Chin Anping, *The China Century: A Photographic History of the Last Hundred Years.* New York: Random House, 1996.

Stalin, J. V. *Sobraniye sochinenii* (Collected Works). Vols. 14–18. Moscow: Izd-vo "Pisatel," 1997.

———. *Works.* 13 vols. Moscow: Foreign Languages Publishing House, 1954.

*Stenograficheskii otchet VI s"ezda Kommunisticheskoi partii Kitaia* (Stenographic Record of the Sixth Congress of the Chinese Communist Party). 6 vols. Moscow: Institute of Chinese Studies Press, 1930.

*Stenograficheskii otchet XX s"ezda KPSS* (Stenographic Report of the 20th Congress of the CPSU). 2 vols. Moscow: Gospolitizdat, 1956.

Stettinius, Edward R., Jr. *Lend-Lease: Weapon for Victory.* New York: Macmillan, 1944.

Stilwell, Joseph W. *The Stilwell Papers.* Arranged and edited by Theodore H. White. New York: Schocken Books, 1972.

Subcommittee to Investigate the Administration of the Internal Security Act and Other Internal Security Laws of the Committee on the Judiciary, United States Senate. *The Amerasia Papers: A Clue to the Catastrophe of China.* 2 vols. Washington, DC: U.S. Government Printing Office, 1970.

Sun Wen (Sun Yat-sen). "Preface." In Chiang Kai-shek, *Sun da zongtong Guangzhou mengnan ji* (Notes on the Kidnapping of Great President Sun in Canton). Shanghai: Minzhi shuju, 1922. Supplementary insert.

Sun Yat-sen. *Izbrannye proizvedeniia* (Selected Works). 2nd ed. revised and expanded. Moscow: Nauka, 1985.

———. *Prescriptions for Saving China: Selected Writings of Sun Yat-sen.* Edited, with an Introduction and Notes, by Julie Lee Wei, Ramon H. Myers, Donald G. Gillin. Translated by Julie Lee Wei, E-su Zen, Linda Chao. Stanford: Hoover Institution Press, [1994].

———. *Sun Zhongshan quanji* (Complete Works of Sun Zhongshan). 16 vols. Beijing: Renmin chubanshe, 1986.

———. *Zhongshan quanji* (Complete Works of [Sun] Zhongshan). 2 vols. Shanghai: Lianyou tushuguan inshuai gongsi, 1931.

"Taiwan Midterm Prospects: Interagency Intelligence Memorandum." https://www.cia.gov/library/readingroom/docs/CIA-RDP84B00049R000701970017–5.pdf.

Tao Chengzhang. *Tao Chengzhang ji* (Works of Tao Chengzhang). Beijing: Zhonghua shuju, 1986.

Teitler, Ger, and Kurt W. Radtke, eds. *A Dutch Spy in China: Reports on the First Phase of the Sino–Japanese War (1937–1939).* Leiden: Brill, 1999.

"Text of Joint Resolution on Defense of Formosa." In Dwight D. Eisenhower, *Mandate for Change: 1953–1956: The White House Years.* Garden City, NY: Doubleday, 1963.

Tigert, John James, ed. *The Doctrines and Discipline of the Methodist Episcopal Church, South, 1902.* Nashville, TN: Publishing House of the Methodist Episcopal Church, South, 1902.

Tikhvinsky, S. L., ed. *Russko–kitaiskie otnosheniia v XX veke: Dokumenty i materialy* (Russo–Chinese Relations in the 20th Century). Vols. 3–5. Moscow: "Pamiatniki istoricheskoi mysli," 2000–2010.

Titarenko, M. L., et al., eds. *Kommunisticheskii Internatsional i kitaiskaia revoliutsiia. Dokumenty i materialy* (The Communist International and the Chinese Revolution: Documents and Materials). Moscow: Nauka, 1986.

———, ed. *VKP (b), Komintern i Kitai: Dokumenty* (The CPSU, the Comintern and China: Documents). 5 vols. Moscow: AO "Buklet," 1994–2007.

Torkunov, A. V. *Zagodnochnaia voina: Koreiskii konflikt 1950–1953* (The Enigmatic War: The Korean Conflict, 1950–1953). Moscow: ROSSPEN, 2000.

Truman, Harry S. *Off the Record: The Private Papers of Harry S. Truman.* Edited by Robert H. Ferrell. Columbia: University of Missouri Press, 1980.

———. *Strictly Personal and Confidential: The Letters Harry Truman Never Mailed.* Edited by Monte M. Poen. Boston: Little, Brown, 1982.

*Tsinan Affair.* Vol. 1. Shanghai: International Relations Committee, 1928.

*United Stated Relations with China: With Special Reference to the Period 1944–1949.* New York: Greenwood Press, 1968.

Van Min (Wang Ming). *Sobranie sochinenii* (Collected Works). 4 vols. Moscow: IDV AN SSSR, 1984–87.

Van Slyke, Lyman P., ed. *The Chinese Communist Movement: A Report of the United States War Department, July 1945.* Stanford: Stanford University Press, 1968.

Vautrin, Minnie. *Terror in Minnie Vautrin's Nanjing: Diaries and Correspondence, 1937–38.* Urbana: University of Illinois Press, 2008.

"Vosstanie Chzhan Siue-liana" (Zhang Xueliang's Uprising). *Izvestiia* (News). December 14, 1936.

Wan Renyuan et al., eds., *Jiang Jieshi yu guomin zhengfu* (Chiang Kai-shek and the National Government). 3 vols. Taipei: Taipei shangwu yinshuguan, 1994.

Wedemeyer, Albert C. *Wedemeyer Reports!* New York: Henry Holt, 1958.

White, Theodore H. "The Desperate Urgency of Flight." *Time*, October 26, 1942.

———. "Until the Harvest Is Reaped." *Time,* March 22, 1944.

Wickert, Erwin, ed. *The Good Man of Nanking: The Diaries of John Rabe.* Translated by John E. Woods. New York: A. A. Knopf, 1998.

Wilbur, C. Martin, and Julie Lian-ying How, eds. *Missionaries of the Revolution: Soviet Advisers and Nationalist China 1920–1927.* Cambridge: Harvard University Press, 1989.

Willkie, Wendell L. *One World.* New York: Simon & Schuster, 1943.

Wu Chao-chu. *The Nationalist Program for China.* New Haven: Yale University Press, 1929.

Wu Zusheng, ed. *Jiang Zhongzheng xiansheng tulu* (Photographs of Mr. Jiang Zhongzheng). Taipei: Guoli Zhongzheng jiniantang guanlichu, 2014.

Wu Zusheng and Chen Liwen, eds. *Jiang Zhongzheng yu Minguo waijiao* (Jiang Zhongzheng and the Foreign Relations of the Republic). 2 vols. Taipei: Guoli Zhongzheng jiniantang guanlichu, 2013.

Xibei daxue lishixi Zhongguo xiandai shi jiaoyanshi, Xi'an dizhi xueyuan zhonggong dangshizu, Balujun Xi'an banshichu jinianguan, eds. *Xi'an shibian ziliao xuanji* (Selected Documents on the History of the Xi'an Incident). Xi'an: Xibei daxue lishixi Zhongguo xiandai shi jiaoyanshi, 1979.

Xie Ruizhi. *Zhonghua minguo xianfa* (Constitution of the Republic of China). 6th ed. Taipei: Huatai chubanshe, 1994.

Yan Xishan. *Yan Xishan riji* (Yan Xishan's Diaries). Taiyuan: San Jin chubanshe, 2011.

Yang You-cheng. "Pis'mo syna Chan Kai-shi k materi" (Chiang Kai-shek's Son's Letter to His Mother). *Leningradskaia Pravda* (Leningrad Truth). February 9, 1936.
Yin, James, and Shi Young. *The Rape of Nanking: An Undeniable History in Photographs.* Chicago: Innovative Publishing Group, 1996.
Yiu, Cody. "A Sad Life Ends for Chiang Fang-liang." *Taipei Times,* December 16, 2004.
Zhang Renjie. *Zhang Jingjiang xiansheng wenji* (Collection of Works of Zhang Jingjiang). Taipei: Zhongguo guomindang zhongyang weiyuanhui dangshi weiyuanhui; Jingxiaochu zhongyang wenwu gongyingshe, 1982.
Zhang Tailei. *Zhang Tailei wenji* (Works of Zhang Tailei). Beijing: Renmin chubanshe, 1981.
Zhang Xianwen, ed. *Nanjing da tusha: zhongyao wenzheng xuanlu* (The Nanjing Massacre: A Collection of Assorted Documentary Evidence). Nanjing: Fenguang chubanshe, 2014.
Zhang Xueliang. "Chang Hsueh-liang's Self-examination over the Sian Incident." In Chiang Kai-shek, *A Fortnight in Sian;* Soong Chiang Mayling (Madame Chiang Kai-shek). *Sian: A Coup d'Etat,* 74–76. 2nd ed. Taipei: China Publishing, 1986.
Zhe Fu, ed. *Ningbo jiu ying* (Old Pictures of Ningbo). Ningbo: Ningbo chubanshe, 2004.
Zhongguo di er lishi dang'anguan, ed. *Zhongguo guomindang di yi di er ci quanguo daibiaohui huiyi shiliao* (Materials on the History of the First and Second Guomindang Congresses). 2 vols. Nanjing: Jiangsu guji chubanshe, 1986.
Zhou Enlai. *Selected Works of Zhou Enlai.* 2 vols. Beijing: Foreign Languages Press, 1981.
Zhu Wenyuan, ed. *Xi'an shibian shiliao* (Documents on the History of the Xi'an Incident). 2 vols. Taipei: Guoshiguan, 1993.

### *MEMOIRS*

Abend, Hallett. *My Life in China: 1926–1941.* New York: Harcourt, Brace, 1943.
———. *Tortured China.* New York: Ives Washburn, 1930.
Acheson, Dean. *Present at the Creation: My Years in the State Department.* New York: W. W. Norton, 1969.
Allen, Henry A. (V. M. Primakov). *Zapiski volontera: Grazhdanskaia voina v Kitae* (Notes of a Volunteer: The Civil War in China). Moscow: Nauka, 1967.
Alliluyeva, Svetlana. *Twenty Letters to a Friend.* Translated by Priscilla Johnson McMillan. New York: Harper & Row, 1967.
Alsop, Joseph, and Stewart Alsop. *The Reporter's Trade.* New York: Reynal, 1958.
Alsop, Joseph W., with Adam Platt. *"I've Seen the Best of It": Memoirs.* New York: W. W. Norton, 1992.

Barrett, David D. *Dixie Mission: The United States Army Observer Group in Yenan, 1944.* Berkeley: University of California Press, 1970.

Bertram, James M. *Crisis in China: The Story of the Sian Mutiny.* London: Macmillan, 1937.

Bisson, T. A. *Yenan in June 1937: Talks with the Communist Leaders.* Berkeley: Center for Chinese Studies, University of California, 1973.

Braun, Otto. *A Comintern Agent in China 1932–1939.* Translated by Jeanne Moore. Stanford: Stanford University Press, 1982.

Burke, James. *My Father in China.* New York: Farrar & Rinehart, 1942.

Candlin, Enid Saunders. *The Breach in the Wall: A Memoir of the Old China.* New York: Macmillan, 1973.

Carlson, Evans Fordyce. *Twin Stars of China: A Behind-the-Scenes Story of China's Valiant Struggle for Existence by a U.S. Marine Who Lived and Moved with the People.* New York: Hyperion Press, 1940.

Carter, Carrole J. *Mission to Yenan: American Liaison with the Chinese Communists 1944–1947.* Lexington: University Press of Kentucky, 1997.

Chang Kuo-t'ao. *The Rise of the Chinese Communist Party. Volumes One & Two of Autobiography of Chang Kuo-t'ao.* Lawrence: University Press of Kansas, 1972.

Chen Bulei. *Chen Bulei huiyilu* (Memoirs of Chen Bulei). Taipei: Zhuanji wenxue chubanshe, 1981.

Ch'en Chieh-ju. *Chiang Kai-shek's Secret Past: The Memoirs of His Second Wife, Ch'en Chieh-ju.* Edited and with an Introduction by Lloyd E. Eastman. Boulder, CO: Westview Press, 1993.

Chen Gongbo. *Kuxiao lu (yi jiu er wu zhi yi jiu san liu)* (Somber Notes [1925–1936]). Beijing: Xiandai shiliao biankanshe, 1981.

Chen Jieru. *Chen Jieru huiyilu quan yi ben: Jiang Jieshi Chen Jieru de hunyin gushi* (Complete Text of Chen Jieru's Reminiscences: The Story of Chiang Kai-shek and Chen Jieru's Family Life). 2 vols. Taipei: Zhuanji wenxue, [1992].

Ch'en Li-fu. *The Storm Clouds Clear over China: The Memoir of Ch'en Li-fu, 1900–1993.* Edited and compiled, with an Introduction and Notes, by Sidney H. Chang and Ramon H. Myers. Stanford: Stanford University Press, 1994.

Chennault, Claire Lee. *Way of a Fighter.* New York: G. P. Putman's Sons, 1949.

Cherepanov, A. I. "Itogi Uhanskoi operatsii" (Notes on the Wuhan Campaign). In Yu. V. Chudodeev, ed., *Po dorogam Kitaia 1937–1945: Vospominaniia,* 14–52 (Along Chinese Roads 1937–1945: Reminiscences). Moscow: Nauka, 1989.

———. *Notes of a Military Adviser in China.* Translated by Alexandra O. Smith. Taipei: Office of Military History, 1970.

———. *Zapiski voennogo sovetnika v Kitae* (Notes of a Military Advisor in China). 2nd ed. Moscow: Nauka, 1976.

Chiang Ching-kuo. *Calm in the Eye of a Storm.* Taipei: Li Ming Cultural Enterprise, 1978.

———. *Jiang Jingguo zizhuan* (The Autobiography of Chiang Ching-kuo). Beijing: Tuanjie chubanshe, 2005.

———. *Mei tai si qin* (Reminiscences of My Parents in the Summer House under the Plum Tree). Taipei: Zhengzhong shuju, 1976.

———. *My Days in Soviet Russia.* [Taipei, 1963].

Chiang Chung-cheng (Chiang Kai-shek). *Soviet Russia in China: Summing-up at 70.* Translated under the direction of Madame Chiang Kai-shek. Revised, enlarged ed. with maps. New York: Farrar, Straus, and Cudahy, 1957.

Chiang Kai-shek. "The Day I Was Kidnapped." In Dun J. Li, ed., *The Road to Communism: China since 1912,* 135–41. New York: Van Nostrand Reinhold, 1969.

Chiang Wego, W. K., General. *How Generalissimo Chiang Kai-shek Won the Eight-Year Sino-Japanese War 1937–1945.* Taipei: Li Ming Culture Enterprise, 1979.

Chiang Wei-Kuo, General. *How the China Mainland was Lost.* Taipei: Armed Forces University, 1979.

Chiang Wei-kuo and Liu Fenghan. *Jiang Weiguo koushu zizhuan* (The Autobiography of Chiang Wei-kuo as Told by Himself). Beijing: Zhongguo dabaike quanshu chubanshe, 2008.

Chudodeev, Yu. V., ed. *Na kitaiskoi zemle: Vospominaniia sovetskikh dobrovol'tsev 1925–1945* (On Chinese Soil: Recollections of Soviet Volunteers 1925–1945). Moscow: Nauka, 1977.

———. *Po dorogam Kitaia 1937–1945: Vospominaniia* (Along Chinese Roads 1937–1945: Reminiscences). Moscow: Nauka, 1989.

Chuikov, V. I. *Missiia v Kitae: Zapiski voennogo sovetnika* (Mission in China: Notes of a Military Advisor). Moscow: Nauka, 1981.

Churchill, Winston S. *Closing the Ring.* Boston: Houghton Mifflin, 1951.

Cowles, Gardner. *Mike Looks Back: The Memoirs of Gardner Cowles, Founder of Look Magazine.* New York: Gardner Cowles, 1985.

Cressy-Marcks, Violet. *Journey into China.* New York: E. P. Dutton, 1942.

Dalin, S. A. *Kitaiskie memuary, 1921–1927* (Chinese Memoirs, 1921–1927). Moscow: Nauka, 1975.

———. *V riadakh kitaiskoi revoliutsii* (In the Ranks of the Chinese Revolution). Moscow–Leningrad: Moskovskii rabochii, 1926.

Davis, John Paton, Jr. *China Hand: An Autobiography.* Philadelphia: University of Pennsylvania Press, 2012.

———. *Foreign and Other Affairs.* New York: W. W. Norton, 1964.

Del Mar, Walter. *Around the World Through Japan.* London: A. and C. Black, 1903.

Djilas, Milovan. *Conversations with Stalin.* Translated by Michael B. Petrovich. New York: Harcourt, Brace & World, 1962.

Dorn, Frank. *Walkout with Stilwell in Burma.* New York: Thomas Y. Crowell, 1971.

Eisenhower, Dwight D. *Waging Peace: 1956–1961: The White House Years.* Garden City, NY: Doubleday, 1965.

Fairbank, John King. *Chinabound: A Fifty-Year Memoir.* New York: Harper & Row, 1982.

Farjenel, Fernand. *Through the Chinese Revolution: My Experience in the South and North: The Revolution of Social Life: Interviews with Party Leaders: An Unconstitutional Loan—The Coup d'État.* New York: Frederick A. Stokes, 1916.

Farmer, Rhodes. *Shanghai Harvest: A Diary of Three Years of the China War.* London: Museum Press, 1945.

Feng Lida. *Wode fuqin Feng Yuxiang jiangjun* (My Father General Feng Yuxiang). Chengdu: Sichuan renmin chubanshe, 1984.

Feng Yuxiang. *Wo de shenghuo* (My Life). Beijing: Zhongguo qingnian chubanshe, 2015.

———. *Wo suo renshi de Jiang Jieshi* (The Chiang Kai-shek as I Remember Him). Harbin: Beifang wenyi chubanshe, 2010.

Fischer, Louis. *Men and Politics: An Autobiography.* Westport, CT: Greenwood Press, 1946.

Fleming, Peter. *News from Tartary: A Journey from Peking to Kashgar.* London: Jonathan Cape, 1936.

———. *One's Company: A Journey to China.* New York: Charles Scribner's Sons, 1934.

Foo Yee Wah. *Chiang Kai-shek's Last Ambassador to Moscow: The Wartime Diaries of Fu Bingchang.* New York: Palgrave Macmillan, 2011.

Franck, Harry A. *Marco Polo Junior: The True Story of an Imaginary American Boy's Travel-adventures All over China.* New York: Century, 1929.

Geil, William Edgar. *Eighteen Capitals of China.* London: Constable, 1911.

Gellhorn, Martha. *Travels with Myself and Another.* New York: Dodd, Mead, 1978.

Greene, Ruth Altman. *Hsiang-Ya Journal.* Hamden, CT: Archon Books, 1977.

Grew, Joseph C. *Turbulent Era: A Diplomatic Record of Forty Years, 1904–1945.* 2 vols. Boston: Houghton Mifflin, 1952.

Gunther, John. *Inside Asia.* New York: Harper & Brothers, 1939.

Hager, Charles R. "Doctor Sun Yat Sen: Some Personal Reminiscences." In Lyon Sharman, *Sun Yat-sen: His Life and Its Meaning: A Critical Biography,* 382–87. New York: John Day, 1934.

Heben Dazuo (Komoto Daisaku) et al. *Wo shasila Zhang Zuolin* (I Killed Zhang Zuolin). Changchun: Jilin wenshi chubanshe, 1986.

Hoover, Herbert. *Freedom Betrayed: Herbert Hoover's Secret History of the Second World War and Its Aftermath.* Stanford: Stanford University Press, 2011.

Hu Qiaomu. *Hu Qiaomu huiyi Mao Zedong: zengdingben* (Hu Qiaomu Remembers Mao Zedong: Expanded ed.). Beijing: Renmin chubanshe, 2014.

Huang Hua. "My Contacts with John Leighton Stuart after Nanjing's Liberation." *Chinese Historians* 5, no. 1 (Spring 1992): 47–56.

Hume, Edward H. *Doctors East, Doctors West: An American Physician's Life in China.* London: George Allen & Unwin, 1949.

Jacobs-Larkcom, Dorothy. *As China Fell: The Experiences of a British Consul's Wife 1946–1953.* Elms Court: Arthur H. Stockwell, 1976.

Jiang Song Meiling (Madame Chiang Kai-shek-Song Meiling). *Yu Baoluoting tanhuade huiyilu* (Recollections of Conversations with Borodin). Taipei: Liming wenhua shiye gufen youxian gongsi, 1976.

Jiang Tingfu. *The Reminiscences of Tsiang T'ing-fu (1895–1965).* New York: Chinese Oral History Project, East Asian Institute of Columbia University, 1975.

Kalinin, V., and D. Kuznetsov. *Tanker "Tuapse": Dokumental'naia povest'* (Tanker Tuapse: A Documentary Novel). Moscow: Molodaia Gvardiia, 1956.

Kalyagin, A. Ya. "Bitva za Uhan" (Battle for Wuhan). In Yu. V. Chudodeev, ed., *Na kitaiskoi zemle: Vospominaniia sovetskikh dobrovol'tsev 1925–1945* (On Chinese Soil: Recollections of Soviet Volunteers 1925–1945), 177–88. Moscow: Nauka, 1977.

———. *Po neznakomym dorogam (Zapiski voennogo sovetnika v Kitae)* (Along Alien Roads [Notes of a Military Advisor in China]). 2nd ed. Moscow: Nauka, 1979.

Kennan, George F. *Memoirs 1925–1950.* Boston: Little, Brown, 1967.

———. *Memoirs 1950–1963.* Boston: Little, Brown, 1972.

Kerr, George H. *Formosa Betrayed.* Boston: Houghton Mifflin, 1965.

Khe Hsian-nin (He Xiangning). *Vospominaniia o Sun Yat-sene* (Reminiscences of Sun Yat-sen). Translated by Yu. M. Garushiants. Moscow: Progress, 1966.

Khrushchev, Nikita S. *Memoirs of Nikita Khrushchev.* 3 vols. Translated by George Shriver. University Park: Pennsylvania State University Press, 2007–8.

———. *Vospominaniia: Izbrannye fragmenty* (Reminiscences: Selected Fragments). Moscow: Vagrius, 1997.

———. *Vremia, Liudi, Vlast': Vospominaniia* (Time, People, Power: Memoirs). 4 vols. Moscow: Moskovskie novosti, 1999.

Kishkina, Elizaveta. *Iz Rossii v Kitai: Put' dlinnoiu v sto let: Memuary* (From Russia to China: A One-Hundred-Year Path: Memoirs). Moscow: OOO Mezhdunarodnaia izdatel'skaia kompaniia "Shans," 2018.

Kissinger, Henry A. *White House Years.* Boston: Little, Brown, 1979.

———. *Years of Upheaval.* Boston: Little, Brown, 1982.

Knight, Margot. "Interviews with Sarah McClendon for the Washington Press Club Foundation as Part of Its Oral History Project Women in Journalism." Washington, DC, 1991.

Knowlton, Winthrop. *My First Revolution.* White Plains, NY: EastBridge, 2001.

La Motte, Ellen N. *Peking Dust.* New York: The Century, 1920.

Lapwood, Ralph, and Nancy Lapwood. *Through the Chinese Revolution.* Westport, CT: Hyperion Press, 1954.

Lattimore, Owen, and Fujiko Isono. *China Memoirs: Chiang Kai-shek and the War Against Japan.* Tokyo: University of Tokyo Press, 1990.

Leonard, Royal. *I Flew for China.* Garden City, NY: Doubleday, Doran, 1942.

Li Zhisui. *The Private Life of Chairman Mao: The Memoirs of Mao's Personal Physician.* Translated by Tai Hung-chao. New York: Random House, 1994.

Lü Fangshang et al. *Jiang Zhongzheng zongtong shicong renyuan fangwen jilu* (Notes of Interviews with Service Personnel for President Jiang Zhongzheng). 2 vols. Taipei: Zhongyang yanjiuyuan, 2012.

Luo Ruiqing, Lü Zhengcao, and Wang Bingnan. *Zhou Enlai and the Xi'an Incident: An Eyewitness Account: A Turning Point in Chinese History.* Beijing: Foreign Languages Press, 1983.

MacArthur, Douglas. *Reminiscences.* New York: McGraw-Hill, 1964.

Marshall, George C. *George C. Marshall: Interviews and Reminiscences for Forrest C. Pogue.* Revised ed. Lexington, VA: George C. Marshall Research Foundation, 1991.

Marshall, Katherine Tupper. *Together: Annals of an Army Wife.* New York: Tupper & Love, 1946.

McLendon, Sarah. *My Eight Presidents.* New York: Wyden Books, 1978.

Minge zhongyang xuanchuanbu, ed. *Huiyi yu huainian—Jinian Sun Zhongshan xiansheng wenzhang xuanji* (Memoirs and Warm Reminiscences—Selected Articles in Memory of Mr. Sun Zhongshan). Beijing: Huaxia chubanshe, 1986.

Misselwitz, Henry Francis. *The Dragon Stirs: An Intimate Sketch-Book of China's Kuomintang Revolution 1927–29.* Westport, CT: Harbinger House, 1941.

Mi Xi et al. *Zai Jiang Jieshi Song Meiling shenbian de rizi* (Days We Served by the Side of Chiang Kai-shek and Song Meiling). Beijing: Tuanjie chubanshe, 2005.

Mo Yongming and Fan Ran. *Chen Yingshi jinian* (Chronology of the Life of Chen Yingshi). Nanjing: Nanjing daxue chubanshe, 1991.

Nie Rongzhen. *Inside the Red Star: The Memoirs of Marshal Nie Rongzhen.* Beijing: New World Press, 1983.

———. *Nie Rongzhen huiyilu* (Reminiscenses of Nie Rongzhen). 3 vols. Beijing: Jiefangjun chubanshe, 1983.

Nixon, Richard. *In the Arena: A Memoir of Victory, Defeat and Renewal.* New York: Simon & Schuster, 1990.

———. *Leaders.* New York: Warner Books, 1982.

———. *RN: The Memoirs of Richard Nixon.* New York: Grosset & Dunlap, 1978.

Paniushkin, A. S. *Zapiski posla: Kitai 1939–1944 gg.* (Notes of the Ambassador: China 1939–1944). Moscow: IDV AN SSSR, 1981.

Parks, Lillian Rogers, with Francez Spatz Leighton. *My Thirty Years Backstairs at the White House.* New York: Fleet, 1961.

Peck, Graham. *Two Kinds of Time.* Boston: Houghton Mifflin, 1950.
Powell, John B. *My Twenty-five Years in China.* New York: Macmillan, 1945.
Pu Yi. *From Emperor to Citizen.* Translated by W. J. F. Jenner. New York: Oxford University Press, 1987.
Rankin, Karl Lott. *China Assignment.* Seattle: University of Washington Press, 1964.
Ransome, Arthur. *The Chinese Puzzle.* Boston: Houghton Mifflin, 1927.
Roosevelt, Eleanor. *This I Remember.* New York: Harper & Brothers, 1949.
Roosevelt, Elliot. *As He Saw It.* Westport, CT: Greenwood Press, 1974.
Rowman, Roy. *Chasing the Dragon: A Veteran Journalist's Firsthand Account of the 1949 Chinese Revolution.* Guilford, CT: Lyons Press, 2004.
Rusk, Dean. *As I Saw It.* New York: W. W. Norton, 1990.
Scaroni, Silvio. *Missione Militare Aeronautica in Cina* (Air Force Military Mission). Maggio: Ufficio storico, 1970.
Schlesinger, Arthur M., Jr. *A Thousand Days: John F. Kennedy in the White House.* Boston: Houghton Mifflin, 1965.
Semenov, G. G. *Tri goda v Pekine: Zapiski voennogo sovetnika* (Three Years in Beijing: Notes of a Military Advisor). Moscow: Nauka, 1978.
Service, John S. *State Department Duty in China, the McCarthy Era, and After, 1933–1977.* An Oral History Conducted 1977–1978 by Rosemary Levinson. Regional Oral History Office. Bancroft Library. University of California, Berkeley, 1981.
Shao Lizi, "Chushi Sulian de huiyi" (Memoirs of My Mission as an Ambassador in the Soviet Union). *Wenshi ziliao xuanji* (Selected Documents of Literature and History): no. 60 (1979): 181–94.
Sliusarev, S. V. "V vozdushnykh boiakh nad Kitaem" (In Air Battles over China). In Yu. V. Chudodeev, ed., *Po dorogam Kitaia 1937–1945: Vospominaniia* (Along Chinese Roads 1937–1945: Reminiscences), 92–148. Moscow: Nauka, 1989.
Smalley, Martha Lund, ed. *American Missionary Eyewitnesses to the Nanking Massacre, 1937–1938.* New Haven: Yale Divinity School Library, 1997.
Smedley, Agnes. *China Fights Back: An American Woman with the Eight Route Army.* New York: Vanguard Press, 1938.
Snow, Edgar. *Journey to the Beginning.* New York: Random House, 1958.
———. *Random Notes on Red China (1936–1945).* Cambridge: East Asian Research Center Harvard University, 1957.
———. *Red Star over China.* London: Victor Gollancz, 1937.
Song Meiling. *Song Meiling zishu* (Song Meiling's Autobiographical Notes). Beijing: Tuanjie chubanshe, 2007.
Soong Chiang Mayling (Madame Chiang Kai-shek). "Sian: A Coup d'État." In General and Madame Chiang Kai-shek, *General Chiang Kai-shek: The Account of the Fortnight in Sian When the Fate of China Hung in the Balance,* 63–117. New York: Doubleday, Doran, 1937.

Stuart, John Leighton. *Fifty Years in China: The Memoirs of John Leighton Stuart, Missionary and Ambassador.* New York: Random House, 1954.

Sudoplatov, Pavel, and Anatoli Sudoplatov, with Jerrold L. Schecter and Leona P. Schecter. *Special Tasks: The Memoirs of an Unwanted Witness: A Soviet Spymaster.* Boston: Little, Brown, 1994.

Sun Yat-sen. *Kidnapped in London: Being the Story of My Capture, Detention at, and Release from the Chinese Legation.* Bristol, UK: Simpkin, Marshall, Hamilton, Kent, 1897.

Tikhvinsky, S. L. *Kitai v moei zhizni (30–90 gg.)* (China in My Life [1930s–1990s]). Moscow: Nauka, 1992.

———. *Vozvrashchenie k "Vorotam nebesnogo spokoistviia"* (Return to "the Gates of Heavenly Peace"). Moscow: "Pamiatniki istoricheskoi mysli," 2002.

Timperley, Harold J. *Japanese Terror in China.* Freeport NY: Books for Libraries Press, 1938.

Tong, Hollington K. *Chiang Kai-shek's Teacher and Ambassador: An Inside View of the Republic of China from 1911–1958: General Stilwell and American Policy Change Towards Free China.* Bloomington, IN: Arthur House, 2005.

Tong Te-kong and Li Tsung-jen. *The Memoirs of Li Tsung-jen.* Boulder, CO: Westview Press, 1979.

Tong Xiaopeng. *Zai Zhou Enlai shenbian sishi nian* (Forty Years I Served by the Side of Zhou Enlai). 2 vols. Beijing: Huawen chubanshe, 2015.

Topping, Seymour. *Journey between Two Chinas.* New York: Harper & Row, 1972.

Truman, Harry S. *The Autobiography of Harry S. Truman.* Edited by Robert H. Ferrell. Boulder, CO: Colorado Associated University Press, 1980.

———. *Memoirs.* 2 vols. Garden City, NY: Doubleday, 1956.

Tszian Chzhunzhen (Chan Kaishi). (Jiang Zhongzheng [Chiang Kai-shek]). *Sovetskaia Rossia v Kitae: Vospominaniia i razmyshlenniia v 70 let* (Soviet Russia in China: Reminiscences and Thoughts at 70). Edited by Alexander V. Pantsov. Moscow: Posev, 2009.

"24 in Plot to Slay Chinese President." *New York Times*, September 7, 1929.

Tyau, Min-Ch'in T. Z. *Two Years of Nationalist China.* Shanghai: Kelly and Walsh, 1930.

Utley, Freda. *China at War.* New York: e John Day, 1939.

Vishniakova-Akimova, V. V. *Dva goda v vostavshem Kitae 1925–1927: Vospominaniia* (Two Years in Revolutionary China, 1925–1927: Memoirs). Moscow: Nauka, 1965.

———. *Two Years in Revolutionary China, 1925–1927.* Translated by Steven I. Levine. Cambridge: East Asian Research Center, Harvard University, 1971.

Vladimirov, P. P. *Osobyi raion Kitaia, 1942–1945* (Special Region of China, 1942–1945). Moscow: APN, 1975.

Voitinsky, G. "Moi vstrechi s Sun Yat-senom" (My Meetings with Sun Yat-sen). *Pravda* (Truth), March 15, 1925.

Wang, Peter Chen-main. "Revising US–China Wartime Relations: A Study of Wedemeyer's China Mission." *Journal of Contemporary China*, no. 18 (59) (March 2009): 233–47.

Wang Shichun. *Qianshan duxing: Jiang Weiguo de ren sheng zhi lü* (The Solitary Path among a Thousand Mountains: The Life Path of Chiang Wei-kuo). Taipei: Tianxia wenhua, 1996.

Weng Yuan. "Jiang Fangliang hao jiuliang" (Jiang Fangliang Loved to Drink). https://tw.ixdzs.com/read/19/19131/p70.html.

Weng Yuan and Wang Feng. *Wo zai Jiang Jieshi fuzi shenbian de rizi* (Days I Served by the Side of Chiang Kai-shek and His Son). Taipei: Shibao wenhua chuban qiye gufen youxian gongsi, 2015.

White, Theodore H. *In Search of History: A Personal Adventure.* New York: Harper & Row, 1978.

Willens, Liliane. *Stateless in Shanghai.* Hong Kong: China Economic Review, 2010.

Witte, Count S. Yu. *Vospominannia: Tsarstvovanie Nikolai II* (Reminiscences: Reign of Nicholas II). 2 vols. 3rd ed. Berlin: "Slovo," 1924.

Xiong Wan. *Jiang Jieshi siren yisheng huiyilu* (Reminiscences of Chiang Kai-shek's Personal Physician). Beijing: Tuanjie chubanshe, 2009.

Ye Bangzong. *Jiang Jieshi shiweizhang huiyilu* (Reminiscences of the Head of Chiang Kai-shek's Bodyguards). Beijing: Tuanjie chubanshe, 2012.

Ye Zilong. *Ye Zilong huiyilu* (Memoirs of Ye Zilong). Beijing: Zhongyang wenxian chubanshe, 2000.

Ying Mengqing. "Fenghua yumin canjia guangfu Hangzhou gansidui ji" (Notes on the Dare to Die Detachment of Fenghua Fishermen that Took Part in the Restoration of Sovereignty in Hangzhou). In Zhongguo renmin zhengzhi xieshanghui Zhejiang sheng weiyuanhui wenshi ziliao yanjiu weiyuanhui, ed., *Zhejiang xinhai geming huiyilu* (Reminiscences of the Xinhai Revolution in Zhejiang), 186–92. Hangzhou: Zhejiang renmin chubanshe, 1981.

Yorke, Gerald. *China Changes*. New York: Charles Scribner's Sons, 1936.

Zang Zhuo. *Wo zai Jiang Jieshi yu Wang Jingwei shenbiande rizi* (Days I Served by the Side of Chiang Kai-shek and Wang Jingwei). Taipei: Duli zuojia, 2013.

———. *Zang Zhuo huiyilu* (Memoirs of Zang Zhuo). Taipei: Duli zuojia, 2015.

Zhang Fakui. *Zhang fakui koushu zizhuan* (The Oral Autobiography of Zhang Fakui). Beijing: Dangdai Zhongguo chubanshe, 2012.

Zhang Xueliang and Wang Shujun. *Zhang Xueliang de jinsheng jinshi* (Life of Zhang Xueliang). 2 vols. Beijing: Tuanjie chubanshe, 2011.

Zhang Xueliang and Tang Degang. *Zhang Xueliang koushu lishi* (History of Zhang Xueliang Told by Himself). Taipei: Yuan liu chubanshe ye gufen youxian gongsi, 2009.

———. *Zhang Xueliang koushu lishi* (History of Zhang Xueliang Told by Himself). Taiyuan: Shanxi renmin chubanshe, 2013.

Zhejiang sheng xinhai geming shi yanjiu hui, Zhejiang sheng tushuguan, eds. *Xinhai geming Zhejiang shiliao xuanji* (Collection of Selected Materials on the History of Zhejiang during the Xinhai Revolution). Hangzhou: Zhejiang renmin chubanshe, 1982.

Zhongguo renmin zhengzhi xieshanghui Zhejiang sheng weiyuanhui wenshi ziliao yanjiu weiyuanhui, ed. *Zhejiang xinhai geming huiyilu* (Reminiscences of the Xinhai Revolution in Zhejiang). Hangzhou: Zhejiang renmin chubanshe, 1981.

### *NEWSPAPERS AND JOURNALS*

*American Journal of Chinese Studies*. 2010.

*Bainian chao* (Century Tides). 2001–20.

*Bolshevik*. 1925–27.

*China Brief*. 2009.

*China Quarterly*. 1960–2020.

*Chinese Historians*. 1992.

*Chinese Historical Review*. 2004–20.

*Cold War History*. 2015.

*Collier's*. 1943.

*Dangshi yanjiu* (Studies on Party History). 1986–87.

*Dangshi yanjiu ziliao* (Study Materials on Party History). 1979–2020.

*Department of State Bulletin*. 1964.

*Diletante* (Dilettante). 2016.

*Diplomat*. 2015.

*Diplomatic History*. 1979.

*English Historical Review*. 2011.

*Er shi yi shiji* (The Twenty-first Century). 2004–20.

*Far Eastern Quarterly*. 1948.

*Far Eastern Survey*. 1937–43.

*Foreign Affairs*. 1967–2020.

*Gazeta Polska* (The Polish Newspaper). 1935.

*Geming shi ziliao* (Materials on Revolutionary History). 1986.

*Guangming ribao* (Enlightenment Daily). 1988.

*Hanxue yanjiu* (Sinological Studies). 2010.

*H-Diplo*. 2011–18.

*Hongqi* (Red Flag). 1981.

*International Journal of Asian Studies*. 2012.

*Istoricheskii arkhiv* (Historical Archive). 1998.

*Izvestiia* (News). 1994.

*Jiefang ribao* (Liberation Daily). 2005.

*Jindaishi yanjiu* (Studies in Modern History). 1985–2020.

*Jindai Zhongguo* (Contemporary China). 2005.
*Jiujiang xueyuan xiebao (shehui kexue ban)* (Bulletin of Jiujiang University [Social Sciences Issue]). 2011.
*Journalism Quarterly.* 1989.
*Journal of Asian Studies.* 1956–2020.
*Journal of Cold War Studies.* 2017.
*Journal of Contemporary China.* 2009.
*Journal of Historical Biography.* 2009.
*Journal of Modern Chinese History.* 2007–20.
*Journal of Modern History.* 1960–2015.
*Journal of Presbyterian History (1962–1985).* 1971.
*Journal of Sport History.* 1999.
*Kangri zhanzheng yanjiu* (Studies on the War of Resistance against Japan). 2000–2001.
*Kommunist* (The Communist). 1964–69.
*Kommunisticheskii Internatsional* (Communist International). 1920–36.
*Komsomol'skaia pravda* (Communist Youth Truth). 2004.
*Leningradskaia pravda* (Leningrad Truth). 1936.
*Life.* 1936–72.
*Military Affairs.* 1979.
*Minguo dang'an* (Republican Archive). 1998–2020.
*Minguo ribao* (Republican Daily). 1917–27.
*Modern Asian Studies.* 1987.
*Moskovskii komsomolets* (Moscow Young Communist). 2002.
*Nanfang dushu bao* (Southern Capital). 2014.
*Nanfang zhoumo* (Southern Weekend). 2006.
*Narody Azii i Afriki* (Peoples of Asia and Africa). 1955–2020.
*The New Republic.* 2011.
*New York Times.* 1927–2020.
*Nezavisimoe voennoe obozrenie* (The Independent Military Review). 2008.
*NIDS Military History Studies Annual.* 2013.
*Novaia i noveishaia istoriia* (Modern and Contemporary History). 1989–2020.
*Pacific Affairs.* 1932–94.
*Palgrave Communications.* 2015.
*Pravda* (Truth). 1917–2020.
*Problemy Dal'nego Vostoka* (Far Eastern Affairs). 1972–2020.
*Qingdao ribao* (Qingdao Daily). 2014.
*Renmin ribao* (People's Daily). 1949–2020.
*Republican China.* 1975–97.
*Russian Review.* 1925.
*San Francisco Chronicle.* 1927.

*Saturday Evening Post.* 1950.
*Shangye zhoukan* (Trade Weekly). 1997.
*Shilin* (History Review). 2012.
*Shixue yuekan* (Historical Science Monthly). 1997–2020.
*Sociological Quarterly.* 2010.
*Taipei Times.* 2004.
*Taiwan Today.* 2018.
*Time.* 1942–44.
*Trud* (Labor). 2000.
*Twentieth-Century China.* 1997–2020.
*Vodnyi transport* (The Water Transport). 1959.
*Voprosy istorii* (Problems of History). 1990–2020.
*War in History.* 2001.
*Xin qingnian* (New Youth). 1919–25.
*Zhonggong chuangjian shi yanjiu* (Studies on the History of Founding the CCP). 2016–20.
*Zilu wanbao* (Independence Evening Newspaper). 1950.

## *SECONDARY SOURCES*

*All about Shanghai and Environs: A Standard Guide Book: Historical and Contemporary Facts and Statistics.* Shanghai: University Press, 1934.

Alsop, Joseph. "The Feud between Stilwell and Chiang." *Saturday Evening Post* 222, no. 28 (January 1, 1950): 16–18, 41, 46–48.

Ambrose, Stephen E. *Eisenhower: Soldier and President.* New York: Simon & Schuster, 1990.

Andrew, Morris. "'I Can Compete!' China in the Olympic Games, 1932 and 1936." *Journal of Sport History*, no. 3 (1999): 550–61.

———. *Marrow of the Nation: A History of Sport and Physical Culture in Republican China.* Berkeley: University of California Press, 2004.

Andreyev, Catherine. *Vlasov and the Russian Liberation Movement: Soviet Reality and Émigré Theories.* Cambridge: Cambridge University Press, 1987.

Bergère, Marie-Claire. *Sun Yat-sen.* Stanford: Stanford University Press, 1998.

Bernd, Martin. *Deutsch–chinesische Beziehungen 1928–1937: "Gleiche" Partner unter "ungleichen" Bedingungen: Eine Quellensammlung* (Sino–German Relations 1928–1937: "Equal" Partners under Dissimilar Conditions: A Source Collection). Berlin: De Gruyter Akademie Forschung, 2003.

Bertke, Donald A., et al. *World War Two Sea War.* Vol. 4. Dayton, OH: Bertke, 2012.

Bian Xuyue. *Kangri zhanzheng shiqi Zhongguo renkou sunshi wenti yanjiu (1937–1945)* (A Study of the Losses of the Chinese Population during the Period of the Anti-Japanese War [1937–1945]). Beijing: Hualing chubanshe, 2010.

Bickers, Robert A., and Jeffrey N. Wasserstrom. "Shanghai's 'Dogs and Chinese Not Admitted' Sign: Legend, History, and Contemporary Symbol." *China Quarterly* 142 (June 1995): 444–66.

Book of the Prophet Ezekiel.

Book of the Prophet Isaiah.

Boorman, Howard, ed. *Biographical Dictionary of Republican China.* 3 vols. New York: Columbia University Press, 1967.

Boyle, John Hunter. *China and Japan at War 1937–1945: The Politics of Collaboration.* Stanford: Stanford University Press, 1972.

Brady, Anne-Marie. "Adventurers, Aesthetes and Tourists: Foreign Homosexuals in Republican China." In Anne-Marie Brady and Douglas Brown, eds., *Foreigners and Foreign Institutions in Republican China,* 146–68. London: Routledge, 2013.

Brinley, Alan. *The Publisher: Henry Luce and His American Century.* New York: Alfred A. Knopf, 2010.

Broomhall, M. *General Feng: "A Good Soldier of Christ Jesus."* London: China Inland Mission, 1923.

Bunker, Gerald E. *The Peace Conspiracy: Wang Ching-wei and the China War, 1937–1941.* Cambridge: Harvard University Press, 1972.

Cai Dejin and Wang Sheng. *Wang Jingwei shengping jishi* (Chronological Biography of Wang Jingwei). Beijing: Zhongguo wenshi chubanshe, 1993.

Cao Lixin. *Taiwan baoye shihua* (Sketches on the History of Newspapers on Taiwan). Hong Kong: Jiuzhou chubanshe, 2015.

Carter, Carrole J. *Mission to Yenan: American Liaison with the Chinese Communists 1944–1947.* Lexington: University Press of Kentucky, 1997.

Chang, Iris. *The Rape of Nanking: The Forgotten Holocaust of World War II.* New York: Basic Books, 1997.

Chang Kia-ngau. *The Inflationary Spiral: The Experience in China, 1939–1950.* Cambridge: MIT Press, 1958.

Chang, Maria Hsia. *The Chinese Blue Shirt Society: Fascism and Developmental Nationalism.* Berkeley: University of California Press, 1985.

———. "'Fascism' and Modern China." *China Quarterly* 79 (September 1979): 553–67.

Chang, Nelson, et al. *The Zhangs from Nanxun: A One Hundred and Fifty Year Chronicle of a Chinese Family.* Denver: CF Press, 2010.

Chavanne, Jonathan B. "The Battle for China: The U.S. Navy, Marine Corps and the Cold War in Asia, 1944–1949." PhD dissertation, Texas A&M University, 2016.

Chen, Leslie H. Dingyan. *Chen Jiongming and the Federalist Movement: Regional Leadership and Nation Building in Early Republican China.* Ann Arbor: University of Michigan Press, 1999.

Chen Bulei. *Jiang Jieshi xiansheng nianbiao* (Chronological Biography of Mr. Chiang Kai-shek). Taipei: Zhuanji wenxue chubanshe, 1978.

Chen Dawei. *Wang Jingwei da zhuan* (Large Biography of Wang Jingwei). Beijing: Huawen chubanshe, 2010.

Chen Fulin and Yu Yanguang. *Liao Zhongkai nianpu* (Chronological Biography of Liao Zhongkai). Changsha: Hunan chubanshe, 1991.

Chen Hongmin. *Si pin Jiang Jieshi: Jiang Jieshi riji yuedu zhaji* (Studying Chiang Kai-shek: Notes Made on Reading Chiang Kai-shek's Diaries). Beijing: Renmin chubanshe, 2016.

Chen Ningjun and Xin Chen. *Minguo zhengyao zuihou de "quan jia fu"* (The Last "Happy Family" of the Republican Politicians). Hangzhou: Zhejiang daxue chubanshe, 2016.

Chen Ruiyun. *Jiang Jieshi yu Wang Jingwei* (Chiang Kai-shek and Wang Jingwei). Beijing: Tuanjie chubanshe, 2009.

Chen San-ching. *Sifenxi ban lunshi* (Articles on History Written on the Bank of Sifen Creek). Hong Kong: Jiuzhou chubanshe, 2013.

Chen Shan. *He Xiangning nianpu* (Chronological Biography of He Xiangning). Nanning: Guangxi renmin chubanshe, 2016.

Chen Tingyi. *Jiang shi jiazu quan zhuan* (Full Biographies of the Members of the Jiang Clan). Beijing: Zhongguo qingnian chubanshe, 2013.

Chen Xiaoqing et al. *Kangri shiwu nian: yige shidai de ceying: Zhongguo 1931–1945* (Fifteen Years of the War of Resistance: A Silhouette of an Epoch: China 1931–1945). 2nd ed. Guilin: Guangxi shifan daxue chubanshe, 2008.

Chen Xiqi, ed. *Sun Zhongshan nianpu changbian* (Large Chronological Biography of Sun Zhongshan). 2 vols. Beijing: Zhonghua shuju, 1991.

Chen Yu, ed. *Huangpu junxiao nianpu changbian* (Large Chronology of the Whampoa Academy). Beijing: Huawen chubanshe, 2014.

Ch'en Yung-fa. "Chiang Kai-shek and the Japanese Ichigo Offensive, 1944." In Laura De Giorgi and Guido Samaranu, eds., *Chiang Kai-shek and His Time: New Historical and Historiographical Perspectives,* 37–74. Venice: Edizioni Ca'Foscari, 2017.

Chen Yunqian. *Chongbai yu jiyi—Sun Zhongshan fuhao de jianguo yu chuanbo* (Worship and Memory—Construction and Dissemination of the Symbol of Sun Yat-sen). Nanjing: Nanjing daxue chubanshe, 2009.

Ch'eng, M. *Marshal Feng—The Man and His Work.* Shanghai: Kelly & Walsh, 1926.

Cheng Shuwei et al. *Jiang Jieshi mishi* (The Secret History of Chiang Kai-shek). Beijing: Tuanjie chubanshe, 2007.

Ch'i Hsi-sheng. *The Much Troubled Alliance: US–China Military Cooperation during the Pacific War, 1941–1945.* Singapore: World Scientific, 2016.

———. *Nationalist China at War: Military Defeats and Political Collapse, 1937–45.* Ann Arbor: University of Michigan Press, 1982.

*The Chinese Classics.* With a Translation, Critical and Exegetical Notes Prolegomena, and Copious Indexes by James Legge. 5 vols. Oxford: Clarendon Press, 1893.

Chou Shun-hsin. *The Chinese Inflation 1937–1949*. New York: Columbia University Press, 1963.

*Chronology of Dr. Sun Yat-sen: The Founding Father of the Republic of China*. Taipei: Dr. Sun Yat-sen Memorial Hall, [1972].

Ch'u Chai and Winberg Chai, eds. *I Ching: Book of Changes*. Translated by J. Legge. New Hyde Park, NJ: University Books, 1964.

———. *Li Chi: Book of Rites: An Encyclopedia of Ancient Ceremonial Usages, Religious Usages, Religious Creeds, and Social Institutions*. Translated by James Legge. Vol. 1. New Hyde Park, NY: University Books, 1967.

Chu, Samuel C., ed. *Madame Chiang Kai-shek and Her China*. Norwalk, CT: EastBridge, 2005.

Chu Shao-kang. "Chiang Kai-shek's Position on Resisting Japan: An Analysis of 'Domestic Stability Takes Precedence Over Resisting Foreign Invasion' Policy, 1928–1936." PhD dissertation, University of British Columbia, 1999.

Clark, Elmer T. *The Chiangs of China*. New York: Abingdon-Cokesbury Press, 1943.

Clinton, Maggie. *Revolutionary Nativism: Fascism and Culture in China: 1925–1937*. Durham: Duke University Press, 2017.

Coble, Parks M. "The Soong Family and Chinese Capitalists." In Samuel C. Chu, ed., *Madame Chiang Kai-shek and Her China*, 69–79. Norwalk, CT: EastBridge, 2005.

Collie, Craig. *The Reporter and the Warlords*. Sydney: Allen & Unwin, 2013.

Combs, Matthew T. "Chongqing 1943: People's Livelihood, Price Control, and State Legitimacy." In Joseph W. Esherick and Matthew T. Combs, eds., *1943: China at the Crossroads*, 282–322. Ithaca: Cornell University, 2015.

Confucius. *The Analects of Confucius*. Translated by Simon Leys. New York: W. W. Norton, 1997.

Courtney, Chris. "The Dragon King and the 1931 Wuhan Flood: Religious Rumors and Environmental Disasters in Republican China." *Twentieth-Century China*, no. 2 (2015): 83–104.

———. *The Nature of Disaster in China: The 1931 Yangzi River Flood*. Cambridge: Cambridge University Press, 2018.

Cowman, Mrs. Charles E. *Streams in the Desert*. Grand Rapids, MI: Zondervan, 1996.

Crozier, Brian, with Eric Chou. *The Man Who Lost China: The First Full Biography of Chiang Kai-shek*. New York: Charles Scribner's Sons, 1976.

Cui Xiaozhong. *Qingnian Jiang Jieshi* (Young Chiang Kai-shek). Beijing: Huawen chubanshe, 2003.

Cullather, Nick. "'Fuel for the Good Dragon': The United States and Industrial Policy in Taiwan, 1950–1965." In Peter L. Hahn and Mary Ann Heiss, eds., *Empire and Revolution: The United States and the Third World since 1945*, 242–68. Columbus: Ohio State University Press, 2001.

Culp, Robert. *Articulating Citizenship: Civic Education and Student Politics in Southeastern China, 1912–1940.* Cambridge: Harvard University Asian Center, 2007.

Dallek, Robert. *Franklin D. Roosevelt and American Foreign Policy, 1932–1945.* New York: Oxford University Press, 1995.

Davies, John Paton, Jr. *Dragon by the Tail: American, British, Japanese, and Russian Encounters with China and One Another.* New York: W. W. Norton, 1972.

Davis, G. *China's Christian Army: A Story of Marshal Feng and His Soldiers.* New York: Christian Alliance, 1925.

DeLong, Thomas A. *Madame Chiang Kai-shek and Miss Emma Mills: China's First Lady and Her American Friend.* Jefferson, NC: McFarland, 2007.

Dickson, Bruce J. "The Lessons of Defeat: The Reorganization of the Kuomintang on Taiwan, 1950–52." *China Quarterly* 133 (March 1993): 56–84.

Dikötter, Frank. *The Age of Openness: China before Mao.* Berkeley: University of California Press, 2008.

Dong, Stella. *Shanghai: The Rise and Fall of a Decadent City.* New York: Perennial, 2000.

Dou Yingtai. *Jiang Jieshi bi xia de fenghu xueyue* (Romantic Themes Under the Pen of Chiang Kai-shek). Hong Kong: Zhonghe chuban, 2015.

———. *Song Meiling yu Liu Jiwen de chulian* (The First Love of Song Meiling and Liu Jiwen). Beijing: Tuanjie chubanshe, 2005.

Du Fu. *Du Fu quanji* (Complete Works of Du Fu). Hong Kong: Guangzhi shuju, [195?].

Duan Yunzhang and Ma Qingzhong, eds. *Sun Zhongshan cidian* (Dictionary of Sun Zhongshan). Guangzhou: Guangdong renmin chubanshe, 1994.

Dubinsky, A. M. *Sovetsko–kitaiskie otnosheniia v period iapono–kitaiskoi voiny 1937–1945* (Soviet–Chinese Relations in the Period of the Japanese–Chinese War 1937–1945). Moscow: "Mysl,'" 1980.

Eastman, Lloyd E. *The Abortive Revolution: China under Nationalist Rule 1927–1937.* Cambridge: Harvard University Press, 1974.

———. "Fascism in Kuomintang China: The Blue Shirts." *China Quarterly* 49 (January–March 1972): 1–31.

———. "Fascism in Modern China: A Rejoinder." *China Quarterly* 80 (December 1979): 838–42.

———. "Who Lost China? Chiang Kai-shek Testifies." *China Quarterly* 88 (1988): 658–68.

Edgerton-Tarpley, Kathryn. "Saving the Nation, Starving the People? The Henan Famine of 1942–1943." In Joseph W. Esherick and Matthew T. Combs, eds., *1943: China at the Crossroads,* 323–64. Ithaca: Cornell University, 2015.

Ehrenburg, G. B. *Sovetskii Kitai* (Soviet China). Moscow: Partizdat, 1933.

———. *Sovetskoe dvizhenie v Kitae* (The Soviet Movement in China). Moscow, 1933.

Elleman, Bruce A. "The End of Extraterritoriality in China: The Case of the Soviet Union, 1917–1960." *Republican China,* no. 2 (1996): 65–89.

Elvin, Mark, and G. William Skinners, eds. *The Chinese City between Two Worlds.* Stanford: Stanford University Press, 1974.

Endicott, Stephen Lyon. *Diplomacy and Enterprise: British China Policy 1933–1937.* Vancouver: University of British Columbia Press, 1975.

Erbaugh, Mary S. "The Secret History of the Hakkas: The Chinese Revolution as a Hakka Enterprise." *China Quarterly* 132 (1992): 937–68.

Esherick, Joseph W. "The Many Faces of Chiang Kai-shek." *Chinese Historical Review* 17, no. 1 (Spring 2010): 16–23.

———. *Reform and Revolution in China: The 1911 Revolution in Hunan and Hubei.* Berkeley: University of California Press, 1976.

Fairbank, John King. *The United States and China.* Cambridge: Harvard University Press, 1948.

Fan Xiaofang, Bao Dongbo, and Li Quanlu. *Jiang Jieshi de guoce guwen Dai Jitao* (Dai Jitao, Political Advisor to Chiang Kai-shek). Beijing: Tuanjie chubanshe, 2011.

Fatica, Michele. "The Beginning and the End of the Idyllic Relations between Mussolini's Italy and Chiang Kai-shek's China (1930–1937)." In Maurizio Marinelli and Giovanni Andornino, eds., *Italy's Encounters with Modern China: Imperial Dreams, Strategic Ambitions.* New York: Palgrave Macmillan, 2014.

Feis, Herbert. *The China Tangle: The American Effort in China from Pearl Harbor to the Marshall Mission.* Princeton: Princeton University Press, 1953.

Fenby, Jonathan. *Chiang Kai-shek: China's Generalissimo and the Nation He Lost.* New York: Carroll & Graff, 2004.

———. *Generalissimo: Chiang Kai-shek and the China He Lost.* London: Free Press, 2003.

Feng Lin. *Zhongguo guomindang zai Tai gaizao yanjiu (1950–1951)* (Studies on the Reform of the Guomindang in Taiwan [1950–1951]). Nanjing: Fenghuang chubanshe, 2013.

Firsov, F. *Sekretnye kody Kominterna 1919–1943* (Secret Codes of the Comintern 1919–1943). Moscow: AIRO-XX/Kraft+, 2007.

Fitzgerald, John, ed. "The Nationalists and Chinese Society 1923–1937: A Symposium." Parkville: History Department, University of Melbourne, 1989.

Fox, John P. *Germany and the Far Eastern Crisis 1931–1938: A Study in Diplomacy and Ideology.* Oxford: Clarendon Press, 1982.

———. "Max Bauer: Chiang Kai-shek's First German Military Adviser." *Journal of Contemporary History* 5, no. 4 (1970): 21–44.

Fung, Edmund S. K. "Chinese Nationalists and Unequal Treaties 1924–1931." *Modern Asian Studies* 21, no. 4 (1987): 793–819.

———. *The Intellectual Foundations of Chinese Modernity: Cultural and Political Thought in the Republican Era.* New York: Cambridge University Press, 2010.

Furuya Keiji. *Chiang Kai-shek: His Life and Times.* New York: St. John's University Press, 1981.

Galitsky, V. P. *Tszian Tszingo: Tragediia i triumf syna Chan Kaishi* (Chiang Ching-kuo: The Tragedy and Triumph of Chiang Kai-shek's Son). Moscow: RAU-Universitet, 2002.

Garver, John W. *Chinese–Soviet Relations, 1937–1945: The Diplomacy of Chinese Nationalism.* New York: Oxford University Press, 1988.

———. *The Sino–American Alliance: Nationalist China and American Cold War Strategy in Asia.* Armonk, NY: M. E. Sharpe, 1997.

Gato-Shibata, Harumi. *Japan and Britain in Shanghai, 1925–1931.* New York: St. Martin's, 1995.

Giles, Robert, Robert W. Snyder, and Lisa DeLisle, eds. *Covering China.* New Brunswick, NJ: Transaction Publishers, 2001.

Gillin, Donald G. *Warlord: Yen Hsi-shan in Shansi Province: 1911–1949.* Princeton: Princeton University Press, 1967.

Goldstein, Melvyn C. *A History of Modern Tibet: 1913–1951: The Demise of the Lamaist State.* Berkeley: University of California Press, 1989.

Goodpasture, H. McKennie. "China in an American Frank Wilson Price: A Bibliographical Essay." *Journal of Presbyterian History (1962–1985)* 49, no. 4 (Winter 1971): 352–64.

The Gospel According to Saint Matthew.

Grieve, William G. *The American Military Mission to China, 1941–1942: Lend-Lease Logistics, Politics and the Tangles of Wartime Cooperation.* Jefferson, NC: McFarland, 2014.

Grigoriev, A. M. *Kommunisticheskaia partiia Kitaia v nachal'nyi period sovetskogo dvizheniia (iul' 1927–sentiabr' 1931)* (The Chinese Communist Party in the Initial Soviet Period [July 1927–September 1931]). Moscow: IDV AN SSSR, 1976.

Gu Siyong. *Liang dai bei ge: Chen Bulei he ta de nüer Chen Lian* (The Sad Song of Two Generations: Chen Bulei and His Daughter Chen Lian). Beijing: Tuanjie chubanshe, 2005.

Harmsen, Peter. *Shanghai 1937: Stalingrad on the Yangtze.* Philadelphia: Casemate, 2013.

Harrison, Henrietta. *The Making of the Republican Citizen: Political Ceremonies and Symbols in China, 1911–1929.* New York: Oxford University Press, 2000.

Hayford, Charles W. "The Final Triumph of Chiang Kai-shek? The Rush to Revisionism." *H-Diplo*. December 21, 2011. http://www.h-net.org/~diplo/essays/.

He Husheng. *Ba nian kangri zhong de Jiang Jieshi 1937–1945* (Chiang Kai-shek during the Eight-Year War of Resistance 1937–1945). Beijing: Taihai chubanshe, 2011.

———. *Jiang Jieshi zhuan* (Biography of Chiang Kai-shek). 3 vols. Beijing: Huawen chubanshe, 2005.

He Husheng and Yu Zejun. *Song Meiling da zhuan* (Large Biography of Song Meiling). 2 vols. Beijing: Wenhua chubanshe, 2007.

He Yizhong. "Da geming shibai hou zhonggongdangyuan de 'zhengshou' yundong" (Movement to "Expand" the Number of Communists after the Failure of the Great Revolution). *Shilin* (History Review), no. 1 (2012): 120–25.

Heinzig, Dieter. *The Soviet Union and Communist China 1945–1950: The Arduous Road to the Alliance.* Armonk, NY: M. E. Sharpe, 2004.

Ho, Samuel P. S. "Economics, Economic Bureaucracy, and Taiwan's Economic Development." *Pacific Affairs* 60, no. 2 (Summer 1987): 226–47.

Hoover Institution Archives Staff. "An Inventory of the Chiang Kai-shek Diaries 1917–1972." (Manuscript).

Hsiao Tseng. *Land Reform in the Republic of China.* Taipei: Conference on the History of the Republic of China, 1981.

Hsiao Tso-liang. *Power Relations within the Chinese Communist Movement, 1930–1934: A Study of Documents.* Seattle: University of Washington Press, 1967.

Hsieh Shou-kang. *President Chiang Kai-shek: His Childhood and Youth.* Taipei: China Cultural Service, [1954].

Hsiung, James, and Steven I. Levine, eds. *China's Bitter Victory: The War with Japan 1937–1945.* Armonk, NY: M. E. Sharpe, 1992.

Hsiung, S. I. *The Life of Chiang Kai-shek.* London: Peter Davies, 1948.

Hu Hua-ling. *American Goddess of the Rape of Nanking: The Courage of Minnie Vautrin.* Carbondale: Southern Illinois University Press, 2000.

Hu Xing. *Jiang Jingguo yu Zhang Yaruo zhi lian* (Love between Chiang Ching-kuo and Zhang Yaruo). Zhengzhou: Zhengzhou wenyi chubanshe, 2009.

Huang Daoxuan. "Jiang Jieshi 'rang wai bi xian an nei' fangzhen yanjiu" (A Study of Chiang Kai-shek's Policy "Before We Fight the External Enemy, We Must First Establish Peace Inside the Country"). *Kangri zhanzheng yanjiu* (Studies on the War of Resistance Against Japan), no. 2 (2000): 28–58.

Huang Fuqing. *Qing mo liu zhi xuesheng* (Chinese Students in Japan in the Late Qing Dynasty). Taipei: Zhongyang yanjiuyuan jindaishi yanjiusuo, 2010.

Huang, Grace C. "Chiang Kai-shek's Uses of Shame: An Interpretive Study of Agency in Chinese Leadership." PhD dissertation, Chicago, 2005.

Huang Kuo-wu. "Retrospect and Prospect of Overseas Studies on Chiang Kai-shek and Related Topics." *Journal of Modern Chinese History* 5, no. 2 (December 2011): 233–46.

Huang Meizhen and Hao Shengchao, eds. *Zhonghua minguo shi shijian renwu lu* (Dictionary of Events and Persons in the History of the Republic of China). Shanghai: Shanghai renmin chubanshe, 1987.

Huang Zijin. *Jiang Jieshi yu Riben: Yi bu jindai Zhong–Ri guanxi shi de suoying* (Chiang Kai-shek and Japan: Reflection of the History of Japan–Chinese Relations in Modern Times). Taipei: Zhongyang yanjiuyuan jindaishi yanjiusuo, 2012.

Huang Zijin and Pan Guangzhe, eds. *Jiang Jieshi yu xiandai Zhongguo de xingsu* (Chiang Kai-shek and the Formation of Contemporary China). 2 vols. Taipei: Zhongyang yanjiuyuan jindaishi yanjiusuo, 2013.

"Huanqiu renwu" zazhishe, ed. *Jiang shi jiazu bainian midang* (Secret Archives of Jiang's Clan for 100 Years). Beijing: Xiandai chubanshe, 2017.

Hutchisson, James M. *Ernest Hemingway: A New Life.* University Park: Pennsylvania State University Press, 2016.

Irvine, E. Eastman, ed. *The World Almanac and the Book of Facts for 1940.* New York: New York World-Telegram, 1940.

Isaacs, Harold R. *The Tragedy of the Chinese Revolution.* With an Introduction by Leon Trotsky. London: Secker and Warburg, 1938.

Israel, John. *Student Nationalism in China 1927–1937.* Stanford: Stanford University Press, 1966.

Israel, John, and Donald Klein. *Rebels and Bureaucrats: China's December 9ers.* Berkeley: University of California Press, 1976.

Ivin, A. *Ocherki partizanskogo dvizheniia v Kitae, 1927–1930* (Sketches of the Guerrilla Movement in China, 1927–1930). Moscow-Leningrad: GIZ, 1930.

———. *Sovietskii Kitai* (Soviet China). Moscow: Molodaia gvardiia, 1931.

Jacobs, Dan N. *Borodin: Stalin's Man in China.* Cambridge: Harvard University Press, 1981.

Jacoby, Neil H. *Evaluation of U. S. Economic Aid to Free China, 1951–1956.* Washington, DC: Bureau of the Far East, Agency for International Development, 1966.

Jaffe, Philip. "The Secret of 'China's Destiny.'" In Chiang Kai-shek, *China's Destiny and Chinese Economic Theory,* 11–25. With Notes and Commentary by Philip Jaffe. New York: Roy Publishers, 1947.

Jansen, Marius B. *Japan and China: From War to Peace, 1894–1972.* Chicago: Rand McNally College, 1975.

———. *The Japanese and Sun Yat-sen.* Cambridge: Harvard University Press, 1954.

Jesperson, T. Christopher. *American Images of China: 1931–1949.* Stanford: Stanford University Press, 1996.

Jiajin Liangzi (Ieshika Ryuko). *Jiang Jieshi yu Nanjing guomin zhengfu* (Chiang Kai-shek and the Nanjing National Government). Beijing: Shehui kexue wenxian chubanshe, 2005.

Jiang Huaxuan. "Dangde minzhu geming gangling de tichu he guogong hezuo celüede jige wenti" (Several Questions Connected with the Party's Program for the Democratic Revolution and Defining the Strategy for Guomindang–CCP Cooperation). *Jindaishi yanjiu* (Studies in Modern History), no. 2 (1985): 111–26.

"Jiang Jieshi quan kao zong mu hao fengshui" (Chiang Kai-shek Buried His Mother Strictly According to Fengshui). http://www.csxxly.com/lywh_detail/newsId=6.html.

Jiang Xiaoyan. *Jiang jia men wai de haizi* (The Children Behind the Gates of the Chiang House). 3rd ed. Hong Kong: Jiuzhou chubanshe, 2012.

Jiang Yihua. *Guomindang zuopai qizhi—Liao Zhongkai* (The Banner of the Left Guomindang—Liao Zhongkai). Shanghai: Shanghai renmin chubanshe, 1985.

Jiang Yongjing. *Baoloting yu Wuhan zhengquan* (Borodin and the Wuhan Government). Taipei: Zhongguo xueshu zhuzuo jiangzhu weiyuanhui, 1963.

Jiang Yongjing and Liu Weikai. *Jiang Jieshi yu guogong he zhan: 1945–1949* (Chiang Kai-shek, Peace Negotiations and War between the Guomindang and the CCP: 1945–1949). Taiyuan: Shanxi renmin chubanshe, 2013.

Jin Chongji, ed. *Mao Zedong zhuan (1893–1949)* (Biography of Mao Zedong [1893–1949]). Beijing: Zhongyang wenxian chubanshe, 2004.

———. *Mao Zedong zhuan (1949–1976)* (Biography of Mao Zedong [1949–1976]). 2 vols. Beijing: Zhongyang wenxian chubanshe, 2003.

———. *Zhou Enlai zhuan (1898–1976)* (Biography of Zhou Enlai [1898–1976]). 2 vols. 2nd ed. Beijing: Zhongyang wenxian chubanshe, 2009.

Jin Guo. *Jiang Jieshi yu Jiang Jingguo, Jiang Weiguo* (Chiang Kai-shek and Chiang Ching-kuo, Chiang Wei-kuo). Beijing: Dongfang chubanshe, 2009.

Jin Yilin. *Guomindang gao ceng de paixi zhengzhi: Jiang Jieshi "zuigao lingxiu" diwei shi ruhe quelide* (Fractional Politics at the Top: How Chiang Became the GMD's Supreme Leader). Beijing: Shehui kexue wenxian chubanshe, 2009.

Jocelyn, Ed, and Andrew McEwan. *The Long March: The True Story behind the Legendary Journey that Made Mao's China.* London: Constable, 2006.

Joiner, Lynne. *Honorable Survivor: Mao's China, McCarthy's America, and the Persecution of John S. Service.* Annapolis, MD: Naval Institute Press, 2009.

Jordan, Donald A. *China's Trial by Fire: The Shanghai War of 1932.* Ann Arbor: University of Michigan Press, 2001.

———. *Chinese Boycotts versus Japanese Bombs: The Failure of China's "Revolutionary Diplomacy," 1931–32.* Ann Arbor: University of Michigan Press, 1991.

———. *The Northern Expedition: China's National Revolution of 1926–1928.* Honolulu: University Press of Hawaii, 1976.

Keeley, Joseph. *The China Lobby Man: The Story of Alfred Kohlberg.* New Rochelle, NY: Arlington House, 1969.

Kirby, William. *Germany and Republican China.* Stanford: Stanford University Press, 1984.

———. "The Internationalization of China: Foreign Relations at Home and Abroad in the Republican Era." In Frederic Wakeman Jr. and Richard Louis Edmonds, eds., *Reappraising Republican China,* 179–204. New York: Oxford University Press, 2000.

———. "The Nationalist Regime and the Chinese–Party State, 1928–1958." In Merle Goldman, and Andrew Gordon, *Historical Perspectives on Contemporary East Asia,* 211–37, 339–43. Cambridge: Harvard University Press, 2000.

Klein, Donald, and Anne Clark. *Biographic Dictionary of Chinese Communism: 1921–1969.* 2 vols. Cambridge: Harvard University Press, 1971.

Korean Institute of Military History. *The Korean War.* Vol. 1. Lincoln: University of Nebraska, 2000.

Kuo Tai-chun. "A Strong Diplomat in a Weak Polity: T. V. Soong and Wartime US–China Relations, 1940–1943." *Journal of Contemporary China,* no. 18 (29) (March 2009): 219–31.

Kuo Tai-chun and Hsiao-ting Lin. *T. V. Soong in Modern Chinese History: A Look at His Role in Sino–American Relations in World War II.* Stanford: Stanford University Press, 2006.

Lai, Sherman Xiaogang. "Chiang Kai-shek versus Guomindang's Corruption in the Republic Era." In Qiang Fang, and Xiaobing Li, eds., *Corruption and Anticorruption in Modern China,* 73–99. Lanham, MD: Lexington Books, 2018.

Lai Tse-han, Ramon H. Myers, and Wei Wou. *A Tragic Beginning: The Taiwan Uprising of February 28, 1947.* Stanford: Stanford University Press, 1991.

Landis, Richard D. *The Origins of Whampoa Graduates Who Served in the Northern Expedition.* Seattle: Far Eastern and Russian Institute, University of Washington, 1964.

Lary, Diana. *China's Republic.* New York: Cambridge University Press, 2007.

———. *The Chinese People at War: Human Suffering and Social Transformation, 1937–1945.* New York: Cambridge University Press, 2010.

———. "Drowned Earth: The Strategic Breaching of the Yellow River Dyke, 1938." *War in History* 8, no. 2 (2001): 191–207.

———. *Region and Nation: The Kwangsi Clique in Chinese Politics, 1925–1937.* London: Cambridge University Press, 1974.

———. "The Waters Covered the Earth: China's War-induced Natural Disasters." In Mark Selden et al., eds., *War and State Terrorism: The United States, Japan, and the Asia–Pacific in the Long Twentieth Century.* Lanham, MD: Rowman & Littlefield, 2004.

Lary, Diana, and Stephen MacKinnon, eds. *Scars of War: The Impact of Warfare on Modern China.* Vancouver: UBC Press, 2001.

Lee, Frederic E. *Currency, Banking, and Finance in China.* Washington, DC: U.S. Government Printing Office, 1926.

Lee Hun-ju. *A Brief Biography of the Late President Chiang Kai-shek.* [Taipei, 1987].

Lensen, George Alexander. *The Damned Inheritance: The Soviet Union and the Manchurian Crisis 1924–1935.* Tallahassee, FL: Diplomatic Press, 1974.

Leung, Edwin Pak-wah, ed. *Political Leaders of Modern China: A Biographic Dictionary.* Westport, CT: Greenwood Press, 2002.

Levich, Eugene William. *The Kwangsi Way in Kuomintang China 1931–1939.* Armonk, NY: M. E. Sharpe, 1993.

Levine, Steven I. *Anvil of Victory: The Communist Revolution in Manchuria, 1945–1948.* New York: Columbia University Press, 1987.

———. "A New Look at American Mediation in the Chinese Civil War: The Marshall Mission in Manchuria." *Diplomatic History*, no. 3 (1979): 349–75.

Leviticus.

Lew, Christopher R. *The Third Chinese Revolutionary Civil War, 1945–1949: An Analysis of Communist Strategy and Leadership.* London: Routledge, 2009.

Li Gongzhong. *Zhongshanling: Yige xiandai zhengzhi fuhao de dansheng* (Sun Yat-sen's Mausoleum: The Birth of a Modern Political Symbol). Beijing: Shehui kexue wenxian chubanshe, 2009.

Li Maosheng et al. *Yan Xishan quan zhuan* (Complete Biography of Yan Xishan). 2 vols. Beijing: Dangdai Zhongguo chubanshe, 1997.

Li Qunshan. "Jiang Jieshi zai Tai xingguan zhi chutan (1919–1975)" (Initial Analysis of Chiang Kai-shek's Villas on Taiwan [1919–1975]). In Lü Fangshang, ed., *Jiang Jieshi de richang shenghuo* (Chiang Kai-shek's Daily Life), 163–214. Taipei: Zhengda chubanshe, 2012.

Li Songlin. *Jiang Jieshi de wannian suiyue* (The Last Years of Chiang Kai-shek). Beijing: Tuanjie chubanshe, 2013.

———, eds. *Zhongguo guomindang dashiji (1894.11–1986.12)* (Chronology of the Chinese Guomindang [November 1894–December 1986]). Beijing: Jiefangjun chubanshe, 1988.

Li Songlin and Chen Taixian. *Jiang Jingguo da zhuan 1910–1988* (Large Biography of Chiang Ching-kuo 1910–1988). 2 vols. Beijing: Tuanjie chubanshe, 2011.

Li Songlin and Zhu Zhinan. *Zhonggong heping jiejue Taiwan wenti de lishi kaocha* (A Historical Analysis of How the CCP Will Resolve the Taiwan Question via Peaceful Means). Beijing: Jiuzhou chubanshe, 2014.

Li Xiaobing. "Anticorruption Policy and Party Politics: The Lost Political Battle and the Fate of the GMD." In Fang Qiang and Xiaobing Li, eds., *Corruption and Anticorruption in Modern China,* 101–18. Lanham, MD: Lexington Books, 2018.

Li Xiaobing and Hongshan Li, eds. *China and the United States: A New Cold War History.* Lanham, MD: University Press of America, 1998.

Li Yiping et al. *Shilin guandi* (Shilin Residence). 3rd ed. Taipei: Taipei shi wenhua ju, 2016.

Li Yongming and Fan Xiaofang. *43 zhanfan de houbansheng* (The Second Half of the Lives of 43 War Criminals). Wuhan: Hubei renmin chubanshe, 2008.

Liang Hsi-Huey. *The Sino–German Connection: Alexander von Falkenhausen between China and Germany 1900–1941.* Amsterdam: Van Gorcum, 1978.

Liao Yanbo and Chen Yiming. *Jiang shi jiazu shenghuo mishi* (Secret History of the Life of the Jiang Clan). Taipei: Haodu chuban, 2007.

Lin Bowen. *Zhang Xueliang, Song Ziwen dang'an da jiemi* (Big Secrets Uncovered in the Archives of Zhang Xueliang and Song Ziwen). Taipei: Shibao wenhua chuban qiye gufen youxian gongsi, 2007.

Lin Hongnuan. "Zhang Tailei." In Hu Hua, ed., *Zhonggongdang shi renwu zhuan* (Biographies of Persons in the History of the CCP). Vol. 4:62–108. Xian: Shaanxi renmin chubanshe, 1985.

Lin Hsiao-ting. *Accidental State: Chiang Kai-shek, the United States, and the Making of Taiwan.* Cambridge: Harvard University Press, 2016.

———. "Chiang Kai-shek and the Cairo Summit." In Joseph W. Esherick and Matthew T. Combs, eds., *1943: China at the Crossroads,* 426–58. Ithaca: Cornell University, 2015.

———. "Reassessing Wartime U.S.–China Relations: Leadership, Foreign Aid, and Domestic Politics, 1937–1945." *NIDS Military History Studies Annual*, no. 16 (2013): 117–38.

Lin Youhua, *Lin Sen nianpu* (Chronological Biography of Lin Sen). Beijing: Zhongguo wenshi chubanshe, 2011.

Lin Yutang. "Introduction." In Chiang Kai-shek, *China's Destiny,* 11–25. Translated by Wang Chung-hui. With an Introduction by Lin Yutang. New York: Macmillan, 1947.

Linebarger, Paul Myron Anthony. *Government in Republican China.* Westport, CT: McGraw-Hill, 1938.

———. *The Political Doctrines of Sun Yat-sen: An Exposition of the San min chu i.* Baltimore: Johns Hopkins University Press, 1937.

Litten, Frederick S. "The Noulens Affair." *China Quarterly* 138 (June 1994): 492–512.

Liu Hongzhe. "1927 nian Jiang Jieshi yu Song Ailing 'Jiujiang tanhua' tanwei—Qian lun 'Chen Jieru huyilu' de shixue jiazhi" (Brief Analysis of the "Jiujiang Conversations" of Chiang Kai-shek and Song Ailing in 1927, or On the Historical Value of the "Reminiscences of Chen Jieru"). *Jiujiang xueyuan xuebao (shehui kexue ban)* (Bulletin of Jiujiang University [Social Sciences Issue]) 30, no. 2 (161) (2011): 63–65.

Liu Keqi. *Liang Jiang jilupian* (Two Chiangs Documentary). Taipei, [2017].

Liu Weikai. "Guofang huiyi yu guofang lianxi huiyi zhi zhaokai yu yingxiang" (Convening the Conference on National Defense Issues and the Joint

Conference on Issues of Defense and Their Influence). *Jindai Zhongguo* (Contemporary China), no. 163 (2005): 32–52.

———. *Zhongguo guomindang zhiming lu (1894–1994)* (List of Officials of the Chinese Guomindang [1894–1994]). Beijing: Zhonghua shuju, 2014.

Liu Yisheng. "Guomindang kaichu dangji xianxiang shulun" (Brief Essay on the Phenomenon of Guomindang Expulsion from the Party). *Shixue yuekan* (Historical Science Monthly), no. 5 (1997): 45.

Loh, Pichon P. Y. *The Early Chiang Kai-shek: A Study of His Personality and Politics, 1887–1924*. New York: Columbia University Press, 1971.

Lorenzo, David J. *Conceptions of Chinese Democracy: Reading Sun Yat-sen, Chiang Kai-shek and Chiang Ching-kuo.* Baltimore: Johns Hopkins University Press, 2013.

Lowe, Peter. *The Origins of the Korean War.* 2nd ed. London: Longman, 1997.

Lü Fangshang, ed. *Zhanzheng de lishi yu jiyi* (War in History and Memory). 4 vols. Taipei: Guoshiguan, 2015.

———. "Zongcai de 'shounao waijiao': 1949 nian Jiang Zongzheng chufang Fei Han" (The Zongcai's "Summit Diplomacy": Jiang Zhongzheng's 1949 Visits to the Philippines and South Korea). In Wu Zusheng and Chen Liwen, eds., *Jiang Zongzheng yu Minguo waijiao* (Jiang Zhongzheng and the Foreign Relations of the Republic). Vol. 2. Taipei: Guoli Zhongzheng jiniantang guanlichu, 2013.

Lu [Lü] Fang-shang and Hsiao-ting Lin. "Chiang Kai-shek's Diaries and Republican China: New Insights on the History of Modern China." *Chinese Historical Review* 15, no. 2 (Fall 2008): 331–39.

Lü Fangshang et al., eds. *Jiang Jieshi de qinqing, aiqing yu youqing* (Chiang Kai-shek's Family Members, Lovers, and Friends). Taipei: Shibao wenhua chuban qiye gufen youxian gongsi, 2011.

———. *Jiang Jieshi de richang shenghuo* (Chiang Kai-shek's Daily Life). Taipei: Zhengda chubanshe, 2012.

———. *Jiang Zhongzheng xiansheng nianpu changbian* (Large Chronological Biography of Mr. Jiang Zhongzheng). 6 vols. Taipei: Guoshiguan, 2014.

Lu Xingsheng. *Xiang qian zou, bie huigu: Lu Xingsheng baogao wenxue xuan* (March Forward, Don't Look Back: Selected Reports by Lu Xingsheng on Literature). Beijing: Duli zuojia, 2015.

Lutze, Thomas D. *China's Inevitable Revolution: Rethinking America's Loss to the Communists.* New York: Palgrave Macmillan, 2007.

Ma Quanzhong, ed. *Taiwan ji shi liushi nian* (Sixty-Year Chronicle of Taiwan). Taipei: Taiwan xuesheng shuju, 2010.

Ma Zhendu. "Chiang Kai-shek's Diary: A Comparison between the Original and Copies Compiled by Mao Sicheng—Using Entries from July 1926 as Examples." *Journal of Modern Chinese History* 5, no. 2 (December 2011): 247–60.

———, ed. *Kangri zhong de Jiang Jieshi* (Chiang Kai-shek during the War of Resistance). Beijing: Jiuzhou chubanshe, 2013.

"MAAG—Saga of Service." *Taiwan Today.* March 13, 2018.

Macdonald, Douglas J. *Adventures in Chaos: American Intervention for Reform in the Third World.* Cambridge: Harvard University Press, 1992.

MacKinnon, Janice R., and Stephen R. MacKinnon. *Agnes Smedley: The Life and Times of an American Radical.* Berkeley: University of California Press, 1988.

MacKinnon, Stephen R. *Wuhan. 1938: War, Refugees, and the Making of Modern China.* Berkeley: University of California Press, 2008.

MacKinnon, Stephen R., and Oris Friesen. *China Reporting: An Oral History of American Journalism in the 1930s and 1940s.* Berkeley: University of California Press, 1987.

MacKinnon, Stephen R., Diana Larry, and Ezra F. Vogel. *China at War: Regions of China, 1937–1945.* Stanford: Stanford University Press, 2007.

Maliavin, V. V. *Kitaiskaia tsivilizatsiia* (Chinese Civilization). Moscow: Astrel', 2004.

Malraux, André. *Man's Fate.* Translated by Haakon Maurice Chevalie. New York: Modern Library, 1934.

"Mao Fumei." *Zhongguo baike zai xian* (Chinese Internet Encyclopedia). http://www.zwbk.org/MyLemmaShow.aspx?zh=zh-tw&lid=263253.

Mao Jiaqi. *Jiang Jingguo de yisheng he ta de sixiang yanbian* (The Life of Chiang Ching-kuo and the Evolution of His Views). Taipei: Taiwan shangwu yinshuguan, 2003.

Mao Sicheng, *Minguo shiwu nian yilai zhi Jiang Jieshi xiansheng* (Mr. Chiang Kai-shek Before 1926). Hong Kong: Long men shudian, 1965.

Marinelli M., and Andornino G., eds. *Italy's Encounters with Modern China: Imperial Dreams, Strategic Ambitions.* New York: Palgrave Macmillan, 2014.

Martin, Brian G. *The Shanghai Green Gang: Politics and Organized Crime, 1919–1937.* Berkeley: University of California Press, 1996.

Maslov, S. "Drug sovetskoi razvedki" (A Friend of Soviet Intelligence Service). In V. N. Karpov, ed., *Rassekrecheno vneshnei razvedkoi* (Declassified by Foreign Intelligence Service). Moscow: OLMA-PRESS, 2003.

———. "Kak nashi s drugom Gitlera v rasvedku khodili" (How Our People Cooperated in Intelligence Work with a Friend of Hitler). *Komsomol'skaia pravda* (Communist Youth Truth). April 18, 2004.

Matsusaka, Yoshihisa Tak. *The Making of Japanese Manchuria, 1904–1932.* Cambridge: Harvard University Asian Center, 2001.

May, Ernest. *The Truman Administration and China, 1945–1949.* Philadelphia: J. D. Lippincott, 1975.

Mayakovsky, Vladimir. *The Bedbug and Selected Poetry.* Translated by Max Hayward and George Reavey. Cleveland: Meridian Books, 1960.

McClain, James L. *Japan, A Modern History.* New York: W. W. Norton, 2002.

McCullough, David. *Truman.* New York: Simon & Schuster, 1992.

McDonald, Angus W., Jr. *The Urban Origins of Rural Revolution: Elites and the Masses in Hunan Province, China, 1911–1927*. Berkeley: University of California Press, 1978.

McLaughlin, John J. *General Albert C. Wedemeyer: America's Unsung Strategist in World War II*. Philadelphia: Casemate, 2012.

Meliksetov, A. V., ed. *Istoriia Kitaia* (History of China). Moscow: Izdatel'stvo MGU, 1998.

———. *Sotsial'no-ekonomicheskaia politika Gomindana v Kitae (1927–1949)* (The Socioeconomic Policy of the Guomindang in China [1927–1949]). Moscow: Nauka, 1977.

Mencius. *The Works of Mencius*. Translated with Critical and Exegetical Notes, Prolegomena, and Copious Indexes by James Legge. New York: Dover, 1970.

Metzler, John J. *Taiwan's Transformation: 1895 to the Present*. New York: Palgrave Macmillan, 2017.

Meyers, Jeffrey. *Hemingway: A Biography*. New York: Harper & Row, 1985.

Miller, John R. "The Chiang–Stilwell Conflict, 1942–1944." *Military Affairs* 43, no. 2 (April 1979): 59–62.

Mirovitskaia, R. A. "Sovetskii Soiuz i Kitai v period razryva i vosstanovleniia otnoshenii (1928–1936 gg.)" (The Soviet Union and China during the Period of the Rift and the Restoration of Relations [1928–1936]). *Informatsionnyi biulleten' IDV AN SSSR* (Information Bulletin of the Institute of the Far East, Academy of Sciences, USSR), no. 67. Moscow: IDV AN SSSR, 1975.

Mitter, Rana. *Forgotten Ally: China's World War II, 1937–1945*. Boston: Houghton Mifflin Harcourt, 2013.

Mlechin, L. M. *Istoriia vneshnei razvedki: Kar'ery i sud'by* (The History of Foreign Intelligence: Careers and Fates). Moscow: ZAO Tsentrpoligrapf, 2008.

Moeller, Hans-Georg. *Daodejing (Laozi): A Complete Translation and Commentary*. Chicago: Open Court, 2007.

Moreira, Peter. *Hemingway on the China Front: His WWII Spy Mission with Martha Gellhorn*. Washington, DC: Potomac Books, 2006.

Morris, Andrew D. *Marrow of the Nation: A History of Sport and Physical Culture in Republican China*. Berkeley: University of California Press, 2004.

Morton, William Fitch. *Tanaka Giichi and Japan's China Policy*. New York: St. Martin's Press, 1980.

Moss, George Donelson. *Vietnam: An American Ordeal*. 6th ed. Upper Saddle River, NJ: Prentice Hall, 2006.

Muscolino, Micah S. *The Ecology of War in China: Henan Province, the Yellow River and Beyond*. New York: Cambridge University Press, 2015.

Musgrove, Charles D. *China's Contested Capital: Architecture, Ritual, and Response in Nanjing*. Honolulu: University of Hawai'i Press, 2013.

Neal, Steve. *Dark Horse: A Biography of Wendell Willkie.* Garden City, NY: Doubleday, 1984.

Neils, Patricia. *China Images in the Life and Times of Henry Luce.* Savage, MD: Rowman & Littlefield, 1990.

Nester, William R. *Japanese Industrial Targeting: The Neomercantilist Path to Economic Superpower.* New York: St. Martin's Press, 1991.

Newman, Robert P. *Owen Lattimore and the "Loss" of China.* Berkeley: University of California Press, 1992.

Niu Jun. "The Origins of the Sino–Soviet Alliance." In O. Arne Westad, ed., *Brothers in Arms: The Rise and Fall of the Sino-Soviet Alliance: 1945–1963,* 47–89. Stanford: Stanford University Press, 1998.

O'Brien, Neil L. *An American Editor in Early Revolutionary China: John William Powell and the China Weekly/Monthly Review.* New York: Routledge, 2003.

Odani, Akira. "Wang Ching-wei and the Fall of the Chinese Republic, 1905–1935." PhD dissertation, Brown University, 1976.

Ogata, Sadako N. *Defiance in Manchuria: The Making of Japanese Foreign Policy, 1931–1932.* Berkeley: University of California Press, 1964.

Osinsky, Pavel. "Modernization Interrupted? Total War, State Breakdown, and the Communist Conquest of China." *Sociological Quarterly* 51, no. 4 (September 2010): 576–99.

Pakula, Hannah. *The Last Empress: Madame Chiang Kai-shek and the Birth of Modern China.* New York: Simon & Schuster, 2009.

Pan Ling. *In Search of Old Shanghai.* Hong Kong: Joint Publishing, 1983.

Pan Qichang. *Bainian Zhong–De guanxi* (One Hundred Years of Sino–German Relations). Beijing: Shijie zhishi chubanshe, 2006.

Pang Xianzhi, ed. *Mao Zedong nianpu, 1893–1949* (Chronological Biography of Mao Zedong, 1893–1949). 3 vols. Beijing: Renmin chubanshe/Zhongyang wenxian chubanshe, 2002.

Pantsov, Alexander. *The Bolsheviks and the Chinese Revolution, 1919–1927.* Honolulu: University of Hawai'i Press, 2000.

———. "Karl Radek—Sinilogist." In Alexander V. Pantsov, ed., *Karl Radek on China: Documents from the Former Secret Soviet Archives,* 1–15. Leiden: Brill, 2021.

———. *Mao Tsze-dun* (Mao Zedong). 2nd, rev. ed. Moscow: Molodaia gvardiia, 2012.

———. "Obrazovaniie opornykh baz 8-i Natsional'no-revoliutsionnoi armii v tylu iaponskikh voisk v Severnom Kitae" (Establishment of the Eighth Route Army Base Areas in the Japanese Rear in North China). In M. F. Yuriev, *Voprosy istorii Kitaia* (Problems of Chinese History), 39–43. Moscow: Izdatel'stvo MGU, 1981.

———. "Pochemy Iaponiia ne napala na Sovetskii Soiuz?" (Why Did Japan Not Attack the Soviet Union?). https://echo.msk.ru/programs/victory/560650-echo/.

Pantsov, Alexander V., and Daria A. Arincheva. "'Novaiia demokratiia' Mao Tszeduna i Novyi avtoritaizm Chan Kaishi: Dve paradigmy obshchestvennogo progressa Kitaia serediny 20-go veka" (Mao Zedong's "New Democracy" and Chiang Kai-shek's New Authoritarianism: Two Paradigms of Social Progress in Mid-Twentieth Century China). *Problemy Dal'nego Vostoka* (Far Eastern Affairs), no. 1 (2014): 109–18.

———. *Zhizni i sud'by pervykh kitaiskikh kommunistov: Sbornik statei k 100-letiiu Kompartii Kitaia* (Lives and Fates of the First Chinese Communists: A Collection of Articles Dedicated to the 100th Anniversary of the Chinese Communist Party). Moscow: IDV RAN, 2021.

Pantsov, Alexander V., and Steven I. Levine, "Chinese Comintern Activists: An Analytic Biographic Dictionary." Manuscript.

Pantsov, Alexander V., with Steven I. Levine. *Deng Xiaoping: A Revolutionary Life.* New York: Oxford University Press, 2016.

———. *Mao: The Real Story.* New York: Simon & Schuster, 2012.

Pantsov, A. V., and M. F. Yuriev. "Ustanovlenie sotrudnichstva mezhdu KPK i Sun Yat-sen v 1921–1924 gg.: K istorii obrazovaniia edinogo antiimperialisticheskogo fronta" (Establishment of Cooperation between the CCP and Sun Yat-sen in 1921–1924: On a History of the Formation of the Anti-imperialist United Front). In L. S. Tikhvinsky, ed., *Sun Yat-sen, 1866–1986: K 120-letiyu so dnia rozhdeniia: Sbornik statei, vospominanii i materialov* (Sun Yat-sen, 1866–1986: On the 120th Anniversary of His Birth: Collection of Articles, Reminiscences and Materials), 129–71. Moscow: Nauka, 1987.

Panzuofu, Yalishanda (A. V. Pantsov). *Dui Yang Kuisong jiaoshou guanyu "Mao Zedong zhuan" shuping de huiying* (Reply to Professor Yang Kuisong's Review of "Biography of Mao Zedong"). *Jindaishi yanjiu* (Studies in Modern History), no. 6 (2017): 105–21.

Payne, Robert. *Chiang Kai-shek.* New York: Weybright and Talley, 1969.

Pepper, Suzanne. *Civil War in China: The Political Struggle 1945–1949.* 2nd ed. Lanham, MD: Rowman & Littlefield, 1999.

Perelomov, L. S. *Konfutsii: "Lun yu"* (Confucius: "Lun yu"). Moscow: Vostochnaia literatura RAN, 1998.

Pisarev, A. A. *Gomindan i agrarno-krest'ianskii vopros v Kitae v 20–30-e gody XX v.* (The Guomindang and the Agrarian-Peasant Question in China in the 1920s–1930s). Moscow: Nauka, 1986.

Polo, Marco. *The Book of Ser Marco Polo, the Venetian Concerning the Kingdoms of Marvels of the East.* Translated by Colonel Sir Henry Yule. 2 vols., 3rd ed. New York: Charles Scribner's Sons, 1929.

Prokhorov, Dmitrii. "Liternoe delo' marshala Zhan Zolinia" (The "Lettered File" of Marshal Zhang Zuolin). *Nezavisimoe voennoe obozrenie* (The Independent Military Review), no. 21 (2003): 5.

Pronin, A. "Sovetnik Chan Kaishi" (Chiang Kai-shek's Advisor). *Trud* (Labor). March 11, 2000.

Prudnikova, E. *Rikhard Zorge: Razvedchik No. 1?* (Richard Sorge: Spy No. 1?). Saint Petersburg: Neva, 2004.

Qi Pengfei. *Jiang Jieshi jia shi* (Generations of the Ching Kai-shek's Family). Beijing: Tuanjie chubanshe, 2007.

Qiang Fang and Xiaobing Li, eds. *Corruption and Anticorruption in Modern China.* Lanham, MD: Lexington Books, 2018.

Qin Xiaoyi, ed. *Chen Yingshi xiansheng jinian ji* (Collection in Memory of Chen Yingshi). Taipei: Jingxiao chu zhongyang wenwu gongyingshe, 1977.

———, ed. *Zongtong Jiang gong dashiji changbian chugao* (First Draft of Large Chronological Biography of Mr. President Chiang). 13 vols. Taipei: Zhongzheng wenjiao jijinhui chubanshe, 1978.

Radchenko, Sergey. "Lost Chance for Peace: The 1945 CCP–Kuomintang Peace Talks Revisited." *Journal of Cold War Studies* 19, no. 2 (Spring 2017): 84–114.

Rand, Peter. *China Hands: The Adventures and Ordeals of the American Journalists Who Joined Forces with the Great Chinese Revolution.* New York: Simon & Schuster, 1995.

Rankin, Mary Backus. *Early Chinese Revolutionaries: Radical Intellectuals in Shanghai and Chekiang, 1902–1911.* Cambridge: Harvard University Press, 1971.

Remer, C. F., and William B. Palmer. *A Study of Chinese Boycotts: With Special Reference to Their Economic Effectiveness.* Baltimore: Johns Hopkins Press, 1933.

Ritchie, John, ed. *Australian Dictionary of Biography.* Vol. 8:317–18. Carton, Victoria: Melbourne University, 1981.

Roberts, Geoffrey. *The Soviet Union and the Origins of the Second World War: Russo–German Relations and the Road to War, 1933–1941.* New York: St. Martin's Press, 1995.

Rodriguez, Robyn L. "Journey to the East: The German Military Mission in China, 1927–1938." PhD dissertation, Ohio State University, 2011.

Romanus, Charles F., and Riley Sunderland. *Stilwell's Command Problems.* Washington, DC: Office of the Chief of Military History, Department of the Army, 1956.

———. *Stilwell's Mission to China.* Washington, DC: Office of the Chief of Military History, Department of the Army, 1953.

Rottman, Gordon F. *Korean War Order of Battle: United States, United Nations, and Communist Ground, Naval, and Air Forces, 1950–1953.* Westport, CT: Praeger, 2002.

*The Sacred Books of China: The Texts of Taoism.* Book 1. Translated by James Legge. Oxford: Clarendon Press, 1891.

Sainsbury, Keith. *The Turning Point: Roosevelt, Stalin, Churchill, and Chiang Kai-shek, 1943: The Moscow, Cairo, and Teheran Conferences.* Oxford: Oxford University Press, 1985.

Samarani, Guido. "The Evolution of Fascist Italian Diplomacy during the Sino–Japanese War, 1937–1943." In David P. Barrett and Larry N. Shyu, eds., *China in the Anti-Japanese War, 1937–1945: Politics, Culture, and Society,* 65–88. New York: Peter Lang, 2001.

———. "Italians and Nationalist China (1928–1945): Some Case Studies." In Anne-Marie Brady and Douglas Brown, eds., *Foreigners and Foreign Institutions in Republican China,* 234–50. London: Routledge, 2013.

Sandilands, Roger J. *The Life and Political Economy of Lauchlin Currie: New Dealer, Presidential Adviser, and Development Economist.* Durham: Duke University Press, 1990.

Sang Tse-lan, D. *The Emerging Lesbian: Female Same-Sex Desire in Modern China.* Chicago: University of Chicago Press, 2003.

Sapozhnikov, B. G. *Kitai v ogne voiny (1931–1950)* (China in the Fires of War [1931–1950]). Moscow: Nauka, 1977.

Schafferer, Christian. *The Power of the Ballot Box: Political Development and Election Campaigning in Taiwan.* Lanham, MD: Lexington Books, 2003.

Schaller, Michael. *The U.S. Crusade in China, 1938–1945.* New York: Columbia University Press, 1979.

Schechter, Jerrold, and Leona Schechter. *Sacred Secrets: How Soviet Intelligence Operations Changed American History.* Washington, DC: Brassey's, 2002.

Schivelbusch, Wolfgang. *Three New Deals: Reflections on Roosevelt's America, Mussolini's Italy, and Hitler's Germany, 1933–1939.* New York: Metropolitan Books, 2006.

Schoppa, R. Keith. *Chinese Elites and Political Change: Zhejiang Province in the Early Twentieth Century.* Cambridge: Harvard University Press, 1982.

Selden, Mark, et al., eds. *War and State Terrorism: The United States, Japan, and the Asia-Pacific in the Long Twentieth Century.* Lanham, MD: Rowman & Littlefield, 2004.

Selle, Earl Albert. *Donald of China.* New York: Harper & Brothers, 1948.

Sergeant, Harriet. *Shanghai.* London: Jonathan Cape, 1991.

Shai, Aron. *Zhang Xueliang: The General Who Never Fought.* New York: Palgrave Macmillan, 2012.

Shao Minghuan, ed. *Jiang Zhongzheng yu dangzheng guanxi* (Jiang Zhongzheng's Relations with the Party and the Government). Taipei: Guoli Zhongzheng jiniantang guanlichu, 2013.

Sharman, Lyon. *Sun Yat-sen: His Life and Its Meaning: A Critical Biography.* New York: John Day, 1934.

Shaw, Henry I., Jr. *The United States Marines in North China 1945–1949.* Washington, DC: Historical Branch, G-3 Division, Headquarters, U.S. Marine Corps, 1968.

Shen Shiming and Xu Yong, eds. *Sun Zhongshan yu Huzhou ren* (Sun Zhongshan and People from Huzhou). Beijing: Tuanjie chubanshe, 2001.

Sheng Yonghua, ed. *Song Qingling nianpu (1893–1981)* (Chronological Biography of Song Qingling [1893–1981]). 2 vols. Guangzhou: Guangdong renmin chubashe, 2006.

Sheridan, James E. *China in Disintegration: The Republican Era in Chinese History, 1912–1949*. London: Free Press, 1975.

———. *Chinese Warlord: The Career of Feng Yü-hsiang*. Stanford: Stanford University Press, 1966.

Shewmaker, Kenneth E. *Americans and Chinese Communists, 1927–1945: A Persuading Encounter*. Ithaca: Cornell University Press, 1971.

Shi Quansheng et al. *Nanjing guomin zhengfu de jianli* (Formation of the Nanjing National Government). Zhengzhou: Henan renmin chubanshe, 1987.

Shi Yonggang and Fang Xu. *Jiang Jieshi hou zhuan: Jiang Jieshi Taiwan 26 nian zhengzhi dili* (The Last Part of Chiang Kai-shek's Biography: The Political Geography of Chiang Kai-shek's Twenty-six Year Sojourn on Taiwan). Beijing: Tuanjie chubanshe, 2013.

———. *Jiang Jingguo hua zhuan* (Illustrated Biography of Chiang Ching-kuo). Changsha: Hunan wenyi chubanshe, 2013.

Shi Yonggang and Lin Bowen. *Song Meiling hua zhuan* (Illustrated Biography of Song Meiling). Beijing: Zuojia chubanshe, 2015.

Shi Yonggang and Yang Su. *Jiang Jieshi 1887–1975 tu zhuan* (Illustrated Biography of Chiang Kai-shek). Wuhan: Changjiang wenyi chubashe, 2016.

Shiroyama, Tomoko. *China during the Great Depression: Market, State, and the World Economy, 1929–1937*. Cambridge: Harvard University Asian Center, 2008.

Short, Philip. *Mao: A Life*. New York: Henry Holt, 1999.

Sidorov, A. "Problema zakliucheniia pakta of nenapadenii v sovetsko-kitaiskikh otnosheniiakh (1932–1937 gg.)" (The Problem of Concluding the Sino–Soviet Non-Aggression Pact [1932–1937])." *Problemy Dal'nego Vostoka* (Far Eastern Affairs), no. 1 (2009): 122–39.

Sladkovsky, M. I., ed. *Noveishaia istoriia Kitaia 1917–1927* (Contemporary History of China 1917–1927). Moscow: Nauka, 1983.

———. *Noveishaia istoriia Kitaia 1928–1949* (Contemporary History of China 1928–1949). Moscow: Nauka, 1984.

Slavinsky, B. N. *The Japanese–Soviet Neutrality Pact: A Diplomatic History, 1941–1945*. Translated by Geoffrey Jukes. London: RoutledgeCurzon, 2004.

———. *Pakt o neitralitete mezhdu SSSR i Iaponiei: Diplomaticheskaia istoriia, 1941–1945* (The Pact on Neutrality between the USSR and Japan: A Diplomatic History, 1941–1945). Moscow: TOO "Novina," 1995.

Smith, Jean Edward. *FDR*. New York: Random House, 2007.

Smith, Shirley Ann. *Imperial Designs: Italians in China, 1900–1947*. Madison, NJ: Fairleigh Dickenson University Press, 2012.

Sokolov, V. V. "Dve vstrechi Sun Fo s I. V. Stalinym v 1938–1939 gg." (Sun Fo's Two Meetings with Stalin in 1938–1939). *Novaia i noveishaia istoriia* (Modern and Contemporary History), no. 6 (1999): 18–26.

———. "'Zabytii diplomat' D. V. Bogomolov (1890–1938)" (A "Forgotten Diplomat" D. V. Bogomolov [1890–1938]). *Novaia i noveishaia istoriia* (Modern and Contemporary History), no. 3 (2004): 165–95.

Spence, Jonathan D. *The Search for Modern China.* 3rd ed. New York: W. W. Norton, 2013.

Spichak, D. A. *Kitaiskii avangard Kremlia: Revoliutsionery Kitaia v moscovskikh shkolakh Kominterna (1921–1939)* (The Chinese Vanguard of the Kremlin: Revolutionaries of China in the Moscow Schools of the Comintern [1921–1939]). Moscow: "Veche," 2011.

Steenberg, Sven. *Vlasov.* New York: Knopf, 1970.

Stranahan, Patricia. *Underground: The Shanghai Communist Party and the Politics of Survival, 1927–1937.* Lanham, MD: Rowman & Littlefield, 1998.

Strand, David. *Rickshaw Beijing: City People and Politics in the 1920s.* Berkeley: University of California Press, 1989.

———. *An Unfinished Republic: Leading by Word and Deed in Modern China.* Berkeley: University of California Press, 2011.

Su Zhiliang, ed. *Zuoerge zai Zhongguo de mimi shiming* (Sorge's Secret Mission in China). Shanghai: Shanghai shehui kehui chubanshe, 2014.

Sukharchuk, G. D. *Sotsial'no-ekonomicheskie vzgliady politicheskikh liderov Kitaia pervoi poloviny XX v.: sravnitel'nyi analiz* (Socioeconomic Views of Political Leaders in China in the First Half of the Twentieth Century: A Comparative Analysis). Moscow: Nauka, 1983.

———. "Sun Yat-sen." In M. L. Titarenko, ed., *Dukhovnaiia kul'tura Kitaia: Entsiklopediia* (Spiritual Culture of China: Encyclopedia). 2nd ed. Vol. 1. Moscow: Izdatel'stvo "Vostochnaia literatura," 2011.

Sun Zhaiwei, ed. *Nanjing da tusha* (The Nanjing Massacre). Beijing: Beijing chubanshe, 1997.

Sutton, Donald S. "German Advice and Residual Warlordism in the Nanking Decade: Influences on Nationalist Military Training and Strategy." *China Quarterly* 91 (September 1982): 386–410.

———. *Provincial Militarism and the Chinese Republic: The Yunnan Army, 1905–25.* Ann Arbor: University of Michigan Press, 1980.

Tai, Paul H., and Tai-chun Kuo. "Chiang Kai-shek Revisited." *American Journal of Chinese Studies* 17 (April 2010): 81–86.

Tang Peiji, ed. *Zhongguo lishi dashi nianbiao: Xiandai* (Chronology of Events in Chinese History: Contemporary History). Shanghai: Shanghai cishu chubanshe, 1997.

Tang Tsou. *America's Failure in China 1941–50.* Chicago: University of Chicago Press, 1963.

Tanner, Harold M. *The Battle for Manchuria and the Fate of China: Siping, 1946.* Bloomington: Indiana University Press, 2013.

———. *Where Chiang Kai-shek Lost China: The Liao–Shen Campaign, 1948.* Bloomington: Indiana University Press, 2015.

Tao Baichuan, ed. *Jiang zhuxi de shenghuo he shengguan* (Life and the Life Views of Chairman Chiang). Chongqing: Zhong zhou chubanshe, 1944.

Tao Tailai and Tao Jinsheng. *Tao Xisheng nianbiao* (Chronological Biography of Tao Xisheng). Taipei: Lianjing, 2017.

Tao Yuanming. "Guiqiu lai xici" (Return Home). https://baike.baidu.com/item/%E5%BD%92%E5%8E%BB%E6%9D%A5%E5%85%AE%E8%BE%9E.

Taylor, Jay. *The Generalissimo: Chiang Kai-shek and the Struggle for Modern China.* Cambridge: Harvard University Press, 2009.

———. *The Generalissimo's Son: Chiang Ching-kuo and the Revolutions in China and Taiwan.* Cambridge: Harvard University Press, 2000.

Taylor, Jeremy E. "The Production of the Chiang Kai-shek Personality Cult, 1929–1975." *China Quarterly* 185 (2006): 96–110.

Taylor, Jeremy E., and Grace C. Huang. "'Deep Changes in Interpretive Currents?' Chiang Kai-shek Studies in the Post–Cold War Era." *International Journal of Asian Studies* 9, no. 1 (January 2012): 99–121.

Tertitsky K. M., and A. E. Belogurova. *Taivanskoe kommuniusticheskoe dvizhenie i Komintern (1924–1932 gg): Issledovanie: Dokumenty* (The Taiwanese Communist Movement and the Comintern [1924–1932]: Research: Documents). Moscow: AST, Vostok-Zapad, 2005.

Thomas, James C. "The Secret Wheat Deal." http://thislandpress.com/2016/12/06/the-secret-wheat-deal/.

Tiezzi, Shannon. "How Eisenhower Saved Taiwan." *The Diplomat,* July 29, 2015.

Tikhvinsky, S. L., ed. *Novaia istoriia Kitaia* (Modern History of China). Moscow: Nauka, 1972.

Titov, A. S. *Iz istorii bor'by i raskola v rukovodstve KPK 1935–1936 gg.* (On the History of Struggle and Split in the Leadership of the CCP 1935–1936). Moscow: Nauka, 1979.

———. *Materialy k politicheskoi biografii Mao Tsze-duna* (Materials for a Political Biography of Mao Zedong). 3 vols. Moscow: IDV AN SSSR, 1970.

Tong, Hollington K. *Chiang Kai-shek: Soldier and Statesman: Authorized Biography.* 2 vols. Shanghai: China Publishing, 1937.

Tsang, S. "Chiang Kai-shek's 'Secret Deal' at Xian and the Start of the Sino–Japanese War." *Palgrave Communications* 1, 14003 (2015). https://doi.org/10.1057/palcomms.2014.3.

Tsui, Brian. *China's Conservative Revolution: The Quest for a New Order, 1928–1949.* Cambridge: Cambridge University Press, 2018.

Tuchman, Barbara W. *Stilwell and the American Experience in China, 1911–45*. New York: Macmillan, 1971.

Tyson Li, Laura. *Madame Chiang Kai-shek: China's Eternal First Lady*. New York: Atlantic Monthly Press, 2006.

Van de Ven, Hans J. *China at War: Triumph and Tragedy in the Emergence of the New China*. Cambridge: Harvard University Press, 2018.

———. *War and Nationalism in China 1925–1945*. London: RoutledgeCurzon, 2003.

Wakabayashi Masahiro, Liu Jinqin, and Matsunaga Masaesu. *Taiwan baike* (Taiwan Encyclopedia). Tokyo: Yiqiao chubanshe, 1996.

Wakeman, Frederic, Jr. *Policing Shanghai 1927–1937*. Berkeley: University of California Press, 1995.

———. "A Revisionist View of the Nanjing Decade: Confucian Fascism." In Frederic Wakeman, Jr., and Richard Louis Edmonds, eds., *Reappraising Republican China*, 141–78. New York: Oxford University Press, 2000.

Wakeman, Frederic, Jr., and Richard Louis Edmonds, eds. *Reappraising Republican China*. New York: Oxford University Press, 2000.

Waldheim, Harald von. "Germany's Economic Position in the Far East." *Far Eastern Survey* 6, no. 6 (1937): 59–65.

Walker, Michael M. *The 1929 Sino–Soviet War: The War Nobody Knew*. Lawrence: University Press of Kansas, 2017.

Walsh, Billie K. "The German Military Mission in China, 1928–38." *Journal of Modern History* 46, no. 3 (September 1974): 502–13.

Wan Renyuan and Fang Qingqiu, eds. *Jiang Jieshi nianpu chugao* (Draft Chronological Biography of Chiang Kai-shek). 2 vols. Beijing: Dang'an chubanshe, 1992.

Wang Chaoguang. "Kangzhan yu jianguo: Guomindang linshi quanguo daibiao dahui yanjiu" (The War of Resistance and State Construction: A Study of the All-China Emergency Congress of the Guomindang). In Lü Fangshang, ed., *Zhanzheng de lishi yu jiyi* (War in History and Memory). Vol. 2:191–210. Taipei: Guoshiguan, 2015.

———. *1945–1949: Guogong zhengzheng yu Zhongguo mingyun* (1945–1949: The GMD–CCP Political Struggle and the Fate of China). Beijing: Shehui kexue wenxian chubanshe, 2010.

Wang Chaoguang, Wang Qisheng, and Jin Yilin. *Tianxia deshi: Jiang Jieshi de rensheng* (Success and Failure under Heaven: Jiang Kai-shek's Life). Taiyuan: Shanxi renming chubanshe, 2012.

Wang Chengzhi and Chen Su. *Archival Resources of Republican China in North America*. New York: Columbia University Press, 2016.

Wang Feng. *Jiang Jishi siwang zhi mi* (The Riddle of Chiang Kai-shek's Death). Beijing: Tuanjie chubanshe, 2009.

Wang Guangyuan. *Jiang Jieshi zai Huangpu* (Chiang Kai-shek at Whampoa). Beijing: Zhongguo wenshi chubashe, 2009.

———. *Jiang Jieshi zai Taiwan* (Chiang Kai-shek on Taiwan). Beijing: Zhongguo wenshi chubashe, 2008.

Wang Jianying, ed. *Zhongguo gongchandang zuzhi shi ziliao huibian—lingdao jigou yange he chengyuan minglu* (Collection of Documents on the History of the CCP Organizations—the Evolution of Leading Organs and Their Personal Composition). Beijing: Hongqi chubanshe, 1983.

Wang Ke-wen. "Wang Jingwei and the Policy Origins of the 'Peace Movement,' 1932–1937." In David P. Barrett and Larry N. Shyu, eds., *Chinese Collaboration with Japan, 1932–1945: The Limits of Accommodation*, 21–37. Stanford: Stanford University Press, 2001.

Wang, L. Sophia. "The Independent Press and Authoritarian Regimes: The Case of the Dagong bao in Republican China." *Pacific Affairs* 67, no. 2 (Summer 1994): 216–41.

Wang Liangjing. "Zhongguo guomindang zongcai zhidu de zhan qian yunnian yu zhan shi jianli" (Establishment of the Zongcai System in the Chinese Guomindang before the War and Its Creation during the War). In Lü Fangshang, ed., *Zhanzheng de lishi yu jiyi* (War in History and Memory). Vol. 2:211–34. Taipei: Guoshiguan, 2015.

Wang Liping. "Creating a National Symbol: The Sun Yat-sen Memorial in Nanjing." *Republican China*, no. 2 (1996): 23–63.

Wang Meiyu. *Caimei rongyao yixiang lu: Jiang Fangliang zhuan* (The Lonely, Beautiful, and Glorious Road in a Foreign Land: Biography of Jiang Fangliang). Taipei: Shibao wenhua chuban qiye gufen youxian gongsi, 1997.

Wang Qisheng. "Kangzhan chuqi de 'he' sheng" (Voice about "Peace" in the Initial Period of the War of Resistance). In Lü Fangshang, ed., *Zhanzheng de lishi yu jiyi* (War in History and Memory). Vol. 1:123–62. Taipei: Guoshiguan, 2015.

Wang Taidong. *Jiang Jieshi de di yi wendan Chen Bulei* (Jiang Jieshi's First Speechwriter Chen Bulei). Beijing: Tuanjie chubanshe, 2011.

Wang Tiancang. *Xikou fengguang* (Xikou Scenery). Ningbo: Ningbo chubanshe, 2003.

Wang Xiaobo, ed. *Chen Yi yu er er ba shijian* (Chen Yi and the February 28 Incident). Taipei: Haixia xueshu chubanshe, 2004.

Wang Xingfu. *Zhengzhi shashou Chen Lifu* (Political Killer Chen Lifu). Shijiazhuang: Hebei renmin chubanshe, 2006.

Wei, Betty Peh-t'i. *Old Shanghai*. Hong Kong: Oxford University Press, 1993.

Wei Hongyun. *Sun Zhongshan nianpu (1866–1925)* (Chronological Biography of Sun Zhongshan [1866–1925]). Tianjin: Tianjin renmin chubanshe, 1979.

Wen Shaohua. *Wang Jingwei zhuan* (Biography of Wang Jingwei). Beijing: Tuanjie chubanshe, 2016.

West, Philip. "Liberal Persuasions and China: Soong Meiling and John Leighton Stuart." In Samuel C. Chu, ed., *Madame Chiang Kai-shek and Her China*, 59–68. Norwalk, CT: EastBridge, 2005.

Westad, Odd Arne, ed. *Brothers in Arms: The Rise and Fall of the Sino–Soviet Alliance, 1945–1963*. Stanford: Stanford University Press, 1998.

———. *Cold War and Revolution: Soviet–American Rivalry and the Origins of the Chinese Civil War: 1944–1946*. New York: Columbia University Press, 1993.

———. *Decisive Encounters: The Chinese Civil War: 1946–1950*. Stanford: Stanford University Press, 2003.

Whiting, Allen S. *Soviet Policies in China, 1917–1924*. New York: Columbia University Press, 1954.

Wilbur, C. Martin. *The National Revolution in China, 1923–1928*. Cambridge: Harvard University Press, 1983.

———. *Sun Yat-sen: Frustrated Patriot*. New York: Columbia University Press, 1976.

Wilson, Stephen L. *Advising Chiang's Army: An American Soldier's World War II Experience in China*. Minneapolis: Mill City Press, 2016.

Woodhead, H. G. W., ed. *The China Year Book 1928*. Tientsin: Tientsin Press, 1928.

———. *The China Year Book 1929–30*. Tientsin: Tientsin Press, 1930.

———. *The China Year Book 1932*. Nendeln/Liechtenstein: Kraus Reprint, 1969.

———. *The China Year Book 1933*. Nendeln/Liechtenstein: Kraus Reprint, 1969.

———. *The China Year Book 1934*. Nendeln/Liechtenstein: Kraus Reprint, 1969.

———. *The China Year Book 1936*. Nendeln/Liechtenstein: Kraus Reprint, 1969.

———. *The China Year Book 1938*. Nendeln/Liechtenstein: Kraus Reprint, 1969.

———. *The China Year Book 1939*. Shanghai: North China Daily News and Herald, 1939.

Worthing, Peter. *General He Yingqin: The Rise and Fall of Nationalist China*. Cambridge: Cambridge University Press, 2016.

Wright, Tim. "Coping with the World Depression: The Nationalist Government's Relations with Chinese Industry and Commerce, 1932–1936." In John Fitzgerald, ed., *The Nationalists and Chinese Society 1923–1937: A Symposium*, 133–63. Parkville: History Department, University of Melbourne, 1989.

Wu Dianyao. *Liu Ding zhuan* (Biography of Liu Ding). Beijing: Zhongyang wenjiao chubanshe, 2012.

Wu Jinliang and Zhu Xiaoping. *Jiang shi jiazu quan zhuan* (Full Biographies of the Members of the Jiang Clan). 2 vols. Beijing: Zhongguo wenshi chubanshe, 1997.

Wu Qinjie, ed. *Mao Zedong guanghui dicheng dituji* (Atlas of Mao Zedong's Glorious Historical Path). Beijing: Zhongguo ditu chubanshe, 2003.

Wu Tien-wei. *The Sian Incident: A Pivotal Point in Modern Chinese History*. Ann Arbor: Center for Chinese Studies, University of Michigan, 1976.

Xiang Zhai and Ruping Xiao. "Shifting Political Calculation: The Secret Taiwan–Soviet Talks, 1963–1971." *Cold War History* 15, no. 4 (2015): 533–56.

Xiao Jie. *Jiang Jieshi yu Hu Hanmin* (Chiang Kai-shek and Hu Hanmin). Beijing: Tuanjie chubanshe, 2009.

Xiao Ruping. *Jiang Jingguo zhuan* (Biography of Chiang Ching-kuo). Hangzhou: Zhejiang daxue chubanshe, 2012.

Xie Rudi. *Jiang Jieshi de peidu suiyue: 1937–1946* (Chiang Kai-shek's Sojourn in the Provisional Capital: 1937–1946). Shanghai: Wenhui chubanshe, 2010.

Xin Hua. *"Jiban" yu fuchi de kunjing: Lun Kennidi yu Yuehanxun shiqi de Meiguo dui Tai zhengce (1961–1968)* (Between "Encumbrance" and "Support": On the US Policy on Taiwan during the Kennedy and Johnson Administrations [1961–1968]). Shanghai: Shanghai renmin chubanshe, 2008.

Xiong Zongren. " 'Rang wai bi xian an nei' " zai pipan" (New Critique of the Expression "Before We Fight the External Enemy, We Must First Establish Peace Inside the Country"). *Kangri zhanzheng yanjiu* (Studies on the War of Resistance against Japan), no. 4 (2001): 30–44.

Xu Haoran. *Jiang Jingguo zai Gan'nan* (Chiang Ching-kuo in Southern Jiangxi). Taipei: Xinchao she, 1993.

Xu Yuandong et al. *Zhongguo gongchandang lishi jianghua* (Lectures on the History of the CCP). Beijing: Zhongguo qingnian chubanshe, 1982.

Yamada Tatsuo. "Jiang Jieshi jiyi zhong zhi Riben liuxue" (Chiang Kai-shek's Reminiscences about Studying in Japan). In Huang Zijin and Pan Guangzhe, eds., *Jiang Jieshi yu xiandai Zhongguo de xingsu* (Chiang Kai-shek and the Formation of Contemporary China). Vol. 1:3–38. Taipei: Zhongyang yanjiuyuan jindaishi yanjiusuo, 2013.

Yan Lu. *Pre-understanding Japan: Chinese Perspectives, 1895–1945*. Honolulu: University of Hawai'i Press, 2004.

Yang Bichuan. *Taiwan xiandai shi nianbiao (1945 8 yue–1994 9 yue)* (Chronological Tables of Contemporary Taiwan History [August 1945–September 1994]). Taipei: Yiqiao chubanshe, 1996.

Yang Daqing. "Convergence or Divergence: Recent Historical Writings on the Rape of Nanjing." *American Historical Review* 104, no. 3 (June 1999): 840–65.

Yang Fan. *Guomindang qutai gaoguan dajieju* (The End of the Guomindang Top Officials Who Fled to Taiwan). Beijing: Tuanjie chubanshe, 2010.

Yang Han. *Xi'an shibian, banian kangzhan yu Yang Hucheng* (The Xi'an Incident, the Eight-Year War of Resistance, and Yang Hucheng). Taipei: Fengyun shidai, 2016.

———. *Yang Hucheng yu Xi'an shibian* (Yang Hucheng and the Xi'an Incident). Beijing: Dangdai Zhongguo chubanshe, 2014.

Yang Kuisong. "Jiang Jieshi bing fei 'Li Wen can'an' de muhou zhushizhe" (Chiang Kai-shek Was Not the Man Who Gave a Secret Order to Kill Li and Wen). https://read01.com/aEQGKO.html#.YOVX8C-cbxs.

———. *Shiqu de jihui? Kangzhan qianhou guogong tanpan shilu* (Lost Chance? Notes on Negotiations between the Guomindang and the CCP Before and After the War of Resistance Against Japan). Beijing: Xinxing chubanshe, 2010.

———. *Xi'an shibian xin tan: Zhang Xueliang yu zhonggong guanxi yanjiu* (A New View of the Xi'an Incident: A Study of Zhang Xueliang's Links with the CCP). Xi'an: Shaanxi renmin chubanshe, 2012.

Yang Lianfu. *Jiang jia wangchao: Taipei: 1975* (The Jiang Dynasty: Taipei: 1975). Taipei: Boyang wenhua, 2012.

Yang Shengqun and Yan Jianqi, eds. *Deng Xiaoping nianpu: 1904–1974* (Chronological Biography of Deng Xiaoping: 1904–1974). 3 vols. Beijing: Zhongyang wenxian chubanshe, 2010.

Yang Shubiao and Yang Jing. *Jiang Jieshi zhuan (1887–1949)* (Biography of Chiang Kai-shek [1887–1949]). Hangzhou: Zhejiang daxue chubanshe, 2008.

Yang Tianshi. *Dizhi de zhongjie: Jianming Xinhai geming shi* (End of Imperial Rule: Brief History of the Xinhai Revolution). Changsha: Yuelu shushe, 2011.

———. *Jiang Jieshi yu guomin zhengfu* (Chiang Kai-shek and the National Government). Beijing: Zhongguo renmin daxue chubanshe, 2007.

———. *Jiang Jieshi zhenxiang zhi er: Fenqi: Kangzhan ji zhanhou* (The True Face of Chiang Kai-shek. Vol. 2 of Upsurge: The War of Resistance and After). Taipei: Fengyun shidai, 2009.

———. *Jiang Jieshi zhenxiang zhi san: Fenqi: Kangzhan ji zhanhou (xu).* (The True Face of Chiang Kai-shek. Vol. 3 of Upsurge: The War of Resistance and After. [Continuation]). Taipei: Fengyun shidai, 2009.

———. *Jiang Jieshi zhenxiang zhi yi: Nanjing zhengfu* (The True Face of Chiang Kai-shek. Vol. 1. The Nanjing Government). Taipei: Fengyun shidai, 2009.

———. *Jiang shi midang yu Jiang Jieshi zhenxiang* (Chiang's Secret Archive and the True Face of Chiang Kai-shek). Beijing: Shehui kexue wenxian chubanshe, 2002.

———. *Jiang shi midang yu Jiang Jieshi zhenxiang* (Chiang's Secret Archive and the True Face of Chiang Kai-shek). Chongqing: Chongqing chubanshe, 2015.

———. "Perspectives on Chiang Kai-shek's Early Thoughts from His Unpublished Diary." In Mechthild Leutner et al., eds., *The Chinese Revolution in the 1920s: Between Triumph and Disaster*, 77–97. London: RoutledgeCurzon, 2002.

———. *Taiwan shiqi Jiang Jieshi yu Meiguo zhengfu maodun* (Contradictions between Chiang Kai-shek and the American Government during Chiang's Time on Taiwan). A Lecture Delivered at Zhejiang University, May 31, 2017.

———. "Zai lun Long Yun he Wang Jingwei chutao shijian: qian shu Long Yun de huangyan yu liangmian xingwei" (Once More on Long Yun and Wang Jingwei's Fleeing the Country: or about the Lies and Duplicity of Long Yun). In Lü Fangshang, ed., *Zhanzheng de lishi yu jiyi* (War in History and Memory). Vol. 2:385–417. Taipei: Guoshiguan, 2015.

———. *Zhaoxun zhenshi de Jiang Jieshi: Jiang Jieshi riji jielu* (In Search of the True Chiang Kai-shek: Analyzing Chiang Kai-shek's Diaries). 3 vols. Hong Kong: Sanlian shudian, 2008–14.

———. *Zhaoxun zhenshi de Jiang Jieshi: Jiang Jieshi riji jielu* (In Search of the True Chiang Kai-shek: Analyzing Chiang Kai-shek's Diaries). Vol. 1. Chongqing: Chongqing chubanshe, 2015.

Yao Fan. *Hu jun dudu—Xinhai geming zhong de Chen Yingshi* (Military Dudu of Shanghai—Chen Yingshi during the Xinhai Revolution). Shanghai: Shanghai wenyi chubanshe, 1982.

Young, Arthur N. *China and the Helping Hand 1937–1945*. Cambridge: Harvard University Press, 1963.

———. *China's Wartime Finance and Inflation, 1937–1945*. Cambridge: Harvard University Press, 1965.

Yu Fangde. "Dai Jitao yu ta de san qiqin" (Dai Jitao and His Three Lovers). http://www.sjfx.com/qikan/bkview.asp?bkid=39447&cid=69428.

Yu, George T. *Party Politics in Republican China: The Kuomintang, 1912–1924*. Berkeley: University of California Press, 1966.

Yu Maochun. *The Dragon's War: Allied Operations and the Fate of China, 1937–1947*. Annapolis, MD: Naval Institute Press, 2006.

Yu Yang-Chou and Daniel Riffe. "Chiang and Mao in U.S. News Magazines." *Journalism Quarterly* (Winter 1989): 913–19.

Yuan Tengyu (Homare, Endo). *Mao Zedong goujie rijun de zhenxiang: lai zi ri die de huiyi yu dang'an* (The True Story of Mao Zedong's Secret Collaboration with the Japanese Army: From the Memoirs of Japanese Spies and Archives). Deer Park, NY: Mingjing chubanshe, 2016.

Yuan Xiaolun. *Zhou Enlai yu Jiang Jieshi* (Zhou Enlai and Chiang Kai-shek). Beijing: Guangming ribao chubanshe, 1994.

Yuriev, M. F. *Revoliutsiia 1925–1927 gg. v Kitae* (The Revolution of 1925–1927 in China). Moscow: Nauka, 1968.

Yurkevich, A. G. *Moskva–Kanton, 1920-e: Pomoshch' SSSR Gomindanu i dve strategii ob"edineniia Kitaia* (Moscow–Canton, 1920s: USSR Aid to the Guomindang and Two Strategies for Uniting China). Moscow: OOO "Variant," 2013.

Zanasi, Margherita. *Saving the Nation: Economic Modernity in Republican China*. Chicago: University of Chicago Press, 2006.

Zeng Jingzhong. "Youguan guomindang linshi quanguo daibiaodahui zhi yantao" (Study of the All-China Emergency Congress of the Guomindang). *Minguo dang'an* (Republican Archive), no. 4 (2001): 81–89.

Zhang Hong. *Jiang Jieshi jiating de nürenmen: Yi lu fengyu tuo si sheng* (Women of the Chiang Kai-shek's Family: Through the Wind and Rain until Death). Beijing: Taihai chubanshe, 2013.

Zhang Jiangzhi. *Zhang Jingjiang zhuan* (Biography of Zhang Jingjiang). Wuhan: Hubei renmin chubanshe, 2004.

Zhang Jin. "'Xin du' yihuo 'jiu du': Kangzhan shiqi Chingqing de chengshi xingxiang" ("New Capital" or "Old Capital": The Urban Appearance of Chongqing during the War of Resistance). In Lü Fangshang, ed., *Zhanzheng de lishi yu jiyi* (War in History and Memory). Vol. 3:25–58. Taipei: Guoshiguan, 2015.

*Zhang Jingjiang xiansheng baisui jinian ji* (Memorial Collection on the Centenary of Zhang Jingjiang). Taipei: Shijie she, 1976.

Zhang Mei. *Du Mu.* Beijing: Wuzhou chuanbo chubanshe, 2006.

Zhang Qingjun. *Jiang Jieshi midang yu xinhan* (Chiang Kai-shek's Secret Archive and Correspondence). Taipei: Fengyun shidai chuban gufen youxian gongsi, 2014.

Zhang Rong. "Jiang Jieshi ceng liang ci lai Qingdao haibin sanbu youren renchu" (Chiang Kai-shek Visited Qingdao Twice, Walked along the Beach, Nobody Recognized Him). *Qingdao ribao* (Qingdao Daily), May 23, 2014.

Zhang Ruide. *Kangzhan shiqi de guojun renshi* (The Personnel of National Army during the War of Resistance). Taipei: Zhongyang yanjiuyuan jindaishi yanjiusuo, 1993.

———. *Wusheng de yaojiao: Jiang Jieshi de shicongshi yu zhang shi Zhongguo* (Silent Key Point: Chiang Kai-shek's Personal Secretariat and Wartime China). Taipei: Taiwan shangwu, 2017.

Zhang Shanke. *Taiwan wenti da shiji: 1945.8–1987.12* (Chronology of the Taiwan Question: August 1945–December 1987). Beijing: Wenhua chubanshe, 1988.

Zhang Shiying. "Kangzhan shiqi guojun tongshibu duiyu youjizhan de gouxiang yu zhixing" (Concepts of the Unified Command of the National Army Relating to Guerrilla Warfare and Its Implementation during the War of Resistance). In Lü Fangshang, ed., *Zhanzheng de lishi yu jiyi* (War in History and Memory). Vol. 1:195–221. Taipei: Guoshiguan, 2015.

Zhang Su. "Jiang Jingguo yu Zhang Yaruo" (Chiang Ching-kuo and Zhang Yaruo). In Zhengxie Jiangxi sheng weiyuanhui, Zhengxie Ganzhou shi weiyuanhui wenshi ziliao yanjiu weiyuanhui, eds., *Jiang Jingguo zai Gan'nan* (Chiang Ching-kuo in Southern Jiangxi), 347–66. Nanchang: Zhengxie Jiangxi sheng wei yuan hui, Zhengxie Ganzhou shi weiyuanhui wenshi ziliao yanjiu weiyuanhui, 1989.

Zhang Xianwen, ed. *Zhonghua minguo shigang* (Studies in the History of the Republic of China). Zhengzhou: Henan renmin chubanshe, 1985.

Zhang Xiuzhang. *Jiang Jieshi riji jiemi* (Chiang Kai-shek's Diaries Reveal Secrets). Beijing: Tuanjie chubanshe, 2007.

Zhang Xueji and Xu Kaifeng. *Bai Chongxi da zhuan* (Large Biography of Bai Chongxi). Hangzhou: Zhejiang daxue chubanshe, 2012.

Zhang Yongbin. *Zhang Xueliang da zhuan* (Large Biography of Zhang Xueliang). 2 vols. Beijing: Tuanjie chubanshe, 2001.

Zhang Zhenhua. *Minguo di yi jiating—Jiang shi jiazu* (The First Family of the Republic—The Jiang Clan). Beijing: Zhongguo wenshi chubanshe, 2013.

Zhang Zuyan. *Jiang Jieshi yu zhanzheng shi waijiao yanjiu (1931–1945)* (A Study of Chiang Kai-shek and the Foreign Policy during the War [1931–1945]). Hangzhou: Zhejiang daxue chubanshe, 2013.

Zhao Suisheng. *Power by Design: Constitution-Making in Nationalist China.* Honolulu: University of Hawai'i Press, 1996.

Zheng Canhui. "Zhongguo guomindang di yi ci quanguo daibiaodahui" (The First All-China Congress of the Chinese Guomindang). *Geming shi ziliao* (Materials on Revolutionary History), no. 1 (1986): 113–26.

Zheng Chuangqi. *Jiang Jieshi quan jilu: 1887–1975* (Complete Collection of Writings about Chiang Kai-shek: 1887–1975). 3 vols. Beijing: Huawen chubanshe, 2009.

Zheng Wenxin. "Sun Yat-sen and Japan, 1895–1915." MA thesis, Bowling Green, OH, 1998.

Zhengxie Jiangxi sheng weiyuanhui, Zhengxie Ganzhou shi weiyuanhui wenshi ziliao yanjiu weiyuanhui, eds. *Jiang Jingguo zai Gan'nan* (Chiang Ching-kuo in Southern Jiangxi). Nanchang: Zhengxie Jiangxi sheng wei yuan hui, Zhengxie Ganzhou shi weiyuanhui wenshi ziliao yanjiu weiyuanhui, 1989.

Zhonggong zhongyang wenxian yanjiu shi, ed. *Zhou Enlai nianpu (1898–1949)* (xiudingben) (Chronological Biography of Zhou Enlai [1898–1949]. [Revised ed.]). Beijing: Zhongyang wenxian chubanshe, 1998.

———. *Zhou Enlai nianpu: 1949–1976* (Chronological Biography of Zhou Enlai: 1949–1976). 3 vols. Beijing: Zhongyang wenxian chubanshe, 1997.

———. *Zhu De nianpu* (Chronological Biography of Zhu De). Beijing: Renmin chubanshe, 1986.

*Zhongguo geming shi jiangyi* (Lectures on the History of the Chinese Revolution). Beijing: Zhongguo renmin daxue chubanshe, 1983.

Zhongguo guomindang zhongyang weiyuanhui dangshi weiyuanhui, ed. *Zhongguo guomindang zhiming lu* (List of Officials of the Chinese Guomindang). Taipei: Guomindang dangshihui chuban, 1994.

Zhongguo renmin zhengzhi xieshang huiyi quanguo weiyuanhui wenshi ziliao yanjiu weiyuanhui bangongshi, ed. *Heping laoren Shao Lizi* (Peaceful Oldster Shao Lizi). Beijing: Wenshi ziliao chubanshe, 1985.

Zhou Xiuming. *Si da jiazu houdai miwen* (Secrets of Descendants of the Four Big Families). Beijing: Taihai chubanshe, 2011.

Zhou Yan et al. *Chen Yu zhuan* (Biography of Chen Yu). Beijing: Gongren chubanshe, 1988.

*Zhou Yi.* [Song] Zhu Xi zhu ([Book] of Changes of the Zhou Era). With Commentary by [Song] Zhu Xi. Shanghai: Shanghai guji chubanshe, 1995.

Zhou Yue and Chen Hongmin. *Hu Hanmin pingzhuan* (Biography of Hu Hanmin). Guangzhou: Guangdong renmin chubanshe, 1989.

Zhu Baoqin and Li Nin. *Song Mailing nianpu* (Chronological Biography of Song Meiling). Beijing: Dongfang chubanshe, 2019.

Zhu Wenyuan et al., eds. *Zhonghua minguo jianguo bainian dashiji* (Large Chronology of the Republic of China for One Hundred Years from Its Founding). 2 vols. Taipei: Guoshiguan, 2012.

Zhu Xiaoping. *Jiang shijia quan zhuan* (Complete Biography of the Chiang Family). 2 vols. Beijing: Zhongguo wenshi chubanshe, 1997.

Zhu Yuzhi and Cai Lesu, eds. *Mao Zedong yu 20 shiji Zhongguo* (Mao Zedong and 20th Century China). Beijing: Qinghua daxue chubanshe, 2000.

Zhuangzi. *The Complete Works of Chuang Tsu.* Translated by Burton Watson. New York: Columbia University Press, 1968.

Zhuge Liang and Liu Ji. *Mastering the Art of War.* Translated and edited by Thomas Cleary. Boston: Shambhala, 1989.

Zipp, Samuel. *The Idealist: Wendell Willkie's Wartime Quest to Build One World.* Cambridge: Harvard University Press, 2020.

Zou Lu. *Zhongguo guomindang gaishi* (General History of the Chinese Guomindang). Taipei: Zhongzheng shuju, 1958.

———. *Zhongguo guomindang shigao* (An Outline History of the Chinese Guomindang). Changsha: Minzhi shuju, 1931.

# Index